THE LIBRARY

OF

LITERARY CRITICISM

OF

ENGLISH AND AMERICAN AUTHORS

VOLUME IV
1785 – 1824

EDITED BY CHARLES WELLS MOULTON
ASSISTED BY A CORPS OF ABLE CONTRIBUTORS

GLOUCESTER, MASS.
PETER SMITH
1959

To

Professor William Torrey Harris, LL. D.

INTRODUCTION.

POETS AND POETRY

He could songes make, and wel endite.
—CHAUCER, GEOFFREY, 1387–93? *Canterbury Tales.*

Having bene in all ages, and even amongst the most barbarous, always of singular accounpt and honour, and being indede so worthy and commendable an arte; or rather no arte, but a divine gift and heavenly instinct not to bee gotten by laboure and learning, but adorned with both; and poured into the witte by a certain Ἐνθουσιασμός and cellestial inspiration.—SPENSER, EDMUND, 1579, *The Shepherd's Calendar, Argument, Oct.*

Nature never let forth the earth in so rich tapistry, as divers Poets have done, neither with pleasant rivers, fruitful trees, sweet smelling flowers: nor whatsoever els may make the too much loved earth more lovely. Her world is brasen, the Poets only deliver a golden.—SIDNEY, SIR PHILIP, 1595, *An Apologie for Poetrie.*

I had rather be a kitten, and cry—mew,
Than one of these same metre ballad-mongers;
I had rather hear a brazen canstick turn'd,
Or a dry wheel grate on an axle-tree;
And that would set my teeth nothing on edge,
Nothing so much as mincing poetry;
'Tis like the forc'd gait of a shuffling nag.
—SHAKESPEARE, WILLIAM, 1596–97, *King Henry IV., Part I, Act iii, Sc. i.*

When Heav'n would strive to do the best it can,
And puts an Angel's Spirit into a Man,
The utmost power in that great work doth spend
When to the World a Poet it doth intend.
—DRAYTON, MICHAEL, 1597, *England's Heroical Epistles.*

It was ever thought to have some participation of divineness, because it doth raise and erect the mind, by submitting the shews of things to the desires of the mind.—BACON, FRANCIS LORD, 1605, *Advancement of Learning, bk. ii.*

A verse may finde him who a sermon flies,
And turn delight into a sacrifice.
—HERBERT, GEORGE, 1633, *The Temple, Church Porch.*

Lift not thy spear against the Muses' bower:
The great Emathian conqueror bid spare
The house of Pindarus, when temple and tower
Went to the ground; and the repeated air
Of sad Electra's poet had the power
To save the Athenian walls from ruin bare.
—MILTON, JOHN, 1642, *When the Assault was intended to the City.*

For rhyme the rudder is of verses,
With which, like ships, they steer their courses.
—BUTLER, SAMUEL, 1663, *Hudibras.*

. . . the fate of verses, always prized
With admiration, or as much despised;
Men will be less indulgent to their faults,
And patience have to cultivate their thoughts,
Poets lose half the praise they should have got,
Could it be known what they discreetly blot;
Finding new words, that to the ravished ear
May like the language of the gods appear,
Such as, of old, wise bards employed, to make
Unpolished men their wild retreats forsake;
Law-giving heroes, famed for taming brutes,
And raising cities, with their charming lutes;
For rudest minds with harmony were caught,
And civil life was by the Muses taught.
—WALLER, EDMUND, 1670, *Upon the Earl of Roscommon's Translation of Horace "de Arte Poetica."*

Fame from science, not from fortune, draws.
So poetry, which is in Oxford made
An art, in London only is a trade.
There haughty dunces, whose unlearned pen
Could ne'er spell grammar, would be reading men.
Such build their poems the Lucretian way;
So many huddled atoms make a play;
And if they hit in order by some chance,
They call that nature which is ignorance.
—DRYDEN, JOHN, 1673, *Prologue to the University of Oxford.*

True Poets are the Guardians of a State,
And, when they fail, portend approaching Fate.
For that which Rome to conquest did inspire,
Was not the Vestal, but the Muses' fire.
—ROSCOMMON, EARL OF, 1684, *An Essay on Translated Verse.*

If he have a poetic vein, 'tis to me the strangest thing in the world that the father should desire or suffer it to be cherished or improved. Methinks the parents should labour to have it stifled and suppressed as much as may be; and I know not what reason a father can have to wish his son a poet, who does not desire to have him bid defiance to all other callings and business; which is not yet the worst of the case; for if he proves a successful rhymer, and gets once the reputation of a wit, I desire it may be considered what company and places he is like to spend his time in,— nay, and estate too. . . . Poetry and gaming, which usually go together, are alike in this too, that they seldom bring any advantage but to those who have nothing else to live on. . . . If therefore you would not have your son the fiddle to every jovial company, without whom the sparks could not relish their wine nor know how to pass an afternoon idly; if you would not have him to waste his time and estates to divert others, and contemn the dirty acres left him by his ancestors,—I do not think you will much care he should be a poet, or that his schoolmaster should enter him in versifying.—LOCKE, JOHN, 1693, *Some Thoughts concerning Education.*

True ease in writing comes from art, not chance,
As those move easiest who have learned to dance.
'Tis not enough no harshness gives offence,
The sound must seem an echo to the sense,
Soft is the strain when zephyr gently blows,
And the smooth stream in smoother numbers flows;
But when loud surges lash the sounding shore,
The hoarse rough verse should like the torrent roar:
When Ajax strives some rock's vast weight to throw,
The line too labors, and the words move slow:
Not so, when swift Camilla scours the plain,
Flies o'er th' unbending corn, and skims along the main.
—POPE, ALEXANDER, 1711, *Essay on Criticism, pt.* ii, *v.* 162–173.

True poets can depress and raise,
Are lords of infamy and praise;
They are not scurrilous in satire,
Nor will in panegyric flatter,
Unjustly poets we asperse ·
Truth shines the brighter clad in verse,
And all the fictions they pursue
Do but insinuate what is true.
—SWIFT, JONATHAN, 1720, *To Stella.*

Rhymes are difficult things—they are stubborn things, sir.—FIELDING, HENRY, 1751, *Amelia.*

The bard, nor think too lightly that I mean
Those little, piddling witlings, who o'erween
Of their small parts, the Murphys of the stage,
The Masons and the Whiteheads of the age,
Who all in raptures their own works rehearse,
And drawl out measured prose, which they call verse.
—CHURCHILL, CHARLES, 1764, *Independence.*

The essence of poetry is invention; such invention as, by producing something unexpected, surprises and delights.—JOHNSON, SAMUEL, 1779, *Waller, Lives of the Poets.*

There is a pleasure in poetic pains,
Which only poets know.
—COWPER, WILLIAM, 1785, *The Task, bk.* ii, *v.* 285–286.

Not mine the soul that pants not after fame—
Ambitious of a poet's envied name,
I haunt the sacred fount, athirst to prove
The grateful influence of the stream I love.
—GIFFORD, WILLIAM, 1791, *The Baviad.*

The poet must be alike polished by an intercourse with the world as with the studies of taste; one to whom labour is negligence, refinement a science, and art a nature.—DISRAELI, ISAAC, 1796–1818, *Vers de Société, Literary Character of Men of Genius.*

Call it not vain:—they do not err,
Who say that when the poet dies
Mute Nature mourns her worshipper
And celebrates his obsequies;
Who say tall cliff and cavern lone
For the departed bard makes moan;
That mountains weep in crystal rill;
That flowers in tears of balm distil;
Through his loved groves that breezes sigh,
And oaks in deeper groan reply,
And rivers teach their rushing wave
To murmur dirges round his grave.
—SCOTT, SIR WALTER, 1805, *Lay of the Last Minstrel, Canto* v, *St.* i.

Sweet are the pleasures that to verse belong,
And doubly sweet a brotherhood in song.
—KEATS, JOHN, 1815, *Epistle to George
Felton Mathews.*

Poetry is the blossom and the fragrance
of all human knowledge, human thoughts,
human passions, emotions, language.—
COLERIDGE, SAMUEL TAYLOR, 1817, *Biographia Literaria, ch.* xv.

What must a Muse of strength, of force, of
fire,
In the true Poet's ample mind inspire?
What must he feel, who can the soul express,
Of saint or hero?—he must be no less.
Nor less of evil minds he knows the pain,
But quickly lost the anguish and the stain;
While with the wisest, happiest, purest, best,
His soul assimilates and loves to rest.
—CRABBE, GEORGE, 1819, *Tales of the
Hall, bk.* vi, *note.*

Poetry is found to have a few stronger
conceptions, by which it would affect or
overwhelm the mind, than those in which
it presents the moving and speaking image
of the departed dead to the senses of the
living.—WEBSTER, DANIEL, 1820, *Discourse Delivered at Plymouth on the 22nd
of December.*

Poetry is not like reasoning, a power
to be exerted according to the determination of the will. A man cannot say, "I
will compose poetry." The greatest poet
even cannot say it; for the mind in creation is as a fading coal, which some invisible
influence, like an inconstant wind, awakens
to transitory brightness; this power
arises from within, like the colour of
a flower which fades and changes as it is
developed, and the conscious portions of
our nature are unprophetic either of its
approach or its departure. . . . Poetry
is the record of the best and happiest
moments of the happiest and best minds.
We are aware of evanescent visitations of
thought and feeling, sometimes associated
with place or person, sometimes regarding our own mind alone, and always arising
unforseen and departing unbidden, but elevating and delightful beyond all expression:
so that even in the desire and the regret

they leave, there cannot but be pleasure,
participating as it does in the nature of
its object. It is, as it were, the inter-
penetration of a diviner nature through
our own; but its footsteps are like those
of a wind over the sea, which the morning
calm erases, and whose traces remain only,
as on the wrinkled sand which paves it.—
SHELLEY, PERCY BYSSHE, 1821, *A Defence
of Poetry.*

Poetry produces an illusion on the eye
of the mind, as a magic lantern produces
an illusion on the eye of the body. And,
as a magic lantern acts best in a dark
room, poetry effects its purpose most completely in a dark age. As the light of
knowledge breaks in upon its exhibitions,
as the outlines of certainty become more
and more definite, and the shades of probability more and more distinct, the hues
and lineaments of the phantoms which it
calls up grow fainter and fainter. We
cannot unite the incompatible advantages
of reality and deception, the clear discernment of truth and the exquisite enjoyment of fiction.—MACAULAY, THOMAS
BABINGTON, 1825, *Milton, Edinburgh Review; Critical and Miscellaneous Essays.*

The poet, we cannot but think, can never
have far to seek for a subject: the elements of his art are in him and around
him on every hand; for him the ideal world
is not remote from the actual, but under
it and within it; nay, he is a poet, precisely
because he can discern it there. Wherever there is a sky above him, and a world
around him, the poet is in his place, for
here too is man's existence, with its definite longings and small acquirings; its
ever-thwarted, ever-renewed endeavors;
its unspeakable aspirations, its fears and
hopes that wander through eternity; and
all the mystery of brightness and of gloom
that it was ever made of, in any age or
climate, since man first began to live. Is
there not the fifth act of a tragedy in
every death-bed, though it were a peasant's
and a bed of heath? And are wooings

and weddings obsolete, that there can be comedy no longer? Or are men suddenly grown wise, that Laughter must no longer shake his sides, but be cheated of his farce? Man's life and nature is as it was, and as it will ever be. But the poet must have an eye to read these things, and a heart to understand them, or they come and pass away before him in vain. He is a *vates*, a seer; a gift of vision that has been given him. Has life no meanings for him which another cannot equally decipher? Then he is no poet, and Delphi itself will not make him one.—CARLYLE, THOMAS, 1828, *The Life of Robert Burns.*

The poet in a golden clime was born,
  With golden stars above;
Dower'd with the hate of hate, the scorn of
    scorn,
  The love of love.
. . . .
And bravely furnish'd all abroad to fling
  The wingéd shafts of truth,
To throng with stately blooms the breathing
  spring,
  Of hope and youth.
—TENNYSON, ALFRED LORD, 1830, *The Poet.*

        The words
He utters in his solitude shall move
Men like a swift wind—that tho' dead and
  gone,
New eyes shall glisten when his beauteous
  dream
Of love come true in happier frames than his.
—BROWNING, ROBERT, 1833, *Pauline.*

Poetry is itself a thing of God;
He made his prophets poets; and the more
We feel of poesie do we become
Like God in love and power,—under-makers.
—BAILEY, PHILIP JAMES, 1839, *Festus, Proem.*

. . . these were poets true,
Who did for Beauty as martyrs do
For Truth—the ends being scarcely two.
God's prophets of the Beautiful
These poets were; of iron rule,
The rugged cilix, serge of wool.
—BROWNING, ELIZABETH BARRETT, 1844, *A Vision of Poets.*

Poetry is the breath of beauty, flowing around the spiritual world, as the winds that wake up the flowers do about the material.—HUNT, LEIGH, 1844, *Of States- men Who have Written Verses; Men, Women and Books.*

Blessings be with them—and eternal praise,
Who gave us nobler loves, and nobler cares—
The Poets, who on earth have made us heirs
Of truth and pure delight by heavenly lays!
—WORDSWORTH, WILLIAM, 1846, *Personal Talk.*

All that is best in the great poets of all countries is not what is national in them, but what is universal.— LONGFELLOW, HENRY WADSWORTH, 1849, *Kavanagh, ch.* xx.

One more royal trait properly belongs to the poet. I mean his cheerfulness, without which no man can be a poet,—for beauty is his aim. He loves virtue, not for its obligation, but for its grace; he delights in the world, in man, in woman, for the lovely light that sparkles from them. Beauty, the spirit of joy and hilarity, he sheds over the universe.—EMERSON, RALPH WALDO, 1850, *Shakespeare; or the Poet.*

        Poetry is
The grandest chariot wherein king-thoughts
  ride;—
One who shall fervent grasp the sword of
  song
As a stern swordsman grasps his keenest
  blade,
To find the quickest passage to the heart.
— SMITH, ALEXANDER, 1852, *A Life Drama.*

      —Doth not song
To the whole world belong!
Is it not given wherever tears can fall,
Wherever hearts can melt, or blushes glow,
Or mirth and sadness mingle as they flow,
A heritage to all?
—CRAIG-KNOX, ISA, 1859, *Ode on a Centenary of Burns.*

We call those poets who are first to mark
  Through earth's dull mist the coming of
    the dawn,—
Who see in twilight's gloom the first pale
  spark,
  While others only note that day is gone.
— HOLMES, OLIVER WENDELL, 1864, *Shakespeare Tercentennial Celebration, April* 23.

. . . there dawneth a time to the Poet,
  When the bitterness passes away,
With none but his God to know it,
  He kneels in the dark to pray;
And the prayer is turn'd into singing,

And the singing findeth a tongue,
And Art, with her cold hands clinging,
　Comforts the soul she has stung.
Then the Poet, holding her to him,
　Findeth his loss is his gain :
The sweet singing sadness thrills through
　him,
　Though nought of the glory remain ;
And the awful sound of the city,
　And the terrible faces around,
Take a truer, tenderer pity,
　And pass into sweetness and sound ;
The mystery deepens to thunder,
　Strange vanishings gleam from the cloud,
And the Poet, with pale lips asunder,
　Stricken, and smitten, and bow'd,
Starteth at times from his wonder,
　And sendeth his Soul up aloud!
—BUCHANAN, ROBERT, 1864, *London.*

　　　The earth is given
To us : we reign by virtue of a sense
Which lets us hear the rhythm of that old
　verse,
The ring of that old tune whereto she spins.
Humanity is given to us : we reign
By virtue of a sense which lets us in
To know its troubles ere they have been told,
And take them home and lull them into rest
With mournfullest music.　Time is given
　to us,—
Time past, time future.　Who, good sooth,
　beside
Have seen it well, have walked this empty
　world
When she went steaming, and from pulpy
　hills
Have marked the spurting of their flamy
　crowns?
—INGELOW, JEAN, 1867, *Gladys and Her
Island.*

Verse-makers' talk! fit for a world of rhymes
Where facts are feigned to tickle idle ears,
Where good and evil play at tournament,
And end in amity,—a world of lies,—
A carnival of words where every year
Stale falsehoods serve fresh men.
—ELIOT, GEORGE, 1868, *The Spanish
Gypsy, bk.* i.

The busy shuttle comes and goes
Across the rhymes, and deftly weaves
A tissue out of autumn leaves,
With here a thistle, there a rose.
—ALDRICH, THOMAS BAILEY, 1874, *The
Cloth of Gold.*

We are the music makers,
　And we are the dreamers of dreams,
Wandering by lone sea-breakers,
　And sitting by desolate streams;—
World-losers and world-forsakers,
　On whom the pale moon gleams:
Yet we are the movers and shakers

Of the world for ever, it seems.
With wonderful deathless ditties
We build up the world's great cities,
　And out of a fabulous story
　We fashion an empire's glory :
One man with a dream, at pleasure,
　Shall go forth and conquer a crown ;
And three with a new song's measure
　Can trample a kingdom down.
— O'SHAUGHNESSY, ARTHUR, 1874, *Ode,
Music and Moonlight.*

There are few delights in any life so
high and rare as the subtle and strong delight of sovereign art and poetry ; there
are none more pure and more sublime.　To
have read the greatest works of any great
poet, to have beheld or heard the greatest
works of any great painter or musician, is
a possession added to the best things of
life.—SWINBURNE, ALGERNON CHARLES,
1875, *Victor Hugo, Essays and Studies.*

All days are birthdays in the life,
　The blessed life that poets live,
Songs keep their own sweet festivals,
　And are the gifts they come to give.
The only triumph over Time,
　That Time permits, is his who sings ;
The poet Time himself defies
　By secret help of Time's own wings.
—JACKSON, HELEN HUNT, 1879, *To O.
W. Holmes on his* 70*th Birthday.*

A Poem consists of all the purest and
most beautiful elements in the poet's
nature, crystallised into the aptest and
most exquisite language, and adorned with
all the outer embellishment of musical
cadence or dainty rhyme.　Hence it presents us with the highest and noblest product of the æsthetic faculty, embracing
as it does in their ideal forms the separate
beauties of all its sister arts.　Whatever
loveliness in face or feature, in hill or
stream or ocean, the painter can place
before us on his breathing canvas, that
loveliness the poet can body forth in his
verse, with the superadded touches of his
vivid imagination.　Whatever glorious
floods of sound the singer can pour out
from his ever-welling fountain of liquid
treble and thundering bass, that glory the
poet can reproduce for us in his graphic
delineation of all things seen or heard.

Even more than this the poet can do. For while painting can only portray for us the forms and colours of the human face or of external nature, with at best some pregnant suggestion of the passions and emotions at work within it—while music can only play upon our inner cords by dim hints and half-comprehended touches, "telling us of things we have not seen, of things we shall not see"—the supreme art of all can utter in clear and definite language every feeling, external or internal, which makes up the sum of human life.—ALLEN, GRANT, 1879, *A Fragment from Keats, The Gentleman's Magazine, vol.* 244, *p.* 676.

He is a poet strong and true
Who loves wild thyme and honey-dew;
And like a brown bee works and sings,
With morning freshness on his wings,
And a gold burden on his thighs,—
The pollen-dust of centuries!
—THOMPSON, MAURICE, 1883, *Wild Honey.*

I sometimes doubt
If they have not indeed the better part—
These poets, who get drunk with sun, and weep
Because the night or a woman's face is fair.
—LEVY, AMY, 1884, *A Minor Poet.*

She comes like the husht beauty of the night,
But sees too deep for laughter;
Her touch is a vibration and a light
From worlds before and after.
— MARKHAM, CHARLES EDWIN, 1889, *Prize Quatrain, Magazine of Poetry, vol.* 1, *p.* 488.

Oh, we who know thee know we know thee not,
Thou Soul of Beauty, thou Essential Grace!
Yet undeterr'd by baffled speech and thought,
The heart stakes all upon thy hidden face.
—BATES, KATHARINE LEE, 1889, *Prize Quatrain, Magazine of Poetry, vol.* 1, *p.* 488.

. . . the great gods of Song, in clear white light,
The radiance of their godhead, calmly dwell
And with immutable cold starlike gaze
Scan both the upper and the under world,
As it revolves, themselves serenely fixed.
Their bias is the bias of the sphere,
That turns all ways, but turns away from none,
Save to return to it. They have no feud
With gods or men, the living or the dead,
The past or present, and their words complete
Life's incompleteness with a healing note.
For they are not more sensitive than strong,

More wise than tender; understanding all,
At peace with all, at peace with life and death,
And love that gives a meaning unto life
And takes from death the meaning and the sting:
At peace with hate, and every opposite.
—AUSTIN, ALFRED, 1889, *A Dialogue at Fiesole.*

We name thee not the Angel of the Tomb:
O'er that, vain-glory fleets, waning wrath:
God's light alone dispels the churchyard's gloom:
Yet whisperings hast thou with God's Daughter, Faith.
—DE VERE, AUBREY THOMAS, 1889, *Prize Quatrain, Magazine of Poetry, vol.* 1, *p.* 490.

God placed a solid rock man's path across,
And bade him climb; but that it might not be
Too rough, He wrapped it o'er with tender moss:
The rock was Truth, the moss was Poetry.
—INGLISS, BERT, 1889, *Prize Quatrain, Magazine of Poetry, vol.* 1, *p.* 488.

The poet dies as dies the barren mind,
It is in death his deathless days begin.
To him of what avail? But he has willed
His wealth to every dweller on the soil,
That so shall ages drifting by be filled
With lustrous reminiscence of his toil.
Through him man's spirit quits its baser pleasures,
Beholding Nature's world as now his own,
Astonished at his newly-gotten treasures,—
Into his lap the wealth of ages thrown!
—HAKE, THOMAS GORDON, 1890, *The New Day, Sonnet* xxxi.

He walks with God upon the hills!
And sees, each morn, the world arise
New-bathed in light of Paradise.
He hears the laughter of her rills,
Her melodies of many voices,
And greets her while her heart rejoices.
She, to his spirit undefiled,
Makes answer as a little child;
Unveiled before his eyes she stands,
And gives her secrets to his hands.
—COOLBRITH, INA D., 1891, *The Poet.*

Poets must ever be their own best listeners.
No word from man to men
Shall sound the same again;
Something is lost through all interpreters.
Never for finest thought
Can crystal words be wrought
That to the crowd afar
Shall show it—more than a telescope a star.
—SPENCER, CARL, 1891, *Half Heard.*

CONTENTS.

ENGRAVINGS.

The
Library of Literary Criticism
of
English and American Authors

VOLUME IV.

Richard Glover

1712–1785

Born at London, 1712: Died there, Nov. 25, 1785. An English Poet. He was the son of a Hamburg merchant, and entered into business with his father. His chief work, an epic poem, "Leonidas," appeared in 1737. He enlarged it and republished it in 1770, and it has been translated into French and German. Its success was partly due to its usefulness to the opponents of Walpole. He also published "London, etc." (1739), "Boadicea" (a tragedy, 1753), "Medea" (1761), and "The Athenaid," an epic in 30 books, published in 1787 by his daughter.—SMITH, BENJAMIN E., *ed.*, 1894–97, *The Century Cyclopedia of Names, p.* 443.

PERSONAL

The greatest coxcomb and the greatest oaf that ever met in blank verse or prose.—WALPOLE, HORACE, 1742, *To Sir Horace Mann, March* 3; *Letters, ed. Cunningham, vol.* I, *p.* 136.

We spent the evening with Miss Hamilton; who, I fancy, will have another name by the time you get this letter. I was much amused with hearing old Leonidas Glover sing his own fine ballad of "Hosier's Ghost," which was very affecting. He is past eighty. Mr. Walpole coming in just afterward, I told him how highly I had been pleased. He begged me to entreat for a repetition of it. I suppose you recollect that it was the satire conveyed in this little ballad upon the conduct of Sir Robert Walpole's ministry, which is thought to have been a remote cause of his resignation. It was a very curious circumstance to see his son listening to the recital of it with so much complacency. Such is the effect of the lapse of time. I have rarely heard a more curious instance of the absence of mind produced by poetic enthusiasm, than that which occurred when the author of "Leonidas" made one of a party of literati

assembled at the house of Mr. Gilbert West, at Wickham. Lord Lyttleton, on opening his window one morning, perceived Glover pacing to and fro with a whip in his hand, by the side of a fine bed of tulips just ready to blow, and which were the peculiar care of the lady of the mansion, who worshiped Flora with as much ardour as Glover did the Muses. His mind was at that instant teeming with the birth of some little ballad, when Lord Lyttleton, to his astonishment and dismay, perceived him applying his whip with great vehemence to the stalks of the unfortunate tulips; all of which, before there was time to awaken him from his revery, he had completely levelled with the ground: And when the devastation he had committed was afterward pointed out to him, he was so perfectly unconscious of the proceeding that he could with difficulty be made to believe it.—MORE, HANNAH, 1785, *Letter to her Sister, June* 16; *Memoirs, ed. Roberts, vol.* I, *p.* 229.

At the age of twenty-five he published nine books of his "Leonidas." The poem was immediately taken up with ardour by Lord Cobham, to whom it was inscribed, and by all the readers of verse, and leaders of politics, who professed the strongest attachment to liberty. It ran rapidly through three editions, and was publicly extolled by the pen of Fielding, and by the lips of Chatham. Even Swift in one of his letters from Ireland, drily inquires of Pope, "*who is this Mr. Glover, who writ 'Leonidas,' which is reprinting here, and hath great vogue?*" Overrated as "Leonidas" might be, Glover stands acquitted of all attempts or artifice to promote its popularity by false means. He betrayed no irritation in the disputes which were raised about its merit; and his personal character appears as respectable in the ebb as in the flow of his poetical reputation.—CAMPBELL, THOMAS, 1819, *Specimens of the British Poets.*

LEONIDAS
1737

Some contemporary writers, calling themselves critics, preferred "Leonidas" in its day to "Paradise Lost;" because it had smoother versification, and fewer hard words of learning. The re-action of popular opinion, against a work that has been once over-rated, is apt to depress it beneath its just estimation. It is due to "Leonidas" to say, that its narrative, descriptions, and imagery, have a general and chaste congruity with the Grecism of its subject. It is far, indeed, from being a vivid or arresting picture of antiquity; but it has an air of classical taste and propriety in its design; and it sometimes places the religion and manners of Greece in a pleasing and impressive light. . . . The undeniable fault of the entire poem is, that it wants impetuosity of progress, and that its characters are without warm and interesting individuality. What a great genius might have made of the subject, it may be difficult to pronounce by supposition; for it is the very character of genius to produce effects which cannot be calculated. But imposing as the names of Leonidas and Thermopylæ may appear, the subject which they formed for an epic poem was such, that we cannot wonder at its baffling the powers of Glover.—CAMPBELL, THOMAS, 1819, *Specimens of the British Poets.*

We are not without our literary talk either. It did not extend far, but as far as it went, it was good. It was bottomed well; had good grounds to go upon. In *the cottage* was a room, which tradition

authenticated to have been the same in which Glover, in his occasional retirements, had penned the greater part of his "Leonidas." This circumstance was nightly quoted, though none of the present inmates, that I could discover, appeared ever to have met with the poem in question. But that was no matter. Glover had written there, and the anecdote was pressed into the account of the family importance. It diffused a learned air through the apartment.—LAMB, CHARLES, 1824, *Captain Jackson, Essays of Elia.*

Glover's "Leonidas," though only party spirit could have extolled it as a work of genius, obtained no inconsiderable sale, and a reputation which flourished for half a century. It has a place now in the two great general collections, and deserves to hold it. The author has the merit of having departed from bad models, rejected all false ornaments and tricks of style, and trusted to the dignity of his subject. And though the poem is cold and bald, stately rather than strong in its best parts, and in general rather stiff than stately, there is in its very nakedness a sort of Spartan severity that commands respect.—SOUTHEY, ROBERT, 1835, *Life of Cowper, vol.* II, *ch.* XII.

Nor probably was Glover's blank verse epic of "Leonidas" which appeared so early as 1737, much read when he himself passed away from among men, in the year 1785, at the age of seventy-four, although it had had a short day of extraordinary popularity, and is a performance of considerable rhetorical merit.—CRAIK, GEORGE L., 1861, *A Compendious History of English Literature and of the English Language, vol.* II, *p.* 287.

It is not altogether deficient in poetical merit, but as an epic it is a decided failure.—BALDWIN, JAMES, 1882, *English Literature and Literary Criticism, Poetry, p.* 287.

Power is visible in this epic, which displays also a large amount of knowledge, but the salt of genius is wanting, and the poem, despite many estimable qualities, is now forgotten.—DENNIS, JOHN, 1894, *The Age of Pope, p.* 244.

GENERAL

The "Athenaid," which could not be included in Anderson's collection, is contained in this.. It ought always to accompany the "Leonidas." Mr. Chalmers censures it because, he says, the events of history are so closely followed as to give the whole the air of a poetical chronicle. To this opinion we may oppose the fact of having ourselves repeatedly perused it in early youth, for the interest which the story continually excited. Glover endeavoured to imitate the ancients, but wanted strength to support the severe style which he had chosen. He has, however, many and great merits, this especially among others, that instead of treading in the sheep-track wherein the writers of modern epics, till his time, *servum pecus*, had gone one after the other, he framed the stories of both his poems according to their subject, without reference to any model, or any rule but that of propriety and good sense.—SOUTHEY, ROBERT, 1814, *Chalmers's English Poets, Quarterly Review, vol.* 11, *p.* 498.

Believe me, I walked with an impression of awe on my spirits, as W—— and myself accompanied Mr. Klopstock to the house of his brother, the poet, which stands about a quarter of a mile from the city gate. . . . He then talked of Milton and Glover, and thought Glover's blank verse superior to Milton's. W—— and myself expressed our surprise; and my friend gave his definition and notion of harmonious verse, that it consisted (the English iambic blank verse above all) in the apt arrangement of pauses and cadences, and the sweep of whole paragraphs,

—"with many a winding bout
Of linked sweetness long drawn out,"

and not even in the flow, much less in the prominence or antithetic vigor, or single lines, which were indeed injurious to the total effect, except where they were introduced for some specific purpose. Klopstock assented, and said that he meant to confine Glover's superiority to single lines.—COLERIDGE, SAMUEL TAYLOR, 1817, *Satyrane's Letters, Biographia Literaria.*

His Epic Poem rather disappointed the world. The critic showed it to be replete with poetic excellence, and the patriot bosom glowed at the very name of Leonidas; yet it faded away as deficient in its interest, and too narrow in its plan. What has been said tauntingly of the French, may be more liberally and not

less justly put:—*Les modernes n'ont pas la tête epique.* Mr. Glover wrote three tragedies, two of which were upon the subject of Medea and Jason; the other had for its heroine, Boadicea. Mrs. Yates was fond of Glover's cold declamation, and frequently displayed herself in the character of Medea. Glover, like Mason, loved and preferred the classic model, and would not see the incompatibility of the Greek chorus with the modern stage.— BOADEN, JAMES, 1825, *Memoirs of the Life of John Philip Kemble, vol.* I, *p.* 303.

The Greek plays differ so much from those we are accustomed to, that it is extremely difficult to adapt them to the taste of a modern audience—Glover has succeeded much better than anybody else —the character of Medea is, on the whole, drawn in a masterly manner—but Glover has softened the violence of her temper rather too much—the thought of making her kill her children in a temporary fit of phrenzy is a very happy one—the scenes in which Medea is not concerned have little to recommend them.— GENEST, P., 1832, *Some Account of the English Stage from the Restoration in* 1660 *to* 1830, *vol.* V, *p.* 123.

The elegant but cold Epics of Glover. —SPALDING, WILLIAM, 1852–82, *A History of English Literature, p.* 356.

He published two elaborate poems in blank verse, "Leonidas" and the "Athenaid"—the former bearing reference to the memorable defence of Thermopylæ, and the latter continuing the war between the Greeks and Persians. The length of these poems, their want of sustained interest, and lesser peculiarities not suited to the existing poetical taste, render them next to unknown in the present day. But there is smoothness and even vigour, a calm moral dignity and patriotic elevation in "Leonidas," which might even yet find admirers. Thomson is said to have exclaimed, when he heard of the work of Glover: "He write an epic poem, who never saw a mountain!" . . . His chief honour is that of having been an eloquent and patriotic city merchant, at the same time that he was eminent as a scholar and man of letters.— CHAMBERS, ROBERT, 1876, *Cyclopædia of English Literature, ed. Carruthers.*

Glover was a man of considerable powers, but he was stronger on the side of politics and practical life than in the field of literature. In his poems the rhetoric of party warfare is more conspicuous than the inspiration of genius. His best-known poem, "Leonidas," was based it is true on his reading of Herodotus and Plutarch; but in reality it is the utterance of one who wished to stir his fellow-citizens to an anti-Walpole "patriotic" policy. So far as the form is concerned it may be called a blank-verse echo of Pope's version of Homer, the influence of which may continually be traced; and under the inspiration of this model Glover expands a few simple chapters of his authority Herodotus into the dimensions of an epic by inventing various characters, love-affairs, and thrilling episodes. Campbell remarks that the want of "impetuosity of progress" is the chief fault in the poem. It does not seem clear that this censure is just. The action moves on swiftly enough, and is sufficiently varied by epoch-making or decorative incidents. The personages introduced are not inactive, or long-winded; they have only the damning fault of being dull. The reader does not much care what they do, nor what becomes of them. A sort of glossy rhetoric is the general characteristic of the poem, which accordingly is not without striking passages, but the lack of human interest mars the total effect. . . . Of the "Athenaid," a sequel to "Leonidas," with its thirty books, it is enough to say that it is simply unreadable. It appears to be a florid reproduction, with new incidents and scenery, of the story of Græco-Persian war, from Thermopylæ to Platæa. The opposition to Sir Robert Walpole found in Glover an enthusiastic ally. One of his chief objects in writing "London" is said to have been to exasperate the public mind against Spain, a power to which Walpole was held to have truckled. In the same year, after the news came of Vernon's success at Porto Bello, Glover wrote the spirited ballad of "Hosier's Ghost," rather perhaps with the design of damaging Walpole than exalting Vernon. The political aim interests us no more; but the music and swing of the verse,—perhaps also the naval cast of the imagery and the diction,—will keep this ballad popular with Englishmen for many a year to come.—ARNOLD, THOMAS, 1880, *English Poets, ed. Ward, vol.* III.

Narrative poetry in the eighteenth century was of the slenderest dimensions and the most modest temper. Poems of description and sentiment seemed to leave no place for poems of action and passion. . . . That estimable London merchant, Glover, had indeed written an heroic poem containing the correct number of Books; its subject was a lofty one; the sentiments were generous, the language dignified; and inasmuch as Leonidas was a patriot and a Whig, true Whigs and patriots bought and praised the poem. But Glover's poetry lacks the informing breath of life. His second poem, "The Athenaid," appeared after his death, and its thirty books fell plumb into the water of oblivion. It looked as if the narrative poem *à longue haleine* was dead in English literature.—DOWDEN, EDWARD, 1880, *Southey (English Men of Letters), p.* 51.

Another and more ambitious Thomsonian. . . . A politician whom indignation against Walpole hurried into copious blank verse. There must be few men now alive who can boast a more than fragmentary acquaintance with the epics of Glover. "Leonidas" (in nine books, afterwards enlarged), 1737, begins his poetical career, and "The Athenaid" (positively in thirty books), 1788, closed it. Glover is only remembered by his extremely spirited ballad of "Admiral Hosier's Ghost," which, however, he might have improved by shortening to five syllables the last line of each octet. —GOSSE, EDMUND, 1888, *A History of Eighteenth Century Literature, p.* 228.

His ponderous "Athenaid," an epic poem in thirty books, was published in 1787 by his daughter, Mrs. Halsey. It is much longer and so far worse than "Leonidas," but no one has been able to read either for a century. . . . The "Memoirs" are of little value, though they contribute something to our knowledge of the political intrigues of the time.— STEPHEN, LESLIE, 1890, *Dictionary of National Biography, vol.* XXII, *p.* 7.

There is one poem of Glover's,—"London, or the Progress of Commerce,"—that illustrates the fashionable poetical style of the Queen Anne time—the prevalent idea as to how Nature was to be dressed to advantage. As a London merchant, Glover no doubt felt his heart swell within him as he looked at the bustle of many nations on the London wharves, and saw ships from many distant regions crowding up the Thames. How did he give expression to this exaltation of mind? He could not present the coarse and vulgar details of trade to a fine Queen Anne gentleman; he asks his reader to look at them through a fine allegorical veil, transports us to the regions of mythology, and gives a long narrative of a love affair between the sea-god Neptune and the nymph named Phœnice, the guardian spirit of the Phœnicians. The beautiful nymph Commerce was the offspring of this Union. This is the poet's way of relating the prosaic fact that the Phœnicians were the first great traders by sea; and the events in the subsequent history of Commerce are given as incidents in the life of the nymph Commerce, from her cradle and nursery till the time when she fixed her abode in Great Britain.—MINTO, WILLIAM, 1894, *The Literature of the Georgian Era, ed. Knight, p. 89.*

William Whitehead

1715-1785

William Whitehead, 1715-1785. Born, at Cambridge, Feb., 1715. Early education at Winchester School, July, 1728 to Sept., 1735. Matric. Clare Hall, Cambridge, as Sizar, 1735; B. A., 1739; Fellow, 1742-46; M. A., 1743. Appointed tutor to son of Lord Jersey, 1745; travelled on Continent with him, June, 1754, to Sept., 1756. Was an inmate of Lord Jersey's household till 1769. Play, "The Roman Father," produced at Drury Lane, 24 Feb., 1750; "Creusa," Drury Lane, 20 April, 1754; "The School for Lovers," Drury Lane, 1762; "A Trip to Scotland," Drury Lane, 1770. Contrib. to "The World," 1753. Registrar of Order of Bath, 1755. Poet-Laureate, 1757. Died, in London, 14 April, 1785. Buried in South Audley Street Chapel. *Works:* "On the Danger of Writing in Verse," 1741; Epistle of Anne Boleyn to Henry VIII., 1743; "Essay on Ridicule," 1743; "On Nobility," 1744; "Atys and Adrastus," 1744; "The Roman Father," 1750; "A Hymn to the Nymph of Bristol Spring," 1751; "Creusa," 1754; "Poems on Several Occasions," 1754; "Elegies," 1757; "Verses to the People of England," 1758; "A Charge to the Poets," 1762; "The School for Lovers," 1762 (adapted from the French of Le Bovier de Fontenelle); "A Trip to Scotland" (anon.), 1770; "Plays and Poems" (2 vols.), 1774; "Variety" (anon.), 1776; "The Goat's Beard" (anon.), 1777.—SHARP, R. FARQUHARSON, 1897, *A Dictionary of English Authors, p. 299.*

PERSONAL

The following fact is true
From nobler names, and great in each degree,
The pension'd laurel had devolv'd to me,
To me, ye bards; and what you'll scarce conceive,
Or, at the best, unwillingly believe,
Howe'er unworthily I wear the crown,
Unask'd it came, and from a hand unknown.
—WHITEHEAD, WILLIAM, 1762, *A Charge to the Poets.*

In the same year [1762] the rabid satire of Churchill sorely smote his reputation. Poor Whitehead made no reply. Those who, with Mason, consider his silence as the effect of a pacific disposition, and not of imbecility, will esteem him the more for his forebearance, and will apply it to the maxim, *Rarum est eloquenter loqui varias eloquenter tacere.* Among his unpublished MSS. there were even found verses expressing a compliment to Churchill's talents. There is something, no doubt, very amiable in a good and candid man taking the trouble to cement rhymes upon the genius of a blackguard, who had abused him; but the effect of all this candor upon his own generation reminds us how much more important it is, for a man's own advantage, that he should be formidable than harmless. His candour could not prevent his poetical character from being completely killed by Churchill. Justly, some will say; he was too stupid to resist his adversary. I have a different opinion, both as to the justice of his fate, and the cause of his abstaining from retaliation. He certainly wrote too many insipid things; but a tolerable selection might be made from his works, that would discover his talents to be no legitimate object of contempt; and there is not a trait of arrogance or vanity in any one of his compositions, that deserved to be publicly humiliated. He was not a satirist; but he wanted rather the gall than the ingenuity that is requisite for the character. If his heart had been full of spleen, he was not so wholly destitute of humour as not to have been able to deal some hard blows at Churchill, whose private character was a broad mark, and even whose writings had many vapid parts that were easily assailable. Had Whitehead done so, the world would probably have liked him the better for his pugnacity. As it was, his name sunk into such a by-word of contempt, that Garrick would not admit his "Trip to Scotland" on the stage, unless its author was concealed. He also found it convenient to publish his pleasing tale, entitled "Variety," anonymously. The public applauded both his farce and his poem, because it was not known that they were Whitehead's.—CAMPBELL, THOMAS, 1819, *Specimens of the British Poets.*

He died April 14, 1785, at the age of seventy, and was buried in South Audley Street chapel.

An Epitaph on W. Whitehead, Esq.
Intended for His Monument in Westminster Abbey.
"Beneath this stone a Poet Laureat lies,
Nor great, nor good, nor foolish, nor yet wise;
Not meanly humble, nor yet swell'd with pride.
He simply liv'd—and just as simply died:
Each year his Muse produced a Birth Day Ode,
Compos'd with flattery in the usual mode:
For this, and but for this, to George's praise,
The Bard was pension'd, and receiv'd the Bays."
—HAMILTON, WALTER, 1879, *The Poets Laureate of England, p.* 189.

The boy showed his good sense by not being ashamed to win an education at the expense of his pride. Entering Cambridge as a sizar, he graduated with honours and was elected a fellow of his college. He then became tutor to the son of the Earl of Jersey. He travelled with him, and then settled down with him in his quiet, beautiful home, where many happy years were passed. Whitehead had leisure for literary studies, and he enjoyed not only the friendship and confidence of his employers, but formed many close connections with the nobility who treated him with respect and deference. Whitehead became very popular among his friends, winning their regard, and keeping it, too. His manners were not only polished, but were the outward expression of a sincere and kind heart. Though fond of society, he indulged in no dissipation. He visited the theatres frequently, and this finally led him to try his hand at dramatic writing, and his success was greater than he had himself anticipated.—HOWLAND, FRANCES LOUISE (KENYON WEST), 1895, *The Laureates of England, p.* 108.

GENERAL

Come, Method, come in all thy pride,
Dullness and Whitehead by thy side;
Dullness and Method still are one,
And Whitehead is their darling son.
. . . .
But he, who in the Laureate chair,
By grace, not merit, planted there,
In awkward pomp is seen to sit,
And by his patent proves his wit.
. . . .
But he—who measures, as he goes,
A mongrel kind of tinkling prose,
And is too frugal to dispense,
At once, both poetry and sense;
Who, from amidst his slumbering guards,
Deals out a charge to subject bards,
Where couplets after couplets creep
Propitious to the reign of sleep;
Yet every word imprints an awe,
And all his dictates pass for law
With beaus, who simper all around,
And belles, who die in every sound.
—CHURCHILL, CHARLES, 1762, *The Ghost, bk.* iii.

Mr. Whitehead has just published a pretty poem called "Variety," in which there is humour and ingenuity, but not more poetry than is necessary for a Laureate; however, the plan is one, and is well wound up.—WALPOLE, HORACE, 1776, *To Rev. William Mason, Feb.* 18; *Letters, ed. Cunningham, vol.* VI, *p.* 310.

Will. Whitehead bad the reign commence
Of Birth-Day Odes and Common-Sense:
And there his efforts rested:
True Poetry, by Genius fir'd,
Billy's cold bosom ne'er inspir'd;
For *Bill* was chicken-breasted.
—COLMAN, GEORGE, 1786, *The Laureat, An Ode, April* 11.

He will be most advantageously known to posterity as a dramatic writer; his "Roman Father" and "Creusa," tragedies, and his "School for Lovers" a comedy, possessing considerable merit.—DRAKE, NATHAN, 1810, *Essays, Illustrative of the Rambler, Adventurer, and Idler, vol.* II, *p.* 294.

A play ["Creusa"] which, though seldom read, and never acted, is by no means destitute of dramatic feeling and conception. . . . The piece contains some strong situations; its language is unaffected; and it fixes the attention (if I may judge from my own experience) from the first to the last scene. The pure and holy character of the young Ilyssus is brought out, I have no hesitation to say, more interestingly than in Euripides, by the display of his reverential gratitude to the queen, upon the first tenderness which she shows him, and by the agony of his ingenuous spirit, on beholding it withdrawn. And, though Creusa's character is not unspotted, she draws our sympathy to some of the deepest conceivable agonies of human nature. I by no means wish to deny that the tragedy has many defects, or to speak of it as a great production, but it does not deserve to be consigned to oblivion. — CAMPBELL, THOMAS, 1819, *Specimens of the British Poets.*

The most accomplished tuft-hunter of his time. . . . The writings of Whitehead, Cambridge, Coventry, and Lord Bath are forgotten.—MACAULAY, THOMAS BABINGTON, 1833, *Walpole's Letters to Sir Horace Mann, Critical and Miscellaneous Essays.*

He was the author of several successful plays—"The Roman Father," "Creusa," and "The School for Lovers;" and of miscellaneous poems, that have scarce any individualizing characteristics, but are in the manner of writers of the time of Queen Anne. On his return from travelling with noble pupils he published an "Ode to the Tiber" and six "Elegiac Epistles," which were applauded at first, and in course of time neglected; the usual fate of poems produced by Talent apart from Genius: the Junonian offspring of a female parent alone. This "Ode to the Tiber" is an excellent specimen of such poetry as may be written by a clever man, on command, having everything that is to be desired, except a soul *of its own;* it reads like a first-rate school exercise, or such an exercise as might be produced in an adult *School* of Poetry.—COLERIDGE, SARA, 1847, *ed. Coleridge's Biographia Literaria, Appendix.*

An elegant poet and a nervous writer. —MILLS, ABRAHAM, 1851, *The Literature and the Literary Men of Great Britain and Ireland, vol.* II, *p.* 333.

He wrote the usual official poems, which had the negative merit of being considered superior to those of his predecessor; and he was engaged in the composition of a birthday ode when he died. . . . Whitehead was more successful as a dramatist than as a poet. . . . As Laureate, Whitehead did not escape the usual fate of being lampooned by the envious wits, and small poets of his day.—HAMILTON, WALTER, 1879, *The Poets Laureate of England, pp.* 184, 185, 186.

His poetry is for the most part tame and conventional enough; yet here and there he emerges from the ruck of Georgian poetasters and becomes noticeable. "Variety, a Tale for Married People," which is too long for quotation, is an excellent story in verse—with a moral, of course, as a *conte* should have—told in a light and flowing style not unworthy of Gay.—WARD, THOMAS HUMPHRY, 1880, *English Poets, vol.* III, *p.* 337.

He was always fond of the theatre, and his first effort was a little farce which was never published, but which tempted him to compose heavy tragedies which were. Of these tragedies it would be absurd to speak; they never enjoyed any popularity, either on the stage or in the closet. He owed his appointment—which he did not obtain till Gray had refused it—entirely to his noble friends.—BIRRELL, AUGUSTINE, 1894, *Essays about Men, Women and Books, p.* 164.

Sprung from the ranks, he had the good fortune to secure the favour of the great, until he became tutor to Lord Jersey. Whitehead's knowledge of books was considerable, and he became a man of cultured taste. Though he possessed little originality of thought, he had a musical ear, and found it comparatively easy to produce poetry of a certain order. He even indulged in writing dramas; but Macaulay, in his time, said his works were forgotten. He himself confessed that his verses would not bear criticism, and apologized for them by remarking that his muse would not be "obliged by sack and pension." The fact is he was a metre-making machine.—WRIGHT, J. C., 1896, *The Poets Laureate, p.* 28.

Whitehead was no poet. He simply reflected in a turbid fashion what more original men were saying. His tolerably full statement of the romantic attitude towards nature, with his subsequent assertion of the triumphant good sense of Classicism is, therefore, valuable testimony to the two-fold spirit of the age.—REYNOLDS, MYRA, 1896, *The Treatment of Nature in English Poetry, p.* 130.

At Cambridge, Whitehead had published his first more important poetic efforts, which showed him to have deliberately formed his style as a writer of verse upon Pope, at a time when English poetical literature was at last on the very point of widening its range as to both form and subjects. His epistle "On the Danger of writing in Verse" (1741) is elegant in versification and diction, and modest in tone—two merits which are rarely absent in Whitehead. . . .   In form Whitehead's versatility was remarkable.— WARD, ADOLPHUS WILLIAM, 1900, *Dictionary of National Biography, vol.* LXI, *p.* 107.

John Hall Stevenson
1718–1785

Originally John Hall, was born in Durham, England, in 1718. Was admitted as a fellow-commoner of Jesus College, Cambridge, in 1735, but left the university without a degree about 1738. He owes his chief fame to his connection with Sterne. He published a number of literary and political pamphlets of a rather coarse nature during his lifetime, and his collected works were issued in three volumes in 1795. His most important single work is "Crazy Tales," which was reprinted privately in 1854. —MOULTON, CHARLES WELLS, 1902.

PERSONAL

Hall-Stevenson's sole aim in life was, he repeatedly declared, to amuse himself. He had no liking for field sports, and divided his energies at Skelton between literature and hospitality. He collected a library, largely consisting of facetiæ, and wrote with fatal fluency verse in imitation chiefly of La Fontaine, whose "Contes" attracted him by their obscenity. At the same time he gathered round him a crew of kindred spirits, drawn chiefly from the squirearchy and clergy of Yorkshire, whom he formed into "a club of demoniacks." The members met under his roof at Skelton several times a year, and indulged by night in heavy drinking and obscene jesting. . . . Their orgies seem to have been pale reflections of those practised by Wilkes and his friends at Medmenham. . . .   Hall-Stevenson's relations with Sterne give his career its only genuine interest. Sterne introduces him into both "Tristram Shandy" and "Sentimental Journey" under the name of Eugenius. He represented him as a prudent counsellor, and gratefully acknowledged the readiness with which Hall-Stevenson often put his purse at a friend's service. Hall-Stevenson returned the compliment by flattering references to Sterne as "Cousin Shandy," and often signed himself "Anthony Shandy."—LEE, SIDNEY, 1898, *Dictionary of National Biography, vol.* LIV, *p.* 239.

GENERAL

I have met with no account of this writer's life, nor have I been very anxious to seek for it, as a volume of poems, which bears his name, is disgraced by obscenity.—CAMPBELL, THOMAS, 1819, *Specimens of the British Poets.*

Author of the witty and indecent collection entitled "Crazy Tales," where there is a very humorous description of his ancient residence, under the name of Crazy Castle.—SCOTT, SIR WALTER, 1821, *Laurence Sterne.*

The clever but licentious productions of John Hall Stevenson.—MOORE, THOMAS, 1825, *Memoirs of the Life of Sheridan.*

We see nothing clever even in John Hall Stevenson himself.—CROKER, JOHN WILSON, 1826, *Memoirs of Sheridan, Quarterly Review, vol.* 33, *p.* 565.

Thomas Tyrwhitt
1730–1786

Born, in London, 1730. Educated at Eton. Matriculated Queen's College, Oxford, 9 May 1747; B. A., 1750. Fellow of Mer..n College, 1755; M. A., 1756. Called to Bar at Middle Temple, 1755. Under-Secretary, War Dept., 1756. Clerk of House of Commons. 1762–68. Curator of British Museum, 1784. F. R. S., F. S. A.   Died, 15 Aug., 1786. *Works:* "Epistle of Florio at Oxford" (anon.), 1749; "Translations in Verse," 1752; "Observations and Conjectures on some Passages of Shakespeare" (anon.), 1766; "Dissertatio de Babrio" (anon.), 1776. *Posthumous:* "Conjecturæ in Strabonem" [1783]; "Conjecturæ in Æschylum, Euripidem et Aristophanem," 1822. He *edited:* "Proceedings and Debates in the House of Commons, 1620–21" (2 vols.), 1766; H. Elsynge's "The Manner of holding Parliaments in England," 1768; "Fragmenta duo Plutarchi," 1773; Chaucer's "Canterbury Tales," 1775–78; "Rowley's Poems," 1777; "Aristotelis De Poetica liber," 1794.—SHARP, R. FARQUHARSON, 1897, *A Dictionary of English Authors.*

PERSONAL

He was an honour to his age and country, not more for his extensive erudition, his fine genius, and deep and solid judgment, than for the candour, elegance, and probity of his manners, his unassuming modesty and simplicity of character, and distinguished virtues.—PERCY, THOMAS, 1786, *Nichols's Illustrations of Literature, vol.* VIII, *p.* 222.

The life of the greater editor of Chaucer is hardly better known than that of Chaucer himself. He was born at London in 1730; he was educated at Eton and at Merton College, Oxford; he became master of arts in 1756; he filled one or two political positions; he wrote a few treatises, and edited two or three works; he was made curator of the British Museum, and while holding that office died in Welbeck Street, Cavendish Square, on the fifteenth of August, 1786. This barren record contains nearly all the facts that can be easily gathered in reference to one of the most accomplished and successful students of our literature. . . . One of the greatest scholars England has ever produced.—LOUNSBURY, THOMAS R., 1892, *Studies in Chaucer, vol.* I, *p.* 301.

Charles Burney, D. D., ranked Tyrwhitt among the greatest critics of the last century. Glowing tributes were paid to him by Wyttenbach in his life of Ruhnken (p. 71), by Kraft in the "Epistolæ Selectæ" (p. 313), by Schweighäuser in his edition of Polybius (i. p. xxvi of preface), by Kidd in the "Opuscula Ruhnkeniana" (p. viii, and in pp. lxiii–lxx is a list of his works), and by Bishop Copleston in the "Reply to the Calumnies of the 'Edinburgh Review'" (2nd edit. 1810). Mathias thought that his learning and sagacity were often misapplied ("Pursuits of Literature," 7th edit. pp., 88 and 96).—COURTNEY, W. P., 1899, *Dictionary of National Biography, vol.* LVII, *p.* 446.

EDITION OF CHAUCER
1775–78

I am obliged to you for your intelligence concerning the late edition of Chaucer. I find it true in all particulars. Your alarm however for my property, as you call it, is groundless. As I have not entered my book at Stationers-Hall, I have, it seems, no legal property in it. But if I had, would you advise me to go to law for a property unattended by any profit? A certain philosopher, when his gouty shoes were stolen, only wished that they might fit the thief as well as they fitted himself; and for my own part I shall be contented, if my book shall prove just as lucrative to Mr. Bell, as it has been to me.—TYRWHITT, THOMAS, 1783, *Letter, June* 12; *Gentleman's Magazine, vol.* 53, *p.* 461.

Tyrwhitt, a scholar as well as an antiquary, was an expert philologer: His extensive reading in the lore of our vernacular literature and our national antiquities promptly supplied what could not have entered into his more classical studies; and his sagacity seems to have decided on the various readings of all the manuscripts by piercing into the core of the poet's thoughts.—DISRAELI, ISAAC, 1841, *Chaucer, Amenities of Literature.*

It is truly to be lamented that a text of Chaucer so utterly corrupt as that of Tyrwhitt should continue to be reprinted. Tyrwhitt fell into the error of attempting to *make up* the text of an author, when he was totally ignorant of the grammatical construction of his language, and equally incompetent to appreciate the comparative value of the manuscripts. The consequence is that there is not perhaps a single line in Tyrwhitt's edition of the "Canterbury Tales" which Chaucer could possibly have written. The very worst manuscript in existence contains a better text, because it was at least grammatically correct for the time in which it was written, whereas in Tyrwhitt all grammar is set at defiance.—WRIGHT, THOMAS, 1844, *Anecdote Literaria.*

It has been said with much force that Tyrwhitt, whose services to the study of Chaucer remain uneclipsed by those of any other scholar, would have composed a quite different biography of the poet, had he not been confounded by the formerly (and here and there still) accepted date of Chaucer's birth, the year 1328.—WARD, ADOLPHUS WILLIAM, 1880, *Chaucer (English Men of Letters), p.* 2.

Tyrwhitt's edition of the "Canterbury Tales"—the only work of Chaucer he ever edited—appeared in four volumes in March, 1775. A fifth volume, containing a glossary to all of the poet's writings, followed in 1778. In the preparation of this work Tyrwhitt collated twenty-six manuscripts, to five of which he attached a special value. His duty was not done perfunctorily. No more thorough and conscientious editing had ever before been applied to the elucidation of a great English classic. He neglected nothing that lay in his power to perfect it. Wherever he failed it was not from lack of insight or industry, but from the general diffusion of ignorance about the English language that then prevailed, and from the influence of which he could by no possibility be wholly free. On the other hand, he was in many respects extraordinarily well fitted for the task he assumed, both by mental equipment and special acquirement. His acquaintance with the authors of the Middle Ages, who constituted no small share of Chaucer's reading, was far greater than that of any one who has since endeavored to illustrate the poet's writings; at least what he did alone in this one matter has much surpassed the combined labors of all who have since followed in his footsteps, valuable as have been the services of some. Many of the most loudly vaunted modern discoveries were anticipated a century ago by this quiet scholar. They have usually escaped attention because they were packed away in few sentences, and relegated to a position in some obscure note. A modern investigator would have made out of some of them a pamphlet or a volume. In so doing he would often have been fully justified by the value of what he had brought to light. . . . He had by nature that

judicial cast of mind which rendered it impossible for him to frame assumptions of his own or adopt those of others under the impression either that they were fact or were evidence of fact. The sanest of English poets had the good fortune to meet with the sanest of editors. Tyrwhitt was animated by but one desire, that of ascertaining the truth; not what he would like to have the truth, nor what he had argued himself into believing before hand was the truth. He was never led astray by captivating conjectures. . . . In all doubtful matters, indeed, he was wholly free from that confidence of conviction and positiveness of assertion to which easy omniscience is so generously addicted.—LOUNSBURY, THOMAS R., 1892, *Studies in Chaucer, vol.* I, *pp.* 301, 304.

GENERAL

I have often wondered, how so deeply learned a scholar as Mr. Tyrwhitt ever suffered himself to be enrolled with these note-makers on Shakspeare.—MATHIAS, THOMAS JAMES, 1794–98, *The Pursuits of Literature, Eighth ed., p.* 89, *note.*

Certain it is, that no such attempt has been made since, except in the single and minute, but very successful instance of Aristotle's *Poetics,* which was produced by an auxiliary volunteer, residing in the metropolis, engaged in business, and never secluded from the avocations of society. By not enjoying the leisure, perhaps, he never contracted the indolence or apathy of a monk, but preserved his activity even by the distraction of his faculties. His name stands in the title-page plain Thomas Tyrwhitt—without any decorative adjunct or title of degree—though it would have done honour to the proudest, which the most exalted seat of learning could bestow.—COPLESTON, EDWARD, 1810, *A Reply to the Calumnies of the Edinburgh Review Against Oxford, p.* 34.

One of the most eminent of modern critics.—ALLIBONE, S. AUSTIN, 1871, *A Critical Dictionary of English Literature, vol.* III, *p.* 2493.

Tyrwhitt is the only writer among those that handled the subject [ed. Chatterton] who had a real critical knowledge of the language of the fourteenth and fifteenth centuries, and who, in fact, had on that account a real claim to be heard.— SKEAT, W. W., 1871, *Chatterton's Poems, vol.* II, *p.* ix.

Gilbert Stuart

1742-1786

Historian and reviewer, born at Edinburgh in 1742. He was educated at the grammar school and University of Edinburgh. His principal works are "A View of Society in Europe" (1778), "Observations on the Public Law and Constitutional History of Scotland" (1779), "History of the Establishment of the Reformation in Scotland" (1780), "The History of Scotland from the Establishment of the Reformation till the Death of Queen Mary" (1782). He died, Aug. 13, 1786.—MOULTON, CHARLES WELLS, 1902.

PERSONAL

It is my constant fate to be dissappointed in every thing I attempt: I do not think I ever had a wish that was gratified, and never dreaded an event that did not come. . . . I mortally detest and abhor this place [Edinburgh] and everybody in it. . . . A curse on the country, and all the men, women, and children of it. . . . The publication is too good for the country.—STUART, GILBERT, 1774, *Letter, June 17.*

Henry and his history long survived Stuart and his *critiques;* and Robertson, Blair, and Kaimes, with others he assailed, have all taken their due ranks in public esteem. What niche does Stuart occupy? His historical works possess the show, without the solidity, of research; hardy paradoxes, and an artificial style of momentary brilliancy, are none of the lasting materials of history. This shadow of "Montesquieu," for he conceived him only to be his fit rival, derived the last consolations of life from an obscure corner of a Burton ale-house—there, in rival potations, with two or three other disappointed authors, they regaled themselves on ale they could not always pay for, and recorded their own literary celebrity, which had never taken place. Some time before his death, his asperity was almost softened by melancholy; with a broken spirit, he reviewed himself; a victim to that unrighteous ambition which sought to build up its greatness with the ruins of his fellow-countrymen; prematurely wasting talents which might have been directed to literary eminence. And Gilbert Stuart died as he had lived, a victim to intemperance, physical and moral!—DISRAELI, ISAAC, 1812-13, *Literary Hatred, Calamities of Authors.*

Stuart was known, while engaged on his historical treatises, to have confined himself to his library for several weeks, scarcely ever leaving his house for air and exercise. But these periods of intense labour were always followed by bouts of dissipation lasting for equal periods of time. When in England he often spent whole nights in company with his boon companions at the Peacock in Gray's Inn Lane. These habits destroyed a strong constitution. . . . A writer of great talent and learning his excesses and want of principle ruined his career.—COURTNEY, W. P., 1898, *Dictionary of National Biography, vol.* LV, *p.* 84.

GENERAL

Here the author has made a great, and indeed a splendid, effort to eclipse the reputation of Robertson, whom he both envied and hated. As the one historian considered Mary guilty of some of the foulest crimes laid to her charge, it was almost an obvious consequence that the other should represent her as innocent.—IRVING, DAVID, 1827-42, *Encyclopædia Britannica, Seventh ed., vol.* XX.

A very able ["Antiquity of British Constitution,"] though somewhat impetuous inquirer into the earlier parts of history.—SMYTH, WILLIAM, 1840, *Lectures on Modern History, Lecture* v.

He also published in 1779, 1780, and 1782, three works: one on the "Constitutional History of Scotland," being an attack on Dr. Robertson's first book; another on the "History of the Reformation in Scotland," and the third on the "History of Queen Mary," being also an elaborate attack upon the Principal. The ability and the learning of these works, and their lively and even engaging style, has not saved them from the oblivion to which they were justly consigned by the manifest indications prevailing throughout them all, of splenetic temper, of personal malignity, and of a constant disturbance of the judgment by these vile, unworthy passions.—BROUGHAM, HENRY LORD, 1845-6, *Lives of Men of Letters of the Time of George III.*

All displaying both research and acuteness, but the two last-mentioned ["History of the Establishment of the Reformation in Scotland" and his "History of Scotland from the establishment of the Reformation till the death of Queen Mary"], deformed by the author's violent personal animosity against Robertson, for the purpose of confuting certain of whose statements or views, they were mainly written.—CRAIK, GEORGE L., 1861, *A Compendious History of English Literature and of the English Language, vol.* II, *p.* 359.

Robert Lowth
1710–1787

Robert Lowth (1710–87), born at Winchester, was educated there and at New College, Oxford. In 1741 he became professor of Poetry, in 1750 Archdeacon of Winchester, in 1753 rector of East Woodhay, in 1755 a prebendary of Durham and rector of Sedgefield, in 1765 F. R. S., in 1766 Bishop of St. Davids and of Oxford, and in 1777 of London. He published *De Sacra Poesi Hebræorum* (1753), a Life of William of Wykeham, and a new translation of Isaiah. He was one of the first to treat the Bible poetry as literature.—PATRICK AND GROOME, *eds.*, 1897, *Chambers's Biographical Dictionary, p.* 605.

PERSONAL

For myself, on the contrary, it is well if I can acquit myself of the burden of being responsible for the great advantages which I enjoyed. For, my lord, I was educated in the University of Oxford; I enjoyed all the advantages, both public and private, which that famous seat of learning so largely affords. I spent many happy years in that illustrious society, in a well-regulated course of useful discipline and studies, and in the agreeable and improving commerce of gentlemen and scholars; in a society where emulation without envy, ambition without jealousy, contention without animosity, incited industry and awakened genius; where a liberal pursuit of knowledge, and a generous freedom of thought, was raised, encouraged, and put forward by example, by commendation, and by authority. I breathed the same atmosphere that the Hookers, the Chillingworths, and the Lockes had breathed before. . . . And do you reproach me with my education in this place, and this most respectable body, which I shall always esteem my greatest advantage and my highest honour? —LOWTH, ROBERT, 1765, *Letter to Warburton.*

Lowth is said to have been well and stoutly built, with a florid countenance and animated expression. His conversation was easy and refined, and his manners were courtly. Of a sympathetic disposition, he was more inclined to melancholy than mirth. His temper was hasty but kept under control. His taste was fine, and he was an industrious student. He was an accomplished and elegant scholar, well versed in Hebrew, and with a keen appreciation of the poetic beauty of the Old Testament scriptures. Hebrew was, he believed, the language spoken in Paradise; he studied it critically, and his knowledge of it gained him a European reputation. He wrote both Latin and English verse with some success. In controversy he was a dangerous antagonist, with great power of polished sarcasm which he employed against his opponents personally, as well as against their arguments.—HUNT, WILLIAM, 1893, *Dictionary of National Biography, vol.* XXXIV, *p.* 215.

DE SACRA POESI HEBRÆORUM
1753

Bishop Lowth prepared the way for a more accurate knowledge of this important part of divine revelation [the Prophetical Books] by his admirable "Prelections," and by his amended translations of the prophecies of Isaiah.—WILLIAMS, EDWARD, 1800, *The Christian Preacher.*

It is an elegant and interesting book, though somewhat calculated to lead the mind to admire the poetical beauties of Scripture rather than their spiritual tendency and design. It is not distinguished so much for its philological criticisms as for the felicity of its illustrations. . . . Lowth was himself a poet, and deeply versant in the poetry of the Hebrews, as well as in the poetical writers of Greece and Rome.—ORME, WILLIAM, 1824, *Bibliotheca Biblica.*

Before the appearance of his volume, scarcely any thing had been accomplished in the whole wide range of sacred literature which it occupies. . . . Lowth was fortunate indeed in being the first adventurer to investigate a region so delightful. . . . He has displayed in the execution of his task much sound judgment and research. All the notes he has selected are of sterling value; and those which are the results of his own investigations exhibit originality and learning.—CHEEVER, GEORGE BARRELL, 1830, *Lowth's Hebrew Poetry, North American Review, vol.* 31, *pp.* 366, 367, 375.

If you have not read Bishop Lowth's "Prælections on Hebrew Poetry," let me commend its perusal to you. It opened to me, some years ago, quite a new view of the beauties of the prophetical and poetical part of the Old Testament.— WEBSTER, DANIEL, 1844, *Letter to Mrs. Paige, March* 27; *Private Correspondence, vol.* II, *p.* 186.

In the year 1753 the Clarendon Press at Oxford brought out, in a splendid quarto with all the honours of typography, the series of Lectures which Lowth had delivered during his ten years' occupancy of the chair of poetry in that University. It was not the externals only of the volume of which the University was proud. It was no less remarkable for its matter. It was the first sign of the awakening of Oxford from that torpor under which two generations had now lain, under the besotting influence of Jacobite and high-church politics. The Lectures "De Sacra Poesi Hebræorum" seemed to combine the polish of a past generation, long gone, with the learning of a new period to come. The lore of Michaelis was here dressed not in Latin as classical as, and more vigorous than, that of Addison. Kocher has indeed shown that Lowth's Hebrew skill was not equal to his pretensions; and Parr has pointed out that the professor was capable of writing *poterit* after *ut.* Still the effect of the Lectures was great. The Jacobite University had at last produced a work which might vie in solidity with anything that proceeded from Hanoverian Göttingen, and with the finished style of which Göttingen had nothing to compare. The "classic elegance of Lowth" became a standard phrase, and continued to be so till into the present century; and German Hebraists occupied themselves in refuting the temerity of his numerous emendations of the Hebrew text. —PATTISON, MARK, 1863-89, *Life of*

Bishop Warburton, Essays, ed. Nettleship, vol. II, *p.* 135.

Lowth's lectures on the Sacred Poetry of the Hebrews (1753) encouraged the study of the Old Testament from the purely literary point of view, and opened up anew all the grandeur and imagery of Hebrew poetry. The critical side of his work helped also in forming true ideas on the nature of poetry. His chapter on "Poetic Imagery from the Objects of Nature" must have been especially suggestive in those days.—PHELPS, WILLIAM LYON, 1893, *The Beginnings of the English Romantic Movement, p.* 172.

GENERAL

A sublime and admirably-executed version ["Isaiah"].—HORNE, THOMAS HARTWELL, 1818-39, *A Manual of Biblical Bibliography.*

No former translator ["Isaiah"] has expressed the meaning and spirit of the evangelical prophet so felicitously as Lowth. . . . Lowth is, perhaps, too partial to conjectural criticism, and the version is too highly wrought for common use; but it is a valuable specimen of sacred criticism, and indispensable to the interpretation of Isaiah.—ORME, WILLIAM, 1824, *Bibliotheca Biblica.*

The reflections are sparing ["Life of William of Wykeham"] and the style is languid. Even in antiquarian lore there is a dearth of intelligence; but the subject was not suited to the taste, habits, and learning, of Lowth.—DIBDIN, THOMAS FROGNALL, 1824, *The Library Companion, p.* 523.

He gave to England the first regular grammar of his native tongue [?]. We are somewhat surprised that Murray's grammar, which is but an enlarged copy of Lowth's, should so generally have occupied its place; and that, too, with little acknowledgment to the individual, from whom were derived its plan and most of its materials. Although Lowth's treatise was written so early as the year 1758, yet we doubt whether there is at the present day a single work of equal excellence in the same compass.—CHEEVER, GEORGE BARRELL, 1830, *Lowth's Hebrew Poetry, North American Review, vol.* 31, *p.* 377.

The writings by which Bishop Lowth is most known are, "A Short Introduction to English Grammar," for many years a text-book in the schools and colleges in England and in this country; his "Translation of the Prophet Isaiah," with a large body of valuable notes; and his "Lectures on the Poetry of the Hebrews." The latter is a work which unites a depth of learning to a discriminating criticism and a refined taste, in a very unusual degree; and while it is of inestimable value to the professed Biblical student, it affords equal pleasure and instruction to the general reader.—CLEVELAND, CHARLES D., 1848, *A Compendium of English Literature, p.* 673.

In polished dexterity of argument, tinged, and not more than tinged, with the raillery of one who knows exactly what is due both to himself and his antagonists, this short piece has perhaps never been surpassed in literary warfare. At that period of paper ruffianism, when the courtesies of legitimate warfare were unpractised and unknown, such moderate language, combined with such superiority of demeanour, was wholly new. Even the mere English composition of the "Letter" was an event which opened a new era in writing, and made the public wonder that it could ever have admired the lame sentences and clumsy English of Warburton and his followers.—PATTISON, MARK, 1863–89, *Life of Bishop Warburton, Essays,* ed. Nettleship, *vol.* II, *p.* 139.

Although an excellent critic of poetry, had no creative gift.—PHELPS, WILLIAM LYON, 1893, *The Beginnings of the English Romantic Movement, p.* 72.

Soame Jenyns

1704–1787

Born at London, Jan. 1, 1704: Died there, Dec. 18, 1787. An English miscellaneous writer. In 1722 he entered St. John's College, Cambridge, leaving without a degree in 1725. He published anonymously "The Art of Dancing: a poem" (1727) and a collection of poems (1752). He was returned to Parliament in 1742. In 1757 he published a "Free Enquiry into the Nature and Origin of Evil," and in 1765 "The Objections to the Taxation of our American Colonies by the Legislature of Great Britain briefly considered." His "View of the Internal Evidences of the Christian Religion" was published in 1776.—SMITH, BENJAMIN E., *ed.,* 1894–97, *The Century Cyclopedia of Names, p.* 544.

PERSONAL

Here lies a little ugly nauseous elf,
Who judging only from its wretched self,
Feebly attempted, petulant and vain,
The "Origin of Evil" to explain.
A mighty Genius at this elf displeas'd,
With a strong critick grasp the urchin squeez'd.
For thirty years its coward spleen it kept,
Till in the dust the mighty Genius slept;
Then stunk and fretted in expiring snuff,
And blink'd at Johnson with its last poor puff.
—BOSWELL, JAMES, 1778? *Epitaph Prepared for a Creature not quite Dead Yet.*

Mr. Soame Jenyns, who died a few days ago, had (as Mr. Wm. Gerard Hamilton, who sat for six years at the Board of Trade with him, informed me) no notion of ratiocination, no rectitude of mind; nor could he be made without much labour to comprehend an argument. If however there was anything weak, or defective, or ridiculous in what another said, he always laid hold of it and played upon it with success. He looked at everything with a view to pleasantry alone. This being his grand object, and he being no reasoner, his best friends were at a loss to know whether his book upon Christianity was serious or ironical. He twice endeavoured to speak in the House of Commons, and every one was prepared with a half-grin before he uttered a word; but he failed miserably. He had a most inharmonious voice, and a laugh scarcely human. He laughed all his life at patriotism and public spirit; and supposed all oppression of the people by those in power was merely imaginary.—MALONE, EDMOND, 1787, *Maloniana,* ed. *Prior, p.* 375.

He was a man of great mildness, gentleness, and sweetness of temper, which he manifested to all with whom he had concerns, either in the business of life or its social intercourse. His earnest desire, so far as possible, was never to offend any person; and he made such allowances for those whose disposition differed from his own, that he was rarely offended with others. He was strict in the performance of religious duties in public, and a constant practiser of them in private. His conversation among his equals was most amiable and engaging; for he possessed a well informed mind, accompanied by an uncommon vein of the most lively, spirited, and genuine wit, which always flowed copiously, but was ever tempered by the most perfect kindness. To his inferiors he was most kind and courteous, not only in his expressions and behaviour, but in assisting them in all their wants and distresses, ever considering his poor neighbours in the country as part of his own family; and that he might give them his care and protection, he spent his summers on his estate, saying, "I can do more good in my own parish at that time than in any other situation." It is also no ordinary or misplaced eulogium which we read in the obituary of that parish:— "Decr. 18, 1787, Soame Jenyns, Esq., in the eighty-third year of his age, one of the most amiable of men and one of the truest Christians, in whom was united one of the finest understandings to one of the best hearts."—COLE, CHARLES NELSON, 1790, *ed.*, *The Works of Soame Jenyns, Life.*

He was the man who bore his part in all societies with the most even temper and undisturbed hilarity of all the good companions, whom I ever knew. He came into your house at the very moment you had put upon your card; he dressed himself to do your party honour in all the colours of the jay; his lace indeed had long since lost its lustre, but his coat had faithfully retained its cut since the days when gentlemen wore embroidered velvets with short sleeves, boot cuffs, and buckram shirts. As nature had cast him in the exact mould of an ill-made pair of stiff stays, he followed her so close in the fashion of his coat, that it was doubted if he did not wear them. Because he had a protuberant wen just under his poll, he wore a wig that did not cover above half his head. His eyes were protruded like the eyes of the lobster, who wears them at the end of his feelers, and yet there was room between one of these and his nose for another wen, that added nothing to his beauty; yet I heard this good man very innocently remark,

when Gibbon published his history, that he wondered any body so ugly could write a book. Such was the exterior of a man, who was the charm of the circle, and gave a zest to every company he came into; his pleasantry was of a sort peculiar to himself; it harmonised with everything; it was like the bread to our dinner; you did not perhaps make it the whole, or principal part, of your meal, but it was an admirable and wholesome auxiliary to your other viands. Soame Jenyns told you no long stories, engrossed not much of your attention, and was not angry with those that did; his thoughts were original, and were apt to have a very whimsical affinity to the paradox in them: he wrote verses upon dancing, and prose upon the origin of evil, yet he was a very indifferent metaphysician, and a worse dancer; ill-nature and personality, with the single exception of his lines upon Johnson, I never heard fall from his lips; those lines I have forgotten, though I believe I was the first person to whom he recited them; they were very bad, but he had been told that Johnson ridiculed his metaphysics, and some of us had just then been making extemporary epitaphs upon each other.— CUMBERLAND, RICHARD, 1806, *Memoirs Written by Himself, vol.* I, *p.* 336.

His appearance, dress, manner, and conversation, were very eccentric, and those of his wife, who generally accompanied him on his visits, were no less so. The lady here alluded to was his second wife, who entertained so exalted an idea of her husband's accuracy and propriety of conversation, that she acquired the habit of always repeating the last sentence of any thing he said. Thus when the gentleman observed, we had a disagreeable journey to town, the roads were bad, we were sadly jolted, the lady would immediately repeat the observation "Yes, as Mr. Jenyns says, we were sadly jolted." —BELOE, WILLIAM, 1817, *The Sexagenarian, vol.* II, *p.* 214.

Soame Jenyns appears to have been an amiable country gentleman, rather bigoted in his political tendencies, but not without acuteness and elegance of style. He could write pretty verses after the model of Prior; that he "gave his days and nights to the study of Addison" was inferred from two or three papers contributed to the "World"; and he is said to have been the charm of every social circle which he entered.—STEPHEN, LESLIE, 1876, *History of English Thought in the Eighteenth Century, vol.* I, *p.* 385.

Soame Jenyns once expressed a wonder that anybody so ugly as Gibbon could write a book ; the real marvel would have been if that monumental work, the "Decline and Fall," had been produced by a handsome man. The remark was still stranger, coming, as it did, from one who was himself a writer of books, and of good books too, although he was disfigured by an immense wen under his head, and had eyes protruding like a lobster's, yet allowing room for another wen between them and his nose.—MATHEWS, WILLIAM, 1887, *Men, Places and Things, p.* 242.

Here lies poor Jenyns, whose good taste and wit
In Johnson emphasized the "cough and spit,"
Held cheap the sweetness of that monarch mind,
And found delight in mocking at the rind;
Rude was the Doctor, yet in kindly wise ;
In Jenyns, sooth, the case is otherwise,
For he, whom Jenyns rudely called a "brute"
Is all that makes important this dispute;
Well had it been for Jenyns, if *his* art
Supplied such lack of manners with such heart!
—MAHANY, ROWLAND B., 1891, *On Soame Jenyns, Life, Apr.* 30.

INTERNAL EVIDENCE OF THE CHRISTIAN RELIGION
1776

Soame Jenyns has published a confirmation of the Christian Religion from internal evidence. Pray was not his Origin of Evil a little heterodox? I have dipped a little into this new piece, and thought I saw something like irony, but to be sure I am wrong, for the *Ecclesiastical Court* are quite satisfied.—WALPOLE, HORACE, 1776, *To Rev. William Mason, May* 4; *Letters, ed. Cunningham, vol.* VI, *p.* 335.

Dr. Mayo having asked Johnson's opinion of Soame Jenyns's "View of the Internal Evidence of the Christian Religion," —JOHNSON : "I think it a pretty book; not very theological, indeed ; and there seems to be an affectation of ease and carelessness, as if it were not suitable to his character to be very serious about the matter."—JOHNSON, SAMUEL, 1778, *Life by Boswell, ed. Hill, vol.* III., *p.* 327.

A work of very considerable shrewdness and ingenuity, in which many striking views of Christianity are adduced in support of its heavenly origin.—ORME, WILLIAM, 1824, *Bibliotheca Biblica.*

The last and best work of Mr. Jenyns, was the dissertation on "the Internal Evidence of the Christian Religion." The literary history of this work is not without interest. Originally impressed with deep convictions of the truth of Christianity, its author allowed himself to be seduced into doubts, and finally settled in Deism. Renewed inquiry re-established his mind in a rational faith. He subsequently endeavored to arrange in this treatise the arguments and considerations which had most weight in his case. Immediately on its first appearance, it became popular with all parties, and yet every party in religion and literature expressed the most decided dissatisfaction with some particular portion of the argument, or some special view of the author. Such has continued to be its reception up to the present hour. As a whole, it is admitted to be the best treatise, in its particular range, yet given to the world, but in some respect—differing according to the source whence the censure comes— the disapproval of its individual doctrines and reasonings is almost universal. We have hinted that the circumstances of the author may be pleaded as offering at once an apology and a distinction in favour of his work. They go far also to account for this mixed estimate of its merits. With a more experienced theology, he would have conducted his argument more technically, and without the reckless admissions which offend divines; but, at the same time, he might thus have rendered his treatise less popular with ordinary readers. Let the man of the world, again, who turns away from the evangelical seriousness, and scriptural earnestness of other parts, remember, that these are the sentiments of one who, amid the gay literature and selfish business of the world, thus felt, and thus recommends the power of Christianity.—MEMES, JOHN S., 1849, *ed., Christian Literature : Evidences, Prefatory Memoirs, p.* 18.

GENERAL

I have read the little wicked book about Evil, that settled Mr. Dodsley's conscience in that point, and find nothing in it but absurdity.—GRAY, THOMAS, 1757, *Letter to Rev. William Mason, April* 23; *Works, ed. Gosse, vol.* II, *p.* 310.

When specious sophists with presumption scan
The source of evil hidden still from man;
Revive Arabian tales, and vainly hope
To rival St. John, and his scholar Pope:
Though metaphysicks spread the gloom of night,
By reason's star he guides our aching sight;
The bounds of knowledge marks, and points the way
To pathless wastes, were wilder'd sages stray;
Where, like a farthing link-boy, Jenyns stands,
And the dim torch drops from his feeble hands.
—COURTENAY, JOHN, 1786, *A Poetical Review of the Literary and Moral Character of the Late S. Johnson.*

His poetry does not rise above mediocrity : indeed, it scarcely deserves the name; but the style of his prose is smooth and lucid, his turns of thought are neat and unexpected ; and when he sports in irony, in which he apparently delights to indulge, he is uncommonly playful and airy. . . . Jenyns has evidently a predilection for paradoxical opinions; and why, he might reasonably urge in his defence, should a man address the Public, who has nothing new to offer to it?—GREEN, THOMAS, 1779–1810, *Diary of a Lover of Literature.*

In a literary point of view he obtained a considerable degree of temporary celebrity, occasioned principally by the bold and paradoxical nature of his disquisitions. . . . To any distinguished rank as a poet he has no claim; it may be said, however, that his versification is smooth, and sometimes elegant, though deficient in vigour ; and that several of his smaller productions effervesce with humour and well chosen satire. As a writer in prose, he is entitled to more estimation, whether his matter or manner be considered.—DRAKE, NATHAN, 1810, *Essays, Illustrative of the Rambler, Adventurer, and Idler, vol.* II, *p.* 286.

His poems were published collectively in the volumes of Dodsley, and whoever pleases, may judge of their value. But they excited no great interest when originally written; they excite less at the present period, and will probably glide down the stream of time, till, with the mob of gentlemen who write with ease, they sink into the waters of oblivion.—BELOE, WILLIAM, 1817, *The Sexagenarian, vol.* II, *p.* 215.

We venture to assert, that there are few books in the language, of the same size as the little volume before us, containing more acute and ingenious reasoning, abounding in more lively illustration or more elegant and polished composition. . . . To those who do not possess this little volume we fearlessly recommend them to procure it, and unhesitatingly promise them a rich, though small, store of instruction and entertainment. . . . The first Essay, on the chain of universal being, is chiefly remarkable for the complete and elegant manner in which this mysterious connection is shewn to exist. The reasoning in it is of that sort which carries conviction, by the method of stating and setting forth the bearings of the question. It may, perhaps, be not unfitly called the reasoning of development, which requires nothing more than an unveiling or disclosing of the hidden link of circumstances, and not an invention of arguments, but a mere opening of the eyes to the nature of things.—SOUTHERN, H., 1820, *Soame Jenyns's Disquisitions, Retrospective Review, vol.* 2, *pp.* 291, 292.

Read the works of Soame Jenyns and of Locke. Would not both of these men, for instance, while they retained their integrity, have been seen always on the opposite sides of any question that could affect the constitution and government of a free country.—SMYTH, WILLIAM, 1840, *Lectures on Modern History, Lecture* XXIV.

Some divines rejoiced that Jenyns had discarded his early scepticism and embraced orthodoxy; others questioned his sincerity and disliked his ingenious paradoxes. . . . Jenyns's prose style was regarded by his contemporaries as a model of ease and elegance. It was highly commended by Burke, and Boswell allowed that "Jenyns was possessed of lively talents . . . and could very happily play with a light subject." His metaphysical speculations were not profound, and his political views were short-sighted; but he wrote some agreeable essays (though Charles Lamb entered his works on the list of "books which are no books").—BULLEN, A. H., 1892, *Dictionary of National Biography, vol.* XXIX, *p.* 333.

Charles Wesley

1707-1788

Born at Epworth, Lincs., 29 Dec., 1707. At Westminster School, 1716–26. Matric. Ch. Ch., Oxford, 13 June, 1726; B. A., 1730; M. A., 1733. One of founders of "Methodist" Society at Oxford, 1730. Ordained Deacon and Priest, 1735. To Georgia, as Sec. to Gen. Oglethorpe, 1735. Returned to England, 1736. Active life as religious missionary in England, 1736–56. Married Sarah Gwynne, 8 April, 1749. Lived in Bristol, 1749–71; in London, 1771–88. Died, in London, 29 March, 1788. Buried in Marylebone Parish Churchyard. *Works:* His publications consist almost entirely of hymns; for the most part written with his brother John, and published anonymously, between 1744 and 1782. His "Hymns and Sacred Poems" (2 vols.) were pubd. in 1729; his "Sermons" (posthumously) in 1816; his "Journal" (2 vols.) in 1849. *Life:* by J. Telford, 1886.—SHARP, R. FARQUHARSON, 1897, *A Dictionary of English Authors, p.* 296.

PERSONAL

We find and present CHARLES WESLEY to be a person of ill-fame, a vagabond, and a common disturber of his Majesty's peace, and we pray that he may be transported!—REPORT OF GRAND JURY OF CORK, IRELAND, 1749.

Persuaded two or three young scholars to accompany me, and to observe the method of study prescribed by the statutes of the university. This gained me the harmless nickname of Methodist.—WESLEY, CHARLES, 1785, *Letter to Thomas Bradbury Chandler, Apr.* 28.

Mr. Wesley was of a warm and lively disposition; of great frankness and integrity, and generous and steady in his friendships. His love of simplicity, and utter abhorrence of hypocrisy, and even of affectation in the professors of religion, made him sometimes appear severe on those who assumed a consequence, on account of their experience, or, were pert and forward in talking of themselves and others. These persons were sure of meeting with a reproof from him, which some, perhaps, might call precipitate and imprudent, though it was evidently founded on a knowledge of the human heart. In conversation he was pleasing, instructive, and cheerful; and his observations were often seasoned with wit and humor. His religion was genuine and unaffected. As a minister, he was familiarly acquainted with every part of divinity; and his mind was furnished with an uncommon knowledge of the Scriptures. His discourses from the pulpit were not dry and systematic, but flowed from the present views and feelings of his own mind. He had a remarkable talent of expressing the most important truths with simplicity and

energy; and his discourses were sometimes truly apostolic, forcing conviction on the hearers in spite of the most determined opposition. As a husband, a father, and a friend, his character was amiable. Mrs. Wesley brought him five children, of whom two sons and a daughter are still living. The sons discovered a taste for music, and a fine musical ear, at an early period of infancy, which excited general amazement; and are now justly admired by the best judges for their talents in that pleasing art.—WHITEHEAD, JOHN, 1793, *Life of the Rev. Charles Wesley, vol.* I., *p.* 227.

The character of Mr. Charles Wesley has been beautifully drawn by one of his daughters, in a letter to a friend. In speaking of some remarks made by a certain author in reference to her deceased father, she says: "Mr. Moore seems to think that my father preferred rest to going about doing good. He had a rising family, and considered it his duty to confine his labors to Bristol and London, where he labored most sedulously in ministerial affairs, and judged that it was incumbent upon him to watch over the youth of his sons, especially in a profession which nature so strongly pointed out, but which was peculiarly dangerous. He always said his brother was formed to lead, and he to follow. No one ever rejoiced more in another's superiority, or was more willing to confess it. Mr. Moore's statement of his absence of mind in his younger days is probably correct, as he was born impetuous, and ardent, and sincere. But what a change must have taken place when we were born! For his exactness in his accounts, in his manuscripts, in his bureau, &c., equalled my uncle's. Not

JOHN WESLEY

*Engraving by J. Cochran. From
a Scarce Print published in 1743.*

CHARLES WESLEY

*Engraving by Dick, from an Original
Painting in the Possession of the Family.*

in his dress indeed; for my mother said, if she did not watch over him, he might have put on an old for a new coat, and marched out. Such was his power of abstraction, that he could read and compose with his children in the room, and visitors talking around him. He was nearly forty when he married, and had eight children, of whom we were the youngest. So kind and amiable a character in domestic life can scarcely be imagined. The tenderness he showed in every weakness, and the sympathy in every pain, would fill sheets to describe. But I am not writing his eulogy; only I must add, with so warm a temper, he never was heard to speak an angry word to a servant, or known to strike a child in anger,—and he knew no guile!"—GORRIE, P. DOUGLASS, 1853, *The Lives of Eminent Methodist Ministers, p.* 47.

In studying their biographies, one cannot well avoid the conclusion that though Charles was less aggressive than his brother, and though his fame, in part on this account, has been wholly overshadowed by that of the latter, his was the steadier and better rounded character of the two; and that to him their common success as religious leaders is largely due. Charles was the forerunner in the movement at Oxford, and again, though only by a few days, in his "conversion"; and above all, Charles was the hymn-writer of Methodism, and the influence of the service of song upon the Methodist movement it is almost impossible to exaggerate. Charles Wesley, it is said, wrote more than six thousand hymns; and though in this vast flux of words he sometimes—nay, often—"ran to emptins," there are among his sacred songs some which appeal to people of every faith, and promise to live as long as Divine service is continued. The strong musical bias in his blood is shown in the fact that his son Samuel played on the organ at three, and composed an oratorio at eight.—POTTS, WILLIAM, 1897, *Library of the World's Best Literature, ed. Warner, vol.* XXVII, *p.* 15791.

Tender and sensitive, his family affections were strong; his warmth of temper never led him into angry heats; to his brother he looked up with a loving reverence, undisturbed by their differences. In defensive repartee he was as ready, though not so pungent, as his brother. He had no faculty for government.

Though he had plenty of courage, he was swayed by conflicting feelings, with the result that his half-measures conveyed an impression of timidity.—GORDON, ALEXANDER, 1899, *Dictionary of National Biography, vol.* LX, *p.* 300.

HYMNS

I do not at all desire to discourage your publication. But when you tell me you write, not for the critic, but for the Christian, it occurs to my mind that you might as well write for *both;* or in such a manner that the critic may, by your writing, be moved to turn Christian, rather than the Christian turn critic. I should be wanting, I fear, in speaking freely and friendly upon this matter, if I did not give it as my humble opinion that, before you publish, you might lay before some experienced Christian critics the design which you are upon. But I speak this with all submission. It is very likely that, in these matters, I may want a spur more than you want a bridle.—BYROM, JOHN, 1738, *Letter to Charles Wesley, March* 3.

In these Hymns there is no doggerel, no botches, nothing put in to patch up the rhyme, no feeble expletives. Here is nothing turgid or bombast on the one hand, or low and creeping on the other. Here are no cant expressions, no words without meaning. Here are (allow me to say) but the purity, the strength, and the elegance of the English language, and at the same time the utmost simplicity and plainness, suited to every capacity.—WESLEY, JOHN, 1779, ed., *Collection of Hymns, Preface, Oct.* 20.

I write this, my dear Mary, in a situation that would make your soul freeze with horror; it is on the last projecting point of rock of the "Land's End," upwards of two hundred feet perpendicular above the sea, which is raging and roaring most tremendously, threatening destruction to myself and the narrow point of rock on which I am now sitting. On my right hand is the Bristol Channel, and before me the vast Atlantic Ocean. There is not one inch of land, from the place on which my feet rest, to the vast American continent! This is the place, though probably not so far advanced on the tremendous cliff, where Charles Wesley composed those fine lines,—

"Lo! on a narrow neck of land,
Twixt two unbounded seas I stand," etc.

The point of rock itself is about three feet broad at its termination, and the fearless adventurer will here place his foot, in order to be able to say that he has been on the uttermost inch of land in the British empire westward; and on this spot the foot of your husband now rests, while he writes the following words in the same hymn:

"O God! my inmost soul convert,
And deeply on my thoughtful heart
    Eternal things impress;
Give me to feel their solemn weight,
And tremble on the brink of fate,
    And wake to righteousness."

—CLARKE, ADAM, 1819, *Letter to his Wife, Oct.* 11*th.*

Next to Dr. Watts, as a hymn-writer, undoubtedly stands the Rev. Charles Wesley. He was probably the author of a greater number of compositions of this kind, with less variety of matter or manner, than any other man of genius that can be named.—MONTGOMERY, JAMES, 1825, *The Christian Psalmist, Introduction.*

It is as a writer of devotional poetry, that Mr. Charles Wesley will be permanently remembered, and that his name will live in the annals of the Church. In the composition of hymns adapted to Christian worship, he certainly has no equal in the English language, and is perhaps superior to every other uninspired man that ever lived. It does not appear, that any person beside himself, in any section of the universal Church, has either written so many hymns, or hymns of such surpassing excellence. . . . During the last fifty years few Collections of Hymns, designed for the use of evangelical congregations, whether belonging to the Established Church, or to the Dissenting bodies, have been made, without a considerable number of his compositions, which are admired in proportion as the people are spiritually-minded. His hymns are, therefore, extensively used in secret devotion, in family-worship, and in public religious assemblies. Every Sabbath day, myriads of voices are lifted up, and utter, in the hallowed strains which he has supplied, the feelings of penitence, of faith, of grateful love, and joyous hope, with which the Holy Ghost, the Lord and Giver of life, has inspired them; and are thus in a course of training for the more perfect worship of heaven. . . . As long as

the language in which they are written is understood, and enlightened piety is cherished, the hymns of this venerable man will be used as a handmaid to devotion. —JACKSON, THOMAS, 1841, *Life of Charles Wesley.*

Charles and John Wesley seemed to fulfill toward their great family of disciples the offices commonly assigned to Woman and Man. Charles had a narrower, tamer, less reasoning mind, but great sweetness, tenderness, facility and lyric flow. "When successful in effecting the spiritual good of the most abject, his feelings rose to rapture." Soft pity fired his heart, and none seemed so near to him as the felon and the malefactor, because for none else was so much to be done. His habitual flow of sacred verse was like the course of a full fed stream.—OSSOLI, MARGARET FULLER, 1850?-59, *Papers on Literature and Art, ed. Fuller, p.* 350.

No hymn-writer is more *intellectual*: none puts more doctrine, thought, solid mental pabulum, into his poems. And certainly none is more awakening and edifying; few others, in fact, approach him in native moral earnestness, force, fire; and none possesses a higher, purer, more consistent, uniform, and positive spirituality. How and why then does it happen, all this being so, that his writings are not more largely known, honored, and used? . . . It has been considered a difficult point to decide which is entitled to stand first among hymn-writers, Charles Wesley or Dr. Watts. The difficulty lies simply here, that Dr. Watts was merely a hymn-writer, and could and did, most naturally, put all his powers within the proper limits of a song suited to public worship. The only question to ask relative to anything of his is, is it good enough? Whereas twenty reasons may unfit Wesley's poems for that use. If a piece of the Doctor's is unfit to sing, it is probably unfit to read: not so with the other; for Wesley was a poet in a larger sense. Their relative claims *as poets* will soon be settled, by the good taste of competent judges, whenever Wesley's poetry becomes sufficiently known. Dr. Watts's confession that his rival's "Wrestling Jacob" was worth all his own effusions, proves nothing but the modesty and generosity of the speaker; but there are other grounds for believing that Wesley excelled him in originality, variety, intensity, and elevation. Dr. Watts has been appreciated within the church at large; Charles Wesley has not. Let him not be judged further than as he is known. It is an easy task to compare our poet with the other more eminent hymnists. Doddridge and Steele are diluted reproductions of Dr. Watts. Montgomery, a professed and lifelong poet, is inferior to Wesley in all the qualities mentioned above, and in no respect above him in propriety, harmony, and grace of style. Heber, the most elegant and mellifluous of sacred poets, is not more polished and fluent than his Methodist predecessor; nor has he anything of his solidity, strength, and fire. Cowper is the greatest name in the hymn books; but Cowper's best poems, which are very few, are but equal, not superior, to Wesley's best, which are very many. Toplady approaches most nearly to the Methodist poet; but Toplady borrowed his inspiration from Wesley, and reproduced his style; and it is the Calvinist's highest praise that his finest pieces are undistinguishable from those of his Arminian neighbor. No other names in British sacred lyric poetry can be mentioned with that of Charles Wesley; and when it is remembered that all these counted their poems by dozens or hundreds, while he by thousands; and that *his* thousands were in power, in elegance, in devotional and literary value above *their* few, we call him, yet more confidently, great among poets, and prince of English hymnists.—BIRD, FREDERIC M., 1864, *Charles Wesley and Methodist Hymns, The Bibliotheca Sacra, vol.* 21, *pp.* 311, 317.

In Charles Wesley's verses we trace the influence of his careful classical training, though this is less manifest than we might have expected. . . . Neither Wesley nor Watts has left any one great poem. Wesley will, perhaps, be judged to have best maintained his claim to the name of poet, but the question of which is the better hymn-writer must still, we think, be left undecided. Even the greatest admirers of Charles Wesley admit that Watts excels him in the sweeter flow of his numbers, and in those of his hymns which are designed to administer comfort to the afflicted.—MILLER, JOSIAH, 1866–69, *Singers and Songs of the Church, pp.* 187, 188.

I do not say that many of these songs possess much literary merit, but many of them are real lyrics; they have that essential element, song, in them. The following, ["Wrestling Jacob",] however, is a very fine poem. That certain expressions in it may not seem offensive, it is necessary to keep the allegory of Jacob and the Angel in full view—even better in view, perhaps, than the writer does himself.—MACDONALD, GEORGE, 1868, *England's Antiphon, p.* 297.

We love and honor Charles Wesley, not only as a hymn writer, but as a man and a preacher. He has made the church and the world forever his debtor. It is doubtful indeed whether the Methodist church could have been established, it certainly could not have grown and flourished as it has without his hymns. The author of "Jesus, lover of my soul," "O, for a thousand tongues to sing," "A charge to keep I have," and others of this character, need have no fear of being eclipsed; nor should his friends and admirers betray any want of confidence in the justness of the claims they make in his behalf, by being over-sensitive at honors paid at another shrine.—ROBINSON, R. T., 1868, *Dr. Watts's Hymns, Hours at Home, vol.* 7, *p.* 519.

Charles Wesley, with higher poetical gifts than his brother, produced several of the finest hymns known to the language. His "Jesus, lover of my soul," has no equal in modern, perhaps in ancient, sacred song; and the poet has expressed in tuneful numbers the last aspiration of all undoubting faith.—LAWRENCE, EUGENE, 1872, *John Wesley and his Times, Harper's Magazine, vol.* 45, *p.* 119.

Charles Wesley, a Christ-Church student, came to add sweetness to this sudden and startling light. He was the "sweet singer" of the movement. His hymns expressed the fiery conviction of its converts in lines so chaste and beautiful that its more extravagant features disappeared. The wild throes of hysteric enthusiasm passed into a passion for hymn-singing, and a new musical impulse was aroused in the people which gradually changed the face of public devotion throughout England.—GREEN, JOHN RICHARD, 1874, *A Short History of the English People, p.* 708.

What John Wesley said of Charles

Wesley's Hymns on the Nativity might well have been extended to many dozens. "Omit one or two of them and I will thank you. They are namby-pambical." But Charles nevertheless had within him a poetic fervour, perhaps a scholar-like polish, which his brother wanted. These gifts showed themselves in the closer tenacity with which he clung to the Church of his fathers, and also gave to his hymns a literary character which redeems many of them from the pedestrian and argumentative style which disfigures so large a part of his own and his brother's poems. Secondly, there is a redeeming quality in the subjects themselves round which hymns have clustered: although it is true that polemics and over-strained metaphors and sounding words are dangerous pitfalls, yet when a genuine religious soul strikes on one of the greater themes of religion, either touching the simpler emotions of the human heart or the more unquestionable doctrines of Christianity, is struck a spark which not unfrequently rises into true and lasting poetry.—STANLEY, ARTHUR PENRHYN, 1880, *English Poets, ed. Ward, vol.* III, *p.* 258.

It is as a hymn writer that the name of Charles Wesley will live, and live for long. It is said that he composed altogether above six thousand hymns. He was writing and publishing them almost to the day of his death. They are of all kinds, and for all occasions. He contributed the great majority of the hymns in the Wesleyan *Collection.* From the year 1741 onwards, he published very many volumes of hymns. Some are of remarkable excellence, and are justly popular with nearly all bodies of Christians. It is said that some were written on cards, as he rode on horseback. At times, he would hasten home, and rush for pen and ink, that he might put down the words which were burning within him.—PRESCOTT, J. E., 1883, *Christian Hymns and Hymn Writers, p.* 122.

Among our English hymnists, the Wesleys—Charles and John—shine as twin stars, and stars also of the first magnitude. . . . Charles composed the multitude of beautiful hymns that bear the name of Wesley. He at least equalled Watts, in the average excellence of his hymns; in these respects, he stands foremost among the priesthood of Christian minstrelsy.—SAUNDERS, FREDERICK, 1885, *Evenings with the Sacred Poets, pp.* 309, 310.

It was Charles who sang the doctrines of the Methodists into the hearts of believers—and his evangelical fervor is such that he has made all Christendom his parish in a grander sense even than his administrative brother, John.—DUFFIELD, SAMUEL WILLOUGHBY, 1886, *English Hymns, p.* 350.

"Jesu, Lover of my Soul." This is Charles Wesley's masterpiece. "I would rather have written this hymn," says Henry Ward Beecher, "than to have the fame of all the kings that ever sat on the earth. . . . That hymn will go on singing until the last trump brings forth the angel-band; and then, I think, it will mount up on some lip to the very presence of God." . . . Round this hymn are gathering the delightful traditions which convert the driest facts into fascinating fairy tales. There is no end to the stories which good Methodists will tell you as to how this hymn has helped poor mortals in the hour and article of death. Shipwrecked captains read it before they perish in the deep. A mother and child lashed upon a spar float down the Channel, the poor woman lifts her feeble voice singing this hymn, and she is rescued. Passengers on board a steamer in the heart of a thunderstorm allay panic and prepare for death amid blinding sheets of flame and bursts of thunder by raising the familiar tune. Dr. Lyman Beecher dies listening to the first two lines as they were read to him by his wife. It is, they say, the finest heart hymn in the English language. As befits a poem so freely incrusted with traditions, it has a suitable legendary origin. It is said that "Charles Wesley was sitting at his desk when a bird pursued by a hawk flew into the open window. The baffled hawk did not dare to follow, and the poet took his pen and wrote this immortal song."—STEAD, WILLIAM T., 1897, *Hymns That Have Helped, pp.* 151, 153.

Whatever subject disturbed the public mind, his prolific muse took up, and a hymn or a poem was the result. In 1749 a collection of hymns and sacred poems in two volumes was published, with the name of Charles Wesley alone as the author. Many thousand singing marvelously fervent descriptions of religious experience in every stage from conviction to the highest attainments of Christian life—the whole sustained by a framework of doctrine rigorously clear and logical in definition, expressed in vigorous English—produced an effect hardly second to that of the preaching. It was alike instructive and inspiring, afforded the materials for maintaining services in the absence of preachers, and attracted many to the meetings who would never have been drawn to hear any minister, however renowned.—BUCKLEY, JAMES M., 1898, *A History of Methodism in the United States, vol. I, p.* 105.

Among the many services rendered by Charles Wesley to the cause of religion, his work as a hymn-writer stands preeminent. Exercising an hereditary gift, he had early written verses both in Latin and English, but the opening of the vein of his spiritual genius was a consequence of the inward crisis of Whit-Sunday, 1738. Two days later his hymn upon his conversion was written. He doubted at first whether he had done right in even showing it to a friend. The first collection of hymns issued by John Wesley (1737) contains nothing by Charles. From 1739 to 1746, the brothers issued eight collections in their joint names. Some difficulty has been felt in assigning to each his respective compositions. To John are usually given all translations from German originals, as it is doubtful whether Charles could read that language; and if this is not conclusive (as the originals might have been interpreted for him), a strong argument may be found in his constant inability to write on subjects proposed to him, and not spontaneously suggested by his own mind. All original hymns, not expressly claimed by John in his journals and other writings, are usually given to Charles. But it must be remembered that these were edited by John, who adapted his brother's pieces for public use, both by omission and by combination. Charles Wesley's untouched work is to be seen in publications issued in his sole name, and in posthumous prints from his manuscript.—GORDON, ALEXANDER, 1899, *Dictionary of National Biography, vol.* LX, *p.* 301.

The poet of the movement, the "sweet singer" of Methodism, was, there is no gainsaying, Charles Wesley. John might be—he was—a competent translator, a correct and elegant verse-writer. But Charles was more; he had flaming in him something of the true poetic fire. Himself familiar with the varied phases of Methodist experience he could describe with equal truth and equal sympathy the feelings of a weeping sinner and a rejoicing saint; and all the intermediate emotions were to him as A, B, C. Methodism, John Wesley defined as religion of the heart. Charles gave to the Methodist people a transfused and transfigured theology, theology rememberable as verse. Not didactic verse, though didaxis was in it, but verse that was passionate—perhaps too passionate. . . . If another criticism may be permitted, it is that many of Charles Wesley's hymns are better adapted for private devotional study than for public worship. They are concerned with the fears and the failings, the hopes and the aspirations of the individual. No doubt, congregations are made up of individuals, but the individuals that make up congregations are not Wesleys, and it is undesirable that they should be asked to express, as *I* or *me*, what they probably do not feel and may not sympathise with.—SNELL, F. J., 1900, *Wesley and Methodism, pp.* 224, 228.

GENERAL

As a hymnist, this author is widely famous, though either beyond or beneath his merit, according to sectarian accidents of creed and name; but as a *poet*, he is scarce heard of or suspected; for the critical world is yet but half-persuaded that a hymn can be poetry. To remedy this injustice, which lies alike on the fame of him departed, and on the living that are robbed of many a gem of sacred song, is in some degree attempted in this book: for it is believed that, whatever eccentricities of temper, habit, or opinion may have marred the Methodist preacher's verses, there is in them the genuine fire, and that in such portion as has been bestowed on few that used the English tongue. . . . We should take the Methodist poet, as it is attempted to present him here: fairly, yet at his best; with appreciation, but discriminating; not allowing sympathy and admiration to run into blind worship, nor difference of creed to hide from us his merits and his uses. There does not exist in America or England that Christian Church, sect, or man, that can afford to forget his obligations to Charles Wesley; and we can acknowledge those obligations best by increasing them—BIRD, FREDERIC M., 1866, *Charles Wesley seen in his Finer and Less Familiar Poems*, pp. iii, vi.

William Julius Mickle

1735–1788

Born in Langholm manse, and educated at Edinburgh High School, failed as a brewer, and turned author in London. In 1765 he published a poem, "The Concubine" (or "Syr Martyn"), and in 1771–75 his version rather than translation of the "Lusiad" of Camoens. In 1779 he went to Lisbon as secretary to Commodore Johnstone, but his last years were spent in London. His ballad of "Cumnor Hall" (which suggested "Kenilworth" to Scott) is poor stuff, but "There's nae luck about the house" is assured of immortality. See Life by Sim prefixed to Mickle's Poems (1806). —PATRICK AND GROOME, eds., 1897, *Chambers's Biographical Dictionary*, p. 655.

PERSONAL

Mickle was a man of genius, who had ventured upon the chance of living by his literary labours,—an experiment always perilous, generally injurious, and often fatal, in the worst acceptation of the word. Mickle, however, did not overrate the powers which he was conscious of possessing, and knew that he could rely upon himself for their due exertion; and he had sufficient worldly prudence to look out for a subject which was likely to obtain notice and patronage. That he was actuated by this motive in fixing upon the Lusiad, appears evidently by the manner in which his translation is executed, and the matter with which it is accompanied. In saying this, no reproach is intended to a man whom we admire and respect; whose memory is without a spot, and whose name will live among the English poets.—SOUTHEY, ROBERT, 1822, *Life and Writings of Camoens*, Quarterly Review, vol. 27, p. 29.

THE MARINER'S WIFE

Mickle assisted in Evans's "Collection of Old Ballads"—in which "Cumnor Hall" and other pieces of his first appeared; and though in this style of composition he did not copy the direct simplicity and unsophisticated ardour of the real old ballads, he had much of their tenderness and pathos. A still stronger proof of this is afforded by a Scottish song, "The Mariner's Wife," but better known as "There's nae Luck about the House," which was claimed by a poor school-mistress, named Jean Adams, who died in the town's Hospital, Glasgow, in 1765. It is probable that Jean Adams had written some song

with the same burthen ("There's nae luck about the house"), but the popular lyric referred to seems to have been the composition of Mickle. An imperfect, altered, and corrected copy was found among his manuscripts after his death; and his widow being applied to, confirmed the external evidence in his favour, by an express declaration that her husband had said the song was his own, and that he had explained to her the Scottish words. It is the fairest flower in his poetical chaplet. The delineation of humble matrimonial happiness and affection which the song presents, is almost unequalled.— CHAMBERS, ROBERT, 1876, *Cyclopædia of English Literature*, ed. Carruthers.

Mickle's ballad of "Cumnor Hall," which suggested to Scott the groundwork of his romance of "Kenilworth," is a tame production compared with the charming little poem of "The Mariner's Wife," in regard to which much doubt has been expressed whether Mickle was really its author. It first appeared as a broad-sheet, sold in the streets of Edinburgh. Mickle did not include it in an edition of his poems, published by himself; but Allan Cunningham claims it for him on the ground that a copy of the poem, with alterations marking the text as in process of formation, was found among Mickle's papers, and in his handwriting; also, that his widow declared that he said the song was his. Beattie added a stanza, which mars its flow, and is omitted in our version. The poem was claimed by Jean Adams, a poor school-mistress, who died in 1765. Chambers thinks that it must, on the whole, be credited to Mickle.

Dean Trench does not feel at liberty to disturb the ascription of this "exquisite domestic lyric" to Mickle. Burns, not too strongly, characterized it as "one of the most beautiful songs in the Scotch or any other language."—SARGENT, EPES, 1880–81, *Harper's Cyclopædia of British and American Poetry, p.* 217.

To Mickle has been attributed the Scottish song "There's na'e luck about the hoose," which of itself is sufficient to establish a poetical reputation. Internal evidence is rather against the likelihood of his authorship and in favour of that of Jean Adams (1710–1765), but there is no definite external evidence, and the doubt on the subject cannot be resolved.— BAYNE, THOMAS, 1894, *Dictionary of National Biography, vol.* XXXVII, *p.* 337.

One cannot be quite sure that Mickle wrote this delightful poem, but I like to believe he did, rather than to keep his name out of the collection altogether, for to my knowledge he has achieved nothing else to come near it.—CRAWFURD, OSWALD, 1896, *ed., Lyrical Verse from Elizabeth to Victoria, p.* 432, *note.*

LUSIAD
1775

Nor let the critic, if he finds the meaning of Camoens in some instances altered, imagine that he has found a blunder. It was not to gratify the dull few, whose greatest pleasure in reading a translation is to see what the author exactly says,— it was to give a poem that might live in the English language,—which was the ambition of the translator.—MICKLE, WILLIAM JULIUS, 1775, *Note to the Lusiad.*

A man of genius, and of great poetical powers. He translated the "Lusiad" of Camoens in a free paraphrastick manner, but with the spirit of an original poet. I never could account for the neglect of so very poetical a work.—MATHIAS, THOMAS JAMES, 1794–98, *The Pursuits of Literature, Eighth ed., p.* 55.

No poet perhaps has ever been so greatly indebted to a Translator as Camöens, whose "Lusiad," in the very elegant and spirited version of Mr. Mickle, has perfectly the air of an English original; its defects are concealed or mitigated, while its beauties catch double lustre from the British dress.—DRAKE, NATHAN, 1798–1820, *Literary Hours, vol.* II, *No.* 29, *p.* 122.

Mickle's version of the Lusiad offers an affecting instance of the melancholy fears which often accompany the progress of works of magnitude, undertaken by men of genius. Five years he had buried himself in a farmhouse, devoted to the solitary labour; and he closes his preface with the fragment of a poem, whose stanzas have perpetuated all the tremblings and the emotions, whose unhappy influence the author had experienced through the long work. Thus pathetically he addresses the Muse:—

—Well thy meed repays thy worthless toil;
Upon thy houseless head pale want descends
In bitter shower; and taunting scorn still rends
And wakes thee trembling from thy golden dream:
In vetchy bed, or loathly dungeon ends
Thy idled life—

And when, at length, the great and anxious labour was completed, the author was still more unhappy than under the former influence of his foreboding terrors. The work is dedicated to the Duke of Buccleugh. Whether his Grace had been prejudiced against the poetical labour by Adam Smith, who had as little comprehension of the nature of poetry as becomes a political economist, or from whatever cause, after possessing it for six weeks the Duke had never condescended to open the volume.—DISRAELI, ISAAC, 1812–13, *The Miseries of Successful Authors, Calamities of Authors.*

The translation of the "Lusiad" is that by which he is best known. In this, as in his original poems, the expression is sometimes very faulty; but he is never flat or insipid. In the numbers, there is much sweetness and freedom: and though they have somewhat of the masculine melody of Dryden, yet they have something also that is peculiarly his own. He has in a few instances enriched the language of poetry by combinations unborrowed from any of his predecessors. It is doubtful whether as much can be said for Pope's translation of Homer.—CARY, HENRY FRANCIS, 1821–24–45, *Lives of the English Poets, p.* 285.

In the execution of his task, treated Camoens with as little ceremony as the French used towards the Italian pictures which they re-painted in the Louvre; but with this difference, that the original was not destroyed by the process, and that he undertook nothing more than he was well qualified to perform. Some things he kept out of sight, others he softened, others he elevated and enriched. Wherever he thought any thing could be inserted with advantage, he inserted it.—SOUTHEY, ROBERT, 1822, *Life and Writings of Camoens; Quarterly Review, vol.* 27, *p.* 31.

The "Lusiad" is best known in England by the translation of Mickle, who has been thought to have done something more than justice to his author, both by the unmeasured eulogies he bestows upon him, and by the more substantial service of excelling the original in his unfaithful delineation. The style of Mickle is certainly more poetical, according to our standard, than that of Camoens; that is, more figurative and emphatic: but it seems to me replenished with common-place phrases, and is wanting in the facility and sweetness of the original; in which it is well known that he has interpolated a great deal without a pretence.—HALLAM, HENRY, 1837–39, *Introduction to the Literature of Europe, pt.* ii, *ch.* v, *par.* 42.

That poem, in Mickle's translation, is as little like the work of Camoens as Pope's "Iliad" is like the "Iliad" of Homer. Mickle has made it declamatory where Camoens is simple, and all the rapidity of the narrative is lost in the diffuse verses of the translator.—BRYANT, WILLIAM CULLEN, 1869, *Orations and Addresses, p.* 185.

GENERAL

Mickle's story of Syr Martyn is the most pleasing of his original pieces. The object of the narrative is to exhibit the degrading effects of concubinage, in the history of an amiable man, who is reduced to despondency and sottishness, under the domination of a beldam and a slattern. The defect of the moral is, that the same evils might have happened to Syr Martyn in a state of matrimony. The simplicity of the tale is also, unhappily, overlaid by a weight of allegory and of obsolete phraseology, which it has not importance to sustain. Such a style, applied to the history of a man and his housekeeper, is like building a diminutive dwelling in all the pomp of Gothic architecture.—CAMPBELL, THOMAS, 1819, *Specimens of the British Poets.*

Mickle was a man of strong natural

powers, which he had not always properly under controul. When he is satisfied to describe with little apparent effort what he has himself felt or conceived, as in his ballads and songs, he is at times eminently happy. He has generally erred on the side of the too much, rather than of the too little. His defect is not so much want of genius as of taste. His thoughts were forcible and vivid; but the words in which he has clothed them, are sometimes illchosen, and sometimes awkardly disposed. He degenerates occasionally into mere turgidness and verbosity. . . . When his stanza forced him to lop off his vain superfluity of words, that the sense might be brought within a narrow compass, he succeeded better.—CARY, HENRY FRANCIS, 1821–24–45, *Lives of the English Poets, pp.* 281, 282.

A schoolfellow, who was now, like himself, a writer's apprentice, recollects the eagerness with which he thus made himself master of Evans's Ballads, shortly after their publication; and another of them, already often referred to, remembers, in particular, his rapture with Mickle's "Cumnor Hall," which first appeared in that collection. "After the labours of the day were over," says Mr. Irving, "we often walked in *the Meadows*" —(a large field intersected by formal alleys of old trees, adjoining George's Square)—"especially in the moonlight nights; and he seemed never weary of repeating the first stanza." . . . I have thought it worth while to preserve these reminiscences of his companions at the time, though he has himself stated the circumstance in his Preface to "Kenilworth." "There is a period in youth," he there says, "when the mere power of numbers has a more strong effect on ear and imagination than in after life. At this season of immature taste, the author was greatly delighted with the poems of Mickle and Langhorne. The first stanza of 'Cumnor Hall' especially had a peculiar enchantment for his youthful ear—the force of which is not yet (1829) entirely spent." Thus that favourite elegy, after having dwelt on his memory and imagination for forty years, suggested the subject of one of his noblest romances.—LOCKHART, JOHN GIBSON, 1836, *Life of Sir Walter Scott, ch.* v.

Mickle would have excelled in the

Scottish dialect, and in portraying Scottish life, had he known his own strength, and trusted to the impulses of his heart, instead of his ambition.—WILSON, JAMES GRANT, 1876, *The Poets and Poetry of Scotland, vol.* I, *p.* 250.

Mickle had not power to produce any long and sustained work, though he could, on the rare occasions when he designed to be simple and natural, write a few graceful and pleasing verses. His odes of the Pindaric type have gone the way of nearly all such odes. Some of his songs have fared and have deserved to fare no better. If indeed we could credit him with that exquisite one, "There's nae luck about the house," it must be admitted that he for once rose high; but if there is any force in internal evidence, scepticism on that point is justified. He has nothing else approaching it in merit, nothing at all resembling it in style.—WALKER, HUGH, 1893, *Three Centuries of Scottish Literature, vol.* II, *p.* 119.

John Logan
1748–1788

John Logan, 1748–1788, a native of Fala, county of Edinburgh, minister of South Leith, 1773, displeased his parishoners by writing for the stage and by his intemperance, and removed to London in 1786, where he became a writer for the "English Review." It is asserted that he reformed his habits before his death. 1. "Michael Bruce's Poems," 1770. Several pieces in this collection are by Logan and others, and some of Bruce's are omitted. . . . 2. "Elements of the Philosophy of History," Part I, 1781. 3. "Essay on the Manners of Asia," 1781. 4. "Poems," 1781–82. 5. "Runnimede; a Tragedy," 1783. Founded on the history of Magna Charta. 6. "Review of the Principal Charges against Warren Hastings," 1788. 7. "A View of Ancient History," &c., 1788. 8. "Sermons," 1790–91. Logan was a contributor to, and a reviser of, the Psalmody of the Church of Scotland, of which the collection of translations and paraphrases was first published in 1781.—ALLIBONE, S. AUSTIN, 1854–58, *A Critical Dictionary of English Literature, vol.* I, *p.* 1122.

PERSONAL

Mr. Logan, a clergyman of uncommon learning, taste, and ingenuity, but who cannot easily submit to the puritanical spirit of this country, quits his charge and proposes to settle in London, where he will probably exercise what may be called the trade of a man of letters. He has published a few poems, of which several have great merit, and which are probably not unknown to you. He has likewise published a tragedy, which I cannot say I admire in the least. He has another in manuscript, founded and almost translated from a French drama, which is much better. But the best of all his works which I have seen are some lectures upon universal history, which were read here some years ago, but which, notwithstanding they were approved and even admired by some of the best and most impartial judges, were run down by the prevalence of a hostile literary faction, to the leaders of which he had imprudently given some personal offence. Give me leave to recommend him most earnestly to your countenance and protection. — SMITH, ADAM, 1785, *Letter to Andrew Strahan.*

From one of his executors, Mr. Donald Grant, who wrote the life prefixed to his poems, I heard of the state of his numerous MSS.; the scattered, yet warm embers of the unhappy bard. Several tragedies, and one on Mary Queen of Scots, abounding with all that domestic tenderness and poetic sensibility which formed the soft and natural feature of his muse; these, with minor poems, thirty lectures on the Roman History, and portions of a periodical paper, were the wrecks of genius! He resided here, little known out of a very private circle, and perished in his fortieth year, not of penury, but of a broken heart. Such noble and well-founded expectations of fortune and fame, all the plans of literary ambition overturned: His genius, with all its delicacy, its spirit, and its elegance, became a prey to that melancholy which constituted so large a portion of it.—DISRAELI, ISAAC, 1812–13, *Literary Scotchmen, Calamities of Authors.*

His connection with the stage was deemed improper in a clergyman. His literary pursuits interfered with his pastoral diligence; and, what was worse, he was constitutionally subject to fits of depression, from which he took refuge in inebriety. Whatever his irregularities were (for they have been differently described), he was obliged to compound for them, by resigning his flock, and retiring upon a small annuity. He came to London, where his principal literary employments were, furnishing articles for the English Review, and writing in vindication of Warren Hastings. He died at the age of forty, at his lodgings, in Marlborough-street. His Sermons, which were published two years after his death, have obtained considerable popularity.—CAMPBELL, THOMAS, 1819, *Specimens of the British Poets.*

In the course of my literary researches I have been brought pretty near to Logan, by his own letters, by letters of contemporaries, by anecdotes, and other data, and know not that a more *false* life has ever been lived—the worst of all falsity, moreover, seeing it is a serving the devil while wearing Christ's livery. It may be needful, some day, to reveal all, though personally I should prefer silence, save only where Bruce's claims come in for defence.—GROSART, ALEXANDER B., 1865, ed., *Works of Michael Bruce*, p. 108, *note.*

Whatever may have been the amount of Logan's weaknesses or errors, they were of a kind, and in a degree, not unusual in the history of the sons of genius. Admitting that he was the victim of intemperance, even to a greater extent than what traditional stories of the usual cast have portrayed him, and admitting the lowering moral tendency of such a condition, yet to make it the ground of a charge of dishonourable conduct is not the part of an unbiased judge. We have already, in the life of his fellow-student Michael Bruce, referred to the charges brought against Logan's character; and the kind of proceeding which we have condemned is unsparingly used to give—what we must admit to have been a most unfortunate and serious error of judgment on his part —a dishonourable character. But like most intemperate charges, it overreaches itself; for there is no evidence of Logan's having contracted those habits for years after his being entrusted with Bruce's manuscripts. . . . To deprive Logan of the credit of what he himself claimed as his own, on such evidence as has been produced on behalf of Bruce, would be yielding to clamour that which only can be given up on the most convincing proofs of Logan's fraud.—ROSS, J., 1884, *The Book of Scottish Poems*, pp. 586, 588.

Logan was one of the most popular preachers of the time; his historical productions evince wide knowledge, comprehensive views, and a philosophic mind; his poetical versions of scripture are singularly felicitious, and the "Ode to the Cuckoo" was pronounced by Edmund Burke "the most beautiful lyric in our language." In his better days he won the friendship and esteem of some of the most eminent clergymen of the time, and when he disappointed their hopes they made allowance for the temperament he had inherited.—SPROTT, G. W., 1893, *Dictionary of National Biography*, vol. XXXIV, p. 85.

GENERAL

This elegant philosopher has impressed on all his works the seal of genius; and his posthumous compositions became even popular; he who had with difficulty escaped excommunication by Presbyters, left the world after his death two volumes of sermons, which breathe all that piety, morality, and eloquence admire. His unrevised lectures, published under the name of a person, one Rutherford, who had purchased the MS., were given to the world in "A View of Ancient History." But one highly-finished composition he had himself published; it is a philosophical review of Despotism: Had the name of Gibbon been affixed to the title-page, its authenticity had not been suspected.— DISRAELI, ISAAC, 1812–13, *Literary Scotchmen, Calamities of Authors.*

Sweet rung the harp to Logan's hand. —HOGG, JAMES, 1813, *The Queen's Wake, Conclusion.*

A tithe of Logan's talents would make ten Lord Woodhouselees.—SOUTHEY, ROBERT, 1814, *Chalmers's English Poets, Quarterly Review*, vol. 11, p. 501.

He has left little behind him; but that little (excepting the hymn taken from the Bible) is his own. It is purely the offspring of soft affections, tuning his verse to a correspondent softness. Neither the thoughts nor the expressions are borrowed from others; or prompted by study and reflection. But in saying this, all is said. He has none of the higher faculties of the poet. His only gem is the "Ode to the

Cuckoo," which procured him the honour of a visit from Burke. . . . His sermons are more poetical than his poems.— CARY, HENRY FRANCIS, 1823, *Notices of Miscellaneous English Poets; Memoir, ed. Cary, vol.* II, *pp.* 293, 294.

His sermons are smooth and pleasing in composition, but never very forcible or striking. The same merits mark his verse, and the same limitations. It is sweet, but cloying. His mind was elegant, not powerful. Effeminacy of taste is perceptible in his work generally, and especially in the melodramatic tragedy of "Runnamede." But even if the "Ode" is not his, he deserves a niche in memory as the author of the fine song, "The Braes of Yarrow," which, although it owes much to the older and more exquisite "Willie drowned in Yarrow," has likewise high merits of its own.—WALKER, HUGH, 1893, *Three Centuries of Scottish Literature, vol.* II, *p.* 121.

One of the visits Burke paid in Edinburgh was to a charming poet, to whom fortune has been singularly unkind, not only treating him cruelly when alive, but instead of granting the usual posthumous reparation, treating him more cruelly after his death. I mean John Logan, the author of the "Ode to the Cuckoo," which Burke thought the most beautiful lyric in the language. Logan was at the moment in the thick of his troubles. He had written a tragedy called "Runnymede," which, though accepted by the management of Covent Garden, was prohibited by the Lord Chamberlain, who scented current politics in the bold speeches of the Barons of King John, but is was eventually produced in the Edinburgh theatre in 1783. Its production immediately involved the author, as one of the ministers of Leith, in difficulties with his parishioners and the ecclesiastical courts similar to those which John Home had encountered twenty years before, and the trouble ended in Logan resigning his charge in December, 1786, on a pension of £40 a year. . . . The lectures which Smith praises so highly were published in 1779, and are interesting as one of the first adventures in what was afterwards known as the philosophy of history. But his memory rests now on his poems, which Smith thought less of, and especially on his "Ode to the Cuckoo," which he has been accused so

often of stealing from his deceased friend, Michael Bruce, but to which his title has at last been put beyond all doubt by Mr. Small's publication of a letter, written to Principal Baird in 1791, by Dr. Robertson of Dalmeny, who acted as joint editor with him of their common friend Bruce's poems. —RAE, JOHN, 1895, *Life of Adam Smith, pp.* 396, 397.

Logan's tragedy of "Runnimede," like most of his authentic poetry, is lacking in force. His two volumes of "Sermons," however, were recommended by Sir Walter Scott, and are still read. Certainly his finest poem is "The Braes of Yarrow," though one verse, "She sought him east," &c., is borrowed from the ancient ballad of "Willie drowned in Yarrow."—EYRE-TODD, GEORGE, 1896, *Scottish Poetry of the Eighteenth Century, vol.* II, *p.* 93.

"The Cuckoo," a poem well worth the sharp controversy waged over it by the respective friends of the two authors. There is nothing else in this period that rings so fresh and clear as this little ode. One stanza may be quoted to illustrate its beauty, its simplicity, and naturalness. . . . Logan's other poems, though he has nothing equal to the cuckoo song in spontaneity and exquisite simplicity, are yet of real value. His "Braes of Yarrow" is an effective presentation of the ancient, sorrow-laden Yarrow *motif.* As is fitting in a ballad, the touches of description are of the briefest sort, but the forest, the bonny braes, and the sounding stream, are felt through all the plaintive story. "Ossian's Hymn to the Sun" is a poetical paraphrase of the famous apostrophe in "Balclutha." It has some fine lines, but is inferior in strength to the original.—REYNOLDS, MYRA, 1896, *The Treatment of Nature in English Poetry, pp.* 144, 145.

Another bird, the Cuckoo, acted up to its reputation by inspiring a good, though not consummate, copy of verses, which has been challenged by the champions of Bruce and Logan for both those writers. In such a quarrel, especially as the authorship is of infinitesimal importance, no wise man takes a side. Bruce died young, and certainly wrote some pleasing verse; Logan, his friend, literary executor, and (as one theory holds) supplanter, died in early middle age, and seems to have had rather more talent than conduct. But all the poets of the paragraph must rest their main claim to historic interest on the fact that they exemplify, and that they handed on, the vague poetic inspiration which was to take definite form in Burns.— SAINTSBURY, GEORGE, 1898, *A Short History of English Literature*, p. 594.

Thomas Sheridan
1719–1788

Born in 1721, at Quilca, in Ireland. and was educated at Westminster School, and at Trinity College, Dublin. In 1742 he went upon the stage, and gained much celebrity as a tragedian, both in his native country and in England. He became manager of the Dublin company; but being ruined by the opposition of a rival theatre and by riots in his own, he relinquished the profession, commenced as a lecturer on elocution, and for a time was very successful. During the ministry of Lord Bute, he obtained a pension of £200. He subsequently became manager of Drury Lane Theatre; but some disputes taking place, he retired, and resumed his attention to oratory. His principal works are his "Dictionary of the English Language," and a "Life of Swift." Died, 1788.—CATES, WILLIAM L. R., ed, 1867, *A Dictionary of General Biography*, p. 1026.

PERSONAL

His action's always strong, but sometimes such
That Candour must declare he acts too much.
Why must impatience fall three paces back?
Why paces three return to the attack?
Why is the right leg, too, forbid to stir
Unless in motion semicircular?
Why must the hero with the nailor vie,
And hurl the close-clenched fist at nose or eye?
In royal *John*, with *Philip* angry grown,
I thought he would have knocked poor Davies down.
Inhuman tyrant! was it not a shame,
To fright a king so harmless and so tame?
But, spite of all defects, his glories rise;
And art, by judgment form'd, with nature vies.
Behold him sound the depths of *Hubert's* soul,
Whilst in his own contending passions roll;
View the whole scene, with critic judgment scan,
And then deny him merit if you can,
Where he falls short, 'tis Nature's fault alone;
Where he succeeds, the merit's all his own.
—CHURCHILL, CHARLES, 1761–63, *The Rosciad.*

A pension of two hundred pounds a year had been given to Sheridan. Johnson, who, as has been already mentioned, thought slightingly of Sheridan's art, upon hearing that he was also pensioned, exclaimed: "What! have they given *him* a pension? Then it is time for me to give up mine!" . . . Johnson complained that a man who disliked him repeated his sarcasm to Mr. Sheridan, without telling him what followed, which was that after a pause he added: "However,

I am glad that Mr. Sheridan has a pension, for he is a very good man." Sheridan could never forgive this hasty, contemptuous expression. It rankled in his mind; and though I informed him of all that Johnson said, and that he would be very glad to meet him amicably, he positively declined repeated offers which I made, and once went off abruptly from a house where he and I were engaged to dine, because he was told that Dr. Johnson was to be there. . . . This rupture with Sheridan deprived Johnson of one of his most agreeable resources for amusement in his lonely evenings, for Sheridan's well informed, animated and bustling mind never suffered conversation to stagnate, and Mrs. Sheridan was a most agreeable companion to an intellectual man.—BOSWELL, JAMES, 1791–93, *Life of Johnson, ed. Hill*, vol. I., pp. 446, 448, 450.

His appearance on the boards of Smock Alley Theatre on the 29 January, 1743, in the character of *Richard III.*, caused considerable sensation in the town. He was in the twenty-third year of his age; his appearance was handsome, his voice mellow and expressive, and his *début* was a decided success. He next played *Othello, Hamlet, Cato* and *Brutus*, and his acting gained so rapidly on the town that he became the rage; his name was on all men's lips.—MOLLOY, J. FITZGERALD, 1884, *The Life and Adventures of Peg Woffington*, vol. I, ch. 9.

Mr. Sheridan kept a tight hand over his children. He was a strict disciplinarian, and he managed his household as sternly as he did a theatre. He exacted unquestioning obedience from those dependent upon him, while he took great offence if his superiors required submission from him. He "poured lava," as he said, upon those who had offended him. He was very methodical and precise in all his ways. He had morning prayers regularly, and on Sunday evenings he either commented on the sermon of the day or expounded a passage in the Bible. He was fond of Dr. Johnson's "Ramblers," and his daughters were often wearied and disheartened with the task of reading them aloud, because he was exacting with regard to enunciation and cadence, and careful in correcting what he deemed their faults of speech.—RAE, W. FRASER, 1896, *Sheridan, A Biography, vol.* I, *p.* 78.

GENERAL

"Unpretending mediocrity is good, and genius is glorious; but the weak flavor of genius in a person essentially common is detestable," so the Autocrat of the Breakfast-Table tells us; and although Thomas Sheridan cannot fairly be called a person essentially common, yet it is not to be denied that he had but a weak flavor of genius.—MATTHEWS, BRANDER, 1886, *Actors and Actresses of Great Britain and the United States, eds. Matthews and Hutton, vol.* I, *p.* 165.

Thomas Amory

1691?–1788

Thomas Amory (c. 1691–1788), an eccentric author of Irish descent, who was living in Westminster about 1757, seldom stirred out till dark, and was doubtless somewhat insane. His chief works are: "Lives of Several Ladies of Great Britain: A History of Antiquities, Productions of Nature," &c. (1755); and the "Life of John Buncle" (1756-66)—an odd combination of autobiography, fantastic descriptions of scenery, deistical theology, and sentimental rhapsody.—PATRICK AND GROOME, *eds.*, 1897, *Chambers's Biographical Dictionary, p.* 27.

PERSONAL

If the writings of Thomas Amory were at times suggestive of a disturbed brain, the singular habits of his life supported that impression. For, although he had the appearance, manners, honourable conduct of a gentleman, he led a most secluded and bat-like existence, shunning all company, and never stirring abroad until the fall of the evening, when he would wander in the streets in abstract meditation, possessed of nothing in common with those who surged around him. . . . A noteworthy feature in Amory's case is that, although he led a life apart from the human family generally, he was not a morose man, nor in any degree a misanthrope; on the contrary, as far as his writings reveal his true character, he was keenly alive to the pleasures of society, love, and friendship. He intensely enjoyed the beauties of nature, and was not in the least indifferent to what are termed the good gifts of Providence; he was full of sympathy and kindly feeling for others, goodwill to man being an essential article of his creed.—BAILEY, JOHN BURN, 1888, *Modern Methuselahs, pp.* 196, 197.

If this is not a person of whom we would like to know more, I know not what the romance of biography is. Thomas Amory's life must have been a streak of crimson on the grey surface of the eighteenth century. It is really a misfortune that the red is almost all washed off.— GOSSE, EDMUND, 1891, *Gossip in a Library, p.* 218.

LIFE OF JOHN BUNCLE

1756–66

John Buncle is the English Rabelais. . . . The soul of Francis Rabelais passed into John Amory, the author of the "Life and Adventures of John Buncle." Both were physicians, and enemies of too much gravity. Their great business was to enjoy life. Rabelais indulges his spirit of sensuality in wine, in dried meat-tongues, in Bologna sausages, in botorgas. John Buncle shows the same symptoms of inordinate satisfaction in tea and bread-and-butter. While Rabelais roared with Friar John and the monks, John Buncle gossiped with the ladies.—HAZLITT, WILLIAM, 1817, *Round Table, No.* xiv.

The "Life of John Buncle, Esq.; containing various Observations and Reflections made in several parts of the World, and many Extraordinary Relations," is a book unlike any other in the language, perhaps in the world; and the introduction of passages from it into the present volume must be considered as being, like itself, an exception to rules; for it will resemble rather a notice in a review, than our selections in general. John's Life is not a classic; it contains no passage which is a general favourite; no extract could be made from it of any length, to which readers of good taste would not find objections. Yet there is so curious an interest in all its absurdities; its jumble of the gayest and gravest considerations is so founded in the actual state of things; it draws now and then such excellent portraits of life; and above all, its animal spirits are at once so excessive and so real, that we defy the best readers not to be entertained with it, and having had one or two specimens, not to desire more. Buncle would say, that there is "cut and come again" in him, like one of his luncheons of cold beef and a foaming tankard. —HUNT, LEIGH, 1849, *A Book for a Corner, p.* 137.

In the "Life of John Buncle" and his seven wives, Amory discusses the subject of earthquakes, phlogiston, then a popular theme, fluxions, the Asthanasian Creed, and muscular motion. The whole is such a farrago as Burton or Rabelais might have collected, with something of the odd thoughts and quaint humour that distinguish those writers. One object of both books is to illustrate the truth and the influence of Unitarian principles of religion. The ladies he visits and the ladies he won are all represented as models of beauty and intelligence, who largely owe their high qualities to their religious faith.—ANGUS, JOSEPH, 1865, *The Handbook of English Literature, p.* 472.

A great part of the work is devoted to the theological disquisition, showing considerable reading, in defence of "Christian deism." Much of his love-making and religious discussion takes place in the north of England, and there is some interest in his references to the beauty of the lake scenery. His impassable crags, fathomless lakes, and secluded valleys, containing imaginary convents of unitarian monks and nuns, suggest the light-headed ramblings of delirium. Amory was clearly disordered in his intellect, though a writer in the "Retrospective Review" is scandalised at the imputation and admires him without qualification.—STEPHEN, LESLIE,

1885, *Dictionary of National Biography, vol.* I, *p.* 365.

Hazlitt has said that "the soul of Rabelais passed into John Amory." His name was Thomas, not John, and there is very little that is Rabelaisian in his spirit. One sees what Hazlitt meant—the voluble and diffuse learning, the desultory thread of narration, the mixture of religion and animalism. But the resemblance is very superficial, and the parallel too complimentary to Amory. It is difficult to think of the soul of Rabelais in connection with a pedantic and uxorious Unitarian. To lovers of odd books, "John Buncle" will always have a genuine attraction. Its learning would have dazzled Dr. Primrose, and is put on in glittering spars and shells, like the ornaments of the many grottoes that it describes. It is diversified by descriptions of natural scenery, which are often exceedingly felicitous and original, and it is quickened by the human warmth and flush of the love passages, which, with all their quaintness, are extremely human. It is essentially a "healthy" book, as Charles Lamb, with such a startling result, assured the Scotchman. . . . The style of the book is very careless and irregular, but rises in its best pages to an admirable picturesqueness.—GOSSE, EDMUND, 1891, *Gossip in a Library, pp.* 225, 226.

The book, which is entirely *sui generis,* fascinated Hazlitt, and has been reprinted, but never widely read.—SAINTSBURY, GEORGE, 1898, *A Short History of English Literature, p.* 610.

GENERAL

His works may be said to be unknown to the general reader; they are familiar to those only who delight to wander in the bye-paths of literature, and to seek out the peculiarities and follies of authors. Amory's claims are sufficient, however, to entitle him to a little nook in this gallery of those who have a higher right to be remembered than the mere fact of extraordinary tenure of life confers. As he attained to his ninety-seventh year, and gave to the world several volumes marked by some literary ability, originality of thought, extensive knowledge of theology, and close observation of nature, he has the double qualification demanded of those whose lives are here sketched.—BAILEY, J. B., 1888, *Modern Methuselahs.*

Thomas Day
1748-1789

Born, in London, 22 June, 1748. Succeeded to family estate of Bear Hill, Berkshire, July, 1749. Mother removed with him to Stoke Newington; soon afterwards married again, and settled at Bear Hill, 1755. At school at Stoke Newington, and at Charterhouse, 1755–63. Matriculated Corpus Christi College, Oxford, 1 June, 1764; left, without degree, 1766. Admitted to Middle Temple, 12 Feb., 1765; called to Bar, 14 May, 1775; never practised. After disappointments in love, endeavoured to train two orphan girls on his own principles, in order that he might marry one of them. Scheme failed. Visit to France. On return, after other love disappointments, settled in London; engaged in literary work, with occasional travelling. Married Esther Milnes, 7 Aug., 1778; spent the winter in Hampstead. Bought house at Abridge, Essex, 1779. Removed to Anningsley, Surrey, 1781. Life of great seclusion and asceticism. Killed by accident on horseback, 28 Sept., 1789. Buried at Wargrave. *Works:* "The Dying Negro" (anon., with J. Bicknell), 1773; "Ode for the New Year" (anon.), 1776; "The Devoted Legions," 1776; "The Desolation of America" (anon.), 1777; "Two Speeches," 1780; "Reflexions on the Present State of England," 1782 (2nd edn. same year); "Letters of Marius," 1784; "Fragments of Original Letters on the Slavery of Negroes," 1784; "Dialogue between a Justice of the Peace and a Farmer," 1785; "Four Tracts," 1785; "Letter to Arthur Young," 1788; "History of Little Jack," 1788; "History of Sandford and Merton"(anon.), vol. i., 1783; vol. ii., 1787; vol. iii., 1789. *Life:* by J. Keir, 1791; by Blackman, 1862.—SHARP, R. FARQUHARSON, 1897, *A Dictionary of English Authors, p.* 75.

PERSONAL

In memory of Thomas Day, Esq., who died the 28th September, 1789, *aged* 41, *after having promoted by the energy of his writings and encouraged by the uniformity of his example the unremitted exercise of every public and private virtue.*
Beyond the rage of time or fortune's power,
Remain, cold stone, remain and mark the hour
When all the noblest gifts which Heaven e'er gave
Were centred in a dark untimely grave.
Oh, taught on Reason's boldest wings to rise
And catch each glimmering of the opening skies,
Oh, gentle bosom! Oh, unsullied mind!
Oh, friend to truth, to virtue and mankind,
Thy dear remains we trust to this sad shrine,
Secure to feel no second loss like thine.
—INSCRIPTION ON TOMB, 1789.

Edgeworth calls Day the "most virtuous human being" he had ever known. His friend and biographer Keir speaks with equal warmth. His amusing eccentricities were indeed only the symptoms of a real nobility of character, too deeply in earnest to submit to the ordinary compromises of society.—STEPHEN, LESLIE, 1888, *Dictionary of National Biography, vol.* XIV, *p.* 241.

Mr. Keir tells us that Day was tall, strong, erect, and of a manly deportment, deeply marked with small-pox; voice clear, expressive, and fit for public elocution.

Mrs. Ritchie says: "He was tall and stooped in the shoulders, full made but not corpulent, and in his meditations and melancholy airs a degree of awkardness and dignity were blended." He talked like a book and always thought in the same full dress style, which must have rendered his society rather oppressive, and even Mr. Keir confesses that in conversation he entered into the subject more deeply and fully than was agreeable to the fashionable tone of the day. The picture of him by Wright, of Derby, shows him as a man with a heavy jaw, dark and abundant hair—in the original, the lightning is depicted as passing through it—nor does it seem that he paid that attention to his personal appearance that would be expected of a society author in these days. Mr. Edgeworth says of him, that at the very commencement of their acquaintance, when the Days were living at Bear Hill, in Berkshire, "His appearance was not prepossessing! He seldom combed his raven locks, though he was remarkably fond of washing in a stream."—LOCKWOOD, M., 1897, *Thomas Day, The Nineteenth Century, vol.* 42, *p.* 76.

SANDFORD AND MERTON
1783-89

Altogether "Sandford and Merton" affected me the wrong way; and for the first time my soul revolted from the pretentious virtues of honest poverty. It is to the malign influence of that tale that I owe my sneaking preference for the drones and butterflies of earth. I do not now believe that men are born equal; I do not love universal suffrage; I mistrust all popular agitators, all intrusive legislation, all philanthropic fads, all friends of the people and benefactors of their race. I cannot even sympathize with the noble theory that every man and woman should do their share of the world's work; I would gladly shirk my own if I could. And this lamentable, unworthy view of life and its responsibilities is due to the subtle poison instilled into my youthful mind by the too strenuous counter-teaching of "Sandford and Merton."—REPPLIER, AGNES, 1891, *Books that have Hindered Me, Points of View, p.* 69.

GENERAL

Utility rather than display of talent was the motive of his writing.—KEIR, J., 1791, *Life of Thomas Day.*

He is one of our best composers in that style of antithetic and declamatory couplets which we learned from the French. The resolute enemy of political bondage, he put on without reluctance the closest shackles of the poet. Disdaining to torture his looks in conformity with the reigning fashion, he curled up his verses so as to adapt them to most arbitrary modes. The difference between the stiff couplet measure, as it is formed on the French model, and that looser disposition of it, which was practised by our elder writers, and which we have lately seen restored, reminds one of the comparison which the historian makes between the Macedonian armies and the Roman. "In each the soldier was stationary, preserving his ranks; the phalanx of the former was immovable, and of but one kind; the Roman force more distinct, consisting of several parts; and easily disposable for the purposes either of separation or of junction." Of his three poems in this style, "The Dying Negro," "The Devoted Legions," and "The Desolation of America," the second ("The Devoted Legions") is the best. It is a satire against our national degeneracy and the supposed avarice which made us engage in the American war, conveyed under a description of the Parthian expedition setting out under Crassus, and the prophecy of its ruin. There was something novel in the design, and it is executed with extraordinary vigour.—CARY, HENRY FRANCIS, 1823, *Notices of Miscellaneous English Poets; Memoir, ed. Cary, vol.* II, *p.* 294.

Sir John Hawkins
1719–1789.

Born, in London, 30 March, 1719. Articled to an attorney. Contrib. to "Gentleman's Mag.," from 1739. Mem. of Madrigal Soc., 1741 (?). Perhaps contrib. anonymously to "Universal Spectator," 1747. Mem. of Academy of Ancient Music. Married Sidney Storer, 1753. Gave up business as attorney, 1769. J. P. for Middlesex, 1761; Chairman of Quarter Sessions, 19 Sept., 1765. Knighted, 23 Oct., 1772. Died, in Westminster, 21 May, 1789; buried in cloisters of Westminster Abbey. *Works:* "Observations on the State of the Highways," 1763; "The Principles and Power of Harmony" (anon.), 1771; "The General History of the Science and Practice of Music" (5 vols.), 1776; "Dissertation on the Armorial Ensigns of the County of Middlesex," 1780; "The Life of Samuel Johnson," 1787. *Posthumous:* Contribution to "Poetical Miscellanies" (anon.), 1790. He *edited:* Walton's "Compleat Angler," 1760; Johnson's Works, 1787–89.—SHARP, R. FARQUHARSON, 1897, *A Dictionary of English Authors, p.* 127.

PERSONAL

"Why really I believe him to be an honest man at the bottom; but to be sure he is penurious, and he is mean, and it must be owned he has a degree of brutality, and a tendency to savageness, that cannot easily be defended."—JOHNSON, SAMUEL, 1778, *Mme. D'Arblay's Diary, vol.* I.

The fiddling Knight. — WOLCOT, JOHN (PETER PINDAR), 1787, *a Poetical and Congratulatory Epistle to James Boswell, Esq.*

I met Dr. Percy, Bishop of Dromore, at Sir Joshua Reynolds'. . . . The bishop concurred with every other person I have heard speak of Hawkins, in saying that he was a most detestable fellow. He was the son of a carpenter, and set out in life in the very lowest line of the law. Dyer knew him well at one time, and the bishop heard him give a character of Hawkins once that painted him in the blackest colours; though Dyer was by no means apt to deal in such portraits. Dyer said he was a man of the most mischievous, uncharitable, and malignant disposition, and that he knew instances of his setting a husband against a wife, and a brother against a brother; fomenting their animosity by anonymous letters. . . . Sir Joshua observed that Hawkins, though he assumed great outward sanctity, was not only mean and groveling in disposition but absolutely dishonest. After the death of Dr. Johnson, he as one of his executors laid hold of his watch and several trinkets, coins, etc., which he said he should take to himself for his trouble — a pretty *liberal* construction of the rule of law, that an executor may satisfy his own demands in the first instance. Sir Joshua and Sir Wm. Scott, the other executors, remonstrated against this, and with great difficulty *compelled* him to give up the watch, which Dr. Johnson's servant, Francis Barber, now has; but the coins and old pieces of money they could never get. — MALONE, EDMOND, 1791, *Maloniana, ed. Prior, pp.* 424, 425, 426.

Sir John Hawkins was originally bred a lawyer, in which profession he did not succeed. Having married a gentlewoman who by her brother's death proved a considerable fortune he bought a house at Twickenham, intending to give himself up to his studies and music, of which he was very fond. He now commenced a justice of peace; and being a very honest, moral man, but of no brightness, and very obstinate and contentious, he grew hated by the lower class and very troublesome to the gentry, with whom he went to law both on public and private causes; at the same time collecting materials indefatigably for a "History of Music." — WALPOLE, HORACE, 1797 (?), *Memoirs of the Reign of King George III., vol.* I, *p.* 421.

"And Sir John Hawkins," exclaimed Uncle Timothy, with unwonted asperity, "whose ideas of virtue never rose above a decent exterior and regular hours! calling the author of the 'Traveller' an idiot! It shakes the sides of splenetic disdain to hear this Grub Street chronicler of fiddling

and fly-fishing libelling the beautiful intellect of Oliver Goldsmith!" — DANIEL, GEORGE, 1842-81, *Merrie England in the Olden Time, p.* 233.

He had been an attorney for many years, affecting literary tastes, and dabbling·in music at the Madrigal Club; but, four years before the present, so large a fortune had fallen to him in right of his wife, that he withdrew from the law, and lived and judged with severe propriety as a Middlesex magistrate. Within two years he will be elected chairman of the sessions; after seven years more, will be made a knight; and, in four years after that will deliver himself of five quarto volumes of a history of music, in the slow and laborious conception of which he is already painfully engaged. Altogether, his existence was a kind of pompous, parsimonious, insignificant drawl, cleverly ridiculed by one of the wits in an absurd epitaph: "Here lies Sir John Hawkins, Without his shoes and stauckins." To him belonged the original merit, in that age of penal barbarity and perpetual executions, of lamenting that in no less that fourteen cases it was still possible to cheat the gallows. Another of his favorite themes was the improvidence of what he called sentimental writers, at the head of whom he placed the author of "Tom Jones;" a book which he charged with having "corrupted the rising generation," and sapped "the foundation of that morality which it is the duty of parents and all public instructors to inculcate in the minds of young people." This was his common style of talk. He would speak contemptuously of Hogarth as a man who knew nothing out of Covent-garden. Richardson, Fielding, Smollett, and Sterne, he looked upon as "stuff;" and for the last three, as men "whose *necessities* and abilities were nearly commensurate," he had a special contempt. — FORSTER, JOHN, 1848, *The Life and Times of Oliver Goldsmith, vol.* I, *p.* 312.

Hawkins was as mean and parsimonious as he was pompous and conceited. He forebore to partake of the suppers at the club, and begged therefore to be excused from paying his share of the reckoning. — IRVING, WASHINGTON, 1849, *Oliver Goldsmith, p.* 164.

Hawkins was a man of coarse fibre, absurdly proud of "my coach," rough to

inferiors, and humble to men like Walpole,
but not without solid good qualities.—
STEPHEN, LESLIE, 1891, *Dictionary of
National Biography, vol.* XXV, *p.* 221.

HISTORY OF MUSIC
1776

I have been three days at Strawberry,
and have not seen a creature but Sir John
Hawkins's five volumes, the two last of
which, thumping as they are, I literally
did read in two days. They are old books
to all intents and purposes, very old books;
and what is new, is like old books, too,
that is, full of minute facts that delight
antiquaries. . . . My friend, Sir
John, is a matter-of-fact man, and does
now and then stoop very low in quest of
game. Then he is so exceedingly religious
and grave as to abhor mirth, except it is
printed in the old black letter, and then
he calls the most vulgar ballad pleasant
and full of humour. He thinks nothing
can be sublime but an anthem, and
Handel's choruses heaven upon earth.
However, he writes with great moderation, temper and good sense, and the book
is a very valuable one. I have begged his
Austerity to relax in one point, for he
ranks comedy with farce and pantomime.
Now I hold a perfect comedy to be the
perfection of human composition, and believe firmly that fifty Iliads and Æneids
could be written sooner than such a character as Falstaff's.—WALPOLE, HORACE,
1776, *To the Countess of Ossory, Dec.* 3;
Letters, ed. Cunningham, vol. VI, *p.* 395.

In which, however, there is much original and valuable information, as in all his
other works, so unjustly censured in my
opinion. Sir John's principal fault was
digression from his subject; but if you
excuse that, you are well repaid by
the information you receive.—MATHIAS,
THOMAS JAMES, 1794–98, *The Pursuits of
Literature, Eighth ed., p.* 98.

Contemporary judgment awarded the
palm of superiority to Burney and neglected Hawkins. Evidence of the feeling
is found in a catch which was formerly
better known than it is now:—

" Have you Sir John Hawkins' History?
Some folks thing it quite a mystery.
Music fill'd his wondrous brain.
How d'ye like him? Is it plain?
Both I've read and must agree,
That Burney's history pleases me."

Which in performance is made to sound:—
" Sir John Hawkins!
Burn his history!
How d'ye like him?
Burn his history!
Burney's history pleases me,"

Posterity, however, has reversed the
decision of the wits; Hawkins' "History" has been re-printed, but Burney's
never reached a second edition. The
truth lies between the extremes. Burney,
possessed of far greater musical knowledge than Hawkins, better judgment, and
a better style, frequently wrote about
things which he had not sufficiently examined; Hawkins, on the other hand, more
industrious and painstaking than Burney,
was deficient in technical skill, and often
inaccurate.—HUSK, WILLIAM H., 1879, *A
Dictionary of Music and Musicians, ed.
Grove, vol.* I, *p.* 699.

Hawkins, though a worse writer than
Burney, was a more painstaking antiquary,
and his book has therefore a more perma-
nent value for students of musical history.
—STEPHEN, LESLIE, 1891, *Dictionary of
National Biography, vol.* XXV, *p.* 221.

LIFE OF SAMUEL JOHNSON
1787

Mr. Urban:— Have you read that divine book, the "Life of Samuel Johnson,
LL.D., by Sir John Hawkins, Knt.?"
Have you done anything but read it since
it was first published? For my own part,
I scruple not to declare that I could not
rest till I had read it quite through, notes,
digressions, index and all; then I could
not rest till I had gone over it a second
time. I begin to think that increase of
appetite grows by what it is fed on; for
I have been reading it ever since. I am
now in the midst of the sixteenth perusal;
and still I discover new beauties. I can think
of nothing else; I can talk of nothing else.
In short, *my mind is become tumid, and longs
to be delivered of those many and great conceptions* with which it has laboured since I
have been through a course of this most
perfect *exemplar* of biography. The compass of learning, the extent and accuracy
of information, the judicious criticism, the
moral reflections, the various opinions,
legal and political, to say nothing of that
excess of candour and charity that breathe
throughout the work, make together such
a collection of sweets that the sense aches
at them. To crown all, *the language is*

refined to a degree of immaculate purity, and displays the whole force of turgid eloquence. . . .

Read Hawkins once, and you can read no more,

For all books else appear so mean, so poor, Johnson's a dunce; but still persists to read, And Hawkins will be all the books you need. —PORSON, RICHARD, 1787, *Letters to the Gentleman's Magazine.*

He has thrown a heap of rubbish of his own over poor Johnson, which would have smothered any less gigantic genius—EDGEWORTH, MARIA, 1809, *Letters, vol.* I, *p.*167.

Sir John Hawkins, whose "Life of Samuel Johnson, LL.D.," 1787, comes next in importance to Mrs. Piozzi's "Anecdotes," has suffered considerably; and his book, which immediately after Johnson's death was advertised as "forthcoming," is, to use the words of a recent writer, "spoken of with contempt by many who have never taken the trouble to do more than turn over its leaves." That the author seems to have been extremely unpopular can scarcely be denied. —DOBSON, AUSTIN, 1898, *Boswell's Predecessors and Editors, Miscellanies, p.* 116.

Adam Smith
1723-1790

He was the son of Adam Smith (lawyer and Customs' comptroller at Kirkcaldy), and Margaret Douglas of Strathendry; and he was born probably at the beginning of June, 1723. He was a student at Glasgow University from 1737 to 1740, and at Balliol College, Oxford (as Snell Exhibitioner) from 1740 to 1747. After a year and a half at Kirkcaldy he came to Edinburgh and lectured on *belles lettres* (1748–50). In 1751 he was made Professor of Logic at Glasgow University, and in 1752 Professor of Moral Philosophy. In 1759 he published his "Theory of Moral Sentiments." In 1764 he was persuaded by Charles Townshend to go abroad with the young Buccleuch to Toulouse, Geneva, and Paris, resigning his chair of Moral Philosophy. He was back in London in 1766 and at Kirkcaldy in 1767, devoting himself to his "Inquiry Into the Nature and Causes of the Wealth of Nations," which appeared in 1776, just before the death of Hume. In 1778 he became a Commissioner of Customs in Edinburgh. In 1787 he was chosen Rector of his old University, and on 17th July, 1790, he died at his residence, Panmure House, Canongate. He is buried in Canongate Churchyard. His last years were saddened by the loss of his mother and his cousin (Miss Jane Douglas), the former of whom died in 1784, and the latter in 1788.—BONAR, JAMES, 1894, *A Catalogue of the Library of Adam Smith, Introduction, p.* ix.

PERSONAL

Adam Smith, though perhaps only second to David in learning and ingenuity, was far inferior to him in conversational talents. In that of public speaking they were equal—David never tried it, and I never heard Adam but once, which was at the first meeting of the Select Society, when he opened up the design of the meeting. His voice was harsh and enunciation thick, approaching to stammering. His conversation was not colloquial, but like lecturing, in which I have been told he was not deficient, especially when he grew warm. He was the most absent man in company that I ever saw, moving his lips, and talking to himself, and smiling, in the midst of large companies. If you awaked him from his reverie, and made him attend to the subject of conversation, he immediately began a harangue, and never stopped till

he told you all he knew about it, with the utmost philosophical ingenuity. He knew nothing of characters, and yet was ready to draw them on the slightest invitation. But when you checked him or doubted, he retracted with the utmost ease, and contradicted all he had been saying. His journey abroad with the Duke of Buccleuch cured him in part of these foibles; but still he appeared very unfit for the intercourse of the world as a travelling tutor. But the Duke was a character, both in point of heart and understanding, to surmount all disadvantages — he could learn nothing ill from a philosopher of the utmost probity and benevolence. If he [Smith] had been more a man of address and of the world, he might perhaps have given a ply to the Duke's fine mind, which was much better when left to its own energy. Charles Townshend had chosen Smith, not for his fitness for the purpose, but for his own glory in having sent an eminent Scottish philosopher to travel with the Duke.—CARLYLE, ALEXANDER, 1753-56-1860, *Autobiography, p.* 226.

Sir, I was once in company with Smith, and we did not take to each other; but had I known that he loved rhyme so much as you tell me he does I should have hugged him.—JOHNSON, SAMUEL, 1763, *Life by Boswell, ed. Hill, vol.* I, *p.* 495.

Poor Smith! We must soon lose him, and the moment in which he departs will give a heart-pang to thousands. Mr. Smith's spirits are flat, and I am afraid the exertions he sometimes makes to please his friends do him no good. His intellect as well as his senses are clear and distinct. He wishes to be cheerful, but nature is omnipotent. His body is extremely emaciated, and his stomach cannot admit of sufficient nourishment; but, like a man, he is perfectly patient and resigned.—SMELLIE, W., 1790, *Letter to Patrick Clason, Memoirs of Smellie, ed. Kerr, vol.* I, *p.* 295.

I have been surprised, and I own a little indignant, to observe how little impression his death has made here. Scarce any notice has been taken of it, while for above a year together, after the death of Dr. Johnson, nothing was to be heard of but panegyrics of him. Lives, Letters, and Anecdotes, and even at this moment there are two more lives of him about to start into existence. Indeed one ought not, perhaps, to be very much surprised that the public does not do justice to the works of A. Smith, since he did not do justice to them himself, but always considered his "Theory of Moral Sentiments" as a much superior work to his "Wealth of Nations."—ROMILLY, SIR SAMUEL, 1790, *Letter to M. Dumont, Aug.* 20; *Memoirs, vol.* I, *p.* 404.

There was no situation in which the abilities of Mr. Smith appeared to greater advantage than as a professor. In delivering his lectures he trusted almost entirely to extemporary elocution. His manner, though not graceful, was plain and unaffected, and as he seemed to be always interested in his subject, he never failed to interest his hearers. Each discourse consisted commonly of several distinct propositions, which he successively endeavoured to prove and illustrate. These propositions, when announced in general terms, had, from their extent, not unfrequently something of the air of a paradox. In his attempts to explain them, he often appeared, at first, not to be sufficiently possessed of the subject, and spoke with some hesitation. As he advanced, however, the matter seemed to crowd upon him, his manner became warm and animated, and his expression easy and fluent. On points susceptible of controversy you could easily discern, that he secretly conceived an opposition to his opinions, and that he was led upon this account to support them with greater energy and vehemence. By the fulness and variety of his illustrations the subject gradually swelled in his hands and acquired a dimension which, without a tedious repetition of the same views, was calculated to seize the attention of his audience, and to afford them pleasure, as well as instruction, in following the same object, through all the diversity of shades and aspects in which it was presented, and afterwards in tracing it backwards to that original proposition or general truth, from which this beautiful train of speculation had proceeded.—MILLAR, JOHN, c 1793, *Letter, Stewart's Works, vol.* VII, *p.* 10.

Of the intellectual gifts and attainments by which he was so eminently distinguished; —of the originality and comprehensiveness of his views; the extent, the variety, and the correctness of his information; the inexhaustible fertility of his invention; and the ornaments which his rich and beautiful imagination had borrowed from classical culture;—he has left behind him lasting monuments. To his private worth the most certain of all testimonies may be found in that confidence, respect, and attachment, which followed him through all the various relations of life. The serenity and gaiety he enjoyed, under the pressure of his growing infirmities, and the warm interest he felt to the last, in everything connected with the welfare of his friends, will be long remembered by a small circle, with whom, as long as his strength permitted, he regularly spent an evening in the week; and to whom the recollection of his worth still forms a pleasing, though melancholy bond of union. The more delicate and characteristical features of his mind, it is perhaps impossible to trace. That there were many peculiarities, both in his manners, and in his intellectual habits, was manifest to the most superficial observer; but although, to those who knew him, these peculiarities detracted nothing from the respect which his abilities commanded; and although, to his intimate friends, they added an inexpressible charm to his conversation, while they displayed, in the most interesting light, the artless simplicity of his heart; yet it would require a very skillful pencil to present them to the public eye. He was certainly not fitted for the general commerce of the world, or for the business of active life. The comprehensive speculations with which he had been occupied from his youth, and the variety of materials which his own invention continually supplied to his thoughts, rendered him habitually inattentive to familiar objects, and to common occurrences; and he frequently exhibited instances of absence, which have scarcely been surpassed by the fancy of La Bruyère. Even in company, he was apt to be ingrossed with his studies; and appeared, at times, by the motion of his lips, as well as by his looks and gestures, to be in the fervor of composition. I have often, however, been struck, at the distance of years, with his accurate memory of the most trifling particulars; and am inclined to believe, from this and some other circumstances, that he possessed a power, not perhaps uncommon among absent men, of recollecting, in consequence of subsequent efforts of reflection, many occurrences which, at the time when they happened, did not seem to have sensibly attracted his notice. . . . In his external form and appearance, there was nothing uncommon. When perfectly at ease, and when warmed with conversation, his gestures were animated, and not ungraceful; and, in the society of those he loved, his features were often brightened with a smile of inexpressible benignity. In the company of strangers, his tendency to absence, and perhaps still more his consciousness of this tendency, rendered his manner somewhat embarrassed, an effect which was probably not a little heightened by those speculative ideas of propriety, which his recluse habits tended at once to perfect in his conception, and to diminish his power of realizing. He never sat for his picture; but the medallion of Tassie conveys an exact idea of his profile,

and of the general expression of his countenance. — STEWART, DUGALD, 1793, *Account of the Life and Writings of Adam Smith.*

Those persons who have ever had the pleasure to be in his company may recollect that even in his common conversation the order and method he pursued, without the smallest degree of formality or stiffness, were beautiful and gave a sort of pleasure to all who listened to him. — PLAYFAIR, WILLIAM, 1805, *Life of Adam Smith.*

At the age of twenty-nine, he filled the chair of Moral Philosophy in the University of Glasgow; a place for which he was admirably suited by his power of communication as well as by the habits of his mind, as he spoke with great fluency when once engaged in his subject, and was listened to with the enthusiasm which his ability, accompanied by a popular manner, might be expected to inspire. It is much to be regretted, that his lectures were destroyed by his own hand before he died. The course of Natural Theology was one which would have great interest for readers of the present day; and such was the variety of suggestions always flowing from his active and fertile mind, that every part must have contained much to interest and instruct mankind. — PEABODY, WILLIAM B. O., 1846-50, *Men of Letters and Science, Art.* II, *Literary Remains*, ed. Peabody, p. 262.

When a young man [in 1789], I went to Edinburgh, carrying letters of introduction (from Dr. Kippis, Dr. Price, &c.,) to Adam Smith, Robertson, and others. When I first saw Smith, he was at breakfast, eating strawberries; and he descanted on the superior flavour of those grown in Scotland. I found him very kind and communicative. He was (what Robertson was not) a man who had seen a great deal of the world. Once, in the course of conversation, I happened to remark of some writer, that "he was rather superficial, — *a* Voltaire." "Sir," cried Smith, striking the table with his hand, "there has been but *one* Voltaire!" — ROGERS, SAMUEL, 1855? *Table Talk.*

In person he was a grave, preoccupied-looking man, of a stout middle size, with large features and large grey eyes, absent-minded in company, often incontinently talking to himself, and keeping up his rather poor constitution by strict regularity and temperance. He was warm and affectionate in disposition, exceedingly unreserved, with simple frankness expressing the thoughts of the moment, and with ready candour retracting his opinion if he found that he had spoken without just grounds. His intellectual proceedings were calm, patient and regular; he mastered a subject slowly and circumspectly, and carried his principles with steady tenacity through multitudes of details that would have checked many men of greater mental vigour unendowed with the same invincible persistence.—MINTO, WILLIAM, 1872–80, *Manual of English Prose Literature, p.* 476.

In 1778 he was appointed, at the request of the Duke of Buccleuch, one of the commissioners of his majesty's customs in Scotland, and removed to Edinburgh, taking his mother with him; it is scarcely necessary to mention that he continued all his life a bachelor. Here he spent the last twelve years of his life. Henceforth he became an object of curiosity to all people of literary culture; and his person was scrutinized, as he walked the streets, by the curious, and his peculiar habits reported. Many a youth, studying in Edinburgh, was proud to relate in after years that he had seen him—a fine gentleman of the old school, a little above the ordinary size, with a manly countenance lighted by large gray eyes, wearing a cap, a long, wide great-coat, breeches, and shoebuckles.—MCCOSH, JAMES, 1874, *The Scottish Philosophy, p.* 166.

Adam Smith, who taught the nations economy, could not manage the economy of his own house. Choked with books and absorbed in abstractions, he was feeble and inefficient in active life—incapable of acting on his own conclusions.—MATHEWS, WILLIAM, 1887, *Men, Places and Things, p.* 134.

There is much, besides the contents of his published works, to draw to Adam Smith the attention of those who are attracted by individual power. Scotchmen have long been reputed strong in philosophic doctrine, and he was a Scot of Scots. But, though Scotland is now renowned for her philosophy, that renown is not of immemorial origin; it was not till the last century was well advanced that she began to add great speculative

thinkers to her great preachers. Adam Smith, consequently, stands nearly at the opening of the greatest of the intellectual eras of Scotland; and yet by none of the great Scotch names, which men have learned since his day, has his name been eclipsed. The charm about the man consists, for those who do not regard him with the special interest of the political economist, in his literary method, which exhibits his personality and makes his works thoroughly his own, rather than in any facts about his eminency among Scotchmen. You bring away from your reading of Adam Smith a distinct and attractive impression of the man himself, such as you can get from the writings of no other author in the same field, and such as makes you wish to know still more of him. . . . Unhappily, we know very little of Adam Smith as a man, and it may be deplored, without injustice to a respected name, that we owe that little to Dugald Stewart.—WILSON, WOODROW, 1888, *An Old Master, The New Princeton Review, vol.* VI, *pp.* 211, 212.

A common misconception regarding Smith is that he was as helpless as a child in matters of business. One of his Edinburgh neighbors remarked of him to Robert Chambers that it was strange a man who wrote so well on exchange and barter was obliged to get a friend to buy his horse corn for him. This idea of his helplessness in the petty transactions of life arose from observing his occasional fits of absence and his habitual simplicity of character, but his simplicity, nobody denies, was accompanied by exceptional acuteness and practical sagacity, and his fits of absence seem to have been neither so frequent or prolonged as they are commonly represented. Samuel Rogers spent most of a week with him in Edinburgh the year before his death, and did not remark his absence of mind all the time. Anyhow, during his thirteen years' residence at Glasgow College, Smith seems to have had more to do with the business of the College, petty or important, than any other professor, and his brethren in the Senate of that University cannot have seen in him any marked failing or incapacity for ordinary business. They threw on his shoulders an ample share of the committee and general routine work of the place, and set him to audit accounts, or inspect the drains in the College Court, or see the holly hedge in the College garden uprooted, or to examine the encroachments on the College lands on the Molendinar Burn, without any fear of his forgetting his business on the way. They entrusted him for years with the post of College Quæstor or Treasurer, in which inattention or the want of sound business habits might inflict injury even on their pecuniary interests. They made him one of the two curators of the College chambers, the forty lodgings provided for students inside the College gates. And when there was any matter of business that was a little troublesome or delicate to negotiate, they seem generally to have chosen Smith for their chief spokesman or representative.—RAE, JOHN, 1895, *Life of Adam Smith, p.* 66.

In Edinburgh, where better things might have been expected, the public interest, or rather apathy, was reflected in two meagre paragraphs of his death in the newspapers. Lord Cockburn has left it on record that in his day all that seemed to be known of the founder of the science of Political Economy was that he had been Commissioner of Customs and had written a sensible book. . . . When Adam Smith's personality is carefully analysed the reason of the public apathy at the time of his death becomes obvious. A solitary thinker, out of touch with the theological sympathies of his countrymen, and indifferent to the prevailing parochialism, Smith was an intellectual alien. A sensitive plant, he shrank from uncongenial influences by which he was surrounded. In the public mind his friend Hume bulked considerably, but that was not because he was more in touch with Scottish sympathies than Smith, but because of his greater intellectual aggressiveness. On the all-absorbing theme of human destiny Smith was silent; consequently he lived in a state of mental isolation. In this attitude he was confirmed by his temperament, which was not favourable to social expansion. . . . At this distance we can readily detect the limitations of the Smithsonian type of mind. Within its limitations, however, the genius of Smith was a potent influence, and had far-reaching issues. In the sphere of international economics his place is with the immortals. If his personality lacked the dramatic

element, it was eminently harmonious. In the midst of his intellectual absorption he kept the fountains of his heart ever open. Adam Smith was no dry-as-dust speculator on mundane affairs; his emotional interest in humanity was intense. To outsiders he might seem cold and reserved, but those who knew him intimately record that he was not only a great thinker but a good man. — MACPHERSON, HECTOR C., 1899, *Adam Smith (Famous Scots Series), pp.* 135, 139, 141.

With all drawbacks, Adam Smith must be counted not only one of the greatest influences, but also one of the most characteristic figures of the age. He was a man of simple life, wrapt in abstract thought, a stranger to all the baser ambitions of ordinary life, yet devoting himself, with singular tenacity of purpose, and with singular boldness, to work out a theory which had a profound effect upon the most practical side of human life. In another age than his, the recluse student, who struck his contemporaries as one utterly lacking even ordinary discernment of character, would have hung back in timidity from propounding views which were to be effectual only by moulding the action of men. His artlessness, his modesty, his occasional wayward eccentricity of view, which appeared to his intimates as almost childish, gave additional interest to the concentrated perseverance with which he worked out his system. His ordinary conversation consisted of long philosophical harangues, varied by fits of silence and reverie, and by the utterance of paradoxical opinions which he was ready to retract upon a show of opposition.—CRAIK, SIR HENRY, 1901, *A Century of Scottish History, vol.* II, p. 201.

His figure was one of the most familiar in the High Street—dressed in a light-coloured coat, in cocked hat or broad-brimmed beaver, white silk stockings, and silver-buckled shoes, a bamboo cane held over his shoulder, as a soldier carries his musket, with one hand, while the other might hold a bunch of flowers from his garden. Thus he walked, with eyes gazing vacantly, and lips moving as if in inaudible converse, a placid smile occasionally wreathing his countenance, his body swaying, as an acquaintance describes it, "vermicularly, as if at every step he meant to alter his direction or to turn back.'' No wonder the Musselburgh fish-wife, as she watched the punctiliously attired, vacant-eyed, amiable man pass along the street, mistook him for a demented but harmless old gentleman, and sighed to her sister vender of haddocks, "Hech! and he is weel put on tae!'' His very unpracticalness in little affairs of life only endeared him the more to friends, who were comforted at feeling they were at least in some things superior to a genius. In political matters he was, like most of his Scots brethren, on the side of liberalism; in religion he did not pronounce his opinions, and his friends did not question him, though they knew his convictions were deep. — GRAHAM, HENRY GREY, 1901, *Scottish Men of Letters in the Eighteenth Century, p.* 169.

THE THEORY OF MORAL SENTIMENTS
1759

I give you thanks for the agreeable present of your Theory. Wedderburn and I made presents of our copies to such of our acquaintances as we thought good judges, and proper to spread the reputation of the book. I sent one to the Duke of Argyle, to Lord Lyttleton, Horace Walpole, Soame Jenyns, and Burke, an Irish gentleman, who wrote lately a very pretty treatise on the Sublime. Millar desired my permission to send one in your name to Dr. Warburton. I have delayed writing to you till I could tell you something of the success of the book, and could prognosticate with some probability, whether it should be finally damned to oblivion, or should be registered in the temple of immortality. Though it has been published only a few weeks, I think there appear already such strong symptoms, that I can almost venture to foretell its fate. . . . Three Bishops called yesterday at Millar's shop in order to buy copies, and to ask questions about the author. The Bishop of Peterborough said he had passed the evening in a company where he heard it extolled above all books in the world. The Duke of Argyle is more decisive than he used to be in favor. I suppose he either considers it as an exotic, or thinks the author will be serviceable to him in the Glasgow elections. Lord Lyttleton says, that Robertson and Smith and Bower are the glories of English literature. Oswald protests he does not know whether

he has reaped more instruction or entertainment from it. But you may easily judge what reliance can be put on his judgment, who has been engaged all his life in public business, and who never sees any faults in his friends. Millar exults and brags that two-thirds of the edition are already sold, and that he is now sure of success. You see what a son of the earth that is, to value books only by the profit they bring him. In that view, I believe it may prove a very good book. Charles Townshend, who passes for the cleverest fellow in England, is so taken with the performance, that he said to Oswald he would put the Duke of Buccleugh under the author's care, and would make it worth his while to accept of that charge.—HUME, DAVID, 1759, *Letter to Adam Smith, April* 12.

The author seeks for the foundation of the just, the fit, the proper, the decent, in our most common and most allowed passions, and making approbation and disapprobation the tests of virtue and vice, and showing that these are founded on sympathy, he raises from this simple truth one of the most beautiful fabrics of moral theory that has perhaps ever appeared. The illustrations are numerous and happy, and show the author to be a man of uncommon observation. His language is easy and spirited, and puts things before you in the fullest light; it is rather painting than writing.—BURKE, EDMUND, 1776, *Annual Register.*

The system to which I allude, is that which is delivered by Dr. Smith, in his "Theory of Moral Sentiments,"—a work, unquestionably of the first rank, in a science which I cannot but regard as to man the most interesting of sciences. Profound in thought, it exhibits, even when it is most profound, an example of the graces with which a sage imagination knows how to adorn the simple and majestic form of science; that it is severe and cold, only to those who are themselves cold and severe,—as in those very graces, it exhibits in like manner, an example of the reciprocal embellishment which imagination receives from the sober dignity of truth. In its minor details and illustrations, indeed, it may be considered as presenting a model of philosophic beauty, of which all must acknowledge the power, who are not disqualified by their very nature for the admiration and enjoyment of intellectual excellence,—so dull of understanding, as to shrink with a painful consciousness of incapacity at the very appearance of refined analysis—or so dull and cold of heart, as to feel no charm in the delightful varieties of an eloquence, that in the illustration and embellishment of the noblest truths seems itself to live and harmonize with those noble sentiments which it adorns. It is chiefly in its minor analyses, however, that I conceive the excellence of this admirable work to consist. Its leading doctrine I am far from admitting. Indeed it seems to me as manifestly false, as the greater number of its secondary and minute delineations appear to me faithful, to the fine lights and faint and flying shades, of that moral nature which they represent.— BROWN, THOMAS, 1820, *Lectures on the Philosophy of the Human Mind, Lecture* lxxx.

The "Theory of Moral Sentiments," although it be not the work by which Dr. Smith is best known, and for which he is most renowned, is yet a performance of the highest merit. The system has not, indeed, been approved by the philosophical world, and it seems liable to insuperable objections when considered even with an ordinary degree of attention, objections which never could have escaped the acuteness of its author but for the veil so easily drawn over an inquirer's eyes when directed to the weak points of his own supposed discovery. . . . There are whole compartments of the work which are of inestimable value, without any regard to the theory, and independent of those portions more connected with it, of which we have admitted the value. Thus the copious and accurate and luminous account of the other systems of morals, forming the seventh part, which occupies a fourth of the book, would have been a valuable work detached from the rest. . . . The admirable felicity, and the inexhaustible variety of the illustrations in which the book everywhere abounds, sheds a new and strong light upon all the most important principles of human nature; and affords an explanation of many things which are wholly independent of any theory whatever, and which deserves to be known and understood, whatever theory may obtain our

assent. The beauty of the illustrations, and the eloquence of the diction, are indeed a great merit of this work.— BROUGHAM, HENRY LORD, 1846–55, *Lives of Philosophers of the Time of George III.,* pp. 197, 200, 201.

In a history of Scotch philosophy it would become us to notice the "Theory of Moral Sentiments" of Hume's illustrious friend, Adam Smith. Even in such a history, a notice of them would be rather due to the fame which their author has earned in another direction, than to any influence which has proceeded from his "Ethics."— MAURICE, FREDERICK DENISON, 1862, *Moral and Metaphysical Philosophy, vol.* II, *p.* 578.

In Smith's "Essay," the purely scientific enquiry is overlaid by practical and hortatory dissertations, and by eloquent delineations of character and of beau-ideals of virtuous conduct. His style being thus pitched to the popular key, he never pushes home a metaphysical analysis, so that even his favourite theme, Sympathy, is not philosophically sifted to the bottom.— BAIN, ALEXANDER, 1868, *Moral Science, p.* 219.

His "Theory of Moral Sentiments" has commonly been a favorite with students, because of the eloquence of its language, modelled after the best philosophic writers of ancient Rome and modern France, and of the fertility of his resources in confirming his positions from his varied observation and reading. But his theory has gained the assent of few, and has often been prescribed by professors as a subject on which to exercise the critical acumen of their pupils. Adam Smith is always a discursive writer, and in the work now before us he wanders like a river amidst luxuriant banks, and it is not easy to define his course.—McCOSH, JAMES, 1874, *The Scottish Philosophy, p.* 168.

Was his most important contribution to Ethical Philosophy, and is characterized by consummate ingenuity in its analyses of ethical phenomena, and by the affluence of its interesting illustrations, and the elegance of its somewhat elaborate diction. The theory of Smith is an offshoot of the theory of Hume.—PORTER, NOAH, 1874, *Philosophy in Great Britain and American, Ueberweg History of Philosophy, vol.* II, *p.* 393.

Smith's ingenious and discursive intellect pours itself out in streams of diffuse eloquence, often brilliant with felicitous illustrations, and quick flashes of historical insight, and yet wide rather than deep, rather dextrous in new combinations than penetrating the essence of the subject, and, therefore, apt to disappoint us by a certain superficiality and flimsiness. Smith's ingenuity in tracing the working of the mechanism of human nature is so marked and so delightful to himself that he almost forgets to enquire. into the primary forces which set it in action. He describes the mutual action and reaction of the passions with more fidelity than the passions themselves. Smith, in fact, is a thorough representative of that optimistic Deism which we have seen illustrated by Shaftesbury and Hutcheson. . . . The name of Adam Smith should be mentioned with high respect; but I think that the respect is due chiefly to his economical labours. It may be fully admitted that he shows great ingenuity, and great fertility of illustration, and that he calls mention to a fact which must be taken into account by the moralist. But it is impossible to resist the impression, whilst we read his fluent rhetoric, and observe his easy acceptance of theological principles already exposed by his master Hume, that we are not listening to a thinker really grappling with a difficult problem, so much as to an ambitious professor who has found an excellent opportunity for displaying his command of language, and making brilliant lectures. The whole tone savours of that complacent optimism of the time which retained theological phrases to round a paragraph, and to save the trouble of genuine thought. Smith's main proposition was hardly original, though he has worked it out in detail, and it is rather calculated to lead us dexterously round difficult questions than to supply us with a genuine answer.— STEPHEN, LESLIE, 1876, *History of English Thought in the Eighteenth Century*, vol. II, pp. 70, 77.

Soon became popular, as one of the most interesting and attractive books in the circle of ethical literature. . . . Analytically, his treatise is not remarkable; its merits rather lie in the practical and hortatory discourse, in the eloquent criticisms of character, and the fine illustrations of virtuous conduct with which it abounds, and are presented in a naturally copious, easy, flowing, and fascinating style. The chief blemish of his style is an excess of language—a running into redundance. — MACKINTOSH, JOHN, 1878–96, *The History of Civilisation in Scotland*, vol. IV, pp. 45, 46.

Critics who have rejected the "Theory" as a whole, have been uniformly loud in their praises of its minor details and illustrations. Brown, for instance, who has been the most successful perhaps of all the adverse critics of the "Theory," speaks of it as presenting in these respects "a model of philosophic beauty." Jouffroy, too, allows that the book is one of the most useful in moral science, because Adam Smith, "deceived as he undoubtedly was as to the principle of morality," brought to light and analyzed so many of the facts of human nature. Dugald Stewart and Mackintosh both say much the same thing; so that it is evident no account of Adam Smith's work can be complete which omits from consideration all the collateral inquiries he pursues or all the illustrations he draws, either from history or from his imagination.—FARRER, J. A., 1881, *Adam Smith* (*English Philosophers*), p. 17.

If precariously based, is a model of ingenious system-making. — SAINTSBURY, GEORGE, 1886, *Specimens of English Prose Style*, p. 216.

The essays are finely written, full of subtle analysis and truthful illustration. The book is least significant, however, as philosophy; because it lacks any profound examination of the foundation upon which the author's views rest.—ELY, RICHARD T., 1897, *Library of the World's Best Literature, ed. Warner*, vol. XXIII, p, 13521.

Adam Smith was one of the least metaphysical persons that ever wrote, but in some respects he anticipated a theory which some people would regard as metaphysical in the highest degree, that of the "social self," and it is a social self which enables us to effect not only an imaginary change of situation with the persons chiefly concerned, but a complete identification of our own person and character with that of another person. Yet he does not ignore the influence of common interest, and, if sympathy with the motives of the agent is the source of our idea of propriety, sympathy with the gratitude of the person acted on is the source of our idea of merit; but the latter sympathy does not arise unless there be, first, propriety in the motives of the agent. He is thus enabled to recognize the undeniable element of utility in moral institutions, to which the selfish school had confined its view, and also to preserve those other elements which distinguish moral approval from the approval which we bestow on a well-contrived machine. His deliverance of moral approbation from the dead level imposed on it by the selfish and benevolent schools alike, and his restoration of variety and elasticity to that function, would alone be a considerable achievement. His theory of sympathy is rather a preservative than a solvent. His system, however, is a "closed system," and he refused to recognize the existence of any question which necessarily leads beyond it, and, however useful for practical purposes, as a theory of the moral criterion it is insufficient.—SELBY-BIGGE, L. A., 1897, *ed., British Moralists,Introduction,vol.* I. *p.* lxi.

As a literary production it holds a high place, but its philosophic value is slight.—MACPHERSON, HECTOR C., 1899, *Adam Smith (Famous Scots Series), p.* 38.

THE WEALTH OF NATIONS
1776

The life which I led at Glasgow was a pleasurable, dissipated life in comparison to that which I lead here at present. I have begun to write a book, in order to pass away the time.— SMITH, ADAM, 1764, *Letter to David Hume, Geneva, July* 5.

Euge! Belle! Dear Mr. Smith: I am much pleased with your performance, and the perusal of it has taken me from a state of great anxiety. It was a work of so much expectation, by yourself, by your friends, and by the public, that I trembled for its appearance; but am now much relieved. Not but that the reading of it necessarily requires so much attention, and the public is disposed to give so little, that I shall still doubt for some time of its being at first very popular. But it has depth and solidity and acuteness, and is so much illustrated by curious facts, that it must at last take the public attention. It is probably much improved by your last abode in London. If you were here at my

fire-side, I should dispute some of your principles. . . . But these, and a hundred other points, are fit only to be discussed in conversation. I hope it will be soon; for I am in a very bad state of health, and cannot afford a long delay.——HUME, DAVID, 1776, *Letter to Adam Smith, April* 1.

But there is still another cause, even more satisfactory than these, because it is of a still more extensive and permanent nature; that constant accumulation of capital, that continual tendency to increase, the operation of which is universally seen in a greater or less proportion, whenever it is not obstructed by some public calamity, or by some mistaken or mischievous policy, but which must be conspicuous and rapid indeed in any country which has once arrived at an advanced state of commercial prosperity. Simple and obvious as this principle is, and felt and observed as it must have been in a greater or less degree, even from the earliest periods, I doubt whether it has ever been fully developed and sufficiently explained, but in the writings of an author of our times, now, unfortunately, no more (I mean the author of a celebrated treatise on the wealth of nations), whose extensive knowledge of detail and philosophical research will, I believe, furnish the best solution to every question connected with the history of commerce or with the systems of political economy.—PITT, WILLIAM, 1792, *Debate in House of Commons, Feb.* 17.

Did not Adam Smith judge amiss, in his premature attempt to form a sort of system upon the wealth of nations, instead of presenting his valuable speculations to the world under the form of separate dissertations? As a system, his work is evidently imperfect; and yet it has so much the air of a system, and a reader becomes so fond of every analogy and arrangement, by which a specious appearance of system is made out, that we are apt to adopt erroneous opinions, because they figure in the same fabric with approved and important truths. That illustrious philosopher might therefore have contributed more powerfully to the progress of political science, had he developed his opinions in detached essays; nor would he have less consulted the real interests of his reputation, which indeed may have been more brilliant at first, by his appearance as the author of a comprehensive theory, but will ultimately be measured by what he shall be found to have actually contributed to the treasures of valuable knowledge.—HORNER, FRANCIS, 1800, *Journal Dec.* 1; *Memoirs, ed. Horner, p.* 126.

It is only a promiscuous assemblage of the soundest principles of political economy, supported by the clearest illustrations and ingenious statistical speculations, blended with instructive reflections; it is not a complete treatise on either science, but an ill-digested mass of enlightened views and accurate information.—SAY, JEAN-BAPTISTE, 1803–21, *A Treatise on Political Economy, Introduction.*

The writer in combating received opinions, has found it necessary to advert more particularly to those passages in the writings of Adam Smith from which he sees reason to differ; but he hopes it will not, on that account, be suspected that he does not, in common with all those who acknowledge the importance of the science of Political Economy, participate in the admiration which the profound work of this celebrated author so justly excites. —RICARDO, DAVID, 1817, *Principles of Political Economy and Taxation, Preface.*

The fact that the distinct statement of several of the most important of these principles, and that traces of them all, may be found in the works of previous writers, does not detract in any, or but in a very inconsiderable degree, from the real merits of Dr. Smith. In adopting the discoveries of others, he has made them his own; he has demonstrated the truth of principles on which his predecessors had, in most cases, stumbled by chance; has separated them from the errors by which they were encumbered, traced their remote consequences, and pointed out their limitations; has shewn their practical importance and real value, their mutual dependence and relation; and has reduced them into a consistent, harmonious, and beautiful system. —McCULLOCH, JOHN RAMSAY, 1825–30, *Principles of Political Economy, p.* 58.

The great defect of Adam Smith, and of our economists in general, is the want of definitions.—WHATELY, RICHARD, 1826, *Elements of Logic.*

Dr. Franklin once told Dr. Logan that the celebrated Adam Smith when writing his "Wealth of Nations" was in the habit of bringing chapter after chapter as he composed it to himself, Dr. Price, and others of the literati; then patiently hear their observations and profit by their discussions and criticisms, sometimes submitting to write whole chapters anew, and even to reverse some of his propositions.—WATSON, JOHN FANNING, 1830–68, *Annals of Philadelphia, vol.* I.

The great name of Adam Smith rests upon the "Inquiry into the Nature and Causes of the Wealth of Nations;" perhaps the only book which produced an immediate, general, and irrevocable change in some of the most important parts of the legislation of all civilized states. The works of Grotius, of Locke, and of Montesquieu, which bear a resemblance to it in character and had no inconsiderable analogy to it in the extent of their popular influence, were productive only of a general amendment,—not so conspicuous in particular instances as discoverable, after a time, in the improved condition of human affairs. The work of Smith, as it touched those matters which may be numbered, and measured and weighed, bore more visible and palpable fruit. In a few years it began to alter laws and treaties; and has made its way through the convulsions of revolution and conquest to a due ascendant over the minds of men, with far less than the average of those obstructions of prejudice and clamour, which ordinarily choke the channel through which truth flows into practice. The most eminent of those who have since cultivated and improved the science will be the foremost to address their immortal master,

Tenebris tantis tam clarum extollere lumen
Qui primus potuisti, inlustrans commoda vitæ
Te sequor!

—MACKINTOSH, SIR JAMES, 1830, *Dissertation on the Progress of Ethical Philosophy.*

It is not less agreeable in form than it is valuable in substance; and, instead of being—as is supposed by some who have not read it—dry and repulsive, is undoubtedly, to every reader of mature taste and liberal accomplishments, one of the most interesting as well as instructive books which he can take up.—EVERETT, ALEXANDER H., 1831, *Phillips's Manual of*

Political Economy, North American Review, vol. 32, p. 216.

Far superior to Arthur Young—superior as the researches of a Newton are above, though supporting and supported by, the observations of an Astronomical Table—stands the name of Adam Smith. . . . To say of the "Wealth of Nations" that it has faults and errors is only to say, in other words, that it is the work of man. But not merely did Adam Smith found the science of Political Economy; we might almost say of him that he completed it, leaving, at least as some have thought, to his successors, not so much any new discoveries to make, or any further principles to prove, but far rather conjectures to hazard and consequences to pursue.— STANHOPE, PHILIP HENRY (LORD MAHON), 1836-54, *History of England from the Peace of Utrecht to the Peace of Versailles, pp.* 335, 336.

The great work of A. Smith is not an elementary book,—very far from it; and your best chance of understanding it is to read of each chapter as much as you can, then go to the next chapter, and so on; and when you have got to the end of the book, begin the book again; and you will at length comprehend the whole sufficiently for any general purpose. I have lately seen a treatise by Mr. Boileau, which I hoped I might recommend to you on this occasion; but I do not think that it will be found either more simple or more intelligible, than A. Smith's original work, from which it is avowedly borrowed.— SMYTH, WILLIAM, 1840, *Lectures on Modern History*, Lecture xxx.

In the sense of a comprehensive aggregate, gathering into the unity of one edifice the total architecture of Political Economy, there are even at this day but few systems besides the "Wealth of Nations,"—none which approaches it in philosophic beauty.—DE QUINCEY, THOMAS, 1842-90, *Ricardo and Adam Smith, Works,* ed. *Masson, vol.* IX, *p.* 116.

The "Wealth of Nations" combines both the sound and enlightened views which had distinguished the detached pieces of the French and Italian Economists, and above all, of Mr. Hume, with the great merit of embracing the whole subject, thus bringing the general scope of the principles into view, illustrating all

the parts of the inquiry by their combined relations, and confirming their soundness in each instance by their application to the others. The copiousness of the illustrations keeps pace with the closeness of the reasoning; and wherever the received prejudices of lawgivers are to be overcome, or popular errors to be encountered, the arguments, and the facts, and the explanations are judiciously given with extraordinary fullness, the author wisely disregarding all imputations of prolixity or repetition, in pursuit of the great end of making himself understood and gaining the victory over error. The chapter on the Mercantile System is an example of this; but the errors of that widely-prevailing theory and its deeply rooted prejudices are also encountered occasionally in almost every other part of the work. It is a lesser, but a very important merit that the style of the writing is truly admirable. There is not a book of better English to be anywhere found. The language is simple, clear, often homely like the illustrations, not seldom idiomatic, always perfectly adapted to the subject handled. Besides its other perfections, it is one of the most entertaining of books. There is no laying it down after you begin to read. You are drawn on from page to page by the strong current of the arguments, the manly sense of the remarks, the fullness and force of the illustrations, the thickly-strewed and happily-selected facts. Nor can it ever escape observation, that the facts, far from being a mere bede-roll of details unconnected with principle and with each other, derive all their interest from forming parts of a whole, and reflecting the general views which they are intended to exemplify or to support.—BROUGHAM, HENRY LORD, 1846-55, *Lives of Philosophers of the Time of George III. p.* 263.

Twenty years have elapsed since Mackintosh pronounced this opinion; and during these twenty years, the influence of Adam Smith's science of political economy has been even more conspicuous and direct than it was during the period of which he spoke. It has shaped the polity of nations; its principles are embodied on almost every page of commercial law; it has guided the most important applications of national industry; it has done more than all other causes united to put a stop to the practice of international war. Though its doctrines have been somewhat modified, and large additions have been made to it, it is still, in the main, what we have called it, Adam Smith's science. His successors have built mainly upon the foundations which he laid, and the structure has risen in general conformity with the plan which he sketched out. Among all the moral sciences, there is no other which bears the name of its founder so distinctly engraven upon its front, or which retains so large a proportion of the doctrines that he first promulgated.—BOWEN, FRANCIS, 1851, *Phillips on Protection and Free Trade, North American Review, vol.* 72, *p.* 398.

Adam Smith is the distinguished man, by common consent, referred to as the Father of that School which has long claimed pre-eminence in Political Economy. Whatever ground there may be for ascribing to him this paternity, it is very safe to say, that were he to revisit the world, he would find it difficult to recognise his offspring. We prefer giving all the honor of this fatherhood to J. B. Say, who, though he may have taken his inspiration from Adam Smith, was certainly the first to give the doctrines of Political Economy a shape and degree of consistency sufficient to form the rallying points of a School. Regarded as a treatise upon industry, wealth, and trade, and the other subjects to which it refers, and considering the time at which it appeared, the "Wealth of Nations" must be admitted to be one of the most successful works of modern times. It has, beyond question, been the chief stimulus to the extraordinary discussions which have since ensued upon the subjects of which it treats. Its leading ideas made a great impression, and have since been the subjects of interminable discussion; but the "Wealth of Nations," though often referred to, is seldom studied.—COLWELL, STEPHEN, 1856, *ed., List's National System of Political Economy, p.* xxvii.

Looking at its ultimate results, is probably the most important book that has ever been written, and is certainly the most valuable contribution ever made by a single man towards establishing the principles on which government should be based. . . . Well may it be said of Adam Smith, and said too without fear of contradiction, that this solitary Scotchman has, by the publication of one single work, contributed more toward the happiness of men, than has been effected by the united abilities of all the statesmen and legislators of whom history has preserved an authentic account.—BUCKLE, HENRY THOMAS, 1857, *History of Civilisation in England, vol.* I. *ch.* IV.

The great text-book in political economy, "The Wealth of Nations." In every page of that work its readers found themselves presented with the evidence of the superior advantages of commerce over trade; and of the absolute necessity of commerce at home if they would have it abroad. . . . In every page of that great work they found evidence that if they would prosper they could do so on one condition only,—that condition which requires that the consumer and the producer take their places by each other's side, and thus approximate as nearly as possible the prices of raw materials and manufactured commodities. . . . Dr. Smith was not always right, but he was very generally so. Modern political economy, as has before been said, has very generally rejected him when he was right, or has so used him as to cause him to stand responsible for the correctness of views, that, had he been alive, he would indignantly have denounced as utterly erroneous.—CAREY, HENRY C., 1858, *Principles of Social Science, vol.* II, *pp.* 108, 109, 127, *note.*

When Adam Smith first stated the truth that one nation does not gain by the poverty of another, but that all are gainers by the prosperity of all, no one suspected that a sagacious despot of great power [Napoleon III.] would on this very year pronounce the great truth on his imperial throne to the assembled deputies of his nation.—LIEBER, FRANCIS, 1860, *Speech on the Hayes Arctic Expedition, New York, March* 22.

It is even at the present day important to direct careful attention to an erroneous conception of wealth, which was universal until the appearance of Adam Smith's great work, in 1775.—FAWCETT, HENRY, 1863–88, *Manual of Political Economy, p.* 8.

A glance at the index of the "Wealth of Nations" will suffice to show that its author possessed just that kind of knowledge of the American Colonies which

Franklin was of all men the best fitted to impart. The allusion to the Colonies may be counted by hundreds; illustrations from their condition and growth occur in nearly every chapter. We may go further and say that the American Colonies constitute the experimental evidence of the essential truth of the book, without which many of its leading positions had been little more than theory.—PARTON, JAMES, 1864, *Life and Times of Benjamin Franklin, vol.* I, *p.* 537.

That which Adam Smith got from the French economists was the habit of analytical research, exercised upon economical phenomena. I do not say that political economy began with him, but I can assert that its method does. His teachers argued from *à priori,* or what they believed to be *à priori,* principles, and examined the facts by these principles. Smith applied an inductive method to his facts, and, as far as possible, verified his hypotheses by observation. Hence his work is full of illustrations, is copious in examples, whenever illustration or example could be obtained. And just as succeeding economists have used his method, and in so far as they have gone to history and statistics, so they have been able to correct Smith; for in his day, history was uncritical, statistics were imperfect and inexact. But in so far as they have departed from his method, and suffered themselves to evolve the science from their own theories, they have, even the ablest among them, fallen into notorious fallacies.—ROGERS, JAMES E. THOROLD, 1869, *Historical Gleanings, p.* 119.

If books are to be measured by the effect which they have produced on the fortunes of mankind, the "Wealth of Nations" must rank among the greatest of books.— GREEN, JOHN RICHARD, 1874, *A Short History of the English People, p.* 755.

We may, however, admit that no more important book than the "Wealth of Nations" was published in Great Britain during the last half of the eighteenth century. Few writers have ever done for any study what Smith did for Political Economy. If he did not found a science, he brought a great body of theory into close relation with facts, and may be said to have first brought about a union between abstract reasoners and practical statesmen. To marry science to practice is the

great problem of politics; and from the appearance of the "Wealth of Nations" the main outlines and the chief methods of one important branch of political science were distinctly marked out. Much had been done, and much still remained to do; but Smith took the significant step and is rightly regarded as the intellectual ancestor of a race of theorists, whose influence, though not uniformly beneficial, has at least been of great importance towards constituting the still rudimentary science of sociology.—STEPHEN, LESLIE, 1876, *History of English Thought in the Eighteenth Century, vol.* II, *p.* 316.

It is just a hundred years since "An Inquiry into the Nature and Causes of the Wealth of Nations," appeared from the pen, not of a statesman, a banker, or a merchant, but of a Scottish professor of Ethics, of the somewhat ubiquitous name of Smith. It can hardly be said to have been an attractive subject; in all polite societies, its topics—labor, capital, wages, profits, rent and taxation—would have been voted dry, if mentioned at all; and even able editors of the day, who, of course, knew everything, save their own ignorance, must have despised its long disquisitions on real and nominal prices and the mercantile system. The prevalent conceptions of the wealth of nations at that day were of the resources of a prince, to raise armies, equip fleets, subsidize allies, pension poets, and build ostentatious monuments. As to useful labor as wealth, as to free labor as the chief glory of nations and the source of their power, it was a thing still undreamed. Yet the book which argued in this strain, soon made its way into men's minds: it penetrated the cabinets as well as the counting houses; it created a school; it grew in fame with the revolving seasons, until now, in this great land, which had then just sprung into distinct national existence, it is held in honor among our best centennial memories.—GODWIN, PARKE, 1876, *The Adam Smith Centennial, Address.*

It is interesting and pertinent to this year and to this occasion to call attention to the circumstance, not generally known, that months before the Declaration of American Independence, Adam Smith was led by his reasoning and investigations to advocate the peaceful abandonment, on grounds of purely economic advantage to the mother country, of the American colonies; and while pointing out, during the very first year of the war, the great improbability of conquering the Americans by force, predicted that the new transAtlantic States would ultimately form one of the greatest and most powerful empires that ever existed. And if to-day we fail to make good this prediction, it will be more than from any other one cause, because as a nation, we neglect and despise the economic laws developed in the "Wealth of Nations;" under and through the influence and intelligent application of which, the maximum of abundance and the highest intellectual, moral and religious development are capable of attainment by our countrymen.—WELLS, DAVID A., 1876, *The Adam Smith Centennial, Address.*

By nature, Smith was wholly unfitted to conduct a scientific discussion of any kind. He was a dreamer, not a reasoner. He evolved, to use a cant phrase, his systems from his own consciousness. He knew nothing of affairs, and could learn nothing from others. In his antipathy to merchants, or in a freak of passion, he lost sight of his principles altogether. . .

It is not strange that a person so wholly wanting in practical sense should be equally wanting in the perception of principles, in method, and in originality. He borrowed his ideas of money very largely from Law; following him, like Hume, where he was wrong, and rejecting him where he was right. In urging the advantages of freedom of trade, he was fully anticipated by Hume, "whose political discourses," says Stewart, "were of greater use to him than any other works which had appeared prior to his lectures." Had neither of them lived, the whole question of Free-Trade and Protection would have been precisely where it is to-day. . . . When the ignorance of Smith upon the subject upon which he wrote, his want of scientific method, the groundlessness of his assumptions and conclusions, especially in reference to money, are considered, the influence he has exerted over succeeding generations is well fitted to excite astonishment.— POOR, HENRY V., 1877, *Money and Its Laws, pp.* 168, 169.

Adam Smith may be said to have changed the whole theory of government, and in this way to have contributed more than any other person to the great revolutions of the nineteenth century.—WALPOLE, SPENCER, 1878, *A History of England from the Conclusion of the Great War in* 1815, *vol.* I, *p.* 327.

Had the great Scotchman taken this as the initial point of his reasoning, and continued to regard the produce of labor as the natural wages of labor, and the landlord and master but as sharers, his conclusions would have been very different, and political economy to-day would not embrace such a mass of contradictions and absurdities; but instead of following the truth obvious in the simple modes of production as a clue through the perplexities of the more complicated forms, he momentarily recognizes it, only to immediately abandon it, and stating that "in every part of Europe twenty workmen serve under a master for one that is independent," he re-commences the inquiry from a point of view in which the master is considered as providing from his capital the wages of his workmen. . . . Now, such men have not been led into such confusion of thought without a cause. If they, one after another, have followed Dr. Adam Smith, as boys play "follow my leader," jumping where he jumped, and falling where he fell, it has been that there was a fence where he jumped and a hole where he fell.—GEORGE, HENRY, 1879, *Progress and Poverty, pp.* 45, 142.

Although it at first attracted no great attention and had little political influence for at least a generation after its appearance, it has ultimately proved one of the most important events in the economical, and indeed in the intellectual, history of modern Europe. . . . Adam Smith showed by an exhaustive examination that the liberty of commerce which England allowed to her colonies, though greatly and variously restricted, was at least more extensive than that which any other nation conceded to its dependencies, and that it was sufficient to give them a large and increasing measure of prosperity.— LECKY, WILLIAM EDWARD HARTPOLE, 1882, *A History of England in the Eighteenth Century, vol.* III, *ch.* xii, *p.* 423.

The epoch-making "Wealth of Nations." —SIDGWICK, HENRY, 1883, *The Principles of Political Economy, p.* 15.

Is undoubtedly the Bible of political economy.—SAINTSBURY, GEORGE, 1886, *Specimens of English Prose Style, p.* 216.

The "Wealth of Nations" is, without doubt, the greatest existing book on that department of knowledge, the only attempt to replace and so antiquate it—that of John Stuart Mill—having, notwithstanding its partial usefulness, on the whole decidedly failed. Buckle, however, goes too far when he pronounces it "the most important book ever written," just as he similarly exceeds due measure when he makes its author superior as a philosopher to Hume. Mackintosh more justly said of it that it stands on a level with the treatise "De Jure Belli et Pacis," the "Essay on the Human Understanding," and the "Spirit of Laws," in the respect that these four works are severally the most conspicuous landmarks in the progress of the sciences with which they deal. And, when he added that the "Wealth of Nations" was "perhaps the only book which produced an immediate, general, and irrevocable change in some of the most important parts of the legislation of all civilized states," he scarcely spoke too strongly if we understand him as referring to its influence as an agent of demolition. It certainly operated powerfully through the harmony of its critical side with the tendencies of the half-century which followed its publication to the assertion of personal freedom and "natural rights."—INGRAM, J. K., 1887, *Encyclopædia Britannica, vol.* XXII.

Not only have we here a full disquisition on the comparative claims of Free-trade and Reciprocity; State regulation and unlimited competition; the importance of liberating industry, and the marvellous results of a division of labour; the sources of wealth in nature and the secret springs of human action, stimulating its production and determining distribution; but we have here, also, sage remarks on the decay of foreign trade and the causes of commercial depression, on the advantages of colonial enterprize, and an extension of Imperial possessions from an economic point of view; we have allusions to the co-existence of progress and poverty when the "age of industry" had scarcely commenced, and remarks on depopulation of the country districts and over-crowding of the towns; on landlordism and peasant proprietorship; on education and Church Establishment; on the just principles of taxation and local government—all subjects which at this present moment are occupying the public mind, and on which Adam Smith's views throw interesting and instructive side lights, whilst on such topics as the functions of capital, and the relationship of rent, profit, and wages, his authority, though questioned by some, cannot be ignored by any in the settlement of the long-standing controversy between capital and labour.—KAUFMANN, M., 1887, *Adam Smith and his Foreign Critics, The Scottish Review, vol.* 10, *p.* 388.

Adam Smith's book, as will be readily seen, was based upon the manufacture-industry which had as yet not been supplanted by the great machine-industry of modern times. It is important to bear this in mind in considering many of the views advanced in the work. Those who followed in his footsteps had necessarily to take into account the great industrial revolution which supervened but a few years after his death. The more immediate result of his teaching and the one which has maintained itself until the present day was the complete overthrow, in this country at least, of the doctrine of protection, and the establishment of free-trade as the basis of orthodox middle-class economics on their practical side.—BAX, ERNEST BELFORT, 1887, *ed., The Wealth of Nations, Introduction, vol.* I, *p.* xxxiii.

To the practical politician and social reformer, Adam Smith ought to be a hero, no less than he is to the economist. To both he appears in the light of one of the greatest vanquishers of error on record, the literary Napoleon of his generation. No man in modern times has said more with so much effect within the compass of one book. Yet it is not probable that any competent person could now be found to repeat without hesitation the assertion, made more than once by Buckle in his "History of Civilization," that "The Wealth of Nations" is the most important book ever written. As we become removed by an ever-increasing distance from the prejudices and opinions which Adam Smith once for all shattered, their magnitude and importance appear to grow smaller.—HALDANE, R. B., 1887, *Life of Adam Smith (Great Writers), p.* 12.

Adam Smith left the love of wealth in human minds, not rebuked but enlightened. Little more than a century has elapsed, yet mankind have made greater progress toward humane and mutually advantageous international relations in that time than during all the other centuries of human history.—WALKER, FRANCIS A., 1888, *Political Economy, p.* 2.

The chief merit of the "Wealth of Nations," and that which enables it still to hold its place at the head of the politico-economic literature of the world, is not any very great originality in detail, but an extraordinary grasp of all parts of the subject, and a marvellous ability in illustrating theoretical propositions by apt instances from practical life. Adam Smith is usually spoken of as the first prophet of Free Trade.—GOSSE, EDMUND, 1888, *A History of Eighteenth Century Literature, p.* 306.

One of the most remarkable books which bear a Scotchman's name—and that is saying much for it, and for him.— HUTTON, LAWRENCE, 1891, *Literary Landmarks of Edinburgh, p.* 26.

"Adam Smith on Wealth of Nations,"
Love is lost in calculations.
Bees whose bags are full of money
Do not gather love for honey;
  Business, enter if you dare!
  What is gold to golden hair!
—SLADEN, DOUGLAS, c1893, *Confessio Amantis, Amator: Amata: Mater.*

In reality I owe far more to Adam Smith than to Mill. The great defect of Mill's work is the want of historical knowledge, whilst a large part of the "Wealth of Nations" is history of the highest order. I have availed myself of the authority of the older master to include a much greater amount of history than is usual in a statement of principles. —NICHOLSON, J. SHIELD, 1893, *Principles of Political Economy, Preface, p.* vi.

It is not too much to say that Franklin's influence on economic education is illustrative of his whole educational doctrine. He gave to Adam Smith apt illustrations of the utility of the ideas of the "Wealth of Nations." So great had been the changes in America due to its development that the illustrations in the "Wealth of Nations" which bear particularly upon the American colonies are now hardly estimated at their original value; it should

be remembered that this book, which Buckle calls "the most important book ever written," and "the most valuable contribution ever made by a single man toward establishing the principles on which governments should be based," was the first work by an European scholar which made use of the American colonies as apt illustrations of its doctrines and pointed to those colonies as the country where the new political economy should develop in all its strength. Had Franklin done nothing else in the world but contribute these illustrations to Adam Smith's book, he would have had a high place among the great educators of mankind. As the first book on the economy basis of modern government in America, the "Wealth of Nations" should be classed with the "Federalist," De Tocqueville's "Democracy in America," and Bryce's "American Commonwealth." — THORPE, FRANCIS NEWTON, 1893, *Benjamin Franklin and the University of Pennsylvania, p.* 100.

The nature of his subject demanded clearness more than elegance; and the "Wealth of Nations" is always clear, often homely, even at times ungrammatical. . . . He will not keep up his dignity at the cost of the smallest obscurity; and, like Socrates, he takes his illustrations rather from the courtyard than the court. . . . His examples are almost always from actual life and history; he is fanciful only in his similes. . . . He is a hard hitter, and a good hater, though his heaviest strokes are levelled at bad laws and false doctrines, and his hatred is usually kept for classes, not individuals.—BONAR, JAMES, 1895, *English Prose, ed. Craik, vol.* IV, *p.* 318.

The value of the book can hardly be exaggerated. It consists largely in its practicality. He was writing, not for students only, but for statesmen and financiers and business men. . . . His book is full of acute practical suggestions. No wonder Pulteney said, in 1797, it is converting this generation and will conquer the next. What also aided it was the arrangement and plan of the book, so informal and unpedantic; its combination of deductive and inductive method, so well fitted to be the source of an historical as well as of an abstract school of economics; the broad view it takes of human life, so contrasted with "the economic man" of some later writers. It is remarkable that while his great aim was the demolition of abuses, he should have succeeded also in constructing so much that has proved permanent; and that, practical writer as he was, the one thing of supreme importance in him should be his contribution to the theory of his subject; for it has been noted that it was he who first showed how "value" measures human motive—that is, how much of human activity is measurable, and, therefore, open to science. Much of his influence was due to the exact date at which his book appeared—early enough to administer the *coup de grâce* to the old system of obstruction and to champion the cause of land and of labour, but not too soon to ride on the advancing wave of a new industrial epoch.—SMITH, A. L., 1895, *Social England, ed. Traill, vol.* 5, *p.* 335.

A good book to read in these times, or in any times. He may indeed say rash things about "that crafty animal called a Politician," and the mean rapacity of capitalists; but he is full of sympathy for the poor, and for those who labor; and is everywhere large in his thought and healthy and generous. I am glad to pay this tribute, though only in a note.— MITCHELL, DONALD G., 1895, *English Lands Letters and Kings, Queen Anne and the Georges, p.* 148, *note.*

By a course of masterly reasoning, far superior to that of Condillac, he demonstrated that in commerce both sides gain; and, therefore, that nations in multiplying their commercial relations, multiply their profits, and multiply their wealth; and that, as a necessary consequence, the labour of artisans, manufactures and commerce, all enrich a nation, and, therefore, that those who engage in them are productive labourers. Perhaps it may seem that the doctrine is so plain that it needs no proof; but that is far from being the case. At the time Smith proved it, it was a perfect paradox, contrary to the universal opinion of centuries. Even if Adam Smith had never done anything else for Economics than this, he would have been entitled to immortal glory. Smith's doctrine is now the very corner-stone of Economics, and made a complete change in public opinion, and in international policy, which has forever removed a

perennial source of war from the world. —MACLEOD, HENRY DUNNING, 1896, *The History of Economics, p.* 75.

It was not by mere chance that the Declaration of Independence and the "Wealth of Nations" were published at so nearly the same time. Each involved the recognition of the same principle in different fields of human activity. In modern politics we have seen that society is better governed by allowing individuals, as far as possible to govern themselves. In modern economics we have seen that society is made richer by allowing individuals, as far as possible, freedom to get rich in their own ways. Each of these principles has its limits; but each marks an immeasurable advance in politics and in economics, over the system of police government which had preceded it.—HAD-LEY, ARTHUR TWINING, 1896, *Economics, p.* 13.

To speak of Adam Smith as the author of "The Wealth of Nations" brings before us at once his chief claim to a place among the immortals in literature. The significance of this work is so overwhelming that it casts into a dark shadow all that he wrote in addition to this masterpiece. His other writings are chiefly valued in so far as they may throw additional light upon the doctrines of this one book. Few books in the world's history have exerted a greater influence on the course of human affairs; and on account of this one work, Adam Smith's name is familiar to all well-educated persons in every civilized land. . . . All the economists before the time of Adam Smith must be regarded as his predecessors; all the economists who have lived since Adam Smith have carried on his work: and his position in economics is therefore somewhat like that of Darwin in natural science. There are many schools among modern economists, but their work all stands in some relation to that large work of this "old master." —ELY, RICHARD T., 1897, *Library of the World's Best Literature, ed. Warner, vol.* XXIII, *pp.* 13519, 13523.

Too often the blood of the martyred thinker has been the seed of civilisation. To this general experience Adam Smith was a notable exception. As the founder of Political Economy, the systematiser and expounder of those economic ideas which lie at the root of civilisation, Adam

Smith escaped alike the violent opposition and the contemptuous indifference of his contemporaries; he had the good fortune to reap in his lifetime the reward of his greatness. Upon his brow ere he died was placed the wreath of immortality. When Adam Smith began to meditate upon economic problems the world was wedded to the great delusion of Protection. What could a solitary thinker do single-handed to overthrow a system which for centuries held the foremost intellects of the world in thraldom? Only an intellectual Don Quixote could hope by philosophic tilting to destroy a world-wide delusion. And yet the modest, retiring philosopher of Kirkcaldy, from his obscure study, sent forth ideas which, by moulding afresh the minds of statesmen, have changed the economic history of the world. In view of the grandeur of his work and the far-reaching nature of his influence, it is surely meet that in Scotland's temple of fame a niche should be found for her illustrious son, Adam Smith. . . . The remarkable features of Adam Smith's work was, that long before political emancipation was conceded, the Governments of the day, under the influence of the "Wealth of Nations," made concessions which paved the way for Free Trade. Pitt, whose economic ideas were somewhat advanced, made a sympathetic reference to the "Wealth of Nations" in the House of Commons in 1792, and his successors did much to purify the tariff on Smithian principles. By Cobden and Gladstone the ideas of the "Wealth of Nations" were still further translated into practical life in the direction of complete Free Trade. Under the guidance of the idea of Freedom which dominates that book, Liberalism set itself to the work of emancipation in all departments of the national life. A reformed commercial policy in the direction of Free Trade, a reformed foreign policy in the direction of national independence, a reformed legal code in the direction of equality before the law and freedom from feudal restraints, a reformed ecclesiastical policy in the direction of freedom from religious tests—these, and numerous emancipatory movements, were inspired by the idea of natural liberty, which, on the economic side, came from Adam Smith, and on the political side from the principles of the Revolution of 1688

as formulated by John Locke.—MAC-PHERSON, HECTOR C., 1899, *Adam Smith (Famous Scots Series), pp.* 9, 66.

GENERAL

Smith, who called into existence a new science, fraught with the dearest interests of humanity, and unfolded many of its principles in a single lifetime.—ALISON, SIR ARCHIBALD, 1833–42, *History of Europe During the French Revolution, vol.* XIV, *p.* 3.

The greatest man his county has ever produced. — BUCKLE, HENRY THOMAS, 1862–66, *History of Civilization in England, vol.* III, *p.* 338, *note.*

One consideration to be carried in mind in the interpretation of the "Wealth of Nations," is that its author's system of philosophy ought to be studied as a whole; his economic system was part of a complete system of social, or, as he called it, moral philosophy. Mr. Buckle, who on other points has much misconceived the "Wealth of Nations," properly says of it, and the "Theory of Moral Sentiments," that the two must be taken together and considered as one, both forming parts of the scheme embraced in his course of moral philosophy at Glasgow—a course which, it is important to observe, began with Natural Theology, and included, along with Ethics and Political Economy, the Philosophy of Law. Again, as his social philosophy should be considered as a whole, so the whole should be considered in connection with the philosophical systems, or methods, of investigation of his time.—LESLIE, T. E. CLIFFE, 1870, *The Political Economy of Adam Smith, Fortnightly Review, vol.* 14, *p.* 550.

He created the Science of Political Economy, and started the theory and practice of Free Trade.—BROOKE, STOPFORD, 1876, *English Literature (Primer), p.* 136.

Adam Smith, the first (alas! perhaps the last) real economist, did not devote his life to polishing up a theory of rent. Astronomy, society, education, government, morals, psychology, language, art, were in turns the subject of his study, and in all he was master; they all moved him alike, as part of man's work on earth. He never would have founded Political Economy if he had been merely an economist.—HARRISON, FREDERIC, 1883, *The*

Choice of Books and Other Literary Pieces,
p. 373.

The breadth and comprehensiveness of treatment characteristic of the utterances of such a teacher are inseparable attributes of his manner of thought. He has the artist's eye. For him things stand in picturesque relations; their great outlines fit into each other; the touch of his treatment is necessarily broad and strong. The same informing influence of artistic conception and combination gives to his style its luminous and yet transparent qualities. His sentences cannot retain the stiff joints of logic; it would be death to them to wear the chains of formal statement; they must take leave to deck themselves with eloquence.—WILSON, WOODROW, 1888, *An Old Master, The New Princeton Review, vol.* 6, *p.* 220.

It is needless, for these general and other reasons, to speak in detail of Smith's exposition of justice. Enough has been said about it and about the "Lectures" in general to show how far Adam Smith was from being a dogmatist, an exponent of some one uncritical and uncriticised view of human economic or social activity. The man had a complete "social philosophy," if we are obliged to put matters in this way, and these "Lectures" establish the fact that the "Wealth of Nations" was written as illustrative of merely one phase of human activity—not the ultimate and only phase. And the originality of Adam Smith's genius is more apparent after their perusal and after consideration of the facts and considerations they make apparent. What he learned in France was not enough to make him wholly recast what he had evolved as the natural result of the workings of his own independent, and great, original mind along the lines laid down for him largely by his British predecessors.—CALDWELL, WILLIAM, 1897, *Smith's Lectures on Justice, etc., Journal of Political Economy, vol.* 5, *p.* 257.

There can in any case be no doubt that Smith was a sincere theist, and that he especially lays great stress upon the doctrine of final causes. It is probably as clear that he was not an orthodox believer. His characteristic shrinking from "clamour" explains his reticence as to deviations from accepted opinions. But his warm admiration for Hume, Voltaire, and Rousseau, was scarcely compatible with complete disapproval of their religious doctrines; and not to express such disapproval, had he felt it, would have been cowardly rather than reticent. He no doubt shared the rationalism of most contemporary philosophers, though in the sense of optimistic deism. Smith argues, in the "Wealth of Nations," that society is so constituted that each man promotes the interests of all by attending to his own interests, and in the "Moral Sentiments," that sympathy induces us to approve such conduct as tends to this result. In both cases a belief in the argument from design is clearly implied.—STEPHEN, LESLIE, 1898, *Dictionary of National Biography, vol.* LIII, *p.* 8.

Thomas Warton

1728–1790

Born, at Basingstoke, 1728. Matric. Trin. Coll., Oxford, 16 March, 1744; B. A., 1747; M. A., 1750; Fellow, 1751; Professor of Poetry, 1756–66; B. D., 7 Dec., 1767. Rector of Kiddington, 1771. F. S. A., 1771. Camden Prof. of Ancient Hist., Oxford, 1785–90. Poet Laureate, 1785–90. Died, at Oxford, 21 May 1790. Buried in Trin. Coll. Chapel. *Works:* "The Pleasures of Melancholy" (anon.), 1747; "Poems on several Occasions," 1747; "The Triumph of Isis," (anon.), 1749; "A Description of . . . Winchester" (anon.), 1750; "Newmarket," 1751; "Ode for Music," 1751; "Observations on the Faerie Queene," 1754; "A Companion to the Guide, and a Guide to the Companion" (anon.), 1760; "Life . . . of Ralph Bathurst" (2 vols.), 1761; "Life of Sir Thomas Pope," 1772; "The History of English Poetry" (4 vols.), 1774–81; "Poems," 1777; "Enquiry into the authenticity of the poems attributed to Thomas Rowley," 1782; "Specimen of a History of Oxfordshire" (priv. ptd.), 1782; "Verses on Sir Joshua Reynolds' Painted Window at New College" (anon.), 1782. He *edited:* "The Union," 1753; "Inscriptionum Romanorum Metricarum Delectus," 1758; "The Oxford Sausage," 1764; C. Cephalas' "Anthologiæ

Græcæ," 1766; Theocritus' Works, 1770; Milton's "Poems upon Several Occasions," 1785. *Collected* Works: "Poetical Works," ed. by R. Mant, with *memoir* (2 vols.), 1802.—Sharp, R. Farquharson, 1897, *A Dictionary of English Authors, p.* 294.

PERSONAL

The grestest clod I ever saw, and so vulgar a figure with his clunch wig that I took him for a shoemaker at first.—Burney, Charlotte Ann, 1783, *Journal, ed. Ellis, Jan.* 14, *p.* 301.

His disposition, with some appearance of indolence, was retired and studious, and he fortunately acquired such preferments as enabled him to pursue his natural bent, and rove unmolested among the treasures of learning which his *alma mater* contains in such profusion. . . . He had less polish in his manner than his brother, Dr. Joseph, but the conversation of the two together was a rich banquet.— Chalmers, Alexander, 1808–23, *The British Essayists, Preface to the Idler.*

His person was short and thick, though in the earlier part of his life he had been thought handsome. His face, latterly, became somewhat rubicund, and his utterance so confused, that Johnson compared it to the gobbling of a turkey. The portrait of him by Reynolds, besides the resemblance of the features, is particularly characterized by the manner in which the hand is drawn, so as to give it a great air of truth. He was negligent in his dress; and so little studious of appearances, that having despatched his labours, while others were yet in bed, he might have been found, at the usual hours of study, loitering on the banks of his beloved Cherwell, or in the streets, following the drum and fife, a sound which was known to have irresistible attraction for his ears,—a spectator at the military parade, or even one amongst a crowd at a public execution. —Cary, Henry Francis, 1821–24–45, *Lives of the English Poets, p.* 158.

There are few characters on which I look with so much complacent interest as Warton's. His temper was so sunshiny and benevolent; his manners were so simple; his erudition was so classical and various; his learning was so illuminated by fancy; his love of the country was so unaffected; his images were so picturesque; his knowledge of feudal and chivalrous manners was so minute, curious and lively; his absence of all worldly ambition and show was so attractive; his humour was so good-natured and innocent; his unaffected love of literature was so encouraging and exemplary—that I gaze upon his memory with untired satisfaction. What life can be more innocent, or more full of enjoyment, than a life spent among books, under the control of taste and judgment! I do not think that Warton was of the highest order of genius; he had not enough of warmth and invention; nor dare I say that he was the more happy for this want. But still what pure pleasure must have been continually experienced by him who could write the "Ode on Leaving Wynslade!"—Brydges, Sir Samuel Egerton, 1834, *Autobiography, vol.* ii, *p.* 194.

HISTORY OF ENGLISH POETRY
1774–81

I am extremely pleased with T. Warton's new edition of his Observations, and have let him know as much by Balguy. I am glad he is in earnest with his project of the History of English Poetry; he will do it well.—Warburton, William, 1762, *Letters from a Late Eminent Prelate, Nov.* 30, *p.* 338.

To develope the dawnings of genius, and to pursue the progress of our national poetry, from a rude origin and obscure beginnings to its perfection in a polished age must prove interesting, instructive, and be productive of entertainment and utility. . . . The object being to faithfully record the features of the time, and preserve the picturesque representations of manners. . . . I have chose to note but the history of our poetry in a chronological series, and often to deviate into incidental digressions to notice the contemporaneous poetry of other nations. . . . My performance exhibits without transportation the gradual improvement of our poetry to the time that it uniformly represents the progression of our language. In the earlier sections of the work are numerous citations extracted from ancient MSS. never before printed, and which may illustrate the darker periods of the history of our poetry.— Warton, Thomas, 1774–81, *The History of English Poetry, Preface, p.* v.

Well, I have read Mr. Warton's book; and shall I tell you what I think of it?

I never saw so many entertaining particulars crowded together with so little entertainment and vivacity. The facts are overwhelmed by one another, as Johnson's sense is by words: they are all equally strong. Mr. Warton has amassed all the parts and learning of four centuries, and all the impression that remains is, that those four ages had no parts or learning at all. There is not a gleam of poetry in their compositions between the Scalds and Chaucer. . . . I have dipped into Mr. Warton's second volume, which seems more unentertaining than the former. . . . I have very near finished Warton, but, antiquary as I am, it was a tough achievement. He has dipped into an incredible ocean of dry and obsolete authors of the dark ages, and has brought up more rubbish than riches; but the latter chapters, especially on the progress and revival of the theatre, are more entertaining; however, it is very fatiguing to wade through the muddy poetry of three or four centuries that had never a poet.—WALPOLE, HORACE, 1774–78, *Letters to Rev. W. Cole and Rev. W. Mason; Letters, ed. Cunningham, vols. VI, p. 72, VII, pp. 50, 54.*

The progress of romance, and the state of learning, in the middle ages, are illustrated by Mr. Thomas Warton, with the taste of a poet, and the minute diligence of an antiquarian.—GIBBON, EDWARD, 1776–78, *Decline and Fall of the Roman Empire, ch. xxxviii, note.*

His diligence is indefatigable, and his learning stupendous; but I believe every reader, except a mere antiquary, will regret that, instead of a regular progressive history, he did not adopt the form of a critical dissertation, interspersed with anecdotes. His taste, which is frequently buried under piles of cumbrous erudition, would have had a freer scope.—GREEN, THOMAS, 1779–1810, *Diary of a Lover of Literature.*

In this latter author's (Warton) antiquarian mud we are already above knee-deep, and we must on as fast as we are able. . . . I trust that posterity (if posterity deserves it) will be blessed with some future anecdotist like one I could name . . . that will select out of those three quartos, Anecdotes of English Poetry, in two or three small octavos, about the size, for instance, of the "Royal and Noble Authors"; and should this be

the case, our Oxonian will not have written in vain.—MASON, REV. WILLIAM, 1781, *to Horace Walpole, March 20; Walpole's Letters, ed. Cunningham, vol. VIII, p. 18, note.*

An immense treasury of materials.— GODWIN, WILLIAM, 1803, *Life of Chaucer.*

The late Mr. Warton, with a poetical enthusiasm which converted toil into pleasure, and gilded, to himself and his readers, the dreary subjects of antiquarian lore, and with a capacity of labour apparently inconsistent with his more brilliant powers, has produced a work of great size, and, partially speaking, of great interest, from the perusal of which we rise, our fancy delighted with beautiful imagery, and with the happy analysis of ancient tale and song, but certainly with very vague ideas of the history of English poetry. The error seems to lie in a total neglect of plan and system; for, delighted with every interesting topic which occurred, the historical poet perused it to its utmost verge, without considering that these digressions, however beautiful and interesting in themselves, abstracted alike his own attention, and that of the reader, from the professed purpose of his book. Accordingly, Warton's "History of English Poetry" has remained, and will always remain, an immense commonplace book of *memoirs to serve for such an history.* No antiquary can open it, without drawing information from a mine which, though dark, is inexhaustible in its treasures; nor will he who reads merely for amusement ever shut it for lack of attaining his end; while both may probably regret the desultory excursions of an author, who wanted only system, and a more rigid attention to minute accuracy, to have perfected the great task he has left incomplete.—SCOTT, SIR WALTER, 1804, *Critical and Miscellaneous Essays, vol. I, p. 11.*

Compared with this, how different was Menander's case! Careless himself about examining and quoting authorities with punctilious accuracy, and trusting too frequently to the *ipsedixits* of good friends —with a quick discernment—a sparkling fancy—great store of classical knowledge, and a never ceasing play of colloquial wit, he moved right onwards in his manly course; the delight of the gay, and the admiration of the learned. —'DIBDIN,

THOMAS FROGNALL, 1811, *Bibliomania, or Book Madness.*

He loved poetry dearly—and he wrote its history well; that book being a mine. —WILSON, JOHN, 1831, *An Hour's Talk about Poetry, Blackwood's Magazine, vol.* 30, *p.* 483.

We have nothing historical as to our own poetry but the prolix volumes of Warton. They have obtained, in my opinion, full as much credit as they deserve: without depreciating a book in which so much may be found, and which has been so great a favourite with the literary part of the public, it may be observed that its errors as to fact, especially in names and dates, are extraordinarily frequent, and that the criticism, in points of taste, is not of a very superior kind.—HALLAM, HENRY, 1837–39, *Introduction to the Literature of Europe, Preface.*

It is pretty clear, from his observation upon the rhimes, and also from his notice of the contents, that Warton never read the poem ["Hule and Nightengale"]. He seems, indeed, but seldom to have opened a MS.; and when he gives an extract, or ventures a criticism, both extract and criticism will generally be found in the *Catalogue.*—GUEST, EDWIN, 1838, *A History of English Rhythms, vol.* II, *p.* 135, *note.*

The work has so much both of antiquarian learning, of poetical taste, and of spirited writing, that it is not only an indispensable and valuable authority, but in many parts an interesting book to the mere amateur. Not without many errors, and presenting a still larger number of deficiencies, it has yet little chance of being ever entirely superseded. — SPALDING, WILLIAM, 1852–82, *A History of English Literature, p.* 350.

A very curious and valuable work. It has had the reputation of a classic ever since its first publication, in 1774.— ADAMS, CHARLES KENDALL, 1882, *A Manual of Historical Literature, p.* 501.

His work, indeed, is one which it will perhaps be always necessary to consult for its facts, its references, and its inferences; and though in many points it needs to be corrected, a long time will certainly elapse before it will be superseded. All this can be said, and be said truly. But while the substantial merits of the chapters on Chaucer need not be denied, they are very far from being perfectly satisfactory. They were marked in particular by the defects which invariably characterized the writings of both the Wartons. In certain ways these two scholars were the most irritating of commentators and literary critics. Their object was never so much to illustrate their author as to illustrate themselves. Instances of this disposition occur constantly in those sections of the "History of English Poetry" which treat of Chaucer. Warton is constantly wandering away from his legitimate subject to furnish information about matters that concerned very remotely, if at all, the business in hand. Much of the material he collected is introduced not to throw light upon the question under consideration, but to parade his knowledge. Still, it is the spirit that pervades the work which is especially objectionable. About it lingered the apologetic air of the eighteenth century, which talked as if it had something of a contempt for itself for taking interest in an age when neither language nor poetry had reached the supreme elegance by which both were then distinguished. Warton's words make upon the mind the impression that he admired Chaucer greatly, and was ashamed of himself for having been caught in the act. Whenever he abandons conventionally accepted ground, we recognize at once the timid utterance of the man who feels called upon to put in a plea in extenuation of the appreciation he has manifested.—LOUNSBURY, THOMAS R., 1891, *Studies in Chaucer, vol.* III, *p.* 246.

Warton's work may be looked upon as a kind of classic fragment, the incompleteness of which has been emphasised by the glosses and alterations of three generations of commentators. . . . Had Warton chosen to follow the course contemplated by Pope and Gray, few men would have been better qualified to bring the undertaking to a successful issue. His reading was wide, his scholarship sound, his taste fine and discriminating; and though he had no pretensions to be called a great poet, his verse is at least marked by genuine poetic sensibility. Unfortunately he set about his work in the spirit of an antiquary, and in the patience, the industry, and the accuracy, required for this branch of knowledge, he was inferior to men who could not compare with him in capacity as a literary critic.—COURTHOPE, W. J., 1895, *A History of English Poetry, vol.* I, *pp.* xi, xii.

His cumbrous and amorphous learning, too vast to be exact, and too tenacious to be discriminating, might seem likely to submit its vigorous independence to any environment, however strong. But yet, as a fact, the work that Warton achieved would not have been possible to him had he lived in any previous age. His learning would have run into abstruse divagations, where pedantry and fancy would have overwhelmed all sense of proportion. To such abberations he was by nature only too prone. But the scientific sense of his age revealed to him just the questions in literary history which called for solution. He saw, by anticipation, some of the fruits which the comparative method might be made to yield; and, as a consequence, although he essayed a task too large for any man, and achieved what is doubtless an ill-arranged and ill-proportioned fragment, yet he left the impress of his independent thought and of his vigorous grasp upon our literature, and traced the lines upon which its history must be written.—CRAIK, HENRY, 1895, *ed., English Prose, Introduction, vol.* IV, *p.* 8.

Warton's "History of English Poetry" marks, and to some extent helped to produce an immense change for the better in the study of English literature; and he deserved the contemptuous remarks of some later critics as little as he did the savage attacks of the half-lunatic Ritson. But he was rather indolent; his knowledge, though wide, was very desultory and full of scraps and gaps; and, like others in his century, he was much too fond of hypothesis without hypostasis, of supposition without substance.—SAINTS-BURY, GEORGE, 1897, *The Flourishing of Romance and the Rise of Allegory, p.* 139.

But Warton's learning was wide, if not exact; and it was not dry learning, but quickened by the spirit of a genuine man of letters. Therefore, in spite of its obsoleteness in matters of fact, his history remains readable, as a body of descriptive criticism, or a continuous literary essay. The best way to read it is to read it as it was written—in the original edition—disregarding the apparatus of notes, which modern scholars have accumulated about it, but remembering that it is no longer an

authority and probably needs correcting on every page. Read thus, it is a thoroughly delightful book, "a classic in its way," as Lowell has said.—BEERS, HENRY A., 1898, *A History of English Romanticism in the Eighteenth Century, p.* 205.

At the outset, Warton's great undertaking was cautiously received. In so massive a collection of facts and dates, errors were inevitable. Warton's arrangement of his material was not flawless. Digressions were very numerous. His translation of old French and English was often faulty. In 1782 Ritson attacked him on the last score with a good deal of bitterness, and Warton, while contemptuously refusing to notice the censures of the "black-letter dog," was conscious that much of the attack was justified. Horace Walpole found the work unentertaining, and Mason echoed that opinion. Subsequently Sir Walter Scott, impressed by its deficiencies of plan, viewed it as "an immense commonplace book of memoirs to serve for" a history; and Hallam deprecated enthusiastic eulogy. On the other hand, Gibbon described it as illustrating "the taste of a poet and the minute diligence of an antiquarian," while Christopher North wrote appreciatively of the volumes as "a mine." But, however critics have differed in the past, the whole work is now seen to be impregnated by an intellectual vigor which reconciles the educated reader to almost all its irregularities and defects. Even the mediæval expert of the present day, who finds that much of Warton's information is superannuated and that many of the generalisations have been disproved by later discoveries, realises that nowhere else has he at his command so well furnished an armoury of facts and dates about obscure writers; while for the student of sixteenth century literature, Warton's results have been at many points developed, but have not as a whole been superseded. His style is unaffected and invariably clear. He never forgot that he was the historian and not the critic of the literature of which he treated. He handled with due precision the bibliographical side of his subject, and extended equal thoroughness of investigation to every variety of literary effort. No literary history discloses more comprehensive learning in classical and foreign literature, as well as in that of Great Britain.—LEE, SIDNEY, 1899, *Dictionary of National Biography*, vol. LIX, *p.* 434.

GENERAL

You have shewn to all, who shall hereafter attempt the study of our ancient authours, ["Observations on the Faerie Queene"] the way to success; by directing them to the perusal of the books which those authours had read.—JOHNSON, SAMUEL, 1754, *Letter to Warton, July* 16; *Life by Boswell, ed. Hill, vol.* I, *p.* 314.

This is a very splendid edition; [ed. Theocritus] and, after a careful perusal, I can pronounce it as correct as splendid. Every lover of Greek literature is under great obligations to the very learned and ingenious Mr. Warton for this magnificent edition of Theocritus, and for several other immortal productions. Everybody allows the Preface to be a beautiful and interesting composition.—HARWOOD, EDWARD, 1775–90, *A View of the Classics.*

One of the most beautiful ["Ode on Spring"] and original descriptive poems in our language, and strongly shews the force of poetical imitation in rendering objects that have no beauty in themselves highly beautiful in description. I suppose there are few scenes less pleasing and picturesque in themselves than the view from Catherine Hill, near Winchester, over the bare adjacent downs, and on the Itchin at its feet, formed into a navigable canal, and creeping through a wide valley of flat water-meadow, intersected often at right angles by straight narrow water-courses. But hear the poet, and observe how the scene appears in the picture he has given of it, without changing the features of the original.—PYE, HENRY JAMES, 1788, *Commentary on Aristotle's Poetic.*

Nor, amid the choir
Of pealing minstrelsy, was thy own lyre,
Warton, unheard;—as Fancy pour'd the song,
The measur'd music flow'd along,
Till all the heart and all the sense
Felt her divinest influence. . . .
—BEATTIE, JAMES, 1790, *Monody on the Death of Dr. Warton.*

He was a *genuine* poet, in its strictest sense. I remember some years ago, when it was the fashion to deny him *genius:* but I am utterly at a loss to guess what

meaning those, who denied genius to T. Warton, could affix to the word.—BRYDGES, SIR SAMUEL EGERTON, 1800, *Phillips's Theatrum Poetarum Anglicanorum, p.* lxi, *note.*

In one department he is not only unequalled, but original and unprecedented: I mean in applying to modern poetry the embellishment of Gothic manners and Gothic arts; the tournaments and festivals, the poetry, music, painting, and architecture of "elder days." Nor can I here refrain from repeating, that, though engaged in the service, his talents were never prostituted to the undue praise of royalty; nor from adding as a topic of incidental applause, that, though he wanders in the mazes of fancy, he may always be resorted to as supplying at least an harmless amusement; and that with Milton and Gray, whom he resembled in various other points, he shares also this moral commendation, that his laurels, like theirs, are untainted by impurity, and that he has uniformly written (to use the words of another unsullied bard)
Verse that a Virgin without blush may read.
—MANT, RICHARD, 1802, *Poetical Works of Thomas Warton, Life, vol.* I, *p.* clxi.

The poems of Thomas Warton are replete with a sublimity, and richness of imagery, which seldom fail to enchant: every line presents new beauties of idea, aided by all the magic of animated diction. From the inexhaustible stores of figurative language, majesty, and sublimity, which the ancient English poets afford, he has culled some of the richest and sweetest flowers. But, unfortunately, in thus making the use of the beauties of other writers, he has been too unsparing; for the greatest number of his ideas and nervous epithets cannot, strictly speaking, be called his own; therefore, however we may be charmed by the grandeur of his images, or the felicity of his expression, we must still bear in our recollection, that we cannot with justice bestow upon him the highest eulogium of genius—that of originality.—WHITE, HENRY KIRKE, 1806–13, *Remains, ed. Southey, vol.* II, *p.* 207.

This beautifully romantic poem ["Pleasures of Melancholy"], though executed at a period so early in life, betrays almost immediately the tract of reading, and the school of poetry, to which its author had, even then, sedulously addicted himself. Every page suggests to us the disciple of Spenser and Milton, yet without servile imitation; for, though the language and style of imagery whisper whence they were drawn, many of the pictures in this poem are so bold and highly coloured, as justly to claim no small share of originality. . . . On the genius of Warton, as a Poet, an adequate value has not yet been placed; for in consequence of a sedulous imitation of the diction of our elder bards, especially of Spenser and Milton, originality of conception has been very unjustly denied him. To his brother Joseph, with whom he has been commonly ranked, he is greatly superior, both in vigour and fertility of imagination, though, perhaps, less sweet and polished in his versification. In the rhymed pentameter, indeed, and in blank verse, in point of versification, to Dryden, Pope, and Milton; but in the eight-syllable metre, to which he was particularly partial, he has exhibited, almost uniformly, great harmony and sweetness. The mixture of *trochaics* of seven syllables, and *iambics* of eight, which has been objected to him as a fault, in this species of verse, I am so far from considering as a defect, that, as in Milton and Gray, I esteem it productive of much beauty and much interesting variety.—DRAKE, NATHAN,1810, *Essays, Illustrative of the Rambler, Adventurer, and Idler, vol.* II, *pp.* 169, 174.

In the best of Warton's there is a stiffness, which too often gives them the appearance of imitations from the Greek.— COLERIDGE, SAMUEL TAYLOR, 1817, *Biographia Literaria, ch.* I.

Warton was a poet and a scholar, studious with ease, learned without affectation. He had a happiness which some have been prouder of than he, who deserved it less— he was a poet-laureate.
"And that green wreath which decks the bard when dead,
That laurel garland,crown'd his living head."
But he bore his honours meekly, and performed his half-yearly task regularly. I should not have mentioned him for this distinction alone (the highest which a poet can receive from the state), but for another circumstance; I mean his being the author of some of the finest sonnets in the language—at least so they appear to me; and as this species of composition

has the necessary advantage of being short (though it is sometimes both "tedious and brief"), I will here repeat two or three of them, as treating pleasing subjects in a pleasing and philosophical way.—HAZLITT, WILLIAM, 1818, *Lectures on the English Poets, Lecture* VI.

Every Englishman who values the literature of his country, must feel himself obliged to Warton as a poetical antiquary. As a poet, he is ranked by his brother Joseph in the school of Spenser and Milton; but this classification can only be admitted with a full understanding of the immense distance between him and his great masters. He had, indeed, "spelt the fabled rhyme;" he abounds in allusions to the romantic subjects of Spenser, and he is a sedulous imitator of the rich lyrical manner of Milton: but of the tenderness and peculiar harmony of Spenser he has caught nothing; and in his resemblance to Milton, he is the heir of his phraseology more than of his spirit. His imitation of manner, however, is not confined to Milton. . . . If we judge of him by the character of the majority of his pieces, I believe that fifty out of sixty of them are such, that we should not be anxious to give them a second perusal. From that proportion of his works, I conceive that an unprejudiced reader would pronounce him a florid, unaffecting describer, whose images are plentifully scattered, but without selection of relief. To confine our view, however, to some seven or eight of his happier pieces, we shall find, in these, a considerable degree of graphic power, of fancy, and animation. His "Verses to Sir Joshua Reynolds" are splendid and spirited. There is also a softness and sweetness in his ode entitled "The Hamlet," which is the more welcome, for being rare in his productions; and his "Crusade," and "Grave of Arthur," have a genuine air of martial and minstrel enthusiasm. . . . The spirit of chivalry, he may indeed be said to have revived in the poetry of modern times. His memory was richly stored with all the materials for description that can be got from books: and he seems not to have been without an original enthusiasm for those objects which excite strong associations of regard and wonder. Whether he would have looked with interest on a shepherds' cottage, if he had not found it described by Virgil or Theocritus, may be fairly doubted; but objects of terror, splendour and magnificence, are evidently congenial to his fancy.—CAMP-BELL, THOMAS, 1819, *Specimens of the British Poets.*

His style in prose, though marked by a character of magnificence, is at times stiff and encumbered. He is too fond of alliteration in prose as well as in verse; and the cadence of his sentences is too evidently laboured.—CARY, HENRY FRAN-CIS, 1821–24–45, *Lives of the English Poets. p.* 162.

Tom Warton was one of the finest fellows that ever breathed—and the gods had made him poetical, but not a poet.—WIL-SON, JOHN, 1831, *An Hour's Talk about Poetry, Blackwood's Magazine, vol.* 30, *p.* 483.

Thomas Warton, although not one of our greatest, is still a most respectable literary name. He was an elegant scholar, if not a Bentley; a refined and genial critic, if not a Johnson; a tender and true poet, if not a Milton. If we may substitute comparison for contrast, he may be called, as a poet, a diffuser Gray, or even a weaker and less versatile Scott. . . . Altogether, looking at his poems in the light of effusions poured out in the intervals of laborious research and critical discussion, they are worthy of all acceptation; and we feel justified in binding the Poetical Works of Warton in the same volume with those of Goldsmith and Collins. They are certainly three among the truest and most refined of our minor poets. —GILFILLAN, GEORGE, 1854, *The Poetical Works of Goldsmith, Collins and T. Warton, pp.* 152, 154.

That robust scholar and genial poet.—LOWELL, JAMES RUSSELL, 1858–64–90, *Library of Old Authors; Prose Works, Riverside ed., vol.* I, *p.* 320.

Some of them express real feelings with an elegance so scholarly, so simple, and so full of faith, that no universalist in the love of poetry who has once read them chooses to part with them.—HUNT, LEIGH, 1859?–67, *An Essay on the Sonnet, ed. Lee.*

The scholia [Ed. Theocritus] are not conveniently disposed for the purpose of reference; and, in the opinion of Harles, as well as Brunck, the editor has not to the

full extent availed himself of all the valuable materials that were within his reach. —IRVING, DAVID, 1860, *Life of Warton, Encyclopædia Britannica, Eighth ed.*

Warton's numerous sonnets cover a wide range; but are particularly noteworthy for the increased attention they give to natural objects, and for the transition in the application of the sonnet to poetical subjects of a descriptive kind which this increase denotes. Instead of being confined, as the sonnet had been very generally, to amatory, elegiac, or complimentary subjects, or to the sublimation of some abstract sentiment or idea, his sonnets largely celebrate historical or familiar scenes and places, chosen by him for the picturesqueness of their environments, or for the interesting associations that were clustered around them. Many of the local descriptions in these brief poems are very attractive; and, indeed, there is scarcely one of his sonnets, whatever their theme, but will reward us by the gracefulness and delicacy of its sentiments, and the correctness of its diction and structure. It is true they make no great pretensions, but the level plain on which they travel reveals so many inviting bits of retired loveliness, and affords so many charming glimpses of quiet beauty, that we wonder his poems are so little known and prized. Probably, however, the neglect into which they have fallen is due to an excess of correctness of finish and an over-refinement of taste, which impart to them an air of stiffness and effeminacy that a closer inspection would measurably dissipate. To my mind, the transcripts of English sights and scenes in Warton's sonnets are extremely pleasing, and will bear close scrutiny.—DESHLER, CHARLES D., 1879, *Afternoons with the Poets, p.* 178.

Thomas Warton is in his poetry chiefly imitative, as was natural in so laborious a student of our early poetical literature. The edition of his poems which was published by his admirer and his brother's devoted pupil, Richard Mant, offers a curious example of a poet "killed with kindness;" for the apparatus of parallel passages from Spenser, Shakespeare, Milton, and others, is enough to ruin any little claim to originality which might have been put forward for him. . . . There are reasons why his genial figure should

GEORGE WASHINGTON

*From the Original Painting by Stuart
in the Boston Atheneum.*

BENJAMIN FRANKLIN

*From Original Painting by
Alonzo Chappel.*

not be altogether excluded from a representative English anthology. It has often been said that his "History of English Poetry." with Percy's "Reliques," turned the course of our letters into a fresh channel; but what is more noticeable here is that his own poetry—or much of it, for he is not always free from the taint of psuedo-classicalism — instinctively deals with materials like those on which the older writers had drawn. In reaction against the didactic and critical temper of the earlier half of his century, he is a student of nature; he is even an "enthusiast," in Whitehead's sense.—WARD, THOMAS HUMPHRY, 1880, *English Poets, vol. III, p. 382.*

Warton's style has no very special characteristics, and he does not conform to any marked convention in the structure of his sentences. But it is at all times forcible, clear, and free from pedantry; and he unquestionably added something to the recourses of English prose, in being the first to treat literary questions from the historical point of view.—CRAIK, HENRY, 1895, *English Prose, vol. IV, p. 331.*

Of all the laureates, with the exception of Rowe, Warton suffered the least from satirical attacks. His unmistakable claim to greatness seemed to impress the small buzzing gnats that usually swarmed about the poets of the day. Warton's first official ode was composed in haste and was not at all equal to the poetry he has been writing for many years, and it excited more or less ridicule; but after that, his official work was done with such genuine power that even the famous Wolcot, who under the name of Peter Pindar, produced such biting, brilliant, and unmerciful satires, contented himself with a few harmless thrusts. Warton was too great a poet and too amiable a man to treat such attacks with anything but composure and dignity. — HOWLAND, FRANCES LOUISE (KENYON WEST), 1895, *The Laureates of England, p. 124.*

Fourth-rate men like the two Wartons.

—BROOKE, STOPFORD A., 1896, *English Literature, p. 220.*

His books furnish ample evidence of that extraordinary industry in the discovery and examination of manuscript authorities which characterizes the antiquaries of the period; and though the accuracy of his learning was severely impugned by Ritson in 1782, in the anonymous "Observations on the History of English Poetry, in a Familiar Letter to the Author," yet the majority of the mistakes acridly corrected in the pamphlet are far from inexcusable in a work compiled from notes taken under all sorts of difficulties, and Ritson's attack was considered merely malignant. Warton's notebooks and papers, a box full of which is in the library of Trinity College, though often elaborate, are generally very slovenly and illegible, and the want of method which they display would sufficiently account for many *errata*. But while one is bound to make every allowance for accidental mistakes and immaterial inaccuracies, the interests of historical truth demand that one should expose without hesitation misstatements which appear to be intentional; and, unpleasant as the task is, it is a duty to call public attention to some facts which must seriously impair the confidence so long reposed in the trustworthiness of Warton's historical work.— BLAKISTON, HERBERT E. D., 1896, *Thomas Warton and Machyn's Diary, English Historical Review, vol. 11, p. 282.*

He had also an appreciation of wild nature, as we see from the descriptions in "The Grave of King Arthur." Warton's work is of interest because of the many attractive details scattered through his poems, but there is little unity of effect. The general impression is that he saw nature first through Milton's eyes, and that when he afterwards made many charming discoveries for himself he tried to express them in the *Il Penseroso* manner.— REYNOLDS, MYRA, 1896, *The Treatment of Nature in English Poetry, p. 128.*

Benjamin Franklin

1706–1799.

Born at Boston, Mass., Jan. 17, 1706: Died at Philadelphia, April 17, 1790. A celebrated American philosopher, statesman, diplomatist, and author. He learned the printer's trade in the office of his elder brother James, and in 1729 established himself at Philadelphia as editor and proprietor of the "Pennsylvania Gazette."

He founded the Philadelphia library in 1731; began the publication of "Poor Richard's Almanac" in 1732; was appointed clerk of the Pennsylvania assembly in 1736; became postmaster of Philadelphia in 1737; founded the American Philosophical Society and the University of Pennsylvania in 1743 and in 1752 demonstrated by experiments made with a kite during a thunderstorm that lightning is a discharge of electricity, a discovery for which he was awarded the Copley medal by the Royal Society in 1753. He was deputy postmaster-general for the British colonies in America 1753-74. In 1754, at a convention of the New England colonies with New York, Pennsylvania, and Maryland, held at Albany, he proposed a plan, known as the "Albany Plan," which contemplated the formation of a self-sustaining government for all the colonies, and which, although adopted by the convention, failed of support in the colonies. He acted as colonial agent for Pennsylvania in England 1757-62 and 1764-75; was elected to the second Continental Congress in 1775; and in 1776 was a member of the committee of five chosen by Congress to draw up a declaration of independence. He arrived at Paris, Dec. 21, 1776, as ambassador to the court of France; and in conjunction with Arthur Lee and Silas Deane concluded a treaty with France, Feb. 6, 1778, by which France recognized the independence of America. In 1782, on the advent of Lord Rockingham's ministry to power, he began a correspondence with Lord Shelburne, secretary of state for home and colonies, which led to negotiations for peace; and in conjunction with Jay and Adams concluded with England the treaty of Paris, Sept, 3, 1783. He returned to America in 1785; was president of Pennsylvania 1785-88; and was a delegate to the constitutional convention in 1787. He left an autobiography, which was edited by John Bigelow in 1868. His works have been edited by Jared Sparks (10 vols., 1836-40) and John Bigelow (10 vols., 1887-1888).— SMITH, BENJAMIN E., 1894-97, *The Century Cyclopedia of Names*, p. 408.

PERSONAL

The Body
Of
Benjamin Franklin,
Printer,
(Like the cover of an old book,
Its contents torn out,
And stript of its lettering and gilding),
Lies here, food for worms.
Yet the work itself shall not be lost,
For it will, as he believed, appear once more,
In a new
And more beautiful edition,
Corrected and amended
By
The Author.
—FRANKLIN, BENJAMIN, 1726? *Proposed Epitaph.*

There was a circumstance that I shall never forget, which passed in one of our conversations. Dr. Wight and I had seen Dr. Franklin at Edinburgh, as I have formerly related; we mentioned this philosopher to Mr. Allen with the respect we thought due, and he answered, "Yes, all you have said of him is true, and I could add more in his praise; but though I have now got the better of him, he has cost me more trouble since he came to reside in our State than all mankind besides; and I can assure you that he is a man so turbulent, and such a plotter, as to be able to embroil the three kingdoms, if he ever

has an opportunity." Franklin was after this for several weeks in Edinburgh, with David Hume, but I did not see him, having been from home on some jaunt. In 1769 or '70 I met him at an invited dinner in London, at John Stuart's, the Provost's son, I think it was, where he was silent and inconversible, but this was after he has been refused the office of Postmaster-General of America, and had got a severe dressing from Wedderburn, then Solicitor or Attorney-General.—CARLYLE, ALEXANDER, 1763-1860, *Autobiography*, p. 353.

An Epitaph &c. | To the much esteem'd Memory of | B . . . F . . . Esq., LL.D. | . . . | Possessed of many lucrative Offices | Procured to him by the Interest of Men | Whom he infamously treated | And receiving enormous sums | from the Province | For Services | He never performed | After betraying it to Party and Contention | He lived, as to the Appearance of Wealth | In moderate circumstances; | His principal Estate, seeming to consist | In his Hand Maid Barbara | A mostvaluable Slave | The Foster Mother | of his last offspring | Who did his dirty Work | And in two Angelic Females | Whom Barbara also served | As Kitchen Wench and Gold Finder | But alas the Loss! | Providence for wise tho' secret ends | Lately deprived him of his Mother

| of Excellency | His Fortune was not however impaired | For he piously withheld from her | Manes | The pitiful stipend of Ten pounds per Annum | On which he had cruelly suffered her | To starve | Then stole her to the Grave in Silence | Without a Pall, the covering due to her dignity | Without a tomb or even | A Monumental Inscription.—WILLIAMSON, HUGH, 1764, *What is Sauce for the Goose is also Sauce for the Gander.*

There is a general union among the colonies, which no artifices of a mininstry will be able to break. Dr. Franklin is a very popular character in every part of America. He will be received, and carried in triumph to his house, when he arrives amongst us. It is to be hoped he will not consent to hold any more offices under government. No step but this can prevent his being handed down to posterity among the first and greatest characters in the world.—RUSH, BENJAMIN, 1774, *Letter to Arthur Lee, May 4.*

A man who makes a figure in the learned world.—KAMES, HENRY HOME LORD, 1774, *Sketches of the History of Man, vol. III, p. 435.*

After dinner we went to the Academy of Sciences, and heard M. d'Alembert, as perpetual secretary, pronounce eulogies on several of their members, lately deceased. Voltaire and Franklin were both present, and there presently arose a general cry that M. Voltaire and M. Franklin should be introduced to each other. This was done, and they bowed and spoke to each other. This was no satisfaction; there must be something more. Neither of our philosophers seemed to divine what was wished or expected; they, however, took each other by the hand. But this was not enough; the clamor continued, until the explanations came out. "Il faut s' embrasser, à la Françoise." The two aged actors upon this great theatre of philosophy and frivolity then embraced each other, by hugging one another in their arms, and kissing each other's cheeks, and then the tumult subsided. And the cry immediately spread through the whole kingdom, and, I suppose, over all Europe—"Qu' il était charmant de voir embrasser Solon et Sophocle!"—ADAMS, JOHN, 1778, *Diary, Paris, Apr. 29.*

Mr. Fragonard, the king's painter at Paris, has lately displayed the utmost efforts of his genius in an elegant picture dedicated to the genius of Franklin. Mr. Franklin is represented in it opposing with one hand the ægis of Minerva to the thunderbolt, which he first knew how to fix by his conductors, and with the other commanding the god of war to fight against avarice and tyranny whilst America, nobly reclining upon him, and holding in her hand the fasces, a true emblem of the union of the American States, looks down with tranquility on her defeated enemies. The painter, in this picture, most beautifully expressed the idea of the Latin verse, which has been so justly applied to Mr. Franklin:

Eripuit cœlo fulmen sceptrumque tyrannis.

(He snatched the thunderbolt from heaven and the scepter from the hands of tyrants). —GAZETTE OF AMIENS, 1779, *on the Painting of Franklin.*

In a gallery of paintings in the Louvre, I was much gratified in perceiving the portrait of Franklin, near those of the king and queen, placed there as a mark of distinguished respect, and, as was understood, in conformity with royal directions. Few foreigners have been presented to the court of St. Cloud who have acquired so much popularity as Dr. Franklin. I have seen the populace attend his carriage, in the manner they followed the king's. His venerable figure, the ease of his manners, formed in an intercourse of fifty years with the world, his benevolent countenance, and his fame as a philosopher, all tended to excite love, and to command influence and respect. He had attained, by the exercise of these qualities, a powerful interest in the feelings of the beautiful queen of France. She held at that time a powerful political influence. The exercise of that influence, adroitly directed by Franklin, tended to produce the acknowledgment of our independence, and the subsequent efficient measures pursued by France in its support.—WATSON, ELKANAH, 1779, *Memoirs, p. 106.*

What diff'rence then can virtue claim
　From vice, if it oblivious lie?
While I can sing your spotless name,
　Your worthy deeds shall never die.
Nor shall oblivion's livid power
　Your patriotic toils conceal:
Alike in good, or adverse hour,
　A patron of the common-weal.
Forever faithful and sincere,

Your hands from gilded baits are free:
The public villain stands in fear
    You should perpetual counsel be.
The knave possest of shining pelf,
    Can never sway your honest choice:
For justice, emblem of yourself,
    Exalts above the rabble's voice.
—PARKE, JOHN, 1781, *To Lollius.*

Of all the celebrated persons whom in my life I have chanced to see, Dr. Franklin, both from his appearance and his conversation, seemed to me the most remarkable. His venerable patriarchal appearance, the simplicity of his manner and language, and the novelty of his observations, at least the novelty of them at that time to me, impressed me with an opinion of him as of one of the most extraordinary men that ever existed.—ROMILLY, SIR SAMUEL, 1783, *Journal, Life by his Sons, vol.* I, *p.* 69.

A new town in the state of Massachusetts having done me the honor of naming itself after me, and proposing to build a steeple to their meeting-house, if I would give them a bell, I have advised the sparing themselves the expense of a steeple for the present, and that they would accept of books instead of a bell, sense being preferable to sound. These are therefore intended as a commencement of a little parochial library for the use of a society of intelligent, respectable farmers, such as our country people generally consists of.—FRANKLIN, BENJAMIN, 1785, *Letter to Richard Price.*

DEAR SIR: Amid the public gratulation on your safe return to America, after a long absence, and the many eminent services you had rendered it—for which as a benefited person I feel the obligation —permit an individual to join the public voice in expressing his sense of them; and to assure you, that as no one entertains more respect for your character, so none can salute you with more sincerity or with greater pleasure than I do on this occasion. I am—dear sir, Your most obt. and most Hble. Servt.—WASHINGTON, GEORGE, 1785, *Letter to Benjamin Franklin, Sep.* 25.

Dr. Franklin lives in Market street. His house stands up a court, at some distance from the street. We found him in his garden, sitting upon a grass-plot, under a very large mulberry tree, with several other gentlemen and two or three ladies. When Mr. Gerry introduced me, he rose from his chair, took me by the hand, expressed his joy at seeing me, welcomed me to the city, and begged me to seat myself close to him. His voice was low, but his countenance open, frank, and pleasing. . . He seemed exceedingly fond, through the course of the visit, of dwelling on philosophical subjects and particularly that of Natural History; while the other gentlemen were swallowed up with politics. This was a favorable circumstance for me; for almost the whole of his conversation was addressed to me, and I was highly delighted with the extensive knowledge he appeared to have of every subject, the brightness of his memory, and clearness and vivacity of all his mental faculties, notwithstanding his age. His manners are perfectly easy, and everything about him seems to diffuse an unrestrained freedom and happiness. He has an incessant vein of humor, accompanied with an uncommon vivacity, which seems as natural and involuntary as his breathing.—CUTLER, MANASSEH, 1787, *Journal, July* 13; *Sparks' Life of Franklin, vol.* I, *pp.* 520, 523.

Be it remembered
In honor of the Philadelphia Youth,
(then chiefly artificers)
that in MDCCXXXI.,
they cheerfully,
at the instances of Benjamin Franklin,
one of their number,
instituted the Philadelphia Library,
which, though small at first,
is become highly valuable and extensively
useful
and which the walls of this edifice
are now destined to contain and preserve,
the first stone of whose foundation
was here placed,
the thirty-first day of August, 1789.
—CORNER STONE, PHILADELPHIA LIBRARY, 1789.

About sixteen days before his death he was seized with a feverish indisposition, without any particular symptoms attending it, till the third or fourth day, when he complained of a pain in the left breast, which increased till it became extremely acute, attended with a cough and laborious breathing. During this state when the severity of his pains drew forth a groan of complaint, he would observe—that he was afraid he did not bear them as he ought— acknowledged his grateful sense of the many blessings he had received from that

Supreme Being, who had raised him from small and low beginnings to such high rank and consideration among men—and made no doubt but his present afflictions were kindly intended to wean him from a world, in which he was no longer fit to act the part assigned him. In this frame of body and mind he continued till five days before his death, when his pain and difficulty of breathing entirely left him, and his family were flattering themselves with the hopes of his recovery, when an imposthumation, (abscess) which had formed itself in his lungs suddenly burst, and discharged a great quantity of matter, which he continued to throw up while he had sufficient strength to do it; but, as that failed, the organs of respiration became gradually oppressed—a calm lethargic state succeeded—and, on the 17th of April, 1790, about eleven o'clock at night, he quietly expired, closing a long and useful life of eighty-four years and three months.— JONES, DR. JOHN, 1790, *Account of the Illness and Death of Dr. Franklin.*

Mr. Speaker : As we have been informed, not only through the channel of the newspapers, but by a more direct communication, of the decease of an illustrious character, whose native genius has rendered distinguished services to the cause of science and of mankind in general; and whose patriotic exertions have contributed in a high degree to the independence and prosperity of this country in particular; the occasion seems to call upon us to pay some tribute to his memory expressive of the tender veneration his country feels for such distinguished merit. I therefore move the following resolution: "The House being informed of the decease of Benjamin Franklin, a citizen whose native genius was not more an ornament to human nature than his various exertions of it have been precious to science, to freedom, and to his country, do resolve, as a mark of the veneration due to his memory, that the members wear the customary badge of mourning for one month."— MADISON, JAMES, 1790, *Resolution of Congress, April 22.*

Franklin is dead! The genius that freed America and poured a flood of light over Europe has returned to the bosom of the Divinity. The sage whom two worlds claim as their own, the man for whom the history of science and the history of

empires contend with each other, held, without doubt, a high rank in the human race. Too long have political cabinets taken formal note of the death of those who were great only in their funeral panegyrics. Too long has the etiquette of courts prescribed hypocritical mourning. Nations should wear mourning only for their benefactors. The representatives of nations should recommend to their homage none but the heroes of humanity. The Congress has ordained, throughout the United States, a mourning of one month for the death of Franklin, and at this moment America is paying this tribute of veneration and gratitude to one of the fathers of her Constitution. Would it not become us, gentlemen, to join in this religious act, to bear a part in this homage, rendered, in the face of the world, both to the rights of man and to the philosopher who has most contributed to extend their sway over the whole earth? Antiquity would have raised altars to this mighty genius, who, to the advantage of mankind, compassing in his mind the heavens and earth, was able to restrain alike thunderbolts and tyrants. Europe, enlightened and free, owes at least a token of remembrance and regret to one of the greatest men who has ever been engaged in the service of philosophy and liberty. I propose that it be decreed that the National Assembly, during three days shall wear mourning for Benjamin Franklin.—MIRABEAU, HONORÉ GABRIEL RIQUETI COMTE DE, 1790, *Speech Before the National Legislature of France, June* 11.

As soon as his country was so well established that she had no need of seeking for partisans, his life became more retired and peaceable. In his retreat at Passy, there formed around him a circle, not large, of a few friends; and their company, with simple pursuits, occupied the close of a noble life. The course of it was broken by a painful illness, however, and from this moment his mind turned toward his own country. He left France, giving her, as the reward of her service, a great example, and lessons which could not long remain without profit. He sailed from an English port, to which he was accompanied by M. Le Veillard, who, while he lived at Passy, had lavished all the cares of filial tenderness upon him, and wished to postpone to the last moment what was to be an eternal separation. Franklin only stopped on the shores of England. He was so generous that he spared his humiliated enemies the spectacle of his glory. The French were his friends; the English were relatives,— whose faults one is glad to forget,—with regard to whom we still respect the bonds of nature, though they have broken them by their injustice.—CONDORCET, MARIE JEAN MARQUIS DE, 1790, *Address before the French Academy, Nov.* 13.

On Wednesday, King the American minister, Eliot, Montagu, and Henry Thornton dined with me, Rational day. . . Franklin seems, from King, not to be in good estimation in America. Thought a dishonest, tricking, hypocritical character; a free-thinker really, yet pretending to believe in the authority of Scripture. —WILBERFORCE, WILLIAM, 1796, *Table Talk, Life by his Sons, vol.* II, *p.* 179.

This self-taught American is the most rational, perhaps, of all philosophers. He never loses sight of common sense in any of his speculations. . . . No individual, perhaps, ever possessed a juster understanding, or was so seldom obstructed in the use of it by indolence, enthusiasm, or authority. Dr. Franklin received no regular education; and he spent the greater part of his life in a society where there was no relish and no encouragement for literature. On an ordinary mind, these circumstances would have produced their usual effects, of repressing all sorts of intellectual ambition or activity, and perpetuating a generation of incurious mechanics; but to an understanding like Franklin's, we cannot help considering them as peculiarly propitious, and imagine that we can trace back to them distinctly almost all the peculiarities of his intellectual character. — JEFFREY, FRANCIS LORD, 1806, *The Works of Dr. Franklin, Edinburgh Review, vol.* 8, *p.*328.

His reputation was more universal than that of Leibnitz or Newton, Frederick or Voltaire, and his character more beloved and esteemed than any or all of them. . . His name was familiar to government and people, to kings and courtiers, nobility, clergy and philosophers, as well as plebeians, to such a degree that there was scarcely a peasant or a citizen, a *valet de chambre:* a coachman or footman, a lady's chambermaid or a scullion in the kitchen who was not familiar with it, and who did not consider him as a friend to human kind. . . Nothing, perhaps, that ever occurred upon the earth was so well calculated to give any man an extensive and universal celebrity as the discovery of the efficacy of iron points and the invention of lightning-rods. The idea was one of the most sublime that ever entered a human imagination, that a mortal should disarm the clouds of heaven, and almost "snatch from his hand the sceptre and the rod." The ancients would have enrolled him with Bacchus and Ceres, Hercules and Minerva. His *Paratonnères* erected their heads in all parts of the world, on temples and palaces no less than on cottages of peasants and the habitations of ordinary citizens. These visible objects reminded all men of the name and character of their inventor; and, in the course of time, have not only tranquilized the minds; and dissipated the fears of the tender sex and their timorous children, but have almost annihilated that panic terror and superstitious horror which was once almost universal in violent storms of thunder and lightning.—ADAMS, JOHN, 1811, *Works, vol.* I, *Appendix, pp.* 660, 661.

An independence of thought, a constant and direct reference to utility, a consequent abstinence from whatever is merely curious and ornamental, or even remotely useful, a talent for ingeniously betraying vice and prejudice into an admission of reason, and for exhibiting their sophisms in that state of undisguised absurdity in which they are ludicrous, and with a singular power of striking illustration from homely objects, would justify us in calling Franklin The American Socrates. —MACKINTOSH, SIR JAMES, 1812, *Life by Mackintosh, vol.* II, *p.* 203.

Benjamin Franklyn, who, by bringing a spark from heaven, fulfilled the prophecies he pretended to disbelieve; Franklyn, who wrote a profane addition to the Book of Genesis, who hissed on the colonies against their parent country, who taught men to despise their Sovereign and insult their Redeemer; who did all the mischief in his power while living, and at last died, I think, in America; was beside all the rest, a plagiarist, as it appears; and the curious epitaph made *on* himself, and as we long believed, *by* himself, was, I am informed, borrowed without acknowledgment, from one, upon Jacob Tonson, to whom it was more appropriate, comparing himself to an old book, eaten by worms; which on some future day, however, should be new *edited*, after undergoing *revisal* and *correction* by the *Author*. —PIOZZI, HESTER LYNCH, 1815, *Notes on Wraxall, Autobiography*.

As to the charge of subservience to France, . . . two years of my own service with him at Paris, daily visits, and the most friendly and confidential conversations, convinced me it had not a shadow of foundation. He possessed the confidence of that government in the highest degree, insomuch that it may truly be said, that they were more under his influence than he under theirs. The fact is, that his temper was so amiable and conciliatory, his conduct so rational, never urging impossibilities, or even things unreasonably inconvenient to them, in short so moderate and attentive to their difficulties as well as our own, that what his enemies called subserviency I saw was only that reasonable disposition which, sensible that advantages are not all to be on one side, yielding what is just and liberal, is the more certain of obtaining liberality and justice. Mutual confidence produces of course mutual influence, and this was all which subsisted between Dr. Franklin and the government of France. —JEFFERSON, THOMAS, 1818, *Letter to Robert Walsh, Dec. 4.*

Franklin enjoyed, during the greater part of his life, a healthy constitution, and excelled in exercises of strength and activity. In stature he was above the middle size; manly, athletic and well proportioned. His countenance, as it is represented in his portrait, is distinguished by an air of serenity and satisfaction, the natural consequence of a vigorous temperament, of strength of mind, and conscious integrity. It is also marked, in visible characters, by deep thought and inflexible resolution. Very rarely shall we see a combination of features, of more agreeable harmony; an aspect in which the human passions are more happily blended or more favourably modified, to command authority, to conciliate esteem, or to excite love and veneration. His colloquial accomplishments are mentioned by those who knew him, in terms of the highest praise.—SANDERSON, JOHN,

1820–28, *Biography of the Signers to the Declaration of Independence, vol. III, p. 132.*

Our Franklin happily passes his time, in pleasing sobriety, with the illustrious sages and philosophers of all nations and ages. Though uniformly cheerful, he seldom or never laughs; and, with all the engaging simplicity of a child, he pours forth the matured and comprehensive wisdom of experience. Uniting the essence of wit, quickness of thought and facility of combination, with that brevity which is its appropriate garb, he charms without effort and teaches without appearing the master. It is delightful to see him in simple dress and simple language, like one of the primitive instructors of mankind, condensing some fine moral in the compass of a single sentence, or illustrating some glorious precept by a happy allegory that embodies, and gives life and being to the truth. The weight of wisdom and benignity united with good temper and unaffected manners, was never more strikingly exemplified than in the influence of this immortal Printer upon the country to which he was a benefactor, and the age to which he was an ornament.—PAULDING, JAMES K., 1821, *National Intelligencer, Jan. 20; Literary Life, ed. Paulding, p.* 155.

Dr. Franklin appeared at court in the costume of an American cultivator; his hair plainly brushed, without powder. His round hat and plain coat of brown cloth contrasted strongly with the powdered *coiffures* and the bespangled and embroidered coats of the perfumed courtiers of Versailles. His simple and novel, yet dignified appearance charmed the ladies of the court, and many were the *fêtes* given him, not only for his fame as a philosopher, but in acknowledgment of his patriotic virtues, which led him to enroll himself among the noble supporters of the cause of liberty. I assisted at one of these entertainments, where the most beautiful from among three hundred ladies was designated to place a crown of laurel on the gray head, and to salute with a kiss each cheek of the American philosopher. —CAMPAN, JEANNE LOUISE HENRIETTE, 1823, *Memoirs of Marie Antoinette.*

His qualities were those of a sterling practical Englishman; he directed his whole attention to the real and substantial objects of life, and therefore at a later period in France he laughed at the sentimentality, ideality and enthusiasm of the French in favour of the freedom which he announced, and even at the manner in which he himself was idolized; but he was prudently silent, and availed himself of the Parisian *mode* for the promotion of his objects. He had now been for thirty years renowned in America as the founder of a printing establishment, the originator of widely circulated newspapers and journals, as a popular writer and moralist; and in Europe for fifteen years as a natural philosopher, an acute observer and discoverer of some of the grand phænomena of the physical world. He had become strictly moral as soon as he renounced the sins of his youth, and was no longer straitened or weighted down by the pressure of poverty; he however knew the ways of men too well to feel himself always bound to walk on the narrow path, or to renounce the course of crooked policy when the attainment of an important object invited him to pursue it, provided he was not required to commit any flagrant violations of propriety. — SCHLOSSER, FRIEDRICH CHRISTOPH, 1823, *History of the Eighteenth Century, tr. Davison, vol.* v, *p.* 60.

The incorruptible integrity, sagacious intellect, and philosophic spirit of Franklin.—ALISON, SIR ARCHIBALD, 1833–42, *History of Europe During the French Revolution, vol.* XIV, *p.* 2.

No man in Paris, was more *à la mode*, more sought after than was Dr. Franklin. The crowd used to run after him in the walks and in the public resorts; hats, canes, snuff-boxes, everything was *à la Franklin*. Men and women considered it a piece of good fortune to be invited to a dinner at which this celebrated man was to be present.—LEBRUN, MADAME VIGÉE, 1835, *Memoirs, vol.* I, *p.* 251.

Sage Franklin next arose in cheerful mien,
And smil'd, unruffled, o'er the solemn scene;
High on his locks of age, a wreath was brac'd,
Palm of all arts that e'er a mortal grac'd;
Beneath him lay the sceptre kings had borne,
And crowns and laurels from their temples torn.
—WEEMS, MASON L., 1835, *Title Page to Life of Franklin.*

One of the most remarkable men certainly, of our times, as a politician, or of any age, as a philosopher, was Franklin; who also stands alone in combining together these two characters, the greatest that man can sustain, and in this, that having borne the first part in enlarging science, by one of the greatest discoveries ever made, he bore the second part in founding one of the greatest empires in the world. . . . In domestic life he was faultless, and in the intercourse of society, delightful. There was a constant good humour and a playful wit, easy and of high relish, without any ambition to shine, the natural fruit of his lively fancy, his solid, natural good sense, and his cheerful temper, that gave his conversation an unspeakable charm, and alike suited every circle, from the humblest to the most elevated. With all his strong opinions, so often solemnly declared, so imperishably recorded in his deeds, he retained a tolerance for those who differed with him, which could not be surpassed in men whose principles hang so loosely about them as to be taken up for a convenient cloak, and laid down when found to impede their progress. In his family he was everything that worth, warm affections, and sound prudence could contribute, to make a man both useful and amiable, respected and beloved. In religion, he would by many be reckoned a latitudinarian; yet it is certain that his mind was imbued with a deep sense of the Divine perfections, a constant impression of our accountable nature, and a lively hope of future enjoyment.—BROUGHAM, HENRY LORD, 1839, *Statesmen of the Time of George III.*

With placid tranquility, Benjamin Franklin looked quietly and deeply into the secrets of nature. His clear understanding was never perverted by passion, or corrupted by the pride of theory. The son of a rigid Calvinist, the grandson of a tolerant Quaker, he had from boyhood been familiar not only with theological subtilities, but with a catholic respect for freedom of mind. Skeptical of tradition as the basis of faith, he respected reason, rather than authority; and, after a momentary lapse into fatalism, escaping from the mazes of fixed decrees and free will, he gained, with increasing years, an increasing trust in the overruling providence of God. Adhering to none "of all the religions" in the colonies, he yet devoutly, though without form, adhered to religion. But though famous as disputant, and having a natural aptitude for metaphysics, he obeyed the tendency of his age, and sought by observation to win an insight into the mysteries of being. . . Never professing enthusiasm, never making a parade of sentiment, his practical wisdom was sometimes mistaken for the offspring of selfish prudence; yet his hope was steadfast, like that hope which rests on the Rock of Ages, and his conduct was as unerring as though the light that led him was a light from heaven. He ever anticipated action by theories of self-sacrificing virtue; and yet, in the moments of intense activity, he, from the highest abodes of ideal truth, brought down and applied to the affairs of life the sublimest principles of goodness, as noiselessly and unostentatiously as became the man who, with a kite and hempen string, drew the lightning from the skies.—BANCROFT, GEORGE, 1844, *History of the United States, vol.* III, *p.* 378.

Franklin was the greatest diplomatist of the eighteenth century. He never spoke a word too soon; he never spoke a word too late; he never spoke a word too much; he never failed to speak the right word at the right season.—BANCROFT, GEORGE, 1852, *New York Historical Society Lecture, Dec.* 9.

The historic image of Benjamin Franklin, does not so vividly impress the mind as the grander, more colossal figures which, instinct with the glory of brilliant genius, star-stud the vista of the dim past —but its paler, less dazzling light, is— we may be permitted to repeat—a more hopeful and cheering one to the masses of mankind, for it shines upon a path to eminence which it requires no seraph's wing,—no transcendant mental power— to oversweep or climb,—nothing but the qualities, prudently but courageously exercised, which he himself possessed,—a clear intellect,—firm purpose,—self-denial,— energetic labour,—and perhaps the moral of his life is all the more pertinent and instructive, inasmuch that he stumbled heavily upon the threshold of his career, and recovered himself unaided save by God and his own brave honesty of will.—RUSSELL, WILLIAM, 1853, *Extraordinary Men,* p. 102.

To-morrow we are to inaugurate Greenough's Franklin with a tremendous procession—which I look at solely from a Mabelian point of view. Did I say solely? Well, let it stand. But I may just mention that the American Academy comes in before the governor, and Charles perhaps can tell you who *some* of the fellows are. *It is thought* that they will find carriages provided for them. That under these circumstances I should find composure to write to you is a curious biological (I believe that's the word now) fact. There are to be two addresses and an oration. Only think how interesting! And we shall find out that Franklin was born in Boston, and invented being struck with lightning and printing and the Franklin medal, and that he had to move to Philadelphia because great men were so plenty in Boston that he had no chance, and that he revenged himself on his native town by saddling it with the Franklin stove, and that he discovered the almanac, and that a penny saved is a penny lost, or something of the kind. So we put him up a statue. *I* mean to invent something—in order to encourage sculptors.— LOWELL, JAMES RUSSELL, 1856, *Letters, ed. Norton, vol.* I, *p.* 271.

Go forth then, Benjamin Franklin, printer, to thy great calling; master, not of arts, but of the art of arts; graduate, not of academic halls, but of the three great faculties of temperance, industry, and generous ambition. There is a conflict before thee long and sharp, but the press has taught thy hands to war and thy fingers to fight; the victory is certain, the reward is glorious. Seas of trouble shall stretch before thee, but they shall roll up their crystal walls on thy right hand and on thy left, and thou shall pass through on dry ground. Events of unexampled magnitude for thee and thy country attend thy career; great wars are to be fought; oppressive rulers set at defiance; arduous negotiations conducted; alliances contracted abroad, confederacies entered into at home, constitutions framed, and governments administered;—and in all these vast concerns thou, even thou, Benjamin Franklin, printer, shalt bear a responsible and even a leading part, with the sages, the patriots, and the monarchs of Europe, with the most honoured and trusted of thy own counntry, with Adams, with Jefferson, with Jay, with Laurens, and above all, with Washington.

Boston now sends thee forth a penniless fugitive; Philadelphia receives thee a homeless adventurer; but ere thou shalt taste of death, America, Europe, shall be too narrow for thy fame; and in times to come, the friendly strife of the city of thy birth and the city of thy adoption shall be which best, which most, shall do honor to thy memory.—EVERETT, EDWARD, 1859, *Franklin the Boston Boy, Orations and Speeches, vol. IV, p.* 128.

Well, Sir, this part of the town, I think, should have an interest for people from your side of the water, for it has associations connected with a certain countryman of yours named Benjamin Franklin. When he was toiling as a journeyman printer in the metropolis, more than a century ago, he was accustomed to stroll upon the Sunday afternoon along the banks of Father Thames, and this end of this Cheyne Row was usually his goal. One day, as he walked discoursing with a friend, he declared himself able to swim from here to London Bridge, distant about five miles. His friend offered a wager that it was impossible; and he, upon the instant stripping, plunged boldly in, and started for his mark, while his friend, bearing the clothes, strode down the bank; and a great multitude of spectators, growing ever greater as he proceeded, followed to see the feat. He, with brave stroke and lusty sinew buffeting the tide, gained the bridge and the wager. Whereupon, amidst great acclamations, the people suggested that he should start a swimming school. But God had other work for him to do: for in later years he was to teach the people of your continent how, by Frugality and Labor, and Patience and Courage, any man might buffet the waves of Fortune, and swim straight on to prosperity and success. And that was the swimming-school which he was to establish.—CARLYLE, THOMAS, 1860? *Conversation with Dr. Milburn; Guernsey's Life of Carlyle, p.* 17.

Dr. Sprague, of Albany, who has collected a great number of autographs, made application, some time since, to a certain gentleman for that of Dr. Franklin. "Oh, you have one already," said the person referred to. "No matter," replied the determined collector. "I want it for exchange. One Benny Franklin in Europe is worth *two kings!*"—NORTON, JOHN N., 1861, *Life of Doctor Franklin, p.* 177, *note.*

Of the men whom the world currently terms *Self-Made*—that is, who severally fought their life-battles without the aid of inherited wealth, or family honors, or educational advantages, perhaps our American Franklin stands highest in the civilized world's regard. . . . I think I adequately appreciate the greatness of Washington, yet I must place Franklin above him as the consummate type and flowering of human nature under the skies of colonial America. Not that Washington was born to competence and all needful facilities for instruction, so that he began responsible life on vantage ground that Franklin toiled twenty arduous, precious years to reach; I can not feel that this fact has undue weight with me. I realize that there are elements of dignity, of grandeur, in the character of Washington for which that of Franklin affords no parallel. But when I contemplate the immense variety and versatility of Franklin's services to his country and to mankind; when I think of him as a writer whose first effusions commanded attention in his early boyhood; as a monitor and teacher of his fellow journeymen in a London printing office; as almost from the outset a prosperous and influential editor when journalism had never before been a source of power; as taking his place naturally at the head of the postal service in America, and of the earliest attempts to form a practical confederation of the colonies; when I see him, never an enthusiast, and now nearly three-score-and-ten, renouncing office, hazarding fame, fortune, everything, to struggle for the independence of his country, he having most to lose by failure of any American, his only son a bitter Loyalist, he cheerfully and repeatedly braving the dangers of an ocean swarming with enemies, to render his country the service as ambassador which no other man could perform, and finally, when more than eighty years old, crowning a life of duty and honor by helping to frame that immortal Constitution which made us one nation forever, I cannot place Franklin second to any other American. He could not have done the work of Washington—no other man could; but then he did so many admirable things which Washington had too sound a judgment even to attempt. And, great as Washington was, he was not great enough to write and print after he had achieved power and world-wide fame, a frank, ingenuous confession of his youthful follies and sins for the instruction and admonition of others. Many a man can look calmly down the throats of roaring cannon who lacks the courage and true philanthropy essential to those called to render this service to mankind.—GREELEY, HORACE, 1862, *Self-Made Men.*

Men have lived who were more magnificently endowed than Franklin. Men have lived whose lives were more splendid and heroic than his. If the inhabitants of the earth were required to select, to represent them in some celestial congress composed of the various orders of intelligent beings, a specimen of the human race, and we should send a Shakespeare, the celestials would say, He is one of *us;* or a Napoleon, the fallen angels might claim him. But if we desired to select a man who could present in his own character the largest amount of human worth with the least of human frailty, and in his own lot on earth the largest amount of enjoyment with the least of suffering; one whose character was estimable without being too exceptionally good, and his lot happy without being too generally unattainable; one who could bear in his letter of credence, with the greatest truth, *This is a Man, and his life on earth was such as good men may live*, I know not who, of the renowned of all ages, we could more fitly choose to represent us in that high court of the universe, than Benjamin Franklin, printer, of Philadelphia.—PARTON, JAMES, 1864, *Life and Times of Benjamin Franklin, vol.* II, *p.* 655.

No one began lower than the poor apprentice of Boston; no one raised himself higher, by his own energy, than did the inventor of the lightning-rod; no one has rendered more splendid services to his country than the diplomatist who signed the peace of 1783 and secured the independence of the United States.—LABOULAYE, EDOUARD, 1866, *Memoir of Franklin.*

The ideal American, as he has been painted for us of late, is a man who has shaken off the yoke of definite creeds, while retaining their moral essence, and finds the highest sanctions needed for the conduct of human life in experience tempered by common sense. Franklin is generally supposed to have reached this ideal by anticipation, and there is a half-truth in the supposition. But whoever will study this great master of practical life in the picture here painted by himself, will acknowledge that it is only superficially true, and that if he never lifts us above the earth or beyond the domain of experience and common-sense, he retained himself a strong hold on the invisible which underlies it, and would have been the first to acknowledge that it was this which enabled him to control the accidents of birth, education, and position, and to earn the eternal gratitude and reverence of the great nation over whose birth he watched so wisely and whose character he did so much to form.—HUGHES, THOMAS, 1879, *Benjamin Franklin, The Contemporary Review, vol.* 35, *p.* 594.

The Declaration did its work; the representative of America in Paris was doing his. Edmund Burke was right when, in a letter to a friend, he remarked that Franklin's presence in France was in itself a triumph for the Colonies. The man who it was said had "snatched the thunderbolt from heaven and the sceptre from tyrants" received such men as Turgot, who had resigned his portfolio, and Vergennes who was still in power; naturalists, such as Buffon; nobles, such as La Rochefoucauld; philosophers, such as D'Alembert and Helvétius; physicians, such as Cabanis and Vicq d'Azyr; men of letters, such as Rynal, Morellet, and Mably; jurists, such as Malesherbes, the admirer of a country that sent a tallow-chandler's son as its envoy to a court. All these Franklin charmed and captivated by a power so subtle and magnetic as to be well-nigh indefinable. The people read with admiration the "Science du Bonhomme Richard." At Paris they called it with praise "a very little book treating great subjects." Many purchased and read a thin volume which then appeared and which contained the American Colonies' Constitution. Numbers called on Franklin at his house and discussed public affairs with him. Those who came, those who discussed, those who read were equally ardent for the American struggle. — ROSENTHAL, LEWIS, 1882, *America and France, p.* 32.

To say that his life is the most interesting, the most uniformly successful, yet lived by any American, is bold. But it is nevertheless, strictly true. Not the least of the many glories of our country is the long list of men who, friendless, half-educated, poor, have, by the sheer force of their own abilities, raised themselves from the humblest beginnings to places of eminence and command. Many of these have surpassed him. Some have speculated more deeply on finance, have been more successful as philanthropists, have made greater discoveries in physics, have written books more commonly read than his. Yet not one of them has attained to greatness in so many ways, or has made so lasting an impression on his countrymen. His face is as well known as the face of Washington, and, save that of Washington, is the only one of his time that is now instantly recognized by the great mass of his countrymen. His maxims are in every man's mouth. His name is, all over the country, bestowed on counties and towns, on streets, on societies, on corporations.—McMASTER, JOHN BACH, 1887. *Benjamin Franklin as a Man of Letters* (*American Men of Letters*), *p.* 281.

To this day Franklin is cordially remembered in France. Nor can any one well study the history of the years of his life, which proved so important to his country, without constant reference to the archives of that other country which he loved next to his own.—HALE, EDWARD EVERETT, AND HALE, JR., EDWARD EVERETT, 1888, *Franklin in France, pt.* ii, *p.* 416.

One cannot rise from a perusal of these documents without entertaining a higher regard for Benjamin Franklin as a man of feeling. He is generally considered to have been one in whom excess of intellectual activity and Yankee shrewdness overbalanced the exercise of his emotional nature. That he is capable of warm and enduring friendship, however, becomes at once apparent in these genial letters, written by the American printer to his brother printer across the seas.—BENJAMIN, S. G. W., 1888, *Unpublished Letters of Franklin to Strahan, Atlantic Monthly, vol.* 61, *p.* 21.

He was sanguine by nature, by resolution, and by policy; and his way of alluring good fortune was to welcome it in advance.—MORSE, JR., JOHN T., 1889, *Benjamin Franklin* (*American Statesmen*), *p.* 264.

The Frenchman's American is Benjamin Franklin. It was so when they first began to know him, when he went in and out among them a living man, and it is so to-day, when an even century has closed around his simple tomb. There is something grand in the personality of this man who was able to inspire such deep admiration and such sinister hatred by the same act. Benjamin Franklin was, without doubt, a strong man—a man of strong and positive character, whose friends and enemies were equally strong in their feelings of like and dislike. The men who were ranged as his enemies have been relegated to a second place on the page of history, while those who were his friends stand out boldly in the front rank of the notable characters of the past. If we were asked to say what was the characteristic in Franklin that made him an idol among the French nation, we should answer his versatility. He was the adroit diplomat and the simple bourgeois, the learned philosopher and scientist, and the gay *bon vivant* and *bonhomme*. He could write a dispatch or an epigram with equal facility, and he could control the electric fluid and a smoky chimney with equal success. He at turns could be the chivalric courtier or the simple representative of the infant republic, and whatever he did or whatever pose he assumed he was the same peerless Franklin: and now that he has been at rest these hundred years he stands forth on the page of history as the first American—not even second to Washington himself.—HART, CHARLES HENRY, 1890, *Franklin in Allegory, The Century, vol.* 19, *p.* 197.

While Thomas Jefferson, with that breadth of statesmanship which characterized all of his labors, kept unceasingly before his view the importance of popular education to reinforce and make effective the operations of the principle of local self-government, on the other hand, Dr. Franklin, himself a noteworthy example of a self-educated man, kept in view the importance of education as the foundation of thrift and social development. These two men seem to have furnished more than any other two men the guiding principles which have prevailed in our civilization, political and social. . . . Benjamin Franklin stands somewhat in contrast to Jefferson in the fact that he looks more to the social welfare than to the political function of the people. His most pronounced idea is that of thrift. He wishes to have it impressed on each man or woman or child that industry and economy are prime sources of power. But he is in agreement with Thomas Jefferson as to the importance of an elementary education to prepare the citizen for intelligent application of the lessons of industry and thrift.—HARRIS, WILLIAM T., 1893, *Benjamin Franklin and The University of Pennsylvania, ed. Thorpe, Introduction, pp.* 1, 2.

The difficulty of a study of Franklin is intensified by the fact that he was the most-sided man that ever appeared in our history, if not, indeed, in history at all. To be comprehended we must know him, not only as a diplomatist, but as the foremost scientist in the world; a most remarkable financier and business manager; an author whose work has a fixed place among the higher classics; a philosopher who found rank with Voltaire and Leibnitz; as Kant expressed it, "the Prometheus of modern days." John Adams, whose jealousy was irrepressible, wrote from Paris that Franklin's reputation was "more universal than that of Newton." Nor do we find our task minified by the fact that Franklin was a man as simple as he was great, as childlike as he was philosophic. Like Lincoln, he loved a joke, but, unlike Lincoln, he put his jokes into state papers. It has been hinted that for this reason no great historic document of the period was intrusted to his pen. His economy was not only political, it was domestic; and in "Poor Richard" popular estimation cannot easily recognize the controlling mind of the world's affairs and the builder of democracy. He wrote alamnacs instead of constitutions. He was as marked for his toleration in theology as for his democracy in statecraft. In both he was clearsighted and even prophetic, far beyond his age.—POWELL, E. P., 1893, *A Study of Benjamin Franklin, The Arena, vol.* 8, p. 477.

Those persons who knew Franklin, the inventor, only as the genius to whom we owe the lightning rod, will be amazed at the range of his activity. For half a century his mind seems to have been on the alert concerning the why and wherefore of every phenomenon for which the explanation was not apparent. Nothing in nature failed to interest him. Had he lived in an era of patents he might have rivalled

Edison in the number of his patentable devices, and had he chosen to make money for such devices, his gains would certainly have been fabulous. As a matter of fact, Franklin never applied for a patent, though frequently urged to do so, and he made no money by his inventions. . . . The complete list of inventions, devices, and improvements of which Franklin was the originator, or a leading spirit and contributor, is so long a one that a dozen pages would not suffice for it.—HUBERT, JR., PHILIP G., 1893, *Inventors, pp.* 9, 10.

A characteristic as well as a memorable product of colonial civilization at this epoch was Benjamin Franklin, by birth and education a New Englander, by adoption a Pennsylvanian. He cannot be said to have been an offspring of the theocracy, inasmuch as he was a latitudinarian in religion and had a natural son. But he was an offspring of New England Puritanism grown mellow. His commercial shrewdness, his practical inventiveness, his fundamental integrity, his public spirit, his passion for improvement, were native to his community in the phase which it had now reached, no less than were his "Poor Richard" philosophy of life and the absence in him of anything spiritual or romantic. He it was who in his boyhood had suggested to his father that much time might be saved by saying grace at once over a whole barrel of red herrings. He leads up the mighty army of American inventors. At the same time though no revolutionist by nature he was the destined harbinger of the Revolution. He had been the first projector of a general union of the colonies. His figure marks the transition to the revolutionary and national period which is now opening from that of the Puritan commonwealth.—SMITH, GOLDWIN, 1893, *The United States, An Outline of Political History, 1492–1871, p.* 62.

Humor, indeed, he had so abundantly that it was almost a failing. Like Abraham Lincoln, another typical American, he never shrank from a jest. Like Lincoln, he knew the world well and accepted it for what it was, and made the best of it, expecting no more. But Franklin lacked the spirituality, the faith in the ideal, which was at the core of Lincoln's character. And here was Franklin's limitation: what lay outside of the bounds of common sense he did not see—probably he did not greatly care to see; but common sense he had in a most uncommon degree. One of his chief characteristics was curiosity—in the wholesome meaning of that abused word. He never rested till he knew the why and wherefore of all that aroused his attention.—MATTHEWS, BRANDER, 1896, *An Introduction to the Study of American Literature*, p. 36.

One of the first men to exhibit this American spirit with an unmistakable touch of greatness and distinction was Benjamin Franklin. It was characteristic of America that this self-made man should become a philosopher, a founder of philosophical societies, an authoritative man of science; that his philosophy of life should be so homely and so practical in its maxims, and uttered with so shrewd a wit; that one region should be his birthplace and another his home; that he should favor effective political union among the colonies from the first, and should play a sage and active part in the establishment of national independence and the planning of a national organization; and that he should represent his countrymen in diplomacy abroad. They could have had no spokesman who represented more sides of their character. Franklin was a sort of multiple American. He was versatile without lacking solidity; he was a practical statesman without ceasing to be a sagacious philosopher. He came of the people, and was democratic; but he had raised himself out of the general mass of unnamed men, and so stood for the democratic law, not of equality, but of self-selection in endeavor. One can feel sure that Franklin would have succeeded in any part of the national life that it might have fallen to his lot to take part in. He will stand the final and characteristic test of Americanism: he would unquestionably have made a successful frontiersman, capable at once of wielding the axe and of administering justice from the fallen trunk.—WILSON, WOODROW, 1896, *Mere Literature*, p. 200.

He was the Abou ben Adhem of his times. If service is the test of love, few men have loved their fellows better than did this unsentimental, unspiritual homely old body, American's patron saint of common sense.—BATES, KATHARINE LEE, 1897, *American Literature* p. 58.

In the long and angry disputes of the American Revolution, the part taken in them by Franklin was very much like that which Socrates might have taken had he been born in Boston in the early part of the eighteenth century, had he been for many years a printer and a politician in Philadelphia, and had he filled at London and Paris the diplomatic stations that were filled by Franklin. Indeed, the likeness between Franklin and Socrates was more than superficial; for, besides the plebeian origin of both and some trace of plebeian manners which clung to both, and the strain of animal coarseness from which neither was ever entirely purified, they both had an amazing insight into human nature in all its grades and phases, they were both indifferent to literary fame, they were both humorists, they both applied their great intellectual gifts in a disciplinary but genial way to the improvement of their fellow-men, and in dealing controversially with the opinions of others they both understood and practised the strategy of coolness, playfulness, an unassuming manner, moderation of statement, the logical parallel, and irony.—TYLER, MOSES COIT, 1897, *The Literary History of the American Revolution*, 1763–1783, *vol.* II, *p.* 371.

There are, I conceive, two chief reasons why the name of Franklin is so constantly on our lips and his memory so impressed upon our hearts—why, in other words, he really lives for us instead of being a mere fossil in the strata of history. One is that as an embodiment of practical learning, shrewd mother wit, honesty, and patriotism he is a typical and in many respects unapproachable product of true Americanism. The other is that he is the most complete representative of his century that any nation can point to. With regard to the typical character of his Americanism few cavils will be raised, but with regard to the claim that he best represents the eighteenth century there will probably be not a little dissension. Washington, Dr. Johnson, Frederick the Great, and Voltaire might each and all be put in competition with the sage who snatched the lightning from heaven and the sceptre from tyrants, and would have many supporters. But in none of these does the age of prose and reason seem to find such adequate and complete expression as in Franklin. Washington is beyond his own or any century. Dr. Johnson does not sufficiently represent the age on its rational side; Frederick is too extreme a combination of daring and sublime seriousness of purpose and petty affectation; while Voltaire is at once too intense and not radical enough, and is, after all, too entirely a man of letters. Franklin, on the other hand, thoroughly represents his age in its practicality, in its devotion to science, in its intellectual curiosity, in its humanitarianism, in its lack of spirituality, in its calm self-content—in short, in its exaltation of prose and reason over poetry and faith.—TRENT, W. P., 1897, *The Makers of the Union, McClure's Magazine, vol. 8, p. 273.*

Franklin was now well in the way of prosperity, aged twenty-four, with a little printing business; plans plus, and ambitions to spare. He had had his little fling in life, and had done various things of which he was ashamed; and the foolish things that Deborah had done were no worse than those of which he had been guilty. So he called on her, and they talked it over and made honest confessions that are good for the soul. The potter disappeared—no one knew where—some said he was dead, but Benjamin and Deborah did not wear mourning. They took rumor's word for it, and thanked God, and went to a church and were married. Deborah brought to the firm a very small dowry; and Benjamin contributed a bright baby boy, aged two years, captured no one knows just where. This boy was William Franklin, who grew up into a very excellent man, and the worst that can be said of him is, that he became Governor of New Jersey. He loved and respected his father, and called Deborah mother, and loved her very much. And she was worthy of all love and ever treated him with tenderness and gentlest considerate care. Possibly a blot on the 'scutcheon may, in the working of God's providence, not always be a dire misfortune, for it sometimes has the effect of binding broken hearts as nothing else can, a citatrice toughens the fibre. Deborah had not much education, but she had good, sturdy common sense, which is better if you are forced to make choice. She set herself to help her husband in every way possible and so far as I know, never sighed for one of those things you call "a

career." She even worked in the printing office, folding, stitching, and doing up bundles. Long years afterward, when Franklin was Ambassador of the American Colonies in France, he told with pride that the clothes he wore were spun, woven, cut out, and made into garments all by his wife's own hands. Franklin's love for Deborah was very steadfast. Together they became rich and respected, won worldwide fame, and honors came that way such as no American before or since has ever received.—HUBBARD, ELBERT, 1898, *Little Journeys to the Homes of American Statesmen, p. 58.*

Franklin was a rather large man, and is supposed to have been about five feet ten inches in height. In his youth he was stout, and in old age corpulent and heavy, with rounded shoulders. The portraits of him reveal a very vigorous-looking man, with a thick upper arm and a figure which, even in old age, was full and rounded. In fact, this rounded contour is his most striking characteristic . . . Franklin's figure was a series of harmonious curves, which make pictures of him always pleasing. These curves extended over his head and even to the lines of his face, softening the expression, slightly veiling the iron resolution, and entirely consistent with the wide sympathies, varied powers, infinite shrewdness, and vast experience which we know he possessed.—FISHER, SYDNEY GEORGE, 1899, *The True Benjamin Franklin, p. 17.*

Benjamin Franklin is considered all over the world a polyhistor of the foremost rank. Nothing escaped his attention. However, it was not merely of a receptive kind. Like Leonardo da Vinci, our "patriot and sage," as he was called in eulogies, never received without giving. Whoever went through John Bigelow's edition of Franklin's complete works knows that he suggested inventions and improvements, not only in electricity, printing, flying machines—the latter in the modern sense, not of fast stage coaches, as in the terminology of the eighteenth century—optics, chemistry, submarine boats, but also in very many other directions. Strangely enough, the invention of the musical glasses, or harmonica, which since more than a hundred and thirty years has been attributed to Franklin, was not his invention. He only

suggested some important improvements.
. . . Benjamin Franklin possessed a
keen interest for music and a certain
knowledge of its literature. But so far,
with exception of his traditional invention of the musical glasses, he did not
surpass the many other lovers of music in
colonial America. . . . He can justly
be classified among the most critical and
boldest writers on musical declamation of
that period. Very few critics and professional musicians had or have equally
independent esthetical reasoning powers,
and certainly the contemporaneous artists,
when "talking shop" with Franklin,
have haughtily sneered at the ideas of the
musical greenhorn from the American
prairies and backwoods.—SONNECK, O.
G., 1900, *Benjamin Franklin's Relation
to Music, Music, vol.* 19, *pp.* 1, 7, 11.

He acted at one time as a commander
of troops, yet cannot be called a soldier; he
was a great statesman, yet not among the
greatest; he made famous discoveries in
science, yet was scarcely a professional
scientist; he was lauded as a philosopher,
yet barely outstepped the region of common sense; he wrote ever as a moralist,
yet in some respects lived a free life; he
is one of the few great American authors,
yet never published a book; he was a
shrewd economist, yet left at his death
only a moderate fortune; he accomplished
much as a philanthropist, yet never sacrificed his own weal. Above all and in
all things he was a man, able to cope with
every chance of life and wring profit out
of it; he had perhaps the alertest mind of
any man of that alert century. In his
shrewdness, versatility, self-reliance, wit,
as also in his lack of the deeper reverence
and imagination, he, I think, more than
any other man who has yet lived, represents the full American character.—MORE,
PAUL ELMER, 1900, *Benjamin Franklin
(Riverside Biographical Series), p.* 1.

THE HUTCHINSON LETTERS

Sir,—Finding that two gentlemen have
been unfortunately engaged in a duel
about a transaction and its circumstances
of which both of them are totally ignorant
and innocent, I think it incumbent upon
me to declare (for the prevention of
further mischief, as far as such a declaration may contribute to prevent it) that I
alone am the person who obtained and

transmitted to Boston the letters in question. Mr. Whately could not communicate them, because they were never in his
possession; and for the same reason they
could not be taken from him by Mr.
Temple. They were not of the nature
of *private* letters between friends. They
were written by public officers to persons
in public stations on public affairs, and
intended to procure public measures; they
were therefore handed to other public
persons, who might be influenced by them
to produce those measures. Their tendency was to incense the mother country
against her colonies, and, by the steps recommended, to widen the breach which they
effected. The chief caution expressed
with regard to privacy was, to keep their
contents from the colony agents, who, the
writers apprehended, might return them,
or copies of them, to America. That
apprehension was, it seems, well founded,
for the first agent who laid his hands on
them thought it his duty to transmit them
to his constituents.—FRANKLIN, BENJA-
MIN, 1773, *To the Printer of the "Public
Advertiser," Dec.* 25.

I hope, my lords, you will mark and
brand the man, for the honour of this
country, of Europe, and of mankind.
Private correspondence has hitherto been
held sacred in times of the greatest party
rage, not only in politics, but in religion.
The betrayer of it has forfeited all the
respect of the good, and of his own associates. Into what companies will the fabricator of this iniquity hereafter go with an
unembarassed face, or with any semblance
of the honest intrepidity of virtue? Men
will watch him with a jealous eye—they
will hide their papers from him, and lock
up their escritoires. Having hitherto aspired after fame by his writings, he will
henceforth esteem it a libel to be called *a
man of letters*—"*homo trium literarum.*"
But he not only took away these papers
from one brother,—he kept himself concealed till he nearly occasioned the murder of another. It is impossible to read
his account, expressive of the coolest and
most deliberate malice, without horror.
Amidst these tragical events, of one person nearly murdered—of another answer-
able for the issue—of a worthy governor
hurt in the dearest interests—the fate of
America in suspense—here is a man who,
with the utmost insensibility or remorse,

stands up and avows himself the author of all. . I can compare him only to Zanga in Dr. Young's Revenge—
——"Know, then, 'twas I.
I forged the letter—I disposed the picture—
I hated, I despised—and I destroy!"
I ask, my Lords, whether the revengeful temper attributed by poetic fiction only to the bloody-minded African, is not surpassed by the coolness and apathy of the wily New Englander? — WEDDERBURN, ALEXANDER (LORD LOUGHBOROUGH), 1774, *Speech before the Committee of the Privy Council, Jan. 29.*

The character of the inquiry, and the dignity of the tribunal to whose investigation it was submitted, were not duly considered. Ministers, taught by experience, ought to have known the degradation which they must inevitably incur when they elevated an individual into the rank of a personal opponent. . . . Dr. Franklin, who had recently completed his sixty-seventh year, who was known and honoured in the most eminent philosophical and literary societies in Europe, sat with his grey, unadorned locks, a hearer of one of the severest invectives that ever proceeded from the tongue of man, and an observer of a boisterous and obstreperous merriment and exultation, which added nothing to the dignity of his judges. He had sufficient self-command to suppress all display of feeling; but the transactions of the day sunk deeply into his mind, and produced an unextinguishable rancour against this country, which coloured all the acts of his subsequent life, and occasioned extensive and ever memorable consequences.—ADOLPHUS, JOHN, 1802, *History of England During the Reign of George III, vol.* II, *pp.* 46, 47.

The conduct of Franklin in the affair of the letters was unworthy a man of honour and a gentleman.—MASSEY, WILLIAM, 1855, *A History of England during the reign of George III, vol.* II, *p.* 145.

As we review the whole story of the transaction of this day, in cool blood, we can hardly understand how it occurred; and there are those on the other side of the ocean, if not on our own side, who fail to perceive how it could have been justified, as it was, by so many of our calmest, wisest, and most conscientious patriots. For, certainly, the men who were intrusted with the letters were second

to none in Massachusetts for integrity and principle. Chauncy and Cooper, as we all know, were Doctors of Divinity, who could hardly have been invited to take part in an unworthy act. Doctor Winthrop—very remotely connected with myself, and of whom I may therefore speak without delicacy—was the foremost man of science at Harvard University, a member, too, of the Royal Society, and a gentleman of the highest character. And Bowdoin, who stands first on the list, would have been singled out among all the patriots of that period as a man of the greatest moderation, of inflexible principle, and of the nicest sense of honor. Yet Bowdoin, in a letter to Franklin of Sept. 6, 1774, calls the sending of the letters "that most meritorious act;" and I am not aware of any other view of the affair having been expressed, at the time it occurred, by him, or by any other of our Revolutionary Fathers. —WINTHROP, ROBERT C., 1878, *The Hutchinson Letters, Addresses and Speeches, vol.* IV, *p.* 3.

It must be confessed that the question whether Franklin should have sent these letters to be seen by the leading men of Massachusetts involves points of some delicacy. The very elaborateness and vehemence of the exculpations put forth by American writers indicate a lurking feeling that the opposite side is at least plausible. I add my opinion decidedly upon Franklin's side, though I certainly see force in the contrary view. Yet before one feels fully satisfied he would wish to know from whom these letters came to Franklin's hands, the information then given him concerning them, and the authority which the giver might be supposed to have over them, in a word, all the attendant and qualifying circumstances and conversation upon which presumptions might have been properly founded by Franklin. Upon these essential matters there is absolutely no evidence. Franklin was bound to secrecy concerning them, at whatever cost to himself. But it is evident that Franklin never for an instant entertained the slightest doubt of the entire propriety of his action, and even in his own cause he was wont to be a fairminded judge.—MORSE, JR., JOHN T., 1889, *Benjamin Franklin (American Statesmen), p.* 182, *note.*

POOR RICHARD'S ALMANAC
1733.

COURTEOUS READER:—I might attempt in this place to gain thy favor by declaring that I write Almanacs with no other view than that of the public good, but in this I should not be sincere. . . . The plain truth of the matter is, I am excessive poor, and my wife, good woman, is, I tell her, excessive proud: she cannot bear, she says to sit spinning in her shift of tow, while I do nothing but gaze at the stars; and has threatened more than once to burn all my books and rattling traps (as she calls my instruments) if I do not make some profitable use of them for the good of my family. The printer has offered me some considerable share of the profits, and I have thus begun to comply with my dame's desire.—SAUNDERS, DR. RICHARD, 1733, *Poor Richard's Almanac.*

While in this weary state of suspense, a prey to impatience, anxiety, and mortification, Jones happened one day to be looking over an old number of Franklin's Pennsylvania Almanac, when his attention was struck with the saying of Poor Richard: "If you would have your business done, go; if not, send." It immediately occurred to him, that the delay of his own business was in no slight degree owing to his having so long remained at a distance, sending letters to court, instead of going to attend to it in person. He set out forthwith for the capital, and made such good speed in his errand, that, ere many days had elapsed, he received from the reluctant M. de Sartine, the following conclusive letter, dated at Versailles, on the 4th of February, 1779. . . . Feeling that his final success in obtaining a command had been owing to his having adopted the good advice which he had met with in Dr. Franklin's Almanac, and out of compliment to the sage, for whom his veneration was so unbounded, Paul Jones had asked leave, as appears by M. Sartine's letter, to give the ship of which the command was now conferred upon him, the name of the *Bon Homme Richard*, the *Poor Richard:* a name which his heroism was destined to render as enduring as his own.—MACKENZIE, ALEXANDER SLIDELL, 1841, *The Life of Paul Jones, vol.* I, *pp.* 133, 136.

"But, pray, dear father, tell us what made him so famous," said George. "I have seen his portrait a great many times. There is a wooden bust of him in one of our streets; and marble ones, I suppose in some other places. And towns, and ships of war, and steamboats, and banks, and academies, and children, are often named after Franklin. Why should he have grown so very famous?" "Your question is a reasonable one, George," answered his father. "I doubt whether Franklin's philosophical discoveries, important as they were, or even his vast political services, would have given him all the fame which he acquired. It appears to me that 'Poor Richard's Almanac' did more than anything else towards making him familiarly known to the public. As the writer of those proverbs which Poor Richard was supposed to utter, Franklin became the counsellor and household friend of almost every family in America. Thus it was the humblest of all his labors that has done the most for his fame."—HAWTHORNE, NATHANIEL, 1842, *Biographical Stories, Works, Riverside ed., vol.* XII, *p.* 202.

Some of the best fun Franklin ever wrote, occurs in the prefaces to "Poor Richard." . . . "Poor Richard," at this day, would be reckoned an indecent production. All great humorists were more or less indecent before Charles Dickens; *i. e.,* they used certain words which are now never pronounced by polite persons, and are never printed by respectable printers; and they referred freely to certain subjects which are familiar to every living creature, but which, it is now agreed among civilized beings, shall not be topics of conversation. In this respect, "Poor Richard" was no worse, and not much better, than other colonial periodicals, some of which contained things incredibly obscene; as much so as the broadest passages of Sterne, Smollett, Fielding, and Defoe.—PARTON, JAMES, 1864, *Life and Times of Benjamin Franklin, vol.* I, *pp.* 228, 234.

The almanac went year after year, for a quarter of a century, into the house of nearly every shopkeeper, planter, and farmer in the American provinces. Its wit and humor, its practical tone, its shrewd maxims, its worldly honesty, its morality of common sense, its useful information, all chimed well with the national character. It formulated in homely phrase and with droll illustration what the colonists more vaguely knew, felt, and believed upon a thousand points of life and conduct. In so doing it greatly trained and invigorated the natural mental traits of the people. "Poor Richard" was the revered and popular schoolmaster of a young nation during its period of tutelage. His teachings are among the powerful forces which have gone to shaping the habits of Americans. His terse and picturesque bits of the wisdom and the virtue of this world are familiar in our mouths today; they moulded our great-grandparents and their children; they have informed our popular traditions; they still influence our actions, guide our ways of thinking, and establish our points of view, with the constant control of acquired habits which we little suspect. If we were accustomed still to read the literature of the almanac, we should be charmed with its humor. The world has not yet grown away from it, nor ever will. Addison and Steele had more polish but vastly less humor than Franklin. "Poor Richard" has found eternal life by passing into the daily speech of the people, while the "Spectator" is fast being crowded out of the hands of all save scholars in literature.—MORSE, JR., JOHN T., 1889, *Benjamin Franklin* (*American Statesmen*), p. 22.

"Poor Richard's Almanac" was so much the best that it soon took the place of all others, and its wise maxims were in people's mouths nearly as often as Bible verses. Indeed, I have heard people quote Franklin's proverbs as Solomon's, though they are generally very different. These homely sayings had a wonderful effect on the New England colonists: they helped to make them sharp, business-like, active, cautious, hard-working, saving. Franklin was the first well-known type and the best type of the true "Yankee."—WATKINS, MILDRED CABELL, 1894, *American Literature*, p, 20.

Franklin's Almanack, his crowning work in the sphere of journalism, published under the pseudonym of Richard Saunders, —better known since as Poor Richard, —is still one of the marvels of modern literature. Under one or another of many titles the contents of this publication, exclusive of its calendars, have been translated into every tongue having any

pretensions to a literature; and have had more readers, probably, than any other publication in the English or indeed in any other language, with the single exception of the Bible. It was the first issue from an American press that found a popular welcome in foreign lands, and it still enjoys the special distinction of being the only almanac ever published that owed its extraordinary popularity entirely to its literary merit. What adds to the surprise with which we contemplate the fame and fortunes of this unpretentious publication, is the fact that its reputation was established by its first number, and when its author was only twenty-six years of age. For a period of twenty-six years, and until Franklin ceased to edit it, this annual was looked forward to by a larger portion of the colonial population and with more impatience than now awaits a President's annual message to Congress.—BIGELOW, JOHN, 1897, *Library of the World's Best Literature*, ed. *Warner, vol.* x, *p.* 5926.

And thus for a quarter of a century or more Poor Richard preached his little lifelong sermons, year after year; sermons from very old texts, many of them—waifs of common knowledge or tradition—Biblical many of them and as old as Solomon, but given a new twang by quaint or sharp wording, which set them upon new and wider flight. Let us not speak reproachfully of the stealing; 'tis a good sort of stealing, like Chaucer's in his "Canterbury Tales;" whoever can put new force and new beauty into an old truth by his method of re-stating it, is doing good work—doing indeed what most of the good sermonizers are bent upon. No matter what old metal you may use, if you can put enough of your own powder behind it 'twill reach the mark.—MITCHELL, DONALD G., 1897, *American Lands and Letters, The Mayflower to Rip-Van-Winkle,* p. 107.

It was in "Poor Richard," indeed, that we see Franklin in his most striking light as a philosopher of the people—a hardheaded, practical thinker, an epigrammatic moralist, and an exploiter or adapter of adages, almost any one of which might have made him famous. For Mr. Saunders had a terse way of telling plain truths, and while his sayings were not, for the most part, exactly original, nearly every one of them, even when a more modern setting to an ancient saw, bore the hall-mark of Franklin's genius for apt expression.—ROBINS, EDWARD, 1898, *Benjamin Franklin (American Men of Energy)*. *p.* 44.

AUTOBIOGRAPHY

From the poverty and obscurity in which I was born, and in which I passed my earliest years, I have raised myself to a state of affluence and some degree of celebrity in the world. As constant good fortune has accompanied me even to an advanced period of life, my posterity will perhaps be desirous of learning the means which I employed, and which, thanks to Providence, so well succeeded with me. They may also deem them fit to be imitated, should any of them find themselves in similar circumstances. This good fortune, when I reflect on it, which is frequently the case, has induced me sometimes to say, that if it were left to my choice, I should have no objection to go over the same life from its beginning to the end: requesting only the advantage authors have, of correcting in a second edition the faults of the first. So would I also wish to change some incidents of it for others more favourable. Notwithstanding, if this condition was denied, I should still accept the offer of recommencing the same life.' But as this repetition is not to be expected, that which resembles most living one's life over again, seems to be to recall all the circumstances of it; and, to render this remembrance more durable, to record them in writing. In thus employing myself I shall yield to the inclination so natural to old men, of talking of themselves and their own actions; and I shall indulge it without being tiresome to those who, from respect to my age, might conceive themselves obliged to listen to me, since they will be always free to read me or not. —FRANKLIN, BENJAMIN, 1771, *Memoirs Written by Himself.*

There is a simplicity in this book which charms us in the same way with the humorous touches of nature in the "Vicar of Wakefield." Franklin's Boston brother in the printing-office,—irascible, jealous, and mortified on the return of the successful adventurer, who is playing off his prosperity before the workmen, is an artist's picture of life, drawn in a few conclusive touches. So, too, is Keimer as happily hit off as any personage in Gil Blas, particularly in that incident at the break-up of Franklin's system of vegetable diet, which he had adopted; he invites his journeymen and two women friends to dine with him, providing a roast pig for the occasion, which being prematurely served up, is devoured by the enthusiast, before the company arrives; in that effective sketch, in a paragraph of the Philadelphia City Croaker, whose ghost still walks every city in the world, mocking prosperity of every degree,—"a person of note, an elderly man, with a wise look and a very grave manner of speaking."— DUYCKINCK, EVERT A., AND GEORGE L., 1855-65-75, *Cyclopædia of American Literature,* ed. Simons, vol. I, *p.* 117.

Of this fragment of "Autobiography" I have sometimes been imprudent enough to say, that it is the only piece of writing yet produced on the continent of America which is likely to be generally known two centuries hence.—PARTON, JAMES, 1864, *Life and Times of Benjamin Franklin, vol.* I, *Preface, p.* 6.

It is now eighty years since the death of Dr. Franklin, and during this time his "Autobiography" has been more extensively read in this country than any other historical work. It was, perhaps, the earliest American book that acquired and sustained a great popularity.—GREENE, SAMUEL A., 1871, *The Story of a Famous Book, Atlantic Monthly, vol.* 27, *p.* 207.

Wherever he lived he was the inevitable centre of a system of influences always important and constantly enlarging; and dying, he perpetuated it by an autobiography which to this day not only remains one of the most widely read and readable books in our language, but has had the distinction of enriching the literature of nearly every other. No man has ever lived whose life has been more universally studied by his countrymen or is more familiar to them.—BIGELOW, JOHN, 1879, *Franklin, A Sketch.*

A greater Autobiography than Edward Gibbon's is our own Benjamin Franklin's. Franklin had exactly the genius and temperament of an autobiographer. He loved and admired himself; but he was so bent upon analysis and measurement that he could not let even himself pass without discrimination. The style is like Defoe.

Indeed we are pleased to find that he placed great value both on Defoe and Bunyan, whose stories are told so like his own. He watches his own life as he watched one of his own philosophical experiments. He flies his existence as he flew his kite, and tells the world about it all just as a thoughtful boy might tell his mother what he had been doing—sure of her kindly interest in him. The world is like a mother to Ben Franklin always: so domestic and familiar is his thought of her. He who has read this book has always afterward the boy-man who wrote it clear and distinct among the men he knows.—BROOKS, PHILLIPS, 1880–94, *Biography, Essays and Addresses, p.* 441.

But to Benjamin Franklin's "Autobiography" I feel that I owe more than to any other book, and the greatest literary treasure I own is an old edition of this work, in two tiny volumes, printed in London in 1799. I picked it up at a book sale some years ago for fifty cents. It is a very rare edition, I believe, and is not to be found in the Stevens collection of Franklin's works, now in the possession of our government.—GILDER, JEANNETTE L., 1888, *Books That Have Helped Me, p.* 72.

The style of this work is inimitable; it is as simple, direct, and idiomatic as Bunyan's; it is a style which no rhetorician can assist us to attain, and which the least touch of the learned critic would spoil.—UNDERWOOD, FRANCIS H., 1893, *The Builders of American Literature, First Series, p.* 46.

GENERAL

I am very sorry that you intend soon to leave our hemisphere. America has sent us many good things,—gold, silver, sugar, tobacco, indigo, and so forth; but you are the first philosopher, and indeed the first great man of letters, for whom we are beholden to her.—HUME, DAVID, 1762, *Letter to Franklin, May* 10.

One of the first philosophers, one of the most eminent literary characters, as well as one of the most important in the political world, that the present age can boast of.—COWPER, WILLIAM, 1782, *Letter to the Rev. William Unwin, May* 27, *Works, vol.* II, *p.* 426.

The peculiar charm of his writings, and his great merit also in action, consisted in the clearness with which he saw his object,—and the bold and steady pursuit of it, by the surest and the shortest road. He never suffered himself, in conduct, to be turned aside by the seductions of interest or vanity, or to be scared by hesitation and fear, or to be misled by the arts of his adversaries. Neither did he, in discussion, ever go out of his way in search of ornament, or stop short from dread of the consequences. He never could be caught, in short, acting absurdly, or writing nonsensically:—at all times, and in every thing he undertook, the vigour of an understanding, at once original and practical, was distinctly perceivable. But it must not be supposed that his writings are devoid of ornament or amusement. The latter especially abounds in almost all he ever composed; only nothing is sacrificed to them. On the contrary, they come most naturally into their places; and they uniformly help on the purpose in hand, of which neither writer nor reader ever loses sight for an instant. Thus, his style has all the vigour and even conciseness of Swift, without any of his harshness. It is in no degree more flowery, yet both elegant and lively. The wit, or rather humour, which prevails in his works, varies with the subject. Sometimes he is bitter and sarcastic; oftener gay, and even droll; reminding us, in this respect, far more frequently of Addison than of Swift, as might be naturally expected from his admirable temper, or the happy turn of his imagination. . . . There is nothing more delightful than the constancy with which those amiable feelings, those sound principles, those truly profound views of human affairs, make their appearance at every opportunity, whether the immediate subject be speculative or practical—of a political, or of a general, description. . . . We have said little respecting his language, which is pure, and English. A few, and but a few, foreign expressions may be traced, and these French, rather than American; as, for instance, *influential.* Indeed, we cannot reckon him more as an American than an European. — JEFFREY, FRANCIS LORD, 1817, *Franklin's Correspondence, Edinburgh Review, vol.* 28, *pp.* 276, 277.

Taken all together, this collection of letters would, we think, in the absence of all other documents and representations, afford sufficient means for a competent estimate of the writer. The character displayed by them is an unusual combination of elements. The main substance of the intellectual part of it is a superlative good sense, evinced and acting in all the modes of that high endowment; such as an intuitively prompt and perfect, and steadily continuing appprehension; a sagacity which with admirable ease strikes through all superficial and delusive appearances of things to the essence and the true relations; a faculty of reasoning in a manner marvelously simple, direct, and decisive; a power of reducing a subject or question to its plainest principles; an unaffected daring to meet whatever is to be opposed, in an explicit, direct manner, and in the point of its main strength; a facility for applying familiar truths and self-evident propositions, for resolving the most uncommon difficulties; and a happy adroitness of illustration, by parallel cases, supposed or real, the real ones being copiously supplied by a large and most observant acquaintance with the world. It is obvious how much this same accurate observation of the world would contribute to that power of interpreting the involuntary indications of character, and of detecting motives and designs in all sorts of persons he had to deal with, and to that foresight of consequences in all practical concerns, in which he was probably never surpassed.—FOSTER, JOHN, 1818, *Benjamin Franklin, Critical Essays, ed. Ryland, vol. II, p.* 413.

Though after the first conception of an electrical charge as a disturbance of equilibrium, there was nothing in the development or details of Franklin's views which deserved to win for them any peculiar authority, his reputation, and his skill as a writer, gave a considerable influence to his opinions. Indeed, for a time he was considered, over a large part of Europe, as the creator of the science, and the terms, *Franklinism, Franklinist, Franklinian system,* occur in almost every page of continental publications on the subject. Yet the electrical phenomena to the knowledge of which Franklin added least, those of induction, were those by which the progress of the theory was most promoted.—WHEWELL, WILLIAM, 1837, *History of the Inductive Sciences, vol. II, p.* 202.

Few writers have been so regardless of literary reputation as Franklin. Scarcely any of his compositions were published under his own eye; many of them were not written for the press; and the fame of authorship appears rarely to have been among the motives by which he was induced to employ his pen. It is true, that, in early life and afterwards, he cultivated with uncommon assiduity the art of writing, till he attained a mastery over the language, which has raised his name to the first rank in English literature. Yet it was his primary object, not so much to become distinguished by this accomplishment; as to acquire the power of acting on the minds of others, and of communicating, in the most attractive and effectual manner, such discoveries as he might make, and his schemes for the general improvement, the moral culture, the comfort, the happiness of mankind. He seldom affixed his name to any of his writings. They were mostly designed for a particular purpose; and, when they had answered the end for which they were intended, he seems to have given himself little concern about their future destiny. —SPARKS, JARED, 1840, *ed., Works of Benjamin Franklin, Preface, vol.* I, *p.* v.

The beginner of this literature, amiable and subtle scholar of Defoe and Addison, was Benjamin Franklin. He announced the advent of a milder and more indulgent civilization. Addison's apologue and delicacy; the popular, plain-speaking of Defoe and Bunyan, were softened and melted into a pleasant composition, which characterized the first essays of colonial literature, essays remarkable for the sobriety of their tone, and the absence of high color. Imagination, magnificent and dangerous gift, is not found in the works of Franklin, nor do any of his contemporaries or friends possess it.—CHASLES, PHILARÈTE, 1852, *Anglo-American Literature and Manners, p.* 3.

If ever the doctrine of saving has attained a sort of homely poetry of expression, by dint of contentment and liveliness, it is in Franklin that we must seek for it. An inner warmth of sentiment animates his prudence; a ray of sunshine illumines and enlivens his honesty. . . . Franklin's correspondence in these years is most agreeable and soothing reading; the perfect balance, the precision, the absence of all evil passion and of all heat, the good use to which he puts even his enemies, an affectionate sentiment which mingles with a correct appreciation of things, and which banishes dryness, an elevated sentiment whenever necessary, a certain lightsome air diffused over the whole, compose a real treasure of morality and wisdom. Compared with the Correspondence of Voltaire, that of Franklin gives rise to many reflections; everything there is wholesome, upright, and animated as it were with a lively and constant serenity. Franklin possessed gay, clear, and brilliant good sense; he called bad temper *the uncleanliness of the mind.*—SAINTE-BEUVE, C. A., 1852, *English Portraits, pp.* 63, 104.

He wrote no elaborate histories, or learned treatises, or stately tomes. Short essays or tracts, thrown off at a heat to answer an immediate end,—letters to his associates in science or politics,—letters to his family and friends,—these make up the great bulk of his literary productions; and under the admirable editorship of Mr. Sparks, nine noble volumes do they fill, —abounding in evidences of a wisdom, sagacity, ingenuity, diligence, freshness of thought, fullness of information, comprehensiveness of reach, and devotedness of purpose, such as are rarely to be found associated in any single man.—WIN-THROP, ROBERT C., 1856, *Address at the Inauguration of the Franklin Statue at Boston.*

The pervading trait of Franklin's character was allegiance to the practical. Few devotees of knowledge have so consistently manifested this instinct, the more remarkable because united to speculative tendencies which quickened his intelligence and occupied his leisure to the very close of his existence. For the intangible aims of the metaphysician, the vagaries of the imaginative, the "airy bubble reputation," he exhibited no concern; but the application of truth to the facts of nature and of life, the discovery of material laws and their conversion to human welfare, the actual influence of morals, economy, politics, and education, upon civil society and individual development, were problems upon which he never failed to think, read, talk, write, and experiment.—TUCKERMAN, HENRY T., 1857, *Essays, Biographical and Critical, p.* 456.

Wrote several miscellaneous papers, scientific and political, which have doubtless had no small influence in forming American style. . . . His writings are remarkable for simplicity, terseness, and force. Both the language and the illustrations fit the meaning with emphatic closeness. He affects no graces of style: a hard-headed, practical man, he seeks to convey his meaning as briefly and as emphatically as possible. —MINTO, WILLIAM, 1872–80, *A Manual of English Prose Literature, p.* 434.

The venerable Nestor of three generations; born in the old puritan time, with the shades of the past hanging about his home; traversing the military period of two wars, from Wolfe to Washington, from Quebec to Yorktown; privileged to partake of the new era of laws and legislation—the old sage, full of years and honors, has now at length finished his work. He has inaugurated a new period in philosophy; he has heralded new principles in politics, he has shown his countrymen how to think and write; he has embalmed the wisdom of his life in immortal compositions; he has blessed two great cities with associations of pleasure and profit clustering about his name; he has become the property of the nation and the world; there is nothing further but retirement and death. — DUYCKINCK, EVERT A., 1873, *Portrait Gallery of Eminent Men and Women, vol.* I, *p.* 203.

Franklin is not often spoken of as a witty man, but his wit was as remarkable as his statesmanship. I think that he would have had as much wit as Swift or as Voltaire if he had but cultivated this talent. Only his clear, practical good sense predominated, and he never showed himself in the capacity of a humorist save when some practical purpose was to be affected by it.—BRYANT, WILLIAM CULLEN, 1874, *Franklin as Poet, Prose Writings, ed. Godwin, vol.* II, *p.* 330.

Our humorous writers, with a few exceptions, are not strictly national. Even Franklin, our first, best humorist, stifled his humor in the Addisonian style. His was too earnest a character to make the humorous trait very prominent; but his sly, shining threads of observation, intertwisted into the strong strand of his practical sense, have had their effect on the older men of this generation.—COX, S. S., 1875, *American Humor, Harper's Magazine, vol.* 50, *p.* 699.

In whom the acuteness of the philosopher

was curiously blended with the cunning of the trader.—STEPHEN, LESLIE, 1876, *History of English Thought in the Eighteenth Century, vol.* II, *p.* 299.

Of Franklin then it must be said, that he not only did not advance the growth of economic science, but that he seems not even to have mastered it as it was already developed; and little more can be said for any of our public men or writers during the period of Franklin's activity.—DUNBAR, CHARLES F., 1876, *Economic Science in America, 1776–1876, North American Review, vol.* 122, *p.* 130.

He employed his admirable style, his lucid thought, in defending before the world the rights of man. Calmness was the chief trait of his intellect; his political pieces have a weight and clearness that few others have attained; the fierce but clouded reasoning of Junius, the rude splendor of Johnson, the thoughtful verbiage of Burke, grow feeble and overstrained when placed by the side of one of Franklin's irrefutable arguments. His was the voice of humanity, the opening of an age of reason.—LAWRENCE, EUGENE, 1880, *A Primer of American Literature, p.* 32.

I intended in these pages to limit my remarks to Franklin's scientific position, but that would be to represent very inadequately the whole life of this great man. Let us remember that his electrical researches, on which his scientific celebrity must mainly depend, occupied at the most only seven or eight years, and then were abandoned because of the pressure of political affairs. Not by his scientific life, but by his political, will Franklin be judged of by his countrymen. In that his true grandeur is seen. He conducted the foreign affairs that gave independence to America. No other American could have stood in his place, and have done what he did. Very true, his scientific reputation gave him position before the eyes of the French court, and added force to his urgent entreaties for money and an army and a fleet to aid his struggling countrymen. No one can rise from a perusal of his political writings, from the time of the Albany Commission to the close of his eventful life, without recognizing his great intellectual ability, his political foresight. To meet the trained statesmen of England, to conduct successfully to a close negotiations which were

the most important in which they could engage, since the partition, the disruption, of the British Empire was involved, demanded a clear head, a piercing eye, a calm judgment. The result he accomplished was of far more importance to mankind than any philosophical experiment he ever made—a vast continent dedicated to human freedom. Contemplated from this point of view, Franklin appears as one of the greatest men of his generation. His electrical discoveries, brilliant as they were, were only embellishments of his life.—DRAPER, JOHN WILLIAM, 1880, *Franklin's Place in the Science of the Last Century, Harper's Magazine, vol.* 61, *p.* 275.

Franklin is, indeed, one of the very small class of men who can be said to have added something of real value to the art of living. Very few writers have left so many profound and original observations on the causes of success in life, and on the best means of cultivating the intellect and the character. To extract from surrounding circumstances the largest possible amount of comfort and rational enjoyment, was the ideal he placed before himself and others, and he brought to its attainment one of the shrewdest and most inventive of human intellects, one of the calmest and best balanced of human characters.—LECKY, WILLIAM EDWARD HARTPOLE, 1882, *A History of England in the Eighteenth Century, vol.* III, *p.* 407.

Edwards would doubtless have considered Franklin a child of wrath, but Francis Bacon would have hailed him as one of that band of explorers, who, by serving Nature, will in the end master her mysteries, and use their knowledge for the service of man. Indeed, the cheerful, hopeful spirit which runs through Franklin's writings, even when he was tried by obstacles which might have tasked the proverbial patience of Job, is not one of the least of his claims upon the consideration of those who rightfully glory in having such a genius for their countrymen. The spirit which breathes through Franklin's life and works is that which has inspired every pioneer of our Western wastes, every poor farmer who has tried to make both ends meet by the exercise of rigid economy, every inventor who has attempted to serve men by making machines do half the drudgery of their work, every statesman who has striven to introduce large principles into our somewhat confused and contradictory legislation, every American diplomatist who has upheld the character of his country abroad by sagacity in managing men, as well as by integrity in the main purpose of his mission, and every honest man who has desired to diminish the evil there is in the world, and to increase every possible good that is conformable to good sense. Franklin is doubtless our Mr. Worldly Wiseman, but his worldly wisdom ever points to the Christian's prayer that God's will shall be done on earth as it is done in heaven.—WHIPPLE, EDWIN PERCY, 1886, *American Literature and Other Papers, ed. Whittier, p.* 8.

The truth about Franklin as a miscellaneous writer—a truth which any one may verify by a day's reading in his collected works—is that most of his productions, while respectable, of wide range, well-written, sensible, and telling, are not of the highest rank, and that, measured by the tests of English literature between 1725 and 1775, they are commonplace. From the several editions of his works but three things stand out because of inherent literary merit: his "Autobiography," his highly important papers on electricity, and the maxims in "Poor Richard's Almanac"—the last being chief and sufficient in themselves to perpetuate his fame as a writer.—RICHARDSON, CHARLES F., 1887, *American Literature,* 1607–1885, *vol.* I, *p.* 159.

Franklin was admirably equipped as a popular teacher. Long study of the best models of English prose, aided by his fine literary sense, gave him a style unsurpassed for clearness and directness; while his rich vein of humor, his command of satire, of anecdote, and of terse, sententious phrase, enabled him to convey large truths in such portable and attractive forms, that his teachings soon spread far and wide, and fixed themselves in the memory and speech of men. But here, as in all cases, that which gave most weight to his teachings were the character and the life of the teacher. He made the newspaper press a power for good, as it had never been before; and he set the example, and adhered to it throughout his editorial career, of preserving the columns of his paper free from all libelling and personal abuse, and all purveying to the prurient taste of a section of the community.—PEPPER, WILLIAM, 1887, *An Address on Benjamin Franklin, p.* 8.

The place to be allotted Franklin among American men of Letters is hard to determine. He founded no school of literature. He gave no impetus to letters. He put his name to no great work of history, of poetry, of fiction. Till after his day, no such thing as American literature existed. To place him, with respect to Irving, Bryant, Cooper, Prescott, and the host of great men that came after him, is impossible. There is no common ground of comparison. Unlike them, he never wrote for literary fame. Had he cared for such fame, he would not have permitted friends and strangers to gather and edit his writings during his lifetime; he would not have suffered death to overtake him when the Autobiography was but half done; he would not have made it an invariable rule to never send anything to the press over his own name. His place is among that giant race of pamphleteers and essayists most of whom went before, but a few of whom came immediately after, the war for independence. And among them he is easily first. Their merit lies in what they said: the merit of Franklin lies not only in what he said, but in the way in which he said it. . . . No other writer has left so many just and original observations on success in life. No other writer has pointed out so clearly the way to obtain the greatest amount of comfort out of life. What Solomon did for the spiritual man that did Franklin for the earthlyman. The Book of Proverbs is a collection of receipts for laying up treasures in heaven. "Poor Richard" is a collection of receipts for laying up treasures on earth.—McMASTER, JOHN BACH, 1887, *Benjamin Franklin as a Man of Letters* (*American Men of Letters*), *pp.* 272, 277.

By far the most eminent of the early American writers was Benjamin Franklin. . . . Franklin's style is notoriously graceful and charming, but he is almost the only American writer before the Independence who can be named with the recognised masters of eighteenth-century English.—GOSSE, EDMUND, 1888, *A History of Eighteenth Century Literature, p.* 398.

Franklin is perhaps the real starting-point of American literature. As he was the first American scientific discoverer of renown, the first American diplomatist, the founder of the first public library and the first permanent philosophical society in this country, so he was the first writer in the field of general literature. His writings are full of acute thought on practical themes, and suited to the genius of a busy people engrossed with their outward affairs.—EGGLESTON, EDWARD,1888–92, *The Household History of the United States and its People, p.* 373.

He could so marry words to things as to make them seem one; he expressed positive thoughts and emotions, without ornament or amplification; his style was the true reflection of his intellectual and moral stature. He was, it is true, the first American to cultivate the art of literary phrasing; but this was an instinct of his temperament, which loved pith, point, clearness and homely symbolism. . . . Humor was another of Franklin's literary gifts, and literary, in his case, because it was first personal. It was not the thin, smirking artifice which is regarded as humor by some of our contemporary writers, and which is as carefully studied as a new dialect or a recondite title; it was the native, ineradicable quality of the man, the natural armor of his strength, his worldly wisdom, his kindly human sympathy and his shrewd Yankee insight. Many a portentous predicament had he faced in his day, but he was never for a moment scared out of his humor. It forms the predominating flavor of his writings, which are almost always in earnest,but seldom quite solemn; the demure twinkle of the eye is there, though the hasty or the foolish miss it. It was sometimes a trifle broad for modern taste, but it is of itself enough to preserve his productions from oblivion.—HAWTHORNE, JULIAN, AND LEMMON, LEONARD, 1891, *American Literature, pp.* 16, 17.

He had a gift for putting much prudence into few words. His low ideals and the self-complacence which appear in his autobiography do him little credit, but as a counselor in matters of expediency he was much needed by his excitable, extravagant, and often over-sanguine countrymen.—MABIE, HAMILTON W., 1892, *The Memorial Story of America, p.* 586.

It is the tradition of his life that has survived rather than any wide knowledge of what he wrote. No figure in our history is more generally remembered, nor any more deservedly; for whatever his merits on a moral scale, the man was in his life first, last, and always an American. Shrewd common-sense never had a more palpable incarnation; nor that peculiar, ever-present, not needlessly obtrusive personal independence which so generally makes a native Yankee, wherever he goes, a troublesome match for people who assume to be his betters. Himself, then, we remember first; and if we are suddenly asked what he was besides being himself, our impulse would be in conveniently general terms to answer that he was a statesman and a philosopher.— WENDELL, BARRETT, 1893, *Stelligeri and Other Essays Concerning America, p.* 123.

Either we must be willing to give a place in economic science to Franklin, or we must deny the same privilege to all writers on economic matters who preceded Adam Smith. It is true that Franklin was largely a man of expedients, if by that we mean that he was interested in that truth which could be immediately applied for the good of mankind. But we maintain also that Franklin was a man who understood thoroughly the working of certain economic principles. No one else saw more clearly than he did the injurious effect of the many trade restrictions prevalent in the civilized world in his day. In that "great reaction of the eighteenth century against artificial conditions of life," in that movement of liberty, industrial as well as political, we claim that Franklin was one of the first as well as one of the leading factors. And it must be admitted that on the subject of population he did not always indulge in the "crudest speculations as to the operation of causes in any degree remote." No one knew better than he did the causes both of the increase of population and of the adjustment of people among the nations of the earth.—WETZEL, W. A., 1895, *Benjamin Franklin as an Economist, p.* 54.

We might be led to believe at first thought that the extraordinary repute into which he rose was relative, and that the world's appreciation of him, and particularly the feeling of his own countrymen, was exaggerated by the surprise that the colonies, then so young and primitive, should have produced so able and versatile a man. But this would be an incorrect view. Franklin's fame was a tribute to his real eminence. The more his life and achievements are studied the more clearly does it appear that Franklin's greatness was of the whole world and would have been as prominent in any age; and that in any group of leaders of progress, from whatever time or nation they might be selected, he would find his place near the head.—YOUMANS, WILLIAM JAY, 1896, ed., *Pioneers of Science in America, p. 1.*

The Doric simplicity of his style; his incomparable facility of condensing a great principle into an apologue or an anecdote, many of which, as he applied them, have become the folk-lore of all nations: his habitual moderation of statement, his aversion to exaggeration, his inflexible logic, and his perfect truthfulness,—made him one of the most persuasive men of his time, and his writings a model which no one can study without profit. A judicious selection from Franklin's writings should constitute a part of the curriculum of every college and high school that aspires to cultivate in its pupils a pure style and correct literary taste.—BIGELOW, JOHN, 1897, *Library of the World's Best Literature, vol. x, p.* 5933.

He was one of the best American prose writers of the century.—MORRIS, CHARLES, 1897, *A History of the United States of America, p.* 176.

Undoubtedly, his best work in letters was done after the year 1764, and thence forward down to the very year of his death; for, to a degree not only unusual but almost without parallel in literary history, his mind grew more and more vivacious with his advancing years, his heart more genial, his inventiveness more sprightly, his humor more gay, his style brighter, keener, more deft, more delightful. Yet even in these earlier writings of his, Franklin is always Franklin. . . . It is only by a continuous reading of the entire body of Franklin's Revolutionary writings, from grave to gay, from lively to severe, that any one can know how brilliant was his wisdom, or how wise was his brilliance, or how humane and gentle and helpful were both. No one who, by such a reading, procures for himself such a pleasure and such a benefit,

will be likely to miss the point of Sydney Smith's playful menace to his daughter, —"I will disinherit you, if you do not admire everything written by Franklin." —TYLER, MOSES COIT, 1897, *The Literary History of the American Revolution, 1763–1783, vol.* II, *pp.* 365, 381.

The peculiar dryness especially characteristic of Yankee drollery is better illustrated from Franklin's shrewd proverbs than from Irving's spontaneous and sparkling descriptions. — BATES, KATHARINE LEE, 1897, *American Literature, p.* 285.

Franklin's individualism ultimately found political application in the essential doctrines of that great party of which Jefferson is commonly called the founder. His influence for this reason has been, and to this day is, confounded with that of Jefferson and Voltaire. It differed from theirs in being more conservative. Its conservatism consisted in its sanity. His conception of government was one based on experience and "adapted to such a country as ours."—THORPE, FRANCIS NEWTON, 1898, *A Constitutional History of the American People, 1776–1850, vol.* I, *p.* 42.

Franklin was indeed read, and exercised a good deal of influence, especially in his own city; and Franklin was a writer of no small literary abilities. Still, his popularity was due largely to his labors in behalf of his country, his interest in scientific matters, and the common-sense practicality of his maxims, which appealed to the shrewd commercial instincts of his countrymen.—CAIRNS, WILLIAM B., 1898, *On the Development of American Literature from 1815 to 1833, p.* 24.

Jonathan Edwards and Benjamin Franklin are like enormous trees (say a pine and an oak), which may be seen from a great distance dominating the scrubby, homely, second growth of our provincial literature. They make an ill-assorted pair,—the cheery man of the world and the intense man of God—but they owe their preëminence to the same quality. Franklin, it is true, is remarkable for his unfailing common sense, a quality of which Edwards had not very much, his keenest sense being rather uncommon. But it was not his common sense, but the cause of his common sense, namely, his faculty of realization, that made Franklin eminent. This faculty is rare among men, but it was possessed by Franklin to a great degree. His perceptions of his surroundings—material, intellectual, personal, social, political—had power to affect his mind and action. He took real account of his circumstances.—HALE, EDWARD EVERETT, JR., 1898, *American Prose, ed. Carpenter, p.* 13.

Almost every event of his life has been distorted until, from the great and accomplished man he really was, he has been magnified into an impossible prodigy. Almost everything he wrote about in science has been put down as a discovery. His wonderful ability in expressing himself has assisted in this; for if ten men wrote on a subject and Franklin was one of them, his statement is the one most likely to be preserved, because the others, being inferior in language, are soon forgotten and lost. Every scrap of paper he wrote upon is now considered a precious relic and a great deal of it is printed, so that statements which were but memoranda or merely his way of formulating other men's knowledge for his own convenience or for the sake of writing a pleasant letter to a friend, are given undue importance. Indeed, when we read one of these letters or memoranda it is so clearly and beautifully expressed and put in such a captivating form that, as the editor craftily forbears to comment on it, we instinctively conclude that it must have been a gift of new knowledge to mankind.—FISHER, SYDNEY GEORGE, 1899, *The True Benjamin Franklin, Preface, p.* 7.

To judge Franklin from the literary standpoint is neither easy nor quite fair. It is not to be denied that as a philosopher, as a statesman, and as a friend, he owed much of his success to his ability as a writer. His letters charmed all, and made his correspondence eagerly sought. His political arguments were the joy of his party and the dread of his opponents. His scientific discoveries were explained in language at once so simple and so clear that plow-boy and exquisite could follow his thought or his experiment to its conclusion. Yet he was never a literary man in the true and common meaning of the term. Omitting his uncompleted autobiography and his scientific writings, there is hardly a line of his pen which was not privately or anonymously written, to exert a transient influence, fill an empty column, or please a friend. The larger part of his work was not only done in haste, but never revised or even proof-read. Yet this self-educated boy and busy, practical man gave to American literature the most popular autobiography ever written, a series of political and social satires that can bear comparison with those of the greatest satirists, a private correspondence as readable as Walpole's or Chesterfield's; and the collection of Poor Richard's epigrams has been oftener printed and translated than any other production of an American pen.—FORD, PAUL LEICESTER, 1899, *The Many-Sided Franklin.*

Franklin was the best letter-writer of his day in America. In comparison with Washington's uniform epistolary style, Franklin's is striking for its flexibility—dignified in weighty matters, in familiar letters, playful as a kitten, frequently witty and fanciful, pleasing always by clearness, naturalness and ease.—BRONSON, WALTER C., 1900, *A Short History of American Literature, p.* 56.

Robert Henry

1718–1790

Robert Henry, the author of the "History of Great Britain written on a new plan," was the son of a farmer, and was born in the parish of St. Ninians, near Stirling, 18th February 1718. He received his early education at the school of his native parish, and at the grammar school of Stirling, and after completing a course of study at Edinburgh University became master of the grammar school of Annan. In 1746 he was licensed to preach by the Annan presbytery, shortly after which he was chosen minister of a Presbyterian congregation at Carlisle, where he remained until 1760, when he was removed to a similar charge at Berwick-on-Tweed. It was during his stay at Berwick that the idea of his "History" first occurred to him, but the dearth of books and the difficulty of consulting original authorities compelled him to postpone the execution of his design till his removal to Edinburgh, as minister of New Greyfriars, in 1768. The first volume of his "History" appeared in 1771, and the others followed at irregular intervals until 1785, when the fifth was published, bringing down the narrative to the Tudor dynasty. The work was virulently assailed by Gilbert Stuart, but the attack was overdone, and although it for a time hindered the sale, the injury effected was only temporary. For the volumes published in his lifetime Henry realized as much as £3300, and through the influence of Lord Mansfield he was in 1781 rewarded with a pension of £100 a year from George III. In 1784 he received the degree of D. D. from the university of Edinburgh. He died in 1790 before his tenth volume was quite ready for the press. Four years after his death it was published under the care of Malcolm Laing, who supplied the entire chapters v. and vii., and added an index.—BAYNES, THOMAS SPENCER, ed., 1880, *Encyclopædia Britannica, vol.* XI.

PERSONAL

To-morrow morning Henry sets off for London, with immense hopes of selling his history. I wish he had delayed till our last review of him had reached your city. But I really suppose that he has little probability of getting any gratuity. The trade are too sharp to give precious gold for perfect nonsense. I wish sincerely that I could enter Holborn the same hour with him. He should have a repeated fire to combat with. I entreat that you may be so kind as to let him feel some of your thunder. I shall never forget the favour. If Whitaker is in London, he could give a blow. Patterson will give him a knock. Strike by all means. The wretch will tremble, grow pale, and return with a consciousness of his debility. I entreat I may hear from you a day or two after you have seen him. He will complain grievously of me to Strahan and Rose. I shall send you a paper about him—an advertisement from Parnassus, in the manner of Boccalini.— STUART, GILBERT, 1774, *Letter, March* 21, *Disraeli's Calamities of Authors.*

To proceed with our *Literary Conspiracy,* which was conducted by Stuart with a pertinacity of invention perhaps not to be paralleled in literary history. That the peace of mind of such an industrious author as Dr. Henry was for a considerable time destroyed; that the sale of a work on which Henry had expended much of his fortune and his life was stopped; and that, when covered with obloquy and ridicule, in despair he left Edinburgh for London, still encountering the same hostility; that all this was the work of the same hand perhaps was never even known to its victim. The multiplied forms of this Proteus of the Malevoli were still but one devil; fire or water, or a bull or a lion; still it was the same Proteus, the same Stuart.—DISRAELI, ISAAC, 1812–13, *Literary Hatred, Calamities of Authors.*

Dr. Henry was one of those characteristic Moderates of the old school who were genial in society, humorous at table, and deplorably dry—and deliciously conscious of being dry—in the pulpit. He belonged to that class of ministers who, according to Lord Robertson, of facetious memory, "are better in bottle than in wood."—GRAHAM, HENRY GREY, 1901, *Scottish Men of Letters in the Eighteenth Century, p.* 429.

HISTORY OF GREAT BRITAIN

1771–90

He neither furnishes entertainment nor instruction. Diffuse, vulgar, and ungrammatical, he strips history of all her ornaments. As an antiquary, he wants accuracy and knowledge; and, as an historian, he is destitute of fire, taste, and sentiment. His work is a gazette, in which we find actions and events without their causes, and in which we meet with the names, without the characters, of personages. He has amassed all the refuse and lumber of the times he would record. . . . The mind of his reader is affected with no agreeable emotions; it is awakened only to disgust and fatigue.—STUART, GILBERT, 1773, *Edinburgh Review and Magazine, vol.* I, *pp.* 266, 270.

His historical narratives are as full as those remote times seem to demand, and, at the same time, his inquiries of the antiquarian kind omit nothing which can be an object of doubt or curiosity. The one as well as the other is delineated with great perspicuity, and no less propriety, which are the true ornaments of this kind of writing; all superfluous embellishments are avoided; and the reader will hardly find in our language any performance that unites together so perfectly the two great points of entertainment and instruction. —HUME, DAVID, 1773, *Review of Henry's History.*

DR. JOHNSON.—"I have heard Henry's

'History of Britain' well spoken of: I am told it is carried on in separate divisions, as the civil, the military, the religious history: I wish much to have one branch well done, and that is the history of manners of common life." DR. ROBERTSON.—"Henry should have applied his attention to that alone, which is enough for any man; and he might have found a great deal scattered in various books, had he read solely with that view. Henry erred in not selling his first volume at a moderate price to the booksellers, that they might have pushed him on till he had got reputation." — BOSWELL, JAMES, 1791–93, *Life of Johnson, ed. Hill, vol.* III, *p.* 379.

The work of Dr. Henry is an ornament and an honour to his country. — DIBDIN, THOMAS FROGNALL, 1809, *The Bibliomania; or Book Madness.*

Those parts of Henry's history which profess to trace the progress of government are still more jejune than the rest of his volumes.—HALLAM, HENRY, 1818, *View of the State of Europe During the Middle Ages, Preface.*

Much of this sort of information [respecting the early constitutional history of England], and of every other historical information, may be found in the "History" of Dr. Henry; but the same facts, when collected and printed in a modern dress, properly arranged, and to be read without difficulty, as they are in the work of Dr. Henry, no longer excite the same reflection nor obtain the same possession of the memory which they do when seen in something like their native garb, in their proper place, and in all the simplicity, singularity, and quaintness which belong to them.—SMYTH, WILLIAM, 1840, *Lectures on Modern History.*

Considerable merit in the execution, and complete originality in the plan, of his history.—COCKBURN, HENRY THOMAS LORD, 1854? *Memorials of his Times, ch.* I.

To this great work Henry devoted the anxious labour of nearly thirty years; and he has certainly accumulated a vast store of useful information. But to write philosophically and entertainingly upon so many heterogeneous subjects exceeds man's might. Even when the scope is far less ambitious, the charm of style possessed by a Hume, a Robertson, a Macaulay, a Prescott, or a Bancroft, can alone interest the desultory reader in historical details. For all practical purposes, Henry's history has been superseded by the noble work published by Charles Knight.—ALLIBONE, S. AUSTIN, 1854–58, *A Critical Dictionary of English Literature, vol.* I, *p.* 825.

A work valuable for the numerous facts it contains illustrative of manners and the state of society, which are not to be found in any of our previous general historians, but chiefly meritorious as having been our first English history compiled upon that plan.—CRAIK, GEORGE L., 1861, *A Compendious History of English Literature and of the English Language, vol.* II, *p.* 359.

For this history, Henry received the sum of 3200*l.* from the booksellers, and from the Crown a pension of 100*l.* a year —a reward not due to his style or even to the accuracy of the research, but to the growing interest among all classes in the domestic life of our ancestors and in the condition of the people. Henry was the first to direct attention to these themes. His idea has been carried out with a large amount of corrected and additional information in the popular history of England by Charles Knight.— ANGUS, JOSEPH, 1865, *The Handbook of English Literature, p.* 573.

As a popular and comprehensive history it has much merit, but it lacks original research; while its style and method detracts from its literary value.—HENDERSON, T. F., 1891, *Dictionary of National Biography, vol.* XXVI, *p.* 127.

William Livingston
1723–1790

An eminent statesman who was governor of New Jersey, 1776-90. "Philosophic Solitude," a poem; "Review of the Military Operations in North America," 1757; "Digest of the Laws of New York."—ADAMS, OSCAR FAY, 1897, *A Dictionary of American Authors, p.* 232.

PERSONAL

Livingston appears to have had but little vanity, either as a private or public man. His real learning and the quaint style of the day, sometimes give his writings an air of formality, which might be mistaken for pedantry; but on a close examination, his character bears few, if any traces of affectation. His conversation was entirely free of egotism. As governor, he despised, and altogether threw off the state, which his predecessors under the crown had assumed, and thus early adapted himself to the rapidly changing tastes of the people. Nor does this appear to have sprung so much from necessity as inclination. He was plain and indifferent, almost to slovenliness, in his dress. . . . In his family, Livingston was a fond husband, and a generous father, ready at all times to make every sacrifice which the welfare of his children demanded; while at the same time it is not to be denied that a temper, originally irritable, and rendered more so by the difficulties and responsibility of his situation, was sometimes less restrained in his domestic circle, than where it was checked by the presence of strangers. An extreme sensitiveness to noise; an occasional unwillingness to converse when not excited by society; and a sensibility more quickly manifested with regard to trifling vexations than serious evils, sometimes threw a gloom over the fireside of Liberty Hall. . . . He was considerably above the middle stature, and in early life, so very thin as to receive from some female wit of New-York, perhaps in allusion to his satirical disposition, the nickname of the "whipping-post." In later years he acquired a more dignified corpulency. Speaking of himself, in the language of one of his opponents in the American Whig (1768), he says, "The Whig is a long-nosed, long-chinned, ugly-looking fellow." . . . Of his scholarship, it may be said that it was distinguished in days when scholarship was more common. Greek he abandoned early in life, but of the Latin he retained a familiar knowledge; the French and Dutch he read with great facility, writing them both with considerable ease, though without elegance. With the literature of his own language, he was intimately acquainted. In polemical divinity, a study now fallen

into considerable disrepute, he was also well read. His religious taste and readings tinge most of his literary productions, which often borrow point and eloquence from the rich treasure-house of scriptural allusions and quotations. His skill in literature was not confined to the closet or his own gratification; we have seen it rendering more effective his exertions directed to Holland; and in his own country, he was active in supplying the want of instruction in the different States, to do which he was more than once requested; while at the same time as trustee *ex-officio* of Princeton and Rutgers Colleges, he exercised a supervision over the literary interests of New Jersey. — SEDGWICK, THEODORE, 1833, *A Memoir of the Life of William Livingston, pp.* 443, 445, 446, 447.

In person he was, in middle life, tall and spare, later slightly corpulent; in dress, careless, almost slovenly, but his biographer informs us that he was a capital fisherman and wrote a bad hand, two unerring marks of a gentleman. He was an excellent Latin scholar, read and wrote French and Dutch with ease, and was thoroughly acquainted with English literature. . . . Among the men of this historic period, no one affords a more interesting study than this staunch, original and devoted friend of the liberties and rights of man.—STEVENS, JOHN AUSTIN, 1878, *William Livingston, Magazine of American History, vol.* 2, *pp.* 487, 488.

At the head of the New Jersey delegation stood her famous war governor, William Livingston, who had reached his sixty-fifth year. He had been an eminent member of the New York bar as early as 1752, and was one of the most caustic and forcible essayists in the country; he was also one of the few poets of his time. It was next to impossible for him to make a speech that was not seasoned with dry humor and stinging satire. He was probably the best classical scholar in the assemblage. He had through a long career of active public and political service acquitted himself with honor.—LAMB, MARTHA J., 1885, *The Framers of the Constitution, Magazine of American History, vol.* 13, *p.* 338.

PHILOSOPHIC SOLITUDE
1747

This poem is obviously the effort of a rhyming apprentice, still in bondage to the methods of his master, Alexander Pope; yet he catches the knack of his master, with a cleverness proving the possibility of original work, on his own account, by and by. It illustrates, likewise, a trait of human nature, that this young lawyer and politician, having given himself to a practical career in the thick of the world's affairs, and one made tumultuous by his own aggressive spirit, should have begun it by depicting, in enthusiastic verse, his preference for a life of absolute retirement and serene meditation. . . . He would have books for his most intimate friends. . . . The voluptuous languors of this poem, report a quality in the author that did not control him; and henceforward, through nearly half a century, his real life was a battle for stern and great ideas.—TYLER, MOSES COIT, 1878, *A History of American Literature*, 1676–1765, *vol.* II, *pp.* 218, 220.

A poem on "Philosophic Solitude" which reproduces the trick of Pope's antitheses and climaxes with the imagery of the "Rape of the Lock," and the didactic morality of the "Imitations from Horace" and the "Moral Essays."—BEERS, HENRY A., 1887, *An Outline Sketch of American Literature, p.* 66.

Written in the conventional eighteenth-century manner, but is smooth and pretty. —BRONSON, WALTER C., 1900, *A Short History of American Literature, p.* 40.

John Wesley
1703–1791

1703, June 17, John Wesley born. 1707 (end of), Charles Wesley born. 1709, Fire at Epworth rectory. 1714, John Wesley goes to the Charterhouse. George Whitefield born. 1716–17, December 2—end of January, Epworth ghost. 1720, John Wesley goes up to Christchurch, Oxford. 1725, September 19, Ordained deacon. 1726, March 17, Elected Fellow of Lincoln College, Oxford. Charles Wesley goes up to Chirstchurch, Oxford, from Westminster School. 1727–29, August, 1727, November, 1729, Curate to his father at Wroote, Epworth. 1728, September 22, Ordained priest. 1729, John Wesley becomes "Father of the Holy Club." 1732, Whitefield servitor at Pembroke College. 1733 (*circa*), John Wesley makes William Law's acquaintance. 1735, April 25, the Rev. Samuel Wesley, John's father, died. Charles Wesley ordained. October 14, John and Charles Wesley sail from Gravesend for Georgia. 1736, Charles Wesley returns. 1738, February 1, John returns to England, landing at Deal. George Whitefield leaves for Georgia. Wesley's conversion and visit to the Moravians at Herrnhut. Whitefield returns from Georgia. 1739, February 17, Whitefield begins field preaching. Wesley begins field preaching. Whitefield returns to Georgia. May 12, Stone of first Methodist meeting-house laid. 1740, Wesley's breach with the Moravians. 1740-48, Wesley separates from Whitefield on predestination. Breach with Calvinists. 1740-90, Period of Wesley's itinerant preaching. 1741–45, Opposition and violence of mobs and magistrates to itinerant preaching. 1742, July, Susannah Wesley, John's mother, dies. 1744, June 25, First Methodist Conference. 1748, Whitefield returns from Georgia. 1751, John Wesley marries Mrs. Vazeille. 1768, Regular Methodist society formed in New York, U. S. 1770, Whitefield dies at Newburyport, Mass. 1777, April 1, Foundation stone of City Road Chapel laid. 1784, Legal settlement of Conference effected. September 2, Wesley ordains Dr. Coke a bishop, and so founds Methodist Episcopal Church. 1788, March 29, Charles Wesley died. 1791, March 2, John Wesley died. —BANFIELD, FRANK, 1900, *John Wesley, p.* xiii.

PERSONAL

Dear Son,—I came hither to-day because I cannot be at rest till I make you easier. I could not possibly manufacture any money for you here sooner than next Saturday. On Monday I design to wait on Dr. Morley, and will try to prevail with your brother to return you £8, with interest. I will assist you in the charges for ordination, though I am just now struggling for life. This £8 you may depend on the next week, or the week after. Your affectionate father.—WESLEY, SAMUEL, 1725, *Letter to John Wesley, Sept.* 1.

In the evening I went to a house in Aldersgate Street (London), where one was reading Luther's preface to the Epistle to the Romans. About a quarter before nine, while he was describing the change which God works in the heart through faith in Christ, I felt my heart strangely warmed. I felt I did trust in Christ, Christ alone, for salvation; and an assurance was given me that he had taken away *my* sins, even *mine*, and saved *me* from the law of sin and death. I began to pray with all my might for those who had, in a more especial manner, despitefully used me, and persecuted me. I then testified openly to all there, what I now first felt in my heart.—WESLEY, JOHN, 1738, *Journal, May* 24.

The regard I have always had for you and your brother, is still as great as ever; and I trust we shall give this and future ages an example of true Christian love abiding, notwithstanding difference in judgment. Why our lord has permitted us to differ as to some points of doctrine, will be discovered at the last day. I have had the pleasure of reading the continuance of your Appeal; and pray, that God would prosper every labour of your pen and lip.—WHITEFIELD, GEORGE, 1746, *Letter to John Wesley.*

Here lieth the Body
of
JOHN WESLEY,
A Brand plucked out of the burning;
Who died of a Consumption in the Fifty-first
Year of his Age,
not leaving, after his Debts are paid,
Ten Pounds behind him:
Praying
God be merciful to me, an unprofitable
Servant!
He ordered, that this, if any, inscription
should be placed on his tombstone.
—WESLEY, JOHN, 1753, *Proposed Epitaph.*

I was once a kind of oracle with Mr. Wesley. I never suspected anything bad of him, or ever discovered any kind or degree of falseness or hypocrisy in him. But during all the time of his intimacy with me, I judged him to be much under the power of his own spirit, which seemed to have the predominance in every good thing or way that his zeal carried him to. It was owing to his unwillingness or inability to give up his own spirit that he was forced into that false and rash censure which he published in print against the mystics:—as enemies to good works, and even tending to atheism. A censure so false, and regardless of right and wrong, as hardly anything can exceed it; which

is to be found in a preface of his to a book of hymns.—LAW, WILLIAM, 1756, *Works, vol.* IX, *p.* 123.

A lean, elderly man, fresh colored, his hair smoothly combed, but with a *soupçon* of curls at the ends. Wondrous clean, but as evidently an actor as Garrick.—WALPOLE, HORACE, 1766, *To John Chute, Oct.* 10; *Letters, ed. Cunningham, vol.* V, *p.* 16.

By only erasing about half-a-dozen lines from the whole, I might defy the shrewdest of his readers to discover whether the *lying apostle* of the Foundery be a Jew, a papist, a pagan, or a Turk. . . . As unprincipled as a rook, and as silly as a jackdaw, first pilfering his neighbour's plumage, and then going proudly forth, displaying his borrowed tail to the eyes of a laughing world. . . . Persons that are toad eaters to Mr. John Wesley stand in need of very wide throats, and that which he wishes them to swallow is enough to choke an elephant. . . . Wesley is a crafty slanderer, an unfeeling reviler, a liar of the most gigantic magnitude, a Solomon in a cassock, a wretch, a disappointed Orlando Furioso, a miscreant apostate, whose perfection consists in his perfect hatred of all goodness and good men.—HILL, ROWLAND, 1777, *Imposture Detected, and the Dead Vindicated; in a Letter to a Friend: containing some gentle Strictures on the false and libellous Harangue, lately delivered by Mr. John Wesley, upon his laying the first stone of his new Dissenting meeting-house, near the City Road.*

He said, "John Wesley's conversation is good, but he is never at leisure. He is always obliged to go at a certain hour. This is very disagreeable to a man who loved to fold his legs and have out his talk, as I do."—JOHNSON, SAMUEL, 1778, *Life by Boswell, ed. Hill, vol.* III, *p.* 261.

Very lately I had an opportunity, for some days together, of observing Mr. Wesley with attention. I endeavoured to consider him, not so much with the eye of a friend, as with the impartiality of a philosopher; and I must declare, every hour I spent in his company afforded me fresh reasons for esteem and veneration. So fine an old man I never saw! The happiness of his mind beamed forth in his countenance: every look showed how fully he enjoyed
The gay remembrance of a life well spent.

Wherever he went he diffused a portion of his own felicity. Easy and affable in his demeanour, he accommodated himself to every sort of company; and showed how happily the most finished courtesy may be blended with the most perfect piety. In his conversation, we might be at a loss whether to admire most his fine classical taste, his extensive knowledge of men and things, or his overflowing goodness of heart. While the grave and serious were charmed with his wisdom, his sportive sallies of innocent mirth delighted even the young and thoughtless; and both saw in his uninterrupted cheerfulness the excellency of true religion. No cynical remarks on the levity of youth embittered his discourses. No applausive retrospect to past times marked his present discontent. In him even old age appeared delightful, like an evening without a cloud; and it was impossible to observe him without wishing fervently, "May my latter end be like his!"—KNOX, ALEXANDER, 1789, *Letter.*

Sacred to the Memory
Of the Rev. John Wesley, M. A.
SOMETIME FELLOW OF LINCOLN COLLEGE, OXFORD;
A Man in Learning and sincere Piety
Scarcely inferior to any;
In Zeal, Ministerial Labours, and extensive Usefulness,
Superior, perhaps, to all Men,
Since the days of ST. PAUL.
Regardless of fatigue, personal Danger, and Disgrace,
He went out into the highways and hedges
Calling Sinners to Repentance.
And Publishing the GOSPEL of Peace.
He was the Founder of the Methodist Societies,
And the chief Promoter and Patron
Of the Plan of Itinerant preaching,
Which he extended through GREAT BRITAIN and IRELAND,
The WEST INDIES, and AMERICA,
With unexampled Success.
He was born the 17th of June, 1703;
And died the 2d of March, 1791,
In sure and certain hope of Eternal Life,
Through the Atonement and Mediation of a Crucified Saviour.
He was sixty-five Years in the Ministry,
And fifty-two an Itinerant Preacher:
He lived to see, in these Kingdoms only,
About three hundred Itinerant,
And one thousand Local Preachers,
Raised up from the midst of his own People;
And eighty thousand Persons in the Societies under his care.

His Name will be ever had in grateful Remembrance
By all who rejoice in the universal Spread
Of the Gospel of CHRIST.
Soli Deo Gloria.
—INSCRIPTION ON TABLET, CITY ROAD CHAPEL.

His face for an old man was one of the finest I have seen A clear, smooth forehead, an aquiline nose, an eye the brightest and most piercing that can be conceived, and a freshness of complexion scarcely ever to be found at his years and impressive of the most perfect health, conspire to render him a venerable and interesting figure. . . . A narrow plaited stock, a coat with a small upright collar, no buckles at his knees, no silk or velvet in any part of his apparel, and a head as white as snow, gave an idea of something primitive and apostolical; while an air of neatness and cleanliness was diffused over his whole person. . . . In social life Mr. Wesley was lively and conversible, and of exquisite companionable talents. He had been much accustomed to society, was well acquainted with the rules of good breeding; and in general perfectly attentive and polite. The abstraction of a scholar did not appear in his behaviour. He spoke a good deal in company; and as he had seen much of the world, and in the course of his travels through every corner of the nation had acquired an infinite fund of anecdote and observation, he was not sparing in his communications, and the manner in which he related them was no inconsiderable addition to the entertainment they afforded. His manner in private life was the reverse of cynical or forbidding. It was sprightly and pleasant to the last degree, and presented a beautiful contrast to the austere deportment of many of his preachers and people, who seemed to have ranked laughter among the mortal sins. It was impossible to be long in his company without partaking his hilarity. Neither infirmities of age nor the approach of death had any apparent influence on his manners. His cheerfulness continued to the last, and was as conspicuous at fourscore as at one-and-twenty.— HAMPSON, JOHN, 1791, *Memoirs of the Late Rev. John Wesley.*

His indefatigable zeal in the discharge of his duty has been long witnessed by the world; but, as mankind are not always inclined to put a generous construction on the exertions of singular talents, his motives were imputed to the love of popularity, ambition, and lucre. It now appears that he was actuated by a disinterested regard to the immortal interests of mankind. He laboured, and studied, and preached, and wrote, to propagate what he believed to be the gospel of Christ. The intervals of these engagements were employed in governing and regulating the concerns of his numerous societies; assisting the necessities, solving the difficulties, and soothing the afflictions of his hearers. He observed so rigid a temperance, and allowed himself so little repose, that he seemed to be above the infirmities of nature, and to act independent of the earthly tenement he occupied. The recital of the occurrences of every day of his life would be the greatest encomium. Had he loved wealth, he might have accumulated it without bounds. Had he been fond of power, his influence would have been worth courting by any party. I do not say he was without ambition; he had that which Christianity need not blush at, and which virtue is proud to confess. I do not mean that which is gratified by splendour and large possessions; but that which commands the hearts and affections, the homage and gratitude of thousands. For him they felt sentiments of veneration, only inferior to those which they paid to Heaven: to him they looked as their father, their benefactor, their guide to glory, and immortality: for him they fell prostrate before God, with prayers and tears, to spare his doom, and prolong his stay. Such a recompense as this is sufficient to repay the toils of the longest life. Short of this, greatness is contemptible impotence. Before this, lofty prelates bow, and princes hide their distinguished heads.—WOODFALL, WILLIAM, 1791, *Diary, June 17.*

Mr. Wesley had most exquisite talents to make himself agreeable in company, and having been much accustomed to society the rules of good breeding were habitual to him. . . . He never travelled alone; and the person who attended him had the charge of his letters and papers, which, of course, lay open to his inspection. The preachers, likewise, who were occasionally with him, had access to his letters and papers, especially if he had confidence in their sincerity and zeal in religion, which it was not very difficult to obtain. It was easy for these persons to see the motive that influenced him, and the end he had in view in every action of his life, however remote from public observation; and he took no pains to conceal them, but seemed rather to court the discovery.—WHITEHEAD, JOHN, 1793–96, *Life of the Rev. John Wesley, Sometime Fellow of Lincoln College, Oxford.*

Oh I have seen (nor hope perhaps in vain,
Ere life go down, to see such sights again)
A veteran warrior in the Christian field,
Who never saw the sword he could not wield;
Grave without dulness, learnèd without pride,
Exact, yet not precise, though meek, keen-eyed;
A man that would have foil'd at their own play
A dozen would-bes of the modern day.
Who, when occasion justified its use,
Had wit as bright as ready to produce,
Could fetch from records of an earlier age,
Or from philosophy's enlighten'd page,
His rich materials, and regale your ear
With strains it was a privilege to hear;
Yet above all his luxury supreme,
And his chief glory was the gospel theme;
There he was copious as old Greece or Rome,
His happy eloquence seem'd there at home,
Ambitious not to shine or to excel,
But to treat justly what he loved so well.
—COWPER, WILLIAM, c1798, *Conversation.*

During his last illness he said: "Let me be buried in nothing but what is woollen; and let my corpse be carried in my coffin into the chapel." . . . In his will he directed that six poor men should have 20 shillings each for carrying his body to the grave; "for I particularly desire," said he, "that there may be no hearse, no coach, no escutcheon, no pomp, except the tears of them that love me, and are following me to Abraham's bosom." . . . Wesley's body lay in the chapel in a kind of state becoming the person, dressed in his clerical habit, with gown, cassock, and band, the old clerical cap on his head, a Bible in one hand, and a white handkerchief in the other. . . . The crowds who flocked to see him were so great that it was thought prudent, for fear of accident, to accelerate the funeral, and perform it between five and six in the morning. The intelligence, however, could not be kept entirely secret, and several hundred persons attended at that unusual hour.—SOUTHEY, ROBERT, 1820, *The Life of Wesley and the Rise and Progress of Methodism.*

In dress, he was a pattern of neatness and simplicity. A narrow plaited stock, a coat with a small upright collar, no buckles at his knees, no silk or velvet in any part of his apparel, and his thin silver locks gave to his whole person an air of something primitive and apostolic. The same neatness and simplicity was manifest in every circumstance of his life. In his chamber and study, during his winter months of residence in London I never observed that a book was misplaced, or even a scrap of paper left unheeded. He could enjoy every convenience of life; and yet, he acted in the smallest things like a man who was not to continue an hour in one place. He seemed at home in every place, settled, satisfied, and happy: and yet was ready every hour to take a journey of a thousand miles. His conversation was always pleasing, and frequently interesting and instructive in the highest degree. By reading, traveling, and continual observation, he had acquired a fund of knowledge, which he dispensed with a propriety and perspicuity that has been rarely equalled. The Greek and Latin classics were as familiar to him as the most common English authors; and also many of the best French writers. Yet though so richly furnished, we believe those of the most improved taste have never observed in him the affectation of learning. He joined in every kind of discourse that was innocent.—MOORE, HENRY, 1824, *The Life of the Rev. John Wesley, vol.* II, *p.* 358.

He is spoken of as credulous, as hoping good of men naturally, and able to hope it again from those that had deceived him. This last is weakness unless allied with wise decision and force, generosity when it is thus tempered. To the character of John Wesley it imparted a persuasive nobleness, and hallowed his earnestness with mercy. He had in a striking degree another of those balances between opposite forces which mark the great man. He kept himself open to new inspirations, was bold in apprehending and quick in carrying them out. Yet with a resolve once taken he showed a steadiness of purpose beyond what the timid scholars of tradition can conceive.— OSSOLI, MARGARET

FULLER, 1850?-59, *Papers on Literature and Art, ed. Fuller, p.* 350.

As I was walking home one day from my father's bank, I observed a great crowd of people streaming into a chapel in the City Road. I followed them; and saw laid out upon a table the dead body of a clergyman in full canonicals. It was the corpse of John Wesley; and the crowd moved slowly and silently round and round the table to take a last look at that most venerable man.—ROGERS, SAMUEL, 1855? *Table-Talk, p.* 120.

Taking him altogether, Wesley is a man *sui generis.* He stands alone; he has had no successor; no one like him went before; no contemporary was a coequal. There was a wholeness about the man, such as is rarely seen. His physique, his genius, his wit, his penetration, his judgment, his memory, his beneficence, his religion, his diligence, his conversation, his courteousness, his manners, and his dress,—made him as perfect as we ever expect man to be on this side heaven.—TYERMAN, L., 1866, *The Life and Times of the Rev. John Wesley, vol.* III, *p.* 660.

It was indeed evident to the most cursory reader that the "enthusiasm" charged against him was that inner wellspring of power without which he could never have accomplished his great work; and that the "love of authority" is that quality which is actually necessary to a great leader of men. That Wesley was too apt to credit all that people told him may be true; himself sincere by nature, he gave too much credit for sincerity to all others. His nature, although calm and tranquil, was of the believing rather than of the doubting order; and this cannot be better illustrated than by the fact that while discussing some modern miracles, stated to have been wrought at the tomb of a French Abbé, he remarked that to doubt would be to unsettle all foundations based on human testimony. So slight defects as these could detract little from the intellectual and the moral stature of one of the very ablest and best men of modern times. — URLIN, R. DENNY, 1869, *John Wesley's Place in Church History, p.* 136.

Wesley, when a young man, was distinguished for his long flowing hair, which he wore to save the expense of a periwig, that he might give the money to the poor.

—FORSYTH, WILLIAM, 1871, *The Novels and Novelists of the Eighteenth Century, p.* 67.

Wesley was a scholar, an Oxford student, and he believed in the devil; he attributes to him sickness, nightmare, storms, earthquakes. His family heard supernatural noises; his father had been thrice pushed by a ghost; he himself saw the hand of God in the commonest events of life. One day at Birmingham, overtaken by a hailstorm, he felt that he received this warning, because at table he had not sufficiently exhorted the people who dined with him; when he had to determine on anything, he looked out by chance for a text of Scripture, in order to decide. . . . He lived the life of an apostle, giving away all that he earned, travelling and preaching all the year, and every year, till the age of eighty-eight; it has been reckoned that he gave away thirty thousand pounds, travelled about a hundred thousand miles, and preached forty thousand sermons.—TAINE, H. A., 1871, *History of English Literature, tr. Van Laun, vol.* II, *bk.* iii, *ch.* iii, *p.* 58.

In power as a preacher he stood next to Whitefield; as a hymn writer he stood second to his brother Charles. But while combining in some degree the excellences of either, he possessed qualitites in which both were utterly deficient; an indefatigable industry, a cool judgment, a command over others, a faculty of organization, a singular union of patience and moderation with an imperious ambition, which marked him as a ruler of men. He had, besides, a learning and skill in writing which no other of the Methodists possessed; he was older than any of his colleagues at the start of the movement, and he outlived them all. His life, indeed, from 1703 to 1791, almost covers the century, and the Methodist body had passed through every phase of its history before he sank into the grave at the age of eighty-eight. It would have been impossible for Wesley to have wielded the power he did, had he not shared the follies and extravagance as well as the enthusiasm of his disciples. Throughout his life his asceticism was that of a monk. At times he lived on bread only, and often slept on the bare boards. He lived in a world of wonders and divine interpositions. It was a miracle if the rain stopped and allowed him to set forward on a journey. It was a judgment of Heaven if a hailstorm burst over a town which had been deaf to his preaching. One day, he tells us, when he was tired and his horse fell lame, "I thought—can not God heal either man or beast by any means or without any? Immediately my headache ceased and my horse's lameness in the same instant." With a still more childish fanaticism he guided his conduct, whether in ordinary events or in the great crises of his life, by drawing lots or watching the particular texts at which his Bible opened. But with all this extravagance and superstition, Wesley's mind was essentially practical, orderly, and conservative. No man ever stood at the head of a great revolution whose temper was so anti-revolutionary. —GREEN, JOHN RICHARD, 1874, *A Short History of the English People, p.* 709.

He belonged to an unbroken ancestral succession of English gentlemen, of whom at least his three immediate predecessors were scholars and divines. . . . No fibre of hereditary connection between himself and the artisan classes, or the peasantry of England, can be traced in all his long pedigree; and yet this was the man whose words were to take hold of colliers and weavers, of tinners and stone-masons, and hardhanded workers generally, as no man's words had done before for centuries, if ever, or have done since. —RIGG, JAMES HARRISON, 1875, *The Living Wesley.*

He was a man who had made religion the single aim and object of his life, who was prepared to encounter for it every form of danger, discomfort, and obloquy; who devoted exclusively to it an energy of will and power of intellect that in worldly professions might have raised him to the highest positions of honour and wealth. Of his sincerity, of his self-renunciation, of his deep and fervent piety, of his almost boundless activity, there can be no question. Yet with all these qualities he was not an amiable man. He was hard, punctilious, domineering, and in a certain sense even selfish. —LECKY, WILLIAM EDWARD HARTPOLE, 1878, *History of England in the Eighteenth Century, vol.* II, *p.* 602.

There must be many a field in Great Britain thick-sown with stones which have been thrown at John Wesley and his proto-Methodists. Traveling from four to five thousand miles every year, and preaching from two to four times nearly every day to audiences of thousands; often disturbed by mobs of men more savage than wild beasts; keeping an eye on all his preachers, and receiving their reports; starting a publishing house, and carrying it on, that his people everywhere might have wholesome intellectual fare within their scanty means; taking no money but just what would suffice for his bare expenses; stopping for no storms or floods, fires or frosts; reading and studying on horseback, and answering innumerable assaults through the press, from bishops, archbishops, and ecclesiastical foes of all ranks; compiling grammars in Greek, and Hebrew, and French, and Latin, for his students; editing, writing, translating, or abridging not less than two hundred different publications; eager only, in it all, to save men and to extend the kingdom of God. Half a million souls were to be numbered as his adherents at the close of that fifty years; and outside of this, a vast multitude that no man can number, morally and spiritually benefited by his movement. He is, I think, the finest illustration of consecrated, unselfish, wholehearted devotion, for fifty solid years of this world's dark history, that the Church of Christ has ever offered to the vision of men, perhaps to that of the angels.—HERRICK, S. E., 1884, *Some Heretics of Yesterday, p.* 313.

The illustrious personage now known in history under the modest title of the Rev. John Wesley, without any of the more ambitious affixes or prefaces of the present day, would have been reverenced as a great man in any age or country. . . . Wesley was always a very conscientious man. He was ambitious, also, but not for place. His ambition was for work, for enterprise, for doing something useful,—something which could not, or would not, be done by any other person. The very fact that nobody else would undertake a good thing was to him its best recommendation. The more strange, unusual, difficult, the scheme for doing good, the more his adventurous spirit was likely to be devoted to it. To such a mind, the regular, common-place, monotonous glory of living at his ease, as the acknowledged primate of the British

world, would have presented no attractions. He preferred some impossible job, some Herculean labour, something to do where the most resolute would scarcely dare to go; and it is equally certain that his keen, sensitive, commanding consciousness, his imperial characteristic, pushed him in the same direction.—TEFFT, BENJAMIN F., 1885, *Evolution and Christianity, pp.* 266, 268.

A life which was all but commensurate with the eighteenth century, and which was certainly the busiest, and in some respects the most important life in that century—a life about which the most divers views have been taken, and in which the interest, so far from having slackened through lapse of time, is as keen if not keener than ever it was.— OVERTON, J. H., 1891, *John Wesley (English Leaders of Religion), p.* v.

Between the founder of the Society of Jesus and the creator of Wesleyan Methodism there is a parallel much closer than many good Methodists care to admit. Loyola was a Spaniard and a soldier. Wesley an Englishman and a parson, but after allowing for that initial difference there is much resemblance between the man who saved the Papacy in the sixteenth century and the man who saved Protestantism in the eighteenth. Loyola is, no doubt, a much more picturesque and a more heroic figure. The brilliant cavalier whose leg was smashed by a cannon ball at the siege of Pampeluna, set about the task of rallying the forces of Catholic Christendom in a manner more worthy of a countryman of the Cid and of Cervantes than did the trim little man who was reared in Epworth parsonage. But both had the same central idea at heart, both were inflamed with a passion for souls, and both sought to save souls by organizing a Religious Order. The English Church in those days, being a distinctly non-spiritual and Erastian institution, drove out the man whose labors might have reared an invulnerable rampart for Anglicanism throughout the world. The Roman church being wiser in its day and generation, has garrisoned its outposts with the followers of Loyola. The story is old and trite, but those who care to pursue the subject will find the parallel between Loyola and Wesley and Gen. Booth much closer than fervent Protestants generally recognize.—STEAD, WILLIAM T., 1891, *St. John of England, Review of Reviews, vol. 3, p. 250.*

Although the world and the Church have learned to be comparatively generous to Wesley now that a hundred years have sped away, and though the roar of contemporary scandal has long since ceased, I doubt whether even now he is at all adequately appreciated. I doubt whether many are aware of the extent to which to this day the impulse to every great work of philanthropy and social reformation has been due to his energy and insight. . . . The bust placed in Westminster Abbey to the memory of John Wesley, more than twenty years ago, was a very tardy recognition of the vast debt of gratitude which England owes to him. It stands hard by the cenotaph of that other illustrious Nonconformist, Isaac Watts, and gives the beautiful presentment of the aged face of the evangelist and the fine features of Charles, his poet-brother. In the solemn aisle thousands of visitors to our great Temple of Silence and Reconciliation may read three of his great sayings—one, so full of holy energy, "I look on all the world as my parish;" another, so full of bright and holy confidence, "God buries his workmen, but continues his work;" the third, when, on his death-bed, uplifting victoriously his feeble and emaciated arm, he said: "The best of all is, God is with us." "Yes!" he exclaimed again, in a tone of victorious rapture," the best of all is, God is with us." —FARRAR, F. W., 1896, *The Prophets of the Christian Faith, pp.* 139, 144.

In 1899, when the map of England looks like a gridiron of railways, none but the sturdiest of pedestrians, the most determined of cyclists can retrace the steps of Wesley and his horse and stand by the rocks and the natural ampitheatres in Cornwall and Northumberland, in Lancashire and Berkshire, where he preached his gospel to the heathen. Exertion so prolonged, enthusiasm so sustained, argues a remarkable man, while the organization he created, the system he founded, the view of life he promulgated, is still a great fact among us. No other name than Wesley's lies embalmed as his does. Yet he is not a popular figure. Our standard historians have dismissed him curtly. The fact is, Wesley puts your

ordinary historian out of conceit with himself. How much easier to weave into your page the gossip of Horace Walpole, to enliven it with a heartless jest of George Selwyn's, to make it blush with sad stories of the extravagance of Fox, to embroider it with the rhetoric of Burke, to humanize it with the talk of Johnson, to discuss the rise and fall of administrations, the growth and decay of the constitution, than to follow John Wesley into the streets of Bristol, or on to the bleak moors near Burslem, when he met, face to face in all their violence, all their ignorance, and all their generosity, the living men, women, and children who made up the nation.—BIRRELL, AUGUSTINE, 1899, *John Wesley, Scribner's Magazine, vol.* 26, *p.* 756.

No new facts about John Wesley are likely to be brought to light. He left abundant materials for his biographers in his journals, and his volumes of sermons are sufficiently exhaustive and clear as to the substance of his religious opinions. One of Wesley's great merits was his lucidity in thought, speech, and style, so that he is not a man whose obscurity in expression might generate mistakes about him. Moreover, he admitted the world into the secrets of the inner motions of his soul and mind as far as he was able. In a word, there is no new thing, in the literal sense, to be learned about Wesley. . . . Wesley was a man of limitations, but without those limitations of mind and character he would not have accomplished the work he did. To dominate the serious middle-class intelligence of the eighteenth century, he was admirably adapted. The proof of his adaptation is in his achievement. He was, I take it, in a specially manifest way, an instrument of Providence; and this is further shown by the fact that so many of the earnest men who have been prominent in the great religious revival of the nineteenth century are the lineal descendants of those who in the eighteenth were identified with the general Methodist movement. Wesley helped materially in the gradual lifting of Anglo-Saxondom out of the Paganism in which it was wallowing part of the way on the road back towards a perfect Christianity. He is plainly a man of whom every educated person should have some knowledge; and I hope I have succeeded in telling his story, in comparatively few words, fairly, squarely, and readably.—BANFIELD, FRANK, 1900, *John Wesley, pp.* vii, x.

Wesley was a glorious being. His zeal was matchless; and he accomplished, by prodigies of mental and physical effort, a vast and necessary work. The physic may have been nasty,—those fits, especially,—but Methodism arrested national decay and infused new life into Christianity. In the political sphere, though Wesley's direct intervention was not happily conceived, it is in every way probable that the influence of that high Tory over the masses did much to prevent an English analogue of the French Revolution by absorbing into the ranks of Methodism those who would naturally have been its leaders. The emancipation of the slaves, and, after that, other emancipations were the reflexion and the fruit of that inward emanciaption of which Wesley was the preacher. The Evangelical movement, and the Oxford movement, in the Church of England, were both founded on the principle that religion was something other, something higher, than an aspect of civil life. This principle, which in the eighteenth century had been fairly lost, Wesley and his companions were bold enough to reassert. For this all English-speaking men, irrespective of creed, have cause to be thankful. To take a single illustration—may we not trace the abolition of the duel in England to Wesley's influence? In every other European country the obligations of honour prescribe this reckless mode of settling certain disputes. Why is England exempt? The episode of the fashionable tailor is not an adequate explanation. The true reason is that the English conscience, as remodelled by Wesley, will not tolerate the making of widows and orphans on a frivolous pretext. However, Wesley was not precisely a saint. He was too active, too full of fight, to merit that description. But he was, pre-eminently a man.—SNELL, F. J., 1900, *Wesley and Methodism, p.* 242.

In his eighty-fifth year he acknowledges that he is not so agile as formerly, that he has occasional twinges of rheumatism and suffers slight dimness of sight, his other senses remaining unimpaired. "However, blessed be God," he says, "I do not slack from my labour, and can

preach and write still." From being one of the worst hated he became one of the best loved men in the Kingdom. At Cork, where he had been mobbed and burned in effigy, he was met by a cortège of mounted horsemen. At Falmouth, where he had been taken prisoner by an immense mob, "roaring like lions," high and low lined the street from one end of the town to the other, "out of love and kindness, gaping and staring as if the king were going by." At Burslem the people gathered so early in the morning that he began to preach at half-past four. At Newgate he preached to forty-seven men under sentence of death, "the clink of whose chains was very awful." He now ceased recording his receipts and expenditures in his account-book. His last entry is a remarkable one : "For upwards of eighty years I have kept my accounts exactly; I will not attempt it any longer, being satisfied with the continual conviction that I save all I can, and give all I can—that is, all I have." It is estimated that he gave away over thirty thousand pounds which he had earned with his pen. His was a serene and sunny old age which mellowed as the years passed by. His early asceticism had long disappeared. One of his pious helpers complained that by Wesley's witty proverbs he was tempted to levity. To a blustering fellow who attempted to throw him down, saying, "Sir, I never make way for a fool," Wesley replied "I always do," and politely stepped aside.—WITHROW, W. H., 1901, *The Wesleys and the New Portraits, The Outlook, vol.* 69, *p.* 318.

MARRIAGE

February 19.—Rev. Mr. John Wesley, to Mrs. Vazel, of Threadneedle Street, a widow lady of large fortune.—LONDON MAGAZINE, 1751, *Marriages.*

The connection was unfortunate. There never was a more preposterous union. It is pretty certain that no loves lighted their torches on this occasion ; and it is as much to be presumed, that neither did Plutus preside at the solemnity. Mrs. Wesley's property was too inconsiderable to warrant the supposition that it was a match of interest. Besides, had she been ever so rich, it was nothing to him; for every shilling of her fortune remained at her own disposal; and neither the years, nor the temper of the parties, could give any reason to suppose them violently enamoured. That this lady accepted his proposals, seems much less surprising than that he should have made them. It is probable, his situation at the head of a sect, and the authority it conferred, was not without its charms in the eyes of an ambitious female. But we much wonder, that Mr. Wesley should have appeared so little acquainted with himself and with human nature. He certainly did not possess the conjugal virtues. He had no taste for the tranquility of domestic retirement: while his situation, as an itinerant, left him little leisure for those attentions which are absolutely necessary to the comfort of married life.—HAMPSON, JOHN, 1791, *Life of John Wesley,* vol. II, p. 124.

Mr. Wesley's constant habit of traveling. . . . the number of persons who came to visit him wherever he was, and his extensive correspondence with the members of the society were circumstances unfavourable to that social intercourse, mutual openness and confidence, which form the basis of happiness in the married state. These circumstances, indeed, would not have been so very unfavourable, had he married a woman who could have entered into his views, and have accommodated herself to his situation. But this was not the case. Had he searched the whole kingdom on purpose he would hardly have found a woman more unsuitable in these respects, than she whom he married. —WHITEHEAD, JOHN, 1793-96, *The Life of the Rev. John Wesley, Some Time Fellow of Lincoln College, Oxford.*

She seemed truly pious, and was very agreeable in her person and manners. She conformed to every company, whether of the rich or the poor; and she had a remarkable facility and propriety in addressing them concerning their true interests.—MOORE, HENRY, 1824, *The Life of Rev. John Wesley,* vol. II, p. 144.

Neither in understanding nor in education was she worthy of the eminent man to whom she was united; and her temper was intolerably bad. During the lifetime of her first husband, she appears to have enjoyed every indulgence; and, judging from some of his letters to her, which have been preserved, he paid an entire deference to her will. Her habits and spirit were ill adapted to the privations and inconveniences which were incident to her new mode of life, as the traveling companion of Mr. John Wesley.—JACKSON, THOMAS, 1841, *Life of Charles Wesley.*

His wife traveled with him for some time, but soon very naturally grew dissatisfied with a life so restless and so incompatible with the taste and convenience of her sex. Unwilling to travel herself, she became equally dissatisfied with her husband's habitual absence. Her discontent took at last the form of a monomaniacal jealousy. During twenty years she persecuted him with unfounded suspicions and intolerable annoyances, and it is among the most admirable proofs of the genuine greatness of his character that his public career never wavered, never lost one jot of its energy or success, during this protracted domestic wretchedness. She repeatedly deserted him, but returned at his own earnest instance. She opened, interpolated, and then exposed to his enemies his correspondence, and sometimes traveled a hundred miles to see, from a window, who accompanied him in his carriage. At last, taking with her portions of his journals and papers, which she never restored, she left him with the assurance that she would never return. His allusion to the fact in his journal is characteristically laconic. He knew not, he says, the immediate cause of her determination, and adds, "*Non eam reliqui, non dimissi, non revocabo*"—I did not forsake her, I did not dismiss her, I will not recall her. She lived about ten years after leaving him. Her tombstone commemorated her virtues as a parent and a friend, but not as a wife.—STEVENS, ABEL, 1866, *The Women of Methodism,* p. 128.

His marriage was ill advised as well as ill assorted. On both sides, it was, to a culpable extent, hasty, and was contracted without proper and sufficient thought. Young people entering into hurried marriages deserve and incur censure; and if so, what shall be said of Wesley and his wife? They married in haste and had leisure to repent. Their act was, in a high degree, an act of folly; and, properly enough, to the end of life, both of them were made to suffer a serious penalty. It is far from pleasant to pursue the subject: but perhaps it is needful. In a world of danger like this, we must look at beacons as well as beauties.—TYERMAN, L., 1869, *The Life and Times of the Rev. John Wesley, vol.* II, *p.* 106.

Her first marriage had been full of happiness from the simple cause that it was a union of two loving, sympathetic hearts, whereas there is abundant evidence to show that her subsequent wedding was the outcome of motives which, under the circumstances and peculiar conditions in which they both lived, could hardly have resulted otherwise than it did. . . . Absorbed by the work he had in hand, he failed to offer to his second love those demonstrations of affection to which she had been accustomed, and which alone make matrimony desirable. She, on the other hand, a highly-educated and sensitive lady, endowed with a considerable fortune, accustomed, as she had been, to the most devoted attentions of an affectionate husband, feeling the neglect of his successor (whether that neglect was unavoidable or not), and witnessing the honor and warm expressions of friendship lavished upon him by his admirers of both sexes, often riding with him in the carriage purchased with her money while she was left alone, could hardly fail to feel neglected by him who had vowed to "love and comfort, to honor and keep her in sickness and in health." One does not wonder that marriage under such circumstances should turn out unhappily. What I wish to point out to your readers is that the fault was not solely on the side of the lady, as has been and still is, I fear, the fashion to affirm in this case—at any rate, the letter which you have published does not evidence much of that "softness" which Mr. Wesley says is the only influence by which "Love can be won." I am not aware that man's greatness tends to develop marital affection. Perhaps John Wesley was too great a man to cultivate such insignificant qualifications! There can be no doubt that the marriage turned out unfortunately; in fact, it was an instance of "marrying in haste and repenting at leisure." Further, there is much better ground for believing that Mr. Wesley's estrangement from his brother Charles was due rather to the intended marriage with his first love than his consummated union with Mrs. Vazeille.— STOCKS, EDWARD VAZEILLE, 1885, *To the Editor of the London Evening Mail.*

No doubt it was not an easy thing to be the wife of such a tireless enthusiast as John Wesley, especially when he was a second husband, when the marriage was barren of children. But no apology can excuse and no stretch of charity can condone the conduct of Mrs. Wesley. She was emphatically unworthy of the supreme position to which she was called.—STEAD, WILLIAM T., 1891, *St. John of England, Review of Reviews, vol.* 3, *p.* 257.

From the time of this wedding John Wesley seems to have experienced a kind of unrest. He had been used to take a severely ascetic view of marriage. At twenty-seven, he tells us, he held it unlawful for a priest to marry; and, at a later period, he could not disassociate a suspicion of impurity from the marriage bed. Whether he was still affected by this prejudice when he was wooing Miss Sophy, or thought it better to take her, impurity and all, rather than go without her agreeable society, is an enigma, and a difficult one. Anyhow, at forty-six, he had vanquished this scruple, and to wed or not to wed had come to be a question, not of lawfulness, but of expediency. By expediency must not be understood worldly prudence. Wesley, disregarding scriptural advice, hardly ever sat down to count the cost. But he saw no reason why he should not do as other men, and it was reasonable to conclude that he would make a much better husband, father, citizen, and friend than the vast majority of those who assumed marital responsibilities from worldly or carnal motives. Tyerman maintains that, if the woman he married had been worthy of him, he would have been one of the most loving husbands that ever lived. Perhaps so. No doubt he was, in his awkward way, affectionate. But sentiment, though too much disparaged by professional match-makers, is no adequate basis for marriage. To do him justice, Wesley never supposed that it was, but other considerations presented themselves when he was morally or actually committed to a choice recommended by sentiment alone.—SNELL, F. J., 1900, *Wesley and Methodism, p.* 188.

AS A PREACHER

My health advances faster than my amusement. However, I have been at one opera, Mr. Wesley's. They have boys and girls with charming voices, that sing hymns, in parts, to Scotch ballad tunes; but indeed so long, that one would think they were already in eternity, and knew how much time they had before them. The chapel is very neat, with true Gothic windows; (yet I am not converted); but I was glad to see that luxury is creeping in upon them before persecution. . . . He spoke his sermon, but so fast, and with so little accent, that I am sure he has often uttered it, for it was like a lesson. There were parts and eloquence in it; but towards the end he exalted his voice, and acted very ugly enthusiasm. . . . Except a few from curiosity, and some honorable women, the congregation was very mean.—WALPOLE, HORACE, 1766, *To John Chute, Oct.* 10; *Letters, ed. Cunningham, vol.* V, *p.* 16.

I felt great satisfaction last week in hearing that veteran in the service of God, the Rev. John Wesley. At another time, and not knowing the man, I should almost have ridiculed his figure. Far from it now. I looked upon him with a respect bordering upon enthusiasm. After the people had sung one verse of a hymn, he arose and said: "It gives me a great pleasure to find that you have not lost your singing; neither men nor women. You have not forgotten a single note. And I hope, by the assistance of God, which enables you to sing well, you may do all other things well." A universal "Amen" followed. At the end of every head or division of his discourse, he finished by a kind of prayer, a momentary wish as it were, not consisting of more than three or four words, which was always followed by a universal buzz. His discourse was short. The text I could not hear. After the last prayer, he rose up and addressed the people on liberality of sentiment, and spoke much against refusing to join with any congregation on account of difference in opinion.—ROBINSON, HENRY CRABB, 1790, *Letter, Oct.* 18; *Diary, Reminiscences and Correspondence, vol.* I. *p.* 20.

The travels of Mr. Wesley in the work of the ministry, for fifty years together, are I apprehend without precedent. During this period he traveled about four thousand five hundred miles every year, one year with another. . . . It had been impossible for him to perform this almost incredible degree of labor without

great punctuality and care in the management of his time. He had stated hours for every purpose, and his only relaxation was a change of employment. . . . For fifty-two years or upward, he generally delivered two, frequently three or four, sermons in a day. But calculating at two sermons a day, and allowing as a writer of his life has done, fifty annually for extraordinary occasions, the whole number of sermons he preached during this period will be forty thousand five hundred and sixty. To these may be added an infinite number of exhortations to the societies after preaching, and in other occasional meetings, at which he assisted.—WHITEHEAD, JOHN, 1793–96, *Life of the Rev. John Wesley, Some Time Fellow of Lincoln College, Oxford.*

Wesley you alone can touch; but will you not have the hive about you? When I was about twelve years old, I heard him preach more than once, standing on a chair, in Kelso churchyard. He was a most venerable figure, but his sermons were vastly too colloquial for the taste of Saunders. He told many excellent stories. —SCOTT, SIR WALTER, 1815, *Letter to Robert Southey, April* 4; *Life by Lockhart.*

Wesley's own temperament was rather cold, and he had probably from that cold and calm nature, and the great self-control and presence of mind which he possessed, the power to awe, subdue, and thrill an audience. While Whitefield on many occasions preached dissolved in tears, and so moved vast numbers, the strong and determined will of Wesley was almost electrical in its influence and even frightful in its effects on the assemblages he preached before. Frequently, when he had concluded his discourse, the whole of his congregation appeared to be riveted to the ground, and not a person moved till he had retired.—ELLIS, G. A., 1871, *John Wesley, Atlantic Monthly, vol.* 27, *p.* 330.

Wesley was not a pictorial or dramatic preacher like his great preaching contemporary, Whitefield; but whereas Whitefield, powerful preacher as he was, was yet more popular than powerful; Wesley, popular preacher as he was, was yet more powerful, in comparison with his fellows, than he was popular.—RIGG, JAMES HARRISON, 1875, *The Living Wesley.*

He always preached in gown and cassock. He lacked the pathetic tone and the dramatic delivery of Whitefield. He had an essentially calm and logical mind. His speech, like Cobden's, was conspicuously "unadorned." He preached the Gospel with the least possible admixture of individual colouring. His very language was unusually Biblical, and he constantly used the *ipsissima verba* of Scripture. On the other hand, he had a sweet and penetrating voice, which could be distinctly heard at a measured distance of one hundred and forty yards. He had an ample command of the plainest, purest, and most powerful English. Beneath his calm exterior slept a very volcano of devotion to God and love to man. And his appeal was always directly and unmistakably to the human conscience.—HUGHES, HUGH PRICE, 1891, *John Wesley, The Nineteenth Century, vol.* 29, *p.* 486.

When the storm passed over, the "Symmonds" cast anchor in the Savannah River, near Coxpur Island, and one or two days aftewards the voyagers reached the town in safety, on February 5, 1736. On the seventh of March following John Wesley preached the first Methodist sermon every preached on this continent, not far from the site of the present Christ Church, Savannah, of which he subsequently was the third rector. It was addressed to a mixed assemblage. His congregation hardly exceeded four hundred persons, including children and adults, reënforced, however, by one hundred or more of the neighboring Indians. Wesley was then in the prime of his stalwart manhood. He was not robust in his physique, but shapely in his figure, measuring five feet ten inches in stature, and with a Roman physiognomy and a bearing not unbefitting a Roman Senator. He was, at this time, about thirty-four years old, and as he stood before his strange congregation he was an impressive figure. He discussed in a most eloquent manner the principles of Christian charity as argued by Saint Paul in the thirteenth chapter of First Corinthians. Dr. Nunes, a Spanish physician and a Jew, was an interested listener to the sermon. He was frequently known in after life to say that this chapter of Saint Paul's as expounded by Mr. Wesley, deserved to be written in letters of gold.—SCOTT, W. J., 1897, *When John Wesley Preached in Georgia, The Ladies' Home Journal, vol.* 14, *June.*

Wesley's fame as a preacher was somewhat obscured by the extraordinary power of Whitefield, whose dramatic eloquence attracted all classes. Yet the severity and overwhelming religious power of Wesley was such that men who would not submit to the claims of God as expounded by him did not dare to hear him. He attracted even larger congregations than Whitefield, and produced a more powerful and permanent impression. . . . No preacher since the days when Paul reasoned of righteousness, temperance, and judgment to come, equaled him, on extraordinary occasions, in moral power, of which many instances are given by Southey.—BUCKLEY, JAMES M., 1897, *A History of Methodism in the United States, vol.* I, *p.* 329.

WESLEYISM

My brothers are now become so notorious, that the world will be curious to know when and where they were born, what schools bred at, what colleges of in Oxford, and when matriculated, what degrees they took, and where, when, and by whom ordained. I wish they may spare so much time as to vouchsafe a little of their story. For my own part, I had much rather have them picking straws within the walls, than preaching in the area of Moorfields. It was with exceeding concern and grief, I heard you had countenanced a spreading delusion, so far as to be one of Jack's congregation. Is it not enough that I am bereft of both my brothers, but must my mother follow too? I earnestly beseech the Almighty to preserve you from joining a schism at the close of your life, as you were unfortunately engaged in one at the beginning of it. It will cost you many a protest, should you retain your integrity, as I hope to God you will. They boast of you already as a disciple. They design separation. They are aready forbidden all the pulpits in London; and to preach in that diocese is actual schism. In all likelihood, it will come to the same all over England, if the bishops have courage enough. They leave off the liturgy in the fields; and though Mr. Whitefield expresses his value for it, he never once read it to his tatterdemalions on a common. Their societies are sufficient to dissolve all other societies but their own. . . . As I told Jack, I am not afraid the Church should excommunicate him (discipline is at too low an ebb), but, that he should excommunicate the Church. It is pretty near it.—WESLEY, SAMUEL, 1739, *Letter to Susannah Wesley.*

A man of great views, great energy, and great virtues. That he awakened a zealous spirit, not only in his own community, but in a Church which needed something to quicken it, is acknowledged by the members of that Church itself; that he encouraged enthusiasm and extravagance, lent a ready ear to false and impossible relations, and spread superstition as well as piety, would hardly be denied by the candid and judicious among his own people. In its immediate effects the powerful principle of religion, which he and his preachers diffused, has reclaimed many from a course of sin, has supported many in poverty, sickness, and affliction, and has imparted to many a triumphant joy in death.—SOUTHEY, ROBERT, 1820, *The Life of Wesley and the Rise and Progress of Methodism, p.* 589.

Wesley's object was to revive the spirit of religion in the Church of England. To this he thought himself called; for this he commenced and continued his labours. —WATSON, RICHARD, 1820, *Observations of Southey's Life of Wesley, p.* 125.

My present theme is Southey's "Life of Wesley"—a theme much more copious, and one which interests me a good deal. How I shall succeed in it I do not yet know; it is no easy matter to give Wesley his due praise, at the same time that I am to distinguish all that was blamable in his conduct and doctrines; and it is a very difficult matter indeed to write on such a subject at all without offending one or both of the two fiercest and foolishest parties that ever divided a Church—the High Churchmen and the Evangelicals. —HEBER, REGINALD, 1820, *Letter to R. J. Wilmot Horton, May* 26; *Bishop Heber, ed. Smith, p.* 98.

Metastasio: Strange stories are reported of one Wesley, who is permitted by the authorities to preach in the open fields.

Alfieri. Were not those whom you most venerate permitted by the Pagan authorities to preach both in the fields and in the cities? Wesley gave out no new Commandments: he opened before the eyes of the assembled thousands the small volume which contains them, and cried aloud, "*Read! Read!*" I know an Italian who would have spoken to them words of far different import in their own vernacular, and have said, "*If you dare to read, go and be damned.*" I am not highly fanatical, but I do bear veneration toward this saintly man, commanding by meekness and humility. He found the members of the Anglican Church putrescent, as Luther found the Papal; he used no knife of cautery.—LANDOR, WALTER SAVAGE, 1828, *Alfieri and Metastasio, Imaginary Conversations, Third Series, vol.* V, *p.* 132.

The first of theological statesman.— BUCKLE, HENRY THOMAS, 1857, *History of Civilization in England, vol.* I, *p.* 421.

No wonder that the clergy were corrupt and indifferent amid this indifference and corruption. No wonder that skeptics multiplied and morals degenerated, so far as they depended on the influence of such a king. No wonder that Whitfield cried out in the wilderness,—that Wesley quitted the insulted temple to pray on the hill-side. I look with reverence on those men at that time. Which is the sublimer spectacle,—the good John Wesley, surrounded by his congregation of miners at the pit's mouth, or the queen's chaplains mumbling through their morning office in their ante-room, under the picture of her great Venus, with the door opened into the adjoining chamber, where the queen is dressing, talking scandal to Lord Hervey, or uttering sneers at Lady Suffolk, who is kneeling with the basin at her mistress's side? — THACKERAY, WILLIAM MAKEPEACE, 1861, *The Four Georges.*

Wesley died at the head of a thoroughly organized host of 550 itinerant preachers, and 140,000 members of his societies, in the United Kingdom, British North America, in the United States, and West Indies. —STEVENS, ABEL, 1861, *History of Methodism, vol.* III.

Wesley, nursed in the most exclusive church principles, kindled the flame of his piety by the devout reading of mystic books, when our university was marked by the half-heartedness of the time; and afterwards, when instructed by the Pietists of Germany, devoted a long life to wander over the country, despised, ill-treated, but still untired; teaching with indefatigable energy the faith which he loved, and introducing those irregular agencies of usefulness which are now so largely adopted even in the church. He too was an accomplished scholar, and possessed great gifts of administration; but whatever good he effected, in kindling the spiritual Christianity which checked the spread of infidelity, was not so much by argument as by stating the omnipotent doctrine of the Cross, Christ set forth as the propitiation for sin through faith in his blood.—FARRAR, ADAM STOREY, 1862, *A Critical History of Free Thought, Lecture* iv, *p.* 161.

John Wesley, the founder of Methodism, with all his eccentricities and puerilities, was a man in whom there was much that was great and noble. He cannot, indeed, be ranked with some of those apostles of Christianity whose single object was to do good. He loved excitement, power, and praise. He allowed himself to think that he was the constant subject of miraculous interpositions, and that when his horse fell lame, or his head ached, a special interposition was wrought in his favour. He believed that people could be converted in dreams, or by visions to their waking senses, and that erring and fallible mortals could attain sinless perfection in this life. He seemed to suppose himself to have the power of healing diseases by faith and prayer; and though St. Paul was obliged to see Epaphroditus "sick nigh unto death," yet that the health of his friends was a matter he could boldly claim of God. He allowed himself to fall into the foolish and reprehensible practice of divination and sortilege, and to entertain the absurd notion that every sort of diversion was sinful. He was inconsistent in his teaching, holding at one time that men were justified by faith, "including no good work;" and at another, that "repentance and works meet for repentance" must go before faith. But though inconsistencies may be found in his teaching, and littlenesses and follies in his conduct, yet Wesley was essentially an honest man, who laboured almost beyond example for the good of his fellow-creatures. For fifty years he continued his unabating, ungrudging toil, and the results were enormous. At his death, the members of his flock in England exceeded 71,000, in America 48,000, and he had 500 traveling preachers under his control. — PERRY,

GEORGE G., 1864, *The History of the Church of England, vol.* III, *p.* 457.

There are probably few names familiar to all Englishmen which have gathered round them associations so misleading as those which surround John Wesley. For those who take their impressions from hearsay, it is no more than a symbol for the religion of the illiterate. Others, to whom it is familiar through cursory mentions in the literature of the day, recall, on hearing a name coupled with Richelieu by Lord Macaulay, and with Luther by Mr. Buckle, vague notions of able ecclesiastical origination and controversial zeal. Neither view (if the following delineation be correct) can be accepted without large modification. Wesley reached the age of thirty-six without any exclusive devotion to the religious teaching of a particular class; his organizing power, great as it was, does not exhibit his character on its strongest side, while his advocacy of particular doctrines brings forward his weakest. Perhaps the founder of a sect is especially liable to misconception. The true representatives of a reformer are never those who call themselves by his name: what is remarkable in him is that he breaks through conventional barriers, what is remarkable in them is that they take the beaten track; and it is necessary, in order to understand him, to connect him with his cotemporaries rather than with his followers.—WEDGWOOD, JULIA, 1870, *John Wesley, p.* 1.

He was not exactly a man of genius or a great writer; and in his younger days he would have seemed chiefly remarkable to the common observer for a certain degree of eccentricity and want of sense. Even good men would have remarked of him that he was always pushing his opinion to extremes. And his opinions were changing, for in the course of life he seems to have passed almost from one pole of theology to the other. Yet this was the man who has a greater present influence on the religion of the Christian world than any apostle or saint or prophet since the Reformation, perhaps it may be said with truth since St. Paul himself.—JOWETT, BENJAMIN, 1881, *Sermons Biographical and Miscellaneous,* ed. *Fremantle, p.* 112.

It is remarkable that Wesleyanism has found so little favour in its founder's own family. With the exception of some of their sisters, who became connected with the Society, John and Charles stood alone during their lifetime, so far as their relatives were concerned, and the majority of those who have since borne their name have adhered staunchly to the Church of England. This is as John himself would have had it, for he was no Separatist, though he could not stop the movement of which he was the mainspring; nor did he wish to do so, but he did not see that it would necessarily lead to secession. Blood, however, will tell, and a vast amount of talent and energy are still manifested in all the descendants of the Epworth family. Impetuous and quick-witted, and, perhaps, not overmuch given to take thought for the morrow, they must all be up and doing, and in these characteristics they vindicate their lineage, and the vigour of that original strain which is still so far from being worn out.—CLARKE, ELIZA, 1886, *Susanna Wesley (Eminent Women Series), p.* 238.

His wise catholicity and broad and liberal sympathies are exemplified in the admiration which, at a time when the name excited detestation and disgust, Wesley expressed for Ignatius Loyola. Yet Wesley may, in some respects, be called the Loyola of the eighteenth century. . . . Like Loyola, Wesley was inflamed by an ardent zeal for religion; like him again he saw keenly the evils of the time and framed a remedy that could never be a panecea. His systematic mind was gifted with a peculiar power of giving permanent form to the excitement or enthusiasm of the moment. He began his career with no other project than that of raising up "a holy people;" but as his work grew beneath his hand, his intellect proved comprehensive enough to conceive a gigantic plan, and yet sufficiently minute to grasp the smallest details. And his organizing capacity was not greater than his administrative power. The structure of his Society was admirable, and his management of the machine in all the earlier years of his life showed a happy union of tact, firmness, and flexibility. He was not a dogmatic theologian, and he took no pleasure in philosophical speculation.—PROTHERO, R. E., 1891, *John Wesley, Good Words, vol.* 32, *p.* 195.

Of that work, it has been well said, Methodism itself is one the of least significant

results. True, at his death in 1791, his followers were counted by the thousand, and to-day are counted by the million. But even they were the least result of the Methodist revival. For its effects were felt far and wide in other directions. The Church of England awoke once more from its apathy and sloth, and its clergy roused themselves from lifelessness and contempt to a practical religious energy of which we still feel the force. And in the nation at large appeared a new moral enthusiasm which, rigid and pedantic though it often seemed, was still healthy in social tone, and whose power was seen in the partial disappearance of the open profligacy which disgraced the early Georgian era. Philanthropy, and social reform generally, received a fresh stimulus among the mass of the nation, a stimulus whose effects were afterwards seen in an amelioration of our penal code, more humanity in our prison life, and a feeling of indignation against negro slavery. Wesley helped also, we believe, very largely the growth of the national consciousness of the English people, by giving men something more to think about than their own individual aims and their own individual life. Especially was this the case among the poorer people, and it is curious to note how many leaders of the working classes have sprung from the ranks of Methodism.—GIBBINS, H. DE B., 1892, *English Social Reformers, p.* 92.

If Whitefield was the most persuasive and eloquent preacher of the early Methodists, John Wesley was incomparably the greatest man. He was a trained scholar, as well as an effective preacher, and he was an organizer, in this respect on a level with the most renowned leaders of the mediæval monastic orders.—FISHER, GEORGE PARK, 1896, *History of Christian Doctrine, p.* 390.

He came to see that the Spirit of God was not merely in the Bible, but in the souls of living men, giving light and life to the men of the eighteenth century as to those of the first. If this was fanaticism, it was fanaticism that for more than fifty years bore the strain of one of the most strenuous and perfectly organised lives ever lived.—BROWN, J., 1896, *Social England, ed. Traill, vol.* V, *p.* 237.

The Oxford methodists were assiduous in study (in 1731 John and Charles Wesley began a lifelong practice of conversing with each other in Latin); every night they met for consultation before supper; they relieved the poor, and looked after the clothing and training of school children; they daily visited the prisoners in the castle, read prayers there on Wednesdays and Fridays, preached there on Sundays, and administered the communion once a month. Their religion was formed on the prayer-book; next to the bible in point of doctrine they valued the books of homilies. Nor did they deny themselves recreation; it would be unjust to charge their temper as morbid; their philanthropy kept them in touch with real life; Wesley's strong sense, his cheerfulness (he did not disdain a game of cards, as his private accounts show), and his knowledge of human nature, gave a manly tone to their zeal. The marked divergence of their subsequent careers, while showing reaction in some cases from an ideal overstrained, proves also that the discipline of strictness was not ruinous to the independence of individual minds. Wesley himself was little of an ascetic; to be methodical and exact was with him an essential part of happiness. He rose at four to cure himself of lying awake at night. At five, morning and evening, he spent an hour in private prayer. His diary and accounts were kept with constant precision. One day a week he allowed for friendly correspondence.—GORDON, ALEXANDER, 1899, *Dictionary of National Biography, vol.* LX, *p.* 304.

Few men have more genuine claims to greatness than John Wesley, a many sided man, but in all things the reformer. That really was his great work, although usually he is thought of only as the leader of an evangelistic movement, the preacher and crusader who founded the Methodist church. As a preacher, a critic, a teacher, and an organizer, Wesley was truly remarkable. Measured by what he accomplished, he was colossal. He was true to his own ideals, and his capacity for work is not to be measured by ordinary standards. Wesley earned two hundred thousand dollars by his writings, which is the smallest part of what he did in his long life. He gave away every penny of this. Spurgeon said of him: "When John Wesley died he left behind him two silver spoons in London, two in Bristol, a teapot,

and the great Methodist church." This church, with its seven million members—nine tenths of them in America—and its mission work extending throughout the world, is the magnificent monument of the great man who founded it.—JOHNSON, J. WESLEY, 1900, *The Last of the Great Reformers, Munsey's Magazine, vol.* 23, *p.* 757.

GENERAL

He never wrote merely to please, or to get money. His object constantly was, to inform the understanding, and mend the heart: to discourage vice, and promote virtue. He never published anything with a view to promote a party-spirit. A great degree of candor and liberality runs through all his publications; and in matters of mere speculation, he endeavored to show the necessity of christian love, and mutual forbearance among those who differ in opinion. In his controversies, he combated opinions, not men. And this he did, in general, with great moderation. He maintained, that even right opinions, make but a small part of religion: that, a man may hold the truth in unrighteousness, and therefore perish with the greater condemnation. But, a man whose heart, from a living faith in Christ operating as a practical principle, is influenced to the love of God and man, and whose life is correspondent to it, cannot err dangerously, though he may hold some erroneous opinions. And he thought, that we ought to contend for this christian temper and practice, much more earnestly, than for any speculative notions, not essentially necessary to obtain them. This made him earnest to contend for practical truth; and had a happy influence on all his writings. . . . Mr. Wesley's treatise on "Original Sin," is, perhaps, the most labored performance that he published. He knew, and respected the abilities and character of Dr. Taylor, his opponent. He bestowed much time and attention in a careful investigation of the subject; but avoided entering into minute metaphysical disquisitions. He knew that nothing could be affirmed in this way of reasoning, however true, but what another might deny with some degree of plausibility. His treatise therefore is, an animated defence of the orthodox doctrine, in a deduction from the actual state of morality in all ages, and under every kind of restraint from evil that has been imposed on mankind; or, as he expresses it, "from Scripture, reason, and experience."— WHITEHEAD, JOHN, 1793–96, *The Life of the Rev. John Wesley, Some Time Fellow of Lincoln College, Oxford.*

As a logician he piqued himself, as we have seen, on his skill; and it must be allowed that his writings in general are distinguished by a remarkable force, acuteness, and vivacity of conception and expression. Yet, it is also remarkable that the doctrines which he most anxiously insisted on through life, were not only incapable of being moulded into any consistent system, but were, many of them, in direct opposition to each other. His tenet of assurance was decidedly Calvinistic; and one which could not, without great violence to common sense, be separated from the notion of absolute election. His doctrine of Christian perfection had as direct a tendency to make men Mystics or Antinomians; for what can be the use of ordinances to him who needs no further grace; and what is law to him who cannot sin? Yet Wesley was too good a logician to be a Calvinist; he was too pure and holy to fall into the Antinomian errors, and he had too cool a head to remain long a Mystic. How strange that he did not perceive that his eclectic divinity could not stand by itself, and that if he went thus far he must go farther! Nor is it easy to apprehend how his powerful mind, while it honestly lamented the disorders and vices, the pride, envy, and slander which prevailed in his societies, should not have perceived that the details of his discipline were of themselves calculated to generate such a spirit, and to undo, in a great measure, in the minds of his followers, the good which his preaching and example had produced in them. — HEBER, REGINALD, 1820, *Southey's Life of Wesley, Quarterly Review, vol.* 24, *p.* 53.

Mr. Wesley was a voluminous writer; and as he was one of the great instruments in reviving the spirit of religion in these lands, so he led the way in those praiseworthy attempts which have been made to diffuse useful information of every kind, and to smooth the path of knowledge to the middle and lower ranks of society.—WATSON, RICHARD, 1831, *The Life of the Rev. John Wesley.*

Wesley ["Journal"], you will find pleasant to dip into, I think: of course, there is much sameness; and I think you will allow some absurdity among so much wise and good.—FITZGERALD, EDWARD, 1868, *Letters, vol.* I, *p.* 317.

Whether men like Methodist doctrine or not, I think they must honestly concede that the old Fellow of Lincoln was a scholar and a sensible man. The world, which always sneers at evangelical religion, may please itself by saying that the men who shook England a hundred years ago were weak-minded, hot-headed enthusiasts, and unlearned and ignorant men. The Jews said the same of the apostles in early days. But the world cannot get over facts. The founder of Methodism was a man of no mean reputation in Oxford, and his writings show him to have been a well-read, logical-minded, and intelligent man.—RYLE, J. C., 1869, *The Christian Leaders of the Last Century, p.* 104.

His own poetical powers were considerable; his verses are sometimes melodious, and often vigorous; but far above the trammels of art is their bold and grand sincerity. Music and poetry were to him only the means of expressing the joys and triumphs of faith.—LAWRENCE, EUGENE, 1872, *John Wesley and His Times, Harper's Magazine, vol.* 45, *p.* 119.

When one looks at his travelling, he may well wonder how Wesley found time to write; when one looks at his writings, the marvel is how he found time to do anything else.—GUERNSEY, ALFRED H., 1874, *John Wesley, Galaxy, vol.* 17, *p.* 212.

Wesley's was a singular blending of strength and weakness. His strength lies almost entirely in the sphere of practice. He shows remarkable literary power; but we feel that his writings are means to a direct practical end, rather than valuable in themselves, either in form or substance. It would be difficult to find any letters more direct, forcible, and pithy in expression. He goes straight to the mark without one superfluous flourish. He writes as a man confined within the narrowest limits of time and space, whose thoughts are so well in hand that he can say everything needful within those limits. The compression gives emphasis and never causes confusion. The letters, in other words, are the work of one who for more than half a century was accustomed to turn to account every minute of his eighteen working hours.—STEPHEN, LESLIE, 1876, *History of English Thought in the Eighteenth Century, vol.* II, *p.* 409.

The poetical works of John and Charles Wesley extend through ten volumes, edited lately with scrupulous care by Dr. G. Osborn. Such a demand as he thus imposed on his own poetical powers was too extensive even for a great poet to have met; but in his case the difficulty was aggravated partly by the nature of the subject, partly by his own deficiencies. . . . Nevertheless there are two sources of inspiration from which hymn-writers in general and John Wesley in particular have derived a fire which makes it impossible to overlook the claims of the Wesleyan hymnology to be ranked as part of our national literature. First, however prosaic might be the soul of John Wesley himself, he had sufficient appreciation of the grandeur of the gift in others to appropriate it in some degree for his purposes. Such are some beautiful passages adopted or adapted from Gambold the Moravian and from George Herbert. —STANLEY, ARTHUR PENRHYN, 1880, *English Poets, ed.* Ward, *vol.* III, *pp.* 255, 258.

As a poet, John Wesley, though correct and classical, does not compare with his brother Charles. While in college, he indulged in versification as a recreation, but confined himself almost exclusively to translations from other languages.—HATFIELD, EDWIN F., 1884, *The Poets of the Church, p.* 663.

The very last thing of which John Wesley was ambitious was literary fame. In nothing does the intensely practical character of his mind come out more strongly than in his writings. Whether it is long treatise or short tract, whether it is prose or poetry, whether it is original composition or the reprinting or abridging of the works of others, whether it is a simple school-book or one on controversial divinity, whether it is a sermon or a commentary or a journal, it is all the same; he has always some immediate practical end in view; and in almost every case we can trace the reason of his writing what he did write in the particular circumstances which were at that particular time before him. . . . It would, of course, be absurd to contend that anything which

John Wesley wrote is of the same calibre as the great works of his contemporaries, such as Butler or Waterland; but if we are content to ignore his writings as obsolete works out of which all the virtue is gone, we are ignoring a very vivid and complete picture of the times, as well as a very life-like portrait of one of the most interesting and influential men *of* those times. So that merely from the historical, to say nothing of the religious, point of view, it would be a great mistake to be satisfied with regarding Wesley as he appears when filtered through the mind of any critic or biographer, however able, without contemplating him as he appears in his own pages.—OVERTON, J. H., 1891, *John Wesley (English Leaders of Religion), pp.* 169, 170.

His mind was not without something of the mysticism that dominated Law; it has a strain of melancholy which does not lessen our interest, and he presents the rare spectacle of a scholar who dreaded lest his own scholarship might interfere with the popular work which was the supreme aim of his life. There was a certain Puritanism in the conscious simplicity of his style; but he could not divorce himself altogether from that literary sympathy that linked him to his age, and that made him the friend of one with whom he stands in many respects so much in contrast as Johnson.—CRAIK, HENRY, 1895, *ed., English Prose, Introduction, vol.* IV, *p.* 5.

There is a peculiar interest attached to this hymn. ("Thou Hidden Love of God"). John Wesley is said to have translated it in Savannah, in the United States, where he suffered much and was grievously tormented by his ill-starred passion for a certain Miss Sophy. It was with special reference to the continually obtruding thoughts of this Miss Sophy that the Rev. John composed the verse "Is there a thing beneath the sun?" It seems to have been efficacious, and the lovelorn poet came home to meet a worse fate at the hands of her whom, for his Karma, he was allowed to make Mrs. Wesley. The Hymn has helped thousands who never knew of Wesley and his ill-fated loves to acts of consecration and self-sacrifice from which they would otherwise have shrunk. —STEAD, W. T., 1897, *Hymns that Have Helped, p.* 191.

Where the reader of the journal will be shocked is when his attention is called to the public side of the country—to the state of the jails—to Newgate, to Bethlehem, to the criminal code—to the brutality of so many of the judges, and the harshness of the magistrates, to the supineness of the bishops, to the extinction in high places of the missionary spirit. . . . No man lived nearer the centre than John Wesley. Neither Clive nor Pitt, neither Mansfield nor Johnson. You cannot cut him out of our national life. No single figure influenced so many minds, no single voice touched so many hearts. No other man did such a life's work for England. As a writer he has not achieved distinction, he was no Athanasius, no Augustine, he was ever a preacher and an organizer, a laborer in the service of humanity; but happily for us his journals remain, and from them we can learn better than from anywhere else what manner of man he was, and the character of the times during which he lived and moved and had his being.—BIRRELL, AUGUSTINE, 1899, *John Wesley, Scribner's Magazine, vol.* 26, *p.* 761.

Thomas Blacklock

1721-1791

Thomas Blacklock, D. D., the blind poet, was born of humble parentage at Annan, and lost his sight through small-pox before he was six months old. Educated at Edinburgh, he was minister of Kirkcudbright (1762-64), and then took pupils to board with him in Edinburgh till his death. It was a letter of his that arrested Burns on the eve of his departure for the West Indies. The first volume of his own poor poems appeared in 1746; and a collected edition in 1793.—PATRICK AND GROOME, *eds.,* 1897, *Chambers's Biographical Dictionary, p.* 102.

PERSONAL

He soon appeared what I have ever since found him, a very elegant Genius, of a most affectionate grateful disposition, a modest backward temper, accompanied with that delicate Pride, which so naturally *attends Virtue in Distress. His great Moderation and Frugality,* along with the Generosity of a few persons, particularly Dr. Stevenson and Provost Alexander, had hitherto enabled him to subsist. All his good qualities are diminished, or rather perhaps embellished by a great *want of Knowledge of the World.*— HUME, DAVID, 1754, *Letter to Joseph Spence, Oct.* 15; *Spence's Anecdotes, ed. Singer, p.* 351.

He never could dictate till he stood up: and as his blindness made walking about without assistance inconvenient or dangerous to him, he fell insensibly into a vibratory sort of motion with his body, which increased as he warmed with his subject and was pleased with the conception of his mind.—SPENCE, JOSEPH, 1754, *Life of Blacklock.*

Doctor Blacklock belonged to a set of critics, for whose *applause* I had not *dared to hope.*—BURNS, ROBERT, 1786, *Letters.*

All those who ever acted as his amanuenses agree in this rapidity and ardour of composition which Mr. Jameson ascribes to him.—MACKENZIE, HENRY, 1793, *Life of Thomas Blacklock.*

Through the genial society of Edinburgh, with its vigorous speaking and drinking, its stalwart race of men of letters, law, and fashion, flits the somewhat pathetic figure of the gentle and helpless Dr. Blacklock. He was to be seen led along the crowded High Street, every one making way respectfully for the blind man, and led carefully up the slippery staircases, whose dirt and darkness could not vex his sight, though the odours might afflict his acuter sense of smell. In the best company he was welcomed, and all forgot the plainness of that pock-pitted face in the amiable expression that gave it charm. In the Meadows friends would find him in the forenoon, leaning on the arm of Robert Heron, the discarded assistant to Dr. Blair—a versatile literary hack, a threadbare taper, who, after an evening's debauch on a meagre supply of potatoes and green peas, with large potations of whiskey, had risen from his garret bed to take his venerated friend out for a stroll. Blacklock's reputation was considerable for genius and for fine literary judgment. To-day we must deny him genius, but may allow him taste.

. . . To everybody Blacklock endeared himself; for he was a very good man, though a very poor poet. Young men he drew from obscurity, educated, and started in life, who never forgot the unhumorous, guileless man, who knew nothing of the world except its goodness. With a temper which nothing could ruffle, he worked with his boarders over Greek and Latin, and entered into all their entertainments with childlike pleasure, while the keenest pleasure of his boarders was to do kindly services for him. In his placid home there would meet at breakfast or in the evening all who had any pretence to wit and culture. There were heard the chatter of Mrs. Cockburn, the lively tongue of the Duchess of Gordon, with the voices of Adam Ferguson, Lord Monboddo, Dr. Robertson, as they sat at tea; while the boarders handed scones and cookies to the company, and listened eagerly as great men and bright women discussed and jested, making the little room noisy with their talk and merry with their laughter.—GRAHAM, HENRY GREY, 1901, *Scottish Men of Letters in the Eighteenth Century, pp.* 139, 145.

GENERAL

The 104th Psalm is esteemed one of the most sublime in the whole book, [A New Version of the Psalms of David]. . . . There have not been less than forty different Versions, and Paraphrases of this Psalm, by poets of very considerable eminence, who seem to have vied with one another for the superiority. Of all these attempts, if we may trust our own judgment, none have succeeded so happily as Mr. Blacklock, a young gentleman now resident at Dumfries in Scotland. This Paraphrase is the more extraordinary, as the author of it has been blind from his cradle, and now labours under that calamity; it carries in it such elevated strains of poetry, such picturesque descriptions, and such a mellifluent flow of numbers, that we are persuaded the reader cannot be displeased at finding it inserted here. —CIBBER, THEOPHILUS, 1753, *Lives of the Poets, vol.* IV, *p.* 63.

Few men blessed with the most perfect sight can describe visual objects with more spirit and justness than this blind man.—BURKE, EDMUND, 1757, *A Philosophical Enquiry into the Origin of our Ideas of the Sublime and the Beautiful.*

He [Dr. Johnson] talked of Mr. Blacklock's poetry, so far as it was descriptive of visible objects; and observed that, "as its authour had the misfortune to be blind, we may be absolutely sure that such passages are combinations of what he has remembered of the works of other writers who could see. That foolish fellow,Spence, has laboured to explain philosophically how Blacklock may have done, by means of his own faculties, what it is impossible he should do. The solution, as I have given it, is plain. Suppose, I know a man to be so lame that he is absolutely incapable to move himself, and I find him in a different room from that in which I left him; shall I puzzle myself with idle conjectures, that perhaps his nerves have by some unknown change all at once become effective? No, Sir, it is clear how he got into a different room: he was *carried.*"— JOHNSON, SAMUEL, 1763, *Life by Boswell, ed. Hill, vol.* I, *p.* 539.

As an author, under disadvantages which seem unsurmountable to nature, Blacklock has eminently distinguished himself. Though blind from his infancy, the impulse of curiosity and the vigorous exertion of his talents conducted him to uncommon knowledge. He acquired tongues and arts by the ear, in many of which he excelled. There was no science with which he was not acquainted; he was familiar with the learned languages, and he knew with accuracy those of modern Europe that are the most cultivated. Among philosophers he has attained a conspicuous rank. . . . As a poet, though not of the highest rank, he is entitled to a rank not inferior to Addison, Parnell, and Shenstone.—ANDERSON, ROBERT, 1799, *The Works of the British Poets, vol.* XI.

His verses are extraordinary for a man blind from his infancy; but Mr. Henry Mackenzie, in his elegant biographical account of him, has certainly over-rated his genius; and when Mr. Spence, of Oxford, submitted Blacklock's descriptive powers as a problem for metaphysicians to resolve, he attributed to his writings a degree of descriptive strength which they do not possess. Denina carried exaggeration to the utmost when he declared that Blacklock would seem a fable to posterity, as he had been a prodigy to his contemporaries. It is no doubt curious that his memory should have retained so many forms of expression for things which he had never seen; but those who have conversed with intelligent persons who have been blind from their infancy, must have often remarked in them a familiarity of language respecting the objects of vision which, though not easy to be accounted for, will be found sufficiently common to make the rhymes of Blacklock appear far short of marvelous. Blacklock on more than one occasion, betrays something like marks of blindness.—CAMPBELL, THOMAS, 1819, *Specimens of the British Poets.*

The series of conjectures by which Mr. Spence has endeavoured to account for this poet's capability of producing animated descriptions of external nature, can scarcely be regarded as altogether satisfactory; when such a faculty is displayed by a poet blind from his infancy, it is chiefly to be referred to his accurate recollection of the descriptive language employed by other poets; but what notions he himself attaches to words expressive of the visible qualities of objects, it might be extremely difficult for a blind poet to explain.—IRVING, DAVID, 1861, *The History of Scotish Poetry, ed. Carlyle, p.* 189.

We read all concerning him with strong interest *except his poetry,* for this is generally tame, languid, and commonplace.—CHAMBERS, ROBERT, 1876, *Cyclopædia of English Literature, ed. Carruthers.*

In the short memoir which we have of him, written by Mackenzie, there are a great many special quotations made, and lines selected, to show that, notwithstanding his blindness, he was capable of describing nature. This, of course, must have been simply in imitation of the lavish colours, the purple evenings and rosy mornings of the poets: but there is a pathetic correctness in his enumeration of the yellow crocuses and purple hyacinths, which touches the heart.— OLIPHANT, MARGARET O. W., 1882, *Literary History of England in the End of the Eighteenth Century and Beginning of the Nineteenth Century, vol.* I, *p.* 149.

Blacklock's poems are mere echoes of the poetical language of his time, and show little more than a facility for stringing together rhymes. He would, we are told, dictate thirty or forty verses as fast as they could be written down. Whilst doing so he acquired a trick of nervous vibration of his body which became habitual. By Hume's advice Blacklock abandoned a project of lecturing on oratory, and studied divinity.—STEPHEN, LESLIE, 1886, *Dictionary of National Biography, vol.* V, *p.* 128.

He has in truth little claim to remembrance except such as can be founded upon a pathetic story and an amiable and virtuous character.—WALKER, HUGH, 1893, *Three Centuries of Scottish Literature, vol.* II, *p.* 101.

Francis Hopkinson
1737–1791

Few pens of the day effected more than Hopkinson's in educating the American people for political independence. The brevity, wit, and vivacity of his pieces gave them portability, currency, and popular favour. Of this class—the most important —of his writings we may specify "The Pretty Story," 1774; "The Prophecy," 1776; "The Political Catechism," 1777. But the collector of American History (a large class these collectors have now become!) must secure for his shelves, if he can, (which is more than doubtful), "The Miscellaneous Essays and Occasional Writings of Francis Hopkinson," Philadelphia, pub. by Dobson, 1792, 3 vol. 8vo.—ALLIBONE, S. AUSTIN, 1854–58, *A Critical Dictionary of English Literature, vol.* I, *p.* 886.

PERSONAL

At this shop I met Mr. Francis Hopkinson, late a mandamus councillor of New Jersey, now a member of the Continental Congress, who, it seems, is a native of Philadelphia, . . . was liberally educated, and is a painter and a poet. I have a curiosity to penetrate a little deeper into the bosom of this curious gentleman, and may possibly give you some more particulars concerning him. He is one of your pretty, little, curious, ingenious men. His head is not bigger than a large apple, less than our friend Pemberton, or Doctor Simon Tufts. I have not met with anything in natural history more amusing and entertaining than his personal appearance,—yet he is genteel and well bred, and is very social.—ADAMS, JOHN, 1776, *Letters Addressed to His Wife, August.*

Sir:—I have the pleasure to inclose to you a commission as judge of the United States for the District of Pennsylvania, to which office I have nominated, and, by and with the advice and consent of the Senate, have appointed you. In my nomination of Persons to fill offices in the Judicial Department, I have been guided by the importance of the object—considering it as of the first magnitude, and as the Pillar upon which our political fabric must rest. I have endeavoured to bring into the high offices of its administration such characters as will give stability and dignity to our National Government,—and I persuade myself they will discover a due desire to promote the happiness of our Country by a ready acceptance of their several appointments. The laws which have passed, relative to your office, accompany the commission. I am, Sir, with very great esteem, Your most obedient Servant.—WASHINGTON, GEORGE, 1789, *Letter to Francis Hopkinson, Sept. 30.*

He was the author of several fugitive pieces, which were very popular in their day. His well known ballad, called "The Battle of the Kegs," gives evidence of a rich and exhaustless fund of humor, and will probably last the wear of centuries. He excelled in music, and had some knowledge of painting. His library was extensive, and his stock of knowledge constantly accumulating. In stature, Mr. Hopkinson was below the common size. His countenance was animated, his speech fluent; and motions were unusually rapid. Few men were kinder in their dispositions, or more benevolent in their lives.—LINCOLN, ROBERT W., 1833, *Lives of the Presidents of the United States with Biographical Notices of the Signers of the Declaration of Independence, p.* 383.

Even in these days, Francis Hopkinson would have been regarded as a man of quite unusual cultivation, having in reality many solid as well as shining accomplishments. He was a distinguished practitioner of the law; he became an eminent judge; he was a statesman trained by much study and experience; he was a mathematician, a chemist, a physicist, a mechanician, an inventor, a musician and a composer of music, a man of literary knowledge and practice, a writer of airy and dainty songs, a clever artist with pencil and brush, and a humorist of unmistakable power. For us Americans, the name of Francis Hopkinson lives—if indeed it does live—chiefly on account of its presence in the august roll-call of the signers of the Declaration of Independence; and through all the strenuous years which preceded and followed that great avowal, this man served the cause therein set forth, not only as a patriot of austere principle, as a statesman of genuine sagacity, as a citizen of high civic courage, but as a wit and a satirist,—the edge of his sarcasm cutting into the enemy as keenly as any sword, and the ruddy glow of his mirth kindling good cheer over all the land on many a grim day when good cheer was a hard thing to be had on his side of the fight.—TYLER, MOSES COIT, 1897, *The Literary History of the American Revolution,* 1763–1783, *vol.* I, *p.* 163.

GENERAL

A poet, a wit, a patriot, a chemist, a mathematician, and a judge of the admirality; his character was composed of a happy union of qualities and endowments commonly supposed to be discordant; and, with the humour of Swift and Rabelais, he was always found on the side of virtue and social order. — WHARTON, THOMAS I., 1825, *Notes on the Provincial Literature of Pennsylvania.*

Great as Judge Hopkinson's reputation was as an advocate while at the bar, and distinguished as he was for learning, judgment, and integrity when upon the bench, he was, perhaps, more celebrated as a man of letters, of general knowledge, of fine taste, but, above all, for his then unrivaled powers of wit and satire. Dr. Rush, after speaking of his varied attainments, says:—"But his forte was humour and satire, in both of which he was not surpassed by Lucian, Swift, or Rabelais. These extraordinary powers were consecrated to the advancement of the interests of patriotism, virtue, and science." This praise may be too strong; and yet we hardly know where to find papers of more exquisite humour than among the writings of Francis Hopkinson. His paper on the "Ambiguity of the English Language," to show the ridiculous mistakes that often occur from words of similar sounds, used the one for the other: on "White-Washing" on "A Typographical Method of

Conducting a Quarrel," which made friends of two fierce newspaper combatants; "The New Roof," an allegory in favor of the Federal Constitution; the "Specimen of a Collegiate Examination," to turn certain branches, and the modes of studying them, into ridicule; and "The Battle of the Kegs," are all pieces which, while they are fully equal to any of Swift's writings for wit, have nothing at all in them of Swift's vulgarity.—CLEVELAND, CHARLES D., 1859, *A Compendium of American Literature, p. 60.*

His pen was not distinguished for depth, but there was a genuine humor in his productions, which made him widely popular. A majority of his poetical effusions were of an ephemeral nature, and were forgotten, in a degree, with the occasion which called them forth; yet a few have been preserved, among which may be mentioned "The Battle of the Kegs," a ballad, or sort of epic, of inimitable humor. —LOSSING, BENSON J., 1870, *Lives of the Signers of the Declaration of American Independence, p. 86, note.*

All through the war Hopkinson's fertile brain was busy devising arguments in prose and verse to strengthen and cheer the hearts of his countrymen, and by the able discharge of his duties in the administration of naval affairs and as treasurer of loans he rendered special service to the good cause.—HILDEBURN, CHARLES R., 1878, *Francis Hopkinson, The Pennsylvania Magazine, vol. II, p. 320.*

Francis Hopkinson was another of the writers who served the popular cause by seizing every occasion to make the British pretensions to rule ridiculous as well as hateful. His "Battle of the Kegs" probably laughed a thousand men into the Republican ranks. — WHIPPLE, EDWIN PERCY, 1886, *American Literature and Other Papers, ed. Whittier, p. 23.*

Hopkinson has some title to rank as one of the earliest American humorists. Without the keen wit of "McFingal" some of his "Miscellaneous Essays and Occasional Writings" published in 1792, have more geniality and heartiness than Trumbull's satire. His "Letter on Whitewashing" is a bit of domestic humor that foretokens the *Danbury News* man, and his "Modern Learning," 1784, a burlesque on college examinations, in which a saltbox is described from the point of view of metaphysics, logic, natural philosophy, mathematics, anatomy, surgery and chemistry, long kept its place in school readers and other collections.—BEERS, HENRY A., 1887, *An Outline Sketch of American Literature, p. 74.*

The ballad was immensely popular; perhaps more so than any ballad of Revolutionary times; and I can well remember how (after the first quarter of this century had passed) patriotic schoolboys used to love to reel off, in brilliant recitation, that story of the trick of the Yankees upon the obtuse Britishers. But Hopkinson wrote much better things; he was master of a quiet satire and of a dry humor. — MITCHELL, DONALD G., 1897, *American Lands and Letters, The Mayflower to Rip-Van-Winkle, p. 121.*

Catherine Macaulay

(Neé Graham)

1731–1791

Mrs. Catherine Macaulay, 1733–1791, was a writer of some notoriety. She wrote on historical, moral, and political subjects, and was an avowed republican. She was so much of a partisan that her historical writings are regarded as of doubtful credit. She wrote "A History of England from the Accession of James II. to that of the Brunswick Line," 8 vols., 4to; "A History of England from the Revolution to the Present, Time," only one volume finished; "Moral Truth," 8vo. ; "Letters on Education," 4to. ; several political pamphlets.—HART, JOHN S., 1872, *A Manual of English Literature, p. 343.*

PERSONAL

I would behave to a nobleman as I should expect he would behave to me, were I a nobleman and he Sam. Johnson. Sir, there is one Mrs. Macaulay in this town, a great republican. One day when I was at her house, I put on a very grave countenance, and said to her, "Madam, I am now become a convert to your way of thinking. I am convinced that all mankind are upon an equal footing; and to give you an unquestionable proof, Madam, that I am in earnest, here is a very sensible, civil, well-behaved fellow-citizen, your footman; I desire that he may be allowed to sit down and dine with us." I thus, Sir, shewed her the absurdity of the leveling doctrine. She has never liked me since.—JOHNSON, SAMUEL, 1763, *Life by Boswell, ed. Hill, vol.* I, *p.* 518.

Was much pleased with her good sense and liberal turn of mind.—QUINCY, JR., JOSIAH, 1774, *Memoirs, p.* 243.

HISTORY OF ENGLAND

To Mrs. Macaulay I did give a letter, but am ashamed of it, as she ought to be of her foolish and absurd "Summary," which is a wretched compilation from magazines, full of gross mistakes, and confounding all characters, leveling all for no end or purpose, but to support so silly an hypothesis, as that no king can be a good king, because he is a king. She defends James II. for the nonsensical pleasure of abusing King William, and has no more idea of general merit than Sir John Dalrymple. In short, whom does she approve but herself and her idolater—that dirty disappointed hunter of a mitre, Dr. Wilson, and Alderman Heathcote, a paltry worthless Jacobite, whom I remember, and her own grandfather Sawbridge, who, *she has been told*, was a mighty worthy man though dipped in the infamous job of the South Sea? In short I ran through the book, had forgotten it, and only recollect it now to answer your question.—WALPOLE, HORACE, 1778, *To Rev. William Mason, March* 16; *Letters, ed. Cunningham, vol.* VII, *p.* 42.

The very word respect brings Mrs. Macaulay to my remembrance. The woman of the greatest abilities, undoubtedly, that this country has ever produced. —And yet this woman has been suffered to die without sufficient respect being paid to her memory. Posterity, however, will be more just; and remember that Catherine Macaulay was an example of intellectual acquirements supposed to be incompatible with the weakness of her sex. In her style of writing, indeed, no sex appears, for it is like the sense it conveys, strong and clear. I will not call her's a masculine understanding, because I admit not of such an arrogant assump-

tion of reason; but I contend that it was a sound one, and that her judgment, the matured fruit of profound thinking, was a proof that a woman can acquire judgment, in the full extent of the word. Possessing more penetration than sagacity, more understanding than fancy, she writes with sober energy and argumentative closeness; yet sympathy and benevolence give an interest to her sentiments, and that vital heat to arguments, which forces the reader to weigh them.—WOLLSTONECRAFT, MARY (NEÉ GODWIN), 1792, *A Vindication of the Rights of Woman, p.* 235.

Combining Roman admiration with English faction, she violated truth in her English characters, and exaggerated romance in her Roman.—DISRAELI, ISAAC, 1795, *On the Literary Character.*

Strafford's Letters . . . furnished materials to Harris and Macaulay; but the first is little read at present, and the second not at all.—HALLAM, HENRY, 1827-46, *The Constitutional History of England.*

When any doubt is entertained of the character of Charles, Mrs. Macaulay may be referred to; and a charge against him, if it can possibly be made out, will assuredly be found, and supported with all the references that the most animated diligence can supply.—SMYTH, WILLIAM, 1840, *Lectures on Modern History, Lecture* xvi.

Catherine, though now forgotten by an ungrateful public, made quite as much noise in her day as Thomas does in ours. —CROKER, J. WILSON, 1849, *Mr. Macaulay's History of England, Quarterly Review, vol.* 84, *p.* 561.

Mrs. Macaulay, as an historian, is placed by Horace Walpole. very nearly on a level with Robertson, and far beyond the partial and unreliable Hume. She was certainly a woman of remarkable intelligence; enthusiastic, well read, laborious, and sincere in her passion for freedom. In her own age she found many admirers. . . . Her numerous works show the ardor with which she pursued her literary labors. She wrote a History of England from the reign of James I. to the Accession, in which she supports her liberal views by a violent attack upon the Stuarts. With no delicacy of taste or novelty of manner, this work could only have gained reputation as a severe and unreliable partisan history. It is evidently, however, the production of a person of considerable reflection, of great ardor and sincerity, and of a warm and enthusiastic temperament. Mrs. Macaulay's mind seemed to turn resolutely towards politics, as if assured that there was its natural bent. . . . In all these writings Mrs. Macaulay showed unusual ability, without ever rising to the excellence of a fine writer. And the name of the author is hardly remembered, except among historical inquirers.—LAWRENCE, EUGENE, 1855, *The Lives of the British Historians, vol.* II, *pp.* 230, 231.

The ablest writer of the New Radical School.—LECKY, WILLIAM EDWARD HARTPOLE, 1882, *A History of England in the Eighteenth Century, vol.* III, *p.* 224.

Richard Price
1723–1791

Richard Price (1723–91) carries forward the intellectualist tradition in morals. Of the earlier English moralists, he most resembles Cudworth. He was an intimate friend of Priestley; but in a correspondence between them, published in 1778, Price appears as the champion of free-will and of the unity and immateriality of the human soul. Among his friends was Franklin, to whom he addressed some observations on statistical questions published in the "Philosophical Transactions," 1769. His "Appeal to the People on the Subject of the National Debt" (1771) is supposed to have influenced Pitt in re-establishing the sinking fund created by Walpole in 1716 and abolished in 1733. In his ethical treatise entitled "Review of the Principal Questions in Morals" (1757), he maintains against Hutcheson that ideas of right and wrong are perceived by the reason, or understanding, and not by a "sense."—WHITTAKER, T., 1896, *Social England, vol.* V, *p.* 245.

PERSONAL

The Corporation of London—then, as in so many parts of its previous history, a really popular body, representative of the best Liberal feeling of the time—presented him with the freedom of the city in a gold box, in "testimony of their approbation of his principles and of the high sense they entertained of the excellence of his observations on the justice and policy of the war with America." Fame brought its inconveniences together with its pleasures. Anonymous letters were sent threatening his life, and he was obliged to decline correspondence with Dr. Franklin on the ground that he had become so marked and obnoxious that prudence required him to be extremely cautious. The populace, however, loved and reverenced the courageous advocate of popular rights. As he rode in the streets of London, on his old white horse blind in one eye, clothed, as Rogers remembered him, "in a great coat and black spatter dashes," Rogers says that, like Demosthenes, he was often diverted by hearing the carmen and orange-women say, "There goes Dr. Price!" "Make way for Dr. Price!" The seriousness and gentle mildness of his character surprised those who only knew him from his works. When the Duchess of Bedford met him, at her own request, at Shelburne House, his quiet aspect and unassuming manners caused her great astonishment. "I expected to meet a Colossus," she afterwards said, "with an eye like Mars, to threaten and command." Gibbon is reported to have expressed similar surprise when he met him in Mr. Cadell's shop. The services he had rendered to freedom were acknowledged in France and the United States, and in most unexpected quarters at home. Congress passed a resolution inviting him to become a citizen of the United States, and to assist them in the regulation of their finances. In later years Turgot corresponded with him, Pitt repeatedly consulted him on great questions of national finance, and a speech of his in proposing the toast of union between England and France was read twice in the National Assembly, the members standing. He was one day at the Bar of the House of Lords, when the Duke of Cumberland came up and told him he had read his "Essay on Civil Liberty" till he was blind. "It is remarkable," replied Lord Ashburton, who was standing near, "that your royal highness should have been blinded by a book which has opened the eyes of all mankind."— CLAYDEN, P. W., 1887, *The Early Life of Samuel Rogers, p.* 30.

If a man could be judged by his friends, Price's deserts would be high. He was intimate with Benjamin Franklin and John Howard; he corresponded with Hume and Turgot. He was visited by Lyttelton, Shelbourne, and Mrs. Montague. The now nearly-forgotten Mrs. Chapone has written high praise of him in the character of "Simplicius" ("Miscellanies," Essay I.); Simplicius is modest, learned and candid. Nevertheless he has not left a name worthy to be called great in our literature. He was a man of vigorous, independent judgment, who did good public service in his generation. He stimulated discussion on philosophical, theological, and political questions, and showed taste and sobriety in dealing with opponents. He had the moral courage to advocate unpopular causes.—BONAR, JAMES, 1895, *English Prose, ed. Craik, vol.* IV, *p.* 293.

GENERAL

He investigated with acuteness and ability many important questions relative to morals, and controverted the doctrine of a Moral Sense, as irreconcilable with the unalterable character of fundamental moral conceptions, which, as well as those of Substance and Cause, he maintained to be eternal and original principles of the intellect itself, independent of the Divine Will. He has admirably illustrated the differences existing between Morality and Sensation, Virtue and Happiness; at the same time that he points out the intimate connection existing between the two last. —TENNEMANN, WILLIAM GOTTLEIB, 1812–52, *A Manual of the History of Philosophy, tr. Johnson, ed. Morrell, p.* 376.

Dr. Price was *not* a Socinian, but an Arian; he wrote professedly in confutation of Socinianism; and though I disapprove of his religious principles, I feel no hesitation in affirming, in spite of the frantic and unprincipled abuse of Burke, that a more ardent and enlightened friend of his country never lived than that venerable patriarch of freedom.— HALL, ROBERT, 1822, *Reply to the Review of the Apology for the Freedom of the Press.*

If in England you only look at London in the eighteenth century, you will doubtless there see little else than sensualism.

But even at London, you would find, by the side of Priestley, Price, that ardent friend of liberty, that ingenious and profound economist, who renewed and brilliantly sustained the Platonic idealism of Cudworth. I know that Price is an isolated phenomenon at London; but the whole Scotch school is more or less spiritualistic.—COUSIN, VICTOR, 1828–29, *History of Modern Philosophy, tr. Wight.*

Almost the only writer of this [the rationalistic] school whose works are likely to form a part of our standard philosophy, is Dr. Richard Price. . . . In his controversy with Priestley, particularly, he showed how strongly he viewed the philosophical aberration of the age, and how earnestly he desired to place moral and metaphysical truth upon its deeper and truer foundation.—MORELL, J. D., 1846, *Speculative Philosophy in the Nineteenth Century.*

His style displays in no eminent degree either of the cardinal virtues of a philosophical work; he is not remarkably perspicuous, and he is far from being remarkably precise. His numerous political and economical pamphlets are written with considerable energy, "not unfitly typified by the unusual muscular and nervous activity of his slender person."—MINTO, WILLIAM, 1872–80, *Manual of English Prose Literature, p.* 473.

It is comparatively plausible to say that the intellect is the sole agent in framing the criterion. His language upon this subject may sometimes remind us of Kant's "Categorical Imperative;" and he seems to have been blundering round the same truths or errors from which the great German elaborated a moral theory far more ingenious, though involving the same fundamental fallacy.— STEPHEN, LESLIE, 1876, *History of English Thought in the Eighteenth Century, vol.* II, *p.* 12.

A veteran who had nearly reached his sixtieth year when our period commences, chiefly belongs to literature as an antagonist of Burke, as does Priestley, whose writing was very extensive, but who was as much more a "natural philosopher" than a man of letters as Price was much less a man of letters than a moralist and a statistician. — SAINTSBURY, GEORGE, 1896, *A History of Nineteenth Century Literature, p.* 26.

SIR JOSHUA REYNOLDS

EDMUND BURKE

From a Painting by Himself.

From Painting by Alonzo Chappel.
Original by Sir Joshua Reynolds.

Price's reputation at the present time rests mainly upon the position which he occupies in the history of moral philosophy. His ethical theories are mostly contained in "A Review of the Principal Questions in Morals," of which the first edition was published in 1757, and the third, expressing "the author's latest and maturest thoughts," in 1787. . . . The English moralist with whom Price has most affinity is Cudworth. The main point of difference is that, while Cudworth regards the ideas of right and wrong as νοηματα or modifications of the intellect itself, existing first in germ, and afterwards developed by circumstances, Price seems rather to regard them as acquired from the contemplation of actions, though acquired necessarily, immediately, and intuitively. The interest of his position, however, in the history of moral philosophy, turns mainly on the many points of resemblance, both in fundamental ideas and in modes of expression, which exist between his writings and those of Kant, whose ethical works are posterior to those of Price by nearly thirty years.—T.F. (THE REVEREND PRESIDENT OF CORPUS CHRISTI COLLEGE OXFORD), 1896, *Dictionary of National Biography, vol.* XLVI, *p.* 336.

Sir Joshua Reynolds
1723–1792

Born at Plympton Earl, Devonshire, July 16, 1723: Died at London, Feb. 23, 1792. A celebrated English portrait-painter. He was educated by his father, a schoolmaster and clergyman. In Oct., 1741, he went to London and studied under Thomas Hudson. In 1746 he established himself as a portrait-painter in London. By invitation of his friend, Commodore (afterward Admiral) Keppel, he sailed for Italy on the Centurion, arriving in Rome at the close of 1749. Owing to a cold which he took there, he became deaf and never recovered his hearing. After two years in Rome he visited Parma, Florence, Venice, and other Italian cities. He returned to London in 1752, and was intimately associated with Johnson, Burke, Goldsmith, Garrick, and others. The "Literary Club" was established at his suggestion in 1764. In 1768 The Royal Academy was founded, with Reynolds as its first president. His annual addresses form its well-known "Discourses." In 1784, on the death of Allan Ramsay, he was made painter to the king. Reynolds wrote three essays in the "Idler" (1759–60). His most famous works are his portraits of Johnson, Garrick, Sterne, Goldsmith, the little Lady Penelope Boothby, Mrs. Siddons as the "Tragic Muse," the "Infant Hercules," the "Strawberry Girl," "Garrick between Tragedy and Comedy," etc.—SMITH, BENJAMIN E., *ed.*, 1894–97, *The Century Cyclopedia of Names, p.* 852.

PERSONAL

Of Reynolds all good should be said, and no harm;
Though the heart is too frigid, the pencil too warm;
Yet each fault from his converse we still must disclaim,
As his temper 'tis peaceful, and pure as his fame.
Nothing in it o'erflows, nothing ever is wanting,
It nor chills like his kindness, nor glows like his painting.
When Johnson by strength overpowers our mind,
When Montagu dazzles, and Burke strikes us blind;
To Reynolds well pleased for relief we must run,
Rejoice in his shadow, and shrink from the sun.
—PIOZZI, HESTER LYNCH, 1773? *The Streatham Portraits, Autobiography, ed. Hayward, p.* 254.

Here Reynolds is laid, and to tell you my mind,
He has not left a wiser or better behind:
His pencil was striking, resistless and grand;
His manners were gentle, complying, and bland;
Still born to improve us in every part,
His pencil our faces, his manners our heart:
To coxcombs averse, yet most civilly steering,
When they judg'd without skill, he was still hard of hearing;
When they talk'd of their Raphaels, Corregios, and stuff,
He shifted his trumpet, and only took snuff.
—GOLDSMITH, OLIVER, 1774, *The Retaliation.*

I heard yesterday of your late disorder, and should think ill of myself if I had heard of it without alarm. I heard likewise of your recovery, which I sincerely wish to be complete and permanent. Your country has been in danger of

losing one of its brightest ornaments, and
I of losing one of my oldest and kindest
friends; but I hope you will still live long,
for the honour of the nation: and that
more enjoyment of your elegance, your
intelligence, and your benevolence is still
reserved for, dear Sir, your most affectionate, &c.—JOHNSON, SAMUEL, 1782,
Letter to Sir Joshua Reynolds, Nov. 14.

His native humility, modesty, and candour never forsook him, even on surprise
or provocation; nor was the least degree
of arrogance or assumption visible to the
most scrutinizing eye in any part of his
conduct or discourse. His talents of
every kind, powerful from nature, and
not meanly cultivated by letters, his social
virtues in all the relations and all the
habitudes of life, rendered him the centre of a very great and unparalleled variety of agreeable societies, which will be
dissipated by his death. He had too
much merit not to excite some jealousy,
too much innocence to provoke any enmity. . . . Sir Joshua Reynolds was
on very many accounts one of the most
memorable men of his time. . . . He
was the first Englishman who added the
praise of the elegant arts to the other
glories of his country. In taste, in
grace, in facility, in happy invention, and
in the richness and harmony of colouring,
he was equal to the great masters of the
renowned ages. In portrait he went
beyond them; for he communicated to
that description of the art in which English artists are the most engaged, a variety, a fancy, and a dignity derived from
the higher branches, which even those
who professed them in a superior manner
did not always preserve when they delineated individual nature. His portraits
remind the spectator of the invention of
history and of the amenity of landscape.
In painting portraits, he appeared not to
be raised upon that platform, but to descend to it from a higher sphere. . . .
Few individuals have proved themselves
so capable of illustrating the theory of
the science they professed, by their practice and their discourses. . . . To be
such a painter, he was a profound and
penetrating philosopher. . . . The
loss of no man of his time can be felt
with more sincere, general, and unmixed
sorrow.—BURKE, EDMUND, 1791, *London
Gentleman's Magazine, vol.* I, *p.* 190.

Poor Sir Joshua! How good—how
kind—how truly amiable and respectable!
The best of men—whose talents, though
an honour to his country, were the least
of his qualifications!—CHARLEMONT,LORD,
1792, *Letter to Edmond Malone, March*
1; *Malone's Life by Prior, p.* 189.

I became first acquainted with him in
1778, and for these twelve years past we
have lived in the greatest intimacy. . .
He was blessed with such complacency
and equality of temper, was so easy, so
uniformly cheerful, so willing to please
and be pleased, so fond of the company
of literary men, so well read in mankind,
so curious an observer of character, and
so replete with various knowledge and
entertaining anecdotes, that not to have
loved as well as admired him would have
shown great want of taste and sensibility.
He had long enjoyed such constant health,
looked so young, and was so active, that
I thought, though he was sixty-nine years
old, he was as likely to live eight or ten
years longer as any of his younger friends.
. . . I cannot help thinking that we
should not have lost this most amiable
man for some years, had there not been
want of exertion, combined with some
want of skill in his physicians. . . .
On his body being opened, his liver which
ought to have weighed about five pounds,
had attained the great weight of eleven
pounds. It was also somewhat scirrhus.
The optic nerve of the left eye was quite
shrunk, and more flimsy than it ought to
have been. The other, which he was so
apprehensive of losing, was not affected.
In his brain was found more water than
is usual in men of his age.—MALONE,
EDMOND, 1792, *Life by Prior, pp.* 190,
191, 192.

He had none of those eccentric bursts
of action, those fiery impetuosities, which
are supposed by the vulgar to characterize
genius, and which frequently are found to
accompany a secondary rank of talent,
but are never conjoined with the first. His
incessant industry was never wearied into
despondency by miscarriage, nor elated
into negligence by success. All nature
and all art combined to form his academy.
. . . In conversation he preserved an
equable flow of spirits, which had rendered
him at all times a most desirable companion,—ever ready to be amused, and
to contribute to the amusement of others.

He practised the minute elegancies, and, though latterly a deft companion, was never troublesome.—NORTHCOTE, JAMES, 1813, *Memoirs of Sir Joshua Reynolds.*

In his stature, Sir Joshua Reynolds was rather under the middle size. He was in height nearly five feet six inches, of a florid complexion, roundish, blunt features, and a lively, pleasing aspect; not corpulent, though somewhat inclined to it, but extremely active. With manners highly polished and agreeable, he possessed an uncommon flow of spirits, but always under the strictest regulation, which rendered him, at all times, a most pleasing and desirable companion. Such was the undeviating propriety of his deportment, that wherever he appeared, he invariably, by his example, gave a tone of decorum to the society. With a carriage the most unassuming, he always commanded that personal respect which was shown him on all occasions. No man was more fitted for the seat of authority. When acting in a public capacity, he united dignity with ease; in private society he was ever ready to be amused, and to contribute to the amusement of others; and was always attentive to receive information on every subject that presented itself; and by the aid of an ear-trumpet he was enabled to partake of the conversation of his friends with great facility and convenience.—FARINGTON, JOSEPH, 1819, *Memoirs of Sir Joshua Reynolds.*

Sir Joshua Reynolds had no real or affected peculiarities, which distinguished him from the plain English gentleman: He was subject to no fits of hysteric enthusiasm, asserted no undue pretensions, and thought nothing beneath his consideration which the rank that he held in society appeared to require at his hands. The history of his life will afford but little scope to those who look for romance as inseparable from genius, and think it unbecoming, in men of lofty minds, to climb to fame by a path which might be trodden by others.—BEECHEY, HENRY WILLIAM, 1835–55, *The Literary Works of Sir Joshua Reynolds, Memoir, vol.* I, *p.* 32.

The good-humour of Reynolds was a different thing from that of Hogarth. It had no antagonism about it. Ill-humour with any other part of the world had nothing to do with it. It was gracious and diffused; singling out some, it might be, for special warmth, but smiling blandly upon all. He was eminently the gentleman of his time; and if there is a hidden charm in his portraits, it is that. His own nature pervades them, and shines out from them still.—FORSTER, JOHN, 1848–71, *The Life and Times of Oliver Goldsmith, vol.* I, *p.* 306.

I am afraid Sir Joshua, though a bachelor, is not very particular about his studio being kept neat; for I observe, evidently left from yesterday's campaign, a great ring of brown dust, which I believe to be the Famous Hardham's 37, the snuff from 37, Fleet Street, that Garrick uses and puffs. There it is all round the easel, dropped in lavish slovenliness—a trail of it marking the artist's walk between the easel and the throne. It is rather a weakness of Sir Joshua's, and, in fact, he sometimes sets his wits and beauties sneezing, so that they lose their expression and spoil their attitudes. The six sitters of to-day will not like it. I know he, Sir Joshewa, is so bland and courteous, they will not like to say anything, remembering the story at Blenheim, of how he refused to let the servant the duchess sent sweep up the snuff till he had finished painting, observing that his picture would suffer more injury by the dust than the carpet could possibly do with the snuff.—THORNBURY, WALTER, 1860, *British Artists from Hogarth to Turner, vol.* I, *p.* 199.

I declare, I think, of all the polite men of the age, Joshua Reynolds was the finest gentleman.—THACKERAY, WILLIAM MAKEPEACE, 1861, *George III, The Four Georges.*

Sir Joshua, in Miss Burney's "Diary," appears bland, amiable, sensible, unaffected, and essentially kindly. In this the "Diary" is borne out by all the reliable contemporary evidence to character. The conception of him as a cold, calculating, politic, selfish being, a smoulderer instead of a blazer, is a figment of later biographers and critics. Its best foundation is an occasional splenetic remark of Northcote's, made when he was old, ailing, and querulous, but contradicted by the general tenor of Northcote's own account of the painter he reverenced, and whom he was always holding up as a pattern to young men.— LESLIE, CHARLES ROBERT, AND TAYLOR, TOM, 1865, *Life and Times of Sir Joshua Reynolds, vol.* II, *p.* 205.

It was while studying Raphael's frescos in the Vatican that Reynolds caught the cold which resulted in his deafness; and thereafter the ear-trumpet of Sir Joshua was as characteristic a part of himself as was the wooden leg a part of the redoubtable Governor Peter Stuyvesant. He even painted his own portrait with his trumpet held to his ear; though, when about the same time he painted Dr. Johnson holding a book very close to his eyes, the great man did not relish this vivid evidence of his extreme near-sightedness, but said to Boswell: "Sir, he may paint himself as deaf as he chooses, but I *will not* go down to posterity as 'Blinking Sam.'"—KEPPEL, FREDERICK, 1894, *Sir Joshua Reynolds, Scribner's Magazine, vol.* 15, *p.* 98.

His personal life is indicative of the spirit that influenced his art. There was nothing erratic, venturesome, or impulsive about either. It is difficult to believe that the man at any time, either in life or in art, possessed such things as fire, passion, romance. He was too calm for either love or hatred, too conservative for brilliancy, too philosophical for enthusiasm. In art he placed less reliance upon inspiration than upon intelligent knowledge, believed the gospel of genius to be work, and thought originality a new way of saying old truths. Such ideas as these form the chief counts in his discourses to the students of the Royal Academy.—VAN DYKE, JOHN C., 1897, *Old English Masters, The Century, vol.* 54, *p.* 817.

The beauty of his disposition and the nobility of his character were equal to his talents. Without any physical advantages—for he was neither tall nor handsome, and had the great social drawback of deafness—he secured without seeking, and maintained without effort, a position in society which is almost unrivalled. Treating all men on the plain level of common human nature and unactuated by any prejudice, he mixed, as by natural charter, with all classes. His principal passports were kindliness, sincerity, and tolerance; but these were aided by a ready sympathy, of a well-informed mind, gentle manners, and invariable tact and commonsense. The charm of his presence and conversation was all the more irresistible because it was unforced and unfeigned.

He was a born diplomatist, and avoided friction by natural instinct; a philosopher who early learnt and consistently acted on the principle not to concern himself about matters of small importance.—MONKHOUSE, COSMO, 1896, *Dictionary of National Biography, vol.* XLVIII, *p.* 66.

ART

One of the most interesting exhibitions of this season is of Sir Joshua Reynolds' pictures, which have been sent from all parts of the kingdom by the owners, and which are remarkable, not only for the genius of the master, but as a gallery of all the beauties, wits, and heroes of the last sixty years, who have almost all been painted by Sir Joshua.—MACKINTOSH, SIR JAMES, 1813, *Letters to his Daughters, May* 11; *Life, ed. Mackintosh, vol.* II, *ch.* iv.

Having emptiness for breadth, plastering for surface, and portrait individuality for general nature. Reynold's tone is too much toned. Raffaele is pure and inartificial in comparison. Reynolds is a man of strong feeling, labouring to speak in a language he does not know, and giving a hint of his idea by a dazzling combination of images—Raffaele a master of polished diction who conveys in exquisite phraseology certain perceptions of truth. . . . It may take its place triumphantly by any borreggio on earth. It is very lovely. The whole series are unequaled by an English master.—HAYDON, BENJAMIN ROBERT, 1821, *On the Sir Joshua Reynolds Sale.*

If I was to compare him with Vandyke and Titian, I should say that Vandyke's portraits are like pictures (very perfect ones no doubt), Sir Joshua's like the reflection in a looking-glass, and Titian's like the real people. There is an atmosphere of light and shade about Sir Joshua's which neither of the others have in the same degree, together with a vagueness that gives them a visionary and romantic character, and makes them seem like dreams or vivid recollections of persons we have seen. I never could mistake Vandyke's for anything but pictures; and I go up to them as such; when I see a fine Sir Joshua, I can neither suppose it to be a mere picture nor a man, and I almost involuntarily turn back to ascertain if it is not some one behind me reflected in the glass; when I see a Titian I am riveted to it, and I can no more take my eye off from it than if it were the very individual in the room.— NORTHCOTE, JAMES, 1826–27, *Conversations, ed. Hazlitt, p. 257.*

The influence of Reynolds on the taste and elegance of the island was great, and will be lasting. The grace and ease of his compositions were a lesson for the living to study, while the simplicity of his dresses admonished the giddy and the gay against the hideousness of fashion. He sought to restore nature in the looks of his sitters, and he waged a thirty years' war against the fopperies of dress. His works diffused a love of elegance, and united with poetry in softening the asperities of nature, in extending our views, and in connecting us with the spirits of the time. His cold stateliness of character, and his honourable pride of art, gave dignity to his profession: the rich and the far-descended were pleased to be painted by a gentleman as well as a genius.—CUNNINGHAM, ALLAN, 1830–33, *The Lives of the Most Eminent British Painters and Sculptors, vol.* I, *p.* 279.

The colouring of Sir Joshua Reynolds in his best works combines the highest qualities of Correggio and Titian with the brilliancy and luxuriance of the Dutch and the Flemish schools, deprived of their tumidities. The common error that his colours all fail, ought by this time to be entirely effaced. It is too true that this is the case with the colouring of many pictures painted by him during a short period of his life; he thought that he had discovered a mode of rendering colouring *more* vivid, and employed it without duly considering the chemical qualities of his materials. But he was soon made acquainted with the mistake he had committed, reassumed his durable system with increased beauty and vigour, and continued to employ it till the termination of his valuable labours.—PHILLIPS, THOMAS, 1833, *Lectures on Painting, p.* 372.

That the portraits of Reynolds were the best of all likenesses I have no manner of doubt. I know several of his pictures of children, the originals of whom I have seen in middle and old age, and in every instance I could discover much likeness. —LESLIE, CHARLES, 1855, *Hand-Book for Young Painters.*

But there is likewise a window, lamentable to look at, which was painted by Sir Joshua Reynolds, and exhibits strikingly the difference between the work of a man who performed it merely as a matter of taste and business, and what was done religiously and with the whole heart; at least, it shows that the artists and public of the last age had no sympathy with Gothic art. In the chancel of this church there are more painted windows, which I take to be modern, too, though they are in much better taste, and have an infinitely better effect, than Sir Joshua's.— HAWTHORNE, NATHANIEL, 1856, *Oxford, English Note Books, Aug.* 31.

Considered as a painter of individuality in the human form and mind, 1 think him even as it is, the prince of portrait painters. Titian paints nobler pictures and Vandyck has nobler subjects, but neither of them enter so subtly as Joshua did into the minor varieties of human heart and temper.—RUSKIN, JOHN, 1859, *The Two Paths, Lecture,* ii.

With Reynolds the assurance of the master never bordered on impertinence. He was searching always and to the end, and even those melancholy experiments with pigments and colours which have served to hasten the ruin of many of his pictures, are but the outward sign of a higher intellectual curiosity which is of the very essence of his genius. To the close of his long career his painting preserved the interesting characteristics that in the work of other men belong only to the season of youth and progress: he is little of a mannerist, because he has none of the settled confidence of style which begets mannerism: with each new subject he is moved to new effort and experiment: and though the measure of his success is not always the same, even his failures are not the failures of audacity or self-assurance.—CARR, J. COMYNS, 1884, *Sir Joshua Reynolds, English Illustrated Magazine, vol.* I. *p.* 342.

The individual portrait was the portrait of Sir Joshua. In him the gift of painting men and women was supreme. Not only did he paint them in their habit as they lived, but with such masterly suggestion of character as was practically unknown amongst the men of his generation. . . . A singularly calm and genial temper was joined to an astonishing alertness of observation, and these gifts were trained by constant and varied practice.

Always on the watch for the turn of the head, the uplifting of the hand, the bending or stiffness of the figure, he never seems to have failed to recognise the really differential note of character. And he indicated these things with extraordinary subtlety. In particular, he divined the character of children with unfailing accuracy and sympathy. As has been very perfectly said, Reynolds has the secret of all the characteristic graces of women and children.—HUGHES, R., 1896, *Social England, ed. Traill, vol. v, p.* 283.

The name of Sir Joshua Reynolds holds a place of honor among the world's great portrait painters. To appreciate fully his originative power one must understand the disadvantages under which he worked. His technical training was of the meagrest kind, and all his life he was hampered by ignorance of anatomy. But on the other hand he combined all those peculiar qualities of the artist without which no amount of technical skill can produce great portrait work. He had, in the first place, that indefinable quality of taste, which means so much in portraiture. His was an unerring instinct for poise, drapery, color, and composition. Each of his figures seems to assume naturally an attitude of perfect grace; the draperies fall of their own accord in beautiful lines. Reynolds knew, too, the secret of imparting an air of distinction to his sitters. The meanest subject was elevated by his art to a position of dignity. His magic touch made every child charming, every woman graceful, and every man dignified. Finally, he possessed in no small degree, though curiously enough entirely disclaiming the quality, the gift of presenting the essential personality of the sitter, that which a critic has called the power of "realizing an individuality." This is seen most clearly in his portraits of men, and naturally in the portraits of the men he knew best, as Johnson.—HURLL, ESTELLE M., 1900, *Sir Joshua Reynolds, p.* 7.

GENERAL

I cannot think that the theory here [in his "Discourses"] laid down is clear and satisfactory, that it is consistent with itself, that it accounts for the various excellences of art from a few simple principles, or that the method which Sir Joshua has pursued in treating the subject is, as he himself expresses it, "a plain and honest method." It is, I fear, more calculated to baffle and perplex the student in his progress, than to give him clear lights as to the object he should have in view, or to furnish him with strong motives of emulation to attain it.—HAZLITT, WILLIAM, 1824-43-44, *Criticism on Art, Second Series, p.* 84.

Then, as to Sir Joshua's writings, their spirit is all in delightful keeping with his pictures. One of the few painters he —such as Leonardo Da Vinci, Michael Angelo, and so on—our own Barry, Opie, Fuseli, and so on—who could express by the pen the principles which guide the pencil. 'Tis the only work on art which, to men not artistis, is entirely intelligible.—WILSON, JOHN, 1829, *Noctes Ambrosianæ, April.*

Sir Joshua Reynolds, who has the good fortune to be remembered alike by his pencil and his pen, and whose discourses still remain the most sensible and judicious work on the principles of painting, in our language. — HILLARD, GEORGE STILLMAN, 1853, *Six Months in Italy, p.* 78.

A word as to his style. There is a clearness and perspicuity about it which enables us at once to perceive the drift of his remarks; he does not conceal himself in a dense mass of verbiage, nor does he write ambiguously, hinting at this and suggesting that, but arrow-like goes straight to his point. Withal, there is no baldness; every sentence is carefully constructed, and there are everywhere marks of the *labor limæ;* perhaps here and there it savours somewhat too much of elaboration. Still, it is a very graceful style; just what we should expect from a cultured, well-tempered mind,—scholarly without pedantry, easy without vulgarity.—PULLING, F. S., 1880, *Sir Joshua Reynolds, p.* 100.

The earliest art-criticisms of any value published in this country were contained in the annual and biennial "Discourses" which Sir Joshua Reynolds, F. R. A., delivered from January 1759 to his retirement in December 1790. They were issued year by year, and collected after his death. . . . It was, doubtless, through his lifelong companionship with Johnson, Burke, and Goldsmith that Reynolds learned to write in the English language only a little less brilliantly than they.—GOSSE, EDMUND, 1888, *A History of Eighteenth Century Literature, pp.* 308, 309.

Nothing is more remarkable in the great career of our master than the genuine literary ability which he developed by degrees, side by side with, yet quite independently of, his artistic capacity. And we must wonder the more when we remember that he received not more than the education of the average school-boy of his time, and in the course of his well-filled and practically uninterrupted career was unable to supplement early deficiencies by any sustained course of reading or study.— PHILLIPS, CLAUDE, 1894, *Sir Joshua Reynolds, p.* 389.

The personal charm and strength of character, which doubtless assisted the universal recognition of his genius, may account in part for the great influence of his writings. His style, though somewhat formal, was graceful, simple, and urbane. He had been trained in the classical school of Dr. Johnson, who "qualified him to think justly," but fortunately his admiration of the master did not tempt him to forget, in composition, the true principles of imitation which he expounded in the "Discourses."—JOHNSON, REGINALD BRIMLEY, 1895, *English Prose, ed. Craik, vol.* IV, *p.* 301.

The fame of Sir Joshua's Discourses is at first sight a little difficult to understand. For a hundred years it has been the fashion to treat them as models of literature and monuments of critical profundity. Their style has been thought so much too good for their putative author, that the great shades of Burke and Johnson have been descried at Sir Joshua's elbow, controlling his expression and even suggesting his ideas. Again, their reasoning on the foundations of art has been so far accepted by those who ought to know, that

they have been put, as a text-book, into the hands of some twenty generations of students. And yet Sir Joshua's style is good only through its sincerity; and his teaching sound only if meant to be superficial. . . . To us who have the advantage of a distant perspective, it seems extraordinary that any one should ascribe the eminently human, but somewhat invertebrate periods of Sir Joshua first to Johnson and afterwards to Burke. As a writer Reynolds was, of course, an amateur. He had never been drilled in the use of language, or compelled to notice how the practised writer avoids those involutions and cacophonies which spring from the unguarded expression of complex ideas. He piles relative on relative and participle on participle, until his sentences become so long drawn out that we have to read them twice to grasp their meaning. As interpreted by a good speaker, they would, no doubt, be clear enough. Vocal modulations would bring out the sense. But Reynolds, we are told, had a very bad delivery, and so it is not surprising that his colleagues paid him the compliment of a request to print his sermons ! . . . In reading Sir Joshua, we feel that he is inside his subject, groping his way out. His guesses are often unhappy, and lead him to conclusions which are little else than absurd. But there he is, nevertheless, inside, and doing his best to understand his *milieu*, and to get a right conception of the whole matter. His methods of expression are imperfect, and leave us with the idea that his conceptions are too complicated to be rendered in such words as he can command.—ARMSTRONG, SIR WALTER, 1900, *Sir Joshua Reynolds First President of the Royal Academy, pp.* 175, 177, 179.

George Horne

1730–1792

George Horne was born (November 1, 1730) at Otham, near Maidstone, in Kent. At the age of 13, he was sent to school at Maidstone; and at 15, entered University College, Oxford. He graduated B. A. in 1749, was afterwards elected a fellow of Magdalen College, graduated M. A. in 1752, became B. D. in 1759, and D. D. in 1764, and in 1768 was appointed principal of Magdalen. Pious, of thoughtful disposition ; contented in mind, and devoted to learning ; Dr. Horne resided year after year in his college, happy in his family circle, and devoting himself, chiefly, to the study of Hebrew and sacred literature, and engaging in Biblical works, especially the preparation of his "Commentary on the Book of Psalms," which he had commenced in 1758. It appeared in two volumes, in 1776, and has been frequently reprinted. Its value is thought, by some, to be lessened, through the influence the author allowed to be exercised over him, in its preparation, by those erroneous philological and philosophical principles of Hutchinson, which have long since been exploded. In the year of the publication of this work, he was appointed Vice-Chancellor of his University; in 1781, Dean of Canterbury; and, in 1791, Bishop of Norwich. But he did not long enjoy his episcopal honour. He died January 17, 1792, in his sixty-second year.—MILLER, JOSIAH, 1866–69, *Singers and Songs of the Church, p.* 250.

PERSONAL

Bishop Horne, whose literary feelings were of the most delicate and lively kind, has beautifully recorded them in his progress through a favourite and lengthened work—his "Commentary on the Psalms." He alludes to himself in the third person; yet who but the self-painter could have caught those delicious emotions which are so evanescent in the deep occupation of pleasant studies?—DISRAELI, ISAAC, 1796–1818, *Enthusiasm of Genius, The Literary Character.*

Like many earnest men of the day, Horne fell under the imputation of methodism. He adopted the views of John Hutchinson (1674—1737), and wrote his defence, although he disagreed with his fanciful interpretations of Hebrew etymology. Hutchinsonianism had some points in common with methodism, notably its intense appreciation of holy scripture, and its insistence upon spiritual religion. But Horne was distinctly what would now be called a high churchman, and he publicly protested from the university pulpit against those who took their theology from the Tabernacle and the Foundry (Whitefield's and Wesley's headquarters) instead of from the great divines of the church. Nevertheless, apart from his position as a Hutchinsonian, Horne personally showed a sympathy with the methodists. He strongly disapproved of the expulsion of the six methodist students from St. Edmund Hall, Oxford. He would not have John Wesley, "an ordained minister of the Church of England," forbidden to preach in his diocese, and John Wesley thoroughly appreciated Horne's action.—OVERTON, J. H., 1891, *Dictionary of National Biography, vol.* XXVII, *p.* 356.

COMMENTARY ON THE PSALMS
1771

A delightful amplification of the music of Zion, wherein every phrase is spiritualized, every prophetic and recondite meaning pointed out.—GRANT, JOHNSON, 1811–25, *A Summary of the History of the English Church.*

It is a truly evangelical and most valuable work, generally commended and admired for the vein of spirituality and devotion which runs through it, as well as for the elegant taste displayed in the illustration of difficult passages. The author's design is to illustrate the historical sense of the Psalms as they relate to King David and the people of Israel; and to point out their application to the Messiah, to the Church, and to individuals as members of the Church.—LOWNDES, WILLIAM THOMAS, 1839, *British Librarian.*

His "Commentary on the Psalms" is his capital performance, and the one by which he will be known so long as piety and elegant learning are loved in England. It is altogether a beautiful work. The preface is a masterpiece of composition and good sense. The exposition implies more learning and research than it displays; and the views of Christian doctrine contained in it are generally very correct. Perhaps he carries his applications to the Messiah and his Church occasionally rather far; but this is less hurtful than the opposite extreme, which has more generally been adopted.—ORME, WILLIAM, 1824, *Bibliotheca Biblica.*

GENERAL

Mr. Warburton has seen a thing against the Newtonian philosophy in favour of Hutchinson by one Horne, of Oxford, and thinks it would be a good employment for some Cambridge Soph to answer it.—HURD, RICHARD, 1753, *Letter to Rev. Mr. Balguy, Memoirs, ed. Kilvert, p.* 48.

This writer seems to have had as much devotion and regard for the grand principles of Christianity as command respect; but few evangelical preachers, notwithstanding, would like to take him for a pattern.—WILLIAMS, EDWARD, 1800, *The Christian Preacher.*

Bishop Horne's views of preaching, not always (alas! such is our common infirmity!) fully illustrated by his own sermons, are instructive. . . . His sermons are polished, and have many beautiful and excellent thoughts; but they are wanting in the full declaration of justification by faith, and therefore meet not adequately the distresses of an awakened conscience. . . . His sermons are devotional and elegant. He and others of his school have brought some important truths before men who would not have listened to those writing more in the spirit of the Reformers.—BICKERSTETH, EDWARD,1844, *The Christian Student.*

George Horne was very soon described as "without exception the best preacher in England," a judgment which his sermons which remain to us go far to justify. By these and his other writings, especially his devotional work on the Psalms, Horne may be regarded as the founder of the Scriptural school, which towards the end of the century received so great a development. . . . The praise of attempting to overthrow this lifeless and unedifying treatment of Scripture is due to Horne, and the great success which his truly Christian writings obtained, was of the highest service to the cause of religion. —PERRY, GEORGE G.,1864, *The History of the Church of England, vol.* III, *pp.* 382,383.

Sir David Dalrymple

Lord Hailes

1726-1792

Sir David Dalrymple, Lord Hailes, historical antiquary, born at Edinburgh, 28th October 1726, was the great grandson of the first Lord Stair. He was called to the Scottish bar in 1748, and in 1766 became a judge of the Court of Session as Lord Hailes, in 1776 a justiciary lord. At his country-seat of New Hailes, near Edinburgh, he gave his leisure to uninterrupted literary activity. He died 29 November 1792. Among his books are "A Discourse on the Gowrie Conspiracy" (1757); "Memorials relating to the Reigns of James I. and Charles I." (1762-66); and "Annals of Scotland, 1057-1371" (1776-79). He wrote besides on legal antiquities and ancient church history, edited old Scotch poems, &c.—PATRICK AND GROOME, *eds.*, 1897, *Chambers's Biographical Dictionary, p.* 450.

PERSONAL

The indefatigable Sir David is translating Minutius Felix, and writing notes. Of the *last*, I have a large farrago in my hands, and am to keep them, I suppose, till his Arch-Critic arrives. This Sir David is a good, well-intentioned man, has learning and sense, but is withal immoderately vain; which I conclude, not from his writings so much (for then how should another friend of yours escape?) but from his teasing his friends so immoderately with his MSS. However, with all his imperfections upon his head, give me a writer—an animal that is now become a *rara avis,* and much to be stared at, even in our learned universities.—HURD, RICHARD, 1780, *Letter to Dr. Balguy, Dec.* 14, *Memoirs, ed. Kilvert, p.* 140.

He was called to the bar at Edinburgh, February 23d, 1748, and was much admired for the elegant propriety of the Cases he drew. Though he had not attained to the highest rank as a practising lawyer, his character for sound knowledge and probity in the profession was so great that he was appointed one of the Judges of the Court of Session, in the room of Lord Nesbit, March 6th, 1766, and in May, 1776, one of the Lord Commissioners of Justiciary, in the room of Lord Coalston, who resigned. He died on the 29th of November.—SAVAGE, JAMES, 1808, *The Librarian, vol.* I, *p.* 85.

As an oral pleader he was not successful. A defect in articulation prevented him from speaking fluently, and he was naturally an impartial critic rather than a jealous advocate. Much of the business of litigation in Scotland at this time was conducted, however, by writing pleadings, and he gained a solid reputation as a learned and accurate lawyer. There is no better specimen of such pleadings than the case for the Countess of Southerland in her claim for the peerage in the House of the Lords, which was drawn by Hailes as her guardian after he became judge. It won the cause, and is still appealed to by peerage lawyers for the demonstration of the descent of the older Scottish titles to and through females. . . . The solemnity of his manner in administering oaths and pronouncing sentences specially struck his contemporaries. As a judge in the civil court he was admired for diligence and patience, keeping under restraint his power of sarcasm. In knowledge of the history of law he was surpassed by none of his brethren, though among them were Elchies, Kaimes, and Monboddo.—MACKAY, ÆNEAS, 1888, *Dictionary of National Biography, vol.* XIII, *pp.* 403, 404.

An estimable man was this scholar; but a little less self-consciousness would have improved his lordship, who kept aloof from the genial society of Edinburgh lest it might impair his flawless dignity. Distant in manner, he was seldom met with even in the company of Ferguson and Blair and Adam Smith, for such friendly comradeship would jar on his prim punctiliousness, and vex his due regard for what was "becoming."—GRAHAM, HENRY GREY, 1901, *Scottish Men of Letters in the Eighteenth Century, p.* 201.

GENERAL

"Lord Hailes's 'Annals of Scotland' have not that painted form which is the taste of this age; but it is a book which will always sell, it has such a stability of dates, such a certainty of facts, and such a punctuality of citation. I never before read Scotch history with certainty."—JOHNSON, SAMUEL, 1776, *Life by Boswell, ed. Hill, vol.* III, *p.* 67.

His "Annals of Scotland" is a masterly performance; in which, and in some detached pieces of historical research, he was the first to elucidate properly the early part of the history of our country, and it is only to be regretted that he has not brought his work down to a later period, as it stops at a time when the history was becoming more and more interesting, and his materials more copious. "The Case of the Sutherland-peerage," although originally a law-paper, written professionally when he was at the bar, at the time when the title of the young Countess, to the honours of her ancestors, was called in question, is one of the most profound disquisitions on the ancient peerages of Scotland anywhere to be met with.—FORBES, SIR WILLIAM, 1806-7, *An Account of the Life and Writings of James Beattie, vol.* II, *p.* 10, *note.*

The erudition of Lord Hailes was not of a dry and scholastic nature: he felt the beauties of the composition of the ancients; he entered with taste and discernment into the merits of the Latin poets, and that peculiar vein of delicate and ingenious thought which characterizes the Greek epigrammatists; and a few specimens which he has left of his own composition in that style, evince the hand of a master. . . . Lord Hailes was a man of wit, and possessed a strong feeling of the absurd and ridiculous in human conduct and character, which gave a keen edge of irony both to his conversation and writings. To his praise, however, it must be added, that that irony, if not always untinctured with prejudice, was never prompted by malignity, and was generally exerted in the cause of virtue and good morals. How much he excelled in painting the lighter weaknesses and absurdities of mankind, may be seen from the papers of his composition in the *World* and the *Mirror*. His private character was everything that is praiseworthy and respectable. In a word, he was an honour to the station which he filled, and to the age in which he lived.—TYTLER, ALEXANDER FRASER, 1806-14, *Memoirs of the Life and Writings of Henry Home of Kames, vol.* I, *pp.* 251, 252, *note.*

These works by Lord Hailes ["Remains of Christian Antiquity'] are among the most elegant specimens of translation, and discover a profound acquaintance with the most minute circumstances of early Christian antiquity. . . . He was one of the most formidable antagonists of Gibbon. His "Inquiry into the Secondary Causes" is a most triumphant exposure of the sophistry and misrepresentations of that artful writer. The preceding works are now become scarce; but I know not a higher treat which can be enjoyed by a cultivated and curious mind than that which they afford.—ORME, WILLIAM, 1824, *Bibliotheca Biblica.*

The "Annals" of Hailes, written with the accuracy of a judge, which far exceeds the accuracy of the historian, has been the text-book of all subsequent writers on the period of Scottish history it covers. The earlier Celtic sources had not in his time been explored, except by Father Innes, and were imperfectly understood. Nor could he have carried on his work much further without encountering political and religious controversies. He was thus enabled to maintain throughout his whole work a conspicuous impartiality. —MACKAY, ÆNEAS, 1888, *Dictionary of National Biography, vol.* XIII, *p.* 405.

Many a venerable [in his "Annals"] story and cherished tradition were demolished or banished to mythland. Hitherto the field had been the preserve of unconscionable pedants like Ruddiman, who warred with party animosity, and in temper as atrocious as their style, over charters and "claims" and pedigrees. Now this "restorer of Scottish History," as Sir Walter Scott has called him, lifted research into the domain of history. The "Annals" are dry, deplorably dry; but invaluable still for facts—a quarry in which later writers have dug for material out of which to build more artistic works. In the fine library at New Hailes the judge was busy editing and compiling; composing careful pieces of elegance for the *World;* translating Church Fathers, with erudite disquisitions dedicated to Anglican bishops; writing a learned answer to Gibbon's famous Fourteenth Chapter of his "Decline and Fall," with a learning and ability which are more than respectable. The fastidious accuracy of mind which spoiled Hailes as a lawyer and made him tedious as a judge suited him well as an antiquary.—GRAHAM, HENRY GREY, 1901, *Scottish Men of Letters in the Eighteenth Century, p.* 201.

Gilbert White

1720-1793

Born, at Selborne, Hants, 18 July, 1720. Early education at a school at Basingstoke. Matric. Oriel Coll., Oxford, 17 Dec., 1739; B. A., 1743; Fellow Oriel Coll., 1744-93; M. A., 1746; Proctor, 1752-53. Ordained Deacon, 1747; Priest, 1749. Curate at Swarraton, 1747-51; at Selborne, 1751-52; at Durley, 1753-55. Returned to Selborne, 1755. Vicar of Moreton-Pinkney, Northamptonshire (sinecure), 1757-93. Curate at Faringdon, 1762-84; at Selborne, 1784. Died, at Selborne, 26 June, 1793. *Works:* "The Natural History and Antiquities of Selborne" (anon.), 1789. *Posthumous:* "A Naturalist's Calendar," 1795; "Extracts from the unpublished MSS. of Mr. White," in the second series of E. Jesse's "Gleanings in Natural History," 1834. *Collected Works:* in 2 vols., ed. by J. Aikin, 1802.—SHARP, R. FARQUHARSON, 1897, *A Dictionary of English Authors, p.* 299.

PERSONAL

Your work, upon the whole, will immortalize your place of abode as well as yourself.—MULSO, JOHN, 1776, *Letter to Gilbert White, July* 16; *Life and Letters,* ed. Holt-White, *vol.* I, *p.* 324.

And lastly to close all I do desire that I may be buried in the churchyard belonging to the parish Church of Selborne aforesaid in as plain and private a way as possible without any pall bearers or parade and that six honest day labouring men respect being had to such as have bred up large families may bear me to my grave to whom I appoint the sum of ten shillings each for their trouble.—WHITE, GILBERT, 1793, *Will.*

IN THE FIFTH GRAVE FROM THIS WALL ARE BURIED THE REMAINS OF THE REV. GILBERT WHITE, M. A., FIFTY YEARS FELLOW OF ORIEL COLLEGE, IN OXFORD, AND HISTORIAN OF THIS HIS NATIVE PARISH. HE WAS ELDEST SON OF JOHN WHITE, ESQUIRE, BARRISTER-AT-LAW, AND ANNE, HIS WIFE, ONLY CHILD OF THOMAS HOLT, RECTOR OF STREATHAM, IN SURREY, WHICH SAID JOHN WHITE WAS THE ONLY SON OF GILBERT WHITE, FORMERLY VICAR OF THIS PARISH. HE WAS KIND AND BENEFICIENT TO HIS RELATIONS, BENEVOLENT TO THE POOR, AND DESERVEDLY RESPECTED BY ALL HIS FRIENDS AND NEIGHBOURS. HE WAS BORN JULY 18TH, 1720, O. S., AND DIED JUNE 26TH, 1793. NEC BONO QUICQUAM MALI EVENIRE POTEST, NEC VIVO, NEC MORTUO. —INSCRIPTION ON MONUMENT, *Selborne Churchyard.*

He was widely known as a philosopher, in the highest sense of the word, but he was so known only to the world without. His own village could not understand him, and little did its inhabitants suppose that their insignificant little Selborne should

become a world-known name by means of him, whose peaceful life was spent in retirement, and whose only eulogy, from a surviving fellow-parishioner, was, "That he was a still, quiet body, and there wasn't a bit of harm in him, there wasn't indeed."
—WOOD, J. G., 1853, ed., *The Natural History of Selborne, Biography*, p. vii.

There are few, perhaps, who have so extensively and so pleasantly occupied the mind of contemporaries and of posterity, and yet have left such scanty materials for a biography of corresponding interest, as the estimable and accomplished author of the "Natural History and Antiquities of Selborne."—BELL, THOMAS, 1877, ed., *The Natural History of Selborne*.

Most men must have marvelled at White's always remaining a bachelor in spite of being endowed with exceptionally domestic tastes. And perhaps some have surmised that a disappointment in love had caused his single life. We learn from Mr. Bell that this was the case. White had in early life been attached to no less a person than Mrs. Chapone. . . . Her maiden name was Hester Mulso. She preferred a barrister to our naturalist; and although she was left a widow ten months after marriage, and continued to correspond with White on the most friendly terms, they never married. It is amusing to see White's anger at any calumny on her fair fame after fourteen years of widowhood. . . . A sensitive nature like White's, capable of strong attachment and yet somewhat diffident as becomes a recluse and scholar, seldom gets the better of such a love-sorrow.—WATKINS, M. G., 1879, *White of Selborne, Fraser's Magazine*, vol. 99, p. 338.

To visit Selborne had been sweet
　No matter what the rest might be;
But some good genius led my feet
　Thither in such fit company,
As trebled all its charms for me.
With them to seek his headstone grey,
　The lover true of birds and trees,
Added strange sunshine to the day.
My eye a scene familiar sees,
And Home! is whispered by the breeze.
My English blood its right reclaims;
　In vain the sea its barrier rears;
Our pride is fed by England's fame,
　Ours is her glorious length of years;
Ours, too, her triumphs and her tears.
—LOWELL, JAMES RUSSELL, 1880, *On Gilbert White*.

Ghosts of great men in London town
　Confuse the brains of such as dream,
But here betwixt this hanging down
And this great moorland, waste and brown,
　One only reigns supreme.
In Wolmer Forest, old and wide,
　Along each sandy pine-girt glade
And lonesome heather-bordered ride,
A gentle presence haunts your side,
　A gracious reverend shade.
And as you pass by Blackmoor grim,
　And stand at gaze on Temple height,
Methinks the fancy grows less dim:
Methinks you really talk with him
　Who once was Gilbert White.
.　.　.　.　.　.　.　.　.
We know it all! Familiar, too,
　Seems this quaint hamlet 'neath the steeps—
House, "Pleystor," church, and churchyard
　yew,
And the plain headstone, hid from view,
　Where their historian sleeps.
—PLARR, VICTOR, 1893, *In the Country of Gilbert White, The Speaker*, June 17.

Our country has changed; old institutions have passed away; the railway and electric telegraph have transformed society. Yet in Selborne, whatever change there may be, is almost imperceptible. We are told that White preached a favourite sermon of his no less than fifty times, and that his text bore on the duty of love to man. Were he with us again he would be gratified to find that the passage of time had left unchanged the natural objects he so dearly loved; that the general aspect of his beloved village, as affected by the hand of man, was as he knew it; and that any changes in social and domestic life were such as are based on the duty of loving others and trying to improve the condition of mankind.—PALMER, H. P., 1896, *Selborne and Gilbert White, Temple Bar*, vol. 109, p. 117.

At the top of the Plestor, in cheerful proximity to the living, lies the ancient church-yard about the quaint Norman church where Gilbert White addressed his ordinary parishioners, in distinction from those winged and singing ones, the four-footed ones, and those even who modestly crawled, who all filled up his calm life. The church is a good deal renovated, of necessity; but, with Norman traditions, it is not quite at its ease in the presence of nineteenth-century pews and a nineteenth-century organ. Human beings, however, are pretty much the same, and the little boys are marched out just before the sermon with the same subdued yet hilarious clatter as in the days when those were living and young who now lie in the church-yard under the moss-grown head-stones from which the centuries have softly wiped out the dates. Even the five bell-ropes hanging under the belfry of the church are pulled as they were centuries ago; for as soon as the vicar has pronounced the benediction, five Selborne men grasp the ropes and pull with a will, and the chimes ring into the peaceful landscape. Beside the weather-beaten church-tower stands the venerable tenant of the cemetery, a yew-tree so old that it is respectfully mentioned in the Domesday Book. Tradition gives it twelve hundred years; and amazingly young and vigorous it looks, and its mighty branches make a grateful shade on a summer's day; and, sitting on the bench about its gnarled trunk, somehow one feels that to lie under a lichen-grown stone, with the summer sun beating the waving grass on the gentle slope towards the Lythe, within the sound of a bird singing joyously in the old chest-nut-tree and the passing patter of a child's little feet, might not be the saddest of fates. On the north side of the church lies Gilbert White under a moss-grown head-stone, the long grass swaying lightly, just as he would have wished, with no futile word to praise him. Some one has suggested a nice new monument for the old naturalist—think of it! So far, thank Heaven! his grave has mercifully been spared that fatal honor.—LANE, MRS. JOHN, 1899, *The Home of Gilbert White of Selborne, Lippincott's Magazine, vol.* 64, *p.* 593.

On the 26th an express messenger was sent to Salisbury for Dr. John White. He posted to Selborne at once, but can hardly have found his uncle alive; since on the latter day the White family lost its amiable head; Selborne a highly respected neighbour; and the world a singularly observant and original naturalist. What is the happy life? It is a true, if trite, saying that few men attain their ideal of a career in life; or, having attained it, realise that it is the ideal career. But the man who lay dead at Selborne, fascinated from boyhood by the study of Nature, had longed for life and leisure in his wild, woodland, native country—not from any merely indolent wish to shirk the

responsibilities of life, to cope with which he was by character and attainments amply equipped—of him it may be truly said that he had realised his ideal, and as much as any man had lived a happy life.— HOLT-WHITE, RASHLEIGH, 1901, *The Life and Letters of Gilbert White of Selborne, vol.* II, *p.* 271.

THE NATURAL HISTORY AND AN-TIQUITIES OF SELBORNE
1789

The | Natural History | and | Antiquities | of | Selborne, | in the | County of Southampton: | with | Engravings, and an Appendix. London: | printed by T. Bensley; | for B. White and Son, at Horace's Head, Fleet Street. | M, DCC, LXXXIX. —TITLE PAGE TO FIRST EDITION.

If this author should be thought by any to have been too minute in his researches, be it remembered that his studies have been in the great book of nature. It must be confessed, that the economy of the several kinds of crickets, and the distinction between the stock-dove and the ring-dove, are humble pursuits, and will be esteemed trivial by many; perhaps by some to be objects of ridicule. However, before we condemn any pursuits which contribute so much to health by calling us abroad, let us consider how the studious have employed themselves in their closets. In a former century, the minds of the learned were engaged in determining whether the name of the Roman poet should be spelt Vergilius or Virgilius; and the number of letters in the name of Shakespear still remains a matter of much solicitude and criticism. Nor can we but think that the conjectures about the migration of Hirundines are fully as interesting as the Chattertonian controversy.— WHITE, THOMAS, 1789, *Gentleman's Magazine.*

One of the most delightful books in the English language!— KNIGHT, CHARLES, 1847–48, *Half-Hours with the best Authors.*

No lover of the country or of country-things can pass him by without cordial recognition and genial praise. There is not so much of incident or of adventure in his little book as would suffice to pepper the romances of one issue of a weekly paper in our day. The literary mechanicians would find in him no artful contrivance of parts and no rhetorical jangle of language. It is only good Parson White, who, wandering about the fields and the brook-sides of Selborne, scrutinizes with rare clearness and patience a thousand miracles of God's providence, in trees, in flowers, in stones, in birds,—and jots down the story of his scrutiny with such simplicity, such reverent trust in His power and goodness, such loving fondness for almost every created thing, that the reading of it charms like Walton's story of the fishes. We Americans, indeed, do not altogether recognize his chaffinches and his titlarks; his daws and his fern-owl are strange to us; and his robin-redbreast, though undoubtedly the same which in our nursery-days flitted around the dead "Children in the Wood" . . . Notwithstanding, however, the dissimilarity of species, the studies of this old naturalist are directed with a nice particularity, and are colored with an unaffected homeliness, which are very charming; and I never hear the first whisk of a swallow's wing in summer but I feel an inclination to take down the booklet of the good old Parson, drop into my library-chair, and follow up at my leisure all the gyrations and flutterings and incubations of all the *hirundines* of Selborne. Every country-liver should own the book, and be taught from it—nicety of observation.—MITCH-ELL, DONALD G., 1864, *Wet Days at Edgewood, pp.* 262, 263.

One of the most delightful books in my father's library was White's "Natural History of Selborne." For me it has rather gained in charm with years. I used to read it without knowing the secret of the pleasure I found in it, but as I grow older I begin to detect some of the simple expedients of this natural magic. Open the book where you will, it takes you out of doors. In our broiling July weather one can walk out with this genially garrulous Fellow of Oriel and find refreshment instead of fatigue. You have no trouble in keeping abreast of him as he ambles along on his hobby-horse, now pointing to a pretty view, now stopping to watch the motions of a bird or an insect, or to bag a specimen for the Honourable Daines Barrington or Mr. Pennant. In simplicity of taste and natural refinement he reminds one of Walton; in tenderness toward what he would have called the brute creation, of Cowper. I do not know whether his descriptions of scenery are good or not, but they have made me familiar with his neighborhood. Since I first read him, I have walked over some of his favorite haunts, but I still see them through his eyes rather than by any recollection of actual and personal vision. The book has also the delightfulness of absolute leisure. Mr. White seems never to have had any harder work to do than to study the habits of his feathered fellow-townsfolk, or to watch the ripening of his peaches on the wall. No doubt he looked after the souls of his parishioners with official and even friendly interest, but, I cannot help suspecting, with a less personal solicitude.—LOWELL, JAMES RUSSELL, 1869–90, *My Garden Acquaintance, Prose Works, Riverside ed., vol.* III, *p.* 192.

The work of the Selborne naturalist belongs to the class of books that one must discover for himself: their quality is not patent; he that runs may not read them. Like certain fruits they leave a lingering flavor in the mouth that is much better than the first taste promised. In some congenial mood or lucky moment you find them out. . . . There was no other book of any merit like it for nearly a hundred years. It contains a great deal of good natural history and acute observations upon various rural subjects, put up in a cheap and portable form. The contemporary works of Pennant are voluminous and costly,—heavy sailing-craft that come to port only in the great libraries, while this is a nimble light-draught vessel that has found a harbor on nearly every man's book-shelf. Hence we say that while it is not one of the great books, it is one of the very *real* books, one of the very *live* books, and has met and supplied a tangible want in the English reading world. It does not appeal to a large class of readers, and yet no library is complete without it. It is valuable as a storehouse of facts, it is valuable as a treatise on the art of observing things, and it is valuable for its sweetness and charm of style.—BURROUGHS, JOHN, 1889, *Gilbert White's Book, Indoor Studies, pp.* 162, 164.

White's book has taken possession of the English mind as securely as the "Complete Angler," or even as "Robinson Crusoe." At the distance of a century one may well ask why this is so, and what has given the book its enduring quality.

. . . He was White of Selborne,
not White of Oxford. If natural history
has lost anything by his want of adventure, it has after all gained more; for
the unique value of his book is mainly
due to the persistence with which he
followed his own instinct, and to the
complete ease and isolation in which his
acute mind worked at home. . . .
Though his records are confined to his own
district, White's conception of the work
of the naturalist was as broad and rational
as that of Aristotle. He took mankind
into his view, and nothing escaped him
that was worth recording of the economy,
the superstitions, the language, of the
people who lived around him.—FOWLER,
W. WARDE, 1893, *Gilbert White of Selborne, Macmillan's Magazine, vol.* 68, *pp.*
183, 184, 187.

To the majority of those who do not
know him personally, a perusal of the volume, it is not improbable, would prove
somewhat of a disappointment. For despite the praise it has received and justly
merits, it is a book unlikely to please the
average reader,—the less so if he is not
an ardent orinthologist or zoölogist.
Embracing mineralogy, zoölogy, meteorol-
ogy, orinthology, etomology, and botany,
with constant reference to ætiology, it
may be termed a cyclopædia of English
natural history, presented in epistolary
form. . . . Strictly speaking, Gilbert White was not a poet or an idyllist,
but rather an observer and investigator,
with a strong trend toward science in its
less arid and technical forms. And yet
he possesses an unquestionable charm of
his own, apart from that of a mere scientific recorder,—if the reader be but sympathetic and responsive to the spell. . . .
Yet although he may not be termed an
idyllist, his book deserves to be classed
among country idyls, if only for its reflex
character in having fostered a closer ac-
quaintanceship with outward Nature,—a
work that has paved the way to Jesse,
Kingsley, Thoreau, Jefferies, Burroughs,
and Gibson, and the choir that has hailed
the sun upon the upland lawn. It has
taught when and how to observe, and
made us more responsive to a life that
enters into intimate relationship with our
own. It is as such that White deserves
lasting recognition, apart from his valuable labours as a naturalist during his own
generation. . . . Re-reading "Selborne," one comes to appreciate it the
more, and to perceive in the letters of
the learned Hampshire parson those qualities that one must ever cherish in fond
regard. Its fresh and simple style, its
modest, unassuming grace cling to and
permeate its leaves like the fragrance of
the ferny lanes and shade of the beech-
woods it leads to. To remember it is to
enter a region of rest and quietude, with
nothing more important than to watch the
churn-owl's flight and hearken to the
cricket's cry. And if read in the right
mood, it will, after all, seem eminently
deserving of being classed among rustic
idyllia, and returned to the library shelves
to be enshrined with Theocritus and "The
Georgics."— ELLWANGER, GEORGE H.,
1895, *Idyllists of the Country-Side, pp.*
48, 52, 54, 80.

His seeing eye and gentle heart are
imaged in his fresh and happy style.—
BROOKE, STOPFORD A., 1896, *English
Literature, p.* 200.

That White's "Selborne" is the only
work on natural history which has attained
the rank of an English classic is admitted
by general acclamation, as well as by
competent critics, and numerous have
been the attempts to discover the secret
of its ever-growing reputation. Scarcely
two of them agree, and no explanation
whatever offered of the charm which invests it can be accepted as in itself satisfactory. If we grant what is partially
true, and that it was the first book of its
kind to appear in this country, and therefore had no rivals to encounter before its
reputation was established, we find that
alone insufficient to account for the way
in which it is still welcomed by thousands
of readers, to many of whom—and this
especially applies to its American admirers—scarcely a plant or an animal mentioned in it is familiar, or even known
but by name. White was a prince among
observers, nearly always observing the
right thing in the right way, and placing
before us in a few words the living being
he observed. Of the hundreds of statements recorded by White, the number
which are undoubtedly mistaken may be
counted almost on the fingers of one
hand. . . . In addition White was
"a scholar and a gentleman," and a philosopher of no mean depth. But it seems

as though the combination of all these qualities would not necessarily give him the unquestioned superiority over all other writers in the same field. The secret of the charm must be sought elsewhere; but it has been sought in vain. Some have ascribed it to his way of identifying himself in feeling with the animal kingdom, though to this sympathy there were notable exceptions. Some, like Lowell, set down the "natural magic" of White to the fact that, "open the book where you will, it takes you out of doors," but the same is to be said of other writers who yet remain comparatively undistinguished. White's style, a certain stiffness characteristic of the period being admitted, is eminently unaffected, even when he is "didactic," as he more than once apologises for becoming, and the same simplicity is observable in his letters to members of his family, which could never have been penned with the view of publication, and have never been retouched. Then, too, there is the complete absence of self-importance or self-consciousness. The observation or the remark stands on its own merit, and gains nothing because he happens to be the maker of it, except it be in the tinge of humour that often delicately pervades it. The beauties of the work, apart from the way in which they directly appeal to naturalists, as they did to Darwin, grow upon the reader who is not a naturalist, as Lowell testifies, and the more they are studied the more they seem to detect analysis.—NEWTON, ALFRED, 1900, *Dictionary of National Biography, vol.* LXI, *p.* 45.

I have pondered a hundred times on the wonderful fact that the world should take such a heart-felt interest in the work of a retiring and modest eighteenth-century clergyman! . . . Apart from Westminster Abbey, Windsor Castle, and other places of historical interest in the British Islands, there is probably no place, save Stratford-on-Avon, to which the pilgrims of the Anglo-Saxon race render more respectful tribute than to the lowly headstone which marks the grave of Gilbert White of Selborne. The occupant of that simple grass-grown grave would probably have been the most astonished of all people in the world could he have realized that his celebrity as an Englishman would have come near to equalling that of

Shakespeare; and yet there exists at the present date as much affection, among naturalists at least, for the sayings and doings of Gilbert White as is felt for the records of Shakespeare and his time.— SHARPE, R. BOWDLER, 1901, *ed., The Natural History and Antiquities of Selborne.*

GENERAL

A | Naturalist's Calendar, | with | Observations in various branches | of | Natural History; | extracted from the papers | of the late | Rev. Gilbert White, M. A. | of Selborne, Hampshire, | Senior Fellow of Oriel College, Oxford. | Never before published. | London: | printed for B. and J. White, Horace's Head, | Fleet Street. | 1795.—TITLE PAGE TO FIRST EDITION.

His Diaries were kept with unremitting diligence; and in his annual migrations to Oriel College, and other places, his man Thomas, who seems to have been well qualified for the office, recorded the weather journal. The state of the thermometer, barometer, and the variations of the wind are noted as well as the quantity of rain which fell. We have daily accounts of the weather, whether hot or cold, sunny or cloudy: we have, also information of the first tree in leaf, and even of the appearance of the first fungi, and of the plants first in blossom. We are told when mosses vegetate, and when insects first appear and disappear. There are also remarks with regard to fish and other animals; with miscellaneous observations and memoranda on various subjects. For instance, we are told that on the 21st of June, house-martins, which had laid their eggs in an old nest, had hatched them, and that when this is the case they get the start of those that build new ones by ten days or a fortnight. He speaks with some degree of triumph to having ricked his meadow hay in *delicate* order, and that Thomas had seen a pole-cat run across his garden. He records the circumstance of boys playing at *taw* on the Plestor; and that he had set *Gunnery*, one of his bantam hens, on nine of her own eggs. He complains that dogs come in to his garden at night and eat his goose-berries, and gives a useful hint to farmers and others, when he says that rooks and crows destroy an immense number of chaffers, and that were it not for these birds the chaffers would destroy everything. . . . Insignificant as these little details may appear, they were not thought to be so by a man whose mind was evidently stored with considerable learning, who possessed a cultivated and elegant taste for what is beautiful in nature, and who has left behind him one of the most delightful works in the English language,—a work which will be read as long as that language lasts, and which is equally remarkable for its extreme accuracy, its pleasing style, and the agreeable and varied information it contains.— JESSE, EDWARD, 1849, *ed., The Natural History of Selborne, Biography, pp.* xv, xvii.

He had a wide range of knowledge, he was the master of a good Latin style, and he knew the literature of his country well, having an extensive acquaintance with it, and a keen perception of its spirit. It is very pleasant when the old naturalist stops to point a reflection with a line from the Latin or the British poets.—NADEL, E. S., 1877, *White of Selborne, Scribner's Monthly, vol.* XIII, *p.* 506.

Who that lives in this busy, noisy age has not envied the lot of Gilbert White, watching with keen, quiet eyes the little world of Selborne for more than fifty uneventful years? To a mind so tranquil and a spirit so serene the comings and goings of the old domesticated turtle in the garden were more important than the debates in Parliament. The pulse of the world beat slowly in the secluded hamlet, and the roar of change and revolution, beyond the Channel were only faintly echoed across the peaceful hills. The methodical observer had as much leisure as Nature herself, and could wait patiently on the moods of the seasons for those confidences which he always invited, but which he never forced; and there grew up a somewhat platonic but very loyal friendship between him and the beautiful rural world about him. How many days of happy observation were his, and with what a sense of leisure his discoveries were set down in English as devoid of artifice or strain or the fever of haste as the calm movements of the seasons registered there! There was room for enjoyment in a life so quietly ordered; time for meditation and for getting acquainted with one's self. — MABIE, HAMILTON WRIGHT, 1894, *My Study Fire, Second Series, p.* 23.

White may be regarded as the founder of a new branch of English literature, and few of those who have followed him have had so much to tell, or have succeeded in conveying so much in so short a space. In the narration of the features of events so as to give a clear idea of the details, as well as of the whole, White, in the natural world, shows skill comparable to that of Cowper in the description of his domestic circle and its incidents. The letters of White are less numerous and briefer than those of Cowper, and of somewhat less literary power, but they have the same kind of merit, and while making clear what the writer saw, unconsciously furnish a portrait of his own mind.—MOORE, NORMAN, 1895, *English Prose, ed. Craik, vol.* IV, *p.* 247.

Gilbert White strikes us at first only by his homeliness and simplicity, by his lucid and unpretentious narrative, by the sincerity and piety of his unwearied study of nature. But in truth the scholar never forgets his books. The simplicity is the effect of the highest art; his narrative impresses us because it is arranged with the skill of a trained thinker, who never allows his induction to be slovenly or inexact, who knows exactly how to buttress a theory with an unassuming anecdote, and who can bring a scientific reminiscence, or a recondite classification, into the midst of the homely story of some everyday incident.—CRAIK, HENRY, 1895, *English Prose, Introduction, vol.* IV, *p.* 8.

Books he shall read in hill and tree;
    The flowers his weather shall portend.
The birds his moralists shall be,
    And everything his friend.
—COURTHOPE, W. J., 1900, *Gilbert White.*

Not an aspect or a mood of Nature passed him unnoted, and each, marked by a feature of importance, was stamped with minute particularity upon his retentive memory. There was an incessant gathering of incessant facts which had not before been reported for the benefit of science at large. The gentle curate had no means of measuring the value of his investigations. He was following the bent of his inclinations in single-heartedness and purity of aim. Love set him on to the work, and the honesty of his mind kept him true to the performance of it.— HUBBARD, SARA A., 1901, *Gilbert White of Selborne, The Dial, vol.* 30, *p.* 304.

William Robertson

1721-1793

Born, at Borthwick, Midlothian, 19 Sept., 1721. Early education at Borthwick parish school and at Dalkeith Grammar School. To Edinburgh Univ., 1733. Licensed by Presbytery as preacher, June, 1741. Minister of Gladsmuir, 1743. Served in volunteers against Pretender's army, 1745. Mem. of General Assembly, 1746. Married Mary Nisbet, 1751. Part ed. of "Edinburgh Rev.," 1755. Visit to London, 1758. Minister of Lady Yester's Chapel, Edinburgh, June 1758 to April 1761. Created D. D., Edinburgh, 1758. Chaplain of Stiring Castle, 1759. Minister of Old Greyfriars, Edinburgh, April, 1761. Chaplain to the King, Aug. 1761. Principal of Edinburgh Univ., 1762-92. Moderator of General Assembly, 1763-80. Mem. of Royal Acad. of History, Madrid, Aug. 1777. Mem. of Acad. of Science, Padua, 1781. Mem. of Imperial Acad., St. Petersburg, 1783. Historiographer for Scotland, 6 Aug. 1783. Died at Grange House, near Edinburgh, 11 June, 1793. *Works:* "The Situation of the World at the time of Christ's Appearance," 1755; "History of Scotland" (2 vols.), 1759; "History of the Reign of the Emperor Charles V." (3 vols.), 1769; "History of America" (2 vols.), 1777; "Historical Disquisition concerning the Knowledge which the Ancients had of India," 1791. *Collected Works:* in 12 vols., ed. by Dugald Stewart, with *memoir*, 1817; in 11 vols., ed. by R. A. Davenport, with *memoir*, 1824.—SHARP, R. FARQUHARSON, 1897, *A Dictionary of English Authors, p.* 240.

PERSONAL

His speeches in church courts were admired by those whom they did not convince, and acquired and preserved him an influence over a majority in them, which none before him enjoyed: though his measures were sometimes new, and warmly, and with great strength of argument opposed, both from the press, and in the general assembly. To this influence many causes contributed: his firm adherence to the general principles of church policy, which he early adopted; his sagacity in forming plans; his steadiness in executing them; his quick discernment of whatever might hinder or promote his designs; his boldness in encountering difficulties; his presence of mind in improving every occasional advantage; the address with which, when he saw it necessary, he could make an honorable retreat; and his skill in stating a vote, and seizing the favorable moment for ending a debate, and urging a decision. He guided and governed others, without seeming to assume any superiority over them. . . . Deliberate in forming his judgment, but, when formed, not easily moved to renounce it, he sometimes viewed the altered plans of others with too suspicious an eye. Hence, there were able and worthy men, of whom he expressed himself less favorably, and whose latter appearances in church judicatories, he censured as inconsistent with principles which they had formerly professed; while they maintained, that the system of managing church affairs was changed, not their opinions or conduct. Still, however, keen and determined opposition to his schemes of ecclesiastical policy, neither extinguished his esteem, nor forfeited his friendly offices, when he saw opposition carried on without rancor, and when he believed that it originated from conscience and principle, not from personal animosity, or envy, or ambition.— ERSKINE, JOHN, 1793, *Funeral Sermon, Discourses, p.* 271.

He delighted in good-natured, characteristical anecdotes of his acquaintance, and added powerfully to their effect by his own enjoyment in relating them. He was, in a remarkable degree, susceptible of the ludicrous; but, on no occasion did he forget the dignity of his character, or the decorum of his profession; nor did he even lose sight of that classical taste which adorned his compositions. His turn of expression was correct and pure; sometimes, perhaps, inclining more than is expected in the carelessness of a social hour, to formal and artificial periods; but it was stamped with his own manner no less than his premediated style: it was always the language of a superior and a cultivated mind, and it embellished every subject on which he spoke. In the company of strangers, he increased his exertions to amuse and to inform; and the splendid variety of his conversation was commonly the chief circumstance on which they dwelt in enumerating his talents; and yet, I must acknowledge, for my own part, that, much as I always admired his powers when they were thus called forth, I enjoyed his society less, than when I saw him in the circle of his intimates, or in the bosom of his family. . . . In point of stature Dr. Robertson was rather above the middle size; and his form though it did not convey the idea of much activity, announced vigor of body and a healthful constitution. His features were regular and manly; and his eye spoke at once good sense and good humor. He appeared to greatest advantage in his complete clerical dress; and was more remarkable for gravity and dignity in discharging the functions of his public stations, than for ease or grace in private society.—STEWART, DUGALD, 1796–1801, *Account of the Life and Writings of William Robertson.*

The history of the author is the history of the individual, excepting as regards his private life and his personal habits: these were in the most perfect degree dignified and pure. Without anything of harshness or fanaticism, he was rationally pious and blamelessly moral. His conduct, both as a christian minister, as a member of society, as a relation, and as a friend, was wholly without a stain. His affections were warm; they were ever under control, and therefore equal and steady. . . . His conversation was cheerful, and it was varied. Vast information, copious anecdote, perfect appositeness of illustration,—narration or description wholly free from pedantry or stiffness, but as felicitous and as striking as might be expected from such a master, —great liveliness, and often wit, and often humour, with a full disposition to enjoy the merriment of the hour, but the most scrupulous absence of every thing like coarseness of any description,—these formed the staples of his talk. . . . His very decided opinions on all subjects of public interest, civil and religious, never interrupted his friendly and familiar intercourse with those who held different principles. . . . His manner was not graceful in little matters, though his demeanour was dignified on the whole. —BROUGHAM, HENRY LORD, 1845–6, *Lives of Men of Letters of the Time of George III.*

Dr. Robertson was a Christian in character, and therefore a gentleman in his manners; he did not think himself bound to treat an unbeliever, who never insulted his faith, as a profane and graceless enemy of man. Though he was firm, or perhaps we should say *because* he was firm, in his own conviction, he could look upon one whose opinions were different without the least feeling of hatred and revenge; in which respects he had the advantage of some over-zealous Christians, both in the peace and happiness of his own temper, and in the influence he exerted to bring unbelieving wanderers home.—PEABODY, W. B. O., 1845, *Brougham's Lives of Men of Letters and Science, North American Review, vol.* 61, *p.* 405.

Principal Robertson and his family were very intimate with the family of my father. . . . He was a pleasant-looking old man; with an eye of great vivacity and intelligence, a large, projecting chin, a small hearing-trumpet fastened by a black ribbon to a button-hole of his coat, and a rather large wig, powdered and curled. He struck us boys, even from the side-table, as being evidently fond of a good dinner, at which he sat with his chin near his plate, intent upon the real business of the occasion. This appearance, however, must have been produced partly by his deafness; because, when his eye told him that there was something interesting, it was delightful to observe the animation with which he instantly applied his trumpet, when, having caught the scent, he followed it up, and was the leader of the pack.—COCKBURN, HENRY LORD, 1854–56, *Memorials of his Time, ch.* I

On 26 May 1763 he was elected moderator of the general assembly, the administration of which he continued to direct with a firm hand for upwards of sixteen years. As a manager of the business of the general assembly, he acquired an influence greater than any moderator since Andrew Melville. By him were laid the foundations of that system of polity—the independence of the church as opposed to a fluctuating dependence upon the supposed views of the government of the day, the exaction of obedience by the inferior judicatories, and the enforcement of the law of patronage, except in flagrant cases of erroneous doctrine or immoral conduct—by means of which peace and unity were preserved in the

Scottish church until a new principle was established by the assembly of 1834. Despite a zealous and able opposition, Robertson's statemanship, skill as a debater, and high character gave him paramount influence over "the moderates," and rendered his power over all parties irresistible. . . . In Robertson's as in Gibbons domestic life, pomposity was but skin deep. . . . He was very fond of claret.— SECCOMBE, THOMAS, 1896, *Dictionary of National Biography, vol.* XLVIII, *pp.* 427, 429.

Dr. Robertson lived till he became Principal in a house at the head of the Cowgate, now the most squalid of Edinburgh squalid districts. There he kept boarders, like most city ministers and professors in those impecunious days, for English noblemen were in the habit of sending their sons to Edinburgh for the efficient and sedate college training they could not get at Oxford or Cambridge. In society he was prominent, as befitted his position of importance. Courteous and pleasing, with his bland and intelligent face and keen eyes, his presence gave an air of propriety to any company, as he sat in his well-fitting garments, his prim clerical bands, his legs crossed, displaying the neatest of silver-buckled shoes. His talk, agreeable but rather too instructive, came forth in strong Scots tongue, with a fluency which at times was too flowing for those who wished to speak as well as he. Friends rather resented his propensity, which increased with years, to lead the talk, and they murmured that whenever the cloth was removed after dinner and the wine appeared on the shining mahogany, the doctor would settle himself with deliberation in his chair, introduce some topic, and discourse thereon till general talk ceased. He would take the opinions and thoughts that his friends uttered yesterday and present them in elegant paraphrase—"the greatest plagiary in conversation that I ever knew," says "Jupiter" Carlyle. His admiring biographer, Dugald Stewart, hints delicately at such colloquial defects, speaking of "his formal and artificial periods, the language of a strong and superior mind, which embellished every subject." —GRAHAM, HENRY GREY, 1901, *Scottish Men of Letters in the Eighteenth Century, p.* 92.

THE SITUATION OF THE WORLD AT THE TIME OF CHRIST'S APPEARANCE
1755

This sermon, the only one he ever published, has been long ranked, in both parts of the Island, among the best models of pulpit eloquence in our language. It has undergone five editions, and is well known, in some parts of the continent, in the German translation of Mr. Ebeling.— STEWART, DUGALD, 1796–1801, *Account of the Life and Writings of William Robertson.*

This view of the question may derive confirmation, or at least illustration, from comparing Gibbon's two chapters with Dr. Robertson's "Sermon on the state of the world at the time of the appearance of Christ." The sound and rational observations of the reverend historian on certain facilities afforded to the diffusion of the gospel by the previous state of the public mind, and of public affairs, in the hands of Gibbon, or of any other author more disposed to sneer than to argue candidly on such subjects, would admit of a perversion nearly similar to that given to the accidental causes which he has enumerated; while several of Gibbon's natural causes, changing the offensive language in which they are conveyed, might fairly have been expounded, as perfectly true and efficient, from any pulpit.— MACKINTOSH, SIR JAMES, 1805, *Journal, April* 25; *Life, ed. Mackintosh, vol.* I, *ch.* v, *note.*

The subject of the sermon is one peculiarly suited to his habits of inquiry. . . . The merits of this piece, as a sermon, are very great; and it is admirable as an historical composition, in that department which Voltaire first extended to all the records of past times. It was written and published before the appearance of the "Essai sur les Mœurs," though as has been already said, detached portions of that work had appeared in a Paris periodical work.—BROUGHAM, HENRY LORD, 1845–6, *Lives of Men of Letters of the Time of George III.*

HISTORY OF SCOTLAND
1759

David Hume so far indulged my patience as to allow me to carry to the country during the holidays the loose sheets which he happened to have by him. In that condition I read it quite through with the greatest satisfaction, and in much less time than I ever employed on any portion of history of the same length. . . . Your work will certainly be ranked in the highest historical class; and, for my own part, I think it, besides, a composition of uncommon genius and eloquence.—ELLIOT, GILBERT, 1759, *Letter to Dr. Robertson, Jan. 20th.*

I have not heard of one who does not praise it warmly. . . . Must fatigue your ears, as much as ours are in this place [London] by endless and repeated and noisy praises of the "History of Scotland." . . . Mallet told me that Lord Mansfield is at a loss whether he shall most esteem the matter or the style. Elliot told me, that being in company with George Grenville, that gentleman was speaking loud in the same key. . . . Lord Lyttelton seems to think that since the time of St. Paul there scarce has been a better writer than Dr. Robertson. Mr. Walpole triumphs in the success of his favourites the Scotch.—HUME, DAVID, 1759, *Letter to Robertson.*

Having finished the first volume, and made a little progress in the second, I cannot stay till I have finished the latter to tell you how exceedingly I admire the work. . . . In short, Sir, I don't know where or what history is written with more excellences; and when I say this, you may be sure I do not forget your impartiality.—WALPOLE, HORACE, 1759, *To Dr. Robertson; Letters, ed. Cunningham, vol.* III, *p.* 202.

Upon my word, I was never more entertained in all my life; and, though I read it aloud to a friend and Mrs. Garrick, I finished the three first books at two sittings. I could not help writing to Millar and congratulating him upon this great acquisition to his literary treasures.—GARRICK, DAVID, 1759, *Letter to Dr. Robertson.*

I have received and read with great pleasure the new "History of Scotland," and will not wait for the judgment of the public to pronounce it a very excellent work. From the author's apparent love of civil and religious liberty, I suppose, that were it not for fear of offence (which every wise man in his situation would fear to give) he would have spoken with much more freedom of the hierarchical principles of the infant church of Scotland.— WARBURTON, WILLIAM, 1759, *Letter to Mr. Millar.*

I am very proud of being instrumental in contributing to the translation [by J. B. Suard], of the valuable work you are going to publish. The excellent work you have published already is a sure sign of the reception your "History of Charles V." will meet with in the continent.—D'HOL-BACH, BARON, 1768, *Letter to Dr. Robertson, May* 30.

The fourteenth edition of your "Scotland" will be published in the course of the winter, during which it is our intention to advertise all your works strongly in all the papers. And we have the satisfaction of informing you that, if we may judge by the sale of your writings, your literary reputation is daily increasing.— STRAHAN, ANDREW, 1792, *To Dr. Robertson, Nov.* 19.

I think the merit of Robertson consists in a certain even and well-supported tenour of good sense and elegance. There is a formality and demureness in his manner, his elegance has a primness, and his dignity a stiffness, which remind one of the politeness of an old maid of quality standing on all her punctilios of propriety and prudery. These peculiarities are most conspicuous in his introductory book. As we advance, his singular power of interesting narrative prevails over every defect. His reflections are not uncommon; his views of character and society imply only sound sense. . . . During the trial of Dustergool, my mind was full of Mary, Queen of Scots, in whose history I had just read, for the thousandth time, efforts more successful than those of the Armenian Mary, by a vicious and beautiful wife, to murder a bad husband. As soon as Mary gets into England, Robertson is tempted, by the interest of his story, into constant partiality to her. Her abilities are exaggerated to make her story more romantic: she was a weak girl of elegant accomplishments.—MACKINTOSH, SIR JAMES, 1811, *Journal, July* 13 *and* 16, *Life, vol.* II, *ch.* ii.

His "History of Scotland" is doubtless, by far, the most popular history extant. —DIBDIN, THOMAS FROGNALL, 1824, *The Library Companion, note, p.* 271.

The "History of Scotland," the only one of his works which approaches the perfect plan of a history, is the best of his productions, the most interesting, and the most naturally written. Although he asserts that he was ten years engaged on it, the size of the work would hardly seem to require so much labor. It hardly exceeds nine hundred pages octavo, and in order to swell it to two volumes he was obliged to add, afterwards, by a few months' labor, a large body of notes. He was always fond of referring to many authorities, and was careful in his researches; yet he seldom discovered any new facts and does little more than relate gracefully the more interesting portions of a well-known narrative.—LAWRENCE, EUGENE, 1855, *The Lives of the British Historians, vol.* I, *p.* 360.

In the following year, the reading public—especially the literary men of London—were electrified by the appearance of "A History of Scotland" from this unknown minister's pen. Dealing with the reigns of Mary Stuart and her son, down to the accession of the latter to the English throne, he described, in pure, pathetic, and dignified language, the sorrows of that wretched Scotchwoman with a French soul, who saw so little of Holyrood and so much of English jails. He stands midway between those who believe her to have been a beautiful martyr, and those who brand her as a beautiful criminal. Agreeing with all writers as to the great loveliness of this beheaded Scottish queen, he considers that the intensity and long continuance of the sorrows, darkening over her whole life until the bloody catastrophe of Fotheringay, have blinded us to her faults, and that we therefore "approve of our tears, as if they were shed for a person who had attained much nearer to pure virtue."— COLLIER, WILLIAM FRANCIS, 1861, *A History of English Literature, p.* 330.

Notwithstanding the immense materials which have been brought to light since the time of Robertson, his "History of Scotland" is still vauable; because he possessed a grasp of mind which enabled him to embrace general views, that escape ordinary compilers, however industrious they may be.—BUCKLE, HENRY THOMAS, 1862–66, *History of Civilization in England, vol.* III, *ch.* I, *note.*

Hume criticised some peculiarities of Robertson's vocabulary. But, after all deductions, the purity of Robertson's English cannot be seriously impugned. He modelled his style upon Swift, after exhaustively studying that of Livy and Tactius. By way of practice in the writing of English he had, long before the appearance of his "History," prepared a translation of Marcus Aurelius, the manuscript of which belonged to Lord Brougham. Later and more exhaustive methods of research have deprived Robertson's "History" of most of its historical value. But its sobriety, fairness, and literary character give it a permanent interest to a student of the evolution of historical composition.—SECCOMBE, THOMAS, 1896, *Dictionary of National Biography, vol.* XLVIII, *p.* 426.

CHARLES V.
1769

I got yesterday from Strahan about thirty sheets of your history to be sent over to Suard. . . . To say only that they are very well written is by far too faint an expression, and much inferior to the sentiments I feel: they are composed with nobleness, with dignity, with elegance, and with judgment to which there are few equals. They even excel, and, I think, in a sensible degree, your "History of Scotland." I propose to myself great pleasure in being the only man in England during some months who will be in the situation of doing you justice, after which you may certainly expect that my voice will be drowned in that of the public.—HUME, DAVID, 1769, *Letter to Dr. Robertson.*

I think that the historian of Mary, Queen of Scots, cannot fail to do justice to any great subject. . . . Go on, dear sir, to enrich the English language with more traits of modern history.— LYTTELTON, LORD, 1769, *Letter to Dr. Robertson.*

Robertson is your Livy; his "Charles V." is written with truth.—VOLTAIRE, FRANÇOIS MARIE AROUET, 1778? *Martin Sherlock's Letters from an English Traveller.*

Finished the 1st vol. of Robertson's "Charles the Fifth," obeying the references to proofs and illustrations. I am confounded at the immense researches which furnished material for this preliminary volume.—GREEN, THOMAS, 1779–1810, *Diary of a Lover of Literature.*

Robertson, if he had applied to Monsieur Gerard of Brussels, keeper of the archives, and many other persons in the Austrian Netherlands, might have procured documents and information which would have rendered the "History of Italy" something more than a bare splendid relation of facts already known to every common historical reader.—THICKNESSE, PHILIP, 1792? *Journey through the Austrian Netherlands, vol.* III, *p.* 53.

In no part of Dr. Robertson's works has he displayed more remarkably than in this introductory volume, his patience in research; his penetration and good sense in selecting his information; or that comprehension of mind, which, without being misled by system, can combine with distinctness and taste the dry and scattered details of ancient monuments. In truth, this dissertation, under the unassuming title of an Introduction to the "History of Charles V." may be regarded as an introduction to the History of Modern Europe. It is invaluable, in this respect, to the historical student; and it suggests, in every page, matter of speculation to the politician and the philosopher.— STEWART, DUGALD, 1796–1801, *Account of the Life and Writings of William Robertson.*

The subject of private warfare is treated so exactly and perspicuously by Robertson, that I should only waste the reader's time by dwelling so long upon it as its extent and importance would otherwise demand. Few leading passages in the monuments of the middle ages, relative to this subject, have escaped the penetrating eye of that historian; and they are arranged so well as to form a comprehensive treatise in small compass.—HALLAM, HENRY, 1818–48, *View of the State of Europe During the Middle Ages, ch.* II, *pt.* II, *note.*

Robertson's State of Europe in his "Charles the Fifth" is another of my great favourites; it contains an epitome of information. Such works . . . are the railroads to learning.—BYRON, LORD, 1823–34, *Countess of Blessington's Conversations with Byron.*

Robertson received four thousand and five hundred pounds for the "History of Charles V.;" and it is no disrespect to the memory of Robertson to say that the "History of Charles V." is both a less valuable and a less amusing book than the "Lives of the Poets." — MACAULAY, THOMAS BABINGTON, 1843, *Samuel Johnson, Critical and Historical Essays.*

The first volume of his "Charles V." may justly be regarded as the greatest step which the human mind had yet made in the philosophy of history. Extending his views beyond the admirable survey which Montesquieu had given of the rise and decline of the Roman Empire, he aimed at giving a view of the *progress of society* in modern times.—ALISON, SIR ARCHIBALD, 1844, *Guizot, Blackwood's Magazine, vol.* 56, *p.* 790.

For the "History of Charles V." Robertson received £4500, then supposed to be the largest sum ever paid for the copyright of a single work.—CURWEN, HENRY, 1873, *A History of Booksellers, p.* 66.

"A View of the Progress of Society in Europe, from the Subversion of the Roman Empire to the Beginning of the Sixteenth Century." 8vo., Edinburgh, 1818. This volume is properly an introduction to the author's "History of the Reign of the Emperor Charles V.," and is usually to be found in the various editions of that work. This was perhaps the first really philosophical view of the Middle Ages ever written. In calmness of judgment, in breadth of scholarship, and in comprehensiveness of treatment it still has no superior among the shorter treatises on the Middle Ages. . . . The "proofs and illustrations" form nearly half of the whole volume, and are not the least important and interesting portion of the work. They abound in facts of the utmost interest and importance. It is difficult to discriminate against any portion of this excellent piece of historical writing; but the first and the third section will be found by most students more interesting, if not more valuable than the third.—ADAMS, CHARLES KENDALL, 1882, *A Manual of Historical Literature, pp.* 156, 157.

In 1769 he issued the three volumes of his "History of the Reign of Charles V.," one of the best paid pieces of literary labour ever undertaken by a human pen, and this was followed by several historical works of minor importance. Robertson was not more impressed than Hume with the necessity of close, independent, and impartial research, but he was no less graceful in style, and he diffused over his best work an even milder radiance of philosophic reflection. Hume and Robertson are strangely alike as historians. Neither descends the hill to survey the country at his feet, but each has exceedingly long sight, and the power of taking wide and harmonious Pisgah-views from his self-adopted eminence. Robertson, however, is certainly superior to Hume in his skill in making general estimates of history. It is not the least of Robertson's claims to our consideration that the opening chapters of his "Charles V." had the effect of awakening a historic sense in the childhood of Carlyle, supplying him with "new worlds of knowledge, vistas in all directions."—GOSSE, EDMUND, 1888, *A History of Eighteenth Century Literature, p.* 304.

His "History of the Emperor Charles V." is written with a general sagacity of truth which is hardly affected by several faulty details.—ROBERTSON, J. LOGIE, 1894, *A History of English Literature, p.* 239.

HISTORY OF AMERICA
1777

I could not go through your work at one breath at that time, though I have done it since. I am now enabled to thank you, not only for the honor you have done me, but for the great satisfaction, and the infinite variety and compass of instruction I have received from your incomparable work. Everything has been done which was so naturally to be expected from the author of the "History of Scotland," and of the age of Charles V. I believe few books have done more than this, towards clearing up dark points, correcting errors, and removing prejudices. You have too the rare secret of rekindling an interest on subjects that had so often been treated, and in which every thing which could feed a vital flame appeared to have been consumed. I am sure I read many parts of your history with that fresh concern and anxiety which attend those who are not previously apprised of the event. You have besides, thrown quite a new light on the present state of the Spanish provinces, and furnished both materials and hints for a rational theory of what may be expected from them in future. The part which I read with the greatest pleasure is, the discussion on the manners and character of the inhabitants of that New World. I have always thought with you that we possess at this time very great advantages towards the knowledge of human nature. We need no longer go to history to trace it in all stages and periods.—BURKE, EDMUND, 1777, *Letter to Dr. Robertson.*

I have seen enough to convince me that the present publication will support, and, if possible, extend the fame of the author ; that the materials are collected with care, and arranged with skill ; that the progress of discovery is displayed with learning and perspicuity ; that the dangers, the achievements, and the views [?] of the Spanish adventurers, are related with a temperate spirit ; and that the most original, perhaps the most curious portion of human manners is at length rescued from the hands of sophists and declaimers.—GIBBON, EDWARD, 1777, *Letter to Robertson, July* 14.

After all, however, the principal charm of this, as well as of his other histories, arises from the graphical effect of his narrative, wherever his subject affords him materials for an interesting picture. What force and beauty of painting in his circumstantial details of the new voyage of Columbus; of the first aspect of the new Continent; and of the interviews of the natives with the Spanish adventurers ! With what animation and fire does he follow the steps of Cortes through the varying fortunes of his vast and hazardous career ; yielding, it must be owned, somewhat too much to the influence of the passions which his hero felt ; but bestowing, at the same time, the warm tribute of admiration and sympathy on the virtues and fate of those whom he subdued ! The arts, the institutions, and the manners of Europe and of America ; but above all, the splendid characters of Cortes and of Guatimozin, enable him, in this part of his work, to add to its other attractions that of the finest contrasts which occur in history.—STEWART, DUGALD, 1796–1801, *Account of the Life and Writings of William Robertson.*

Robertson. . . . in what he calls his "History of America," is guilty of such omissions and consequent misrepresentations as to make it certain that he had not read some of the most important documents to which he refers, or that he did not chuse to notice the facts which are to be found there, because they were not in conformity to his own preconceived opinions. . . . The reputation of this author must rest upon his "History of Scotland." . . . if that can support it. His other works are grievously deficient.—SOUTHEY, ROBERT, 1810, *History of Brazil, vol.* I, *p.* 639.

Robertson's "History of America," admirable for the sagacity with which it has been compiled; but too much abridged in the part relating to the Toltecks and Aztecks.-HUMBOLDT, FRIEDRICH HEINRICH ALEXANDER, 1814–34, *Researches in America, vol.* II, *p.* 248.

Robertson's "History of America," published in 1777, is entirely unequal to the claims it makes. Simancas was closed to him, and the admirable collection at the Lonja of Seville was not yet imagined, so that he had not the materials needful for his task; besides which, his plan was not only too vast, but, in its separate parts, was ill proportioned and ill adjusted.—DUYCKINCK, EVERT A., AND GEORGE L., 1855–75, *Cyclopædia of American Literature, ed. Simons, vol.* I, *p.* 977.

After receiving the warm approbation of the Royal Academy of History at Madrid, was about to be translated into Spanish, when the Government, not wishing their American administration to be brought under discussion, interfered with a prohibition.—ARNOLD, THOMAS, 1862–87, *A Manual of English Literature, p.* 285.

The "History of America" is accurate but dull. He has none of the qualifications of an excellent historian. He keeps up the dignity of history, and never descends from his stilts. His style is sonorous, dignified, and sometimes very eloquent.—EMERY, FRED PARKER, 1891, *Notes on English Literature, p.* 74.

His "History of America" must always remain a classic.—ROBERTSON, J. LOGIE, 1894, *A History of English Literature, p.* 239.

Its vivid descriptions and philosophical disquisitions on aboriginal society captivated the literary world, while the outbreak of the American war lent the book pertinent public interest and rendered it more popular than either of its predecessors. Keats, who read it with enthusiasm many years after, owed to it the suggestion of his famous simile of "Cortez and his men." — SECCOMBE, THOMAS, 1896, *Dictionary of National Biography, vol.* XLVIII, *p.* 428.

HISTORY OF INDIA
1791

Dr. Robertson's book amused me pretty well, madam, though very defective from the hiatuses in his materials. It is a genealogy with more than half the middle descents wanting; and thence his ingenious hypothesis of Western invaders importing civilization from the East is not ascertained. Can one be sure a peer is descended from a very ancient peer of the same name, though he cannot prove who a dozen of his grandfathers were?—WALPOLE, HORACE, 1791, *To the Countess of Ossory, Nov.* 23; *Letters, ed. Cunningham, vol.* IX, *p.* 361.

Nothing can be more unjust than the notion that this work is so incorrect, or grounded on information so imperfect, as to have been superseded by more full and accurate books since published. It is, from its accuracy, its knowledge of the ancient writings, its judicious reasoning and remarks, as well as its admirable composition, quite worthy of a place by the author's former and more celebrated writings; and it proves his great faculties to have continued in their entire vigour to the latest period of his life.—BROUGHAM, HENRY LORD, 1845–6, *Lives of Men of Letters of the Time of George III.*

GENERAL

BOSWELL. "Will you not admit the superiority of Robertson, in whose 'History' we find such penetration—such painting?" JOHNSON. "Sir, you must consider how that penetration and that painting are employed. It is not history, it is imagination. He who describes what he never saw, draws from fancy. Robertson paints minds as Sir Joshua paints faces in a history-piece: he imagines an heroic countenance. You must look upon Robertson's work as romance, and try it by that standard. History it is not. Besides, Sir, it is the great excellence of a writer to put into his book as much as his book will hold. Goldsmith has done this in his "History." Now Robertson might have put twice as much into his book. Robertson is like a man who has packed gold in wool: the wool takes up more room than the gold. No, Sir; I always thought Robertson would be crushed by his own weight,—would be buried under his own ornaments. Goldsmith tells you shortly all you want to know: Robertson detains you a great deal too long. No man will read Robertson's cumbrous detail a second time; but Goldsmith's plain narrative will please again and again. I would say to Robertson what an old tutor of a college said to one of his pupils: 'Read over your compositions, and whenever you meet with a passage which you think is particularly fine, strike it out.' —JOHNSON, SAMUEL, 1773, *Life by Boswell*, ed. *Hill, vol.* II, *p.* 272.

A disciple of the old school of slander— a liar—and one for whom bedlam is no bedlam.—WHITAKER, JOHN, 1787, *Mary Queen of Scots Vindicated.*

Dr. Robertson shone when he wrote the History of his own country, with which he was acquainted. All his other works are collections tacked together for the purpose; but as he has not the genius, penetration, sagacity, and art of Mr. Gibbon, he cannot melt his materials together, and make them elucidate and even improve and produce new discoveries; in short, he cannot, like Mr. Gibbon, make an *original* picture with some bits of Mosaic.—WALPOLE, HORACE, 1791, *To the Countess of Ossory, Nov.* 23; *Letters,* ed. *Cunningham, vol.* IX, *p.* 361.

The perfect composition, the nervous language, the well-tuned periods of Dr. Robertson, inflamed me to the ambitious hope that I might one day tread in his footsteps: the calm philosophy, the careless inimitable beauties of his friend and rival, often forced me to close the volume with a mixed sensation of delight and despair.—GIBBON, EDWARD, 1793, *Autobiography.*

None of Dr. Robertson's periods with three members.—LAMB, CHARLES, 1800, *Letters,* ed. *Ainger, March* 1, *vol.* I, *p.* 115.

The histories of Robertson abound in the finest descriptions, the most pleasing delineations of character, the most dignified and judicious mixture of reflections; and more especially they are distinguished by a style of narration at once manly, copious, and easy. But all these descriptions, delineations, reflections, and even this narrative itself, are too general for practical use and application. The politician and political œconomist will search these writings in vain for the accurate details of fact which they have a right to expect from one who investigates the subjects of particular men and nations. . . . In plain terms, Dr. Robertson appears to have studied grace and dignity more than usefulness. He has chosen those features of every figure which he could best paint, rather than those which were most worthy of the pencil. . . . The charms of Robertson's style, and the full flow of his narration, which is always sufficiently minute for ordinary readers, will render his works immortal in the hands of the bulk of mankind. But the scientific reader requires something more than periods which fill his ear, and general statements which gratify by amusing; he even requires more than a general text-book,—a happy arrangement of intricate subjects, which may enable him to pursue them in their details. . . . When we repair to the works of Robertson for the purpose of finding facts, we are instantly carried away by the stream of his narrative, and forget the purpose of our errand to the fountain. As soon as we can stop ourselves, we discover that our search has been vain, and that we must apply to those sources from which he drew and culled his supplies. — BROWN, THOMAS, 1803, *Stewart's Account of Dr. Robertson, Edinburgh Review, vol.* 2, *pp.* 240, 241.

Robertson's style is most attractive: his language ornate, and, though ornate, yet lucid and unaffected. His weak side is that which has regard to research and import, certainly the most important of all historic qualities. It is now universally admitted, even in England, that he is unreliable, superficial, and often full of errors as to facts: yet his style is wont to be held up as a pattern, owing, probably, to the degeneracy of taste. But even his style is, in my opinion, too verbose and antithetical.—SCHLEGEL, FREDERICK, 1815–59, *Lectures on the History of Literature, Lecture* xiv.

Do you like Robertson? I used to find in him a shrewd, a systematic, but not a great understanding; and no more heart than in my boot. He was a kind of deist in the guise of a Calvinistic priest; a portentous combination.—CARLYLE, THOMAS, 1824, *Early Letters, ed. Norton, p.* 307.

Robertson, who first threw over the maze of human events the light of philosophic genius, and the spirit of enlightened reflection.—ALISON, SIR ARCHIBALD, 1833–42, *History of Europe During The French Revolution, vol.* XIV, *p.* 3.

Yet there was a power of arrangement in Robertson: no one knew better where to begin a story and where to stop. This was the greatest quality in him, that and a soft sleek style. On the whole, he was merely a politician, open to the common objection to all the three, that total want of belief; and worse in Robertson, a minister of the Gospel, preaching, or pretending to preach.—CARLYLE, THOMAS, 1838, *Lectures on the History of Literature, p.* 185.

In Adam Smith's day all poetical criticism not contained in Dr. Blair's Lectures or Lord Kames's Elements would have been hooted out of reasonable society; now those books themselves, and the school which they represent, have sunk into the lowest estimation. Robertson and Hume would of course have been Smith's standards of historical writing; now the world can listen with great complacency to Charles Lamb's assertion that their books have the same title to the character of histories as the chess-boards which we see inscribed in gilt letters with the same honourable name.—MAURICE, FREDERICK DENISON, 1839, *Lectures on National Education, p.* 115.

The pages of Dr. Robertson have not the unwearied splendour of Gibbon, nor the sudden flashes of sagacity which so charm us in the historical writings of Hume; but Robertson is always an historian, with all the important merits which belong to the character.—SMYTH, WILLIAM, 1840, *Lectures on Modern History, Lecture* xxi.

The public has been hitherto indebted for its knowledge of the reign of Charles the Fifth to Robertson,—a writer who, combining a truly philosophical spirit with an acute perception of character, is recommended, moreover, by a classic elegance of style which has justly given him a pre-eminence among the historians of the Great Emperor.—PRESCOTT, WILLIAM

HICKLING, 1855–58, *The History of the Reign of Philip II.*

Robertson, admirable for gravity and shrewd sense.—MORISON, JAMES COTTER, 1878, *Gibbon (English Men of Letters),p.*102.

He was the Macaulay of his times. His successive works were as eagerly anticipated, and kindled the same enthusiasm. The fame he reaped in the field of letters added weight to his position as a leader in the Church. He reflected the honours he won on the Church he served. As an author of high merit he was brought into contact with, and honoured by the intimacy of men of light and leading; statesmen, ministers, men of letters, and dignitaries of the Church, were counted amongst his friends. The highest personage of the realm interested himself in his persuits, and proposals from that quarter were made to him of the most flattering kind. Since the days of the Reformation he was the first minister of the Church who in the field of letters won for himself a European fame. He elevated the Church from a position of comparative obscurity, lifted her into the presence of foremost men of the world, and won for her history their consideration and esteem.—ROBERTSON, FREDERICK LOCKHART, 1883, *St. Giles' Lectures, Third Series, Scottish Divines, p.* 223.

Robertson's style is essentially a made one. . . . Taken at his best, in narrative, Robertson is admirable. His prose flows easily, carrying the reader along by the studied but concealed art by which one sentence is made to seem the necessary sequel to its predecessor. The general style is, indeed, too smooth for modern taste. As Robertson never allowed himself to pass a certain limit of fervency in his sermons, through fear of being dubbed "Highflyer," so he always wrote, so to speak, with the drag on. His facts are skilfully marshalled in their proper sequence; his tone is kept exceptionally low. . . . The best quality of Robertson's style is its easy motion. He constantly strives after grace and dignity. The balanced phrase, the period, the tautological adjective are perpetually employed.—WALLACE, WILLIAM, 1895, *English Prose, ed. Craik, vol.* IV, *p.* 276.

His style is, in the merely correct, but not merely jejune, kind, singularly good; his conception of history, though not answering to that of more modern times, and tinged with the idiosyncrasies of his age, is philosophical and shrewd; and above all, he had, what modern historians, with all their pretensions and all their equipment, have too often lacked, a thorough sense of rhetorical fitness in the good, not the empty, sense, and could make his histories definite works of art and definite logical presentments of a view. Nor was he by any means careless of research according to his own standard, which was already a severer one than that of Hume.—SAINTSBURY, GEORGE, 1898, *A Short History of English Literature, p.* 624.

Posterity, we fear, has confirmed Johnson's verdict, and the history which pleased the polite readers of last century, and appeared to them as even more correct and dignified than that of Gibbon, is not likely to come again into vogue. But none the less he performed a work and achieved a fame which added immensely to the influence of his Church, and enhanced the position of her clergy.—CRAIK, SIR HENRY, 1901, *A Century of Scottish History, vol.* I, *p.* 405.

John Hunter
1728–1793

Physiologist and surgeon; born at Long Calderwood, Glasgow, Scotland, July 14, 1728; youngest of ten children of whom one was the afterward celebrated William Hunter. John received very imperfect instruction at school; was apprenticed to a cabinetmaker; went in 1748 to study anatomy with his brother; studied at Oxford 1753–54; became a surgical pupil at St. Bartholomew's 1751, and St. George's 1754; studied surgery under Cheselden and Pott; lectured upon anatomy 1754–59; attained great knowledge of human and comparative anatomy; served in France and Portugal as staff-surgeon 1761–63; began to practice surgery in London 1763; was made F. R. S. 1767, in consequence of the publication of important papers containing new discoveries in pathology and physiology; became surgeon to St. George's Hospital 1768; surgeon extraordinary to the king 1776; surgeon-general of the forces and inspector-general of hospitals 1790 . . . He was an anatomist of marvelous knowledge, and one of the fathers of zoölogical science. He was author of "Natural History of the Human Teeth" (1771–78); On "Venereal Disease" (1786); "Observations on Certain Parts of the Animal Economy" (1786); "On the Blood, Inflammation, and Gunshot Wounds" (1794). He was the collector of the great Hunterian Museum, chiefly of pathological and anatomical specimens, purchased by the British Government and presented to the Royal College of Surgeons. Died in London, Oct. 16, 1793.—ADAMS, CHARLES KENDALL, *ed.*, 1897, *Johnson's Universal Encyclopædia, vol.* IV, *p.* 415.

PERSONAL

JOHN HUNTER, ESQ., F. R. S.,
Surgeon-General to the Army, and
Inspector-General of Hospitals;
Surgeon to St. George's Hospital;
Surgeon-Extraordinary to the King;
&c., &c., &c.,
DIED OCTOBER 16th, 1793,
On the same day, and perhaps hour,
that the unfortunate Marie Antoinette
Queen of France was beheaded in
Paris.
—CLIFT, WILLIAM, 1793, *Account-Book.*

It was a truly interesting thing to hear Dr. Jenner, in the evening of his days, descanting from all the fervour of youthful friendship and attachment, on the commanding and engaging peculiarities of Mr. Hunter's mind. He generally called him the "dear man," and when he described the honesty and warmth of his heart, and his never-ceasing energy in the pursuit of knowledge, it was impossible not to be animated by the recital.—BARON, JOHN, 1827, *Life of Edward Jenner, p.* 10.

He was fond of company and mixed much in the society of young men of his own standing, and joined in that sort of dissipation which men at his age, and freed from restraint, are but too apt to indulge in. Nor was he always very nice in the choice of his associates, but sometimes sought entertainment in the coarse, broad humour to be found amid the lower ranks of society. He was employed by his brother to cater for the dissecting-room, in the course of which employment he became a great favorite with that certainly not too respectable class of persons the resurrection-men and one of the amusements in which he took special pleasure, was to mingle with the gods in the shilling gallery, for the purpose of assisting to damn the productions of unhappy authors, an office in which he is said to have displayed peculiar tact and vigour.—OTTLEY, DREWRY, 1835, *Life of John Hunter, ed. Palmer.*

"O Lord, how manifold are thy works."
Beneath
are deposited the remains
of
JOHN HUNTER,
Born at Long Calderwood, Lanarkshire,N.B.,
on the 13th of February, 1728,
Died in London on the 16th of October, 1793
His remains were removed
from the Church of St. Martin-in-the-Fields
to this Abbey on the 28th of March, 1859.
—INSCRIPTION ON TABLET, *Westminster Abbey*, 1859.

John Hunter's coffin was, I knew, among this mass of coffins in No. 3 vault somewhere. It was my self-imposed task to find it; and the only way to do this was to inspect each coffin as it was brought out on its way to the catacombs outside the church. I therefore stationed myself at the door of the vault, and examined by the light of the lamp hung on to the door-post, every coffin as it came sliding down the plank, occasionally climbing on to the top of them, and looking about among them with my policeman's bull's-eye lamp to see if I could find the much-wished-for name of John Hunter inscribed on any of the brass coffin-plates. We worked away at this vault No. 3 for *eight* days, when, the Hunterian oration being so near, Mr. Burstall decided to go on moving the coffins at another part of the . vault. . . . We worked on in No. 3 vault for seven days more, and, as may be imagined, I got very nervous towards the last, especially as I found the engraved brass coffin-plates loosened from the tops of the older coffins, and was very fearful that John Hunter's coffin-plate might also have got loose. . . . The total number of coffins in No. 3 vault was over two hundred. The total number of coffins removed was three thousand two hundred and sixty. This will give some idea of the task that had to be undertaken. If one of these coffins, therefore was not John Hunter's, our labours would have

been in vain. The workmen stood at the head and foot of the uppermost coffin of the three, and slowly moved it away that I might see the name upon that immediately below it. As it moved slowly off I discerned first the letter J and the O, and at last the whole word "John." My anxiety was now at its height, and I quickly running to one end, Mr. Burstall at the other, moved the coffin away. At last I got it completely off, and to my intense delight read upon the brass-plate the following inscription:

John Hunter
Esq.,
Died 16th Octr.,
1793,
Age 64 Years.

. . . .
Though I had worked hard to gain the object I desired, I was not sorry that I had taken the entire responsibility, as well as the carrying out of the task, upon myself; for from my discovery arose two important events, viz. :—1. The reinterment of John Hunter in Westminster Abbey. 2. And then out of this the erection of a marble statue to his memory in the Museum, at the College of Surgeons.—BUCKLAND, FRANK, 1866, *Discovery of the Remains of John Hunter in St. Martin's Church, Leisure Hour, vol. 15, pp.* 566, 567.

He allowed himself four hours' sleep by night, and a short nap after dinner. He rose early to his dissections, experiments, and preparation-making, and was so busied for a couple hours, or more, prior to commencing the routine work of the day by the reception of his patients at half-past eight. His evenings were devoted to recording the thoughts and expanding the brief notes of the day. The social obligations which Hunter's high position involved were mainly fulfilled, and admirably by his accomplished wife, whose words are wedded to the music of the immortal canzonets of Haydn, the great composer of the period. The four-windowed drawing-room which still looks upon the renovated square was crowded weekly by the beauty, rank and fashion of the season. My father-in-law described to me the scene he often stayed to witness with sleep-laden eyes, when the master could no longer dictate, and issued from his study on the ground floor to seek his much needed repose, on one of Mrs. Hunter's reception nights. With difficulty stemming the social stream on the staircase he would stop to give a kindly greeting to the beauty of the year, had a smart reply to the passing joke of the man of fashion, or a more serious to the question of an administrator, all hurrying away to some later gathering westward, while the weary philosopher sought to lay his head upon the pillow.—OWEN, RICHARD, 1874, *Hunter's Scientific Character and Works, Leicester Square by Tom Taylor, p. 429.*

In person Hunter was of middle height, vigorous, and robust, with high shoulders and rather short neck. His features were strongly marked, with prominent eyebrows, pyramidal forehead, and eyes of light blue or gray. His hair in youth was a reddish yellow, and in later years white. . . . Hunter often rose at five or six to dissect, breakfasted at nine, saw patients till twelve, and visited his hospital and outdoor patients till four. He was most punctual and orderly in his visits, leaving a duplicate of his visiting-book at home, so that he could be found at any time. He dined at four. For many years he drank no wine, and sat but a short time at table, except when he had company. He slept for an hour after dinner, then read or prepared his lectures, made experiments, and dictated the results of his dissections. He was often left at midnight with his lamp freshly trimmed, still at work. He wrote his first thoughts and memorandums on odd scraps of paper. These were copied and arranged, and formed many folio volumes of manuscript. Hunter would often have his manuscripts rewritten many times, making during the process endless corrections and transpositions. In manners Hunter was impatient, blunt, and unceremonious, often rude and overbearing, but he was candid and unreserved to a fault. He read comparatively little, and could never adequately expound the information already accessible on any subject. Most of what he knew he had acquired himself, and he attached perhaps undue importance to personal investigation. Few men have ever done so much with so little book-learning. His detachment from books, combined with his patient search for facts, gave him a vital grip of subjects most needing to be studied in the concrete. His opinions were always in process of improvement, and he never clung to former opinions through conservatism.—BETTANY, G. T., 1891, *Dictionary of National Biography, vol.* XXVIII, *p.* 290.

GENERAL

His experiments, if they be true, carry with them no manner of information:—if they be true, no effect for the benefit of man can possibly be derived from them.—FOOT, JESSE, 1794, *Life of Hunter, p.* 116.

The moral sense has often been found too weak to temper the malignancy of literary jealousy, and has impelled some men of genius to an incredible excess. A memorable example offers in the history of the two brothers, Dr. William and John Hunter, both great characters fitted to be rivals; but Nature, it was imagined in the tenderness of blood, had placed a bar to rivalry. John, without any determined pursuit in his youth, was received by his brother at the height of his celebrity; the doctor initiated him into his school; they performed their experiments together; and William Hunter was the first to announce to the world the great genius of his brother. After this close connexion in all their studies and discoveries, Dr. William Hunter published his magnificent work—the proud favorite of his heart, the assertor of his fame. Was it credible that the genius of the celebrated anatomist, which had been nursed under the wing of his brother, should turn on that wing to clip it? John Hunter put in his claim to the chief discovery; it was answered by his brother. The Royal Society, to whom they appealed, concealed the documents of this unnatural feud. The blow was felt, and the jealousy of literary honour forever separated the brothers—the brothers of genius.—DISRAELI, ISAAC, 1796–1839, *Jealousy of Authors, The Literary Character.*

He appears to me as a new character in our profession; and, briefly to express his peculiar merit, I may call him the first and great physionosologist, or expositor of the nature of disease.—ABERNETHY, JOHN, 1819, *Hunterian Oration, p.* 29.

I had the happiness of hearing the first course of lectures which John Hunter delivered. I had been at that time for some years in the profession, and was tolerably well acquainted with the opinions held by the surgeons most distinguished for their talents, then residing in the metropolis; but having heard Mr. Hunter's lectures on the subject of disease, I found them so far superior to everything I had conceived or heard before, that there seemed no comparison between the great mind of the man who delivered them and all the individuals, whether ancient or modern, who had gone before him.—CLINE, HENRY, 1824, *Hunterian Oration.*

Those who have traced the progress of modern surgery to its true source, will not fail to have discerned, in the principles which Hunter established, the germs of almost all the improvements which have been since introduced.—PALMER, JAMES F., 1835, *ed. Hunter's Works, vol.* I, *p.* vii.

The majority of Hunter's contemporaries considered his pursuits to have little connexion with practice, charged him with attending to physiology more than surgery, and looked on him as little better than an innovator and an enthusiast. —OTTLEY, DREWRY, 1835, *Life of Hunter, Works of Hunter, ed. Palmer, p.* 126.

With many ideas to tell, and most of them new, had a difficulty of expressing himself. With more need than any man before him for additional facilities in this way, he had a restricted vocabulary: again, in making use of it, his style was seldom easy, often obscure; so that things which, when thoroughly understood, had no feature more striking than their simplicity, were often made to appear difficult, and by many readers, no doubt, had often been left unexamined.— MACILWAIN, GEORGE, 1853, *Memoirs of John Abernethy, p.* 364.

I have now only one more name to add to this splendid catalogue of the great Scotchmen of the eighteenth century. But it is the name of a man, who, for comprehensive and original genius, comes immediately after Adam Smith, and must be placed far above any other philosopher whom Scotland has produced. I mean, of course, John Hunter, whose only fault was, an occasional obscurity, not merely of language, but also of thought. In this respect, and, perhaps, in this alone, Adam Smith had the advantage; for his mind was so flexible, and moved so freely, that even the vastest designs were unable to oppress it. With Hunter, on the

contrary, it sometimes seemed as if the understanding was troubled by the grandeur of his own conceptions, and doubted what path it ought to take. He hesitated; the utterance of his intellect was indistinct. Still, his powers were so extraordinary, that, among the great masters of organic science, he belongs, I apprehend, to the same rank as Aristotle, Harvey, and Bichat, and is somewhat superior either to Haller or Cuvier. As to this classification, men will differ, according to their different ideas of the nature of science, and, above all, according to the extent to which they appreciate the importance of philosophic method. It is from this latter point of view that I have, at present, to consider the character of John Hunter; and, in tracing the movements of his most remarkable mind, we shall find, that, in it, deduction and induction were more intimately united than in any other Scotch intellect, either of the seventeenth or eighteenth century. The causes of this unusual combination, I will now endeavour to ascertain.—BUCKLE, HENRY THOMAS, 1862–66, *History of Civilization in England, vol.* III, *ch.* V.

In 1776, Hunter delivered his first course of surgical lectures at St. George's. The sense of his deficiencies as a speaker led him to read his lectures. He seldom looked up from his book; and his written style was not happy. His doctrines were new, and their obscurity and difficulty was little relieved by his exposition. He used to compare the preparation of a lecture to a tradesman's taking stock. His sole object was truth. He was pitiless in demolishing fallacies or exposing errors, even his own.—TAYLOR, TOM, 1874, *Leicester Square, its Associations and its Worthies, p.* 396.

All intelligent readers of biography are more or less familiar with the labors and writings of John Hunter, his marvellous genius, and his vast contributions to science. In the medical profession his name is, and always will be, a household word throughout the civilized world; it is spoken with respect and reverence in every college amphitheatre, and is deeply ingraved on the mind of every student of surgery. . . . With the exceptions of Hippocrates, the father of medicine, John Hunter is the grandest figure in the history of our profession. . . . He was not only a great surgeon, a wise physician and a great anatomist and physiologist, human and comparative, but above all, he was a philosopher whose mental grasp embraced the whole range of nature's works, from the most humble structure to the most complex and the most lofty. He was emphatically the Newton of the medical profession, and what Pope said of that great philosopher may, by pharaphrase, be said with equal force and truth of Hunter:

"Nature and Nature's laws lay hid in night;
God said 'Let Hunter be,' and all was light."

Hunter is peerless in the history of British surgery; and after the lapse of nearly a century the profession turns to his memory with increased reverence for his transcendent genius, his matchless ability, and his unequalled services. To say that he was simply the founder of scientific surgery would fall far short of his great deserts; to do him full justice we must add that he was the father also of scientific zoology and of comparative physiology.—GROSS, S. D., 1881, *John Hunter and his Pupils, pp.* 9, 10.

Medical science owes much to John Hunter, who by his researches in animal and vegetable Physiology, made a vast number of discoveries, which, considered singly, are curious, but which, collectively, constitute an invaluable body of new truths. His museum, at the time of his death, contained upwards of ten thousand preparations illustrative of the phenomena of nature. His great object was to show that nature is a vast and united whole, that nothing is irregular, that nothing is perturbed, that in every change there is order, that all things are done according to never-failing law.—WELSH, ALFRED H., 1883, *Development of English Literature and Language, vol.* II, *p.* 187.

The genius of one man—John Hunter—created English pathology, and took it at once almost to the highest position, for he fortified it with clinical, anatomical, and experimental observations which are unassailable when they are combined. John Hunter was in some respects even more remarkable than William, his elder brother. He possessed greater singleness of purpose, and therefore greater concentration, greater depth of knowledge, greater determination, and that minute

attention to detail associated with the power of generalisation which only co-exist in the highest intellects.—POWER, D'ARCY, 1896, *Social England, ed. Traill, vol.* V, *p.* 423.

It is impossible to include in one view the multitudinous forms of Hunter's work; you cannot see the wood for the trees. He was anatomist, biologist, naturalist, physician, surgeon, and pathologist, all at once, and all in the highest. Nor is it possible to reproduce the lights and shadows of that aspect of his life which was not turned toward science. . . . He is like Vesalius; he made his name immortal by the labour of his own hands outside the sphere of surgery. Apart from all his hospital and private practice, and all his writing and lecturing, the actual manual work that he accomplished in dissections and *post-mortem* examinations is past all telling. Twelve years before he died, at Captain Donellan's trial, he was asked, "You have been long in the habit of dissecting human subjects; I presume you have dissected more than any man in Europe?" and he answered, "I have dissected some thousands during these thirty-three years." His dissections of animals must also be reckoned in thousands. Literary work was uncongenial to him, and against the grain; he took no pleasure in style and no pains over spelling, submitted his writings to the corrections of his friends, adopted at their suggestion Greek words, and that most foolish phrase "materia vitæ diffusa." But in anatomy and experiment he had the strength and patience of ten; and Clift often saw him, in his old age, standing like a statue for hours over some delicate bit of dissection. The whole output of his working life is fourfold—literary, surgical, anatomical, physiological and experimental; but the multiplication together of these factors does not give the whole result of his work. He brought surgery into closer touch with science. Contrast him with Ambroise Paré, a surgeon in some ways like him, shrewd, observant, ahead of his age; the achievements of Paré, side by side with those of Hunter, are like child's play in comparison with the serious affairs of men; Paré advanced the art of surgery, but Hunter taught the science of it.—PAGET, STEPHEN, 1897, *John Hunter (Masters of Medicine), pp.* 220, 233.

William Murray
Lord Mansfield
1705-1793

William Murray, Earl of Mansfield, lord-chief-justice of the king's bench, was the fourth son of Andrew, viscount Stormont, and was born at Perth, Mar. 2, 1705. He studied at Christ-church, Oxford, took the degree of M. A. in 1730, and was called to the bar in 1731. He soon acquired an extensive practice—mainly, it would seem, on account of his facility and force as a speaker, for neither then nor at any subsequent period of his career was he reckoned a very erudite lawyer—and was often employed on appeal cases before the house of lords. In 1743 he was appointed by the ministry solicitor-general, entered the house of commons as member for Boroughbridge, and at once took a high position. In 1746 he acted, *ex officio*, as counsel against the rebel lords, Lovat, Balmerino and Kilmarnock; was appointed king's attorney in 1754; and at this time stood so high that, had not the keenness of his ambition been mitigated by a well-founded distrust of his fitness for leading the house, he might have aspired to the highest political honors. He became chief-justice of the king's bench in 1756, and entered the House of Lords under the title of baron Mansfield of Mansfield in the county of Nottingham. Still his political *rôle* has little interest for posterity. As his opinions were not those of the popular side, he was exposed to much abuse and party hatred. Junius, among others, bitterly attacked him; and during the Gordon riots of 1780, his house, with all his valuable books and manuscripts, was burned. He declined, with much dignity, indemnification by parliament. In 1776 Murray was made earl of Mansfield. He worked hard as a judge till 1788, when age and ill-health forced him to resign. He died Mar. 20, 1793, in the 89th year of his age. —PECK, HARRY THURSTON, *ed.*, 1898, *The International Cyclopædia, vol.* IX, *p.* 454.

PERSONAL

To number five direct your doves,
There spread round Murray all your blooming loves;
Noble and young, who strikes the heart
With every sprightly, every decent part;
Equal the injured to defend,
To charm the mistress, or to fix the friend;
He, with a hundred arts refined,
Shall stretch thy conquests over half the kind:
To him each rival shall submit,
Make but his riches equal to his wit.
—POPE, ALEXANDER, 1738, *Imitation of Horace's Ode to Venus.*

Your fate depends upon your success there as a speaker; and, take my word for it, that success turns much more upon Manner than Matter. Mr. Pitt, and Mr. Murray the Solicitor-General, are, beyond comparison, the best speakers. Why? Only because they are the best orators. They alone can inflame or quiet the House; they alone are attended to in that numerous and noisy assembly, that you might hear a pin fall while either of them is speaking. Is it that their matter is better, or their arguments stronger, than other people's? Does the House expect extraordinary information from them? Not in the least; but the House expects pleasure from them, and therefore attends; finds it, and therefore approves.—STANHOPE, PHILIP DORMER (EARL CHESTERFIELD), 1751, *Letters to his Son, Feb.* 11*th.*

In all debates of consequence Murray, the attorney general, had greatly the advantage over Pitt in point of argument; and, abuse only excepted, was not much his inferior in any part of oratory.—WALDEGRAVE, LORD, 1755, *Memoirs, p.* 53.

As a speaker in the House of Lords, where was his competitor? The grace of his action, and the fire and vivacity of his looks, are still present to imagination; and the harmony of his voice yet vibrates in the ear of those who have been accustomed to listen to him. His Lordship possessed the strongest powers of discrimination; his language was elegant and perspicuous, arranged with the happiest method, and applied with the utmost extent of human ingenuity; his images were often bold, and always just; but the character of his eloquence is that of being flowing, perspicuous, convincing, and affecting.—BURTON, EDMUND, 1763, *Character Deduced from Classical Remains.*

This gentleman had raised himself to great eminence at the bar by the most keen, intuitive spirit of apprehension, that seemed to seize every object at first glance; an innate sagacity, that saved the trouble of intense application; and an irresistible stream of eloquence, that flowed pure and classical, strong and copious, reflecting in the most conspicuous point of view the subject over which it rolled, and sweeping before it all the slime of formal hesitation and all the intangling weeds of chicanery.—SMOLLET, TOBIAS GEORGE, 1763–65, *History of England, Reign of George II.*

Our language has no term of reproach, the mind has no idea of detestation, which has not already been applied to you, and exhausted. Ample justice has been done by abler pens than mine to the separate merits of your life and character. Let it be *my* humble office to collect the scattered sweets until their united virtue tortures the sense. . . . Yet you continue to support an Administration which you know is universally odious, and which on some occasions you yourself speak of with contempt. You would fain be thought to take no share in government, while, in reality, you are the mainspring of the machine. Here, too, we trace the *little*, prudential policy of a Scotchman. Instead of acting that open, generous part, which becomes your rank and station, you meanly skulk into the closet and give your Sovereign such advice as you have not spirit to avow or defend. You secretly engross the power while you decline the title of minister; and though you dare not be Chancellor, you know how to secure the emoluments of the office. Are the seals to be forever in commission, that you may enjoy five thousands pounds a year. —JUNIUS, 1770, *Letter to Lord Mansfield, Nov.* 14.

At Lady Colvill's, to whom I am proud to introduce any stranger of eminence, that he may see what dignity and grace is to be found in Scotland, an officer observed, that he had heard Lord Mansfield was not a great English lawyer. JOHNSON. "Why, Sir, supposing Lord Mansfield not to have the splendid talents which he possesses, he must be a great English lawyer, from having been so long at the bar, and having passed through so many of the great offices of the law. Sir, you may as well maintain that a carrier, who has driven a packhorse between Edinburgh and Berwick for thirty years, does not know the road, as Lord Mansfield does not know the law of England."— BOSWELL, JAMES, 1785, *The Journal of a Tour of the Hebrides with Samuel Johnson, Nov.* 11–20, ed. Hill, vol. v, p. 450.

I cannot recollect the time, when, sitting at the table with Lord Mansfield, I ever failed to remark that happy and engaging art, which he possessed, of putting the company present in good humour with themselves; I am convinced they naturally liked him the more for his seeming to like them so well: this has not been the general property of all the witty, great, and learned men; whom I have looked up to in my course of life. . . . Lord Mansfield would lend his ear most condescendingly to his company, and cheer the least attempt at humour with the prompt payment of a species of laugh, which cost his muscles no exertion, but was merely a subscription that he readily threw in towards the general hilarity of the table. He would take his share in the small talk of the ladies with all imaginable affability; he was in fact, like most men, not in the least degree displeased at being incensed by their flattery.—CUMBERLAND, RICHARD, 1806, *Memoirs Written by Himself, vol.* ii, *pp.* 344, 346.

In private Lord Mansfield appears to have been much and justly beloved. His moral character was blameless. In his friendships he was warm and constant; in his charities judicious and discriminating, not bestowing small sums to relieve himself from present importunities, but assisting in a more substantial manner those who were capable of benefiting by such kindness. In society and especially at his own table, he was remarkable for the liveliness and intelligence of his conversation, in which, however, he never indulged to the exclusion of others. One of his most distinguishing characteristics was the decorum and propriety that pervaded not only his actions but his manners, his personal appearance and even his domestic establishment, in every department of which good sense and good taste were seen conjoined. Lord Mansfield's features were regular and expressive, and his presence graceful and dignified.—ROSCOE, HENRY, 1830, *Eminent British Lawyers, p.* 224.

In closeness of argument, in happiness of illustration, in copiousness and grace of diction, the oratory of Murray was unsurpassed; and, indeed, in all the qualities which conspire to form an able debater, he is allowed to have been Pitt's superior. When measures were attacked, no one was better capable of defending them; when reasoning was the weapon employed, none handled it with such effect; but against declamatory invective his very temperament incapacitated him from contending with so much advantage. He was like an accomplished fencer, invulnerable to the thrusts of a small sword, but not equally able to ward off the downright stroke of a bludgeon.—WELSBY, W. N., 1846, *Lives of Eminent Judges of the Seventeenth and Eighteenth Centuries, p.* 392.

Even the learned on the continent of Europe, who had hitherto looked upon English lawyers as very contracted in their views of jurisprudence, and had never regarded the decisions of our courts as settling any international question, acknowledged that a great jurist had at last been raised up among us, and they placed his bust by the side of Grotius and D'Aguesseau. In his own lifetime, and after he had only a few years worn his ermine, he acquired the designation by which he was afterwards known, and by which he will be called when, five hundred years hence, his tomb is shown in Westminster Abbey—that of "THE GREAT LORD MANSFIELD." . . . Lord Mansfield must, I think, be considered the most prominent legal character, and the brightest ornament to the profession of the law, that appeared in England during the last century.—CAMPBELL, JOHN LORD, 1849, *Lives of the Chief Justices of England, vol.* II, *pp.* 397, 562.

At the bar his mere statement of a case, by its extreme lucidity, was supposed to be worth the argument of any other man. As a statesman his fame is tarnished by his blind adhesion to the policy of coercing America, nor is his name associated with any statute of first-rate importance. Macaulay terms him, however, "the father of modern toryism, of toryism modified to suit an order of things in which the House of Commons is the most powerful body in the state." As a judge, by his perfect impartiality, inexhaustible patience, and the strength and acumen of his understanding, he ranks among the greatest who have ever administered justice. Such was his ascendency over his colleagues, that during the first twelve years of his tenure of office they invariably, though by no means insignificant lawyers, concurred in his judgment.. —RIGG, J. M., 1894, *Dictionary of National Biography, vol.* XXXIX, *p.* 414.

GENERAL

He excelled in the *statement of a case.* One of the first orators of. the present age said of it "that it was of itself worth the argument of any other man."—BUTLER, CHARLES, 1804, *Horæ Juridicæ Subsecivæ.*

The Reports of Burrow, Cowper, and Douglass contain the substance of Lord Mansfield's judicial decisions; and they are among the most interesting reports in the English law. . . . We should have known but very little of the great mind and varied accomplishments of Lord Mansfield if we had not been possessed of the faithful reports of his decisions. It is there that his title of the character of "founder of the Commercial Law of England" is verified.—KENT, JAMES, 1826–54, *Commentaries, vol.* I.

If we possess hardly any remains of Lord Mansfield's speeches at the bar or in parliament, we have considerable materials from which to form an estimate of his judicial eloquence. The Reports of Sir James Burrows are carefully corrected, to all appearance; probably by the learned Judges themselves. Many of the judgments of the Chief Justice are truly admirable in substance, as well as composition; and upon some of the greater questions, his oratory rises to the full height of the occasion. It would be difficult to overrate the merit of the celebrated address to the public, then in a state of excitement almost unparalleled, with which he closed his judgment upon the application to reverse Wilkes's outlawry. Great elegance of composition, force of diction, just and strong but natural expression of personal feelings, a commanding attitude of defiance to lawless threats, but so assumed and so tempered with the dignity which was natural to the man, and which here as on all other occasions, he sustained throughout, all render this one of the most striking productions on record.— BROUGHAM, HENRY LORD, 1839–43, *Historical Sketches of Statesmen who Flourished in the Time of George III.*

Though, besides the three judges whom

he found on the bench of his court, there were no less than eight who took their places afterwards as his colleagues, it is a strong evidence of the soundness of his law that during the thirty-two years of his presidency there were only two cases in which the whole bench were not unanimous: and, what is still more extraordinary, two only of his judgments were reversed on appeal: but some of them were not entirely approved by the legal community. The system on which he acted was censured as introducing too much of the Roman law into our jurisprudence; and he was charged with overstepping the boundary between equity and law, and of allowing the principles of the former to operate too strongly in his legal decisions. How far these criticisms were justified still remains a question: but recent legislation proves how little his system deserved censure.—Foss, Edward, 1864, *The Judges of England, vol.* viii, *p.* 343.

Lord Mansfield's chief intellectual merit as a judge is, that in a great measure, he created the law which he pronounced. He made the commercial law of England. To him we owe the settled form and principles of the law of negotiable paper and insurance. He was accused by some of his contemporaries of confounding equitable with legal principles in his administration, and certainly he did brush away the artificial and trivial notions of old time with an unsparing hand. But he cast the legal future of England in a grand horoscope. He judged rightly of the necessities of a more modern state of society, and of the rapidly growing grandeur of his country's commerce. He built for the future as well as the then present, and we in our day have not out-grown or distanced his wise provisions. Only two of his decisons were reversed during his tenure of judicial office, and his authority is higher to-day than it was then. So truly was he the creator of the law of bills that it is almost laughable to read of his laying down for the first time principles which are now as certain and familiar "as those which guide the planets in their orbits." He also adorned the law of evidence to an unprecedented extent: as one has said of him, "he found it brick, he layed it of marble." He pronounced against the legality of employing "puffers" at an action. He exploded the dogma of escheat in case of wrecks, where no living thing comes ashore.— Browne, Irving, 1878, *Short Studies of Great Lawyers, p.* 17.

Edward Gibbon

1737–1794

Born, at Putney, 27 April, 1737. To school in Putney; afterwards at school at Kingston-on-Thames, Jan. 1746 to 1748 (?). At Westminster School, Jan. 1748 to 1750. To Bath for health 1750. To school at Esher, Jan., 1752. At Magdalen Coll., Oxford, 3 April, 1752 to June 1753. To Lausanne, as pupil of M. Pavillard, June 1753. Returned to England, Aug. 1758. Held commission in Hampshire militia, 12 June 1759 to 1770. In Paris, 28 Jan. to 9 May 1763; at Lausanne, May 1763 to April 1764; in Italy, April, 1764 to May, 1765. Returned to England; lived with father at Buriton. After father's death settled in London, 1772. Prof. of Ancient History at Royal Academy, 1774. M. P. for Liskeard, 11 Oct. 1774 to Sept. 1780. Lord Commissioner of Trade and Plantations, 1779. M. P. for Lymington, June 1781 to March 1784. Settled at Lausanne, Sept. 1783. Visit to England, 1788 and 1793. Died, in London, 16 Jan. 1794. Buried at Fletching, Sussex. *Works:* "Essai sur l'étude de la Littérature" (in French, 1761 Eng. trans., 1764); "Mémoires Littéraires de la Grande-Bretagne" (with Deyverdun), 2 vols., 1767–68; "Critical Observations on the Sixth Book of the Æneid" (anon.), 1770; "History of the Decline and Fall of the Roman Empire" (6 vols.), 1776–88 (2nd and 3rd edns. in same period). *Posthumous:* "An Historical View of Christianity" (with Bolingbroke, Voltaire, and others), 1806; "Antiquities of the House of Brunswick," ed. by Lord Sheffield, 1814; "Memoirs," ed. by Lord Sheffield, 1827; "Life" (autobiog.), ed. by H. H. Milman, 1839; "The Autobiographies of Edward Gibbon," ed. J. Murray, 1896; "Private Letters," ed. by R. E. Prothero, 1896. *Collected Works:* "Miscellaneous Works," in 2 vols., 1796; in 5 vols. 1814.—Sharp, R. Farquharson, 1897, *A Dictionary of English Authors, p.* 111.

WILLIAM ROBERTSON

Engraving by F. A. Dean.
From a Painting by Sir Joshua Reynolds.

EDWARD GIBBON

From a Painting by Alonzo Chappel.
After a Likeness by Sir Joshua Reynolds.

PERSONAL

They have had great doings here at the christening of Mr. Gibbon's son. . . . Our landlady says that his lady had no fortune, but was a young lady of good family and reputation, and that old Mr. Gibbon led her to church and back again. —BYROM, JOHN, 1737, *Diary, May* 15.

Gibbon is an ugly, affected, disgusting fellow, and poisons our literary club to me.—BOSWELL, JAMES, 1779, *Letter to Temple, May* 8.

Fat and ill-constructed, Mr. Gibbon has cheeks of such prodigious chubbiness, that they envelope his nose so completely, as to render it, in profile, absolutely invisible. His look and manner are placidly mild, but rather effeminate; his voice,— for he was speaking to Sir Joshua at a little distance,—is gentle, but of studied precision of accent. Yet, with these Brobdignatious cheeks, his neat little feet are of a miniature description; and with these, as soon as I turned around, he hastily described a quaint sort of circle, with small quick steps, and a dapper gait, as if to mark the alacrity of his approach, and then, stopping short when full face to me, he made so singularly profound a bow, that—though hardly able to keep my gravity—I felt myself blush deeply at its undue, but palpably intended obsequiousness.—D'ARBLAY, MADAME (FANNY BURNEY), 1782, *Letter to Samuel Crisp, Memoirs of Dr. Burney, p.* 170.

Mr. Gibbon, the historian, is so exceedingly indolent that he never even pares his nails. His servant, while Gibbon is reading, takes up one of his hands, and when he has performed the operation lays it down and then manages the other—the patient in the meanwhile scarcely knowing what is going on, and quietly pursuing his studies. The picture of him painted by Sir. J. Reynolds, and the prints made from it, are as like the original as it is possible to be. When he was introduced to a blind French lady, the servant happening to stretch out her mistress's hand to lay hold of the historian's cheek, she thought, upon feeling its rounded contour, that some trick was being played upon her with the *sitting* part of a child, and exclaimed, "Fidonc!"— MALONE, EDMOND, 1787, *Maloniana, ed. Prior, p.* 382.

The publication of Gibbon's "Memoirs" conveyed to the world a faithful picture of the most fervid industry; it is in *youth*, the foundations of such a sublime edifice as his history must be laid. The world can now trace how this Colossus of erudition, day by day, and year by year, prepared himself for some vast work. . . . Of all our popular writers the most experienced reader was Gibbon.—DISRAELI, ISAAC, 1791–1824, *Literary Composition, Curiosities of Literature.*

Went to the library of Mr. Gibbon; it still remains here, though bought seven years ago by Mr. Beckford, of Fonthill, for 950*l*. It consists of nearly 10,000 volumes, and, as far as I could judge by a cursory and (from its present situation) a very inconvenient examination of it, it is, of all the libraries I ever saw, that of which I should most covet the possession—that which seems exactly everything that any gentleman or gentlewoman fond of letters could wish. Although it is in no particular walk of literature a perfect collection, in the classical part perhaps less than any other, and in the Greek less than in the Latin classics, still there are good editions of all the best authors in both languages. The books, though neither magnificent in their editions nor in their bindings, are all in good condition, all clean, all such as one wishes to read, and could have no scruple in using. They are under the care of Mr. Scott, a physician of this place, who made the bargain for Mr. Beckford with Gibbon's heirs in England, and are placed in two small and inconvenient rooms hired for the purpose, and filled with rows of shelves so near as scarcely to admit of looking at the books on the back side of them. Mr. Beckford, when last here in 179—, packed up about 2,500 vols. of what he considered as the choicest of them, in two cases, which he then proposed sending to England directly, but which still remain in their cases with the others.—BERRY, MARY, 1803, *Lausanne, July* 6; *Journal, ed. Lewis, p.* 260.

I enclose you a sprig of Gibbon's acacia and some rose-leaves from his garden, which, with part of his house, I have just seen. You will find honourable mention, in his *Life*, made of this acacia, when he walked out on the night of concluding his history. The garden and summer-house, where he composed, are neglected, and the last utterly decayed; but they still show it as his "cabinet," and seem perfectly aware of his memory.— BYRON, LORD, 1816, *Letter to John Murray, June* 27.

I invited the four military gentlemen, our committee, and six other persons the best qualified I could meet with, among whom were my father, Lord Carmarthen, and Mr. Gibbon, the historian, who was then at the zenith of his fame, and who certainly was not at all backward in availing himself of the deference universally shown to him, by taking both the lead, and a very ample share of the conversation, in whatever company he might honour with his presence. His conversation was not, indeed, what Dr. Johnson would have called *talk.* There was no interchange of ideas, for no one had a chance of replying, so fugitive, so variable, was his mode of discoursing, which consisted of points, anecdotes, and epigrammatic thrusts, all more or less to the purpose, and all pleasantly said with a French air and manner which gave them great piquancy, but which were withal so desultory and unconnected that, though each separately were extremely amusing, the attention of his auditors sometimes flagged before his own resources were exhausted.—BURGES, SIR JAMES BLAND, 1824? *Letters and Correspondence, p.* 54.

On the day I first sat down with Johnson, in his rusty brown, and his black worsteads, Gibbon was placed opposite to me in a suit of flower'd velvet, with a bag and sword. . . . The costume was not extraordinary at this time (a little overcharged, perhaps, if his *person* be considered), when almost every gentleman came to dinner in full dress. . . . Each had his measured phraseology; and Johnson's famous parallel, between Dryden and Pope, might be loosely parodied, in reference to himself and Gibbon. Johnson's style was grand, and Gibbon's elegant; the stateliness of the former was sometimes pedantick, and the polish of the latter was occasionally finical. Johnson march'd to kettle-drums and trumpets; Gibbon moved to flutes and hautboys; Johnson hew'd passages through the Alps, while Gibbon levell'd walks through parks and gardens. Maul'd as I had been by Johnson, Gibbon pour'd balm upon my bruises, by condescending, once or twice, in the course of the evening, to talk with me; the great historian was light and

playful, suiting his matter to the capacity of the boy;—but it was done *more suâ* (sic); still his mannerism prevail'd;—still he tapp'd his snuff-box,—still he smirk'd, and smiled; and rounded his periods with the same air of good-breeding, as if he were conversing with men.—His mouth, mellifluous as Plato's, was a round hole, nearly in the centre of his visage.—COLMAN, GEORGE (THE YOUNGER), 1830, *Random Records, p.* 121.

The author of the great and superb "History of the Roman Empire" was scarcely four feet seven to eight inches in height; the huge trunk of his body, with a belly like Silenus, was set upon the kind of slender legs called *drumsticks;* his feet, so much turned in that the point of the right one could often touch the point of the left, were long and broad enough to serve as a pedestal to a statue of five feet six inches. In the middle of his face, not larger than one's fist, the root of his nose receded into the skull more deeply than the nose of a Calmuck, and his very bright but very small eyes were lost in the same depths. His voice, which had only sharp notes, could only reach the heart by splitting the ears. If Jean-Jacques Rousseau had met Gibbon in the Province of Vaud, it is probable that he would have made of him a companion portrait to his funny one of the *Chief Justice.* M. Suard, who cared little to look at, and still less to produce, caricatures, often drew Gibbon, and always as Madam Brown.—GARAT, M., 1820, *Dominique Joseph, Memoirs, vol.* II.

Gibbon has remarked, that his history is much the better for his having been an officer in the militia and a member of the House of Commons. The remark is most just. We have not the smallest doubt that his campaign, though he never saw an enemy, and his parliamentary attendance, though he never made a . speech, were of far more use to him than years of retirement and study would have been. If the time that he spent on parade and at mess in Hamshire, or on the Treasury-bench and at Brookes's during the storms which overthrew Lord North and Lord Shelburne had been passed in the Bodleian Library, he might have avoided some inaccuracies; he might have enriched his notes with a greater number of references; but he never would have produced so lively a picture of the court, the camp, and the

senate-house.—MACAULAY, THOMAS BAB-
INGTON, 1834, *Mackintosh's History, Edin-
burgh Review; Critical and Miscellaneous
Essays.*

Southey, like Gibbon, was a miscellaneous scholar; he, like Gibbon, of vast
historical research; he, like Gibbon, signally industrious, and patient, and elaborate in collecting the materials for his
historical works. Like Gibbon, he had
dedicated a life of competent ease, in a
pecuniary sense, to literature; like Gibbon he had gathered to the shores of a
beautiful lake, remote from great capitals,
a large, or, at least sufficient library (in
each case I believe, the library ranged, as
to numerical amount, between seven and
ten thousand); and, like Gibbon, he was
the most accomplished *littérateur* amongst
the erudite scholars of his time, and the
most of an erudite scholar amongst the accomplished *littérateurs.* After all these
points of agreement known, it remains as a
pure advantage on the side of Southey—a
mere *lucro ponatur*—that he was a poet;
and by all men's confession, a respectable
poet, brilliant in his descriptive powers,
and fascinating in his narration, however
much he might want of

"The vision and the faculty divine."

It is remarkable amongst the series of
parallelisms that have been or might be
pursued between two men, that both had
the honour of retreating from a parliamentary life. — DE QUINCEY, THOMAS,
1839, *The Lake Poets; Southey, Wordsworth, and Coleridge; Works, ed. Masson,
vol.* II, *p.* 338.

Thus converted firstly to the Romish
communion at Oxford in June, 1753, at
the age of sixteen years and two months,
he renounced it at Lausanne in December
1754, at the age of seventeen years and
eight months. This was precisely, within
a few years, what Bayle had done in his
youth. In Gibbon's case everything was
performed in his head and within the lists
of dialectics; one argument had carried it
off. He could say, for his own satisfaction, that he owed both the one change
and the other to his reading and his solitary meditation alone. Later, when he
flattered himself with being wholly impartial and indifferent concerning beliefs, it
is allowable to suppose that, even without avowing it, he cherished a secret and
cold spite against religious thought, as if
it had been an adversary which had one
day struck him in the absence of his
armour and had wounded him.—SAINTE-
BEUVE, C. A., 1853, *English Portraits,
p.* 124.

Respecting Dr. Franklin's journey from
Nantes to Paris, Cobbett has preserved
from the old newspapers, an anecdote of
some point, and not too improbable for
belief. I know not whether there is any
truth in it. The story is, that at one of
the inns at which he slept on the road, he
was informed that Gibbon (the first volume of whose History had been published
in the spring of that year) was also stopping. "Franklin sent his compliments,
requesting the pleasure of spending the
evening with Mr. Gibbon. In answer he
received a card, importing that, notwithstanding Mr. Gibbon's regard for the
character of Dr. Franklin, as a man and a
philosopher, he could not reconcile it with
his duty to his king, to have any conversation with a revolted subject! Franklin
in reply wrote a note, declaring, that
'though Mr. Gibbon's principles had compelled him to withhold the pleasure of his
conversation, Dr. Franklin had still such
a respect for the character of Mr. Gibbon,
as a gentleman and a historian, that when,
in the course of his writing the history of
the *decline and fall* of empires, the *decline
and fall* of the British Empire should
come to be his subject, as he expects
it soon would, Dr. Franklin would be happy
to furnish him with ample materials which
were in his possession.'"—PARTON, JAMES,
1864, *Life and Times of Benjamin Franklin, vol.* II, *p.* 209.

Gibbon's political career is the side of
his history from which a friendly biographer would most readily turn away. Not
that it was exceptionally ignoble or self-
seeking if tried by the standard of the
time, but it was altogether commonplace
and unworthy of him. The fact that he
never even once opened his mouth in the
House is not in itself blameworthy, though
disappointing in a man of his power. It
was indeed laudable enough if he had
nothing to say. But why had he nothing
to say? His excuse is timidity and want
of readiness. We may reasonably assume
that the cause lay deeper. With his mental vigour he would soon have overcome
such obstacles if he had really wished and
tried to overcome them. The fact is that

he never tried because he never wished. It is a singular thing to say of such a man, but nevertheless true, that he had no taste or capacity whatever for politics.—MORISON, JAMES COTTER, 1878, *Gibbon, (English Men of Letters), p.* 77.

The face and figure of Gibbon are familiar to us from the profile usually found at the beginning of his collected works. The testimony of foreigners as well as of Englishmen, both sufficiently prove its accuracy. To corroborate it farther, there is the well-known story of the blind French old lady, and Charles Fox's coarse lines, neither of which testimonies could be well produced here. This great man was a lover—a lover when he was old as well as when he was young. The style of his letters was rather pedantic and like a page of his history, and the result proved that he was not what is called a successful lover.—FITZGERALD, PERCY, 1883, *Kings and Queens of an Hour, vol.* I, *p.* 340.

To an Englishman at Lausanne, Gibbon is still the prime subject of local interest. . . . We were favoured with a sight of the portraits: one of the usual Kit-cat in pastels—Lausanne then containing sundry famous pastellistes—a cameo-bust on wedgewood (much idealized), and an *aquarelle* of "The Historian" (hideous exceedingly), sitting before the facade of his house at Lausanne, afterwards removed to make way for the Hôtel Gibbon. This, by the way, is a fraud, boasting that its garden contains the identical chestnut tree under which the last lines of a twenty-years' work were written. Unfortunately, the oft-quoted passage describing that event assigns it to "a summer-house in my garden," near a *berceau*, or covered walk of acacias; all of which have long disappeared to make way for the Rue du Midi. Upon the strength of this being "Gibbon Castle," we are somewhat overcharged and underfed.—BURTON, SIR RICHARD F., 1889, *Letters, Life by His Wife, vol.* II, *p.* 371.

One of the relics which will attract most public attention, lent us by General Meredith Read, is Gibbon's Bible, which is said always to have lain in his bedroom at Lausanne. Undoubtedly his attitude to Christianity is the feature in his great work which has done most to dimish its influence, and all educated men, to whatever school they belong, would now admit

with his masterly biographer, Mr. Cotter Morison, that this is a most serious blemish. It is, however, only fair to remember that Christianity, as it presented itself to Gibbon's mind, was something very different from what we are accustomed to associate with the name.—DUFF, SIR M. E. GRANT, 1894, *Proceedings of the Gibbon Commemoration, Nov.* 15, *p.* 15.

During these hundred years the reputation of the historian has been continually growing larger and more firm; his limitations and his errors have been so amply acknowledged that they have ceased to arouse the controversy and the odium which they naturally invited in former generations; and the civilised world, making full allowance for differences of party and of creed, has agreed to honour the historian for his grand success, and no longer to censure that wherein he failed. But hardly any Englishman, with a world-wide fame, has received so little of public honour, or has fallen so completely out of the eye of the world as a personality. Our National Portrait Gallery contains not a single likeness of any kind; there is no record of him in any public institution, no tablet, inscription, bust, or monument; his name figures in no public place; and the house which he inhabited in London bears no mark of its most illustrious inmate. Though masses of his original manuscripts exist, our British Museum contains nothing of them but a single letter; his memoirs, his diaries, his notes, his letters, in his own beautiful writing, are extant in perfect condition. But they are all in private hands, and for some generations they have never been examined or collated by any student or scholar. . . . Much less will any one claim for Edward Gibbon the character of a hero, the name of a great man, the spirit of a martyr or leader of men. No one will ever call him *ultimus Romanorum*, or the thunder-god; no one pretends that he is one of the great souls who inspire their age. We do not set him on any moral pinnacle, either as man or as teacher; nor do we rank him with the master spirits who form the conscience of generations. Without unwisely exaggerating his intellectual forces, without weakly closing our eyes upon his moral shortcomings, we can do full justice to the magnificent literary art, to the lovable nature, the indomitable industry, the noble equanimity of the man. We come, then, to-day, neither to praise nor to criticise; we offer round his tomb no idle encomium, nor do we presume to weigh his ashes in our critical scales. We come to meditate again over all that recalls the charm and sweet sociability of a warm and generous friend; to study with rekindled zest the cherished remnants which friendship has preserved of one of the greatest masters of historical research that has ever adorned the literature of Europe. . . . Edward Gibbon had his worries like other men— worries hardly ever the consequence of any error of his own—but how little of repining or of irritation does he display! He was bitterly and unjustly attacked; but how little is there of controversy; and even in his replies to Priestley and to Davies his language is measured, dignified, and calm. No one pretends that Edward Gibbon had any trace in his nature of passionate impulse or of spiritual nobility. His warmest affection is cast into a Ciceronian mould; and his imperturbable good sense always remains his dominant note. Gibbon was neither a Burke nor a Shelley, still less was he a Rousseau or a Carlyle. He was a delightful companion, a hearty friend, an indomitable student, and an infallible master of that equanimity which stamps such men as Hume, Adam Smith, and Turgot. It is the *mitis sapientia Læli* which breathes through every line of these elaborate letters.—HARRISON, FREDERIC, 1894, *Gibbon Commemoration, Nov.* 15.

There is usually a tendency to underrate Gibbon's military experiences. . . . He was evidently an officer of more than ordinary intelligence, and possessed some military aptitude. He went beyond the requirements of an infantry captain by closely studying the language and science of tactics; indeed all that pertained to the serious side of soldiering he studied with a perseverance which might have been expected of a man that wrote his memoirs nine times before he was satisfied. While acquiring personal experience he was studying the campaigns of all the great masters of the art of war, in exactly the manner which Napoleon half a century later laid down as the only means of becoming a great captain.— HOLDEN, R., 1895, *Gibbon as a Soldier, Macmillan's Magazine, vol.* 71, *p.* 38.

He was one of those happiest of mortals who do not need the "preponderance from without," for whose guidance Wilhelm Meister longed; for him the preponderance within spoke clear enough. The call to be a scholar was in him from the first, the special call to history came later. Both were promptly, strenuously, unwearyingly obeyed; and to that cheerful and long-sustained obedience the historian owed one of the happiest of lives, and we owe the greatest work of history in a modern language.—BAILEY, J. C., 1897, *The Man Gibbon, Fortnightly Review, vol.* 67, *p.* 455.

Gibbon's service in Parliament covered the period of the American Revolution, and during the latter part of the time he was a member of the Board of Trade. The complete correspondence of these years sets his political career in a much better light than did the selections published by Lord Sheffield. We find that Gibbon made a serious attempt to inform himself on the American question, and that he really appreciated the importance of the crisis. Mr. Cotter Morison, relying on the fragmentary letters, has depicted Gibbon's parliamentary career much too unfavourably.—BOURNE, EDWARD GAYLORD, 1897, *American Historical Review, vol.* 2, *p.* 728.

He was a little slow, a little pompous, a little affected and pedantic. In the general type of his mind and character he bore much more resemblance to Hume, Adam Smith, or Reynolds, than to Johnson or Burke. A reserved scholar, who was rather proud of being a man of the world; a confirmed bachelor, much wedded to his comforts though caring nothing for luxury, he was eminently moderate in his ambitions, and there was not a trace of passion or enthusiasm in his nature. Such a man was not likely to inspire any strong devotion. But his temper was most kindly, equable, and contented; he was a steady friend, and he appears to have been always liked and honored in the cultivated and uncontentious society in which he delighted. His life was not a great one, but it was in all essentials blameless and happy. He found the work which was most congenial to him. He pursued it with admirable industry and with brilliant success, and he left behind him a book which is not likely to be forgotten while the English

language endures.—LECKY, WILLIAM ED-
WARD HARTPOLE, 1897, *Library of the
World's Best Literature*, ed. *Warner, vol.*
XI, *p.* 6278

MADEMOISELLE CURCHOD

The cooling-off of Mr. Gibbon has made
me think meanly of him. I have been
going over his book, and he seems to me
to be straining at *esprit*. He is not the
man for me; nor can I think that he will
be the one for Mademoiselle Curchod.
Any one who does not know her value is
not worthy of her; but a man who has
come to that knowledge and then with-
draws himself, is only worthy of contempt.
. . . I would sooner a thousand times
that he left her poor and free among you
than that he brought her rich and miserable away to England.—ROUSSEAU, JEAN
JACQUES, 1763, *Letter to Moulton.*

I should be ashamed if the warm season
of youth had passed away without any
sense of friendship or love; and in the
choice of their objects I may applaud the
discernment of my head or heart. . . .
The beauty of Mademoiselle Curchod, the
daughter of a country clergyman, was
adorned with science and virtue: she listened to the tenderness which she had inspired; but the romantic hopes of youth
and passion were crushed, on my return,
by the prejudice or prudence of an English parent. I sighed as a lover, I obeyed
as a son; my wound was insensibly healed
by time, absence, and the habits of a new
life; and my cure was accelerated by a
faithful report of the tranquility and
cheerfulness of the Lady herself. Her
equal behaviour under the tryals of indigence and prosperity has displayed the
firmness of her character. A citizen of
Geneva, a rich banker of Paris, made himself happy by rewarding her merit; the
genius of her husband has raised him to a
perilous eminence; and Madame Necker
now divides and alleviates the cares of the
first minister of the finances of France.—
GIBBON, EDWARD, C 1789, *Autobiography,
Memoir C.*, ed. *Murray, p.* 238.

The letter in which Gibbon communicated to Mademoiselle Curchod the opposition of his father to their marriage still
exists in manuscript. The first pages are
tender and melancholy, as might be expected from an unhappy lover; the latter
becomes by degrees calm and reasonable,

and the letter concludes with these words:
—*C'est pourquoi, Mademoiselle, j'ai l'hon-
neur d'être votre très humble et très obéis-
sant serviteur, Edward Gibbon.* He truly
loved Mademoiselle Curchod; but every
one loves according to his character, and
that of Gibbon was incapable of a despairing passion.—SUARD, M., 1828, *Life.*

His love affair—his first and only one—
was transient enough. . . . She was, as
Gibbon declares (and we know it on better
testimony than a lover's eyes), beautiful,
intelligent, and accomplished. Her charms,
however, do not seem to have made any
indelible impression on our young student,
whose sensibility, to the truth, was never
very profound. On his father's expressing his disapprobation, he surrendered
the object of his affection with as little
resistance as he had surrendered his
Romanism.—ROGERS, HENRY, 1857, *Encyclopœdia Britannica, Eighth edition.*

That the passion which she inspired in
him was tender, pure, and fitted to raise
to a higher level a nature which in some
respects was much in need of such elevation will be doubted by none but the hopelessly cynical; and probably there are few
readers who can persue the paragraph in
which Gibbon "approaches the delicate
subject of his ealry love," without discerning in it a pathos much deeper than that
of which the writer was himself aware.—
BLACK, J. SUTHERLAND, 1879, *Encyclopœdia Britannica, Ninth edition.*

It becomes a kind of "Ring and the
Book," but a Gibbonian "Ring and the
Book"—every voice is the voice of Gibbon, and as we turn the pages we always
see the same short fat figure explaining
and pronouncing, and hear no echoes from
the market-place, or the law-courts.
When the historian treats of his early
love affair, it is especially entertaining to
have his feelings described in many ways
and at different periods of his life. Gibbon's love-story, told by himself, has always interested and amused his fellows—it
is a literary curiosity—a perennial joke—
but even here we might welcome another
point of view. In the original collection
edited by Gibbon's friend, several letters
from his correspondents were inserted—
all worth reading in their way. But far
the most interesting were a number of
letters written by Mme. Necker to her
former lover. They extend over a long

stretch of time, and bear witness to an extraordinary loyal and faithful tenderness on her part. Some of the love for him, which Gibbon has disregarded, seems to have always remained in the bottom of her heart, and while she learned to realize that his genius lay in friendship and not in courtship, she adapted herself to his temperament and gave him to the last day of his life an unswerving affection.— LYTTELTON, EDITH, 1897, *The Sequel to Gibbon's Love-Story, National Review, vol.* 29, *p.* 904.

The tone in which Gibbon generally refers to love affairs in his history is not altogether edifying, and hardly implies that his passion had purified or ennobled his mind.—STEPHEN, LESLIE, 1898, *Studies of a Biographer, vol.* I, *p.* 169.

DECLINE AND FALL OF THE ROMAN EMPIRE
1776–88

You have, unexpectedly, given the world a classic history. The fame it must acquire will tend every day to acquit this panegyric of flattery.—WALPOLE, HORACE, 1776, *To Edward Gibbon, Feb.* 14; *Letters, ed. Cunningham, vol.* VI, *p.* 308.

As I ran through your volume of History with great avidity and impatience, I cannot forbear discovering somewhat of the same impatience in returning you thanks for your agreeable present, and expressing the satisfaction which the performance has given me. Whether I consider the dignity of your style, the depth of your matter, or the extensiveness of your learning, I must regard the work as equally the object of esteem, and I own that, if I had not previously had the happiness of your personal acquaintance, such a performance from an Englishman in our age would have given me some surprize. —HUME, DAVID, 1776, *Letter to Edward Gibbon, March* 18.

Gibbon I detect a frequent poacher in the "Philosophical Essays" of *Bolingbroke:* as in his representation of the unsocial character of the Jewish religion; and in his insinuation of the suspicions cast by succeeding miracles, acknowledged to be false, on prior ones contended to be true. Indeed it seems not unlikely that he caught the first hint of his theological chapters from this work.—GREEN, THOMAS, 1779-1810, *Diary of a Lover of Literature.*

Another d—mn'd thick, square book! Always scribble, scribble, scribble! eh! Mr. Gibbon?—GLOUCESTER, DUKE OF?, 1781, *On Presentation of the Second Volume of the Decline and Fall.*

I can recollect no historical work from which I ever received so much instruction, and when I consider in what a barren field you had to glean and pick up materials I am truly astonished at the connected and interesting story you have formed.— ROBERTSON, WILLIAM, 1781, *Letter to Edward Gibbon, May* 12.

You will be diverted to hear that Mr. Gibbon has quarrelled with me. He lent me his second volume in the middle of November. I returned it with a most civil panegyric. He came for more incense; I gave it, but alas! with too much sincerity; I added, "Mr. Gibbon, I am sorry *you* should have pitched on so disgusting a subject as the Constantinopolitan History. There is so much of the Arians and Eunomians, and semi-Pelagians; and there is such a strange contrast between Roman and Gothic manners, and so little harmony between a Consul Sabinus and a Ricimer, Duke of the Palace, that though you have written the story as well as it could be written, I fear few will have patience to read it." He coloured: all his round features squeezed themselves into sharp angles; he screwed up his button-mouth, and rapping his snuff-box, said, "It had never been put together before"—*so well,* he meant to add—but gulped it. He meant *so well* certainly, for Tillemont, whom he quotes in every page, has done the very thing. Well, from that hour to this, I have never seen him, though he used to call once or twice a week; nor has he sent me the third volume, as he promised. I well knew his vanity, even about his ridiculous face and person, but thought he had too much sense to avow it so palpably. —WALPOLE, HORACE, 1781, *To Rev. William Mason, Jan.* 27; *Letters, ed. Cunningham, vol.* VII, *p.* 505.

If there be any certain method of discovering a man's real object, yours has been to discredit Christianity in fact, while in words you represent yourself as a friend to it; a conduct which I scruple not to call highly unworthy and mean; an insult on the common sense of the Christian world. — PRIESTLEY, JOSEPH,

1782, *A Letter to Edward Gibbon on the Decline and Fall.*

I now feel as if a mountain was removed from my breast; as far as I can judge, the public unanimously applauds my compliment to Lord North, and does not appear dissatisfied with the conclusion of my work, I look back with amazement on the road which I have travelled, but which I should never have entered had I been previously apprized of its length.—GIBBON, EDWARD, 1788, *Private Letters, vol.* II, *p.* 170.

I cannot express to you the pleasure it gives me to find, that, by the universal assent of every man of taste and learning whom I either know or correspond with, it sets you at the very head of the whole literary tribe at present existing in Europe.—SMITH, ADAM, 1788, *Letter to Edward Gibbon, Dec.* 10.

You desire to know my opinion of Mr. Gibbon. I can say very little about him, for such is the affectation of his style, that I could never get through the half of one of his volumes. If anybody would translate him into good classical English, (such, I mean, as Addison, Swift, Lord Lyttelton, &c., wrote), I should read him with eagerness; for I know there must be much curious matter in his work. His cavils against religion, have, I think, been all confuted; he does not seem to understand that part of his subject: indeed I have never yet met with a man, an author, who both understood Christianity, and disbelieved it.—BEATTIE, JAMES, 1788, *Letter to Duchess of Gordon, November 20th; Works, ed. Forbes, vol.* III, *p.* 56.

It is a most wonderful mass of information, not only on history, but almost on all the ingredients of history, as war, government, commerce, coin, and what not. If it has a fault, it is in embracing too much, and consequently in not detailing enough, and in striding backwards and forwards from one set of princes to another, and from one subject to another; so that, without much historic knowledge, and without much memory, and much method in one's memory, it is almost impossible not to be sometimes bewildered: nay, his own impatience to tell what he knows, makes the author, though commonly so explicit, not perfectly clear in his expressions. The last chapter of the fourth volume, I own, made me recoil,

and I could scarcely push through it. So far from being Catholic or heretic, I wished Mr. Gibbon had never heard of Monophysites, Nestorians, or any such fools! But the sixth volume made ample amends; Mahomet and the Popes were gentlemen and good company. I abominate fractions of theology and reformation.— WALPOLE, HORACE, 1788, *To Thomas Barrett, June* 5; *Letters, ed. Cunningham, vol.* IX, *p.* 126.

His reflections are often just and profound. He pleads eloquently for the rights of mankind, and the duty of toleration; nor does his humanity ever slumber unless when women are ravished, or the Christians persecuted. . . . He often makes, when he cannot readily find, an occasion to insult our religion, which he hates so cordially that he might seem to revenge some personal insult. Such is his eagerness in the cause, that he stoops to the most despicable pun, or to the most awkward perversion of language, for the pleasure of turning the Scriptures into ribaldry, or of calling Jesus an impostor.—PORSON, RICHARD, 1790, *Letters to Archdeacon Travis, Preface.*

I am at a loss how to describe the success of the work without betraying the vanity of the writer. The first impression was exhausted in a few days; a second and third edition were scarcely adequate to the demand; and the bookseller's property was twice invaded by the pyrates of Dublin. My book was on every table, and almost on every toilette; the historian was crowned by the taste or fashion of the day; nor was the general voice disturbed by the barking of any profane critic. . . . It was on the day, or rather, night of the 27th of June, 1787, between the hours of eleven and twelve, that I wrote the last lines of the last page, in a summerhouse in my garden. After laying down my pen, I took several turns in a berceau, or covered walk of acacias, which commands a prospect of the country, the Lake, and the mountains. The air was temperate, the sky was serene, the silver orb of the moon was reflected from the waters, and all nature was silent. I will not dissemble the first emotions of joy on the recovery of my freedom, and perhaps the establishment of my fame. But my pride was soon humbled, and a sober melancholy was spread over my mind, by the idea that I had taken an everlasting leave of an old and agreeable companion, and that, whatsoever might be the future date of my history, the life of the historian must be short and precarious.—GIBBON, EDWARD, 1793, *Autobiography, Memoir E., ed. Murray, pp.* 311, 333.

The work of Gibbon excites my utmost admiration; not so much by the immense learning and industry which it displays, as by the commanding intellect, the keen sagacity, apparent in almost every page. The admiration of his ability extends even to his manner of showing his hatred to Christianity, which is exquisitely subtle and acute, and adapted to do very great mischief, even where there is not the smallest avowal of hostility. It is to be deplored that a great part of the early history of the Christian Church was exactly such as a man like him could have wished.—FOSTER, JOHN, 1805, *Letters, ed. Ryland, vol.* I, *p.* 262.

The author of the "History of the Decline," &c., appears to have possessed a considerable share of sense, ingenuity, and knowledge of his subject, together with great industry. But these qualities or talents are disgraced,—by *a false taste of composition*, which prompts him continually to employ a verbose, inflated style, in order to obtain the praise of force and energy,—by *a perpetual affectation of wit, irony,* and *satire*, altogether unsuited to the historic character,—and, what is worse, by *a freethinking, licentious spirit,* which spares neither morals nor religion, and must make every honest man regard him as a bad citizen and pernicious writer. All these miscarriages may be traced up to one common source, an excessive vanity. —HURD, RICHARD, 1808? *Commonplace Book, ed. Kilvert, p.* 250.

The uncommon sum Gibbon received for copyright, though it excited the astonishment of the philosopher himself, was for the continued labour of a *whole life,* and probably the *library* he had purchased for his work equalled at least in cost the produce of his *pen;* the tools cost the workman as much as he obtained for his work. Six thousand pounds gained on these terms will keep an author indigent. —DISRAELI, ISAAC, 1812-13, *Laborious Authors, Calamities of Authors.*

Gibbon is a writer full of thoughts; his language is in general powerful and exquisite, but it has, to a great excess, the faults of elaborateness, pompousness, and monotony. His style is full of Latin and French words and phrases. . . . The work of Gibbon, however instructive and fascinating it may be, is nevertheless at bottom an offensive one, on account of his deficiency in feeling, and his propensity to the infidel opinions and impious mockeries of Voltaire. These are things extremely unworthy of a historian, and in the periodic and somewhat cumbrous style of Gibbon they appear set off to far less advantage than in the light and airy compositions of his master. He never seems to be naturally a wit, but impresses us with the idea that he would very fain be one if he could.—SCHLEGEL, FREDERICK, 1815-59, *Lectures on the History of Literature.*

But the high estimation in which Mr. Gibbon's outline is held on the continent, where the Roman Law has for so many centuries been thoroughly studied, and elaborately written on, will be regarded as strong evidence of its high merit.— HOFFMAN, DAVID, 1817, *A Course of Legal Study.*

A work of immense research and splendid execution. . . . Alternately delighted and offended by the gorgeous colouring with which his fancy invests the rude and scanty materials of his narrative; sometimes fatigued by the learning of his notes, occasionally amused by their liveliness, frequently disgusted by their obscenity, and admiring or deploring the bitterness of his skilful irony—I toiled through his massy tomes with exemplary patience. His style is exuberant, sonorous, and epigrammatic to a degree that is often displeasing. He yields to Hume in elegance and distinctness—to Robertson in talents for general disquisition—but he excels them both in a species of brief and shrewd remark for which he seems to have taken Tacitus as a model, more than any other that I know of.—CARLYLE, THOMAS, 1818, *Early Letters, ed. Norton, pp.* 68, 69.

Arrived at Bury before tea. My brother and sister were going to hear an astronomical lecture. I stayed alone and read a chapter in Gibbon on the early history of the Germans. Having previously read the first two lectures of

Schlegel, I had the pleasure of comparison, and I found much in Gibbon that I had thought original in Schlegel.—ROBINSON, HENRY CRABB, 1820, *Diary, ed. Sadler, vol.* I, *p.* 430.

Gibbon was not, like Hume, a self-thinking, deep-fathoming man, who searched into the nature of things, existence and thought, but was in these respects like the French, or like the Scotchman Brougham, who has also attained this Franco-Genevese capacity, of quickly making other people's thoughts and investigations his own, and propounding them in an admirable manner. Like the great French writers, he can take a quick and comprehensive view of various departments of knowledge, and we can therefore learn most readily through his instrumentality the results of the learned labours of the great collectors of materials upon the theology, philosophy, and jurisprudence of the times of declining antiquity, and of the rising middle ages. Because his eloquence and his great skill in representation give a charm and splendour to the thoughts which he wishes to disseminate, he has the full right of all men who are great in politics and literature to claim, that nobody should ask, whether he was really in earnest, or how his language and his conduct harmonized.—SCHLOSSER, FRIEDRICH CHRISTOPH, 1823–64, *History of the Eighteenth Century, tr. Davison, vol.* II, *p.* 85.

I have had occasion, during my labors, to consult the writings of philosophers, who have treated on the finances of the Roman Empire; of scholars, who have investigated the chronology; of theologians, who have searched the depths of ecclesiastical history; of writers on law, who have studied with care the Roman jurisprudence; of Orientalists, who have occupied themselves with the Arabians and the Koran; of modern historians, who have entered upon extensive researches touching the crusades and their influence; each of these writers has remarked and pointed out, in the "History of the Decline and Fall of the Roman Empire," some negligences, some false or imperfect views, some omissions, which it is impossible not to suppose voluntary; they have rectified some facts, combated with advantage some assertions; but in general they have taken the researches and the

ideas of Gibbon, as points of departure, or as proofs of the researches or of the new opinions which they have advanced.—GUIZOT, FRANÇOIS PIERRE GUILLAUME, 1828, *ed. Gibbon's Works, Preface.*

There is no writer who exhibits more distinctly the full development of the principles of modern history, with all its virtues and defects, than Gibbon. . . . Gibbon was a more vivacious draughtsman than most writers of his school. He was, moreover, deeply versed in geography, chronology, antiquities, verbal criticism— in short, in all the sciences in any way subsidiary to his art. The extent of his subject permitted him to indulge in those elaborate disquisitions so congenial to the spirit of modern history on the most momentous and interesting topics, while his early studies enabled him to embellish the drier details of his narrative with the charms of a liberal and elegant scholarship. What, then, was wanting to this accomplished writer? Good faith. His defects were precisely of the class of which we have before been speaking, and his most elaborate efforts exhibit too often the perversion of learning and ingenuity to the vindication of preconceived hypotheses. He cannot, indeed, be convicted of ignorance or literal inaccuracy, as he has triumphantly proved in his discomfiture of the unfortunate Davis. But his disingenuous mode of conducting the argument leads precisely to the same unfair result. Thus, in his celebrated chapters on the "Progress of Christianity," which he tells us were "reduced by three successive revisals from a bulky volume to their present size," he has often slurred over in the text such particulars as might reflect most credit on the character of the religion, or shuffled them into a note at the bottom of the page, while all that admits of a doubtful complexion in its early propagation is ostentatiously blazoned, and set in contrast to the most amiable features of paganism. At the same time, by a style of innuendo that conveys "more than meets the ear," he has contrived, with Iago-like duplicity, to breathe a taint of suspicion on the purity which he dares not openly assail.—PRESCOTT, WILLIAM HICKLING, 1829, *Irving's Conquest of Granada, Biographical and Critical Miscellanies, pp.* 102, 103.

Gibbon, the architect of a bridge over

the dark gulf which separates ancient from modern times, whose vivid genius has tinged with brilliant colours the greatest historical work in existence.—ALISON, SIR ARCHIBALD, 1833–42, *History of Europe During the French Revolution, vol.* XIV, *p.* 3.

Gibbon's style is detestable, but his style is not the worst thing about him. His history has proved an effectual bar to all real familiarity with the temper and habits of imperial Rome. Few persons read the original authorities, even those which are classical; and certainly no distinct knowledge of the actual state of the empire can be obtained from Gibbon's rhetorical sketches. He takes notice of nothing but what may produce an effect; he skips on from eminence to eminence, without ever taking you through the valleys between: in fact, his work is little else but a disguised collection of all the splendid anecdotes which he could find in any book concerning any persons or nations from the Antonines to the capture of Constantinople. When I read a chapter in Gibbon I seem to be looking through a luminous haze or fog :—figures come and go, I know not how or why, all larger than life, or distorted or discoloured; nothing is real, vivid, true; all is scenical, and as it were, exhibited by candlelight. And then to call it a History of the Decline and Fall of the Roman Empire! Was there ever a greater misnomer? I protest I do not remember a single philosophical attempt made throughout the work to fathom the ultimate causes of the decline or fall of that empire. How miserably deficient is the narrative of the important reign of Justinian! And that poor scepticism, which Gibbon mistook for Socratic philosophy, has led him to misstate and mistake the character and influence of Christianity in a way which even an avowed infidel or atheist would not and could not have done. Gibbon was a man of immense reading; but he had no philosophy; and he never fully understood the principle upon which the best of the old historians wrote. He attempted to imitate their artificial construction of the whole work—their dramatic ordonnance of the parts—without seeing that their histories were intended more as documents illustrative of the truths of political philosophy than as mere chronicles of events.— COLERIDGE, SAMUEL TAYLOR, 1833, *Table Talk, Aug.* 15, *ed. Ashe, p.* 245.

We have ourselves followed the track of Gibbon through many parts of his work; we have read his authorities with constant reference to his pages, and we must pronounce our deliberate judgment in terms of the highest admiration of his general accuracy. Many of his seeming errors are almost inevitable from the close condensation of his matter. From the immense range of his history it was sometimes necessary to compress into a single sentence, a whole vague and diffuse page of a Byzantine chronicler. Perhaps something of importance may thus escape, and his expressions may not quite contain the whole substance of the quotation. His limits, at times, compel him to sketch; where that is the case, it is not fair to expect the full details of the picture. At times he can only deal with important results; and in his account of a war, it sometimes requires great attention to discover that the events, which seem to be comprehended in a single campaign, occupy several years. But this admirable skill in selecting and giving prominence to the points which are of real weight and importance—this distribution of light and shade—though perhaps it may occasionally betray him into vague and imperfect statements, is one of the highest excellencies of Gibbon's historic manner. It is the more striking, when we pass from the works of his chief authorities, where, after labouring through long, minute and wearisome descriptions of the accessary and subordinate circumstances, a single unmarked and undistinguished sentence, which we may overlook from the inattention of fatigue, contains the great moral and political result.—MILMAN, HENRY HART, 1834, *Guizot's Edition of Gibbon, Quarterly Review, vol.* 50, *p.* 290.

Perhaps the most masterly and elaborate account of the Civil Law which is extant is to be found in the forty-fourth chapter of Gibbon's "Decline and Fall of the Roman Empire." Lord Mansfield characterised it as "beautiful and spirited." — WARREN, SAMUEL, 1835, *Law Studies.*

Another very celebrated historian, we mean Gibbon—not a man of mere science and analysis, like Hume, but with some (though not the truest or profoundest) artistic feeling of the picturesque, and from whom, therefore, rather more might have been expected—has with much pains succeeded in producing a tolerably graphic picture of here and there a battle, a tumult, or an insurrection; his book is full of movement and costume, and would make a series of very pretty ballets at the Opera house, and the ballets would give us fully as distinct an idea of the Roman empire, and how it declined and fell, as the book does. If we want that, we must look for it anywhere but in Gibbon. One touch of M. Guizot removes a portion of the veil which hid from us the recesses of private life under the Roman empire, lets in a ray of light which penetrates as far even as the domestic hearth of a subject of Rome, and shews us the Government at work making that desolate; but no similar gleam of light from Gibbon's mind ever reaches the subject; *human life*, in the times he wrote about, is not what he concerned himself with.— MILL, JOHN STUART, 1837, *The French Revolution, Early Essays, ed. Gibbs, p.* 276.

A greater historian than Robertson, but not so great as Hume. With all his swagger and bombast, no man ever gave a more futile account of human things than he has done of the decline and fall of the Roman Empire; assigning no profound cause for these phenomena, nothing but diseased nerves, and all sorts of miserable motives, to the actors in them.— CARLYLE, THOMAS, 1838, *Lectures on the History of Literature, p.* 185.

The great work of Gibbon is indispensable to the student of history. The literature of Europe offers no substitute for "The Decline and Fall of the Roman Empire." It has obtained undisputed possession, as rightful occupant, of the vast period which it comprehends. However, some subjects which it embraces may have undergone more complete investigation, on the general view of the whole period, this history is the sole undisputed authority to which all defer, and from which few appeal to the original writers, or to more modern compilers. The inherent interest of the subject; the inexhaustible labor employed upon it; the immense condensation of matter; the luminous arrangement; the general accuracy; the style, which, however monotonous from its uniform stateliness, and

sometimes wearisome from its elaborate art, is throughout vigorous, animated, often picturesque, always commands attention, always conveys its meaning with emphatic energy, describes with singular breadth and fidelity, and generalizes with unrivalled felicity of expression; all these high qualifications have secured, and seem likely to secure, its permanent place in historic literature.—MILMAN, HENRY HART, 1838–39, *ed., The History of the Decline and Fall of the Roman Empire, Preface.*

I read a good deal of Gibbon. He is grossly partial to the pagan persecutors; quite offensively so. His opinion of the Christian fathers is very little removed from mine; but his excuses for the tyranny of their oppressors give to his book the character which Porson describes. He writes like a man who had received some personal injury from Christianity, and wished to be revenged on it and all its professors. — MACAULAY, THOMAS BABINGTON, 1838, *Diary, Dec.* 22; *Life and Letters, ed. Trevelyan, vol.* I, *p.* 26.

He had three hobbies which he rode to the death (stuffed puppets as they were), and which he kept in condition by the continual sacrifice of all that is valuable in language. These hobbies were *Dignity— Modulation—Laconism.* Dignity is all very well; and history demands it for its general tone; but the being everlastingly on stilts is not only troublesome and awkward, but dangerous. He who falls *en homme ordinaire*—from the mere slipping of his feet—is usually an object of sympathy; but all men tumble now and then, and this tumbling from high sticks is sure to provoke laughter. His modulation, however, is always ridiculous; for it is so uniform, so continuous, and so jauntily kept up, that we almost fancy the writer waltzing to his words. With him, to speak lucidly was a far less merit than to speak smoothly and curtly. There is a way in which, through the nature of language itself, we may often save a few words by talking backwards; and this is, therefore, a favorite practice with Gibbon.—POE, EDGAR ALLAN, 1839– 49, *Marginalia, Works, ed. Woodberry, vol.* VII, *p.* 338.

If his work be not always history, it is often something more than history, and above it: it is philosophy, it is theology, it is wit and eloquence, it is criticism the most masterly upon every subject with which literature can be connected. If the style be so constantly elevated as to be often obscure, to be often monotonous, to be sometimes even ludicrously disproportioned to the subject; it must at the same time be allowed, that whenever an opportunity presents itself, it is the striking and adequate representation of comprehensive thought and weighty remark. It may be necessary no doubt to warn the student against the imitation of a mode of writing so little easy and natural. But the very necessity of the caution implies the attraction that is to be resisted; and it must be confessed that the chapters of the "Decline and Fall" are replete with paragraphs of such melody and grandeur as would be the fittest to convey to a youth of genius the full charm of literary composition; and such as, when once heard, however unattainable to the immaturity of his own mind, he would alone consent to admire, or sigh to emulate. . . . When such is the work, it is placed beyond the justice or the injustice of criticism; the Christian may have, but too often, very just reason to complain, the moralist to reprove, the man of taste to censure,—even the historical inquirer may be fatigued and irritated by the unseasonable and obscure splendour through which he is to discover the objects of his research. But the whole is, notwithstanding, such an assemblage of merits so various, so interesting, and so rare, that the "History of the Decline and Fall" must always be considered as one of the most extraordinary monuments that has appeared of the literary powers of a single mind, and its fame can perish only with the civilization of the world.—SMYTH, WILLIAM, 1840, *Lectures on Modern History, vol. I.*

The great merit of Gibbon is his extraordinary industry, and the general fidelity of his statements, as attested by the constant references which he makes to his numerous and varied authorities—references which enable the "most faithful of historians" to ascertain clearly their accuracy, that is, the truth of his narrative. This is the very first virtue of the historical character; and that merit, therefore, is fully possessed by Gibbon. In it he is the worthy rival of Robertson, and in it he forms a remarkable contrast to Hume.

The next great merit of Gibbon is the judgment with which he weighs conflicting authorities and the freedom with which he rejects improbable relations. His sagacity is remarkable; and his attention seems ever awake. . . . The third excellence of his work is its varied learning, distributed in the vast body of notes which accompany the text, and which contain no small portion of a critical abstract, serving for a *catalogue raisonné*, of the works referred to in the page. . . . It must, lastly, be allowed, that the narrative is as lucid as the confused nature of the subject will admit; and that, whatever defects may be ascribed to it, there is nothing tiring or monotonous, nothing to prevent the reader's attention from being kept ever awake. When the nature of the subject is considered, perhaps there may some doubt arise, if the chaster style of Livy, of Robertson, or even of Hume, could have rendered this story as attractive as Gibbon's manner, singularly free from all approach to monotony, though often deviating widely from simplicity and nature. —BROUGHAM, HENRY LORD, 1845–6, *Lives of Men of Letters of the Time of George III.*

Every intelligent reader felt that only a most uncommon sagacity could have seen through the confusion of the chaotic variety of his materials, estimating their claims and merits, and their often obscure relations with each other. So far from complaining of any want of clearness in the narrative, the wonder is, that he should ever have been able to subdue them into tolerable harmony and order. He seems never to have been weary of searching into the endless range of subjects presented, balancing authorities and determining their accuracy with a precision and faithfulness which few will venture to impeach.—PEABODY, WILLIAM B. O., 1846–49, *Men of Letters and Science, Article II., Literary Remains, ed. Peabody, p.* 280.

It is acknowledged that Gibbon wrote with a preconceived, speculative object. Cold design overlays every page. His work is rather an elegant oration, pronounced with sustained diction, than a living picture of the past. The order into which he reduced an immense quantity of chaotic material is, perhaps, its most striking charm.—TUCKERMAN, HENRY T., 1849, *Characteristics of Literature, p.* 188.

Fox used to say that Gibbon's history was immortal, because nobody could do without it; nobody, without vast expense of time and labour, could get elsewhere the information which it contains. I think, and so Lord Grenville thought, that the introductory chapters are the finest part of that history: it was certainly more difficult to write *them* than the rest of the work.—ROGERS, SAMUEL,1855, *Table Talk.*

There is no more solid book in the world than Gibbon's history. Only consider the chronology. It begins before the year *one* and goes down to the year 1453, and is a schedule or series of schedules of important events during that time. Scarcely any fact deeply affecting European civilisation is wholly passed over, and the great majority of facts are elaborately recounted. Laws, dynasties, churches, barbarians, appear and disappear. Everything changes; the old world—the classical civilisation of form and definition—passes away, a new world of free spirit and inward growth emerges; between the two lies a mixed weltering interval of trouble and confusion, when everybody hates everybody, and the historical student leads a life of skirmishes, is oppressed with broils and feuds. All through this long period Gibbon's history goes with steady consistent pace; like a Roman legion through a troubled country—*hæret pede pes;* up hill and down hill, through marsh and thicket, through Goth or Parthian—the firm defined array passes forward—a type of order, and an emblem of civilisation. Whatever may be the defects of Gibbon's history, none can deny him a proud precision and a style in marching order. . . . . Gibbon's reflections connect the events; they are not sermons between them. But, notwithstanding, the manner of the "Decline and Fall" is the last which should be recommended for strict imitation. It is not a style in which you can tell the truth. A monotonous writer is suited only to monotonous matter. Truth is of various kinds—grave, solemn, dignified,petty, low, ordinary; and an historian who has to tell the truth must be able to tell what is vulgar as well as what is great, what is little as well as what is amazing. Gibbon is at fault here.— BAGEHOT, WALTER, 1856, *Edward Gibbon, Literary Studies,* ed. Hutton, *vol.* II, *pp.* 35, 36.

"Gibbon's Decline and Fall" has now been jealously scrutinized by two generations of eager and unscrupulous opponents; and I am only expressing the general opinions of competent judges when I say that by each successive scrutiny it has gained fresh reputation. Against his celebrated fifteenth and sixteenth chapters, all the devices of controversy have been exhausted; but the only result has been, that while the fame of the historian is untarnished, the attacks of his enemies are falling into complete oblivion. The work of Gibbon remains; but who is there who feels any interest in what was written against him?—BUCKLE, HENRY THOMAS, 1857, *History of Civilization in England, vol.* I, *p.* 308, *note.*

Guizot and Milman have both subjected the original authorities, consulted by Gibbon in his history of the Decline and Fall of the Roman Empire, to the intensest scrutiny, to see if the historian has perverted, falsified, or suppressed facts. Their judgment is in favor of his honesty and his conscientious research. Yet this by no means proves that we can obtain through his history the real truth of persons and events. The whole immense tract of history he traverses he has thoroughly *Gibbonized.* The qualities of his character steal out in every paragraph; the words are instinct with Gibbon's nature; though the facts may be obtained from without, the relations in which they are disposed are communicated from within; and the human race for fifteen centuries is made tributary to Gibbon's thought, wears the colors and badges of Gibbon's nature, is denied the possession of any pure and exalted experiences which Gibbon cannot verify by his own; and the reader, who is magnetized by the historian's genius, rises from the perusal of the vast work, informed of nothing as it was in itself, but everything as it appeared to Gibbon, and especially doubting two things,—that there is any chastity in women, or any divine truth in Christianity. —WHIPPLE, EDWIN P., 1857, *Character, Character and Characteristic Men, p.* 27.

The student must have perceived at once that this unbeliever, however he might adopt the cant of the philosophers, was no mere philosophical historian in the Hume and Voltaire sense of the word; that he had devoted intense labour to his task; that he had succeeded in presenting a picture of the past ages such as had not been presented before. He might detect many sophisms in the arguments of his fifteenth and sixteenth chapters. But what are all these arguments to the actual vision of the evils of human society under the Christian dispensation? It is these that give the special pleas for secondary causes their weight. It is these that tempt to the notion that those secondary causes were many of them not divine, but devilish. If that conviction is truly followed out, Gibbon himself will be the best of preachers. He will be the brilliant and eloquent witness for a divine power which has been at work in all ages to counteract the devilish power; which has been stronger to support a righteous kingdom on earth than all evil influences, proceeding from those who call themselves divine ministers, have been to destroy it. But if his reasoning and facts are merely brought face to face with arguments, to prove that at a certain moment there was launched into the world, with miraculous sanctions, a religion the outward displays of which, through subsequent ages, have been so mixed,—which has apparently prompted so many evil deeds—the result must be, in a multitude of cases, a negative indifferent scepticism, in not a few, a positive infidelity.—MAURICE, FREDERICK DENISON, 1862, *Moral and Metaphysical Philosophy, vol.* II, *p.* 600.

He did not write expressly against Christianity; but the subject came across his path in travelling over the vast space of time which he embraced in his magnificent "History of the Decline and Fall of the Roman Empire." It is a subject of regret to be compelled to direct hostile remarks against one who has deserved so well of the world. That work, though in the pageantry of its style it in some sense reflects the art and taste of the age in which it was written, yet in its love of solid information and deep research is the noblest work of history in the English tongue. Grand alike in its subject, its composition, and its perspective, it has a right to a place among the highest works of human conception; and sustains the relation to history which the works of Michael Angelo bear to art.—FARRAR, ADAM STOREY, 1863, *A Critical History of Free Thought, p.* 196.

Gibbon has planted laurels long to bloom
Above the ruins of sepulchral Rome.
He sang no dirge, but mused upon the land
Where Freedom took his solitary stand.
To him Thucydides and Livius bow,
And Superstition veils her wrinkled brow.
—LANDOR, WALTER SAVAGE, 1863, *Heroic Idyls, with Additional Poems, Works, vol.* VIII, *p.* 351.

The famous XVIth chapter of Gibbon's "Decline and Fall of the Roman Empire" was assailed furiously, but in vain, each assault exposing the weakness of the assailants; and it was only by adopting his history, and editing it with judicious notes, that the church silenced the enemy it could not crush.—FROTHINGHAM, OCTAVIUS BROOKS, 1876, *Transcendentalism in New England, p.* 185.

I have finished Gibbon, with a great deduction from the high esteem I have had of him ever since the old Kirkcaldy days, when I first read the twelve volumes of poor Irving's copy in twelve consecutive days. A man of endless reading and research, but of a most disagreeable style, and a great want of the highest faculties (which indeed are very rare) of what we could call a classical historian, compared with Herodotus, for instance, and his perfect clearness and simplicity in every part.—CARLYLE, THOMAS, 1877? *Letters; Life in London, ed.* Froude, *vol.* II, *p.* 395.

A man of genius; not for what he has done for history, but what he has done for literature, in showing that no theme is so huge but that art may proportion it and adorn it till it charms,—the work which lastingly charms being always and alone the proof of genius. When one turns from other histories to his mighty achievement, one feels that it is really as incomparable for its noble manner as for the grandeur of the story it narrates. That story assumes at his touch the majestic forms, the lofty movement, of an epic; its advance is rhythmical; in the strong pulse of its antitheses is the fire, the life of a poetic sense; its music, rich and full, has a martial vigor, its colors are the blazons of shields and banners.—HOWELLS, WILLIAM DEAN, 1878, *Edward Gibbon, Atlantic Monthly, vol.* 41, *p.* 100.

It would be difficult to name any writer in our language, especially among the few who deserve to be compared with him, who is so un-English, not in a bad sense of the word, as implying objectionable qualities, but as wanting the clear insular stamp and native flavour. If an intelligent Chinese or Persian were to read his book in a French translation, he would not readily guess that it was written by an Englishman. It really bears the imprint of no nationality, and is emphatically European. . . . An indefinable stamp of weightiness is impressed on Gibbon's writing; he has a baritone manliness which banishes everything small, trivial, or weak. When he is eloquent (and it should be remembered to his credit that he never affects eloquence, though he occasionally affects dignity), he rises without effort into real grandeur. On the whole we may say that his manner, with certain manifest faults, is not unworthy of his matter, and the praise is great.—MORISON, JAMES COTTER, 1878, *Gibbon (English Men of Letters), pp. 26, 167.*

Gibbon's "Decline and Fall" leaves a reader cold who cares only to quicken his own inmost being by contact with what is most precious in man's spiritual history; one chapter of Augustine's "Confessions," one sentence of the "Imitation"—each a live coal from off the altar—will be of more worth to such an one than all the mass and laboured majesty of Gibbon. But one who can gaze with a certain impersonal regard on the spectacle of the world will find the "Decline and Fall of the Roman Empire," more than almost any other single book, replenish and dilate the mind.— DOWDEN, EDWARD, 1880, *Southey (English Men of Letters), p. 20.*

Though Gibbon's history was completed nearly a century ago, its great importance has not declined, and it is probably still entitled to be esteemed as the greatest historical work ever written. . . . The minuteness and comprehensiveness of Gibbon's historical knowledge are somewhat appalling to the scholarship of the present day. . . . So thorough were his methods that the laborious investigations of German scholarship, the keen criticisms of theological zeal, and the steady researches of a century have brought to light very few important errors in the results of his labours. But it is not merely the learning of the work, learned as it is, that gives it character as a history. It is also that ingenious skill by which the vast erudition, the boundless range, the infinite variety, and the gorgeous magnificence of the details are all wrought together into a symmetrical whole. Two objections to Gibbon's history have often been urged. The one is to the stately magnificence of his style, the other to his strong bias against Christianity. In both of these objections there is considerable reason. The majestic periods with which the author describes even the least important events are a source either of annoyance or of amusement to nearly every modern reader. The other characteristic not only leads the author to describe the origin and growth of Christianity without sympathy, but it throws a gloomy hue over the whole, and gives to events as they pass before the reader something of the melancholy pomp of a funeral procession. But whatever objections different minds may raise, either to the unbending stateliness of his style or to the stinging sarcasm of his spirits, these peculiarities will prevent no genuine scholar from studying the work and profiting by it.—ADAMS, CHARLES KENDALL, 1882, *A Manual of Historical Literature, p. 138.*

No Christian, therefore, but will rejoice that, with its great faults on this side, a history like that of Gibbon has been written; and Christianity needs too much to have its infirmities, as a human product, displayed for its own correction, to quarrel even with its severest censor who challenges historical evidence for his accusations. In particular allegations Gibbon may have failed, but many of his charges hit some weak point, where Christianity is the better for the criticism; and if his general spirit be complained of, as, for example, in his sympathy with Mohammedanism rather than with so much higher a faith, this teaches the Church of Christ to remember its own corruption as the precursor of its defeat, while there is no more striking moral which Gibbon has unconsciously helped to point than the divine vitality, as since tested, of the one religion, while the other has been sinking into senility and exhaustion. In this point of view, or as a permanent measure of the strength and enduring resource of Christianity, the celebrated inquiry of Gibbon as to Secondary Causes of the success of Christianity has a special interest.— CAIRNS, JOHN, 1881, *Unbelief in the Eighteenth Century, p.* 113.

If you want to know where the world was, and how it fared with it during the first ten centuries of our era, read Gibbon. No other writer can do for you just what he does. No one else has had the courage to attempt his task over again. The laborious student of history may go to the many and obscure sources from which Gibbon drew the materials for his great work, and correct or supplement him here and there, as Milman has done; but the general reader wants the completed structure, and not the mountain quarries from which the blocks came; and the complete structure you get in Gibbon. To omit him is to leave a gap in your knowledge of the history of the world which nothing else can fill. As Carlyle said to Emerson, he "is the splendid bridge which connects the old world with the new;" very artificial, but very real for all that, and very helpful to any who have business that way. The case may be even more strongly stated than that. To read Gibbon is to be present at the creation of the world—the modern world. . . . Ruskin objects to Gibbon's style as the "worst English ever written by an educated Englishman." It was the style of his age and country brought to perfection, the stately curvilinear or orbicular style; every sentence makes a complete circle; but it is always a real thought, a real distinction that sweeps through the circle. Modern style is more linear, more direct and picturesque; and in the case of such a writer as Ruskin, much more loose, discursive and audacious. The highly artificial buckram style of the age of Gibbon has doubtless had its day, but it gave us some noble literature, and is no more to be treated with contempt than the age which produced it is to be treated with contempt.— BUR-ROUGHS, JOHN, 1886, *Ruskin's Judgment of Gibbon and Darwin, The Critic, May* 1.

Gibbon has a good deal to answer for. You can find nearly every fact in him, but he began by making the subject ridiculous, by trotting out some absurd and, if possible, indecent anecdote, as if it were a summary of the whole reign. It is that chapter which gives the impression, and those which follow never take it away. I believe that Pipin was made patrician by authority of Constantine Kopronymos, but that Pope Stephen bamboozled them all round.—FREEMAN, EDWARD A., 1888, *Letter to Goldwin Smith, April* 25; *Life and Letters, ed. Stephens, vol.* II, *p.* 380.

In accuracy, thoroughness, lucidity, and comprehensive grasp of a vast subject, the "History" is unsurpassable. It is the one English history which may be regarded as definitive. The philosophy is of course that of the age of Voltaire and implies a deficient insight into the great social forces. The style, though variously judged, has at least the cardinal merit of admirable clearness, and if pompous is always animated. Whatever its shortcomings the book is artistically imposing as well as historically unimpeachable as a vast panorama of a great period. Gibbon's fortunate choice of a subject enabled him to write the one book in which the clearness of his own age is combined with a thoroughness of research which has made it a standard for his successors.—STE-PHEN, LESLIE, 1890, *Dictionary of National Biography, vol.* XXI, *p.* 255.

It is no personal paradox, but the judgment of all competent men, that the "Decline and Fall" of Gibbon is the most perfect historical composition that exists in any language: at once scrupulously faithful in its facts; consummate in its literary art; and comprehensive in analysis of the forces affecting society over a very long and crowded epoch. In eight moderate volumes, of which every sentence is compacted of learning and brimful of thought, and yet every page is as fascinating as romance, this great historian has condensed the history of the civilised world over the vast period of fourteen centuries—linking the ancient world to the modern, the Eastern world to the Western, and marshalling in one magnificent panorama the contrasts, the relations, and the analogies of all. If Gibbon has not the monumental simplicity of Thucydides, or the profound insight of Tacitus, he has performed a feat which neither has attempted. "Survey mankind," says our poet, "from China to Peru!" And our historian surveys mankind from Britain to Tartary, from the Sahara to Siberia, and weaves for one-third of all recorded time the epic of the human race.—HARRISON, FREDERIC, 1894, *Some Great Books of History, The Meaning of History, p.* 101.

A great work then, and a great work

now, measured by what standard we will. To say that one approaches the accuracy of Gibbon is to exhaust praise; to say that one surpasses him in reach of learning is to deal in hyperbole.—MITCHELL, DONALD G., 1895, *English Lands Letters and Kings, Queen Anne and the Georges,* p. 128.

Gibbon gave a new impetus to the study of the history of Roman law through the celebrated 44th chapter of his "Decline and Fall of the Roman Empire." It was translated by Professor Hugo of Göttingen and Professor Warnkönig of Liège, and has been used as the text-book on Civil Law in some of the foreign universities. . . . Herder, Savigny, and Niebuhr stand all under the immediate influence of Gibbon, and Lessing saw in him kindred tendencies, though in a different direction. —MERZ, JOHN THEODORE, 1896, *A History of European Thought in the Nineteenth Century, vol.* I, *p.* 169, *note.*

Gibbon was the first to write a complete history on the largest scale, with a magnificent sense of proportion, and with profound original research; tracing the complex, stormy evolution of the modern world out of the ancient, and the momentous transitions from polytheism and slavery to monotheism and free industry. It is the history of civilization during thirteen centuries. The vast canvas is filled without confusion, without apparent effort, and without discord by one glowing, distinct, harmonious composition. He was not a philosophic historian, nor did he profess the profound insight of Thucydides, of Tacitus, of Bacon, or of Hume, into the springs of human action; but he was great in research, and his work remains as the initial triumph of a great historical method. Allowing for manifest defects, arising from its ornate and elaborate style; from his perverse misconception of Christianity; from his disbelief in heroism, in popular enthusiasm, and in self-devotion; and from his own epicurean and aristocratic habit of mind, his "Decline and Fall" stands alone and unrivalled for breadth, knowledge, unity of conception, and splendour of form. It resembles the stately, solid, irresistible march of a Roman Legion; and is characterized by Niebuhr as the greatest achievement of human thought and erudition in the department of history.— AUBREY,

W. H. S., 1896, *The Rise and Growth of the English Nation, vol.* III, *p.* 254.

Permanently established its author in that position of supremacy as a historian of which each succeeding generation renders his tenure more secure. . . . On the merits and demerits of his style it cannot be pretended that the same consensus of competent opinion prevails. It has been reprehended by many who had some right to criticise it, and by more who had not. Coleridge, whose own prose style, with all its eloquence, left much to be desired, condemned it in terms so extravagant as to discredit the critic rather than the criticised; but others, reviewing it with less bias, and expressing themselves with more moderation, have managed to draw up a pretty long list of objections to it. It has been pronounced monotonous, inelastic, affected, pompous; it has been called exotic in its spirit, and un-English in its structure. The most serious of these charges is, perhaps the second.—TRAILL, HENRY DUFF, 1896, *Social England, vol.* V, *pp.* 448, 449.

One who is, all things told and all things allowed for, the greatest historian of the world.—SAINTSBURY, GEORGE, 1896, *Social England, ed. Traill, vol.* V, *p.* 268.

If we continue Gibbon in his fame, it will be for love of his art, not for worship of his scholarship. We some of us, nowadays, know the period of which he wrote better even than he did; but which one of us shall build so admirable a monument to ourselves, as artists, out of what we know? The scholar finds his immortality in the form he gives to his work. It is a hard saying, but the truth of it is inexorable: be an artist, or prepare for oblivion.— WILSON, WOODROW, 1896, *Mere Literature, p.* 22.

To Edward Gibbon, who timidly deprecated comparison with Robertson and Hume, criticism is steadily awarding a place higher and higher above them. He is, indeed, one of the great writers of the century, one of those who exemplify in the finest way the signal merits of the age in which he flourished. The book by which he mainly survives, the vast "Decline and Fall of the Roman Empire," began to appear in 1776, and was not completed until 1788. It was at once discovered by all who were competent to judge, that here was a new thing introduced into the literature of the world.—GOSSE, EDMUND, 1897, *Short History of Modern English Literature, p.* 258.

Gibbon excels all other English historians in symmetry, proportion, perspective, and arrangement, which are also the pre-eminent and characteristic merits of the best French literature. We find in his writing nothing of the great miscalculations of space that were made by such writers as Macaulay and Buckle; nothing of the awkward repetitions, the confused arrangement, the semi-detached and disjointed episodes that mar the beauty of many other histories of no small merit. Vast and multifarious as are the subjects which he has treated, his work is a great whole, admirably woven in all its parts. On the other hand, his foreign taste may perhaps be seen in his neglect of the Saxon element, which is the most vigorous and homely element in English prose. Probably in no other English writer does the Latin element so entirely predominate. Gibbon never wrote an unmeaning and very seldom an obscure sentence; he could always paint with sustained and stately eloquence an illustrious character or a splendid scene: but he was wholly wanting in the grace of simplicity, and a monotony of glitter and of mannerism is the great defect of his style. He possessed, to a degree which even Tacitus and Bacon had hardly surpassed, the supreme literary gift of condensation, and it gives an admirable force and vividness to his narrative; but it is sometimes carried to excess. Not unfrequently it is attained by an excessive allusiveness, and a wide knowledge of the subject is needed to enable the reader to perceive the full import and meaning conveyed or hinted at by a mere turn of phrase. But though his style is artificial and pedantic, and greatly wanting in flexibility, it has a rare power of clinging to the memory, and it has profoundly influenced English prose.—LECKY, WILLIAM EDWARD HARTPOLE, 1897, *Edward Gibbon, Library of the World's best Literature, ed. Warner, vol.* XI, *p.* 6273.

The author's profits for the "Decline and Fall of the Roman Empire," by Gibbon, are put down at £10,000.—ANDREWS, WILLIAM, 1898, *The Earnings of Authors, Literary Byways, p.* 56.

AUTOBIOGRAPHY

1796-1896

Papa has read us several parts of Mr. Gibbon's Memoirs, written so exactly in the style of his conversation that, while we felt delighted at the beauty of the thoughts and elegance of the language, we could not help feeling a severe pang at the idea we should never hear his instructive and amusing conversation any more.—HOLROYD, MARIA JOSEPHA, 1793, *Girlhood, p.* 273.

The most important part consists of Memoirs of Mr. Gibbon's life and writings, a work which he seems to have projected with peculiar solicitude and attention, and of which he left six different sketches, all in his own hand-writing. One of these sketches, the most diffuse and circumstantial, so far as it proceeds, ends at the time when he quitted Oxford. Another at the year 1764, when he travelled to Italy. A third, at his father's death, in 1770. A fourth, which he continued to a short time after his return to Lausanne in 1788, appears in the form of Annals, much less detailed than the others. The two remaining sketches are still more imperfect. It is difficult to discover the order in which these several pieces were written, but there is reason to believe that the most copious was the last. From all these the following Memoirs have been carefully selected, and put together.—SHEFFIELD, JOHN LORD, 1795, *ed., The Miscellaneous Works of Edward Gibbon, Introduction.*

The private memoirs of Gibbon the historian have just been published. In them we are able to trace with considerable accuracy the progress of his mind. While he was at college, he became reconciled to the Roman Catholic faith. By this circumstance he incurred his father's displeasure, who banished him to an obscure situation in Switzerland, where he was obliged to live upon a scanty provision, and was far removed from all the customary amusements of men of birth and fortune. If this train of circumstances had not taken place, would he ever have been the historian of the "Decline and Fall of the Roman Empire?" Yet how unusual were his attainments in consequence of these events, in learning, in acuteness of research, and intuition of genius.—GODWIN, WILLIAM, 1797, *The Enquirer, p.* 25.

We are now "in the thick and bustle" of living biographers; but let a tribute of literary respect be paid to the recent dead. The *autobiography* of Gibbon, attached to his Posthumous Works edited by Lord Sheffield, has been perhaps the most popular production, of its kind, of modern times. It is winning in an unusual degree. The periods flow with a sort of liquid cadence. The facts are beautifully brought together, and ingeniously argued upon; and the life of a studious Recluse has something about it of the air of a romantic Adventurer. This is attributable to the charm—the polish—the harmony of the style. But the autobiography of Gibbon is, in fact, the consummation of Art: and never were pages more determinedly and more elaborately written for the admiration of posterity.— DIBDIN, THOMAS FROGNALL, 1824, *The Library Companion*, p. 529.

Read Gibbon's autobiography again; it rouses me like a bugle.—ALEXANDER, JAMES W., 1825, *Familiar Letters, May 28, vol.* I, *p.* 78.

The most imposing of domestic narratives, the model of dignified detail.— BAGEHOT, WALTER, 1856, *Edward Gibbon, Literary Studies*, ed. Hutton, vol. II, *p.* 53.

English literature is rich in autobiography. It has, indeed, no tale so deep and subtle as that which is told in the "Confessions of St. Augustine." It has no such complete and unreserved unbosoming of a life as is given by the strange Italian, Benvenuto Cellini, who is the prince of unconcealment. But there is hardly any self-told life in any language which is more attractive than the autobiography of Edward Gibbon, in which he recounts the story of his own career in the same stately, pure prose in which he narrates the "Decline and Fall of Rome." It must have needed a great faith in a man's self to write those sonorous pages. Two passages in them have passed into the history of man. One is that in which he describes how, in Rome, on the 15th of October, 1764, as he sat musing amid the ruins of the Capitol, while the barefooted friars were singing vespers in the Temple of Jupiter, the idea of writing the decline and fall of the city first started in his mind. The other is the passage in which the great historian records how, on the night of the 27th of June, 1787,

between the hours of eleven and twelve, he wrote the last lines of the last page in a summer-house at Lausanne, and how then, laying down his pen, he "took several turns in a berceau, or covered walk of acacias, which commanded a prospect of the country, the lake, and the mountains." The story is all very solemn and exalted. It is full of the feeling that the beginning and ending of a great literary work is as great an achievement as the foundation and completion of an empire—as worthy of record and of honor; and as we read we feel so too.—BROOKS, PHILLIPS, 1880-94, *Biography, Essays and Addresses*, p. 440.

He had written a magnificent history of the Roman Empire. It remained to write the history of the historian. Accordingly we have the autobiography. These two immortal works act and react upon one another; the history sends us to the autobiography, and the autobiography returns us to the history. . . . He made six different sketches of the autobiography. It is a most studied performance, and may be boldly pronounced perfect.—BIRRELL, AUGUSTINE, 1892, *Res Judicatœ*, p. 50.

Lord Sheffield executed his editorial task with extreme judgment, singular ingenuity, but remarkable freedom. . . . Quite a third of the whole manuscript is omitted, and many of the most piquant passages that Gibbon ever wrote were suppressed by the caution or the delicacy of his editor and his family. The result is a problem of singular literary interest. A piece, most elaborately composed by one of the greatest writers who ever used our language, an autobiography often pronounced to be the best we possess, is now proved to be in no sense the simple work of that illustrious pen, but to have been dexterously pieced together out of seven fragmentary sketches and adapted into a single and coherent narrative.—SHEFFIELD, EARL OF, 1896, *The Autobiographies of Edward Gibbon, Introduction*, p. ix.

It is one of the best specimens of self-portraiture in the language, reflecting with pellucid clearness both the life and character, the merits and defects, of its author.—LECKY, WILLIAM EDWARD HARTPOLE, 1897, *Library of the World's Best Literature*, ed. Warner, vol. XI, p. 6278.

All critics agree that Gibbon's autobiography is a model in its way.—STEPHEN,

LESLIE, 1998, *Studies of a Biographer, vol.* I, *p.* 148.

Gibbon's miscellaneous work, both in English and French, is not inconsiderable, and it displays his peculiar characteristics; but the only piece of distinct literary importance is his "Autobiography." This, upon which he seems to have amused himself by spending much pains, was left unsettled for press. Edited with singular judgment and success under the care of his intimate friend and literary executor Lord Sheffield, it has been for three generations one of the favourite things of its kind with all good judges, and is likely to continue so in the *textus receptus,* for which the fussy fidelity of modern literary methods will probably try in vain to substitute a chaos of rough drafts.—SAINTS-BURY, GEORGE, 1898, *A Short History of English Literature, p.* 626.

If, as Johnson said, there had been only three books "written by man that were wished longer by their readers," the eighteenth century was not to draw to its close without seeing a fourth added. With "Don Quixote," "The Pilgrim's Progress" and "Robinson Crusoe," the "Autobiography of Edward Gibbon" was henceforth to rank as "a work whose conclusion is perceived with an eye of sorrow, such as the traveller casts upon departing day." It is indeed so short that it can be read by the light of a single pair of candles; it is so interesting in its subject, and so alluring in its turns of thought and its style, that in a second and a third reading it gives scarcely less pleasure than in the first. Among the books in which men have told the story of their own lives it stands in the front rank.—HILL, GEORGE BIRKBECK, 1900, *ed. The Memoirs of the Life of Edward Gibbon, Preface, p.* v.

LETTERS AND MISCELLANEOUS WORKS
1796–1897

I shall thus give more satisfaction, by employing the language of Mr. Gibbon, instead of my own; and the public will see him in a new and admirable light, as a writer of letters. By the insertion of a few occasional sentences, I shall obviate the disadvantages that are apt to arise from an interrupted narration. A prejudiced or a fastidious critic may condemn, perhaps, some parts of the letters as

trivial; but many readers, I flatter myself, will be gratified by discovering, even in these, my friend's affectionate feelings, and his character in familiar life. His letters in general bear a strong resemblance to the style and turn of his conversation: the characteristics of which were vivacity, elegance, and precision, with knowledge astonishingly extensive and correct. He never ceased to be instructive and entertaining; and in general there was a vein of pleasantry in his conversation which prevented its becoming languid, even during a residence of many months with a family in the country. It has been supposed that he always arranged what he intended to say, before he spoke; his quickness in conversation contradicts this notion: but it is very true, that before he sat down to write a note or letter, he completely arranged in his mind what he meant to express.—SHEFFIELD, JOHN LORD, 1795, *ed., The Autobiography of Edward Gibbon, Illustrated from his Letters with Occasional Notes and Narratives.*

On the style and spirit of Mr. Gibbon's own letters it were vain to comment. They rank in the first class of epistolary composition, equally honourable to the head and heart of the writer. Ease, vigour, spirit, and the very soul of friendship pervade the whole. On the subject of religion, they maintained a general silence, which was obviously the effect of indifference; and on another subject they contain nothing that would put a Vestal to blush. On one or two occasions, however, enough is disclosed to shew, that with the proofs of Revelation, Gibbon rejected the probabilities of natural religion. Born with a constitution naturally incredulous, he had refined it into a systematic rejection of almost everything beyond the reach of the senses; and this state of the understanding, after the example of his school, he dignified with the name of Philosophy.—WHITAKER, T. D., 1815, *Gibbon's Miscellaneous Works, Quarterly Review, vol.* 12, *p.* 384.

I have finished reading the first volume of "Gibbon's Miscellaneous Works," published by Lord Sheffield. Of mere worldly production, it is the most interesting that I have read for many years, more especially Gibbon's own memoirs of himself. I have been acquainted with Lord Sheffield above forty years, and more than once met Gibbon at his house; and, if I remember rightly, the first time I was at Sheffield Place, which, I think, was in 1770, being invited by him on my advertising the intentions of the Eastern tour. . . . But, alas! the whole volume has not one word of Christianity in it, though many which mark the infidelity of the whole gang. Lord Sheffield never had a grain of religion, and his intimate connections with Gibbon would alone account for it.—Young, Arthur, 1816, *Autobiography, ed., Betham-Edwards, pp. 468, 469.*

His letters have the faults of his conversation; they are not easy or natural; all is constrained, all for effect. No one can suppose in reading them that a word would have been changed, had the writer known they were to be published the morning after he dispatched them, and had sent them to the printing-office instead of the post-office.— Brougham, Henry Lord, 1845-6, *Lives of Men of Letters of the Time of George III.*

If the Memoirs give us Gibbon in the full dress of a fine gentleman of letters, the correspondence reveals to us the man as he was known to his valet and his housekeeper. The letters have the ease and freshness of conversations with intimate friends, and, considering the character of the century in which they were written, they present one feature which deserves special notice. Only one short sentence has been omitted as too coarse to be printed. With this solitary exception, the reader knows the worst as well as the best of Gibbon, and there are scarcely a dozen phrases, scattered over 800 pages, which will offend good taste or good feeling.—Prothero, Rowland E., 1896, *ed., Private Letters of Edward Gibbon, Preface, vol.* i, *p.* xii.

It is Gibbon's letters that will most interest the reader. With very few exceptions, they were addressed to his father, his stepmother, and his friend Lord Sheffield. The character of the man shines in them all. As a son he was constantly dutiful, devoted, obedient, and sympathetic.—Halsey, Francis W., 1897, *The New Memoirs of Gibbon, The Book Buyer, vol.* 14, *p.* 178.

Gibbon's Letters may be said to derive more interest from him than he derives

from them. They have not the audacious fun and commanding force of Byron's, the full-blooded eloquence of Burns's, the manly simplicity of Cowper's, the profound humour and pathos of Carlyle's. They are without the radiant geniality of Macaulay's. They do not touch the high literary water-mark of Gray's. They express the mundane sentiments of an earthly sage, in love, if the phrase may be pardoned, with peace and wealth. The secret of the charm which most of them undoubtedly have is that they reveal the inner homely side of the richest and most massive intellect which the eighteenth century produced. Gibbon was an indefatigable student, and so far as he could rise to enthusiasm, an enthusiastic admirer of Cicero. Peahaps the rather monotonous flow of the Ciceronian rhythm is too evident in his prose.—Paul, Herbert, 1897, *Gibbon's Life and Letters, The Nineteenth Century, vol.* 41, *p.* 304.

But now that we have the intimate records of his daily life from youth to death in their original form, one wonders anew how so gigantic a work as the "Decline and Fall" was ever completed in about sixteen years amidst all the distractions of country squires, London gaieties, Parliamentary and official duties, interminable worries about his family and property, social scandals and importunate friends. In all these six hundred letters there is not very much about his studies and his writings, but a great deal about politics, society, and pecuniary cares. We are left to imagine for ourselves when the great scholar read, how he wrote, and why he never seemed to exchange a thought with any student of his own calibre of learning. One would think he was a man of fashion, a dilettante man of the world, a wit, a *bon vivant,* and a collector of high-life gossip. All this makes the zest of his "Letters," which at times seem to recall to us the charm of a Boswell or a Horace Walpole. The world can now have all the fun, as Maria Holroyd said. But it leaves us with the puzzle even darker than before—how did Gibbon, whose whole epoch of really systematic study hardly lasted twenty-five years, acquire so stupendous a body of exact and curious learning?—Harrison, Frederic, 1897, *The New Memoirs of Edward Gibbon, The Forum, vol.* 22, *p.* 751.

GENERAL

I prefer your style, as an historian, to that of the two most renowned writers of history the present day has seen. That you may not suspect me of having said more than my real opinion will warrant, I will tell you why. In your style I see no affectation. In every line of theirs I see nothing else. They disgust me always, Robertson with his pomp and his strut, and Gibbon with his finical and French manners.—COWPER, WILLIAM, 1783, *To Rev. John Newton, July* 27; *Works, ed. Southey, vol.* III, *p.* 33.

Though his style is in general correct and elegant, he sometimes "draws out the thread of his verbosity finer than the staple of his argument." In endeavouring to avoid vulgar terms he too frequently dignifies trifles, and clothes common thoughts in a splendid dress that would be rich enough for the noblest ideas. In short we are too often reminded of that great man, Mr. Prig, the auctioneer, whose manner was so inimitably fine that he had as much to say on a ribbon as on a Raphael.—PORSON, RICHARD, 1790, *Letters to Archdeacon Travis.*

Heard of the death of Mr. Gibbon, the calumniator of the despised Nazarene, the derider of Christianity. Awful dispensation! He too was my acquaintance. Lord, I bless Thee, considering how much infidel acquaintance I have had, that my soul never came into their secret! How many souls have his writings polluted! Lord preserve others from their contagion! —MORE, HANNAH, 1794, *Diary, Jan.* 19.

None of the cursed Gibbonian fine writing, so fine and composite! — LAMB, CHARLES, 1800, *Letters, ed. Ainger, March* 1, *vol.* I, *p.* 115.

I hear Gibbon's artificial style still commended by a few; but it is his matter which preserves him.—BRYDGES, SIR SAMUEL EGERTON, 1824, *Recollections of Foreign Travel, July* 20, *vol.* I, *p.* 86.

His way of writing reminds one of those persons who never dare look you full in the face.—WHATELY, RICHARD, 1826, *Elements of Logic, note.*

There can be no gainsaying the sentence of this great judge. To have your name mentioned by Gibbon, is like having it written on the dome of St. Peter's. Pilgrims from all the world admire and behold it.—THACKERAY, WILLIAM MAKEPEACE, 1853, *The English Humourists of the Eighteenth Century.*

Gibbon, however excellent an authority for facts, knew nothing about philosophy, and cared less.—KINGSLEY, CHARLES, 1854, *Alexandria and her Schools.*

Gibbon's literary ambition was never pure. It was rather a longing for temporary distinction than a desire to become of use to his age and his fellow men. He sought fame rather as a means of personal advantage than for any great and noble purpose. Even his love for literature was never that high and honorable passion which filled all the nature of Hume, and he seems now, abandoning the common professions as unsuited to his habits, to have betaken himself to his studies as a means of self-aggrandizement, rather than as the source of purest satisfaction. . . . Gibbon had none of the qualities of a good biographer. His style, heavy and sonorous, was never suited to convey the delicate painting of character, or to unfold a simple tale of domestic life and manners. . . . Gibbon is of all the historians the most learned. His rivals, Hume and Robertson, by whose side he modestly refused to place himself, sink into insignificance before the vast range of his acquirements. But his learning is not his chief excellence; his highest was that he was suited exactly to his theme. By nature, by the inclination of his taste, by his fondness for learned disquisition, by his clear method, by his grand and powerful style, by his imagination rising with his subject, by his accuracy and honesty of research, by his untiring labor, and above all by his single and unfaltering devotion to one absorbing theme, he was fitted above all men to become the historian of the "Decline and Fall of the Roman Empire." On this field he can never have a rival. There may, perhaps, be written a history of England, possessing greater research and purer honesty, if not the simple and perfect manner of Hume; but we can hope for no second "History of the Decline and Fall of Rome." The subject is fully occupied, and like the Coliseum or the Pyramids, Gibbon's vast work must stand alone for ever.—LAWRENCE, EUGENE, 1855, *The Lives of the British Historians, vol.* II, *pp.* 256, 262, 310.

These will bring him to Gibbon, who will take him in charge and convey him with abundant entertainment down—with notice of all remarkable objects on the way—through fourteen hundred years of time. He cannot spare Gibbon, with his vast reading, with such wit and continuity of mind, that, though never profound, his book is one of the conveniences of civilization, like the new railroad from ocean to ocean,— and I think, will be sure to send the reader to his "Memoirs of Himself," and the "Extracts from my Journal," and "Abstracts from my Readings," which will spur the laziest scholar to emulation of his prodigious performance.— EMERSON, RALPH WALDO, 1870–83, *Books; Works, Riverside ed., vol.* VII, *p.* 195.

He possessed in the largest measure the author's first great requisites—a full command of words, and the power of striking out fresh combinations. His chief mechanical peculiarities are an excessive use of the abstract noun, and an unusually abundant employment of descriptive and suggestive epithets. This last peculiarity is the main secret of what is often described as the "pregnancy" of his style; it forms one of the principal arts of condensation, brevity, compression. He conveys incidentally, by a passing adjective, information that Macaulay would have set forth in a special sentence: from its form, the expression seems to take for granted that the reader is already acquainted with the facts referred to, but substantially in an allusive way it adds to the knowledge of the most uninitiated.—MINTO, WILLIAM, 1872–80, *Manual of English Prose Literature, p.* 480.

His English the worst ever written by an educated Englishman.—RUSKIN, JOHN, 1886, *Pall Mall Magazine.*

He is retrogressive in the matter of sentence-length. Only 10 per cent. of his sentences fall below the 15-mark. His stately and sonorous periods have a harmony of their own, but it is not paragraph harmony. His sentences have much proportion; his paragraphs little. We admire the comprehensive analysis of the discourse into chapters and paragraphs, but we do not quite feel that the paragraph is an organism. It is a well-defined cage in which the splendid sentence is confined. His movement is not rapid, but the sequence is in general sure.

Demonstratives are numerous. When an introductory pronoun would be ambiguous he adds a noun, seldom a repeated one, but rather a synonym. Inversions, so frequent in Burke, are infrequent here. Conjunctions the author utterly despises, depending on the sheer inertia of his rolling sentences to carry the thought ahead. No other writer examined shows so small a list of sentence-connectives. The abandonment of them is Gibbon's only contribution to the development; and it may be questioned if the contribution is a real or a permanent one, depending as it does on balance in the sentence.—LEWIS, EDWIN HERBERT, 1894, *The History of the English Paragraph, p.* 124.

Just in so far as Gibbon was not so great a man as Johnson, does his style fall below Johnson's level. The strain of affectation, the undue elaboration, the tone of artificial irony are always unduly marked in that style. But the massiveness of Gibbon's intellect, the largeness of his grasp, his unfailing sense of literary proportion, the fearless vigour of his historical conception,—all these are too great to be buried beneath the affectation. He towers above all competitors as a giant amongst the pigmies.—CRAIK, HENRY, 1895, *ed., English Prose, Introduction, vol.* IV, *p.* 10.

To those who insist upon extreme ornamentation, or extreme simplicity of style, Gibbon's, of course, must be distasteful. But to those who judge a thing by its possession of its own excellences, and not by its lack of the excellences of others, it must always be the subject of an immense admiration. In the first place it is perfectly clear, and for all its stateliness so little fatiguing to the reader that true Gibbonians read it, by snatches or in long draughts, as others read a newspaper or a novel for mere pastime. Although full of irony and epigram it is never uneasily charged with either; and the narrative is never broken, the composition never interrupted for the sake of a flourish or a "point." It may be thought by some to abuse antithesis of sense and balance of cadence; but I should say myself that there is fully sufficient variety in the sentences and in the paragraph arrangement to prevent this. — SAINTSBURY, GEORGE, 1895, *English Prose, ed. Craik, vol.* IV, *p.* 458.

Sir William Jones
1746–1794.

Born, in Westminster, 28 Sept. 1746. At Harrow School, 1753–64. Matric., Univ. Coll., Oxford, 15 March 1764; Scholar, 31 Oct. 1764; Fellow, 1766; B. A., 1768; M. A., 1773. Private tutor to Lord Althorp, 1765–70. F. R. S., 1772. Mem. of Literary Club, 1773. Called to Bar at Middle Temple, 1774. Commissioner of Bankruptcy, 1776. Judge of High Court at Calcutta, 1783–94. Knighted, 19 March 1783. Married Anna Maria Shipley, April 1783. Arrived at Calcutta, Dec. 1783. Founded Bengal Asiatic Soc., Jan. 1784. Edited "The Asiatic Miscellany," 1787. Wife returned to Europe, owing to ill-health, Dec. 1793. He died, at Calcutta, 27 April 1794. Buried there. *Works:* "Traité sur la Poésie Orientale," 1770; "Dissertation sur la littérature Orientale," (anon.), 1771; "Grammar of the Persian Language," 1771; "Lettre à Monsieur A * * * du P. * * *" (anon.), 1771; "Poems, consisting chiefly of translations from the Asiatick Languages" (anon.), 1772; "Poeseos Asiaticæ Commentariorum libri sex," 1774; "A Dialogue between a Country Farmer and a Gentleman" (anon), 1778; "A Speech." 1780; "An Inquiry into the Legal Mode of Suppressing Riots" (anon.), 1780; "An Essay on the Law of Bailments," 1781; "The Muse Recalled," 1781; "An Ode in imitation of Alcæus" (anon.), (1782); "The Principles of Government" (anon.), 1782; "A Letter to a Patriot Senator" (anon.), 1783; "On the Orthography of Asiatick Words," 1784. "On the Gods of Greece, Italy and India," 1785; "On the Hindus," 1786; "On the Arabs," 1787; "On the Tartars," 1788; "On the Persians," 1789; "On the Chinese," 1790; "On the Borderers, Mountaineers and Islanders of Asia," 1791; "On the Origin and Families of Nations," 1792; "On Asiatick History," 1793; "On the Philosophy of the Asiaticks," 1794. He *translated:* "Life of Nader Shah" (into French), 1770 (English version, 1773); "The Moallakat," 1782; "The Mahomedan Law of Succession," 1782; "Sacontalá," 1789; "Al-Sirájiyyah, or Mahomedan Law of Inheritance," 1792; Manu's "Institutes," 1796. *Collected Works:* "Works," ed. by A. M. Jones (6 vols.), 1799; two supplemental vols., 1801; "Poetical Works," 1810; "Discourses, etc.," 1821. *Life:* "Memoirs," by Lord Teignmouth, 1804.—SHARP, R. FARQUHARSON, 1897, *A Dictionary of English Authors, p.* 151.

PERSONAL

I knew him from the early age of eight or nine, and he was always an *uncommon* boy. Great abilities, great particularity of thinking, fondness for writing verses and plays of various kinds, and a degree of integrity and manly courage, of which I remember many instances, distinguished him even at that period. I loved him and revered him, and, though one or two years older than he was, was always instructed by him from my earliest age. In a word, I can only say of this amiable and wonderful man, that he had more virtues, and less faults, than I ever yet saw in any human being; and that the goodness of his head, admirable as it was, was exceeded by that of his heart. I have never ceased to admire him from the moment I first saw him; and my esteem for his great qualities, and regret for his loss, will only end with my life. — BENNET, WILLIAM (BISHOP OF CLOYNE), 1795, *Letter to the Dean of St. Asaph, November.*

His intercourse with the Indian natives of character and abilities was extensive: he liberally rewarded those by whom he was served and assisted, and his dependents were treated by him as friends. Under this denomination, he has frequently mentioned in his works the name of Bahman, a native of Yezd, and follower of the doctrines of Zoroaster, whom he retained in his pay, and whose death he often adverted to with regret. Nor can I resist the impulse which I feel to repeat an anecdote of what occurred after his demise; the pundits who were in the habit of attending him, when I saw them at a public *durbar,* a few days after that melancholy event, could neither refrain their tears for his loss, nor find terms to express their admiration at the wonderful progress which he had made, in the sciences which they professed. — TEIGNMOUTH, LORD, 1804, *The Life of Sir William Jones, vol.* II, *p.* 306.

The name of Sir William Jones is associated, not only with the splendour of a great reputation, but with almost all the amiable and exemplary virtues; and the gentler affections, which were a little chilled by the aspect of his vast literary attainments, are won sweetly back, and rest with delight upon the view, which is here exhibited, of the purity, the integrity, and the mildness, of his private manners. His life, indeed, seems, from his earliest youth, not only to have been undefiled by those coarser blemishes of excess and debauchery, which are generally excluded by an addiction to letters, but to have been distinguished for all that manly exertion, and varied activity, which so rarely escapes unimpaired from the langour of an academical retirement; while it was adorned by the polished manners and elegant accomplishments which are still more frequently neglected by the man of business and the scholar. The most remarkable features in his character, indeed, seem to have resulted from the union of this gentleness and modesty of disposition, with a very lofty conception of his own capability and destination. Without ever appearing to presume upon the force of his genius or the vigour of his understanding, he seems to have thought nothing beyond the reach of his industry and perseverance.—JEFFREY, FRANCIS LORD, 1805, *Lord Teignmouth's Life of Sir W. Jones, Edinburgh Review, vol.* 5, *p.* 329.

"Know him, sir!" exclaimed the friend of his boyhood, Samuel Parr,—who, with all his pompous affectation, had a warm heart under his Roman mail,—"Know him, sir! Who did not know him? Who did not bend in devout respect at the variety and depth of his learning, the integrity of his principles, and the benevolence of his heart?"—BARKER, EDMUND HENRY, 1828–29, *Parriana, p.* 322.

When I entered the Temple [1782], Sir William Jones was in high fame as a commentator and translator of Oriental poetry, and as a classical scholar; but the lawyers, rightly or wrongly, held him in little estimation for his skill in their own profession; nor was he considered then to have the talents of an original writer. I had not the good luck to be acquainted with him, nor even to know his person.— —BRYDGES, SIR SAMUEL EGERTON, 1834, *Autobiography, vol.* I, *p.* 190.

His acquaintance with the history, philosophy, laws, religion, science, and manners of nations, was most extensive and profound. As a linguist, he has scarcely, if ever, been surpassed; he had made himself acquainted with no fewer than twenty-eight different languages, and was studying the grammars of several of the Oriental dialects up to within a week of his lamented death. In accordance with a determination to which we have already referred, he perfected himself in Greek, Latin, Italian, French, Spanish, Portuguese, Hebrew, Arabic, Persian, Turkish, German and English; made himself master of Sanscrit, and less completely of Hindostanee and Bengalee, and also of the dialects called the Tibetian, the Pâli, the Phalavi, and the Deri. The other languages which he studied more or less completely were the Chinese, Russian, Runic, Syriac, Ethiopic, Coptic, Dutch, Swedish, and Welsh.—SEYMOUR, CHARLES C. B., 1858, *Self-Made Men, p.* 477.

GENERAL

He too, whom Indus and the Ganges mourn,
The glory of their banks, from Isis torn,
In learning's strength is fled, in judgment's prime,
In science temp'rate, various, and sublime;
To him familiar every legal doom,
The courts of Athens, or the halls of Rome,
Or Hindoo Vedas taught; for him the Muse
Distill'd from *every* flow'r Hyblæan dews;
Firm, when exalted, in demeanour grave,
Mercy and truth were his, he lov'd to save.
His mind collected; at opinion's shock
JONES stood unmov'd, and from the Christian rock,
Coelestial brightness beaming on his breast,
He saw the STAR, and worshipp'd in the East.
—MATHIAS, THOMAS JAMES, 1794–98, *The Pursuits of Literature, Eighth ed., p.* 424.

The death of this great man is an irreparable loss to Christianity, to science, and to literature.— DRAKE, NATHAN, 1798–1820, *Literary Hours, No.* xxix, *vol.* II, *p.* 122, *note.*

I close with a retrospect of the works of Sir William Jones, who, by establishing the affinity between the Indian language and the Latin, Greek, German, and Persian, first threw a light on this obscure study, and consequently on the earliest popular history which before his time was everywhere dark and confused. Yet he has extended the affinity to some other instances infinitely less important, tracing back the exhaustless abundance of language to three chief families—the Indian, Arabic, and Tartar; and, finally, after having himself so finely exhibited the total difference of the Arabic and Indian languages, seeking, from a love of unity, to derive all from one common source: I have, therefore, been unable to adhere closely in every particular to this excellent and learned man, since his arguments being directed to support an opposite theory, would unquestionably militate against my own opinions.—SCHLEGEL, FREDERICK VON, 1808, *On the Indian Language, Literature and Philosophy, tr. Millington, p.* 464.

The doctrine of bailments (which lies at the foundation of the law of shipments) was almost struck out at a single heat by Lord Holt who had the good sense to incorporate into the English code that system which the text and the commentaries of the civil law had already built up on the continent of Europe. What remained to give perfect symmetry and connexion to all the parts of that system, and to refer it to its principles, has been accomplished in our times by the incomparable essay of Sir William Jones, a man, of whom it is difficult to say, which is most worthy of admiration, the splendour of his genius, the rareness and extent of his acquirements, or the unspotted purity of his life. Had he never written any thing but his "Essay on Bailments," he would have left a name unrivalled in the common law, for philosophical accuracy, elegant learning, and finished analysis. Even cold and cautious as is the habit, if not the structure, of a professional mind, it is impossible to suppress enthusiasm, when we contemplate such a man.— STORY, JOSEPH, 1817, *Hoffman's Course of Legal Study, North American Review, vol.* 6, *p.* 46.

In the course of a short life, Sir William Jones acquired a degree of knowledge which the ordinary faculties of men, if they were blest with antediluvian longevity, could scarcely hope to surpass. His learning threw light on the laws of Greece and India, on the general literature of Asia, and on the history of the family of nations. He carried philosophy, eloquence, and philanthropy into his character of a lawyer and a judge. Amid the driest toils of erudition, he retained a sensibility to the beauties of poetry, and a talent for transfusing them into his own language, which has seldom been united

with the same degree of industry. Had he written nothing but the delightful ode from Hafiz,

"Sweet maid, if thou wouldst charm my sight,"

it would alone testify the harmony of his ear, and the elegance of his taste. When he went abroad, it was not to enrich himself with the spoils of avarice or ambition; but to search, amid the ruins of Oriental literature, for treasures which he would not have exchanged

"For all Bokhara's gold,
Or all the gems of Samarcand."

It is, nevertheless, impossible to avoid supposing, that the activity of his mind spread itself in too many directions to be always employed to the best advantage. The impulse that carried him through so many pursuits, has a look of something restless, inordinate, and ostentatious. Useful as he was, he would in all probability have been still more so, had his powers been concentrated to fewer objects. His poetry is sometimes elegant; but altogether, it has too much of the florid luxury of the East.—CAMPBELL, THOMAS, 1819, *Specimens of the British Poets.*

To the name of poet, as it implies the possession of an inventive faculty, Sir William Jones has but little pretension. He borrows much; and what he takes he seldom makes better. Yet some portion of sweetness and elegance must be allowed him. In the hymns to the Hindu deities, the imagery which is derived chiefly from Eastern sources, is novel and attractive. —CARY, HENRY FRANCIS, 1821–45, *Lives of English Poets, p.* 384.

Need I dwell a moment on the recommendation of the works of Sir William Jones? . . . A scholar, a critic, philosopher, lawyer, and poet,—where shall we find, in the work of the same man, greater demonstration of pure and correct feelings, and cultivated and classical taste, than in the volumes here noticed and recommended? The piety of Sir William Jones was not inferior to his learning. A thoroughly good and great-minded man,—his caution, humility, and diffidence were equal to his learning and multifarious attainments; and there is a vigour and raciness in his translations of Persian poetry which give them the enchanting air of original productions.—DIBDIN, THOMAS FROGNALL, 1824, *Library Companion, p.* 413, *note.*

The professional acquirements of Sir William Jones were undoubtedly of a very high order. He commenced the study of the law at a later period of life than is usual; and he brought with him to the task powers of mind polished to the finest brilliancy by unremitting exercise, and tempered and proved in a variety of pursuits. With these advantages, he applied himself to the study of his profession as to that of a science, resting upon principles, and to be mastered, like other sciences, by an exact and orderly method. His "Essay on the Law of Bailments" affords an instance of the logical manner in which his mind was accustomed to deal with legal subjects; and it has been already stated that he had treated several other branches of the law upon the same model. His acquaintance with legal writers was doubtless very extensive; and his admirable memory enabled him to preserve the greater portion of whatever he pursued. As a judge his character stood stainless and unreproached.—ROSCOE, HENRY, 1830, *Lives of Eminent British Lawyers, p. 327.*

There are few authors to whom Oriental literature is under more deep obligations than to Sir William Jones; few who, like him, have not merely pointed out original and important sources of knowledge, but contributed in no inconsiderable degree to render them accessible. He was equally remarkable for his ardour and industry in philological pursuits, from a very early period of his life, until its premature and lamented close.—WELSFORD, HENRY, 1845, *On Origin and Ramifications of the English Language.*

The Admirable Crichton of his day. . . . The poetry of Sir William Jones is very sonorous and imposing; and in his happiest efforts there is not wanting nobleness of thought, or glow of passion, as well as pomp of words. He cannot, however, be called a poet of an original genius; any peculiarty, of inspiration that may seem to distinguish some of his compositions is for the most part only the Orientalism of the subject, and of the figures and images. He is a brilliant translator and imitator rather than a poet in any higher sense.— CRAIK, GEORGE L., 1861, *A Compendious History of English Literature, vol.* II.

Many Englishmen, notably Warren Hastings, who had spent long years in India, had become profoundly versed in the languages and literature of the country; but they were too much occupied with the practical work of administration to embody their knowledge and researches in literary and scientific form. Jones, on the other hand, came to India with a mind imbued not only with enthusiasm for oriental studies, but with a wider knowledge of classical and other literatures than men sent to India in their early manhood ordinarily possessed. Moreover, he could express himself in writing with rapidity and elegance. No subject was too abstruse or too trifling for Jones to investigate. Hindu chronology, music, and chess were all studied and described by him. He planned an exhaustive work on the botany of India, and paid attention to the local zoology. The famous asoka tree of Indian mythology and poetry is known to botanists as *Jonesia asoka* and was so named by Dr. William Roxburgh (1759–1815) in honor of Sir William Jones.—STEPHENS, H. MORSE, 1892, *Dictionary of National Biography, vol.* XXX, *p.* 175.

George Colman

The Elder

1732–1794.

Born, in Florence, March (or April?), 1732. At Westminster School, 1746–51. To Ch. Ch., Oxford, 5 June 1751; B. A., 18 April 1755; M. A., 18 March 1758. Contributed to "The Student," 1751; to Hawkesworth's "The Adventurer," Sept. 1753; ed. "The Connoisseur," with Bonnell Thornton, Jan. 1754 to Sept. 1756. Called to Bar at Lincoln's Inn, 1755. On Oxford Circuit, 1759. Farce, "Polly Honeycombe," produced at Drury Lane, 5 Dec. 1760; "The Jealous Wife" produced, 12 Feb. 1761. Started "St James's Chronicle," with Bonnell Thornton and Garrick, 1761. . . . Purchased Covent Garden Theatre (with Powell, Harris, and Rutherford), and opened it, 14 Sept. 1767. Married Miss Ford, 1767 (?); she died, 29 March 1771. . . . Resigned management, 26 May 1774, and retired to Bath. Contrib. a series of papers called "The Gentleman" to "The London Packet," July to Dec. 1775. A version of Ben Jonson's

"Epicœne," produced at Drury Lane, 13 Jan. 1776; "The Spleen," 7 March, 1776; "New Brooms," 21 Sept. 1776. Manager of Haymarket, 1777-85. . . . Pall-bearer at Dr. Johnson's funeral, 20 Dec., 1784. Paralytic stroke, 1785. Mind gradually gave way. Died, in Paddington, 14 Aug. 1794. Buried in vaults of Kensington Church. *Works:* "Polly Honeycombe" (anon.), 1760; "Ode to Obscurity" (anon.), 1760; "The Jealous Wife," 1761; "Critical Reflections on the Old English Dramatick Writers" (anon.), 1761; "The Clandestine Marriage" (with Garrick), 1761; "The Musical Lady" (anon.), 1762; "The Deuce is in Him" (anon.), 1763; "Terræ Filius" (4 nos., anon.), 1764; "The English Merchant," 1767; "T. Harris Dissected," 1768; "True State of the Differences, etc.," 1768 (2nd edn. same year); "Occasional Prelude," 1768; "The Portrait, (anon.; date misprinted MCCCLXX.), 1770; "Man and Wife" (anon.), 1770; "The Oxonian in Town" (anon.), 1769; "The Fairy Prince" (anon.), 1771; "The Man of Business," 1774; "The Spleen," 1776; "The Occasional Prelude," 1776; "New Brooms," 1776; "Dramatic Works," 1777; "A Fairy Tale" (adapted, with Garrick, from "A Mid-summer Night's Dream"), 1777; "The Sheep-shearing" (adapted from "Winter's Tale"), 1777; "The Manager in Distress," 1780; "Prose on Several Occasions," 1787; "Tit for Tat" (anon.), 1788; "Ut Pictura Poesis," 1789. *Posthumous:* "Some Particulars of the Life of the late George Colman, written by himself" (ed. by R. Jackson), 1795; "Miscellaneous Works," 1797. He *translated:* Terence's "Comedies," 1765; Horace's "Art of Poetry," 1783; and *edited:* "Poems by Eminent Ladies" (with Bonnell Thornton), 1755; Beaumont and Fletcher's "Philaster," with alterations, 1763; "Comus," altered from Milton, 1772; Jonson's "Epicœne," with alterations, 1776; Beaumont and Fletcher's "Dramatic Works," 1778; Foote's "Devil Upon Two Sticks," 1778; Foote's "Maid of Bath," 1788; Foote's "The Nabob," 1778; Foote's "A Trip to Calais," 1778; Lillo's "Fatal Curiosity," with alterations, 1783. *Life:* In Peake's "Memoirs of the Colman Family," 1841.—SHARP, R. FARQUHARSON, 1897, *A Dictionary of English Authors*, p. 63.

PERSONAL

MY DEAR SIR.—I have this moment taken a peep at the house, for the author of Polly Hon. The pit and galleries are crammed—the boxes full to the last rows —and every thing as you and I could wish for our friend. I am most happy about it, and could not help communicating it to one I so much love and esteem. Pray let me see you at your arrival—the second music—and time for me to put on my fool's coat. *Yours ever and most affectionately.*—GARRICK, DAVID, 1760, *Letter to Colman, Dec.* 31.

And Colman too, that little sinner,
That essay weaver, drama spinner,
Too much the comic sock will use,
For 'tis the law must find him shoes;
And though he thinks on fame's wide ocean
He swims, and has a pretty notion,—
Inform him, Lloyd, for all his grin,
That Harry Fielding holds his chin.
—COLMAN, GEORGE, 1763, *Cobbler of Cripplegate's Letter to Robert Lloyd, A. M., St. James's Magazine, April.*

He is one of the best tempered (though I believe very passionate) of men, lively, agreeable, open-hearted, and clever.— BURNEY, FRANCES, 1771, *Early Diary, ed. Ellis, vol.* I, *p.* 105.

I correspond again with Colman, and upon the most friendly footing, and find in his instance, and in some others, that an intimate intercourse which has been only casually suspended, not forfeited on either side by outrage, is capable not only of revival, but improvement.—COWPER, WILLIAM, 1786, *Letter to Joseph Hill, June* 9; *Life by Hayley, vol.* I, *p.* 116.

They never admitted Colman as one of the set; Sir Joshua did not invite him to dinner. If he had been in the room Goldsmith would have flown out of it, as if a dragon had been there. I remember Garrick once saying, "D—n his *dishclout* face! His plays would never do, if it were not for my patching them up and acting in them." Another time he took a poem of Colman's and read it backwards to turn it into ridicule. Yet some of his pieces keep possession of the stage, so that there must be something in them.—NORTHCOTE, JAMES, 1826-27, *Conversations, ed. Hazlitt, p.* 402.

His case was simply this; that he had gout in his habit, which had been indicated so slightly, that he neglected the hints to take care of himself which nature had mildly thrown out. Cold bathing is perhaps one of the most dangerous luxuries in which an elderly man can indulge, when so formidable an enemy is lurking in his constitution. The gout having been repelled by repeated submersion in the sea, not only paralyzed the body, but distempered the brain, and Reason was subverted. But, from the earliest sparks of his disorder at the end of 1785, till it blazed forth unequivocally in June, 1789, an interval of rather more than three years and a half, and again from the last mentioned year to the time of his decease, there was nothing of that "second childishness and mere oblivion," which his biographers have attached to his memory. The assertion that his gradually increasing derangement left him in "a state of idiotism," is directly the reverse of fact. His mind, instead of having grown progressively vacant till it became a blank, was, in the last stages of his malady, filled, like a cabalistic book, with delusions, and crowded with the wildest flights of morbid fancy; it was always active, always on the stretch; and, so far from his exhibiting that moping fatuity which obscured the last sad and silent days of Swift, it might have been said of him, "how pregnant sometimes his replies are! a happiness which reason and sanity would not so prosperously be delivered of."—COLMAN, GEORGE (THE YOUNGER), 1830, *Random Records*.

GENERAL

I believe his Odes sell no more than mine did, for I saw a heap of them lie in a bookseller's window, who recommended them to me as a very pretty thing.— GRAY, THOMAS, 1760, *Letter, July*.

I have read Colman's "Ars Poetica;" he is much too negligent a versifier, but easy and elegant.—MORE, HANNAH, 1783, *Letter to Her Sister, Memoirs, ed. Roberts, vol.* I, *p.* 165.

It is very much to the credit of that excellent writer Mr. Colman, that, while other dramatists were lost in the fashion of sentiment, his comedies always present the happiest medium of nature; without either affectation of sentiment, or affectation of wit. That the able translator of Terence should yet have sufficient force of mind to keep his own pieces clear of the declamatory dullness of that ancient, is certainly a matter deserving of much applause. The "Jealous Wife," and the

"Clandestine Marriage," with others of his numerous dramas, may be mentioned as the most perfect models of comedy we have: to all the other requisites of fine comic writing they always add just as much sentiment and wit as does them good. This happy medium is the most difficult to hit all composition, and most declares the hand of a master.—PINKERTON, JOHN (ROBERT HERON), 1785, *Letters of Literature, p.* 47.

This elegant simplicity of Terence has met with an admirable vehicle in the well chosen and familiar blank verse of Colman. —DRAKE, NATHAN, 1798-1820, *Literary Hours, No.* XXIX, *vol.* II, *p.* 120.

This comedy, by Colman the elder, was written in his youth; and, though he brought upon the stage no less than twenty-five dramas, including those he altered from Shakspeare and other writers, subsequent to this production, yet not one of them was ever so well received by the town, or appears to have deserved so well, as "The Jealous Wife." To this observation, "The Clandestine Marriage," may possibly be an exception; but, in that work, Mr. Garrick was declared his joint labourer. It therefore appears, that Mr. Colman's talents for dramatic writing declined, rather than improved, by experience—or, at least, his ardour abated; and all works of imagination require, both in conception and execution, a degree of enthusiasm. . . . Mrs. Oakly is, indeed, so complete a character from life, and so ably adapted to the stage by the genius of the writer, that, performed by an actress possessed of proper abilities for the part, the play might be well supported, were the wit, humor, and repartee, of every other character in the piece annihilated.—INCHBALD, ELIZABETH, 1808, *ed., The Jealous Wife, The British Theatre, vol.* I.

In respect to the report of Garrick having written the entire character of Lord Ogleby, my father once told me that it was not true; that, as an instance to the contrary, he (my father) wrote the whole of Ogleby's first scene. He also informed me that one of Garrick's greatest merits in this work (and it is a very good one) was planning the incidents in the last act; the alarm of the families, through the means of Mrs. Heidelberg and Miss Sterling, and bringing forward the various characters from their beds to produce an explanation, and the catastrophe. I regret that when my father imparted this, I did not make further inquiry; but I was then "a moonish youth," and troubled my head little or nothing about the matter. He always talked, however, of the play as a joint production. . . . It would be strange if Garrick robbed, or were accessory to his colleague's robbing his friend Townley. In the two pieces, there may be some coincidence, without theft; but the ground work of "The Clandestine Marriage" was professedly suggested by Hogarth's prints. At the worst, there is no great literary crime in catching hints, if any were caught, from an apparently stillborn farce, and improving upon them in a play of lasting vitality.—COLMAN, GEORGE (THE YOUNGER), 1820, *On The Clandestine Marriage.*

His abilities as a dramatist were not more the subject of praise, than his punctuality as a manager, and his liberal encouragement to other writers for the stage. From the lamentable condition into which he had sunk, both mentally and bodily, his death must have been considered a happy release. A few hours before he expired, he was sized with violent spasms, and these were succeeded by melancholy stupor, in which he drew his last breath. . . . These dramas have considerable merit. In his petite pieces the plots are simple, yet they contain strong character, and aim at ridiculing fashionable and prevailing follies. His comedies have the same merit with the others, as to the preservation of character. The estimation in which the entertainments exhibited under his direction were held by the public, the reputation which the Haymarket Theatre acquired, and the continual concourse of the fashionable world during the height of summer, sufficiently spoke the praises of Mr. Colman's management.—PEAKE, RICHARD BRINSLEY, 1841, *Memoirs of the Colman Family, vol.* II, *p.* 220.

Among the respectable dramatists of this period who exerted an influence in leading the public taste away from the witty and artificial schools of the Restoration, the two Colmans deserve mention.— COPPÉE, HENRY, 1872, *English Literature,* p. 366.

In 1760 he produced a farcical piece in one act, entitled "Polly Honeycombe," in which the novel-reading propensities of the young ladies of the age were goodhumouredly satirised. Honeycombe was the pseudonym of the editor of the "Royal Female Magazine," which was chiefly made up of the silliest and most vapid sentimental novels. The skit was a complete success; but the author, on account of his relations with his uncle Bath, did not consider it prudent to declare himself. Early in the ensuing year he placed "The Jealous Wife" in Garrick's hands; the underplot and the characters of Russet, Charles, Lord Trinket, and Lady Freelove were borrowed from "Tom Jones," but Mr. and Mrs. Oakley and the Major are original creations. Probably the absurd side of jealousy has never been more felicitously ridiculed than in the best scenes of this comedy; but it appears to have gone through much revision, pruning, and condensation from the manager's pen before it assumed its present shape. Garrick himself played Oakley, but he was not much at home in the part, and its success on the first night, which during the earlier part of the performance seemed rather doubtful, was ascribed entirely to Mrs. Pritchard's fine acting as the wife. The comedy is still familiar to old playgoers, and perhaps the two leading characters were never more admirably performed than they were some few years ago at Drury Lane by Phelps and Mrs. Hermann Vezin.—BAKER, H. BARTON, 1881, *George Colman, Elder and Younger, Belgravia, vol.* 46, *p.* 189.

Colman was a man of tact, enterprise, and taste; his plays are ingenious and occasionally brilliant, and more than one of them remains on the acting list. The characters are as a rule well drawn, and types of living eccentricity are well hit off.—KNIGHT, JOSEPH, 1887, *Dictionary of National Biography, ed. Stephen, vol.* XI, *p.* 393.

It occurred to Garrick and to George Colman that an entertaining drama might be drawn up on the lines of Hogarth's "Marriage à la Mode," and the result of their joint labours was "The Clandestine Marriage" (1766), a play now wholly neglected, but worthy of revival as much on the stage as in the study.—GOSSE, EDMUND, 1888, *A History of Eighteenth Century Literature, p.* 318.

Susanna Blamire
1747–1794.

Miss Susanna Blamire was born at Cardew Hall, near Carlisle, and remained there from the date of her birth (1747) till she was twenty years of age, when she accompanied her sister—who had married Colonel Graham of Duchray, Perthshire—to Scotland, and continued there some years. She became enamoured of Scottish music and poetry, and thus qualified herself for writing such sweet lyrics as "The Nabob" and "What ails this heart o' mine?" On her return to Cumberland, she wrote several pieces illustrative of Cumbrian manners. She died unmarried in 1794. Her poetical pieces, some of which had been floating through the country in the form of popular songs, were collected by Mr. Patrick Maxwell, and published in 1842.—GILFILLAN, GEORGE, 1860, *ed. The Less-Known British Poets, vol.* III, *p.* 290.

PERSONAL

Of graceful form, somewhat above the middle size, and a countenance—though slightly marked with the smallpox—beaming with good nature. Her dark eyes sparkled with animation, and won every heart at the first introduction.—MAXWELL, PATRICK, 1842, *ed., Poems of Susanna Blamire.*

Judging from her portrait, and from descriptions which are extant of the person of Sukey Blamire (whose sister Sarah was one of the greatest beauties in Cumberland), we gather that she was slightly marked from small-pox, but not so much as to disfigure her features or mar her complexion. She had berry-brown hair, of which she professed to be very vain. She wore it thrown back from her high forehead, and hanging down on her shoulders in a long roll, formed of one thick curl, disposed with studied negligence somewhat in the style of the present day. Her nose was large, and too *pronouncé*, but her mouth was very sweet in its firmness, and her eyes and brows were fine. She was tall and slender, with a shapely neck, bust, and shoulders. Her dress (in the portrait) is a marvel of simple elegance. The body of the gown is cut square and low, with a full white edging around the bosom. A single rose is worn at one side.—TYTLER, SARAH AND WATSON, J. L., 1871, *The Songstresses of Scotland, vol.* I, *p.* 243.

Susanna Blamire's life was uneventful, and there are scarcely any records of it left. She lived in an obscure part of England amongst her own relatives, and her correspondence has not been preserved. Her poems were fugitives pieces, some of which appeared in magazines, but were never signed by her name. They were not collected till long after her death, when her memory had almost faded away, and personal details were vague. She is described as of "graceful form, somewhat above the middle size, and a countenance, though slightly marked with the smallpox, beaming with good nature; her dark eyes sparkled with animation." Her country neighbours called her a "bonnie and varra lish young lass." She lived among the rustics, entered into their enjoyments, and sympathized with their troubles. She was fond of society, and was in great request at the "merrie-neets," or social gatherings, where she mixed with every class. A good farmer said sadly after her death: "The merrie-neets won't be worth going to since she is no more." The genuine gaiety and sprightliness of her disposition may be judged by the fact that if she met a wandering musician on the road she was known to dismount from her pony, ask for the music of a jig, and dance, till she was weary, on the grass.—CREIGHTON, MANDELL, 1886, *Dictionary of National Biography, vol.* V, *p.* 191.

GENERAL

The characteristics of Miss Blamire's poetry are considerable tenderness of feeling, very gracefully expressed, and a refined delicacy of imagination, which, whilst it never thrills, always pleases. Her poem called "The Nabob," which describes the return of an Indian adventurer to the home of his youth, is a very effecting and delightful production. Her songs, though not without marks of elaboration, display great simplicity and force of feeling.—ROWTON, FREDERIC, 1848, *The Female Poets of Great Britain, p.* 237.

Susanna Blamire reached by keen observation what Lady Nairne arrived at instinctively. As a result which might be looked for from the two processes, Lady Nairne's studies of ploughmen, fish-wives, and gude-wives have more of the large framework of common humanity, are more delicate and idealised; while Susanna Blamire's are narrower, and more literal. —TYTLER, SARAH, AND WATSON, J. L., 1871, *The Songstresses of Scotland, vol.* I, *p.* 238.

Susanna Blamire was a true poet, and deserves more recognition than she has yet received. Her sphere is somewhat narrow, but everything that she had written is genuine and truthful. She has caught the peculiar humour of the Cumbrian folk with admirable truth, and depicts it faithfully so far as was consistent with her own refinement. As a song-writer she deserves to rank very high. She pre-

ferred to write songs in the Scottish dialect, and three at least of her songs are exquisite, "What ails this heart o' mine?" "And ye shall walk in silk attire," and "The Traveller's Return."— CREIGHTON, MANDELL, 1886, *Dictionary of National Biography, vol.* V, *p.* 192.

She wrote a variety of pieces in English, but is chiefly remembered by her Scottish songs. These were for long merely handed about in manuscript, and it was only in 1842 that they were collected and published at Edinburgh, the authoress being designated on the title-page the "Muse of Cumberland."— EYRE-TODD, GEORGE, 1896, *Scottish Poetry of the Eighteenth Century, vol.* II, *p.* 81.

James Bruce
1730–1794.

Born, at Kinnaird, Stirlingshire, 14 Dec. 1730. At Harrow School, 21 Jan. 1742, to 8 May 1746; then with tutor till April, 1747. Returned to Scotland, May 1747; to Edinburgh Univ., Nov. 1747, to study Law. Left Univ., owing to ill-health, spring of 1748. To London, July 1753. Married Adriana Allan, 3 Feb. 1754. Took share in her father's wine business. Wife died in Paris, 9 Oct. 1754. In Spain and Portugal, Aug. to Dec. 1757; in France and Holland, 1758. Succeeded to family estates on father's death, and returned to England, July 1758. Withdrew from wine business, Aug. 1761. Appointed Consul-General at Algiers, Feb. 1762. In Italy, July 1762, to March 1763; arrived at Algiers, 20 March 1763. Resigned Consulship, Aug. 1765. Travelled in Barbary, Africa, Crete, Syria. To Egypt, July 1768. To Abyssinia, Sept. 1769; reached Goudar, 14 Feb. 1770. Lived. at court of King of Abyssinia, with various expeditions of exploration, till Dec. 1771. Through Nubia to Assouan; reached there 29 Nov. 1772. Arrived at Marseilles, March 1773. Returned to England, July 1774. To Scotland, Autumn of 1774. Married Mary Dundas, 20 May 1776; she died spring of 1785. Engaged in compiling his "Travels." Died at Kinnaird, from an accident, 27 April 1794; buried in Larbert churchyard. *Works:* "Travels to Discover the Source of the Nile" (5 vols), 1790.—SHARP, R. FARQUHARSON, 1897, *A Dictionary of English Authors, p.* 35.

PERSONAL

In this tomb are deposited the remains
of
JAMES BRUCE, ESQ., OF KINNAIRD,
who died on the 27th of April, 1794,
in the 64th year of his age.
his life was spent in performing
useful and splendid actions.
he explored many distant regions.
he discovered the sources of the nile.
he traversed the deserts of nubia.
he was an affectionate husband,
an indulgent parent,
an ardent lover of his country.
by the unanimous voice of mankind
his name is enrolled with those
who were conspicuous
for genius, for valour, and for virtue.
—INSCRIPTION ON TOMB, 1794, *Churchyard of Larbert.*

BRUCE appears to have been seen once, and once only, by our Sexagenarian, who nevertheless expresses, in various parts of his manuscript, a general confidence in his veracity, and a great admiration of his prowess and intrepidity. He lived intimately with some of Bruce's most familiar friends, and had frequent opportunities of ascertaining that many assertions made by the traveller, like those of Herodotus, were confirmed by subsequent observation and examination. But it was Bruce's peculiar character, that if he discerned, or ever suspected any want of confidence in his auditors, he disdained all explanation, and could not be prevailed upon to enter upon any further discussion. . . . Though very partial, on the whole, to this most extraordinary man, he was by no means blind to his errors, or insensible of his inaccuracies. His confidence in him was very materially, diminished latterly, from having discovered, that Bruce, in all probability, never was at the battle of Sebraxos, which he nevertheless describes with circumstantial minuteness, and of which he has introduced plans, drawn up with the precision of one well versed in military tactics. There was also something remarkably mysterious and suspicious, as our friend seemed to think, in the circumstance and character of Luigi Balugani, who accompanied Bruce as a draughtsman. He owed more to his talents than he was willing to acknowledge, and the story of his death is glossed over in a very unsatisfactory manner. — BELOE, WILLIAM, 1817, *The Sexagenarian, vol.* II, *pp.* 45, 48.

The last act of Bruce's life was one of gentleman-like, refined, and polite attention. A large party had dined at Kinnaird, and while they were about to depart, Bruce was gaily talking to a young lady in the drawing-room, when, suddenly observing that her aged mother was proceeding to her carriage unattended, he hurried from the drawing-room to the great staircase. In this effort, the foot which had safely carried him through all his dangers happened to fail him; he fell down several of the steps—broke some of his fingers—pitched on his head—and never spoke again! . . . Thus perished, in the sixty-fourth year of his age, in the healthy winter of his life, in vigour of mind and body, James Bruce of Kinnaird, a Scotchman, who was religious, loyal, honourable, brave, prudent, and enterprizing. He was too proud of his ancestors, yet his posterity have reason to be proud of him. His temper was eager, hasty, and impetuous; yet he himself selected for the employment of his life enterprizes of danger in which haste, eagerness, and impetuosity were converted into the means of serving science and his country. The eagerness with which he toiled for the approbation of the world, and the pain he suffered from its cruelty and injustice, exclude him from ranking among those great men, who, by religion, or even by philosophy, may have learnt to despise both; yet it must be observed, that, had he possessed the equanimity of mind, he would never have undertaken the race which he won.— HEAD, SIR F. B., 1830, *The Life of Bruce the African Traveller, p.* 533.

The really honourable and superior points of Bruce's character—such as his energy and daring, his various knowledge and acquirements, and his disinterested zeal in undertaking such a journey at his own expense—were overlooked in this petty war of the wits. Bruce felt their attacks keenly; but he was a proud-spirited man, and did not deign to reply to pasquinades impeaching his veracity. He survived his publication only four years. The foot which had trod without failing the deserts of Nubia, slipped one evening on his own staircase, while handing a lady to her carriage, and he died in consequence of the injury then received, April 16, 1794. — CHAMBERS, ROBERT, 1876, *Cyclopædia of English Literature, ed. Carruthers.*

TRAVELS TO DISCOVER THE SOURCE OF THE NILE
1790

I have only to add, that were it probable, as in my decayed state of health it is not, that I should live to see a second edition of this work, all well-founded, judicious remarks suggested should be gratefully and carefully attended to; but I do solemnly declare to the public in general, that I never will refute or answer any cavils, captious, or idle objections, such as every new publication seems unavoidably to give birth to, nor ever reply to those witticisms and criticisms that appear in newspapers and periodical writings. What I have written I have written. My readers have before them, in the present volumes, all that I shall ever say, directly or indirectly, upon the subject; and I do, without one moment's anxiety, trust my defence to an impartial, well-informed, and judicious public.—BRUCE, JAMES, 1790, *Travels to Discover the Source of the Nile, Introduction, vol.* I, *p.* lxxv.

Everybody is looking into Bruce's Travels. Part takes the attention, but they are abominably abused. Banks objects to the Botany, Reynell to the Geography, Cambridge to the History, The Greeks to the Greek, &c., &c.; yet the work is to be found on every table. Bruce printed the work, and sold 2,000 copies to Robertson for £6000. He sells

to the booksellers at 4 guineas, and
they to their customers at 5 guineas.—
SHEFFIELD, LORD, 1790, *Letter to Gibbon,
Sept.* 21, *Private Letters, ed. Prothero, vol.*
II, *p.* 226.

O Bruce, I own, all candour, that I look
With envy, downright envy, on the book;
A book, like Psalmanazar's, formed to last,
That gives th' historic eye a sweet repast;
A book like Mandeville's, that yields delight,
And puts more probability to flight;
A book that even Pontopidan would own;
A book most humbly offered to the throne;
A book, how happy, which the king of isles
Admires (says rumour), and received with
 smiles!
—WOLCOT, JOHN (PETER PINDAR), 1790?
*A Complimentary Epistle to James Bruce,
Poetical Works.*

It was the misfortune of that traveller
(Bruce) who is now no more, to have
known that his veracity had too often
captiously, and sometimes capriciously,
been called in question, owing, besides
the nature of his adventures, partly, I believe, to a certain manner in conversing
as well as in writing, which alienated
many who were less than himself disposed
to take offence. He is now beyond the
reach of flattery or humiliation; and I
trust it will not be imputed merely to the
partiality of friendship, if, as a small but
just tribute to his memory, I repeat here
what I have often before asserted in occasional conversation, that however I might
regret a constitutional irritability of temper, so injurious to its owner, or however
I might wish to have seen him at times
condescend to explanations which I have
reason to think would have removed prejudices, I never, either in course of our acquaintance, or in the perusal of his book,
found myself disposed to supect him of
any intentional deviation from the truth.
—RUSSEL, PATRICK, 1794, *Natural History of Aleppo, by Alexander,* 2nd ed., *with
Notes.*

Bruce sunk into his grave defrauded of
that just fame which his pride and vivacity perhaps too keenly prized, at least for
his happiness, and which he authoritatively
exacted from an unwilling public. Mortified and indignant at the reception of his
great labour by the cold-hearted scepticism of little minds, and the maliciousness
of idling wits, he, whose fortitude had
toiled through a life of difficulty and danger, could not endure the laugh and scorn

of public opinion; for Bruce there was a
simoon more dreadful than the Arabian,
and from which genius cannot hide its
head. Yet Bruce only met with the fate
which Marco Polo had before encountered;
whose faithful narrative had been condemned by his contemporaries, and who
was long thrown aside among legendary
writers.—DISRAELI, ISAAC, 1796–1818,
*Sensitiveness to Criticism, The Literary
Character.*

Who has not heard of Bruce,—the
romantic, the intrepid, the indefatigable
Bruce? His *"tale"* was once suspected;
but suspicion has sunk into acquiescence
of its truth. . . . A more enterpris-
ing, light, but lion-hearted traveller never
left his native hills for the accomplishment of such purposes as those which
Bruce accomplished.— DIBDIN, THOMAS
FROGNALL, 1824, *The Library Companion,
p.* 445.

Frank and open in society, Bruce, in describing his adventures, generally related
those circumstances which he thought
were most likely to amuse people by
the contrast they afforded to the European fashions, customs, and follies of the
day. Conscious of his own integrity, and
not suspecting that in a civilized country
the statements of a man of honour would
be disbelieved, he did not think it necessary gradually and cautiously to prepare
his hearers for a climate and scenery altogether different from their own, but, as if
from a balloon, he at once landed them in
Abyssinia, and suddenly shewed them a
vivid picture to which he himself had been
long accustomed. They had asked for
novelty; in complying with their request,
he gave them good measure, and told them
of people who wore rings in their lips instead of their ears—who annointed themselves not with bear's grease or pomatum,
but with the blood of cows—who, instead
of playing tunes upon them, wore the en-
trails of animals as ornaments—and who,
instead of eating hot putrid meat, licked
their lips over bleeding living flesh. He
described debauchery dreadfully disgusting, because it was so different from their
own.—He told them of men who hunted
each other—of mothers who had not seen
ten winters—and he described crowds of
human beings and huge animals retreating in terror before an army of little flies!
In short, he told them the truth, the whole

truth and nothing but the truth, but the mind of man, like his stomach, can only contain a certain quantity, and the dose which Bruce gave to his hearers was more than they had power to retain.—HEAD, SIR F. B., 1830, *The Life of Bruce the African Traveller, p.* 511.

One of the most romantic and persevering of our travellers. . . . The strangeness of the author's adventures at the court at Gondar, the somewhat inflated style of the narrative, and the undisguised vanity of the traveller, led to a disbelief of his statements, and numerous lampoons and satires, both in prose and verse, were directed against him. . . . The style of Bruce is prolix and inelegant, though occasionally energetic. He seized upon the most prominent points, and coloured them highly. The general accuracy of his work has been confirmed from different quarters.— CHAMBERS, ROBERT, 1876, *Cyclopædia of English Literature, ed. Carruthers.*

Bruce's character is depicted with incomparable liveliness by himself. It is that of a brave, magnanimous, and merciful man, endowed with excellent abilities, though not with first-rate intellectual powers, but swayed to an undue degree by self-esteem and the thirst for fame. The exaggeration of these qualities, without which even his enterprise would have shrunk from his perils, made him uncandid to those whom he regarded as rivals, and brought inputations, not wholly undeserved, upon his veracity. As regards the bulk and general tenor of his narrative, his truthfulness has been sufficiently established; but vanity and the passion for the picturesque led him to embellish minor particulars, and perhaps in some few instances to invent them. The circumstances under which his work was produced were highly unfavorable to strict accuracy. Instead of addressing himself to his task immediately upon his return, with the incidents of his travels fresh in his mind and his journals open before him, Bruce delayed for twelve years, and then dictated to an amanuensis, indolently omitting to refer to the original journals, and hence frequently making a lamentable confusion of facts and dates, which only came to light upon examination of his original manuscripts. "In the latter part of his days," says his biographer, Murray, "he seems to have viewed the numerous

adventures of his active life as in a dream, not in their natural state as to time and place, but under the pleasing and arbitrary change of memory melting into imagination." . . . His method of composition, moreover, if unfavorable to the strictly historical, was advantageous to the other literary qualities of his work. Fresh from the author's lips, the tale comes with more vividness than if it had been compiled from journals; and scenes, characters, and situations are represented with more warmth and distinctness. Bruce's character portraits are masterly; and although the long conversations he records are evidently highly idealised, the essential truth is probably conveyed with as much precision as could have been attained by a verbatim report. Not the least of his gifts is an eminently robust and racy humour. He will always remain the poet, and his work the epic, of American travel.—GARNETT, RICHARD, 1886, *Dictionary of National Biography, vol.* VII, *p.* 102.

As to travel, it has rarely produced books which may be called literature, but the works of biographers and travellers have brought together the materials of literature. Bruce left for Africa in 1762, and in the next seventy years Africa, Egypt, Italy, Greece, the Holy Land, and the Arctic Regions were made the common property of literary men.— BROOKE, STOPFORD A., 1896, *English Literature, p.* 209.

No traveller is more dear to the Scottish geographer than James Bruce of Kinnaird. It was owing to a perusal of his travels in 1848 that I was induced to go to Egypt; there I met Outram, as I have already narrated; so that it is hardly too much to say that Bruce laid the foundation of whatever fortune has followed me during my political career. . . . I might prolong indefinitely an account of the good work Bruce did in North Africa; but enough has been said to show what great reason we have to be proud of our distinguished countryman. If he had never been to Abyssinia at all, his explorations in North Africa would have sufficed to place him in the foremost rank of travellers, artists, and archæologists.— PLAYFAIR, SIR R. LAMBERT, 1899, *Reminiscences, Chambers's Journal, vol.* 76, *pp.* 369, 372.

James Boswell

1740-1795.

Born, at Auchinleck, 29 Oct. 1740. Educated by private tutor; then at private school in Edinburgh; then at Edinburgh High School and Edinburgh Univ. To Glasgow as Student of Civil Law, 8 Jan., 1759. To London, March 1760. In Edinburgh, April, 1761 to Nov. 1762; then returned to London. Contrib. poems to "Collections of Original Poems by Mr. Blacklock," 1762. First met Johnson, 16 May 1763. In Berlin, July 1764. To Italy, Dec. 1764. To Utrecht, to study Law, Aug. 1765. Tour in Italy and Corsica. Returned to Scotland, Feb. 1766. Admitted Advocate, 26 July 1766. To London on publication of "Account of Corsica," May 1768. Married Margaret Montgomerie, 25 Nov. 1769. Contrib. to "London Magazine," 1769-70, 1777-79. Frequent visits to Johnson, mostly in London, between 1772 and 1784. Elected Member of Literary Club, 30 April 1773. Voyage to Hebrides with Johnson, Aug. to Nov. 1773. Began to keep terms at Inner Temple, 1775. Auchinleck estate entailed on him, 7 Aug. 1776. Father died, 30 Aug. 1782. Called to Bar, 1786. Appointed Recorder of Carlisle, 1788. Took chambers in Temple, 1790. "Life of Johnson" appeared, 16 May 1791. Appointed Secretary of Foreign Correspondence to Royal Academy July, 1791. Died, in London, 19 May 1795. Buried at Auchinleck. *Works:* "Ode to Tragedy" (anon.), 1761; "Elegy upon the Death of an amiable Young Lady" (anon.), 1761; "The Cub at Newmarket" (anon.), 1762; "Correspondence with Hon. A. Erskine," 1763; "Critical Strictures on Mallet's 'Elvira' " (with Erskine and Dempster), 1763; "Speeches, Arguments and Determinations" in the Douglas case (anon.), 1767; "Essence of the Douglas Cause" (anon.), 1767; "Dorando," 1767; Prologue for the Opening of Edinburgh Theatre, 1767; "An Account of Corsica," 1768; "British Essays in favour of the Brave Corsicans," 1769; "Decision in the Cause of Hunter *v.* Donaldson," 1774; "A Letter to the People of Scotland on the Present State of the Nation," 1783; "Ode by Samuel Johnson to Mrs. Thrale" (by Boswell; anon.), 1784; "The Journal of a Tour to the Hebrides," 1785 (2nd ed. same year); "Letter to the People of Scotland on the alarming Attempt to infringe the Articles of Union," 1786; "The Celebrated Letter from Samuel Johnson, LL. D., to Phillip Dormer Stanhope, Earl of Chesterfield," 1790; "Conversation between George III. and Samuel Johnson," 1790; "No Abolition of Slavery" (probably suppressed), 1791; "Life of Johnson," 1791; (another edn., pirated, 1792; 2nd authorised edn., 1793); "Principal Corrections and Additions to First Edition," 1793. *Posthumous:* "Letters to Rev. J. W. Temple," 1857; "Boswelliana: the Common-place Book of J. Boswell," published by Grampian Club, 1874.—SHARP, R. FARQUHARSON, 1897, *A Dictionary of English Authors, p.* 29.

PERSONAL

I have just seen a very clever letter to Mrs. Montagu, to disavow a jackanapes who has lately made a noise here, one Boswell, by anecdotes of Dr. Johnson.— WALPOLE, HORACE, 1786, *To Sir Horace Mann, March* 16; *Letters, ed. Cunningham, vol.* IX, *p.* 45.

I fancy Boswell, from some things I heard of him, and it seems confirmed by various passages in his "Life of Johnson," has a sort of rage for knowing all sorts of public men, good, bad, and indifferent, all one if a man renders himself known he likes to be acquainted with him.—YOUNG, ARTHUR, 1790, *Autobiography, Oct.* 24, *ed. Betham-Edwards, p.* 191.

I loved the man; he had great convivial powers and an inexhaustible fund of good humour in society; no body could detail the spirit of a conversation in the true style and character of the parties more happily than my friend James Boswell, especially when his vivacity was excited, and his heart exhilarated by the circulation of the glass, and the grateful odour of a well-broiled lobster.—CUMBERLAND, RICHARD, 1806, *Memoirs Written by Himself, vol.* II, *p.* 228.

Of those who were frequently at Sir Joshua Reynolds's parties, Mr. Boswell was very acceptable to him. He was a man of excellent temper, and with much gaiety of manner, possessed a shrewd understanding, and close observation of character. He had a happy faculty of dissipating that reserve, which too often damps the pleasure of English society.

His good-nature and social feeling always inclined him to endeavour to produce that effect; which was so well known, that when he appeared, he was hailed as the harbinger of festivity. Sir Joshua was never more happy than when, on such occasions, Mr. Boswell was seated within his hearing. The Royal Society gratified Sir Joshua by electing Mr. Boswell their Secretary of Foreign Correspondence; which made him an Honorary Member of that body.—FARRINGTON, JOSEPH, 1819, *Memoirs of Sir Joshua Reynolds, p.* 83.

With the usual ill hap of those who deal in *mauvaise plaisanterie,* old Bozzy was often in the unpleasant situation of retreating from expressions, which could not be defended. He was always labouring at notoriety, and, having failed in attracting it in his own person, he hooked his little bark to them whom he thought most likely to leave harbour, and so shine with reflected light, like the rat that eat the malt that lay in the house that Jack built.—SCOTT, SIR WALTER, 1829, *Letter to Mr. Croker, Jan.* 30; *The Croker Papers, ed. Jennings, vol.* II, *p.* 32.

He united lively manners with indefatigable diligence, and the volatile curiosity of a *man about town* with the drudging patience of a *chronicler.* With a very good opinion of himself, he was quick in discerning, and frank in applauding, the excellencies of others. Though proud of his own name and lineage, and ambitious of the countenance of the great, he was yet so cordial an admirer of merit, wherever found, that much public ridicule, and something like contempt, were excited by the modest assurance with which he pressed his acquaintance on all the notorieties of his time, and by the ostentatious (but, in the main, laudable) assiduity with which he attended the exile Paoli and the low-born Johnson! These were amiable, and, for us, fortunate inconsistencies. His contemporaries indeed, not without some colour of reason, occasionally complained of him as vain, inquisitive, troublesome, and giddy; but his vanity was inoffensive—his curiosity was commonly directed towards laudable objects—when he meddled, he did so, generally, from good-natured motives—and his giddiness was only an exuberant gaiety, which never failed in the respect and reverence due to literature, morals, and religion; and posterity gratefully acknowledges the taste, temper, and talents with which he selected, enjoyed, and described that polished and intellectual society which still lives in his work, and without his work had perished.—CROKER, JOHN WILSON, 1831, *ed. Boswell's Life of Johnson, Preface.*

He was, if we are to give any credit to his own account, or to the united testimony of all who knew him, a man of the meanest and feeblest intellect. Johnson described him as a fellow who had missed his only chance of immortality, by not having been alive when the Dunciad was written. Beauclerk used his name as a proverbial expression for a bore. He was the laughing-stock of the whole of that brilliant society which has owed to him the greater part of its fame. He was always laying himself at the feet of some eminent man, and begging to be spit upon and trampled upon. . . . Servile and impertinent—shallow and pedantic— a bigot and a sot—bloated with family pride, and eternally blustering about the dignity of a born gentleman, yet stooping to be a talebearer, an eavesdropper, a common butt in the taverns of London— so curious to know everybody who was talked about, that, Tory and High Churchman as he was, that, he manœuvered, we have been told, for an introduction to Tom Paine. . . . All the caprices of his temper, all the illusions of his vanity, all the hypochondriac whimsies, all his castles in the air, he displayed with a cool self-complacency, a perfect unconsciousness that he was making a fool of himself, to which it is impossible to find a parallel in the whole history of mankind. He has used many people ill, but assuredly he has used nobody so ill as himself.—MACAULAY, THOMAS BABINGTON, 1831, *Boswell's Life of Johnson, Edinburgh Review; Critical and Miscellaneous Essays.*

In that cocked nose, cocked partly in triumph over his weaker fellow-creatures, partly to snuff up the smell of coming pleasure, and scent it from afar; in those bag-cheeks, hanging like half-filled wine-skins, still able to contain more; in that coarsely-protruded shelf-mouth, that fat dewlapped chin; in all this, who sees not sensuality, pretension, boisterous imbecility enough; much that could not have been ornamental in the temper of a great man's overfed great man (what the Scotch name *flunky*), though it had been more natural there? The under part of Boswell's face is of a low, almost brutish character. — CARLYLE, THOMAS, 1832, *Boswell's Life of Johnson.*

"Who *is* this Scotch cur at Johnson's heels?" asked some one, amazed at the sudden intimacy. "He is not a cur," answered Goldsmith; "You are too severe. He is only a bur. Tom Davies flung him at Johnson in sport, and he has the faculty of sticking."—PRIOR, SIR JAMES, 1836, *The Life of Oliver Goldsmith.*

He [Carlyle] rescued poor Boswell from the unmerited obloquy of an ungrateful generation, and taught us to see something half-comically beautiful in the poor, weak creature, with his pathetic instinct of reverence for what was nobler, wiser, and stronger than himself.—LOWELL, JAMES RUSSELL, 1866–90, *Carlyle, Prose Works, Riverside ed., vol.* II, *p.* 87.

Matching his vanity was his love for wine and his admiration of the other sex. This latter was a terrible failing, and brings him fairly within our list of lovers. Some years ago were published the Boswell-Temple letters, as to whose genuineness there arose a controversy. As to this point there can be no question now. These were said to be found, under rather suspicious circumstances, in a shop at Boulogne, wrapping up articles. This conventional shape of introduction for spurious papers might excite reasonable doubts; but since their publication they have been traced with reasonable exactness from hand to hand to France. In these we have all his amatory raptures set out with charming candour. He began when he was only eighteen, and before he had left Edinburgh he began his amatory course, which corresponded not a little, both in tone and finale, with that of Mr. Sterne.—FITZGERALD, PERCY, 1872, *The Loves of Famous Men, Belgravia, vol.* 16, *p.* 222.

Boswell's tastes, however, were by no means limited to sensual or frivolous enjoyments. His appreciation of the bottle was combined with an equally hearty sensibility to more intellectual pleasures. He had not a spark of philosophic or poetic power, but within the ordinary range of such topics as can be discussed at a dinner-party, he had an abundant share of liveliness and intelligence. His palate was as keen for good talk as for good wine. He was an admirable recipient, if not an originator, of shrewd or humorous remarks upon life and manners. What in regard to sensual enjoyment was mere gluttony, appeared in higher matters as ah insatiable curiosity.—STEPHEN, LESLIE, 1879, *Samuel Johnson (English Men of Letters), p.* 84.

"Ambitious Thane," "The Bear-Leader," "Bozzy," "Corsica Boswell," "Curious Scrapmonger," "Dapper Jemmy," "A Feather in the Scale," "Thou Jackall," "Lazarus," "Will-o'-th'-Wisp."—FREY, ALBERT R., 1888, *Sobriquets and Nicknames, p.* 381.

It is peevish to refuse credit to those who do things admirably well, because there is something incomprehensible in their capacity. Those who think that James Boswell was a vain and shallow coxcomb of mediocre abilities, without intellectual gifts of any eminence, are confronted with the fact that this supposed fool was the unaided author of two of the most graphic and most readable works which the eighteenth century has left us. It is right that Boswell's claim to a high independent place in literature should be vindicated, and the fact is that, after Burke and Goldsmith, he is by far the most considerable of the literary companions of Johnson. That he has risen into fame on the shoulders of that great man is true, but the fact has been insisted upon until his own genuine and peculiar merits have been most unduly overlooked. —GOSSE, EDMUND, 1888, *A History of Eighteenth Century Literature, p.* 358.

What a wonderful fellow was James Boswell.—LOCKER-LAMPSON, FREDERICK, 1896, *My Confidences, p.* 307.

"Love," wrote Madame de Stael, "is with man a thing apart, 'tis woman's whole existence." This is not true at least of Boswell, for his love affairs fill as large a part in his life as in that of Benjamin Constant. A most confused chapter withal, and one that luckily was not known to Macaulay, whose colours would otherwise have been more brilliant. We find Bozzy paying his addresses at one and the same time to at least eight ladies, exclusive as this is of sundry minor divinities of a fleeting and more temporary nature not calling here for allusion.—LEASK, W. KEITH, 1897, *James Boswell (Famous Scots)*, p. 76.

That this garrulous, vain, wine-bibbing tattler should ally himself with the great moralist, may be explained by his love of notoriety and of notables; but that the austere, intolerant veteran of letters should like—indeed love such a companion, is a curious problem. Yet, moralist though he was, he liked, as he said, to "frisk it" now and then,—he loved the Honourable Tom Hervey, the rake, and Topham Beauclerc, whose morals were far to seek. Boswell, though not learned, and needing his mentor's advice to "read more and drink less," knew something of his letters, knew much of the world, was clever, entertaining, good-natured, and loyal. . . . Meanwhile his wife, a woman of sense and some wit, had much to endure—her society neglected for "good company," where he got tipsy, with the usual sequels of fits of depression and tearful sentiment. He reminds us of Sir Richard Steele with his bibulous indulgence, and protestations of affection in notelets to his much suffering spouse: "I am, dear Prue, a little in drink, but all the time your faithful husband, Richard Steele." All his characteristics remained unchanged; his alternate hypochondria and joviality; his moods of piety and his lapses from it; his superstitions; his love of excitement—especially for a hanging, in which he was as keen a connoisseur as George Selwyn himself. He was ready to kneel down and join in the chaplain's prayers in the prison cells with the convict in profoundest devotion, and to see him turned off at Tyburn with the greatest gusto,—to witness fifteen men hanged at once filled him with the keenest pleasure and the finest moral reflections. Vain as poor Goldsmith, whose pride in his plum-coloured coat from Filbey's he laughed at, he would rush in his Court dress from a levee at St. James's to dazzle compositors at the printing-offices with his magnificence. Few figures were better known in London artistic and literary society than his—paunchy and puffy, with red face, long, cocked nose, protuberant mouth and chin, with mock solemnity of manner and voice, with slow gait and slovenly dress—the clothes being loose, the wig untidy, the gestures restless so as to resemble his

great master, of whom he incessantly spoke, and whose big manner and oddities he mimicked with infinite drollery, making listeners convulse with laughter at the exquisite, but irreverent copy of his "revered friend."—GRAHAM, HENRY GREY, 1901, *Scottish Men of Letters in the Eighteenth Century*, pp. 221, 223.

Of the kind of man Boswell was he himself has given us the most abundant evidence. His pages are autobiographic in their self-delineation. We see his extraordinary want of tact; his amazing folly, egotism, self-obtrusion, and excessive freedom of manners; his want of self-respect, amounting almost to self-debasement (he did not hestitate to liken himself to a dog); his conceit, vanity, absurd pomposity, and serene self-complacency. He was easily enamored, and was no Moslem when the wine was circulating; for he frequently succumbed to the material good things, and admits that he was unable to recollect the intellectual good things that flowed around him.—SILLARD, P. A., 1901, *The Prince of Biographers*, *Atlantic Monthly*, vol. 88, p. 214.

AN ACCOUNT OF CORSICA
1768

Jamie had taen a toot on a new horn. —BOSWELL, ALEXANDER, 1768, *Father of James Boswell.*

Mr. Boswell's book I was going to recommend to you, when I received your letter: it has pleased and moved me strangely, all (I mean) that relates to Paoli. He is a man born two thousand years after his time! The pamphlet proves what I have always maintained, that any fool may write a most valuable book by chance, if he will only tell us what he heard and saw with veracity. Of Mr. Boswell's truth I have not the least suspicion, because I am sure he could not invent nothing of this kind. The true title of this part of his work is, a Dialogue between a Green-Goose and a Hero. —GRAY, THOMAS, 1768, *Letter to Horace Walpole*, Feb. 25; *Works, ed. Gosse*, vol. III, p. 310.

He came to my country, and he fetched me some letter of recommending him; but I was of the belief he might be an impostor, and I supposed in my minte he was espy; for I look away from him, and in a moment I look to him again, and I behold his tablets. Oh! he was to the work of writing down all I say. Indeed I was angry. But soon I discover he was no impostor and no espy; and I only find I was myself the monster he had come to discern. Oh! he is a very good man; I love him indeed; so cheerful, so gay, so pleasant! but at the first, oh! I was indeed angry.—PAOLI, PASCAL, 1782, *To Miss Burney, Diary and Letters*, Oct. 15, *vol.* II, *p.* 155.

The personal part of which is far better written than the hasty critic is wont to acknowledge.— GOSSE, EDMUND, 1888, *A History of Eighteenth Century Literature, p.* 358.

Mrs. Barbauld regarded him as no ordinary traveller, with

"Working thoughts which swelled the breast
Of generous Boswell, when with noble aim
And views beyond the narrow beaten track
By trivial fancy trod, he turned his course
From polished Gallia's soft delicious vales."

Such thoughts were perhaps really foreign to that traveller, yet Dr. Hill assures us that by every Corsican of education the name of Boswell is known and honoured. One curious circumstance is given. At Pino, when Boswell fancying himself "in a publick house" or inn, had called for things, the hostess had said *una cosa dopo un altra, signore,* "one thing after another, sir." This has lingered as a memento of Bozzy in Corsica, and has been found by Dr. Hill to be preserved among the traditions in the Tomasi family. Translations of the book in Italian, Dutch, French, and German, spread abroad the name of the traveller who, if like a prophet without honour in his own country, has not been without it elsewhere. — LEASK, W. KEITH, 1897, *James Boswell (Famous Scots), p.* 52.

JOURNAL OF A TOUR TO THE HEBRIDES
1785

O Boswell, Bozzy, Bruce, whate'er thy name,
Thou mighty shark for anecdote and fame.
. . . .
Triumphant, thou through Time's vast gulf shalt sail,
The pilot of our literary whale. . . .
Thou, curious scrapmonger, shalt live in song,
When death has stilled the rattle of thy tongue;
Even future babes to lisp thy name shall learn,
And Bozzy join with Wood and Tommy Hearn,

Who drove the spiders from much prose and rhyme,
And snatched old stories from the jaws of time. . . .
What tasteless mouth can gape, what eye can close,
What head can nod, o'er thy enlivening prose? . .
Yes! whilst the Rambler shall a comet blaze,
And gild a world of darkness with his rays,
Thee, too, that world with wonderment, shall hail,
A lively, bouncing cracker at his tail!
—WOLCOT, JOHN (PETER PINDAR), 1787, *A Poetical and Congratulatory Epistle to James Boswell, Esq., on His Journal of a Tour to the Hebrides, with the Celebrated Doctor Johnson.*

I return you many thanks for Boswell's Tour. I read it to Mrs. Unwin after supper, and we find it amusing. There is much trash in it, as there must always be in every narrative that relates indiscriminately all that passed. But now and then the Doctor speaks like an oracle, and that makes amends for all. Sir John was a coxcomb, and Boswell is not less a coxcomb, though of another kind.—COWPER, WILLIAM, 1789, *Letter to Samuel Rose, June* 5; *Life, ed.* Hayley, *vol.* I, *p.* 188.

In my "Tour," I was almost unboundedly open in my communications, and from my eagerness to display the wonderful fertility and readiness of Johnson's wit, freely showed to the world its dexterity, even when I was myself the object of it. I trusted that I should be liberally understood; as knowing very well what I was about, and by no means as simply unconscious of the pointed effects of the satire. I own, indeed, that I was arrogant enough to suppose that the tenour of the rest of the book would sufficiently guard me against such a strange imputation. But it seems I judged too well of the world; for, though I could scarcely believe it, I have been undoubtedly informed, that many persons, especially in distant quarters, not penetrating enough into Johnson's character, so as to understand his mode of treating his friends, have arraigned my judgment, instead of seeing that I was sensible of all that they could observe. It is related of the great Dr. Clarke, that when, in one of his leisure hours, he was unbending himself with a few friends in the most playful and frolicsome manner, he observed Beau Nash approaching; upon which he suddenly stopped:—"My boys," said he, "let us be grave; here comes a fool." The world, my friend, I have found to be a great fool as to that particular on which it has become necessary to speak very plainly.—BOSWELL, JAMES, 1791, *The Life of Samuel Johnson, Dedication to Sir Joshua Reynolds.*

Never, I think, was so unimportant a journey so known of men. Every smart boy in every American school, knows now what puddings he ate, and about the cudgel that he carried, and the boiled mutton that was set before him. The bare mention of these things brings back a relishy smack of the whole story of the journey. Is it for the literary quality of the book which describes it? Is it for our interest in the great, nettlesome, ponderous traveller; or is it by reason of a sneaking fondness we all have for the perennial stream of Boswell's gossip? I cannot tell, for one: I do not puzzle with the question; but I enjoy.—MITCHELL, DONALD G., 1895, *English Lands Letters and Kings, Queen Anne and the Georges,* p. 137.

No better book of travels in Scotland has ever been written than Boswell's "Journal of a Tour to the Hebrides." The accuracy of his description, his eye for scenes and dramatic effects, have all been fully borne witness to by those who have followed in their track, and the fact of the book being day by day read by Johnson, during its preparation, gives it an additional value from the perfect veracity of its contents—"as I have resolved that the very journal which Dr. Johnson read shall be presented to the publick, I will not expand the text in any considerable degree".—LEASK, W. KEITH, 1897, *James Boswell (Famous Scots),* p. 109.

LIFE OF JOHNSON

1791–93

Boswell tells me he is printing *anecdotes* of Johnson, not his *life*, but, as he has the vanity to call it, his *pyramid.* I besought his tenderness for our virtuous and most revered departed friend, and begged he would mitigate some of his asperities. He said, roughly, "He would not cut off his claws, nor make a tiger a cat, to please anybody." It will, I doubt not, be a very amusing book, but I hope not

an indiscreet one; he has great enthusiasm, and some fire.—MORE, HANNAH, 1785, *Letter, Memoirs, ed. Roberts.*

Boswell's book will be curious, or at least whimsical; his hero, who can so long detain the public curiosity, must be no common animal.—GIBBON, EDWARD, 1791, *Letter to Cadell.*

The labour and anxious attention with which I have collected and arranged the materials of which these volumes are composed, will hardly be conceived by those who read them with careless felicity. The stretch of mind and prompt assiduity by which so many conversations were preserved, I myself, at some distance of time, contemplate with wonder; and I must be allowed to suggest that the nature of the work in other respects, as it consists of innumerable detached particulars, all which, even the most minute, I have spared no pains to ascertain with a scrupulous authenticity, has occasioned a degree of trouble far beyond that of any other species of composition. Were I to detail the books which I have consulted, and the inquiries which I have found it necessary to make by various channels, I should probably be thought ridiculously ostentatious. Let me only observe, as a specimen of my trouble, that I have sometimes been obliged to run half over London, in order to fix a date correctly; which, when I had accomplished I well knew would obtain me no praise, though a failure would have been to my discredit. And after all, perhaps, hard as it may be, I shall not be surprised if omissions or mistakes be pointed out with invidious severity. I have also been extremely careful as to the exactness of my quotations; holding that there is a respect due to the public, which should oblige every author to attend to this, and never to presume to introduce them with, "I think I have read," or, "If I remember right," when the originals may be examined.— BOSWELL, JAMES, 1791, *The Life of Samuel Johnson, Advertisement.*

Boswell has at last published his long-promised "Life of Dr. Johnson," in two volumes in quarto. I will give you an account of it when I have gone through it. I have already perceived, that in writing the history of Hudibras, Ralpho has not forgot himself—nor will others, I believe, forget *him!*—WALPOLE, HORACE, 1791,

To Miss Berry, May 19; *Letters, ed. Cunningham, vol.* IX, *p.* 317.

Highly as this work is now estimated, it will, I am confident, be still more valued by posterity a century hence, when the excellent and extraordinary man, whose wit and wisdom are here recorded, shall be viewed at a still greater distance; and the instruction and entertainment they afford will at once produce reverential gratitude, admiration, and delight.—MALONE, EDMOND, 1804, *ed. Boswell's Life of Johnson, Preface.*

The circle of Mr. Boswell's acquaintance among the learned, the witty, and indeed among men of all ranks and professions, was extremely extensive, as his talents were considerable, and his convivial powers made his company much in request. His warmth of heart towards his friends, was very great; and I have known few men who possessed a stronger sense of piety, or more fervent devotion (tinctured, no doubt, with some little share of superstition which had, probably in some degree, been fostered by his habits of intimacy with Dr. Johnson), perhaps not always sufficient to regulate his imagination, or direct his conduct, yet still genuine, and founded both in his understanding and his heart. His "Life" of that extraordinary man, with all the faults with which it has been charged, must be allowed to be one of the most characteristic and entertaining biographical works in the English language.—FORBES, SIR WILLIAM, 1806, *Account of the Life and Writings of James Beattie, vol.* II, *p.* 378, *note.*

His "Life of Samuel Johnson" exhibits a striking likeness of a confident, overweening, dictatorial pedant, though of parts and learning; and of a weak, shallow, submissive admirer of such a character, deriving a vanity from that very admiration.—HURD, RICHARD, 1808? *Commonplace Book, ed. Kilvert, p.* 254.

Boswell was probably an inferior man to Spence;—but he was a far better collector of anecdotes, and the very prince, indeed, of retail wits and philosophers; so that, with all possible sense of the value of what he has done, we sometimes can hardly help wishing that he had lived in the time of Pope, instead of our own.—HAZLITT, WILLIAM, 1820, *Spence's Anecdotes, Edinburgh Review, vol.* 33, *p.* 306.

Considering the eminent persons to whom it relates, the quantity of miscellaneous information and entertaining gossip which it brings together, may be termed, without exception, the best parlour-window book that ever was written.—SCOTT, SIR WALTER, 1823, *Samuel Johnson.*

I now approach, with a keen recollection of the pleasure which, in common with every tolerably well-educated Englishman, I have felt, and shall continue to my very latest hour to feel, in the perusal of it the biography of Dr. Samuel Johnson, by James Boswell, his companion, his chronicler, and his friend. This fascinating, and I may add truly original, composition, is a work for all times. In reading it, we see the man—

"Vir ipse. . . .
Sic oculos, sic ille manus, sic ora ferebat."

We even hear his voice, and observe his gesticulations. The growth of discontent and the shout of triumph equally pervades our ears. Walking, sitting, reading, writing, talking, all is Johnsonian. Such another piece of domestic painting, in black and white, is, perhaps, no where to be seen. We place Boswell's Johnson in our libraries, as an enthusiast hangs up his Gerard Dow in his cabinet—to be gazed at again and again; to feed upon, and to devour.—DIBDIN, THOMAS FROGNALL, 1824, *Library Companion, p.* 523.

Of above *twenty years,* therefore, that their acquaintance lasted, periods equivalent in the whole to about three-quarters of a year only, fell under the personal notice of Boswell. . . . It appears from the Life, that Mr. Boswell visited England a dozen times during his acquaintance with Dr. Johnson, and that the number of days on which they met were about 180, to which is to be added the time of the *Tour,* during which they met daily from the 18th August, to the 22d November, 1773; in the whole about 276 days. The number of pages in the separate editions of the two works is 2528, of which 1320 are occupied by the history of these 276 days; so that a *little less than an hundredth part* of Dr. Johnson's life occupies *above one-half* of Mr. Boswell's works. Every one must regret that his personal intercourse with his great friend was not more frequent or more continued.—CROKER, JOHN WILSON, 1831, *ed. Boswell's Life of Johnson, Preface.*

"The Life of Johnson" is assuredly a great, a very great work. Homer is not more decidedly the first of heroic poets, Shakspeare is not more decidedly the first of dramatists, Demosthenes is not more decidedly the first of orators, than Boswell is the first of biographers. He has no second. He has distanced all his competitors so decidedly, that it is not worth while to place them. Eclipse is first, and the rest nowhere. We are not sure that there is in the whole history of the human intellect so strange a phenomenon as this book. Many of the greatest men that ever lived have written biography. Boswell was one of the smallest men that ever lived; and he has beaten them all.—MACAULAY, THOMAS BABING-TON, 1831, *Boswell's Life of Johnson, Edinburgh Review, Critical and Miscellaneous Essays.*

Out of the fifteen millions that then lived, and had bed and board in the British Islands, this man has provided us a greater *pleasure* than any other individual, at whose cost we now enjoy ourselves; perhaps has done us a greater *service* than can be specially attributed to more than two or three: yet, ungrateful that we are, no written or spoken eulogy of James Boswell anywhere exists; his recompense as solid pudding (so far as copyright went) was not excessive; and as for the empty praise, it has altogether been denied him. Men are unwiser than children; they do *not* know the hand that feeds them. . . . As for the Book itself, questionless the universal favour entertained for it is well merited. In worth as a Book we have rated it beyond any other product of the eighteenth century: all Johnson's own Writings, laborious and in their kind genuine above most, stand on a quite inferior level to it; already, indeed, they are becoming obsolete for this generation; and for some future generation may be valuable chiefly as Prolegomena and expository Scholia to this *Johnsoniad* of Boswell. Which of us but remembers, as one of the sunny spots in his existence, the day when he opened these airy volumes, fascinating him by a true natural magic! It was as if the curtains of the Past were drawn aside, and we look mysteriously into a kindred country, where dwelt our Fathers; inexpressibly dear to us, but which had seemed forever hidden from our eyes.—CARLYLE, THOMAS, 1832, *Boswell's Life of Johnson.*

Do you know our English "Boswell's Life of Johnson?" If not, read it. There are not ten books of the eighteenth century so valuable.—CARLYLE, THOMAS, 1834, *Letter to Eckermann, May 6; Correspondence Between Goethe and Carlyle, ed. Norton, Appendix, p.* 342.

Really, the ambition of the man to illustrate his mental insignificance, by continually placing himself in juxtaposition with the great lexicographer, has something in it perfectly ludicrous. Never, since the days of Don Quixote and Sancho Panza, has there been presented to the world a more whimsically contrasted pair of associates than Johnson and Boswell.—IRVING, WASHINGTON, 1845, *Oliver Goldsmith, p.* 157.

Content not only to be called, by the object of his veneration, a dunce, a parasite, a coxcomb, an eavesdropper, and a fool, but even faithfully to report what he calls the "keen sarcastic wit," the "variety of degrading images," the "rudeness," and the "ferocity," of which he was made the special object: bent all the more firmly upon the one design which seized and occupied the whole of such faculties as he possessed, and living in such a manner to achieve it as to have made himself immortal as his hero. "You have but two topics, sir," exclaimed Johnson; "yourself and me. I am sick of both." Happily for us, nothing could sicken Boswell of either; and by one of the most moderately wise men that ever lived, the masterpiece of English biography was written.—FORSTER, JOHN, 1848-54, *The Life and Times of Oliver Goldsmith, vol.* II, *p.* 296.

The greatest work of the class which exists in the world. The "Tour to the Hebrides" had shown what was to be expected from a man who seems to have been better fitted for his vocation than anybody else who ever lived, and whose name has supplied the English language with a new word. Every year increases the popularity of Boswell's marvellous work. The world will some day do more justice to his talents, which those who cannot forgive his Toryism are far too prone to run down; for he possessed great dramatic talent, great feeling for humour, and a very keen perception of all the kinds of colloquial excellence. With these men, —and they are not a few,—nine-tenths of whose affected contempt of him rests on the mean foundation that they dislike the very pardonable pride he took in his ancient birth, who would condescend to reason? But if any unprejudiced person doubts the real talent required for doing what Boswell did, let him make the experiment by attempting to describe somebody's conversation himself. Let him not fancy that he is performing a trivial or undignified task; for which of us, in any station, can hope to render a tithe of the service to the world that was conferred on it by the Laird of Auchinleck? —HANNAY, JAMES, 1856-61, *Table-Talk, Essays from the Quarterly Review, p.* 27.

Hard names have been freely applied to what has unquestionably proved to be disinterested attachment. Yet who has contributed so much to our amusement? Where shall we find in our own or any other language one who has shown equal talent and industry in recording so much wit, wisdom, and acquaintance with life for the instruction and amusement of mankind? Such a book is not the product of chance. He had no model to follow; but with that happiness of thought, which if it does not imply genius certainly falls little short of it, struck out one for himself. As there has been but one Johnson, so there certainly is but one Boswell. He stands alone in the plan and execution of a work which has won the admiration of every description of reader.—PRIOR, SIR JAMES, 1860, *Life of Edmond Malone, p.* 124.

That altogether unvenerable yet profoundly-verating Scottish gentleman,— that queerest mixture of qualities, of force and weakness, blindness and insight, vanity and solid worth,—has written the finest book of its kind which our nation possesses. It is quite impossible to overstate its worth. You lift it, and immediately the intervening years disappear, and you are in the presence of the Doctor. You are made free of the last century, as you are free of the present. You double your existence. The book is a letter of introduction to a whole knot of departed English worthies. In virtue of Boswell's labours, we know Johnson—the central man of his time — better than Burke did, or Reynolds, — far better even than

Boswell did. We know how he expressed himself, in what grooves his thoughts ran, how he dressed, how he ate, drank, and slept. Boswell's unconscious art is wonderful, and so is the result attained. This book has arrested, as never book did before, time and decay. Bozzy is really a wizzard : he makes the sun stand still. Till his work is done, the future stands respectfully aloof.—SMITH, ALEXANDER, 1863, *Dreamthorp, p.* 204.

Boswell's "Life of Johnson" not only holds an undisputed place among the classical achievements of English Literature, but belongs to that group within the classical group which may be distinguished as consisting of works both well-reputed and *read*, the other classics being well-reputed and unopened. No one who has this book is content to have it on his shelves, a mere respectability in calf-gilt —one of Charles Lamb's favourite aversions, "a book which no gentleman's library should be without." If it is on his shelves, it is often on his table. . . . "Boswell's Johnson" is for me a sort of test-book : according to a man's judgment of it, I am apt to form my judgment of him. It may not always be a very good test, but it is never a very bad one. In spite, however, of its great reputation, the book is less read now-a-days than its admirers imagine ; and I have often been surprised to find how many cultivated men and women, who would assuredly be able to do it full justice, were satisfied with vague second-hand knowledge of it, simply because they had allowed the idle trash of the hour to come between them and it— preferring to read what "every one" is reading to-day, and no one will read to-morrow. . . . No one has ever reported conversations with a skill comparable to that of Boswell—a skill which appears marvellous when compared with the attempts of others ; and although there may have been talkers as good as Johnson, no man's reported talk has the variety and force of his. . . . It is Boswell's eternal merit to have deeply reverenced the man whose littlenesses and asperities he could keenly discern, and has courageously depicted ; and his work stands almost alone in Biography because he had this vision and this courage. The image of Johnson is not defaced by these revelations, it only becomes more intelligible in

becoming more human.—LEWES, GEORGE
HENRY, 1873, *Life and Conversations of
Dr. Samuel Johnson*, ed. *Main, Preface,
pp.* vii, viii, x, xii.

Johnson entirely depends on Boswell's
life of him for his fame. The fond Boswell, with all his Scotch affection, and
Scotch strength of diligence, gathered the
gleanings from the fields, and picked up
the heads of grain, long after the reaper
had fulfilled his work. The pickings and
gatherings, so carefully preserved, have
fed many a hungry and empty mind since,
and enriched the gallery of English literature.— PURVES, JAMES, 1874, *James
Boswell, Dublin Magazine, vol.* 84, *p.* 704.

His singular gifts as an observer could
only escape notice from a careless or inexperienced reader. Boswell has a little
of the true Shaksperian secret. He lets
his characters show themselves without obtruding unnecessary comment. He never
misses the point of a story, though he
does not ostentatiously call our attention to it. He gives just what is wanted
to indicate character, or to explain the
full meaning of a repartee. It is not till
we compare his reports with those of less
skilful hearers, that we can appreciate the
skill with which the essence of a conversation is extracted, and the whole scene
indicated by a few telling touches. We
are tempted to fancy that we have heard
the very thing, and rashly infer that Boswell was simply the mechanical transmitter of the good things uttered. Any one
who will try to put down the pith of a
brilliant conversation within the same
space, may soon satisfy himself of the absurdity of such an hypothesis, and will
learn to appreciate Boswell's powers not
only of memory but artistic representation.
Such a feat implies not only admirable
quickness of appreciation, but a rare literary faculty. Boswell's accuracy is remarkable; but it is the least part of his
merit.—STEPHEN, LESLIE, 1879, *Samuel
Johnson* (*English Men of Letters*), *p.* 91.

Johnson, Goldsmith, and all the rest of
them are only ghosts until the pertinacious young laird of Auchinleck comes on
the scene to give them color, and life,
and form.—BLACK, WILLIAM, 1879, *Goldsmith* (*English Men of Letters*), *p.* 41.

The most remarkable biography written in the English language—or indeed,
in any language. . . . Filled with

admiration for the works and the character
of Dr. Johnson, and desiring to gratify
his own vanity and insatiable thirst for
notoriety, Boswell attached himself to
Johnson as a kind of a humble hanger-on
and satellite. He diligently cultivated
the acquaintance of the great literary
dictator, sought his society on every possible occasion, and took copious notes of
everything that he saw or heard. . . .
It was not until 1791 that he gave to the
world that wonderful collection of sketches
and anecdotes which compose his great
masterpiece of biography. — BALDWIN,
JAMES, 1883, *English Literature and Literary Criticism, Prose, p.* 96.

A paradox in himself, Boswell has been
a great cause of paradoxes. The virtue
of his incomparable "Life of Johnson,"
though apparently parasitic, has been recognized by the best judges as original.
—SAINTSBURY, GEORGE, 1886, *Specimens
of English Prose Style, p.* 239.

With me the preparation of these volumes has, indeed, been the work of many
years. Boswell's "Life of Johnson" I
read for the first time in my boyhood,
when I was too young for it to lay any
hold on me. When I entered Pembroke
College, Oxford, though I loved to think
that Johnson had been there before me,
yet I cannot call to mind that I ever
opened the pages of Boswell. . . .
Such was my love for the subject that
on one occasion, when I was called upon
to write a review that should fill two columns of a weekly newspaper, I read a new
edition of the "Life" from beginning to
end without, I believe, missing a single
line of the text or a single note. At
length, "towering in the confidence" of
one who as yet has but set his foot on the
threshold of some stately mansion in which
he hopes to find for himself a home, I was
rash enough more than twelve years ago
to offer myself as editor of a new edition
of Boswell's "Life of Johnson." Fortunately for me another writer had been
already engaged by the publisher to whom
I applied, and my offer was civilly declined.
From that time on I never lost sight of
my purpose but when in the troubles of
life I well-nigh lost sight of every kind of
hope. Everything in my reading that
bore on my favourite author was carefully
noted, till at length I felt that the materials which I had gathered from all sides

were sufficient to shield me from a charge of rashness if I now began to raise the building. . . . I have now come to the end of my long labours. "There are few things not purely evil," wrote Johnson, "of which we can say without some emotion of uneasiness, *this is the last.*" From this emotion I cannot feign that I am free. My book has been my companion in many a sad and many a happy hour. I take leave of it with a pang of regret, but I am cheered by the hope that it may take its place, if a lowly one, among the works of men who have laboured patiently but not unsuccessfully in the great and shining fields of English literature.—HILL, GEORGE BIRKBECK, 1887, *ed. Boswell's Life of Johnson, Preface, vol.* I, *pp.* xi, xiii, xxix.

The universal verdict of mankind has placed this work among the five or six most interesting and stimulating of the world's books.—GOSSE, EDMUND, 1888, *A History of Eighteenth Century Literature, p.* 358.

Did he (Macaulay) recognise to the full the fact of Boswell's pre-eminence as an artist? Was he really conscious that the "Life" is an admirable work of art as well as the most readable and companionable of books? As, not content with committing himself thus far, he goes on to prove that Boswell was great because he was little; that he wrote a great book because he was an ass, and that if he had not been an ass his book would probably have been at least a small one, incredulity on these points becomes repectable. — HENLEY, WILLIAM ERNEST, 1890, *Views and Reviews, p.* 197.

How much the literary Jupiter owes to his literary satellites, particularly to the first one, it is not easy, at this distance of time, to tell. But who reads his "Journey to the Western Islands of Scotland" in these days? How often is his "Dictionary" consulted? What influence has his "Rambler" upon modern letters? What sweet girl graduate or cultivated Harvard "man" of to-day can quote a line from "The Vanity of Human Wishes," or knows whether that production is in prose or verse? What would the world have thought of Samuel Johnson at the end of a hundred years if a silly little Scottish laird had not made a hero of him, to be worshipped as no literary man was

ever worshipped before or since, and if he had not written a biography of him which is the best in any language, and the model for all others.—HUTTON, LAURENCE, 1891, *Literary Landmarks of Edinburgh, p.* 20.

Boswell, then, possessed in perfection some essential qualifications for the biographer—discernment, discrimination, the eye of an artist, a keen sense of literary proportion. His way was made easy for him by good humour, and an unbounded love of society, and his vanity made him impervious to any rebuff, however crushing. His keen sympathy enabled him to penetrate the motives of men, and he had enough of literary skill to convey the impression of a character or of an incident with dramatic reality. In spite of all his weakness, his folly, his dissipation, and the essential shallowness of his character, he had earnestness of purpose enough to force him to untiring perseverance in his task. . . . Wonderful as it is that a man so compact of folly and vanity, so childish and so weak as Boswell, should have produced a book which has enforced the admiration of the world, yet we need not explain that book as a literary miracle. Its success is achieved by the usual means—insight, sympathy, skill, and perseverance; and its author had served an apprenticeship to his art before he began his greatest work.—CRAIK, HENRY, 1895, *English Prose, vol.* IV, *p.* 479.

Boswell's book itself may now, in Parliamentary language, be taken for "read." As Johnson said of Goldsmith's "Traveller," "its merit is established, and individual praise or censure can neither augment nor diminish it." . . . What is most distinctive in Boswell is Boswell's method and Boswell's manner. . . . This faculty of communicating his impressions accurately to his reader is Boswell's most conspicuous gift. Present in his first book, it was more present in his second, and when he began his great biography it had reached its highest point. So individual is his manner, so unique his method of collecting and arranging his information, that to disturb the native character of his narrative by interpolating foreign material, must of necessity impair its specific character and imperil its personal note.—DOBSON, AUSTIN, 1898, *Boswell's Predecessors and Editors, Miscellanies, pp.* 110, 124, 125.

It is refreshing to turn to Boswell. We shall confine ourselves to Boswell's character, which has been little studied. If the "Journal to Stella" is a diary of two worlds, Boswell's "Life" is an atmosphere of one—that of his hero. Yet through this atmosphere his own personality emerges clear and palpable.—SICHEL, W., 1899, *Men who Have Kept A Diary, Blackwood's Magazine, vol.* 165, *p.* 80.

It was through having his attention almost always alert that he was enabled to give us those vivid pictures which make his book a veritable literary cinematograph; for in truth his pages may be said to live; with a few simple but subtle strokes the living scene is dramatically brought before us, and we can almost fancy that we hear the loud voice of Johnson and the sonorous tones of Burke, that we see the quaint figure of Goldsmith and the sedate deportment of Gibbon.—SILLARD, P. A., 1901, *The Prince of Biographers, Atlantic Monthly, vol.* 88, *p.* 214.

GENERAL

That he was a coxcomb and a bore, weak, vain, pushing, curious, garrulous, was obvious to all who were acquainted with him. That he could not reason, that he had no wit, no humour, no eloquence, is apparent from his writings. And yet his writings are read beyond the Mississippi, and under the Southern Cross, and are likely to be read as long as the English exists, either as a living or as a dead language.—MACAULAY, THOMAS BABINGTON, 1843, *Samuel Johnson, Critical and Historical Essays.*

With all the praise that is lavished upon his biography, the author himself is rather an underrated man. It is pretty generally supposed that little intellectual power was required for such a production —that it is merely an affair of memory and observation. Now such powers of memory and observation are certainly no common endowment. . . . Macaulay, who dilates upon the meanness of spirit shown in the drawing out of Johnson's opinions, gives no credit to the ingenuity. Boswell was undoubtedly a man of much social tact, possessing great general knowledge of human nature, and a most penetrating insight into the thoughts and intents of his habitual companions.—MINTO, WILLIAM, 1872–80, *Manual of English Prose Literature, p.* 481.

James Boswell has been treated with the greatest injustice and ingratitude by nearly all the literary men who have recorded their opinions concerning him and his work. Sir Walter Scott alone, with characteristic good sense, stands aloof from the rest in his respectful treatment of the distinguished biographer. He does not, indeed, seem to be aware that Boswell requires defence, or that there is anything particular in a kindly and respectful demeanour towards the author of Johnson's Life. He knows that Boswell, in spite of his faults, was a high-spirited and honourable gentleman, warm-hearted, and of a most candid and open nature, a sunny temper, and the most unusual and genuine literary abilities. Accordingly, when Sir Walter happens to allude to the Laird of Auchinleck it is always in a friendly and frequently admiring tone — a tone very different from the brutal vituperation of Macaulay or the superior compassion and humane condescension of the great Herr Teufelsdrock. James Boswell did not deserve the hatred of the one or the pity of the other. In standing contrast with the resolute vituperation of the rhetorician and the determined compassion of the prophet, the honest student of English literature will be always glad to encounter the kindly, grateful, and admiring language which flows so gracefully and naturally from the pen of Sir Walter in dealing with the character and the literary performances of Boswell.—CLIVE, ARTHUR, 1874, *Boswell and his Enemies, Gentleman's Magazine, n. s., vol.* 13, *p.* 68.

The unique character of Boswell is impressed upon all his works. The many foibles which ruined his career are conspicuous but never offensive; the vanity which makes him proud of his hypochondria and his supposed madness is redeemed by his touching confidence in the sympathy of his fellows; his absolute good-nature, his hearty appreciation of the excellence of his eminent contemporaries, though pushed to absurdity, is equalled by the real vivacity of his observations and the dramatic power of his narrative. Macaulay's graphic description of his absurdities, and Carlyle's more penetrating appreciation of his higher qualities, contain all that can be said.—STEPHEN, LESLIE, 1885, *Dictionary of National Biography, vol.* V, *p.* 437.

WILLIAM COWPER

Engraving by S. Fillman.

ROBERT BURNS

From a Painting by Alonzo Chappel.
Original by Nasmyth.

Robert Burns

1759–1796

January 25, 1759, Birth at Ayr, parish of Alloway. 1765, School at Alloway Mill; with Murdoch. 1766–1777, At Mount Oliphant, parish of Ayr (1766). 1768, Early associations on the farm. Taught at home by his father. 1769, Books. Love and song. Jenny Wilson. 1777–84, At Lochlea, parish of Tarbolton. 1778, School at Kirkoswald. 1780, The Bachelor's Club. 1781, Flax-dressing at Irvine. 1782, Finds Fergusson's Poems. 1783. A Freemason. February 1784, His father's death. 1784–1786, At Mossgiel, parish of Mauchline. 1785, Early friends: Gavin Hamilton, Robert Aiken. Struggle with Auld Lichts. Poetic Springtide. Epistles. Satirical Poems. Descriptive Poems. Songs. August 1786, Kilmarnock (first) edition of poems published. Literary friendships: Dr. Blacklock, Dugald Stewart, Dr. Blair, Rev. Mr. Laurie, Mrs. Dunlop. Visits Katrine, meets Lord Daer and Mrs. Stewart. November 1786, Visits Edinburgh. Among the celebrities. April 1787, Second edition of poems. Travels in Scotland, May, Border Tour. June, Returns to Mossgiel. First Highland Tour. Second Highland Tour. Third Highland Tour. September, Returns to Edinburgh. Johnson's Museum. March 1788, Leaves Edinburgh. 1788–1791, At Ellisland. August 1788, Marries Jean Armour, At Friar's Carse. 1790, Appointed Excise Officer. 1791–1796, At Dumfries. Bank Vennel. Dumfries Volunteers. Thomson's Collection. 1792, Patriotic Songs. 1793, Visits Galloway. 1794, Removes to Mill Hill Brae. Failing Health. July 21, 1796, Death. —GEORGE, ANDREW J., 1896, *ed.*, *Select Poems of Robert Burns*, p. 231.

PERSONAL

This kind of life—the cheerless gloom of a hermit, with the unceasing moil of a galley-slave, brought me to my sixteenth year; a little before which period I first committed the sin of Rhyme. You know our country custom of coupling a man and woman together as partners in the labours of harvest. In my fifteenth autumn my partner was a bewitching creature, a year younger than myself. My scarcity of English denies me the power of doing her justice in that language; but you know the Scottish idiom—she was a *bonnie sweet, sonie lass*. In short, she altogether, unwittingly to herself, initiated me in that delicious passion, which, in spite of acid disappointment, gin-horse prudence, and book-worm philosophy, I hold to be the first of human joys, our dearest blessing here below! How she caught the contagion, I cannot tell: you medical people talk much of infection from breathing the same air, the touch, &c.; but I never expressly said I loved her, indeed, I did not know myself why I liked so much to loiter behind with her, when returning in the evening from our labours; why the tones of her voice made my heart-strings thrill like an Æolian harp; and particularly my pulse beat such a furious ratan when I looked and fingered over her little hand to pick out the cruel nettle-stings and thistles. Among her other love-inspiring qualities, she sung sweetly; and it was her favourite reel to which I attempted giving an embodied vehicle in rhyme. I was not so presumptuous as to imagine that I could make verses like printed ones, composed by men who had Greek and Latin; but my girl sung a song, which was said to be composed by a small country laird's son, on one of his father's maids, with whom he was in love! and I saw no reason why I might not rhyme as well as he; for, excepting that he could smear sheep, and cast peats, his father living in the moor-lands, he had no more scholar-craft than myself.—BURNS, ROBERT, 1787, *Letter to Dr. Moore, Aug. 2*; *Burns's Works, ed. Currie.*

After all my boasted independence, curst necessity compels me to implore you for five pounds. A cruel scoundrel of a haberdasher, to whom I owe an account, taking it into his head that I am dying, has commenced a process, and will infallibly put me into jail. Do, for God's sake, send me that sum, and that by return of post. Forgive me this earnestness; but the horrors of a jail have made me half distracted. I do not ask all this gratuitously; for, upon returning health, I hereby promise and engage to furnish you with five pounds' worth of the neatest song-genius you have seen. I tried my hand on *Rothermurchie* this morning. The measure is so difficult, that it is impossible to infuse much genius into the lines; they are on the other side. Forgive, forgive me!— BURNS, ROBERT, 1796, *Letter to George Thomson, July 12.*

If others have climbed more successfully to the heights of Parnassus, none certainly out-shone Burns in the charms—the sorcery I would almost call it, of fascinating conversation; the spontaneous eloquence of social argument, or the unstudied poignancy of brilliant repartee. His personal endowments were perfectly correspondent with the qualifications of his mind. His form was manly; his action energy itself; devoid, in a great measure, however, of those graces, of that polish, acquired only in the refinement of societies, where in early life he had not the opportunity to mix; but, where, such was the irresistible power of attraction that encircled him, though his appearance and manners were always peculiar, he never failed to delight and to *excel*. His figure certainly bore the authentic impress of his birth and original station in life; it seemed rather moulded by nature for the rough exercises of agriculture, than the gentler cultivation of the *belles lettres*. His features were stamped with the hardy character of independence, and the firmness of conscious, though not arrogant pre-eminence. I believe no man was ever gifted with a larger portion of the *vivida vis animi:* the animated expressions of his countenance were almost peculiar to himself. The rapid lightenings of his eye were always the harbingers of some flash of genius, whether they darted the fiery glances of insulted and indignant superiority, or beamed with the impassioned sentiment of fervent and impetuous affections. His voice alone could improve upon the magic of his eye; sonorous, replete with the finest modulations, it alternately captivated the ear with the melody of poetic numbers, the perspicuity of nervous reasoning, or the ardent sallies of enthusiastic patriotism.— RIDDELL, MARIA, 1796, *Letter to Dumfries Journal, Aug. 7, Burns's Works, ed. Curry.*

My pupil, Robert Burns, was then between six and seven years of age; his preceptor about eighteen. Robert, and his younger brother, Gilbert, had been grounded a little in English before they were put under my care. They both made a rapid progress in reading, and a tolerable

progress in writing. In reading, dividing words into syllables by rule, spelling without book, phrasing sentences, &c., Robert and Gilbert were generally at the upper end of the class, even when ranged with boys by far their seniors. The books most commonly used in the school were the "Spelling Book," the "New Testament," the "Bible," "Masson's Collection of Prose and Verse," and "Fisher's English Grammar." They committed to memory the hymns, and other poems of that collection, with uncommon facility. This facility was partly owing to the method pursued by their father and me in instructing them, which was, to make them thoroughly acquainted with the meaning of every word in each sentence that was to be committed to memory. . . . Gilbert always appeared to me to possess a more lively imagination, and to be more of the wit, than Robert. I attempted to teach them a little church-music. Here they were left far behind by all the rest of the school. Robert's ear, in particular, was remarkably dull, and his voice untunable. It was long before I could get them to distinguish one tune from another. Robert's countenance was generally grave, and impressive of a serious, contemplative, and thoughtful mind. Gilbert's face said, *Mirth, with thee I mean to live ;* and certainly, if any person who knew the two boys, had been asked which of them was the most likely to court the muses, he would surely never have guessed that Robert had a propensity of that kind. — MURDOCH, JOHN, 1799, *Letter to Joseph Cooper Walker, Feb. 22, Burns's Works, ed. Currie.*

The first time I saw Robert Burns was on the 23d of October, 1786, when he dined at my house at Ayrshire, together with our common friend Mr. John Mackenzie, surgeon, in Mauchline, to whom I am indebted for the pleasure of his acquaintance . . . . His manners were then, as they continued ever afterwards, simple, manly, and independent; strongly expressive of conscious genius and worth; but without any thing that indicated forwardness, arrogance, or vanity. He took his share in conversation, but not more than belonged to him; and listened with apparent attention and deference, on subjects where his want of education deprived him of the means of information. If there had been

a little more of gentleness and accommodation in his temper, he would, I think,
have been still more interesting; but he
had been accustomed to give law in the
circle of his ordinary acquaintance; and
his dread of any thing approaching to
meanness or servility, rendered his manner somewhat decided and hard. Nothing,
perhaps, was more remarkable among his
various attainments, than the fluency, and
precision, and originality of his language,
when he spoke in company; more particularly as he aimed at purity in his turn of
expression, and avoided more successfully
than most Scotchmen, the peculiarities of
Scottish phraseology. . . . The attentions he received during his stay in
town from all ranks and descriptions of
persons, were such as would have turned
any head but his own. I cannot say that
I could perceive any unfavourable effect
which they left on his mind. He retained
the same simplicity of manners and appearance which had struck me so forcibly
when I first saw him in the country; nor
did he seem to feel any additional self-
importance from the number and rank of
his new acquaintance. His dress was perfectly suited to his station, plain and unpretending, with a sufficient attention to
neatness. If I recollect right he always
wore boots; and, when on more than
usual ceremony, buck-skin breeches.
. . . All the faculties of Burns's mind
were, as far as I could judge, equally vigorous; and his predilection for poetry was
rather the result of his own enthusiastic
and impassioned temper, than of a genius exclusively adapted to that species of
composition. From his conversation I
should have pronounced him to be fitted
to excel in whatever walk of ambition he
had chosen to exert his abilities.—STEW-
ART, DUGALD, 1800, *Letter to James Currie, Currie's Life of Burns.*

Burns died in great poverty; but the
independence of his spirit, and the exemplary prudence of his wife, had preserved
him from debt. He had received from his
poems a clear profit of about nine hundred
pounds. Of this sum, the part expended
on his library (which was far from extensive) and in the humble furniture of his
house, remained; and obligations were
found for two hundred pounds advanced by
him to the assistance of those to whom he
was united by the ties of blood, and still

more by those of esteem and affection.
When it is considered, that his expenses
in Edinburgh, and on his various journeys,
could not be inconsiderable; that his agricultural undertaking was unsuccessful;
that his income, from the Excise was for
some time as low as fifty, and never rose
to above seventy pounds a year; that his
family was large and his spirit was liberal
—no one will be surprised that his circumstances were so poor, or that, as his
health decayed, his proud and feeling heart
sunk under the secret consciousness of
indigence, and the apprehensions of absolute want. Yet poverty never bent the
spirit of Burns to any pecuniary meanness. Neither chicanery nor sordidness
ever appeared in his conduct. He carried
his disregard of money to blameable excess.
Even in the midst of distress he bore himself loftily to the world, and received with
a jealous reluctance every offer of friendly
assistance. . . . Burns, as has already
been mentioned, was nearly five feet ten
inches in height, and of a form that indicated agility as well as strength. His
well-raised forehead, shaded with black
curling hair, indicated extensive capacity.
His eyes were large, dark, full of ardour
and intelligence. His face was well
formed; and his countenance uncommonly
interesting and expressive. His mode of
dressing which was often slovenly, and a
certain fulness and bend in his shoulders,
characteristic of his original profession,
disguised in some degree the natural symmetry and elegance of his form. The external appearance of Burns was most
strikingly indicative of the character of
his mind.—CURRIE, JAMES, 1800, *ed.,
Works of Robert Burns, Life.*

We turned again to Burns's house. Mrs.
Burns was gone to spend some time by
the seashore with her children. We spoke
to the servant-maid at the door, who invited us forward, and we sate down in the
parlour. The walls were coloured with a
blue wash; on one side of the fire was a
mahogany desk, opposite to the window a
clock, and over the desk, a print from
"Cotter's Saturday Night," which Burns
mentions in one of his letters having received as a present. The house was cleanly
and neat in the inside, the stairs of stone,
scoured white, the kitchen on the right
side of the passage, the parlour on the
left. In the room above the parlour the

poet died, and his son after him in the same room.— WORDSWORTH, DOROTHY, *Aug.* 18, 1803, *Journals.*

Till he fixed his residence in Dumfries, his irregularities, though by no means unfrequent, had not become *inveterately habitual ;* the temptations, however, to which he was now exposed proved too powerful for his better impressions; after various struggles against the stream of dissipation which was gradually surrounding him, he at length suffered himself to be rapidly carried along by its fatal current. A large proportion of the more genteel, or more idle inhabitants of Dumfries, consists of men connected with the profession of law : and in some of these, as well as in other inhabitants of the town and its vicinity, Burns found associates from whom it was not to be expected that he should learn sobriety. The fame of his literary character also exposed him to the company of every stranger who professed a respect for poetry. As their interviews commonly took place in taverns, his familiarity with riotous excess was daily increasing. In the midst of such distractions, it *must have been impossible* for him to discharge the duties of his office with that regularity which is almost indispensable.—IRVINE, DAVID, 1810, *The Lives of the Scottish Poets.*

I was not much struck with his first appearance, as I had previously heard it described. His person, though strong and well knit, and much superior to what might be expected in a ploughman, was still rather coarse in its outline. His stature, from want of setting up, appeared to be only of the middle size, but was rather above it. His motions were firm and decided, and though without any pretentions to grace, were at the same time so free from clownish constraint, as to show that he had not always been confined to the society of his profession. His countenance was not of that elegant cast, which is most frequent among the upper ranks, but it was manly and intelligent, and marked by a thoughtful gravity which shaded at times into sternness. In his large dark eye the most striking index of his genius resided. It was full of mind; and would have been singularly expressive, under the management of one who could employ it with more art, for the purpose of expression. . . . In conversation he was powerful. His conceptions and expression were of corresponding vigour, and on all subjects were as remote as possible from common places. Though somewhat authoritative, it was in a way which gave little offence, and was readily imputed to his inexperience in those modes of smoothing dissent and softening assertion, which are important characteristics of polished manners. After breakfast I requested him to communicate some of his unpublished pieces, and he recited his farewell song to the Banks of Ayr, introducing it with a description of the circumstances in which it was composed, more striking than the poem itself. I paid particular attention to his recitation, which was plain, slow, articulate, and forcible, but without any eloquence or art. He did not always lay the emphasis with propriety, nor did he humour the sentiment by the variations of his voice. He was standing, during the time, with his face towards the window, to which, and not to his auditors, he directed his eye— thus depriving himself of any additional effect which the language of his composition might have borrowed from the language of his countenance.— WALKER, JOSIAH, 1811, *Life of Burns.*

No person can regret more than I do the tendency of *some* of my Brother's writings to represent irregularity of conduct as a consequence of genius, and sobriety the effect of dulness ; but surely more has been said on that subject than the fact warrants : and it ought to be remembered that the greatest part of his writings, having that tendency, *were not published by himself, nor intended for publication.* But it may likewise be observed, and every attentive reader of Burns's Works, must have observed, that he frequently presents a caricature of his feelings, and even of his failings—a kind of mock-heroic account of himself and his opinions, which he never supposed could be taken literally. I dare say it never entered into his head, for instance, that when he was speaking in that manner of Milton's Satan, any one should gravely suppose that was the model on which he wished to form his own character. Yet on such rants, which the author evidently intends should be considered a mere play of imagination, joined to some abstract reasoning of the critic, many of the heavy accusations brought against the Poet for bad taste and worse morals, rest.—BURNS, GILBERT, 1814, *Letter to Alexander Peterkin, Sep.* 29; *Life and Works of Robert Burns, ed. Peterkin.*

IN AETERNUM HONOREM
ROBERTI BURNS
POETARUM CALEDONIAE SUI AEVI LONGE
PRINCIPIS
CUJUS CARMINA EXIMIA PATRIO SERMONE
SCRIPTA
ANIMI MAGIS ARDENTIS VIQUE INGENII
QUAM ARTE VEL CULTU CONSPICUA
FACETIIS JUCUNDITATE LEPORE AFFLUENTIA
OMNIBUS LITTERARUM CULTORIBUS
SATIS NOTA
CIVES SUI NECNON PLERIQUE OMNES
MUSARUM AMANTISSIMI MEMORIAMQUE VIRI
ARTE POETICA TAM PRAECLARI FOVENTES
HOC MAUSOLEUM
SUPER RELIQUIAS POETAE MORTALES
EXTRUENDUM CURAVERE
PRIMUM HUJUS AEDIFICII LAPIDEM
GULIELMUS MILLER ARMIGER
REIPUBLICAE ARCHITECTONICAE APUD
SCOTOS
IN REGIONE AUSTRALI CURIO MAXIMUS
PROVINCIALIS
GEORGIO TERTIO REGNANTE
GEORGIO WALLIARUM PRINCIPE
SUMMAM IMPERII PRO PATRE TENENTE
JOSEPHO GASS ARMIGERO DUMFRISIAE
PRAEFECTO
THOMA F. HUNT LONDINENSI ARCHITECTO
POSUIT
NONIS JUNIIS ANNO LUCIS VMDCCCXV
SALUTIS HUMANAE MDCCCXV.
—INSCRIPTION ON TOMB, 1815.

The truth is, that the convivial excesses or other errors of Robert Burns, were neither greater nor more numerous than those which we every day see in the conduct of men who stand high in the estimation of society;—of some men, who, like Burns, have, in their peculiar spheres, conferred splendid gifts of genius on their country, and whose names are breathed in every voice, with pride and enthusiasm, as the benefactors of society. Are their errors officiously dragged from the tomb, or emblazoned amidst the trophies of victory without universal reprobation? All we ask is the same measure of justice and of mercy for Burns.—PETERKIN, ALEXANDER, 1815, *ed., The Life and Works of Robert Burns, vol.* I, *p.* xlix.

One song of Burns's is of more worth to you than all I could think for a whole year in his native country. His misery is a dead weight upon the nimbleness of one's quill; I tried to forget it—to drink toddy without any care—to write a merry sonnet—it won't do—he talked with bitches, he drank with blackguards; he was miserable. We can see horribly clear, in the works of such a man, his whole life, as if we were God's spies.— KEATS, JOHN, 1818, *Letters.*

He had a strong mind, and a strong body, the fellow to it. He had a real heart of flesh and blood beating in his bosom—you can almost hear it throb. Some one said, that if you had shaken hands with him, his hand would have burnt yours. The gods, indeed, "made him poetical;" but nature had a hand in him first. His heart was in the right place. He did not "create a soul under the ribs of death," by tinkling siren sounds, or by piling up centos of poetic diction; but for the artificial flowers of poetry, he plucked the mountain-daisy under his feet; and a field mouse, hurrying from its ruined dwelling, could inspire him with the sentiments of terror and pity. He held the plough or the pen with the same firm, manly grasp; nor did he cut out poetry as we cut out watch-papers, with finical dexterity, nor from the same flimsy materials. Burns was not like Shakspeare in the range of his genius; but there is something of the same magnanimity, directness, and unaffected character about him. He was not a sickly sentimentalist, a namby-pamby poet, a mincing metre ballad-monger, any more than Shakspeare. He would as soon hear "a brazen candlestick tuned, or a dry wheel grate on the axletree." He was as much of a man—not a twentieth as much of a poet—as Shakspeare. With but little of his imagination or inventive power, he had the same life of mind: within the narrow circle of personal feeling or domestic incidents, the pulse of his poetry flows as healthily and vigorously. He had an eye to see; a heart to feel:—no more.—HAZLITT, WILLIAM, 1818, *Lectures on the English Poets, Lecture* vii.

To-day our Burns's dinner. . . . Burns's son was brought forward, and spoke sensibly: very like the father to judge by the engravings, and worthy of him in the manly sentiments he expressed about politics; too manly and free, poor fellow, for his advancement as a placeman.—MOORE, THOMAS, 1819, *Journal, June* 5; *Memoirs, ed. Russell, vol.* II, *p.* 322.

Dumfries was like a besieged place. It was known that he was dying, and the anxiety, not of the rich and the learned only, but of the mechanics and peasants, exceeded all belief. Wherever two or three people stood together, their talk was of Burns, and of him alone. They spoke of his history—of his person—of his works—of his family—of his fame— and of his untimely and approaching fate, with a warmth and an enthusiasm which will ever endear Dumfries to my remem- berance. All that he said or was saying— the opinions of the physicians (and Maxwell was a kind and a skillful one), were eagerly caught up and reported from street to street, and from house to house. . . . His good humour was unruffled, and his wit never forsook him. He looked to one of his fellow volunteers with a smile, as he stood by the bed-side with his eyes wet, and said, "John, don't let the awkward squad fire over me." He repressed with a smile the hopes of his friends, and told them he had lived long enough. As his life drew near a close, the eager, yet decorous solicitude of his fellow-towns- men, increased. It is the practice of the young men of Dumfries to meet in the streets during the hours of remission from labour, and by these means I had an oppor- tunity of witnessing the general solici- tude of all ranks and of all ages. His difference with them on some important points were forgotten and forgiven; they thought only of his genius—of the delight his compositions had diffused—and they talked of him with the same awe as of some departing spirit, whose voice was to gladden them no more. . . . I went to see him laid out for the grave, several elder people were with me. He lay in a plain unadorned coffin, with a linen sheet drawn over his face, and on the bed, and around the body, herbs and flowers were thickly strewn, according to the usage of the country. He was wasted somewhat by long illness; but death had not increased the swarthy hue of his face, which was uncommonly dark and deeply marked—his broad and open brow was pale and serene, and around it his sable hair lay in masses, slightly touched with grey. The room where he lay was plain

and neat, and the simplicity of the poet's humble dwelling pressed the presence of death more closely on the heart than if his bier had been embellished by vanity, and covered with the blazonry of high ancestry and rank. We stood and gazed on him in silence for the space of several minutes—we went, and others succeeded us—not a whisper was heard. This was several days after his death. . . . The multitude who accompanied Burns to the grave went step by step with the chief mourners. They might amount to ten or twelve thousand. Not a word was heard. . . . It was an impressive and mournful sight to see men of all ranks and persuasions and opinions ming- ling as brothers, and stepping side by side down the streets of Dumfries, with the remains of him who had sung of their loves and joys and domestic endearments, with a truth and a tenderness which none perhaps have since equalled.—CUNNING- HAM, ALLAN, 1824, *Robert Burns and Lord Byron, London Magazine.*

I was a lad of fifteen in 1786–7, when he came first to Edinburgh, but had sense and feeling enough to be much interested in his poetry, and would have given the world to know him; but I had very little acquaintance with any literary people, and still less with the gentry of the west country, the two sets that he most fre- quented. Mr. Thomas Grierson was at that time a clerk of my father's. He knew Burns, and promised to ask him to his lodgings to dinner, but had no oppor- tunity to keep his word, otherwise I might have seen more of this distinguished man. . . . His person was strong and robust: his manners rustic, not clownish; a sort of dignified plainness and simplicity which received part of its effect perhaps from one's knowledge of his extraordinary talents. His features are represented in Mr. Nasmyth's picture, but to me it con- veys the idea that they are diminished as if seen in perspective. I think his coun- tenance was more massive than it looks in any of the portraits. I would have taken the poet, had I not known what he was, for a very sagacious country farmer of the old Scotch school—*i. e.* none of your modern agriculturists, who keep labour- ers for their drudgery, but the *douce gude- man* who held his own plough. There was a strong expression of sense and shrewdness in all his lineaments; the eye alone, I think, indicated the poetical character and temperament. It was large, and of a dark cast, and glowed (I say literally *glowed*) when he spoke with feeling or interest. I never saw such another eye in a human head, though I have seen the most distinguished men in my time. His conversation expressed perfect self-confidence, without the slightest presumption. Among the men who were the most learned of their time and country, he expressed himself with perfect firmness, but without the least intrusive forwardness; and when he differed in opinion, he did not hesitate to express it firmly, yet at the same time with modesty. I do not remember any part of his conversation distinctly enough to be quoted, nor did I ever see him again, except in the street, where he did not recognize me, as I could not expect he should. He was much caressed in Edinburgh, but (considering what literary emoluments have been since his day) the efforts made for his relief were extremely trifling.—SCOTT, SIR WALTER, 1827, *Letter to Lockhart, Memoirs by Lockhart, vol.* I, *pp.* 166, 167.

Burns, eager of temper, loud of tone, and with declamation and sarcasm equally at command, was, we may easily believe, the most hated of human beings, because the most dreaded, among the provincial champions of the administration of which he thought fit to disapprove. But that he ever, in his most ardent moods, upheld the principles of those whose applause of the French Revolution was but the mask of revolutionary designs at home, after these principles had been really developed by those that maintained them, and understood by him, it may be safely denied. There is not in all his correspondence, one syllable to give countenance to such a charge. . . . Here, then, as in most other cases of similar controversy, the fair and equitable conclusion would seem to be, "truth lies between." To whatever Burns's excesses amounted, they were, it is obvious, and that frequently, the subject of rebuke and remonstrance even from his own dearest friends—even from men who had no sort of objection to potations deep enough in all conscience. That such reprimands, giving shape and form to the thoughts that tortured his own bosom, should have been received at times with

a strange mixture of remorse and indignation, none that have considered the nervous susceptibility and haughtiness of Burns's character, can hear with surprise.—LOCKHART, JOHN GIBSON, 1828, *Life of Robert Burns, pp.* 308, 341.

To the ill-starred Burns was given the power of making man's life more venerable, but *t*hat of wisely guiding his own was not given. Destiny—for so in our ignorance we must speak—his faults, the faults of others, proved too hard for him; and that spirit, which might have soared, could it but have walked, soon sank to the dust, its glorious faculties trodden under foot in the blossom, and died, we may almost say, without ever having lived. And so kind and warm a soul; so full of inborn riches, of love of all living and lifeless things! . . . He has a just self-consciousness, which too often degenerates into pride; yet it is a noble pride, for defence, not for offence, no cold, suspicious feeling, but a frank and social one. The peasant poet bears himself, we might say, like a king in exile: he is cast among the low, and feels himself equal to the highest; yet he claims no rank that none may be disputed to him. . . . And this was he for whom the world found no fitter business than quarreling with smugglers and vintners, computing excise dues upon tallow, and gauging ale barrels! In such toils was that mighty spirit sorrowfully wasted: and a hundred years may pass on before another such is given us to waste. . . . We had something to say on the public moral character of Burns, but this also we must forbear. We are far from regarding him as guilty before the world, as guiltier than the average; nay, from doubting that he is less guilty than one of ten thousand. Tried at a tribunal far more rigid than that where the *plebiscita* of common civic reputations are pronounced, he had seemed to us even there less worthy of blame than of pity and wonder.—CARLYLE, THOMAS, 1828, *Essay on Burns.*

In early life he laboured under a disorder of the stomach, accompanied by palpitations of the heart, depression of the spirits, and nervous pains in the head, the nature of which he never appears to have understood, but which evidently arose from dyspepsia. These sufferings, be it remembered, are complained of in his letters years before he had committed any excess; and so far from being the consequence of intemperance, as they are generally considered to have been, the exhaustion they produced was probably the cause which drove him in his moments of hypochondria, to the excitement of the bottle for a temporary palliation of his symptoms.—MADDEN, R. R., 1833, *Infirmities of Genius, vol.* I, *p.* 276.

The cranial bones were perfect in every respect, if we except a little erosion of their external table, and firmly held together by their sutures; even the delicate bones of the orbits, with the trifling exception of the *os unguis* in the left, were sound, and uninjured by death and the grave. The superior maxillary bones still retained the four most posterior teeth on each side, including the dentes sapientiae, and all without spot or blemish; the incisores, cuspidati, &c., had in all probability recently dropped from the jaw, for the alveoli were but little decayed. The bones of the face and palate were also sound. Some small portions of black hair, with a very few gray hairs intermixed, were observed while detaching some extraneous matter from the occiput. Indeed, nothing could exceed the high state of preservation in which we found the bones of the cranium, or offer a fairer opportunity of supplying what has so long been desiderated by phrenologists—a correct model of our immortal poet's head: and in order to accomplish this in the most accurate and satisfactory manner, every particle of sand, or other foreign body, was carefully washed off, and the plaster of Paris applied with all the tact and accuracy of an experienced artist. The cast is admirably taken, and cannot fail to prove highly interesting to phrenologists and others. Having completed our intention, the skull, securely enclosed in a leaden case, was again committed to the earth, precisely where we found it.— BLACKLOCK, DR. ARCHIBALD, 1834, *Report on the Cranium of Robert Burns.*

I. DIMENSIONS OF THE SKULL.

Greatest circumference . . . inches 22¼
From Occipital Spine to Individuality,
    over the top of the head, . . . 14
.........Ear to Ear vertically over the
    top of the head, ... 13
.........Philoprogenitiveness to Individu-
    ality (greatest length) . . . 8

.........Concentrativeness to Comparison 7⅛
.........Ear to Philoprogenitiveness, . 4⅞
.............Individuality, ... 4¾
...............Benevolence, ... 5½
...............Firmness, ... 5½
.........Destructiveness to Destructive-
    ness, ... 5¾
.........Secretiveness to Secretiveness, . 5⅞
.........Cautiousness to Cautiousness, . . 5½
.........Ideality to Ideality, ... 4⅝
.........Constructiveness to Constructive-
    ness, ... 4½
.........Mastoid Process to Mastoid Pro-
    cess, ... 4¾
—COMBE, GEORGE, 1834, *Report on the Cast of Burns's Skull.*

A £10 bank note, by way of subscription for a few copies of an early edition of his poems—this the outside that I could ever see proof given of Burns having received anything in the way of *patronage*; and doubtless this would have been gladly returned, but from the dire necessity of dissembling. Lord Glencairn is the "patron" for whom Burns appears to have felt the most sincere respect. Yet even he—did he give him more than a seat at his dinner table? Lord Buchan again, whose liberalities are by this time pretty well appreciated in Scotland, exhorts Burns, in a tone of one preaching upon a primary duty of life, to exemplar gratitude towards a person who had given him absolutely nothing at all. The man has not yet lived to whose happiness it was more essential that he should live unencumbered by the sense of obligation; and, on the other hand, the man has not lived upon whose independence as professing benefactors so many people practised, or who found so many others ready to ratify and give value to their pretences. Him, whom beyond most men nature had created with the necessity of conscious independence, all men beseiged with the assurance that he was, must be, ought to be dependent; nay, that it was his primary duty to be grateful for his dependence . . . not merely that, with his genius, and with the intellectual pretentions generally of his family, he should have been called to a life of early labour, and of labour unhappily not prosperous, but also that he, by accident about the proudest of human spirits, should have been by accident summoned, beyond all others, to eternal recognitions of some mysterious gratitude which he owed to some mysterious patrons little and great, whilst yet, of all men, perhaps, he reaped the least obvious or known benefit from any patronage that has ever been put on record.—DE QUINCEY, THOMAS, 1837, *Literary Reminiscences, Collected Writings,* ed. *Masson, vol.* II, *pp.* 133, 134.

Altogether independently of his writings, the character of Burns, like that of Johnson, was one of great massiveness and power. There was a cast of true tragic greatness about it. There was a largeness in his heart, and a force in his passions, that corresponded with the mass of his intellect and the vigour of his genius. We receive just such an impression from reading his life as we do from perusing one of the greater tragedies of Shakspeare. Like the Othellos or Macbeths of the dramatist,—characters that fasten upon the imagination and sink into the memory from causes altogether unconnected with either literary taste or moral feeling,—we feel in him, perforce, an interest which exists and grows alike independently of the excesses into which his passions betrayed him, or the trophies which his genius enabled him to erect. Burns was not merely a distinguished poet,—he was a man on a large scale.— MILLER, HUGH, 1844, *The Burns Festival and Hero Worship, Essays, p.* 148.

He married his Jean, and chose his farm on the banks of the Nith, as Allan Cunningham's father remarked to him at the time, not with a farmer's, but a poet's choice. But here, half farmer, half exciseman, poverty came rapidly upon him once more; in three years' time only he quitted it, a man ruined in substance and constitution, and went to depend on his excise salary of £70 a year in the town of Dumfries. I visited this farm in August, 1845. . . . The farm, as I have said, is a very pleasant one. Burns is supposed to have chosen the particular situation of his house not only for its fine situation on the banks of the river, and overlooking the vale and country round, but on account of a beautiful spring which gushes from the slope just below the house. The ground-plan of his house is very much like that of most Scotch farms. The buildings form three sides of a quadrangle. The house and buildings are only one story high, white, and altogether a genuine Scotch steading. The house is on the lower side, next to the

river. Burns's bedroom has yet two beds in it, of that sort of cupboard fashion, with check curtains, which are so often seen in Scotch farm-houses. The humble rooms are much as they were in his time. Near the house, and running parallel with the river, is a good large garden which he planted. The side of the farm-yard opposite to the house is pleasantly planted off with trees. The farm is just as it was, about one hundred acres. By places it exhibits that stony soil which made Burns call it "the riddlings of creation," and say that when a ploughed field was rolled it looked like a paved street; but still it carries good crops. Burns had it for £50 a year, or ten shillings an acre. I suppose the present tenant pays three times the sum, and is proud of his bargain. He observed that it was an ill wind that blew nobody any profit. "Mr. Burns," said he, "had the farm on lease for ninety years, and had he not thrown it up, I should not have been here now." . . . The view from the house is very charming. The river runs clear and fleet below, broad as the Thames at Hampton Court, or the Trent at Nottingham, and its dark trees hang far along it over its waters. Beyond the stream lie the broad, rich meadows and house of Dalswinton, a handsome mansion of red freestone aloft amid its woods, and still beyond and higher up the river rise still bolder hills. — HOWITT, WILLIAM, 1847, *Homes and Haunts of the Most Eminent British Poets, vol.* I, *pp.* 424, 428, 431.

Could he have remained always at the plough, and worn always the mantle of inspiration which fell on him there, and enjoyed ever the lawful intoxication of natural scenery and solitary thought, he had been as happy as he was glorious. But night came, and found him weary and jaded in mind and body, thirsting for some new excitement, and eager to pass (O human nature! O hideous anti-climax!) from an Elisha-like plough—to a penny-wedding! There the lower part of his nature found intense gratification and unrestricted play. There the "blood of John Barleycorn" furnished him with a false and hollow semblance of the true inspiration he had met in the solitary field, or on "the side of a plantain, when the wind was howling among the trees, and raving over the plain." And there, through the misty light of the presiding punch-bowl, he saw the most ordinary specimens of female nature transformed into angels; and fancied that, like divinities they should be adored.—GILFILLAN, GEORGE, 1856, *ed., The Poetical Works of Robert Burns, vol.* I, *p.* xii.

Burns was a grand *Man.* I am not going to *praise* him; I leave *that* to Scotland and to *you;* supported, and sympathised with, by the universal heart of humanity. All this is so very well known that it has almost degenerated into common-place. Miss Edgeworth once remarked to me that such or such a thing "had been said till it was *not* believed!" A splendid remark, as I thought at the time but the fame of your Burns can survive it.—HAMILTON, SIR WILLIAM ROWAN, 1859, *Letter to John Nichol, Jan.* 22; *Life, ed. Graves, vol.* III, *p.* 109.

Beholding his poor, mean dwelling and its surroundings, and picturing his outward life and earthly manifestations from these, one does not so much wonder that the people of that day should have failed to recognize all that was admirable and immortal in a disreputable, drunken, shabbily clothed, and shabbily housed man, consorting with associates of damaged character, and, as his only ostensible occupation, gauging the whiskey, which he too often tasted. . . . For my part, I chiefly wonder that his recognition dawned so brightly while he was still living. There must have been something very grand in his immediate presence, some strangely impressive characteristic in his natural behavior, to have caused him to seem like a demigod so soon. . . . There is no writer whose life, as a man, has so much to do with his fame, and throws such a necessary light upon whatever he has produced.—HAWTHORNE, NATHANIEL, 1863, *Some of the Haunts of Burns, Our Old Home.*

Mighty is the hallowing of death to all, —to him more than to most. As he lay stretched, his dark locks already streaked with unnatural gray, all unworthiness fell away from him—every stain of passion and debauch, every ignoble word, every ebullition of scorn and pride—and left pure nobleness. Farmer no longer, exciseman no longer, subject no longer to criticism, to misrepresentation, to the malevolence of mean natures and evil

tongues, he lay there the great poet of his country, dead too early for himself and for it. He had passed from the judgments of Dumfries, and made his appeal to Time.—SMITH, ALEXANDER, 1865, *The Poetical Works of Robert Burns, Life, p.* xxxvi.

In 1856 I spent an afternoon with Mrs. Begg, the poet's sister. She said that Robert took their father's place in conducting household worship, and that he instructed her in the Shorter Catechism. "He was a father to me," said Mrs. Begg, "and my knowedge of the Scriptures in my youth I derived from his teachings."— ROGERS, CHARLES, 1871, *A Century of Scottish Life.*

Another happy man, after all, seems to be Allingham, for all his want of "success." Nothing but the most absolute calm and enjoyment of outside Nature could account for so much gadding hither and thither on the soles of his two feet. Fancy carrying about grasses for hours and days from the field where Burns ploughed up a daisy! Good God, if I found the daisy itself there, I would sooner swallow it than be troubled to carry it twenty yards.—ROSSETTI, DANTE GABRIEL, 1871, *Letter to Scott, Letters and Memoir, ed. Rossetti, vol.* I, *p.* 418.

This is the cottage room as 'twas of old:
> The window four small panes, and in the wall
> The box-bed, where the first daylight did fall
Upon their new-born infant's narrow fold
And poor, when times were hard and winds were cold,
As they were still with him. Lo! now close by
Above Corinthian columns mounted high
The old Athenian Tripod shines in gold!
The lumbering carriages of these dull years
Have passed away: their dust has ceased to whirr
About the footsore: silent to our ears
> Is that maelstrom of Scottish men; this son
Of all that age we count the kingliest one:
Such is Time's justice, Time the harvester.
—SCOTT, WILLIAM BELL, 1871, *On Visiting Burns's Cottage and Monument, Autobiographical Notes of the Life of Scott, ed. Minto, vol.* II, *p.* 164.

But, not frae Life's rough work was brought
> For him, the least exemption:
At his ain task, he painfu' wrought,
He strugglit, suff'rit, felt, and thought,
Aschewin' name, and shrinkin' naught,
> Till Death brought him redemption.

Nae thornless road through Life he sought,
     Just where he was, he entered:
He dealt his blows, where ithers fought,
     There where the battle centered!
Frae early dawn, ahint the plew,
     Until the sun was settin':
The mornin' an' the 'enen dew
     His fit right manly wettin'.
—RANKIN, J. E., 1872–87, *Ingleside Rhaims, Verses in the Dialect of Burns, p.* 127.

The name of Robert Burns is a well-understood signal for an overflow of all sorts of commonplaces from the right-minded critic. These commonplaces run mainly in three channels:—ecstatic astonishment at finding that a ploughman was also a poet; wringing of hands over the admission that the ploughman and poet was like-wise a drunkard, and a somewhat miscellaneous lover; and caustic severity upon the lionizers and "admirers of native genius" who could find no employment more appropriate than that of excise-officer for the brightest and finest mind of their country and generation. All these commonplaces must stand confessed as warranted by the facts: they are truths, but they are also truisms. We have heard them very often, and have always sat in a meek acquiescence and unfeigned concurrence. But the time comes when they have been repeated frequent enough to make the enlarging upon them a weariness, and the profuse and argumentative re-enforcement of them a superfluity.—ROSSETTI, WILLIAM MICHAEL, 1878, *Lives of Famous Poets, p.* 189.

Here was a man, a son of toil, looking out on the world from his cottage, on society low and high, and on nature homely or beautiful, with the clearest eye, the most piercing insight, and the warmest heart; touching life at a hundred points, seeing to the core all the sterling worth, nor less the pretence and hollowness of the men he met, the humour, the drollery, the pathos, and the sorrow of human existence; and expressing what he saw, not in the stock phrases of books, but in his own vernacular, the language of his fireside, with a directness, a force, a vitality that tingled to the finger tips, and forced the phrases of his peasant dialect into literature, and made them for ever classical. Large sympathy, generous enthusiasm, reckless abandonment, fierce indignation, melting compassion,

rare flashes of moral insight, all are there. Everywhere you see the strong intellect made alive, and driven home to the mark, by the fervid heart behind it. And if the sight of the world's inequalities, and some natural repining at his own obscure lot, mingled from the beginning, as has been said, "some bitterness of earthly spleen and passion with the workings of his inspiration, and if these in the end ate deep into the great heart they had long tormented," who that has not known his experience may venture too strongly to condemn him?—SHAIRP, JOHN CAMPBELL, 1879, *Robert Burns (English Men of Letters), p.* 190.

He was born poor, he lived poor, he died poor, and he always felt his poverty to be a curse. He was fully conscious of himself and of his intellectual superiority. He disdained and resented the condecension of the great, and he defiantly asserted his independence. I do not say that he might not or ought not to have lived tranquilly and happily as a poor man. Perhaps, as Carlyle suggests, he should have divided his hours between poetry and virtuous industry. We only know that he did not. Like an untamable eagle he dashed against the bars he could not break, and his life was a restless, stormy alternation of low and lofty moods, of pure and exalted feeling, of mad revel and impotent regret. . . . Distracted by poetry and poverty and passion, and brought to public shame, he determined to leave the country, and in 1786, when he was twenty-seven years old, Burns published his poems by subscription, to get the money to pay his passage to America. Ah! could that poor, desperate ploughman of Mossgiel have forseen the day, could he have known that because of those poems—an abiding part of literature, familiar to every people, sung and repeated in American homes from sea to sea—his genius would be honored and his name blessed, and his statue raised with grateful pride to keep his memory in America green forever, perhaps the amazing vision might have nerved him to make his life as noble as his genius; perhaps the full sunshine of assured glory might have wrought upon that great, generous, wilful soul to

     "tak' a thought an' men'."
—CURTIS, GEORGE WILLIAM, 1880, *Robert Burns, an address Delivered at the Unveiling*

*of the Statue of the Poet, in Central Park,
New York, October* 2; *Orations and Addresses, vol.* III, *pp.* 309, 310.

He set out for Edinburgh on a pony he
had borrowed from a friend. The town
that winter was "agog with the ploughman poet." Robertson, Dugald Stewart,
Blair, "Duchess Gordon and all the gay
world," were of his acquaintance. Such
a revolution is not to be found in literary
history. He was now, it must be remembered, twenty-seven years of age; he had
fought since his early boyhood an obstinate battle against poor soil, bad seed,
and inclement seasons, wading deep in
Ayrshire mosses, guiding the plough in
the furrow, wielding "the thresher's
weary flingin'-tree;" and his education,
his diet, and his pleasures, had been those
of a Scotch countryman. Now he stepped
forth suddenly among the polite and
learned. We can see him as he then was,
in his boots and buckskins, his blue coat
and waistcoat striped with buff and blue,
like a farmer in his Sunday best; the heavy
ploughman's figure firmly planted on its
burly legs; his face full of sense and
shrewdness, and with a somewhat melancholy air of thought, and his large dark
eye "literally glowing" as he spoke. "I
never saw such another eye in a human
head," says Walter Scott, "though I have
seen the most distinguished men of my
time." With men, whether they were
lords or omnipotent critics, his manner
was plain, dignified, and free from bash-
fulness or affectation. If he made a slip
he had the social courage to pass on and
refrain from explanation.—STEVENSON,
ROBERT LOUIS, 1882, *Some Aspects of
Robert Burns, Familiar Studies of Men and
Books, p.* 62.

That night, at my lonely dinner in the
King's Arms, I had the Edinburgh papers.
There were in them three editorials headed
with quotations from Burns's poems, and
an account of the sale in Edinburgh, that
week, of an autograph letter of his for
ninety-four pounds! Does he think sadly,
even in heaven, how differently he might
have done by himself and by Earth, if
Earth had done for him then a tithe of
what it does now? Does he know it?
Does he care? And does he listen when,
in lands he never saw, great poets sing of
him in words simple and melodious as his
own?—JACKSON, HELEN HUNT, 1883, *A
Burns Pilgrimage, The Century, vol.* 26,
p. 761.

It was at a slightly earlier date than I
have been referring to that our first visit
to Scotland was paid. Our tour was limited as to extent, and was made without
any special purpose, except to describe and
report "the Burns Festival" held at Ayr
on the 6th of August, 1844. I had been
engaged by Mr. Herbert Ingram of the
Illustrated London News, to write the descriptive article, which was to be illustrated by wood-engravings. . . .
THE BURNS FESTIVAL! I do not think,
if we ransacked the annals of the world
from the earliest ages, they would furnish
the record of a ceremonial more truly
glorious. Was it a stretch of fancy to
believe the poet was present on that day,
to receive part of his reward? It was
not in "the Pavilion," when two thousand guests drank in silence the toast,
"The memory of Robert Burns," and with
cheers that shook the canvas of the tent,
the healths of his three sons, seated at
the side of the chairman, the Earl of
Eglinton, that the real business of the
day, was, so to speak, transacted. The
glory and the triumph were for the prodigious crowd of peasants and artisans
who passed slowly and in order before the
platform, where the family of the poet
had their seats, bowing or courtesying as
each passed on receiving in return a recognition the memory of which, no doubt,
all of them carried to their graves. It
was the cheers in Gaelic and "broad
Scotch," and the waving of Glengarry
bonnets, tartan shawls and shepherd
plaids, that made the triumph and glory
of that marvelous day, when one continually asked, "Was it only a man who had
written verses, who was of no account in
the world's estimation during his earth-
life, who was born in the hovel within ken,
lived in a continual struggle with poverty,
and, to say the least, died needy—was it
really to commemorate such a man that
these plaudits went up from a Scottish
field to a Scottish sky?"—HALL, S. C.,
1883, *Retrospect of a Long Life; from* 1815
to 1883, *pp.* 467, 468.

I had come to Dumfries because it was
for some time the home of Robert Burns,
because here he had found his death-bed,
and here lay buried. I had been at Ayr, and
stood in the small cottage where the

baby-poet was tossed up and down, like an ordinary child, by his thrifty, loving mother, who little dreamed that this tiny, nervous, weird-eyed creature was to make her name remembered as long as mothers exist. . . . "Yon building across the way" proved to be a hospital,—in fact, a kind of more genteel poorhouse,—established by some wealthy men of the town. To this institution poor people were admitted, who by birth, talents, or other cause, were considered too good for the common work-house. And here I found him,—a grandson of Robert Burns, a man of the same given name, a man whose father was of the same given name, and, in truth, resembling wonderfully the best pictures of the poet. . . . He was a stout, soldierly-looking old man, with a considerable appearance of neatness peeping out through all his poverty. His face was cleanly shaven, except that he wore closely trimmed side-whiskers: his eyes were large and bright, and his manners and language those of a gentleman. Throughout the interview, he maintained what might be called a nervous, restless sort of dignity, although evidently feeling the awkwardness of his position; for few really sensitive and proud people like to be exhibited as some distinguished person's descendant, unless they themselves have done something to add to the family renown. . . . I could almost fancy that the poetic hero of my boy-days had come back for an hour into this old town of Dumfries, had met me in some rude inn, and was modestly telling his own trials and triumphs as those of another person. But, at last, the old man came to speak of the squalor and wretchedness that marked the last months of the poet's life, —a state of which his own must often have reminded him. It was then that he burst forth in a torrent of eloquence that showed him to be possessed of some of the talent, and much of the fire, of his immortal ancestor. . . . As I parted with this interesting acquaintance of an hour, there came a pang of hopeless pity for this poor man, who, with the warning before him of his grandfather's misery and early death, had all his days followed the same broad, misery-seeking road.—CARLETON, WILL, 1885, *A Grandson of Robert Burns, Some Noted Princes, Authors, and Statesmen of Our Time.*

In fancy, as wi' dewy een,
I part the clouds aboon the scene
Where thou wast born, and peer atween,
I see nae spot
In a' the Hielands half sae green
And unforgot!
—RILEY, JAMES WHITCOMB, 1888, *To Robert Burns, Afterwhiles.*

He was utterly incapable of anything like baseness. No man could be more jealous of his honour; no man had a greater pride in being largely and loftily a man.—BLACKIE, JOHN STUART, 1888, *Life of Robert Burns (Great Writers), p.* 163.

"The Ayrshire Bard," "The Ayrshire Ploughman," "The Ayrshire Poet," "The Bard of Ayrshire," "The Glory and Reproach of Scotland," "The Peasant Bard."—FREY, ALBERT R., 1888, *Sobriquets and Nicknames, p.* 385.

Burns was but a visitor, the lion of a season and therefore we are not called upon to associate with Edinburgh the whole tragic story of his life. And yet his appearance was one of the most remarkable that had distinguished the ancient town. . . . All the accounts we have of his appearance in Edinburgh agree in this. He was neither abashed nor embarrassed; no rustic presumption or vulgarity, but quite as little any timidity or awkwardness, was in the Ayrshire ploughman. His shoulders a little bent with the work to which he had been accustomed, his dress like a countryman, a rougher cloth perhaps, a pair of good woollen stockings rig and fur, his mother's knitting, instead of the silk which covered limbs probably not half so robust—but so far as manners went, nothing to apologise for or smile at. The accounts all agree in this. If he never put himself forward too much, he never withdrew with any unworthy shyness from his modest share in the conversation. Sometimes he would be roused to eloquent speech, and then the admiring ladies said he carried them "off their feet" in the contagion of his enthusiasm and emotion. But this was a very strange phenomenon for the Edinburgh professors and men of letters to deal with: a novice who had not come humbly to be taught, but one who had come to take up his share of the inheritance, to sit down among the great, as in his natural place. He was not perhaps altogether unmoved by their insane advices to him, one of the greatest of lyrical poets, a singer above all—to write a tragedy, to give up the language he knew and write his poetry in the high English which, alas! he uses in his letters. Not unmoved, and seriously inclining to a more lofty measure, ᵗᵉ compounded addresses to Edinburgh:

"Edina, Scotia's darling seat!"

and other such intolerable effusions.— OLIPHANT, MARGARET O. W., 1890, *Royal Edinburgh*, pp. 476, 481.

Robert Burns was a great man and a great poet, and the influence of his truly tremendous satiric lyrical genius has been one of the great factors in the disintegration of Scottish superstition. . . . He was a convivial creature, and his conviviality was that of a fearless and liberal nature, overflowing with love, and honest as the day. But what was to some extent a virtue in him has become to my mind, a very curious vice in his disciples. The fact is, Scotchmen seem to have granted Burns his apotheosis chiefly on account of its being an excuse for the consumption of Whiskey. So they celebrate his Birthday. So they fill their glasses, hiccup "Auld Langsyne," and cry in chorus:

"Robin was a rovin' boy,
    Rantin' rovin', rantin' rovin';
Robin was a rovin' boy,
    Rantin' rovin' Robin!"

The drunken squirearchy, whose progenitors broke the poet's heart, and who, if the poet were alive now, would break his heart again, are full of enthusiasm for his memory. Even some of the more liberal-minded ministers of the Gospel join in the acclaim. Farmers and shepherds, factors and ploughmen, all come together on the one great occasion to honour the bard whom everybody can understand, because his synonym is the Whiskey Bottle. They weep over his woes; they smack their lips over his satire; they shriek at his denunciations and they murmur his songs. Burns or Bacchus—it is all one. The chief point is that, now or never, there is an excuse for getting "reeling ripe" or "mortal drunk." It is poetic, it is literary, it is—hiccup?—honouring the Muses. Any frenzy, however maniacal, is justifiable under the circumstances. "Glorious Robin!" Pledge him again and again, pledge him and bless him; and when you can't pledge him upright,

pledge him prone, as you lie, with your fellow Burns-worshippers, under the table. —BUCHANAN, ROBERT, 1891, *The Coming Terror and Other Essays and Letters*, p. 315.

When it is remembered how much he suffered, how much he vanquished, and how much he accomplished, with what misery his genius had to fight to be born and to live, the perseverance of his years of apprenticeship, his intellectual exploits, and, after all, his glory; one cannot help saying that what he did not succeed in, or what he did not undertake, was as nothing compared to what he achieved, and he was a man who achieved much. What remains to be said except that the clay of which he was made was full of diamonds, and that his life was one of the bravest and proudest ever lived by a poet?— ANGELLIER, AUGUSTE, 1893, *Robert Burns*.

Adequate length of days is indispensable to the production of any monumental work. Milton spent nearly as much time as was granted for the whole mortal career of Burns in what he regarded as a mere apprenticeship to the art of poetry. It is indispensable too, opportunity should be granted as well as time. Those Greek philosophers, whose superb wisdom, discredited for a while by the youthful self-assurance of modern science, is again enforcing recognition, insist upon nothing so much as the need of σχολή to the noble mind. In this respect Burns was still more unfortunate than in the matter of time. His thirty-seven years of life were shorter for effective purposes of art than the nine-and-twenty of Shelley, hardly longer than five-and-twenty of Keats. The crushing weight of circumstance becomes evident when we contemplate his career from his first introduction to the world till his death. A period of ten years passed between the publication of the Kilmarnock edition and the closing of the grave. For the purposes of poetry they ought to have been far more valuable than all the time that went before. They did not prove so. The cause must lie either in the man or his environment. The man was not blameless; but it was not he who was chiefly to blame. Few probably who study Burns will arrive at the conclusion that his was one of those minds which bloom early and fade early. A shrewd observer remarked of his great countryman and successor,

Scott, that his sense was even more extraordinary than his genius. Strange as it may seem to many, the same assertion may be made with only a little less truth of Burns. He possessed a clear, penetrating, logical intellect, a sound and vigorous judgment. Once and again in his poems he delights the idealist with his flashes of inspiration; but just as frequently he captivates the man of common sense, who finds his own sober views of life expressed by the poet with infinitely more of force and point than he could give them.—WALKER, HUGH, 1893, *Three Centuries of Scottish Literature, vol.* II, *p.* 147.

The picture [Nàsmyth Portrait] has been painted with a careful and a loving hand. It renders the ripe contours of cheek and chin, the fine arching of the eyebrows, the rippling lines of the lips and the exquisite dimples that end them; and it seems to catch not a little of what must have been the normal look of the poet's rich brown, widely-opened eyes, which were so memorable a feature in his face, and which, when an impassioned moment arrived, actually "glowed"— "I say literally *glowed*"—as Sir Walter Scott has so emphatically recorded. Yet we feel here that the kindly painter has a little softened down the actual man; we miss something of the rustic strength that must have been visible in the peasant-bard.—GRAY, J. M., 1894, *The Authentic Portraits of Robert Burns, Magazine of Art, vol.* 17, *p.* 239.

In his family Burns was the watchful, kindly, diligent father,—not to be spoken of in the same day with the father who neglects his household for himself, who forgets their need, and loses their love; and the man who degrades him as an habitual drunkard, unable to meet life's daily duties, does not know what he is speaking of.—HALE, EDWARD EVERETT, 1896, *Address at the Burns Centennial, Boston, July* 21.

"On the fourth day," we are told, "when his attendant held a cordial to his lips, he swallowed it eagerly, rose almost wholly up, spread out his hands, sprang forward nigh the whole length of the bed, fell on his face and expired." I suppose there are many who can read the account with composure. They are more fortunate than I. There is nothing much more

melancholy in all biography. The brilliant poet, the delight of all society, from the highest to the lowest, sits brooding in silence over the drama of his spent life; the early innocent home, the plough and the savour of fresh turned earth, the silent communion with nature and his own heart, the brief hour of splendour, the dark hour of neglect, the mad struggle for forgetfulness, the bitterness of vanished homage, the gnawing doubt of fame, the distressful future of his wife and children — and endless witch-dance of thought without clew or remedy, all perplexing, all soon to end while he is yet young, as men reckon youth; though none know so well as he that his youth is gone, his race is run, his message is delivered. — ROSEBERY, ARCHIBALD PHILIP PRIMROSE LORD, 1896, *Address at Dumfries July* 21.

At least 50,000 people celebrated the centenary of Robert Burns's death, at Dumfries, on Tuesday. In the morning a long procession, accompanied by bands, filed through the streets, and hundreds of persons visited the poet's grave, on which wreaths were laid, many being sent by Scottish societies in the most distant parts of the world. At two o'clock within the Drill Hall a conversazione, attended by 4,000 persons was held. . . . Burns has become the patron saint of Dumfries, and he had borne aloft the banner of the essential equality of man. At St. Michael's Church-yard, wreaths presented by 130 Burns and other societies were handed to Lord Rosebery, who placed them on the poet's tomb. The first wreath laid on the tomb was that of Lord Rosebery, consisting of arum lilies and eucharis. The most modest wreath, and yet, probably, the most interesting, was that from the Glasgow Mauchline Society. It consisted of holly and gowans, the latter grown on the field at Mossgiel, celebrated by Burns in his poem "To a Mountain Daisy." The wreath was made up by the granddaughters of Burns, the daughters of Col. James Glencairn Burns.—ANON, 1896, *Publisher's Circular, July* 25.

The farm of Mossgiel is situated in the parish of Mauchline, from the town of which name it is about a mile distant. Whatever it may have been in the poet's time, it strikes the visitor in these days as a most desirable home. . . . Its walls have been considerably raised since it was Burns's home, and the roof of thatch has given place to one of slates. When Hawthorne visited it in 1857, and forced his way inside in the absence of the family, he found it remarkable for nothing so much as its dirt and dunghill odour. There is neither dirt nor odour to-day. The good wife of the present occupant of Mossgiel, Mr. Wyllie, keeps her house spotlessly clean notwithstanding the demands made upon her time by innumerable inquisitive visitors. On the parlour table lies the copious visitors' book, and in the same room hang the manuscript of "The Lass o' Ballochmyle," and the letter in which Burns asked Miss Alexander's permission to publish the song. At the back of the house lies the field where Burns turned down the daisy, and the soil "seems to have been consecrated to daisies by the song which he bestowed on that first immortal one." Over the hedge, there is the other field where the poet's ploughshare tore up the mouse's nest.—SHELLEY, HENRY C., 1897, *The Ayrshire Homes and Haunts of Burns, pp.* 28, 30.

During his own lifetime Thomson suffered keenly from the charge that he had taken an unfair advantage of Burns, in accepting so much from the poet without making him any substantial pecuniary return. The charge still hangs about Thomson's name in a vague sort of way, for in affairs of this kind the dog who has once acquired a bad repute is likely to retain it. The unfortunate editor, as he puts it himself was assailed, "first anonymously, and afterwards, to my great surprise, by some writers who might have been expected to possess sufficient judgment to see the matter in its true light." He defended himself, in the words of one of his calumniators, "about once every seven years;" but it is not until the appearance of Professor Wilson's onslaught in the "Land of Burns" (1838) that his correspondence begins to show the full extent of his suffering under the lash. . . . The truth is that Burns declined to write deliberately for money. He would—in a patriotic undertaking of this kind at any rate—write for love, or not write at all. If his poems brought him a profit—well, they were not written with that profit directly in view; the pecuniary return

was, as it were, but an accident, not affecting in any way the inception of the work. This was practically his view of the matter as expressed to Thomson. It appears that he expressed the same view also to others.—HADDEN, J. CUTHBERT, 1898, *George Thomson the Friend of Burns, pp.* 139, 145.

Home life was poor in the little two-roomed cottage, and toil hard on the farm, on which the family did all the work. Robert and Gilbert, as each reached the age of thirteen, would weed the furrows and thresh the corn; at fifteen they would act as ploughman and shearers, working from daybreak till late evening, when they were ready to go weary to their chaff beds. The fare, like the home life, was mean and monotonous—sowans and kail and milk, with little variations at the meals; no meat appearing on the board except when a cow or sheep died of old age or infirmity. . . . While engaged on the farm, which did not pay much, and composing poems, which paid still less, he had time for his favourite wooing, which paid worst of all. His relations with the "sex" were many and migratory. He was no sooner off with the old love than he was on with the new, and even for that he often did not wait. In his tastes he was not fastidious as to the position, quality, or even looks of his entrancer. "He had always a particular jealousy of people who were richer than himself, or had more consequence," says his brother Gilbert. "His love therefore seldom settled on persons of this description." A buxom barn-door beauty, a servant girl was enough, although she was as devoid of romance as of stockings. He must be the superior. A "fine woman," especially among his humble acquaintance, he could not resist; and seldom could she resist the masterful wooer, with his winning ways, his bewitching talk, his eyes that "glowed like coals of fire."—GRAHAM, HENRY GREY, 1901, *Scottish Men of Letters in the Eighteenth Century, pp.* 383, 394.

JEAN

Poor ill-advised ungrateful Armour came home on Friday last. You have heard of all the particulars of that affair, and a black affair it is. What she thinks of her conduct now, I don't know; one thing I do know, she has made me completely miserable. Never man loved, or rather adored, a woman, more than I did her; and to confess a truth between you and me, I do still love her to distraction after all, although I won't tell her so if I were to see her, which I don't want to do. My poor, dear, unfortunate Jean, how happy I have been in thy arms! It is not the losing her that made me so unhappy, but for her sake I feel most severely; I forsee she is on the road to—I am afraid —eternal ruin. May Almighty God forgive her ingratitude and perjury to me, as I from my soul forgive her; and may His grace be with her and bless her in all her future life! I can have no nearer idea of the place of eternal punishment than what I have felt in my own heart on her account. I have tried often to forget her. I have run into all kinds of dissipation and riots, mason meetings, drinking matches, and other mischief, to drive her out of my head, but all in vain. And now for a grand cure: the ship is on her way home that is to take me out to Jamaica; then farewell, dear old Scotland; and farewell, dear, ungrateful Jean, for never, never, will I see you more.—BURNS, ROBERT, 1786, *Letter to David Brice.*

Compared Robert Burns, with Jean Armour, his alleged spouse. They both acknowledged their irregular marriage, and their sorrow for that irregularity, and desiring that the Session will take such steps as may seem to them proper, in order to the solemn confirmation of the said marriage. The Session, taking this affair under their consideration, agree that they both be rebuked for this acknowledged irregularity, and that they be solemnly engaged to adhere faithfully to one another as man and wife all the days of their life. In regard the Session have a title in law to some fine for behoof of the poor, they agree to refer to Mr. Burns his own generosity. The above sentence was accordingly executed, and the Session absolved the said parties from any scandal on this account.—AULD, WILLIAM (MODERATOR), 1788, *Mauchline Kirk-Session Books, Aug. 5.*

She still survives to hear her name, her early love, and her youthful charms, warbled in the songs of her native land. He, on whom she bestowed her beauty and her maiden truth, dying, has left to her the mantle of his fame. What though

she be now a grandmother? to the fancy, she can never grow old, or die. We can never bring her before our thoughts but as the lovely, graceful country girl, "lightly tripping among the wild flowers," and warbling, "Of a' the airs the win' can blaw,"—and this, O women, is what genius can do for you! Wherever the adventurous spirit of her countrymen transport them, from the spicy groves of India to the wild banks of the Mississippi, the name of Bonnie Jean is heard, bringing back to the wanderer sweet visions of home, and of days of "Auld lang Syne." —JAMESON, ANNA BROWNELL, 1829, *The Loves of the Poets, vol.* II, *p.* 195.

Mrs. Burns through the liberality of her children, spent her latter years in comparative affluence, yet "never changed, nor wished to change her place." In March 1843, at the age of sixty-eight, she closed her respectable life in the same room in which her husband had breathed his last thirty-eight years before.—CHAMBERS, ROBERT, 1851-52, *The Life and Works of Robert Burns.*

Patrick said she was "a decent, weeldoin' lass," full of sprightliness and fun. She was a good-looking brunette, or as Patrick's father (a shoemaker, next door to her father's, in the Cowgate) used to say, "Jean, you're a ticht jaud, but a dun one!" a compliment which she always took in good part, with her usual bright laugh or smile, accompanied by a smart retort. Willie also described her as "ticht i' the legs"—most expressive Scotch, meaning at once, handsome, sprightly, and well-knit, from the idea of being firmly bound. The poet himself uses the same word regarding her; and regarding no less a personage than the Muse, Coila, when she appeared to him in "the spence" at Mossgiel, portraying her as

"A tight outlandish hizzie braw;"

and continuing the picture thus—

"Down flowed her robe, a tartan sheen,
Till half a leg was scrimply seen;
And such a leg! my bonny Jean
    Could only peer it;
Sae straught, sae taper, tight and clean,
    Nane else cam' near it."

—JOLLY, WILLIAM, 1881, *Robert Burns at Mossgiel; With Reminiscences of the Poet by His Herd-Boy, p.* 63.

It may be questionable whether any marriage could have tamed Burns; but it is at least certain that there was no hope for him in the marriage he contracted. He did right, but then he had done wrong before; it was, as I said, one of those relations in life which it seems equally wrong to break or to perpetuate. He neither loved nor respected his wife. "God knows," he writes, "my choice was as random as blind man's buff." He consoles himself by the thought that he has acted kindly to her; that she "has the most sacred enthusiasm of attachment to him;" that she has a good figure; that she has a "wood-note wild," "her voice rising with ease to B natural," no less. The effect on the reader is one of unmingled pity for both parties concerned. This was not the wife who (in his own words) could "enter into his favourite studies or relish his favourite authors;" this was not even a wife, after the affair of the marriage lines, in whom a husband could joy to place his trust. Let her manage a farm with sense, let her voice rise to B natural all day long, she would still be a peasant to her lettered lord, and an object of pity rather than of equal affection. She could now be faithful, she could now be forgiving, she could now be generous even to a pathetic and touching degree; but coming from one who was unloved, and who had scarce shown herself worthy of the sentiment, these were all virtues thrown away, which could neither change her husband's heart nor effect the inherent destiny of their relation. From the outset, it was a marriage that had no root in nature; and we find him, ere long, lyrically regretting Highland Mary, renewing correspondence with Clarinda in the warmest language, on doubtful terms with Mrs. Riddel, and on terms unfortunately beyond any question with Anne Park.—STEVENSON, ROBERT LOUIS, 1882, *Familiar Studies of Men and Books, p.* 72.

Her condition being discovered, Burns, after some strong revulsions of feeling against—not Jean, I hope, but—the estate of marriage, gave her what he presently had every reason to call "an unlucky paper," recognising her as his wife; and, had things been allowed to drift in the usual way, the world had lacked an unforgotten scandal and a great deal of silly writing.—HENLEY, WILLIAM ERNEST, 1897, *Life, Genius, Achievement, The Poetry of Robert Burns, vol.* IV, *p.* 280.

HIGHLAND MARY

He loved Mary Campbell, his "Highland Mary," with as pure a passion as ever possessed a young poet's heart; nor is there so sweet and sad a passage recorded in the life of any other one of all the sons of song. Many such partings there have been between us poor beings—blind at all times, and often blindest in our bliss—but all gone to oblivion. But that hour can never die—that scene will live forever. Immortal the two shadows standing there, holding together the Bible—a little rivulet flowing between—in which, as in consecrated water, they have dipt their hands, water not purer than, at that moment, their united hearts. There are few of his songs more beautiful, and none more impassioned.—WILSON, JOHN, 1844, *The Genius and Character of Burns, p.* 15.

O loved by him whom Scotland loves,
　Long loved, and honoured duly
By all who love the bard who sang
　So sweetly and so truly!
In cultured dales his song prevails;
　Thrills o'er the eagle's aëry—
Has any caught that strain, nor sighed
　For Burns's "Highland Mary?"
I wandered on from hill to hill,
　I feared nor wind nor weather,
For Burns beside me trode the moor,
　Beside me pressed the heather.
I read his verse: his life—alas!
　O'er that dark shades extended:—
With thee at last, and him in thee,
　My thoughts their wanderings ended.
His golden hours of youth were thine;
　Those hours whose flight is fleetest.
Of all his songs to thee he gave
　The freshest and the sweetest.
Ere ripe the fruit one branch he brake,
　All rich with bloom and blossom;
And shook its dews, its incense shook,
　Above thy brow and bosom.
—DE VERE, AUBREY, 1847, *To Burns's Highland Mary.*

All the world has heard of Highland Mary—in life a maid-servant in the family of Mr. Hamilton, after death to be remembered with Dante's Beatrice and Petrarch's Laura. How Burns and Mary became acquainted we have little means of knowing—indeed the whole relationship is somewhat obscure—but Burns loved her as he loved no other woman, and her memory is preserved in the finest expression of his love and grief. Strangely enough, it seems to have been in the fierce rupture between himself and Jean that this white flower of love sprang up, sudden in its growth, brief in its passion and beauty. It was arranged that the lovers should become man and wife, and that Mary should return to her friends to prepare for her wedding. Before her departure there was a farewell scene. "On the second Sunday of May," Burns writes to Mr. Thomson, after an historical fashion which has something touching in it, "in a sequestered spot on the banks of the Ayr the interview took place." The lovers met and plighted solemn troth. According to popular statement, they stood on either side of a brook, they dipped their hands in the water, exchanged Bibles—and parted. Mary died at Greenock, and was buried in a dingy churchyard hemmed by narrow streets—beclanged now by innumerable hammers, and within a stone's throw of passing steamers. Information of her death was brought to Burns at Mossgiel; he went to the window to read the letter, and the family noticed that on a sudden his face changed. He went out without speaking; they respected his grief and were silent. On the whole matter Burns remained singularly reticent; but years after, from a sudden geysir of impassioned song, we learn that through all that time she had never been forgotten.—SMITH, ALEXANDER, 1865, *The Poetical Works of Robert Burns, Life*, p. xiii.

There is no stronger proof of the transcending power of the genius of Burns than is found in the fact that, by a bare half dozen of his stanzas, an humble dairy servant—else unheard of outside her parish and forgotten at her death—is immortalized as a peeress of Petrarch's Laura and Dante's Beatrice, and has been for a century loved and mourned of all the world. . . . How little is known of Highland Mary, the most famous heroine of modern song, is shown by the brief, incoherent, and often contradictory allusions to her which the biographies of the ploughman-poet contain. . . . She first saw the light in 1764, at Ardrossan, on the coast, fifteen miles northward from the "auld town of Ayr." Her parentage was of the humblest, her father being a sailor before the mast, and the poor dwelling which sheltered her was in no way superior to the meanest of those we find to-day on the narrow streets of her

village. . . . He told a lady that he first saw Mary while walking in the woods of Coilsfield, and first spoke with her at a rustic merry-making, and, "having the luck to win her regards from other suitors," they speedily became intimate. . . . The bard's niece, Miss Begg, of Bridgeside, told the writer that she often heard Burns's mother describe Mary as she saw her at Hamilton's: she had a bonnie face, a complexion of unusual fairness, soft blue eyes, a profusion of shining hair which fell to her knees, a *petite* figure which made her seem younger than her twenty summers, a bright smile, and pleasing manners, which won the old lady's heart. . . . All who have written of her have noticed her beauty, her good sense, her modesty and self-respect. . . . Poor Mary is laid in the burial-plot of her uncle in the west kirk-yard of Greenock, near Crawford Street; our pilgrimage in Burnsland may fitly end at her grave. A pathway, beaten by the feet of many reverent visitors, leads us to the spot. It is so pathetically different from the scenes she loved in life,—the heather-clad slopes of her Highland home, the seclusion of the wooded braes where she loitered with her poet-lover. Scant foliage is about her; few birds sing above her here. She lies by the wall; narrow streets hem in the enclosure; the air is sullied by smoke from factories and from steamers passing within a stone's-throw on the busy Clyde; the clanging of many hammers and the discordant din of machinery and traffic invade the place and sound in our ears as we muse above the ashes of the gentle lassie. For half a century her grave was unmarked and neglected; then, by subscription, a monument of marble, twelve feet in height, and of graceful proportions, was raised. It bears a sculptured medallion representing Burns and Mary, with clasped hands, plighting their troth. Beneath is the simple inscription read oft by eyes dim with tears:

Erected over the Grave of
HIGHLAND MARY
1842.

"My Mary, dear departed shade,
Where is thy place of blissful rest?"

—WOLFE, THEODORE F., 1895, *A Literary Pilgrimage*, pp. 194, 195, 196, 197, 205.

There is probably no name in Scottish literature that has so affectingly touched the hearts of her fellow-countrymen as that of Mary Campbell. Though born of an obscure family, brought up in circumstances little fitted to attract attention, and credited with no achievement that invests heroism with permanent or even transient distinction, this Highland girl is now a brilliant star in the galaxy of Fame, and has become an object of unmingled and growing admiration. The lustre of Mary's name, like that of other stars, whether fixed or planetary, borrows its fascination from a luminary brighter and greater than itself. . The very obscurity of her origin and early condition sets off by constrast the halo that now encircles her memory. Moralists have noted and extolled her virtues, critics have lovingly dropped their satiric shafts when commenting on the few but romantic appearances she made on the stage of Time, and poets of several generations, and of almost all countries, have exhausted their poetical resources in their efforts to express their conceptions of her worth, but all their contributions towards the sum of her praise have taken their force and complexion from the picture which inspired genius has given of her to the world. The interest created by the association of the heroine's career with that of the gifted lover who has procured for her the honour of poetical immortality, is not, it is pleasant to know, confined to the little country that gave her birth. In England, Ireland, America, and the Colonies, and even in countries that have less in common with Great Britain, Mary's worth, ill-starred career, and premature death, have found admirers and mourners as cordial and sincere as any that Caledonia has produced. —MUNRO, ARCHIBALD, 1896, *Burns and Highland Mary.*

Little that is positive is known of Mary Campbell except that she once possessed a copy of the Scriptures (now very piously preserved at Ayr), and that she is a subject of a fantasy, in bronze, at Dunoon.— HENLEY, WILLIAM ERNEST, 1897, *Life, Genius, Achievement, The Poetry of Robert Burns, vol.* IV, *pp.* 285.

By all means let us reject the Mary Campbell tradition, immolate the Bible at Ayr, melt down the "fantasy in bronze" at Dunoon, make building material of the monument at Greenock, reduce all get-at-able Highland Mary literature to pulp,

and *for ever more let the story stand as Burns left it.*—LOCKHART, ROBERT M., 1898, *Mr. Henley and Highland Mary, The Westminster Review, vol.* 149, *p.* 336.

CLARINDA

Mrs. M'Lehose originally refused Mr. Syme (who collected for Dr. Currie) permission to publish the Letters, and declined, as has been already stated, various similar applications in her latter years. But the present editor is of opinion, that the time is now come for their publication, and that an authentic edition of the Correspondence will have the effect of removing prejudice, will do honour to the memory of his respected relative, and interest the public, by giving them a new chapter in the life of our immortal poet. This interest, too, is increased by the consideration that these letters are probably the last original composition of his which will ever be made public.—M'LEHOSE, WILLIAM C., 1843, *ed., The Correspondence between Burns and Clarinda, Preface, p.* ix.

She called herself "high-spirited," which meant "unyielding;" she mingled romance and strong Calvinistic principles, an almost incompatible mixture; she was light, vain; a "foolish woman," listening to the rhapsodies of the Ayrshire ploughman when she ought to have been thinking of her children; and her quiet discussion of certain matters relating to her admirer shows her to have been eminently coarse. She also, as one of her family says, "cultivated the Muses." All these elements, combined as it were in one dish, make up a doubtful sort of salad.—FITZGERALD, PERCY, 1870, *The Loves of Famous Men, Belgravia, vol.* 12, *p.* 425.

It was at this time Burns met Clarinda once more. She was about to sail for the West Indies, in search of the husband who had forsaken her; the interview was a brief and hurried one, and no account of it remains, except some letters, and a few lyrics which he addressed to her. One of these is distinguished as one of the most impassioned effusions which Burns ever poured forth. It contains that one consummate stanza in which Scott, Byron, and many more, saw concentrated, "the essence of a thousand love-tales."

Had we never loved so kindly,
Had we never loved so blindly;
Never met, or never parted,
We had ne'er been broken-hearted.

Mrs. Burns is said to have been a marvel of long-suffering and forgiveness, for the way in which she bore the wrongs her husband inflicted upon her by his unfaithfulness. There is no doubt that Burns also tasted self-reproach and

"Self-contempt, bitterer to drink than blood."

—PRICE, CHARLOTTE A., 1895, *Famous Poets, Belgravia, vol.* 87, *p.* 273.

Poor Clarinda! Well for her peace of mind that the poet was leaving her; well for Burns, also, that he was leaving Clarinda and Edinburgh. Only one thing remained for both to do, and it had been wise, to burn their letters. Would that Clarinda had been as much alive to her own good name, and the poet's fair fame, as Peggy Chalmers, who did not preserve her letters from Burns!—SETOUN, GABRIEL, 1896, *Robert Burns* (*Famous Scots Series*), *p.* 109.

So in the beginning of December he falls in with Mrs. M'Lehose; he instantly proposes to "cultivate her friendship with the enthusiasm of religion;" and the two are languishing in Arcady in the twinkling of a cupid's wing. She was a handsome, womanly creature "of a somewhat voluptuous style of beauty:" a style the Bard appreciated—lively but devout, extremely sentimental yet inexorably dutiful: a grass widow with children—nine times in ten a lasting safeguard—and the strictest notions of propriety—a good enough defence for a time; but young (she was the Bard's own age), clever, "of a poetical fabric of mind," and all the rest. . . . In the prime of life, deserted, sentimental, a tangle of simple instincts and as simple pieties, she had the natural woman's desire for a lover and the religious woman's resolve to keep that lover's passion within bounds. . . . She was plainly an excellent creature, bent on keeping herself honest and her lover straight; and it is impossible to read her letters to Sylvander without a respect, a certain admiration even, which have never been awakened yet by the study of Sylvander's letters to her. From Sylvander's point of view, as M'Lehose was still alive, and an open intrigue with a married woman would have been ruin, only one inference is possible: that he longed for the shepherd's hour to strike for the chimes' sake only; so that, when he thought of his future, as

he must have done anxiously and often, he cannot ever have thought of it as Clarinda's, even though in a moment of peculiar exaltation he swore to keep single till that wretch, the wicked husband died.—HENLEY, WILLIAM ERNEST, 1897, *Life, Genius, Achievement, The Poetry of Robert Burns, vol.* IV, *pp.* 304, 305, 306.

MRS. DUNLOP

MADAM,—I have written you so often without recg. any answer, that I would not trouble you again but for the circumstances in which I am. An illness which has long hung about me in all probability will speedily send me beyond that bourne whence no traveller returns. Your friendship with which for so many years you honored me was a friendship dearest to my soul. Your conversation and especially your correspondence were at once highly entertaining and instructive. With what pleasure did I use to break up the seal! The remembrance yet adds one pulse more to my poor palpitating heart! — Farewell!!! —BURNS, ROBERT, 1796, *Last Letter to Mrs. Dunlop.*

The friendship of Mrs. Dunlop was of particular value to Burns. This lady, daughter and sole heiress to Sir Thomas Wallace of Craige, and lineal descendant of the illustrious Wallace, the first of Scottish warriors, possesses the qualities of mind suited to her high lineage. Preserving, in the decline of life, the generous affections of youth; her admiration of the poet was soon accompanied by a sincere friendship for the man; which pursued him in after life through good and evil report; in poverty, in sickness, and in sorrow; and which is continued to his infant family, now deprived of their parent.—CURRIE, JAMES, 1800, *ed., Works of Robert Burns, Life.*

He appears from first to last to have stood somewhat in awe of this excellent lady, and to have been no less sensible of her sound judgment and strict sense of propriety, than of her steady and generous partiality. — JEFFREY, FRANCIS LORD, 1809, *Reliques of Burns, Edinburgh Review, vol.* 13, *p.* 256.

His letters to Mrs. Dunlop form a very large proportion of all his subsequent correspondence, and, addressed as they were to a person, whose sex, age, rank, and benevolence, inspired at once profound respect and a graceful confidence, will ever remain the most pleasing of all the materials of our poet's biography.—LOCKHART, JOHN GIBSON, 1828, *Life of Robert Burns, p.* 122.

The real basis of the friendship was their common warmth and generosity of soul. Mrs. Dunlop's interest in the poet was not purely, or even primarily, intellectual. She was not what would be called a literary lady. She was by no means a pedant. She was simply a woman of good birth and good breeding; old enough and wise enough to have drawn profit from the experiences of life; fond of books and sincerely religious; endowed with good judgment and good sense, with quick womanly sympathy and inextinguishable youthfulness of heart. Being what she was, she won the poet's confidence and sincere affection, and drew out all his finer feelings. His letters to her are not indeed free from that artificiality which characterised the epistolary style of his day, and marred all his correspondence; but they are less disfigured by it than those addressed to some of his patrons, or to his unknown literary correspondents—to say nothing of the effusions to "Clarinda."—ROBERTS, L. M., 1895, *The Burns and Dunlop Correspondence, Fortnightly Review, vol.* 64, *p.* 663.

The Lochryan MSS., now published for the first time, were in all probability never seen by Currie. Manifestly none of them has ever been handled by either editor or printer. They are all in a state of beautiful preservation, and include at least as fine specimens of the poet's handwriting as any that have seen the light in the original or reproduction. . . . Mrs. Dunlop kept the Lochryan MSS. at Dunlop till her death, when she left the estate of Lochryan and the MSS. to her grandson, General Sir John Wallace, from whom the documents descended to his son and heir, the next possessor of Lochryan, who left them by will to his youngest brother the present Colonel F. J. Wallace, from whom they were recently acquired by Mr. Adam. They have thus been continuously in the hands of the Dunlop-Wallace family during the past century. Colonel Wallace states to the best of his knowledge that they have been kept in a box in the safe-room at Lochryan for the last fifty years. The interweaving of this new material with the old makes the Correspondence of Burns and Mrs. Dunlop almost unique in its completeness. A careful search after possible *lacunae* has discovered no more than four places where it can be definitely stated that the letter of Burns is missing, and of the gross sum of Mrs. Dunlop's it appears that Burns had lost or destroyed only nine—a circumstance which must have wiped out the memory of the many proofs the lady had received that he did not always read her communications with the most respectful care, and at the same time must have deepened the remorse she felt for her neglect of the poet during the last eighteen months of his life.—WALLACE, WILLIAM, 1898, *Robert Burns and Mrs. Dunlop, Preface, vol.* I, *pp.* vi, vii.

A curious figure, this Mrs. Dunlop, of Dunlop, and most out of line with one's notion of a Scotch gentlewoman! To be a lady of sensibility was her ideal. To go to posterity as the social and, forsooth, the literary mentor of her gifted neighbor was her ambition. Her religion was of the Genevan type—not Jean Calvin's, but Jean Jacques Rousseau's. The religion of the heart, she called it, and had she not been a Sexagenarian and forever occupied with the births of grandchildren, there is no telling where it would have landed her. In comparison with her solicitude for Burns, the cares of a patriarchal household sat light upon her, and with pen in hand she could say, "as to forming schemes, it is a kind of castle-building that I cannot resign, as it pleases myself and does little harm to anything else." Scolding, questioning, teasing, advising, and spoiling Burns like a grandmother, she is yet irrepressibly youthful. With all her intellectual fire, and with all her provincial awkwardness, it is impossible not to admire her buoyancy, freshness, and hero-worship. She comes near possessing charm, and is almost a romantic figure.—HARPER, GEORGE MCLEAN, 1898, *Burns in his Correspondence, The Book Buyer, vol.* 17, *p.* 20.

THE HOLY FAIR

In Burns's time this poem was much relished by the moderate clergy, and Dr. Blair condescended to suggest the change of a word in order to render its satire more pointed. In these days of better taste, a regret will be generally felt that Burns should have been tempted or provoked into such subjects. This is, however, a general belief in Ayrshire that the "Holy Fair" was attended with a good effect, for since its appearance, the custom of resorting to the "occasion" in neighbouring parishes for the sake of holiday making has been much abated, and a great increase of decorous observance has taken place. — CHAMBERS, ROBERT, 1851-52, *The Life and Works of Robert Burns, vol.* I, *p.* 270.

As a matter of fact, in the history of Scottish literature and religion, this caricature of the Holiest, as some might be inclined to call it, did no harm, but rather good ; for the caricature lay undoubtedly to no small extent in the real facts of the case, not in the mere treatment of the poet. Harm to Burns it certainly did do ; for it tended to raise a wall of partition between him and the reverential sentiment of the country, which stands in the way of his acceptance with not a few of the most worthy of his countrymen even at the present hour. Harm to the people it could not do ; for so far as it was overcharged, the roots of the popular piety had stuck too deep to be shaken by a rude hand ; and so far as it was true, the reproof has been so effective that not a shadow of the abuse remains. Had it not been for the polemical relation in which he found himself to the zealous party in the Church, and for the glaring nature of the abuse of sacred ceremonies that forced itself on his observation, I feel certain that Burns was the last man in the world to have wantonly held so sacred a rite up to public ridicule.—BLACKIE, JOHN STUART, 1888, *Life of Robert Burns (Great Writers), p.* 51.

Of all the series of satires, however, "The Holy Fair" is the most remarkable. It is in a sense a summing up of all the others that preceded it. The picture it gives of the mixed and motley multitude fairing in the church-yard at Mauchline, with a relay of ministerial mountebanks catering for their excitement, is true to the life. It is begging the question to deplore that Burns was provoked to such an attack. The scene was provocation sufficient to any right-thinking man who associated the name of religion with all that was good and beautiful and true. Such a state of things demanded reformation. The church-yard—that holy ground

on which the church was built and sanctified by the dust of pious and saintly men —cried aloud against the desecration to which it was subjected, and Burns, who alone had the power to purify it from such profanities, would have been untrue to himself and a traitor to the religion of his country had he merely shrugged his shoulders and allowed things to go on as they were going.—SETOUN, GABRIEL, 1896, *Robert Burns (Famous Scots Series), p.* 51.

The "Holy Fair," that "joyful solemnity" in which the scandals attending the open-air communions are painted with vivid power and merciless veracity. In these satires there is not *saeva indignatio* at evils he hated, but wild humour over scandals he laughed at. In them he was merely voicing the feelings of the educated classes, and echoing the teaching of the moderate clergy in two-thirds of the Lowland pulpits of Scotland. To say that Burns, by his drastic lines, broke down the despotism of the Church, overthrew the spirit of Puritanism, and dispelled religious gloom in the country, is to speak in ignorance of the real part he played. That work had been begun effectively by others before him, and was to be carried on by others who never felt his influence.—GRAHAM, HENRY GREY, 1901, *Scottish Men of Letters in the Eighteenth Century, p.* 392.

COTTER'S SATURDAY NIGHT

I intended writing you last night, but happening to lift the "Cotter's Saturday Night," it was impossible for me to close the book without reading it, tho' for the five hundred time. Do, I beg you, try if you can make anything now like it. I'm sure no one else I have ever seen can ; but I'll say no more of it, or I could speak of nothing else.—DUNLOP, MRS. FRANCES A., 1789, *Letter to Burns, Sept.* 23 ; *Robert Burns and Mrs. Dunlop, ed. Wallace, vol.* I, *p.* 308.

"The Cotter's Saturday Night" is tender and moral, it is solemn and devotional, and rises at length into a strain of grandeur and sublimity, which modern poetry has not surpassed. The noble sentiments of patriotism with which it concludes, correspond with the rest of the poem. In no age or country have the pastoral muses breathed such elevated accents, if the Messiah of Pope be excepted, which is indeed a pastoral in form only.—CURRIE, JAMES, 1800, ed., *Works of Robert Burns, Life.*

A noble and pathetic picture of human manners, mingled with a fine religious awe.—HAZLITT, WILLIAM, 1818, *Lectures on the English Poets, Lecture* vii.

The "Cottar's Saturday Night" is, perhaps, of all Burns's pieces, the one whose exclusion from the collection, were such things possible now-a-days, would be the most injurious, if not to the genius, at least to the character, of the man. In spite of many feeble lines, and some heavy stanzas, it appears to me, that even his genius would suffer more in estimation, by being contemplated in the absence of this poem, than of any other single performance he has left us. Loftier flights he certainly had made, but in these he remained but a short while on the wing, and effort is too often perceptible; here the motion is easy, gentle, placidly undulating. There is more of the conscious security of power, than in any other of his serious pieces of considerable length; the whole has an appearance of coming in a full stream from the fountain of the heart— a stream that soothes the ear, and has no glare on the surface.—LOCKHART, JOHN GIBSON, 1828, *Life of Robert Burns, p.* 97.

In "the Cottar's Saturday Night," the poet has so varied his dialect that there are scarcely two consecutive stanzas written according to the same model. An hour of winter evening music on the Æolian harp, when all the winds are on the wing, would hardly be more wild, and sweet, and stern, and changeable than the series. Some of the strains are as purely English as the author could reach; others so racily Scottish as often to require a glossary; while in a third class the two are so enchantingly combined, that no poetic diction can excel the pathos and sublimity, blended with beauty and homeliness, that equally mark them.—MONTGOMERY, JAMES, 1833, *Lectures on General Literature, Poetry, etc., p.* 135.

There are a few more *perfect* poems. It is the utterance of a heart whose cords were all tuned to gratitude, "making sweet melody" to the Giver, on a night not less sacred in His eye than His own appointed Sabbath.—WILSON, JOHN, 1844, *The Genius and Character of Burns, p.* 31.

There is an artless beauty and solemnity in the picture of the humble devotions of the farmer and his household which shows that the poet himself felt the influence of such scenes, and inclines us the more to look with pity and leniency on the excesses which ruined the man, and which these stanzas show that he himself, in his better moments, must have both lamented and condemned.—YONGE, CHARLES DUKE, 1872, *Three Centuries of English Literature, p.* 475.

This is true, but the piece as a whole is formed on English models. It is the most artificial and the most imitative of Burns's works. Not only is the influence of Gray's "Elegy" conspicuous, but also there are echoes of Pope, Thomson, Goldsmith, and even Milton; while the stanza, which was taken, not from Spenser, whom Burns had not then read, but from Beattie and Shenstone, is so purely English as to lie outside the range of Burns's experience and accomplishment.—HENLEY, WILLIAM ERNEST, AND HENDERSON, THOMAS F., 1896, ed., *The Poetry of Robert Burns, vol.* I, *p.* 362, *note.*

No nobler tribute to the sturdy virtues of the poor has ever been penned. It is not marred by ranting; in a pure, simple, homely way, it pictures the sweetness of life in honest poverty.—WATROUS, GEORGE A., 1898, ed., *Selections from Dryden, Burns, Wordsworth and Browning, p.* 131, *note.*

TAM O'SHANTER
1793

The humor, the grandeur, and the fancy of that poem will never be equaled.—MITFORD, MARY RUSSELL, 1813, *Letter to Sir William Elford, Nov.* 10; *Life, ed. L'Estrange, vol.* I, *p.* 186.

It is not so much a poem as a piece of sparkling rhetoric; the heart and body of the story still lies hard and dead. He has not gone back, much less carried us back, into that dark, earnest, wondering age, when the tradition was believed, and when it took its rise; he does not attempt, by any new modelling of his supernatural ware, to strike anew that deep mysterious chord of human nature, which once responded to such things, and which lives in us too, and will forever live, though silent, or vibrating with far other notes, and to far different issues. Our German readers will understand us when we say that he is not the Tieck but the Musäus of this tale. Externally it is all green and living; yet look closer, it is no firm growth, but only ivy on a rock. The piece does not properly cohere; the strange chasm which yawns in our incredulous imagination between the Ayr public-house and gate of Tophet is nowhere bridged over; nay, the idea of such a bridge is laughed at; and thus the tragedy of the adventure becomes a mere drunken phantasmagoria painted on ale-vapors, and the farce alone has any reality. We do not say that Burns should have made much more of this tradition; we rather think that, for strictly poetical purposes, not much *was* to be made of it. Neither are we blind to the deep, varied, genial power displayed in what he has actually accomplished; but we find far more "Shakespearean" qualities, as these of "Tam o' Shanter" have been fondly named, in many of his other pieces; nay, we incline to believe that this latter might have been written, all but quite as well, by a man who, in place of genius, had only possessed talent. — CARLYLE, THOMAS, 1828, *Essay on Burns.*

He himself regarded it as his masterpiece of all his poems, and posterity has not, I believe, reversed the judgment.— SHAIRP, JOHN CAMPBELL, 1879, *Robert Burns (English Men of Letters), p. 121.*

Ay, the very house in which Tam and Souter Johnny prolonged their marketnight meetings, the foaming ale growing better with each successive draught, Souter telling his queerest stories, Tam and the landlady growing gracious—a house not less famous than the old Boar's Head in Eastcheap, or the Bell at Edmonton, named in these latter days after that drouthiest of "drouthy neebors," the incorrigible Tam, who elbows Rip Van Winkle, Bailie Nichol Jarvie, and Conn in our vagabond affiliations. It is a plain, plastered, thatched little tavern, tinted yellow, in contrast to the surrounding houses, which are white. Over the door is a signboard with a creditable painting of Tam leaving the house,

"Weel mounted on his gray mare Meg,"

and the Souter grasping his hand with maudlin affection before he plunges through the storm toward Alloway. The landlord holds the history of the tavern precious, and on another sign-board he specifies its associations, with the additional announcement that "a chair and caup are in the house." The "caup" is the identical one drained by Tam, the chair the one he sat in, and it would be a teetotaler of less than usual flexibility who could pass without ordering some mild beverage as an excuse for viewing the interior. The landlord's name is A. Glass, and he is not only a most devoted admirer of Burns, but also a poet in a very small way himself.—RIDEING, WILLIAM H., 1879, *The Land o' Burns, Harper's Magazine, vol. 59, p. 184.*

"Tam O' Shanter" is not so marvellous a creation as "The Dance of the Sevin Deidly Synnis," though we may find it easier to appreciate the modern poem, in which the tipsy hilarity of the hero gives a familiar aspect to the devilry of the witches, and robs it of the weirdness and horror that should mark the spectacle of a supernatural world. Burns's humour plays most freely round the incidents of human life, though none can deny the boldness with which it now and again makes a sweep into the realms of superstition.—ROSS, JOHN MERRY, 1884, *Scottish History and Literature, ed. Brown, p. 214.*

Scarcely excelled in powers of imagination by Shakespeare himself is Burns's weird description of the orgies of the witches, and the infernal scenery in which they are exhibited. . . . The only fault found in this poem is that at the conclusion it falls off in interest. This is said to be owing to Burns having stuck to the popular tale of this hero; for Tam was not a creation of fancy, but a real person. . . . Burns considered "Tam O'Shanter" his masterpiece, and many critics have regarded it in the same light; yet it does not perhaps embody what is brightest and best in his poetry. His address to a mouse on turning up her nest with a plough in November is richer in true poetic light and color. Its companion is that to a daisy. In these and in the "Cotter's Saturday Night" it has been happily remarked that "the poet is seen in his happiest inspiration, his brightest sunshine, and his tenderest tears." The latter poem is familiar to all, and in true and touching description is almost unrivalled.—BROOKS, SARAH WARNER, 1890, *English Poetry and Poets, pp. 289, 290, 291.*

THE JOLLY BEGGARS

Perhaps we may venture to say that the most strictly poetical of all his "poems" is one which does not appear in Currie's edition, but has been often printed before and since under the humble title of "The Jolly Beggars." The subject truly is among the lowest in nature; but it only the more shows our poet's gift in raising it into the domain of art. To our minds this piece seems thoroughly compacted; melted together, refined; and poured forth in one flood of true *liquid* harmony. It is light, airy, and soft of movement, yet sharp and precise in its details; every face is a portrait: that *raucle carlin*, that *wee Apollo*, that *Son of Mars* are Scottish, yet ideal; the scene is at once a dream, and the very Rag-castle of "Poosie-Nansie." Further, it seems in a considerable degree complete, a real self-supporting whole, which is the highest merit in a poem.— CARLYLE, THOMAS, 1828, *Essay on Burns.*

In the world of the "Jolly Beggars" there is more than hideousness and squalor, there is bestiality; yet the piece is a superb poetic success. It has a breadth, truth, and power which make the famous scene in Auerbach's Cellar, of Goethe's "Faust," seem artificial and tame beside it, and which are only matched by Shakespeare and Aristophanes.—ARNOLD, MATTHEW, 1880, *English Poets, ed. Ward, Introduction, vol.* I, *p.* xlv.

That incomparable opera in which critical genius of the highest order has discovered the highest flight of his poetical genius.—SERVICE, JOHN, 1880, *English Poets, ed. Ward, vol.* III, *p.* 521.

In Burns's "Jolly Beggars," it seems to me that Burns touched nearly the highest point of his creative genius, though nothing, except the large licence of the roving vagabond's life, is concentrated into it, and rendered with an almost passionate wealth of vigour and sympathy. —HUTTON, RICHARD HOLT, 1882, *Professor Shairp's "Aspects of Poetry," Criticisms on Contemporary Thought and Thinkers, vol.* II, *p.* 163.

For riotous luxuriance, "The Jolly Beggars" overtops all that Burns ever wrote. Probably no poem more graphic exists in literature. It describes what the writer had actually seen, and not otherwise would its extreme vividness seem to be attainable.

—WALKER, HUGH, 1893, *Three Centuries of Scottish Literature, vol.* II, *p.* 162.

Is an immortal masterpiece of melody and observation. The squalor of the piece is glorified by a style so little rustic that every word and every rhythm is fitted to its purpose. It is the literature of the street, maybe, but the literature of the street made classic for all time.—WHIBLEY, CHARLES, 1898, *Burns, Macmillan's Magazine, vol.* 77, *p.* 183.

HOLY WILLIE'S PRAYER

"Holy Willie's Prayer" is a satirical crucifixion — slow, lingering inexorable. He hated Hypocrisy, he tore its holy robe, and for the outrage Hypocrisy did not forgive him while he lived, nor has it yet learned to forgive him.—SMITH, ALEXANDER, 1865, *The Complete Works of Robert Burns, Life, p.* xxxix.

The unfortunate man, William Fisher, known as "Holy Willie," both Patrick and his wife were little inclined to speak of. When they did so, it was only as a man "neither very bad nor very guid, to ootward appearance." Mrs. Patrick said he must have drawn attention to himself, in his earlier days, as at least a good professor, "to be made an elder o'." Seeing that I knew that the satires of Burns were only too well founded, for he was subsequently dismissed the eldership and died in a ditch after a debauch, they admitted that "he was blaim'd for takin' the kirk bawbees. When standin' at the plate on Sabbath, fowk said, he would boo doon to pat his boots richt, as it were, and slip in a bawbee or so!" Poor man, his punishment has been greater than Burns, with all his indignation against his character, I am sure, meant it to be; for the poet had little anticipation that his fiery words would reach so far and wide when he wrote them, and be so long remembered against their luckless object. Happily, however, in such world-wide pages, the man himself becomes a myth, a mere ideal representative of certain thoughts and actions, which alone remain as the theme of the poem.—JOLLY, WILLIAM, 1881, *Robert Burns at Mossgiel; With Reminiscences of the Poet by His Herd-Boy, p.* 100.

This amazing achievement in satire, this matchless parody of Calvinistic intercession—so nice, so exquisite in detail, so overwhelming in effect. — HENLEY,

WILLIAM ERNEST, AND HENDERSON, THOMAS
F., 1896, *ed.*, *The Poetry of Robert Burns*,
vol. II, *p.* 320, *note.*

LETTERS

The prose works of Burns consist almost
entirely of his letters. They bear, as well
as his poetry, the seal and the impress of
his genius; but they contain much more
bad taste, and are written with far more
apparent labour. His poetry was almost
all written primarily from feeling, and
only secondarily from ambition. His letters seem to have been nearly all composed as exercises, and for display.
There are few of them written with simplicity or plainness; and though natural
enough as to the sentiment, they are generally very strained and elaborate in the
expression. A very great proportion of
them, too, relate neither to facts nor feelings peculiarly connected with the author
or his correspondent—but are made up
of general declamation, moral reflections,
and vague discussions—all evidently composed for the sake of effect, and frequently introduced with long complaints
of having nothing to say, and of the necessity and difficulty of letter-writing.—
JEFFREY, FRANCIS LORD, 1809–44, *Contributions to the Edinburgh Review, vol.* II,
p. 398.

Allen (Lord Holland's Allen—the best
informed and one of the ablest men I know
—a perfect Magliabecchi—a devourer, a
Helluo of books, and an observer of men),
has lent me a quantity of Burns's unpublished and never-to-be published, Letters.
They are full of oaths and obscene songs.
What an antithetical mind!—tenderness,
roughness—delicacy, coarseness—sentiment, sensuality—soaring and grovelling,
dirt and deity—all mixed up in that one
compound of inspired clay!—BYRON,
LORD, 1813, *Journal, Dec.* 13, *ed. Moore.*

His prose-letters are sometimes tinctured with affectation. They seem written by a man who has been admired for
his wit, and is expected on all occasions
to shine. Those in which he expresses
his ideas of natural beauty in reference to
Alison's "Essay on Taste," and advocates
the keeping up the remembrances of old
customs and seasons, are the most powerfully written. — HAZLITT, WILLIAM,
1818, *Lectures on the English Poets, Lecture* vii.

Lord Byron's correspondence exhibits
some of the finest specimens of epistolary
composition in the language; but the
monotony of selfish complaint without
cause, petulant aspersion of his fellow-
creatures, inexcusable accumulation of
oaths, and occasional use of slang, which
disfigures it, are faults that must offend
the most partial reader. Page after
page of sneering, of wilful swearing, or
of petty scandal, with scarcely the relief
of a single tear, or the sunshine of a
single smile, is overwhelming at once to
taste and patience. In variety of topic
there is nothing in him at all like Burns,
and in appropriate diversity of style—on
this, or on that theme, as it occurs—there
is but little approach to him. In Burns
we have sometimes an oath, and sometimes indecorum; but sympathy and sincerity always, and slang never.—WAD-
DELL, HATELY, 1869, *Critical Edition of
the Life and Works of Burns, vol.* II.

The letters are of unequal value, and
have been variously estimated. They
show indeed that, like almost all poets, he
might, if choice and fate had united, have
become a very considerable prose-writer,
and they have immense autobiographic
value. But they are sometimes, and perhaps often, written as much in falsetto as
the division of verse just ruled out; their
artificiality does not take very good models; and their literary attraction is altogether second-rate.—SAINTSBURY, GEORGE,
1896, *A History of Nineteenth Century
Literature, p.* 14.

GENERAL

Unacquainted with the necessary requisites for commencing Poet by rule, he
sings the sentiments and manners he felt
and saw in himself and his rustic compeers around him, in his and their native
language. Though a Rhymer from his
earliest years, at least from the earliest
impulses of the softer passions, it was
not till very lately that the applause, perhaps the partiality, of Friendship, wakened his vanity so far as to make him
think anything of his was worth showing;
and none of the following works were ever
composed with a view to the press. To
amuse himself with the little creations of
his own fancy, amid the toil and fatigues
of a laborious life; to transcribe the
various feelings, the loves, the griefs, the
hopes, the fears, in his own breast; to

find some kind of counterpoise to the struggles of a world, always an alien scene, a task uncouth to the poetical mind; these were his motives for courting the Muses, and in these he found Poetry to be its own reward. . . . To his Subscribers the Author returns his most sincere thanks. Not the mercenary bow over a counter, but the heart-throbbing gratitude of the Bard, conscious how much he is indebted to Benevolence and Friendship for gratifying him, if he deserves it, in that dearest wish of every poetic bosom—to be distinguished. He begs his readers, particularly the Learned and the Polite, who may honour him with a perusal, that they will make every allowance for Education and Circumstances of Life: but if, after a fair, candid, and impartial criticism, he shall stand convicted of Dulness and Nonsense, let him be done by, as he would in that case do by others—let him be condemned without mercy, to contempt and oblivion. —BURNS, ROBERT, 1786, *Poems Chiefly in the Scottish Dialect, Preface.*

I hope I shall not be thought to assume too much, if I endeavour to place him in a higher point of view, to call for a verdict of his country on the merit of his works, and to claim for him those honours which their excellence appears to deserve. In mentioning the circumstance of his humble station, I mean not to rest his pretensions solely on that title, or to urge the merits of his poetry, when considered in relation to the lowness of his birth, and the little opportunity of improvement which his education could afford. These particulars, indeed, might excite our wonder at his productions; but his poetry, considered abstractedly, and without the apologies arising from his situation, seems to me fully entitled to command our feelings, and to obtain our applause.—MACKENZIE, HENRY, 1786, *The Lounger, Dec.* 9.

Many instances have I seen of Nature's force and beneficence exerted under numerous and formidable disadvantages; but none equal to that with which you have been kind enough to present me. There is a pathos and delicacy in his serious poems, a vein of wit and humour in those of a more festive turn, which cannot be too much admired, nor too warmly approved; and I think I shall never open the book without feeling my astonishment renewed and increased. It was my wish

to have expressed my approbation in verse; but whether from declining life, or a temporary depression of spirits, it is at present out of my power to accomplish that agreeable intention. Mr. Stewart, Professor of Morals in this University, had formerly read me three of the poems, and I had desired him to get my name inserted among the subscribers: but whether this was done, or not, I never could learn. I have little intercourse with Dr. Blair, but will take care to have the poems communicated to him by the intervention of some mutual friend. It has been told me by a gentleman, to whom I shewed the performances, and who sought a copy with diligence and ardour, that the whole impression is already exhausted. It were, therefore, much to be wished, for the sake of the young man, that a second edition, more numerous than the former, could immediately be printed: as it appears certain that its intrinsic merit, and the exertion of the author's friends, might give it a more universal circulation than any thing of the kind which has been published within my memory.—BLACKLOCK, THOMAS, 1786, *Letter to Rev. G. Lowrie.*

Some of the poems you have added in this last edition are very beautiful, particularly the "Winter Night," the "Address to Edinburgh," "Green Grow the Rashes," and the two songs immediately following, the latter of which is exquisite. By the way, I imagine you have a peculiar talent for such compositions, which you ought to indulge. No kind of poetry demands more delicacy or higher polishing. Horace is more admired on account of his Odes than all his other writings. But nothing now added is equal to your "Vision" and "Cotter's Saturday Night." In these are united fine imagery, natural and pathetic description, with sublimity of language and thought. It is evident that you already possess a great variety of expression and command of the English language; you ought, therefore, to deal more sparingly for the future in the provincial dialect; why should you, by using that, limit the number of your admirers to those who understand the Scottish, when you can extend it to all persons of taste who understand the English language? In my opinion, you should plan some larger work than any you have as yet attempted. I mean, reflect upon some proper subject, and arrange the plan in your mind, without beginning to execute any part of it till you have studied most of the best English poets, and read a little more of history. —MOORE, JOHN, 1787, *Letter to Burns, May* 23.

I have been much pleased with the poems of the Scottish ploughman, of which you have had specimens in the Review. His "Cotter's Saturday Night," has much of the same kind of merit as the "School-mistress;" and the "Daisy,"and the "Mouse," which I believe you have had in the papers, I think are charming. The endearing diminutives, and the Doric rusticity of the dialect, suit such subjects extremely.—BARBAULD, ANNA LÆTITIA, 1787, *Letter to Dr. Aikin, Works, vol.* II, *p.* 151.

Read Burns's poems, and have read them twice: and though they be written in a language that is new to me, and many of them on subjects much inferior to the author's ability, I think them, on the whole, a very extraordinary production. He is, I believe, the only poet these kingdoms have produced in the lower rank of life since Shakspeare, I should rather say since Prior, who need not be indebted for any part of his praise as a charitable consideration of his origin, and the disadvantages under which he has laboured. It will be pity if he should not hereafter divest himself of barbarism, and content himself with writing pure English, in which he appears perfectly qualified to excel. . . . Poor Burns loses much of his deserved praise in this country, through our ignorance of his language. I despair of meeting with any Englishman who will take the pains that I have taken to understand him. His candle is bright, but shut up in a dark lantern. I lent him to a very sensible neighbour of mine, but his uncouth dialect spoiled all, and before he had half read him through, he was quite *ramfeezled.*—COWPER, WILLIAM, 1787, *Letters to Samuel Rose, July* 24, *and Aug.* 27; *Life, ed. Hayley, vol.* I, *pp.* 138, 139.

Robert Burns, a natural poet of the first eminence, does not, perhaps appear to his usual advantage in song—*non omnia possumus.* The political "fragment," as he calls it, inserted in the second volume of the present collection, has, however, much merit in some of the satirical stanzas,

and could it have been concluded with the spirit with which it is commenced, would indisputably have been entitled to great praise; but the character of his favourite minister seems to have operated like the touch of a torpedo; and after vainly attempting something like a panegyric, he seems under the necessity of relinquishing the task. Possibly the bard will one day see occasion to complete his performance as a uniform satire.—RITSON, JOSEPH, 1794, *Historical Essay on Scottish Songs, p.* 71.

> Rustick Burns,
> And all his artless wood-notes Scotland mourns.

—MATHIAS, THOMAS JAMES, 1797, *The Pursuits of Literature, Eighth ed., p.* 417.

Old and young, high and low, grave and gay, learned or ignorant, all were alike delighted, agitated, transported. I was at that time resident in Galloway, contiguous to Ayrshire: and I can well remember, how that even the plough-boys and maid-servants would have gladly bestowed the wages which they earned and most hardly, and which they wanted to purchase necessary clothing, if they might but secure the works of Burns.—HERON, ROBERT, 1797, *A Memoir of the Life of the Late Robert Burns.*

It was not, indeed, until the appearance of the rustic Burns, that Bard of Nature and of Love, that we could boast of a writer of eminent genius, who had paid due attention to this department of Lyric poetry, and had brought forward numerous specimens of undoubted excellence. —DRAKE, NATHAN, 1798-1820, *Literary Hours, vol.* II, *No.* xliii, *p.* 374.

Now I have to satisfy you as to my favourite poem of Burns. Doubtless the "Daisy" is the most finished and excels in simple elegance; "The De'il himsel" in humour—exquisite, peculiar humour. I confess, if decorous people could be reconciled to blackguardism, John Hornbook is the very Emperor of blackguards. Only think of that despotic power over the fancy, which can unite, what the creative Shakspeare himself never united, the terrible and ludicrous. Yet, where Death is personified meeting the bard, I am sure you would laugh, if you were not afraid. The same power reappears in "Tam O'Shanter," which I allow to possess superior excellence, though not the very sort of excellence most to my taste. But if you talk of my very own taste, I find myself quite at home in "The Epistle to Davy," and "The Cottar's Saturday Night."—GRANT, MRS. ANNE, 1802, *To Miss Dunbar, April 25; Letters from the Mountains, vol.* II, *p.* 176.

> I mourned with thousands, but as one
> More deeply grieved, for He was gone
> Whose light I hailed when first it shone,
>   And showed my youth
> How Verse may build a princely throne
>   On humble truth.

—WORDSWORTH, WILLIAM, 1803, *At the Grave of Burns.*

Much as I admire the exquisite tenderness and moral delicacy of Cowper's temperament, I confess I am still more delighted with the boldness and vehemence of the bard of Caledonia. "His generous affections, his ardent eloquence, his brilliant and daring imagination" make him my idol. His proper regard to the dignity of his own powers, his stern and indignant elevation of manners, and due jealousy and repression of the insolence of rank and wealth, are worthy of inexpressible applause. . . . The genius of Burns was more sublime than that of Cowper. Both excelled in the familiar: but yet the latter was by nature as well as education more gentle, more easy, and delicate: he had also more of tenuity, while Burns was more concise, more bold, and energetic. They both also abounded in humour, which possessed the same characteristics in each; one mild, serene, and smiling; the other daring and powerful, full of fire and imagery. The poems of one fill the heart and the fancy with the soft pleasures of domestic privacy, with the calm and innocent occupations of rural solitude, the pensive musings of the moralist, and the chastised indignation of pure and simple virtue: the poems of the other breathe by turns Grief, Love, Joy, Melancholy, Despair and Terror; plunge us in the vortex of passion, and hurry us away on the wings of unrestrained and undirected fancy.—BRYDGES, SIR SAMUEL EGERTON, 1806, *Censura Literaria, vol.* II, *pp.* 43, 59.

> Yes, Burns, "thou dear departed shade!"
> When rolling centuries have fled,
> Thy name shall still survive the wreck of
>   time,
> Shall rouse the genius of thy native clime;
> Bards yet unborn, and patriots shall come,

> And catch fresh ardour at thy hallow'd
>   tomb!
> There's not a cairn-built cottage on our hills,
> Nor rural hamlet on our fertile plains,
> But echoes to the magic of thy strains,
> While every heart with highest transport
>   thrills.
> Our country's melodies shall perish never,
> For, Burns, thy songs shall live for ever.

—TANNAHILL, ROBERT, 1807, *Ode for the Celebration of the Birthday of Burns, Works,* ed. Ramsay, p. 157.

An earnest wish to possess a scrap of the hand-writing of Burns, originally led to the discovery of most of the papers that compose this volume. In the manner of laying them before the public I honestly declare that I have done my best; and I trust I may fairly presume to hope that the man who has contributed to extend the bounds of literature by adding another genuine volume to the writings of Robert Burns, has some claim on the gratitude of his countrymen. On this occasion, I certainly ·feel something of that sublime and heart-swelling gratification, which he experiences, who cast another stone on the Cairn of a great and lamented chief.—CROMEK, R. H., 1808, *ed., Reliques of Robert Burns, Preface, p.* viii.

The illustrious soul that has left amongst us the name of Burns, has often been lowered down to a comparison with me; but the comparison exists more in circumstances than in essentials. That man stood up with the stamp of superior intellect on his brow; a visible greatness: and great and patriotic subjects would only have called into action the powers of his mind, which lay inactive while he played calmly and exquisitely the pastoral pipe. The letters to which I have alluded in my preface to the "Rural Tales," were friendly warnings, pointed with immediate reference to the fate of that extraordinary man. "Remember Burns," has been the watchword of my friends. I do remember Burns; but I *am not* Burns! I have neither his fire to fan, or to quench; nor his passions to control! Where then is my merit, if I make a peaceful voyage on a smooth sea, and with no mutiny on board.—BLOOMFIELD, ROBERT, 1808, *Reliques of Robert Burns, ed. Cromek.*

Burns is certainly by far the greatest of our poetical prodigies—from Stephen

Duck down to Thomas Dermody. *They are forgotten already; or only remembered for derision.* But the name of Burns, if we are not mistaken, has not yet "gathered all its fame;" and will endure long after those circumstances are forgotten which contributed to its first notoriety. So much indeed are we impressed with a sense of his merits, that we cannot help thinking it a derrogation from them to consider him as a prodigy at all; and are convinced that he will never be rightly estimated as a poet, till that vulgar wonder be entirely repressed which was raised on his having been a ploughman. It is true, no doubt, that he was born in an humble station; and that much of his early life was devoted to severe labour, and to the society of his fellow-labourers. But he was not himself either uneducated or illiterate; and was placed in a situation more favourable, perhaps, to the development of great poetical talents, than any other which could have been assigned him.—JEFFREY, FRANCIS LORD, 1809–44, *Contributions to the Edinburgh Review, vol.* II, *p.* 389.

The sweetest, the sublimest, the most tricksy poet who has blest this nether world since the days of Shakespeare!—MITFORD, MARY RUSSELL, 1813, *Letter to Sir William E. Elford, Nov.* 10; *Life, ed. L'Estrange, vol.* I, *p.* 186.

Whether engaged, or roaming at liberty, Wither never seems to have abated a jot of that free spirit, which sets its mark upon his writings, as much as a predominant feature of independence impresses every page of our late glorious Burns; but the elder poet wraps his proof-armour closer about him, the other wears his too much outwards; he is thinking too much of annoying the foe, to be quite easy within.—LAMB, CHARLES, 1814, *George Wither's Poetical Works, Quarterly Review, Oct.*

It is a remark too trite perhaps to require repetition, that the writings of Robert Burns are, in Scotland, the most popular of any works of fancy, ancient or modern,—that there is scarcely a home in the kingdom which does not contain a copy of his poems—and that there are few individuals elevated above the clods of valley, who are not familiar with the productions of his muse. The tendency of works so widely circulated, and so highly

esteemed, is evidently a matter of no trivial moment. — PETERKIN, ALEXANDER, 1815, ed., *The Life and Works of Robert Burns, vol.* I, *p.* xiii.

Neither the subjects of his poems, nor his manner of handling them, allow us long to forget their author. On the basis of his human character he has reared a poetic one, which with more or less distinctness presents itself to view in almost every part of his earlier, and in my estimation, his most valuable verses. This poetic fabric, dug out of the quarry of genuine humanity, is airy and spiritual: —and though the materials, in some parts, are coarse, and the disposition is often fantastic and irregular, yet the whole is agreeable and strikingly attractive. . . . It is probable that he would have proved a still greater poet if, by strength of reason, he could have controlled the propensities which his sensibility engendered; but he would have been a poet of a different class; and certain it is, had that desirable restraint been early established, many peculiar beauties which enrich his verses could never have existed, and many accessary influences, which contribute greatly to their effect, would have been wanting.—WORDSWORTH, WILLIAM, 1816, *A Letter to a Friend of Robert Burns.*

Burns has given an elixir of life to his native dialect. The Scottish "Tam O'Shanter" will be read as long as any English production of the same century. The impression of his genius is deep and universal; and, viewing him merely as a poet, there is scarcely any other regret connected with his name, than that his productions, with all their merit, fall short of the talents which he possessed. . . . He meets us, in his compositions, undisguisedly as a peasant. At the same time, his observations go extensively into life, like those of a man who felt the proper dignity of human nature in the character of a peasant. The writer of some of the severest strictures that ever have been passed upon his poetry conceives that his beauties are considerably defaced by a portion of false taste and vulgar sentiment, which adhere to him from his low education. That Burns's education, or rather the want of it, excluded him from much knowledge, which might have fostered his inventive ingenuity, seems to be clear; but his circumstances cannot be

admitted to have communicated vulgarity to the tone of his sentiments. They have not the sordid taste of low condition. It is objected to him, that he boasts too much of his own independence; but, in reality, this boast is neither frequent nor obtrusive; and it is in itself the expression of a manly and laudable feeling. So far from calling up disagreeable recollections of rusticity, his sentiments triumph, by their natural energy, over those false and fastidious distinctions which the mind is but too apt to form in allotting its sympathies to the sensibilities of the rich and poor. He carries us into the humble scenes of life, not to make us dole out our tribute of charitable compassion to paupers and cottagers, but to make us feel with them on equals terms, to make us enter into their passions and interests, and share our hearts with them as with brothers and sisters of the human species.
—CAMPBELL, THOMAS, 1819, *Specimens of the British Poets.*

What bird, in beauty, flight, or song,
  Can with the Bard compare,
Who sang as sweet, and soar'd as strong,
  As ever child of air?
His plume, his note, his form, could Burns
  For whim or pleasure change;
He was not one, but all by turns,
  With transmigration strange.

. . . .

Peace to the dead—In Scotia's choir
  Of Minstrels great and small,
He sprang from his spontaneous fire,
  The Phœnix of them all.
— MONTGOMERY, JAMES, 1820, *Robert Burns.*

There have been loftier themes than his,
  And longer scrolls, and louder lyres,
And lays lit up with Poesy's
  Purer and holier fires:
Yet read the names that know not death;
  Few nobler ones than Burns are there;
And few have won a greener wreath
  Than that which binds his hair.
His is that language of the heart,
  In which the answering heart would speak,
Thought, word, that bids the warm tear start,
  Or the smile light the cheek;
And his that music, to whose tone
  The common pulse of man keeps time,
In cot or castle's mirth or moan,
  In cold or sunny clime.
And who hath heard his song, nor knelt
  Before its spell with willing knee,
And listened, and believed, and felt
  The Poet's mastery
O'er the mind's sea, in calm and storm,

O'er the heart's sunshine and its showers,
O'er Passion's moments, bright and warm,
O'er Reason's dark cold hours.

. . . .

Praise to the bard! his words are driven,
  Like flower-seeds by the far winds sown,
Where'er, beneath the sky of heaven,
  The birds of fame have flown.
—HALLECK, FITZ-GREENE, 1822, *Burns.*

"Mr. John Home, the celebrated author of Douglas," says an evening paper of 6th Nov. 1789, "was lately asked his opinion of the poems of Robert Burns. His answer was, 'The encouragement that fellow has met with is a perfect disgrace to the nation.' This anecdote is genuine, and the majority is satisfied the remark is just. His reputation is vastly faded!"
—COLLET, STEPHEN, 1823, *Relics of Literature, p. 260.*

The great Master of lyrical composition, in its purest and most intelligible sense. His ballads, on the simplest, sweetest, and most powerful subjects, are beyond all competition; and the strains of love, friendship, and patriotism, by turn take possession of the heart.—DIBDIN, THOMAS FROGNALL, 1824, *The Library Companion, p. 743, note.*

His native strains each bard may try,
  But who has got his fire?
Why, none—for Nature saw him die,
  Then took away his lyre.
And for that lyre the learned youth
  May search the world in vain;
She vowed she ne'er would lend it more
  To sound on earth again;
But called on Fame to hang it by—
  She took it with a tear,
Broke all the strings to bind the wreath
  That Burns shall ever wear.
—NICHOLSON, JOHN, 1826, *The Birthday of Burns.*

Lyrical poetry admits of less variety than any other species: and Burns, from this circumstance, as well as from the flexibility of his talents, may be considered as the representative of his whole nation. Indeed, his universal genius seems to have concentrated within itself the rays which were scattered among his predecessors: the simple tenderness of Crawford, the fidelity of Ramsay, and careless humour of Ferguson. The Doric dialect of his country was an instrument peculiarly fitted for the expression of his manly and unsophisticated sentiments. But no one is more indebted to the national music than Burns: embalmed in the sacred melody, his songs are familiar to us from childhood, and, as we read them, the silver sounds with which they have been united seem to linger in our memory, heightening and prolonging the emotions which the sentiments have excited.— PRESCOTT, WILLIAM HICKLING, 1826, *Scottish Song, Biographical and Critical Miscellanies.*

If, in spite of Burns, and all his successors, the boundary lines of society are observed with increasing strictness among us—if the various orders of men still, day by day, feel the chord of sympathy relaxing, let us lament over symptoms of a disease in the body politic, which, if it goes on, must find sooner or later a fatal ending: but let us not undervalue the antidote which has all along been checking this strong poison. Who can doubt, that at this moment thousands of "the firstborn of Egypt" look upon the smoke of a cottager's chimney with feelings which would never have been developed within their being, had there been no Burns?— LOCKHART, JOHN GIBSON, 1828, *Life of Robert Burns, p.* 434.

A certain rugged sterling worth pervades whatever Burns has written: a virtue, as of green fields and mountain breezes, dwells in his poetry; it is redolent of natural life, and hardy natural men. There is a decisive strength in him, and yet a sweet native gracefulness: he is tender, and he is vehement, yet without constraint or too visible effort; he melts the heart, or inflames it, with a power which seems habitual and familiar to him. We see in him the gentleness, the trembling pity of a woman, with the deep earnestness, the force, and passionate ardour of a hero. Tears lie in him, and consuming fire, as lightning lurks in the drops of a summer cloud. He has a resonance in his bosom for every note of human feeling: the high and the low, the sad and the ludicrous, the joyful, are welcome in their turns to his "lightly-moved and all-conceiving spirit." . . . No poet of any age or nation is more graphic than Burns: the characteristic features disclose themselves to him at a glance; three lines from his hand, and we have a likeness. And in that rough dialect, in that rude, often awkward meter, so clear and definite a likeness! It seems a draughtsman working with a burnt stick;

and yet the burin of a Retzsch is not more expressive or exact. . . . No one, at all events, is ignorant that in the poetry of Burns keenness of insight keeps pace with keenness of feeling; that his *light* is not more pervading than his *warmth.* He is a man of the most impassioned. temper; with passions not strong only, but noble, and of the sort in which great virtues and great poems take their rise. It is reverence, it is love toward all Nature that inspires him, that opens his eyes to its beauty, and makes heart and voice eloquent in its praise. . . . Burns, indeed, lives in sympathy; his soul rushes forth into all realms of being; nothing that has existence can be indifferent to him. The very Devil he cannot hate with right orthodoxy!—CARLYLE, THOMAS, 1828, *Essay on Burns.*

Porson.—What an admirable Spanish scholar must Mr. Wordsworth be! How completely has he transfused into his own compositions all the spirit of those verses! Nevertheless, it is much to be regretted that, in resolving on simplicity, he did not place himself under the tuition of Burns; which quality Burns could have taught him in perfection; but others he never could have imparted to such an auditor. He would have sung in vain to him

"Scots wha hae wi' Wallace bled."

A song more animating than ever Tyrtæus sang to the fife before the Spartans. But simplicity in Burns is never stale and unprofitable. In Burns there is no waste of words out of an ill-shouldered sack; no troublesome running backward and forward of little, idle, ragged ideas; no ostentation of sentiment in the surtout of selfishness.—LANDOR, WALTER SAVAGE, 1828, *Southey and Porson, Imaginary Conversations, Third Series.*

Burns, whose lofty soul spread its own pathos and dignity over the "short and simple annals of the poor."—ALISON, SIR ARCHIBALD, 1833–42, *History of Europe During The French Revolution, vol.* XIV, *p.* 3.

When we consider the genius of Burns, we see it manifestly moulded and coloured by his agricultural life. It was thus that nothing seemed worthy to engross his attention but the feelings and the passions of the heart of man.—HOGG, JAMES, 1838–40, *Memoir of Burns, ch.* ii.

It is not easy to conceive any two men

more unlike each other, than Cowper and Burns were; and yet, in their genius, there is much similarity. Burns, perhaps, was twice as much a man as Cowper, and the tenth part of the tithe as much a poet as Shakspeare or Scott: he was a giant, nevertheless. *His* Muse was manliness: he was honest and fearless. The Muse of Cowper was conscious; *he* was honest but not fearless; he trembled, and a shadow overthrew him but it was a shadow darker than the shadow of death. He would have been a far greater poet than he was, if disease had not made him a coward. Not that he was insincere: oh no! and yet he dared not whisper to his poor heart that God is merciful. Nor was his despair unpoetical; but the hope of Burns is more poetical than Cowper's despair; and Burns had this further advantage, that he neither despaired of a man as he is, nor of his ultimate destiny. How much more respectable human nature appears in our eyes after reading Burns, than after reading Byron! —ELLIOTT, EBENEZER, 1842, *Cowper and Burns, Edinburgh Magazine, vol. 9, p.* 357.

Read Burns: no one ever compressed so much meaning into so few words. Their beautiful rhythm seems their least beauty. —EASTLAKE, LADY, 1843, *Journal, May* 19; *Memoirs, ed. Smith, vol.* I, *p.* 68.

The divine qualities of Burns would have been lost had he been more lettered. . . . What plant is more frail or delicate than genius, and what a combination of circumstances is necessary for its growth? It is not enough this time to have a passionate heart and an ardent imagination. It was necessary that adversity should flourish and hatch the seed, that ignorance should screen the flower of it. And can we help being astonished that this fruit divine should be so rare, and that, like the marvellous tree in Eastern stories, genius should only flourish once in a hundred years! . . . . Burns is of that family of writers whose power reaches the heart: *Pectus est quod facit disertos*. With him there is no literary preoccupation, none of the beauties of the room; he lives in the pure air amid nature. He is not one of those pastoral muses who only visits the country on fine days to recoup themselves after all their luxuriant winter dissipations; courtly muses who only sing of nature in her pleasant garb,

whose forests like those of Virgil, are dignified as a consul; who transfer their armours from the city to bring them back to the shams of a gravelled walk and an artificial river. The muse of Burns is entirely rustic; she dwells in a cottage; rises with the sun; harnesses herself with the cattle; soaks the furrows with her sweat; lives on oatmeal; willingly frequenting the village hostel; speaking more of poppies than of lillies; of pools than of lakes; of wild ducks than of swans; and only taking her loves in the village—perhaps it is for this reason that she is so constant. With such a guide we are far away from the boudoirs of the warm greenhouses, as we inspire the noble air, as we are animated, interested, impassioned in speaking to the heart, as we are conscious of the intimate harmony with those we love, and in whom we live.—WAILLY, LEON DE, 1843, *Poésies Complètes de Robert Burns, traduites de l'Ecossais.*

Burns is by far the greatest poet that ever sprung from the bosom of the people, and lived and died in an humble condition. Indeed, no country in the world but Scotland could have produced such a man; and he will be for ever regarded as the glorious representative of the genius of his country. He was born a poet, if ever man was, and to his native genius alone is owing the perpetuity of his fame. For he manifestly had never very deeply studied poetry as an art, nor reasoned much about its principles, nor looked abroad with the wide ken of intellect for objects and subjects on which to pour out his inspiration. . . . The strings of his lyre sometimes yield their finest music to the sighs of remorse or repentance. Whatever, therefore, be the faults or defects of the poetry of Burns—and no doubt it has many—it has, beyond all that was ever written, this greatest of all merits, intense, life-pervading, and life-breathing truth. . . . No poet ever lived more constantly and more intimately in the hearts of a people. . . . Of all men that ever lived, Burns was the least of a sentimentalist; he was your true Man of Feeling. He did not preach to Christian people the duty of humanity to animals; he spoke of them in winning words warm from a manliest breast, as his fellow-creatures, and made us feel what we owe.—WILSON, JOHN, 1844, *The Genius and Character of Burns, pp.* 1, 3, 4, 118.

And Burns, with pungent passionings
Set in his eyes: deep lyric springs
Are of the fire-mount's issuings.
—BROWNING, ELIZABETH BARRETT, 1844,
A Vision of Poets.

On, exulting in his magic,
    Swept the gifted peasant on—
Though his feet were on the greensward,
    Light from Heaven around him shone;
At his conjuration demons
    Issued from their darkness drear;
Hovering round on silver pinions,
    Angels stoop'd his songs to hear;
Bow'd the Passions to his bidding,
    Terror gaunt, and Pity calm;
Like the organ pour'd his thunder,
    Like the lute his fairy psalm.
Lo! when clover-swathes lay round him,
    Or his feet the furrow press'd,
He could mourn the sever'd daisy,
    Or the mouse's ruined nest;
Woven of gloom and glory, visions
    Haunting throng'd his twilight hour;
Birds enthrall'd him with sweet music,
    Tempests with their tones of power;
Eagle-wing'd, his mounting spirit
    Custom's rusty fetters spurn'd;
Tasso-like, for Jean he melted,
    Wallace-like, for Scotland burn'd!
—MOIR, DAVID MACBETH, 1844, *Stanzas for the Burns Festival.*

In these poems and letters of Burns, we apprehend, is to be found a truer history than any anecdote can supply, of the things which happened to himself, and moreover of the most notable things which went on in Scotland between 1759 and 1796. . . . Consider the terrible contradiction between faith and practice which must have met the eyes of the man, before he could write with the same pen—and one as honestly as the other—"The Cottar's Saturday Night," and "Holy Willie's Prayer." . . . The field in which Burns's influence has been, as was to be expected, most important and most widely felt, is in the poems of working men. He first proved that it was possible to become a poet and a cultivated man, without deserting his class, either in station or in sympathies; nay, that the healthiest and noblest elements of a lowly born poet's mind might be, perhaps certainly must be, the very feelings and thoughts which he brought up with him from below, not those which he received from above, in the course of his artificial culture. From the example of Burns, therefore, many a working man, who would otherwise have "died and given no sign," has taken courage,

and spoken out the thought within him, in verse or prose, not always wisely and well, but in all cases, as it seems to us, in the belief that he had a sort of divine right to speak and be heard, since Burns had broken down the artificial ice-wall of centuries, and asserted, by act as well as song, that "a man's a man for a' that."—KINGSLEY, CHARLES, 1848? *Burns and his School.*

Burns wrote in this class of poetry at no such length as Ramsay; but he was pastoral poetry itself, in the shape of an actual, glorious peasant, vigorous as if Homer had written him, and tender as generous strength, or as memories of the grave. Ramsay and he have helped Scotland for ever to take pride in its heather, and its braes, and its bonny rivers, and be ashamed of no beauty or honest truth, in high estate or in low;—an incalculable blessing. Ramsay, to be sure, with all his genius, and though he wrote an entire and excellent dramatic pastoral, in five legitimate acts, is but a small part of Burns;—is but a field in a corner compared with the whole Scots pastoral region. He has none of Burns's pathos; none of his grandeur; none of his burning energy; none of his craving after universal good. How universal is Burns! What mirth in his cups! What softness in his tears! What sympathy in his very satire! What manhood in everything! If Theocritus, the inventor of a loving and affecting Polyphemus, could have forseen the verses on the "Mouse" and the "Daisy" turned with plough, the "Tam o' Shanter," "O Willie brew'd a peck o' maut," "Ye banks and braes o' bonnie Doon," &c., (not to mention a hundred others, which have less to do with our subject), tears of admiration would have rushed into his eyes.—HUNT, LEIGH, 1848, *A Jar of Honey from Mount Hybla, ch.* viii.

Burns' Songs are better than Bulwer's Epics.—BRONTE, CHARLOTTE, 1849, *Letter to W. S. Williams, April 2; Charlotte Bronte and Her Circle, ed. Shorter, p.* 392.

I have passed the morning in writing to James Stephen, and reading about fifty of Burns's songs, to the merit of which I remain insensible. A happy verse there may be here and there, and even a few good songs; but I have read nothing today which seems worthy to live for twenty years. I have often in the course of my life taken up Burns to see if I would change my mind about him, but my mind won't be changed. He was a man of highly poetic temperament, and some other attributes of genius, but for one reason or another 99 per cent. of what he wrote was worthless, and I think nothing that he wrote was of such excellence as to found a poet's fame. Perhaps if he had written nothing but his best pieces I should think more highly of him, and with less liability to error; but no man's best lies buried under more of worse, worser, and worsest.— TAYLOR, HENRY, 1850, *Letter to his wife, May* 3; *Correspondence, ed. Dowden, p.* 187.

He rose and sang, and Scotland heard;
　The round world echoed with his song,
And hearts in every land were stirred
　With love, and joy, and scorn of wrong.
Some their cold lips disdainful curled,
　Yet the sweet lays would many learn;
But he went singing through the world,
　In most melodious unconcern.
—PARSONS, THOMAS WILLIAM, 1852, *The Birthplace of Robert Burns, Poems, p.* 81.

We must listen, too, while in homely Scots vernacular we are told by an Ayrshire ploughman authentic tidings of living instincts, of spontaneous belief, which not all the philosophy in the brain of the intellectual can banish from the breast of the human being.—CLOUGH, ARTHUR HUGH, 1852, *Development of English Literature, Prose Remains, p.* 350.

There was one writer of the last century, one who wrote satire but who has done higher things,—who has left a name written upon the earth's surface in flowers; one, in all ways, of the greatest men that the literature of Great Britain boasts,—I mean Robert Burns. Burns wrote satire, as the greatest men do, when that was the natural attitude for him. . . . Burns wrote satirical verses, ballads, squibs, and epigrams, as he wrote everything else,— from his heart. He loved, and hated, and prayed, and drank, in obedience to the instincts of a most vivid and genuine nature, and more absolutely than any writer poured out himself. He is as real as a summer afternoon: and his very faults were as natural as poppies among the corn; and because they glare and are staring in color, you must not forget how few and how light they are, compared in bulk and weight with the masses of most beautiful and nutritious grain in the crop. . . . His satire is a piece of himself; and whether he

produced nettles or roses, they were both fresh. . . . I must leave "Holy Willie's Prayer" to anybody's private perusal, who wishes to see irony as exquisite as Swift's,—bitter and brilliant ridicule; and the "Address to the unco Guid" also, full of humor and of heart. I think the best satire he has written, without doubt, to be the "Holy Fair," which has so much comic painting, besides its cutting wit.—HAN-NAY, JAMES, 1854, *Satire and Satirists, pp.* 198, 200, 202.

Through all his tuneful art, how strong
　The human feeling gushes!
The very moonlight of his song
　Is warm with smiles and blushes!
Give lettered pomp to teeth of Time,
　So "Bonnie Doon" but tarry;
Blot out the Epic's stately rhyme,
　But spare his " Highland Mary!"
— WHITTIER, JOHN GREENLEAF, 1856, *Burns, Poetical Works.*

If scant his service at the kirk,
　He *paters* heard and *aves*
From choirs that lurk in hedge and birk,
　From blackbird and from mavis;
The cowering mouse, poor unroofed thing,
　In him found Mercy's angel;
The daisy's ring brought every spring
　To him Love's fresh evangel!
—LOWELL, JAMES RUSSELL, 1859, *At the Burns Centennial, Jan.*

Not Latimer, not Luther struck more telling blows against false theology than did this brave singer. The Confession of Augsburg, the Declaration of Independence, the French Rights of Man, and the *Marseillaise*, are not more weighty documents in the history of freedom than the songs of Burns. His satire has lost none of its edge. His musical arrows yet sing through the air. He is so substantially a reformer that I find his grand plain sense in close chain with the greatest masters—Rabelais, Shakespeare in comedy, Cervantes, Butler and Burns. . . . Yet how true a poet is he! and the poet, too, of poor men, of gray hodden and the guernsey coat, and the blouse. He has given voice to all the experiences of common life; he has endeared the farm-house and cottage, patches and poverty, beans and barley; ale, the poor man's wine; hardship; the fear of debt; the dear society of weans and wife, of brothers and sisters, proud of each other, knowing so few, and finding amends for want and obscurity in books and thoughts. . . . As he was thus the poet of the poor,

anxious, cheerful, working humanity, so
had he the language of low life. He grew
up in a rural district, speaking a *patois*
unintelligible to all but natives, and he
has made the Lowland Scotch a Doric
dialect of fame. It is the only example
in history of a language made classic by
the genius of a single man.—EMERSON,
RALPH WALDO, 1859, *Address at the
Burns Centenary, Boston, Jan.* 25.

We love him, not for sweetest song,
  Though never tone so tender;
We love him, even in his wrong,—
  His wasteful self-surrender.
We praise him, not for gifts divine,—
  His Muse was born of woman,—
His manhood breathes in every line,—
  Was ever heart more human?
We love him, praise him, just for this:
  In every form and feature,
Through wealth and want, through woe and
    bliss,
  He saw his fellow-creature! .   .   .
The waning suns, the wasting globe,
  Shall spare the minstrel's story,—
The centuries weave his purple robe,
  The mountain-mist of glory!
—HOLMES, OLIVER WENDELL, 1859, *For
the Burns Centennial Celebration, Jan.* 25.

All hail! immortal Robin, hail!
  Thy natal day again returns,
And here the gather'd clans are met
  To crown their Poet—Burns!
A crowded century has pass'd,
  Auld Scotia, a repentant dame,
Kneels at her ploughboy's feet and gives
  A hundred years of fame.
How dear to her his memory now—
  See to his grave how pilgrims wend;
Dear are his haunts, the fields he ploughed
  And every line he penn'd.
Rare bards have borne across the deep
  The wild rose pluck'd from Alloway's aisle,
Sprays from the birks of Ellisland
  And braes o' Ballochmyle.
—LATTO, THOMAS C., 1859, *The Poet's
Jubilee, Jan.* 25.

. . . He learned the touch that speeds
  Right to the natural heart of things;
Struck rootage down to where Life feeds
  At the eternal Springs: . . .
He caught them, Witch and Warlock, ere
  They vanished; all the revelry
Of wizard wonder, we must wear
  The mask of Sleep to see!
Droll Humours came for him to paint
  Their pictures; straight his merry eye
Had taken them, so queer, so quaint,
  We laugh until we cry. . . .
He knew the Sorrows of poor folk,
  He felt for all their patient pain;

And from his clouded soul he shook
  Lark-like the music-rain . . .
Auld Scotland's Music waited long,
  And wandered wailing through the land,
Divinely yearning in her wrong,
  And sorrowfully grand;
And many touched responsive chords,
  But could not tell what She would say;
Till Robin wed her with his words,
  And they were One for aye . . .
. . . now we recognize in him,
  One of the high and shining race;
All gone the mortal mists that dim
  The fair immortal face.
—MASSEY, GERALD, 1859, *Robert Burns.*

To nature's feast,—
  Who knew the noblest guest
  And entertained him best,—
Kingly he came. Her chambers of the east
  She draped with crimson and with gold,
And poured her pure joy-wines
  For him the poet-souled.
For him her anthem rolled,
From the storm-wind among the winter
    pines,
  Down to the slenderest note
Of a love-warble from the linnet's throat.
—KNOX, ISA CRAIG, 1859, *Ode on the
Centenary of Burns.*

The most serious and profound Scotchmen of later days have hailed the appearance of the Ayrshire ploughman poet as an
element of wholesome human reality
brought into the midst of an atmosphere
thick and heavy with notions and book
lore. They say that his songs brought back
to them the belief in green fields and hills,
as well as the fact of their belonging to
a land on which their fathers had dwelt
and suffered before them; and that his life
showed them there is need, in the heart of
every peasant, of a hope to raise him and
protect him against himself, as well as
against his rich patrons, which neither the
divinity nor the philosophy of Scotland at
that time afforded; which was not offered
by old light formalism or new light experiences; which was not found necessary
by the polite circles that Hume frequented,
and which only glimmered faintly through
the consciousness and common sense of
Reid; but of which Burns could see the
pledge and the promise in the domestic
life of his sires, and in the testimony they
bore to a Father whose righteousness the
earthly father was feebly to exhibit in his
own. — MAURICE, FREDERICK DENISON,
1862, *Moral and Metaphysical Philosophy,
vol.* II, *p.* 586.

In his own day the Ballad singer on the

street, chanting the last new Ballad, sought for guerdon and applause by announcing it as a new song by Rabbie Burns; and when the grave had closed over his remains, every scrap written in his noble, manly hand-writing, however unworthy, — and many a Poem and Song, because expressed in the rough quaint Doric, were claimed as his, and forthwith thrown from the press.—M'KIE, JAMES, 1869, *ed., Poems Chiefly in the Scottish Dialect by Robert Burns, Preface, vol.* II, *p.* vi.

Many of those who sit at this table have doubtless heard the report of a cannon discharged among the Highlands that overlook the Hudson, our own "exulting and abounding river." The sound has scarcely left the cannon's mouth before it is re-echoed by one of the majestic mountains— Dunderberg, perhaps—on whose summit the clouds rest and the lightnings are born. Crow Nest rolls it back from his dark precipices and ancient forests. Then some headland more remote receives it, and from its cliffs flings it back to the listener. The sound travels swiftly on, and a response comes from height after height, until it passes away among the hills and shores which lie beyond the sight. . . . So the reverberation is likely to go on from generation to generation, an involuntary tribute of admiration from the world of letters to the genius of Burns.—BRYANT, WILLIAM CULLEN, 1870, *Address at Celebration of the* 111th *Anniversary of Robert Burns' Natal Day.*

Of all the poets, larger and less, not one has been so true to his own thought; so faithful to the sight of his eye, to the sound in his ear, to the emotion of his heart! "A touch of nature makes the whole world kin"—and so it is that Burns is the accredited oracle of the human soul, not only where the Scottish dialect—that beautiful modern Doric—is spoken and best appreciated, but in all lands where men employ our capable English tongue. The memory of Burns! Ah! the *poetry* of Burns has taken care of that, for all time to come! It beams like an *aureole* over every hallowed spot where he suffered and sung; it breathes on the "Banks and Braes of Bonny Doon;" it is renewed with each returning Spring in his own "Mountain Daisy;" it lives in the immortal life of "Mary in Heaven!" So long as love is precious, and bereavement sacred, and

hypocrisy hateful, and pretension ridiculous, and labor honorable, and true manhood noble—so long as poetry, simple, natural, eloquent, is the delight of mankind, alike in the halls of the opulent and by "wee bit ingle bluikies' family," so long shall the memory of Burns endure!— SAXE, JOHN G., 1870, *Address at Celebration of the* 111th *Anniversary of Robert Burns' Natal Day.*

Burns cries out in favour of instinct and joy, so as to seem epicurean. He has genuine gaiety, comic energy; laughter commends itself to him; he praises it and the good suppers of good comrades, where the wine flows, pleasantry abounds, ideas pour forth, poetry sparkles, and causes a carnival of beautiful figures and good-humoured people to move about in the human brain. . . . That, indeed, was natural poetry; not forced in a hothouse, but born of the soil between the furrows, side by side with music, amidst the gloom and beauty of the climate, like the violet gorse of the hillside and woods. We can understand that it gave vigour to his tongue: for the first time this man spoke as men speak, or rather as they think, without premeditation, with a mixture of all styles, familiar and terrible, hiding an emotion under a joke, tender and jeering in the same place, apt to combine taproom trivialities with the high language of poetry, so indifferent was he to rules, content to exhibit his feeling as it came to him, and as he felt it. At last, after so many years, we escape from the measured declamation, we hear a man's voice! much better, we forget the voice in the emotion which it expresses, we feel this motion reflected in ourselves, we enter into relations with a soul. Then form seems to fade away and disappear: I will say that this is the great future of modern poetry; Burns has reached it seven or eight times. —TAINE, H. A., 1871, *History of English Literature, tr. Van Laun, vol.* II, *bk.* iv, *ch.* i, *pp.* 237, 239.

O Burns! where bid? where bide you now?
Where are you in this night's full noon,
Great master of the pen and plough?
Might you not on yon slanting beam
Of moonlight, kneeling to the Doon,
Descend once to this hallow'd stream?
Sure yon stars yield enough of light
For heaven to spare your face one night.
O Burns! another name for song,
Another name for passion—pride;

For love and poesy allied;
For strangely blended right and wrong.
I picture you as one who kneel'd
A stranger at his own hearthstone;
One knowing all, yet all unknown,
One seeing all, yet all conceal'd;
The fitful years you linger'd here,
A lease of peril and of pain;
And I am thankful yet again
The gods did love you, ploughman! peer!
—MILLER, JOAQUIN, 1871, *Songs of the Sierras, p.* 259.

About the time you were writing to me about Burns and Béranger, I was thinking of them "which was the Greater Genius?" —I can't say; but, with all my Admiration for about a Score of the Frenchman's almost perfect Songs, I would give all of them up for a Score of Burns' Couplets, Stanzas, or single Lines scattered among those quite *im*perfect Lyrics of his. Béranger, no doubt, was The *Artist;* which still is not the highest Genius—witness Shakespeare, Dante, Æschylus, Calderon, to the contrary. Burns assuredly had more Passion than the Frenchman; which is not Genius either, but a great Part of the Lyric Poet still. What Béranger might have been, if born and bred among Banks, Braes, and Mountains, I cannot tell: Burns had that advantage over him. And then the Highland Mary to love, amid the heather, as compared to Lise the Grisette in a Parisian Suburb! Some of the old French Virelays and *Vaudevires* come much nearer the Wild Notes of Burns, and go to one's heart like his; Béranger never gets so far as that I think.—FITZGERALD, EDWARD, 1873, *Letters to Fanny Kemble, ed. Wright, p.* 18.

Neither Pope with his smooth verses, nor Lord Bolingbroke with his sceptical wit, nor Dr. Johnson amid his worshippers, gave forth the first truly original note which announced a new phase in the poetry of Great Britain: from the banks of the Doon, out of a cottage in Scotland, rose the wood-lark who uttered it.— SCHERR, J., 1874, *A History of English Literature, tr. M. V., p.* 177.

In Part II. are social and drinking songs, with which latter Scotland is abundantly supplied. In this province, too, Burns has lavishly poured out his splendid genius, with a strange fatality, singing the praises of the Syren that lured him to his own ruin.—AITKEN, MARY CARLYLE, 1874, *ed., Scottish Song, Preface, p.* vii.

As a lyric poet Burns deserves the name of great. In the most essential qualities of this form of verse; in fire, tenderness and naturalness, none have surpassed him. . . . Though Burns stands at the entrance of the new period, none of the great poets that followed surpassed him in individuality of faculties, a freedom which yet left him in full mastery of a varied and most melodious verse.—BASCOM, JOHN, 1874, *Philosophy of English Literature, pp.* 221, 222.

In a company of German critics who were weighing the claims and estimating the rank of the poets, their contemporaries, the leader of their chorus, the genial humorist, Jean Paul Richter, is said to have hushed his audience when the name of Goethe was introduced, exclaiming— "We are not to sit in judgment on that sacred head." Scotsmen are apt to attach the same half superstitious reverence to the name which is, more than any other, that of Scotland condensed in a personality, the representative of what is noblest and also of much that is erring in their race. . . . The affectations of his style are insignificant and rare. His prevailing characteristic is an absolute sincerity. A love for the lower forms of social life was his besetting sin; Nature was his healing power. Burns compares himself to an Æolian harp, strung to every wind of heaven. His genius flows over all living and lifeless things with a sympathy that finds nothing mean or insignificant.—NICOL, JOHN, 1875, *Encyclopædia Britannica, vol.* II.

Three things may be noted as to the influnce of Burns on men's feeling for Nature. First, he was a more entirely open-air poet than any first-rate singer who had yet lived, and as such he dealt with Nature in a more free, close, intimate way than any English poet since the old ballad-singers. He did more to bring the hearts of men close to the outer world, and the outer world to the heart, than any former poet. His keen eye looked directly, with no intervening medium, on the face alike of Nature and of man, and embraced all creation in one large sympathy. With familiar tenderness he dwelt on the lower creatures, felt for their sufferings, as if they had been his own, and opened men's hearts to feel how much the groans of creation are needlessly increased by the indifference or cruelty of man. In Burns, as in Cowper, and in him perhaps more than in Cowper, there was a large going forth of tenderness to the lower creatures, and in their poetry this first found utterance, and in no poet since their time, so fully as in these two. Secondly, his feeling in Nature's presence was not, as in the English poets of his time, a quiet contemplative pleasure. It was nothing short of rapture. Other more modern poets may have been thrilled with the same delight, he alone of all in last century expressed the thrill. In this, as in other things, he is the truest herald of that strain of rejoicing in Nature, even to ecstasy, which has formed one of the finest tones in the poetry of this century. Thirdly, he does not philosophize on Nature or her relation to man; he feels it, alike in his joyful moods and in his sorrowful. It is to him part of what he calls "the universal plan," but he nowhere reasons about the life of Nature as he often does so trenchantly about that of man.—SHAIRP, JOHN CAMPBELL, 1877, *On Poetic Interpretation of Nature, p.* 229.

The vigorous and beautiful poetry which Burns thus produced gave men a new standard of criticism. The decasyllabic metre, which Pope had made fashionable, was at once discarded, and most of the great writers of the period adopted either original or other styles. — WALPOLE, SPENCER, 1878, *A History of England from the Conclusion of the Great War in* 1815, *vol.* I, *p.* 348.

Burns, like Chaucer, comes short of a high seriousness of the great classics, and the virtue of matter and manner which goes with that high seriousness is wanting to his work. . . . We arrive best at the real estimate of Burns, I think, by conceiving his work as having truth of matter and truth of manner, but not the accent or the poetic virtue of the highest masters. . . . The freedom of Chaucer is heightened, in Burns, by a fiery, reckless energy; the benignity of Chaucer deepens, in Burns, into an overwhelming sense of the pathos of things;—of the pathos of human nature, the pathos, also, of non-human nature. Instead of the fluidity of Chaucer's manner, the manner of Burns has spring, bounding swiftness. Burns is by far the greater force, though he has perhaps less charm. The world of Chaucer

is fairer, richer, more significant than that of Burns; but when the largeness and freedom of Burns get full sweep, as in "Tam o' Shanter," or still more in that puissant and splendid production, "The Jolly Beggars," his world may be what it will, his poetic genius triumphs over it.—ARNOLD, MATTHEW, 1880, *English Poets, ed. Ward, Introduction, vol.* I, *pp.* xliv, xlv.

Touched by his hand, the wayside weed
Becomes a flower; the lowliest reed
　　Beside the stream
Is clothed with beauty; gorse and grass
And heather, where his footsteps pass,
　　The brighter seem.
He sings of love, whose flame illumes
The darkness of lone cottage rooms;
　　He feels the force,
The treacherous undertow and stress,
Of wayward passions, and no less
　　The keen remorse.
At moments, wrestling with his fate,
His voice is harsh, but not with hate;
　　The brush-wood, hung
Above the tavern door, lets fall
Its bitter leaf, its drop of gall,
　　Upon his tongue.
But still the music of his song
Rises o'er all, elate and strong;
　　Its master-chords
Are Manhood, Freedom, Brotherhood,
Its discords but an interlude
　　Between the words.

—LONGFELLOW, HENRY W., 1880, *Robert Burns, Harper's Magazine, vol.* 61, *p.* 322; *Ultima Thule.*

Burns' poetry shares with all poetry of the first order of excellence the life and movement not of one age but of all ages, that which belongs to what Wordsworth calls "the essential passions" of human nature. It is the voice of nature which we hear in his poetry, and it is of that nature one touch of which makes the whole world kin. It is doubtful whether any poet, ancient or modern, has evoked as much personal attachment of a fervid and perfervid quality as Burns has been able to draw to himself. It is an attachment the amount and the quality of which are not to be explained by anything in the history of the man, anything apart from the exercise of his genius as a poet. His misfortunes, though they were great, do not account for it—these are cancelled by his faults, from which his misfortunes are not easily separated. What renders it at all intelligible is that human nature, in its most ordinary shapes, is more poetical than it looks, and that exactly at those moments of its consciousness in which it is most truly because most vividly and powerfully and poetically itself, Burns has a voice to give to it.—SERVICE, JOHN, 1880, *English Poets, ed. Ward, vol.* III, *p.* 515.

In no respect do the poems of Wordsworth more strongly contrast with those of Burns than in what I would call, with strict meaning, historical value. The first book of Homer's "Iliad" makes the life of old heroic Greece visible to us. We see it and know it in a sense in which no mere statistical information could place it before us. In this sense Burns is the Scottish historian of his day and generation. His Tam o' Shanter, his Duncan Gray, his Doctor Hornbrook, his lads and lasses frolicking at Halloween, his peasant opening the Bible and reverently reading it to his household in the evening, are as true to the Ayrshire of his time as the weeping Achilles and his divine mother, the mourning Priam and his dead Hector, are to that old Homeric world; and the same ring and shout of human laughter makes ancient and modern kin, when the preternatural potent of Halloween turns out to be "grumphy, asteer that night," and when Ajax, clearing from mouth and nostril the mud into which he had flopped, complains that he had been tripped up in the race by Pallas, and the surrounding Achaians "laugh sweetly" at the notion. Now Wordsworth's poems, as compared with those of Keats and Shelley, are racy of the soil. There is a good deal of Cumberland in them. But, compared with those of Burns, they are outside Cumberland life.—BAYNE, PETER, 1881, *Essay on Poetry, Two Great Englishwomen, p.* lxii.

His humour comes from him in a stream so deep and easy that I will venture to call him the best of humourous poets.—STEVENSON, ROBERT LOUIS, 1882, *Some Aspects of Robert Burns, Familiar Studies of Men and Books p.* 85.

We praised the "Lass o' Ballochmyle,"
We talked of Mary, loved and lost,
Until our spirits touched and crossed,
And melted into tears, the while;
We drank to "Nell," and "Bonnie Jean,"
To "Chloris," and the "Banks o' Cree"—
Blest hour!—I keep its mem'ry green,
The night you quoted Burns to me.
—MATTHEWS, JAMES NEWTON, 1883, *The Night you Quoted Burns to Me.*

He was the final product of a long-continued tendency in one direction, and not a miraculous phenomenon.—PERRY, THOMAS SERGEANT, 1883, *English Literature in the Eighteenth Century, p.* 431.

He found his idea, not in the remote and conventional, but in the familiar and near-at-hand; and, without rant or trick, with genuine feeling, gave it articulate voice— a voice not from the university, but from the heart of Nature. Thus we may understand why no poetry was ever more instantaneously and more widely popular; why in the rural circle he was a delight and an admiration, and in cultured Edinburgh a phenomenon. . . . A playmate to Nature and to Man.—WELSH, ALFRED H., 1883, *Development of English Literature and Language, vol.* II, *pp.* 235, 237.

We saw again the plowman lad,
As by the banks of Ayr he wandered,
With burning eyes and eager heart,
And first on Song and Scotland pondered;
We saw him, as from Nature's soul
His own drew draughts of joy o'erflowing:
The plower's voice, the brier-rose,
The tiny harebell lightly growing,
The wounded hare that passed him by,
The timorous mousie's ruined dwelling,
The cattle cowering from the blast,
The dying sheep her sorrows telling,—
All touched the heart that kept so strong
Its sympathy with humbler being,
And saw in simplest things of life
The poetry that waits the seeing!
—MACHAR, AGNES MAULE, 1884, *An Evening with Burns, The Century, vol.* 27, *p.* 479.

Criticism of Burns is only permitted to Scotchmen of pure blood. Admirable appreciations may be found in the essays of Carlyle and Nichol. Yet it may be said that, if there are more elegant and subtle song-writers in the language, no one even approaches Burns in masculine strength or concentrated utterance of passion. Though all his writings are occasional, he reflects every mood of the national character, its tenderness, its sensuous vigour, and its patriotic fervour. Like Byron, he always wrote at a white heat, but, unlike Byron, he had the highest lyrical power, and, if he sometimes fails, he does not fail by excessive dilution. He is only insipid when he tries to adopt the conventional English of his time, in obedience to foolish advice from Dr. Moore and others.—STEPHEN, LESLIE, 1886, *Dictionary of National Biography, vol.* VII.

A quiet life of song, *fallentis semita vitæ*, was not to be yours. Fate otherwise decreed it. The touch of a lettered society, the strife with the Kirk, discontent with the State, poverty and pride, neglect and success, were needed to make your Genius what it was, and to endow the world with "Tam o' Shanter," the "Jolly Beggars," and "Holy Willie's Prayer." Who can praise them too highly—who admire in them too much the humour, the scorn, the wisdom, the unsurpassed energy and courage?—LANG, ANDREW, 1886, *Letters to Dead Authors, p.* 202.

Dear Rob! Manly, witty, fond, friendly, full of weak spots as well as strong ones— essential type of so many thousands— perhaps the average, as just said, of the decent-born young men and the early mid-aged, not only of the British Isles, but America, too, North and South, just the same. I think, indeed, one best part of Burns is the unquestionable proof he presents of the perennial existence among the laboring classes, especially farmers, of the finest latent poetic elements in their blood. (How clear it is to me that the common soil has always been, and is now, thickly strewn with just such gems.) He is well called the *Ploughman.* . . . There is something about Burns peculiarly acceptable to the concrete, human points of view. He poetizes work-a-day agricultural labor and life (whose spirit and sympathies, as well as practicalities, are much the same everywhere), and treats fresh, often coarse, natural occurrences, loves, persons, not like many new and some old poets in a genteel style of gilt and china, or at second or third removes, but in their own born atmosphere, laughter, sweat, unction. Perhaps no one ever sang "lads and lassies"—that universal race, mainly the same, too, all ages, all lands—down on their own plane, as he has. He exhibits no philosophy worth mentioning; his morality is hardly more than parrot-talk—not bad or deficient, but cheap, shopworn, the platitudes of old aunts and uncles to the youngsters (be good boys and keep your noses clean.) Only when he gets at Poosie Nansie's, celebrating the "barley bree," or among tramps, or democratic bouts and drinking generally, ("Freedom and whiskey gang thegither,") we have, in his own unmistakable color and warmth, those interiors of rake-helly

life and tavern fun—the cantabile of jolly beggars in highest jinks—lights and groupings of rank glee and brawny amorousness, outvying the best painted pictures of the Dutch school, or any school. . . . Never indeed was there truer utterance in a certain range of idiosyncrasy than by this poet. Hardly a piece of his, large or small, but has "snap" and raciness. . . . Finally, in any summing-up of Burns, though so much is to be said in the way of fault-finding, drawing black marks, and doubtless severe literary criticism—(in the present outpouring I have "kept myself in," rather than allow'd any free flow)—after full retrospect of his work and life, the aforesaid "odd-kind chiel" remains to my heart and brain as almost the tenderest, manliest, and (even if contradictory) dearest flesh-and-blood figure in all the streams and clusters of by-gone poets.—WHITMAN, WALT, 1886-88, *Robert Burns as Poet and Person, November Boughs, pp.* 59, 60, 63, 64.

The books that have *most* influenced me are inaccessible to the general reader, Horace, Pindar, and Dante, for instance; but these following are good for everybody:—Scott's "Lady of the Lake" and "Marmion" (the "Lady" first for *me*, though not for Scott). Pope's "Homer's Iliad" Byron, all, but most "Corsair," "Bride of Abydos," and the "Two Foscari." Coleridge and Keats, in my youth. Burns, as I grew older and wiser.—RUSKIN, JOHN, 1887, *Books which Have Influenced Me, p.* 43.

It has always been a mystery to me why Walter Scott stands so low in the estimation of the present race of Scotsmen all over the world, and why Robert Burns, a greatly inferior genius, stands so high. Is it because the majority of the Scotch people are so ultra-democratic that they cannot forgive Scott for being an aristocrat; and that they almost worship Burns because he was born and nurtured and died in poverty, because he was an ultra-plebeian, earning his scanty and precarious bread by the sweat of his brow? Or do the multitude, in all countries, love their heroes all the more because of their conspicuous human frailties, and have nothing but cold respect for the great men who are only virtuous and respectable? —MACKAY, CHARLES, 1887, *Through the Long Day, vol.* I, *p.* 147.

But more than all fond memory turns
And rests on Ayr, the home of Burns.
For there the "Daisy" was uptorn,
　To blossom on a wider field;
And there the "Mousie," kindred born,
　Was first to poesie revealed.
The land of "Auld Lang Syne" is there,
The cotter's home, the evening prayer:
To these, in truth, the memory turns—
To these, which make the Land of Burns.

. . . .

It seemed his mission to bestow
　On humble things the highest worth;
The streams that by his "shieling" flow
Ripple in song o'er all the earth.
The little Kirk of Alloway
Shines forth immortal in his lay,
And, filled with witches, takes its stand,
The ruin of his storied land.

. . . .

His "Scots wha hae" rings out more clear
　Than any song in field or camp;
And others rise more true and dear—
　"The rank is but the guinea-stamp."
For there are grander fields to fight,
Where man proclaims his brother's right;
And Burns of poets leads the van
In simple truth—that man is man.
—BRUCE, WALLACE, 1887, *The Land of
Burns, Old Homestead Poems, pp.* 100,
101, 103.

It is not chiefly the romantic side of the
Scotch character which was represented
to Burns—its imagination, its patriotism,
its zealous affectionateness, its love of the
legendary, the marvelous and the ancient,
that part, in fact, which belongs most to the
highlands; he was more amply furnished
with the stronger lowland qualities, sense,
independence, courageous perseverance,
shrewdness, and humour, a retentive heart,
and a mind truthful alike when fully expressed or when partially reserved. These
qualities were united in his abundant
nature; and his poetic temperament freed
them from the limitations which belonged
to every character formed upon a local
type. The consequence is that his songs
are sung at the hearth and on the moun-
tain-side; his pathos is felt and his humour
applauded by the village circle; his sharp
descriptions and shrewd questions on grave
matters are treated as indulgently by
ministers of the "National Assembly,"
the "Free Kirk," and "orthodox dissenters," as Boccaccio's stories once were
by the Italian clergy; and for the lonely
traveller from the South the one small
volume which contains his works is the
best of guide-books, not indeed to noted
spots, legendary or famed for beauty,—
but to the manners, the moral soul, and
the heart of the Scotch people. Burns is
emphatically the most national of poets.
—DE VERE, AUBREY, 1887, *Essays Chiefly
on Poetry, vol.* II, *p.* 121.

Those who hold that poetry should move
in a realm apart from the actual world
find little to enchant or interest them in
Burns, for it was with the actual world
alone that he sought to deal. The sphere
of his observation was narrow in comparison with that of most great poets.
The only class he knew thoroughly were
the Scottish peasantry, a class born to a
life of labour and anxiety, with few excitements to break the monotony of their toil.
Burns had no wish to transform them into
idyllic figures; he was content to take
them as they were, and in their simple
lives he found all the experiences which,
when touched by imagination, move mankind to laughter or to tears.—SIME,
JAMES, 1887, *Robert Burns, English Illustrated Magazine, vol.* 4, *p.* 339.

The Voice of a wondrous Seer!
　The voice of a soul that is strong!
As true as Love, and as swift as Fear
　In the mazes of marvellous song.
Far over the mountains bare,
　Red heather, and ridges of sea,
It flows in the pulse of the living air,
　And throbs in the veins of the free.
It whispers in Summer's breath,
　It lisps on the creamy shore,
It sings in the lips that smile at death,
　In the storm and cataract's roar.
It murmurs in brae and birk,
　It pleads in the daisy's eye,
Where hands are toughened by honest work,
　And bairns in their cradles lie;
In cottage, in kirk, and bower,
　In hall, in court, and in mart,
In the chirp of the mavis, and hawthorn
　　flower,
　And the maiden's simple heart.
It croons in the blaze of the inn,
　Where the droughty neighbors bide,
It shrieks in the ghastly glare and din,
　Where the witches dance and ride.
Its mirth is a tempest of glee,
　Its grief is the smart of fire,
Its solemn strain is the trump of the sea,
　Its chorus the world's desire!
I listen, and brooklet and wold,
　Wild bird and the darkling wood
And breathing secrets before untold
　Of the perfect and passionless Good.
—POWERS, HORATIO NELSON, 1887, *Ten
Years of Song.*

The one immortal bard of humanity.
—RUSSELL, A. P., 1888, *A Club of One*,
p. 150.

To-night amid Canadian snows,
  In lordly hall and cottage home,
Where'er the blood of Scotsmen flows,
  Where'er the feet of Scotsmen roam;
ONE name upon the lips grows sweet,
  More rich than wine from purple urns,
With thrill electric flashing fleet,
  The name of ROBERT BURNS.
— MACFARLAND, JOHN, 1888, *Robert
Burns, Jan.* 25.

The love poetry of Burns affords an
abundant exemplification of nearly all the
known devices peculiar to the theme.
Consisting of short effusions, mainly songs,
it almost entirely excludes plot-interest;
occasionally there is a slight use of narrative, as in "The Soldier's Return" and
"There was a lass and she was fair." In
regard to description of the object of love,
Burns usually depends on a few unsystem-
atic touches, expressive of the emotion
excited. Sometimes, however, he does
enter on a regular enumeration of the
qualities that charm; but his method even
then is rather to elevate the object by
comparisons, both figurative and literal,
than to give any distinct impression of the
personal appearance.—BAIN, ALEXANDER,
1888, *English Composition and Rhetoric,
Part Second*, p. 157.

In respect of genius, I think it is now
universally admitted that our Ayrshire
bard has gained for himself, by the number,
the variety, and the brilliancy of his productions, a place in the first rank of the
great singers of the intellectual world,—
Pindar, Chaucer, Horace, Hafiz, Goethe,
Béranger, Moore, and if there be any others
who enjoy an equally wide recognition.
. . . If ever there was a song-writer
who could say with the most catholic comprehensiveness in the words of the old
comedian, "*I am a man, and all things
human are kin to me,*" it was Robert Burns.
In this respect he is the Shakespeare of
lyric poetry. . . . If inferior to Coleridge in ideal speculation, to Wordsworth
in harmonious contemplation, and to
Southey in book-learning, in all that concerns living men and human life and human
society he was extremely sharp-sighted
and not only wise in penetrating to the
inmost springs of human thought and sentiment, but in the judgment of conduct
eminently shrewd and sagacious; gifted,

in the highest degree, with that fundamental virtue of all sound Scotsmen,
common-sense, without which great genius
in full career is apt to lead a man astray
from his surroundings, and make him most
a stranger to that with which in common
life he ought to be most familiar.—
BLACKIE, JOHN STUART, 1888, *Life of
Robert Burns* (*Great Writers*), pp. 157,160.

[Song] drooped and fell, and one 'neath north-
  ern skies,
With southern heart, who tilled his father's
  field,
Found Poesy a-dying, bade her rise
  And touch quick nature's hem and go
    forth healed.
On life's broad plain the ploughman's con-
  quering share
Upturned the fallow lands of truth anew,
And o'er the formal garden's trim parterre
  The peasant's team a ruthless furrow drew.
—WATSON, WILLIAM, 1890, *Wordsworth's
Grave.*

To Burns the very air was charged with
poetry, and his heart responded to every
appeal made to his imagination. He saw
Nature with a clear and penetrating vision;
his emotions and experiences were blended
with the world about him, and in a single
line a whole landscape flashes into view.
Burns spoke of Nature without a touch
of self-consciousness and with the intimacy
of one born to the soil: he loved with
infinite tenderness every living thing that
made its home in the fields. His early
familiarity with field and sky, the solitude
that came with that intercourse, the sensitiveness of his imagination, and the passion
of his nature gave his poetry a thrill and
rapture born only of the deepest emotion.
The commonest wild-flower, in the verse of
this passionate singer, has its roots beside
the fountain of tears, and not a leaf stirs
or falls but its image is caught in the
tumultuous sweep and current of life.—
MABIE, HAMILTON WRIGHT, 1891-93, *Short
Studies in Literature*, p. 101.

It is for his service to Scotland in the
matter of songs that we specially delight
to honour him. It was he, more than all
else put together, who made Scottish song
the glorious thing that it is. Prior to
Burns's appearance on the stage of human
existence what was the condition, Sir, of
our national minstrelsy? We had a popular song-book polluted on every page.
Such of the popular songs of the time—if
you except a dozen or so, "The Flower o'

the Forest," "Auld Robin Gray," "Nae
luck about the hoose," "Logie o' Buchan," "Johnnie Cope," "Maggie Lau-
der," and "Down the burn, Davie," and
one or two more—such of them, I say, with
these few exceptions, as were not tainted
with vulgarity and vile innuendo, were
the most puerile and feckless doggerel.
Burns set himself to purify these old songs,
and gave us a song-book which is like a
human psalter by comparison. It is when
we take up Ramsay's "Evergreen" and
the "Tea-Table Miscellany," or Herd's
collection of old songs and ballads, and
look at the original of "Dainty Davie,"
"She rose and loot me in," and "John
Anderson my jo," and some more that we
discover the noble—the God's work—
which he performed. It is for the purifi-
cation of these old songs, and for the
hundred and more original gems which he
added to our song-book, that we regard
Robert Burns as a gift from the gods.
It is for this that we can overlook so many
of his faults and failings. It is for this
that we delight to honour his memory—
for this we are "a' sae prood o' Robin."
—FORD, ROBERT, 1893, *Address Delivered
Before the Barlinnie Burns Club, Jan.* 25;
Burnsiana, vol. IV, *p.* 87.

And the natural greatness of mind that
prompted this ambition was not without
special influences to keep the flame alive.
Had Burns been educated as other local
rhymers were, he might have remained,
like them, content with local fame, ignorant of the great world outside, hungering
for no applause beyond his own small
circle, because he was unaware of anything
more to be desired. But the education of
Burns was different from that of other
local rhymers, and had carried him to
spiritual altitudes, the views from which
were bounded by a much wider horizon.
In common with all the other young men
of the time, rich and poor, Burns had the
advantage for a poet of living in a poetical
atmosphere; but he had the further special
advantage of coming under personal influences that helped powerfully to give his
work the quality of greatness.—MINTO,
WILLIAM, 1894, *The Literature of the
Georgian Era, ed. Knight, p.* 160.

The collective poems of Robert Burns
have been reprinted on a great number
of occasions, and in every variety of form.
It is calculated that by the end of 1816

no less than 22 editions had appeared in
London, 19 in Edinburgh, 16 in the United
States, 4 in Dublin, 4 in Belfast, 3 in
Glasgow, 2 in Berwick-upon-Tweed, 1 at
Kilmarnock, 1 at Paisley, and 9 in other
towns scattered about England and Scotland. The original edition appeared at
Kilmarnock in 1786, and for eighty-four
years from that date, say up to 1870,
only two years are recorded (1791 and
1795), in which at least one edition of
Burns' works was not published. This
record of continuous publication is only
surpassed in the case of three other books,
viz., the Bible, the works of Shakespeare,
and the "De Imitatione Christi." . . .
The most extensive collection of Burnsiana
in existence is probably that in the
museum at Kay Park, Kilmarnock. It consists of nearly 1000 volumes, a large proportion of which comprise various editions
of the poet's works published in the United
Kingdom, and the remainder of books
touching on his life or writing or the
scenes with which he was associated.
. . . In March, 1888, at the sale of
the second portion of the extensive library
of the late Mr. Gibson-Craig, a good copy
of the Kilmarnock edition of "Poems
chiefly in the Scottish Dialect," sold for
£111, and on another occasion a rebound
copy brought £86.—SLATER, J. H., 1894,
Early Editions, pp. 56, 57, 58.

Not his the light of Shakespeare's line,
  Nor Milton's massive splendour;
But Scotland rich in Auld Langsyne
  Needs naething mair to mend her.
And while a "Daisy" decks the soil,
  And while a wrang needs rightin',
The rough, strong-hearted sons of toil,
  Shall still his songs delight in.
—MURDOCH, ALEXANDER G., 1894, *Rhymin'
Robin, Burnsiana, vol.* IV, *p.* 24.

It has been the common responsibility
of his biographers to point out how differently he might have lived, how much more
wisely he might have ordered his days.
More wisely, perhaps, but not so well.
There is a diviner economy in these things
than we have come to allow.— RHYS,
ERNEST, 1895, *ed., The Lyrical Poems of
Burns.*

There is perhaps only one poet of real
power who ever has been in modern
times popular,—Robert Burns.—WALKER,
HENRY L., 1895, *The Greater Victorian
Poets, p.* 47.

John Barleycorn
Prepared his sweetest rose and sharpest
     thorn;
The witches set their heads and hoofs to
     work,
To hunt O'Shanter from the ancient kirk;
The hills began to put themselves in tune
To voice the care that lurked in "Bonnie
     Doon;"
The world would soon a world of love en-
     shrine
Within the golden bars of "Auld Lang Syne;"
The cotter's home produced its greatest grief,
But fame and glory, far beyond belief—
          When Burns was born!
—CARLETON, WILL, 1895, *Rhymes of our
Planet, p.* 32.

All the same, this disability weighs me
down with a sense of hopeless obtuseness
when I consider the deportment of the
average intelligent Scot at a Burns banquet, or a Burns *conversazione*, or a Burns
festival, or the unveiling of a Burns statue,
or the putting up of a pillar on some spot
made famous by Burns. All over the
world—and all under it, too, when their
time comes—Scotsmen are preparing
after-dinner speeches about Burns. The
great globe swings round out of the sun
into the dark; there is always midnight
somewhere; and always in this shifting
region the eye of imagination sees orators
gesticulating over Burns; companies of
heated exiles with crossed arms shouting
"Auld Lang Syne;" lesser groups—if
haply they be lesser—reposing under
tables, still in honour of Burns. And as the
vast continents sweep "eastering out of
the high shadow which reaches beyond the
moon," and as new nations, with *their*
cities and villages, their mountains and
seashores, rise up on the morning-side,
lo! fresh troops, and still fresh troops,
and yet again fresh troops, wend or are
carried out of action with the dawn.
None but a churl would wish this enthusiasm abated. But why is it all lavished
on Burns? That is what gravels the
Southron. Why Burns? Why not Sir
Walter? Had I the honor to be a fellow-
countryman of Scott, and had I command
of the racial tom-tom, it seems to me
that I would tune upon it in honor of that
great man until I dropped.—QUILLER-
COUCH, A. T., 1896, *Adventures in Criticism, p.* 109.

A man of Burns's temperament, born
in the middle of that (the 18th) century,
was almost bound to combine rationalism
in theology with a genuine religious sentiment. It is unnecessary to search very
particularly in his actual theological environment for the origins of his religion.
He had the same bias in reasoning—
towards materialism, empiricism, "common-sense,"—as most of the leading intellect of the age. . . . It would be a mistake to try to trace any very close connection between the thought of Burns, so
far it was dogmatic, and the doctrines
held by the New Light ministers who took
the young farmer by the hand, and eulo-
gised the satires which he wrote for their
side. The doctrine spread by Auld, Russell and their kind disgusted him; but his
polemic against them was purely negative and destructive. . . . The consciousness of the living presence of God
in nature was always stronger in him than
any theory of redemption. An intellectual
sceptic, he was not really interested in
theological dogma, though moral and
emotional causes preserved in him certain
relics of more or less inter-dependant
doctrines.—WALLACE, WILLIAM, 1896,
*rev. The Life and Works of Robert Burns,
ed. by Robert Chambers.*

Rare as was the poetic gift of Burns,
and unique in their quality of pure elemental passion as were his bursts of
song, the poet himself has no place in
what is mainly a history of influences
and tendencies. Writing as he did—so
long at least as he wrote poetry and not
somewhat inferior verse—in the Lowland
Scottish vernacular, he naturally could
not contribute anything directly to the
development of English poetic literature.
Nor does it even appear that he directly
influenced those who were the main contributors to this work.—TRAILL, HENRY
DUFF, 1896, *Social England, vol.* v, *p.* 445.

His ideas are—to use the rough old
Lockian division—ideas of sensation, not
of reflection; and when he goes beyond
them he is sensible, healthy, respectable,
but not deep or high. In his own range
there are few depths or heights to which
he has not soared or plunged. . . . In
the expression of the triumph and despair
of love, not sickled over with any thought
as in most modern poets, only Catullus and
Sappho can touch Burns.—SAINTSBURY,
GEORGE, 1896, *A History of Nineteenth
Century Literature, pp.* 15, 16.

Always a poet, he was more, much

more than a poet. He was a student of man,—of all sorts of men; caring much, as a student, for the baser sort which reveled in Poosie Nansie's dram-shop, and which he celebrated in "The Jolly Beggars;" but caring more as a man, for the better sort which languished in huts where poor men lodged, and which he was the voice of lamentation in "Man was Made to Mourn." He was a student of manners, which he painted with a sure hand, his masterpiece being that reverential reproduction of the family life at Lochlea "The Cotter's Saturday Night." He was a student of nature,—his love of which was conspicuous in his poetry, flushing his words with picturesque phrases and flooding his lines with the feeling of outdoor life. He was a student of animal life,—a lover of horses and dogs, observant of their habits and careful of their comfort. He felt for the little mouse which his plowshare turned out of its nest, and he pitied the poor hare which the unskillful fowler could only wound. The commoners of the earth and air were dear to him; and the flower besides his path, the gowan wet with dew, was precious in his eyes. His heart was large, his mind was comprehensive, and his temper singularly sweet and sunny.—STODDARD, RICHARD HENRY, 1896, *Library of the World's Best Literature, ed. Warner, vol.* V, *p.*2839.

Burns is one of the Immortals. What a fortunate thing for us that he was not educated, let us say at Eton and Balliol! There are many of Burns's poems (humorous and pathetic) which are superb.—LOCKER-LAMPSON, FREDERICK, 1896, *My Confidences, p.* 178.

Other poets may be the favourites of a class or a clique; Burns is the favorite of the whole world. The secret of this universal favor is to be found in the fact that he was born in a lowly condition of life, close to our mother earth, and gave utterance to the rudimentary sentiments, the abiding sorrows, and the constant yearnings of human nature.—AUSTIN, ALFRED, 1896, *Address at the Unveiling of the Statue to Burns at Irvine, July.*

In his love songs we hear again, even more simply, more directly the same natural music which in the age of Elizabeth enchanted the world. . . . It was the strength of his passions and the weakness of his moral will which made his poetry

and spoilt his life.—BROOKE, STOPFORD A., 1896, *English Literature, p.* 226.

I come here as a loyal burgess of Dumfries to do honour to the greatest burgess of Dumfries. . . . Mankind owes him a general debt. But the debt of Scotland is special. For Burns exalted our race, he hallowed Scotland and the Scottish tongue. Before his time we had for a long period been scarcely recognised, we had been falling out of the recollection of the world. From the time of the union of the Crowns, and still more from the time of the legislative union, Scotland has lapsed into obscurity. Except for an occasional riot or a Jacobite rising, her existance was almost forgotten. She had, indeed, her Robertsons and her Humes writing history to general admiration, but no trace of Scottish authorship was discoverable in their works; indeed, every flavour of national idiom was carefully excluded. The Scottish dialect, as Burns called it, was in danger of perishing. Burns seemed at this juncture to start to his feet and re-assert Scotland's claim to national existence; his Scottish notes rang through the world, and he thus preserved the Scottish language forever; for mankind will never allow to die that idiom in which his songs and poems are enshrined. That is a part of Scotland's debt to Burns.—ROSEBERY, ARCHIBALD PHILIP PRIMROSE LORD, 1896, *Address at Dumfries, July* 21.

No poet, probably, excepting Shakespeare, ever owed more than Burns to the suggestions of predecessors in his art. Hardly, indeed, is there anything in his work, down even to details, for which the example is not to be found in the pages of some earlier Scottish poet—Dunbar, Lyndsay, Semple, Ramsay, Fergusson, and countless unnamed song and ballad writers. With the works of all these he was closely familiar. At the same time no poet, excepting Shakespeare, ever proved himself so capable of transmuting the rude ore of earlier suggestion into the fine gold of immortal song. It is difficult at the present day, when all its effects are a common possession, to appreciate the native strength and originality of Burns's work. This, however, may be ventured, that what the Revolution at that time did for France at a cost of untold horror and streams of blood, the poetry of Burns did for Scotland. Who will reckon the clearing of the air that has been made, the shams and affectations and cruel tyrannies that have been killed, and the courage and stamina which have been built into the nation's character by a single poem like "Scots wha ha'e" or " A man's a man for a' that"?—EYRE-TODD, GEORGE, 1896, *Scottish Poetry of the Eighteenth Century, vol.* II, *p.* 172.

The daisy by his ploughshare cleft,
The lips of women loved and left,
The griefs and joys that weave the weft
   Of human time,
With craftsman's cunning, keen and deft,
   He carved in rhyme.

. . . .

But never, since bright earth was born
In rapture of the enkindling morn,
Might godlike wrath and sunlike scorn
   That was and is
And shall be while false weeds are worn
   Find word like his.
Above the rude and radiant earth
That heaves and glows from firth to firth
In vale and mountain, bright in dearth
   And warm in wealth,
Which gave his fiery glory birth
   By chance and stealth,
Above the storms of praise and blame
That blur with mist his lustrous name,
His thunderous laughter went and came,
   And lives and flies;
The roar that follows on the flame
   When lightning dies.
Earth, and the snow-dimmed heights of air,
And water winding soft and fair
Through still sweet places, bright and bare,
   By bent and byre,
Taught him what hearts within them were:
   But his was fire.

—SWINBURNE, ALGERNON CHARLES, 1896, *Robert Burns, The Nineteenth Century, vol.* 39, *pp.* 183, 184.

By virtue of his ardent and undisciplined temperament, by his peasant origin and his experience of the sufferings of the poor, by that pride of manhood and of genius which made him feel himself an equal of prince or peer, by the zeal of his humanitarian sympathies, by his sentimental Jacobitism and his imaginative enthusiasm for the traditions of Scottish independence, by the fact that he belonged to the democratic Presbyterian Church and sympathized with the party of spiritual revolt, Burns was fitted to be a spokesman of the passions of the time.—DOWDEN, EDWARD, 1897, *The French Revolution and English Literature, p.* 146.

Not only does he take whatever the Vernacular School can give in such matters as tone, sentiment, method, diction phrase; but also, he is content to run in debt to it for suggestions as regards ideas and for models in style. . . . It was fortunate for him and for his book, as it was fortunate for the world at large—as, too, it was afterwards to be fortunate for Scots song—that he was thus imitative in kind and thus traditional in practice. He had the sole ear of the Vernacular Muse; there was not a tool in her budget of which he was not master; and he took his place, the moment he moved for it, not so much, perhaps, by reason of his uncommon capacity as, because he discovered himself to his public in the very terms—of diction form, style, sentiment even—with which that public was familiar from of old, and in which it was waiting and longing to be addressed.— HENLEY, WILLIAM ERNEST, 1897, *Life, Genius, Achievement, The Poetry of Robert Burns, vol.* IV, *pp.* 270, 272.

Burns rides the ways of literature hedged by a numerous and terrible guard of devoted Scots, and if any hat is not doffed as he passes the irreverent offender is a marked man. Who dares lay hands on a poet guarded by a nation? . . . Burns, like Homer, is not merely a poet, but a literature. He has succeeded in fulfilling the old savage ideal—he has eaten up all his predecessors, and become possessed of their united powers. It is useless to haggle over much about what he borrowed: one can only envy the gigantic luck of his chance. Such vamps as the one I have analysed from Mr. Henley's notes can only be credited to him as brilliant luck brilliantly used. But the pieces I enumerated of the third class proved that he could write charming songs without such luck; though I think, on the whole, they prove that he wrote still better when he borrowed. . . . Taking him, borrowings and all, the merit of his songs lies in the partly dramatic kind; they display, vividly and pictorially, the life of a whole peasantry, as it has not been displayed in English literature. — THOMPSON, FRANCIS, 1897, *Mr. Henley's Burns, The Academy, vol.* 51, *pp.* 273, 274.

No poet, not even Shakespeare, has been so minutely, lovingly studied as Burns.— DAVIDSON, JAMES, 1897, *New Light on Burns, The Scottish Review, vol.* 29, *p.* 306.

A stranger freak of burgess criticism is every-day fare in the odd world peopled by the biographers of Robert Burns. The nature of Burns, one would think, was simplicity itself; it could hardly puzzle a ploughman, and two sailors out of three would call him brother. But he lit up the whole of that nature by his marvellous genius for expression, and grave personages have been occupied ever since in discussing the dualism of his character, and professing to find some dark mystery in the existence of this, that, or the other trait—a love of pleasure, a hatred of shams, a deep sense of religion. It is common human nature, after all, that is the mystery, but they seem never to have met with it, and treat it as if it were the poet's eccentricity. They are all agog to worship him, and when they have made an image of him in their own likeness, and given it a tin-pot head that exactly hits their taste, they break into noisy lamentation over the discovery that the original was human, and had feet of clay. They deem "Mary in Heaven" so admirable that they could find it in their hearts to regret that she was ever on earth.—RALEIGH, WALTER, 1897, *Style, p. 76.*

It is of importance that we recognize the fact that in Burns the two literary estates, English and Scottish, were united. Until his time there was a sharp distinction between Scottish and English literature; but after him the literature of the two countries became one, both in nature and in name. This was but natural, when we consider that something of the original impulse which moved Burns's genius was English. When the riches of this noble Scottish house, and of that sister house of Chaucer, Spenser, Shakespeare, and Milton, awaited union in a royal heir, there came a peasant lad from the "auld clay biggin' " in Ayrshire, who, with the simple and graceful dignity of one of nature's noblemen, claimed his own, and there was added a new hereditary peer to the House of Fame.—GEORGE, ANDREW J., 1897, *Carlyle's Essay on Burns, p.* 114.

Burns.—The most amazing price ever realised for a modern book was that of £572 for "Poems chiefly in the Scottish dialect. By Robert Burns. *Kilmarnock,* 1786." The original price of this octavo volume was three shillings. The history of the very fine copy sold in Edinburgh in February 1898 is traced back about eighty years by a writer in *Literature.* In 1870 it was sold for six guineas to G. B. Simpson, of Dundee, who sold it in 1879, with some other books, to A. C. Lamb for £124. The price of the Kilmarnock Burns has steadily advanced from £3, 10s. in 1858 to £111 in 1888, and then it made the immense leap to £572.—WHEATLEY, HENRY B., 1898, *Prices of Books, p.* 257.

In his relation to Nature there was this great difference between Burns and his literary contemporaries and immediate predecessors, that whereas even the best of them wrote rather as pleased spectators of the country, with all its infinite variety of form and colour, of life and sound, of calm and storm, he sang as one into whose very inmost heart the power of these things had entered. For the first time in English literature the burning ardour of a passionate soul went out in tumultuous joy towards Nature. The hills and woods, the streams and dells were to Burns not merely enjoyable scenes to be visited and described. They became part of his very being. In their changeful aspects he found the counterpart of his own variable moods; they ministered to his joys, they soothed his sorrows. They yielded him a companionship that never palled, a sympathy that never failed. They kindled his poetic ardour, and became themselves the subjects of his song. He loved them with all the overpowering intensity of his affectionate nature, and his feelings found vent in an exuberance of appreciation which had never before been heard in verse.—GEIKIE, SIR ARCHIBALD, 1898, *Types of Scenery and their Influence on Literature, p.* 26.

I venture to assume that I have advanced enough to vindicate my postulate, that throughout Fergusson's poems saturated the mind, heart, imagination, affection, and memory, and imposed subjects and forms and elect words on Robert Burns. That, when all is said, Robert Burns still stands by head and shoulders above Robert Fergusson and beyond all possible comparison Scotland's supremest singer; that his was the larger, stronger soul, the richer imagination, the more inspired utterance, the more seeing eyes, the broader intellect, does not alter the fact of wide, deep, and pervasive obligations to his precursor. Mentally as physically he was stalwart where Fergusson was fragile; he was dowered with immeasurable resources where Fergusson was soon exhausted; he was master of all moods and passions where Fergusson was only their victim; he was possessor of Elisha's wished-for "double portion" of poetic inspiration where Fergusson was at best fitfully and briefly fired and inspired. But with every limitation of genius and range, it abides that it was a happy day for Robert Burns, and a still happier day for the immortal in Scottish poetry, whereon he fell in with Robert Fergusson's volume of 1773-79.—GRO-SART, ALEXANDER B., 1898, *Robert Fergusson (Famous Scots Series), p.* 147.

When the tom-tit patronises the eagle, one realises how small the little bird is. But though Burns is gone, his immortal poems live and burn themselves into our heart of hearts. When we feel disgusted with the little peddling thoughts of little people; when we feel sick to the soul of the conventional cant of the time, of the false gods in art and literature and music;

we should turn for inspiration to the glowing rapture, the blazing patriotism, the all-conquering humour, and the biting wit and overwhelming irony of Robert Burns. The glorious fire of that mighty genius will warm the coldest heart.—FORSTER, JOSEPH, 1898, *Great Teachers, p.* 3.

The very high rank of Burns depends, in great part, on the fact that he could command a wider range of emotion than most lyrists; humour in almost all its varieties save the cynical, pathos in several forms, love when young and passionate, personal independence and the competence of the individual, patriotism—Burns has sung them all.—WINCHESTER, C. T., 1899, *Some Principles of Literary Criticism, p.* 99.

The genius of Burns was breathing into the Scottish Muse a fire and a vigour that were to be the harbingers of new feelings and new impulses far beyond her borders. —CRAIK, SIR HENRY, 1901, *A Century of Scottish History, vol.* II, *p.* 125.

James Macpherson
1736-1796

Born, at Kingussie, Invernesshire, 27 Oct. 1736. Early education at parish school. Matric., King's Coll., Aberdeen, Feb. 1753. To Marischal Coll., 1755. Probably studied at Edinburgh Univ., winter of 1755-56. After leaving Edinburgh, was master in school at Ruthven; and afterwards private tutor. Contrib. to "Scots Mag.," 1758. Friendship with Home and Dr. Carlyle, who encouraged him in publication of translations of Gaelic poems. Travelled in Highlands, 1760, collecting material. To London, 1761. Sec. to Governor of Pensacola, West Florida, 1764. Returned to England, 1766. Employed by Government to write on political questions. Agent to Nabob of Arcot, 1780. M. P. for Camelford, 1780-96. Died, at Badenoch, Invernesshire, 17 Feb. 1796. Buried in Westminster Abbey. *Works:* "The Highlander" (anon.), 1758; "Fragments of Ancient Poetry, collected in the Highlands" (anon.), 1760; Ossian's "Fingal," translated from the Gaelic, 1762; Ossian's "Temora," translated, 1763; "Introduction to the History of Great Britain and Ireland," 1771; translation of Homer's "Iliad," 1773; "A History of Great Britain, from the Restoration to the Accession of the House of Hanover" (2 vols.), 1775; "Original Papers, containing the Secret History of Great Britain" (2 vols.), 1775; "The Rights of Great Britain asserted against the claims of America" (anon.), 1776; "A Short History of the Opposition during the last Session" (anon.), 1779; "The History and Management of the East India Company" (anon.), 1779. He *edited:* "Letters from Mahommed Ali Chang, Nabob of Arcot, to the Court of Directors," 1779. *Collected Works:* "Poetical Works," 1802. *Life:* by T. B. Saunders, 1894.—SHARP, R. FARQUHARSON, 1897, *A Dictionary of English Authors, p.* 181.

PERSONAL

I received your foolish and impudent note. Whatever insult is offered me, I will do my best to repel, and what I cannot do for myself, the law shall do for me. I will not desist from detecting what I

think a cheat, from any fear of the menaces of a Ruffian. What would you have me retract? I thought your book an imposture; I think it an imposture still. For this opinion I have given my reasons to the public, which I here dare you to refute.

Your rage I defy. Your abilities, since your Homer, are not so formidable; and what I hear of your morals inclines me to pay regard, not to what you shall say, but to what you shall prove. You may print this if you will.* — JOHNSON, SAMUEL, 1775, *Letter to Macpherson, Jan.* 20.

"Why dost thou build the tower, son of the winged days? Soon will thou depart with thy fathers. The blast from the desert shall rush through thy hall, and sound upon the bossy shield." Do you recollect, dear Madam, when I stopped with you at the gate of Belleville, I repeated those lines, and observed what a suitable inscription they might prove for the front of poor James Macpherson's new house. It would appear I was moved by a prophetic impulse when I predicted that he never would see it finished. . . . He felt the approaches of death, and hoped no relief from medicine, though his life was not such that one would like to look back on at that awful period: indeed whose is? It pleased the Almighty to render his last scene most affecting and exemplary. He died last Tuesday evening; and, from the minute he was confined, till a very little before he expired, never ceased imploring the Divine mercy in the most earnest and pathetic manner. People about him were overawed and melted at the fervour and bitterness of his penitence; he frequently and earnestly entreated the prayers of good serious people of the lower class who were admitted. He was a very good-natured man; and now, that he had got all his schemes of interest and ambition fulfilled, he seemed to reflect and grow domestic, and showed, of late, a great inclination to be an indulgent landlord, and very liberal to the poor; of which I could relate various instances, more tender and interesting than flashy or ostentatious. His heart and temper were orignally good; his religious principles were, I fear, unfixed, and fluctuating. But the primary cause that so much genius, taste, benevolence and prosperity, did not produce or diffuse more happiness, was his living a stranger to comforts of domestic life, from which unhappy connexions excluded him.—GRANT, MRS. ANNE, 1796, *To Mrs. Macintosh, Feb.* 20; *Letters from the Mountains, vol.* II.

*The original of this well-known letter was sold by auction in 1875, for £50.—SAUNDERS, BAILEY, 1894, *The Life and Letters of James Macpherson, p.* 250.

A Scottish Chatterton of maturer growth who did *not* commit suicide.— COLLIER, WILLIAM FRANCIS, 1861, *A History of English Literature, p.* 353.

As an original writer Macpherson became more and more discredited, but as an individual more and more wealthy; and, to prove that no honour lies beyond the grasp of unprincipled mediocrity, he was buried in Poet's Corner.—GOSSE, EDMUND, 1888, *A History of Eighteenth Century Literature, p.* 336.

He went up to London—was appointed to go with Governor Johnston to Florida, in America; remained there at Pensacola, a year or more; but quarrelled with his chief (he had rare aptitude for quarrelling) and came back in 1766. Some English historical work followed; but with little success or profit. Yet he was a canny Scotchman, and so laid his plans that he became agent for some rich nabob of India (from these pickings winning a great fortune eventually); entered Parliament in 1780; had a country house at Putney, where he entertained lavishly; and at last built a great show place in the highlands near to his birth-place—which one may see to-day—with an obelisk to his memory, looking down on the valley of the Spey; and not so far away from the old coach-road, that passes through Killiecrankie, from Blair Athol to Inverness, but the coach man can show it—as he did to me— with his whip. . . . Yet if his book of Ossianic poems was ten-fold better than it is, it would hardly give an enduring, or a brilliant gloss to the memory of James Macpherson. — MITCHELL, DONALD G., 1895, *English Lands Letters and Kings, Queen Anne and the Georges, pp.* 224, 228.

If none but the great deserved a biography, this book would not have been written. For Macpherson was in no sense a great man : he was a miscellaneous writer of considerable talent, a busy journalist, a member of Parliament, an agent for an Indian prince, a popular and prosperous citizen; and, beyond the fact that he brought out the Ossianic poems at the age of twenty-five, he did little in the sixty years of his life that would entitle him to permanent remembrance. This work of his youth was, as he declared, translated from Gaelic fragments found in the Scottish Highlands. By its wonderful success, and its no less wonderful influence on literature, both in England and on the Continent, it gave him, in his own day, a world-wide reputation. Literary fashions have suffered many changes in the century that has passed since his death, and Macpherson's reputation no longer exists; but his work retains an historical interest of a curious and unique character. . . . While I believe that, on the whole, he has been greatly slandered, he is certainly no hero; and I hope that I am not afflicted, in regard to him, with what has been called the *lues boswelliana*, or the disease of admiration.—SAUNDERS, BAILEY, 1894, *The Life and Letters of James Macpherson, Preface, pp.* v, vii.

The big, burly politician lived in society. . . . As he grew elderly, rich, and prosperous, Macpherson's heart yearned for his old Highland district, and he turned his eyes to Badenoch; there he resolved to buy land and build a home within sight of his native mountains. Two or three small farms were bought on the banks of the Spey and soon a villa, bearing the cockney title of "Belleville," which had been designed by his friend Adam, the architect, rose in the wilds, two miles from Kingussie. People long remembered the great man from London, who came every year, bedizened with rings and gold seals, and clad in fur-edged coat. They told stories of the grand state he kept up as a Highland chief, his splendid table, his home filled with guests; of his sallying forth in the morning and bringing bibulous lairds from houses far and near, who in the dining-room, from whose walls portraits by Sir Joshua Reynolds looked down, kept high revelry till they and the nights were far spent. But good things, too, were told of Macpherson, pleasant to remember; of his refusing from a grateful Government the forfeited estate of Cluny Macpherson, which was thereupon restored to its rightful owner; his generosity to the poor, whom he employed at high wages, which no Badenoch man had ever dreamed of; his kindly remembrance of all about his native Ruthven. Now that his ambition was satisfied, now that his struggle with poverty and obscurity was over he could be the pleasant, affable man, the kindly landlord, and the genial host. —GRAHAM, HENRY GREY, 1901, *Scottish Men of Letters in the Eighteenth Century,* p. 238.

POEMS OF OSSIAN

Several gentlemen of the Highlands and Isles, generously gave me all the assistance in their power, and it was by their means I was enabled to complete the Epic Poem. How far it comes up to the rules of the Epopœia is the province of criticism to examine. It is only my business to lay it before the reader as I have found it. . . . A man diffident of his abilities might ascribe his own compositions to a person whose remote antiquity and whose situation when alive might well answer for faults which would be inexcusable in a writer of this age. . . . But of this I am persuaded . . . that some will think, notwithstanding the disadvantages with which the works ascribed to Ossian appear, it would be a very uncommon instance of self-denial in me to disown them, were they really of my composition.— MACPHERSON, JAMES, 1762, *Fingal, Preface.*

It is as beautiful as Homer.—GRIMM, FRIEDRICH MELCHIOR, 1762, *Correspondance Littéraire, April.*

There we find the fire and enthusiasm of the most early times, combined with an amazing degree of regularity and art. We find tenderness, and even delicacy of sentiment, greatly predominant over fierceness and barbarity. Our hearts are melted with the softest feelings, and at the same time elevated with the highest ideas of magnanimity, generosity, and true heroism.—BLAIR, HUGH, 1763, *Critical Dissertation on the Poems of Ossian.*

Ossian, sublimest, simplest bard of all
Whom English infidels Macpherson call.
—CHURCHILL, CHARLES, 1763, *The Prophecy of Famine.*

I never was able to discover in his most unguarded moments that he was any other than the collector and translator of the works of Ossian, or assumed any other merit that might be derived from thence. But I have heard him express the greatest contempt and disdain for those who thought him the fabricator of them. If there was any person who asserted that Macpherson had owned it to himself, even that would not shake my faith; for I knew him to be of a temper, when he was teased and fretted, to carry his indignation that far.—CARLYLE, ALEXANDER, 1769-70, *Report of the Highland Society, App. p.* 68.

I have no less zeal for the "Poems of

Ossian," than if I had been born on one of his favourite mountains; and I shall be very glad to see history confirm all that his poetry has set forth.—MONTAGU. ELIZ-ABETH, 1771, *Letter to Lord Kames, Oct.* 3.

Homer has been superseded in my heart by the divine Ossian. Through what a world does this angelic bard carry me! With him I wander over barren wastes and frightful wilds; surrounded by whirlwinds and hurricanes, trace by the feeble light of the moon the shades of our noble ances-tors; hear from the mountainous heights, intermingled with the roaring of waves and cataracts, their plaintive tones steal-ing from cavernous recesses; while the pensive monody of some love-stricken maiden, who heaves her departing sighs over the moss-clad grave of the warrior by whom she was adored, makes up the inarticulate concert. I trace this bard, with his silver locks, as he wanders in the valley and explores the footsteps of his fathers. Alas! no vestige remains but their tombs. His thought then hangs on the silver moon, as her sinking beams play upon the rippling main; and the remem-brance of deeds past and gone recurs to the hero's mind—deeds of times when he gloried in the approach of danger, and emulation nerved his whole frame; when the pale orb shone upon his bark, laden with the spoils of his enemy, and illumi-nated his triumphant return. When I see depicted on his countenance a bosom full of woe; when I behold his heroic great-ness sinking into the grave, and he ex-claims, as he throws a glance at the cold sod which is to lie upon him: "Hither will the traveler who is sensible of my worth bend his weary steps, and seek the soul-enlivening bard, the illustrious son of Fingal; his foot will tread upon my tomb, but his eyes shall never behold me;" at this time it is, my dear friend, that, like some renowned and chivalrous knight, I could instantly draw my sword; rescue my prince from a long, irksome existence of langour and pain; and then finish by plunging the weapon into my own breast, that I might accompany the demi-god whom my hand had emancipated.—GOETHE, JOHANN WOLFGANG, 1774, *Sor-rows of Werther, Letter* lxviii.

Doctor Johnson having asserted in his late publication that the Translator of Ossian's Poems "never could show the

original, nor can it be shown by any other," I hereby declare that the originals of "Fin-gal" and other poems of Ossian lay in my shop for many months in the year 1762, for the inspection of the curious. The public were not only apprised of their lying there for inspection, but even proposals for publishing the originals of the poems of Ossian were dispersed through the king-dom, and advertised in the newspapers. Upon finding that a number of subscribers sufficient to bear the expenses were not likely to appear, I returned the manu-script to the proprietor, in whose hands they still remain.—BECKET, THOMAS, 1775, *To the Public, Jan.* 19.

I see you entertain a great doubt with regard to the authenticity of the poems of Ossian. You are certainly right in so doing. It is indeed strange that any men of sense could have imagined it possible, that above twenty thousand verses, along with numberless historical facts, could have been preserved by oral tradition during fifty generations, by the rudest, perhaps, of all the European nations, the most necessitous, the most turbulent, and the most unsettled. Where a supposition is so contrary to common sense, any posi-tive evidence of it ought never to be re-garded. Men run with great avidity to give their evidence in favour of what flatters their passions and their natural prejudices. You are therefore over and above indulgent to us in speaking of the matter with hesitation.—HUME, DAVID, 1776, *Letter to Gibbon, March* 18; *Gib-bon's Memoirs, ed. Hill, p.* 197.

Mr. Tyrrwhit has at last published the Bristol poems. He does not give up the antiquity, yet fairly leaves everybody to ascribe them to Chatterton, if they please, which I think the internal evidence must force every one to do, unless the amazing prodigy of Chatterton's producing them should not seem a larger miracle than Rowley's and Canning's anticipation of the style of very modern poetry. Psalm-anazar alone seems to have surpassed the genius of Chatterton, and when that lad could perform such feats, as he certainly did, what difficulty is there in believing that Macpherson forged the cold skeleton of an epic poem, that is more insipid than "Leonidas?"—WALPOLE, HORACE, 1777, *To Rev. William Mason, Feb.* 17; *Letters, ed. Cunningham, vol.* VI, *p.* 412.

Mr. Macpherson is by many supposed to be the sole and original author of the compositions which he has published as translations of the works of Ossian; this charge I am enabled to refute, at least in part, having fortunately met with the originals of some of them. Mr. Macpherson, I acknowledge, has taken very great liberties with them; retrenching, adding, and altering as he judged proper: but we must admit that he has discovered great ingenuity in these variations.—YOUNG, MATTHEW, 1784, *Ancient Gaelic Poems respecting the Race of the Fians: Transactions of the Royal Irish Academy, vol.* I, *Autiq. p.* 43.

I look upon M'Pherson's "Fingal" to be as gross an imposition as ever the world was troubled with. Had it been really an ancient work, a true specimen how men thought at that time, it would have been a curiosity of the first rate. As a modern production, it is nothing.—JOHNSON, SAMUEL, 1785, *The Journal of the Tour to the Hebrides, by Boswell.*

I was the first person who brought out to the notice of the world, the poems of Ossian: first, by the "Fragments of Ancient Poetry" which I published, and afterwards, by my setting on foot the undertaking for collecting and publishing the "Works of Ossian;" and I have always considered this as a meritorious action of my life.—BLAIR, HUGH, 1787, *Letter to Robert Burns, May* 4.

Mr. Macpherson must not only be esteemed as one of the first poets, but as exhibiting an attention and skill in the preservation of costume hitherto unparalleled. Ancient or modern, however, these poems must be viewed as pregnant with beauties of the highest rank; uniformly mild and generous in manners and sentiment, uniformly simple, pathetic, and sublime, vivid and picturesque in imagery, in diction rapid, nervous, and concise, they are alike calculated to melt and meliorate the heart, to elevate and fire the imagination. I do not hesitate to affirm that, if in sublimity the palm must be allowed, and I think it must, to our great countryman, yet in the pathetic the Caledonian is far superior, not only to Milton, but to every other poet. Conceiving, therefore, as I firmly do, that *Fingal* and *Temora* are solely indebted to Mr. Macpherson for their form, and for, probably, a very considerable portion of their matter, and as

the bard under whose name they are now published was totally unknown till within these forty years, I have placed them, and wish indeed there to place the whole collection, which is in fact truly epic, at the head of the first department, where I am confident they need not fear comparison with any specimens of our elder poetry.—DRAKE, NATHAN, 1798-1820, *Literary Hours, vol.* II, *No.* xxix, *p.* 102.

After a long interval the poetical genius of the Scots was revived in the tender and luxuriant Thomson; but the spurious poems of Ossian, a recent forgery, still continue to pollute their history, and to corrupt their taste.—LAING, MALCOLM, 1800-4, *The History of Scotland, vol.* IV, *p.* 390.

The Phantom was begotten by the snug embrace of an impudent Highlander upon a cloud of tradition. It traveled southward, where it was greeted with acclamation, and the thin consistence took its course through Europe upon the breath of popular applause. . . . Open this far-famed book! I have done so at random, and the beginning of the "Epic Poem Temora," in eight books, presents itself. . . . Having had the good fortune to be born and reared in a mountainous country, from my very childhood I have felt the falsehood that pervades the volumes imposed upon the world under the name of Ossian. From what I saw with my own eyes, I knew that the imagery was spurious. In nature everything is indistinct, yet nothing defined into absolute, independent singleness. In Macpherson's work it is exactly the reverse: everything (that is not stolen) is in this manner defined, insulated, dislocated, deadened, yet nothing distinct. It will always be so when words are substituted for things. To say that the characters never could exist; that the manners are impossible; and that a dream has more substance than the whole state of society, as there depicted, is doing nothing more than pronouncing a censure which Macpherson defied. . . . Yet, much as these pretended treasures of antiquity have been admired, they have been wholly uninfluential upon the literature of the country. No succeeding writer appears to have caught from them a ray of inspiration; no author in the least distinguished has ventured formally to imitate them, except the boy, Chatterton, on their first appearance.

. . . This incapability to amalgamate with the literature of the Island is, in my estimation, a decisive proof that the book is essentially unnatural; nor should I require any other to demonstrate it to be a forgery, audacious as worthless. Contrast, in this respect, the effect of Macpherson's publication with the "Reliques" of Percy, so unassuming, so modest in their pretensions.—WORDSWORTH, WILLIAM, 1800, *Lyrical Ballads, Second Edition, Essay Supplementary to Preface.*

Under a cloudy sky, on the coast of that sea whose tempests were sung by Ossian, their Gothic architecture has something grand and somber. Seated on a shattered altar in the Orkneys, the traveler is astonished at the dreariness of those places: sudden fogs, vales where rises the sepulchral stone, streams flowing through wild heaths, a few reddish pine trees, scattered over a naked desert studded with patches of snow; such are the only objects which present themselves to his view. The wind circulates among the ruins, and their innumerable crevices become so many tubes, which heave a thousand sighs. Long grasses wave in the apertures of the domes, and beyond these apertures you behold the flitting clouds and the soaring sea-eagle. . . . Long will those four stones which mark the tombs of heroes on the moors of Caledonia, long will they continue to attract the contemplative traveler. Oscar and Malvina are gone, but nothing is changed in their solitary country. 'Tis no longer the hand of the bard himself that sweeps the harp; the tones we hear are the slight trembling of the strings, produced by the touch of a spirit, when announcing at night, in a lonely chamber, the death of a hero. . . . So when he sits in the silence of noon in the valley of his breezes is the murmur of the mountain to Ossian's ear: the gale drowns it often in its course, but the pleasant sound returns again.—CHATEAUBRIAND, FRANÇOIS RENÉ VICOMTE DE, 1802, *Génie du Christianisme, bk.* ii, *ch.* vii, *pt.* iv.

You recall me to some very pleasant feelings of my boyhood when you ask my opinion of Ossian. . . . Ossian and Spenser were two books which the good old bard [Dr. Blacklock] put into my hands, and which I devoured rather than perused. Their tales were for a long time so much my delight, that I could repeat without remorse whole Cantos of the one and Duans of the other; and wo to the unlucky wight who undertook to be my auditor, for in the height of my enthusiasm I was apt to disregard all hints that my recitations became tedious. . . . Ossian's poems, in particular, have more charms for youth than for a more advanced stage. . . . After making every allowance for the disadvantages of a literal translation, and the possible debasement which those *now* collected may have suffered in the great and violent change which the Highlands have undergone since the researches of Macpherson, I am compelled to admit that incalculably the greater part of the English Ossian must be ascribed to Macpherson himself, and that his whole introductions, notes, &c., &c., are an absolute tissue of forgeries.—SCOTT, SIR WALTER, 1805, *Letter to Miss Seward, Lockhart's Life of Scott.*

Little as we participate in the unqualified enthusiasm expressed by some admirers of Ossian, still the influence exercised by these poems on the public taste is certainly very remarkable. . . . My observations of these Ossianic poems have been founded on the principle of conceding to them the highest possible antiquity, which is at all consistent with historical truth, and at the same time acquiescing at once in their relative authenticity. Certainly, unless the contrary be proved by extraneous circumstances, no internal evidence militates against the supposition that such a hero-race as that of Fingal existed on the northwest coast of Scotland in the ninth and tenth centuries; that it actually produced an Ossian, who, as bard and hero, celebrated his own exploits and those of his race. If his constant recurrence to the melancholy remembrance of departed ancestors, and the earlier period of their glory, become by frequent repetition monotonous and wearying, still the continual interweaving of the person of the bard into the history narrated, affords a happy poetical and universal point of union, and greatly contributes to enhance that fascinating interest with which the poems have inspired so many readers and hearers. This circumstance is, indeed, so peculiarly propitious, that many succeeding bards have adopted the form once suggested, and written and sung as if in Ossian's person.—SCHLEGEL, FREDERICK,

1812, *On the Poetry of the North, Æsthetic and Miscellaneous Works, tr. Millington, pp. 248, 256.*

Hail, Bards of mightier grasp! on you
I chiefly call, the chosen Few,
Who cast not off the acknowledged guide,
Who falter'd not, nor turn'd aside;
Whose lofty genius could survive
Privation, under sorrow thrive;
In whom the fiery Muse revered
The symbol of a snow-white beard,
Bedew'd with meditative tears
Dropp'd from the lenient cloud of years.
—WORDSWORTH, WILLIAM, 1824, *Lines written in a blank leaf of Macpherson's Ossian.*

They are utterly worthless, except as an edifying instance of the success of a story without evidence, and of a book without merit. They are a chaos of words which present no image, of images which have no archetype:—they are without form and void; and darkness is upon the face of them. Yet how many men of genius have panegyrised and imitated them!—MACAULAY, THOMAS BABINGTON, 1824, *Criticisms Upon the Principal Italian Writers, Critical and Miscellaneous Essays.*

Homer and Virgil, though the gods of our young idolatry,—sunbright both, in the golden morn of our imagination—were not greater or more glorious "orbs of song" than our own Ossian. Was that belief delusion all? Are the songs of Selma but unmeaning words,—idle as the inarticulate winds, the murmurs of the Harp and the Voice of Cona? Let us return, if we can, to our old creed—let us abjure, if we can, the folly of wisdom.—WILSON, JOHN, 1839, *Have You Read Ossian? Blackwood's Magazine, vol. 46, p. 693.*

It is many years ago since I looked at Ossian, and I never did much delight in him, as that fact proves. Since your letter came I have taken him up again, and have just finished "Carthon." There are beautiful passages in it, the most beautiful beginning, I think, "Desolate is the dwelling of Moina," and the next place being filled by that address to the sun you magnify so with praise. But the charm of these things is the *only* charm of all the poems. There is a sound of wild vague music in a monotone—nothing is articulate, nothing *individual*, nothing various. Take away a few poetical phrases from these poems, and they are colourless and bare. Compare them with the old burning ballads, with a wild heart beating in each. How cold they grow in the comparison! Compare them with Homer's grand breathing personalities, with Æschylus's—nay, but I cannot bear upon my lips or finger the charge of the blasphemy of such comparing, even for religion's sake. . . . And that reminds me of a distinction you suggest between Ossian and Homer. I fashion it in this way: Homer sometimes nods, but Ossian *makes his readers nod.*—BROWNING, ELIZABETH BARRETT, 1843, *To H. S. Boyd; Letters, ed. Kenyon, vol.* I, *pp.* 118, 119.

You ask me about Ossian—now here is truth—the first book I ever bought in my life was Ossian. . . . It is now in the next room. And years before that, the first *composition* I ever was guilty of was something in *imitation* of Ossian, whom I had not read, but *conceived*, through two or three scraps in other books—I never can recollect *not* writing rhymes . . . but I knew they were nonsense even then; *this*, however, I thought exceedingly well of, and laid up for posterity under the cushion of a great armchair. "And now my soul is satisfied"—so said one man after killing another, the death being suggested, in its height of honour, by stars and stars (* * * *). I could not have been five years old, that's one consolation. Years after, when I bought this book, I found a vile dissertation of Laing . . . all to prove Ossian was not Ossian. . . . I would not read it, but could not help knowing the purpose of it, and the pith of the hatefully—irresistible arguments. The worst came in another shape, though . . . an after-gleaning of real Ossianic poems, by a firm believer whose name I forget—"if this is the *real*" —I thought! Well, to this day I believe in a nucleus for all that haze, a foundation of truth to Macpherson's fanciful superstructure—and I have been long intending to read once again those Fingals and Malvinas.—BROWNING, ROBERT, 1846, *To Elizabeth Barrett, Aug.* 25; *The Letters of Robert Browning and Elizabeth Barrett, vol.* II, *p.* 466.

The history of Celtic poetry in Scotland has been invested with a false brilliancy, which time is gradually impairing. The poems ascribed to Ossian, whatever may be their intrinsic merit, have been chiefly admired as the productions of a remote age, and of a nation which, if not utterly barbarous, was, at all events, very imperfectly civilized; and when this charm of antiquity is completely dissolved, they cannot be perused with the same degree of enthusiasm.—IRVING, DAVID, 1861, *History of Scotish Poetry, ed. Carlyle, p. 1*.

One circumstance, which has contributed to keep up the dispute about Ossian so much longer than that about Rowley, no doubt, is, that there was some small portion of truth mixed up with Macpherson's deception, whereas there was none at all in Chatterton's. But the Ossianic poetry, after all that has been said about its falsehood of style and substance as well as of pretention, making it out to be thus a double lie, must still have some qualities wonderfully adapted to allure the popular taste. Both Chatterton and Macpherson wrote a quantity of modern English verse in their own names; but nothing either did in this way was worth much: they evidently felt most at ease in their masks.—CRAIK, GEORGE L., 1861, *A Compendious History of English Literature and of the English Language, vol. II, p. 309*.

When the Gaelic "Fingal," published in 1807, is compared with any one of the translations which purport to have been made from it, it seems to me incomparably superior. It is far simpler in diction. It has a peculiar rhythm and assonance which seem to repel the notion of a mere translation from English as something almost absurd. It is impossible that it can be a translation from MacPherson's English, unless there was some clever Gaelic poet then alive, able and willing to write what Eton schoolboys call "full sense verses."
— CAMPBELL, J. F., 1862-93, *Popular Tales of the West Highlands, vol. IV, p. 132*.

The Celts are the prime authors of this vein of piercing regret and passion, of this Titanism in poetry. A famous book, Macpherson's "Ossian," carried, in the last century, this vein like a flood of lava through Europe. I am not going to criticise Macpherson's "Ossian" here. Make the part of what is forged, modern, tawdry, spurious in the book as large as you please; strip Scotland, if you like, of every feather of borrowed plumes which, on the strength of Macpherson's "Ossian," she may have stolen from that *vetus et major Scotia*,

the true home of the Ossianic poetry, Ireland; I make no objection. But there will still be left in the book a residue with the very soul of the Celtic genius in it, and which has the proud distinction of having brought this soul of the Celtic genius into contact with the nations of modern Europe, and enriched all our poetry by it. Woody Morven, and echoing Sora, and Selma with its silent halls! We all owe them a debt of gratitude, and when we are unjust enough to forget it, may the Muse forget us! Choose any one of the better passages in Macpherson's "Ossian," and you can see, even at this time of day, what an apparition of newness and power such a strain must have been to the eighteenth century.—ARNOLD, MATTHEW, 1867, *On the Study of Celtic Literature, p. 152*.

MacPherson got much from MSS. and much from oral recitation. It is most probable that he has given the minor poems exactly as he found them. He may have made considerable changes in the larger ones in giving them their present form, although I do not believe that he, or any of his assistants, added much, even in the way of connecting-links between the various episodes.—CLERK, ARCHIBALD, 1870, *Poems of Ossian in the Original Gaelic, with a literal translation into English, vol. I, p. 1*.

A Scotchman, a man of wit, of overmuch wit, having written to his cost an unsuccessful rhapsody, wished to recover himself, went amongst the mountains of his country, gathered picturesque images, collected fragments of legends, plastered over the whole an abundance of eloquence and rhetoric, and created a Celtic Homer, Ossian, who, with Oscar, Malvina, and his whole troop, made the tour of Europe, and, about 1830, ended by furnishing baptismal names for French *grisettes* and *perruquiers*. Macpherson displayed to the world an imitation of primitive manners, not overtrue, for the extreme rudeness of barbarians would have shocked the people, but yet well enough preserved or portrayed to contrast with modern civilisation, and persuade the public that they were looking upon pure nature. A keen sympathy with Scotch landscape, so grand, so cold, so gloomy, rain on the hills, the birch trembling to the wind, the mist of heaven and the vagueness of the soul, so that every dreamer found there the emotions of his solitary walks and his philosophical glooms; chivalric exploits and magnanimity, heroes who set out alone to engage an army, faithful virgins dying on the tomb of their betrothed; an impassioned, coloured style, affecting to be abrupt, yet polished; able to charm a disciple of Rousseau by its warmth and elegance : here was something to transport the young enthusiasts of the time, civilised barbarians, scholarly lovers of nature, dreaming of the delights of savage life, whilst they shook off the powder which the hairdresser had left on their coats.—TAINE, H. A., 1871, *History of English Literature, tr. Van Laun, vol.* II, *bk.* iii, *ch.* vii, *p.* 220.

The fate of a poem which excited the enthusiasm of Goethe and Napoleon, and which nobody can read at the present day, certainly suggests some curious problems. Briefly, we may assume that its vague and gigantesque scenery, its pompous mouthing of sham heroics, its crude attempts to represent a social state when great men stalked through the world in haughty superiority to the narrow conventions of modern life, were congenial to men growing weary of an effete formalism. Men had been talking under their breath and in a mincing dialect so long that they were easily gratified, and easily imposed upon, by an affectation of vigorous and natural sentiment.—STEPHEN, LESLIE, 1876, *History of English Thought in the Eighteenth Century, vol.* II, *p.* 447.

Above all, Ossian, that poet of the vague—that northern Dante, as great, as majestic, as supernatural as the Dante of Florence, and who draws often from his phantoms cries more human and more heart-rending than those of the heroes of Homer.—VAN LAUN, HENRI, 1877, *History of French Literature, vol.* III, *p.* 333.

The appearance of this poetry gave to the English-speaking mind the thrill of a new and strange emotion about mountain scenery. Whether the poetry was old, or the product of last century, it describes, as none other does, the desolation of dusky moors, the solemn brooding of the mists on the mountains, the occasional looking through them of sun by day, of moon and stars by night, the gloom of dark cloudy Bens or cairns, with flashing cataracts, the ocean with its storms as it breaks on the West Highland shores or on the headlands of the Hebrides.—SHAIRP, JOHN CAMPBELL, 1877, *On Poetic Interpretation of Nature, p.* 232.

Not into literature only did MacPherson's book pour a new lava-steam, but it initiated, in the domain of Historical Science, the most fruitful new researches. Directly springing from, or indirectly stimulated by, the enthusiasm excited by "Ossian," researches were instituted into the antiquities of all the three great races of Europe—not of the Kelts only, but of the Teutons, and of the Slavs—and collections were made, or edited, of their ancient poesies. It is unnecessary to recall the dates of the several publications. Only this general fact we need here note, that if, in very various degrees, *propter* "Ossian," in every case *post* "Ossian," were such works as the Welsh "Myvyrian Archæology" and "Mabinogion;" Müller's "Collection of German Poems from the 12th, 13th and 14th Centuries," and Grimm's "Teutonic Mythology;" and the numberless Slavonic Folk-lore collections which were the antiquarian bases of the great political fact of Panslavonic aspirations. And considering this, we see that by no means was the scope and bearing of the researches springing from, or stimulated by, MacPherson's "Ossian" confined to the sphere of historical theory, and religious belief. Few things are, in the last hundred years, more remarkable than the direct transformation of historical theories into political forces. Political aspirations of nationalities or races to union or re-union are but the transference into the sphere of practical endeavour of the theories of antiquaries and historians. Yet no forces have in Europe, in this century, shown themselves more powerful. And more particularly events are now indicating, with almost daily increasing clearness, that the Keltic Revival, directly, initiated by MacPherson's "Ossian," will show itself hardly less important as a political force than the Slavonic Revival, indirectly stimulated by "Ossian."—STUART-GLENNIE, J. S., 1880, *MacPherson, Burns, and Scott in their Relation to the Modern Revolution, Fraser's Magazine, vol.* 101, *p.* 521.

Addison had already directed attention to the English ballad-poetry, and Klopstock, Gleim and others had profited by

his example. Bishop Percy's collection
of English ballads was, therefore, received
with general rapture in Germany, and the
sentimental heroic poetry of Celtic origin,
which Macpherson sent forth under the
name of Ossian, was greeted with enthusiastic applause by a race of poets full
of sentiment and warlike sympathies.—
SCHERER, WILHELM, 1883-86, *A History
of German Literature, tr. Conybeare, vol.*
II, *p.* 56.

Space (fortunately) does not permit a
discussion of the Ossianic question. That
fragments of Ossianic legend (if not of
Ossianic poetry) survive in oral Gaelic
traditions, seems certain. How much
Macpherson knew of these, and how little
he used them in the bombastic prose which
Napoleon loved (and spelled "Ocean"),
it is next to impossible to discover.—
LANG, ANDREW, 1886, *Books and Book-
men, p.* 27.

Curiously enough, although Macpherson
died suddenly, his papers were searched
in vain for a scrap of evidence for or
against his culpability. In these days few
will be credulous enough to pin their faith
to the misty songs of Ullin; but there are
probably some persons of intelligence,
especially north of the Tay, who still "indulge the pleasing supposition that Fingal
fought and Ossian sang."—GOSSE, ED-
MUND, 1888, *A History of Eighteenth Century Literature, p.* 337.

It has been seen that among his contemporaries and fellow-countrymen there
were some who showed signs of the coming romantic movement; but he was the
first in the English language who powerfully and decisively expressed it. And
this must be set down as his signal merit.
Far from being a mere translator, he was
peculiarly original. Not that Macpherson
created the spirit of romance. . . .
It does not follow that Macpherson was a
man of great genius. On the contrary,
the range of his ideas was so narrow that
to read any one of his poems is to become
master of almost all that he had to say.
The same expressions, the same images,
and almost identical situations recur again
and again. Repetition was affected no
doubt partly to give an aspect of antiquity;
but in Macpherson it goes deeper and discloses poverty of mind. Still, to deny
him the praise of having well expressed
his few thoughts is unjust. There is much

fustian in his style, and it speedily palls
upon the ear; but the peculiar poetic prose
which he formed for himself has, in little
bits, a powerful charm. His descriptions of
scenery and of aspects of nature are often
very beautiful. We ask again and again
why they are there, but he who can forget
their incongruity with a poem of the third
century must feel their truth.—WALKER,
HUGH, 1893, *Three Centuries of Scottish
Literature, vol.* II, *pp.* 127, 128.

Ossian points as directly to Byron as the
chivalry and ballad revivals point to Scott.
These indicate the two great streams in
the Romantic movement. In Byron's
poetry—sincere or feigned—we see constantly manifest the Ossian feeling. What
Byron himself thought of Ossian I have
had a good opportunity to observe by perusing Byron's own manuscript notes in a
copy of the Ossian poems. The following
notes I copied directly from Byron's hand-
writing: "The portrait which Ossian has
drawn of himself is indeed a masterpiece.
He not only appears in the light of a distinguished warrior—generous as well as
brave—and possessed of exquisite sensibility—but of an aged venerable bard
—subjected to the most melancholy vicissitudes of fortune—weak and blind—the
sole survivor of his family—the last of
the race of Fingal. The character of
Fingal—the poet's own father—is a highly
finished one. There is certainly no hero
in the Iliad—or the Odyssey—who is at
once so brave and amiable as this renowned
king of Morven. It is well known that
Hector—whose character is of all the
Homeric heroes the most complete—
greatly sullies the lustre of his glorious
actions by the insult over the fallen
Patroclus. On the other hand the conduct
of Fingal appears uniformly illustrious
and great—without one mean or inhuman
action to tarnish the splendour of his
fame—He is equally the object of our admiration esteem and love." Speaking of
Ossian's skill in depicting female characters, he writes, "How happily, for instance, has he characterized his own mistress—afterwards his wife—by a single
epithet expressive of that modesty—softness—and complacency—which constitute the perfection of feminine excellence
—'the mildly blushing Everallin.' . . . I
am of opinion that though in sublimity of
sentiment—in vivacity and strength of

description—Ossian may claim a full equality of merit with Homer himself—yet in the invention both of incidents and character he is greatly inferior to the Grecian bard.'' These quotations are interesting as showing how seriously Byron took Ossian and how carefully and thoughtfully he read him. The influence of Ossian lasted long after the immediate excitement caused by its novelty and professed antiquity had passed away.—PHELPS, WILLIAM LYON, 1893, *The Beginnings of the English Romantic Movement, p.* 153.

The problem of Macpherson's true character must now be regarded as depending, not upon any question as to the survival of ancient Celtic poetry in the Highlands—for of the existence there, in Macpherson's day, of even a considerable body of such traditionary remains there seems no longer any room to doubt—but rather upon the particular degree of fidelity and conscientious care displayed in his arrangement and translation of the several "fragments" recovered by him from the Highlanders, and declared by him to be none other than the *disjecta membra* of the long-lost epic of "Fingal."—HUTCHINSON, T., 1894, *The Academy, vol.* 46, *p.* 205.

Ossian was translated into Italian by Cesarotti; there were two versions of him in Spanish, several in German, one in Swedish, one in Danish, and two in Dutch, of which one was by Bilderdyk. In Germany, especially, he created a furor. The true originator of Northern poetry was found at last; "Thou, too, Ossian," cried Klopstock, "wert swallowed up in oblivion; but thou has been restored to thy position; behold thee now before us, the equal and the challenger of Homer the Greek." "What need," wrote Voss to Brückner, "of natural beauty? Ossian of Scotland is a greater poet than Homer of Ionia." Lerse, in a sonorous discourse at Strasburg, acknowledged three guides of the "sacred art of poetry:" Shakespeare, Homer, and Ossian—two Northern poets to a single classic. Herder wrote a comparison between the Homeric and the Ossianic epics, spoke of Ossian as "the man I have sought," and contemplated a journey to Scotland in order to collect the songs of the bards. Bürger imitated him, and Christian Heyne constituted himself champion at the University of Göttingen. Lastly, Goethe, need we remind the reader,

drew inspiration from him in "Werther" and elsewhere. When his spirits are high Werther's taste is for Homer, but in sorrow he feeds upon Ossian, and when "it is autumn within and about him," he cries: "Ossian has completely banished Homer from my heart!"—TEXTE, JOSEPH, 1895-99, *Jean-Jacques Rousseau and the Cosmopolitan Spirit in Literature, tr. Matthews, p.* 319.

In his former works M. d'Arboiss had already drawn up a catalogue of Irish epics; he had examined them and briefly defined their character and their literary importance; he had taught us how to distinguish the cycle of Ulster, which crystallised in the North of Ireland around the heroic figure of King Conchobar or Conor; the cycle of Leinster, which celebrated in the east of Ireland the deeds of Osson, or Ossian, as the moderns have it; and finally the mythological cycle, formed in earth, sea and sky, around the conceptions of a religious imagination. He showed us how the two Epics of the North and the East, artificially combined and quite transformed from their rude, barbarous and fierce antiquity, were idealised out of all semblance by the rhetorical Macpherson till they condensed anew into those pale, vague, nebulous poems of Ossian which appeared so tremendous a revelation of nature to the earlier Romantics. A whole generation found in this mutilated paraphrase a joy for ever. Napoleon, Goethe, Lamartine read and raved of Ossian, as also Baour-Lormian. And Werther was to write: "Ossian has supplanted Homer in my heart." M. d'Arbois and his collaborators, Mm. Dottin, Duvau and Ferdinand Grammont give, in the present volume, numerous specimens of these various epochs, which dwell, still unpublished, in the dusty seclusion of libraries and archives. It is interesting to study them, to turn from Macpherson to his models. Despite his inferior value—for the copy is far below the original—his versions merit our attention, not only on their own merits and as the testimony, however ill-reported, of a forgotten world, but for the indirect and latent action which during more than fifty years they continued to exercise upon the imaginative literature of Europe. In two of the episodes selected: the death of Derdrin and the death of Cûchulain, the editors

give, side by side with the version of
Ossian, a literal translation from the
original epic. One knows not which is
the more surprising, the audacity with
which Macpherson has drowned the brutal,
savage, old legends in a vapour of vague
exclamations, or the innocent good faith
with which our romantic fore-fathers
accepted these tricked-out ecstasies and
insipid, tame tirades which we have not
the patience to read to the end of, as
the unsophisticated voice of Nature. It
is a matter to give pause to the advocates
of an absolute standard in criticism, a
shaft the more in the quiver of the impres-
sionists, *chi oggi han il grido*, till a new
mode arise.—DARMESTETER, JAMES, 1894
—96, *Celtica, English Studies, tr. Mrs.
Darmesteter, p.* 183.

The imposture (for that in the main it
was imposture is certain) of Macpherson
is more interesting as a matter of tendency than of essence. The world wanted
romance; it wanted "the Celtic vague;"
it wanted anything but what it had had:
Macpherson met it with a sort of clumsy
genius. All the others named catered for
the same want, not with the intelligent
scoundrelism of the adulterator, but with
the honest attempt of the still unqualified
artist.—SAINTSBURY, GEORGE, 1896, *Social
England, ed. Traill, vol.* V, *p.* 262.

We do not acquit a man of dishonesty
because he passes a few good half-crowns
amid hundreds of his own coinage. We
know that this is a necessary trick of the
game, and part of the prudential wisdom
of knavery. . . . We certainly believe
that many men, and many women, given
a few Gaelic names and a tale to tell about
them, could, after one perusal of "Fingal"
or "Temora," turn out a poem which,
bating perhaps the felicities which appear
at very rare intervals in Macpherson's compilation, and prove that he had some
poetic gift, would pass for Macpherson-
Ossianic.—TOVEY, DUNCAN C., 1897, *Ossian and his Maker, Reviews and Essays
in English Literature, pp.* 138, 144.

In studying the landscape of Macpherson's "Ossian" we soon learn that it belongs unmistakably to Western Argyle-
shire. Its union of mountain, glen, and
sea removes it at once from the interior
to the coast. Even if it had been more
or less inaccurately drawn, its prominence
and consistency all through the poems

would have been remarkable in the productions of a lad of four-and-twenty, who
had spent his youth in the inland region
of Badenoch, where the scenery is of
another kind. But when we discover that
the endless allusions to topographical
features are faithful delineations, which
give the very spirit and essence of the
scenery, we feel sure that whether they
were written in the eighteenth century or
in the third, they display a poetic genius
of no mean order. The grandeur and
gloom of the Highland mountains, the
spectral mists that sweep round the crags,
the roar of the torrents, the gleams of
sunlight on moor and lake, the wail of
the breeze among the cairns of the dead,
the unspeakable sadness that seems to
brood over the landscape whether the sky
be clear or clouded—these features of
west Highland scenery were first revealed
by Macpherson to the modern world.
This revelation quickened the change of
feeling, already begun, in regard to the
prevailing horror of mountain-scenery.
It brought before men's eyes some of the
fascination of the mountain-world, more
especially in regard to the atmospheric
effects that play so large a part in its
landscape. It showed the titanic forces
of storm and tempest in full activity.
And yet there ran through all the poems
a vein of infinite melancholy. The pathos
of life manifested itself everywhere, now
in the tenderness of unavailing devotion,
now in the courage of hopeless despair.—
GEIKIE, SIR ARCHIBALD, 1898, *Types of
Scenery and their Influence on Literature,
p.* 44.

GENERAL

His "History" is pronounced by Fox to
be full of "impudent" falsehoods; it has
long sunk from public notice, and had no
charm either of style or thought to relieve
it from neglect. Nor is it possible to believe, that one who wrote so dull a history could have produced so wild and
imaginative a poem as that which the
world has generally attributed to him.—
LAWRENCE, EUGENE, 1855, *Lives of the
British Historians, vol.* II, *p.* 238.

Though he never could have become so
important a figure as he thought himself,
we are convinced that he would have
achieved a fame in literature quite as
great and much less sinister if he had been
more honest.—TOVEY, DUNCAN C., 1897,

Ossian and his Maker, Reviews and Essays in English Literature, p. 152.

That a writer of the stamp of James Macpherson should have been destined to approach history at all was, I think, a remarkable freak of nature. That it should be reserved, however, for the author of the "Ossian" fraud to discover and give to the world important facts, tearing to shreds the character of one of the greatest men that this country has ever produced, is, I submit, a little too hard for belief by rational beings. Is it reasonable to suppose that "Original Papers" on English history produced by the inventor of the Gaelic "Originals" of the Ossian poems are likely to be genuine? The point is, indeed, virtually settled at the outset by the fact which I have mentioned that the manuscripts in question, imputing such fearful crimes to Marlborough, Godolphin, and their associated helpers in the work of the Revolution, are *not* original. I must ask my readers to keep this steadily in view; for the whole gist of the position taken up by Dalrymple, Hallam, Macaulay, and all more recent followers of Macpherson lies in the assumption that the Nairne papers in the Bodleian library are original state documents, and therefore not to be gainsaid.—PARNELL, ARTHUR, 1897, *Macpherson and the Nairne Papers, English Historical Review, vol.* 12, p. 274.

Thomas Reid

1710–1796

Born, at Strachan, Kincardineshire, 26 April 1710. Early education at Kincardine parish school. To Marischal College, Aberdeen, 1722; B. A., 1726. Studied for Presbyterian ministry. Licensed preacher, Sept. 1731. Librarian of Marischal Coll., 1733-36. Minister of New Machar, Aberdeen, 1737. Married Elizabeth Reid, 1740. "Regent" (afterwards Prof. of Philosophy) at King's Coll., Aberdeen, Oct. 1751 to May 1764. Founded Philosophical Society, 1758; it existed till 1773. Hon. D. D., Marischal Coll., 18 Jan. 1762. Prof. of Moral Philosophy, Glasgow Univ., May 1764 to Oct. 1796; deputed active duties of professorship to an assistant, 1780. Died, in Glasgow, 7 Oct. 1796. *Works:* "An Inquiry into the Human Mind on the Principles of Common Sense," 1764; "Essays on the Intellectual Powers of Man," 1785; "Essays on the Active Powers of Man," 1788; (He contributed: "An Essay on Quantity" to the "Philosophical Transactions" for 1748; "A Brief Account of Aristotle's Logic" to "Kame's Sketches of the History of Man," vol. ii., 1774; "A Statistical Account of the University of Glasgow" to Sinclair's "Statistical Account of Scotland," 1799.) *Collected Works:* ed. by Sir W. Hamilton (2 vols.), 1846-63. *Life:* by Dugald Stewart, 1803.—SHARP, R. FARQUHARSON, 1897, *A Dictionary of English Authors, p.* 238.

PERSONAL

Reid was below the middle size, but had great athletic power. His portrait, painted by Raeburn during his last visit to Edinburgh, belongs to Glasgow University; and a medallion by Tassie, taken in his eighty-first year, in the National Portrait Gallery, Edinburgh, is said to be a very good likeness. Reid's obvious characteristic was the strong and cautious "common sense" which also dictated his philosophy. He was thoroughly independent, strictly economical, and uniformly energetic in the discharge of his duties. He was amiable in his family, delighted in young children, some of whom, it is said, "noticed the peculiar kindness of his eye;" and was as charitable as his means permitted. Stewart mentions a gift to his former parishioners of New Machar, during the scarcity of 1782, which would have been out of proportion to his means had it not been for his rigid economy, and of which he endeavoured to conceal the origin. From the few letters preserved, he appears to have been remarkable for the warmth and steadiness of his friendships.—STEPHEN, LESLIE, 1896, *Dictionary of National Biography, vol.* XLVII, p. 438.

There was a fine simplicity, a sterling honesty in the old philosophical student, who in controversy was the model of courtesy shocking thereby Dr. Beattie, who was grieved that a controversialist who professed to be a Christian should write like a gentleman. As he grew aged he became very deaf, but not less shrewd; as active at eighty-seven years as at sixty, with his short, sturdy frame, busy in his garden, keen over botany, physiology, or physics. Yet with all his energy he would plaintively say, with a kindly look on his good, plain, common-sense face, which looked like an incarnation of his own philosophy: "I am ashamed of having lived so long after having ceased to be useful." GRAHAM, HENRY GREY, 1901, *Scottish Men of Letters in the Eighteenth Century, p.* 259.

His life had been a singularly calm one, and his chief characteristics had been an indomitable faculty of patient thought and a sincerity of purpose that never wavered. Such influence as he possessed was gained by quiet and persistent effort; and he did not affect his contemporaries either by any marked originality of genius, or by a striking or eccentric personality.—CRAIK, SIR HENRY, 1901, *A Century of Scottish History, vol.* II, *p.* 209.

GENERAL

I have been looking into Dr. Reid's book on "The Active Powers of Man." It is written with his usual perspicuity and acuteness; is in some parts very entertaining; and to me, who have been obliged to think so much on those subjects, is very interesting throughout. The question concerning Liberty and Necessity is very fully discussed, and very ably; and, I think, nothing more needs be said about it. I could have wished that Dr. Reid had given a fuller enumeration of the passions, and been a little more particular in illustrating the duties of morality. But his manner is, in all his writings, more turned to speculation than to practical philosophy; which may be owing to his having employed himself so much in the study of Locke, Hume, Berkeley, and other theorists; and partly, no doubt, to the habits of study and modes of conversation which were fashionable in this country in his younger days. If I were not personally acquainted with the Doctor, I should conclude, from his books, that he was rather too warm an admirer of Mr. Hume. He confutes, it is true, some of his opinions; but he pays them much more respect than they are entitled to.—BEATTIE, JAMES, 1788, *Letter to Sir William Forbes, March 5; Account of the Life and Writings of Beattie, ed. Forbes, vol.* III, *p.* 37.

The merit of what you are pleased to call *my Philosophy,* lies, I think, chiefly, in having called in question the common theory of ideas, or images of things in the mind, being the only objects of thought; a theory founded on natural prejudices, and so universally received as to be interwoven with the structure of language. Yet, were I to give you a detail of what led me to call in question this theory, after I had long held it as self-evident and unquestionable, you would think, as I do, that there was much of chance in the matter. The discovery was the birth of time, not of genius; and Berkeley and Hume did more to bring it to light than the man that hit upon it. I think there is hardly any thing that can be called *mine* in the philosophy of the mind, which does not follow with ease from the detection of this prejudice.—REID, THOMAS, 1790, *Letter to Dr. James Gregory, Works.*

The author of an "Inquiry into the Mind," and of subsequent "Essays on the Intellectual and Active Powers of Man," has great merit in the effect to which he has pursued this history. But, considering the point at which the science stood when he began his inquiries, he has perhaps no less merit in having removed the mist of hypothesis and metaphor with which the subject was enveloped, and in having taught us to state the facts of which we are conscious, not in figurative language, but in the terms which are proper to the subject. In this it will be our advantage to follow him; the more that, in former theories, so much attention had been paid to the introduction of *ideas or images* as the elements of knowledge, that the belief of any external existence or prototype has been left to be inferred from the mere idea or image; and this inference, indeed, is so little founded, that many who have come to examine its evidence have thought themselves warranted to deny it altogether. And hence the criticism of ingenious men, who, not seeing a proper access of knowledge through the medium of ideas, without considering whether the road they had been directed to take was the true or a false one, denied the possibility of arriving at the end.— FERGUSON, ADAM, 1792, *Principles of Moral and Political Science, vol.* I.

With respect to his character; its most prominent features were, intrepid and inflexible rectitude; a pure and devoted attachment to truth; and an entire command, acquired by the unwearied exertions of a long life, over all his passions. —STEWART, DUGALD, 1803, *Account of the Life and Writings of Thomas Reid.*

Dr. Reid's great achievement was, undoubtedly, the subversion of the Ideal system, or the confutation of that hypothesis which represents the immediate objects of the mind in perception as certain *images* or *pictures* of external objects conveyed by the senses to the sensorium. This part of his task, it is now generally admitted that he has performed with exemplary diligence and complete success; but we are by no means so entirely satisfied with the uses he has attempted to make of his victory.—JEFFREY, FRANCIS LORD, 1804, *Stewart's Life of Dr. Reid, Edinburgh Review, vol. 3, p.* 281.

A sincere inquirer after Truth, who maintained indeed the existence of certain principles of knowledge, independent of experience, but considered philosophy as the science of the human mind, which must be founded on the principles of Common Sense, regarding the latter as species of Intellectual Instinct. — TENNEMANN, WILLIAM GOTTLIEB, 1812–52, *A Manual of the History of Philosophy, tr. Johnson,* ed. Morell.

You can read in the translation of one of the best pupils of the Normal School, now my colleague in this faculty, the judicious Reid, with the truly superior commentary of M. Royer-Collard. The Scotch philosophy will prepare you for the German philosophy. It is to Reid and to Kant that I refer in great part the polemics which I have instituted against empiricism in the person of Locke.—COUSIN, VICTOR, 1828–52, *History of Modern Philosophy, tr. Wight.*

A patient, modest, and deep thinker, who in his first work ("Enquiry into the Human Mind") deserves a commendation more descriptive of a philosopher than that bestowed by Professor Cousin, of having made a vigorous protest against scepticism on behalf of common sense. His observations on suggestion, on natural signs, on the connection between what he calls sensation and conception, though perhaps occasioned by Berkeley, whose idealism Reid had once adopted, are marked by the genuine spirit of original observation.—MACKINTOSH, SIR JAMES, 1830, *Second Preliminary Dissertation, Encyclopædia Britannica.*

Reid, who carried into the recesses of the human mind the torch of reason.— ALISON, SIR ARCHIBALD, 1833–42, *History of Europe During The French Revolution, vol.* XIV, *p.* 3.

Dr. Reid has many merits as a speculator, but the only merit which he arrogates to himself,—the principal merit accorded to him by others,—is, that he was the first philosopher, in more recent times, who dared, in his doctrine of immediate perception, to vindicate, against the unanimous authority of philosophers, the universal conviction of mankind. But this doctrine he has at best imperfectly developed, and, at the same time, has unfortunately obscured it, by errors of so singular a character, that some acute philosophers—for Dr. Brown does not stand alone—have never even suspected what his doctrine of perception actually is. . . . But if all he did was merely to explode the cruder hypothesis of representation, and to adopt in its place the finer, —why, in the first place, so far from depriving idealism and scepticism of all basis, he only placed them on one firmer and more secure; and, in the second, so far from originating a new opinion, he could only have added one to a class of philosophers, who, after the time of Arnauld, were continually on the increase, and who, among the contemporaries of Reid himself, certainly constituted the majority. His philosophy would thus be at once only a silly blunder; its pretence to originality only in proclamation of ignorance; and, so far from being an honour to the nation from which it arose, and by whom it was respected, it would, in fact, be a scandal and a reproach to the philosophy of any country in which it met with any milder treatment than derision. . . . I then detailed to you the grounds on which it ought to be held that Reid's doctrine of Perception is one of Natural Realism, and not a form of Cosmothetic Idealism, as supposed by Brown. . . . Having concluded the argument by which I endeavoured to satisfy you that Reid's doctrine is Natural Realism, I should now proceed to show that Natural Realism is a more philosophical doctrine than Hypothetical Realism. — HAMILTON, SIR

WILLIAM, 1836–56, *Lectures on Metaphysics, Lectures*, xiii, xxiv.

It may be here remarked that what Malebranche has properly called the judgment of the mind as to the cause of its sensations, is precisely what Reid denominates perception; a term less clear, and which seems to have led some of his school into important errors. The language of the Scottish philosopher appears to imply that he considered perception as a distinct and original faculty of the mind, rather than what it is, a complex operation of the judgment and memory, applying knowledge already acquired by experience. Neither he nor his disciple Stewart, though aware of the mistakes that have arisen in this province of metaphysics by selecting our instances from the phenomena of vision instead of the other senses, have avoided the same source of error. —HALLAM, HENRY, 1837–39, *Introduction to the Literature of Europe*, pt. iv, ch. iii, *par.* 43.

Reid's philosophy made a great stir at first, but has for some years past been sinking into merited neglect. The appeal to Common Sense as arbiter in Philosophy, is now pretty well understood to be on a par with Dr. Johnson's kicking a stone as a refutation of Berkeley.—LEWES, GEORGE HENRY, 1845–46, *Biographical History of Philosophy*, p. 619.

The great aim of Reid's philosophy, then, was to investigate the true theory of perception; to controvert the representationalist hypothesis, as held in one sense or another by almost all preceding philosophers; and to stay the progress which scepticism, aided by this hypothesis, was so rapidly making. . . . That Reid has done much for the advancement of mental science, is almost universally admitted: to complain that he did not accomplish *more*, or follow out the track which he opened to its furthest results, is perhaps unreasonable; since we ought rather to look for the completion of his labours from the hands of his followers, than demand from himself at once the foundation and the superstructure. — MORELL, J. D., 1846–7, *An Historical and Critical View of the Speculative Philosophy of Europe in the Nineteenth Century*.

The merits of Dr. Reid, then, as a reformer of philosophy, amount in our opinion to this: he was among the first to *say* and to *write* that the representative theory of perception was false and erroneous, and was the fountain head of scepticism and idealism. But this admission of his merits must be accompanied by the qualification that he adopted, as the basis of his philosophy, a principle which rendered nugatory all his protestations. It is of no use to disclaim a conclusion if we accept the premises which inevitably lead to it. Dr. Reid disclaimed the representative theory, but he embraced its premises, and thus he virtually ratified the conclusions of the very system which he clamorously denounced. In his language he is opposed to representationism, but in his doctrine he lends it the strongest support by accepting as the foundation of his philosophy an analysis of the perception of matter.— FERRIER, JAMES FREDERICK, 1847–66, *Reid and the Philosophy of Common Sense, Lectures, vol.* II, *p.* 417.

The positive doctrines of Reid's own system could not be understood without much explanation; and his own exposition of them is very imperfect. Indeed the constant occurrence of polemical matter, and the repetitions which his Essays derived from their original shape of Lectures, are the circumstances that chiefly injure the literary value of the work. He is a bald and dry, but very clear and logical writer; and never was there a more sincere lover of truth, or a more candid and honourable disputant. His slow and patient thinking, notwithstanding a strong aversion to close analysis, led him to some very striking results, out of which his whole scheme is developed. The originality of these is much greater than his own manner of expounding them would lead us to suppose; and their importance in the history of philosophy may be estimated from this fact, that Reid's metaphysical creed does really coincide with the first and most characteristic step in that of his German contemporary Kant.— SPALDING, WILLIAM, 1852–82, *A History of English Literature*, p. 352.

Since the first edition of this work, Sir W. Hamilton has published an edition of Reid, illustrated and enriched by notes and dissertations of incomparable erudition and acuteness. Respecting the interpretation Sir William gives to Reid's doctrines, I will only say that he has shown what a subtle mind can *read into* the philosophy of common sense; but he has not in the least produced the conviction in me of Reid's having meant what the illustrious successor supposed him to have meant. At the same time, I will add that, the limits of my work having restricted me to the consideration of Reid's contributions to Philosophy, (in the narrow sense of the term), I have not done justice to his many excellent qualities as a teacher. His works are well worthy of diligent study, and their spirit is eminently scientific.—LEWES, GEORGE HENRY, 1857, *Biographical History of Philosophy*, p. 629, *note*.

Reid is a bold, dry, but very clear and logical writer, a sincere lover of truth, and a candid and honorable disputant; his system is original and important in the history of philosophy.—BOTTA, ANNE C. LYNCH, 1860, *Hand-Book of Universal Literature*, p. 510.

Was the most eminent among the purely speculative thinkers of Scotland, after Hume and Adam Smith, though in point of merit, he must be placed far below them. For, he had neither the comprehensiveness of Smith, nor the fearlessness of Hume. The range of his knowledge was not wide enough to allow him to be comprehensive; while a timidity, almost amounting to moral cowardice, made him recoil from the views advocated by Hume, not so much on account of their being false, as on account of their being dangerous. . . . With Reid, the main question always is, not whether an inference is true, but what will happen if it is true. He says, that a doctrine is to be judged by its fruits; forgetting that the same doctrine will bear different fruits in different ages, and that the consequences which a theory produces in one state of society, are often diametrically opposed to those which it produces in another. He thus made his own age the standard of all future ones. He also trammelled philosophy with practical considerations; diverting thinkers from the pursuit of truth, which is their proper department, into the pursuit of expediency, which is not their department at all. Reid was constantly stopping to inquire, not whether theories were accurate, but whether it was advisable to adopt them; whether they were favourable to patriotism, or to generosity, or to friendship; in a word, whether they were comfortable, and such as we should at present like to believe. Or else, he would take other ground, still lower, and still more unworthy of a philosopher.—BUCKLE, HENRY THOMAS, 1862–66, *History of Civilization in England, vol.* III, *ch.* V.

The mere fact of his originating a school of philosophy, even though we allow that his conclusions were supported by popular feeling, argues a large measure of intellectual force, in one direction or another; but very different opinions have been expressed as to his capacities for mental analysis. Various particulars in his style and his favourite studies indicate a tendency to dwell by preference upon the concrete. He had no great turn for style; his composition deserves the praise of "ease, perspicuity, and purity;" it is, besides, neat and finished, and often moves with considerable spirit: but it has neither the incisive vigour of Campbell, the copiousness of Smith, nor the original freshness of Tucker.—MINTO, WILLIAM, 1872–80, *Manual of English Prose Literature*, p. 471.

If he was not the founder, he is the fit representative of the Scottish philosophy. He is in every respect, a Scotchman of the genuine type: shrewd, cautious, outwardly calm, and yet with a deep well of feeling within, and capable of enthusiasm; not witty, but with a quiet vein of humour. And then he has the truly philosophic spirit seeking truth modestly, humbly, diligently; piercing beneath the surface to gaze on the true nature of things; and not to be caught by sophistry, or mislead by plausible representations. He has not the mathematical consecutiveness of Descartes, the speculative genius of Leibnitz, the sagacity of Locke, the *spirituel* of Berkeley, or the detective skill of Hume; but he has a quality quite as valuable as any of these, even in philosophy he has in perfection that common-sense which he so commends, and this saves him from the extreme positions into which these great men have been tempted by the soaring nature of their inexorable logic.—MCCOSH, JAMES, 1874, *The Scottish Philosophy*, p. 192.

Reid's appeal to the common-sense of men, was taken without sufficient analysis, and hence bears a dogmatic character. He has left it uncertain, whether he regarded sensation itself as a direct contract with the external world, or whether it is instantly completed by an intuitive action of the mind, and the reference of effects to causes becomes the medium by which this union is effected. We suppose him to have obscurely held this last view. Hamilton ascribes to him the first.—BAS-COM, JOHN, 1874, *Philosophy of English Literature*, p. 315.

The ethical speculations of Reid, the most eminent writer of the Common-Sense school, are contained in his "Essays on the Active Powers," but would scarcely justify a prolonged analysis. They may be described briefly as a combination of the views of Clarke and Shaftsbury, though most resembling those of Butler. Recognising the nugatory character of Clarke's theory, he also thinks that to adopt Shaftesbury's theory would be to make morality arbitrary, as dependent upon a "natural or acquired taste." The conscience, therefore, which guides our moral judgments, is at once, in his language, an intellectual and an active power, and its supremacy is, as with Butler, an ultimate and self-evident fact. This power, which is simply common sense applied to moral questions, is, of course, capable of laying down as many first principles as may be required. Here, as elsewhere, the difficulty of finding an ultimate justification for axioms is evaded by simply declaring that no justification is needed; but there is nothing in Reid's ethical doctrine which has not been more articulately worked out by his predecessors, except that his facility in multiplying first principles is, perhaps, more marked and his philosophy proportionally weaker.—STEPHEN, LESLIE, 1876, *History of English Thought in the Eighteenth Century*, vol. II, p. 62.

The principles which Reid insists upon as every where present in experience evidently correspond pretty closely to the Kantian categories and the unity of apperception.—SETH, ANDREW, 1886, *Encyclopædia Brittanica*, vol. XX.

The works of Reid, from his "Enquiry into the Human Mind" (1763), to his "Active Powers of Man" (1788), show a great clearness of intellect and strictly logical habit, but no great enthusiasm or originality.—GOSSE, EDMUND, 1888, *A History of Eighteenth Century Literature*, p. 295.

The father of Scottish or common-sense philosophy.—ROBERTSON, J. LOGIE, 1894, *A History of English Literature*, p. 252.

On the study of psychology, it is admitted by some who do not think very highly of his general philosophy, Reid had a favourable influence.—WHITTAKER, T., 1896, *Social England*, ed. Traill, vol. V, p. 413.

Edmund Burke

1729–1797

Born, in Dublin, 12 Jan. (?) 1729. Educated at a school at Ballitore, 1741–43; at Trinity Coll., Dublin, 1743–48; scholarship, 1746; B. A., 1748. To Middle Temple to study Law, 1750. Never called to Bar; gave up legal studies by 1755. Took to literary work. Married Jane Nugent, 1756 (or 1757?). Edited "Annual Register," 1759–88. Gradually became known by literary work. Private Sec. to William Gerard Hamilton, 1759–64. To Ireland with Hamilton, 1761. Annual pension of £300, 1763. Threw up pension, April 1764. Private Sec. to Lord Rockingham, July 1765. M. P. for Wendover, Dec. 1765. First speech made, 27 Jan. 1766. To Ireland, summer of 1766; received freedom of city of Galway. Purchased estate near Beaconsfield, 1768. Appointed Agent to the Province of New York, 1771. Visit to Paris, Feb. to March 1773. M. P. for Malton after dissolution of Parliament in Sept. 1774; again after dissolution in Sept. 1780; and again in Nov. 1790. Intimacy with Fox begun. Appointed Paymaster of the Forces, 1782. Lord Rector of Glasgow University, 1784 and 1785. Impeachment of Warren Hastings, 10 May 1787; trial begun, 13 Feb. 1788. Grace for conferring Hon. LL.D. degree passed, Dublin Univ., 11 Dec. 1790. Burke apparently never attended to take the degree. Again elected M. P. for Malton, Nov. 1790. Rupture with Fox, 1791. Retired from Parliament, July 1794. Two pensions of £1,200 and £2,500 granted him, Aug. 1794. Interested in foundation of Maynooth Catholic College, 1795. Established, at Beaconsfield, school for sons of French emigrants, 1796. Died at Beaconsfield, 6 July 1797.

Buried in Beaconsfield parish church. *Works:* Burke's chief literary works are: "A Vindication of Natural Society" (anon.), 1756; "A Philosophical Inquiry into the Origin of our Ideas of the Sublime and the Beautiful" (anon.), 1757; "An Account of the European Settlements in America" (anon. probably edited by Burke, and written by himself and his cousin, William Burke), 1757; "A Short Account of a Short Administration" (anon.), 1766; "Observations on a late Publication intituled 'The Present State of the Nation'" (anon.), 1769; "Thoughts on the Causes of the Present Discontents" (anon.), 1770; "Political Tracts and Speeches," 1777; "Reflections on the Revolution in France," 1790 (2nd edn. same year); "Appeals from the New to the Old Whigs" (anon.), 1791 (2nd edn. same year); "Thoughts on the Prospect of a Regicide Peace" (anon), 1796 (11th edn. same year). [Burke published a number of his speeches, also of political pamphlets and letters, beween 1774 and 1791, and many were published posthumously. A complete collection is the "Works and Correspondence" (8 vols.), London, 1852]. *Posthumous:* "Correspondence with Dr. Laurence," 1827; "Letters, 1744-97" (4 vols.), 1844; "Speeches, with Memoir," 1854; "Letters, Speeches, and Tracts on Irish Affairs," 1881. *Collected Works:* in 8 vols., 1792–1827; in 8 vols., 1852. *Life:* by MacCormick, 1798; by Bisset, 1798; by Sir James Prior, 5th edn. 1854; by MacKnight, 1858; by Morley ("English Men of Letters" series), 1879.—SHARP, R. FARQUHARSON, 1897, *A Dictionary of English Authors, p.* 39.

PERSONAL

It is time I should say who my friend is. His name is Edmond Burke. As a literary man he may possibly be not quite unknown to you. He is the author of a piece which imposed on the world as Lord Bolingbroke's, called, "The Advantages of Natural Society," and of a very ingenious book published last year, called, "A Treatise on the Sublime and Beautiful." I must farther say of him, that his chief application has been to the knowledge of public business, and our commercial interests; that he seems to have a most extensive knowledge, with extraordinary talents for business, and to want nothing but ground to stand upon to do his country very important services.—MARKHAM, W., 1759, *Letter to the Duchess of Queensbury, Sep.* 25; *Chatham Correspondence, vol.* I, *p.* 432.

An Irishman, Mr. Burke, is sprung up, in the House of Commons who has astonished every body with the power of his eloquence, and his comprehensive knowledge in all our exterior and internal politics, and commercial interests. He wants nothing but that sort of dignity annexed to rank and property in England to make him the most considerable man in the Lower House.—LEE, ARTHUR, 1766, *To the Prince Royal of Poland, Life, p.* 290.

At Beaconsfield, Mr. Burke is an industrious farmer, a polite husband, a kind master, a charitable neighbour, and a most excellent companion. The demons of ambition and party who hover about Westminster do not extend their influences as far as the villa. I know not why it is, but these busy spirits seem more tranquil and pleased in their days of retreat than the honest, dull justice of the quorum, who never stretched forth his hand to snatch the sceptre of power, or raised his voice in publick to fill the trumpet of fame. — MONTAGU, ELIZABETH, 1772, *Letters, Aug.* 9; *A Lady of the Last Century, ed. Doran, p.* 175.

Here lies our good Edmund, whose genius was such,
We scarcely can praise it, or blame it too much;
Who, born for the universe, narrow'd his mind,
And to party gave up what was meant for mankind;
Though fraught with all learning, yet straining his throat
To persuade Tommy Townshend to lend him a vote;
Who, too deep for his hearers, still went on refining,
And thought of convincing, while they thought of dining;
Though equal to all things, for all things unfit,
Too nice for a statesman, too proud for a wit;
For a patriot, too cool; for a drudge, disobedient;
And too fond of the *right* to pursue the *expedient.*
In short, 'twas his fate, unemploy'd, or in place, sir,
To eat mutton cold, and cut blocks with a razor.
—GOLDSMITH, OLIVER, 1774, *The Retaliation.*

No expectation that I had formed of Mr. Burke, either from his works, his speeches, his character, or his fame, had anticipated to me such a man as I now met. He appeared, perhaps, at this moment, to the highest possible advantage in health, vivacity, and spirits. Removed from the impetuous aggravations of party contentions, that, at times, by inflaming his passions, seem, momentarily at least, to disorder his character, he was lulled into gentleness by the grateful feelings of prosperity; exhilarated, but not intoxicated, by sudden success: and just risen, after toiling years of failures, disappointments, fire and fury, to place, affluence, and honours; which were brightly smiling on the zenith of his powers. He looked, indeed as if he had no wish but to diffuse philanthropy, pleasure, and genial gaiety all around. His figure, when he is not negligent in his carriage, is noble; his air commanding; his address graceful; his voice clear, penetrating, sonorous, and powerful; his language copious, eloquent, and changefully impressive; his manners are attractive; his conversation is past all praise. You will call me mad, I know ;— but if I wait till I see another Mr. Burke for such another fit of extasy—I may be long enough in my very sober good senses!
—D'ARBLAY, MADAME (FANNY BURNEY), 1782, *Letter to Samuel Crisp, Memoirs of Doctor Burney, p.* 172.

Fox never talks in private company; not from any determination not to talk, but because he has not the first motion. A man who is used to the applause of the House of Commons has no wish for that of a private company. A man accustomed to throw for a thousand pounds, if set down to throw for sixpence, would not be at the pains to count his dice. Burke's talk is the ebullition of his mind. He does not talk from a desire of distinction, but because his mind is full.—JOHNSON, SAMUEL, 1783, *Life by Boswell, ed. Hill, vol.* IV, *p.* 192.

So lively, and so foolish, and so good-humoured was he, and so like the agreeable Mr. Burke I once knew and admired, that I soon forgot his malefactions, and how often I had been in a passion with him for some of his speeches.—MORE, HANNAH, 1784, *Letter to her Sister, Memoirs, ed. Roberts.*

He must again repeat that all he ever knew of men, that all he ever read in books, that all his reasoning faculties informed him of, or his fancy suggested to him, did not impart that exalted knowledge, that superior information, which he had acquired from the lessons of his right honourable friend. To him he owed all his fame, if fame he had any. And if he (Mr. Fox) should now, or at any time, prevail over him in discussion, he could acknowledge his gratitude for the capability and pride of the conquest in telling him "Hoc ipsum quod vincit id est tuum."
—FOX, CHARLES JAMES, 1791, *Speech in the House of Commons on the occasion of his rupture with Mr. Burke.*

We trust thy liberal views, thy generous
    heart;
We think of those who, naked, pale, and
    poor,
Relieved and blessed, have wandered from
    thy door;
We see thee with unwearied step explore
Each track of bloodshed on the farthest shore
Of injured Asia, and thy swelling breast
Harrowing the oppressor, mourning for the
    oppressed.
—BOWLES, WILLIAM LISLE, 1792? *The Right Honourable Edmund Burke.*

Burke is, indeed, a young man of his years. But the reason I take to be, that if age should deprive him of one half of his ideas he would have still more left him than any man of five-and-twenty.—CHARLEMONT, LORD, 1792, *Letter to Edmond Malone, Aug.* 20; *Life by Prior, p.* 196.

As late I lay in Slumber's shadowy vale,
    With wetted cheek and in a mourner's
        guise,
    I saw the sainted form of Freedom rise:
She spake! not sadder moans the autumnal
        gale—
"Great Son of Genius! sweet to me thy name,
    Ere in an evil hour with altered voice
    Thou badst Oppression's hireling crew re-
        joice,
Blasting with wizard spell my laurelled fame.
Yet never, BURKE! thou drank'st Corrup-
        tion's bowl!
    Thee stormy Pity and the cherish'd lure
    Of Pomp, and proud precipitance of soul
Wildered with meteor fires. Ah spirit pure!
That error's mist had left thy purged eye:
So might I clasp thee with a Mother's joy!"
—COLERIDGE, SAMUEL TAYLOR, 1794, *Sonnet to Burke, Dec.* 9.

Mrs. Burke presents her compliments to Mr. Fox, and thanks him for his obliging inquiries. Mrs. Burke communicated his letter to Mr. Burke, and, by his desire, has to inform Mr. Fox that it has cost Mr. Burke the most heart-felt pain to obey the stern voice of his duty in rendering asunder a long friendship, but that he deemed his sacrifice necessary; that his principles remained the same; and that in whatever his life yet remained to him, he conceives that he must live for others and not for himself. Mr. Burke is convinced that the principles which he has endeavoured to maintain are necessary to the welfare and dignity of his country, and that these principles can be enforced only by the general persuasion of his sincerity. For herself, Mrs. Burke has again to express her gratitude to Mr. Fox for his inquiries.—BURKE, MRS. EDMUND, 1797, *Letter to C. J. Fox*

His end was suited to the simple greatness of his mind, which he displayed through life, every way unaffected, without levity, without ostentation, full of natural grace and dignity.—LAURENCE, FRENCH, 1797, *Gentleman's Magazine, vol.* 67.

There never was a more beautiful alliance between virtue and talents. All his conceptions were grand, all his sentiments generous. The great leading trait of his character, and that which gave it all its energy and its colour, was that strong hatred of vice which is no other than the passionate love of virtue. It breathes in all his writings; it was the guide of all his actions. But even the force of his eloquence was sufficient to transfuse it into the weaker or perverted minds of his contemporaries. This has caused much of the miseries of Europe; this has rendered of no effect towards her salvation the sublimest talents, the greatest and rarest virtues that the beneficence of Providence ever concentrated in a single character for the benefit of mankind. But Mr. Burke was too superior to the age in which he lived. His prophetic genius only astonished the nation which it ought to have governed.—CAZALÉS, M., 1797, *On the Death of Edmund Burke.*

Had a long and interesting conversation with Mr. Mackintosh, turning principally on Burke and Fox. Of Burke he spoke with rapture, declaring that he was, in his estimation, without any parallel, in any age or country, except, perhaps, Lord Bacon and Cicero: that his works contained an ampler store of political and moral

wisdom than could be found in any other writer whatever; and that he was only not esteemed the most severe and sagacious of reasoners, because he was the most eloquent of men, the perpetual force and vigour of his arguments being hid from vulgar observation by the dazzling glories in which they were enshrined. In taste alone he thought himself deficient; but to have possessed that quality in addition to his other, would have been too much for man.—Passed the last Christmas (of Mr. Burke's Life) with Burke at Beaconsfield, and described, in glowing terms the astonishing effusions of his mind in conversation: perfectly free from all taint of affectation; would enter, with cordial glee, into the sports of children, rolling about with them on the carpet, and pouring out, in his gambols, the sublimest images, mingled with the most wretched puns.— Anticipated his approaching dissolution with due solemnity but perfect composure; —minutely and accurately informed, to a wonderful exactness, with respect to every fact relative to the French Revolution. . . . Of Gibbon, Mackintosh neatly remarked that he might have been cut out of a corner of Burke's mind without his missing it.—GREEN, THOMAS, 1797–1810, *Diary of a Lover of Literature.*

NEAR THIS PLACE LIES INTERRED ALL THAT WAS MORTAL OF THE RIGHT HONOURABLE EDMUND BURKE, WHO DIED ON THE 9TH OF JULY, 1797, AGED 68 YEARS.

IN THE SAME GRAVE ARE DEPOSITED THE REMAINS OF HIS ONLY SON, RICHARD BURKE, ESQ., REPRESENTATIVE IN PARLIAMENT FOR THE BOROUGH OF MALTON, WHO DIED THE 2ND OF AUGUST, 1794, AGED 35.

OF HIS BROTHER, RICHARD BURKE, ESQ., BARRISTER-AT-LAW, AND RECORDER OF THE CITY OF BRISTOL, WHO DIED ON THE 4TH OF FEBRUARY, 1794: AND OF HIS WIDOW, JANE MARY BURKE, WHO DIED THE 2ND OF APRIL, 1812, AGED 78. —TABLET TO THE BURKE FAMILY, 1812, *Beaconsfield Church.*

Burke's conversation was rambling, but splendid, rich and instructive beyond comparison.—BUTLER, CHARLES, 1822, *Reminiscences, vol.* I, *p.* 168.

In person, he was five feet ten inches

high, erect, well-formed, never very robust; when young, expert in the sports of his country and time, active in habits suited to his years until his last illness, and always, it scarcely need be added, particularly active in mind, having nothing of what he called "the master-vice, sloth," in his composition. His countenance in early life possessed considerable sweetness, and by his female friends was esteemed handsome. At a later period, it did not appear to be marked, particularly when in a state of quiescence, by that striking expression which, from the well-known qualities of his mind, many persons expected to see; but the lines of thought were evident, and when excited by discussion, there was an occasional working of the brow, occasioned partly by being near-sighted, which let the attentive observer into the secret of the powerful workings within. From this defective state of vision, he almost constantly, from about the year 1780, wore spectacles. . . . Like Mr. Fox, Mr. Burke was somewhat negligent in common dress, being latterly distinguished by a tight brown coat, which seemed to impede all freedom of motion, and a little bob-wig with curls, which, in addition to his spectacles, made his person be recognized by those who had never previously seen him, the moment he rose to speak in the House of Commons. . . . His address in private life possessed something of a chivalrous air— noble, yet unaffected and unreserved, impressing upon strangers of every rank, imperceptibly and without effort, the conviction of his being a remarkable man. —PRIOR, SIR JAMES, 1824, *Memoir of the Life and Character of the Right Hon. Edmund Burke, vol.* II, *pp.* 374, 377, 378.

It was a great pity that Burke accepted a pension, because as he turned out so right about the Revolution it dimmed the glory of genius. Lord Mulgrave said: "Mr. Fox acknowledged afterwards that Burke was right *too soon.*" It was cruel to break up his friendship with Sheridan and Fox, but Burke had no other way of becoming again an isolated object of public astonishment. Sheridan and Fox had rather dulled his fame, and his only chance of self-applause, the only chance of soothing his wounded vanity left him, was to burst like a fiery star from his regular orbit, and become the object of wonder and abuse, enthusiasm and admiration, which he was no longer in the ordinary progress. Love of power was at the bottom of his heart, depend upon it; to be sure, the weakness of the greatest minds. To think that Burke was always giving Barry caution about his temper, while he was such a signal instance of violence himself.—HAYDON, BENJAMIN ROBERT, 1825, *To Miss Mitford, Dec.* 10; *Life, Letters and Table Talk, ed. Stoddard, p.227.*

I saw a letter or two of Burke's in which there is an *épanchement du cœur* not visible in those of Pitt, who writes like a Premier to his colleague. Burke was under the strange hallucination that his son, who predeceased him, was a man of greater talents than himself. On the contrary, he had little talent and no resolution.—SCOTT, SIR WALTER, 1828, *Journal, May* 24.

What a guardian angel he proved to the nation. There are two individuals who have adorned and benefited our country, whom it is a pleasure to trace into the very recesses of private life: there are no discoveries to make;—all is so fair, so clear, so honourable—the milk of human kindness flows forth so abundantly. I speak of Edmund Burke and Walter Scott. How delightful it is to find those diamonds without a flaw.—GRANT, ANNE, 1834, *Letters, Apr.* 17; *Memoir and Correspondence, ed. Grant, vol.* III, *p.* 237.

It is strange, considering the eminence of the man, and how early his biographers were in the field, what an impenetrable cloud hangs over the life of Edmund Burke, from the time when he left college to his avowed entrance into a public career. The same observation was made long years since by one who knew him personally and well. "It always appeared to Mr. West ('Life of West') that there was about Mr. Burke *a degree of mystery connected with his early life* which their long intercourse never tended to explain." This mystery was not only maintained during life, but prepared for after death. There is not in existence, as far as we know or have a right to infer from the silence of the biographers, one single letter, paper, or document of any kind, —except a mysterious fragment of one letter,—relating to the domestic life of the Burke's, until long after Edmund Burke became an illustrious and public man,—from brothers to brother, or brothers to sister. Such letters could not, of course, find a place in the formal "Correspondence of the Right Honourable,"—but they were the best possible material for the biographer—for the *man* Burke must grow in and out of them. These letters and documentary evidence must have been intentionally collected and destroyed; and the probabilities are, that they were destroyed by Edmund himself, for he was the last survivor of the family.—DILKE, SIR CHARLES WENTWORTH, 1853, *Burke, The Papers of a Critic, vol.* II, *p.* 330.

I confess that he does not interest me chiefly as either statesman, essayist, or orator—that I should not care for him in any of these characters if I did not perceive that he was first of all a Man. I may disagree with a number of his opinions; I shall not tell you with how many I agree or disagree. But he himself, I think, is a subject worthy of all study, and of very sincere affection.—MAURICE, FREDERICK DENISON, 1857, *Edmund Burke, The Friendship of Books and Other Lectures, ed. Hughes, p.* 305.

A few months after her [Mrs. Burke] death, the house which she had occupied to the last was destroyed by fire. All that was pleasant and beautiful in the abode became a dream of the past. Some blackened walls and charred timbers alone remained to tell the tale of desolation. Perhaps it was better so. No stranger was long to inhabit the mansion which had been the scene of so much pure enjoyment, so much domestic affection, so many noble aspirations. Its fate was symbolical of the sad family history of which it had been the scene. The blackened ruins were a fitting memorial of blighted hopes, and of a broken heart.—MACKNIGHT, THOMAS, 1860, *History of the Life and Times of Edmund Burke, vol.* III, *p.* 718.

He was well versed in Greek and Latin literature, was familiar with the great masters of his own language, and had read the best models of the French. Ancient and modern history he had deeply studied; he was an admirable connoisseur in art; and he was not unfamiliar with some of the natural sciences. To theology and philosophy he paid considerable attention. His acquaintance with English law astonished professional men themselves, while from the Roman jurisprudence

he not unfrequently drew happy illustrations; and, as is said of Shakespeare, he loved to converse with laborers and mechanics about their trades. He was a skilful, practical agriculturist; in matters of commerce and finance he was exceedingly well versed, and in the whole science of economics he was far beyond his age.—ROBERTSON, J. B., 1875, *Lectures on the Life of Burke.*

He sits erect and firm, his head thrown somewhat back as if conscious of his intellectual strength. His face is one that a painter would find it hard adequately to portray, for its expression is constantly varying, but full of benevolence; now darkened by the shadow of deep thought, now marked by vigorous intellect, softened by sensibility.—WALLER, J. F., 1881, *Boswell and Johnson, Their Companions and Contemporaries, p.* 7.

There is no public man whose character is more clearly reflected in his life and in his intimate correspondence; and it may be confidently said that there is no other public man whose character was in all essential respects more transparently pure. Weak health, deep and fervent religious principles, and studious habits, saved him from the temptations of youth; and amid all the vicissitudes and corruption of politics his heart never lost its warmth, or his conscience its sensitiveness. There were faults indeed which were only too apparent in his character as in his intellect—an excessive violence and irritability of temper; personal antipathies, which were sometimes carried beyond all the bounds of reason; party spirit, which was too often suffered to obscure his judgment, and to hurry him into great intemperance and exaggeration of language. But he was emphatically a good man; and in the higher moral qualities of public as of private life he has not often been surpassed.—LECKY, WILLIAM EDWARD HARTPOLE, 1882, *A History of England in the Eighteenth Century, vol.* III, *ch.* xi, *p.* 201.

So wide and various are the genius and career of Burke that you might as well attempt to exhaust the character of Shakespeare in a speech of this kind as attempt to deal adequately with the genius of Burke. . . . There was no stronger party man than Burke. He was a Whig of the Whigs. He glorified Whigs. He inspired Whigs. He was, if I may so express myself, the prose Poet Laureate of Whiggery. And yet, without hesitation or murmur, he forsook all and followed what he believed to be the truth. He loved Charles Fox and all his other political associates. His eulogy on Charles Fox in his speech on his Indian Bill is perhaps the noblest tribute ever paid in eloquence by one politician to another. But he forsook them all, Charles Fox and all, to follow what he believed to be the truth. The wrench was terrible. It brought tears to the eyes of all who witnessed it. But Burke never flinched and never blenched. He went home to his lonely country home. He went home to see his son die, and all his hopes and future die with that son, and then to die in solitude and sorrow himself. And what of him? Is he a shadow? No, he is, in my opinion, the one figure of the time which is likely never to be a shadow. He brightens on the historic canvas—as the other figures fade—by his speeches, which, as I have said, were read and not listened to. He will be remembered as long as there are readers to read, when those orators on whose lips Parliaments and people hung enthralled are forgotten with the tongue that spoke and the ears that listened to them.—ROSEBERY, LORD ARCHIBALD P. P., 1894–1900, *Life and Speeches, ed. Coates, vol.* II, *pp.* 1010, 1013.

He became a statesman and great Parliamentary orator, so to speak, in spite of himself. But he must have early discovered the great barrier to complete success created by his poverty. He may be said to have passed his life in pecuniary embarrassment. This alone might not have shut him out from the Whig official Paradise, for the same thing might have been said of Pitt and Fox: but they had connections; they belonged by birth and association to the Whig class. Burke's relatives were no help or credit to him. In fact, they excited distrust of him. They offended the fastidious aristocrats with whom he associated, and combined with his impecuniousness to make him seem unsuitable for a great place. These aristocrats were very good to him. They lent him money freely, and settled a pension on him, and covered him with social adulation; but they were never willing to put him beside themselves in the

government. His latter years therefore had an air of tragedy. He was unpopular with most of those who in his earlier years had adored him, and was the hero of those whom in earlier years he had despised. His only son, of whose capacity he had formed a strange misconception, died young, and he passed his own closing hours, as far as we can judge, with a sense of failure. But he left one of the great names in English history. There is no trace of him in the statue book, but he has, it is safe to say, exercised a profound influence in all succeeding legislation, both in England and America. He has inspired or suggested nearly all the juridical changes which distinguish the England of to-day from the England of the last century, and is probably the only British politician whose speeches and pamphlets, made for immediate results, have given him immortality.—GODKIN, E. L., 1896, *Library of the World's Best Literature, ed. Warner, vol.* V, *p.* 2787.

The genius of Burke is platonically democratic in its multifariousness. . . . While the mind is fascinated by the mere enumeration of the attributes of his prodigal genius, curiosity and controversy, have been ceaselessly attracted to such questions as to the reason why his youth is so enveloped in obscurity, to the interminable dispute as to whether or not he was Junius, and how he managed to purchase the Beaconsfield estate. Many of the rumours on these subjects are, no doubt, mere *contes en l'air*. Some thirty years ago, according to Mr. Lecky, the last word was said about the purchase of Beaconsfield estate, and the same eminent authority considers that the account rendered was satisfactory enough, and that it is idle to pursue the subject. Mr. Morley even takes the trouble to deny the rumour that Burke ever went to America, or that he was a *cavaliere servente* of Peg Woffington. The evidence that Burke paid a visit to America seems, perhaps, worth a little more consideration than Mr. Morley gives it, since it rests on the highly respectable evidence of Benjamin West, a President of the Royal Academy, who was himself an American.—SIBLEY, N. W., 1897, *Edmund Burke, The Westminster Review, vol.* 148, *p.* 496.

Edmund Burke gave the most strikin'; proofs of his character and genius in the evil days in which his life ended—not when he was a leader in the Commons, but when he was a stricken old man at Beaconsfield. That Burke was a great statesman, no thinking man could read his pamphlets and speeches can deny; but a man may be a great statesman and yet fall very short of being a great man. Burke makes as deep an impression upon our hearts as upon our minds. We are taken captive, not so much by his reasoning, strongly as that moves to its conquest, as by the generous warmth that steals out of him into our hearts. There is a tonic breath of character and of generous purpose in which he writes—the fine sentiment of a pure man; and we are made aware that he who could write thus was great, not so much by reason of what he said or did, as by reason of what he was. What a man was you may often discover in the records of his days of bitterness and pain better than in what is told of his seasons of cheer and hope; for if the noble qualities triumph then and show themselves still sound and sweet, if his courage sink not, if he show himself still capable of self-forgetfulness, if he still stir with a passion for the service of causes and policies which are beyond himself, his stricken age is even greater than his full-pulsed years of manhood. This is the test which Burke endures—the test of fire. It has not often been judged so, I know; but let any man of true insight take that extraordinary "Letter to a Noble Lord," which was written in 1796, and which is Burke's *apologia pro vita sua*, consider the circumstances under which it was written, its tone, its scope, its truth, its self-revelations, and the manner of man revealed, and say whether this be not the real Burke, undaunted, unstained, unchanged in purpose and in principle.—WILSON, WOODROW, 1901, *Edmund Burke and the French Revolution, The Century Magazine, vol.* 62, *p.* 784.

SPEECHES AND ORATORY

Burke also abounds with these fine passages, and he soars also as much out of the lower regions of discourse and infinitely further into those of imagination and fancy; but no man could ever perceive in him the least trace of preparation, and he never appears more incontestably inspired by the moment and transported with the fury of the god within him

than in those finished passages which it would cost Shakespeare long study and labour to produce.—ELLIOT, SIR GILBERT, 1751–1806, *Life of Elliot by Lady Minto, vol.* I, *p.* 215.

His performance ["Conciliation with America"] was the best I have heard from him in the whole winter. He is always brilliant to an uncommon degree, and yet I believe it would be better he were less so. I don't mean to join with the cry which will always run against shining parts, when I say that I sincerely think it interrupts him so much in argument that the House are never sensible that he argues as well as he does. Fox gives a strong proof of this, for he makes use of Burke's speech as a repertory, and by stating crabbedly two or three of those ideas which Burke has buried under flowers, he is thought almost always to have had more argument.—FLOOD, HENRY, 1775, *Letter to Charlemont.*

While we are waiting at Trinity Lodge for the deputation from the Senate to conduct the Chancellor, I had a conversation with Lord Erskine upon the qualifications of Burke as an orator. Lord Erskine said that his defect was *episode.* "A public speaker," said he, "should never be *episodical*—it is a very great mistake. I hold it to be a rule respecting public speaking, which ought never to be violated, that the speaker should not introduce into his oratory insular brilliant passages—they always tend to call off the minds of his hearers, and to make them wander from what ought to be the main business of his speech. If he wish to introduce brilliant passages, *they should run along the line of his subject-matter,* and never quit it. Burke's episodes were highly beautiful—I know nothing *more* beautiful, but they were his defects in speaking." . . . Lord Erskine also told me that Burke's manner was *sometimes* bad—"*it was like* that of an Irish chairman." "*Once,*" said he, "I was so tired of hearing him in a debate upon the India Bill, that not liking he should see me leave the House of Commons while he was speaking, I crept along under the benches and got out, and went to the Isles of Wight. Afterwards that very speech of his was published, and I found it to be so extremely beautiful *that I actually wore it into pieces by reading it.*"—CLARKE, E.

D., 1819, *Journal, July* 5; *Prior's Life of Burke, vol.* II, *p.* 431.

The variety and extent of his power in debate was greater than that of any other orator in ancient or modern times. No one ever poured forth such a flood of thought—so many original combinations of inventive genius; as much knowledge of man and the working of political systems; so many just remarks on the relation of government to the manners, the spirit, and even the prejudices of a people; so many wise maxims as to a change in constitutions and laws; so many beautiful effusions of lofty and generous sentiment; such exuberant stores of illustration, or ornament, and apt allusion; all intermingled with the liveliest sallies of wit or the boldest flights of a sublime imagination. In actual debate, as a contemporary informs us, he passed more rapidly from one exercise of his powers to another, than in his printed productions. During the same evening, sometimes in the space of a few moments, he would be pathetic and humorous, acrimonious and conciliating, now giving vent to his indignant feelings in lofty declamation, and again, almost in the same breath, convulsing his audience by the most laughable exhibitions of ridicule or burlesque. —GOODRICH, CHAUNCEY A., 1852, *ed., Select British Eloquence, p.* 237.

Burke always dissappointed me as a speaker. I have heard him, during his speeches in the House, make use of the most vulgar expressions, such as "three nips of a straw," "three skips of a louse," &c.; and, on one occasion when I was present, he introduced, as an illustration, a most indelicate story about a French king, who asked his physician why his natural children were so much finer than his legitimate. —MALTBY, WILLIAM, 1854, *In The Recollections of the Table-Talk of Samuel Rogers, p.* 79.

Sheridan once said to me, "When posterity read the speeches of Burke, they will hardly be able to believe that, during his life-time, he was not considered as a first-rate speaker, not even as a second-rate one." —ROGERS, SAMUEL, 1855, *Table-Talk, p.* 66.

Burke is rescued from the usual doom of orators, because his learning, his experience, his sagacity are rimmed with a halo by this bewitching light behind the

intellectual eye from the highest heaven of the brain.—LOWELL, JAMES RUSSELL, 1871, *Carlyle, My Study Windows, p.* 118.

His speeches on the Stamp Acts and the American War soon lifted him into fame. The heavy Quaker-like figure, the little wig, the round spectacles, the cumbrous roll of paper which loaded Burke's pocket, gave little promise of a great orator and less of the characteristics of his oratory—its passionate ardor, its poetic fancy, its amazing prodigality of resources; and dazzling succession in which irony, pathos, invective, tenderness, and the most brilliant word-pictures, the coolest argument followed each other. It was an eloquence indeed of a wholly new order in English experience. . . . The philosophical cast of Burke's reasoning was unaccompanied by any philosophical coldness of tone or phrase. The groundwork, indeed, of his nature was poetic. His ideas, if conceived by the reason, took shape and color from the splendor and fire of his imagination. A nation was to him a great living society, so complex in its relations, and whose institutions were so interwoven with glorious events in the past, that to touch it rudely was a sacrilege.—GREEN, JOHN RICHARD, 1874, *A Short History of the English People, pp.* 761, 762.

Burke, before the spectre of the French Revolution shot across his path, was listened to as a seer by the House of Commons; but, after that event, his Cassandra-like croakings bored his hearers, and his rising to speak was a signal for a stampede from the benches. . . . Greater as a thinker than Chatham or Fox, but inferior as an orator, was Edmund Burke, who, in the variety and extent of his powers, surpassed every other orator of ancient or modern times. He was what he called Charles Townshend, "a prodigy," and ranks not merely with the eloquent speakers of the world, but with the Bacons, Newtons, and Shakespeares. His speeches and pamphlets are saturated with thought; they absolutely swarm, like an ant-hill, with ideas, and, in their teeming profusion, remind one of the "myriad-minded" author of Hamlet. To the broadest sweep of intellect, he added the most surprising subtlety, and his almost oriental imagination was fed by a vast and varied knowledge,—the stores of a memory that held everything in its grasp. The only man who, according to Adam Smith, at once comprehended the total revolution the latter proposed in political economy, he was at the same time the best judge of a picture that Sir Joshua Reynolds ever knew; and while his knowledge was thus boundless, his vocabulary was as extensive as his knowledge. Probably no orator ever lived on whose lips language was more plastic and ductile.—MATHEWS, WILLIAM, 1878, *Oratory and Orators, pp.* 134, 268.

There is much in the oratory of Edmund Burke to suggest the amplitude of mind and the power and scope of intellectual grasp that characterized SHAKESPEARE. He surveyed every subject as if standing on an eminence and taking a view of it in all its relations, however complex and remote. United with this remarkable comprehensiveness was also a subtlety of intellect that enabled him to penetrate the most complicated relations and unravel the most perplexed intricacies. Why? Whence? For what end? With what results? were the questions that his mind seemed always to be striving to answer. The special objects to which he applied himself were the workings of political institutions, the principles of wise legislation, and the sources of national security and advancement. *Rerum cognoscere causas,*—to know the causes of things—in all the multiform relations of organized society, was the constant end of his striving. More than any other one that has written in English he was a political philosopher. But he was far more than that. He had a memory of extraordinary grasp and tenacity; and this, united with a tireless industry, gave him an affluence of knowledge that has rarely been equalled. He had the fancy of a poet, and his imagination surveyed the whole range of human experience for illustrations with which to enrich the train of his thought.—ADAMS, CHARLES KENDALL, 1884, *ed. Representative British Orations, p.* 172.

Tall and vigorous, of dignified deportment, with massive brow and stern expression, he had an air of command. His voice was of great compass; his words came fast, but his thoughts seemed almost to overcome even his powers of utterance. Invective, sarcasm, metaphor, and argument followed hard after one another; his powers of description were gorgeous, his scorn was sublime, and in the midst of a discussion of some matter of ephemeral importance came enunciations of political wisdom which are for all time, and which illustrate the opinion that he was, "Bacon alone excepted, the greatest political thinker who has ever devoted himself to the practice of English politics" (Buckle, "Civilization in England," c. VII). Although he spoke with an Irish accent, with awkward action, and in a harsh tone, his "imperial fancy" and commanding eloquence excited universal admiration. No parliamentary orator has ever moved his audience as he now and again did. His speech on the employment of the Indians in war, for example, is said at one time to have almost choked Lord North, against whom it was delivered, with laughter, and at another to have drawn "iron tears down Barré's cheek." (Walpole to Mason, 12 Feb., 1778, Letters, vii, 29.) Unfortunately, his power over the house did not last; his thoughts were too deep for the greater part of the members, and were rather exhaustive discussions than direct contributions to debate (Morley, Life, 209), while the sustained loftiness of his style and a certain lack of sympathy with his audience marred the effect of his oratory.—HUNT, WILLIAM, 1886, *Dictionary of National Biography, vol.* VII, *p.* 348.

Burke's prose is as prominent an example as there is in English Letters of the oratorical style, in the best sense of that term. The reported speeches of Fox and Grattan, Pitt and Sheridan—his great contemporaries, evince occasional passages of equal excellence, but as to the entire body of oratorical prose produced, Burke is the superior of any one of them and marks the highest point as yet attained in England in forensic prose.— HUNT, THEODORE W., 1887, *Representative English Prose and Prose Writers, p.* 342.

To Burke has already been assigned the honour of being the first statesman and orator who used the Platform at election time as a real instrument in political power. The occasions on which he so used it were few, but his speeches at Bristol in 1774 and 1780 recognised clearly the claims of constituents to the fullest explanation of the conduct of their representative, and his full accountability to them. That was the most important matter to have put so prominently on record. Though taking part in the Economy Agitation he does not appear to have actually spoken from the Platform in its support, but in the crisis of the struggle between Pitt and the Coalition he had recourse to the Platform at Aylesbury in 1784. After that, however, his voice from the Platform was silent.—JEPHSON, HENRY, 1891, *The Platform, Its Rise and Progress, vol. I, p. 223.*

It is in his oratory that Burke's paragraphs are remarkable. He exhibits here such qualities as make him the best paragrapher our literature produced before the present century. His unity is simple (as opposed to that of compound paragraphs) and organic. His paragraph bears the test, as Wendell has pointed out, of having its substance expressed in one organic sentence. For purposes of oratorical emphasis and oratorical rhythm, he has completely mastered the short sentence. His percentage of sentences of less than fifteen words is higher than the highest yet reached. . . . The great orator had, to a degree uncommon even in the most eminent orators, the power of marshalling his propositions in a specious order. His emotion never ran away with him; he drove straight at his hearer's intellect—did so too constantly for his highest immediate success. There is always the impression of a convincing chain of logic. In short, Burke is the earliest great master of the paragraph, and in impassioned prose he still remains a master of the paragraph. But for his lingering sense of the prime importance of balancing and rounding the sentence he is a nineteenth century paragrapher, and one of the best.—LEWIS, EDWIN HERBERT, 1894, *The History of the English Paragraph, pp. 122, 123.*

A VINDICATION OF NATURAL SOCIETY
1756

The book is a parody upon the style and manner of Lord Bolingbroke. . . . The wit of Burke's essay is that he supposes this very aristocratic man to maintain the advantage of a purely natural society upon the very same ground upon which he had maintained the advantages of a purely natural religion. The imitation of style was so skilful, that many are

said to have been deceived by it. I cannot understand how such a mistake could have been possible for any who had the very slightest acquaintance with the designs or character of Bolingbroke. The outside resemblance only makes the internal contrast more striking. . . . Burke did not appear in his first conspicuous work merely or chiefly as a successful jester. A parody may be very amusing; but he had as distinct and serious a purpose in this as in any of his writings.—MAURICE, FREDERICK DENISON, 1857, *Edmund Burke, The Friendship of Books and Other Lectures, ed. Hughes, p. 311.*

Intended as a parody of Bolingbroke's reasonings on religion, is sometimes praised as a successful piece of mimicry; but it contains more of the real Burke than of the sham Bolingbroke. It may be viewed as an exercise in the style that the author ultimately adopted as his habitual manner of composition. The "Essay on the Sublime and Beautiful" has much less glow and sweep of style; the writer's flow of words seems to be painfully embarrassed by the necessity of observing order and proportion of statement.—MINTO, WILLIAM, 1872-80, *Manual of English Prose Literature, p. 437.*

From the very beginning Burke was drawn to the deepest of all the currents in the thought of the eighteenth century. . . . What is remarkable in Burke's first performance is his discernment of the important fact, that behind the intellectual disturbances in the sphere of philosophy, and the noisier agitations in the sphere of theology, there silently staked a force that might shake the whole fabric of civil society itself. In France, as all students of its speculative history are agreed, there came a time in the eighteenth century when theological controversy was turned into political controversy. Innovators left the question about the truth of Christianity, and busied themselves with questions about the ends and means of government. The appearance of Burke's "Vindication of Natural Society" coincides in time with the beginning of this important transformation. Burke foresaw from the first what, if rationalism were allowed to run an unimpeded course, would be the really great business of the second half of his century.— MORLEY, JOHN, 1879, *Burke (English Men of Letters).*

THE SUBLIME AND BEAUTIFUL
1757

I began to-day, as a natural supplement to Longinus, a philosophical inquiry into the nature of our ideas of the sublime and beautiful, and read the introduction upon Taste, p. 1–40, which, like all other researches into our primary ideas, is rather loose and unsatisfactory. The division, however, of the passive impression which is common to all men, and relates chiefly to positive beauty or faultiness, and the active judgment which is founded on knowledge, and exercised mostly on comparison, pleased me; perhaps because very like an idea of my own. . . . The author writes with ingenuity, perspicuity, and candour.—GIBBON, EDWARD, 1762, *Journal, Nov.* 1, 4.

As I walked out before breakfast with Mr. B., I proposed to him to revise and enlarge his admirable book on the "Sublime and Beautiful," which the experience, reading, and observation of thirty years could not but enable him to improve considerably. But he said the train of his thoughts had gone another way, and the whole bent of his mind turned from such subjects; that he was much fitter for such speculations at the time he published that book (about 1758) than now. Besides, he added, the subject was then new, but several writers have since gone over the same ground, Lord Kames and others. The subject he said had been long rolling in his thoughts before he wrote his book, he having been used from the time he was in college to speculate on the topics which form the subjects of it. He was six or seven years employed on it, and when it was produced he was about 28 or 29 years old—a prodigious work for such a period of life.—MALONE, EDMOND, 1789, *Maloniana, ed. Prior, July* 28, p. 154.

Burke's "Essay on the Sublime and Beautiful" seems to me a poor thing; and what he says upon Taste is neither profound nor accurate.—COLERIDGE, SAMUEL TAYLOR, 1827, *Table Talk, ed. Ashe, July* 12, p. 54.

The essay on the Sublime and Beautiful fell in with a set of topics, on which the curiosity of the better minds of the age, alike in France, England, and Germany, was fully stirred. In England the essay has been ordinarily slighted; it has perhaps been overshadowed by its author's fame in weightier matters. The nearest approach to a full and serious treatment of its main positions is to be found in Dugald Stewart's lectures. The great rhetorical art-critic of our own day refers to it in words of disparagement, and in truth it has none of the flummery of modern criticism. It is a piece of hard thinking, and it has the distinction of having interested and stimulated Lessing, the author of "Laoköon" (1766), by far the most definitely valuable of all the contributions to æsthetic thought in an age which was not poor in them.—MORLEY, JOHN, 1879, *Burke (English Men of Letters), p.* 17.

In the great Mr. Burke's "Essay on the Sublime and the Beautiful"—a singularly modern book, considering how long ago it was wrote (as the great Mr. Steele would have written the participle a little longer ago), and full of a certain well-mannered and agreeable instruction. In some things it is of that droll little eighteenth-century world, when philosophy had got the neat little universe into the hollow of its hand, and knew just what it was, and what it was for; but it is quite without arrogance.—HOWELLS, WILLIAM DEAN, 1891, *Criticism and Fiction, p.* 6.

REFLECTIONS ON THE REVOLUTION IN FRANCE
1790

Waving all discussion concerning the substance and general tendency of this printed letter, I must declare my opinion, that what I have seen of it is very loosely put together. In point of writing, at least, the manuscript you showed me first was much less objectionable. Remember that this is one of the most singular, that it may be the most distinguished, and ought to be one of the most deliberate acts of your life. Your writings have hitherto been the delight and instruction of your own country. You now undertake to correct and instruct another nation, and your appeal, in effect, is to all Europe. Allowing you the liberty to do so, in an extreme case, you cannot deny that it ought to be done with special deliberation in the choice of the topics, and with no less care and circumspection in the use you make of them. Have you thoroughly considered whether it be worthy of Mr. Burke—of a privy-counsellor—of a man so high and considerable in the House of Commons as you are—and holding the station you have obtained in the opinion of the world, to enter into a War of pamphlets with Dr. Price? If he answered you, as assuredly he will (and so will many others), can you refuse to reply to a person whom you have attacked? If you do, you are defeated in a battle of your own provoking, and driven to fly from ground of your own choosing. If you do not, where is such a contest to lead you, but into a vile and disgraceful, though it was ever so victorious, an altercation? "Dî meliora." But if you will do it, away with all jest, and sneer, and sarcasm; let every thing you say be grave, direct, and serious. In a case so interesting as the errors of a great nation, and the calamities of great individuals, and feeling them so deeply as you profess to do, all manner of insinuation is improper, all gibe and nickname prohibited.—FRANCIS, SIR PHILIP, 1790, *To Edmund Burke, Feb.* 19; *The Francis Letters, ed. Francis and Keary, vol.* II, *p.* 378.

I wish Mr. Burke would publish what he intended on the present state of France. He is a man of principle, and a friend to religion, to law, and to monarchy, as well as to liberty.—BEATTIE, JAMES, 1790, *Letter to Robert Arbuthnot, April* 25.

His pamphlet came out this day se'n-night, and is far superior to what was expected, even by his warmest admirers. I have read it twice; and though of three hundred and fifty pages, I wish I could repeat every page by heart. It is sublime, profound, and gay. The wit and satire are equally brilliant; and the whole is wise, though in some points he goes too far: yet in general there is far less want of judgment than could be expected from *him.* If it could be translated,—which, from the wit and metaphors and allusions, is almost impossible,—I should think it would be a classic book in all countries, except in *present* France. To their tribunes it speaks daggers; though, unlike them, it uses none. Seven thousand copies have been taken off by the booksellers already, and a new edition is preparing. I hope you will see it soon.— WALPOLE, HORACE, 1790, *To the Miss Berrys, Nov.* 8; *Letters, ed. Cunningham, vol.* IX, *p.* 260.

Burke's book is a most admirable

medicine against the French disease, which has made too much progress even in this happy country. I admire his eloquence, I approve his politics, I adore his chivalry, and I can forgive even his superstition.— GIBBON, EDWARD, 1791, *To Lord Sheffield; Private Letters, ed. Prothero, vol.* II, *p.* 237.

The Revolution of France does not astonish me as much as the Revolution of Mr. Burke. I wish I could believe the latter proceeded from as pure motives as the former. But what demonstration could scarcely have established before, less than the hints of Dr. Priestley & Mr. Paine established firmly now. How mortifying that this evidence of the rottenness of his mind must oblige us now to ascribe to wicked motives those actions of his life which wore the mark of virtue & patriotism.—JEFFERSON, THOMAS, 1791, *To Benjamin Vaughan, May* 11; *Writings, ed. Ford, vol.* V, *p.* 333.

An author whose splendid and unequalled powers have given a vogue and fashion to certain tenets which from any other pen would have appeared abject and contemptible. In the field of reason the encounter would not be difficult, but who can withstand the fascination and magic of his eloquence? The excursions of his genius are immense. His imperial fancy has laid all nature under tribute, and has collected riches from every scene of the creation and every walk of art. His eulogium on the Queen of France is a masterpiece of pathetic composition; so select are its images, so fraught with tenderness, and so rich with colours "dipt in heaven," that he who can read it without rapture may have merit as a reasoner, but must resign all pretentions to taste and sensibility. His imagination is, in truth, only too prolific; a world of itself, where he dwells in the midst of chimerical alarms, is the dupe of his own enchantments, and starts, like Prospero, at the spectres of his own creation. His intellectual views in general, however, are wide and variegated, rather than distinct; and the light he has let in on the British constitution in particular, resembles the coloured effulgence of a painted medium, a kind of mimic twilight, solemn and soothing to the senses, but better fitted for ornament than use.—HALL, ROBERT, 1796, *An Apology for the Freedom of the Press.*

I conceive there is not to be found in all

the writings of my day, perhaps I may say not in the English language, so brilliant a cluster of fine and beautiful passages in the declamatory style, as we are presented with in Edmund Burke's inimitable tract upon the French Revolution. It is most highly coloured and most richly ornamented, but there is elegance in its splendour, and dignity in its magnificence. The orator demands attention in a loud and lofty tone, but his voice never loses its melody, nor his periods their sweetness. —When he has aroused us with the thunder of his eloquence, he can at once, Timotheus-like, chuse a melancholy theme, and melt us into pity: there is grace in his anger; for he can inveigh without vulgarity; he can modulate the strongest bursts of passion, for even in his madness there is music. I was so charmed with the style and matter of his pamphlet, that I could not withstand the pleasure of intruding upon him with a letter of thanks. —CUMBERLAND, RICHARD, 1806, *Memoirs Written by Himself, vol.* II, *p.* 271.

This was Dodsley's book for authors' receipts; in that he showed me William Burke's receipt for 6*l.* 6*s.* on account of Edmund Burke, for the copy of the "Vindication of Natural Society." That book, said Nicoll, was so much admired in France by d'Alembert, Diderot, &c., &c., that it made them mad, and really produced the Revolution. "And now" (he added) "I have shown you what Burke had for kindling the Revolution, let me also show you what he had for putting it out," and then he pointed out his (Burke's) own receipt for 1,000*l.* for the profits of his famous volume.—YOUNG, ARTHUR, 1806, *Autobiography, Feb.* 25, *ed. Betham-Edwards, p.* 428.

The publication proved one of the remarkable events of the year, perhaps of the century; for it may be doubted whether any previous political production ever excited so much attention, so much discussion, so much praise from one party, so much animadversion from another, but ultimately, among the great majority of persons, such general conviction of the correctness of his views, as to have fully succeeded in turning the stream of public opinion to the direction he wished, from the channel in which it had hitherto flowed. . . . The interest which it excited did not cease with the moment,

for it was sought after then and since by persons little prone to political discussion, for the wisdom of the lessons it taught; by many for its literary beauties; by many in order to retrace the outline of fearful and extraordinary events there in great measure foretold; and it will ever be a source of deep interest to the practical statesman, and of unfeigned admiration to the man of taste and genius.—PRIOR, SIR JAMES, 1824, *Memoir of the Life and Character of the Right Hon. Edmund Burke, vol.* II, *pp.* 91, 92.

The very greatest writers write best when calm, and exerting themselves upon subjects unconnected with party. Burke rarely shows all his powers, unless where he is in a passion. The French Revolution was alone a subject fit for him.—COLERIDGE, SAMUEL TAYLOR, 1823, *Table Talk, ed. Ashe, Jan.* 4, *p.* 22.

The merits of his production are, we think, greatly enhanced by the simplicity of the vehicle in which its thoughts ride. The book is a letter; but such a letter! In this simplest shape of literature, we find philosophy the most subtle; invective the most sublime; speculation the most farstretching; Titanic ridicule, like the cachinnation of a Cyclops; piercing pathos; powerful historic painting; and eloquence the most dazzling that ever combined depth with splendor.—GILFILLAN, GEORGE, 1855, *A Third Gallery of Portraits, p.* 308.

Not a single weak point in the position of the French Revolutionists escaped his glance. We doubt whether modern critics have discovered a single revolutionary error or fallacy which he overlooked, but to the good, or the better side of the revolutionary movement he was as blind as the stupidest of Tory squires.—DICEY, A. V., 1879, *Morley's Burke, The Nation, vol.* 29, *p.* 245.

When Mr. Windham received his copy of Burke's "Reflections," and came to read it, he pronounced the work to be "capable of overturning the National Assembly, and turning the stream of opinion throughout Europe." So thought very many worthy persons who had hoped much from the first prospects of the French Revolution, but, ignorant of the signs of the times, had at length become thoroughly scared. Mr. Burke, indeed, "turned the stream" of opinion; for the stream, which had hitherto flowed with at least some aspect of peacefulness, as over a flat alluvial basin, was at once diverted into two opposite channels of torrent-like character. Mr. Burke may be credited with having evoked one of the most violent conflicts of opinion in English history; and, of the rival parties, those who had expected much from the early stages of the Revolution, and had become frightened at its later, untoward aspects, who forgot that a too sudden disruption must, under any circumstances, leave a certain amount of wreck, were perhaps the most unreasonable.—SMITH, EDWARD, 1881, *The Story of the English Jacobins, p.* 11.

This extraordinary book was published near the outbreak of the French Revolution and justly takes rank as one of the master-pieces of English literature. It is at once a condemnation of the Revolution, and a prophecy of the evils the Revolution would produce. As a specimen of denunciatory writing, it is probably one of the most remarkable ever produced in any language. It pours out torrent after torrent, Niagara after Niagara. But though it is repetitious, and therefore somewhat monotonous, it abounds in shrewd judgments, in brilliant pictures, and in prophecies that seem inspired. At times it is so unfair and so unjust that some have attempted to explain its excesses by the presumption that Burke had lost his reason. There is no need, however, of resorting to this violent hypothesis. Burke's mind was always essentially denunciatory in its nature; and he was never able to be quite just either to men or to political methods he disliked. Moreover, though he was a passionate friend of liberty, he never believed liberty was to be secured or preserved by submitting political affairs to the control of masses of ignorant men. These characteristics of his mind and of his political doctrines are quite sufficient to account for the peculiarities of what, with all its drawbacks, must probably be considered the greatest work of the greatest writer of English prose.—ADAMS, CHARLES KENDALL, 1882, *A Manual of Historical Literature, p.* 363.

Burke though of all rhetoricians the most philosophic was still a rhetorician and presented only one side of a case. Of this his essay on the French Revolution is the memorable and disastrous proof.

Though he goes deep into everything he seldom goes to the bottom.—SMITH, GOLDWIN, 1893, *The United States, an Outline of Political History, p.* 69.

Because Burke broke away in the "Reflections" from the judicial self-restraint which usually characterized him we are apt to forget that, in that wonderful composition, he deviates again and again into his earlier and better manner, and rewards the persevering reader with passages of calm wisdom and solid, fruitful speculation.—POWER, J. O'CONNOR, 1897, *Edmund Burke and His Abiding Influence, North American Review, vol.* 165, *p.* 677.

GENERAL

The most eloquent and rational madman that I ever knew.—GIBBON, EDWARD, 1791, *To Lord Sheffield, May* 31; *Private Letters, ed. Prothero, vol.* II, *p.* 251.

With Mr. Burke's book I do not mean to find fault, but to distinguish between what delights me, and what I only respect. I adore *genius;* to *judgment* I pull off my hat, and make it a formal bow; but as I read only to amuse myself, and not to be informed or convinced, I had rather (for my private pleasure) that in his last pamphlet he had flung the reins on the neck of his boundless imagination, as he did in the first. *Genius* creates enthusiasts or enemies; *judgment* only cold friends; and cold friends will sooner go over to your enemies than to your bigots.—WALPOLE, HORACE, 1791, *To the Countess of Ossory, Aug.* 22; *Letters, ed. Cunningham, vol.* IX, *p.* 338.

Burke's pamphlets and speeches have lost nothing of their attraction by time.—BRYDGES, SIR SAMUEL EGERTON, 1793, *Autobiography, vol.* I, *p.* 168.

When I have revolved the various labours of EDMUND BURKE and THE CAUSE HE HAS MAINTAINED (as it *generally* regards government, religion, and society, not the details of the war and its conduct), I say, with this allowance for the feverous frailties of the passions, and the taint of mortality in all our best actions, I could record in lasting characters, and in our holiest and most honourable temple, the departed Orator of England, the Statesman, and the Christian, EDMUND BURKE! "*Remuneratio ejus* CUM ALTISSIMO!"— MATHIAS, THOMAS JAMES, 1797, *The Pursuits of Literature, Eighth ed., p.* 423.

Eloquent statesman and sage, who, though
  late, broke loose from his trammels,
Giving then to mankind what party too
  long had diverted.
—SOUTHEY, ROBERT, 1821, *A Vision of
Judgment*, x.

I have been assured by a person who had
the best means of knowing, that the "Letter to a Noble Lord" (the most rapid,
impetuous, glancing, and sportive of all
his works) was printed off, and the proof
sent to him; and that it was returned to
the printing-office with so many alterations and passages interlined, that the
compositors refused to correct it as it
was—took the whole matter in pieces,
and re-set the copy. This looks like
elaboration and after-thought.—HAZLITT,
WILLIAM, 1821–22, *Table Talk.*

To our imperfect notice of some of the
benefits, not less durable than numerous,
which Burke achieved for the civil liberties, the national welfare of his country,
we cannot neglect to add—and to rank in
the highest degree—the marked and still
living influence of his writings,—an influence derived not only from the personal
character, and the earnest and impressive
language of the writer, but from the
gradual and conclusive testimony of
events. If we supposed their value to
be confined to the refutation of the doctrines, and the exposure of the tendency
of the French Revolution, we should underrate the matter most unjustly. Great and
useful as may be this merit, the works of
Burke would possess, if entirely stripped
of it, undoubted claims to the gratitude
of Englishmen. The honesty of his
alarms at the danger of the contagion of
French doctrines, and of jacobinical anarchy, has been, and will continue to be,
questioned; but it can scarcely be disputed
that, in pursuing his purpose of denouncing the influence of revolutionary France,
he did profoundly examine the true principles of the British constitution, and
explain its genuine excellence with a force
of argument and a wealth of illustration
of which our preceding political literature
had exhibited no example. He made it
an object of affection and of reverence on
the higher grounds of reason and of philosophy; and by displaying in the strongest
light the value of the possession, he rendered the possible loss of it a more active
and more general cause of apprehension.
. . . Henceforth it was as easy to

disprove the existence of that constitution,
as its value; and in the merit of having
rooted this principle of national faith and
personal devotion more firmly in the hearts
of his countrymen, Burke stands alone
and far above all competition.—CROKER,
JOHN WILSON, 1826, *Prior's Life of Burke,
Quarterly Review, vol.* 34, *pp.* 480, 481.

Burke was, indeed, a great man. No
one ever read history so philosophically
as he seems to have done. Yet, until he
could associate his general principles
with some sordid interest, panic of property, Jacobinism, &c., he was a mere
dinner bell. Hence you will find so many
half truths in his speeches and writings.
Nevertheless, let us heartily acknowledge
his transcendent greatness. He would
have been more influential if he had less
surpassed his contemporaries, as Fox and
Pitt, men of much inferior minds in all
respects.—COLERIDGE, SAMUEL TAYLOR,
1833, *Table Talk, ed. Ashe, Apr.* 8, *p.* 207.

Yesterday I read Burke's appeal from
the new to the old Whigs, which contains
astonishing coincidences with the present
times. His definition of the people is
somewhat tumid and obscure, and involved
in a splendid confusion of generalities
and abstruse doctrine; but it is a wonderful monument of his genius, and exhibits
that extent of knowledge and accuracy of
insight into the nature of parties and the
workings of political ambition which make
him an authority for all times, and show
him to be in the political what Shakespeare was in the moral world. But his
writings, however as objects of study
they may influence the opinions or form
the judgment of young men, would have
no more power than a piece of musty
parchment to arrest the tide of present
violence, and superinduce reflection and
calmness. A speech of Tom Duncombe's
would produce far greater effect than the
perusal of a discourse of Burke's.—GREV-
ILLE, CHARLES C. F., 1835, *A Journal of
the Reigns of King George IV. and King
William IV., Feb.* 17, *vol.* II, *p.* 349.

He was a writer of the first class, and
excelled in almost every kind of prose
composition. Possessed of most extensive
knowledge, and of the most various description; acquainted alike with what
different classes of men knew, each in his
own province, and with much that hardly
any one ever thought of learning; he

could either bring his masses of information to bear directly upon the subjects to which they severally belonged—or he could avail himself of them generally to strengthen his faculties and enlarge his views—or he could turn any portion of them to account for the purpose of illustrating his theme or enriching his diction. Hence, when he is handling any one matter, we perceive that we are conversing with a reasoner or a teacher, to whom almost every other branch of knowledge is familiar. His views range over all the cognate subjects; his reasonings are derived from principles applicable to other matters as well as the one in hand; arguments pour in from all sides, as well as those which start up under our feet, the natural growth of the path he is leading us over; while to throw light round our steps, and either explore its darker places or serve for our recreation, illustrations are fetched from a thousand quarters; and an imagination marvellously quick to descry unthought-of-resemblances pours forth the stores which a lore yet more marvellous has gathered from all ages and nations and arts and tongues.—BROUGHAM, HENRY LORD, 1839–43, *Historical Sketches of Statesmen who Flourished in the Time of George III.*, vol. I, p. 231.

His oratorical impressiveness was strongly connected with the weight of those maxims which he had formed from a long and profound study of the heart of man. And it is the force and abundance of those fine reflections which give an immortal value to his works on topics of the most temporary nature.—CROLY, GEORGE, 1840, *The Political Life of Burke*.

A sufficiently poetical politician to interest one just when one's sonnetteering age is departing, but before one has come down quite to arid fact.—FITZGERALD, EDWARD, 1841, *Letters*, vol. I, p. 72.

Burke's words are continually practising the broad-sword exercise, and sweeping down adversaries with every stroke.— WHIPPLE, EDWIN PERCY, 1845, *Words, Essays and Reviews*.

His most universal charm is a style so copious as to enrich the student's vocabulary by the aptitude and flow of words, to gratify the taste by its elegance, and the ear by its musical periods. Withal it is a manly style. Burke is not fastidious in his choice of epithets or illustrations to

the extent of weakening his force of statement. He can use the most homely as well as the most classic phrases and figures. He does not sacrifice truth to beauty, but aims to render them mutually illustrative. Few English writers boast passages that exhibit so clearly the dignity of the language, its facility of application, and its persuasive grace.—TUCKERMAN, HENRY T., 1849, *Characteristics of Literature, p.* 225.

On the subject of Irish Catholic freedom he wrote fully in letters to Sir Hercules Langrishe and others. He also dealt with this important theme in the defence of his parliamentary conduct, which will be found in this volume amongst his speeches delivered at Bristol. His support of the Catholic side of the question was one of the causes of his unpopularity with the electors of that city. Respecting the liberty of the press he was in advance of his age. . . . On the subject of the toleration of Dissenters, Burke was large-minded and liberal, and supported the principle on several occasions. . . . On questions connected with Irish Trade and with Irish Parliamentary freedom, Burke took the side of his native country. —BURKE, JAMES, 1853, ed., *The Speeches of Edmund Burke, Memoir, pp.* xxii, xxiii.

I have now finished reading again most of Burke's works. Admirable! The greatest man since Milton.—MACAULAY, THOMAS BABINGTON, 1854, *Journal, Feb.* 6; *Life and Letters*, ed. *Trevelyan*.

The contrast between the manner of his characteristic writings and their matter is very remarkable. He too threw over the detail of business and of politics those graces and attractions of manner which seems in some sort inconsistent with them; which are adapted for topics more intrinsically sublime and beautiful. It was for this reason that Hazlitt asserted that no woman ever cared for Burke's writings: the matter, he said, was "hard and dry," and no superficial glitter or eloquence could make it agreeable to those who liked what is in its very nature fine and delicate. . . . His mind was the reverse of historical: although he had rather a coarse, incondite temperament, not finely susceptible to the best influences, to the most exquisite beauties of the world in which he lived, he yet lived in that world thoroughly and completely. He did not take an interest, as a poet does, in the sublime because it is sublime, in the beautiful because it is beautiful; but he had the passions of more ordinary men in a degree, and of an intensity, which ordinary men may be most thankful that they have not. In no one has the intense faculty of intellectual hatred—the hatred which the absolute dogmatist has for those in whom he incarnates and personifies the opposing dogma—been fiercer or stronger; in no one has the intense ambition to rule and govern—in scarcely any one has the daily ambition of the daily politician—been fiercer and stronger: he, if any man, cast himself upon his time.—BAGEHOT, WALTER, 1856, *Thomas Babington Macaulay, Works, ed. Morgan, vol.* II, *pp.* 83, 84.

The slightest sketch of the reign of George III. would indeed be miserably imperfect if it were to omit the name of Edmund Burke. The studies of this extraordinary man not only covered the whole field of political inquiry, but extended to an immense variety of subjects, which, though apparently unconnected with politics, do in reality bear upon them as important adjuncts; since, to a philosophic mind, every branch of knowledge lights up even those that seem most remote from it. The eulogy passed upon him by one who was no mean judge of men, might be justified, and more than justified by passages from his works, as well as by the opinions of the most eminent of his contemporaries. Thus it is, that while his insight into the philosophy of jurisprudence has gained the applause of lawyers, his acquaintance with the whole range and theory of the fine arts has won the admiration of artists; a striking combination of two pursuits, often, though erroneously, held to be incompatible with each other. At the same time, and notwithstanding the occupations of political life, we know on good authority, that he had paid great attention to the history and filiation of languages, a vast subject, which within the last thirty years has become an important resource for the study of the human mind, but the very idea of which had, in its large sense, only begun to dawn upon a few solitary thinkers. And, what is even more remarkable, when Adam Smith came to London full of those discoveries which have immortalized his name, he found to his amazement that Burke had anticipated conclusions the maturing of which cost Smith himself many years of anxious and unremitting labour.—BUCKLE, HENRY THOMAS, 1857, *History of Civilization in England, vol.* I.

Burke's acknowledged writings I had studied diligently many years before I thought of writing anything on his career. They have ever appeared to me as a treasure in English literature, only second in genius and worth to Shakespeare's Plays; and it is through the noble arch-way they afford, that all men must, as an indispensable condition, enter into the spirit of his life. Until we can raise ourselves to the elevation of his mind, and accustom ourselves to look at the events of his time through his own medium, any criticism on his character or political career can be of little worth. We may otherwise complacently remonstrate with him, rebuke him, wonder at him, and misjudge him; but we shall certainly not understand him.—MACKNIGHT, THOMAS, 1858, *History of the Life and Times of Edmund Burke, vol.* I, *Preface p.* xii.

All hail to Edmund Burke, the supreme writer of his century, the man of the largest and finest understanding! Upon that word *understanding*, we lay a stress: for, oh! ye immortal donkeys who have written "about him and about him," with what an obstinate stupidity have ye brayed away for one-third of a century about that which ye are pleased to call his "fancy." Fancy in your throats, ye miserable twaddlers! As if Edmund Burke were the man to play with his fancy for the purpose of separable ornament! He was a man of fancy in no other sense than as Lord Bacon was so, and Jeremy Taylor, and as all large and discursive thinkers are and must be; that is to say, the fancy which he had in common with all mankind, and very probably in no eminent degree, in him was urged into unusual activity under the necessities of his capacious understanding. His great and peculiar distinction was that he viewed all objects of the understanding under more relations than other men, and under more complex relations.—DE QUINCEY, THOMAS, 1859, *Rhetoric, Collected Writings, ed. Masson, vol.* X, *p.* 114.

The freedom of Burke's style in all his more characteristic writings would be altogether strange and startling in a writer

of the present day.—CRAIK, GEORGE L.,
1861, *A Compendious History of English
Literature and of the English Language,
vol.* II, *p.* 565.

Burke has not only loftier qualities of
the mind than Bolingbroke—a knowledge
of books, though not of men, more accurate, comprehensive, and profound—a reasoning more subtle, an imagination more
splendid—but this superiority in gifts and
acquirements is accompanied by an equal
superiority over Bolingbroke in the very
beauties for which Bolingbroke is most
remarkable. He excels him in luxury
and pomp of language; he excels him in
discipline and art of style. The most
sovereign genius will be always that,
whether in prose or verse, which unites in
the highest degree the faculty of reasoning with the faculty of imagination; the
most beautiful writing, either in prose or
verse, will be that which unites the logical
arrangement that satisfies our reason with
the splendour of language that delights
our imagination. And it appears to me
that, in this felicitious union, we have no
prose-writer who is the equal of Burke.
—LYTTON, EDWARD BULWER LORD, 1863–
68, *Caxtoniana, Miscellaneous Prose Works,
vol.* III, *p.* 98.

Burke is so great because, almost
alone in England, he brings thought to
bear upon politics, he saturates politics
with thought; it is his accident that his
ideas were at the service of an epoch of
concentration, not of an epoch of expansion; it is his characteristic that he so
lived by ideas, and had such a source of
them welling up within him, that he could
float even an epoch of concentration and
English Tory politics with them. It does
not hurt him that Dr. Price and the Lib-
erals were enraged with him; it does not
even hurt him that George the Third and
the Tories were enchanted with him. His
greatness is that he lived in a world which
neither English Liberalism nor English
Toryism is apt to enter,—the world of
ideas, not the world of catch words and
party habits.—ARNOLD, MATTHEW, 1865,
*The Function of Criticism at the Present
Time, Essays in Criticism, p.* 14.

With a fertility of fancy sufficient to
make a poet of the rank of Milton, and a
power of general reasoning which might
have furnished a philosopher of the rank
of Bacon, he devoted these rare gifts to

political pursuits. He was not indeed the
ivory paper-knife which Swift considers
as the true measure of sharpness of intellect for a practical statesman, and was
rather the razor to which Goldsmith compares him.—RUSSELL, JOHN LORD, 1866,
*The Life and Times of Charles James Fox,
vol.* III, *p.* 122.

Read him only several pages at a time :
only thus he is great; otherwise all that
is exaggerated, commonplace, and strange
will arrest and shock you; but if you give
yourself up to him, you will be carried
away and captivated. The vast amount
of his work rolls impetuously in a current
of eloquence. Sometimes a spoken or
written discourse needs a whole volume to
unfold the train of his multiplied proofs
and courageous anger.—TAINE, H. A.,
1871, *History of English Literature, tr.
Van Laun, vol.* II, *bk.* iii, *ch.* iii, *p.* 82.

Considered simply as a master of English
prose, Burke has not, in my judgment,
been surpassed in any period of our literature. Critics may point to certain
faults of haste; the evolution of his
thought is sometimes too slow; his majestic march is trammeled by the sweep
of his gorgeous rhetoric; or his imagination takes fire, and he explodes into fierce
denunciations which shock the reader when
the excitement which prompted them has
become unintelligible. But, whatever
blemishes may be detected, Burke's magnificent speeches stand absolutely alone in
the language. They are, literally speaking, the only English speeches which may
still be read with profit when the hearer
and the speaker have long been turned to
dust. His pamphlets, which are written
speeches, are marked by a fervour, a richness, and a flexibility of style which is
but a worthy incarnation of the wisdom
which they embody. It matters little if
we dissent from his appreciations of current events, for it is easy to supply the
corrective for ourselves. The charge
of over-refinement sometimes brought
against him is in great part nothing more
than the unconscious testimony of his
critics that he could see farther than themselves. To a certain degree it is, perhaps,
well founded.—STEPHEN, LESLIE, 1876,
*History of English Thought in the Eight-
eenth Century, vol.* II, *p.* 219.

The varieties of Burke's literary or
rhetorical method are very striking. It

is almost incredible that the superb imaginative amplication of the description of Hyder Ali's descent upon the Carnatic should be from the same pen as the grave, simple, unadorned "Address to the King" (1777), where each sentence falls on the ear with the accent of some golden-tongued oracle of the wise gods. His stride is the stride of a giant, from the sentimental beauty of the picture of Marie Antoinette at Versailles, or the red horror of the tale of Debi Sing in Rungpore, to the learning, positiveness, and cool judicial mastery of the "Report on the Lord's Journals" (1794), which Phillip Francis, no mean judge, declared on the whole to be the "most eminent and extraordinary" of all his productions. Even in the coolest and dryest of his pieces there is the mark of greatness, of grasp, of comprehension. In all its varieties Burke's style is noble, earnest, deep-flowing, because his sentiments were lofty and fervid, and went with sincerity and ardent disciplined travail of judgment. . . . Burke will always be read with delight and edification, because in the midst of discussions on the local and the accidential, he scatters apophthegms that take us into the regions of lasting wisdom. In the midst of the torrent of his most strenuous and passionate deliverances, he suddenly rises aloof from his immediate subject, and in all tranquility reminds us of some permanent relation of things, some enduring truth of human life or society. We do not hear the organ tones of Milton, for faith and freedom had other notes in the seventeenth century. There is none of the complacent and wise-browed sagacity of Bacon, for Burke's were days of eager personal strife and party fire and civil division. . . . The only great English writer of that age whom we can name along with Burke in the literature of enduring power, is Wordsworth, that great representative in another and a higher field, and with many rare elements added that were all his own, of those harmonising and conciliatory forces and ideas that make man's destiny easier to him through piety in its oldest and best sense; through reverence for the past, for duty, for institutions.—MORLEY, JOHN, 1879, *Burke (English Men of Letters), pp.* 210, 211, 212.

Except when dealing with American questions (as to which Burke has the calmness which arises from the sense of being absolutely in the right), he never entirely carries even his admirers with him. You feel that an unknown something spoils what would otherwise be perfect. This "something" is a want of justness of mind. Burke was an enthusiast for justice. He would have sacrificed everything on earth to put an end to any act of oppression, but he was not a just man. The calmness requisite to balance one side against another, the attempt to realize what were the strong points of an opponent's case, the faculty even of showing that kind of appreciation of an enemy's position which is requisite if one is fully to expose its weakness, was the one moral or intellectual gift which Burke did not possess. Hence the persons he assailed suffered from a sense of unfairness which was the greater because of the indubitable force of the assault.—DICEY, A. V., 1879, *Morley's Burke, The Nation, vol.* 29, *p.* 245.

The most distinguished of warriors, the great Burke, the most eloquent and potent champion against whom a young assailant ever tried his powers.—OLIPHANT, MARGARET O. W., 1882, *Literary History of England, XVIII and XIX Centuries, vol.* III, *p.* 270.

In one of his elaborated sentences you will sometimes find words and clauses selected and multiplied and arranged and compacted and qualified and defined and repeated, for the very purpose of extending and limiting the truth to its exact and undoubted measure. He obviously labors to say just what he means, no more, no less, no other. Still, on the whole, he fails, because he is so elaborately precise in details. The thought is suffocated by the multitude of words employed to give it life. It is buried alive. To change the figure, you can divide and subdivide a field into so many, so small, so regular, and so exact patches, that the chief impression it shall leave on your eye is that of the fences. Similar is the impression of an excessively precise style.—PHELPS, AUSTIN, 1883, *English Style in Public Discourse, p.* 91.

To my mind Burke looms up, after the lapse of a century, as a prodigy of thought and knowledge, devoted to the good of his country; an unselfish and disinterested patriot, as wise and sagacious as he was honest; a sage whose moral wisdom shines brighter and brighter, since it was based on the immutable principles of justice and morality. One can extract more profound and striking epigrams from his speeches and writings than from any prose writer that England has produced, if we except Francis Bacon. And these writings and speeches are still valued as among the most precious legacies of former generations; they form a thesaurus of political wisdom which statesmen can never exhaust. Burke has left an example which all statesmen will do well to follow. He was not a popular favorite, like Fox and Pitt; he was not born to greatness, like North and Newcastle; he was not liked by the king or the nobility; he was generally in the ranks of the opposition; he was a new man, like Cicero, in an aristocratic age,—yet he conquered by his genius the proudest prejudices; he fought his way upward, inch by inch; he was the founder of a new national policy, although it was bitterly opposed; and he died universally venerated for his integrity, wisdom and foresight. He was the most remarkable man, on the whole, who has taken part in public affairs, from the Revolution to our times. Of course, the life and principles of so great a man are a study. If history has any interest or value, it is to show the influence of such a man on his own age and the ages which have succeeded,—to point out his contribution to civilization.— LORD, JOHN, 1885, *Beacon Lights of History, vol.* IV, *p.* 288.

Burke spoke well but wrote better, and his political writing has, in the grand style, few equals.—SAINTSBURY, GEORGE, 1886, *Specimens of English Prose Style, p.* 226.

It was Burke's peculiarity and his glory to apply the imagination of a poet of the first order to the facts and the business of life. Arnold says of Sophocles—
"He saw life steadily, and saw it whole." Substitute for the word "life" the words "organised society," and you get a peep into Burke's mind. . . . Wordsworth has been called the High Priest of Nature. Burke may be called the High Priest of Order—a lover of settled ways, of justice, peace, and security. His writings are a storehouse of wisdom, not the cheap shrewdness of the mere man of the world, but the noble, animating wisdom of one

who has the poet's heart as well as the statesman's brain.—BIRRELL, AUGUSTINE, 1887, *Obiter Dicta, Second Series, pp.* 188, 194.

With all due enthusiasm for the majestic merit of his style, that extremity of praise will not be reached here. Notwithstanding all its magnificence it appears to me that the prose of Burke lacks the variety, the delicacy, the modulated music of the very finest writers. When Mr. Leslie Stephen applauds the "flexibility" of Burke's style, he attributes to him the very quality which to my ear he seems most to lack. A robe of brocaded damask is splendid, sumptuous, and appropriate to noble public occasions, but it is scarcely flexible. To be a perfect prose-writer, a man must play sometimes upon thrilling and soul-subduing instruments, but Burke never takes the trumpet from his lips. To those few who may think him humorous, I resign him in despair; and surely still fewer will be found to think him pathetic. The greatest of English prose-writers, we may be sure, would be found to have some command over laughter and tears, but Burke has none—GOSSE, EDMUND, 1888, *A History of Eighteenth Century Literature, p.* 365.

The writer of a prose illumined as with fire; enthusiastic and yet supremely logical; fearless and yet absolutely obedient to order and to law; eloquent and yet restraint; stirred by every popular movement, and yet suggestive and philosophical. More completely than any man he showed, in style no less perfectly than in spirit and in sympathy, all that was most typical of the best genius of his age—its restraint, its philosophy, its obedience to order and to law, and its gift to literary instinct—removed as far from the exaggeration and pedantry of what had gone before, as from the vulgar platitude and superficial complacency of what was to follow.—CRAIK, HENRY, 1895, *ed., English Prose, Introduction, vol.* IV, *p.* ii.

How much of the artist dwelt in the brains of the statesman the record of his indefatigable toil in composition is witness. In answer to the assertion that he is the greatest of English prose writers it is often said that his style lacks restraint and the dignity that accompanies reserve. His temper rather than any lack of taste made him too eager-voiced; he grasped at much that did not fall naturally within his reach, lost *chiaroscuro* in unrelieved emphasis, and attained the massive at the expense of the beautiful. But genius like Burke's declines the selective economy of weaker artists compelled to a choice of material easily handled. He swept into his service all that his excursive imagination took captive, and frequently marshals an unequal array of arguments. But if his touch fails at times to transmute the baser metal into gold, amid such profusion as his we cannot feel ourselves the poorer.—DIXON, W. MACNEILE, 1895, *English Prose, ed. Craik, vol. IV, p. 377.*

Political writers both sagacious and eloquent have flourished at all periods of modern English history. The thought and the expression were often united in the same person, and in some instances with a profundity in the one gift matched worthily with distinction in the other. But it may well be doubted whether any writer on politics and the philosophy of politics has ever combined sagacity and eloquence in such measure, or anything approaching to such measure, as that in which they are combined by Burke.— TRAILL, HENRY DUFF, 1896, *Social England, vol. V, p. 451.*

Burke is the prince of pamphleteers. His great speeches are in reality pamphlets, manifestly written and cast in the pamphlet form. He is a politician among philosophers, a profound philosopher among politicians. He is at his best in the speeches on the American question and the letter on the same question to the sheriffs of Bristol. Here our reason and our moral sense are with him throughout. The elevation of sentiment is noble ; the style is superb ; with all its fervour and force it retains the calmness, the sobriety, the dignity of truth. He hardly ever became declamatory,he is never vituperative. Only once or twice does he lapse into the tasteless extravagant metaphor which defaced his later style. Political writing grander or more full of instruction, moral and prudential, there is none.—SMITH, GOLDWIN, 1896, *Burke, Cornhill, Magazine, vol. 74, p. 18.*

Steeped as we are to-day in evolutionary conceptions, Burke's thought speaks to us in the language we understand best ; it speaks besides with a power that makes it more than simply parallel to already existing influences. Modern evolutionary philosophy has produced no master of political science worthy to be compared for a moment to Burke, in depth of thought, wealth of observation, experience, and research ; and above all, in that primal energy of mind which, baffling all explanation or formulation, in its mighty outflow bears along with it the minds and feelings of men in enforced but willing subdual.—CLAGHORN, KATE HOLLADAY, 1897, *Burke, A Centenary Perspective, Atlantic Monthly, vol. 80, p. 93.*

No account of the great writers of our country could be written without a mention of Edmund Burke and his works. . . . Nearly all he wrote he wrote well, and few men did more to teach and guide the people of his time than Edmund Burke. —FORSTER, H. O. ARNOLD, 1897, *A History of England, p. 791.*

In no part of the world should his name be held more in honor than in this country. He was among the earliest, as he was the greatest, of the defenders of the rights of the American colonies. He gave to the cause of the colonies all the powers of his intellect and the resources of his peculiar and unapproachable knowledge of their affairs and the interests of the empire. No one in England knew the colonial side of the question as he did ; few understood as he did the dangers and difficulties of a vast colonial empire ; no one could unite as he could the interests of the colonies and of the mother country in one comprehensive view, in which rights upon the one hand and duties upon the other would be harmoniously blended. The War of Independence vindicated his statesmanship. — MCDERMOT, GEORGE, 1897, *Edmund Burke the Friend of Human Liberty, Catholic World, vol. 65, p. 473.*

In a well-known canon of style Burke lays it down that the master sentence of every paragraph should involve, first, a thought, secondly, an image, and, thirdly, a sentiment. The rule is certainly not one of universal application ; it is one not always followed by Burke himself, but it expresses the character of his mind. A thought, an image, a sentiment, and all bearing upon action,—it gives us an intimation that the writer who set forth such a canon was a complete nature, no fragment of a man, but a full-formed human spirit, and that when he came to write or

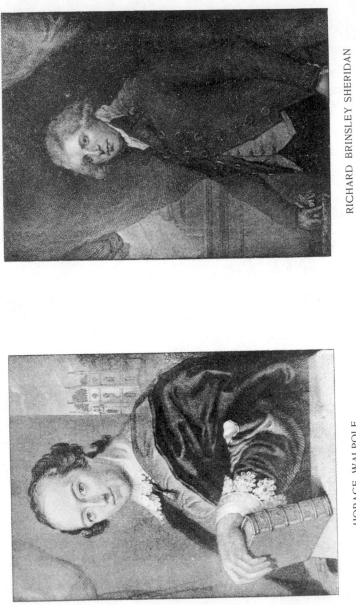

RICHARD BRINSLEY SHERIDAN

Engraving by R. Hicks. Original
Painting by Sir Joshua Reynolds.

HORACE WALPOLE

Engraving by J. Sartain.

speak, he put his total manhood into his utterance. This is, indeed, Burke's first and highest distinction.—DOWDEN, ED-WARD, 1897, *The French Revolution and English Literature, p.* 94.

In the whole scope of political literature there is no writer so often read or so frequently quoted in the present day, and none whose influence has been so deep and lasting, as that of Edmund Burke. . . . He never touched a subject without adorning it with reflections that go to the root of the principles of government in all ages and all nations.—POLLARD, A. F.,

1897,*ed., Political Pamphlets, Introduction, p.* 23.

The times were seeking the man of large and liberal ideas. There existed a reading public. Parliamentary speeches were now allowed to be published. The press was practically free to praise or blame. The post carried the pamphlet and the newspaper to the villages, and thus the English *people* became the audience. At length the man was found, and that man was Edmund Burke.—GEORGE, ANDREW J., 1898, *From Chaucer to Arnold, Types of Literary Art, p.* 642.

Horace Walpole

Earl of Orford

1717–1797

Born, in London, 24 Sept. 1717. Educated at Eton, April 1727 to Sept. 1734. Entered at Lincoln's Inn, 27 May 1731. To King's Coll., Camb., March 1735. Inspector of Imports and Exports, 1737–38; Usher of the Exchequer, 1738; Comptroller of the Pipe, 1738; Clerk of the Estreats, 1738. Left Cambridge, March 1739. Travelled on Continent, 1739–41. M. P. for Callington, 1741–44. Settled at Strawberry Hill, 1747. M. P. for Castle Rising, 1754–57; for King's Lynn, 1757–68. Succeeded to Earldom of Orford, Dec. 1791. Unmarried. Died, in London, 2 March 1797. Buried at Houghton. *Works:* "Lessons for the Day" (anon.), 1742; "Epilogue to Tamerlane" (1746); "Ædes Walpolianæ," 1747; "Letter from Xo-Ho," 1757 (5th edn. same year); "Fugitive Pieces in Verse and Prose," 1758; "Catalogue of the Royal and Noble Authors of England" (2 vols.), 1758; "Observations on the Account given of the Catalogue . . . in . . . the Critical Review," 1759; "Reflections on the Different Ideas of the French and English in regard to Cruelty" (anon.), 1759; "A Counter-Address to the Public" (anon.), 1764; "The Castle of Otranto" (anon.), 1765 (2nd edn. same year); "An Account of the Giants lately discovered," 1766; "The Mysterious Mother" (priv. ptd.), 1768; "Historic Doubts of the Life and Reign of King Richard the Third," 1768 (2nd edn. same year); "Miscellaneous Antiquities" (anon.), 1772; "Description of the Villa . . . at Strawberry Hill," 1772; "Letter to the Editor of the Miscellanies of Thomas Chatterton," 1779; "To Lady H. Waldegrave" (anon.), (1779); "Hieroglyphick Tales" (anon.), 1785; "Essay on Modern Gardening," 1785; "The Press at Strawberry Hill to . . . the Duke of Clarence" (anon.), (1790?); "Hasty Productions." 1791. Posthumous: "Letters to . . . Rev. W. Cole and others," 1818; "Letters to G. Montagu," 1819; "Private Correspondence" (4 vols.), 1820; "Memoirs of the Last Ten Years of the Reign of King George II.," ed. by Lord Holland (2 vols.), 1822; "Letters to Sir H. Mann" (7 vols.), 1833–44; "Letters," ed. by J. Wright (6 vols.), 1840; "Memoirs of the Reign of King George III.," ed. by Sir D. Le Marchant (4 vols.), 1845; "Letters to the Countess of Ossory" (2 vols.), 1848; "Correspondence with W. Mason," ed. by J. Mitford (2 vols.), 1851; "Letters," ed. by P. Cunningham (9 vols.), 1857–58; "Journal of the Reign of King George the Third . . . being a Supplement to his Memoirs," ed. by Dr. Doran (2 vols.), 1859; "Supplement to the Historic Doubts," ed. by Dr. Hawtrey (priv. ptd.), 1860–61. He *edited:* P. Hentzner's "A Journey into England," 1757; G. Vertue's "Anecdotes of Painting in England," 1762; and "Catalogue of Engravers," 1763, Lord Herbert of Cherbury's Life, 1764; Count de Grammont's "Mémoires," 1772. *Collected Works:* in 9 vols., 1798–1825. *Life:* by Austin Dobson, 1890.—SHARP, R. FARQUHARSON, 1897, *A Dictionary of English Authors, p.* 291.

PERSONAL

I find Mr. Walpole then made some mention of me to you; yes, we are together again. It is about a year, I believe, since he wrote to me, to offer it, and there has been (particularly of late), in appearance, the same kindness and confidence almost as of old. What were his motives, I cannot yet guess. What were mine, you will imagine and perhaps blame me. However as yet I neither repent, nor rejoice overmuch, but I am pleased.—GRAY, THOMAS, 1750, *Letter to John Chute, Oct.* 12.

I was well acquainted with Mr. Walpole at Florence, and indeed he was particularly civil to me. I am encouraged to ask a favor of him, if I did not know, that few people have so good memories as to remember, so many years backwards as have passed since I have seen him. If he has treated the character of Queen Elizabeth with disrespect, all the women should tear him in pieces, for abusing the glory of her sex.—MONTAGU, LADY MARY WORTLEY, 1758, *To the Countess of Bute, Oct.* 10; *Works, ed. Dallaway, vol.* v, *p.* 62.

I am certainly the greatest philosopher in the world, without ever having thought of being so: always employed, and never busy; eager about trifles, and indifferent to ever thing serious. Well, if it is not philosophy, at least it is content.—WALPOLE, HORACE, 1774, *To Hon. H. S. Conway, Aug.* 18; *Letters, ed. Cunningham, vol.* VI, *p.* 109.

When Mr. Horace Walpole came from abroad about the year 1746, he was much of a *Fribble* in dress and manner. Mr. Colman, at that time a schoolboy, had some occasion to pay him a visit. He told me he has a strong recollection of the singularity of his manner; and that it was then said that Garrick had him in thought when he wrote the part of *Fribble*, in "Miss in her Teens." But I doubt this much; for there is a character in a play called "Tunbridge Wells," in which that of *Fribble* seems to be evidently formed. However, Garrick might have had Mr. Walpole in his thoughts. This gentleman (Mr. Walpole) is still somewhat singular in manner and appearance; but it seems only a singularity arising from a very delicate and weak constitution, and from living quite retired among his books, and much with ladies. He is always lively and ingenious; never very solid or

energetic. He appears to be very fond of French manners, authors, &c., &c., and I believe keeps up to this day a correspondence with many of the people of fashion in Paris. His love of French manners, and his reading so much of their language, have I think infected his style a little, which is not always so entirely English as it ought to be. He is, I think, a very humane and amiable man.—MALONE, EDMOND, 1782? *Maloniana, ed. Prior, p.* 86.

The letter you sent me of Horace Walpole's is brilliant, and, from its subject, inevitably interesting; but do not expect that I can learn to esteem that fastidious and unfeeling being, to whose insensibility we owe the extinction of the greatest poetic luminary Chatterton, if we may judge from the brightness of its dawn, that ever rose in our, or perhaps any other hemisphere. This fine wit of Strawberry Hill, is of that order of mortals who swarm, always swarmed, and always will swarm in refined states; whose eyes of admiration are in their backs, and who, consequently, see nothing worthy their attention before, or on either side of them; and who, therefore, weary, sicken, and disgust people whose sensibilities are strong and healthy, by their eternal cant about the great *have beens*, and the little *are's*.—SEWARD, MISS, 1787, *Letter to Hardinge, Nov.* 21.

Poor Lord Orford! I could not help mourning for him as if I had not expected it. But twenty years' unclouded kindness and pleasant correspondence cannot be given up without emotion. I am not sorry now that I never flinched from his ridicule or attacks, nor suffered them to pass without rebuke. At our last meeting I made him promise to buy Law's "Serious Call." His playful wit, his various knowledge, his polished manners, alas! what avail they now? The most serious thoughts are awakened. O that he had known and believed the things that belonged to his peace. My heart is much oppressed with this reflection.—MORE, HANNAH, 1797, *Letters.*

When viewed from behind, he had somewhat of a boyish appearance, owing to the form of his person, and the simplicity of his dress. . . . His laugh was forced and uncouth, and even his smile not the most pleasing. His walk was enfeebled by the gout; which, if the editor's memory do not deceive, he mentioned that he had been tormented with since the age of twenty-five; adding, at the same time, that it was no hereditary complaint, his father, Sir Robert Walpole, who always drank ale, never having known that disorder, and far less his other parent. This painful complaint not only affected his feet, but attacked his hands to such a degree that his fingers were always swelled and deformed, and discharged large chalkstones once or twice a year: upon which occasions he would observe, with a smile, that he must set up an inn, for he could chalk up a score with more ease and rapidity than any man in England.— PINKERTON, JOHN, 1799, *Walpoliana.*

The whole spirit of this man was penury. Enjoying an affluent income he only appeared to patronise the arts which amused his tastes,—employing the meanest artists, at reduced prices, to ornament his own works, an economy which he bitterly reprehends in others who were compelled to practise it. He gratified his avarice at the expense of his vanity; the strongest passion must prevail. It was the simplicity of childhood in Chatterton to imagine Horace Walpole could be a patron—but it is melancholy to record that a slight protection might have saved such a youth. Gray abandoned this man of birth and rank in the midst of their journey through Europe; Mason broke with him; even his humble correspondent Cole, this "friend of forty years," was often sent away in dudgeon; and he quarrelled with all the authors and artists he had ever been acquainted with. The Gothic castle at Strawberry-hill was rarely graced with living genius—there the greatest was Horace Walpole himself. — DISRAELI, ISAAC, 1812–13, *The Pain of Fastidious Egotism, Calamities of Authors.*

He certainly was proud of being considered as a sort of patron of literature, and a friend to literary men, but he did not choose to purchase the pre-eminence at a higher price than a little flattery and praise, and a pudding neither over large nor over solid. . . . On his first invitation to dinner with his Lordship, he accompanied Mr. K. There were no other guests. The Sexagenarian presumed that he should for once enjoy the luxury of a splendid dinner, and prepared himself accordingly. Dinner was served, when to the poor author's astonishment, one dish only smoked upon the noble board, and that too, as ill luck would have it, was a species of fish not very agreeable to the palate of the guest. He waited, however, in patience, and the fish was succeeded by a leg of mutton. Wae worth the man, who, in the pride and haughtiness of his heart, presumes to say anything to the disparagement of a leg of mutton. The author, however, thought that he might have a leg of mutton at home, and taking it for granted, that at a nobleman's table, a second course would succeed, where there would be some tit-bit to pamper his appetite, he was very sparingly helped. Alas! nothing else made its appearance. "Well then," exclaimed the disappointed visitor, "I must make up with cheese." His Lordship did not eat cheese. So to the great amusement of his companion, the poor author returned hungry, disconcerted, and half angry. — BELOE, WILLIAM, 1817, *The Sexagenarian, vol.* I, *pp.* 277, 278.

His figure was, as every one knows, not merely tall, but more properly *long,* and slender to excess; his complexion, and particularly his hands, of a most unhealthy paleness. I speak of him before the year 1772. His eyes were remarkably bright and penetrating, very dark and lively: his voice was not so strong; but his tones were extremely pleasant, and (if I may so say) highly gentlemanly. I do not remember his common gait: he always entered a room in that style of affected delicacy which fashion had then made almost natural; *chapeau bras* between his hands, as if he wished to compress it, or under his arm; knees bent; and feet on tiptoe, as if afraid of a wet floor. His dress in visiting was most usually (in summer when I most saw him) a lavender suit; the waistcoat embroidered with a little silver, or of white silk worked in the tambour; partridge silk stockings; and gold buckles; ruffles and frill, generally lace. I remember, when a child, thinking him very much under-dressed if at any time, except in mourning, he wore hemmed cambric. In summer, no powder; but his wig combed straight, and showing his smooth pale forehead, and queued behind; in winter, powder. — HAWKINS, LETITIA MATILDA, 1823, *Anecdotes, Biographical Sketches and Memoirs, vol.* I.

That cold and false-hearted Frenchified coxcomb, Horace Walpole. — WORDSWORTH, WILLIAM, 1833, *Letters, Memoirs by C. Wordsworth, ed. Reed, vol.* II, *p.* 277.

He was, unless we have formed a very erroneous judgment of his character, the most eccentric, the most artificial, the most fastidious, the most capricious of men. His mind was a bundle of inconsistent whims and affectations. His features were covered by mask within mask. When the outer disguise of obvious affectation was removed, you were still as far as ever from seeing the real man. He played innumerable parts, and overacted them all. When he talked misanthropy, he out-Timoned Timon. When he talked philanthropy, he left Howard at an immeasurable distance. He scoffed at courts, and kept a chronicle of their most trifling scandal; at society, and was blown about by its slightest veerings of opinions; at literary fame, and left fair copies of his private letters, with copious notes, to be published after his decease; at rank, and never for a moment forgot that he was an honourable; at the practice of entail, and tasked the ingenuity of conveyancers to tie up his villa in the strictest settlement. The conformation of his mind was such, that whatever was little, seemed to him great, and whatever was great seemed to him little. Serious business was a trifle to him, and trifles were his serious business. To chat with blue-stockings; to write little copies of complimentary verses on little occasions; to superintend a private press; to preserve from natural decay the perishable topics of Ranelagh and White's; to record divorces and bets, Miss Chudleigh's absurdities and George Selwyn's good sayings; to decorate a grotesque house with piecrust battlements; to procure rare engravings and antique chimney-boards; to match odd gauntlets; to lay out a maze of walks within five acres of ground—these were the grave employments of his long life. From these he turned to politics as to an amusement. After the labours of the print-shop and the auction-room, he unbent his mind in the House of Commons. And, having indulged in the recreation of making laws and voting millions, he returned to more important pursuits—to researches after Queen Mary's comb, Wolsey's red hat, the pipe which Van Tromp smoked

during his last sea-fight, and the spur which King William struck into the flank of Sorrel.—MACAULAY, THOMAS BABINGTON, 1833, *Walpole's Letters to Sir Horace Mann, Edinburgh Review, vol.* 58; *Critical and Miscellaneous Essays.*

Mr. Walpole's affection for his mother was so much the most amiable point in his character, and his expressions whenever he names or alludes to her are so touching, come so directly and evidently from the heart, that one would very fain think of her as he did, and believe she had every perfection his partiality assigns to her. But, in truth, there was a contrary version of the matter, not resting solely, nor yet principally, upon the authority of Lady Mary Wortley. It filled so prominent a place in the scandalous history of the time, that the world knew as well which way Captain Lemuel Gulliver was glancing when gravely vindicating the reputation of my Lord *Treasurer* Flimnap's excellent lady, as what he meant by the red, green, and blue girdles of the Lilliputian grandees, or the said Flimnap's feats of agility on the tight-rope. Those ironical lines also, where Pope says that Sir Robert Walpole

"Had never made a friend in private life,
And was besides *a tyrant to his wife*."

are equally well understood as conveying a sly allusion to his good-humoured unconcern about some things which more strait-laced husbands do not take so coolly. Openly laughing at their nicety, he professed it his method "to go his own way, and let madam go hers." . . . That Lady Mary Wortley had been the chief friend and protectress of his step-mother, was alone enough to make him bitter against her.—STUART, LADY LOUISA, 1837, *The Letters and Works of Lady Mary Wortley Montagu, ed. Lord Wharncliffe, Introductory Anecdotes. vol.* I, *pp.* 72, 73.

A vile, malignant, and unnatural wretch, though a very clever writer of Letters.— BROUGHAM, HENRY LORD, 1838, *Selections from the Correspondence of the Macvey Napier, Letter July* 4.

The affections of his heart were bestowed on few; for in early life they had never been cultivated, but they were singularly warm, pure, and constant; characterised not by the ardour of passion, but by the constant preoccupation of real affection. He had lost his mother, to whom he was fondly attached, early in life; and with his father, a man of coarse feelings and boisterous manners, he had few sentiments in common. Always feeble in constitution, he was unequal to the sports of the field, and to the drinking which then accompanied them; so that during his father's retreat at Houghton, however much he respected his abilities and was devoted to his fame, he had little sympathy in his tastes, or pleasure in his society. To the friends of his own selection his devotion was not confined to professions or words: on all occasions of difficulty, of whatever nature his active affection came forward in defence of their character, or assistance in their affairs.—BERRY, MARY, 1840, *Advertisement to the Letters Addressed to the Misses Berry.*

A wit he was of the first water; effeminate too, no doubt, though he prided himself on his open-breasted waistcoats in his old age, and possessed exquisite good sense and discernment, where party-feelings did not blind him. But of the charge of heartlessness, his zeal and painstaking in behalf of a hundred people, and his beautiful letter to his friend Conway in particular, offering, in a way not to be doubted, to share his fortune with him, ought to acquit him by acclamation.—HUNT, LEIGH, 1849, *A Book for a Corner.*

It is said that, latterly, Sir Robert Walpole and his wife did not live happily together, and that Horace, the youngest, was not the son of the great Prime Minister of England, but of Carr, Lord Hervey, elder brother of Pope's antagonist, and reckoned, as Walpole records, of superior parts to his celebrated brother, John. The story rests on the authority of Lady Louisa Stuart, daughter of the minister Earl of Bute, and grand-daughter of Lady Mary Wortley Montagu. She has related it in print in the Introductory Anecdotes to Lady Mary's Works; and there is too much reason to believe that what she says is true.—CUNNINGHAM, PETER, 1858, *ed. Walpole's Letters.*

As for Horace Walpole, he was only a link in the chain of ignoble circumstances that led up to the suicide [of Chatterton] —for which act, however, it is absurd to make any one so responsible as the boy himself. Why should this conceited literary sybarite have been so very forward to befriend a sucking author who had hoaxed

him? It is all fair for a nobleman to amuse himself by elaboratly concocting a series of gossipy letters to be passed off as the offspring of unpremeditated friendly intercourse—and to tell lies about a trumpery "Otranto," writing when he is detected, "the author flatters himself he shall appear excusable"—but when a poor attorney's clerk plays similar pranks in a work of stupendous genius, then the noble "forger" bethinks him that "all of the house of forgery are relations," and that *his younger brother in "Forgery" "must be a consummate villain."*—NOEL, RODEN, 1872–86, *Chatterton, Essays on Poetry and Poets, p. 46.*

"The Autocrat of Strawberry Hill." "The Frenchified Coxcomb." "Lying Old Fox." "A Parasite of Genius." "The Puck in Literature." "Trifler in Great Things." "Tydeus." "Ultimus Romanorum."—FREY, ALBERT R., 1888, *Sobriquets and Nicknames, p. 476.*

The student of English literature can neither overlook Walpole nor treat him as a person of little consequence. He has a marked individuality. If not a great man in the strict sense of the term, he had lived among those who were in the first rank, and he reflected some of their light. His was a complex character which it is easier to criticise than to comprehend. He exhibited in his person a strange compound of foppery and shrewdness, of excessive vanity and of indubitable good sense. He ridiculed and sneered at the follies of his countrymen, and he was the most affected and conceited Englishman of note in his day.—RAE, W. FRASER, 1890, *Horace Walpole's Letters, Temple Bar, vol. 88, p. 188.*

Here, at last, we have the prince of letter-writers drawn for us with a sure and graceful touch. Here is the petted child, who, humored in a foolish whim, was carried privately to court at night, to kiss King George's hand. Here is the clever schoolboy, who preferred reading to fighting; whose friends were lads as precocious as himself, and who, in most unboyish fashion, dubbed his play-fellows Oromasdes and Plato instead of plain Ashton and Gray. Here is the one undergraduate of Cambridge who frankly confesses (for which we love him much) that he never mastered even his multiplication table. Here is the young gentleman of leisure who drew a handsome income from sine-cures, and who was of real service to his country by traveling abroad, and writing admirable letters home. Here is the valued friend of so many brilliant and dis-tinguished people, who has left us in his vivacious pages those matchless portraits that time can never fade. Here, in a word, is Horace Walpole, whom some loved and not a few hated, whose critics have dealt him heavy censure and faint praise, and who now, from a snug corner in the Elysian fields, must secretly rejoice at find-ing himself in hands at once sympathetic, tolerant and impartial.—REPPLIER, AGNES, 1893, *Horace Walpole, A Memoir by Aus-tin Dobson, The Cosmopolitan, vol.* 16, *p.* 250.

He was eleven years younger than the rest of his father's children, a circum-stance which, taken in connection with his dissimilarity, both personally and mentally, to the other members of the family, has been held to lend some countenance to the contemporary suggestion, first revived by Lady Louisa Stuart (Introduction to Lord Wharncliffe's edition of the "Works of Lady Mary Wortley Montagu"), that he was the son not of Sir Robert Walpole, but of Carr, lord Hervey, the "Sporus" of Pope. His attachment to his mother and his life-long reverence for Sir Robert Walpole, of whom he was invariably the strenuous defender, added to the fact that there is nowhere the slightest hint in his writings of any suspicion on his own part as to his parentage, must be held to dis-credit this ancient scandal. — DOBSON, AUSTIN, 1899, *Dictionary of National Biography, vol.* LIX, *p.* 170.

STRAWBERRY HILL

Whether Horace Walpole conferred a benefit upon the public by setting of apply-ing the Gothic style of architecture to domestic purposes, may be doubtful; so greatly has the example he gave been abused in practice since. But, at all events, he thus led the professors of archi-tecture to study with accuracy the princi-ple of the art, which has occasioned the restoration and preservation in such an ad-mirable manner of so many of our finest cathedrals, colleges, and ancient Gothic and conventual buildings. This, it must be at least allowed, was the fortunate re-sult of the *rage* for Gothic, which suc-ceeded the building at Strawberry Hill. For a good many years after that event,

every new building was *pinnacled* and *turreted* on all sides, however little its situation, its size, or its uses might seem to fit it for such ornaments. Then, as fashion is never constant for any great length of time, the taste of the public rushed at once upon castles; and loop-holes, and battlements, and heavy arches, and but-resses appeared in every direction. Now the fancy of the time has turned as madly to that bastard kind of architecture, pos-sessing, however, many beauties, which, compounded of the Gothic, Castellated, and Grecian or Roman, is called *the Elizabethan*, or *Old English*. No villa, no country-house, no lodge in the outskirts of Lon-don, no box of a retired tradesman, is now built, except in some modification of this style.—DOVER, LORD, 1833, *ed. Walpole's Letters to Sir Horace Mann, Life.*

In his multitudinous collection nothing was incongruous, nothing out of place; every thing was well arranged, every thing was complete in its way. Some things might be finical, some trifling; yet all gave evidence of good taste, of refined intellect, and of a range of thought, of occupation, of amusement, far, far higher than could be challenged by any other votarist of fashion of that time. Horace Walpole was himself a living specimen of the rarity which he prized. Strawberry Hill and its master were alike unique.— STONE, ELIZABETH, 1845, *English Society, Chronicles of Fashion.*

The fate of Strawberry was still more lamentable. For four and twenty days the apartments, sacred to the Horatian pleasantries, echoed with the hammer of the auctioneer. Circumstances, that need not be more particularly alluded to, rendered this degradation unavoidable, and it was only with difficulty that the most sacred of the family possessions could be preserved from the relentless or-deal of "a public sale!" The shrine which had been visited with so much interest and veneration, was now overrun by a well dressed mob, who glanced at its treasures, and at the copious catalogue in which they were enumerated, apparently with a like indifference. But at the sale this indiffer-ence, whether feigned or real, changed to the most anxious desire to obtain posses-sion of some relic of the man whose name was invested with so many pleasant as-sociations; and the more interesting portion of "the thousand trifles" created a degree of excitement which would almost have reconciled their proprietor to such a distribution.—WARBURTON, ELIOT, 1852, ed., *Memoirs of Horace Walpole and His Contemporaries, vol.* II, *p.* 568.

If in the history of British art there is one period more distinguished than another for its neglect of Gothic, it was certainly the middle of the eighteenth century. . . . An author appeared . . . to whose writings and to whose influence as an admirer of Gothic art we believe may be ascribed one of the chief causes which induced its present revival. . . . It is impossible to peruse either the letters or the romances of this remarkable man without being struck by the unmistakable evidence which they contain of his Mediæval predilections. . . . The position which he occupies with regard to art resembles in many respects that in which he stands as a man of letters. His labours were not profound in either field. But their result was presented to the public in a form which gained him rapid popularity both as an author and a *dilettante.* As a collector of curiosities he was probably influenced more by a love of old world associations than by any sound appreciation of artistic design.—EAST-LAKE, CHARLES LOCK, 1871, *History of the Gothic Revival, pp.* 42, 43.

Strawberry Hill . . . stands on a gentle elevation about three hundred yards from, and overlooking, the Thames immediately above Twickenham. . . When Walpole rented the house it was little more than a cottage, and the grounds were of narrow compass. As soon as he became its owner, he began to enlarge the house and extend the grounds. The cottage grew into a villa, the villa into a mansion. . . . Strawberry Hill, when completed, was a Gothic building, but Gothic of no particular period, class, or style. Windows, doorways, and mouldings of the thirteenth century stood side by side with others of the fifteenth and sixteenth. Ecclesiastical were co-mingled with secular features, collegiate with baronial or military. Next to an Abbey Entrance was the oriel of an Elizabethan Manor-house, or the keep of a Norman Castle, while battlements and machicolation frowned over the wide bay windows that opened on to the lawn. . . . Walpole was in his thirtieth

year when he took Strawberry Hill; and he spent fifty summers in it, improving the house, adding to his collections, and enjoying the lilacs and nightingales in his grounds. . . . As it now stands, Strawberry Hill is a renewal of Walpole's house, with modern sumptuousness superadded. All the old rooms are there, though the uses of many have been changed. . . . The grounds and gardens are as beautiful and attractive as of old, the trees as verdant, the rosary as bright, the lawn as green, and in their season Walpole's "two passions, lilacs and nightingales," in as full bloom and abundance as ever.—THORNE, JAMES, 1876, *Strawberry Hill, Hand-Book of the Environs of London.*

As a virtuoso and amateur, his position is a mixed one. He was certainly widely different from that typical art connoisseur of his day—the butt of Goldsmith and of Reynolds—who travelled the Grand Tour to litter a gallery at home with broken-nosed busts and the rubbish of the Roman picture-factories. As the preface to the "Ædes Walpolianae" showed, he really knew something about painting, in fact was a capable draughtsman himself, and besides, through Mann and others, had enjoyed exceptional opportunities for procuring genuine antiques. But his collection was not so rich in this way as might have been anticipated; and his portraits, his china, and his miniatures were probably his best possessions. For the rest, he was an indiscriminate rather than an eclectic collector; and there was also considerable truth in that strange "attraction from the great to the little, and from the useful to the odd" which Macaulay has noted. Many of the marvels at Strawberry would never have found a place in the treasure-houses—say of Beckford or Samuel Rogers.—DOBSON, AUSTIN, 1890–93, *Horace Walpole, A Memoir, p.* 286.

He grew old there in his *gim-crack* of a palace, cultivating his flowers and his complexion; tiptoeing while he could over his waxed floors in lavender suit, with embroidered waistcoat and "partridge silk stockings," with *chapeau bas* held before him—very reverent to any visitor of distinction—and afterward (he lived almost into this century), when gout seizes him, I seem to see still—as once before—the fastidious old man, shuffling up and down from the drawing-room to library—stopping here and there to admire some newly arrived bit of pottery—pulling out his golden snuff-box and whisking a delicate pinch into his old nostrils—then dusting his affluent shirt-frills with the tips of his dainty fingers, with an air of gratitude to Providence for having created so fine a gentleman as Horace Walpole, and of gratitude to Horace Walpole for having created so fine a place as Strawberry Hill. —MITCHELL, DONALD G., 1895, *English Lands Letters and Kings, Queen Anne and the Georges, p.* 87.

Horace Walpole's collections were sold at Strawberry Hill by George Robins in April and May 1842, during twenty-four days. The first six days were devoted to the sale of the library, which consisted of 1555 lots, and realised £3900. It was very badly catalogued, and the books and books of prints, collection of portraits, &c., forming the seventh and eight days' sale, were withdrawn, re-catalogued, and extended to a ten days' sale.—WHEATLEY, HENRY B., 1898, *Prices of Books, p.* 162.

ROYAL AND NOBLE AUTHORS
1758

My Catalogue I intended should have been exact enough in style: it has not been thought so by some; I tell you that you may not trust me too much. Mr. Gray, a very perfect judge, has sometimes censured me for parliamentary phrases, familiar to me as your Scotch law is to you.— WALPOLE, HORACE, 1759, *To Dr. William Robertson, Mar.* 4; *Letters, ed. Cunningham, vol.* III, *p.* 213.

A caprice sometimes mingled with affectation, and a prevalent desire of saying a witty thing rather than a wise one, will be obvious to the considerate reader: but his lordship had a liveliness in the manner of conveying his sentiments, an intelligent pertinence in his observations, and a brilliant smartness in his mode of passing critical judgment, which appear to have compensated for many defects, in the eye of the fashionable world.— PARK, THOMAS, 1806, *ed., A Catalogue of the Royal and Noble Authors of England, Scotland and Ireland, vol.* IV, *p.* 438, *note.*

I cannot leave the "Royal and Noble Authors" without exposing the extraordinary chain of errors which an examination of the subject has detected in that work. —NICHOLS, J. G., 1833, *London Gentleman's Magazine, vol.* 2, *p.* 498.

CASTLE OF OTRANTO
1765

Shall I even confess to you, what was the origin of this romance? I waked one morning in the beginning of last June from a dream, of which all I could recover was, that I had thought myself in an ancient castle (a very natural dream for a head filled, like mine, with Gothic story), and that, on the uppermost banister of a great staircase I saw a gigantic hand in armour. In the evening I sat down, and began to write, without knowing in the least what I intended to say or relate. The work grew on my hands. . . . In short, I was so engrossed with my tale, which I completed in less than two months, that one evening I wrote from the time I had drunk my tea, about six o'clock, till half an hour after one in the morning.—WALPOLE, HORACE, 1765, *To Rev. William Cole, March* 9; *Letters, ed. Cunningham, vol.* IV, *p.* 328.

How do you think he has employed that leisure which his political frenzy has allowed of? In writing a novel, entitled the "Castle of Otranto;" and such a novel that no boarding-school Miss of thirteen could get through with without yawning. —WILLIAMS, GILLY, 1765, *Letter to George Selwyn, March* 19.

A series of supernatural appearances, put together under the most interesting form imaginable. Let one be ever so much of a philosopher, that enormous helmet, that monstrous sword, the portrait which starts from its frame and walks away, the skeleton of the hermit praying in the oratory, the vaults, the subterranean passages, the moonshine—all these things make the hair of the sage stand on end, as much as that of the child and his nurse: so much are the sources of the marvellous the same to all men. It is true that nothing very important results at least from all these wonders; but the aim of the author was to amuse, and he certainly cannot be reproached for having missed his aim.— GRIMM, FRIEDRICH MELCHIOR BARON, 1767? *Historical and Literary Memoirs and Anecdotes, vol.* II, *p.* 218.

Read the "Castle of Otranto," which grievously disappointed my expectations.

—GREEN, THOMAS, 1779–1810, *Diary of a Lover of Literature.*

Is, to my notion, dry, meagre, and without effect. It is done upon false principles of taste. The great hand and arm which are thrust into the court-yard, and remain there all day long, are the pasteboard machinery of a pantomime; they shock the senses, and have no purchase upon the imagination. They are a matter-of-fact impossibility; a fixture, and no longer a phantom.—HAZLITT, WILLIAM, 1818, *Lectures on the English Comic Writers, Lecture* vi.

The actors in the romance are strikingly drawn, with bold outlines becoming the age and nature of the story. Feudal tyranny was, perhaps, never better exemplified than in the character of Manfred. . . . The applause due to chastity and precision of style,—to a happy combination of supernatural agency with human interest,—to a tone of feudal manners and language sustained by characters strongly drawn and well discriminated,—and to unity of action, producing scenes alternately of interest and of grandeur;—the applause, in fine, which cannot be denied to him who can excite the passions of fear and of pity, must be awarded to the author of "The Castle of Otranto."—SCOTT, SIR WALTER, 1821, *Horace Walpole.*

By way of experiment, in reviving the more imaginative style of romance, Walpole had bethought himself of a mediæval story of an Italian castle, the human tenants of which should act naturally, but should be surrounded by supernatural circumstances and agencies leading them on to their fate. I confess that on reperusing the story the other day, I did not find my nerves affected as they were when I read it first. The mysterious knockings and voices, the pictures starting from the wainscot, the subterranean vaults, and even the great helmet with the nodding black plumes in the courtyard, had lost their horror; and Walpole seemed to me a very poor master of the Gothic business, or of poetic business of any kind. The attempt, however, is interesting as a harkback to mediævalism, at a time when mediævalism was but little in fashion. As a virtuoso Walpole had acquired a certain artificial taste for the Gothic; and his "Gothic Story," as he called it, did something to bring to the minds of British

readers, on its first publication, the recollection that there had been a time in the world, when men lived in castles, believed in the devil, and did not take snuff, or wear powdered wigs.—MASSON, DAVID, 1859, *British Novelists and Their Styles,* p. 151.

There can, however, be no doubt that this story had a very powerful effect on the writers that followed; nay, that it led, amongst other things, to the study of architecture, mediævalism, the love of the Gothic, the writing of Sir Walter Scott's great romances, and even to the revival of the love of colour, glitter, show, and pictorial decoration observable in the religious services of a large portion of the people of this land.—FRISWELL, JAMES HAIN, 1869, *Essays on English Writers,* p. 294.

This story fills one of the conditions to be found in almost every form of writing that leaves its mark; its main merit is its novelty; it is itself commonplace and nearly unreadable.—PERRY, THOMAS SERGEANT, 1883, *English Literature in the Eighteenth Century,* p. 362.

Originality the work may safely claim. The mountainous helmet, with its waving sable plumes, which crashes down into the courtyard of the Castle of Otranto at the very beginning of the narrative, unheralded and unexplained, may be taken as a symbol and type of the suddenness with which supernatural terror was reintroduced into English fiction by Horace Walpole. Here, with a decisive hand, was struck the keynote of all those later romances which gave only too much ground for Goethe's pithy maxim. "The classical is health; and the romance, disease." The very violence and crudity of Walpole's originality proved an invitation to his imitators to better the instruction he gave them.—RALEIGH, WALTER, 1894, *The English Novel,* p. 223.

It is impossible at this day to take "The Castle of Otranto" seriously, and hard to explain the respect with which it was once mentioned by writers of authority. . . . Walpole's master-piece can no longer make anyone cry even a little; and instead of keeping us out of bed, it sends us there— or would, if it were a trifle longer. For the only thing that is tolerable about the book is its brevity, and a certain rapidity in the action. . . . The book was not an historical romance, and the manners, sentiments, language, all were modern. Walpole knew little about the Middle Ages and was not in touch with their spirit. At bottom he was a trifler, a fribble; and his incurable superficiality, dilettantism, and want of seriousness, made all his real cleverness of no avail when applied to such a subject as "The Castle of Otranto."—BEERS, HENRY A., 1898, *A History of English Romanticism in the Eighteenth Century, pp.* 237, 238, 240.

THE MYSTERIOUS MOTHER
1768

Though the subject of this last piece be singularly horrid and almost disgusting, yet the fable is conducted with such inimitable skill, that it may in this respect be considered as approximating nearer to perfection than any other drama extant, the Œdipus Tyrannus of Sophocles even not excepted.—DRAKE, NATHAN, 1798-1820, *Literary Hours, vol.* II, *No.* xxix, *p.* 109.

He is the *ultimus Romanorum,* the author of the "Mysterious Mother," a tragedy of the highest order, and not a puling love play. He is the father of the first romance, and of the last tragedy, in our language; and surely worthy of a higher place than any living writing, be he who he may.—BYRON, LORD, 1820, *Marino Faliero, Preface.*

"The Mysterious Mother," is a production of higher talent and more powerful genius than any other which we owe to the pen of Horace Walpole.—DOVER, LORD, 1833, ed. *Walpole's Letters to Sir Horace Mann, Life.*

Lord Byron, as quoted by Lord Dover, says, that the "Mysterious Mother" raises Horace Walpole above every author living in his, Lord Byron's, time. Upon which I venture to remark, first, that I do not believe that Lord Byron spoke sincerely; for I suspect that he made a tacit exception in favour of himself at least; secondly, that it is a miserable mode of comparison which does not rest on difference of kind. It proceeds of envy and malice and detraction to say that A. is higher than B., unless you show that they are *in pari materia;*—thirdly, that the "Mysterious Mother" is the most digusting, vile, detestable composition that ever came from the hand of man. No one with a spark of

true manliness, of which Horace Walpole had none, could have written it. As to the blank verse, it is indeed better than Rowe's and Thomson's, which was execrably bad:—any approach, therefore, to the manner of the old dramatists was, of course, an improvement; but the loosest lines in Shirley are superior to Walpole's best.—COLERIDGE, SAMUEL TAYLOR, 1834, *Table Talk, ed. Ashe, March* 20, *p.* 279.

A clever buckram tragedy.—GOSSE, EDMUND, 1888, *A History of Eighteenth Century Literature, p.* 301.

LETTERS

Incomparable letters.—BYRON, LORD, 1820, *Marino Faliero, Preface.*

Read, if you have not read, all Horace Walpole's letters, wherever you can find them;—the best wit ever published in the shape of letters.—SMITH, SYDNEY, 1820, *Letter to Edw. Davenport, Nov.* 19; *Memoir of Rev. Sydney Smith.*

The best letter-writer in the English language.—SCOTT, SIR WALTER, 1821, *Horace Walpole.*

The "Letters" of Mr. Walpole have already attained the highest rank in that department of English literature, and seem to deserve their popularity, whether they are regarded as objects of mere amusement, or as a collection of anecdotes illustrative of the politics, literature, and manners of an important and interesting period.—CROKER, JOHN WILSON, 1825, ed., *Letters from the Hon. Horace Walpole to the Earl of Hertford during his Lordship's Embassy in Paris: to which are added Mr. Walpole's Letters to the Rev. Henry Zouch.*

Walpole's "Letters" are generally considered as his best performances, and we think, with reason. His faults are far less offensive to us in his correspondence than in his books. His wild, absurd, and ever changing opinions about men and things are easily pardoned in familiar letters. His bitter, scoffing, depreciating disposition does not show itself in so unmitigated a manner as in his "Memoirs." A writer of letters must be civil and friendly to his correspondent, at least, if to no other person.—MACAULAY, THOMAS BABINGTON, 1833, *Walpole's Letters to Sir Horace Mann, Edinburgh Review, vol.* 58, *Critical and Miscellaneous Essays.*

Read the new edition of "Horace Walpole's Letters to Sir Horace Mann." There is something I don't like in his style; his letters don't amuse me so much as they ought to do.—GREVILLE, CHARLES C. F., 1833, *A Journal of the Reigns of King George IV and King William IV.*, June 29, *vol.* II, *p.* 170.

The twenty or thirty volumes of Voltaire's correspondence have already furnished a signal example how much a distinguished man will sometimes repeat himself. Yet, as compared with Walpole, he appears to write rather from impulse than meditation, and with the characteristic vivacity of his country. His repeating seems, therefore, to be natural, and like that of a man in conversation upon the same general topics with the succession of individuals. It is not so with Walpole. His phrases are too nicely picked, his anecdotes too carefully told. When they are read the first time, they earn for him the credit of ready wit. But when seen to be transferred from place to place with no essential change, they smack something too much of study. Neither do we detect this solely in his letters. He often produces in his "Memoirs" the counterpart of what he writes to Lord Hertford, or Mann, or Montague. We find the same stories in even the same words. We must, then, already begin to deny him the greatest merit of epistolary composition, its natural and spontaneous flow. But besides this, the repetition of the same thing, however well told, when it is not connected with important events, soon becomes fatiguing.—ADAMS, CHARLES FRANCIS, 1845, *Horace Walpole's Letters and Memoirs, North American Review*, *vol.* 61, *p.* 423.

Of letter-writers by profession we have, indeed, few, although Horace Walpole, bright, fresh, quaint, and glittering as one of his most precious figures of Dresden china, is a host in himself.—MITFORD, MARY RUSSELL, 1851, *Recollections of a Literary Life*, *ch.* xxxii.

I refrain to quote from Walpole regarding George, for those charming volumes are in the hands of all who love the gossip of the last century. Nothing can be more cheery than Horace's "Letters." Fiddles sing all through them; wax-lights, fine dresses, fine jokes, fine plates, fine equipages, glitter and sparkle there; never was such a brilliant, jigging, smirking Vanity Fair as that through which he leads us. Hervey, the next great authority, is a darker spirit.—THACKERAY, WILLIAM MAKEPEACE, 1860, *George the Second, The Four Georges.*

One evergreen still flourishes among all the garlands of flowers which Mudie hourly scatters in our path. Horace Walpole is ours, and ours for ever. Who will ever cease now and then to dip into those numerous volumes, edited, and re-edited, and every now and then coming out with new notes and fresh portraits, and new prefaces and a new index?—THOMSON, KATHARINE (GRACE WHARTON), 1862, *The Literature of Society, vol.* II, *p.* 236.

As to the upper classes, I know few books that leave a more painful impression upon the reader than the volumes which contain the letters of Horace Walpole, in which we see all the froth and scum that floated to the surface of what is called Good Society, and can form a tolerable idea of what was fermenting in the mass below. With all his persiflage and cynicism, he at all events may be trusted as a witness who does not invent, but retails the current scandals of the day.—FORSYTH, WILLIAM, 1871, *The Novels and Novelists of the Eighteenth Century, p.* 19.

The affectations of Horace Walpole sit so gracefully upon him, and are so much a part of the man, that they lend a lustre and reality to the pictures he is drawing. —PATTISON, MARK, 1872-89, *Pope and His Editors, Essays, ed. Nettleship, vol.* II, *p.* 361.

His forte lay in chronicling the gossip of Courts, or in transporting his readers behind the scenes when a political intrigue was in progress. He was more of a Saint-Simon than a Bayard. Although he counted a suit of Francis I.'s armour amongst his choicest treasures, he would have been more in his element handing Louis XIV. a shirt at Versailles than in helping Francis to a fresh horse at Pavia. —HAYWARD, A., 1876, *Strawberry Hill, Sketches of Eminent Statesmen and Writers with other Essays, vol.* II, *p.* 283.

For variety of anecdote and scandal, malicious humour, pleasant cynicism, and lively tittle-tattle, couched in a style at once piquant and graceful, his epistles are quite incomparable. We must bear in mind, however, that Walpole's aim in life was to be amused, and that he gratified this propensity by playing the part of a fashionable critic and thoroughbred virtuoso. His social position, his wealth, his extensive connection with courtiers and aristocrats, littérateurs, and blue-stockings, and his great powers of observation, afforded him unequalled opportunites for gratifying his whim. But he was too unsparing a judge of the vanities and foibles of his own age to escape being placed in the stocks himself; and Macaulay has done it. —SCOONES, W. BAPTISTE, 1880, *Four Centuries of English Letters*, p. 259.

Due allowance made for the superiority of French idiom and French finesse in a department where they appear to most advantage, it may safely be affirmed that, if variety and interest of topics be regarded as well as style, Walpole's letters are unrivalled. It was only by degrees that Horace attained to the perfection of easy engaging writing. His earlier letters betray signs of considerable labour. It is said that a summary prepared beforehand of one of his letters to Montagu was found in looking over some of his correspondence. In later days he wrote with the greatest facility, even carrying on a conversation the while. But he continued to the last the habit of putting down on the backs of letters or slips of paper, a note of facts, of news, of witticisms, or of anything he wished not to forget for the amusement of his correspondents. —SEELEY, L. B., 1884, *Horace Walpole and His World*, p. 32.

These letters have always ranked high since Byron and Scott said they were classic. They are excellently written, and when the subject is good they are delightful, being vivid, amiable, quick, seasoned with allusion, point, and anecdote. But whether they will keep their rank may be questioned. . . . The defect in these letters, as classical compositions, is their lack of freshness. They are a chronicle of faded things—finery, ambitions, sentiments, gossip, criticisms, beaux, dames, and nephews, all musty, and dry, and rubbishy. They do not reveal a nature like Cowper's, nor treasure up refinement, sense, and scholarly associations like Gray's. Invaluable to the historian, and to lovers of old French memoirs, they are not classic in the sense that Cowper's

and Grav's letters are—in the sense of being invaluable to the highly-cultivated man. So far as the society they picture is concerned, the candles were burnt out and the play was done long ago. They are the quintessential spirit of the worldliness—the form and feature of the world of which it was anciently said the fashion of it passeth away. They belong to the antiquary; they no longer touch life.— WOODBERRY, GEORGE E., 1884, *Seeley's Walpole, The Nation*, vol. 38, p. 261.

It is as a letter-writer that he survives; and it is upon the vast correspondence, of which, even now, we seem scarcely to have reached the limits, that is based his surest claim *volitare per ora virum*. The qualities which are his defects in more serious productions become merits in his correspondence; or, rather, they cease to be defects. . . . Among the little band of those who have distinguished themselves in this way, Walpole is in the foremost rank; nay, if wit and brilliancy, without gravity or pathos, are to rank highest, he is first. It matters nothing whether he wrote easily or with difficulty; whether he did, or did not, make minutes of apt illustrations or descriptive incidents: the result is delightful. For diversity of interest and perpetual entertainment, for the constant surprises of an unique species of wit, for happy and unexpected turns of phrase, for graphic characterization and clever anecdote, for playfulness, pungency, irony, persiflage, there is nothing in English like his correspondence. And when one remembers that, in addition, this correspondence constitutes a sixty-years' social chronicle of a specially picturesque epoch by one of the most picturesque of picturesque chroniclers, there can be no need to bespeak any further suffrage for Horace Walpole's "incomparable letters."—DOBSON, AUSTIN, 1890–93, *Horace Walpole, A Memoir*, pp. 293, 294.

Walpole's Letters delight each successive generation. Nor, indeed, can one imagine any abatement of their inextinguishable charm. No student of the eighteenth century, however perfunctorily he may take himself, can afford to neglect that wonderful canvas whereon are posed, in undress, so many great personages, such vital and terrible events. For that matter, the philosopher, the man of affairs, the politician, and the philanthropist—unless his philanthropy shall have deprived him of his natural vision,—may find grave instruction in these light pages. They are instinct with the lessons of other men's experience. — THANET, OCTAVE, 1890, *The Letters of Horace Walpole, The Dial,* vol. 11, *p.* 66.

Walpole's most heinous literary fault was his absurd though not at all remarkable disposition to gauge his estimate of a book according to the rank or gentility of the author. He actually seemed to think a plebeian incapable of meritorious effort in literature, and his opinion as to any performance anonymously published was probably held in suspense until the fact of its authorship had been clearly established. . . . He makes few illusions to the writers contemporaneous with him who were making the real literature of the time; they were all too vulgar to engage his pen, except when he went out of his way to write adversely of them, when he perpetrated some precious bits of most nonsensical critical coxcombry.— ROSSMAN, VINCENT D., 1895, *A Prince of Scriblers, Catholic World,* vol. 60, *p.* 810.

Is sprightly, lively, intolerant, even to nervousness, of dulness or heaviness, speaking the opinion or impression of the hour, superficial, it is true, but yet sincere in his individuality, and with a certain freshness in his freedom from conventionality.— CRAIK, HENRY, 1895, *ed., English Prose, Introduction,* vol. IV, *p.* 7.

The title of coxcomb, which has been scornfully awarded and indignantly repudiated, is too surely his; he had the faults to which those born on the fringe of the purple, as he was, are more liable than those born in the purple itself; he was (chiefly through wilfulness) a bad critic of other men's work, and for this or other reasons not too good a one of his own. But his work is delightful as literature and invaluable as history. Taken with Boswell's "Johnson," it supplies almost a complete view of the intellectual, social, and literary life of this period, certainly an indispensable companion to the due enjoyment and the due understanding of the "Ode on the Passions" and the "Elegy in a Country Churchyard," of "Tom Jones" and "Clarissa," and "Humphry Clinker" and "Tristram Shandy," of the "Rambler" and the "Decline and Fall," of "She Stoops to Conquer" and the "School for Scandal."— SAINTSBURY, GEORGE, 1896, *Social England, ed. Traill,* vol. V, *p.* 270.

It was an out-patient of Bedlam who first suggested that Mr. Walpole's were written with an eye on posterity. . . . He did not write his charming letters for posterity. He wrote them because he had parts and was good-natured, and wished to amuse his friends. . . . Horace Walpole is for every humor. If you are wise he confirms you with a pleasant philosophy, though he hated the name; if you are flippant, he tells you a comical, perhaps a wicked story; if you are complaisant, he charms you with agreeable courtesies; if you would rail at your age, he turns you many a contemptuous text from his.— STREET, G. S., 1899, *After Reading Horace Walpole; Fortnightly Review,* vol. 71, *pp.* 124, 128.

GENERAL

An author who has illustrated many passages in the English History, and adorned more.— ROBERTSON, WILLIAM, 1759, *History of Scotland, bk.* viii, *note.*

The lively and curious acuteness of Walpole.— GIBBON, EDWARD, 1762, *Memoirs of my Life and Writings, July* 26.

I have my fribbles as well as you. In the "Anecdotes of Painting," just published, the author, by the most unprovoked malice, has a fling at your friend obliquely, and puts him in company where you would not expect to find him, with Tom Hearne and Browne Willis. It is about Gothic edifices, for which I shall be about *his pots,* as Bentley said to Lord Halifax of Rowe. But I say it is better; I mean the galley-pots and washes of his toilet. I know he has a fribble-tutor at his elbow, as sicklied over with affectation as himself.— WARBURTON, WILLIAM, 1762, *Letter to Garrick, Feb.* 17.

Walpole had by nature a propensity, and by constitution a plea, for being captious and querulential, for he was a martyr to the gout. He wrote prose and published it; he composed verses and circulated them; and was an author, who seemed to play at *hide-and-seek* with the public. —There was a mysterious air of consequence in his private establishment of a domestic printing press, that seemed to augur great things, but performed little.

—CUMBERLAND, RICHARD, 1806, *Memoirs Written by Himself, vol.* I, *p.* 23.

His taste was highly polished; his vivacity attained to brilliancy; and his picturesque fancy, easily excited, was soon extinguished; his playful wit and keen irony were perpetually exercised in his observations on life, and his memory was stored with the most amusing knowledge, but much too lively to be accurate; for his studies were but his sports. But other qualities of genius must distinguish the great author, and even him who would occupy that leading rank in the literary republic our author aspired to fill. He lived too much in that class of society which is little favourable to genius; he exerted neither profound thinking, nor profound feeling; and too volatile to attain to the pathetic, that higher quality of genius, he was so imbued with the petty elegancies of society that every impression of grandeur in the human character was deadened in the breast of the polished cynic. . . . All his literary works, like the ornamented edifice he inhabited, were constructed on the same artificial principle; an old paper lodging-house, converted by the magician of taste into a Gothic castle, full of scenic effects.—DISRAELI, ISAAC, 1812–13, *The Pains of Fastidious Egotism, Calamities of Authors.*

His judgment of literature, of contemporary literature especially, was altogether perverted by his aristocratical feelings. No writer surely was ever guilty of so much false and absurd criticism. He almost invariably speaks with contempt of those books which are now universally allowed to be the best that appeared in his time; and, on the other hand, he speaks of writers of rank and fashion as if they were entitled to the same precedence in literature which would have been allowed to them in a drawing-room. . . . It is easy to describe him by negatives. He had not a creative imagination. He had not a pure taste. He was not a great reasoner. There is indeed scarcely any writer, in whose works it would be possible to find so many contradictory judgments, so many sentences of extravagant nonsense. Nor was it only in his familiar correspondence that he wrote in this flighty and inconsistent manner; but in long and elaborate books, in books repeatedly transcribed and intended for the public eye.—MACAULAY, THOMAS BABINGTON, 1833, *Walpole's Lettters to Sir Horace Mann, Edinburgh Review, vol.* 58; *Critical and Miscellaneous Essays.*

I must guard you against the historical publications of the celebrated Horace Walpole. Look for entertainment in them if you please, and you will not be disappointed; but give him not your confidence: indeed you will soon see, from his lively and epigrammatic style of invective, that he cannot deserve it.—SMYTH, WILLIAM, 1840, *Lectures on Modern History, Lecture* xxxiii.

The affectation of his style has its roots in the affectation of his nature, and it is an admirable style for him.—WHIPPLE, EDWIN P., 1849, *Use and Misuse of Words, Literature and Life, p.* 247.

Horace Walpole illustrates his knowledge of the world by anecdote and witticism, by the authority of his own empirical opinion, by a fancy so wanton and discursive that it cannot fail to be sometimes just; but he never fatigues himself by seeking, like Rochefoucauld, to dissect and analyse. He prides himself on being frivolous, and, if he is wise, he takes care to tell you that he is only so for his own amusement. We cannot dispute his knowledge of the world in breadth of surface, as we may do that of the French Court-philosophers; but he very rarely dives to the depth which they explore, though it be but the depth of a garden fountain. — LYTTON, EDWARD BULWER LORD, 1863–68, *Caxtoniana, Miscellaneous Prose Works, vol.* III, *p.* 427.

Horace Walpole's pungent prose.— BURTON, JOHN HILL, 1880, *A History of the Reign of Queen Anne, vol.* II, *p.* 131

Without a spark of genius, he has a taste, bright and intelligent, for the arts; he understands their principles, and dabbles in them all. He revives Gothic architecture in Strawberry Hill—a toy house; he makes an experiment in romance in "The Castle of Otranto"—a toy novel; he writes sketchy Lives of the Painters, and composes an ingenious "Essay on Landscape Gardening."—COURTHOPE, WILLIAM JOHN, 1885, *The Liberal Movement in English Literature, p.* 120.

"Unhealthy and disorganised mind," "a bundle of whims and affectations,"

RICHARD CUMBERLAND

*Engraving by Scrieven, from a
Painting by Clover.*

WILLIAM MASON

*Engraving by R. Cooper, from Original
by Sir Joshua Reynolds, at Pembroke
Hall, Cambridge.*

"mask within mask;" these are the phrases that go to make up the popular estimate of a writer who was distinguished by the sincerity of his taste and judgment, and by the quickness and truth of his response to all impressions. Horace Walpole wrote and thought exactly as he pleased; his letters are the expression, direct and clear, of a mind that could not condescend to dull its reflections by any compromise about the values of things, or any concession to opinion. He never tampered with his instinctive appreciation of anything. Whether his judgments are sound in themselves is a question of small importance in comparison with his virtue of self-respect and self-restraint. It is because he had a mind of his own and would not pretend to like what he could not like, that he has been pointed out by the literary demagogue.—KER, W. P., 1895, *English Prose*, ed. *Craik, vol.* IV, *p.* 233.

William Mason

1724-1797

An English divine who gained some reputation by his poetry, but more by the friendship of Gray, was the son of the Vicar of St. Trinity Hall, in the East Riding of Yorkshire; educated at St. John's College, Cambridge, and elected a Fellow of Pembroke College in 1747. In 1754, he took holy orders; became Rector of Aston, Yorkshire, and chaplain to the king, and at the time of his death had been thirty-two years Precentor and Canon Residentiary of York. His principal works are "Elfrida, a Dramatic Poem, written on the Model of the Antient Greek Tragedy," 1752; "Odes on Memory, Independence, Melancholy, and the Fate of Tyranny," 1756; "Caractacus, a Dramatic Poem, written on the Model of the Antient Greek Tragedy," 1759; "The English Garden, a Poem in Four Books," 1772-82; "Collection of Anthems for Church Music," 1782; "Secular Ode in Commemoration of the Glorious Revolution, 1688," 1788; "Essays, Historical and Critical, on English Church Music," 1795, "Memoirs of Thomas Gray," 1775.—ALLIBONE, S. AUSTIN, 1870, *Critical Dictionary of English Literature, vol.* II, *p.* 1238.

PERSONAL

Mr. Mason is my acquaintance: I liked the ode very much, but have found no one else that did. He has much fancy, little judgment, and a good deal of modesty. I take him for a good and well-meaning creature; but then he is really *in simplicity a child*, and loves everybody he meets with: he reads little or nothing, writes abundance, and that with a design to make his fortune by it.—GRAY, THOMAS, 1748, *Letter to Thomas Wharton, June* 5; *Works, ed. Gosse, vol.* II, *p.* 184.

Whence is that groan? no more Britannia sleeps,
But o'er her lost Musæus bends and weeps.
Lo, every Grecian, every British, Muse
Scatters the rarest flowers, and gracious dews,
Where Mason lies.
—MATHIAS, THOMAS JAMES, 1797, *The Pursuits of Literature, Eighth ed., p.* 421.

During the whole progress of the American war, Mason continued unchanged in his Whig principles; and took an active share in the association for parliamentary reform, which began to be formed in the year 1779. . . . Among his accomplishments, his critical knowledge of painting must have been considerable, for his translation of DuFresnoy's poem on that art, which appeared in 1783, was finished at the particular suggestion of Sir Joshua Reynolds, who furnished it with illustrative notes. . . . Mason's learning in the arts was of no ordinary kind. He composed several devotional pieces of music for the choir of York cathedral; and Dr. Burney speaks of an "Historical and Critical Essay on English Church Music," which he published in 1795, in very respectful terms. It is singular, however, that the fault ascribed by the same authority to his musical theory, should be that of Calvinistical plainness. In verse he was my Lord Peter; in his taste for sacred music, Dr. Burney compares him to Jack, in the "Tale of a Tub."—CAMPBELL, THOMAS, 1819, *Specimens of the British Poets.*

Mason's private character is said to have been distinguished by the most fervid affection for his friends, and by the most universal philanthropy, though there was something in his manners which appeared more than the mere dignity of conscious talent. Warton, whose character was

marked by an unaffected simplicity and
easy carelessness, used to say "Mason is
not in my way, he is a *buckram* man;" and
this has been repeated by those who were
not partial to him for political or other
reasons. He had the misfortune to survive most of his early friends, and he does
not appear to have been desirous of forming new connexions; this did not proceed
from misanthropic cynicism, but from
natural reserve; yet it caused the superficial observer to deem him proud and unsocial. That he possessed the Christian
virtues in an eminent degree, and fulfilled
the duties of his sacred character in an
exemplary manner cannot be doubted.—
SINGER, S. W., 1822, *The British Poets*,
Chiswick ed.

ELFRIDA
1752

One of the best poets of the present
age, the ingenious Mr. Mason of Cambridge, has not long ago published a
Tragedy upon the model of the ancients,
called "Elfrida;" the merit of this piece,
as a poem has been confessed by the general reading it has obtained; it is full of
beauties; the language is perfectly poetical, the sentiments chaste, and the moral
excellent; there is nothing in our tongue
can much exceed it in the flowry enchantments of poetry, or the delicate flow of
numbers, but while we admire the poet,
we pay no regard to the character; no
passion is excited, the heart is never
moved, nor is the reader's curiosity ever
raised to know the event.—CIBBER, THE-
OPHILUS, 1753, *Lives of the Poets, vol.* I,
p. 316.

My friend Mason is much chagrined at
his daughter Elfrida's having eloped without his consent. I knew when I heard it
was brought on the stage that he was not
consulted, and they say it is sadly performed. It vexes one to think that a
poem of such delicacy and dignity should
be prostituted, and the charms of virgins
represented by the abandoned nymphs of
Drury Lane. Such a poem would have
been represented in days of yore by the
youthful part of the Royal family, or those
of the first rank. — GRANVILLE, MARY
(MRS. DELANY,), 1772, *Letter to Mrs.
Port, Dec.* 30; *Autobiography and Correspondence, ed. Llanover, Second series, vol.*
I, *p.* 488.

Mr. Mason, in his "Elfrida," has wantonly

misrepresented historical fact,—for which
no man could be forgiven, and for which
no beauties in his poetry can compensate.
—HEADLEY, HENRY, 1787, *Select Beauties
of Ancient English Poetry.*

The conduct of this regular drama is
the most irregular thing in the world.—
BOADEN, JAMES, 1825, *Memoirs of the
Life of John Philip Kemble, vol.* I, *p.* 265.

"Elfrida" is very, very far from a contemptible piece of workmanship: it is
manifestly the production of a scholar and
a gentleman, of an ardent lover of poetry,
and platonic inamorato of abstract virtue:
but impossible as it is to approve our conjecture by experiment, we do shrewdly
suspect that it is nothing like what
Sophocles or Euripides would have written
had they risen from the dead in the pleni-
tude, or, if you will, with only a tithe of
their powers, and an inspired mastery of
the English language, to exhibit to the
eighteenth century the marvel of a modern
ancient drama. . . . As an accommodation of the ancient drama to modern habits
and sympathies, "Elfrida" must be pronounced a decided failure. . . . With
the great poets in any department of
poetry, Mason cannot be numbered, yet
for many years of his life he was England's *greatest* living Poet.—COLERIDGE,
HARTLEY, 1833, *Biographia Borealis, pp.*
406, 427, 462.

There are two sorts of simplicity in the
natural history of poets—the right sort,
the manly simplicity that makes him write
like Burns and Crabbe, from the forcible
dictates of nature; and the wrong sort,
perhaps, better entitled to the name of
credulity, that gulls them to believe in
the false resources of their art. The
worthy and single-hearted Mason was of
the latter description: he was one of
those, to use Burns's words,
"Who think to climb Parnassus' hill
By dint o' Greek."
He was not only persuaded himself that
he could incorporate the Attic chorus
with the modern drama—an attempt like
that of ingrafting a dead branch on a
living tree, but he made his experiment
with a play that is without action and
without interest. We might forgive him
for perverting history, and showing off
"Elfrida," who was a barbarous traitress,
as a tender wife, but it defies all patience
to find her employed in nothing but making

speeches, and calling on her waiting-maids to strike up odes to the rising sun. In order to save her husband, and divert the king's affection, she makes a promise to stain and deform her beauty, but she never performs it; and, when her lord is killed, she hurries off her poor maids into a nunnery, without consulting their inclinations. All this time he dreamed himself, and wrote to his friends, that he was imitating Sophocles! — CAMPBELL, THOMAS, 1834, *Life of Mrs. Siddons, p.*143.

GENERAL

I intended writing to you on "Gray's Life," if you had not prevented me. I am charmed with it, and prefer it to all the biography I ever saw. The style is excellent, simple, unaffected; the method admirable, artful, and judicious. He has *framed* the fragments (as a person said), so well, that they are fine drawings, if not finished pictures. For my part, I am so interested in it, that I shall certainly read it over and over.—WALPOLE, HORACE, 1775, *To Rev. William Cole, April* 11; *Letters, ed. Cunningham, vol.* VI, *p.* 199.

With many other virtues he possessed a fine genius for poetry, and was indeed the best poet of his time, as appears from his Works of that sort published by himself at different times in three volumes.— HURD, RICHARD, 1808? *Commonplace Book, ed. Kilvert, p.* 247.

Mr. Chalmers's character of this poet is expressed as usual with laboured and inaccurate pomposity; its import however is just, he censures the finical profuseness of his ornaments, the epithets which encumber what they do not illustrate, and the stiff and strained alliteration which he so perpetually affected: and he does justice to the bold and original conceptions of a writer who aimed at nobler and better things than any of his contemporaries.— SOUTHEY, ROBERT, 1814, *Chalmers's English Poets, Quarterly Review, vol.* 11, *p.*502.

I cannot bring myself to think much of Mason's poetry. I may be wrong; but all those passages in the Caractacus which we learn to admire at school, now seem to me one continued *falsetto.*—COLERIDGE, SAMUEL TAYLOR, 1833, *Table Talk, ed. Ashe, Jan.* 3, *p,* 184.

Prim, in spruce parti-colours, Mason shone,
His Muse lookt well in gall-dyed crape alone.
—LANDOR, WALTER SAVAGE, 1846, *Satirists, Miscellaneous Poems,* cxvi.

Mason's poetry cannot be said to be popular, even with poetical readers. His greatest want is simplicity, yet at times his rich diction has a fine effect. In his "English Garden," though verbose and languid as a whole, there are some exquisite images. — CHAMBERS, ROBERT, 1876; *Cyclopædia of English Literature, ed. Carruthers.*

Grateful as we must be to Mason for his affection and good-heartedness, we cannot refrain from wishing that his poems had been fastened to a mill-stone and cast into the river Cam. They are not only barren and pompous to the very last degree, but to the lovers of Gray they have this disadvantage, that they constantly resolve that poet's true sublime into the ridiculous, and leave on the ear an uncomfortable echo, as of a too successful burlesque or parody. Of this Gray himself was not unconscious, though he put the thought behind him, as one inconsistent with friendship.—GOSSE, EDMUND, 1882, *Gray (English Men of Letters), p.* 87.

The most pretentious poetical prig that the eighteenth century produced. This was Mason, who still lingers in literary history, after a vicarious fashion, as the friend of Gray. He was himself, however, not actually devoid of poetical ability. At least at one period of his life spitefulness gave a vigor to his pen which inspiration was never able to impart, and he produced, as a result, some abusive and therefore still readable satires. . . . No student of Chaucer needs to be told that language [of "Musæus"] is hardly contemptuous enough to set forth satisfactorily the contemptible character of this imitation. It is an outrage both upon the memory of the poet and of the speech in which he wrote. Yet there is no question that it was generally thought at the time to be a successful reproduction of the diction of Chaucer. Mason was hailed by some as the coming poet upon the strength of this one production. Even as late as 1806 Bowles in his edition of Pope styled it "the exquisite Musæus." That this cuckoo song could so long have been mistaken for the note of a nightingale is one of those perversities of criticism which leave the reader in doubt whether there is in reality anything that can be deemed even remotely a standard of taste. The affirmative view can only be maintained in this case upon the ground that knowledge is essential to any proper literary judgment, and that then knowledge of our early speech did not exist.—LOUNSBURY, THOMAS R., 1891, *Studies in Chaucer, vol. III, pp. 126, 128.*

It is rather difficult to classify the poet William Mason, except to say that he was first, last, and all the time an imitator. . . . His connection with Gray, and the fact that he edited Gray's literary remains have kept Mason alive; his poetry is not altogether without merit, but it "smells of mortality." Lowell said that Gray and Mason together could not make the latter a poet.—PHELPS, WILLIAM LYON, 1893, *The Beginnings of the English Romantic Movement, p. 97.*

Mason was a man of considerable abilities and cultivated taste, who naturally mistook himself for a poet. He accepted the critical canons of the day, taking Gray and Hurd for his authorities, and his serious attempts at poetry are rather vapid performances, to which his attempt to assimilate Gray's style gives an air of affectation. The "Heroic Epistle" gives him a place among the other followers of Pope's school in satire.—STEPHEN, L., 1893, *Dictionary of National Biography.*

Was a very small poet and a somewhat absurd person. He aped, first Milton and afterward Gray, so closely that his work often seems like parody.—BEERS, HENRY A., 1898, *A History of English Romanticism in the Eighteenth Century, p. 151.*

Mary Wollstonecraft Godwin

1759–1797

Mary Wollstonecraft was born 27 April 1759. Companion to a lady, 1778–80. Kept school at Newington Green with her sister, 1783–85. Acquaintance with Dr. Johnson. Governess in Lord Kingsborough's family, 1787–88. To London; worked as reader and translator for Dr. Johnson, 1788–92. Met William Godwin, Nov. 1791. To Paris, 1792. Lived with Gilbert Imlay, 1793–96. Attempted suicide, 1796. Intimacy with William Godwin begun, 1796; married to him, 29 March 1797. Died, in London, 10 Sept. 1797. *Works:* "Thoughts on the Education of Daughters," 1787; "Original Stories" (anon.), 1788; "Vindication of the Rights of Men," 1790; "Vindication of the Rights of Woman," vol. i., 1792 (no more pub.); "Historical and Moral View of . . . the French Revolution," vol. i., 1794 (no more pub.); "Letters written in Norway," 1796. *Posthumous:* "Posthumous Works," ed. by Wm. Godwin (4 vols.), 1798; "Letters to Imlay," ed. by C. Kegan Paul, 1879. She *translated:* Salzmann's "Elements of Morality," 1790.—SHARP, R. FARQUHARSON, 1897, *A Dictionary of English Authors, p. 114.*

PERSONAL

I never wanted but your heart—that gone, you have nothing more to give. Had I only poverty to fear, I should not shrink from life. Forgive me then, if I say, that I shall consider any direct or indirect attempt to supply my necessities, as an insult which I have not merited, and as rather done out of tenderness for your own reputation, than for me. My child may have to blush for her mother's want of prudence, and may lament that the rectitude of my heart made me above vulgar precautions; but she shall not despise me for meanness. You are now perfectly free. God bless you!—WOLLSTONECRAFT, MARY, 1793, *Letters to Imlay, Nov.*

Adieu, thou excellent woman! thou reverse of that hyæna in petticoats, Mrs.

Wolstoncroft, who to this day discharges her ink and gall on Maria Antoinette, whose unparalleled sufferings have not yet stanched that Alecto's blazing ferocity. —WALPOLE, HORACE, 1795, *To Hannah More; Letters, ed. Cunningham, vol. IX, p. 452.*

Of all the lions or *literati* I have seen here, Mary Imlay's countenance is the best, infinitely the best: the only fault in it is an expression somewhat similar to what the prints of Horne Tooke display— an expression indicating superiority; not haughtiness, not sarcasm, in Mary Imlay, but still it is unpleasant. Her eyes are light brown, and although the lid of one of them is affected by a little paralysis, they are the most meaning I ever saw.— SOUTHEY, ROBERT, 1797, *Letter to J. Cottle, March 13.*

Mrs. Godwin died on Sunday, Sept. 10, about eight in the morning. I was with her at the time of her delivery, and with very little intermission until the moment of her death. Every skilful effort that medical knowledge of the highest class could make, was exerted to save her. It is not possible to describe the unremitting and devoted attentions of her husband. Nor is it easy to give you an adequate idea of the affectionate zeal of many of her friends, who were on the watch night and day to seize on an opportunity of contributing towards her recovery, and to lessen her sufferings. . . . I know of no consolations for myself, but in remembering how happy she had lately been, and how much she was admired, and almost idolized, by some of the most eminent and best of human beings.—FENWICK, ELIZA, 1797, *Letter to Everina Wollstonecraft, Sept.* 12.

The loss of the world in this admirable woman, I leave to other men to collect; my own I well know, nor can it be improper to describe it. I do not here allude to the pleasures I enjoyed in her conversation: these increased every day, in proportion as we knew each other better, and as our mutual confidence increased. They can be measured only by the treasures of her mind, and the virtues of her heart. But this is a subject for meditation, not for words. What I purposed alluding to, was the improvement that I have forever lost.—GODWIN, WILLIAM, 1798, *Memoirs of the Author of a Vindication of the Rights of Woman, p.* 199.

They say that thou wert lovely from thy birth,
Of glorious parents, thou aspiring child!
I wonder not—for One then left this earth
Whose life was like a setting planet mild,
Which clothed thee in the radiance undefiled
Of its departing glory; still her fame
Shines on thee, through the tempests dark and wild,
Which shake these latter days.
— SHELLEY, PERCY BYSSHE, 1817, *To Mary, Revolt of Islam.*

An Ariel imprisoned in a brickbat! It is a real tragedy and of the deepest. Sublimely virtuous endowment; in practice, misfortune, suffering, death . . . by destiny, and also by desert. An English Mignon; Godwin an honest boor that loves her, but cannot guide or save her.

—CARLYLE, THOMAS, 1831, *Journal, Life by Froude, vol.* II, *p.* 167.

Fuseli found in her a philosophical sloven: her usual dress being a habit of coarse cloth, black worsted stockings, and a beaver hat, with her hair hanging lank about her shoulders. When the Prince Talleyrand was in this country, in a low condition with regard to his pecuniary affairs, and visited her, they drank their tea, and the little wine they took, indiscriminately from tea-cups.— KNOWLES, JOHN, 1831, *The Life and Writings of Henry Fuseli.*

No woman (with the exception of the greatest woman, Madame de Staël) has made any impression on the public mind during the last fifty years, to be compared with Mrs. Godwin. This was perhaps more especially true in the provinces, where her new and startling doctrines were seized with avidity, and acted upon in some particulars to considerable extent, particularly by married women. . . . She was, I have been told by an intimate friend, very pretty and feminine in manners and person; much attached to those very observances she decries in her works; so that if any gentleman did not fly to open the door as she approached it, or take up the handkerchief she dropped, she showered on him the full weight of reproach and displeasure; an inconsistency she would have doubtless despised in a disciple. I have heard the late Miss Jewsbury express an intention of so remodelling the Rights of Women, that it would not fail to become attractive, and she thought useful.—ELWOOD, MRS. A. K., 1842, *Memoirs of the Literary Ladies of England.*

Mary Wollstonecraft was one of those beings who appear once perhaps in a generation, to gild humanity with a ray which no difference of opinion nor chance of circumstances can cloud. Her genius was undeniable. She had been bred in the hard school of adversity, and having experienced the sorrows entailed on the poor and the oppressed, an earnest desire was kindled within her to diminish these sorrows. Her sound understanding, her intrepidity, her sensibility and eager sympathy, stamped all her writings with force and truth, and endowed them with a tender charm that enchants while it enlightens. She was one whom all loved who had ever seen her. Many years are passed since that beating heart has been laid in the cold still grave, but no one who has ever seen her speaks of her without enthusiastic veneration. Did she witness an act of injustice, she boldly came forward to point it out, and induce its reparation. Was there discord among friends or relatives, she stood by the weaker party, and by her earnest appeals and kindliness awoke latent affection, and healed all wounds. "Open as day to melting charity," with a heart brimful of generous affection, yearning for sympathy, she had fallen on evil days, and her life had been one course of hardship, poverty, lonely struggle, and bitter disappointment. — SHELLEY, MARY WOLLSTONE-CRAFT, 1851, *Fragmentary Notes, Paul's Life of Godwin, vol.* I, *p.* 231.

Mary Wollstonecraft went to live with Imlay without going through any preliminary ceremony of marriage, because she believed that the enforced permanence of wedlock was inexpedient or immoral; and yet, curiously enough, those who are most eager to justify her in acting out one half of the theory are most severe upon Imlay for acting out the other half. The deserted woman, naturally enough, set the example of injustice, and it has been followed by all her admirers. Mrs. Pennell quotes Southey's saying that "Mary Wollstonecraft was but beginning to reason when she died." She had certainly not begun to reason when she blamed Imlay, and considered herself a wronged woman because he had acted as her disciple, and owned no obligation save to his own emotional instincts. He may have been worthy of blame; and for my part I, with probably the majority of my readers, must regard him as a heartless brute; but I do not think that any one who echoes my verdict with one breath, and justifies Mary Wollstonecraft's theory and practice in another, can be credited with a severely logical mind.—NOBLE, JAMES ASHCROFT, 1885, *Mary Wollstonecraft Godwin, The Academy, vol.* 28, *p.* 55.

Who shall paint her as she was, without distortion, without idealization? This beautiful woman, with her "Titianesque" coloring, her careless dress, and habits frugal that she might be generous—with her quick temper, sensitiveness, pride, inconsistency, deep personal tenderness; with her melancholy, and her misunderstood religious enthusiasm; this daughter of the Revolution, her strong head crowded with theories—some of them, one would think, to be beaten out of it by all the waves and billows that went over her. But not so; the circumstances of her marriage with Godwin, the tendency of the work done during the brief remainder of her life, show us that we must add tenacity to her characteristics. This creature, now coarse, now fine, now harsh, and now all pity,—who shall explore her strength and weakness, her deeps and shallows? It is natural that in an age better calculated to understand her motives than that in which she lived, a vindicator should have arisen to call up out of the past, by the name of Mary Wollstonecraft, a spirit radiant and purified, like the soul of Ianthe in "Queen Mab," from every stain of earthliness. But to make the woman herself live before us, as she lived in Paris, in London, in those strange days of the close of the eighteenth century—that would be a task for a pen that has dealt with character under somewhat similar conditions — the pen of Ivan Turgenef.— CONE, HELEN GRAY, AND GILDER, JEANNETTE L., 1887, *Pen-Portraits of Literary Women, vol.* I, *p.* 84.

Her books show some genuine eloquence, though occasionally injured by the stilted sentimentalism of the time. The letters are pathetic from the melancholy story which they reveal. Her faults were such as might be expected from a follower of Rousseau, and were consistent with much unselfishness and nobility of sentiment, though one could wish that her love-affairs had been more delicate.—STEPHEN, LES-LIE, 1890, *Dictionary of National Biography, vol.* XXII, *p.* 61.

She was rather hardly treated in her own time; Horace Walpole calling her, it is said (I have not verified the quotation), a "hyena in petticoats:" it would be at least as just to call Lord Orford a baboon in breeches. And though of late years she has been made something of a heroine, it is to be feared that admiration has been directed rather to her crotchets than to her character. This last appears to have been as lovable as her hap was ill. . . . She had but ill luck in her life, and perhaps showed no very good judgment in letters, but she had neither bad brains nor bad blood; and the references to her, long after her death, by such men as Southey, show the charm which she exercised.— SAINTSBURY, GEORGE, 1896, *A History of Nineteenth Century Literature, pp.* 37, 38.

VINDICATION OF THE RIGHTS OF WOMAN
1792

I have seen Mary Woolstonecroft's book, which is much run after here. . . . It has produced no other conviction in my mind, but that of the author's possessing considerable abilities, and greatly misapplying them. To refute her arguments would be to write another and a larger book; for there is more pains and skill required to refute ill-founded assertions, than to make them. Nothing can be more specious and plausible, for nothing can delight Misses more than to tell them they are as wise as their masters. Though, after all, they will in every emergency be like Trinculo in the storm, when he crept under Caliban's gaberdine for shelter. I consider this work as every way dangerous. First, because the author, to considerable powers adds feeling, and I dare say a degree of rectitude of intention. She speaks from conviction on her own part, and has completely imposed on herself before she attempts to mislead you. Then because she speaks in such a strain of seeming piety, and quotes Scripture in a manner so applicable and emphatic, that you are thrown off your guard, and surprised into partial acquiescence, before you observe that the deduction to be drawn from her position, is in direct contradiction, not only to Scripture, reason, the common-sense and universal custom of the world, but even to parts of her own system, and many of her own assertions. — GRANT, ANNE, 1794, *To Miss Ourry, Jan.* 2; *Letters from the Mountains, vol.* II, *p.* 268.

"The Vindication of the Rights of Woman" is a very unequal performance, and eminently deficient in method and arrangement. When tried by the hoary and long-established laws of literary composition, it can scarcely maintain its claim to be placed in the class of finished productions. But, when we consider the importance of its doctrines, and the eminence of genius it displays, it seems not very improbable that it will be read as long as the English language endures. The publication of this book forms an epocha in the

subject to which it belongs; and Mary Wollstonecraft will perhaps hereafter be found to have performed more substantial service for the cause of her sex, than all the other writers, male or female, that ever felt themselves animated by the contemplation of their oppressed and injured state.—GODWIN, WILLIAM, 1798, *Memoirs of the Author of a Vindication of the Rights of Woman, p.* 83.

The faults of the book are grave over and above those of the time; it is ill-considered, hasty, and rash, but its merits are great also; there is much that is valuable for these days also—it is fresh, vigorous, and eloquent, and most remarkable as the herald of the demand not even yet wholly conceded by all, that woman should be the equal and friend, not the slave and the toy of man. . . . Opposed as were her views to those of the majority of women in her own, and even in this day, yet they were those which now are, except on one point, held by very many cultivated women, without a shadow of blame attaching to them. Her opinions on the equality of the sexes, on the social and political position of women, might now be held without remark, and it would not be too much to say that she was simply in advance of her age in giving expression on those subjects to thoughts which are held increasingly by men and women of advanced political views, but of many shades of devout religion. On the question alone of the relation of the sexes, there is no indication of any approximation to her theories. Her view had now become that mutual affection was marriage, and that the marriage tie should not bind after the death of love, if love should die.—PAUL, C. KEGAN, 1876, *William Godwin: His Friends and Contemporaries, vol.* I, *pp.* 203, 213.

To say that her drunken father was the reason why Mary Wollstonecraft wrote the "Rights of Women" would be too strong an accusation; but this circumstance evidently brought a painful struggle into her life. And one of her sisters, the pretty one, the beauty of the family, "poor Bess," made an unhappy marriage, and had to be taken out of her husband's clutches almost in a state of frenzy by Mary herself. Thus degraded by the besotted folly of one man, and driven into energetic action by the unkindness of another, she certainly was. And it was not till after nearly ten years' experience of the "slings and arrows of outrageous fortune" that she put forth the book which was the first word of a long controversy. . . . The woman who wrote this book was not an abstract personage, or one of the class which is called strong-minded. . . . Mary Wollstonecraft's plea for women is of the mildest description. She vindicates their right to be considered as human creatures, bound by the general laws of truth and honour, and with a generous vehemence assails the sentimental teachings of Rousseau and of the more virtuous moralists—Gregory, Fordyce, and even Mrs. Chapone—who take it for granted that the highest mission of a woman is "to please," and excuse in her, nay, recommend to her, those arts by which she can govern while appearing to obey. All that Mary Wollstonecraft asks is education for her clients and an exemption from that false and mawkish teaching specially addressed to "the fair," in which the eighteenth century was so rich, and which has not quite died out, even among ourselves.— OLIPHANT, MARGARET O. W., 1882, *The Literary History of England, XVIII-XIX Century, pp.* 209, 210.

A plainness of speech, amounting in some places to coarseness, and a deeply religious tone, are to many modern readers the most curious features of the book. . . . A century ago men and women were more straightforward in their speech than we are to-day. They were not squeamish. . . . Therefore, when it came to serious discussions for moral purposes, there was little reason for writers to be timid. . . . Hers is the plain speaking of the Jewish law-giver, who has for end the good of man; and not that of an Aretino, who rejoices in it for its own sake. Even more remarkable than this boldness of expression is the strong vein of piety running through her arguments. Religion was to her as important as it was to a Wesley or a Bishop Watts. The equality of man, in her eyes, would have been of small importance had it not been instituted by man's Creator. . . . If women were without souls, they would, notwithstanding their intellects, have no rights to vindicate. If the Christian heaven were like the Mahometan paradise, then they might indeed be looked upon as slaves and playthings of beings who

are worthy of a future life, and hence are infinitely their superiors. But, though sincerely pious, she despised the meaningless forms of religion as much as she did social conventionalities, and was as free in denouncing them.—PENNELL, ELIZABETH ROBINS, 1884, *Mary Wollstonecraft (Famous Women), pp.* 162, 163.

The "Vindication of the Rights of Woman," on which Mary Wollstonecraft's fame as an author almost wholly rests, is in some ways a book nearly as faulty as it can be. It is not well-written; it is full of prejudices quite as wrong-headed as those it combats; it shows very little knowledge either of human nature or of good society; and its "niceness," to use the word in what was then its proper sense, often goes near to the nasty. But its protest on the one hand against the "proper" sentimentality of such English guides of female youth as Drs. Fordyce and Gregory, on the other against the "improper" sentimentality of Rousseau, is genuine and generous. Many of its positions and contentions may be accepted unhesitatingly to-day by those who are by no means enamoured of advanced womanhood; and Mary, as contrasted with most of her rights-of-woman followers, is curiously free from bumptiousness and the general qualities of the virago.—SAINTSBURY, GEORGE, 1896, *A History of Nineteenth Century Literature, p.* 38.

It was not an able book, and grave faults and frailties that clouded that later life of the authoress did much to discredit it, but in its general tendency it is far from extravagant or revolutionary. Mary Wollstonecraft indulges in none of those attacks on marriage which have sometimes been connected with the movement. She speaks of it with reverence, as "the foundation of almost every social virtue." She dwells on the transcendent importance of chastity and morality, and on the essentially domestic character of the chief duties of women; and although she desires to assimilate in a great measure the tastes and studies of the two sexes, it is worthy of notice that she expresses a strong antipathy to women who are addicted to field sports. . . . These views would not now appear very startling, and it is difficult to realise the indignaiton they aroused. The political aspect of the case was only touched at rare intervals.—LECKY, WILLIAM EDWARD

HARTPOLE, 1896, *Democracy and Liberty,* vol. II, *pp.* 507, 509.

GENERAL

The story that follows is an old one. Captain Imlay, whose name no generous mind who reads the following letters can ever hear mentioned without execration, took advantage of the ardent and tender heart which threw itself trustfully into his keeping. She considered herself his wife until death. He also addressed her, both by letters of affection and business, as his "beloved wife." But when absence, and other attractions which came during absence, asserted themselves over the shallow and base nature of the man, his affection began to wane. It is touching to trace the heart of the woman in these letters, and to see how it asserts itself over all her theories. She pours out to him her love, her reproaches, her fears, in words that seem written in "heart's blood turned to tears." It is touching also to read her first vague consciousness of the distinction between such a love as she felt and that of which he was only capable. . . . There is nothing outside Hood's "Bridge of Sighs" which can parallel in sadness the description of the poor wretch as she stood on Putney Bridge, in a soaking rain, waiting till her clothes should be so saturated that they would more quickly "drag her down to muddy death." She was rescued, however, by a Thames boatman before life was gone, and was restored to her misery. . . . Like the letters of Vanessa to Swift, or of Keats to Fanny Brawne, they are too sacred for the vulgar eye, and ought to be read only by those who have hearts to feel for such suffering and such heart-break as is here made palpable upon the lifeless pages.—RICHARDSON, ABBY SAGE, 1882, *ed., Old Love-Letters, pp.* 110, 111, 112.

Few women have worked so faithfully for the cause of humanity as Mary Wollstonecraft, and few have been the objects of such bitter censure. She devoted herself to the relief of her suffering fellow-beings with the ardor of a Saint Vincent de Paul, and in return she was considered by them a moral scourge of God. Because she had the courage to express opinions new to her generation, and the independence to live according to her own standard of right and wrong, she was denounced as another Messalina. The young were bidden not to read her books, and the more mature warned not to follow her example, the miseries she endured being declared the just retribution of her actions. Indeed, the infamy attached to her name is almost incredible in the present age, when new theories are more patiently criticised, and when purity of motive has been accepted as the vindication of at least one well-known breach of social laws. . . . The mere admiration of Southey and Shelley had little weight against popular prejudice. Year by year Mary's books, like so many other literary productions, were less frequently read, and the prediction that in another generation her name would be unknown bade fair to be fulfilled. But the latest of her admirers, Mr. Kegan Paul, has, by his zealous efforts in her behalf, succeeded in vindicating her character and reviving interest in her writings. By his careful history of her life, and noble words in her defence, he has re-established her reputation. . . . She lived a century too soon.— PENNELL, ELIZABETH ROBINS, 1884, *Life of Mary Wollstonecraft (Famous Women), pp.* 1, 10, 269.

Some of the coarseness of this censor of her sex may, no doubt, be regarded as a mere affair of superficial style, and was referable to the tone of the coteries in which she had been living for several years:—the coteries of Philosophical Radicalism, where speech was even more free than thought. But some of Mary Wollstonecraft's coarseness was due to natural want of refinement and a vein of vulgarity that, instead of playing only on the surface of her life, had its source in the depths of her soul. Her view of men and their feelings was as sordid as her view of women and their failings. Her conception of love as a force in human affairs would have discredited a chambermaid.—JEAFFRESON, JOHN CORDY, 1885, *The Real Shelley, vol.* II, *p.* 25.

The works of Mary Wollstonecraft display unusual versatility of mental powers. She was able to turn her mind to new tasks in a way that made her eminent in several directions. She may be classed among pedagogical writers, but she also wrote on historical subjects and took part in discussions in political principles. She wrote fiction, and her letters descriptive of experiences in travel, and letters personal, take a high rank even to this day, among productions of that kind. And more than all this, her genius furnished, in her "Vindication of the Rights of Woman," the motive power, derived from originality of conception, which helped to carry forward an historic movement. — RAUSCHENBUSCH - CLOUGH, EMMA, 1898, *A Study of Mary Wollstonecraft and the Rights of Woman, p. 24.*

John Wilkes
1727–1797

Born, in Clerkenwell, 17 Oct. 1727. Early education at schools at Hertford and Thame. Afterwards at Leyden University. Returned to England, 1749. Married Miss Mead, Oct. 1749; separated from her soon afterwards. M. P. for Aylesbury, 1757–64. Edited (and wrote) "The North Briton," 1762–63. Expelled from House of Commons (for attack on the king in No. 45 of "The North Briton"), 19 Jan. 1764. M. P. for Middlesex, 1768. Expelled from House for his part in the publication of a letter of Lord Weymouth's, 27 Jan. 1769. Re-elected M. P. for Middlesex, 16 Feb. 1769; re-expelled, 17 Feb. Re-elected, 16 March; re-expelled, 17 March. Re-elected, 13 April; unseated, 15 April. Alderman of Farringdon Without, 2 Jan. 1769. Sheriff, 1771. M. P. for Middlesex, 1774. Lord Mayor, 1774; Chamberlain of London, 1779–97. Died in London, 25 Dec. 1797. Buried in South Audley Street Church. *Works:* (Exclusive of separate speeches): "Observations on the Papers relative to the Rupture with Spain" (anon.), 1762; "The North Briton" (2 vols.), 1763; "An Essay on Woman" (anon. ; priv. ptd.), 1763; "Recherches sur l'origine du Despotisme Oriental," 1763; "The Present Crisis" (anon.), 1764; "Letter to the Worthy Electors of . . . Aylesbury," 1764; "Letter to a Noble Member of the Club in Albemarle Street," 1764; "Letter to . . . the Duke of Grafton" (anon.), 1767 (8th edn. same year) ; "The History of England" (only the "Introduction" pubd.), 1768; "Addresses to the Gentlemen . . . of Middlesex," 1769; "A Letter to Samuel Johnson, LL.D." (anon.), 1770; "Controversial Letters," 1771 ; "Speeches," 1786. *Posthumous:* "Letters . . . to his Daughter" (4 vols.), 1804; "Correspondence," ed. by J. Almon, 1805. He *edited* "Catullus" (priv. ptd.), 1788; "Θεοφραστου Χαραχτηρες 'Ηθικοι'" (priv. ptd.), 1790; "Supplement to the Miscellaneous Works of Mr. Gibbon," 1796. *Life:* by P. Fitzgerald, 1888.—SHARP, R. FARQUHARSON, 1897, *A Dictionary of English Authors, p. 301.*

PERSONAL

On the first Sunday evening I was in Leyden, I walked round the Cingle—a fine walk on the outside of the Rhine, which formed the wet ditch of the town—with John Gregory, who introduced me to the British students as we met them, not without giving me a short character of them, which I found in general a very just outline. When we came to John Wilkes, whose ugly countenance in early youth was very striking, I asked earnestly who he was. His answer was, that he was the son of a London distiller or brewer, who wanted to be a fine gentleman and man of taste, which he could never be, for God and nature had been against him. I came to know Wilkes very well afterwards, and found him to be a sprightly, entertaining fellow,—too much so for his years, as he was but eighteen; for even then he showed something of daring profligacy, for which he was afterwards notorious. Though he was fond of learning, and passionately desirous of being thought something extraordinary, he was unlucky in having an old, ignorant pedant of a dissenting parson for his tutor.— CARLYLE, ALEXANDER, 1745–1860, *Autobiography, p.* 137.

He had such a flow of spirits that it was impossible ever to be a moment dull in his company. His wit gave charm to every subject he spoke upon, and his humour displayed the foibles of mankind in such colours as to put folly even out of countenance. But the same vanity which had first made him ambitious of entering into this society, only because it was composed of persons superior to his own in life, and still kept him in it, though upon acquaintance he despised them, sullied all these advantages. His spirits were often stretched to extravagance to overcome competition. His humour was debased into buffoonery, and his wit was so prostituted to the lust of applause that he would sacrifice his best friend for a scurvy jest, and wound the heart of him whom he would at the very moment hazard his life and fortune to serve, only to raise a laugh. —JOHNSTONE, CHARLES, 1760, *The Adventures of a Guinea.*

Colonel Wilkes, of the Buckinghamshire Militia, dined with us. . . . I scarcely ever met with a better companion; he has inexhaustible spirits, infinite wit and humour, and a great deal of knowledge. . . . He told us himself, that in this time of public dissension, he was resolved to make his fortune.—GIBBON, EDWARD, 1762, *Memoirs, Journal, Sep.* 23.

With good and honest men
His actions speak much stronger than my pen,
And future ages shall his name adore,
When he can act and I can write no more.
England may prove ungrateful and unjust,
But fostering France shall ne'er betray her trust:
'Tis a brave debt which gods on men impose,
To pay with praise the merit e'en of foes.
When the great warrior of Amilcar's race
Made Rome's wide empire tremble to her base,
To prove her virtue, though it gall'd her pride,
Rome gave that fame which Carthage had denied.
—CHURCHILL, CHARLES, 1764, *The Candidate, Poems, ed. Hannay, vol.* II, *p.* 200.

Wilkes is here, and has been twice to see me in my illness. He was very civil, but I cannot say entertained me much. I saw no wit; his conversation shows how little he has lived in good company, and the chief turn of it is the grossest bawdy.— WALPOLE, HORACE, 1765, *To George Montagu, Oct.* 16; *Letters, ed. Cunningham, vol.* IV, *p.* 421.

Bristol, April 14th.—We hear that on Wednesday next, being the day of Mr. Wilkes' enlargement, forty-five persons are to dine at the "Crown," in the passage leading from Broad Street to Tower Lane. The entertainment is to consist of two rounds of beef, of 45 lbs. each; two legs of veal, weighing 45 lbs. ; two ditto of pork, 45 lbs. ; a pig, roasted, 45 lbs. ; two puddings of 45 lbs. ; 45 loaves; and, to drink, 45 tankards of ale. After dinner, they are to smoke 45 pipes of tobacco, and to drink 45 bowls of punch. Among others, the following toasts are to be given:—1. Long live the King; 2. Long live the supporters of British Liberty; 3. The Magistrates of Bristol. And the dinner to be on the table exactly 45 minutes after two o'clock.—LONDON PUBLIC ADVENTURER, 1770.

Did we not hear so much said of Jack Wilkes, we should think more highly of his conversation. Jack has great variety of talk, Jack is a scholar, and Jack has the manners of a gentleman. But, after hearing his name sounded from pole to pole as the phœnix of convivial felicity, we are disappointed in his company.— JOHNSON, SAMUEL, 1777, *Life by Boswell, ed. Hill, vol.* III, *p.* 208.

Wilkes desired that his tomb should be inscribed, "J. W., a friend to Liberty." I am glad he was not ashamed to show a little gratitude to her in her old age; for she was a great friend to him.—TOOKE, JOHN HORNE, 1812? *Recollections by Samuel Rogers.*

He was really a sad dog, but most delightfully amusing, facetious, witty, well-informed, and with much various, though not profound learning. He was sometimes so intolerably sarcastic, and more particularly at the expence of his friends in the city, that the wonder is, how he could so long continue in their good graces.— BELOE, WILLIAM, 1817, *The Sexagenarian, vol.* II, *p.* 5.

Wilkes had, till very lately, been known chiefly as one of the most profane, licentious, and agreeable rakes about town. He was a man of taste, reading, and engaging manners. His sprightly conversation was the delight of green-rooms and taverns, and pleased even grave hearers when he was sufficiently under restraint to abstain from detailing the particulars of his amours and from breaking jests on the New Testament. His expensive debaucheries forced him to have recourse to the Jews. He was soon a ruined man, and determined to try his chance as a political adventurer. In Parlianemt he did not succeed. His speaking, though pert, was feeble, and by no means interested his hearers so much as to make them forget his face, which was so hideous that the caricaturists were forced, in their own despite, to flatter him. As a writer he made a better figure. — MACAULAY, THOMAS BABINGTON, 1844, *The Earl of Chatham, Edinburgh Review, vol.* 80, *p.*560.

He was clever, courageous, unscrupulous. He was a good scholar, expert in resource, humorous, witty, and a ready master of the arts of conversation. He could "abate and dissolve a pompous gentleman" with singular felicity. Churchill did not know the crisis of his fortune that had given him to patriotism. He was ignorant, that, early in the preceding year, after loss of his last seven thousand pounds on his seat of Aylesbury, he had made an unsuccessful attempt upon the Board of Trade. He was not in his confidence when, a little later, he offered to compromise with the Government for the embassy to Constantinople. He was dead when, many years later, he settled into a quiet supporter of the most atrocious of "things as they were." What now presented itself in the form of Wilkes to Churchill, had a clear unembarrassed front;—passions unsubdued as his own; principles rather unfettered than depraved; apparent manliness of spirit; real courage; scorn of conventions; an open heart and a liberal hand; and the capacity of ardent friendship. They entered at once into an extraordinary alliance, offensive and defensive. It is idle to deny that this has damaged Churchill with posterity, and that Wilkes has carried his advocate along with him into the Limbo of doubtful reputations. But we will deny the justice of it.—FORSTER, JOHN, 1845-55, *Charles Churchill*, p. 51.

All, then, that we dare now say of him is, that with all his faults he was a true-born Englishman, with the marking characteristics, good and bad; who, having once taken up a position, even though driven to do so by his adversary, would maintain and defend it with bull-dog pertinacity, and at all costs, personal, political and social. His courage amounted almost to reckless daring; and he would resent an insult, whether it came from a Chatham, a Grafton, an Onslow, a Martin, or even a Grenville, though it should cost him the friendship of a Temple. He was a good, kind, and dutiful son,—a gentle, tender, and affectionate father. There is something morally beautiful in the fact that when challenged by Lord Talbot, his last act before the mad moonlight devilry began was, to write to Lord Temple thanking him for the friendship which he had ever shown to him, and entreating as a last and crowning favour, that if he fell his Lordship and Lady Temple would superintend the education of his daughter. Though drinking and gaming were amongst the vices of his age, he was no gambler,—and his abstinence was remarkable and a subject of remark. He rose early and read diligently. Indeed, his reading was extensive and varied beyond that of most men of his age not being professed scholars; not merely in the Classics, which he especially loved, but in most of the modern languages that had a literature—French, Spanish, and Italian. As the amusement of his leisure hours, and of that quiet domestic life which in truth he loved, he published editions of Catullus and Theophrastus, said to be almost unrivalled for accuracy—and translated Anacreon so well, that Dr. Joseph Warton, no bad judge, pressed him to publish it.—DILKE, SIR CHARLES WENTWORTH, 1852, *Wilkes, The Papers of a Critic, vol.* II, *p.* 262.

One morning when I was a lad, Wilkes came into our banking-house to solicit my father's vote. My father happened to be out, and, I as his representative, spoke to Wilkes. At parting, Wilkes shook hands with me; and I felt proud of it for a week after. He was quite as ugly, and squinted as much, as his portraits make him; but he was very gentlemanly in appearance and manners. I think I see him at this moment, walking through the crowded streets of the city, as Chamberlain, on his way to Guildhall, in a scarlet coat, military boots, and a bag-wig,— the hackney-coachman in vain calling out to him, "A coach, your honour?"—ROGERS, SAMUEL, 1855, *Table-Talk*, p. 42.

Wilkes was without morals of any kind; and only fought for "liberty," when there was nothing to be made by jobbing.—HANNAY, JAMES, 1866, *ed., The Poetical Works of Charles Churchill, Memoir,* p. xviii.

To attempt any analysis of such a character would be superfluous; it is so patent in his actions that those who run may read. Trickster, tuft-hunter, bully, humbug, *roué,* false alike to man and woman, friend and foe, a sceptic in morals, politics, and religion, without honour or honesty, what can be said in his favour? Well, he had courage enough to defend his misdeeds, was a jovial boon companion; and ugly, squinting, lying, dishonest, dissolute as he was, he possessed some mysterious kind of fascination which few men or women could resist, and which we feel even in perusing the records of his life. Such was Jack Wilkes, who, although a Model Demagogue, at least had little of the bilious sourness of the tribe.—BAKER, H. BARTON, 1877, *A Model Demagogue, Gentleman's Magazine, vol.* 241, *p.* 492.

John Wilkes, who now became one of the most prominent figures in English politics, was at this time in his thirty-sixth year. . . . His countenance was repulsively ugly. His life was scandalously and notoriously profligate, and he was sometimes guilty of profanity which exceeded even that of the vicious circle in which he lived, but he possessed some qualities which were well fitted to secure success in life. He had a brilliant and ever ready wit, unflagging spirits, unfailing good humour, great personal courage, much shrewdness of judgment, much charm of manner. The social gifts must have been indeed of no common order which half-conquered the austere Toryism of Johnson, extorted a warm tribute of admiration from Gibbon, secured the friendship of Reynolds, and made the son of a London distiller a conspicuous member of the Medmenham Brotherhood, and the favourite companion of the more dissipated members of the aristocracy. — LECKY, WILLIAM EDWARD HARTPOLE, 1882, *A History of England in the Eighteenth Century, vol.* III, *ch.* x, *p.* 78.

What man was ever more successful in laying seige to female hearts than the demagogue John Wilkes? He was so exceedingly ugly that a lottery-office keeper once offered him ten guineas not to pass his window while the tickets were drawing for fear of his bringing ill-luck on the house. Rogers the poet, who had seen him, speaks of his "diabolical squint." Yet, though the ugliest man in England, he was at the same time its most accomplished intriguer. He was the Don Juan of his day, sneering at the very women he subdued. He once boasted to Lord Townshend, whom he admitted to be the handsomest man in the kingdom, that, give him but a half hour's start, he would enter the lists against his lordship with any woman he might choose to name.—MATHEWS, WILLIAM, 1887, *Men, Places and Things, p.* 244.

His part in public life he played with courage and consistency; but there was a deeper sense than appeared on the surface in his arch denial that he was ever a Wilkite. By nature unquestionably he was no demagogue, but a man of fashion and a dilettante; nor did he possess the ready eloquence which is characteristic of the born leader of the masses. His speeches were always carefully prepared, and smelt too much of the oil for popular effect. He retained dilettantism, and especially his interest in French and Italian literature and painting, to the last.— RIGG, J. M., 1900, *Dictionary of National Biography, vol.* LXI, *p.* 249.

GENERAL

That the paper entitled the *North Briton*, No. XLV. was a false, scandalous, and seditious libel, containing expressions of the most unexampled insolence and contumely towards his Majesty, the grossest aspersions on both houses of parliament, and the most audacious defiance of the authority of the whole legislature; and most manifestly tending to alienate the affections of the people from his Majesty, to withdraw them from their obedience to the laws of the realm, and to excite them to traitorous insurrections.—RESOLUTION OF THE HOUSE OF COMMONS, 1763.

The only part of the work ["Correspondence"] we have pursued with any degree of amusement, is that which contains his private letters to Mr. Cotes and his daughter. The former give a very lively and undisguised picture of his feelings during the period of his persecution and popularity; and afford some curious glimpses of constitutional gaiety and Epicurean carelessness, in a mind agitated by a fierce ambition, a distempered vanity, and a rancorous thirst for revenge. The latter are indulgent, cheerful, unconstrained, and every way amiable. Though written in a tone of a man of the world, the morality which they inculcate is entirely unexceptional, and show the author to have been susceptible, in private life, of better feelings and affections than could be guessed at from his public appearances.—JEFFREY, FRANCIS LORD, 1805, *Correspondence and Memoirs of John Wilkes, Edinburgh Review, vol.* 5, *p.* 488.

Wilkes's brilliancy faded away when he proceeded to commit his thoughts to paper, as if it had dissolved itself in the ink. . . . Some of Wilkes's colloquial impromptus that have been preserved are perfect, considered in themselves, and without regard to the readiness with which they may have been struck out,—are so true and deep, and evince so keen a feeling at once of the ridiculous and of the real, —that one wonders at finding so little of the same kind of power in his more deliberate efforts. In all his published writings that we have looked into—and, what with essays and pamphlets of one kind and another, they fill a good many volumes— we scarcely recollect anything that either in matter or manner rises above the veriest commonplace, unless perhaps it be a character of Lord Chatham, occurring in a letter addressed to the Duke of Grafton, some of the biting things in which are impregnated with rather a subtle venom. A few of his verses also have some fancy and elegance, in the style of Carew and Waller. But even his private letters, of which two collections have been published, scarcely ever emit a sparkle. And his House of Commons speeches, which he wrote before hand and got by heart, are equally unenlivened. It is evident, indeed, that he had not intellectual lung enough for any protracted exertion or display. The soil of his mind was a hungry, unproductive gravel, with some gems embedded in it.— CRAIK, GEORGE L., 1861, *A Compendious History of English Literature and of the English Language, vol.* II, *p.* 319.

His literary qualifications have been extolled beyond their desert. He has been called a good classical scholar; but his reading in Latin was not extensive, and his knowledge of Greek was evidently slight. His editorship of Catullus and Theophrastus was merely nominal; such commendation as the volumes merit belongs to the printer. He seems to have been incapable to any sustained literary effort. After his professed determination to give a life and edition of Churchill and a life of Sterne, it might have been thought that very shame would have urged him to produce something of those works; but what he did for Churchill was nought, and Sterne he utterly neglected. Of his promised History of England nothing was written but a short introduction in praise of liberty and the Revolution. His few attempts at verse are poor and dry.—WATSON, JOHN

SELBY, 1870, *Biographies of John Wilkes and William Cobbett, p.* 113.

The story of the "Essay on Woman" is singular. He had a private press at which he ordered that twelve copies only of this brief poem should be struck off, for he seems to have had no idea of publishing it. One of the printers took one sheet of it with him to wrap some butter in. Having unrolled the butter at a friend's house where he was to sup, the friend read some of the verses, and finding them spicy, asked for the paper, which he showed to some one else. The paper, passing from hand to hand, found its way to higher quarters. The eminent enemies of Wilkes, anxious to get hold of some charge against him which would go down with the public better than their political indictments, actually bribed the head printer with a place worth a hundred pounds per annum to give them a copy of the whole poem. The ridicule it heaped on the Athanasian Creed Wilkes justified by quoting Archbishop Tillotson's wish that the Church were fairly rid of that creed; and, with regard to the alleged indecencies of other portions, after making sundry cracks in the glass houses in which many of his accusers dwelt, he confessed that it contained "a few portraits drawn from warm life, with the too high coloring of a youthful fancy; and two or three descriptions, perhaps too luscious, which, though nature and woman might pardon, a Kidgell and a Mansfield could not fail to condemn." Wilkes does not appear to have lost any friends by the publication of the poem either among men or women. . . . Wilkes seems to have employed one-half of his active life writing the memoirs of the other half.—CONWAY, M. D., 1870, *South-coast Saunterings in England, Harper's Magazine, vol.* 40, *pp.* 373, 374.

Less polished as a writer than Addison, less incisive in attack than Junius, as good a classic and as much a man of the world as the former, as reckless and brazen-faced as the latter, he had the art of stating a case with singular lucidity, and of illustrating it in a homely and telling manner. His touch was light, and his sarcasm stinging. He anticipated Cobbett in the skill and daring with which he put and reiterated in plain terms the most unpalatable truths. He was the first political writer who not only applied to things their proper epithets, but also called persons by their proper names. The initials and innuendoes to which timorous journalists had resorted, he discarded and disowned, excepting when an illusion was more effective than a simple statement.—RAE, WILLIAM FRA-SER, 1873, *Wilkes, Sheridan, Fox, p.* 28.

With the exception of the "Essay on Woman," which was never meant to be published, Wilkes had written nothing that was not sound in reason, and respectful in tone. Number forty-five of the *North Briton*, if it had appeared in the *Morning Chronicle* as a leading article at the time when George the Third dismissed Pitt and sent for Addington, or at the time when William the Fourth dismissed the Whigs and sent for Peel, would have been regarded as a very passable effusion, rather old-fashioned in the tenderness with which it treated the susceptibilities of the monarch. Grave statesmen acknowledged that Wilkes in his famous paper had rendered a solid and permanent service to the cause of constitutional government by the clear and attractive form in which he had laid down the doctrine that ministers are responsible for the contents of the royal speech.—TREVEL-YAN, GEORGE OTTO, 1880, *The Early History of Charles James Fox, p.* 143.

Altogether Mr. Wilkes was one of the most important personages of the last century. He wrote many letters of a very free and easy sort to his daughter "Polly," born in the year 1750, to whom he was without doubt very greatly attached. He informed her of his movements and narrated for her entertainment much that was lively and laughable. But his letters are certainly not of the kind Mrs. Hester Chapone would have approved, or the Reverend Dr. Fordyce have addressed to young women, or, for that matter, to young men either.—COOK, DUTTON, 1882, *John Wilkes at Brighton, Belgravia, vol.* 47, *p.* 295.

It has been often repeated that *The North Briton* was scarcely of sufficient importance to have excited the commotion it did, and that it would have been more prudent to have treated it with contempt. But the truth is, as we read it now, it is found to be a very stirring, vigorous and dangerous opponent, written with much pungency, wit, and even vivacity. This may be imagined, when it is stated that Wilkes had found so valuable a coadjutor as Charles Churchill, who contributed not only his prose but also his verse. Wilkes was often absent, and eventually the whole burden of the paper fell upon Churchill. He must at least have written half of the numbers, and, as Mr. Forster says, "wherever it shows the coarse, broad mark of sincerity, there seems to us the trace of his hand." The correspondence between them during the progress of the paper shows Wilkes to be full of an unbounded admiration for his friend's powers, and his gratitude for his assistance corresponds with his generous appreciation, which certainly was beyond the merits of the work.—FITZGERALD, PERCY, 1888, *The Life and Times of John Wilkes, vol.* I, *p.* 74.

James Hutton
1726-1797

One of the founders of geology, was born at Edinburgh. He studied medicine there, in Paris, and at Leyden, but in 1754 settled in Berwickshire and devoted himself to agriculture and chemisty, from which he was led to minerology and geology; in 1768 he removed to Edinburgh. The Huttonian theory, emphasising the igneous origin of many rocks and deprecating the hypothetical assumption of other causes than those we see still at work, was expounded in two papers read before the Royal Society of Edinburgh, "A Theory of the Earth" (1785) and "A Theory of Rain" (1784). The former was afterwards expanded into two volumes (1795). He also wrote "Dissertations in Natural Philosophy" (1792), "Considerations on the Nature of Coal and Culm" (1777), and other works.—PATRICK AND GROOME, *eds.*, 1897, *Chambers's Biographical Dictionary, p.* 515.

PERSONAL

To his friends his conversation was inestimable; as great talents, the most perfect candour, and the utmost simplicity of character and manners, all united to stamp a value upon it. He had, indeed, that genuine simplicity, originating in the absence of all selfishness and vanity, by which a man loses sight of himself altogether, and neither conceals what is, nor affects what is not. This simplicity prevaded his whole conduct; while his manner, which was peculiar, but highly pleasing, displayed a degree of vivacity hardly ever to be found among men of profound and abstract speculation. His great liveliness, added to this aptness to lose sight of himself, would sometimes lead him into little eccentricities, that formed an amusing contrast with the graver habits of a philosophic life. . . . His conversation was extremely animated and forcible, and, whether serious or gay, full of ingenious and original observation. . . . His figure was slender, but indicated activity; while a thin countenance, a high forehead, and a nose somewhat aquiline, bespoke extraordinary acuteness and vigour of mind. His eye was penetrating and keen, but full of gentleness and benignity; and even his dress, plain, and all of one colour, was in perfect harmony with the rest of the picture, and seemed to give a fuller *relief* to its characteristic features.—PLAYFAIR, JOHN, 1805, *Biographical Account of James Hutton, M. D., Works, vol.* IV, *pp.* 110, 111.

Hutton was slender, but active, thin-faced, with a high forehead, acquiline nose, keen and penetrating eyes, and a general expression of benevolence. His dress was very plain. His portrait was painted by Raeburn for John Davidson of Stewartfield. Upright, candid, humane, and a true friend, he was very cheerful in company, whether social or scientific, and was, like Adam Smith and Joseph Black, a leading member of the "Oyster Club." Playfair draws an interesting contrast (*Biography of Hutton*, pp. 58, 59), between Hutton and his friend Black, to whom, as well as to John Clerk of Eldin, he owed many valuable suggestions. — BETTANY, G. T., 1891, *Dictionary of National Biography, vol.* XXVIII, *p.* 355.

GENERAL

It might have been expected, when a work of so much originality as this "Theory of the Earth" was given to the world, a theory which professed to be the result of such an ample and accurate induction, and which opened up so many views, interesting not to mineralogy alone, but to philosophy in general, that it would have produced a sudden and visible effect, and that men of science would have been everywhere eager to decide concerning its real

value. Yet the truth is, that it drew their attention very slowly, so that several years elapsed before any one showed himself publicly concerned about it, either as an enemy or a friend. . . . Truth, however, forces me to add, that other reasons certainly contributed not a little to prevent Dr. Hutton's theory from making a due impression on the world. It was proposed too briefly, and with too little detail of facts, for a system which involved so much that was new, and opposite to the opinions generally received. The descriptions which it contains of the phenomena of geology, suppose in the reader too great a knowledge of the things described. The reasoning is sometimes embarrassed by the care taken to render it strictly logical; and the transitions, from the author's peculiar notions of arrangement, are often unexpected and abrupt. These defects run more or less through all Dr. Hutton's writings, and produce a degree of obscurity astonishing to those who knew him, and who heard him every day converse with no less clearness and precision, than animation and force. From whatever causes the want of perspicuity in his writings proceed, perplexity of thought was not among the number; and the confusion of his ideas can neither be urged as an apology for himself, nor as a consolation to his readers.—PLAYFAIR, JOHN, 1805, *Biographical Account of James Hutton, M. D., Works, vol.* IV, *pp.* 63, 64.

Meanwhile Hutton, a contemporary of Werner, began to teach, in Scotland, that granite as well as trap was of igneous origin, and had at various periods intruded itself in a fluid state into different parts of the earth's crust. He recognized and faithfully described many of the phenomena of granitic veins, and the alterations produced by them on the invaded strata which will be treated of in the thirty-third chapter. He, moreover, advanced the opinion, that the crystalline strata called primitive had not been precipitated from a primæval ocean, but were sedimentary strata altered by heat. In his writings, therefore, and in those of his illustrator, Playfair, we find the germ of that metamorphic theory.—LYELL, SIR CHARLES, 1838-55, *A Manual of Elementary Geology, p.* 92.

By an idea entirely new, the illustrious Scottish philosopher showed the successive co-operation of water and the internal heat of the globe in the formation of the same rocks. It is the mark of genius to unite in one common origin phenomena very different in their nature. . . . Hutton explains the history of the globe with as much simplicity as grandeur. Like most men of genius, indeed, who have opened up new paths, he exaggerated the extent to which his conceptions could be applied. But it is impossible not to view with admiration the profound penetration and the strictness of induction of so clear-sighted a man, at a time when exact observations had been so few, he being the first to recognise the simultaneous effect of water and heat in the formation of rocks, in imagining a system which embraces the whole physical system of the globe. He established principles which, in so far as they are fundamental, are now universally admitted.—DAUBRÉE, GABRIEL AUGUSTE, 1860, *Essays*.

It is not so generally known that he found much satisfaction in the pursuit of metaphysics, and is author of an elaborate work in three large quarto volumes, "An Investigation of the Principles of Knowledge, and of the Progress of Reason from Sense to Science and Philosophy." The work is full of awkwardly constructed sentences and of repetitions, and it is a weariness in the extreme to read it. Yet we are made to feel at times that these thoughts must be profound, if only we could understand them. He certainly speculates on recondite subjects, but does not throw much light on them.—McCosh, JAMES, 1874, *The Scottish Philosophy*, p. 262.

But it was not merely, or even chiefly, for their exposition of the structure and history of the rocks under our feet that the geologists of the Scottish School deserve to be held in lasting remembrance. They could not, indeed, have advanced as far as they did in expounding former and ancient conditions of the planet, had they not, with singular clearness, perceived the order and system of change which is in progress over the surface of the globe at the present day. It was their teaching which first led men to see the harmony and co-operation of the forces of nature which work within the earth, with those which are seen and felt upon its surface. Hutton first caught the meaning of that constant circulation of water which, by means of evaporation, winds, clouds, rain, snow, brooks, and rivers, is kept up between land and sea. He saw that the surface of the dry land is everywhere being wasted and worn away. The scarped cliff, the rugged glen, the lowland valley, are each undergoing this process of destruction; wherever land rises above ocean, there, from mountaintop to sea-shore, degradation is continually going on. Here and there, indeed, the *débris* of the hills may be spread out upon the plains; here and there, too, dark angular peaks and crags rise as they rose centuries ago, and seem to defy the elements. But these are only apparent and not real exceptions to the universal law, that so long as the surface of land is exposed to the atmosphere it must suffer degradation and removal. . . . The men were before their time: and thus, while the world gradually acknowledged the teaching of the Scottish school as to the past history of the rocks, it lent an incredulous ear to that teaching when dealing with the present surface of the earth. Even some of the Huttonians themselves refused to follow their master when he sought to explain the existing inequalities of the land by the working of the same quiet unobtrusive forces which are still plying their daily tasks around us. But no incredulity or neglect can destroy the innate vitality of truth. And so now after the lapse of fully two generations, the views of Hutton have in recent years been revived, and have become the war-cry of a yearly increasing crowd of earnest hardworking geologists.—GEIKIE, ARCHIBALD, 1871, *The Scottish School of Geology, A Lecture, Nov. 6*.

With his true scientific spirit Hutton would have nothing to do with convulsions or with the origin of the globe; he did not want to guess or speculate, but to argue logically on facts which anybody could observe. He took geology out of the age of the marvellous and laid the foundations of the present aspect of the science. He was in no hurry to publish his views, possibly because his temperament was cautious, and possibly he was aware what a furious fuss there would be made about it; how he would be abused, scolded, and anathematized. There is no doubt that the lights of the age and public opinion were perfectly incompetent to judge the merits of such a theory; they were sunken in prejudices, and resisted any change of opinion. He was aware that a great outcry would be made by men whose religious opinions were his own, and whom he respected greatly. In fact, the world, just before the appearance of Hutton's "Theory of the Earth," was less prepared for it than ordinary opinion was for the doctrines of Charles Darwin one hundred years afterwards. The appearance of the work of this last great naturalist made, and is still making, a great stir, but that of Hutton's work was received, as he anticipated, with incredible opposition, by the teachers of the day; and its slow acceptation by the scientific world was remarkable. No abuse could efface its effects; it was true, and the true alone lasts; it was reasonable, and it was to the glory of God.—DUNCAN, P. MARTIN, 1882, *Heroes of Science, p. 230.*

Hutton ranks as the first great British geologist, and the independent originator of the modern explanation of the phenomena of the earth's crust by means of changes still in progress. "No powers,"

he says, "are to be employed that are not natural to the globe, no action to be admitted of except those of which we know the principle." He first drew a marked line between geology and cosmogony. He early observed that a vast proportion of the present rocks are composed of materials afforded by the destruction of pre-existing materials. He realised that all the present rocks are decaying, and their materials being transported into the ocean; that new continents and tracts of land have been formed by elevation, often altered and consolidated, by volcanic heat, and afterwards fractured and contorted; and that many masses of crystalline rocks are due to the injection of rocks among fractured strata in a molten state. His views on the excavation of valleys by denudation, after being largely ignored by Lyell, have been accepted and inforced by Ramsay, A. Geikie, and others. He may be considered as having originated the uniformitarian theory of geology (science modified by that of evolution).—BETTANY, G. T., 1891, *Dictionary of National Biography, vol.* XXVIII, *p.* 355.

Richard Farmer

1735-1797

Shakespearean scholar; born at Leicester, England, in 1735. He was educated in the free grammar school of his native town and at Emmanuel College, Cambridge; became a classical tutor in the latter institution in 1760, and a master in 1775, and was appointed librarian at the university in 1778. He held various benefices at Lichfield, Canterbury, and St. Paul's, but he twice declined the offer of a bishopric, unwilling to give up the free-and-easy life he was used to. The only monument of his learning and industry he has left is his "Essay on the Learning of Shakespeare," published in 1766, and afterward often reprinted. Died at Cambridge, Sept. 8, 1797. —ADAMS, CHARLES KENDALL, *ed.*, 1897, *Johnson's Universal Cyclopædia, vol.* III, *p.* 289.

PERSONAL

When a young man he wrote some "Directions for Studying the English History," which have been printed in the "European Magazine" for 1791 and in Seward's "Biographiana;" but his only work of any importance is the "Essay on the Learning of Shakespeare." Invincible indolence prevented him from achieving other literary triumphs. He was content to be the hero of a coterie, and to reign supreme in a college combination-room amid the delights of the pipe and the bottle. To his ease or his disappointment in love may be attributed a want of attention to his personal appearance, and to the usual

forms of behaviour belonging to his station. In the company of strangers the eccentricity of his appearance caused him sometimes to be taken for a person half crazed. There were three things, it is said, which he loved above all others, namely, old port, old clothes, and old books; and three things which nobody could persuade him to do, namely, to rise in the morning, to go to bed at night, and to settle an account. In his own college he was adored, and in the university he exercised for many years more influence than any other individual. — COOPER, THOMPSON, 1889, *Dictionary of National Biography, vol.* XVIII, *p.* 215.

GENERAL

It ("the Essay on the Learning of Shakespeare") may in truth be pointed out as a master-piece, whether considered with a view to the sprightliness and vivacity with which it is written, the clearness of the arrangement, the force and variety of the evidence, or the compression of scattered materials into a narrow compass; materials which inferior writers would have expanded into a large volume.—REED, ISAAC, 1807? *Life of Farmer.*

How shall I talk of thee, and of thy wonderful collection, O RARE RICHARD FARMER?—and of thy scholarship, acuteness, pleasantry, singularities, varied learning, and colloquial powers! Thy name will live long among scholars in general; and in the bosoms of virtuous and learned bibliomaniacs thy memory shall be ever shrined! The walls of Emanuel College now cease to convey the sounds of thy festive wit; thy volumes are no longer seen, like Richard Smith's "bundles of sticht books," strewn upon the floor; and thou hast ceased, in the cause of thy beloved Shakspeare, to delve into the fruitful ore of black-letter literature. Peace to thy honest spirit; for thou wert wise without vanity, learned without pedantry, and joyous without vulgarity. . . . Farmer had his foragers, his jackals, and his *avant-couriers,* for it was well known how dearly he loved everything that was interesting and rare in the literature of former ages. As he walked the streets of London—careless of his dress, and whether his wig was full-bottomed or narrow-bottomed—he would talk and "mutter strange speeches" to himself, thinking all the time, I ween, of some curious discovery he had recently made in the aforesaid precious black-letter tomes. But the reader is impatient for the BIBLIOTHECA FARMERIANA.—DIBDIN, THOMAS FROGNALL, 1811, *The Bibliomania; or Book-Madness.*

His knowledge is various, extensive and recondite. With much seeming negligence, and perhaps in later years some real relaxation, he understands more and remembers more about common and uncommon subjects of literature, than many of those who would be thought to read all the day and meditate half the night. In quickness of apprehension and acuteness of discrimination I have not often seen his equal.—PARR, SAMUEL, 1825? *On Richard Farmer.*

Farmer had silently pursued an entire chase in this "black" forest, for he had a keen *gusto* for the native venison; and, alluding to his Shakespearian pursuits, exclaimed in the inspiring language of his poet,—

"Age cannot wither them, nor custom stale
Their infinite variety."

His vivacity relieved the drowsiness of mere antiquarianism. This novel pursuit once opened, an eager and motley pack was halloo'd up; but Shakespeare, like Actæon, was torn to pieces by a whole kennel of his own hounds, as they were typified with equal humor and severity. But to be severe, and never to be just, is the penury of the most sordid criticism; and among these—

"Spirits black, white, and gray,"—

are some of the most illustrious in English literature.— DISRAELI, ISAAC, 1841, *Shakespeare, Amenities of Literature.*

There was another cause of the hospitality of Steevens and his school of commentators. FARMER was their Coriphæus. Their souls were prostrate before the extent of his researches in that species of literature which possesses this singular advantage for the cultivator, that, if he studies it in original edition, of which only one or two copies are known to exist (the merit is gone if there is a baker's dozen known), he is immediately pronounced learned, judicious, laborious, acute. And this was Farmer's praise. He wrote, "An Essay on the Learning of Shakspeare," which has not one passage of solid criticism from the first page to the last, and from which, if the name and the works of Shakspere were to perish, and one copy—an unique copy is the affectionate name for these things—could be miraculously preserved, the only inference from the book would be that William Shakspere was a very obscure and ignorant man, whom some misjudging admirers had been desirous to exalt into an ephemeral reputation, and that Richard Farmer was a very distinguished and learned man, who had stripped the mask off the pretender. The first edition of Farmer's pamphlet appeared in 1767. . . . This arrogant pamphlet.—KNIGHT, CHARLES, 1849, *Studies of Shakspere,* p. 546.

Charles Macklin

1699?-1797

Born, in Ireland, 1699 (?). Name originally McLaughlin, but form "Macklin" eventually adopted. At school near Dublin. Ran away from home. Perhaps served in a public house in London, and at Trinity Coll., Dublin, as servant. Joined strolling company of actors in Bristol. Acted in London, 1725-48. Married (i) Grace Purvor (or, Mrs. Ann Grace?), 1735 (?). Play, "King Henry VII," produced at Drury Lane, 18 Jan. 1746; "A Will and no Will," 23 April 1746; "The Suspicious Husband Criticised," Drury Lane, 24 March 1747; "The Fortune Hunters," 1748. Acted in Dublin, 1748-50; in London, 1750-53. Play, "Covent Garden Theatre," produced at Covent Garden, 8 April 1752. Retired from stage, 1753. Kept a tavern in Covent Garden, March 1754 to Jan. 1758. Wife died, 1758 (?). Reappeared on stage, at Drury Lane 12 Dec. 1759, in his "Love à la Mode." Acted in London, 1759-63. Married (ii) Elizabeth Jones, 10 Sept. 1759. "The Married Libertine" produced, Covent Garden, 28 Jan. 1761. In Dublin, 1761-63. "The True-Born Irishman" produced at Smock Alley Theatre, Dublin, 1763 (at Covent Garden, as "The Irish Fine Lady," 28 Nov. 1767); "The True-Born Scotchman," Crow Street Theatre, Dublin, 7 Feb. 1766 (at Covent Garden, as "The Man of the World," 10 May 1781). Acted in London, 1772-89. Died in London, 11 July 1797. Buried in St. Paul's, Covent Garden. *Works:* "Mr. Macklin's Reply to Mr. Garrick's Answer," 1743; "The Genuine Arguments of the Council," etc. (anon.; attrib to Macklin), 1774; "Love à la Mode," 1784; "The Man of the World" (under initials C. M.), 1786. Life by E. A. Parry, 1891.—SHARP, R. FARQUHARSON, 1897, *A Dictionary of English Authors*, p. 180.

PERSONAL

Macklin, who largely deals in half-form'd sounds,
Who wantonly transgresses Nature's bounds,
Whose acting's hard, affected and constrain'd,
Whose features, as each other they disdain'd,
At variance set, inflexible, and coarse,
Ne'er know the workings of united force,
Ne'er kindly soften to each other's aid,
Nor show the mingled powers of light and shade,
No longer for a thankless stage concern'd,
To worthier thoughts his mighty genius turn'd,
Harangued, gave lectures, made each simple elf
Almost as good a speaker as himself,
Whilst the whole town, mad with mistaken zeal,
An awkward rage for elocution feel;
Dull cits and grave divines his praise proclaim,
And join with Sheridan's their Macklin's name.
—CHURCHILL, CHARLES, 1761, *The Rosciad*, v. 633-648, *Poems, ed. Hannay, vol.* I, *p.* 31.

Macklin, whose writing was as harsh and as hard as his conduct was rude and dogmatic, who, though he did not produce many pieces, contrived to make one answer the purpose of many, whose strange peculiarities made him a torment to himself and to everybody else, was, however, a useful, and sometimes a great actor, and very far from an inferior author.—DIBDIN, CHARLES, 1795, *History of the Stage, bk.* ix, *chap.* 7.

Macklin, whose personation of Shylock to its true reading had elicited the impromptu of Pope, "This is the Jew that Shakespeare drew," was my father's theatrical oracle. His portrait hung over the fireplace of our little dining-room, with the inscription, "Charles Macklin, aged 98." In some of his visits to Dublin he had instructed my father in the part of Egerton in his comedy of the "Man of the World;" and on the occasion of his last benefit there he sent for his pupil from Waterford (where my father was playing) to act "Egerton." . . . His manner was generally harsh, as indeed was his countenance. So much so that on some one speaking to Quin of the "strong lines" of Macklin's face, he cut short his remarks with, "The lines of his face, sir? You mean the cordage." My father has described to me his mode of speaking to the players at rehearsal. There was good advice, though conveyed in his gruff voice and imperious tone. "Look at me, sir, look at me! Keep your eye fixed on me when I am speaking to you! Attention is always fixed; if you take your eye from me you rob the audience of my effects, and you rob me of their applause!"—a precept I never forgot, and to which I have been much indebted.—MACREADY, W. C., 1808–11, *Reminiscences, pp.* 21, 22.

He had no respect for the modesty of youth or sex, but would say the most discouraging, as well as grossest things, and felt pleasure in proportion to the pain he gave. It was common of him to ask his pupils, why they did not rather think of becoming bricklayers than players. He was impatient of contradiction to an extreme; and when he found fault, if the person attempted to answer, he stopped him without hearing, by saying, "Ha, you have always a reason for being in the wrong!" This impatience carried him still farther; it often rendered him exceedingly abusive. He could pronounce the word, *scoundrel, fool, blockhead,* familiarly, without the least annoyance to his nervous system. He, indeed, pretended to the strictest impartiality,and while his passions were inconcerned, often preserved it; but these were so extremely irritable, that the least opposition was construed into an unpardonable insult, and the want of immediate apprehension in his pupils subjected them to the most galling contempt, which excited despair instead of emulation. His authority was too severe a climate for the tender plant of genius ever to thrive in. His judgment was, however, in general sound, and his instructions those of a master.—HOLCROFT, THOMAS, 1809? *Memoirs, bk.* ii, *ch.* i.

His conversation among young people was perfectly moral, and always tended to make us better: he was, in my opinion as to intellect, a very shining character, and in all instances I knew him to be a worthy man; but a great sitter-up at nights for sake of conversation: many a morning sun has peeped into our convival parties; he was then between seventy and eighty. From the loss of his teeth his nose and chin were prominent: he took no snuff, and hated swearing, or broad vulgar jests in conversation, though smitten much with repartee.—O'KEEFFE, JOHN, 1826, *Recollections, vol.* II, *ch.* VI.

Everybody, I presume, must have had some information respecting Macklin's person and manners; that he was a broad-breasted, ball-headed, shaggy-browed, hooked-nosed individual, as rough and husky as a cocoa-nut, with a barking or grunting delivery more peculiar than pleasing, which to musical ears made him something like a "bore." . . . If good manners are to be gleaned from a collision with society, Macklin's were bad, because throughout life he had been chiefly his own company. His manners grew out of his mind, which became powerful and profound, cared not for oil or ornament, so long as it could express itself with vigor and conciseness. . . . The terrific effect of his features,when under excitation,have been recorded in his performance of Shylock. The most amusing proof I have heard upon the point was as follows:— When he had established his fame in that character, George the Second went to see him; and the impression he received was so powerful that it deprived him of rest throughout the night. In the morning the premier (Sir Robert Walpole) waited on the king, to express his fears that the Commons would oppose a certain measure then in contemplation. "I wish, your Majesty," said Sir Robert,"it was possible to find a recipe for frightening a House of Commons?" "What do you think," replied the King, "of sending them to the Theatre to see that Irishman play Shylock!"—BERNARD, JOHN, 1830, *Retrospections of the Stage, vol.* II, *ch.* i.

As an actor, he was without trick; his enunciation was clear, in every syllable. Taken as a whole, he probably excelled every actor who had ever played Shylock, say his biographers; but I remember Edmund Kean, and make that exception. He was not a great tragedian, nor a good light comedian, but in comedy and farce, where rough energy is required, and in parts resembling Shylock, in their earnest malignity, he was paramount. He was also an excellent teacher, very impatient with mediocrity, but very careful with the intelligent. Easily moved to anger, his pupils and, indeed, many others stood in awe of him; but he was honorable, generous, and humane; convivial, frank, and not more free in his style than his contemporaries; but naturally irascible, and naturally forgiving. Eccentricity was second nature to him, and seems to have been so with other men of his blood.—DORAN, JOHN, 1863, *Annals of the English Stage, vol.* II, *p.* 191

GENERAL

As a comic writer, Mr. Macklin unquestionably stands high. "The Man of the World," for boldness of satire, and originality of character, may challenge any production, which has been represented on the stage for the last fifty years; and his "Love-a-la-Mode," which is pregnant with much genuine humour, and knowledge of men and manners, demands also an high share of praise. In most of his dramatic pieces, there is to be found real character, discrimination of humour, modish affectation, and fashionable folly. He never offends (from his thorough knowledge of stage œconomy), in the conduct of his plot, and the right management of his scenes. To these dramatic excellencies, he added a strict attention to decency and morality. Mr. Macklin's merit, as an actor and a man, introduced him to persons of high rank.—KIRKMAN, JAMES THOMAS, 1799, *Memoirs of the Life of Charles Macklin, vol.* II, *p.* 433.

But, alas! where shall we look for the foundation of Macklin's authorship? We have already sketched his education, which, taken at its supposable extremity, could amount to no more than a capacity for reading some of the commonest English school-books, with scarcely any knowledge of the habits of civilized life. . . . His next attempt at Authorship was not till the year 1760, when he produced his Farce of "Love a la Mode;" a dramatic *morceau*, which, though it had many enemies to combat with, from personal prejudices, has long since surmounted them, and given to the author the merited rank of an able comic writer. Having now produced a piece which would stand the test of time, he was ambitious of producing a Comedy which would carry the same seeds of longevity; and for this purpose, without

consulting books, which are very often but the multiplied copies of fanciful originals, he sought his principal characters from his own long experience of life, and of the Stage; and with these aids produced a Comedy, which, considered for regularity of plot, strength of character, and knowledge of the world, will remain a favourite on the stock list, whilst there are performers found capable of supporting so arduous and discriminating a part as that of Sir Pertinax Mac Sycophant.— COOKE, WILLIAM, 1804–6, *Memoirs of Charles Macklin, Comedian, pp.* 412, 415.

Macklin, though not a voluminous contributor to scenic representations, has condensed *multum in parvo*, by showing a complete knowledge of the practices of the stage, and an acute perception of human life: his characters are drawn with the hand of a master, who felt no diffidence in the accomplishment of the task which he had proposed to himself to execute.— IRELAND, S. W. H., 1815, *Scribbleomania, p.* 113.

Energy and honesty were the dominant traits of his character. Entirely self-educated, he yet used his alert intelligence so well as to become, after Garrick, the most cultured actor of his time; though when he attempted to lecture on the theatre of the Greeks and the origins of the Shaksperean drama he was doubtless beyond his depth. He wrote with vigor and propriety, though in controversy he carried to extremes the italicized emphasis then in vogue.—ARCHER, WILLIAM, 1886, *Actors and Actresses of Great Britain and the United States, eds. Matthews and Hutton, vol.* I, *p.* 10.

Joseph Black
1728–1799

Joseph Black was born at Bordeaux, in 1728. His father, John Black, was a native of Belfast, a member of a Scottish family settled in Ireland. His mother belonged to the family of Gordon, of Halhead, in Aberdeenshire, and was a cousin of Dr. Adam Ferguson. In 1740 he was sent home and educated at the Grammar School of Belfast. In 1746 he matriculated at the University of Glasgow, where he remained till 1750, studying in the faculties of art and medicine. He then removed to Edinburgh, where he graduated as doctor of medicine in 1754. In 1756 he was appointed Professor of anatomy and Lecturer on Chemistry in the University of Glasgow. He soon exchanged with a colleague the duty of teaching anatomy for that of physiology, and continued to lecture on physiology and chemistry till 1766, when he was called to Edinburgh to succeed his friend and teacher, Dr. Cullen, in the Chair of Chemistry. He died November 26, 1799.—BROWN, CRUM, 1878, *Lecture to the Edinburgh University Chemical Society, Nature, vol.* 18, *p.* 346.

PERSONAL

His personal appearance and manner were those of a gentleman, and peculiarly pleasing. His voice in lecturing was low, but fine; and his articulation so distinct that he was perfectly well heard by an audience consisting of several hundreds. His discourse was so plain and perspicuous, his illustrations by experiment so apposite, that his sentiments on any subject never could be mistaken, even by the most illiterate; and his instructions were so clear of all hypothesis or conjecture, that the hearer rested on his conclusions with the confidence scarcely exceeded in matters of his own experience.—ROBISON, JOHN, 1803, *Black's Lectures on the Elements of Chemistry, Preface, p.* lxii.

The physical sciences have few more illustrious names to boast than that of Joseph Black. With all the habits and the disciplined faculties of a true philosopher, with the temper as well as the capacity of a sage, he possessed that happy union of strong but disciplined imagination, with powers of close undivided attention, and ample resources of reasoning, which forms original genius in scientific pursuits; and, as all these qualities may be combined in an individual without his happening to signalise his investigations of nature by any discovery, we must add that his life was crowned with the good fortune of opening to mankind new paths in which both himself and his followers successfully trod, enlarging to an incalculable extent the bounds of human knowledge. . . . The qualities which distinguished him as an inquirer and as a teacher followed him into all the ordinary affairs of life. He was a person whose opinions on every subject were marked by calmness and sagacity, wholly free from both passion and prejudice, while affectation was only known to him from the comedies he might have read. His temper in all the circumstances of life was unruffled.—BROUGHAM, HENRY LORD, 1845–50, *Lives of Philosophers of the Time of George III., pp.* 1, 21.

Black was a prominent member of the intellectual society by which Edinburgh was then distinguished. Amongst his intimates were his relative and colleague Adam Ferguson, Hume, Hutton, A. Carlyle, Dugald Stewart, and John Robison. Adam Smith with whom he knit a close friendship at Glasgow, used to say that "no man had less nonsense in his head than Dr. Black." He was one of James Watt's earliest patrons, and kept up a constant correspondence with him. Though grave and reserved, Black was gentle and sincere, and it is recorded of him that he never lost a friend. He was at the same time gifted with a keen judgment of character, and with the power of expressing that judgment in an "indelible phrase." In person he is described as "rather above the middle size; he was of a slender make; his countenance was placid and exceedingly engaging" (Thomson). As he advanced in years, Robison tells us, he preserved a pleasing air of inward contentment. Graceful and unaffected in manner, "he was of most easy approach, affable, and readily entered into conversation, whether serious or trivial." Nor did he distain elegant accomplishments. —CLERKE, MISS A. M., 1886, *Dictionary of National Biography, vol.* v, *p.* 111.

GENERAL

The modesty of his nature making him averse to publish his speculations, and the genuine devotion to the investigation of truth, for its own sake, rendering him most open in his communications with all who were engaged in the same pursuits, his incontestable claim to be regarded as the founder of modern chemistry has been oftentimes overlooked; and, while some have endeavoured more or less obscurely to mingle themselves with his discoveries, others have thought it becoming to postdate the new system, that it might seem the produce of a somewhat later age. The interests of truth and justice therefore require that we should minutely examine the facts of the case; and, happily, the evidence is so clear that it only requires an attentive consideration to remove all doubt from the subject. I feel it a duty imperatively cast upon me to undertake a task from which, did I not regard it as less difficult than sacred, I might shrink. But I had the great happiness of being taught by himself, having attended one of the last courses of lectures which he delivered; and the knowledge thus gained cannot be turned to a better use than in recording the glory and in vindicating the fame of my illustrious master. — BROUGHAM, HENRY LORD, 1845–55, *Lives of Philosophers of the Time of George III., p.* 1.

He struck out a theory which, being

eminently original, was violently attacked, but is now generally admitted. With a boldness and reach of thought not often equalled, he arrived at the conclusion, that whenever a body loses some of its consistence, as in the case of ice becoming water, or water becoming steam, such body receives an amount of heat which our senses, though aided by the most delicate thermometer, can never detect. . . . The intellect of Black belonged to a class, which, in the eighteenth century, was almost universal in Scotland, but was hardly to be found in England, and which, for want of a better word, we are compelled to call deductive, though fully admitting that even the most deductive minds have in them a large amount of induction, since, indeed, without induction, the common business of life could not be carried on.— BUCKLE, HENRY THOMAS, 1862–66, *History of Civilization in England, vol.* III, *chap.* v.

James Burnett
Lord Monboddo
1714–1799

A Scottish lawyer and author, was born at Monboddo, in Kincardineshire, in 1714, educated at Marischal College, Aberdeen, where he displayed a great fondness for the Greek philosophers, and afterwards studied law for 3 years at Gronigen in Holland. In 1737 he became a member of the Scottish bar, and soon obtained considerable practice; but the first thing that brought him prominently into notice was his connection with the celebrated Douglas case, in which Mr. Burnet acted as counsel for Mr. Douglas. In 1767 he was raised to the bench by the title of lord Monboddo. He died May 26, 1799. Monboddo's first work, on the "Origin and Progress of Language" (1771–76), is a very learned, heretical, and eccentric production; yet in the midst of its grotesque crotches there occasionally flashes out a wonderfully acute observation, that makes one regret the distorted and misapplied talent of the author. The notion that men have sprung from monkeys, is perhaps that which is most commonly associated with the name of Monboddo, who gravely asserted that the orangoutangs are members of the human species, and that in the bay of Bengal there exists a nation of human creatures with tails, and that we have only worn away ours by sitting on them, but that the stumps may still be felt. Monboddo wrote another work, entitled "Ancient Metaphysics," which was published only a few weeks before his death.—PECK, HARRY THURSTON, *ed.*, 1898, *The International Cyclopædia, vol.* X, *p.* 16.

PERSONAL

The metaphysical and philological Lord Monboddo breakfasted with us yesterday. He is such an extravagant admirer of the ancients that he scarcely allows the English language to be capable of any excellence, still less the French. . . . He said we moderns were entirely degenerated. I asked in what? "In everything," was his answer. "Men are not so tall as they were,—women are not so handsome as they were, nobody can now write a long period, everything dwindles." . . . Among much just thinking and some taste, especially in his valuable third volume on "The Origin and Progress of Language," he entertained some opinions so absurd that they would be hardly credible if he did not deliver them himself, both in writing and conversation, with a gravity which shows that he is in earnest, but which makes the hearer feel that to be grave exceeds all power of face. He is so wedded to system, that, as Lord Barrington said to me the other day, rather than sacrifice his favorite opinion that men were born with tails, he would be contented to wear one himself.—MORE, HANNAH, 1782, *Letter to her Sister, Memoirs, ed. Roberts, vol.* I, *p.* 146.

I was married to the handsomest woman in Scotland, and I believe the best wife in it, with whom I lived most happily seven years. I have been fifteen years a widower, and during all that time I never had the least thought of a second choice, till I saw you at this time in London, so amiable both in mind and person, and your sentiments so much agreeing with mine that I thought, and still think, we are made for one another, and may live most comfortably together. During my widowhood, the affairs of my family have suffered much, chiefly for want of a mother to my children. . . . I am sure I would make a most loving husband to you, and besides I would propose to be a father to that excellent girl who lives with you and whose admirable genius it would give me the greatest pleasure to cultivate and improve, as I think I could do. Now my dear Mrs. Garrick, tell me if you know any three in Britain that you think would be happier together than we three? And if you pleased, I would add a fourth, my young daughter, who is almost as handsome as her mother, a good figure, a very good disposition, and not defective in genius, particularly in painting.—BUR-NETT, JAMES LORD MONBODDO, 1782, *Letter to Mrs. David Garrick.*

The answer I gave you in that moment when you did me the honor of proposing an union between us came from my heart: it was that I never would change my situation; and which you must give me leave to repeat again as a final answer to your letter, I remain, my Lord, Your most obliged and obedient servant.—GARRICK, MRS. DAVID, 1782, *Letter to Lord Monboddo, June 26.*

Lord Monboddo's temper was affectionate, friendly and social. He was fond of convivial intercourse; and it was his daily custom to unbend himself, after his professional labours, amidst a select party of literary friends, whom he invited to an early supper. The entertainment itself partook of the *costume* of the ancients: it had all the variety and abundance of a principal meal; and the master of the feast crowned his wine, like Anacreon, with a garland of roses. His conversation, too, had a *race* and *flavour* peculiarly its own: it was nervous, sententious, and tinctured with genuine wit. His apothegms, (or, as his favourite Greeks would rather term them Γνωμαι), were singularly terse and forcible; and the grave manner in which he often conveyed the keenest irony, and the eloquence with which he supported his paradoxical theories, afforded the highest amusement of those truly attic banquets, which will be long remembered by all who had the pleasure of partaking in them.—TYTLER, ALEXANDER FRASER, 1806–14, *Memoirs of the Life and Writings of Henry Home of Kames, vol.* I, *p.* 250, *note.*

Lord Monboddo was a humorist both in private life and in his literary career. He was, says Sir Walter Scott, a gentleman of the most amiable disposition, and of the strictest honour and integrity. He was deeply read in ancient literature, was a devout believer in the virtues of the heroic ages and the deterioration of civilized mankind, and so great a contemner of luxuries that he would never use a wheel carriage. There were several points of similarity between him and Johnson—great learning, clearness of head, precision of speech, and a love of inquiry on subjects which people in general do not investigate. Foote used to call Lord Monboddo "an Elzevir edition of Johnson."—FORD, EDWARD, 1883, *Lord Monboddo and Mrs. Garrick, National Review, vol.* 2, *p.* 106.

In his judicial capacity he showed himself to be both a profound lawyer and an upright judge, and his decisions were free from those paradoxes which so frequently appeared in his writings as well as in his conversation. He was not, however, without peculiarities, even in the court of sessions, for instead of sitting on the bench with his fellow-judges, he always took his seat underneath with the clerks. Nor was he as a rule inclined to agree with his colleagues in their decisions, but was generally in the minority and sometimes alone. Burnett is, however, best known to the world as a man of letters. . . In private life Burnett was an amiable, generous, and kind-hearted man. Though in his habit he was exceedingly temperate and lived much according to rule, yet he greatly delighted in the convivial society of his friends.—BARKER, G. F. RUSSELL, 1886, *Dictionary of National Biography, vol.* VII, *pp.* 412, 413.

Lord Monboddo was known rather for his quaint eccentricities and social humour than for any consummate mastery of the law.—CRAIK, SIR HENRY, 1901, *A Century of Scottish History, vol.* II, *p.* 148.

The venerable figure of Monboddo was every year seen on horseback posting off to London, to visit old friends and delight old circles. At last, however, such expeditions were too fatiguing for his shrivelled old body. He was on his way in 1799 to make his annual visit, but only got as far as Dunbar, where he was taken ill, and forced to undergo the ignominy of being conveyed home in the despised chaise. "Oh, George," he said plaintively to his nephew, "I find that I am eighty-four." A few days later, in May, the venerable humorist was dead. Then the world gossiped, according to its fashion, of stories true and false about the old man's humours—how he used to fancy that the tails of babies were snipped off by midwives at their birth, and how he would watch at the bedroom door when a child was born, in order to detect the relics of a primeval ancestry. Others more worthily recalled memorable nights in his society, his sayings of curious wit, his sallies which set the table in a roar, while perfect gravity reigned on his ugly old face; his pleasant ways, his courtly, old-fashioned manners. They missed the familiar form which had trotted up innumerable stairs to merry suppers—the worn-out old figure they had daily seen standing at the door of Creech's shop, or pacing the Parliament Close—the owner of a most kindly heart, the author of most unreadable books. —GRAHAM, HENRY GREY, 1901, *Scottish Men of Letters in the Eighteenth Century*, p. 197.

GENERAL

And with Monboddo still believ'd in tails. —MATHIAS, THOMAS JAMES, 1797, *The Pursuits of Literature, Eighth ed., p.* 331.

The writings of Lord Monboddo display a profound acquaintance with the philosophy of the ancients, which he has explored with the ardour, and admired perhaps with the prejudices of an enthusiast; but in so far as they relate to criticism and philology, they are valuable monuments of classical taste, and a sound discriminating judgment in the excellencies and defects of rhetorical composition.—TYTLER, ALEXANDER FRASER, 1806–14, *Memoirs of the Life and Writings of Henry Home of Kames, vol.* I, p. 246.

The writings of the eccentric James Burnet, Lord Monboddo, contain interesting passages, such as his theory about the origin of man, and his humorously extravagant defence of the superiority of ancient over modern writers; but the interest is more in the matter than in any felicity or original force of expression.—MINTO, WILLIAM, 1872–80, *Manual of English Prose Literature, p.* 487.

I confess that I have felt a deep interest in reading the philosophical works of Lord Monboddo,—he is so unlike any other Scotch metaphysician, he is so unlike his age. As appearing among a body of inductive inquirers, and in the middle of the eighteenth century, he looks very much like a megatherium coming in upon us in the historical period. His society is not with the modern empiricists, not even with the Latins, but with Plato and the Neo-Platonists, with Aristotle and his commentators. As regards the higher Greek philosophy, he is the most erudite scholar that Scotland has produced, not excepting even Sir William Hamilton. He had two great philosophic works. . . . He dwells with evident fondness on categories or universal forms. All things are to be known by their causes. The knowledge of first causes belongs to metaphysics. Everything that is to be known falls under one or other of the categories. He shows that God must have ideas. Man is capable of forming ideas. Time is not a cause, but is a necessary adjunct or concomitant of the material world. — McCOSH, JAMES, 1874, *The Scottish Philosophy, pp.* 248, 250, 252.

A brief reference must suffice to one other thinker of considerable ability, who, in attempting to assail the dominant philosophy, produced at least a literary curiosity. Lord Monboddo, following James Harris, the author of "Hermes," attempted to revive the Aristotelian philosophy. His six quartos upon "Antient Metaphysics," and his six octavos upon the progress of language, contain much acute thought amidst huge masses of digression, repetition, and apology for eccentric crochets. His main point is really a criticism of Locke and Hume for their confusion of sensation and perception. He makes many of the criticisms which from this point of view would commend themselves to the metaphysical school of which he professes himself an adherent; but he produced no influence upon thought— partly because his doctrine was an attempt to resuscitate the dead; and even more, perhaps, because it was overlaid with oddities, some of which are remembered when his more serious remarks are forgotten. . . . Reid and Hartley each founded a school; but Monboddo remained an isolated being, annointing himself according to the fashion of the ancients, growling at the degeneracy of mankind, and regarded by them as a semi-lunatic, outside the sphere of practical influence.—STEPHEN, LESLIE, 1876, *History of English Thought in the Eighteenth Century, vol.* I, *pp.* 68, 69.

Patrick Henry

1736-1799

Henry was born at Studley, Virginia, May 29th, 1736. He was of good Scotch and English blood, and was educated by his father; he married at eighteen and went early into business. He became a lawyer when twenty-four, and was successful from the first. When pleading the cause of a clergyman in 1763 in the celebrated tobacco-tax question, he showed himself to be a fine speaker; and from this on, advanced rapidly in public life. Elected in 1765 to the Virginia House, in a fiery speech he advocated resistence to the Stamp Act and became the leader of his colony. He was a delegate to the first Continental Congress, and in 1776, on the adoption of the Constitution, his own state made him four times governor; he declined re-election in 1786, to be again elected in 1796 and again to decline. . . . Retiring from public life in 1791 at the age of fifty-five, he practiced law, preferring to guard his broken health and provide for his large family; although subsequently Washington offered him the post of Secretary of State and that of Chief Justice, and President Adams named him minister to France. In 1799, however, at Washington's appeal he allowed himself to be elected to the Legislature; but died June 6th, before taking his seat.—WARNER, CHARLES DUDLEY, ed., 1897, *Library of the World's Best Literature, vol.* XII, *p.* 7241.

PERSONAL

On the 6th inst. departed this life Patrick Henry, Esquire, of Charlotte Count. Mourn, Virginia, mourn! Your Henry is gone! Ye friends to liberty in every clime, drop a tear. No more will his social feelings spread delight through his happy house. No more will his edifying example dictate to his numerous offspring the sweetness of virtue, and the majesty of patriotism. No more will his sage advice, guided by zeal for the common happiness, impart light and utility to his caressing neighbors. No more will he illuminate the public councils with sentiments drawn from the cabinet of his own mind, ever directed to his country's good, and clothed in eloquence sublime, delightful, and commanding. Farewell, first-rate patriot, farewell! As long as our rivers flow, or mountains stand—so long will your excellence and worth be the theme of homage and endearment, and Virginia, bearing in mind her loss, will say to rising generations, imitate my Henry.—VIRGINIA GAZETTE, 1799, *June* 14

I have not time to compare the characters of Washington and Henry, or I would clearly show that fewer blunders fell to the share of the latter than the former, and yet I have no objection to paying a tribute to the past services and virtues of either. —TYLER, JOHN, 1799, *Letter to James Monroe, Dec.* 27.

His disposition was indeed all sweetness—his affections were warm, kind, and social—his patience invincible—his temper ever unclouded, cheerful and serene— his manners plain, open, familiar, and simple—his conversation easy, ingenious and unaffected, full of entertainment, full of instruction, and irradiated with all those light and softer graces, which his genius threw, without effort, over the most common subjects. It is said that there stood in the court, before his door, a large walnut-tree, under whose shade it was his delight to pass his summer evenings, surrounded by his affectionate and happy family, and by a circle of neighbours who loved him almost to idolatry. Here he would disport himself with all the careless gaiety of infancy. Here, too, he would sometimes warm the bosoms of the old, and strike fire from the eyes of his younger hearers, by recounting the tales of other times; by sketching, with the boldness of a master's hand, those great historic incidents in which he had borne a part; and by drawing to the life, and placing before his audience, in colours as fresh and strong as those of nature, the many illustrious men in every quarter of the continent, with whom he had acted a part on the public stage. . . . Mr. Henry's conversation was remarkably pure and chaste. He never swore. He was never heard to take the name of his Maker in vain. He was a sincere Christian, though after a form of his own; for he was never attached to any particular religious society, and never, it is believed, communed with any church. . . . His morals were strict. As a husband, a father, a master, he had no superior. He was kind and hospitable to the stranger, and most friendly and accommodating to his neighbours. In his dealings with the world, he was faithful to his promise, and punctual in his contracts, to the utmost of his power.—WIRT, WILLIAM, 1817, *Sketches of the Life and Character of Patrick Henry, pp.* 394, 418.

Imagination can present no brighter picture of a happy old age, than is exhibited in the real life of Henry; and, when we compare this charming spectacle with that of the cares and privations which have clouded the closing years of some of our greatest revolutionary patriots, we are forced to acknowledge, that the strict private economy with which Henry has sometimes been reproached as a fault, when combined, as it was in his case, with a genial temperament and a liberal discharge of all the duties of life, was not so much a venial error as an actual, positive, and most important virtue. He had been always strongly impressed with the importance of religion, and had studied with care the best books on the subject that came within his reach. . . . He possessed an instinctive sagacity, which supplied, to a great extent, the deficiencies of his education; a moral courage, which led him to spurn all considerations of mere temporary expediency, when he was once satisfied where the right lay, and a naturally noble and generous heart. To these better qualities he owed his extraordinary efficiency and success as a public speaker. — EVERETT, ALEXANDER H., 1844, *Life of Patrick Henry; The Library of American Biography, ed. Sparks, vol.* I, *pp.* 384, 387.

Mason Locke Weems, with his fun and his fiddle, his imagination and his fluency, had points in common with that most gifted of all such Virginians, Patrick Henry. Without the opportunity which called into exercise Patrick Henry's sublime talent, that great-natured orator might have lived to the end of his days a fiddling stroller and story-teller, like his contemporary, Weems.—PARTON, JAMES, 1879, *The Traditional and Real Washington, Magazine of American History, vol.* 3, *p.* 467.

Such, I think it may fairly be said, was Patrick Henry when, at the age of twenty-four, having failed in every other pursuit, he turned for bread to the profession of the law. There is no evidence that either he or any other mortal man was aware of the extraordinary gifts that lay within him for success in that

career. Not a scholar surely, not even a considerable miscellaneous reader, he yet had the basis of a good education; he had the habit of reading over and over again a few of the best books; he had a good memory; he had an intellect strong to grasp the great commanding features of any subject; he had a fondness for the study of human nature, and singular proficiency in that branch of science; he had quick and warm sympathies, particularly with persons in trouble,—an invincible propensity to take sides with the underdog in any fight. Through a long experience in off-hand talk with the men whom he had thus far chiefly known in his little provincial world,—with an occasional clergyman, pedagogue, or legislator, small planters and small traders, sportsmen, loafers, slaves, and the drivers of slaves, and, more than all, those bucolic Solons of old Virginia, the good-humored, illiterate, thriftless Caucasian consumers of tobacco and whiskey, who, cordially consenting that all the hard work of the world should be done by the children of Ham, were thus left free to commune together in endless debate on the tavern porch or on the shady side of the country store,—young Patrick had learned somewhat of the lawyer's art of putting things; he could make men laugh, could make them serious, could set fire to their enthusiasms. What more he might do with such gifts nobody seems to have guessed; very likely few gave it any thought at all. In that rugged but munificient profession at whose outward gates he then proceeded to knock, it was altogether improbable that he would burden himself with much more of its erudition than was really necessary for a successful general practice in Virginia in his time or that he would permanently content himself with less.—TYLER, MOSES COIT, 1887, *Patrick Henry (American Statesmen), p.* 18.

With no pomp or ceremony, but amid the tears of his devoted family and loving neighbors, Patrick Henry was laid to rest in the quiet graveyard at Red Hill, at the foot of the garden. A plain marble slab covers his grave, on which are inscribed his name, the dates of his birth and death, and the words, "His fame is his best epitaph."—HENRY, WILLIAM WIRT, 1891, *Patrick Henry, vol.* II, *p.* 626.

Beloved and praised without stint by the

men of his time, and since his death strangely maligned by a rival statesman of Virginia.—POOLE, W. F., 1892, *Patrick Henry, The Dial, vol.* 13, *p.* 41.

Among his own countrymen every detail of the career of such a familiar historical figure is of undying interest; but to the notice of most English readers Patrick Henry comes, I think, but as a shadowy name. His life can be divided into two distinct periods. The first has an international interest, and consists of the almost magical transformation of the despised clown, through a series of dramatic situations, to a leading figure and potent factor in one of the greatest struggles in English history. In the second his activity ceases to have any international significance, and is reduced by the march of events to a purely provincial and domestic stage. The former, as a subject of interest to Englishmen, needs no apology. The latter would only be welcome where some sympathy with the personality of Henry, and the conditions of the Southern Colonies after the war, had been awakened. —BRADLEY, A. G., 1892. *Patrick Henry, Macmillan's Magazine, vol.* 65, *p.* 355.

SPEECHES

He is by far the most powerful speaker I ever heard. Every word he says not only engages but commands the attention; and your passions are no longer your own when he addresses them. But his eloquence is the smallest part of his merit. He is, in my opinion, the first man upon this continent, as well in abilities as public virtues, and had he lived in Rome about the time of the first Punic War. . . . Mr. Henry's talents must have put him at the head of that glorious commonwealth. —MASON, GEORGE, 1774, *Letter to Martin Cockburn, Life and Writings.*

The times in which he lived were suited to his genius, in other times we doubt if his peculiar powers would have raised him to a higher distinction, than that of an eloquent speaker at the bar. . . . The secret of his eloquence unquestionably rested in his power of touching the spring of passion and feeling. He had little to do with the understanding or judgment of his hearers.— SPARKS, JARED, 1818, *Mr. Wirt's Life of Patrick Henry, North American Review, vol.* 6, *p.* 322.

They fall, of course, far below his fame;

and it is, after all, on the faith of mere tradition, attested, however, by facts too numerous and of too public a character to leave it in any way doubtful, that the present and future generations will acknowledge the justice of his claim to the proud title, that has been given him, of the greatest orator of the New World.—EVERETT, ALEXANDER H., 1844, *Life of Patrick Henry; The Library of American Biography, vol.* I, *p.* 389.

Mr. Henry seldom used his pen, and has therefore left but little written eloquence authenticated by himself. To form our estimate of his powers, we have mainly to rely on the reports of those who had witnessed the wonders he wrought—those who had felt the magic of his action, trembled at the majesty of his voice, and caught the flashings of his eye,—who had been fascinated by his smile, or repulsed by his terrific frown, and who always found themselves incompetent to express fully the power with which he impressed conviction.—MAGOON, E. L., 1848, *Orators of the American Revolution, p.* 263.

In executing a mission from the Synod of Virginia, in the year 1794, I had to pass through the county of Prince Edward, where Mr. Henry resided. Understanding that he was to appear before the Circuit Court, which met in that county, in defence of three men charged with murder, I determined to seize the opportunity of observing for myself the eloquence of this extraordinary orator. . . . In person, Mr. Henry was lean rather than fleshy. He was rather above than below the common height, but had a stoop in the shoulders which prevented him from appearing as tall as he really was. In his moments of animation, he had the habit of straightening his frame, and adding to his apparent stature. He wore a brown wig, which exhibited no indication of any great care in the dressing. Over his shoulders he wore a brown camlet cloak. Under this his clothing was black, something the worse for wear. The expression of his countenance was that of solemnity and deep earnestness. His mind appeared to be always absorbed in what, for the time, occupied his attention. His forehead was high and spacious, and the skin of his face more than usually wrinkled for a man of fifty. His eyes were small and deeply set in his head, but were of a bright blue color, and twinkled much in their sockets. In short, Mr. Henry's appearance had nothing very remarkable, as he sat at rest. You might readily have taken him for a common planter who cared very little about his personal appearance. In his manners, he was uniformly respectful and courteous. . . . In the countenance, action, and intonation of the speaker, there was expressed such an intensity of feeling, that all my doubts were dispelled; never again did I question whether Henry felt, or only acted a feeling. Indeed, I experienced an instantaneous sympathy with him in the emotions which he expressed; and I have no doubt the same sympathy was felt by every hearer.—ALEXANDER, ARCHIBALD, 1850, *Reminiscences of Patrick Henry, Princeton Magazine; Life by J. W. Alexander.*

Henry rose with an unearthly fire burning in his eye. He commenced somewhat calmly [Speech of March 23, 1775], but the smothered excitement began more and more to play upon his features and thrill in the tones of his voice. The tendons of his neck stood out white and rigid "like whipcords." His voice rose louder and louder, until the walls of the building, and all within them, seemed to shake and rock in its tremendous vibrations. Finally, his pale face and glaring eye became "terrible to look upon." Men "leaned forward in their seats," with their heads "strained forward," their faces pale, and their eyes glaring like the speaker's. His last exclamation, "Give me liberty or give me death!" was like the shout of a leader which turns back the rout of battle. The old clergymen said, when Mr. Henry sat down, he [the auditor] felt "*sick* with excitement." Every eye yet gazed entranced on Henry. It seemed as if a word from him would have led to any wild explosion of violence. "Men looked beside themselves."—RANDALL, HENRY STEPHENS, 1858, *Life of Thomas Jefferson, vol.* I, *p.* 101.

No one spoke so well or reasoned so badly as Henry. He was to the end of his days an orator and an actor, and nothing more. Had he, indeed, gone upon the stage, he would have rivalled Garrick. The attitudes which he struck, the way in which he walked, his gestures, his sonorous voice, and the wonderful play of his features must, if we may trust the descriptions

of those who heard him, have been most remarkable. He would have been fine as Othello, and have done well as Sir Andrew Aguecheek. But a statesman he certainly was not. Whatever could be done by eloquence he could do. He could deliver a fourth-of-July oration, move a jury, conduct a canvass, or entertain the Legislature with tirades on liberty and the rights of man in a way that would have excited the envy of Pitt and Burke. When, however, the end sought was to be gained not by good speaking, but by good reasoning, he was unable to cope with men whose limited vocabulary, whose mouthing and stammering and monotonous tones it was painful to hear.—McMASTER, JOHN BACH, 1883, *A History of the People of the United States, vol.* I, *p.* 490.

Mr. Henry was a man of marked and peculiar power as an orator. He could sway the minds of the cultured and the ignorant with equal ease. He could rouse to action, or quiet the raging passions. He was a born actor, and understood how to use his powers with the best effect. While he was not a wise and accomplished statesman, he exercised a strong influence on the destinies of his country.—WHITMAN, C. M., 1883, *American Orators and Oratory, p.* 32.

For Virginia he was Otis and Adams in one,—both orator and political manager. Not many of his burning speeches have come down to us, but we well know what he was: one of the first orators of the eighteenth century.—RICHARDSON, CHARLES F., 1887, *American Literature, 1607–1885, vol.* I, *p.* 189.

His speeches had an extraordinary vividness, and no speaker of his day is so widely quoted in our time as Henry. He expressed honesty as well as passion, and strong practical ability lay behind his words. He prepared the minds of the people for the inevitableness of war, and was active in devising measures to meet it when it came —HAWTHORNE, JULIAN, AND LEMMON, LEONARD, 1891, *American Literature, p.* 35.

Mr. Henry was happily endowed with that rich imagination which gives vitality to the body of thought, and which is essential to the success of the great orator. He was deeply inbued with that vehemence of conviction, that oratorical action, which modulates the tones, tinges the visage with irresistible power, and suggests to the hearer more than articulate language can express.—HARDWICKE, HENRY, 1896, *History of Oratory and Orators, p.* 332.

His oratory appeals strongly to the emotions. In his legal practice he depended more on the spell which his eloquence threw over the jury, than on a mastery of the legal intricacies of the case. He was fervid rather than weighty; superficial and hasty rather than deep. His oratory abounds in figurative language; it is sometimes overwrought, even turgid, full of exaggerations and extravagant rhapsodies, yet when joined with the

fire, the energy, the flashing eye, the impassioned voice of the man who originated it, was irresistible.—PATTEE, FRED LEWIS, 1896, *A History of American Literature, p.* 73.

The greatest Revolutionary orator of the emotional type was Patrick Henry of Virginia, inferior to many of his contemporaries in learning, judgment, and practical efficiency, but endowed with the gift of passionate eloquence. His famous speech before the Virginia Convention, in 1775, rivals the oratory of Chatham for terse strength and fiery logic.—BRONSON, WALTER C., 1900, *A Short History of American Literature, p.* 46.

George Washington
1732-1799

Born in Westmoreland County, Va., Feb. 22 (O. S. Feb. 11), 1732: died at Mount Vernon, Dec. 14, 1799. A famous American soldier and statesman, the first President of the United States. He was the son of Augustine Washington, a Virginia planter. He was at school until he was about 16 years of age; was engaged in surveying 1748-51; was appointed adjutant of Virginia troops in 1751; inherited Mount Vernon on the death of his brother in 1752; was made by Dinwiddie commander of a military district of Virginia in 1753; was sent on a mission to the French authorities beyond the Allegheny River 1753-54; was appointed lieutenant-colonel in 1754; had a successful skirmish with the French, and defended Fort Necessity, but was obliged to surrender on July 3; was a volunteer aide-de-camp to Braddock in the battle of the Monongahela in 1755, and brought off the Virginians; commanded on the frontier 1755-57; and led the advance-guard in Forbes's expedition for the reduction of Fort Duquesne in 1758. On Jan. 9, 1759, he married Martha Custis (widow of Daniel Parke Custis), and settled as a planter at Mount Vernon. He was a delegate to the Virginia House of Burgesses, and to the Continental Congresses of 1774 and 1775; was appointed commander-in-chief of the Continental forces June 15, 1775; arrived at Cambridge July 2, and took command and compelled the evacuation of Boston on March 17, 1776. His army was defeated at the battle of Long Island Aug. 27, 1776, and at White Plains Oct. 28, 1776; he retreated through New Jersey; surprised the Hessians at Trenton Dec. 26; won the victory of Princeton Jan., 1777; was defeated at Brandywine and Germantown in 1777; was at Valley Forge during the winter of 1777-78; fought the drawn battle of Monmouth in 1778; compelled the surrender of Cornwallis at Yorktown in 1781; resigned his commission as commander-in-chief at Annapolis in 1783; and retired to Mount Vernon. In 1787 he was president of the Constitutional Convention; was unanimously elected President of the United States in Feb. 1789, and inaugurated at New York April 30, 1789; and was unanimously re-ëlected in 1793, serving until 1797. Among the chief events in his administrations were the establishment of the machinery of government, the crystallization of parties, the regulation of commerce and finance, the admission of Vermont, Kentucky, and Tennessee, the Indian wars, the "whiskey insurrection," and the Jay treaty. He issued his farewell address to the people in Sept., 1796. He was appointed lieutenant-general and commander-in-chief of the army in anticipation of a war with France in 1798.—SMITH, BENJAMIN E., *ed.*, 1894-97, *The Century Cyclopedia of Names, p.* 1051.

PERSONAL

George Washington, son to Augustine and Mary his wife, was born y° 11th day of February 173½ about ten in the morning,

and was baptized the 3d of April following; Mr. Beverly Whiting and Captain Christopher Brooks, godfathers, and Mrs. Mildred Gregory godmother.—FAMILY BIBLE, 1732.

Is Mr. Washington among your acquaintances? If not, I recommend you to embrace the first opportunity to form his friendship. He is about twenty-three years of age; with a countenance both mild and pleasant, promising both wit and judgment. He is of comely and dignified demeanor, at the same time displays much self-reliance and decision. He strikes me as being a young man of extraordinary and exalted character, and is destined to make no inconsiderable figure in our country.—BRADDOCK, GEN. EDWARD, 1755, *Letters.*

Washington, the dictator, has shown himself both a Fabius and a Camillus. His march through our lines is allowed to have been a prodigy of generalship. In one word, I look upon a great part of America as lost to this country! — WALPOLE, HORACE, 1777, *To Sir Horace Mann, April 3; Letters, ed. Cunningham, vol.* VI, *p.* 423.

Strike up, hell's music! roar, infernal drums!
Discharge the cannon! Lo, the warrior comes!
He comes, not tame as on Ohio's banks,
But rampant at the head of ragged ranks.
Hunger and itch are with him—Gates and Wayne!
And all the lice of Egypt in his train.
Sure these are Falstaff's soldiers, poor and bare,
Or else the rotten reg'ments of Rag-Fair.
. . . .
Hear thy indictment, Washington, at large;
Attend and listen to the solemn charge:
Thou hast supported an atrocious cause
Against the king, thy country, and the laws;
Committed perjury, encouraged lies,
Forced conscience, broken the most sacred ties;
Myriads of wives and fathers at thy hand
Their slaughtered husbands, slaughtered sons, demand;
That pastures hear no more the lowing kine,
That towns are desolate, all—all is thine;
The frequent sacrilege that pained my sight,
The blasphemies my pen abhors to write,
Innumerable crimes on thee must fall—
For thou maintainest, thou defendest all.
—ODELL, JONATHAN, 1779, *The Loyalist Poetry.*

I have seen General Washington, that most singular man—the soul and support of one of the greatest revolutions that has ever happened, or can happen. I fixed my eyes upon him with that keen attention which the sight of a great man always inspires. We naturally entertain a secret hope of discovering in the features of such illustrious persons some traces of that genius which distinguishes them from, and elevates them above, their fellow mortals. Perhaps the exterior of no man was better calculated to gratify these expectations than that of General Washington. He is of a tall and noble stature, well proportioned, a fine, cheerful, open countenance, a simple and modest carriage; and his whole mien has something in it that interests the French, the Americans, and even enemies themselves in his favor. . . . His reputation has, at length, arisen to a most brilliant height; and he may now grasp at the most unbounded power, without provoking envy or exciting suspicion. He has ever shown himself superior to fortune, and in the most trying adversity has discovered resources until then unknown: and, as if his abilities only increased and dilated at the prospect of difficulty, he is never better supplied than when he seems destitute of everything, nor have his arms ever been so fatal to his enemies, as at the very instant when they thought they had crushed him forever. It is his to excite a spirit of heroism and enthusiasm in a people who are by nature very little susceptible of it; to gain over the respect and homage of those whose interest it is to refuse it, and to execute his plans and projects by means unknown even to those who are his instruments; he is intrepid in dangers, yet never seeks them but when the good of his country demands it, preferring rather to temporize and act upon the defensive, because he knows such a mode of conduct best suits the genius and circumstances of the nation, and all that he and they have to expect, depends upon time, fortitude, and patience; he is frugal and sober in regard to himself, but profuse in the public cause; like Peter the Great, he has by defeats conducted his army to victory; and like Fabius, but with fewer resources and more difficulty, he has conquered without fighting and saved his country.—ROBIN, CLAUDE C., 1781, *Letter from Camp of Phillipsburg, Aug.* 4; *Magazine of American History, vol.* 20, *pp.* 137, 138.

O Washington! how do I love thy name! How have I often adored and blessed thy God, for creating and forming thee the great ornament of human kind! . . . The world and posterity will, with admiration, contemplate thy deliberate, cool, and stable judgment, thy virtues, thy valor and heroic achievements, as far surpassing those of Cyrus, whom the world loved and adored. The sound of thy fame shall go out into all the earth, and extend to distant ages. . . . Such has been thy military wisdom in the struggles of this arduous conflict, such the noble rectitude, amiableness, and mansuetude of thy character, something is there so singularly glorious and venerable thrown by Heaven about thee, that not only does thy country love thee, but our very enemies stop the madness of their fire in full volley, stop the illiberality of their slander at thy name, as if rebuked from Heaven with a—"Touch not mine Annointed, and do my Hero no harm!" Thy fame is of sweeter perfume than Arabian spices in the gardens of Persia. A Baron de Steuben shall waft it to a far greater monarch, and diffuse thy renown throughout Europe. Listening angels shall catch the odor, waft it to heaven, and perfume the universe!—STILES, EZRA, 1783, *The United States Elevated to Glory and Honor, p.* 334.

The name of the Deliverer of America alone can stand in the title-page of the tragedy of the Deliverer of Rome.—To you, most excellent and most rare citizen, I therefore dedicate this: without first hinting at even a part of so many praises due to yourself, which I now deem all comprehended in the sole mention of your name.—ALFIERI, VITTORIO, 1785, *The First Brutus, Dedication.*

My fine crab tree walking stick, with a gold head curiously wrought in the form of the cap of liberty, I give to my friend, and the friend of mankind, *General Washington.* If it were a sceptre he has merited it; and would become it.—FRANKLIN, BENJAMIN, 1790, *Will.*

Illustrious man, deriving honour less from the splendor of his situation than from the dignity of his mind, before whom all borrowed greatness sinks into insignificance, and all the potentates of Europe (excepting the members of our own royal family) become little and contemptible! He has had no occasion to have recourse to any tricks of policy or arts of alarm; his authority has been sufficiently supported by the same means by which it was acquired, and his conduct has uniformly been characterised by wisdom, moderation and firmness.—FOX, CHARLES JAMES, 1794, *Speech in House of Commons, Jan.*

First in war—first in peace—and first in the hearts of his countrymen, he was second to none in the humble and endearing scenes of private life; pious, just, humane, temperate and sincere; uniform, dignified and commanding, his example was as edifying to all around him as were the effects of that example lasting. To his equals he was condescending, to his inferiors kind, and to the dear object of his affections exemplarily tender. Correct throughout, vice shuddered in his presence, and virtue always felt his fostering hand. The purity of his private character gave effulgence to his public virtues. His last scene comported with the whole tenor of his life—although in extreme pain, not a sigh, nor a groan escaped him; and with undisturbed serenity he closed his well-spent life. Such was the man America has lost—such was the man for whom our nation mourns.—LEE, MAJOR GENERAL HENRY, 1799, *Funeral Oration on Washington, Delivered before the Two Houses of Congress, Dec.* 26.

The life of our WASHINGTON cannot suffer by a comparison with those of other countries, who have been most celebrated and exalted by fame. The attributes and declarations of royalty could have only served to eclipse the majesty of those virtues, which made him, from being a modest citizen, a more resplendid luminary. Misfortune, had he lived, could hereafter have sullied his glory only with those superficial minds, who, believing that characters and actions are marked by success alone, rarely deserve to enjoy it. Malice could never blast his honor: and envy made him a singular exception to her universal rule. For himself he had lived enough, to life and glory. For his fellow-citizens, if their prayers could have been answered, he would have been immortal. For me, his departure is at a most unfortunate moment. Trusting, however, in the wise and righteous dominion of Providence over the passions of men, and the results of their councils and actions, as well as over their lives, and nothing remains for me, but humble resignation. His example is now complete, and it will teach wisdom and virtue to magistrates, citizens, and men, not only in the present age, but in future generations, as long as our history shall be read. If a Trajan found a Pliny, a Marcus Aurelius can never want

biographers, eulogists or historians. —
ADAMS, JOHN, 1799, *To the Senate, Dec.* 19.

Born to high destinies, he was fashioned
for them by the hand of nature. His form
was noble—his port majestic. On his
front were enthroned the virtues which
exalt, and those which adorn the human
character. So dignified his deportment,
no man could approach him but with respect—none was great in his presence.
You all have seen him, and you all have
felt the reverence he inspired; it was
such, that to command, seemed to him but
the exercise of an ordinary function, while
others felt a duty to obey, which (anterior
to the injunctions of civil ordinance, or
the compulsion of a military code) was
imposed by the high behests of nature.
He had every title to command—Heaven, in
giving him the higher qualities of the soul,
had given also the tumultous passions which
accompany greatness, and frequently tarnish its lustre. With them was his first
contest, and his first victory was over himself. So great the empire he had there
acquired, that calmness of manner and of
conduct distinguished him through life.
Yet, those who have seen him strongly
moved, will bear witness that his wrath
was terrible; they have seen boiling in his
bosom, passion almost too mighty for
man; yet, when just bursting into act,
that strong passion was controlled by his
stronger mind.—MORRIS, GOUVERNEUR,
1799, *An Oration upon the Death of General Washington, Delivered at the Request
of the Corporation of the City of New York,
on the 31st of December.*

Oh, WASHINGTON! thou hero, patriot,
sage!
Friend of all climes, and pride of every age!
Were thine the laurels, every soil could raise,
The mighty harvest were penurious praise.
Well may our realms thy Fabian wisdom
boast;
Thy prudence sav'd, what bravery had lost.
—PAINE, THOMAS, 1800, *Ode Sung at the
Old South Meeting House, Boston, Jan.* 9.

Washington is no more! The tomb has
claimed him who was the model of Republican perfection. This is not the time to
trace all that this truly great man has
accomplished for the liberties of America,
the number and importance of military
achievements, the generous inspirations
which he imparted to the French who were
attracted to his school of arms; the sublime act which will ever add lustre to his

memory, when, after exerting his talents
in giving liberty to his country, he volun-
tarily relinquished supreme power to conceal his glory in the obscurity of private
life.—FAULCON, FELIX, 1800, *Proceedings
in the French Legislative Assembly, Feb. 4.*

There was indeed in this patriot something that all felt, but could not describe.
A strength of understanding, a keenness of
perception, a loftiness of thought, that
convinced without argument, and subdued
without effort. His language, like his
carriage, was impressive, elegant and
manly. It had secured a grace beyond
the reach of rhetoric; it had created an
illumination beyond the coloring of metaphor. His integrity overruled persuasion;
and his majesty overawed sophistry.
Corruption stood abashed in his presence,
and venality blushed into shame. The administration caught the character of their
leader, and seconded the energies of his
irresistible influence.— STORY, JOSEPH,
1800, *Eulogy on Washington, Delivered at
Marblehead, Mass., Feb.* 22.

There has scarcely appeared a really
great man whose character has been more
admired in his lifetime, or less correctly
understood by his admirers. When it is
comprehended, it is no easy task to de-
lineate its excellence in such a manner as
to give to the portrait both interest and
resemblance; for it requires thought and
study to understand the true ground of the
superiority of his character over many
others, whom he resembled in the principles of an action, and even in the manner of
acting. But perhaps he excels all the
great men that ever lived, in the steadiness
of his adherence to his maxims of life, and
in the uniformity of all his conduct to the
same maxims. . . . His talents were
such as assist a sound judgment, and
ripen with it. His prudence was consummate, and seemed to take the direction of
his powers and passions; for as a soldier,
he was more solicitous to avoid mistakes
that might be fatal, than to perform exploits that are brilliant; and as a statesman, to adhere to just principles, however
old, than to pursue novelties; and therefore, in both characters, his qualities were
singularly adapted to the interest, and
were tried in the greatest perils, of the
country.—AMES, FISHER, 1800, *Eulogy Delivered before the Massachusetts Legislature, Feb.* 8.

Born to direct the destiny of empires, his character was as majestic as the events, to which it was attached, were illustrious. In the delineation of its features, the vivid pencil of genius cannot brighten a trait, nor the blighting breath of a calumny obscure. His principles were the result of organic philosophy, — his success, of moral justice. His integrity assumed the port of command, — his intelligence, the aspect of inspiration. Glory, to many impregnable, he obtained without ambition; popularity, to all inconstant, he enjoyed without jealousy. The one was his from admiration, the other from gratitude. The former embellished, but could not reward; the latter followed, but never could lead him. The robust vigor of his virtue, like the undazzled eye of the eagle, was inaccessible to human weakness; and the unaspiring temperament of his passions, like the regenerating ashes of the phœnix, gave new life to the greatness it could not extinguish. In the imperial dignity of his person was exhibited the august stature of his mind. — PAINE, ROBERT TREAT, JR., 1800, *Eulogy on Washington.*

Exalted Chief—in thy superior mind
What vast resource, what various talents joined!
Tempered with social virtue's milder rays,
There patriot worth diffused a purer blaze:
Formed to command respect, esteem inspire,
Midst statesmen grave, or midst the social choir,
With equal skill the sword or pen to wield,
In council great, unequalled in the field,
Mid glittering courts or rural walks to please,
Polite with grandeur, dignified with ease;
Before the splendours of that high renown
How fade the glowworm lustres of a crown,
How sink diminished in that radiance lost
The glare of conquest, and of power the boast.
—ALSOP, RICHARD, 1800, *Sacred to the Memory of George Washington.*

There was in him that assemblage of qualities which constitutes real greatness; and these qualities were remarkably adapted to the conspicuous part which he was called to perform. He was not tinsel, but gold; not a pebble, but a diamond; not a meteor but a sun. Were he compared with the sages from the Neroes of antiquity, he would gain by the comparison, or rather, he would be found to be free from the blemishes, and to unite the excellencies of them all. Like Fabius, he was prudent; like Hannibal, he was unappalled by difficulties; like Cyrus, he conciliated affection; like Cimon, he was frugal; like Philopemon, he was humble; and like Pompey, he was successful. If we compare him with characters in the Sacred Records, he combined the exploits of Moses and Joshua, not only by conducting us safely across the Red Sea, and through the wilderness, but by bringing us into the promised land; like David, he conquered an insulting Goliath, and rose to the highest honors from an humble station; like Hezekiah, he ruled, and like Josiah at his death, there is a mourning "as the mourning of Hadadrimmon, in the valley of Megiddon." Nor is the mourning confined to us, but extends to all the wise and good who ever heard of his name. The Generals whom he opposed will wrap their hilts in black, and stern Cornwallis drop a tear.—LINN, WILLIAM, 1800, *Funeral Eulogy on Washington, Feb. 22.*

If Washington possessed ambition, that passion was, in his bosom, so regulated by principles, or controlled by circumstances, that it was neither vicious, nor turbulent. Intrigue was never employed as the means of its gratification, nor was personal aggrandizement its object. The various high and important stations to which he was called by the public voice, were unsought by himself; and, in consenting to fill them, he seems rather to have yielded to a general conviction that the interests of his country would be thereby promoted, than to an avidity for power. . . . Endowed by nature with a sound judgment, and an accurate discriminating mind, he feared not that laborious attention which made him perfectly master of those subjects, in all their relations, on which he was to decide: and this essential quality was guided by an unvarying sense of moral right, which would tolerate the employment, only, of those means that would bear the most rigid examination; by a fairness of intention which neither sought nor required disguise: and by a purity of virtue which was not only untainted, but unsuspected.—MARSHALL, JOHN, 1805-35, *The Life of George Washington, vol.* II, *pp.* 447, 448.

He was as fortunate as great and good. Under his auspices, a civil war was conducted with mildness, and a revolution with order. Raised himself above the influence of popular passions, he happily directed these passions to the most useful purposes. Uniting the talents of the soldier with the qualifications of the statesman, and pursuing, unmoved by difficulties, the noblest end by the purest means, he had the supreme satisfaction of beholding the complete success of his great military and civil services, in the independence and happiness of his country.—BANCROFT, AARON, 1807, *The Life of George Washington, vol.* II, *p.* 218.

Of these private deeds of Washington very little has been said. In most of the elegant orations pronounced to his praise, you see nothing of Washington below the clouds—nothing of Washington the dutiful son—the affectionate brother—the cheerful school-boy—the diligent surveyor—the neat draftsman—the laborious farmer—the widow's husband—the orphan's father—the poor man's friend. No! this is not the Washington you see; 'tis only Washington, the HERO, and the Demigod—Washington the sun-beam in council, or the storm in war.—WEEMS, MASON L., 1810, *The Life of George Washington, p.* 5.

Washington had a large thick nose, and it was very red that day, giving me the impression that he was not so moderate in the use of liquors as he was supposed to be. I found afterward that this was a peculiarity. His nose was apt to turn scarlet in a cold wind. He was standing near a small camp-fire, evidently lost in thought and making no effort to keep warm. He seemed six feet and a half in height, was as erect as an Indian, and did not for a moment relax from a military attitude. Washington's exact height was six feet two inches in his boots. He was then a little lame from striking his knee against a tree. His eye was so gray that it looked almost white, and he had a troubled look on his colorless face. He had a piece of woollen tied around his throat and was quite hoarse. Perhaps the throat trouble from which he finally died had its origin about then. Washington's boots were enormous. They were number 13. His ordinary walking-shoes were number 11. His hands were large in proportion, and he could not buy a glove to fit him and had to have his gloves made to order. His mouth was his strong feature, the lips being always tightly compressed.

That day they were compressed so tightly as to be painful to look at. At that time he weighed two hundred pounds, and there was no surplus flesh about him. He was tremendously muscled, and the fame of his great strength was everywhere. . . . His lungs were his weak point, and his voice was never strong. He was at that time in the prime of life. His hair was a chestnut brown, his cheeks were prominent, and his head was not large in contrast to every other part of his body, which seemed large and bony at all points. His finger-joints and wrists were so large as to be genuine curiosities. As to his habits at that period I found out much that might be interesting. He was an enormous eater, but was content with bread and meat, if he had plenty of it. But hunger seemed to put him in a rage. It was his custom to take a drink of rum or whiskey on awakening in the morning. Of course all this was changed when he grew old. I saw him at Alexandria a year before he died. His hair was very gray, and his form was slightly bent. His chest was very thin. He had false teeth, which did not fit and pushed his under lip outward.—ACKERSON, DAVID, 1811, *Letter to his Son.*

Where may the wearied eye repose
Where gazing on the Great;
Where neither guilty glory glows
Nor despicable state?
Yes, one—the first, the last, the best,
The Cincinnatus of the West,
Whom envy dared not hate—
Bequeathed the name of Washington,
To make man blush, there was but one.
—BYRON, LORD, 1814, *Ode to Napoleon.*

Perhaps the strongest feature in his character was prudence, never acting until every circumstance, every consideration, was maturely weighed; refraining if he saw a doubt, but, when once decided, going through with his purpose, whatever obstacles opposed. His integrity was most pure, his justice the most inflexible I have ever known. . . . On the whole, his character was in its mass, perfect; in nothing bad, in few points indifferent; and it may truly be said, that never did nature and fortune combine more perfectly to make a man great, and to place him in the same constellation with whatever worthies have merited from man an everlasting remembrance. For his was the singular destiny and merit, of leading the armies of his country successfully through an arduous war, for the establishment of its independence; of conducting its councils through the birth of a government, new in its forms and principles, until it had settled down into a quiet and orderly train; and of scrupulously obeying the laws through the whole of his career, civil and military, of which the history of the world furnishes no other example.— JEFFERSON, THOMAS, 1814, *Letter to Dr. Walter Jones, Jan. 2.*

Dilke, whom you know to be a Godwin-perfectibility man, pleases himself with the idea that America will be the country to take up the human intellect where England leaves off. I differ there with him greatly: a country like the United States, whose greatest men are Franklins and Washingtons, will never do that: they are great men doubtless; but how are they to be compared to those, our countrymen, Milton and the two Sidneys? The one is a philosophical Quaker, full of mean and thrifty maxims; the other sold the very charger who had taken him through all his battles.—KEATS, JOHN, 1818, *Letter to George Keats, Oct.* 29; *Works, ed. Forman, vol.* III, *p.* 242.

Washington is another of our perfect characters; to me a most limited, uninteresting sort. The thing is not only to avoid error, but to *attain* immense masses of truth. The ultra-sensual *surrounds* the sensual and gives it meaning, as eternity does time. Do I understand this? Yes, partly, I do.—CARLYLE, THOMAS, 1833, *Journal, Life by Froude, vol.* II, *p.* 300.

The disinterested virtue, prophetic wisdom, and imperturbable fortitude of Washington.—ALISON, SIR ARCHIBALD, 1833–42, *History of Europe During The French Revolution, vol.* XIV, *p.* 2.

On my return to Philadelphia in May, 1796, I saw for the first time, in company with my father and uncle, Stuart's portrait. We all agreed that although beautifully painted, and touched in a masterly style, as a *likeness* it was inferior to its merit as a painting—the complexion being too fair and florid, the forehead too flat, eyebrows too high, eyes too full, nose too broad, about the mouth too much inflated, and the neck too long. Such were the criticisms made by artists and others during the life time of Washington. This is truth, and should be a matter of history. After the death of Washington, it was my opinion and deep-felt regret that

there existed no portrait which characteristically recorded the countenance of that great man. With the hope, therefore, of finding something that would at least gratify my own feelings, I made many attempts to combine in a separate picture what I conceived to be the merits of my father's and my own studies, and with various success, always to gratify some willing purchaser, but never to satisfy myself, till the seventeenth trial, which resulted, under extraordinary excitements, in accomplishing the portrait which is now in the Senate chamber at Washington. These efforts were solely to gratify my own feelings and admiration of the character of the great original; and I had every right to do so, without reference to any other artist's claim.—PEALE, REMBRANDT, 1834, *To William Dunlap, Dec.* 27.

He is eminently conspicuous as one of the great benefactors of the human race, for he not only gave liberty to millions, but his name now stands, and will for ever stand, a noble example of high and low. He is a great work of the Almighty Artist, which none can study without receiving purer ideas and more lofty conceptions of the grace and beauty of the human character. He is one that all may copy at different distances, and whom none can contemplate without receiving lasting and salutary impressions of the sterling value, the inexpressible beauty of piety, integrity, courage, and patriotism, associated with a clear, vigorous, and well-poised intellect. . . . He is already become the saint of liberty, which has gathered new honours by being associated with his name; and when men aspire to free nations, they must take him for their model.—PAULDING, JAMES KIRKE, 1835, *Life of George Washington, p.* 283.

To the historian, indeed, there are few characters that appear so little to have shared the common frailties and imperfections of human nature; there are but few particulars that can be mentioned even to his disadvantage. It is understood, for instance, that he was once going to commit an important mistake as a general in the field; but he had at least the very great merit of listening to Lee (a man whom he could not like, and who was even his rival), and of *not* committing the mistake.—SMYTH, WILLIAM, 1839, *Lectures on Modern History, Lecture* xxxvi.

Washington
Doth know no other language than the one
We speak : and never did an English tongue
Give voice unto a larger, wiser mind.
You'll task your judgment vainly to point
out
Through all this desp'rate conflict, in his
plans
A flaw, or fault in execution. He
In spirit is unconquerable, as
In genius perfect.
—CALVERT, GEORGE HENRY, 1840, *Arnold and Andre.*

However, to say nothing of eloquence, Washington had not those brilliant and extraordinary qualities, which strike the imagination of men at the first glance. He did not belong to the class of men of vivid genius, who pant for an opportunity of display, are impelled by great thoughts or great passions, and diffuse around them the wealth of their own natures, before any outward occasion or necessity calls for its employment. Free from all internal restlessness, and the promptings and pride of ambition, Washington did not seek opportunities to distinguish himself, and never aspired to the admiration of the world. This spirit, so resolute, this heart so lofty, was profoundly calm and modest. Capable of rising to a level with the highest destiny, he might have lived in ignorance of his real power, without suffering from it, and have found, in the cultivation of his estates, a satisfactory employment for those energetic faculties, which were to be proved equal to the task of commanding armies and founding a government. But, when the opportunity presented itself, when the exigence occurred, without effort on his part, without any surprise on the part of others, indeed rather, as we have just seen, in conformity with their expectations the prudent planter stood forth a great man. He had, in a remarkable degree, those two qualities which, in active life, make men capable of great things. He could confide strongly in his own views, and act resolutely in conformity with them, without fearing to assume the responsibility.—GUIZOT, FRANÇOIS PIERRE GUILLAUME, 1840, *An Essay on the Character of Washington and his Influence in the Revolution of the United States of America.*

High over all whom might or mind made
great,
Yielding the conqueror's crown to harder
hearts,
Exalted not by politician's arts,
Yet with a will to meet and master fate,
And skill to rule a young, divided State ;
Greater by what was not than what was
done—
Alone on History's height stands Washington ;
And teeming Time shall not bring forth his
mate ;
For only he, of men, on earth was sent,
In all the might of mind's integrity ;
Ne'er as in him truth, strength, and wisdom
blent ;
And that his glory might eternal be,
A boundless country is his monument,
A mighty nation his posterity.
—WHITE, RICHARD GRANT, 1842, *George Washington.*

The nearest approach to universality of genius in intellect is Shakspeare ; in will, Napoleon ; in harmony of combination, Washington. It is singular that Washington is not generally classed among men of genius. Lord Brougham declares him to be the greatest man that ever lived, but of moderate talents,—as if being the soul of a revolution and the creator of a country did not suppose energies equal to those employed in the creation of a poem,—as if there were any other certain test of genius but its influence, any other measure of the power of a cause but the magnitude of its effects !— WHIPPLE, EDWIN P., 1848-71, *Literature and Life, p.* 159.

The picture of a man beside whom, considered physically, any English nobleman whom I have seen would look like common clay.—HAWTHORNE, NATHANIEL, 1855, *English Note-Books, Sep.* 14.

The character of Washington may want some of those political elements which dazzle and delight the multitude, but it possessed fewer inequalities and a rarer union of virtues than perhaps ever fell to the lot of one man. Prudence, firmness, sagacity, moderation, and overruling judgment, an immovable justice, courage that never faltered, patience that never wearied, truth that disdained all artifice, magnanimity without alloy. It seems that if Providence had endowed him in a preëminent degree with the qualities requisite to fit him for the high destiny he was called upon to fulfill. . . . The fame of Washington stands apart from every name in history : shining with a truer light and more benignant glory.— IRVING, WASHINGTON, 1855-59, *Life of George Washington.*

History, which shows us many a more dazzling character, shows none so grandly consistent, so splendid in disinterestedness, so free from conceit, yet so determined in duty, so true and tender in friendship, yet able to put aside every personal consideration when the good of the country and the great cause of Freedom were in question. What manner of people ought we to be in return for this great gift? Let us bless God that America, having produced one such son, may bring forth others like him, when the day of trial shall come, as it may come, even to us, favored as we are above all the nations of the earth. There is more hope, not less, of another Washington, from having had the first.— —KIRKLAND, CAROLINE MATILDA, 1856, *Memoirs of Washington, p. 501.*

In his person, Washington was six feet high, and rather slender. His limbs were long; his hands were uncommonly large, his chest broad and full, his head was exactly round, and the hair brown in manhood, but gray at fifty; his forehead rather low and retreating, the nose large and massy, the mouth wide and firm, the chin square and heavy, the cheeks full and ruddy in early life. His eyes were blue and handsome, but not quick or nervous. He required spectacles to read with at fifty. He was one of the best riders in the United States, but, like some other good riders, awkward and shambling in his walk. He was stately in his bearing, reserved, distant, and apparently haughty. Shy among women, he was not a great talker in any company, but a careful observer and listener. He read the natural temper of men, but not always aright. He seldom smiled. He did not laugh with his face, but in his body, and while calm above, below the diaphragm his laughter was copious and earnest. Like many grave persons, he was fond of jokes and loved humorous stories. He had negro storytellers to regale him with fun and anecdotes at Mount Vernon. He was not critical about his food, but fond of tea. He took beer or cider at dinner, and occasionally wine. He hated drunkenness, gaming, and tobacco. He had a hearty love of farming, and of private life. There was nothing of the politician in him, no particle of cunning. He was one of the most industrious of men. Not an elegant or accurate writer, he yet took great pains with style, and, after the Revolution, carefully corrected the letters he had written in the time of the French War, more than thirty years before. He was no orator, like Jefferson, Franklin, Madison, and others, who had great influence in American affairs. He never made a speech. . . . Cromwell is the greatest Anglo-Saxon who was ever a ruler on a large scale. In intellect, he was immensely superior to Washington; in integrity, immeasurably below him. For one thousand years no king in Christendom has shown such greatness, or gives us so high a type of manly virtue. He never dissembled. He sought nothing for himself. In him there was no unsound spot; nothing little or mean in his character. The whole was clean and presentable. We think better of mankind because he lived, adorning the earth with a life so noble. . . . God be thanked for such a man.—PARKER, THEODORE, 1858-70, *Historic Americans.*

Upon the banks of the Potomac, which for four years have been swept by the desolating storms of war, where tens of thousands of the bravest sons of the Republic have gone down in the shock of fratricidal strife, is one sacred spot in the presence of which war has forgotten its passion, and assumed, for the moment, the virtues of white-robed Peace. A simple tomb there marks the place where Liberty has erected her chosen altar on this earth. Thanks be to God that every American heart that pulsates lovingly towards the Father of his Country—and whose does not?—may claim that altar for his own! Let us, on this day, with reverent step and worshipful feeling, approach it with votive offerings. Let us come as Americans, who still have one country and one destiny, and unite with our countrymen all over the globe, in acts of grateful commemoration. In this land, united to our own by the most cherished traditions, and which from mothers' lips we learned to love, let us unite in devout thanksgiving, that the Temple of Liberty erected by Washington and his compeers, stands to-day, after its fiery trial, more firm in its foundations, more fair in its beauty, its portals thrown more widely open for the solace and refuge of humanity.—PUTNAM, JAMES O., 1866, *Birthday of Washington Celebrated in Paris, Feb. 22, p. 3.*

Soldier and statesman, rarest unison;
High-poised example of great duties done
Simply as breathing, a world's honors worn
As life's indifferent gifts to all men born;
Dumb for himself, unless it were to God,
But for his barefoot soldiers eloquent,
Tramping the snow to coral where they trod,
Held by his awe in hollow-eyed content;
Modest, yet firm as Nature's self; unblamed
Save by the men his nobler temper shamed;
Never seduced through show of present good
By other than unsetting lights to steer
New-trimmed in Heaven, nor than his stead-
    fast mood
More steadfast, far from rashness as from
    fear;
Rigid, but with himself first, grasping still
In swerveless poise the wave-beat helm of
    will;
Not honored then or now because he wooed
The popular voice, but that he still with-
    stood;
Broad-minded, higher-souled, there is but one
Who was all this and ours, and all men's,
—Washington.
—LOWELL, JAMES RUSSELL, 1875, *Under
the Old Elm.*

To the appointment of Washington, far
more than to any other single circumstance, is due the ultimate success of the
American Revolution, though in purely intellectual powers, Washington was certainly inferior to Franklin, and perhaps to
two or three of his colleagues. . . . His
mind was not quick or remarkably original.
His conversation had no brilliancy or wit.
He was entirely without the gift of eloquence, and he had very few accomplishments. He knew no language but his own,
and except for a rather strong turn for
mathematics, he had no taste which can be
called purely intellectual. There was
nothing in him of the meteor or the cataract, nothing that either dazzled or overpowered. A courteous and hospitable
country gentleman, a skilful farmer, a very
keen sportsman, he probably differed little
in taste and habits from the better members of the class to which he belonged; and
it was in a great degree in the administration of a large estate and in assiduous attention to county and provincial business
that he acquired his rare skill in reading
and managing men.—LECKY, WILLIAM
EDWARD HARTPOLE, 1882, *A History of
England in the Eighteenth Century, vol.*
III, *ch.* xii, *pp.* 468, 469.

Of Washington we know at least that
as he gave himself without reserve to the
welfare of his country, as neither ambition

or any personal object animated him, so
his happiness could not have been exposed
to the causes which afflict the aspiring
and self-seeking; that as he was not a man
of genius, so he did not suffer the pains
of genius; and that all the enduring satisfaction which great deeds, wise counsels,
and disinterested services can give to the
heart of man must have been his.—CUR-
TIS, GEORGE TICKNOR, 1882, *Washington's
Acceptance of the First Presidency, Harper's Magazine, vol.* 64, *p.* 523.

George Washington is now a cold statue
enshrouded in Fourth of July smoke; he is
a teashop chromo and a character that
seldom is dragged from unused histories
except to be belittled by comparison with
some smaller man of later days. While
he lived, Washington was a warm-blooded,
clear-headed, clean-hearted man, a hard
working farmer, a conscientious employer,
a loyal husband, a hearty friend, an unselfish soldier, an honest neighbor, a stout-
hearted patriot, a jolly good fellow and a
consistent Christian. He paid close attention to whatever was going on about him
or within his means of information, was
superior to prejudice and partiality, and
apparently believed that any man could do
anything upon which he set his mind.—
HABBERTON, JOHN, 1884, *George Washington (American Worthies), Preface.*

The world has done ample justice to the
character of Washington. His own countrymen, after death had put its solemn
seal upon his career and services, did him
more than justice, and all but idolised his
memory. He was not great in the highest
sense of the word. He was not brilliant.
He was not even successful, except by aids
which he could not have anticipated, and
which it would have been better for the
self-love of his country if he had never
accepted. He wore out evil fortune
mainly by the incapability which he shared
with the English, from whom he sprang,
of never knowing when he was beaten, and
by the dogged pertinacity and perseverance
which are characteristics of the race. He
was essentiality a good man; and though
subject to occasional fits of violence, was
cautious, prudent, just, honourable, unwearied in the pursuit of the right, and
inflexible in his adherence to it when discovered. He was a man of his age—a
little in advance of it, perhaps, but never
so much in advance of it as to incur the

reproach of being rash, impracticable, or utopian. Living, he attracted but little love—as little as Aristides the Just; but dead, he commanded the admiration of Europe and the affectionate veneration of America, as one, "who was first in war, first in peace, and first in the hearts of his countrymen."—MACKAY, CHARLES, 1885, *The Founders of the American Republic*, p. 141.

The stately column that stretches heavenward from the plain whereon we stand bears witness to all who behold it, that the covenant which our fathers made, their children have fulfilled. In the completion of this great work of patriotic endeavor there is abundant cause for national rejoicing, for while this structure shall endure it shall be to all mankind a steadfast token for the affectionate and reverent regard in which this people continue to hold the memory of Washington. Well may he ever keep the foremost place in the hearts of his countrymen.— ARTHUR, CHESTER A., 1885, *On Presenting the Washington National Monument to the People, Feb. 21.*

Washington stands alone and unapproachable, like a snow peak rising above its fellows into the clear air of morning, with a dignity, constancy, and purity which have made him the ideal type of civic virtue to succeeding generations. No greater benefit could have befallen the republic than to have such a type set from the first, before the eye and mind of the people.— BRYCE, JAMES, 1888, *The American Commonwealth, vol.* I, *p.* 641.

"The American Fabius." "The Atlas of America." "The Cincinnatus of the West." "The Deliverer of America." "The Father of his Country." "The Flower of the Forest." "The Lovely Georgius."—FREY, ALBERT R., 1888, *Sobriquets and Nicknames, p.* 477.

He was not perhaps exactly joyous or gay of nature, but he had a contented and happy disposition, and, like all robust, well-balanced men, he possessed strong animal spirits and a keen sense of enjoyment. He loved a wild, open-air life, and was devoted to rough out-door sports. He liked to wrestle and run, to shoot, ride or dance, and to engage in all trials of skill and strength, for which his great muscular development suited him admirably. With such tastes, it followed almost as a matter

of course that he loved laughter and fun. Good, hearty country fun, a ludicrous mishap, a practical joke, all merriment of a simple, honest kind, were highly congenial to him, especially in his youth and early manhood. . . . He knew human nature well, and had a smile for its little weaknesses when they came to his mind. It was this same human sympathy which made him also love amusements of all sorts; but he was as little their slave as their enemy. No man ever carried great burdens with a higher or more serious spirit, but his cares never made him forbidding, nor rendered him impatient of the pleasure of others. . . . He had, indeed, in all ways a thoroughly well-balanced mind and temper. In great affairs he knew how to spare himself the details to which others could attend as well as he, and yet he was in no wise a despiser of small things. . . . He did not have the poetical and imaginative quality so strongly developed in Lincoln. Yet he was not devoid of imagination, although it was here that he was lacking, if anywhere. He saw facts, knew them, mastered and used them, and never gave much play to fancy; but as his business in life was with men and facts, this deficiency, if it was one, was of little moment. . . . I see in Washington a great soldier who fought a trying war to a successful end impossible without him; a great statesman who did more than all other men to lay the foundations of a republic which has endured in prosperity for more than a century. I find in him a marvellous judgment which was never at fault, a penetrating vision which beheld the future of America when it was dim to other eyes, a great intellectual force, a will of iron, an unyielding grasp of facts, and an unequaled strength of patriotic purpose. I see in him too a pure high-minded gentleman of dauntless courage and stainless honor, simple and stately of manner, kind and generous of heart.—LODGE, HENRY CABOT, 1889, *George Washington (American Statesmen), vol.* II, *pp.* 367, 374, 375, 384, 388.

We always gladly concede that Washington was good, but we are not always so sure that he was great. But a man's greatness is measured by his service to mankind. If, without ambition and without crime, righteously to lead a people to independence through a righteous war; then, without precedent and amid vast and incalculable hostile forces, to organize their government, and establish in every department the fundamental principles of the policy which has resulted in marvellous national power and prosperity, and untold service to liberty throughout the world; and to do all this without suspicion or reproach, with perfect dignity and sublime repose,—if this be greatness, do you find it more in Alexander or Pericles, Cæsar or Alfred, in Charlemagne or Napoleon Bonaparte, or in George Washington? As this majestic arch will stand here, through the long succession of years, in the all-revealing light of day, visible at every point and at every point exquisitely rounded and complete, so in the searching light of history stands Washington, strong, simple, symmetrical, supreme, beloved by a filial nation, revered by a grateful world.—CURTIS, GEORGE WILLIAM, 1890, *The Washington Memorial Arch, May* 30; *Orations and Addresses, vol.* III, *p.* 196.

Let us thank God that he has lived, and that he has given to us the highest and best example of American citizenship. And let us especially be grateful that we have this sacred memory, which spanning time, vicissitude, and unhappy ailenation, calls us together in sincere fellowship and brotherly love on "The birthday of George Washington." — CLEVELAND, GROVER, 1890, *The Character of George Washington, Writings and Speeches, ed. Parker, p.* 351.

Washington was to the confederacy all in all. Without him it would have been ten times lost, and the names of the politicians who had drawn the country into the conflict would have gone down to posterity linked with defeat and shame. History has hardly a stronger case of an indispensable man. His form, like all other forms of the revolution, has no doubt been seen through a golden haze of panegyric. We can hardly number among the greatest captains a general who acted on so small a scale and who, though he was the soul of the war, never won a battle. . . . Carlyle, who threatened "to take George down a peg or two," might have made good his threat. But he could not have stripped Washington of any part of his credit for patriotism, wisdom and courage; for the union of enterprise with prudence; for integrity and truthfulness; for

simple dignity of character; for tact and forbearance in dealing with men; above all for serene fortitude in the darkest hour of his cause and under trials from the perversity, insubordination, jealousy and perfidy of those around him severer than any defeat. . . . Wellington might be more of an aristocrat than Washington, less of a democrat he could hardly be. Washington insisted that his officers should be gentlemen, not men fit to be shoeblacks. He drew a most undemocratic distinction between the officer and the private soldier.—SMITH, GOLDWIN, 1893, *The United States, an Outline of Political History, pp.* 96, 97.

He had the English feeling of never knowing when he was beaten; and his own courageous enthusiasm finally infected the men whom he led. His personal influence was greater than any leader on his side. Lee and Gates might have had a certain amount of romantic enthusiasm attached to them when successful, but when they failed their influence failed too. Through success and failure, through want and privation, as well as through victory, Washington, the only general of them all who never left his men through the weary years of war, even to go to his beloved home, save on two brief occasions, won year by year their increasing reverence and regard. It was this that made George Washington one of the leaders of military history. A leader of men; not from victories in the field, but from that higher and nobler leadership of being their sympathetic comrade through pain and toil as well as through success, which is rarer than generalship.—KING, LIEUT.-COLONEL COOPER, 1894, *George Washington, p.* 273.

There have been three distinct eras in Washington-olatry. The generation which fought the Revolution, framed and adopted the Constitution, and established the United States were impressed with the most profound·veneration, the most devoted affection, the most absolute idolatry for the hero, sage, statesman. In the reaction that came in the next generation against "the old soldiers," who for thirty years had assumed all the honors and enjoyed all the fruits of the victory that they had won, accelerated by the division in American sentiment for or against the French Revolution, it came to be felt, as the younger generation always will feel.

that the achievements of the veterans had been greatly overrated and their demigod enormously exaggerated. They thought, as English Harry did at Agincourt, that "Old men forget: yet all shall be forgot, but they'll remember with advantages what feats they did that day." The fierce attacks of the Jeffersonian Democracy on Washington, his principles, his life, and his habits, exercised a potent influence in diminishing the general respect for his abilities felt by the preceding generation; and Washington came to be regarded as a worthy, honest, well-meaning gentleman, but with no capacity for military and only mediocre ability in civil affairs. The estimate continued from the beginning of Jefferson's administration to the first of Grant's. Neither Marshall nor Irving did much during that period to place him in a proper historical light. The official and judicial statement of the case by Chief-Justice Marshall never reached the popular ear, and the laudatory style of Washington Irving did not impress the popular conviction. But in the last twenty-five years there has been a steady drift toward giving Washington his proper place in history and his appropriate appreciation as soldier and statesman. The general who never won a battle is now understood to have been the Revolution itself, and one of the great generals of history. The statesman who never made a motion, nor devised a measure, nor constructed a proposition in the convention of which he was president, is appreciated as the spirit, the energy, the force, the wisdom which initiated, organized, and directed the formation of the Constitution of the United States and the Union by, through, and under it; and therefore it seems now possible to present him as the Virginian soldier, gentleman, and planter, as a man, the evolution of the society of which he formed a part, representative of his epoch, and his surroundings, developed by circumstances into the greatest character of all time—the first and most illustrious of Americans.— JOHNSON, GEN. BRADLEY T., 1894, *General Washington (Great Commanders), Preface, p. vii.*

There can be no doubt that Washington during the whole of his life had a soft heart for women, and especially for good looking ones, and both in his personal intercourse and in his letters he shows himself very much more at ease with them than in his relations with his own sex. . . . The question whether Washington was a faithful husband might be left to the facts already given, were it not that stories of his immorality are bandied about in clubs, a well-know clergyman has vouched for their truth, and a United States senator has given further currency to them by claiming special knowledge on the subjects. Since such are the facts, it seems best to consider the question and show what evidence there actually is for these stories, that at least the pretended "letters," etc., which are always being cited, and are never produced, may no longer have credence put in them, and the true basis for all the stories may be known and valued at its worth.—FORD, PAUL LEICESTER, 1896, *The True George Washington, pp.* 84, 105.

Washington hardly seems an American, as most of his biographers depict him. He is too colorless, too cold, too prudent. He seems more like a wise and dispassionate Mr. Alworthy, advising a nation as he would a parish, than like a man building states and marshaling a nation in a wilderness. But the real Washington was as thoroughly an American as Jackson or Lincoln. What we take for lack of passion in him was but the reserve and self-mastery natural to a man of his class and breeding in Virginia. He was no parlor politician, either. He had seen the frontier, and far beyond it where the French forts lay. He knew the rough life of the country as few other men could. His thoughts did not live at Mount Vernon. He knew difficulty as intimately and faced it always with as quiet a mastery as William the Silent. — WILSON, WOODROW, 1896, *Mere Literature and Other Essays, p.* 201.

I know of no instance in which sectional feelings disturbed his impartiality, nor do I know of a single Southern or Virginia statesman with whom he can be grouped. One reason of this is obvious—he was that *rara avis* in those days, a self-made Virginian; for in his early years he was thrown largely on his own resources. This was not the case with the other great Virginians of the Revolution, save Patrick Henry; and Henry's career showed traces of the shiftlessness that nearly always accompanied Virginian poverty. Washington, then, was always something more than a Virginian or a Southerner. He has always belonged to America and the nation; yet I do not think he could have developed all the features of his rounded character anywhere else than in the Virginia of the eighteenth century.—TRENT, WILLIAM P., 1897, *Southern Statesmen of the Old Regime, p.* 42.

Of the many thousand victims of these heroic methods, the most illustrious was George Washington, who, but for medical treatment, might probably have lived a dozen or fifteen years into the nineteenth century. When Washington in full vigour found that he had caught a very bad cold he sent for the doctors, and meanwhile had half a pint of blood taken from him by one of his overseers. Of the three physicians in attendance, one was his dear friend, the good Scotchman, Dr. James Craik, "who from forty years' experience," said Washington, "is better qualified than a dozen of them put together." His colleague, Dr. Elisha Dick, said, "Do not bleed the General; he needs all his strength." But tradition prevailed over common sense, and three copious bleedings followed, in the last of which a quart of blood was taken. The third attendant, Dr. Gustavus Brown, afterwards expressed bitter regret that Dr. Dick's advice was not followed. Besides this wholesale bleeding, the patient was dosed with calomel and tartar emetic and scarified with blisters and poultices; or, as honest Tobias Lear said, in a letter written the next day announcing the fatal result, "every medical assistance was offered, but without the desired effect." — FISKE, JOHN, 1897, *Old Virginia and Her Neighbours, vol.* II, *p.* 260.

FAREWELL ADDRESS

When last in Philadelphia, you mentioned to me your wish, that I should *redress* a certain paper which you had prepared. As it is important that a thing of this kind should be done with great care, and much at leisure touched and retouched, I submit a wish, that, as soon as you have given it *the body* you mean it to have, it may be sent to me.—HAMILTON, ALEXANDER, 1796, *Letter to Washington, May* 10.

Even if you should think it best to throw the whole into a different form, let me request, notwithstanding, that my draught may be returned to me (along with yours)

with such amendments and corrections as to render it as perfect as the formation is susceptible of; curtailed if too verbose; and relieved of all tautology not necessary to enforce the ideas in the original or quoted part. My wish is that the whole may appear in a plain style, and be handed to the public in an honest, unaffected, simple garb. — WASHINGTON, GEORGE, 1796, *Letter to Alexander Hamilton, May* 15.

With respect to his farewell address, to the authorship of which, it seems, there are conflicting claims, I can state to you some facts. He had determined to decline re-election at the end of his first term, and so far determined, that he had requested Mr. Madison to prepare for him something Valedictory, to be addressed to his constituents on his retirement. This was done, but he was finally persuaded to acquiesce in a second election, to which no one more strenuously pressed him than myself, from a conviction of the importance of strengthening, by longer habit, the respect necessary for that office, which the weight of his character only could effect. When, at the end of his second term, his valedictory came out, Mr. Madison recognized in it several passages of his draught, several others, we were both satisfied, were from the pen of Hamilton, and others from that of the President himself. These he probably put into the hands of Hamilton to form into a whole, and hence it may all appear in Hamilton's hand-writing, as if it were all his composition.—JEFFERSON, THOMAS, 1823, *To Johnson, June* 12; *Writings, ed. Ford, vol.* X, *p.* 228.

Washington's Farewell Address is full of truths important at all times, and particularly deserving consideration at the present. With a sagacity which brought the future before him, and made it like the present, he saw and pointed out the dangers that even at this moment most imminently threaten us. I hardly know how a greater service of that kind could now be done to the community, than by a renewed and wide diffusion of that admirable paper, and an earnest invitation to every man in the country to reperuse and consider it. Its political maxims are invaluable; its exhortations to love of country and to brotherly affection among citizens, touching; and the solemnity with which it urges the observance of moral duties, and impresses the power of religious obligation, gives to it the highest character of truly disinterested, sincere, parental advice.—WEBSTER, DANIEL, 1832, *The Character of Washington, Works, vol. I, p. 227.*

This composition is not unworthy of him, for it is comprehensive, provident, affectionate, and wise.—SMYTH, WILLIAM, 1839, *Lectures on Modern History, Lecture* xxxvi.

The document was in every respect a masterly production, and formed a fitting close to Washington's official career.—CHANNING, EDWARD, 1895, *The United States of America, 1765-1865, p.* 150.

Although no claim seems to have been made for it, Madison has clearly a share with Hamilton in any honor arising from its literary merit. It is to Hamilton's credit that he used Madison's introductory, since it could hardly be improved upon; and this shows that he was not seeking fame for himself in rendering Washington the assistance requested. If the inception of the address and the substance of it were Washington's, and the literary style was largely that of Madison, what was there in it, it may be asked, that was the distinctive work of Hamilton? While the draft prepared by Washington was more than a desultory enumeration of precepts, recommendations, and warnings, while it embodied his thought and feeling upon the subjects touched with some method, and in language dignified and forceful, it was not yet, in form and finish, such a paper as he intended his Farwell Address to be. It was for Hamilton to "form anew," to "redress," and "much at leisure, touch and retouch." His work was that of the lapidary upon the diamond. It was his to transform the draft of Washington, and to reproduce from it a luminous and unique gem which, as a public paper, should, as he said, "wear well, progress in approbation with time, and redound to future reputation." He brought to bear upon that labor the yearning of a patriotic heart and the vast resources of a trained and logical mind. . . . Authorship, in its restricted literary sense, is not a term properly applicable to the Farewell Address, unless joint authorship be accredited to all who in any way participated in it. The thought and the expression of Washington, Madison, and Hamilton were singularly intermingled

in it, besides some suggestions by Judge Jay, to whom, at Washington's request, it was on one occasion shown. But the *origin* of the Address was not in Madison, Hamilton, or Jay. Whatever their subsequent contributions may have been, the Address did not generate in either of them. It was conceived in the mind, and nurtured in the heart, of Washington. Not only did he conceive the intention and nurture the desire to deliver a parting message to his countrymen, but he selected and determined the subjects he intended to press upon their consideration. . . . Great honor is due to Hamilton and Madison for eminent services in the preparation of the Farewell Address; but the evidence is conclusive that Washington was, in the only applicable sense of the term, the author of it.—WASHINGTON, BUSHROD C., 1899, *Was Washington Author of his Farewell Address? Forum, vol.* 27, *pp.* 153, 154,155.

GENERAL

In his letters he is plain; in his public addresses elegant; in all he is correct, expressing in a small compass his clear conception, without tiresome nervosity or any parade of ornament. In attending to what has fallen from his pen the connection between modes of thinking and writing, between character and composition, is apparent. His writings are worded with the strong and pleasing features of sincerity, simplicity and dignity.—DAVIS, JOHN, 1800, *Address Before the Massachusetts Historical Society.*

That he wrote in his own hand all his official letters during the Revolution, it would be as preposterous to suppose, as that Marlborough, or Bonaparte, or Wellington, or any other great commander, was the penman of all the letters to which he subscribed his name. Compositions of this kind are not adduced as evidences of the genius, the rhetorical ingenuity, the brilliant fancy, the felicitous invention, or the literary accomplishments of the persons, whose name they bear. The value to be attached to them, and the high consideration, which they justly claim, are derived from the circumstance of their being records of great events, expressing the opinions and unfolding the designs of men, in whose conduct and motives the destinies of nations are involved. They are the highest and purest fountains of history, and by whatever hand the written language is constructed, the spirit and substance, the principles, facts, arguments, and purposes, must necessarily be considered as flowing from him by whose name they are sanctioned, he is responsible for the whole; his character and reputation, as well as the vital interests of the cause entrusted to him, are at stake.— SPARKS, JARED, 1834, ed., *The Writings of George Washington; being his Correspondence, Addresses, Messages, and Other Papers, Official and Private, With a Life of the Author.*

We deem it unnecessary to make any extracts from the correspondence, as specimens of its style or substantial character. It is more valuable as materials for history, and as illustrating the character of the writer, than from the intrinsic interest of the contents, which relate in general to matters of mere detail. It has all the prominent qualities of the subsequent revolutionary correspondence, and exhibits a complete maturity of mind, as well as style. The latter was probably somewhat improved by revision at a later period of life.—EVERETT, ALEXANDER HILL, 1834, *The Washington Papers, North American Review, vol. 39, p. 494.*

The character of the author transcends all vulgar praise. The interest of the events, which form the subjects of his writings, is inferior to nothing in history. . . . We consider the publication of a standard edition of the writings of Washington, as a matter of importance in a national point of view. Of the auspicious influence of the principles of Washington over public opinion throughout the country, which happily is still highly operative, much must be ascribed to the unexpended force of his personal ascendency and the freshly-remembered power of his personal intercourse. These, with the lapse of time, must daily grow fainter.—EVERETT, EDWARD, 1838, *Sparks's Life and Writings of Washington, North American Review, vol. 47, p. 319.*

The name of Washington may be introduced in a collection of American literature, rather to grace it than to do honor to him. In any strict sense of the word, Washington was not a literary man; he never exercised his mind in composition on any of those topics abstracted from common life, or its affairs, which demanded either art or invention. He prepared no book of elaborate industry.—Yet he was always scrupulously attentive to the claims of literature; elegant and punctilious in the acknowledgment of compliments from authors and learned institutions; and had formed a style which is so peculiar that it may be recognised by its own ear-mark. . . . The handwriting of Washington, large, liberal, and flowing, might be accepted as proof of the honesty of the figures. Indeed this same handwriting is a capital index of the style of all the letters, and may help us to what we would say of its characteristics. It is open, manly, and uniform, with nothing minced, affected, or contracted. It has neither the precise nor the slovenly style which scholars variously fall into; but a certain grandeur of the countenance of the man seems to look through it. Second to its main quality of truthfulness, saying no more than the writer was ready to abide by, is its amenity and considerate courtesy. Washington had, at different times, many unpleasant truths to tell; but he could always convey them in the language of a gentleman. He wrote like a man of large and clear views. . . . In fine, a critical examination of the writings of Washington will show that the man here, as in other lights, will suffer nothing by a minute inspection.—DUYCKINCK, EVERT A. AND GEORGE L., 1855-65-75, *Cyclopædia of American Literature, ed. Simons, vol. I, pp. 189, 191.*

The writings of Washington produced chiefly in the camp surrounded by the din of arms, are remarkable for clearness of expression, force of language, and a tone of lofty patriotism. They are second to none of similar character in any nation, and they display powers which, had they been devoted to literature, would have achieved a position of no secondary character.—BOTTA, ANNE C. LYNCH, 1860, *Hand-Book of Universal Literature, p. 528.*

In the letters and documents known to be his, his style is simple, direct, and explicit, but bald and fragmentary. Successive ideas were arranged by no rhetorical plan, in no logical order, and with no continuous flow of diction, but jotted down abruptly, and without connective clauses, as they occurred spontaneously to his mind, or were called up by casual associations. His military training, and his incessantly busy life through the entire period in which the graces of diction might have been cultivated, precluded the abundant leisure and the careful practice by which alone he could have become a master of sentences, as he was of noble deeds.— PEABODY, A. P., 1860, *Washington's Farewell Address, North American Review, vol.* 90, *p.* 209.

He has been edited into obscurity, like a Greek play. Where the genial and friendly soldier wrote "Old Put," a respectable editor, devoid of the sense of humor, has substituted General Putman; until, at length, a lover of the man has to defend him against the charge of perfection.—PARTON, JAMES, 1879, *The Traditional and the Real Washington, Magazine of American History, vol.* 3, *p,* 465.

Washington himself claims direct personal recognition in the field of letters only by his clear and incisive, though seldom highly-polished, correspondence; for his celebrated "Farewell Address" is understood to have been mainly the joint work of himself, Madison, and Jay.— NICHOL, JOHN, 1880–85, *American Literature, p.* 74.

Was a writer who made some small mark upon incipient American literature, and who at any rate, may be mentioned among the political writers of his time. Without collegiate education, and never paying special attention to the art of style, he wrote plainly and clearly, in a somewhat individual way. Twelve large volumes trimly include his once scattered and desultory manuscripts, chiefly letters and documents.—RICHARDSON, CHARLES F., 1887, *American Literature,* 1607–1885, *vol.* I, *p.* 203.

As a letter writer Washington had few superiors; his journals, notably the account of his famous journey to the Ohio, first published in 1754, are written in clear, concise English; and his farewell addresses are full of a wisdom and a stateliness worthy in every way of the great man who produced them. — PATTEE, FRED LEWIS, 1896, *A History of American Literature, p.* 81.

Of couse, no one goes to the letters of Washington, in the expectation of finding there sprightliness of thought, flexibly, or ease of movement; yet, in point of diligence and productiveness, he was one of the great letter-writers of that age, while all that he ever wrote has the incommunicable worth of his powerful and noble character—sincerity, purity, robustness, freedom from all morbid vapors, soundness of judgment ripened under vast responsibility. Who can hope ever to know the mind and conscience of our Revolution, its motive, its conduct, its stern and patient purpose, or its cost, without studying Washington's letters?—TYLER, MOSES COIT, 1897, *The Literary History of the American Revolution,* 1763–1783, *vol.* I, *p.* 13.

Washington's correspondence and "Farewell Address" would scarcely, from another, constitute a claim to literary renown.—BATES, KATHARINE LEE, 1897, *American Literature, p.* 72.

Josiah Tucker
1712–1799

Born in Wales; graduate of St. John's College, Oxford, rector of St. Stephen's, Bristol; prebend, 1755; dean of Gloucester, 1758 till his death. He was a thorough student, and careful writer on political economy and subjects pertaining to religion, and published several pamphlets in the beginning of the contest between the English government and its American colonies in favor of the colonists.—PECK, HARRY THURSTON, ed., 1898, *The International Cyclopædia, vol.* XIV, *p.* 616.

GENERAL

A case in which the whole *British nation* were, in one particular, manifestly puzzleheaded, except *one* man : who was accordingly derided by all. In the dispute between Great Britain and her American Colonies. . . . Dean Tucker, standing quite alone, wrote a pamphlet to show that the separation would be *no loss* at all, and that we had best give them the independence they coveted, at once, and in a friendly way. Some thought he was writing in jest, the rest despised him as too absurd to be worth answering. But now (and for above half a century) every one admits that he was quite right, and regrets that his view was not adopted. . . . Of all the clever men, then, that at that time existed, and many of whom spoke eloquently on each side, Tucker was the only one who was not puzzle-headed. And he obtained some small share of late credit, but present contempt.—WHATELY, RICHARD, 1856, ed. *Bacon's Essays, with Annotations, Essay* LV.

Josiah Tucker, whose works on Trade anticipated some of the established doctrines on political economy.—BURTON, JOHN HILL, 1860, ed. *Autobiography of Rev. Dr. Alexander Carlyle.*

A bitter Tory, but one of the best living writers on all questions of trade.—LECKY, WILLIAM EDWARD HARTPOLE, 1882, *A History of England in the Eighteenth Century, vol.* III, *ch.* xii, *p.* 421.

Holds a distinguished place among the immediate predecessors of Smith. Most of his numerous productions had direct reference to contemporary questions, and, though marked by much sagacity and penetration are deficient in permanent interest. . . . The most important of his general economic views are those relating to international commerce. He is an ardent supporter of free-trade doctrines, which he bases on the principle that there is between nations no necessary antagonism, but rather a harmony, of interests, and that their several natural advantages and different aptitudes naturally prompt them to exchange. He had not, however, got quite clear of mercantilism, and favored bounties on exported manufactures and the encouragement of population by a tax on celibacy.—INGRAM, J. K., 1885, *Political Economy, Encyclopædia Britannica, Ninth edition, vol.* XIX, *p.* 378.

Tucker was a very shrewd though a rather crotchety and inconsistent writer. He is praised by McCulloch and others who shared his view of the inutility of colonies; and he argued very forcibly that a "shop-keeping nation" would not improve its trade by beating its customers. The war with the colonies would, he said, hereafter appear to be as absurd as the crusades. He retained, as McCulloch complains, a good many of the prejudices which later economists sought to explode. He is not clear about the "balance of trade"; he believes in the wickedness of forestalling and regrating, and wishes to stimulate population by legislation. In spite, however, of his inconsistencies and narrowness of views, he deserves credit, as Turgot preceived, for attacking many of the evils of monopolies, and was so far in sympathy with the French economists and with Adam Smith. He deserves the credit of anticipating some of Adam Smith's arguments against various forms of monopoly, but, though he made many good points, he was not equal to forming a comprehensive system.— STEPHEN, LESLIE, 1899, *Dictionary of National Biography, vol.* LVII, *p.* 283.

William Cowper
1731–1800

Born, at Great Berkhamstead Rectory, 15 Nov. 1731. At a school in Market Street, Herts, 1737–39. Under the care of an oculist, 1739–41. At Westminster School, 1741–49. Student at Middle Temple, 29 April 1748. Articled to a solicitor for three years, 1750. Called to Bar, 14 June 1754. Depression of mind began. Commissioner of Bankrupts, 1759–65. Contrib. nos. 111, 115, 134, 139 to "The Connoisseur," 1756; to Duncombe's "Translations from Horace," 1756–57; to "The St. James's Chronicle," 1761. Symptoms of insanity began to appear; taken to a private asylum at St. Albans, Dec. 1763. Left there and settled in Huntingdon, June 1765. Began to board in house of Mr. and Mrs. Unwin there, Nov. 1765. Removed with Mrs. Unwin and family to Olney, Bucks, autumn of 1767. Assisted John Newton, curate of Olney, in parochial duties. Fresh attack of insanity, 1773–74. On recovery, showed more activity in literary work. Friendship with Lady Austen, 1781–83. Contrib. to "Gentleman's Mag.," June 1784 and Aug. 1785. Removed from Olney to Weston, Nov. 1786. Attack of insanity, 1787. Contrib. to "Analytical Review," Feb. 1789. Crown pension of £300 a year granted, 1794. Visited various places in Norfolk with Mrs. Unwin, summer of 1795. Settled in Dereham Lodge, Oct. 1795. Died there, 25 April 1800. Buried in Dereham Church. *Works:* "Olney Hymns" (anon., with J. Newton), 1779; "Anti-Thelyphthora" (anon.), 1781; "Poems," 1782; "John Gilpin" (anon.), 1783; "The Task," 1785 (the fly-leaf bears the words: "Poems. . . .

Vol. II."); Translation of "Iliad and Odyssey," 1791; "Poems" ("On the receipt of my mother's picture"—"The Dog and the Water Lily"), 1798. *Posthumous:* "Adelphi," 1802; "Life and Posthumous Writings," ed. by Hayley, 1803 (2nd edn., 1804; 3rd. entitled "Life and Letters," 1809); "Memoir of the early life of William Cowper" (autobiographical), 1816; "Table Talk," 1817; "Hymns," 1822; "Private Correspondence" (2 vols.), 1824; "Poems, the early productions of W. Cowper," ed. by J. Croft, 1825; "Minor Poems," 1825;" "The Negro's Complaint," 1826. *He translated:* "Homer," 1791; "The Power of Grace," by Van Lier, 1792; "Poems by Mme. De la Motte Guion" (posth.), 1801; Milton's Latin and·Italian poems (posth.), 1808. *Collected Works:* ed. by Newton (10 vols.), 1817; ed. by Memes (3 vols.), 1834; ed. by Grimshawe (8 vols.), 1835; ed. by Southey (15 vols.), 1836-37. *Life:* by Hayley, 1803; by Bruce, in Aldine edn. of Works, 1865; by Benham, in Globe edn. of Works, 1870.—SHARP, R. FARQUHARSON, 1897, *A Dictionary of English Authors, p.* 67.

PERSONAL

The morning is my writing time, and in the morning I have no spirits. So much the worse for my correspondents. Sleep, that refreshes my body, seems to cripple me in every other respect. As the evening approaches, I grow more alert, and when I am retiring to bed, am more fit for mental occupation than at any other time. So it fares with us whom they call nervous. By a strange inversion of the animal economy, we are ready to sleep when we have most need to be awake, and go to bed just when we might sit up to some purpose. The watch is irregularly wound up, it goes in the night when it is not wanted, and in the day stands still.—COWPER, WILLIAM, 1784, *Letter to John Newton, Feb.* 10.

IN MEMORY
OF WILLIAM COWPER, ESQ.
BORN IN HERTFORDSHIRE, 1731.
BURIED IN THIS CHURCH, 1800.

Ye, who with warmth the public triumph feel
Of talents, dignified by sacred zeal,
Here, to devotion's Bard devoutly just,
Pay your fond tribute due to Cowper's dust!
England, exulting in his spotless fame,
Ranks with her dearest sons his fav'rite name;
Sense, fancy, wit, suffice not all to raise
So clear a title to affection's praise:
His highest honors to the heart belong;
His virtues form'd the magic of his song.
—HAYLEY, WILLIAM, 1800, *Inscription on Monument, St. Edmund's Chapel, East Dereham Church.*

From his figure, as it first appeared to me, in his sixty-second year, I should imagine that he must have been very comely in his youth; and little had time injured his countenance, since his features expressed, in that period of life, all the powers of his mind, and all the sensibility of his heart. He was of a middle stature, rather strong than delicate in the form of his limbs: the colour of his hair was a light brown, that of his eyes a bluish, and his complexion ruddy. In his dress he was neat, but not finical; in his diet temperate and not dainty. He had an air of pensive reserve in his deportment, and his extreme shyness sometimes produced in his manners an indescribable mixture of aukwardness and dignity; but no being could be more truly graceful when he was in perfect health and perfectly pleased with his society. Towards women, in particular, his behaviour and conversation was delicate and fascinating in the highest degree.—HAYLEY, WILLIAM, 1803, *Life and Posthumous Writings of William Cowper, vol.* II, *p.* 124.

It appears to the present writer, from a careful perusal of that instructive piece of biography published by Mr. Hayley, that Cowper, from his infancy, had a tendency to errations of the mind; and without admitting this fact in some degree, it must seem extremely improbable that the mere dread of appearing as a reader in the house of lords should have brought on his first settled fit of lunacy. Much, indeed, has been said of his uncommon shyness and diffidence, and more, perhaps, than the history of his early life will justify. Shyness and diffidence are common to all young persons who have not been early introduced into company, and Cowper, who had not, perhaps, that advantage at home, might have continued to be shy when other boys are forward. But had his mind been, even in this early period, in a healthful state, he must have gradually assumed the free manners of an ingenuous youth, conscious of no unusual imperfection that should keep him back. At school, we are told, he was trampled upon by the ruder boys who took advantage of his weakness, yet we find that he mixed in their amusements, which must in some degree have advanced him on a level with them: and what is yet more extraordinary, we find him associating with men of more gaiety than pure morality admits, and sporting with the utmost vivacity and wildness with Thurlow and others, when it was natural to expect that he would have been glad to court solitude for the purposes of study, as well as for the indulgence of his habitual shyness, if, indeed, at this period it was so habitual as we are taught to believe.—CHALMERS, ALEXANDER, 1814, *English Poets, Life of Cowper.*

I could have wished a stronger tone of severity to have been expressed, in the authority last referred to, against the publication of those "Memoirs of Cowper," 1816, 8vo., which were written by himself, and which betrayed his morbid and unhappy state of feelings in an attempt to commit suicide. There is perhaps no species of mental depravation, connected with a lust of lucre, more deserving of reproof and castigation, than that which led to the publication of these Memoirs. First, this composition could never have been intended for the public eye; and was therefore on every account sacred. Secondly, it could only lead to the debasement of that amiable creature, whom it was the bounden duty of the publisher to have kept as free from all imputation as the pages of Hayley had justly represented him. Thirdly, if the feeling which lead to this publication were a religious one, I must say that it is one of the most perverted and mischievous views of religion with which I am acquainted. Cant, or lucre, in its genuine form, was, I fear, the source or the motive of this highly injudicious publication. We love and respect Cowper too sincerely, to "drag his frailties from their drear abode."—DIBDIN, THOMAS FROGNALL, 1824, *The Library Companion, p. 533, note.*

Had Cowper's mind been sane, no rational views of religion could unquestionably have produced the hallucination; but when his mind was clouded with hypochondria, as in early life before it had taken any definite form, nothing was wanting to convert his melancholy into monomania, and to change the wandering reveries of the former into the settled gloom of the latter, but the exclusive application of

enthusiasm to a single subject. . . . Cowper, from his earliest years, was delicate in constitution, and timid in his disposition. Excessive application to professional studies in the Temple increased the delicacy of his health, the nervous system and the cerebral organs became disturbed or disordered in their functions, and his natural timidity merged into a morbid sensibility which wholly disqualified him for the active duties of that profession in which he had been so improperly placed.—MADDEN, R. R., 1833, *The Infirmities of Genius, vol. II, pp. 47, 99.*

His prevailing insanity, so far as it could be called insanity at all, in those long intervals of many years, during which his mind was serene and active, his habit of thought playful, and his affections more and more fervent, was simply the exclusion of a personal religious hope to such a degree as to seem like habitual despair. This despair was his insanity, for it could be only madness that could produce it, after such a revelation of the glory of God in the face of Jesus Christ as he had been permitted in the outset to enjoy. If Paul had gone deranged after being let down from his trance and vision in the third heavens, and the type of his derangement had been the despair of ever again beholding his Saviour's face in glory, and the obstinate belief of being excluded by Divine decree from heaven, though his affections were all the while *in* heaven, even that derangement would have been scarcely more remarkable than Cowper's. In the case of so delicate and profound an organization as his, it is very difficult to trace the effect of any entanglement or disturbance from one side or the other between the nervous and mental sensibilities of his frame. There was a set of Border Ruffians continually threatening his peace, endeavoring to set up slavery instead of freedom, and ever and anon making their incursions, and defacing the title-deeds to his inheritance, which they could not carry away; and Cowper might have assured himself with the consolation that those documents would not be destroyed, being registered in heaven, and God as faithful to them, as if their record in his own heart had been always visible. — CHEEVER, GEORGE B., 1843, *Lectures on the Life, Genius and Insanity of Cowper, Introduction, p. vii.*

O poets! from a maniac's tongue was poured
    the deathless singing!
O Christians! at your cross of hope, a hope-
    less hand was clinging!
O men! this man in brotherhood your weary
    paths beguiling,
Groaned inly while he taught you peace, and
    died while ye were smiling!
And now, what time ye all may read through
    dimming tears his story,
How discord on the music fell, and darkness
    on the glory,
And how when one by one, sweet sounds
    and wandering lights departed,
He wore no less a loving face because so
    broken-hearted;
He shall be strong to sanctify the poet's high
    vocation,
And bow the meekest Christian down in
    meeker adoration:
Nor ever shall he be, in praise, by wise or
    good forsaken;
Named softly as the household name of one
    whom God hath taken.
—BROWNING, ELIZABETH BARRETT, 1844,
Cowper's Grave.

Here Cowper was fond of coming, and sitting within the hollow boll for hours, around him stretching the old woods, with their solitude and the cries of woodland birds. The fame which he has conferred on this tree has nearly proved its destrucition. Whole arms and great pieces of its trunk have been cut away with knife and axe and saw to prepare different articles from. The Marquis of Northampton, to whom the chase belongs, has had multitudes of nails driven in to stop the progress of this destruction, but, finding that not sufficient, has affixed a board bearing this inscription: "Out of respect to the memory of the poet Cowper, the Marquis of Northampton is particularly desirous of preserving this oak. Notice is hereby given that any person defacing or otherwise injuring it will be prosecuted according to law." In stepping round the Yardley Oak it appeared to me to be, at the foot, about thirteen yards in circumference.—HOWITT, WILLIAM, 1847, *The Homes and Haunts of the Most Eminent British Poets, vol.* I, *p.* 458.

Few things are more touching than the history of Cowper's life, as it is related, with more than feminine grace, innocence, and tenderness, in his own inimitable letters; and we can understand the devotedness with which so many of his friends sacrificed their whole existence to cherish and console a being so gifted, so fascinating, and so unhappy. The dim shadow, too, of an early and enduring, but hopeless love, throws over the picture a soft and pensive tint, like moonlight on some calm landscape.—SHAW, THOMAS B., 1847, *Outlines of English Literature, p.* 305.

Words are wanting to describe the sense of relief with which we close this saddest, most mysterious narrative. The man were granite who could refrain from sympathy, amounting to bitter anguish, with this poor unfortunate. And then, there are questions arising out of his story, which descend into the very depths of those awful relations which connect us with God and Eternity. Why did this man suffer thus? Why was he ever born to endure such wretchedness? What the *rationale* of his long martyrdom and darkness? . . . Truly William Cowper was still more a marvellous, than he was a mild and gentle spirit,—stronger, even, than he was amiable—a very Prometheus chained to his rock, let us call him,—the rock being his rugged, deep-rooted woe; the chain his lengthened life; and himself the Titan, in his earnestness, lofty purpose, and poetic power.—GILFILLAN, GEORGE, 1854, *ed. Cowper's Poetical Works, Life, vol.* I, *pp.* xxv, xxvii.

His talent is but the picture of his character, and his poems but the echo of his life. . . . He was one of those to whom women devote themselves, whom they love maternally, first from compassion, then by attraction, because they find in them alone the contrivances, minute and tender attentions, delicate observances which men's rude nature cannot give them, and which their more sensitive nature nevertheless craves.—TAINE, H. A., 1871, *History of English Literature, tr.* Van Laun, *vol.* II, *bk.* iv, *ch.* i, *pp.* 243-4.

It must have been a disappointment to Cowper that the songs or ballads he wrote on the slave trade, for the express purpose of being sung in the streets, and by that means widely circulated among the people, came to nothing. "If you hear ballads sung in the streets on the hardships of the negroes in the islands," he writes to Mr. Rose, "they are probably mine." But Mr. Rose heard them not, nor was the song writer ever to have that satisfaction himself.—JACOX, FRANCIS, 1872, *Self-Heard in Song, Aspects of Authorship, p.* 48.

So sad and strange a destiny has never before or since been that of a man of genius. With wit and humour at will, he was nearly all his life plunged in the darkest melancholy. Innocent, pious and confiding, he lived in perpetual dread of everlasting punishment: he could only see between him and heaven a high wall which he despaired of ever being able to scale; yet his intellectual vigour was not subdued by affliction. What he wrote for amusement or relief in the midst of "supreme distress," surpasses the elaborate efforts of others made under the most favourable circumstances; and in the very winter of his days, his fancy was as fresh and blooming as in the spring and morning of existence. That he was constitutionally prone to melancholy and insanity, seems undoubted; but the predisposing causes were as surely aggravated by his strict and secluded mode of life.—CHAMBERS, ROBERT, 1876, *Cyclopædia of English Literature, ed. Carruthers.*

If Cowper's retirement was virtuous, it was so because he was actively employed in the exercise of his highest faculties: had he been a mere idler, secluded from his kind, his retirement would not have been virtuous at all. His flight from the world was rendered necessary by his malady, and respectable by his literary work; but it was a flight and not a victory. His misconception was fostered and partly produced by a religion which was essentially ascetic, and which, while it gave birth to characters of the highest and most energetic beneficence, represented salvation too little as the reward of effort, too much as the reward of passive belief and of spiritual emotion.—SMITH, GOLDWIN, 1880, *Cowper (English Men of Letters.)*, p. 52.

The time of William Cowper seems now, so far as Westminster is concerned, equally remote as that of Raleigh. It was in the churchyard of St. Margaret's, while he was a scholar at Westminster, that he received one of those impressions which had so strong an effect on his after life. Crossing the burial-ground one dark evening, towards his home in the school, he saw the glimmering lantern of a grave-digger at work. He approached to look on, with a boyish craving for horrors, and was struck by a skull heedlessly thrown out of the crowded earth. To the mind of William Cowper

such an accident had an extraordinary significance. In after life he remembered it as the occasion of religious emotions not readily suppressed. On the south side of the church, until the recent restorations, there was a stone the inscription of which suggests the less gloomy view of Cowper's character. It marked "The Burial-Place of Mr. John Gilpin;" the date was not to be made out, but it must have been fresh when Cowper was at school, and it would be absurd to doubt that the future poet had seen it, and perhaps unconsciously adopted from it the name of his hero.— LOFTIE, WILLIAM JOHN, 1883–4, *History of London, vol.* II, *ch.* xvi.

William Cowper is one of the strangest and most pathetic figures in the literary history of England. He had much in common with another famous writer, and it would be easy to draw a parallel between William Cowper and Charles Lamb. In nothing is the resemblance closer than in the circumstance that both began by writing poetry and produced much sweet verse, while the prose of each is far more noteworthy than his poetry, and is among the best in the language. If neither had written a line or a sentence, the personal story of each would have ensured his name being remembered. Though the career of both was chequered and painful, yet it has a fascination for every reader, and, of the two, Cowper's is the sadder and the more curious.—RAE, W. FRASER, 1891, *The Bard of Olney, Temple Bar, vol.* 91, *p.* 503.

On the 19th of April it was evident that death was near, and Mr. Johnson ventured to speak of his approaching dissolution as the signal for his deliverance from the miseries of both mind and body. Cowper making fewer objections than might have been supposed, Johnson proceeded to say, "that in the world to which he was hastening, a merciful Redeemer had prepared unspeakable happiness for all His children, and therefore for him." To the first part of this sentence he listened with composure, but upon hearing the concluding words he passionately entreated that no further observations might be made on the subject. He lingered five days longer. On Thursday he sat up as usual in the evening. In the course of the night, when he was exceedingly exhausted, Miss Perowne offered him some refreshment, which he rejected, saying, "What can it signify?" and these were the last words he was heard to utter. At five in the morning a deadly change had taken place in his features, and he remained in an insensible state from that time till about five in the afternoon, when he ceased to breathe, expiring so peacefully that none who stood at his bedside could tell the precise moment of his departure. From the time of his death till the coffin was closed, Mr. Johnson says, "the expression with which his countenance had settled was that of calmness and composure, mingled, as it were, with holy surprise."—WRIGHT, THOMAS, 1892, *The Life of William Cowper*, p. 656.

Intellectually, Cowper is rendered more difficult in appearance, perhaps, than in reality by his malady. He would probably not have been very different as a perfectly sane man; that is to say, he would have at least shown generous sympathies, pure morality, and, above all things, the instincts and conduct of a gentleman, in the very best sense of the word, without joining to them any very vigorous reasoning power or wide faculty of appreciation. His nature, slightly feminine, must always have been more than slightly prejudiced; but his prejudices sometimes contribute to his poetry, and rarely interfere with it. —SAINTSBURY, GEORGE, 1898, *Short History of English Literature*, p. 590.

The country has but little changed in the course of a century. The ruins of Capability Brown's exploits are still traceable at Weston; the square tower of Clifton still looks down upon the spire of Olney; there is still a clump of poplars at Lavendon Mill; there is still a wealth of flowering rushes with their cherry scented blossoms, of broad-leaved plants varying the monotony of the reeds, of purple loosestrife, of blue forget-me-not. An adventurous holiday-maker, who could for a couple of days forego the delights of dusty roads and the rushing wheel, might find a less agreeable pastime than a voyage in a canoe from Newport Pagnell down to Turvey. Thus he might bathe himself in the atmosphere which was breathed by no mean English poet, gliding beneath hills clothed with trees, or between wide meadows; but he would do well not to surrender himself unguardedly to the calm pleasures of plain-sailing, lest he should rue his error lost in the mazes of a reed-bed.—TARVER, J. C., 1900, *Cowper's Ouse, Macmillan's Magazine, vol. 82, p. 144.*

MARY UNWIN

The twentieth year is well-nigh past,
Since first our sky was overcast;
Ah, would that this might be the last!
    My Mary!
Thy spirits have a fainter flow,
I see thee daily weaker grow;
'Twas my distress that brought thee low,
    My Mary!

. . . .

Thy silver locks, once auburn bright,
Are still more lovely in my sight
Than golden beams of orient light,
    My Mary!

. . . .

Partakers of thy sad decline,
Thy hands their little force resign;
Yet, gently prest, press gently mine,
    My Mary!

. . . .

And should my future lot be cast
With much resemblance of the past,
Thy worn-out heart will break at last,
    My Mary!
—COWPER, WILLIAM, 1793, *To Mary.*

I am tedious without being, perhaps, after all, intelligible; but an example may make me so. Mrs. Unwin, the friend of Cowper, felt that the Divine inflictions were mercies, and to be received as such, as sensibly as we feel that the shower, which wets our garment, refreshes the dried up soil. What we regard, in a speculative way, as a thing we ought to believe, was, with her, like the evidence of the senses, and enabled her to bear the severest evils with unshaken and even cheerful patience. In vain would those, who cherish and brood over sorrow, excuse themselves, by depreciating as a kind of apathy the lively faith which supported this Christian heroine, even under the death of her most excellent and only son. What but sensibility of the purest, highest kind led her to do and suffer, in the cause of friendship, more than ever the courage of man or the love of woman achieved? Dying for one's friend was nothing to this. Estranged from all social enjoyments, and having one's sole attention tied down, day after day, and year after year, to the most painful object that heart can conceive—the ghastly form and suspended faculties of a dear friend! What a being must Çowper have been, that could excite such a pure and fervent attachment; and how much beyond the conception of ordinary minds was the tenderness, the constancy, the fortitude, and, above all, the faith of this blessed woman! Lady Hesketh, the good, the generous, and the amiable, tried to fill her place, but sank under it. Miss Fanshawe, who was with Lady H. in the last months of her life, told me that she never recovered the miserable winter she spent with her beloved cousin.— GRANT, ANNE, 1823, *Letters, Sept.* 2; *Memoir and Correspondence, ed. Grant. vol.* III, *p.* 15.

LADY AUSTEN

He was not a famous poet in those days, but a poor invalid recluse, with a shadow of madness and misery about him, whose story was inevitably known to all his neighbours, and about whom there could be no delusion possible; but though all this is against the theory that a brilliant, lively, charming, and very likely fanciful woman, such as Lady Austen seems to have been, meant to marry him, it is quite enough to explain the compassionate interest rapidly ripening into warm friendship which moved her at first. Men like Cowper are always interesting to women, and there can be little doubt that, in the dull neighborhood of Olney, such company and conversation as his would be a godsend to any visitor from livelier scenes. When the new alliance went so far as to induce her to settle in Olney in the adjoining house, with that famous door in the wall first made to facilitate communications between Newton and Cowper, re-opened, a stronger motive is no doubt necessary. But it is a vulgar conclusion that marriage must be thought of wherever a man and woman are concerned, and it was the age for romantic friendships. At all events, whatever was the cause, Lady Austen took up her abode in the deserted vicarage.—OLIPHANT, MARGARET O. W., 1882, *Literary History of England in the End of the Eighteenth and Beginning of the Nineteenth Century, vol.* I, *p.* 55.

The fact now began to dawn upon his mind that Lady Austen was in love with him. The only wonder is that he did not perceive it before. Nobody can blame her for losing her heart to the poet. She saw only the bright and cheerful side of his character, and knew little or nothing of the canker of despair that gnawed continually at his heart. . . . As soon as Cowper discovered in what light Lady Austen regarded him, he perceived that matters could no longer go on as they were. The thought of love—anything more than a brotherly and sisterly love—had never entered his mind, for since his last dreadful derangement at the vicarage he had given up all thoughts of marriage (it should be remembered, too, that he was in his fifty-fourth year), and seeing himself called on to renounce either one lady or the other, he felt it to be his bounden duty to cling to Mrs. Unwin, to whose kindness he had been indebted for so many years. It has been said by some that Mrs. Unwin was jealous of Lady Austen. Very likely she was. When we consider how tenderly and patiently she had watched over Cowper in his dark and dreadful hours, how for so many years she had shared his joys and sorrows, and delighted in his companionship, we need not wonder if some feeling akin to jealousy stirred her when she perceived the danger of her place being taken by one who, though more brilliant, could not possibly love him more. But Mrs. Unwin had no need to fear. Cowper's affections for her, his knowledge of her worth, his gratitude for past services, would not allow him to hesitate. He had hoped that it would be possible to enjoy the friendship of both ladies; but when he discovered that it was necessary to decide between one and the other, he bowed to the painful necessity and wrote Lady Austen "a very tender yet resolute letter, in which he explained and lamented the circumstances that forced him to renounce her society." She in anger burnt the letter, and henceforth there was no more communication between them. — WRIGHT, THOMAS, 1892, *The Life of William Cowper, pp.* 347, 348.

The sprightly Muse, with all her stability of temper, sense of religion, and seriousness of mind, must soon have become disagreeably conscious of the difference between the forced attendance of a wayward and irritable invalid with his thoughts elsewhere, and the effusive *camaraderie* with which he sought her company in the bright days of their first companionship.

"O Love! it is a pleasant thing
A little time, while it is new."

Mrs. Unwin might not have resented the change, but Lady Austen was not Mrs. Unwin, and she "repaired to Bristol." We might have understood the cause of the separation better if the lady had kept Cowper's letter of farewell, but she was so dissatisfied with it that she threw it in the fire—tempted, perhaps, for once in her life, to believe that Methodism was cant. Lady Austen was too exacting, or Cowper was too exacting; anyhow, they could not get on together—any explanation you please except that Mrs. Unwin was jealous. To entertain this explanation for a moment is to commit the most senseless outrage on the memory of a gentle, self-denying woman who bore with all the crazy poet's selfish whims and caprices, and watched over him with more than a mother's love till her own mind gave way under the strain.—MINTO, WILLIAM, 1894, *The Literature of the Georgian Era, ed. Knight, p. 144.*

OLNEY HYMNS
1779

Precious is his memory to every lover of sacred song.—HATFIELD, EDWIN F., 1884, *The Poets of the Church, p. 165.*

Very many of Cowper's hymns, like passages in his longer poems, have become "household words." . . . Cowper—the great Christian poet of England, and, as Willmott justly remarks, pre-eminently the poet of the affections, above any writer in our language—has enriched sacred literature by so many exquisite bursts of poetic inspiration, that it is no easy task to determine which are the best.—SAUNDERS, FREDERICK, 1885, *Evenings with the Sacred Poets, pp. 345, 346.*

As a hymn-writer, except for one very remarkable composition, Cowper scarcely ranks as high as the Wesleys. He might have taken a much higher place than they —a higher place than almost any writer of hymns of his own time or since—if he could have applied his genius to the work. That was certainly not possible to him at the time when the Olney hymns were written, and at the other periods when it might have been possible he was occupied with greater things. The defect of his hymns was their severe doctrinal character. They are statements of religious belief, for the most part narrow and despondent; and only occasionally, when they reflect what may have been a passing mood of cheerfulness, do they express the aspirations or contentments of simple piety.—COTTERELL, GEORGE, 1897, *Cowper's Letters, The Argosy, vol. 64, p. 152.*

"Hark my Soul" is the most beautiful of all English hymns. It emphasises what is the essence of the Christian faith,—the appeal of Christ to the individual man. It describes in language that is exquisitely simple and true the work of the Saviour for the soul in redemption. In words hardly less powerful than those of St. Paul, it brings home to the heart the truth that He who speaks to us through the Gospel is the fulness of Him who filleth all in all, and then it closes by bringing the poor human heart, conscious of its own feebleness, into its true attitude of absolute reliance on the Divine peace, in which it lives and moves, and has its being.—SINCLAIR, WILLIAM MACDONALD, 1897, *Hymns that have Helped, ed. Stead, p. 146.*

"God Moves in a Mysterious Way." Cowper's hymn has helped multitudes to bear up under the blows of apparently adverse fortune. Within a year of the writing of this beautiful and touching hymn, Cowper's reason reeled, and he endeavoured to commit suicide by drowning in the Ouse. It is some poor consolation to know that his attempt at suicide was not a suicide of despair, but rather the perversion of the spirit of resignation and joyful submission which finds expression in the hymn. Newton says that Cowper tried to take his life, believing it was a sacrifice which God required at his hands. The accepted legend is that he had proposed to commit suicide at a certain place, but as the driver of the postchaise could not find it, he returned home without putting his purpose into execution, and there composed this hymn.—STEAD, W. T., 1897, *Hymns that have Helped, p. 115.*

JOHN GILPIN
1783

When I received your account of the great celebrity of "John Gilpin," I felt myself both flattered and grieved. Being man, and having in my composition all the ingredients of which other men are made, and vanity among the rest, it pleased me to reflect that I was on a sudden become so famous, and that all the world was busy inquiring after me; but the next moment, recollecting my former self, and that thirteen years ago, as harmless as John's history is, I should not then have written it, my spirits sank, and I was ashamed of my success. Your letter was followed the next post by one from Mr. Unwin. You tell me that I am rivalled by Mrs. Bellamy; and he, that I have a competitor for fame, nor less formidable, in the Learned Pig. Alas! what is an author's popularity worth, in a world that can suffer a prostitute on one side, and a pig on the other, to eclipse his brightest glories? I am therefore sufficiently humbled by these considerations; and unless I should hereafter be ordained to engross the public attention by means more magnificent than a song, am persuaded that I shall suffer no real detriment by their applause. I have produced many things, under the influence of despair, which hope would not have permitted to spring. But if the soil of that melancholy, in which I have walked so long, has thrown up here and there an unprofitable fungus, it is well, at least, that it is not chargeable with having brought forth poison. Like you, I see, or think I can see, that Gilpin may have his use. Causes, in appearance trivial, produce often the most beneficial consequences; and perhaps my volumes may now travel to a distance, which, if they had not been ushered into the world by that notable horseman, they would never have reached.—COWPER, WILLIAM, 1785, *Letter to Rev. John Newton, April 22.*

The story of John Gilpin has perhaps given as much pleasure to as many people as anything of the same length that ever was written.—HAZLITT, WILLIAM, 1818, *Lectures on the English Poets, Lecture* V.

THE TASK
1785

Is not "The Task" a glorious poem? The religion of "The Task," bating a few scraps of Calvinistic divinity, is the religion of God and Nature; the religion that exalts and ennobles man.—BURNS, ROBERT, 1795, *Letter to Mrs. Dunlop, Dec. 25.*

The "Task," beginning with all the peaceful attractions of sportive gaiety, rises to the most solemn and awful grandeur, to the highest strain of religious solemnity. Its frequent variation of tone is masterly in the greatest degree, and the main spell of that inexhaustible enchantment which hurries the reader through a flowery maze of many thousand verses, without allowing him to feel a moment of languor or fatigue. Perhaps no author, ancient or modern, ever possessed, so completely as Cowper, the nice art of passing,

by the most delicate transition, from subjects to subjects that might otherwise seem but little or not at all allied to each other, the rare talent

"Happily to steer
From grave to gay, from lively to severe."

—HAYLEY, WILLIAM, 1803, *The Life and Posthumous Writings of William Cowper, vol.* II, *p.* 142.

In the "Task" are to be found descriptive powers not inferior to those of Thomson, mingled with a strain of the happiest satiric humour, and interspersed with touches of the most exquisite pathos and sublimity; while the whole inculcates, in versification of unparalleled sweetness and simplicity, the noblest lessons of morality and religion.—DRAKE, NATHAN, 1810, *Essays, Illustrative of the Rambler. Adventurer, and Idler, vol.* II, *p.* 333.

It seems to have been begun without design like a morning's ramble, and to have been continued and completed without labour. Nevertheless, in this walk how many beautiful and even sublime objects rise upon the view. Cowper appears to bear in his style a very great resemblance to the Roman Ovid. There is in both the same elegance of diction and unstudied easiness of expression. But the Christian poet must be allowed to bear the palm from the Pagan in sentiment if he is equalled by him (which I do not think) in other respects. The pious fervour which goes through the page of Cowper will preserve it from oblivion, while the blasphemous scoffings of a witty infidel, should they pass down to another generation, will be viewed only with mingled indignation and contempt.— THIRLWALL, CONNOP, 1810, *To John Candler, Oct.* 24; *Letters, eds. Perowne and Stokes, p.* 16.

Cowper's first volume, partly from the grave character of the longer pieces and the purposely rugged, rambling, slip-shod versification, was long neglected, till "The Task," the noblest effort of his muse, composed under the inspiration of cheerfulness, hope, and love, unbosoming the whole soul of his affections, intelligence, and piety,—at once made our countrymen feel that neither the genius of poesy had fled from our isle, nor had the heart for it died in the breast of its inhabitants. "The Task" was the first long poem from the close of Churchill's brilliant but evanescent career, that awoke wonder, sympathy, and delight by its own ineffable excellence among the reading people of England.— MONTGOMERY, JAMES, 1833, *Lectures on General Literature, Poetry, etc., p.* 303.

Lady Austen has the honor also of having suggested at this time to Cowper the subject of that work which made him the most popular poet of his age, and raised him to a rank in English poetry from which no revolution of taste can detrude him. She had often urged him to try his powers in blank verse: at last he promised to comply with her request, if she would give him a subject. "Oh," she replied, "you can never be in want of a subject; you can write upon any;—write upon this Sofa!" The answer was made with a woman's readiness, and the capabilities of such a theme were apprehended by Cowper with a poet's quickness of perception. —SOUTHEY, ROBERT, 1836-7, *The Life of William Cowper, vol.* I, *p.* 268.

Where is the poem that surpasses the "Task" in the genuine love it breathes, at once towards inanimate and animate existence—in truthfulness of perception and sincerity of presentation—in the calm gladness that springs from a delight in objects for their own sake, without self-reference—in divine sympathy with the lowliest pleasures, with the most short-lived capacity for pain? . . . How Cowper's exquisite mind falls with the mild warmth of morning sunlight on the commonest objects, at once disclosing every detail and investing every detail with beauty! No object is too small to prompt his song—not the sooty film on the bars, or the spotless tea-pot holding the bit of mignonette that serves to chear the dingy town-lodging with a "hint that Nature lives;" and yet his song is never trivial, for he is alive to small objects, not because his mind is narrow, but because his glance is clear and his heart is large.—ELIOT, GEORGE, 1857, *Worldliness and Other-Worldliness: The Poet Young; Essays, pp.* 72, 73.

Incomparably the best poem that any Englishman then living had produced—a poem, too, which could hardly fail to excite in a well constituted mind a feeling of esteem and compassion for the poet, a man of genius and virtue, whose means were scanty, and whom the most cruel of all the calamities incident to humanity had

made incapable of supporting himself by vigorous and sustained exertion.—MACAULAY, THOMAS BABINGTON, 1859, *William Pitt, Critical and Miscellaneous Essays.*

The great beauties of "The Task," and its pure and elevated feeling, can hardly be said to make it a poem of the highest class. The very method of its origin was some bar to success. . . . Towards the end of the First Book he again changes his subject, for the purpose of moralizing. The country and the life therein are contrasted with the town, and this affords the opening for satire, which is just touched in the end of the First Book, but forms the staple for the Second. And splendid satire it is, full of vigour, and energy, and point, sometimes mere good humoured badinage, sometimes full of burning indignation. It is satire of a different kind from that of his former poems; it is less bilious, more free from personality. Yet, Antæus-like, the author loses all his power when he ceases to touch his proper sphere. His faculty of keen observation enables him to lash effectively the false pretentions and follies which he sees. But his reflections upon the world without are of the poorest kind. He foresees the end of the world close at hand. He rails at the natural philosopher who attempts to discover the causes of physical calamities, such as earthquakes and diseases; at the historian who takes the trouble to investigate the motives of remarkable men; at the geologist and the astronomer. For the last especially there is nothing but contempt.—BENHAM, WILLIAM, 1870, *ed., The Poetical Works of William Cowper, Introduction, p.* lvii.

Is the kitchen-garden indeed poetical? To-day perhaps; but to-morrow, if my imagination is barren, I shall see there nothing but carrots and other kitchen stuff. It is my sensation which is poetic, which I must respect, as the most precious flower of beauty. Hence a new style. . . . This is his great poem, "The Task." If we enter into details, the contrast is greater still. He does not seem to dream that he is being listened to; he only speaks to himself. He does not dwell on his ideas, to set them in relief, and make them stand out by repetitions and antitheses: he marks his sensation and that is all. We follow it in him as it is born, and we see it rising from a former one, swelling, falling, remounting, as we see vapour issuing from a spring, and insensibly rising, unrolling and developing its shifting forms. Thought, which in others was curdled and rigid, becomes here mobile and fluent; the rectilinear verse grows flexible; the noble vocabulary widens its scope to let in vulgar words of conversation and life. At length poetry has again become lifelike; we no longer listen to words, but we feel emotions; it is no longer an author but a man who speaks. His life is there perfect, beneath its black lines, without falsehood or concoction; his whole effort is bent on removing falsehood and concoction.—TAINE, H. A., 1871, *History of English Literature, tr. Van Laun, vol.* II, *bk.* iv, *ch.* i, *pp.* 246, 247.

There is a wonderful variety of objects and of thought in this poem; it may be called a universal composition, for the poet gathers up all the phenomena of life, nature, and society, and the colours with which he paints the bright and the dark sides of all things are as brilliant as they are true.—SCHERR, J., 1874, *A History of English Literature, tr. M. V., p.* 164.

Though Cowper sees the outer world as set off against his own personal moods and the interests of man, yet he does not allow these to discolor his scenes or to blur the exactness of their outlines. Fidelity, absolute veracity, characterize his descriptions. He himself says that he took nothing at second-hand, and all his pictures bear witness to this. Homely, of course, flat, tame, was the country he dwelt in and described. But to this day that Huntingdonshire landscape, and the flats by the sluggish Ouse, in themselves so unbeautiful, acquire a charm to the eye of the traveler from the remembered poetry of the "Task" and for the sake of him who wrote it.—SHAIRP, JOHN CAMPBELL, 1877, *On Poetic Interpretation of Nature, p.* 215.

As "Paradise Lost" is to militant Puritanism, so is "The Task" to the religious movement of its author's time. To its character as the poem of a sect it no doubt owed and still owes much of its popularity. Not only did it give beautiful and effective expression to the sentiments of a large religious party, but it was about the only poetry that a strict Methodist or Evangelical could read; while to those whose worship was unritualistic and who were debarred by their principles from the theatre and the concert, anything in the way of art that was not illicit must have been eminently welcome.—SMITH, GOLDWIN, 1880, *Cowper (English Men of Letters), p.* 62.

It is in the second book, "The Timepiece," that the poet takes his highest flight. Nothing finer of its kind has ever been written in the English language than the first half-dozen pages.—HOPE, EVA, 1886, *The Poetical Works of William Cowper (Canterbury Poets), Introduction, p.* xxvi.

Save for a few occasional—and not always fortunate—lapses into familiarity, Cowper's manner of dealing with the domestic is still the manner of the earlier century, still radically opposed to these principles of "natural" poetic diction, on which Wordsworth was afterwards to insist with so much more zeal than discretion, and to delay for many years the acceptance of invaluable truth by exaggerating them in his preaching and rendering them ridiculous in his practice. Cowper is still far from that frank fraternal recognition of the common objects, ideas, and interests of life which is advocated in the famous preface to the "Lyrical Ballads." Poetry in his hands will unbend to common things, but it is always with a too vigilant dignity: she will take notice of the tea-urn and the silk-reels, and the modest indoor pleasures and employments of the country house, but it is all done with the conscious condescension of the squire's wife at the village school treat. And Cowper, moreover, clings still to that leisurely diffuseness of utterance which is so alien to the spirit of the great poetry, pregnant with thought, and eager to bring it to the birth. One reads him sometimes divided between delight in his perfect literary finish and irritation at its prolixity.—TRAILL, HENRY DUFF, 1896, *Social England, vol.* V, *p.* 443.

Cowper's "Task" is almost curiously barren of landscape; and the style does not essentially differ from Thomson's except in that the poet himself is the spectator; whence, naturally, the landscape is more intimate and more devout. This poem, though of much value in its own day, now certainly disappoints. — PALGRAVE, FRANCIS TURNER, 1896, *Landscape in Poetry, p.* 175.

HOMER

1791

My dear friend's Homer is coming abroad. I have received my copy, but the *publication* is not yet. I have cursorily surveyed the first volume; it seems fully equal to what I expected, for my expectations were not high. I do not think it will add to the reputation of the author of the "Task," as a poet; but I hope the *performance* will not be unworthy of him, though the *subject* is greatly beneath the attention of the writer, who has a mind capable of original, great, and useful things; but he could not at the time fix his thoughts upon any thing better—and they who know his state will rather pity than blame him. I hope we shall have no more translations.—NEWTON, JOHN, 1791, *Letter to Hannah More, July* 17; *Memoirs of Hannah More, ed. Roberts.*

You know my admiration for this truly great genius, but I am really grieved that he should lower his aims so far as to stoop to become a mere editor and translator. It is Ulysses shooting from a baby's bow. Why does he quit the heights of Solyma for the dreams of Pindus? "What's Hecuba to him, or he to Hecuba?" In his own original way he has few competitors; in his new walk he has many superiors; he can do the best things better than any man, but others can do middling things better than he.—MORE, HANNAH, 1791, *Letters, ed. Roberts.*

That the translation is a great deal more close and literal, than any that had previously been attempted in English verse, probably will not be disputed by those who are the least disposed to admire it. That the style into which it is translated is a true English style, though not perhaps a very elegant or poetical one, may also be assumed; but we are not sure that a rigid and candid criticism will go farther in its commendation.—JEFFREY, FRANCIS LORD, 1803, *Hayley's Life of Cowper, Edinburgh Review, vol. 2, p.* 85.

No satiety is perceived from reading any quantity of the blank verse of Cowper; and the genius of Homer, the state of manners of the period in which he wrote, and the whole scope and design of his immortal epopees, are infinitely better felt and comprehended in the blank than in the rhymed copy of the venerable bard. The issue will most likely be this, that for insulated passages, Pope will generally be referred to; but that he who wishes to peruse, and for any length of time together, the entire poems of Homer, will have recourse to the labours of Cowper.—DRAKE, NATHAN, 1804, *Essays Illustrative of the Tatler, Spectator and Guardian, vol. III, p.* 94.

I hate Cowper's slow, dry, blank verse, so utterly alien to the spirit of the poem, and the minstrel mode of delivery. How could it have suited any kind of recitative or melody, or the accompaniment of any music? It is like a pursy, pompous, but unpolished man moving laboriously in a stiff dress of office. Those boar and lion hunting similes describing swift motion are dreadfully dragging in this sort of verse. . . . Cowper's poem is like a Camera Lucida portrait—far more unlike in expression and general result than one less closely copied as to lines and features.—COLERIDGE, SARA, 1834, *To Her Husband, Memoir and Letters, ed. Her Daughter, pp.* 92, 93.

Between Cowper and Homer there is interposed the mist of Cowper's elaborate Miltonic manner, entirely alien to the flowing rapidity of Homer.—ARNOLD, MATTHEW, 1861, *Lectures on Homer, p.* 11.

The transition from Pope to Cowper is the change from poetic thraldom to poetic freedom. In the former you are held down to the severest rigor of rhythm, while yet you admire the grace, the finish, and the splendor of the chain which binds you. In the latter you find yourself let loose and range in freedom, unrestrained but by the beautiful order that rules in the very nature of things. In reading Pope, one admires the wonderful subjection of the idea, the thought in its divers phases and relations, its qualities and its measures, to the exactions of the rhyme and the rhythm; in Cowper, one admires the more wonderful incorporation of the idea into the perfect harmonies and melodies of words. One must read Pope with his attention fixed on the rhythm; he must read Cowper with his mind filled and prompted by the thought. There can hardly be supposed a wider contrast than the two present.—DAY, HENRY N., 1868, *Introduction to the Study of English Literature, p.* 340.

Cowper brought such poetic gifts to his work that his failure might have deterred others from making the same hopeless attempt. But a failure his work is; the translation is no more a counterpart of the original, than the Ouse creeping through its meadow is the counterpart of the Ægean rolling before a fresh wind and under a bright sun. Pope delights school-boys; Cowper delights nobody, though, on the rare occasions when he is taken from the shelf, he commends himself, in a certain measure, to the taste and judgment of cultivated men. — SMITH, GOLDWIN, 1880, *Cowper* (*English Men and Letters*), *p.* 93

He brought scholarly tastes and a quick conscience to the work; a boy would be helped more to the thieving of the proper English by Cowper's Homer, than by Pope's; but there was not "gallop" enough in his nature for a live rendering; and he was too far in-shore for the rhythmic beat of the multitudinous waves and too far from the "hollow" ships.—MITCHELL, DONALD G., 1895, *English Lands Letters and Kings, Queen Anne and the Georges, p.* 251.

ON THE RECEIPT OF MY MOTHER'S PICTURE
1798

This is no doubt, as a whole, Cowper's finest poem, at once springing from the deepest and purest fount of passion, and happy in shaping itself into richer and sweeter music than he has reached in any other. It shows what his real originality, and the natural spirit of art that was in him, might have done under a better training and more favorable circumstances of personal situation, or perhaps in another age.—CRAIK, GEORGE L., 1861, *A Compendious History of English Literature and of the English Language, vol.* II, *p.* 381.

Perhaps the most pathetic poem in our language, which the recluse of Olney wrote on the receipt of his mother's picture.— FARRAR, F. W., 1883, *With the Poets, Preface, p.* xviii.

A cousin sent him his mother's portrait. He received it in trepidation, kissed it, hung it where it would be seen last at night, first in the morning, and wrote a poem on it, whose tenderness and pathos, flowing in richer and sweeter music than he had elsewhere reached, are unequalled by anything else he has written, and surpassed by little in the language. Springing from the deepest and purest fount of passion, and shaping itself into mobile and fluent verse, it reveals his true originality, as well as that life-like elegance, that natural spirit of art, wherein consists the great revolution of the modern style.—WELSH, ALFRED H., 1883, *Development of English Literature and Language, vol.* II, *p.* 245.

After reading [Tennyson] Cowper's "Poplar Field," "People nowadays, I believe, hold this style and metre light; I wish there were any one who could put words together with such exquisite flow and evenness." Presently we reached the same poet's stanzas to Mary Unwin. He read them, yet could barely read them, so deeply was he touched by their tender, their most agonizing pathos. And once when I asked him for the "Lines on my Mother's Portrait," his voice faltered as he said he would, if I wished it; but he knew he should break down.—PALGRAVE, FRANCIS TURNER, 1892–97, *Personal Recollections of Tennyson; Alfred Lord Tennyson, A Memoir by His Son, vol.* II, *p.* 501.

SONNETS

Petrarch's sonnets have a more ethereal grace and a more perfect finish; Shakespeare's more passion; Milton's stand supreme in stateliness, Wordsworth's in depth and delicacy. But Cowper's unites with an exquisiteness in the turn of thought which the ancients would have called Irony, an intensity of pathetic tenderness peculiar to his loving and ingenuous nature.—There is much mannerism, much that is unimportant or of now exhausted interest in his poems: but where he is great, it is with that elementary greatness which rests on the most universal human feelings. Cowper is our highest master in simple pathos.—PALGRAVE, FRANCIS TURNER, 1861, *The Golden Treasury, note.*

They never rise to the highest excellence, neither do they fall much below the level of his average compositions. If they embalm no superb thoughts, of which it can be said, as of Herrick's fly in amber:

"The urn was little but the room
More rich than Cleopatra's tomb; "

and if none of them have lines which have become current for their intrinsic beauty or wealth of thought, or for a breadth of application which has caused them to echo alone the decades from his day till ours, they still present refined and elevated sentiments, gracefully, naturally, and poetically, and clothe them in pure and nervous English.—DESHLER, CHARLES D., 1879, *Afternoons with the Poets, p.* 176.

LETTERS

The letters of Cowper . . . form a perfect contrast to Pope's. In the one, I think I see a mind striving to be great, and affecting to be unaffected; in the other, we contemplate, not the studious loftiness, but the playfulness of a mind naturally lofty, throwing at random a ray of sweetness, cheerfulness, and tenderness upon whatever subject occurs, mixed occasionally with severer touches of wisdom, and a mournful, but seldom angry survey of the follies of mankind. We see the playful humour, mingled with melancholy, and the melancholy, mingled with kindness, social feelings, sincerity and tenderness.—BOWLES, WILLIAM LISLE, 1806, *ed. Pope's Works.*

There is something in the letters of Cowper inexpressibly delightful. They possess excellencies so opposite—a naïve simplicity, arising from perfect goodness of heart and singleness of purpose, contrasted with a deep acquaintance with the follies and vices of human nature, and a keen sense of humour and ridicule. They unite the playfulness of a child, the affectionateness of a woman, and the strong sense of a man: they give us glimpses of pleasures so innocent and pure as almost to realise the Eden of our great poet, contrasted with horrors so deep, as even to exceed his power of imagery to express. —HEBER, REGINALD, 1823, *Private Correspondence of Cowper, Quarterly Review, vol.* 30, *p.* 185.

Being neither a blockhead nor conceited, you will take due interest in all that pertains to this saintly sufferer; yet there are blockheads, namely, conceited ones, that will say, "What do the public care for his stockings, or for his oysters, or for the cake that came in its native pan, or the heartless hens that refused to lay eggs to make another cake?" I would have such persons to know that a Cowper, moving in the light of his mental beauty and modest sanctity, irradiates every object that is in contact with him; it is *their* oysters and cakes that are insignificant, because they are so themselves. I wish I knew what kind of garters he wore; how proud and happy I should have been to knit a pair for him: I should have hung

up the wires as Cervantes did his pen, considering them hallowed ever afterwards. —GRANT, ANNE, 1824, *Letters, Apr.* 7; *Memoir and Correspondence, ed. Grant, vol.* III, *p.* 28.

The best of English letter-writers.— SOUTHEY, ROBERT, 1836-7, *The Life of William Cowper.*

The purest and most perfect specimens of familiar letters in the language. Considering the secluded, uneventful course of Cowper's life, the charm in his letters is wonderful; and is to be explained, I believe, chiefly by the exquisite light of poetic truth which his imagination shed upon daily life, whether his theme was man, himself or a fellow-being, or books, or the mute creation which he loved to handle with such thoughtful tenderness. His seclusion did not separate him from sympathy with the stirring events of his time; and, alike in seasons of sunshine or of gloom, there is in his letters an ever-present beauty of quiet wisdom, and a gentle but fervid spirit.—REED, HENRY, 1851-55, *Lectures on English Literature, From Chaucer to Tennyson, p.* 409.

The charm of Cowper's Correspondence consists in this succession of images, of thought, and of shades of meaning unfolded with varying vivacity, but in an equable and peaceful course. In his letters we can best apprehend the true sources of his poetry, of the true domestic poetry of private life: bantering not devoid of affection, a familiarity which disdains nothing which is interesting as being too lowly and too minute, but alongside of them, elevation or rather profundity. Nor let us forget the irony, the malice, a delicate and easy raillery such as appears in the letters I have quoted.—SAINTE-BEUVE, C. A., 1854, *English Portraits, p.* 191.

Cowper's letters are far more than contributions towards his biography. The graceful affectionateness, the shrewd estimate of men and things, the genuine love of fun and appreciation of it in others, all contribute to make his correspondence delightful. In fact, to many readers his prose will be more agreeable than his poetry, though, as in many like cases, his letters were only published because his poetry had made him famous.—BENHAM, WILLIAM, 1883, *ed., Letters of William Cowper, Introduction, p.* xii.

In these select letters, flowing on in the old, sweet, fresh English, one perceives the rare literary faculty, the shy humor, the discrimination, the sound sense, all the many graces of style and many virtues of intrinsic worth that have long been familiar to scholars, and, more than that, one gladly recognizes again the companionable, soft-hearted, pathetic man whose pastimes, whether in gardening, or poetry, or caring for his pets, were a refuge from the most poignant anguish; who played only to escape this terror, and at last failed even in that. . . . Now, it is a very striking fact that while Cowper spent the larger part of his time in religious reading and conversation, and besides meditated in private on the same themes, his letters do not show in any degree that insight into spiritual things which would naturally be looked for from real genius occupied with such subjects. Spirituality should have been his trait if religion was his life, but, in fact, these letters are in this regard barren.—WOODBERRY, GEORGE E., 1884, *Cowper's Letters, The Nation*, vol. 39, p. 57.

His correspondence is unaffected, facile, and often playful. Religion of course forms a substantial part of this, as it so conspicuously did of the author's mind: but it has been noticed, and has been made matter of some reproach from certain quarters, that the religious tone of the letters diminishes very observably after 1785, when Cowper had become an eminent man in literature, and more open consequently to the entanglements of "the world."—ROSSETTI, WILLIAM MICHAEL, 1878, *Lives of Famous Poets*, p. 187.

His letters, like his best poetry, owe their charm to absolute sincerity. . . . His letters are written without an erasure —at leisure but without revision; the spontaneous gaiety is the more touching from the melancholy background sometimes indicated; they are the recreation of a man escaping from torture; and the admirable style and fertility of ingenious illustration make them perhaps the best letters in the language.—STEPHEN, LESLIE, 1887, *Dictionary of National Biography*, vol. XII, p. 401.

Rich mines of pleasure and profit for us all, full to the brim of homely pleasant details which only leisure can find time to note. A man who was even ordinarily busy would never have stopped to observe the things which Cowper tells us about so charmingly.—REPPLIER, AGNES, 1893, *Essays in Idleness*, p. 219.

His letters are his principal work in prose, if not the best of all his work. They differ from most of the prose of the time by the same interval as separates the verse of "The Task" at its best from the verse of "The Botanic Garden." The phrase of Landor, in the preface to the Hellenics, "not prismatic but diaphanous," applies more fitly to the style of Cowper in verse and prose, especially prose, than to any other writer. It is not that the style is insipid or tame; it is alive and light; but it escapes notice, like the prose of Southey, by reason of its perfect accommodation to the matter.—KER, W. P., 1895, *English Prose, ed. Craik*, vol. IV, p. 424.

All good critics have agreed that his letters are not surpassed, perhaps not surpassable. He has more freedom than Gray; he has none of the coxcombry of Walpole and Byron; and there is no fifth name that can be put even into competition with him. Ease, correctness, facility of expression, freedom from convention within his range, truth to nature, truth to art:—these things meet in the hapless recluse of Olney as they had not met for a century—perhaps as they had never met—in English epistles. The one thing that he wanted was strength: as his madness was melancholy, not raving, so was his sanity mild but not triumphant. —SAINTSBURY, GEORGE, 1896, *A History of Nineteenth Century Literature*, p. 6.

GENERAL

I received the letter you did me the honour of writing to me, and am much obliged by your kind present of a book. The relish for reading of poetry had long since left me, but there is something so new in the manner, so easy, and yet so correct in the language, so clear in the expression, yet concise, and so just in the sentiments, that I have read the whole with great pleasure, and some of the pieces more than once.—FRANKLIN, BENJAMIN, 1782, *Letter to Cowper, May 8*.

I am enchanted with this poet; his images so natural and so much his own! Such an original and philosophic thinker! Such genuine christianity! and such a divine simplicity! but very rambling, and the order not very lucid. He seems to put down every thought as it arises, and never to retrench or alter anything.—MORE, HANNAH, 1786, *Letter to Her Sister, Feb; Memoirs. ed. Roberts, vol.* I, *p.* 235.

With England's Bard, with Cowper who
    shall vie?
Original in strength and dignity,
With more than painter's fancy blest, with
    lays
Holy, as saints to heav'n expiring raise.
—MATHIAS, THOMAS JAMES, 1794–98, *The Pursuits of Literature, Eighth ed., p.* 418.

I have been reading "The Task" with fresh delight. I am glad you love Cowper. I could forgive a man for not enjoying Milton; but I would not call that man my friend who should be offended with the "divine chit-chat of Cowper."— LAMB, CHARLES, 1796, *Dec.* 5; *Letters, ed. Ainger, vol.* I, *p.* 52.

It has been thought that Cowper was the first poet who re-opened the true way to nature and a natural style; but we hold this to be a mistake, arising merely from certain negations on the part of that amiable but by no means powerful writer. Cowper's style is for the most part as inverted and artificial as that of the others; and we look upon him to have been by nature not so great a poet as Pope; but Pope, from certain infirmities on his part, was thrown into the society of the world, and thus had to get what he could out of an artificial sphere :—Cowper, from other and more distressing infirmities (which by the way the wretched superstition that undertook to heal, only burnt in upon him) was confined to a still smaller though more natural sphere, and in truth did not much with it, though quite as much perhaps as was to be expected from an organization too sore almost to come in contact with any thing.—HUNT, LEIGH, 1817, *The Examiner.*

The love of nature seems to have led Thomson to a cheerful religion; and a gloomy religion to have led Cowper to a love of nature. The one would carry his fellowmen along with him into nature; the other flies to nature from his fellowmen. In chastity of diction, however, and the harmony of blank verse, Cowper leaves Thomson immeasurably below him; yet still I feel the latter to have been the born poet.—COLERIDGE, SAMUEL TAYLOR, 1817, *Biographia Literaria, note.*

With all his boasted simplicity and love of the country, he seldom launches out into general descriptions of nature : he looks at her over his clipped hedges, and from his well-swept garden-walks; or if he makes a bolder experiment now and then, it is with an air of precaution, as if he were afraid of being caught in a shower of rain, or of not being able, in case of any untoward accident, to make good his retreat home. He shakes hands with nature with a pair of fashionable gloves on, and leads his "Vashti" forth to public view with a look of consciousness and attention to etiquette, as a fine gentleman hands a lady out to dance a minuet. He is delicate to fastidiousness, and glad to get back, after a romantic adventure with crazy Kate, a party of gypsies or a little child on a common, to the drawing-room and the ladies again, to the sofa and the tea-kettle—No, I beg his pardon, not to the singing, well-scoured tea-kettle, but to the polished and loud-hissing urn. . . . Still he is a genuine poet, and deserves all his reputation. His worst vices are amiable weaknesses, elegant trifling. Though there is a frequent dryness, timidity, and jejuneness in his manner, he has left a number of pictures of domestic comfort and social refinement, as well as of natural imagery and feeling, which can hardly be forgotten but with the language itself.—HAZLITT, WILLIAM, 1818, *Lectures on the English Poets, Lecture* v.

His language has such a masculine idiomatic strength, and his manner, whether he rises into grace or falls into negligence, has so much plain and familiar freedom, that we read no poetry with a deeper conviction of its sentiments having come from the author's heart, and of the enthusiasm, in whatever he describes, having been unfeigned and unexaggerated. . . . Considering the tenor and circumstances of his life, it is not much to be wondered at, that some asperities and peculiarities should have adhered to the strong stem of his genius, like the moss and fungus that cling to some noble oak of the forest, amid the damps of its unsunned retirement. It is more surprising that he preserved, in such seclusion, so much genuine power of comic observation. Though he himself acknowledged having written "many things with bile" in his first volume, yet his satire has many legitimate objects: and it is not abstracted and declamatory satire: but it places human manners before us in the liveliest attitudes and clearest colours. There is much of the full distinctness of Theophrastus, and of the nervous and concise spirit of La Bruyè, in his piece entitled "Conversation," with a cast of humour superadded, which is peculiarly English, and not to be found out of England.— CAMPBELL, THOMAS, 1819, *Specimens of the British Poets.*

At last, Cowper threw off the whole trammels of French criticism and artificial refinement; and, setting at defiance all the imaginary requisites of poetical diction and classical imagery—dignity of style, and politeness of phraseology—ventured to write again with the force and the freedom which had characterised the old school of English literature, and been so unhappily sacrificed, upwards of a century before. Cowper had many faults, and some radical deficiencies;—but this atoned for all. There was something so delightfully refreshing, in seeing natural phrases and natural images again displaying their unforced graces, and waving their unpruned heads in the enchanted gardens of poetry, that no one complained of the taste displayed in the selection;—and Cowper is, and is likely to continue, the most popular of all who have written for the present or the last generation.—JEFFREY, FRANCIS LORD, 1819–44, *Contributions to the Edinburgh Review, vol. II, p. 293.*

Of Cowper, how shall I express myself in adequate terms of admiration? The purity of his principles, the tenderness of his heart, his unaffected and zealous piety, his warmth of devotion (however tinctured at times with gloom and despondency), the delicacy and playfulness of his wit, and the singular felicity of his diction, all conspire by turns

To win the wisest, warm the coldest heart.

Cowper is the poet of a well-educated and well-principled Englishman. "Home, sweet home" is the scene—limited as it may be imagined—in which he contrives to concentrate a thousand beauties, which others have scattered far and wide upon objects of less interest and attraction. His pictures are, if I may so speak, conceived with all the tenderness of Raffaelle, and executed with all the finish and sharpness of Teniers. No man, in such few

words, tells his tale, or describes his scene, so forcibly and so justly. His views of Nature are less grand and less generalised than those of Thomson: and here, to carry on the previous mode of comparison, I should say that Thomson was the Gaspar Poussin, and Cowper the Hobbima, of rural poetry.—DIBDIN, THOMAS FROGNALL, 1824, *The Library Companion, p. 735, note.*

Cowper divested verse of its exquisite polish; he thought in metre, but paid more attention to his thoughts than his verse. It would be difficult to draw the boundary of prose and blank verse between his letters and his poetry.—PEACOCK, THOMAS LOVE, 1820, *The Four Ages of Poetry, Calidore and Miscellanea, p. 61.*

Cowper was a good man, and lived at a fortunate time for his works.—BYRON, LORD, 1821, *On Bowles's Strictures on Pope.*

He is allowed, both by Edinburgh and Quarterly Reviews, to be the patriarch and founder of the romantic, or present school of poetry. When we say, *present* we ought to recollect, that there is a Lake, as well as a romantic school. . . . One thing, however, we must say, that a school of which that moonstruck prophet, Cowper, was the founder, is a school of which we should not wish to become disciples. Is poetry run mad? or is that poetry good for nothing, which is not run mad? So it would seem, from making Cowper the founder of that school which established itself on the ruins of the classical. The Quarterly and Edinburgh Reviews give him the credit of being the founder of this school,—a school of which they are themselves admirers, and yet they know he was a fanatic.—M'DERMOT, M., 1824, *The Beauties of Modern Literature, pp. xxii, xxiii.*

Lord Byron unquestionably estimated *Cowper* much too low in calling him *no poet.* But many others have put him much too high, if we are to pay any consistent regard to principles. . . . The consideration of him raises the question of all those evanescent lines that separate the approximations between poetical fancy and poetical imagination. A painter of particular and local landscapes, or portraits, copies directly from external objects; but a describer in words, who means it to be poetry, scarcely ever (if ever) does; he copies from the *internal* impression made on the fancy.—BRYDGES, SIR SAMUEL EGERTON, 1824, *Recollections of Foreign Travel, July 20, vol.* I, *pp.* 268, 269.

Compare the landscapes of Cowper with those of Burns. There is, if we mistake not, the same sort of difference between them, as in the conversation of two persons on scenery, the one originally an enthusiast in his love of the works of nature, the other driven, by disappointment or weariness, to solace himself with them as he might. It is a contrast which every one must have observed, when such topics come under discussion in society; and those who think it worth while, may find abundant illustration of it in the writings of this unfortunate but illustrious pair. The one all overflowing with the love of nature, and indicating, at every turn, that whatever his lot in life, he could not have been happy without her. The other visibly and wisely soothing himself, but not without effort, by attending to rural objects, in default of some more congenial happiness, of which he had almost come to despair. The latter, in consequence, laboriously sketching every object that came in his way : the other, in one or two rapid lines, which operate, as it were, like a magician's spell, presenting to the fancy just that picture, which was wanted to put the reader's minds in unison with the writer's.—KEBLE, JOHN, 1825, *Sacred Poetry, Quarterly Review, vol.* 32, *p.* 217.

Cowper has not Thomson's genius, but he has much more taste. His range is neither so wide, nor so lofty, but, as far as it extends, it is peculiarly his own. He cannot paint the Plague at Carthagena, or the Snow-storm, or the Earthquake, as Thomson has done ; but place him by the banks of the Ouse, or see him taking his "Winter walk at Noon," or accompany him in his rambles through his Flower garden, and where is the Author who can compare with him for a moment? The pictures of domestic life which he has painted are inimitable. It is hard to say whether his sketches of external nature, or of indoor life, are the best. Cowper does not attempt the same variety of scene as Thomson ; but in what he does attempt, he always succeeds.— NEELE, HENRY, 1827–29, *Lectures on English Poetry,* p. 184.

The forerunner of the great restoration of our literature was Cowper.—MACAULAY, THOMAS BABINGTON, 1830, *Moore's Life of Lord Byron, Edinburgh Review ; Critical and Miscellaneous Essays.*

Cowper's bold freedom, though it seemed at first like uncouth roughness, gained much in variety of expression, without losing much in point of sound. It offended, because it seemed careless, and as if he respected little the prevailing taste of his readers : but it was far from being unpolished as it seemed. He tells us, that the lines of his earlier poems were touched and retouched, with fastidious delicacy : his ear was not easily pleased ; and yet, if we may judge from one or two specimens of alterations, his corrections very often injured what they were meant to repair.—PEABODY, W. B. O., 1834, *Life of Cowper, North American Review, vol.* 38, *p.* 27.

The poet of the Cross.—MEMES, JOHN, 1840, ed. *Cowper's Works, Life.*

If Cowper had written songs, such was the honesty of his nature that he would probably have equalled Burns, great as are the disadvantages under which our language would have laid him. . . . Cowper does not, like Burns, write the history of the poor in every page of his works, but his heart was with them. . . . If Cowper had been blessed with the physical strength of Burns, he might have been,— but I don't say he would have been,—at once, one of the greatest of poets and ablest of active men. As it is, I am unable to name a poet whose writings, page for page, can boast an equal amount of original thought and sterling common sense.—ELLIOTT, EBENEZER, 1842, *A Lecture on Cowper and Burns, Tait's Edinburgh Magazine, vol.* 9, *p.* 359.

When the shame of England burns in the heart of Cowper, you must believe him ; for through that heart rolled the best of England's blood.—WILSON, JOHN, 1845, *Supplement to Mac-Flecnoe and the Dunciad, Blackwood's Magazine.*

> Sweet are thy strains, celestial Bard ;
>   And oft, in childhood's years,
> I've read them o'er and o'er again,
>   With floods of silent tears.
>
> . . . .
> Is He the source of every good,
>   The spring of purity?
> Then in thine hours of deepest woe
>   Thy God was still with thee.
> How else, when every hope was fled,

Couldst thou so fondly cling
To holy things and holy men?
And how so sweetly sing,
Of things that God alone could teach?
And whence that purity,
That hatred of all sinful ways—
That gentle charity?

—BRONTË, ANNE, 1846, *To Cowper, Poems by Currer, Ellis and Acton Bell.*

He is emphatically the poet of ordinary and intimate life, of the domestic emotions, of household happiness. His muse is a domestic deity, a familiar Lar, and his countrymen have enshrined his verses in the very holiest penetralia of their hearths. Cowper was one of the first poets —even among the English—who ventured to describe those familiar thoughts, feelings, and enjoyments which are imagined by the word *home*—that word which echoes so deeply in the English heart, that word for which so many cultivated languages have neither synonym nor equivalent. . . . His language is in the highest degree easy, familiar, and consequently impressive; there is no author who so completely *talks* to his reader— none whose works breathe so completely of the individuality and personal character of their writer. He abounds in description of scenery; and we hardly regret that he should have passed his life among the dull levels of the Ouse, when we think that the power of his genius has given an unfading grace and interest to landscapes in themselves neither romantic nor sublime. It appears to us that he is greatly inferior to Thomson in comprehensiveness and rapidity of picturesque perception; but then his mode of expression is simpler, less ambitious, and in purer taste, and he surpasses not only the author of "The Seasons," but perhaps all poets, in the power of communicating interest to the familiar details of domestic life. His humour was very delicate and just, and his descriptions of the common absurdities of ordinary intercourse are masterly. When rising, as he often and gracefully does, into the loftier atmosphere of moral or religious thought, he exhibits a surprising ease and dignity; his mind was of that rare order which can rise without an effort and sink without meanness. He is uniformly earnest and sincere. — SHAW, THOMAS B., 1847, *Outlines of English Literature*, pp. 305, 307.

Cowper is eminently the David of English poetry, pouring forth, like the great Hebrew bard, his own deep and warm feelings in behalf of moral and religious truth.—CELVELAND, CHARLES D., 1848, *A Compendium of English Literature*, p. 737.

Tenderest of tender hearts, of spirits pure
The purest! such, O Cowper! such wert thou,
But such are not the happiest: thou wert not,
Till borne where all those hearts and spirits rest.
Young was I, when from Latin lore and Greek
I play'd the truant for thy sweeter Task,
Nor since that hour hath aught our Muses held
Before me seem'd so precious; in one hour,
I saw the poet and the sage unite,
More grave than man, more versatile than boy!

—LANDOR, WALTER SAVAGE, 1853, *The Last Fruit off an Old Tree*, xxxvii.

Cowper is certainly the sweetest of our didactic poets. He is elevated in his "Table Talk;" acute in detailing the "Progress of Error;" and he chants the praises of "Truth" in more dulcet notes than were ever sounded by the fairest swan in Cayster. His "Expostulation" is made in the tones of a benevolent sage. His "Hope" and his "Charity" are proofs of his pure Christian-like feeling,—a feeling which also pervades his "Conversation" and his "Retirement," and which barbs the shafts of his satire without taking away from their strength.—DORAN, JOHN, 1854, *Habits and Men*, p. 20.

As a scold, we think Cowper failed. He had a great idea of the use of railing, and there are many pages of laudable invective against various vices which we feel no call whatever to defend. But a great vituperator had need to be a great hater; and of any real rage, any such gall and bitterness as great and irritable satirists have in other ages let loose upon men,—of any thorough, brooding, burning, abiding detestation,—he was as incapable as a tame hare. His vituperation reads like the mild man's whose wife ate up his dinner: "Really, sir, I feel quite *angry*!" Nor has his language any of the sharp intrusive acumen which divides in sunder both soul and spirit, and makes fierce and unforgetable reviling.—BAGEHOT, WALTER, 1855, *William Cowper, Works, ed. Morgan, vol.* I, p. 428.

Whatever estimate may be formed of

his poetry in comparison with that of earlier or later writers, everyone must feel that his English is that of a scholar and a gentleman—that he had the purest enjoyment of domestic life, and of what one may call the domestic or still life of nature. One is sure also that he had the most earnest faith, which he cherished for others when he could find no comfort in it for himself. These would be sufficient explanations of the interest which he has awakened in so many simple and honest readers who turn to books for sympathy and fellowship, and do not like a writer at all the worse because he also demands their sympathy with him. Cowper is one of the strongest instances, and proofs, how much more qualities of this kind affect Englishmen than any others. The gentleness of his life might lead some to suspect him of effeminacy; but the old Westminster school-boy and cricketer comes out in the midst of his Meditation on Sofas; and the deep tragedy which was at the bottom of his whole life, and which grew more terrible as the shadows of evening closed upon him, shows that there may be unutterable struggles in those natures which seem least formed for the rough work of the world.—MAURICE, FREDERICK DENISON, 1856, *The Friendship of Books and Other Lectures, p.* 28.

His language is often vulgar, and not least so when his theme is most sublime; and his most successful passages, his minutely touched descriptions of familiar still-life and rural scenery, are indeed strongly suggestive, but have little of the delicate susceptibility of beauty which breathes through Thomson's musings on nature.— SPALDING, WILLIAM, 1852–82, *A History of English Literature, p.* 357.

As the death of Samuel Johnson closes one era of our literature, so the appearance of Cowper as a poet opens another. Notwithstanding his obligations both to Churchill and Pope, a main characteristic of Cowper's poetry is its originality. Compared with almost any one of his predecessors, he was what we may call a natural poet. He broke through conventional forms and usages in his mode of writing more daringly than any English poet before him had done, at least since the genius of Pope had bound in its spell the phraseology and rhythm of our poetry. His opinions were not more his own than

his manner of expressing them.—CRAIK, GEORGE L., 1861, *A Compendious History of English Literature and of the English Language, vol.* II, *p.* 372.

If we compare our English literature to a beautiful garden, where Milton lifts his head to heaven in the spotless chalice of the tall white lily, and Shakspere scatters his dramas round him in beds of fragrant roses, blushing with a thousand various shades—some stained to the core as if with blood, others unfolding their fair pink petals with a lovely smile to the summer sun,—what shall we find in shrub or flower so like the timid, shrinking spirit of William Cowper, as that delicate sensitive plant, whose leaves, folding up at the slightest touch, cannot bear even the brighter rays of the cherishing sun?— COLLIER, WILLIAM FRANCIS, 1861, *A History of English Literature, p.* 379.

William Cowper and Erasmus Darwin were contemporaries: but how has the lowlier russet outlasted the glittering Balmasque costume, a genuine human heart beneath the one, a piece of mechanism, like a skeleton-clock, within the other: the one pure, true, beating, the other movement without life, energy without appliance.— GROSART, ALEXANDER B., 1868, *Giles Fletcher's Poems, Memorial-Introduction, p.* 56.

The gentleness of his temper, and the wide charity of his sympathies, made it natural for him to find good in everything except the human heart. . . . Your muscles grow springy, and your lungs dilate with the crisp air as you walk along with him. You laugh with him at the grotesque shadow of your legs lengthened across the snow by the just-risen sun. I know nothing that gives a purer feeling of out-door exhilaration than the easy verses of this escaped hypochondriac. . . . To me Cowper is still the best of our descriptive poets for every-day wear. And what unobtrusive skill he has! How he heightens, for example, your sense of winter-evening seclusion, by the twanging horn of the postman on the bridge!— LOWELL, JAMES RUSSELL, 1871, *A Good Word for Winter, My Study Windows.*

While his poems have in them much that might be thought didactic, this matter is given in so natural, reflective, and yet more, in so emotional, a manner as quite to escape the censure that might be implied in the word. The thought does not, predetermined, so much seek for the image and rhythm wherewith to enforce itself, as flow out in an incidental living way from the scenes and objects present to the poetic imagination. . . . Cowper has a large measure of that power which brings interpretation to natural objects, and looks upon them with a rapid interplay of suggestions, uniting the visible to the invisible, and lending to passing events a scope otherwise quite beyond them. . . . The quiet, earnest, subtile, pure, pervasive mind of Cowper made him a poet by the innate force and character of its conceptions. There is everything in his history to confirm the view, that art finds its germ in natural endowment, and nothing to sustain the theory, that it can be compassed by external conditions.—BASCOM, JOHN, 1874, *Philosophy of English Literature*, pp. 218, 219.

Cowper is the first of the poets who loves Nature entirely for her own sake. He paints only what he sees, but he paints it with the affection of a child for a flower and with the minute observation of a man. The change in relation to the subject of man is equally great. The idea of mankind as a whole which we have seen growing up is fully formed in Cowper's mind. The range of his interests is as wide as the world, and all men form one brotherhood. —BROOKE, STOPFORD A., 1876, *English Literature (Primer)*, p. 148.

Cowper's diatribes against the growth of luxury have become obsolete; his religious meanings are interesting to those alone who share his creed; but his intense love of calm scenery fell in with a widely-spread sentiment of his age, and has scattered through his pages vignettes of enduring beauty. The pathetic power in which he was unrivalled, and which gives to two or three of his poems a charm quite unique in its kind, seems to belong to no age.—STEPHEN, LESLIE, 1876, *History of English Thought in the Eighteenth Century*, vol. II, p. 454.

The eager, sudden-looking, large-eyed, shaven face of Cowper is familiar to us in his portraits—a face sharp-cut and sufficiently well-moulded, without being handsome, nor particularly sympathetic. It is a high-strung, excitable face; as of a man too susceptible and touchy to put himself forward willingly among his fellows,

but who, feeling a "vocation" upon him, would be more than merely earnest—self-asserting, aggressive, and unyielding. This is in fact very much the character of his writings. He was an enthusiastic lover of Nature, and full of gentle kindliness, and of quiet pleasant good-humour, —and all these lovable qualities appear in ample proportion and measure in passages of his writings: but at the same time his narrow, exclusive, severe, and arbitrary religious creed—a creed which made him as sure that other people were wicked and marked out for damnation as that himself was elected and saved (and even as regards himself this confidence gave way sometimes to utter desperation) —this creed speaks out in his poems in unmistakable tones of harsh judgment and unqualified denunciation. Few writers are more steadily unsparing of the lash than the shrinking sensitive Cowper. It may be that he does not lay it on with the sense of personal power, and indignant paying-off of old scores, which one finds in a Juvenal or a Pope; but the conviction that he is the mouthpiece of Providence, and that, when William Cowper has pronounced a man reprobate, the smoke of his burning is certain to ascend up for ever and ever, stands instead of much, and lends unction to the hallowed strain. In conformity with this inspiration, his writing is nervous and terse, well stored with vigorous stinging single lines; and his power of expressive characterization, whether in moral declaiming or in descriptive work, is very considerable:—and was (at any rate in the latter class of passages) even more noticeable in his own day than it is in ours. Apart from his religion, Cowper (as has just been said) was eminently humane and gentle-hearted; the interest which he took in his tame hares will perhaps be remembered when much of his wielding of the divine thunderbolts against the profane shall have been forgotten. . . . In point of literary or poetic style, Cowper was mainly independent, and the pioneer of a simpler and more natural method than he found prevailing; his didactic or censorial poems may be regarded as formed on the writings of Churchill rather than of any other predecessor.— ROSSETTI, WILLIAM MICHAEL, 1878, *Lives of Famous Poets*, pp. 185, 186.

An amiable piety makes his "Task," a

long moralizing poem in blank verse, attractive to many minds; from the mere literary point of view, it must be allowed to be a feeble production. As he gained more confidence in himself, he developed a curious sort of mild feline humor, which appears in the delightful ballad of "John Gilpin," and in several shorter pieces. The strength which had been wanting all his life came to him near its close, and inspired him to write those stanzas of wondrous majesty and beauty which have the title of "The Castaway;" unhappily it was the strength of spiritual despair. —ARNOLD, THOMAS, 1878, *English Literature, Encyclopædia Britannica, Ninth Edition, vol.* VII.

The pathos of Cowper's life and his position in our poetical history will always lend a special interest to his work, even though it is no longer possible to regard a poet limited as he was as a poet of the first order. He was an essentially original writer, owing much of course as every writer must owe, to the subtle influences of his time, but deriving as little as ever poet derived from literary study. . . . We read Cowper, indeed, not for his passion or for his ideas, but for his love of nature and his faithful rendering of her beauty; for his truth of portraiture, for his humour, for his pathos; for the refined honesty of his style, for the melancholy interest of his life, and for the simplicity and the lovelinesss of his character.—WARD, THOMAS HUMPHRY, 1880, *The English Poets, vol.* III, *pp.* 423, 433.

His pictures of social life are as truthful as they are charming. All is natural, forcible and pathetic, humorous at times, and frequently desponding and gloomy; but through all these is an undertone of unaffected piety that rises occasionally into higher utterances. And so it is that his popularity has never been on the decline. And there are passages, particularly of domestic life, that one hears perpetually quoted. As a letter-writer, no man perhaps has ever excelled him. His epistolary style is the finest in our language, abounding in every phase of sentiment, humour, sadness, pathos, liveliness, yet all spontaneous and natural.—WALLER, J. F., 1881, *Boswell and Johnson, Their Companions and Contemporaries, p.* 148.

This then was the training which made a poet of Cowper, one of the most popular in England—in his way a transforming influence, a new beginning of intellectual life and power. Had we been left to conjecture what lines of education would have been the best on which to raise up for us the precursor of a new poetical age, certainly these are not the lines which we would have chosen. Nor, had we been asked to prophesy what were the works to be expected from a man so exceptionally circumstanced—with a past so strangely chequered, a future so painfully uncertain, a mind so sensitive, and which had passed through so many passionate struggles— could we have hit upon anything half so unlikely as the actual issue. What we should have looked for would have been some profound and morbid study of a despairing soul, some terrible pictures like those of Job, some confusion of gloomy skies and storms, and convulsions of nature. That anatomy of the heart which he gives us in his various narratives of his own feelings, that minute dissection of quivering nerve and tissue, would have been what we should have looked for in his poetry. But lo, when the moment came, and the prophet was softly persuaded and guided into the delivery of his burden, it was no such wild exposition of the terrors and pangs of the soul that came to his lips. These heavy vapours melted and dispersed from the infinite sweet blueness of the heavens: he forgot himself as if he had never been—and forgot all those miseries of the imagination, those bitter pangs and sorrows, the despair and darkness through which he had stumbled blindly for years. A soft and genial freedom entered into his soul, involuntary smiles came to him, light to his eyes, and to his steps such wandering careless grace, such devious gentle ways, as no one had dreamed of.—OLIPHANT, MARGARET O. W., 1882, *Literary History of England in the End of the Eighteenth and Beginning of the Nineteenth Century, vol.* I, *p.* 49.

Cowper is less read than he deserves to be; but he has this glory, that he has ever been the favorite poet of deeply religious minds; and his history is peculiarly touching, as that of one who, himself plunged in despair and madness, has brought hope and consolation to a thousand other souls. —FARRAR, FREDERICK WILLIAM, 1883, *With the Poets, Preface, p.* xviii.

Cowper's poetry will not win hosts of admirers; no societies will be formed for the purpose of reading papers on his verses and expounding his meaning; but the reader who may be interested in other things than the pomp and clatter of contemporary poetry will be rewarded by occasional tender, simple passages. He will detect many attractive qualities in the poems, but he is tolerably sure not to be swept off his feet by enthusiasm. This is generally the fate of a reformer, or the first man who writes under a new impulse. He is like the guide-post where roads divide; he points the way which others are able to make more attractive, and is soon forgotten. We overlook Cowper's simple record of nature while we are under the influence of Wordsworth's mightier verse, and we grow impatient of his philosophy when we see how much further later poets carried the notion of the brotherhood of man which he was one of the first authoritatively to utter.—PERRY, THOMAS SERGEANT, 1883, *English Literature in the Eighteenth Century, p.* 437.

Cowper is a true poet of a very rare type, one of the most important in the development of English poetry.—HARRISON, FREDERIC, 1883-86, *The Choice of Books and Other Literary Pieces, p.* 381.

The greatest things in this world are often done by those who do not know they are doing them. This is especially true of William Cowper. He was wholly unaware of the great mission he was fulfilling; his contemporaries were wholly unaware of it. And so temporal are the world's standards, in the best of times, that spiritual regenerators are not generally recognized until long after they have passed away, when the results of what they did are fully ripe, and philosophers begin to trace the original impulses.—CORSON, HIRAM, 1886, *An Introduction to the Study of Robert Browning's Poetry, p.* 12.

It would be scarcely claiming too much if we set down the whole of Cowper's original poetry (the translation of Homer is of course not included) as belonging to the literature of the Evangelical Revival. No doubt the fire of his genius would have burnt brightly, whatever his religious sentiments might have been. In the productions of his elegant pen we should, under any circumstances, have recognised at least the *disjecti membra poetæ.* But,

as a matter of fact, his Christian convictions were the mainspring which set the whole machinery of his poetical work in motion. It was this which gave coherence and symmetry and soul to it all. Abstract the religious element from his compositions, and they all fall to pieces; but, in fact, it is impossible to do so. With the exception of one or two lighter pieces, there is an undercurrent of Christian sentiment running through and inseparable from them all.—OVERTON, JOHN HENRY, 1886, *The Evangelical Revival in the Eighteenth Century, p.* 127.

The moral meditations of Young had comprised much vigorous declamation of native English growth. Cowper, a far greater poet, expressed in purer and simpler language thoughts with more of substantial worth, as well as a strain of sentiment, manly, religious, and gravely affectionate. In him, too, we find an admirable fidelity to outward nature in detail; although with her grander forms, unendeared by association, he had little sympathy; while ideal representations of scenery are no more to be found in his poetry than ideal conceptions of character.—DE VERE, AUBREY, 1887, *Essays Chiefly on Poetry, vol.* II, *p.* 120.

Cowper is less read than he deserves to be, but he has this glory, that he has ever been the favourite poet of deeply religious minds.— SAUNDERS, FREDERICK, 1887, *The Story of Some Famous Books, p.* 112.

Cowper has probably few readers now. One sometimes meets with an elderly lady, brought up in an Evangelical family, who, having been made to learn the "Moral Satires" and "The Task" by heart when a child, still remembers a good deal of them, and cherishes for the poet of Evangelicism the tender affections which gathers in old age round the things which belongs to childhood. But we have most of us ceased to be Evangelical, and most of us who love poetry having come under the spell of Goethe and of the lesser poets of the nineteenth century, find poor Cowper a little cramped, a little narrow, and, to tell the truth, a little dull. Yet there are passages in Cowper's poetry which deserve to live and will live, and which will secure him a place, not indeed among English poets of the first rank, but high among those of the second. The pity is that they run great risk of being buried and lost forever in the wilderness of sermons which fills up such a large part of "The Progress of Error" and "The Task." It is very hard to write sermons that will live, and, as a writer of sermons, I am afraid Cowper is likely to take his place on the very peaceful and dusty upper shelf in our libraries where the divines of the last century repose. But he deserves a better fate than this, and all lovers of English poetry ought to do what they can to save him from it.— BAILEY, J. C., 1889, *William Cowper, Macmillan's Magazine, vol.* 60, *p.* 261.

Cowper's virtue was in his simplicity and genuineness, rare qualities then; his good fortune was in never belonging to the literary set or bowing to the town taste; hence in a time the most barren in English literature, he gave us a half dozen fine poems that stand far beyond all contemporary rivalry, and some private letters of the best style and temper. When, however, the question comes as to the intrinsic value of these letters, it must be confessed that though they please the taste they do not interest the mind except in a curious and diverting way. They are less the letters of a poet than of a village original, a sort of schoolmaster or clergyman *manqué*, of sound sense, tender heart and humane perception, but the creature of a narrow sphere.—WOODBERRY, GEORGE EDWARD, 1890, *Studies in Letters and Life, p.* 227.

Direct, easeful, chaste—Cowper's best work is all this, and more; he had the foundation of common sense, without which the other gifts of song go for little or nothing. Given common sense together with spontaneity and taste, and genuine poetry is assured. Beyond these qualifications Cowper reveals both humor,— though humor, perhaps, may be an integral part of taste—and pathos, two essential forces seldom found separated. And having enumerated thus far, we have but to add imagination, and we have the outfit for a poet of the first order. But it will not do to claim for Cowper great imaginative power, nor can we credit him with that certainty, that continuity of inspiration which stamps a master of the guild. We shall look to him in vain for the sublime; furthermore, we shall find that if he can move lightly and gracefully on levels not the highest, he can also plod there, and that right heavily. To transfer

the figure from the feet to the hands, the fingers are naturally nimble, but suddenly on go the Methodist mittens, and we are in for a pull of theologic fumbling.— CHENEY, JOHN VANCE, 1892, *A Study of Cowper, The Chautauquan, vol.* 15, *p.* 405.

There is no more interesting poet than Cowper, and hardly one the area of whose influence was greater. No man, it is unnecessary to say, courted popularity less, yet he threw a very wide net, and caught a great shoal of readers. For twenty years after the publication of "The Task" in 1785, his general popularity never flagged, and even when in the eyes of the world it was eclipsed, when Cowper became in the opinion of fierce Byronians and moss-trooping Northerners, "a coddled Pope" and a milksop, our great, sober, Puritan middle-class took him to their warm firesides for two generations more. . . . Had Cowper not gone mad in his thirty-second year, and been frightened out of the world of trifles, we should have had another Prior, a wittier Gay, an earlier Praed, an English La Fontaine.— BIRRELL, AUGUSTINE, 1892, *Res Judicatæ, pp.* 90, 94.

Cowper, the herald of Wordsworth, may perhaps be described as a reformer of poetry, but it is more significant of his historical position to describe him as an essayist in verse.—MINTO, WILLIAM, 1894, *The Literature of the Georgian Era, ed., Knight, p.* 132.

I am in a state of great excitement about Cowper. Reading him right through I was more than ever struck with his innumerable felicities. Yet how very terribly he sinks! The style sinks, but still more the thought. I imagined that his fine taste had piloted him through the theological *mare mortuum* of his age and school with comparative safety. But really, it is not so. He is often quite abominable; so rude, so insolent. He sends his antagonists to the Devil; literally, if I am not mistaken, tells them to go to H—ll; exults over them, sneers, jeers, jokes. His mildest attitude is a "sarve them right," and his idea of God as the owner of some patent sort of peep-show, which, if we don't appreciate, he will d—n our eyes for a set of God knows what, is absolutely Swiftian in its utter vulgarity. What a destestable poison has penetrated his vitals! Mind, it is not the doctrine, but

the swagger and infernal rudeness that
offend me. The style too becomes infected; with all this ghastly machinery
of unreason, he takes it upon him to be
flippant. Such "awful mirth" is almost
unparalleled in literature. He even assumes an athletic, or pseudo-athletic vigour of contemptuous denunciation.—
BROWN, THOMAS EDWARD, 1895, *To S. T.
Irwin, July* 16; *Letters, vol.* II, *p.* 109.

Critics are agreed that we shall not rank
him among the great poets; but he comes
nearer to their rank than anybody in his
day believed possible. He is so true; he
is so tender; he is so natural. If in his
longer poems there is sometimes a lack of
last finish, and an overplus of language—
there is a frankness of utterance and a
billowy undulation of movement that have
compensating charms. He loves Nature
as a boy loves his play; his humanities are
wakened by all her voices. He not only
seizes upon exterior effects with a painter's
eye and hand, but he has a touch which
steals deeper meanings and influences and
transfers them into verse that flows softly
and quietly as summer brooks. He cannot
speak or rhyme but the odors of the country cling to his words.—MITCHELL, DON-
ALD G., 1895, *English Lands Letters and
Kings, Queen Anne and the Georges, p.* 254.

Several of Cowper's short poems are
inimitable. He writes so very like a
gentleman.— LOCKER-LAMPSON, FREDER-
ICK, 1896, *My Confidences, p.* 178.

William Cowper's first poems were some
of the "Olney Hymns," 1779, and in these
the religious poetry of Charles Wesley
was continued. The profound personal
religion, gloomy even to insanity as it
often became, which fills the whole of
Cowper's poetry, introduced a theological
element into English poetry which continually increased till it died out with
Browning and Tennyson. His didactic and
satirical poems in 1782 link him backwards
to the last age. His translation of Homer,
1791, and of shorter pieces from the Latin
and Greek, connects him with the classical
influence, his interest in Milton with the
revived study of the English poets. The
playful and gentle vein of humour which
he showed in "John Gilpin" and other
poems, opened a new kind of verse to poets.
With this kind of humour is connected a
simple pathos of which Cowper is a great
master. The "Lines to Mary Unwin" and

to his "Mother's Picture" prove, with the
work of Blake, that pure natural feeling
wholly free from artifice had returned to
English song. A new element was also
introduced by him and Blake—the love of
animals and the poetry of their relation to
man, a vein plentifully worked by after
poets. His greatest work was the "Task."
—BROOKE, STOPFORD A., 1896, *English
Literature, p.* 223.

Cowper, even more than most writers,
deserves and requites consideration under
the double aspect of matter and form. In
both he did much to alter the generally
accepted conditions of English poetry; and
if his formal services have perhaps received less attention than they merit, his
material achievements have never been denied.—SAINTSBURY, GEORGE, 1896, *A History of Nineteenth Century Literature, p.* 4.

Such were the simple elements of Cowper's landscape. They have no special
attraction that is not shared by hundreds
of other similar scenes in the Oolitic tracts
of England. To the cursory visitor they
may even seem tame and commonplace.
And yet for us, apart from any mere
beauty they may possess, they have been
for ever glorified and consecrated by the
imagination of the poet. We see in them
the natural features which soothed his
sorrow and gladdened his heart, and which
became the sources of an inspiration that
breathed fresh life into the poetry of
England. The lapse of time has left the
scene essentially unchanged. We may
take the same walks that Cowper loved,
and see the same prospects that charmed
his eyes and filled his nature. In so following his steps, we note the accuracy and
felicity of his descriptions, and appreciate
more vividly the poetic genius which, out
of such simple materials, could work such
a permanent change in the attitude of his
countrymen towards nature.— GEIKIE,
SIR ARCHIBALD, 1898, *Types of Scenery
and their Influence on Literature, p.* 13.

The cold indifference of the moderns
towards Cowper is largely due to the fact
that he has left no love poetry behind him.
For this reason they may find him uninteresting, and they regard him pretty
much as he says his contemporaries and
former associates did: "They think of
me as of the man in the moon, and whether
I have a lantern, a dog and a faggot, or
whether I have neither of these desirable

accommodations, is to them a matter of perfect indifference.'' Whether his heart was torn with the agonies of love or not, Cowper does not tell us. He has left no confessions of this nature. His appeal is not to our passionate 'prentice years, but to our maturity, when having suffered, we have learnt our lesson, and profited by it to pass out of the petty circle of ourselves into the study of life's larger whole.—LAW, ALICE, 1900, *William Cowper, Fortnightly Review, vol. 73, p. 777.*

Cowper was pre-eminently a poet of feelings; he may have been melancholy, but he pointed out to his readers how they were themselves subjects of emotion. He owed a debt to Providence, and he rebuked the people for their follies. In doing so he was regardless of his own fame and of their opprobrium. He gave them tolerable advice, and strove to awaken them from their apathy to a sense of their duty towards their neighbours. First, of poets, since the days of Milton, to champion the sacredness of religion, he was the forerunner of a new school that disliked the political satires of the disciples of Pope, and aimed at borrowing for their lines of song from the simple beauties of a perfect nature.—SPENDER, A. EDMUND, 1900, *The Centenary of Cowper, The Westminster Review, vol. 153, p. 545.*

Cowper knew every landmark about Olney and weaved many a one into his verse. He loved Nature in his gentle way, and her influence must often have been a healing one, when thoughts of those dark insane fits, which turned his homely life into a tragedy, hovered about his mind. He did not observe her with so nice an eye as poor Clare the peasant, who beginning in gladness also ended in the despondency and madness which a poet has declared to be the lot of poets; and I have always had my doubts about the nightingale which he believed he heard in full song on New Year's Day. And yet the "Winter Walk at Noon," among other poems, has lines and descriptions worth remembering. The rich laburnum—"laburnum,'' as Tennyson put it, "drooping wells of fire"—and the leafless but lovely mezereon and the myriad blossomed yellow broom of full summertide—these and many other features in the pageant of the spring and summer he noted and set forth with a lover's eye, if in rather stilted language and in somewhat too much the form of a catalogue to please us to-day. Cowper belonged as a poet of nature rather to the Thomson than the Wordsworth school.—DEWAR, GEORGE A. B., 1900, *William Cowper, The Saturday Review, vol. 89, p. 521.*

Joseph Warton
1722-1800

Born at Dunsfold, Surrey, was the son of the Rev. Thomas Warton (1688-1745), vicar of Basingstoke and Oxford professor of Poetry. In 1740 he passed from Winchester to Oriel, and, rector of Winslade from 1748, returned to Winchester as second master in 1755, and was its head 1766-93. His preferments were a prebend of St. Paul's, the living of Thorley, a prebend of Winchester, and the rectories of Easton and Upham. His "Odes" (1746) marked a reaction from Pope. An edition of Virgil (1753), with translation of the "Eclogues" and "Georgics," gained him a high reputation. He was, like his brother Thomas, a member of the Literary Club. In 1756 appeared vol. i. of his "Essay on Pope" (vol. ii. in 1782), with its distinction between the poetry of reason and the poetry of fancy. Later works were editions of Pope (1797) and Dryden. See the panegyrical "Memoir" by Wooll (1806).—PATRICK AND GROOME, *eds.*, 1897, *Chambers's Biographical Dictionary, p. 956.*

That ardent mind which had so eminently distinguished the exercise of his public duties, did not desert him in the hours of leisure and retirement; for inactivity was foreign to his nature. His parsonage, his farm, his garden, were cultivated and adorned with the eagerness and taste of undiminished youth. His lively sallies of playful wit, his rich stores of literary anecdote, and the polished and habitual ease with which he imperceptibly entered into the various ideas and pursuits of men, rendered him an acquaintance both profitable and amusing; whilst his unaffected piety and unbounded charity stamped him a pastor adored by his parishioners. Difficult indeed would it be to decide whether he shone in a degree less, in this social character, than in the closest of criticism or the chair of instruction.—WOOLL, JOHN, 1806, *Memoirs of Warton.*

I knew Joseph Warton well. When Matthias attacked him in "The Pursuits of Literature" for reprinting some loose things in his edition of Pope, Joseph wrote a letter to me, in which he called Matthias "his *pious* critic,"—rather an odd expression to come from a clergyman.—He certainly ought not to have given that letter of Lord Cobham.—ROGERS, SAMUEL, 1855, *Table-Talk*, p. 133.

He remained a schoolmaster for thirty-eight years. As a teacher Warton achieved little success. He was neither an exact scholar nor a disciplinarian. Thrice in his headmastership the boys openly mutinied against him, and inflicted on him ludicrous humiliations. The third insurrection took place in the summer of 1793, and, after ingloriously suppressing it, Warton prudently resigned his post. His easy good nature secured for him the warm affection of many of his pupils, among whom his favourites were William Lisle Bowles and Richard Mant. Although the educational fame of the school did not grow during his régime, his social and literary reputation gave his office increased dignity and importance. In 1778 George III visited the college, Warton's private guests on the occasion included Sir Joshua Reynolds and Garrick.—LEE, SIDNEY, 1899, *Dictionary of National Biography, vol.* LIX, p. 429.

H. S. E.
JOSEPHUS WARTON, S. T. P.
HUJUS ECCLESIÆ
PREBENDARIUS :
SCHOLÆ WINTONIENSIS
PER ANNOS FERE TRIGINTA
INFORMATOR :
POETA FERVIDUS, FACILIS, EXPOLITUS :
CRITICUS ERUDITUS, PRESPICAX, ELEGANS :
OBIIT XXIII° FEB. MDCCC.,
ÆTAT. LXXVIII.
HOC QUALECUNQUE
PIETATIS MONUMENTUM
PRÆCEPTORI OPTIMO,
DESIDERATISSIMO,
WICCAMICI SUI
P. C.
— INSCRIPTION ON TOMB, WINCHESTER CATHEDRAL.

ESSAY AND EDITION OF POPE.

Is, I think, the most extraordinary work I ever read, and is indeed everything but what it promises. The writer seems to have copied, and impudently enough printed, his commonplace book of anecdotes and remarks upon various writers. Some parts are indeed critical, but his criticisms are not in my opinion always just, and there is but little anywhere to be found that can be called new.— CHARLEMONT, LORD, 1782, *Letter to Edmond Malone, Oct.* 4, *Life by Prior*, p. 96.

Though by nature one of the most candid and liberal of critics, continues, as a biographer, to indulge that prejudice which had early induced him, in his popular "Essay" on this illustrious poet, to endeavour to sink him a little in the scale of poetical renown : not, I believe, from any envious motive, but as an affectionate compliment to his friend Young, the patron to whom he inscribed his Essay.—HAYLEY, WILLIAM, 1803, *The Life and Posthumous Writings of William Cowper, vol.* II, *p.* 157.

Dr. Joseph Warton was an exquisite scholar, of very general reading, a man of the purest taste, and of some genius; yet it is obvious that he had not clearly settled in his own mind the theoretic principles of poetry, otherwise he would not have wavered in so feeble a manner, in finally drawing up a summary of the poetical merits of Pope, in his elegant "Essay" on that poet.—BRYDGES, SIR SAMUEL EGERTON, 1824, *Recollections of Foreign Travel, Aug.* 6, *vol.* I, *p.* 257.

He was seventy-five when he published his edition of Pope, and to save himself trouble he apportioned out the old farrago in notes. Profuse in digressions, he is sparing of needful explanations. His turn was for the lighter portions of criticism and biography, and most of his apposite remarks are critical opinions. They are often just, but never profound, for he had neither fervid feelings nor a robust understanding, and his highest qualities are a fair poetical taste, and a tolerable acquaintance with ancient and modern authors.— ELWIN, WHITWELL, 1871, *ed., The Works of Alexander Pope, Introduction, vol.* I, p. xxiii.

His delay in following up the first volume of his "Essay" with a second, and the long period of forty years which elapsed between his first volume and his edition, have led to its being asserted that he abstained, from fear of Warburton. This assertion is not supported by Dr. Johnson, who, when asked the reason of Warton's delay in bringing out the second volume of his "Essay," said, he supposed "it was because he could not persuade the world to be of his opinion about Pope." But Warton may, very likely, have been afraid of Warburton. If he was, such fear would have been no imputation on his courage and honour. He may, nay, he must, have feared Warburton, not as cowed by his superiority, but as a just and reasonable-minded man fears the contact of the irrepressible slanderer. He feared dirt, not confutation. It was impossible to suppress Warburton, and Warton was too refined a scholar to fight him with his own weapons of scurrility and abuse. When a man is incurably wrong-headed, the only resource is to avoid him. If it seems unhandsome in Warton to have spoken his opinion of the Bishop after his death, having preserved silence for so many years, it should be remembered that what might have been presumptuous in him at thirty-five, when he was only beginning to be known, was no longer so at seventy-five, when he had a long and honourable career of a life devoted to learning behind him. . . . Strange to say, though Warton's *Pope* was published in 1797, and though it has been superseded in the market, it has never yet been improved upon. —PATTISON, MARK, 1872–89, *Pope and His Editors, Essays, ed. Nettleship, vol.* II, *pp.* 368, 373.

GENERAL

Have you seen the works of two young authors, a Mr. Warton and a Mr. Collins, both writers of Odes? It is odd enough, but each is the half of a considerable man, and one the counterpart of the other. The first has but little invention, very poetical choice of expression, and a good ear. The second, a fine fancy, modelled upon the antique, a bad ear, great variety of words, and images with no choice at all. They both deserve to last some years but will not.—GRAY, THOMAS, 1746, *Letter to Thomas Wharton, Dec.* 27; *Works, ed. Gosse, vol.* II, *p.* 159.

To every classical reader, indeed, Warton's Virgil will afford the richest fund of instruction and amusement; and as a professional man, I hesitate not to declare,

that I scarcely know a work, to the upper classes of schools, so pregnant with the most valuable advantages: as it imparts information, without the encouragement of idleness; and crowns the exertions of necessary and laudable industry with the acquisition of a pure and unadulterated taste.—WOOLL, JOHN, 1806, *Memoirs of Warton, p.* 28.

The power which feels, and the power which originates poetry, are totally distinct. The former no writer seems to have possessed with more exquisite precision, than Dr. Warton; and I do not mean to deny that he possessed the latter in a considerable degree: I only say that his powers of execution do not seem to have been equal to his taste.—BRYDGES, SIR SAMUEL EGERTON, 1807, *Censura Literaria, vol.* III, *p.* 199.

On this small collection of Lyric verse the fame of Dr. Warton, as a poet, principally rests. Of the seventeen Odes, however, of which it is composed, there are but two entitled to an elevated rank for their lofty tones and high finish; the Odes "To Fancy" and "On reading Mr. West's Pindar," and of these the first is much the superior. It abounds, indeed, in a succession of strongly contrasted and high-wrought imagery, clothed in a versification of the sweetest cadence and most brilliant polish. . . . The studies and propensities of Warton peculiarly fitted him for a translator of this portion of Virgil. His knowledge of the language of his original was intimate and critical; he was well versed in the manners, customs, and mythology of the ancients; he had a strong relish of the tender and sympathetic; his taste was delicately pure and chastised, and his versification correctly harmonious. With these qualifications, he has produced a translation of the Georgics which, in taste, costume, and fidelity, in sweetness, tenderness, and simplicity, has far exceeded any previous attempt, and has only been rivalled by the version of Mr. Sotheby. —DRAKE, NATHAN, 1810, *Essays, Illustrative of the Rambler, Adventurer, and Idler, vol.* II, *pp.* 117, 123.

As a critic, Dr. Warton is distinguished by his love of the fanciful and romantic. He examined our poetry at a period when it appeared to him that versified observations on familiar life and manners had usurped the honours which were exclusively due to the bold and inventive powers of imagination. . . . The school of the Wartons, considering them as poets, was rather too studiously prone to description. The doctor, like his brother, certainly so far realized his own ideas of inspiration, as to burden his verse with few observations on life which oppress the mind by their solidity. To his brother he is obviously inferior in the graphic and romantic style of composition, at which he aimed; but in which, it must nevertheless be owned, that in some parts of his "Ode to Fancy" he has been pleasingly successful.—Campbell, Thomas, 1819, *Specimens of the British Poets.*

His reputation as a critic and a scholar has preserved his poetry from neglect. Of his Odes, that to Fancy, written when he was very young, is one that least disappoints us by a want of poetic feeling. Yet if we compare it with that by Collins, on the Poetical Character, we shall see of how much higher beauty the same subject was capable. In the "Ode to Evening," he has again tried his strength with Collins. There are some images of rural life in it that have the appearance of being drawn from nature, and which therefore please. . . . In his "Dying Indian," he has produced a few lines of extraordinary force and pathos. The rest of his poems, in blank verse, are for the most part of an indifferent structure.—Cary, Henry Francis, 1821-24-45, *Lives of the English Poets, From Johnson to Kirke White, pp.* 177, 178.

One of the ripest scholars and soundest critics England has produced.—Cleveland, Charles D., 1853, *English Literature of the Nineteenth Century, p.* 19.

Joseph Warton was not one of those original men of genius who rouse our curiosity and leave their mark on their age. Johnson, with far less learning, and Gray, who left only a few hundred lines of fragmentary poetry, will count as more remarkable men than Warton. But if, from want of force of character, Warton does not hold a first place among his contemporaries, he will always claim the regard of students of our literature, both for what he was himself, and for the new direction which he impressed on poetical criticism in this country.—Pattison, Mark, 1872-89, *Pope and His Editors, Essays, ed. Nettleship, vol.* ii, *p.* 369.

What Warton laid down as principles in his prose essays, he tried to exemplify in his verse. He turned directly away from Classicism, and drew his inspiration from fresh out-door nature and from meditative melancholy. Perhaps he is the first *consciously* romantic poet in the eighteenth century.—Phelps, William Lyon, 1893, *The Beginnings of the English Romantic Movement, p.* 92.

Warton deserves remembrance as a learned and sagacious critic. He was a literary, not a philological, scholar. His verse, although it indicates a true appreciation of natural scenery, is artificial and constrained in expression. He was well equipped for the rôle of literary historian, but his great designs in that field never passed far beyond the stage of preliminary meditation. It was as a leader of the revolution which overtook literary criticism in England in the eighteenth century that his chief work was done.—Lee, Sidney, 1899, *Dictionary of National Biography, vol.* lix, *p.* 430.

Elizabeth Montagu

1720–1800

Born at York, Oct. 2, 1720: died at Montagu House, London, Aug. 25, 1800. An English author and social leader. On Aug 5, 1742, she married Edward Montagu, grandson of the first Earl of Sandwich. After 1750 she held her salon in Hill street, Mayfair. The epithet "blue-stocking" was first applied to her assemblies. Among her visitors were Lord Lyttelton, Burke, Garrick, and Sir Joshua Reynolds. Her younger associates included Hannah More and Fanny Burney. In 1760 she contributed three dialogues to Lyttelton's "Dialogues of the Dead." She visited Paris after the peace of 1763. In 1769 she wrote an essay on the "Genius of Shakspere" in answer to Voltaire. In 1776 she built Montagu House, now No. 22 Portman Square, where she died. (This was not the Montagu House upon the site of which the British Museum was built.)—Smith, Benjamin E., 1894-97, *The Century Cyclopedia of Names, p.* 700.

PERSONAL

The husband of Mrs. Montagu, of Shakespeareshire, is dead, and has left her an estate of seven thousand pounds a year in her own power. Will you come and be candidate for her hand? I conclude it will be given to a champion at some Olympic games; and were I she, I would sooner marry you than Pindar. — WALPOLE, HORACE, 1775, *Letter to William Mason; Letters, ed. Cunningham, vol.* VI, *p.* 217.

Just returned from spending one of the most agreeable days of my life, with the female Mæcenas of Hill-street; she engaged me five or six days ago to dine with her, and had assembled half the wits of the age. The only fault that charming woman has, is, that she is fond of collecting too many of them together at one time. There were nineteen persons assembled at dinner, but after the repast, she has a method of dividing her guests, or rather letting them assort themselves, into little groups of five or six each. I spent my time in going from one to the other of these little societies, as I happened more or less to like the subjects they were discussing. Mrs. Scott, Mrs. Montagu's sister, a very good writer, Mrs. Carter, Mrs. Barbauld, and a man of letters, whose name I have forgotten, made up one of these little parties. When we had canvassed two or three subjects, I stole off and joined in with the next group, which was composed of Mrs. Montagu, Dr. Johnson, the Provost of Dublin, and two other ingenious men. —MORE, HANNAH, 1776, *Letter to her Sister, Memoirs, ed. Roberts, vol.* I, *p.* 44.

Mrs. Montague wants to make up with me again. I dare say she does; but I will not be taken and left even at the pleasure of those who are much nearer and dearer to me than Mrs. Montague. We want no flash, no flattery. I never had more of either in my life, nor ever lived half so happily : Mrs. Montague wrote creeping letters when she wanted my help, or foolishly *thought* she did, and then turned her back upon me and sent her adherents to do the same.—THRALE, HESTER LYNCH (MRS. PIOZZI), 1789, *Journal, May* 1; *Autobiography, ed. Hayward, p.* 107.

To me, on all occasions, ever since 1771, when I first became acquainted with her, she has been a faithful and affectionate friend especially in seasons of distress and difficulty. You will not wonder, then, that her death afflicts me. For some years past a failure in her eyes had made writing very painful to her; but for not less than twenty years she was my punctual correspondent. She was greatly attached to Montagu, who received his name from her, and not less interested in my other son, and in everything that related to my family. I need not tell you what an excellent writer she was : you must have seen her book on Shakespeare, as compared with the Greek and French dramatic writers. I have known several ladies eminent in literature, but she excelled them all; and in conversation she had more *wit* than any other person, male or female, whom I have ever known. These, however, were her slighter accomplishments : what was infinitely more to her honour, she was a sincere Christian, both in faith and in practice, and took every proper opportunity to show it; so that by her example and influence she did much good.— BEATTIE, JAMES, 1799, *Letter to Rev. Dr. Laing, March* 7; *Forbes' Life of Beattie, vol.* III, *p.* 162.

At the same time of which I speak, the *gens de lettres,* or "Blue Stockings," as they were commonly denominated, formed a very numerous, powerful, compact phalanx in the midst of London. . . . Mrs. Montague was then the Madame du Deffand of the English capital; and her house constituted the central point of union, for all those persons who already were known, or who emulated to become known by their talents and productions. Her supremacy . . . was indeed established on more solid foundations than those of intellect, and rested on more tangible materials than any with which Shakspeare himself could furnish her. Though she had not as yet begun to construct the splendid mansion in which she afterwards resided near Portman Square, but lived in an elegant house in Hill Street . . . Mrs. Montague was accustomed to open her house to a large company of both sexes, whom she frequently entertained at dinner. A service of plate, and a table plentifully covered, disposed her guests to admire the splendour of her fortune, not less than the lustre of her talents. . . . Mrs. Montague, in 1776, verged towards her sixtieth year. But her person, which was thin, spare, and in good preservation, gave her an appearance of less antiquity. From the infirmities often attendant on advanced life, she seemed to be almost wholly exempt. All the lines of her countenance bespoke intelligence, and her eyes, were accommodated to her cast of features, which had in them something satirical and severe, rather than amiable or inviting. . . . Destitute of taste in disposing the ornaments of her dress, she nevertheless studied or affected those aids, more than would seem to have become a woman possessing a philosophic mind, intent on higher pursuits than toilet. Even when approaching to four score, this female weakness still accompanied her; nor could she relinquish her diamond necklace and bows, which . . . formed on evenings the perpetual ornament of her emaciated person. I used to think that these glittering appendages of opulence, sometimes helped to dazzle the disputants, whom her arguments might not always convince. . . . Notwithstanding the defects that I have enumerated, she possessed a masculine understanding, enlightened, cultivated, and expanded by the acquaintance of men, as well as of books. Many of the most illustrious persons in rank, no less than in ability, under the reigns of George II. and III., had been her correspondents, friends, companions and admirers. — WRAXALL, SIR NATHANIEL WILLIAM, 1815, *Historical Memoirs of My Own Time, from* 1772 *to* 1784, *pp.* 64, 65.

She was equal to conversation on every subject; but she assumed that dogmatic and presumptuous tone which is well known as peculiar to learned English ladies, and even to young English tourists.—SCHLOSSER, FRIEDRICH CHRISTOPH, 1823, *History of the Eighteenth Century, tr. Davison, pt.* ii. *ch.* i.

Her conversational powers were of a truly superior order; strong, just, clear, and often eloquent. Her process in argument, notwithstanding an earnest solicitude for pre-eminence, was uniformly polite and candid. But her reputation for wit seemed always in her thoughts, marring their natural flow, and untutored expression. No sudden start of talent urged forth any precarious opinion; no vivacious new idea varied her logical course of ratiocination. Her smile though most generally benignant, was rarely gay; and her liveliest sallies had a something of anxiety rather than of hilarity—till their

success was ascertained by applause. Her form was stately, and her manners were dignified. Her face retained strong remains of beauty throughout life; and though its native cast was evidently that of severity, its expression was softened off in discourse by an almost constant desire to please. . . . Taken for all in all, Mrs. Montagu was rare in her attainments; splendid in her conduct; open to the calls of charity; forward to precede those of indigent genius; and unchangeably just and firm in the application of her interest, her principles, and her fortune, to the encouragement of loyalty, and the support of virtue. —D'ARBLAY, MADAME (FANNY BURNEY), 1832, *Memoirs of Doctor Burney.*

Mrs. Montagu is one of the best specimens on record of that most comprehensive character—a woman of the world, for she was *of* the world, yet not corrupted by it. Her wit, displayed in the girlish effusions of a satire, rather the result of high spirits than of a sarcastic tone, improved as age advanced. Passionately fond of society, a lover of the great, she displayed; nevertheless, a perfect contentment when deprived of excitement by any accident; and, whilst she courted the great, she was courteous and bountiful to the small.—THOMSON, KATHERINE, 1848, *The Literary Circles of the Last Century, Fraser's Magazine, vol.* 37, *p.* 73.

Mrs. Montague's parties were pleasant, no doubt, for she got together the people best worth knowing; and though she liked flattery, and loved to drape and pose herself as the chief Muse of a new British Parnassus, she was essentially a gentlewoman, full of kindness and benevolence, standing stoutly up for her friends, and always ready to help unknown and struggling people with her patronage, her advice, and her money. If she quarrelled with Johnson when in his "Lives of the Poets" he decried one of her idols, Lyttelton, she not the less kept up her annuity to poor blind Miss Williams. If her "Essay on Shakspere" is not very profound, it shows at least sounder appreciation of the great dramatist than the criticisms of Johnson, who abused it.—LESLIE, CHARLES ROBERT AND TAYLOR, TOM, 1865, *Life and Times of Sir Joshua Reynolds, vol.* I, *p.* 452.

But even in the days of her maidenhood, when she was glad in her youth and in her beauty, and conscious of her intellect, yet unconscious of the pleasures, duties, and trials before her, yet when she feared she might live idle and die vain, she said, "If ever I have an inscription over me, it shall be without a name, and only,—Here lies one whom having done no harm, no one should censure ; and, having done no good, no one can commend ; who, for past folly, only asks oblivion." She lived, however, to do much good, to make great amends for small and venial follies, and by the magnificent usefulness, which little Burney has recorded, to merit such pains as it may cost a poor chronicler to rescue her name and deeds from the oblivion which she asked in the pleasant days of her bright youth and her subduing beauty.—DORAN, JOHN, 1873, *A Lady of the Last Century*, p. 356.

Other ladies—Mrs. Montagu's friend the Duchess of Portland, Mrs. Ord, Mrs. Vesey, wife of Agmondesham Vesey, Mrs. Boscawen, wife of the admiral, and Mrs. Greville, wife of Fulke Greville—endeavoured to rival Mrs. Montagu's entertainments ; but for nearly fifty years she maintained a practically undisputed supremacy as hostess in the intellectual society of London, and to her assemblies was, apparently for the first time, applied the now accepted epithet of "blue-stocking." Two explanations of the term have been suggested. According to the ordinary account, which was adopted by Sir William Forbes in his "Life of Beattie," in 1806 (i. 210), full dress was not insisted on at Mrs. Montagu's assemblies, and Benjamin Stillingfleet who regularly attended them, as well as the rival assemblies presided over by Mrs. Vesey or Mrs. Boscawen, habitually infringed social conventions by appearing in blue worsted instead of black silk stockings ; consequently, Admiral Boscawen, a scoffer at his wife's social ambitions, is stated to have applied the epithet "blue-stockings" to all ladies' conversaziones. On the other hand, Lady Crewe, daughter of Mrs. Greville, who was one of Mrs. Montagu's rival hostesses, stated that the ladies themselves at Mrs. Montagu's parties wore "blue-stockings as a distinction," in imitation of a fashionable French visitor, Madame de Polignac.—LEE, SIDNEY, 1894, *Dictionary of National Biography*, vol. XXXVIII, p. 241.

ESSAY ON THE GENIUS OF SHAKESPEARE
1769

Mrs. Montague, a lady distinguished for having written an Essay on Shakspeare, being mentioned,—REYNOLDS : "I think that essay does her honour." JOHNSON. "Yes, sir, it does *her* honour ; but it would do nobody else honour. I have, indeed, not read it all. But when I take up the end of a web, and find it packthread, I do not expect, by looking further, to find embroidery. Sir, I will venture to say there is not one sentence of true criticism in her book." GARRICK : "But, sir, surely it shows how much Voltaire has mistaken Shakspeare,—which nobody else has done." JOHNSON : "Sir, nobody else has thought it worth while. And what merit is there in that ? You may as well praise a schoolmaster for whipping a boy who has construed ill. No, sir ; there is no real criticism in it,—none showing the beauty of thought as formed on the workings of the human heart." . . . One day at Sir Joshua's table, when it was related that Mrs. Montague, in an excess of compliment to the author of a modern tragedy (Braganza ?), had exclaimed, "I tremble for Shakspeare," Johnson said, "When Shakspeare has got—[Jephson ?] for his rival and Mrs. Montague for his defender, he is in a poor state indeed."—JOHNSON, SAMUEL, 1769, *Life by Boswell*.

The most elegant and judicious piece of criticism which the present age has produced.—WARTON, THOMAS, 1778–81, *The History of English Poetry*.

I no longer wonder that Mrs. Montagu stands at the head of all that is called learned, and that every critic veils his bonnet to her superior judgment. I am now reading and have reached the middle of her essay on the genius of Shakspeare —a book of which, strange as it may seem, though I must have read it formerly, I had absolutely forgot the existence. The learning, the good sense, the sound judgment, and the wit displayed in it fully justify, not only my compliment, but all compliments that either have been already paid to her talents or shall be paid hereafter. Voltaire, I doubt not, rejoiced that his antagonist wrote in English, and that his countrymen could not possibly be judges of the dispute. Could they have known how much she was in the right, and by how many thousand miles the Bard of Avon is superior to all their dramatists, the French critic would have lost half his fame among them.—COWPER, WILLIAM, 1788, *Letter to Lady Hesketh, May* 27.

Considering it as a piece of the secondary or comparative species of criticism; and not of that profound species which alone Dr. Johnson would allow to be "real criticism." It is, besides, clearly and elegantly expressed, and has done effectually what it professed to do; namely, vindicated Shakspeare from the misrepresentations of Voltaire; and considering how many young people were misled by his witty, though false observations, Mrs. Montagu's "Essay" was of service to Shakspeare with a certain class of readers, and is, therefore, entitled to praise.—BOSWELL, JAMES, 1791–93, *Life of Samuel Johnson, note.*

Hurd and Lord Kames, especially the former, may be reckoned among the best of this class; Mrs. Montagu, perhaps, in her celebrated Essay, not very far from the bottom of the list.—HALLAM, HENRY, 1837–39, *Introduction to the Literature of Europe, pt.* iii, *ch.* vi, *par.* 54.

Mrs. Montague was the Minerva, for so she was complimented on this occasion, whose celestial spear was to transfix the audacious Gaul. Her "Essay on the Writings and Genius of Shakespeare, compared with the Greek and French dramatic poets," served for a popular answer to Voltaire. This accomplished lady, who had raised a literary coterie about her, which attracted such fashionable notice that its title has survived its institution, found in "the Blue-stocking Club" choral hymns and clouds of incense gathering about the altar in Portman Square! The volume is deemed "a wonderful performance," by those echoes of contemporary pre-possessions, the compilers of dictionary-biography: even the poet Cowper placed Mrs. Montague "at the head of all that is called learned."— DISRAELI, ISAAC, 1841, *Shakespeare, Amenities of Literature.*

LETTERS

Mrs. Montagu's [Letters] are lively and ingenious, but not natural.—MACKINTOSH, SIR JAMES, 1808, *Life, vol.* I, *ch.* viii.

I think very highly of them. One of their chief merits is *series juncturaque.* Nothing can be more easy and natural than the manner in which the thoughts rise one out of the other, even where the thoughts may appear rather forced, nor is the expression ever hard or laboured. I see but little to object to in the thoughts themselves, but nothing can be more natural or graceful than the manner in which they are put together. The flow of her style is not less natural, because it is fully charged with shining particles, and sparkles as it flows.—WINDHAM, WILLIAM, 1809, *Diary, Dec.* 5.

The merit of the pieces before us seems to us to consist mainly in the great gaiety and vivacity with which they are written. The wit, to be sure, is often childish, and generally strained and artificial; but still it both sparkles and abounds; and though we should admire it more if it were better selected, or even if there were less of it, we cannot witness this profuse display of spirits and ingenuity without receiving a strong impression of the talents and ambition of the writer. The faults of the letters, on the other hand, are more numerous. In the first place, they have, properly speaking, no subjects. They are all letters of mere idleness, friendship, and flattery. There are no events,—no reasonings,—no anecdotes of persons who are still remembered,—no literature, and scarcely any original or serious opinions. . . . There are great faults in the volumes before us; and that we do not exactly perceive the necessity of reading the bad letters before we are favoured with the good.—JEFFREY, FRANCIS LORD, 1809, *Mrs. Montagu's Letters, Edinburgh Review, vol.* 15, *pp.* 76, 87.

I am now reading the third and fourth volumes of Mrs. Montague's "Letters." To me, who have lived through all the time she writes of, they are interesting,—independent of the wit and talent,—as recalling a number of persons and events once present to my mind: they are also, I think, very entertaining, though, as letters, somewhat studied. — BARBAULD, ANNA LÆTITIA, 1813, *Works, vol.* II, *p.* 139.

In her own generation Mrs. Montagu was without a superior in the art of letter writing.—SCOONES, W. BAPTISTE, 1880, *Four Centuries of English Letters, p.* 277.

GENERAL

These letters do great credit both to her head and heart; they are written in an easy and perspicuous style; are filled with judicious and pertinent reflections upon the passing events and the great men of the times; and, with her "Essay on Shakspeare," give her no mean rank among English authors. If not a profound critic, she was certainly an acute and ingenious one, possessing judgment and taste as well as learning; and if not of such versatile talents as her namesake, Lady Mary Wortley, she is an example of much higher moral purity both in her writings and character. — CLEVELAND, CHARLES D., 1853, *English Literature of the Nineteenth Century, p. 25.*

Hugh Blair
1718–1800

Born at Edinburgh 7th April 1718, in 1730 entered the university, and in 1741 was licensed as a preacher. After occupying the churches of Collessie in Fife, Canongate, and Lady Yester's, he was promoted in 1758 to one of the charges of the High Church, Edinburgh. In 1759 he commenced a series of university lectures on "Composition;" and in 1762 he was appointed to a new regius chair of Rhetoric and Belles-lettres, with a salary of £70 a year. He resigned this post in 1783, and published his "Lectures," which obtained a reputation far beyond their merits, and one that time has by no means confirmed. His "Sermons" (1777) enjoyed the approval not only of Dr. Johnson, but of George III., who bestowed on Blair in 1780 a pension of £200 a year. Blair died December 27, 1800.—PATRICK AND GROOME, *eds.,* 1897, *Chambers's Biographical Dictionary, p. 103.*

PERSONAL

Dr. Blair was a different kind of man from Robertson, and his character is very justly delineated by Dr. Finlayson, so far as he goes. Robertson was most sagacious, Blair was most naïf. Neither of them could have been said to have either wit or humor. Of the latter Robertson had a small tincture—Blair had hardly a relish for it. Robertson had a bold and ambitious mind, and a strong desire to make himself considerable; Blair was timid and unambitious, and withheld himself from public business of every kind, and seemed to have no wish but to be admired as a preacher, particularly by the ladies. His conversation was so infantine that many people thought it impossible, at first sight, that he could be a man of sense or genius. He was as eager about a new paper for his wife's drawing-room, or his own new wig, as about a new tragedy or a new epic poem.—CARLYLE, ALEXANDER, 1753–56–1860, *Autobiography, p. 236.*

Saturday morning proving rainy, I could not resist the temptation of staying till Sunday, and I heard Dr. Robertson in the morning, and Dr. Blair in the afternoon. They are neither of them orators, but Dr. Robertson has a serious, unaffected manner which pleased me very much. Dr. Blair is very pompous in his delivery, and all the great and fashionable attend his church. He gave us a sermon on censoriousness, which I understand is soon to be published with some others, in a third volume.—ROGERS, SAMUEL, 1784, *Letter, July* 21; *Early Life by Clayden, p.* 79.

With Dr. Blair I am more at ease. I never respect him with humble veneration; but when he kindly interests himself in my welfare, or still more, when he descends from his pinnacle, and meets me on equal ground in conversation, my heart overflows with what is called *liking.*— When he neglects me for the mere carcass of greatness, or when his eye measures the difference of our points of elevation, I say to myself, with scarcely any emotion, What do I care for him, or his pomp either? — BURNS, ROBERT, 1787, *Commonplace Book, Apr.* 9.

In Edinburgh none was more famous in the latter half of the eighteenth century than Dr. Hugh Blair. His dingy church was attended by the most fashionable when he preached; his little, dark class-room at college was full of the most cultured when he lectured; every tea-table was silent when he spoke; every supper-party was deferential as he conversed. An uneventful life of unbroken health and prosperity was the fortune of the preacher-critic of Scotland. . . . He was accepted as the arbiter of taste. Poems and treatises were submitted for his judgment, and his opinion was considered infallible. Home brought to him his "Douglas," Blacklock his poems, Hume his essays, and we know how in later years his verdict on Burns' poems was awaited with anxiety. He was the literary accoucheur of Scotland. At the same time patrons conferred with him on suitable moderate "presentees" for parishes, and town councils consulted him on candidates for professorial chairs. Is it surprising that the popular preacher, the respected critic, the deferred-to guide, had his constitutional vanity strengthened, and that all this homage made him more pompous and certain of his infallibility, especially as he was utterly devoid of any sense of humour?— GRAHAM, HENRY GREY, 1901, *Scottish Men of Letters in the Eighteenth Century*, *pp.* 121, 126.

SERMONS

I love "Blair's Sermons." Though the dog is a Scotchman, and a Presbyterian, and every thing he should not be, I was the first to praise them.—JOHNSON, SAMUEL, 1781, *Life by Boswell, ed. Hill, vol.* IV, *p.* 113.

Great merit they undoubtedly have; but I cannot discover in them that sublime simplicity of manner and style, which I have long thought essential to such compositions.—BEATTIE, JAMES, 1783, *Letter to the Bishop of Worcester, Sept.* 18; *Life, ed. Forbes, vol.* II, *p.* 308.

We have no modern sermons in the English language that can be considered as very eloquent. The merits of Blair (by far the most popular writer of sermons within the last century) are plain good sense, a happy application of scriptural quotation, and a clear harmonious style, richly tinged with scriptural language. He generally leaves his readers pleased with his judgment, and his just observations on human conduct, without ever rising so high as to touch the great passions, or kindle any enthusiasm in favour of virtue. For eloquence we must ascend as high as the days of Barrow and Jeremy Taylor: and even there, while we are delighted with their energy, their copiousness, and their fancy, we are in danger of being suffocated by a redundance which abhors all discrimination, which compares till it perplexes, and illustrates till it confounds.— SMITH, SYDNEY, 1802, *Dr. Rennel, Edinburgh Review, Essays, p.* 6.

No other sermons in Great Britain have been followed by so splendid a success as the once famous, now forgotten, discourses of Hugh Blair. Neither of Tillotson, nor Jeremy Taylor in past times, nor of Arnold or Newman or even Frederick Robertson in our own time, can be recorded, as of Blair, that they were translated into almost all the languages of Europe, and won for their author a public reward from the Crown. Nor was it only the vulgar public that was satisfied. Even the despot of criticism (fastidious judge, zealous High-churchman, fanatically English as he was), the mighty Samuel Johnson, who had a few years before declared that no Scottish clergyman had written any good work on religious subjects, pronounced, after his perusal of Blair's first sermon, "I have read it with more than approbation—to say it is good is to say too little."— STANLEY, ARTHUR PENRHYN, 1872, *Lectures on the History of the Church of Scotland, p.* 143.

They are not so much sermons as essays, composed by a professor of rhetoric to illustrate the principles of his art. For unction there was mere mouthing; instead of the solid common sense of earlier writers, an infinite capacity for repeating the feeblest of platitudes; their style seems to be determined by an attempt at the easy flow of the Addisonian period, disturbed by a recollection of Johnsonian grandiloquence; the morality can scarcely be dignified by the name of prudential, unless all prudence be summed up in the great commandment, be respectable; the theology is retained rather to give a faint seasoning to the general insipidity of moral commonplace than seriously to influence the thought; and the nearest approach to a philosophical argument is some feeble echo of Pope's "Essay on Man." Blair, in short, is in theology what Hayley was in poetry—a mere washed-out retailer of second-hand commonplaces, who gives us the impression that the real man has vanished, and left nothing but a wig and gown.—STEPHEN, LESLIE, 1876, *History of English Thought in the Eighteenth Century, vol.* II, *p.* 346.

They are perhaps grammatically correct in composition, but they are monotonous in style, and as for grasp of thought or reasoning, elevated emotion, or impassioned eloquence, they have none.—MACKINTOSH, JOHN, 1878-96, *The History of Civilisation in Scotland, vol.* IV, *p.* 216.

Of his sermons, which were originally

published in five volumes, it may be said that they were unduly praised at the time of their appearance, and that they are as unduly neglected now. Samuel Johnson called them "auro magis aurei;" and King George the Third, who was a great patron of Blair, and who gave him a pension of two hundred pounds a year, is reported to have often said that he wished to hear that the Bible and Blair's sermons were in the hands of every youth in the United Kingdom. These opinions from the leader of literature and the leader of fashion may perhaps account in some degree for the number of editions through which Blair's sermons passed; while the fact that the distinctive features of the Gospel are largely absent from them may explain the oblivion into which now they have fallen. But for style and method they may still be studied with advantage, though they do not now, of course, hold the same relatively high place in these respects which they did at the date of their publication. They have a distinctively modern cast, and his mode of opening up and dividing a subject is often felicitous and suggestive. In matter, however, they are exceedingly defective. —TAYLOR, WILLIAM M., 1887, *The Scottish Pulpit*, p. 155.

LECTURES ON RHETORIC AND BELLES-LETTRES
1783

They were originally designed for the initiation of youth into the study of belles lettres, and of composition. With the same intention they are now published; and, therefore, the form of Lectures, in which they were at first composed, is still retained. The author gives them to the world, neither as a work wholly original, nor as a compilation from the writings of others. On every subject contained in them, he has thought for himself. He consulted his own ideas and reflections: and a great part of what will be found in these Lectures is entirely his own. At the same time he availed himself of the ideas and reflections of others, as far as he thought them proper to be adopted. To proceed in this manner, was his duty as a public professor. It was incumbent on him to convey to his pupils all the knowledge that could improve them; to deliver not merely what was new, but what might be useful, from whatever quarter

it came. He hopes, that to such as are studying to cultivate their taste, to form their style, or to prepare themselves for public speaking or composition, his Lectures will afford a more comprehensive view of what relates to these subjects than, as far as he knows, is to be received from any one book in our language.— BLAIR, HUGH, 1783, *Lectures on Rhetoric and Belles-Lettres, Preface.*

These "Lectures on Rhetoric" have been for several years known to the public. They were printed by their excellent author, in the latter period of his life, after he had retired from the discharge of his academical duties. They contain an accurate analysis of the principles of literary composition, in all the various species of writing: a happy illustration of those principles by the most beautiful and apposite examples, drawn from the best authors both ancient and modern; and an admirable digest of the rules of elocution, as applicable to the oratory of the pulpit, the bar, and the popular assembly. They do not aim at the character of a work purely original; for this, as the author justly considered, would have been to circumscribe their utility; neither, in point of style, are they polished with the same degree of care that the author has bestowed on some of his other works, as, for example, his "Sermons:" Yet so useful is the object of these lectures, so comprehensive their plan, and such the excellence of the matter they contain, that, if not the most splendid, they will perhaps prove the most durable monument of their author's reputation.—TYTLER, ALEXANDER FRASER, 1806–14, *Memoirs of the Life and Writings of Lord Kames, vol.* I, *p.* 275.

Will always be esteemed valuable as an exercise of correct taste, and an accumulation of good sense, on the various branches of the art of speaking and writing. . . . In the first place, with respect to the language, though the selection of words is proper enough, the arrangement of them in the sentences is often in the utmost degree stiff and artificial. It is hardly possible to depart further from any resemblance to what is called a living or spoken style, which is the proper diction at all events for popular addresses, if not for all the departments of prose composition. Instead of the thought throwing itself into words, by a free, instantaneous, and almost unconscious action, and passing off in that easy form, it is pretty apparent there was a good deal of handicraft employed in getting ready proper cases and trusses, of various but carefully measured lengths and figures, to put the thoughts into, as they came out, in very slow succession, each of them cooled and stiffened to numbness in waiting so long to be dressed. . . . In the second place, there is no texture in the composition. The sentences appear often like a series of little independent propositions, each satisfied with its own distinct meaning, and capable of being placed in a different part of the train, without injury to any mutual connection, or ultimate purpose, of the thoughts. The ideas relate to the subject generally, without specifically relating to one another.—FOSTER, JOHN, 1807–56, *Critical Essays, ed. Ryland, vol. I. pp. 82, 84, 85.*

Though not equal to Campbell's "Philosophy of Rhetoric" in depth of thought or in ingenious original research, they are written in a most pleasing style, convey a large amount of valuable information, suggest many most useful hints, and contain an accurate analysis of the principles of literary composition in almost every species of writing, and an able digest of the rules of eloquence as adapted to the pulpit, the bar, or to popular assemblies. In short, they form an admirable system of rules for forming the style and cultivating the taste of youth; and the time will be far distant, if it ever arrives, when they shall cease to be a text-book in every well-devised course of study for a liberal education.—CLEVELAND, CHARLES D., 1853, *English Literature of the Nineteenth Century, p. 30.*

Deserves special mention for his lectures on "Rhetoric and Belles-Lettres," which for a long time constituted the principal text-book on those subjects in our schools and colleges. A better understanding of the true scope of rhetoric as a science has caused this work to be superseded by later text-books. Blair's lectures treat principally of style and literary criticism, and are excellent for their analysis of some of the best authors, and for happy illustrations from their works.—COPPÉE, HENRY, 1872, *English Literature, Considered as an Interpreter of English History, p. 370.*

His "Rhetoric" is a very vapid performance compared with Campbell's.—MINTO, WILLIAM, 1872–80, *Manual of English Prose Literature, p. 475.*

The chair of Belles-Lettres was filled by the accomplished Dr. Hugh Blair, whose lectures remain one of the best samples of the correct and elegant, but narrow and frigid style, both of sentiment and criticism, which then flourished throughout Europe, and nowhere more than in Edinburgh.—SHAIRP, JOHN CAMPBELL, 1879, *Robert Burns (English Men of Letters), p. 44.*

His position as a critic was improved by the publication in 1783 of his "Lectures on Rhetoric and Belles Lettres," which made him the literary pope of Scotland.—GRAHAM, HENRY GREY, 1901, *Scottish Men of Letters in the Eighteenth Century, p. 129.*

GENERAL

A tiresome critic, in the French style: he was placed far below Johnson.—CHATEAUBRIAND, FRANÇOIS RENÉ VICOMTE DE, 1831, *Sketches of English Literature, vol. II, p. 269.*

Looked at the "Life of Hugh Blair;"— a stupid book, by a stupid man, about a stupid man. Surely it is strange that so poor a creature as Blair should ever have had any literary reputation at all. The "Life" is in that very vile fashion which Dugald Stewart set;—not a life, but a series of disquisitions on all sorts of subjects.—MACAULAY, THOMAS BABINGTON, 1850, *Journal, Nov. 5; Life and Letters, ed. Trevelyan.*

The lectures expressed the canons of taste of the time in which Addison, Pope, and Swift were recognised as the sole models of English style, and are feeble in thought, though written with a certain elegance of manner. A tenth edition appeared in 1806, and they have been translated into French. The same qualities are obvious in the sermons, which for a long time enjoyed extraordinary popularity. . . . The sermons were translated into many languages, and until the rise of a new school passed as the models of the art. They are carefully composed; he took a week over one (Boswell's *Tour,* ch. iii), and they are the best examples of the sensible, if unimpassioned and rather affected, style of the moderate divines of the time. They have gone through many editions.—STEPHEN, LESLIE, 1886, *Dictionary of National Biography, vol.* v, *p.* 160.

The only reason for mentioning Blair amid so many of his betters is that he wrote popular lectures on rhetoric, in which he said a deal about proportioning the sentence, but nothing about the paragraph; and one is curious to see if such men as Blair, Campbell, and Kames, personally followed paragraph law. Blair's smooth Shaftesburian style leads him securely from sentence to sentence; he writes nearly six monotonous sentences to the paragraph; he follows the loose order of procedure in the paragraph, and observes the law of unity. In brief, it is strange that such mildly correct rhetoricians as he, wrote respectable paragraphs, but, amid the multitude of their stylistic theories, had no theory of the process.— LEWIS, EDWIN HERBERT, 1894, *The History of the English Paragraph, p.* 120.

James Macknight
1721–1800

An eminent Scotch divine, was born in Ayrshire in 1721. He studied in the University of Glasgow, but, like many of the Presbyterian divines both of his own country and of England, went abroad, and finished his studies at Leyden. On his return he entered the ministry in the Scotch Church (in 1753) as pastor of Maybole, in Ayrshire. Here he spent sixteen years, during which time he prepared three works: "A Harmony of the Gospels" (Lond. 1756, 2 vols. 4to), with copious illustrations, being, in fact, a life of Christ, embracing everything which the evangelists have related concerning him:—"A New Translation of the Epistles" (published in 1795 in 4 vols. 4to, and later in 6 vols. 8vo.):—and "Truth of Gospel History" (1763, 4to). These works were favorably received, and are to this day highly esteemed. The "Harmony" has been repeatedly printed, and to the later editions there are added several dissertations on curious points in the history or antiquities of the Jews. The theology of them is what is called moderately orthodox. For these his valuable services to sacred literature Dr. Macknight received the rewards in the power of the Presbyterian Church to give. The Degree of D. D. was conferred upon him by the University of Edinburgh. In 1769 he was removed from Maybole to the more desirable parish of Jedburgh, and in 1772 he became one of the ministers at Edinburgh. Here he continued for the remainder of his life, useful in the ministry and an ornament to the Church. He died Jan. 13, 1800.—WORMAN, J. H., 1873, *Cyclopædia of Biblical, Theological and Ecclesiastical Literature*, eds. *M'Clintock and Strong, vol.* v, *p.* 624.

PERSONAL

I think I see his large, square, bony visage, his enormous white wig, girdled by many tiers of curls, his old, snuffy black clothes, his broad, flat feet, and his thread-bare blue greatcoat. . . . He rarely walked without reading. His elbows were stuck, immovably on to his haunches, on which they rested as brackets and enabled him to form a desk for his book. In this attitude he shuffled forward (in the Meadows) at the rate of half an inch each step; moving his rigid, angular bulk straight forward, without giving place to any person or thing, or being aware indeed that there was anything in the world except himself and his volume.—COCKBURN, HENRY THOMAS LORD, 1854–6, *Memorials of His Time.*

An estimable and learned divine, whose "Harmony of the Gospels" was regarded in its day as a marvel of criticism, though simple folk wondered that the doctor should write a book to "make four men agree who never cast oot."—GRAHAM, HENRY GREY, 1901, *Scottish Men of Letters in the Eighteenth Century, p.* 429.

GENERAL

Dr. Macknight closely adheres to the principle of Osiander; but his paraphrase and commentary contain so much useful information that his "Harmony" has long been regarded as a standard book among divines. It is in the lists of Bishops Watson and Tomline. The preliminary disquisitions greatly enhance its value.— HORNE, THOMAS HARTWELL, 1818–39, *A Manual of Biblical Bibliography, p.* 133.

This ["Harmony"] is the most valuable work of the kind in the English language.

Less violence is done to the text of the Evangelists than by most harmonies; and the evangelical narratives, by being minutely compared, often very happily illustrate one another. . . . His preliminary observations contain useful information : his notes are seldom profound : and the paraphrase contains sentiments which do not accord with the doctrine of the Evangelists. . . . This is one of the most useful ["Apostolical Epistles"] and one of the most dangerous books on the New Testament,—which has thrown considerable light on the Epistles, and, at the same time, has propagated most pernicious views of their leading doctrines. . . . As a critical work it is entitled to rank high. . . . His notes discover very considerable acquaintance with sacred criticism, and, had they contained less of his erroneous theology, would have been very valuable.—ORME, WILLIAM, 1824, *Bibliotheca Biblica.*

Nor let the name of Macknight be forgotten. His works are, indeed, the more exclusive property of the disciplined theological student ; but the *general* reader will do well to secure his inviting quartos upon the *Gospels* and *Epistles* of the New Testament. In these he will find learning without pedantry, and piety without enthusiasm. In short, no theological collection can be perfect without them. If any man may be said to have exhausted his subject, it is Macknight.—DIBDIN, THOMAS FROGNALL, 1824, *The Library Companion.*

BALMER—"Pray, sir, do you admire Macknight as a commentator ?" HALL— "Yes, sir, I do, very much : I think it would be exceedingly difficult, indeed, to come after him in expounding the apostolic epistles. I admit, at the same time, that he has grievous deficiencies : there is a lamentable want of spirituality and elevation about him. He never sets his foot in the other world if he can get a hole to step into in this ; and he never gives a passage a meaning which would render it applicable and useful in all ages if he can find in it any local or temporary allusion. He makes fearful havoc, sir, of the text on which you preached to-day. His exposition of it is inimitably absurd." The text referred to was Ephesians i. 8 : "Wherein he hath abounded towards us in all wisdom and prudence ;" and the "wisdom and prudence" are explained by Macknight, not of the wisdom of God as displayed in the scheme of redemption, but of the wisdom and prudence granted to the apostles to enable them to discharge their office.—HALL, ROBERT, 1819–23, *Miscellaneous Gleanings from Mr. Hall's Conversational Remarks by Rev. Robert Balmer, Works*, ed. Gregory, vol. VI, p. 121.

This work ["Truth of Gospel History Shewed"] is admitted by the best judges to be a performance as useful and instructive as any we have on that important subject.—LOWNDES, WILLIAM THOMAS, 1839, *British Librarian.*

McKnight's "Harmony" is one of the standard works in the literature of the subject. . . . McKnight on the "Epistles" is also one of the standard works which every theologian wishes to have in his library. Neither of these works is exhaustive or final. The science of hermeneutics have made great advance since McKnight's day. Yet they are works of great ability and of original research and no interpreter even now can safely pass them by as superseded.—HART, JOHN S., 1872, *A Manual of English Literature, p.* 373.

His style had little elegance or ornament, but it is clear and pertinent to the subject.—MACKINTOSH, JOHN, 1878–96, *The History of Civilisation in Scotland, vol.* IV, p. 216.

George Steevens

1736–1800

Shakspeare scholar ; born at Stepney, London, May 10, 1736 ; was educated at King's College, Cambridge ; devoted himself to Shakspearean studies, and in 1766 published, in 4 vols. 8vo, "Twenty of the Plays of Shakspeare, being the whole number printed in Quarto during his Lifetime," etc., which led to his association with Dr. Johnson in an annotated edition published in 1773 under their joint names. Afterward, in conjunction with Issac Reed, he prepared two new editions (1785 and 1793). His editions remained the standard for the text for almost fifty years. He also assisted in the preparation of the "Biographia Dramatica," and furnished contributions to Nichols's "Biographical Anecdotes of Hogarth." Died at Hampstead, Jan. 22, 1800.—BEERS, HENRY A., *rev.* 1897, *Johnson's Universal Cyclopædia, vol.* VII, *p.* 735.

PERSONAL

His slaver so subtle no med'cine allays,
It kills by kind paragraphs, poisons with
    praise.
The "Chronicle," James, but too truly can
    tell
How the malice of man can fetch poison
    from Hell.
—BRYANT, JACOB, 1789, *Verses to Horace Walpole.*

If we possessed the secret history of the literary life of George Steevens, it would display an unparalleled series of arch deception and malicious ingenuity. He has been happily characterized by Gifford, as "the Puck of Commentators!" Steevens is a creature so spotted over with literary forgeries and adulterations, that any remarkable one about the time he flourished may be attributed to him. They were the habits of a depraved mind, and there was a darkness in his character many shades deeper than belonged to Puck; even in the playfulness of his invention, there was usually a turn of personal malignity, and the real object was not so much to raise a laugh, as to "grin horribly a ghastly smile," on the individual. It is more than rumoured, that he carried his ingenious malignity into the privacies of domestic life; and it is to be regretted, that Mr. Nichols, who might have furnished much secret history of this extraordinary literary forger, has, from delicacy, mutilated his collective vigour.—DISRAELI, ISAAC, 1824, *On Puck the Commentator, Curiosities of Literature.*

I have elsewhere called Steevens the *Puck of Commentators;* and I know not that I could have described him more graphically. Yet in this, strict justice, I fear, is hardly done to Puck. Both delighted to mislead, and both enjoyed the fruits of their mischievous activity; but the frank and boisterous laugh, the jolly hoh! hoh! hoh! of the fairy hobgoblin degenerated in his follower to a cold and malignant grin, which he retired to his cell to enjoy alone. Steevens was an acute and apprehensive mind, cankered by envy and debased. — GIFFORD, WILLIAM, 1827, *ed. Dramatic Works of Ford, Introduction, vol.* I.

George Steevens and Cumberland . . . would have echoed the praises of the man whom they envied, and then have sent to the newspapers anonymous libels upon him. — MACAULAY, THOMAS BABINGTON, 1843, *Oliver Goldsmith, Critical and Historical Essays.*

As a critic, he has several qualifications —a scholar, a wit, of ready perceptions, an appetite for work, and not indisposed to those antiquarian pursuits required by the undertaking. He did not, however, intend so wide a range in research as the subject of this Memoir had in view; nor was he of course so successful. Neither did he in a private capacity win the favourable opinion of contemporaries. He had the unhappy art of making enemies. He is represented as sarcastic, ill-natured, jealous, envious, self-sufficient, and while occasionally prone to a kind of generous action, quite as ready to evince bitter malignity for small or fancied offences. — PRIOR, SIR JAMES, 1861, *Life of Edmond Malone, Editor of Shakespeare, p.* 48.

But Steevens's irrepressible saturnine humour overshadowed his virtues. In conversation, even with intimates, he recklessly sacrificed truth to cynicism. Dr. Parr, who was well disposed towards him, said he was one of the wisest, most learned, but most spiteful of men. Johnson, the most indulgent of his friends, admitted that he was mischievous, but argued that he would do no man an essential injury. When Lord Mansfield remarked that one could only believe half of what Steevens said, the doctor sagely retorted that no one could tell which half deserved credence.—LEE, SIDNEY, 1898, *Dictionary of National Biography, vol.* LIV, *p.* 145.

EDITION OF SHAKESPEARE

Steevens is a dangerous guide for such as do not look well about them. His errors are specious; for he was a man of ingenuity: but he was often wantonly mischievous, and delighted to stumble for the mere gratification of dragging unsuspecting innocents into the mire with him. He was, in short, the very Puck of commentators. — GIFFORD, WILLIAM, 1811, *Ford's Dramatic Works, Quarterly Review, vol.* 6, *p.* 478.

The sources whence they drew their waters were muddy; and STEEVENS, who affected more gayety in his chains than his brothers in the Shakespearian galley, with bitter derision reproached his great coadjutor MALONE, whom he looked on with the evil eye of rivalry for drawing his knowledge from "books too mean to be formally quoted." The commentators have encumbered the poet, who often has been but a secondary object of their lucubrations; for they not only write notes on Shakespeare, but notes, and bitter ones too, on one another. This commentary has been turned into a gymnasium for the public sports of friendly and of unfriendly wrestlers; where some have been so earnest, that it is evident, that, in measuring a cast, they congratulated themselves in the language of Orlando: "If ever he goes alone again, I'll never wrestle for prize more."—DISRAELI, ISAAC, 1841, *Shakespeare, Amenities of Literature.*

And this then is the text of Shakspere that England has rejoiced in for half a century! These are the labours, whether of correction or of critical opinion, that have made Shakspere "popular." The critical opinions have ceased, we believe, to have any effect except amongst a few pedantic persons, who fancy that it is cleverer to dispraise than to admire. But the text as corrupted by Steevens is that which is generally put into the hands of readers of Shakspere. The number of the editions of the text alone of Shakspere printed during the present century is by no means inconsiderable; and of these editions, which are constantly multiplying, there are many thousand copies year by year supplying the large and increasing demand for a knowledge of our greatest poet. With very few exceptions, indeed, all these editions are copies of some edition whose received text is considered as a standard—even the copying of typographical errors. That received text, to use the words of the title-page of what is called the trade edition, is, "From the text of the corrected copies left by the late George Steevens, Esq., and Edmund Malone, Esq." If we were to suppose, from this title, that Steevens and Malone had agreed together to leave a text for the benefit of posterity, we should be signally deceived. The received text is that produced by Steevens, when he fancied himself "at liberty to restore some apparent meaning to Shakspere's corrupted lines, and a decent flow

to his obstructed versification." Malone was walking in his own track, that of extreme caution, and an implicit reliance on the very earliest copies. The text of his edition of 1821, though deformed with abundant marks of carelessness, is an honest text, if we admit the principle upon which it is founded. But the text of Steevens, in which the peculiar versification of Shakspere, especially its freedom, its vigour, its variety of pause, its sweetness, its majesty, are sacrificed to what he called "polished versification," has been received for nearly half a century as the standard text.— KNIGHT, CHARLES, 1849, *Studies of Shakspere, p.* 551.

Steevens is one of the most acute and accomplished of Shakespeare's commentators; but rarely have abilities and acquirements been put to more unfruitful use. To show his ability to suggest "ingenious" readings, he wantonly rejected the obvious significance of the text, and perverted the author's meaning, or destroyed the integrity of his work. He was witty, and not only launched his shafts at his fellow-commentators, but turned them against his author, and, most intolerable of all, attempted to substitute his own smartness for Shakespeare's humor. He had an accurate—mechanically accurate—ear, and ruthlessly mutilated, or patched up Shakespeare's lines to a uniform standard of ten syllables.—WHITE, RICHARD GRANT, 1854, *Shakespeare's Scholar, p.* 18,

The main business of Steevens's life was the systematic study and annotation of Shakespeare's works. . . . The younger man brought to his task exceptional diligence, method, and antiquarian knowledge of literature. His illustrative quotations from rare contemporary literature were apter and more abundant than any to be met with elsewhere. But his achievement exhibited ingrained defects of taste and temper. He spoke scornfully of the labours of many predecessors, and especially of those of Edward Capell, one of the most capable.—LEE, SIDNEY, 1898, *Dictionary of National Biography, vol.* LIV, *p.* 144.

GENERAL

This gentleman, whose memory will be handed down to posterity as long as commentaries on Shakspere exist, followed his usual mode of conduct with respect to the fabricated manuscripts: he did not boldly enter the lists; but, like a mole, worked in secret; and, when occasion served, stung with the subtlety of a viper. —Whether this gentleman lent his friendly aid to Mr. Malone, in the course of his Inquiry, I will not pretend to say, though I rather conceive, that upon that occasion, the rival commentators, like the two kings of Brentford, "smelt at one nosegay," and buried their private feelings in the general attempt to crush that which would have proved so many of their labours of non effect had it passed current with the world.—IRELAND, WILLIAM HENRY, 1805, *Confessions, p.* 227.

He was acute and well read in dramatic literature, but prone to literary mystification and deception.—CHAMBERS, ROBERT, 1876, *Cyclopædia of English Literature.*

Mary Robinson
1758–1800

Mary Robinson, also called Maria, 1758–1800, the daughter of an American sea-captain named Darby, but a native of Bristol, England, was married at fifteen to Mr. Robinson, whose pecuniary difficulties caused his wife to try her fortune on the stage. Whilst performing in the character of Perdita (a name which she subsequently assumed in amatory correspondence), she attracted the attention of the Prince of Wales (afterwards George IV.), then in his 18th year. An intimacy of two years with this person was followed by one equally reprehensible with an officer of the army. She pub. a vol. of "Poems" in 1775, 8vo; "Captivity, a Poem, and Celadon and Lydia, a Tale," 1777, 4to; 2 more vols. of "Poems," 8vo, in 1791; a number of single poems, novels, plays, pamphlets, &c., between 1775 and 1799; and "The False Friend," 1799 4 vols, 12mo. "The Effusions of Love," purporting to be her correspondence with the Prince of Wales, was pub. in 177—, 8vo; her "Lyrical Tales" appeared in 1800, cr. 8vo; her "Memoirs," written by herself, were pub. after her death in 1801, 4 vols. 12mo. (also 1826, 12mo; and again with Charlotte Clarke's "Autobiography," 18mo. and 12mo); her "Poems," 1803, 2 vols, 12mo; and the "Poetical Works of the late Mrs. Robinson, now first collected," were pub. by her daughter, Mary Robinson, in 1806, 3 vols. p. 8vo.—ALLIBONE, S. AUSTIN, 1870, *Critical Dictionary of English Literature, vol.* II, *p.* 1839.

PERSONAL

Charles Fox is languishing at the feet of Mrs. Robinson. George Selwyn says, "Who should the *Man of the People* live with, but with the *Woman of the People?*"—WALPOLE, HORACE, 1782, *To the Earl of Harcourt, Sept.* 7; *Letters, ed. Cunningham, vol.* VIII, *p.* 276.

So melting is thy lute's soft tone,
  Each breast unused to feel desire,
Confesses bliss before unknown,
  And kindles at the sacred fire!
So chaste, so eloquent thy song,
  So *true* each precept it conveys,
That e'en the Sage shall teach the Young
  To take their lesson from thy lays.
And when thy pen's delightful art
  Paints with soft touch Love's tender flame;
Thy verse so melts and mends the heart,
  That, taught by thee, we prize his name.
—BURGOYNE, GEN. JOHN, 1791, *To Mrs. Robinson.*

Farewell to the nymph of my heart!
Farewell to the cottage and vine!
From *these,* with a tear, I depart,
Where pleasure so often was *mine.*

Remembrance shall dwell on her smile,
And dwell on her lute and her song;
That sweetly my hours to beguile,
Oft echoed the valleys along.
Once more the fair scene let me view,
The grotto, the brook, and the grove.
Dear valleys, for ever adieu!
Adieu to the Daughter of Love!
—WOLCOT, JOHN, 1800, *A Pastoral Elegy on the Death of Mrs. Robinson.*

"Nay, but thou dost not know her might,
The pinions of her soul, how strong!
But many a stranger in my height
Hath sung to me her magic song,
Sending forth his ecstasy
In her divinest melody,
And hence I know her soul is free,
She is, where'er she wills to be,
Unfetter'd by mortality!
Now to 'the haunted beach' can fly,
Beside the threshold scourg'd with waves,
Now where the maniac wildly raves,
Pale Moon, thou spectre of the sky!
No wind that hurries o'er my height
Can travel with so swift a flight.
I too, methinks, might merit
The presence of her spirit!

To me too might belong
The honour of her song and witching melody,
    Which most resembles me,
    Soft, various, and sublime,
    Exempt from wrongs of time! "
Thus spake the mighty mount, and I
Made answer, with a deep drawn sigh:—
"Thou ancient SKIDDAW! by this tear,
I would, I would, that she were here!"
—COLERIDGE, SAMUEL TAYLOR, 1800, *A Stranger Minstrel.*

Deathless was to be the young Prince's love, and his munificence was to be equal to his truth. In proof of the latter, he gave her a bond for £20,000, to be paid to her on his coming of age. In a few months he attained his majority, refused to pay the money, and made no secret to the lady of his deathless love having altogether died out. He passed her in the park, affecting not to know her ; and the spirited young woman, who had given up a lucrative profession for his sake, flung a remark at him, in her indignation, that ought to have made him blush, had he been to that manner born. However, she was not altogether abandoned. The patriotic Whig statesman, Charles Fox, obtained for the Prince's cast-off favourite an annuity of £300,—out of the pockets of a tax-paying people! . . .   There was good in this hapless creature. Throughout life, she was the loving and helping child of her mother, the loving and helpful mother of her child, for both of whom she laboured ungrudgingly, to the last. Hannah More, herself, would not harshly construe the conduct of her pupil. "I make the greatest allowance for inexperience and novel passions," was the comment of Horace Walpole. "Poor Perdita!" said Mrs. Siddons, "I pity her from my very heart!" —DORAN, JOHN, 1863, *Annals of the English Stage, vol.* II, *p.* 214.

The actress had made great way in public favour—she was becoming a favourite with the town. She was not powerful, perhaps, but she was certainly pleasing ; not a great artist but a very graceful one. She could not take the public by storm ; but she could win them gradually, holding them just as securely at last. It was difficult to resist the beauty of her face and form—the charm of her voice. More than these was not required in many of her characters. She had no genius, but she had a cultivated cleverness which did nearly as well. She was very lovely,

dressed beautifully, could be arch and sparkling, or tender and pathetic. The good-natured audience demanded no more —they gave her their hands and hearts without further question, thundering their applause.—COOK, DUTTON, 1865–81, *Poor Perdita, Hours with the Players, vol.* I, *p.*73.

Of all the black spots that rest upon the character of this prince, there are few blacker than his treatment of this unfortunate lady ; and how little blame was considered to attach to her, by those whom envy and malice did not render partial judges, is proved by the sympathy and friendship which she obtained from many persons of high standing in society.— BAKER, HENRY BARTON, 1879, *English Actors from Shakespeare to Macready, vol.* II, *p.* 95.

GENERAL

As an authoress, she displays very considerable powers, but, being one of the Della Cruscan school, she was mercilessly attacked by Gifford.—ROWTON, FREDERIC, 1848, *The Female Poets of Great Britain, p.* 166.

There were in her day many admirers of her writings, though they have since sunk into comparative forgetfulness, and justly, as they are not characterized by merit sufficient to warrant praise.—BETHUNE, GEORGE W., 1848, *The British Female Poets, p.* 85.

Perdita was not idle ; she wrote poems and novels : the former, tender in sentiment and expression ; the latter, not without power and good sense. She had undertaken to supply the *Morning Post* with poetry, when she died.—DORAN, JOHN, 1863, *Annals of the English Stage, vol.* II, *p.* 214.

As an author she was credited in her own day with the feeling, taste, and elegance, and was called the English Sappho. Some of her songs, notably "Bounding Billow, cease thy motion," "Lines to him who well understood them," and "The Haunted Beach," enjoyed much popularity in the drawing-room ; but though her verse has a certain measure of facility, it appears, to modern tastes, jejune, affected, and inept. Wolcott (Peter Pindar) and others belauded her in verse, celebrating her graces, which were real, and her talents, which were imaginary.—KNIGHT, JOSEPH, 1897, *Dictionary of National Biography, vol.* XLIX, *p.* 33.

Charles Johnstone

1719?–1800?

Charles Johnstone, novelist, descended from branch of the Johnstones of Annandale, Dumfriesshire, born at Carrigogunnel in the county of Limerick about 1719, was educated in the university of Dublin, where, however, he does not appear to have taken a degree. He was called to the bar, but extreme deafness prevented his practice except as a chamber lawyer, and not succeeding in that branch of the profession, he had recourse to literature for his support. His chief work, entitled "Chrysal, or the Adventures of a Guinea," and frequently reprinted, appeared in 4 vols., London, 1760-5. The first and second volumes had been written during a visit to the Earl of Mount-Edgcumbe in Devonshire. The book pretended to reveal political secrets, and to expose the profligacy of well-known public characters. It soon attracted attention as "the best scandalous chronicle of the day." In May 1782 Johnstone sailed for India, and very narrowly escaped death by shipwreck on the voyage. He found employment in writing for the Bengal newspaper press, under the signature of "Oneiropolos." He became in time joint proprietor of a journal, and is said to have acquired considerable property. He died at Calcutta about 1800. Johnstone was also the author of 1. "The Reverie, or a Flight to the Paradise of Fools," 2 vols. London, 1762. 2. "The History of Arbases, Prince of Betlis," 2 vols. 1774. 3. "The Pilgrim, or a Picture of Life," 2 vols. 1775. 4. "History of John Juniper, Esq., *alias* Juniper Jack," 3 vols. 1781.—BLACKER, B. H., 1892, *Dictionary of National Biography, vol.* xxx, *p.* 73.

GENERAL

His talents were of a lively and companionable sort, and as he was much abroad in the world, he had already, in his youth, kept such general society with men of all descriptions, as enabled him to trace their vices and follies with a pencil so powerful. . . . His language is firm and energetic—his power of personifying character striking and forcible, and the persons of his narrative move, breathe, and speak, in all the freshness of life. His sentiments are, in general, those of the bold, high-minded, and indignant censor of a loose and corrupted age. . . . Feeling and writing under the popular impression of the moment, Johnstone has never failed to feel and write like a true Briton, with a sincere admiration of his country's laws, an ardent desire for her prosperity, and a sympathy with her interests, which more than atone for every error and prejudice. —SCOTT, SIR WALTER, 1821, *Charles Johnstone.*

As Dr. Johnson—to whom the manuscript was shewn by the bookseller—advised the publication of the "Adventures of a Guinea," and as it experienced considerable success, the novel may be presumed to have possessed superior merit. It exhibits a variety of incidents, related in the style of Le Sage and Smollett, but the satirical portraits are overcharged, and the author, like Juvenal, was too fond of lashing and exaggerating the vices of his age.—CHAMBERS, ROBERT, 1876, *Cyclopædia of English Literature, ed. Carruthers.*

A depraved mind only could find any pleasure in reading "Chrysal," and whoever is obliged to read it from cover to cover for the purpose of describing it to others, must find himself, at the end of his task, in sore vexation of spirit. Human depravity is never an agreeable subject for a work of entertainment, and while Swift's genius holds the reader fascinated with the horror of his Yahoos, the ability of a Manley or a Johnstone is not sufficient to aid the reader in wading through their vicious expositions of corruption. It must be said that Johnstone had some excuse. If he were to satirize society at all, it was better that he should do it thoroughly; that he should expose official greed and dishonesty, the orgies of Medenham Abbey, the infamous extortions of trading justices, in all their native ugliness. It must be said that the time in which he lived presented many features to the painter of manners which could not look otherwise than repulsive on his canvas. But his zeal to expose the vices of his age led him into doing great injustice to some persons, and into grossly libelling others. He imputed crimes to individuals of which he could have had no knowledge; and he shamefully misrepresented the Methodists and the Jews. If Johnstone had wished to see how offensive a book he might write, and how disgusting and indecent a book the public of his day would read and applaud, he might well have brought "Chrysal" into the world. If he had intended, by exposing crime, to check it, he had better have burned his manuscript. He has added one other corruption to those he exposed, and one other evidence of the lack of taste and decency which characterized his time.—TUCKERMAN, BAYARD, 1882, *A History of Prose Fiction, p.* 240.

This savage and gloomy book, which, perhaps, took its form from a reminiscence of Addison's "Adventures of a Shilling," in the *Tattler,* was a very clever following of Smollett in his most satiric mood. —GOSSE, EDMUND, 1888, *A History of Eighteenth Century Literature, p.* 271.

Robert Orme
1728–1801

Author of a "History of British India," was the son of John Orme, surgeon in Bombay, and was born at Anjengo, Travancore, in June 1728. He was sent to Harrow school in 1736, and in 1742 to a school near London to obtain an education preparing him for commercial pursuits. In 1744 he became a clerk in the East India Company's service in Calcutta. In 1752 he went to Madras, and in the following year he returned home with Lord Clive, with whom he lived on terms of close intimacy. His knowledge of Indian affairs gave him considerable influence with the company. Returning to Madras in 1755, he was appointed a member of the council, and in this position took an active part in directing the military operations in the Carnatic in 1755–59. By the court of directors he was appointed to succeed Lord Pigot in the government of Madras, and in 1757–59 he was commissary-general. In the latter year bad health compelled him to quit India, and he took up his residence in London, where he occupied himself in writing a "History of the Military Transactions of the British Nation in Indostan from 1745," the first volume appearing in 1763, the second in 1775, and the third in 1778. In acknowledgment of his services he was appointed historiographer to the East India Company with a salary of £400 a year. In 1770 he was chosen a fellow of the Society of Antiquaries. He died at Ealing 13th January 1801.—BAYNES, THOMAS SPENCER, *ed.,* 1884, *The Encyclopædia Britannica, vol.* XVII, *p.* 853.

PERSONAL

A bust of Orme at the age of forty-six, made in 1774 by J. Nollekens, R. A., was bequeathed to the East India Company; an engraving of it forms the frontispiece to Orme's "Historical Fragments," ed. 1805. His face is described as expressing shrewdness and intelligence. Orme had a taste for painting and sculpture, and was a lover of Handel.—WROTH, WARWICK, 1895, *Dictionary of National Biography, vol.* XLII, *p.* 257.

HISTORY OF BRITISH INDIA
1763–78

Orme, inferior to no English historian in style and power of painting, is minute even to tediousness. In one volume he allots, on an average, a closely-printed quarto page to the events of every forty-eight hours. The consequence is that his narrative, though one of the most authentic and one of the most finely written in our language, has never been very popular, and is now scarcely ever read.—MACAULAY,

THOMAS BABINGTON, 1840, *Sir John Malcom's Life of Lord Clive, Edinburgh Review; Critical and Miscellaneous Essays.*

Colonel Newcome's favourite work.— THACKERAY, WILLIAM MAKEPEACE, 1854–5, *The Newcomes.*

As a writer, he had formed his taste in the school of Robertson. He had some imagination, much clearness, a pure diction, and many agreeable qualities. He was truthful, accurate, and desirous in every particular to avoid exaggeration, and to prepare a reliable narrative of a series of remarkable events. . . . Orme's style, manner, and subject seem to have delighted his contemporaries. Robertson and Sir William Jones unite in praising them highly, and Sterne speaks in graceful praise, in a letter to his daughter, of Mr. Orme's agreeable History. Although he was no philosopher, nor gifted with any remarkable learning or originality, he was honest, truthful, and sincere. Some of his descriptions, too, are written with a simplicity and natural power that remind one strongly of Herodotus.—LAWRENCE, EUGENE, 1855, *Lives of the British Historians, vol.* II, *pp.* 314, 316.

Accurate and perspicuous. — CRAIK, GEORGE L., 1861, *A Compendious History of English Literature and of the English Language, vol.* II, *p.* 360.

Gilbert Wakefield

1756–1801

English divine; born at Nottingham, Feb. 22, 1756; died in London, Sept. 9, 1801. He was graduated at Cambridge, 1776, obtained a fellowship; took holy orders, left (1786), and violently assailed the Established Church. He joined no other communion. From 1779 to 1783 he was classical tutor in the dissenting academy at Warrington, and for a year (1790–91) the same in the dissenting academy at Hackney. His later views were Unitarian. Gentle in domestic life, he yet was acrimonious in controversy. He published editions of Bion and Moschus, Virgil and Lucretius, and many original books, of which may be mentioned, "An enquiry into the opinions of the Christian writers of the three first centuries concerning the person of Christ," London, 1784, (only vol. 1 printed); "Enquiry into the expediency and propriety of social worship," 1791 (in which he takes strong ground against it); "Translations of the New Testament," 1791, 3 vols. (2d. ed., 1795, 2 vols. reprinted, Cambridge, Mass., 1820), "An examination of the Age of Reason, by Thomas Paine," 1794.—SHAFF-HERZOG, *eds.*, 1883, *Religious Encyclopædia, vol.* III, *p.* 2470.

PERSONAL

I was *introduced into this planet* on February 22, 1756, in the parsonage house of St. Nicholas, in Nottingham, of which church my father was rector. . . . From my earliest infancy I was endowed with affections unusually composed, with a disposition grave and serious. I was inspired from the first with a most ardent desire of knowledge, such as I believe hath never been surpassed in any breast, nor for a moment impaired in mine. . . . At the age of *three* years, I could spell the longest words, say my catechism without hesitation, and read the gospels with fluency.—WAKEFIELD, GILBERT, 1772, *Autobiography.*

He had the pale complexion and mild features of a saint, was a most gentle creature in domestic life, and a very amiable man; but when he took part in political or religious controversy, his pen was dipped in gall.—ROBINSON, HENRY CRABBE, 1799, *Diary, Reminiscences and Correspondence.*

Porson was never at any pains to conceal his extreme contempt for Wakefield. There was at one time a seeming sort of friendly communication; but whilst Wakefield aimed at being thought on a level with Porson in point of attainments, this latter must unavoidably have felt the consciousness of his own great superiority.—Indeed, the difference between them was immense.

Without disparagement to Wakefield, his warmest advocates must acknowledge, that although he formed his opinions hastily, he never failed to vindicate them with peremptory decision. In consequence of this eagerness and haste, his criticisms were frequently erroneous, and his conclusions false; neither, if detected in error, would his pride allow him either to confess, or retract his fault.—BELOE, WILLIAM, 1817, *The Sexagenarian, vol.* I, *p.* 222.

He did himself less than justice in his writings; but his private life was spotlessly pure, pre-eminently true, and great in qualities which only those who knew him intimately and enjoyed his friendship had the opportunity of knowing. It conveys a disagreeable impression of himself in his autobiography (a work now almost unknown), but this impression those who loved him declare to be quite a false one, due only to his unfortunate manner of expressing himself and a want of moderation and judgment. That stern obedience to conscience which, in the eighteenth century, brought him to Dorchester Goal, would certainly, in the fifteenth, have gained him a martyr's death; since he never hesitated for a moment to sacrifice what he held most dear to his intense and ardent conviction of truth.—MARTIN, MARY E., 1883, *Memories of Seventy Years, by One of a Literary Family, p.* 176.

GENERAL

Wakefield possesses exquisite taste and a most luxuriant fancy, as a critic; and one grieves that he should ever have misapplied his powers to politics and religion. —GREEN, THOMAS, 1779–1810, *Diary of a Lover of Literature.*

His ravages on Virgil and Horace, in his late editions of them are often as shocking to taste as to truth.—MATHIAS, THOMAS JAMES, 1797, *The Pursuits of Literature, Eighth ed., p.* 113, *note.*

The late Gilbert Wakefield is an instance where the political and theological opinions of a recluse student tainted his pure literary works. Condemned as an enraged Jacobin by those who were Unitarians in politics, and rejected because he was a Unitarian in religion by the orthodox, poor Wakefield's literary labours were usually reduced to the value of waste-paper. We smile, but half in sorrow, in reading a letter, where he says, "I meditate a beginning during the winter, of my criticisms on all the ancient Greek and Latin authors, by small piece-meals, on the cheapest possible paper, and at the least possible expense of printing. As I can never do more than barely indemnify myself, I shall print only 250 copies." He half ruined himself by his splendid edition of Lucretius, which could never obtain even common patronage from the opulent friends of classical literature. Since his death it has been reprinted, and is no doubt now a marketable article for the bookseller; so that if some authors are not successful for themselves, it is a comfort to think how useful, in a variety of shapes, they are made so to others. Even Gilbert's "contracted scheme of publication" he was compelled to abandon! Yet the classic erudition of Wakefield was confessed, and is still remembered.—DISRAELI, ISAAC, 1814, *Political Criticism, Quarrels of Authors, note.*

The design of Mr. Wakefield in the plan of this work ["Silva Critica"] was the union of theological and classical learning,—the illustration of the Scriptures by light borrowed from the philology of Greece and Rome, as a probable method of recommending the books of revelation to scholars.—HORNE, THOMAS HARTWELL, 1818–39, *A Manual of Biblical Bibliography.*

Some of the emendations ["Silva Critica"] are too conjectural, and discover the natural boldness of the author; but his criticisms often afford a clear and happy solution of difficulties which have hitherto proved insuperable. The complete work is now become scarce.—ORME, WILLIAM, 1824, *Bibliotheca Biblica.*

A scholar, and an ardent and multifarious one, Gilbert Wakefield undoubtedly was; but, with his talents and attainments, we regret that a more elegant and interesting air is not given to the pages of his biography: and while the sincerity of his religious principles, and the integrity of his private life, cannot fail to be readily admitted, it must be regretted that these excellent qualities did not produce a more placable temper in argument, and a more peaceful tone in literary and political controversies. Why should human beings, gifted as was Gilbert Wakefield, dip their pens in *gall*, when there is abundance of *milk* within their reach? And why do eminently intellectual characters seem to strive their utmost to make us disgusted with the pursuits and consolations of Literature? Nevertheless, let Gilbert Wakefield's biography find a place upon the shelves of the curious—for a sum somewhat less than a sovereign.—DIBDIN, THOMAS FROGNALL, 1824, *The Library Companion, p.* 561.

Porson felt much respect for Gilbert Wakefield's integrity, but very little for his learning. When Wakefield put forth the "Diatribe Extemporalis" on Porson's edition of the "Hecuba," Porson said, "If Wakefield goes on at this rate, he will tempt me to examine his 'Silva Critica.' I hope that we shall not meet; for a violent quarrel would be the consequence."— Wakefield was a very agreeable and entertaining companion. "'My Lucretius,'" he once said to me, "is my most perfect publication,—it is, in fact, 'Lucretius Restitutus.'" He was a great walker; he has walked as much as forty miles in one day; and I believe that his death was partly brought on by excessive walking, after his long confinement in Dorchester goal. What offended Wakefield at Porson was, that Porson had made no mention of him in his notes. Now, Porson told Burney expressly, that out of pure kindness he had forborne to mention Wakefield; for he could not have cited any of his emendations without the severest censure.—MALTBY, WILLIAM, 1854, *Porsoniana.*

Gilbert Wakefield was a man who received scanty justice. His contemporaries condemned him as hot-headed, arrogant, and eccentric, though they contemptuously admitted his honesty. He was weak enough, they declared, to fall in love with the opinions for which he made sacrifices, and would, so they argued, have ceased to love them had they been generally acceptable. He was as dogmatic about trifles as about serious matters; "he was as violent against Greek accents as he was against the Trinity, and anathematised the final *v* as strongly as episcopacy." He had, in short, that love of petty crotchets which distinguishes men of his temperament, and which flourishes in revolutionary periods. He was a teetotaler and vegetarian in the good old days of port wine and roast beef, and had he lived a generation later would doubtless have been at the head of numerous societies for the regeneration of mankind. Our ancestors dealt him shorter and sharper measure.—STEPHEN, LESLIE, 1876, *History of English Thought in the Eighteenth Century, vol.* I, *p.* 441.

Wakefield possessed accurate scholarship and acuteness of intellect, but lacked judgment; he was violent in his prejudices, and bitter in his animosities; and he rebelled against authority, equally in church, in state, and in letters. His writings are valuable, not for his conclusions, but for the sharpness of his criticism.—HART, JOHN S., 1872, *A Manual of English Literature, p.* 359.

He was one of those not very uncommon men who, personally amiable, become merely vixenish when they write: and his erudition was much more extensive than sound. But he edited several classical authors, not wholly without intelligence and scholarship, and his "Silva Critica," a sort of *variorum* commentary from profane literature on the Bible, was the forerunner, at least in scheme, of a great deal of work which has been seen since.—SAINTSBURY, GEORGE, 1896, *A History of Nineteenth Century Literature.*

He holds a distinct position in the history of English scholarship. As a scholar, he had decided merits and conspicuous defects. He had abundance of good taste, extensive general knowledge, and great industry; but these qualifications were counterbalanced by the excessive haste and temerity of his conclusions. His reputation would be higher if he had been a severer critic of himself. He measured swords with Porson with a light heart, and when Porson published his "Hecuba" in 1787, Wakefield immediately assailed the work in a "Diatribe Extemporalis." The result was a more or less discourteous controversy, which went on simmering in Porson's notes to the "Orestes" and in the second edition of the "Hecuba;" and an estrangement followed. . . . Wakefield's best known works are the "Silva Critica" and the editions of "Lucretius," both of which show him alike at his best and his worst. The former is a medley of critical and illustrative comment on classical passages, acute, ingenious, and widely informed, but here and there disfigured by serious blunders that a little thought would have corrected. It was his chief fault as a scholar that he carried his love of emendation to an absurd degree, and fairly justified Porson's remark that "no author escaped his rage for correction." "Lucretius," although Wakefield's greatest work, was published at a loss.—BRODRIBB, A. A., 1899, *Dictionary of National Biography, vol.* LVIII, *pp.* 454, 455.

Hester Chapone

1727–1801

Authoress, daughter of Thomas Mulso, and born at Twywell, Northants, wrote for the "Rambler" (No. 10), "Adventurer," and "Gentleman's Magazine;" but is now chiefly remembered by her "Letters on the Improvement of the Mind," (1772). She married an attorney in 1760, but next year was left a widow. See her Works with Life (4 vols. 1807).—PATRICK AND GROOME, *eds.,* 1897, *Chambers's Biographical Dictionary, p.* 200.

PERSONAL

I went one evening last week to the Dean of Winchester's, where we met Mrs. Chapone, who looked less forbidding than usual; but she is deadly ugly to be sure;—such [an] African nose and lips, and such a clunch figure!—BURNEY, CHARLOTTE ANN, 1781? *Journal, ed. Ellis, June* 21, *p.* 298.

Mrs. Chapone was of a lively and sanguine temperament, possessed of humour and sagacity, and knowledge of the world, which made her an entertaining companion, and a sound adviser. Her disposition was kind and amiable, and her principles were excellent.—BRYDGES, SIR SAMUEL EGERTON, 1807, *Censura Literaria, vol.* V, *p.* 320.

But though the dignity of her mind demanded, as it deserved, the respect of some return to the visits which her love of society induced her to pay, it was a *tête-à-tête* alone that gave pleasure to the intercourse with Mrs. Chapone: her sound understanding, her sagacious observations, her turn to humour, and the candour of her affectionate nature, all then came into play without effort: and her ease of mind, when freed from the trammels of doing the honours of reception, seemed to soften off, even to herself, her corporeal infirmities. It was thus that she struck Dr. Burney with the sense of her worth; and seemed portraying in herself the original example whence the precepts had been drawn, for forming the unsophisticated female character, that are displayed in the author's "Letters on the Improvement of the Mind." —D'ARBLAY, MADAME (FANNY BURNEY), 1832, *Memoirs of Doctor Burney.*

GENERAL

Mrs. Chapone's "'Letters" are written with such good sense, and unaffected humility, and contain so many useful observations, that I only mention them to pay the worthy writer this tribute of respect. I cannot, it is true, always coincide in opinion with her; but I always respect her.— WOLLSTONECRAFT, MARY (MRS. GODWIN), 1792, *Vindication of the Rights of Woman, p.* 234.

Nor was she only diligent in acquiring the accomplishments of elegance and taste; the studies of philosophy and theology occupied a large portion of her time; for her devotion was ardent, and her reasoning powers of uncommon strength. Her enthusiastic love of genius, and her scepticism with regard to dogmatic assertion, led her, while very young, into a warm admiration of Richardson the author of "Clarissa," and into a masterly refutation of his arbitrary opinions on parental authority and filial obedience; a correspondence which has been lately published, and forms a most respectable proof of early proficiency in argumentative discussion.— DRAKE, NATHAN, 1810, *Essays, Illustrative of the Rambler, Adventurer and Idler, vol.* II, *p.* 154.

Her enthusiastic love of genius made her a warm admirer of Richardson, the novelist, to whom, however, she could not surrender her opinions. With him she entered into an able correspondence on the subject of filial obedience; and her letters, though written at the age of twenty-two, display much ability, and strength and clearness of mind.—CLEVELAND, CHARLES D., 1853, *English Literature of the Nineteenth Century, p.* 35.

Robert Bage

1728–1801

Born at Darley, Derbyshire, England, Feb. 29, 1728: died at Tamworth, England, Sept. 1, 1801. An English novelist. He was a paper-manufacturer by trade, and did not begin to write before the age of fifty-three. He wrote "Mount Henneth" (1781), "Barham Downs" (1784), "Hermsprong, or Man as he is not" (1796), etc.—SMITH, BENJAMIN E., 1894–97, *The Century Cyclopedia of Names, p.* 108.

PERSONAL

In his person, Robert Bage was somewhat under the middle size, and rather slender, but well proportioned. His complexion was fair and ruddy; his hair light and curling; his countenance intelligent, mild, and placid. His manners were courteous, and his mind was firm. His integrity, his honour, his devotion to truth, were undeviating and incorruptible; his humanity, benevolence, and generosity, were not less conspicuous in private life than they were in the principal characters in his works. He supplied persons he never saw with money, because he heard they were in want. He kept his servants and his horses to old age, and both men and quadrupeds were attached to him. He behaved to his sons with the unremitting affection of a father; but, as they grew up, he treated them as men and equals, and allowed them that independence of mind and conduct which he claimed for himself. —HUTTON, CATHERINE, 1821, *Novelist's Library, ed. Scott, Life of Bage.*

We have the testimony of Mr. Hutton, his most intimate friend, that in private life Bage was most amiable, but he adds with regret that "he laid no stress upon revelation," and was "barely a christian." His friends were deeply attached to him, and they described his temper as open, mild, and sociable. He was very kind to his domestics, who lived with him till they were old, and even to his horses when they were past work. — SMITH, G. BARNETT, 1885, *Dictionary of National Biography, vol.* II, *p.* 392.

GENERAL

It is scarce possible to read him without being amused, and, to a certain degree instructed. His whole efforts are turned to the development of human character; and, it must be owned, he possessed a ready key to it. The mere story of the novels seldom possesses much interest—in which we are interested; and, contrary to his general case, the reader is seldom or never tempted to pass over the dialogue in order to continue the narrative. . . . A light, gay, pleasing air, carries us agreeably through Bage's novels; and when we are disposed to be angry at seeing the worse made to appear the better reason, we are reconciled to the author by the ease and good-humour of his style.—SCOTT, SIR WALTER, 1821, *Robert Bage.*

Bage's novels are decidedly inferior to those of Holcroft, and it is surprising that Sir Walter Scott should have admitted them into his "British Novelists," and at the same time excluded so many superior works.—CHAMBERS, ROBERT, 1876, *Cyclopædia of English Literature, ed. Carruthers.*

Good Mr. Bage near Tamworth, whom Godwin, about the time when he tried to persecute and argue Miss Harriet Lee into marrying him, went out of his way to see, asking, "Are not such men as much worth visiting as palaces, towns, and cathedrals?" Bage was born a miller, and was a well-to-do person with paper-mills, beside those that ground the grain. To "dissipate his melancholy" under some special trouble, he began to write novels; and afterward, when he had formed the habit, went on producing them methodically one every two years, as children are born in well-regulated families. Where have all those children of the fancy gone? "Hermsprong," which Godwin reports to be "his sixth," very much indeed as if it had been a baby, is the one that is best known.—OLIPHANT, MARGARET O. W., 1882, *The Literary History of England, XVIII-XIX Century, vol.* II, *p.* 316.

The writer in Chambers's "Cyclopædia of English Literature" describes Bage's novels as decidedly inferior to those of Holcroft, with whom Bage had not little in common; and he expresses surprise that Sir Walter Scott should have admitted them into his "Novelists' Library." But the reader will feel inclined to applaud Sir Walter for granting them this distinction. As novels they may not interest strongly by their plot, but there is a distinct originality about them. They were chiefly intended to inculcate certain political and philosophical opinions. Not unfrequently, perhaps, the author's strong convictions betray him into exaggeration. But touching the literary power of his works there can scarcely be two opinions. Considered altogether apart from their moral and social bearings, the novels of Bage display an unquestionable power in drawing and developing character, while their style is always entertaining and frequently incisive.—SMITH, G. BARNETT, 1895, *Dictionary of National Biography, vol.* II, *p.* 392.

It is impossible to say that there is genius in Bage; yet he is a very remarkable writer, and there is noticeable in him that singular *fin de siècle* tendency which has reasserted itself a century later. An imitator of Fielding and Smollett in general plan,—of the latter specially in the dangerous scheme of narrative by letter, —Bage added to their methods the purpose of advocating a looser scheme of morals and a more anarchical system of government. In other words, Bage, though a man well advanced in years at the date of the Revolution, exhibits for us distinctly the spirit which brought the Revolution about. He is a companion of Godwin and of Mary Wollstonecraft; and though it must be admitted that, as in other cases, the presence of "impropriety" in him by no means implies the absence of dulness, he is full of a queer sort of undeveloped and irregular cleverness.—SAINTSBURY, GEORGE, 1896, *A History of Nineteenth Century Literature.*

Erasmus Darwin

1731-1802

Born at Elston Hall, Notts, 12 Dec. 1731. At Chesterfield School, 1741-50; to St. John's Coll., Camb., 1750; Exeter Scholar; B. A., 1754. To Edinburgh to study medicine, 1754. M. B., Cambridge, 1755. Settled in practice in Nottingham, Sept. 1756; removed to Lichfield, Nov. 1756. Married Mary Howard, Dec. 1757; she died, 1770. Married Mrs. Chandos-Pole, 1781; lived, first at her estate, Radbourne Hall; subsequently at Derby, and Breadsall Priory, near Derby. Died suddenly, at Breadsall Priory, 18 April 1802. Buried in Breadsall Church. *Works:* "Loves of the Plants" (anon., pt. ii. of "Botanic Garden"), 1789; "Economy of Vegetation" (anon., pt. i. of "Botanic Garden") 1792; "Zoonomia," 1794-96; "A Plan for the Conduct of Female Education in Boarding Schools," 1797; "Phytologia," 1800. *Posthumous:* "The Temple of Nature," 1803; "Collected Poems," 1807. He *edited:* C. Darwin's "Experiments establishing a Criterion, etc.," 1780. *Life:* by A. Seward, 1804; by E. Krause, trans. by W. S. Dallas, 1879.—SHARP, R. FARQUHARSON, 1897, *A Dictionary of English Authors, p.* 74.

PERSONAL

ERASMUS DARWIN, M. D., F. R. S.
*Born at Elston, near Newark, 12th Dec., 1731,
Died at the Priory, near Derby, 10th April,
1802.*

*Of the rare union of Talents
which so eminently distinguished him
as a Physician, a Poet and Philosopher
His writings remain
a public and unfading testimony.*

*His Widow
has erected his monument
in memory of
the zealous benevolence of his disposition,
the active humanity of his conduct,
and the many private virtues
which adorned his character.*

—INSCRIPTION ON TOMB, *Breadsall Church.*

Five or six times in my life I have seen him angry, and have heard him express that anger with much real, and more apparent vehemence, more than men of less sensibility would feel or show. But then the motive never was personal. When Dr. Darwin beheld any example of inhumanity or injustice, he never could refrain his indignation; he had not learnt, from the school of Lord Chesterfield, to smother every generous feeling.— EDGEWORTH, RICHARD LOVELL, 1802, *Monthly Magazine.*

I think all those who knew him, will allow that sympathy and benevolence were the striking features. He felt very sensibly for others, and, from his knowledge of human nature, he entered into their feelings and sufferings in the different circumstances of their constitution, character, health, sickness, and prejudice. In benevolence, he thought that almost all virtue consisted. He despised the monkish abstinences and the hypocritical

pretentions which so often impose on the world. The communication of happiness and the relief of misery were by him held as the only standard of moral merit. Though he extended his humanity to every sentient being, it was not like that of some philosophers, so diffused as to be of no effect; but his affection was there warmest where it could be of most service to his family and his friends, who will remember the constancy of his attachment and his zeal for their welfare.—KEIR, JAMES, 1802, *Letter to Robert Darwin, May* 12.

He was somewhat above the middle size, his form athletic, and inclined to corpulence; his limbs too heavy for exact proportion. The traces of a severe smallpox; features, and countenance, which, when they were not animated by social pleasure, were rather saturnine than sprightly; a stoop in the shoulders, and the then professional appendage, a large full-bottomed wig, gave, at that early period of life, an appearance of nearly twice the years he bore. Florid health, and the earnest of good humour, a sunny smile, on entering a room, and on first accosting his friends, rendered, in his youth, that exterior agreeable, to which beauty and symmetry had not been propitious. He stammered extremely, but whatever he said, whether gravely or in jest, was always well worth waiting for, though the inevitable impression it made might not always be pleasant to individual self-love. Conscious of great native elevation above the general standard of intellect, he became, early in life, sore upon opposition, whether in argument or conduct, and always revenged it by sarcasm

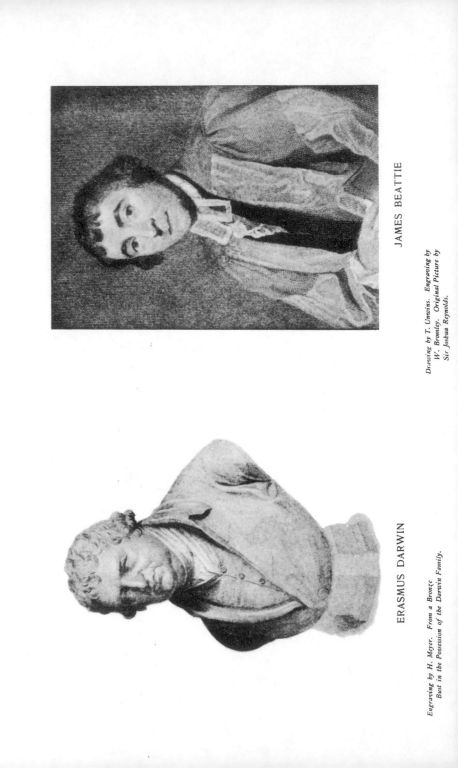

ERASMUS DARWIN

Engraving by H. Meyer. From a Bronze Bust in the Possession of the Darwin Family.

JAMES BEATTIE

Drawing by T. Unwins. Engraving by W. Bromley. Original Picture by Sir Joshua Reynolds.

of very keen edge. Nor was he less impatient of sallies of egotism and vanity, even when they were in so slight a degree, that strict politeness would rather tolerate than ridicule them. Dr. Darwin seldom failed to present their caricature in jocose but wounding irony. If these ingredients of colloquial despotism were discernible in unworn existence, they increased as it advanced, fed by an ever-growing reputation within and without the pale of medicine. —SEWARD, ANNA, 1804, *Memoir of the Life of Dr. Darwin, p.* 1.

We all hastened to the window to see Dr. Darwin, of whom we had heard so much, and whom I was prepared to honor and venerate, in no common degree, as the restorer of my mother's health. What, then, was my astonishment at beholding him, as he slowly got out of the carriage! His figure was vast and massive; his head was almost buried on his shoulders, and he wore a scratch-wig, as he called it, tied up in a little bobtail behind.—SCHIMMEL-PENNICK, MARY ANNE, 1859, *Life, ed. Hankin, p.* 205.

Equally eminent as philanthropist, physician, naturalist, philosopher, and poet, is far less known and valued by posterity than he deserves, in comparison with other persons who occupy a similar rank. It is true that what is perhaps the most important of his many-sided endowments, namely his broad view of the philosophy of nature, was not intelligible to his contemporaries; it is only now, after the lapse of a hundred years, that by the labours of one of his descendants we are in a position to estimate at its true value the wonderful perceptivity, amounting almost to divination, that he displayed in the domain of biology. For in him we find the same indefatigable spirit of research, and almost the same biological tendency, as in his grandson; and we might, not without justice, assert that the latter has succeeded to an intellectual inheritance, and carried out a programme sketched forth and left behind by his grand-father.—KRAUSE, ERNST, 1879, *The Scientific Works of Erasmus Darwin, tr. Dallas, p.* 132.

His correspondence with many distinguished men was large; but most of the letters which I possess or have seen are uninteresting, and not worth publication. Medicine and mechanics alone aroused him to write with any interest. . . . Judging

from his published works, letters, and all that I have been able to gather about him, the vividness of his imagination seems to have been one of his pre-eminent characteristics. This led to his great originality of thought, his prophetic spirit both in science and in the mechanical arts, and to his over-powering tendency to theorise and generalise. Nevertheless, his remarks, hereafter to be given, on the value of experiments and the use of hypotheses show that he had the true spirit of a philosopher. That he possessed uncommon powers of observation must be admitted. The diversity of the subjects to which he tended is surprising. But of all his characteristics, the incessant activity or energy of his mind was, perhaps, the most remarkable.—DARWIN, CHARLES, 1879, *The Scientific Works of Erasmus Darwin by Krause, tr. Dallas, Preliminary Notice, pp.* 27, 48.

THE BOTANIC GARDEN
1781

My father has just returned from Dr. Darwin's, where he has been nearly three weeks. . . . He saw the first part of Dr. Darwin's "Botanic Garden;" £900 was what his bookseller gave him for the whole!—EDGEWORTH, MARIA, 1792, *Letters, vol.* I, *p.* 21.

I wish I could let you have a look at this fashionable style of English book, as I have it before me in large quarto bound in morocco. It weighs exactly five and a half pounds, as I know by having convinced myself of this yesterday. Now as our pocket-books weigh about as much in half-ounces, we may, in this respect, also be as one to thirty-two compared with the English, unless indeed we on our part were able to counterbalance one such fashionable English giant with thirty-two pocket-books. It is splendidly printed on smooth paper, embellished with crazy, allegorical engravings by Fuseli, and in addition to this every now and again adorned with illustrations the subjects of which are taken from botany, antiquarian research, incidents and love-affairs of the day; it has introductions, tables of contents, notes below the text and notes at the end of the text, in which physics, geography, botany, manufacture and commerce, but more especially the names of dead and living celebrities are admirably set forth, so that from ebb and flood down to the sympathetic ink, everything can be readily perceived and understood. . . . Here, therefore, you have the plan of a poem! Such must be the appearance presented by a didactic poem which is not only to teach but to instruct. You will now be able to imagine that a goodly variety of descriptions, of allegories and of similes is to be found roaming about in this book, and that there is not a vestige of poetic feeling to link the poem together. The versification, it seems to me, is not bad, and many passages possess a rhetorical turn peculiar to the metre. In part, the details remind one of many of those English poets whose works are of didactic and narrative order. How pleased the English *blasé* world will be with certain passages when it sees so much theoretical matter—of which it has for long heard faint whisperings—sung aloud to it in the well-known rhythm! I have only had the book in the house since last night, and, in truth, find it beneath my expectation, for I am really in favour of Darwin.—GOETHE, JOHANN WOLFGANG, 1798, *Letter to Schiller, Jan.* 26; *Correspondence Between Schiller and Goethe, tr. Schmitz, vol.* II, *pp.* 26, 27.

Darwin's book would probably have little success in Germany. The Germans like sentiment, and the more trifling it is the more generally welcome it is; but this play of the fancy with ideas, this realm of allegory, this cold intellectuality and learning disguised in verse, could not be attractive to any but the English in their present state of frostiness and unconcern. The work, however, shows what function is wont to be attributed to poetry, and is a new and brilliant triumph to the philistines over their poetical adversaries. Otherwise I do not think the subject-matter inadmissible and wholly inappropriate for poetical treatment. The miscarriage, in this case, I consider altogether the poet's fault. If one were, at the very outset, to relinquish all idea of giving so-called instruction, and merely endeavoured to bring nature, in its rich variety, movement, and co-operation, within reach of the imagination, and· set forth all the products of nature with a certain love and reverence— paying regard to the independent existence of every one and so forth—then a lively interest in the various subjects could not fail to be awakened —SCHILLER, JOHANN CHRISTOPH FRIEDERICH, 1798, *Letter to* Goethe, *Jan.* 30; *Correspondence Between Schiller and Goethe, tr. Schmitz, vol.* II, *p.* 29.

Only a few years have elapsed, since the genius of the author of "The Botanic Garden" first burst on the public notice in all its splendour. The novelty of his plan —an imposing air of boldness and originality in his poetical as well as philosophical speculations—and a striking display of command over some of the richest sources of poetical embellishment, were sufficient to secure to him a large share of approbation, even from the most fastidious readers, and much more than sufficient to attract the gaze and the indiscriminating acclamations of a herd of admirers and imitators. Yet, with all these pretentions to permanent fame, we are much deceived, if we have not already observed, in that of Dr. Darwin the visible symptoms of decay.—THOMSON, T., 1803, *The Temple of Nature, Edinburgh Review, vol.* 1, *p.* 491.

This poem ought not to be considered more than as a capriccio, or sport of fancy, on which he has expended much labour to little purpose. It does not pretend to anything like correctness of design, or continuity of action. It is like a picture of Breughel's where every thing is highly coloured, and every thing out of order.— CARY, HENRY FRANCIS, 1821–24–45, *Lives of English Poets, p.* 265.

When we enter "The Botanic Garden" of Darwin, we find that we have been enticed back into the wilderness of didactic verse: while this masterly versifier exemplifies also, almost everywhere, one of the most common of poetical errors; namely, the attempt to make poetry describe minutely the sensible appearances of corporeal objects, instead of being content with communicating the feelings which those objects awaken.—SPALDING, WILLIAM, 1852–82, *A History of English Literature, p.* 356.

The section on manures, or the food of plants, is the sole part that interests the agriculturist, and it is much too refined for the grossness of the farmer's application of the articles. No new fact was elicited and established, but much light was cast on the processes that had been adopted.—DONALDSON, JOHN, 1854, *Agricultural Biography*.

Strangely enough, in spite of her correct taste, Mrs. Barbauld was quite fascinated by Darwin's "Botanic Garden" when it first appeared, and talked of it with rapture; for which I scolded her heartily. —ROGERS, SAMUEL, 1855, *Recollections of Table-Talk, ed. Dyce.*

Nothing is done in passion and power; but all by filing, and scraping, and rubbing, and other painstaking. Every line is as elaborately polished and sharpened as a lancet; and the most effective paragraphs have the air of a lot of those bright little instruments arranged in rows, with their blades out, for sale. You feel as if so thick an array of points and edges demanded careful handling, and that your fingers are scarcely safe in coming near them. Darwin's theory of poetry evidently was, that it was all a mechanical affair—only a higher kind of pin-making. His own poetry, however, with all its defects, is far from being merely mechanical. The "Botanic Garden" is not a poem which any man of ordinary intelligence could have produced by sheer care and industry, or such faculty of writing as could be acquired by serving an apprenticeship to the trade of poetry. Vicious as it is in manner, it is even there of an imposing and original character; and a true poetic fire lives under all its affectations, and often blazes up through them. There is not much, indeed, of pure soul or high imagination in Darwin; he seldom rises above the visible and material; but he has at least a poet's eye for the perception of that, and a poet's fancy for its embellishment and exaltation. No writer has surpassed him in the luminous representation of visible objects in verse; his descriptions have the distinctness of drawings by the pencil, with the advantage of conveying, by their harmonious words, many things that no pencil can paint. His images, though they are for the most part tricks of language rather than transformations or new embodiments of impassioned thought, have often at least an Ovidian glitter and prettiness, or are striking from their mere ingenuity and novelty.—CRAIK, GEORGE, 1861, *A Compendous History of English Literature and of the English Language, vol. II, p.* 382.

Now the book I mean shows us the scientific faculty and the poetic faculty—and no weak faculties either—working along together, not merged, not chemically united, not lighting up matters like a star,—with the result, as seems to me, of producing the very funniest earnest book in our language. It is "The Loves of the Plants," by Dr. Erasmus Darwin.— LANIER, SIDNEY, 1881, *The English Novel, p.* 191.

For all Wordsworth's exultant prophecy on the harmony of Poetry and Science, it cannot be said that any very assuring illustration of the circumstance has happened before his date or since. The "Botanical Garden" of Erasmus Darwin looms almost tragically alone, like the forlorn desert image of Shelley's famous sonnet, as a warning, if not a menace, to all travellers in this demesne.—BAYNE, WILLIAM, 1898, *James Thomson (Famous Scots Series), p.* 62.

ZOÖNOMIA
1794-6

If, however, the doctrines of the "Zoonomia" are not always infallible, it is a work which must spread the fame of its author over lands and seas, to whatever clime the sun of science has irradiated and warmed. The "Zoonomia" is an exhaustless repository of interesting facts, of curious experiments in natural productions, and in medical effects; a vast and complicated scheme of disquisition, incalculably important to the health and comforts of mankind, so far as they relate to objects merely terrestrial; throwing novel, useful, and beautiful light on the secrets of physiology, botanical, chemical, and aerological.—SEWARD, ANNA, 1804, *Memoirs of the Life of Dr. Darwin, p.* 68.

The second part of the Zoönomia is occupied with an enumeration of diseases, classified on the above principles, illustrated by brief reports of cases, and with suggestions as to their medical treatment. All diseases are morbid motions, and are divided into four classes, as those motions are irritative, sensitive, voluntary, or associative. The four classes are divided into eleven orders, founded on the increased, diminution, or inversion of the motion. The eleven orders are divided into forty-one genera, thirty-seven of which are founded on the part of the system affected, the other four on the fundamental classification. Nothing could have a more admirable simplicity upon paper; and we must pardon those who hailed it with the enthusiastic faith that the Newton of morbid physiology had appeared in Erasmus Darwin. . . . Dr. Darwin's theory of evolution was closely connected with his scheme of classifying diseases; the most signal defect of that scheme was the failure to recognize any other differences than differences of degree. There was no sharpness of definition anywhere. It is, I confess, patent to every eye that some disorders in the human system have this indefinite character. There seems to be no dividing line between the highest state of health and complete disorganization and prostration; the one runs into the other more gradually than the oaks into the chestnuts. But, on the other hand, there are, certainly, some diseases which are sharply defined. The modern microscope, modern chemical reagents, and the modern spirit of experimental science are producing indisputable results in this field. The revulsion from Darwin's method of classifying diseases will, we think, be followed by revulsion from its method of classifying organic beings. — HILL, THOMAS, 1878, *Erasmus Darwin, Bibliotheca Sacra, vol.* 35, *pp.* 470, 480.

Like Buffon, Dr. Darwin had no wish to see far beyond the obvious; he missed good things sometimes, but he gained more than he lost; he knew that it is always on the margin, as it were, of the self-evident that the greatest purchase against the nearest difficulty is obtainable. His life was not one of Herculean effort, but, like the lives of all these organisms that are most likely to develop and transmit a useful modification, it was one of well-sustained activity; it was a long-continued keeping open of the windows of his own mind, much after the advice he gave to the Nottingham weavers. Dr. Darwin knew, and, I imagine, quite instinctively, that nothing tends to oversight like over-seeing. He does not trouble himself about the origin of life; as for the perceptions and reasoning faculties of animals and plants, it is enough for him that animals and plants do things which we say involve sensation and consciousness when we do them ourselves or see others do them. If, then, plants and animals appear as if they felt and understood, let the matter rest there, and let us say they feel and understand —being guided by the common use of language, rather than by any theories

concerning brain and nervous system.— BUTLER, SAMUEL, 1879, *Evolution Old and New, p.* 197.

The "Zoonomia " is largely devoted to medicine, and my father thought that it had much influenced medical practice in England; he was of course a partial, yet naturally a more observant judge than others on this point. The book when published was extensively read by the medical men of the day, and the author was highly esteemed by them as a practitioner.— DARWIN, CHARLES, 1879, *The Scientific Works of Erasmus Darwin, by Krause, tr. Dallas, Preliminary Notice, p.* 105.

GENERAL

Milton is *harmonious* to me, and I absolutely nauseate Darwin's poems.—COLERIDGE, SAMUEL TAYLOR, 1796, *Letters, ed. E. H. Coleridge, vol.* I, *p.* 164.

Meantime the matter and diction seemed to me characterized not so much by poetic thoughts, as by thoughts translated into the language of poetry. On this last point, I had occasion to render my own thoughts gradually more and more plain to myself, by frequent amicable disputes concerning Darwin's "Botanic Garden," which, for some years, was greatly extolled, not only by the reading public in general, but even by those, whose genius and natural robustness of understanding enabled them afterwards to act foremost in dissipating these "painted mists" that occasionally rise from the marshes at the foot of Parnassus. During my first Cambridge vacation, I assisted a friend in a contribution for a literary society in Devonshire: and in this I remember to have compared Darwin's work to the Russian palace of ice, glittering, cold, and transitory.—COLERIDGE, SAMUEL TAYLOR, 1817, *Biographia Literaria.*

Dr. Darwin has splendidly exemplified the effects of his own theory, which certainly includes much truth, but not the whole truth. Endued with a fancy peculiarly formed for picture-poetry, he has limited verse almost within the compass of designing and modelling with visible colours and palpable substances. Even in this poetic painting, he seldom goes beyond the brilliant minuteness of the Dutch school of artists, while his groups are the extreme reverse of theirs, being rigidly classical. His productions are undistinguished by either sentiment or pathos.

He presents nothing but pageants to the eye, and leaves next to nothing to the imagination; every point and object being made out in noonday clearness, where the sun is nearly vertical, and the shadow most contracted. He never touches the heart, nor awakens social, tender, or playful emotions.—MONTGOMERY, JAMES, 1833, *Lectures on General Literature, Poetry, etc., p.* 126.

All optic nerve.—BROWNING, ELIZABETH BARRETT, 1842-63, *The Book of the Poets.*

As a poet, his "Botanic Garden" by its tawdry splendor gained him a tawdry reputation; as a philosopher his "Zoonomia, or, Laws of Organic Life," gained him a reputation equally noisy and fleeting.—LEWES, GEORGE HENRY, 1845-46, *Biographical History of Philosophy, p.* 609.

The poet-laureate of botany.—COLLIER, WILLIAM FRANCIS, 1861, *A History of English Literature, p.* 352.

Almost every single work of the younger Darwin may be paralleled by at least a chapter in the works of his ancestor; the mystery of heredity, adaptation, the protective arrangement of animals and plants, sexual selection, insectivorous plants, and the analysis of the emotions and sociological impulses; nay, even the studies on infants are to be already discussed in the writings of the elder Darwin. But at the same time we remark a material difference in their interpretation of nature. The elder Darwin was a Lamarckian, or, more properly, Jean Lamarck was a Darwinian of the older school, for he has only carried out further the ideas of Erasmus Darwin, although with great acumen; and it is to Darwin therefore that the credit is due of having first established a complete system of the theory of evolution.—KRAUSE, ERNST, 1879, *The Scientific Works of Erasmus Darwin, tr. Dallas, pp.* 132.

He was a poet, in his day a very popular poet, whose works went through many editions. His stately verses are repugnant to modern taste, and it is hard to imagine them ever becoming popular again. Yet this is in a great measure due to the fact that they are written in a language which is wholly gone by, and which in the ears of those educated in this post-Wordsworthian age sounds stilted and pompous. Byron called the author of the "Loves of the Plants" a "mighty master of unmeaning rhyme," but this is unfair. His poetry is anything but unmeaning. It is at times even eloquent. The chief defect that would be found with it nowadays (leaving out of view the Johnsonese vocabulary and style) would be that it is rather rhetorical than poetical.—SEDGWICK, A. G., 1880, *Erasmus Darwin, The Nation, vol.* 30, *p.* 254.

Unfortunately for his lasting fame, Dr. Darwin was much given to writing poetry; and this poetry, though as ingenious as everything else he did, had a certain false gallop of verse about it which has doomed it to become since Canning's parody a sort of warning beacon against the worse faults of the post-Augustan decadence in the ten-syllabled metre. Nobody now reads the "Botanic Garden" except either to laugh at its exquisite extravagances, or to wonder at the queer tinsel glitter of its occasional clever rhetorical rhapsodies. But in his alternative character of philosophic biologist, rejected by the age which swallowed his poetry all applausive, Erasmus Darwin is well worthy of the highest and deepest respect, as a prime founder and early prophet of the evolutionary system. His "Zoonomia," "which, though ingenious, is built upon the most absurd hypothesis"—as men still said only thirty years ago—contains in the germ the whole theory of organic development as understood up to the very moment of the publication of the "Origin of Species."—ALLEN, GRANT, 1885, *Charles Darwin (English Worthies), p.* 21.

The antithesis to Edmund Waller is Erasmus Darwin. . . . He was, indeed, an extraordinary being, and if verve, knowledge, a brilliant vocabulary, and boundless intellectual assurance could make any man a poet, Darwin might have been one. But he has no imagination, and almost every fault of style. When he desires to seem glowing, his verses have the effect of ice; his very versification, for which he was once greatly admired, is so monotonous and so exasperatingly antithetical, that it reads like a parody of the verse of the earlier classicists. His landscapes, his sketches of character, his genre-pieces, his bursts of enthusiasm, are all of them ruined by his excessive insincerity of style, his lack of genuine vivacity, and his unceasing toil and tumidity of phrase. In his abuse of personation, as in many other qualities, he is the typical helot of eighteenth-century poetry, and the great temporary success of his amazing poem led to the final downfall of the school. To rival the *hortus siccus* of Darwin was more than the most ambitious of grandiose poetasters could hope to do.—Gosse, Edmund, 1888, *A History of Eighteenth Century Literature, pp.* 328, 330.

Darwin's poetry would be forgotten were it not for Canning's parody. He followed the model of Pope, just passing out of favour, for his versification, and expounded in his notes the theory that poetry should consist of word-painting. He had great facility of language, but the effort to give an interest to scientific didacticism in verse by elaborate rhetoric and forced personification was naturally a failure. Darwin would not have shrunk from Coleridge's favourite phrase, "Inoculation, heavenly maid." Yet it is remarkable that Darwin's bad poetry everywhere shows a powerful mind. . . . The permanent interest in his writings depends upon his exposition of the form of evolutionism afterwards expounded by Lamarck. He caught a glimpse of many observations and principles, afterwards turned to account by his grandson, Charles Darwin; but though a great observer and an acute thinker, he missed the characteristic doctrine which made the success of his grandson's scheme.—Stephen, Leslie, 1888, *Dictionary of National Biography.*

John Moore
1729–1802

Born at Stirling, a minister's son, studied medicine and practised in Glasgow, travelled with the young Duke of Hamilton 1772–78, and then settled in London. His "View of Society in France, Switzerland, Germany, and Italy" (1779–81) was well received; but the novel "Zeluco" (1789), which suggested Byron's "Childe Harold," is to-day the least forgotten of his works. These include two other novels, "Medical Sketches," and books on the French Revolution. Moore died at Richmond.—Patrick and Groome, eds., 1897, *Chambers's Biographical Dictionary, p.* 672.

PERSONAL

Moore was sagacious as a physician, and throughout life had intense enjoyment in general observation, and in every kind of good literature and good society. He was universally liked, and most of all in his own house. He had a well-built frame and regular features.—Moore, Norman, 1894, *Dictionary of National Biography, vol.* XXXVIII, *p.* 365.

ZELUCO
1789

This character is well contrived to purge the selfish and malignant passions, by exhibiting the hideous effect of their unrestrained indulgence.—Green, Thomas, 1810, *Diary of a Lover of Literature.*

I now leave "Childe Harold" to live his day, such as he is; it had been more agreeable, and certainly more easy, to have drawn an amiable character. It had been easy to varnish over his faults, to make him do more and express less; but he never was intended as an example, further than to show, that early perversion of mind and morals leads to satiety of past pleasures and disappointment in new ones, and that even the beauties of nature, and the stimulus of travel (except ambition, the most powerful of all excitements) are lost on a soul so constituted, or rather misdirected. Had I proceeded with the poem, this character would have deepened as he drew to the close; for the outline which I once meant to fill up for him was, with some exceptions, the sketch of a modern Timon, perhaps a poetical Zeluco.—Byron, Lord, 1813, *Childe Harold's Pilgrimage, Addition to the Preface.*

Dr. Moore, the father of the hero of Corunna, with good narrative power, some sly humour, and much observation of character, would have been, in our day, a writer of the *Peacock* family. Nevertheless, to one who is accustomed to our style of things, it is comic to read the dialogue of a jealous husband, a suspected wife, a faithless maid-servant, a tool of a nurse, a wrong-headed pomposity of a priest, and a sensible physician, all talking Dr. Moore through their masks. Certainly an Irish soldier does say *by Jasus,* and a cockney footman *this here* and *that there;* and this and the like is all the painting of characters which is effected out of the mouths of the bearers by a narrator of great power. I suspect that some novelists repressed their power under a rule that a narrative should narrate, and that the dramatic should be confined to the drama. —DE MORGAN, AUGUSTUS, 1872, *A Budget of Paradoxes, p.* 113.

His novel "Zeluco" (published in 1789) produced a powerful impression at the time, and indirectly, through the poetry of Byron, has left an abiding mark on literature. The novel would in these days be called a psychological novel; it is a close analysis of the motives of a headstrong, passionate, thoroughly selfish and unprincipled profligate. It is full of incident, and the analysis is never prolonged into tedious reflections, nor suffered to intercept the progress of the story, while the main plot is diversified with many interesting episodes. The character took a great hold of Byron's imagination, and probably influenced his life in some of its many moods, as well as his poetry. It is not too much to say that the common opinion that Byron intended "Childe Harold" as a reflection of himself cannot be cleared of its large mixture of falsehood with a study of Moore's "Zeluco." Byron said that he intended the Childe to be "a poetical Zeluco," and the most striking features of the portrait were undoubtedly taken from that character. At the same time it is obvious to everybody acquainted with Moore's novel and Byron's life that the moody and impressionable poet often adopted the character of Zeluco, fancied himself and felt himself to be a Zeluco, although he was at heart a very different man. — BAYNES, THOMAS SPENCER, *ed.,* 1884, *Encyclopædia Brittanica, vol.* XVI, p. 830.

Owing to the praise bestowed on it by Mrs. Barbauld, has been far too generally accepted as one of the most notable of eighteenth-century novels. Zeluco, the Byronic villain, and Laura, his amiable and suffering wife, are highly conventional types of evil and of good.—RALEIGH, WALTER, 1894, *The English Novel,* p. 193.

The book, besides the unlucky drawback that almost all its interest lies in the latter part, has for hero a sort of lifeless monster of wickedness, who is quite as uninteresting as a faultless one and shows little veracity of character except in the minor personages and episodes. In these, and indeed throughout Moore's work,

there is a curious mixture of convention with extreme shrewdness, of somewhat commonplace expression with a remarkably pregnant and humorous conception. But he lacks concentration and finish, and is therefore never likely to be much read again as a whole.—SAINTSBURY, GEORGE, 1896, *A History of Nineteenth Century Literature,* p. 28.

GENERAL

Every reader of extracts from the writings of Dr. Moore must feel a strong desire to become more intimately acquainted with an author so conversant with men and manners and so eminent for the benevolence of his heart and the purity of his morals, and thus be irresistibly induced to purchase all his works and place them in his library by the side of Johnson, Fielding, and Smollett.—PREVOST, F., AND BLAGDON, F., 1803, *Mooriana.*

He is characterised by profound knowledge of the world, admirable good sense, intimate acquaintance with human nature, a lively imagination, a rich vein of original humour, and an incomparable power of representing life and manners with discrimination, force, and delicacy.—ANDERSON, ROBERT, 1820, *Memoirs of the Life and Writings of John Moore,* p. 49.

As an author, Dr. Moore was more distinguished by the range of his information than by its accuracy or extent upon any particular subject, and his writings did not owe their celebrity to any great depth or even originality of thought. As a novelist he showed no extraordinary felicity in the department of invention, no great power of diversifying his characters, or ease in conducting his narrative. The main quality of his works is that particular species of sardonic wit, with which they are indeed perhaps profusely tinctured, but which frequently confers a grace and poignancy on the general strain of good sense and judicious observation that pervades the whole of them.—CARLYLE, THOMAS, 1820–23, *Edinburgh Encyclopædia, Montaigne and other Essays,* p. 44.

The popularity of the work ["View of Society"] was mainly owing to its amusing sketches, to the many good stories which it contains, and to the lively and animated style in which the whole is written.— HILLARD, GEORGE STILLMAN, 1853, *Six Months in Italy.*

James Beattie

1735–1803

Born, at Laurencekirk, Kincardine, 25 Oct. 1735. To Marischal Coll., Aberdeen, 1749; M. A., 1753. Schoolmaster and parish clerk at Fordoun, 1753–58. Contrib. to "Scots' Magazine." Master of Aberdeen Grammar School, 1758–60. Professor of Moral Philosophy and Logic, Marischal Coll., 1760–97. Published first vol. of poems, 1761. First visit to London, 1763. Friendship with Gray begun, 1765. Married Mary Dunn, 28 June 1767. Hon. D. C. L., Oxford, 9 July 1773. Crown pension of £200, Aug. 1773. Refused Professorship of Moral Philosophy at Edinburgh, 1773. Active literary work. Failing health from 1793. Died, 18 Aug. 1803. Buried in St. Nicholas Churchyard, Aberdeen. *Works:* "Original Poems and Translations," 1760; "Judgment of Paris," 1765; "Verses on the Death of Churchill," 1765; "Poems on Several Subjects," 1766; "Essay on Truth," 1770; "The Minstrel," pt. 1. (anon.) 1771; pt. ii., 1774; "Poems on Several Occasions," 1776; "Essays," 1776 (2nd edn. same year); "Letter to the Rev. H. Blair . . . on the Improvement of Psalmody, in Scotland" (anon., privately printed), 1778; "List of Two Hundred Scotticisms" (anon.), 1779; "Dissertations, Moral and Critical," 1783; "Evidences of the Christian Religion," 1786; "The Theory of Language," 1788; "Elements of Moral Science," vol. 1, 1790; vol. 11, 1793; "Notes on Addison (apparently not published), 1790. *Collected Poems:* 1805, 1810, 1822, 1831, etc. He *edited:* "Essays and Fragments," by his son, J. H. Beattie (privately printed), 1794. *Life:* by Bower, 1804; by Sir W. Forbes, 1806.—SHARP, R. FARQUHARSON, 1897, *A Dictionary of English Authors, p.* 20.

PERSONAL

I found him pleasant, unaffected, unassuming, and full of conversable intelligence; with a round, thick, clunch figure, that promised nothing either of his works or his discourse, yet his eye, at intervals, . . . shoots forth a ray of genius that instantly lights up his whole countenance. His voice and his manners are particularly and pleasingly mild, and seem to announce an urbanity of character both inviting and edifying. . . . You would be surprised to find how soon you could forget that he is ugly and clumsy, for there is a sort of perfect good-will in his countenance and his smile, that is quite captivating.—D'ARBLAY, MME. (FANNY BURNEY), 1787, *Diary, July* 13.

> *Memoriæ. Sacrum.*
> JACOBI. BEATTIE. LL.D.
> *Ethices.*
> In Academia. Marescallana. hujus. Urbis.
> Per. XLIII. Annos.
> Professoris. Meretissimi.
> *Viri.*
> Pietate. Probitate. Ingenio. atque. Doctrina.
> *Præstantis.*
> Scriptoris. Elegantissimi. Poetæ. Suavissimi.
> Philosophi. Vere. Christiani.
> Natus. est. V. Nov. Anno. MDCCXXXV.
> Obiit. XVIII. Aug. MDCCCIII.
> Omnibus. Liberis. Orbus.
> Quorum. Natu. Maximus. JACOBUS. HAY.
> BEATTIE.
> Vel. a. Puerilibus. Annis.
> Patrio. Vigens. Ingenio.

> Novumque. Decus. Jam. Addens. Paterno.
> Suis. Carissimus. Patriæ. Flebilis.
> Lenta. Tabe. Consumptus. Periit.
> Anno. Ætatis. XXIII.
> GEO. ET. MAR. GLENNIE.
> H. M. P.

—GREGORY, JAMES, 1803, *Inscription on Monument, Churchyard of St. Nicholas, Aberdeen.*

I am happy to think, that the moral effect of his works is likely to be so powerfully increased by the Memoirs of his exemplary life, which you are preparing for the press, while the respect which the public already entertains for his genius and talents, cannot fail to be blended with other sentiments still more flattering to his memory, when it is known with what fortitude and resignation he submitted to a series of trials, far exceeding those which fall to the common lot of humanity; and that the most vigorous exertions of his mind were made, under the continued pressure of the severest domestic affliction, which a heart like this could be doomed to suffer.—STEWART, DUGALD, 1806, *Letter to Sir William Forbes, Life of Beattie by Forbes, vol.* III, *p.* 255.

Of his conduct towards his unhappy wife, it is impossible to speak in terms of too high commendation. It has already been mentioned, that Mrs. Beattie had the misfortune to inherit from her mother, that most dreadful of all human ills, a distempered imagination, which, in a very few years after their marriage, showed itself in caprices and folly, that embittered every hour of his life, while he strove at first to conceal her disorder from the world, and, if possible, as he has been heard to say, to conceal it even from himself; till at last from whim, and caprice, and melancholy, it broke out into downright insanity, which rendered her seclusion from society absolutely necessary. . . . When I reflect on the many sleepless nights and anxious days, which he experienced from Mrs. Beattie's malady, and think of the unwearied and unremitting attention he paid to her, during so great a number of years, in that sad situation, his character is exalted in my mind to a degree which may be equalled, but I am sure never can be excelled, and makes the fame of the poet and the philosopher fade from my remembrance. . . . In his person, Dr. Beattie was of the middle size, though not elegantly, yet not awkwardly formed, but with something of a slouch in his gait. His eyes were black and piercing, with an expression of sensibility, somewhat bordering on melancholy, except when engaged in cheerful and social intercourse with his friends, when they were exceedingly animated. As he advanced in years, and became incapable of taking his usual degree of exercise, he grew corpulent and unwieldly, till within a few months of his death, when he had greatly decreased in size. When I last saw him, the diminution of his form was but too prophetic of the event that soon followed.—FORBES, SIR WILLIAM, 1806, *An Account of the Life and Writings of James Beattie, vol.* III, *pp.* 176, 177, 187.

Read "Beattie's Life," by Sir Wm. Forbes (from Barjarg, where I was some days ago), *Schneidermässig,* religious "Gigmanity," yet lovable, pitiable, in many respects worthy. Of all literary men, Beattie, according to his deserts, was perhaps (in those times) the best rewarded; yet alas! also, at length, among the unhappiest. How much he enjoyed that is far from *thee!*—converse with minds congenial; an element not of *black cattleism,* but of refinement, plenty, and encouragement. Repine not; or, what is more to be dreaded, *rebel not.*—CARLYLE, THOMAS, 1834, *Journal, Feb.* 9; *Life by Froude, vol.* II, *p.* 327.

Let us recall his black and piercing eyes, "with an expression of sensibility bordering on melancholy" when in repose, but brightening into animation when he addressed those whom he loved. He afterwards—I grieve to say it of any poet—grew corpulent; but at this time he carried with him to those levées of talent a spare person, and the rare qualities of a mind which I shall briefly characterise. His imagination was, perhaps, subservient to his taste. The cultivation of his mind had been carried almost to what human nature can conceive of perfection, his chief acquirements being in moral science. As a professor, he was revered; as a friend and companion, fondly cherished. In literature he held an eminent place. The deepest piety, a true sensibility and gentleness, and a humility sincere as it was rare, softened and elevated all his mental attributes.—THOMSON, KATHERINE (GRACE WHARTON), 1848, *The Literary Circles of the Last Century, Fraser's Magazine, vol.* 37, *p.* 80.

Throughout the whole of the North of Scotland in these days, there was not one that could compete with Dr. Beattie, the recluse professor at Aberdeen, in variety of accomplishments; for he was an excellent classical scholar, a veritable poet, a scientific as well as practical musician, and indefatigable student, and, as a metaphysician, unsurpassed at that epoch, unless it were by his friend and colleague, Dr. Ried.—GILLIES, ROBERT PIERCE, 1851, *Memoirs of a Literary Veteran.*

This excellent and amiable man; for such he was, whatever we may think of him as a writer. Scepticism was at this time fashionable among the wits and men of letters. It was thought a great thing that such a man as Beattie, not a clergyman, should have taken up the pen against Hume and Voltaire. The essay had won him popular fame, royal favour, and a pension. The Edinburgh Town Council had wooed him to the chair of moral philosophy; the Archbishop of York had solicited him to enter the Church of England.—LESLIE, CHARLES ROBERT, AND TAYLOR, TOM, 1865, *Life and Times of Sir Joshua Reynolds, vol.* II, *p.* 56.

During the latter half of the eighteenth century the literary traditions of the most northerly university town of Scotland—the city of John Barbour and of Hector

Boece—were honourably upheld by a small knot of poets. Of these the most academic remains the most famous. Poet and professor, philosopher and man of letters, James Beattie was no less distinguished in his time by his "Minstrel" and his prose "Essay on Truth" than by the encouragement and help which he constantly afforded to men of genius less fortunately placed. Not only were Ross and Blacklock substantially indebted to him for the furtherance of their literary fortunes, but constantly in the literary history of the time one comes upon hints and helps given now to one poet and now to another, which again and again bore valuable fruit. Beattie indeed may be said to have been for forty years a gentle and more generous Johnson, at once the literary dictator and the Mæcenas of the far north.—EYRE-TODD, GEORGE, 1896, *Scottish Poetry of the Eighteenth Century, vol.* II, *p.* 1.

ESSAY ON TRUTH
1770

I am not at all surprised to hear, that your spirited attack on the head-quarters of scepticism has drawn upon you the resentment of Mr. Hume and his followers.—PORTEUS, BIELBY, 1772, *Letter to Beattie May* 22; *Forbes' Life of Beattie, vol.* I, *p.* 293.

I have lately been employed in reading Beattie and Blair's "Lectures." The latter I have not yet finished. I find the former the most agreeable of the two; indeed the most entertaining writer upon dry subjects that I ever met with. His imagination is highly poetical, his language easy and elegant, and his manner so familiar, that we seem to be conversing with an old friend, upon terms of the most social intercourse, while we read him. . . . In Blair we find a scholar; in Beattie both a scholar and an amiable man; indeed so amiable, that I have wished for his acquaintance ever since I read his book.—COWPER, WILLIAM, 1784, *Letter to Rev. John Newton, April* 26; *Works, ed. Southey, vol.* III, *p.* 103.

Dr. Beattie's great work, and that which was undoubtedly the first foundation of his celebrity, is the "Essay on the Nature and Immutability of Truth;" on which such unmeasured praises are bestowed, both by his present biographer, and by all the author's male and female correspondents,

that it is with difficulty we can believe that they are speaking of the performance which we have just been wearying ourselves with looking over. That the author's intentions were good, and his convictions sincere, we entertain not the least doubt: but that the merits of his book have been prodigiously overrated, we think, is equally undeniable. It contains absolutely nothing, in the nature of argument, that had not been previously stated by Dr. Reid in his "Inquiry into the Human Mind;" and, in our opinion, in a much clearer and more unexceptionable form.—JEFFREY, FRANCIS LORD, 1807-44, *Life of Dr. Beattie, Contributions to the Edinburgh Review, vol.* III, *p.* 365.

Beattie is among the philosophers what the Quaker is among religious sectaries. The κοινὸς νοῦς, or common sense, is the spirit whose illapses he sits down and waits for, and by whose whispers alone he expects to be made wise. It has sometimes prompted him well; for there are admirable passages in the Essay. The whole train of his argument, or rather his invective, in the second part, against the sceptics, is irresistible.—CARY, HENRY FRANCIS, 1821-24-45, *Lives of English Poets, p.* 310.

The book was received very favourably, passed through five large editions in four years, and was translated into French, German, Dutch, and Italian. In the history of philosophy it has not the slightest importance. The loose, commonplace character of the professor's reasoning made the essay popular among such readers as wish to be thought acquainted with the philosophy of the day, while they have neither the ability nor inclination to grapple with metaphysical problems. Attacks on Hume in singularly bad taste abound throughout the book. Hume is said to have complained that he "had not been used like a gentleman," and this probably is the only notice that he deigned to take of the professor's labours.—BULLEN, A. H., 1885, *Dictionary of National Biography, vol.* IV, *p.* 23.

The book had an enormous vogue, and procured for its author a renown which, however evanescent, was for the moment astonishing. But it was in England rather than in Scotland that its reception was most flattering. . . . But as a fact the book was but a piece of literary flotsam such as is often cast up by the breaking waves of controversy. As a philosophical disputant Beattie is beneath contempt. Occasionally he scores a good point, but it may almost always be traced to Reid. He makes a sound accusation against the Scottish school, that they were ignorant of the work of the ancient philosophers and blind to their merits; but the accusation is one which he was utterly incapable of pushing home. The book is indeed a commonplace and frothy mixture of popular invective and almost childish argument.—CRAIK, SIR HENRY, 1901, *A Century of Scottish History, vol.* II, *p.* 219.

THE MINSTREL
1771-74

The design was to trace the progress of a Poetical Genius, born in a rude age, from the first dawning of fancy and reason, till that period at which he may be supposed capable of appearing in the world as a Minstrel, that is, as an itinerant Poet and Musician;—a character which, according to the notions of our forefathers, was not only respectable, but sacred. I have endeavoured to imitate Spenser in the measure of his verse, and in the harmony, simplicity, and variety of his composition. Antique expressions I have avoided; admitting, however, some old words, where they seemed to suit the subject; but I hope none will be found that are now obsolete, or in any degree not intelligible to a reader of English poetry. To those who may be disposed to ask, what could induce me to write in so difficult a measure, I can only answer that it pleases my ear, and seems, from its Gothic structure and original, to bear some relation to the subject and spirit of the Poem. It admits both simplicity and magnificence of sound and of language beyond any other stanza that I am acquainted with. It allows the sententiousness of the couplet, as well as the more complex modulation of blank verse. What some critics have remarked, of its uniformity growing at last tiresome to the ear, will be found to hold true only when the poetry is faulty in other respects.— BEATTIE, JAMES, 1771, *The Minstrel, Preface.*

I read the "Minstrel" with as much rapture as poetry, in her noblest, sweetest charms, ever raised in my soul. It seemed to me that my once most-beloved minstrel, Thomson, was come down from heaven, refined by the converse of purer spirits than those he lived with here, to let me hear him sing again the beauties of nature, and the finest feelings of virtue, not with human, but with angelic strains.— LYTTELTON, LORD, 1771, *Letter to Mrs. Montagu, March.*

I am charmed with "The Minstrel," and have circulated its fame. I have enclosed a note, by which you will see how much it pleased Lord Lyttelton. I have sent one into the country to Lord Chatham; and I wrote immediately to a person who serves many gentlemen and ladies with new books, to recommend it to all people of taste. I am very sorry the second edition of Dr Beattie's book is not yet in town. I have recommended it, too, to many of our bishops and others; but all have complained this whole winter, that the booksellers deny having any of either the first or second edition.—MONTAGU, ELIZABETH, 1771, *Letter to Dr. John Gregory, March* 13; *Forbes' Life of Beattie, vol.* I, *p.* 251.

> Nor tremble lest the tuneful art expire,
> While Beattie strikes anew old Spenser's lyre;
> He, best to paint the genuine minstrel knew,
> Who from himself the living portrait drew.
> —MORE, HANNAH, 1782, *Sensibility.*

I thanked you in my last for Johnson; I now thank you, with more emphasis, for Beattie,—the most agreeable and amiable writer I ever met with; the only author I have seen, whose critical and philosophical researches are diversified and embellished by a poetical imagination, that makes even the driest subject and the leanest, a feast for an epicure in books. He is so much at his ease, too, that his own character appears in every page; and, which is very rare, we see not only the writer, but the man; and that man so gentle, so well-tempered, so happy in his religion, and so humane in his philosophy, that it is necessary to love him, if one has the least sense of what is lovely. If you have not his poem called "The Minstrel," and cannot borrow it, I must beg you to buy it for me; for, though I cannot afford to deal largely in so expensive a commodity as books, I must afford to purchase at least the poetical works of Beattie.—COWPER, WILLIAM, 1784, *Letter to Rev. William Unwin, April* 5.

> No gifts have I from Indian coasts
> The infant year to hail;
> I send you more than India boasts,
> In Edwin's simple tale.
> —BURNS, ROBERT, 1787, *To Miss Logan, with Beattie's Poems.*

It was his supreme delight to saunter in the fields the livelong night, contemplating the sky, and marking the approach of day; and he used to describe, with peculiar animation, the pleasure he received from the soaring of the lark in the summer morning. A beautiful landscape which he has magnificently described in the twentieth stanza of the first book of the "Minstrel," corresponds exactly with what must have presented itself to his poetical imagination, on those occasions, at the approach of the rising sun, as he would view the grandeur of that scene from the hill in the neighbourhood of his native village. The high hill which rises to the west of Fordoun, would, in a misty morning, supply him with one of the images so beautifully described in the twenty-first stanza. And the twentieth stanza of the second book of the "Minstrel" describes a night-scene unquestionably drawn from nature, in which he probably had in view Homer's sublime description of the moon, in the eighth book of the Iliad, so admirably translated by Pope, that an eminent critic had not scrupled to declare it to be superior to the original. He used, himself, to tell, that it was from the top of a high hill in the neighbourhood that he first beheld the ocean, the sight of which, he declared, made the most lively impression on his mind.—FORBES, SIR WILLIAM, 1806, *An Account of the Life and Writings of James Beattie, vol.* I, *p.*25.

"Lives there the man," who has a heart to feel, and an understanding to appreciate, who does not even hug the "Minstrel" of Beattie? Most sweet and soothing and instructive is that thoroughly picturesque and sentimental poem, throughout: while the stanza exhibits one of the happiest of modern attempts at that of the Spencerian structure.—DIBDIN, THOMAS FROGNALL, 1824, *The Library Companion,* p. 735, *note.*

His fame now rests upon "The Minstrel" alone. Since its first publication, many poems of a far loftier and more original character have been produced in England; yet still does it maintain its popularity; and still in Edwin, that happy personification of the poetic temperament, do young and enthusiastic readers delight to recognize a picture of themselves. Though we cannot fail to regret that Beattie should have left it incomplete, yet we do not long for the concluding books from any interest which we take in the story, such as is excited by some other unfinished works of genius, the tale of "Cambuscan," for instance, or the legend of "Christabel." In "The Minstrel," indeed, there is but little invention; it is a poem of sentiment and description, conveying to us lessons of true philosophy in language of surprising beauty, and displaying pictures of nature, in her romantic solitudes, painted by a master's hand.—DYCE, ALEXANDER, 1831, *Beattie's Poems, Aldine ed., Memoir.*

No poem has ever given more delight to minds of a certain class, and in a certain stage of their progress . . . that class a high one, and that stage perhaps the most delightful in the course of their pilgrimage. It was to this class that the poet himself belonged; the scenes which he delineated were those in which he had grown up, the feelings and aspirations those of his own boyhood and youth, and the poem derived its peculiar charm from its truth.—SOUTHEY, ROBERT, 1835, *Life of Cowper, p.* 340.

This afternoon I read through Beattie's "Minstrel," which I never read carefully before. It does not seem to me in most parts to possess fire enough—you can't see the "kindling touch" of genius in it.—LOWELL, JAMES RUSSELL, 1837, *To G. B. Loring, April* 14; *Letters, ed. Norton, vol.* I, *p.* 18.

"The Minstrel" is an harmonious and eloquent composition, glowing with poetical sentiment; but its inferiority in the highest poetical qualities may be felt by comparing it with Thomson's "Castle of Indolence," which is perhaps the other work in the language which it most nearly resembles, but which yet it resembles much in the same way as gilding does solid gold, or as colored water might be made to resemble wine.—CRAIK, GEORGE L., 1861, *A Compendious History of English Literature and of the English Language, vol.* II, *p.* 307.

Beattie had not the same power of luscious delineation, nor the same command over language, which belonged to Thomson; yet, on the other hand, he sometimes rises to a strain of manly force and dignity which was beyond the compass of the other.—ARNOLD, THOMAS, 1868-75, *Chaucer to Wordsworth, p.* 362.

Of James Beattie it is enough to record that he published incoherent fragments of a mock-antique "Minstrel," in the Spenserian stanza.—Gosse, Edmund, 1888, *A History of Eighteenth Century Literature, p.* 327.

His thought is nowhere great; it verges on originality, but is never conspicuously fresh and new. "The Minstrel" besides is defective in the execution of its plan. The idea at the root of it was a happy one; and Wordsworth subsequently gave partial proof of what might be done with it. But Beattie did not really carry out his purpose. The figure of Edwin remains a mere shadow; and the reader cannot be said to behold the growth of a mind whose features are nowhere brought before his eye.—Walker, Hugh, 1893, *Three Centuries of Scottish Literature, vol.* ii, *p.* 131.

"The Minstrel," like "The Seasons," abounds in insipid morality, the commonplaces of denunciation against luxury and ambition, and the praise of simplicity and innocence.—Beers, Henry A., 1898, *A History of English Romanticism in the Eighteenth Century, p.* 305.

"The Minstrel or the Progress of Genius" can satisfy only the most moderate expectations, or the least fastidious taste. There is absolutely no story; the expression is seldom or never striking, and the versification (it is Spenserian), though not contemptible, has no distinction. But all the objects of the early, confused, Romantic appetite—country scenes, woods, ruins, the moon, chivalry, mountains— are dwelt upon with a generous emotion, and with at least poetic intention. Above all, Beattie was important "for *them,*" to apply once more one of the most constantly applicable of critical dicta. His time could understand him, as it could not have understood purer Romanticism, and it is probable that, for an entire generation at least, and perhaps longer, "The Minstrel" served to bring sometimes near, and sometimes quite, to poetry, readers who would have found Coleridge too fragmentary, Shelley too ethereal, and both too remote. —Saintsbury, George, 1898, *A Short History of English Literature, p.* 586.

GENERAL

Dr. Beattie's style is singularly free and perspicuous, and adapted in the highest degree to the purpose of familiar lecturing to his pupils; but for the author we should deem it something less than elegant, and something less than nervous. In early life he took great pains to imitate Addison, whose style he always recommended and admired. . . . In many parts of the letters, we are constrained to perceive a degree of egotism inconsistent with the dignity of a philosopher or a man. The writer seems unwilling to lose any opportunity of recounting the attentions, the compliments, the testimonies of admiration, which he has received from individuals or the public. The complacency with which he expatiates on himself and his performances, is but imperfectly disguised by the occasional and too frequent professions of holding himself and those performances cheap. This is a very usual but unsuccessful expedient, with those who have reflection enough to be sensible that they have rather too much ostentation, but not resolution enough to restrain themselves from indulging in it.—Foster, John, 1807, *On Memoir-Writing, Critical Essays, ed. Ryland, vol.* i, *pp.* 27, 28.

He wrote English better than any other of his countrymen, and had formed his style and manner of composition on our Addison; but what he admired in him was his tuneful prose and elegant expression. He had no notion of that writer's original and inimitable humour.—Hurd, Richard, 1808, *Commonplace Book, Memoirs, ed. Kilvert, p.* 244.

The few of his poems which he thought worthy of being selected from the rest, and of being delivered to posterity, have many readers, to whom perhaps one recommendation of them is that they are few. They have, however, and deservedly, some admirers of a better stamp. They soothe the mind with indistinct conceptions of something better than is met with in ordinary life. The first book of the "Minstrel," the most considerable amongst them, describes with much fervour the enthusiasm of a boy "smit with the love of song," and awakened to a sense of rapture by all that is most grand or lovely in the external appearance of nature. It is evident that the poet had felt much of what he describes, and he therefore makes his hearers feel it. Yet at times, it must be owned, he seems as if he were lashing himself into a state of artificial emotion.—Cary, Henry Francis, 1821-24-45, *Lives of English Poets, p.* 313.

On the whole, Beattie may be ranked beside, or near, Campbell, Collins, Gray, and Akenside. Deficient in thought and passion, in creative power, and copious imagination, he is strong in sentiment, in mild tenderness, and in delicate description of nature. Whatever become of his Essay on Truth, or even of his less elaborate and more pleasing Essays on Music, Imagination, and Dreams, the world can never, at any stage of its advancement, forget to read and admire the "Minstrel" and the "Hermit," or to cherish the memory of their warm-hearted and sorely-tried author.— GILFILLAN, GEORGE, 1854, *ed. The Poetical Works of Beattie, Blair and Falconer, p.* xxiv.

Beattie, a metaphysical moralist, with a young girl's nerves and an old maid's hobbies.—TAINE, H. A., 1871, *History of English Literature, tr, Van Laun, vol.* II, *bk.* iii, *ch.* vii, *p.* 220.

His style has considerable power of the rotund declamatory order ; copious, high-sounding, and elegant ; occasionally in its appeals to established feeling throwing out rhetorical interrogations, followed by brief, abrupt answers.—MINTO, WILLIAM, 1872-80, *Manual of English Prose Literature, p.* 474.

His poems will ever hold a place among the classical writings of Great Britain. His "Minstrel" and his "Hermit" are exquisite poems of their kind: simple, graceful, tender, and leaving a peaceful and peace-giving impression on the mind ; and therefore not likely to be appreciated by those whose tastes were formed by the passionate and startling style of poetry introduced in the next page by Byron, who was at school in Aberdeen while Beattie was in his declining years. His prose works do not exhibit much grasp or depth of thought, but are characterized by much ease and elegance. — McCosH, JAMES, 1874, *The Scottish Philosophy, p.* 234.

Beattie also wrote odes, but any interference with the dust that has settled upon them would be officious and unnecessary ; it is by his "Minstrel" that he lives, so far as he can be said to live at all, for there is no great delight to be got from his other poems. "The Minstrel," however, has real merit. It was due in good part to the influence of Spenser, whom he greatly admired, but even in beautiful passages we find such conventional phrases as "glittering waves and skies in gold arrayed." Yet in the first book we find very genuine love of nature expressed with real poetical skill.—PERRY, THOMAS S., 1880, *Gray, Collins and Beattie, Atlantic Monthly, vol.* 46, *p.* 816.

Beattie is perhaps the most difficult poet of the eighteenth century for a nineteenth-century reader to criticise sympathetically. His original poetical power was almost *nil.* But he had a delicate and sensitive taste, and was a diligent student of the works of Gray and Collins on the one hand, and of the ballads which Percy had just published on the other. His earlier poems are merely so many variations on the "Elegy" and the "Ode on the Passions." His "Judgment of Paris" and his "Lines on Churchill" are perhaps those of his works in which he was least indebted to others, and they are almost worthless intrinsically, besides being (at least the Churchill lines) in the worst possible taste. —SAINTSBURY, GEORGE, 1880, *The English Poets, ed. Ward, vol.* III, *p.* 396.

Beattie's odes are feeble echoes of "The Bard" of Gray and "The Passions" of Collins ; his "Judgment of Paris" is mere rhetoric ; his imitation of Shakespeare's "Blow, blow, thou winter wind" is chiefly remarkable for the number of technical faults compressed within so narrow compass. "The Minstrel" itself is more noteworthy as a symptom than for its intrinsic merits.—WALKER, HUGH, 1893, *Three Centuries of Scottish Literature, vol.* II, *p.* 130.

The author of the "Minstrel" was an honest man and a respectable poet, but he prided himself too much on what he called common sense, and failed to see that in the search after truth other and even higher faculties may be also needed.— DENNIS, JOHN, 1894, *The Age of Pope, p.* 226.

His fame to-day is as a tale that is told. His prose works, so lauded in their generation, are forgotten. His "Minstrel" lingers still with a slender reputation after its days of glory, and its author is stamped with that disastrous title of mediocrity—"a pleasing poet."—GRAHAM, HENRY GREY, 1901, *James Beattie, Scottish Men of Letters in the Eighteenth Century, p.* 272.

Joseph Ritson
1752–1803

Antiquary, born at Stockton-on-Tees, came to London in 1775, and practised as a conveyancer, but was enabled to give most of his time to antiquarian studies. He was as notorious for his vegetarianism, whimsical spelling, and irreverence as for his attacks on bigger men than himself. His first important work was an onslaught on Warton's "History of English Poetry" (1782). He assailed (1783) Johnson and Steevens for their text of Shakespeare, and Bishop Percy in "Ancient Songs" (1790); in 1792 appeared his "Cursory Criticisms" on Malone's Shakespeare. Other works were "English Songs" (1783); "Ancient Popular Poetry" (1791); "Scottish Songs" (1794); "Poems," by Laurence Minot (1795); "Robin Hood Ballads" (1795); and "Ancient English Metrical Romances" (1802).—PATRICK AND GROOME, *eds.*, 1897, *Chambers's Biographical Dictionary, p.* 792.

PERSONAL

As bitter as gall, and as sharp as a razor,
And feeding on herbs as a Nebuchadnezzar,
His diet too acid, his temper too sour,
Little Ritson came out with his two volumes
     more.
—SCOTT, SIR WALTER, 1823, *Song of One Volume More.*

Coarse, caustic, clever; and, am I to suppose, not amiable.—LAMB, CHARLES, 1823, *Ritson Versus John Scott, the Quaker, p.* 437.

This narrow-minded, sour, and dogmatical little word-catcher had hated the very name of a Scotsman, and was utterly incapable of sympathizing with any of the higher views of his new correspondent. Yet the bland courtesy of Scott disarmed even this half-crazy pedant; and he communicated the stores of his really valuable learning in a manner that seems to have greatly surprised all who had hitherto held any intercourse with him on antiquarian topics.—LOCKHART, JOHN GIBSON, 1836, *Life of Sir Walter Scott, ch.* x.

Whose wild temper and vegetarian crotchets have found a more permanent place in history than his collections.—OLIPHANT, MARGARET O. W., 1882, *The Literary History of England, XVIIIth-XIXth Century, vol.* II, *p.* 189.

One of the most interesting spots in all London to me is Bunhill Fields cemetery, for herein are the graves of many whose memory I revere. I had heard that Joseph Ritson was buried here, and while my sister, Miss Susan, lingered at the grave of her favorite poet, I took occasion to spy around among the tombstones in the hope of discovering the last resting-place of the curious old antiquary whose labors in the field of balladry have placed me under so great a debt of gratitude to him.

But after I had searched in vain for somewhat more than an hour one of the keepers of the place told me that in compliance with Ritson's earnest desire while living, that antiquary's grave was immediately after the interment of the body levelled down and left to the care of nature, with no stone to designate its location. So at the present time no one knows just where old Ritson's grave is, only that within that vast enclosure where so many thousand souls sleep their last sleep the dust of the famous ballad-lover lies fast asleep in the bosom of mother earth.—FIELD, EUGENE, 1895, *The Love Affairs of a Bibliomaniac, p.* 93.

Ritson combined much pedantry with his scholarship; but he sought a far higher ideal of accuracy than is common among antiquaries, while he spared no pains in accumulating information. Sir Walter Scott wrote that "he had an honesty of principle about him which, if it went to ridiculous extremities, was still respectable from the soundness of the foundation." But Scott did not overlook his friend's peculiarities, and in verses written for the Bannatyne Club in 1823 he referred to "Little Ritson"

As bitter as gall, and as sharp as a razor,
And feeding on herbs as a Nebuchadnezzar.

Ritson's impatience of inaccuracy led him to unduly underrate the labours of his contemporaries, and his suspicions of imposture were often unwarranted. But his irritability and eccentricity were mainly due to mental malady. He showed when in good health many generous instincts, and he cherished no personal animosity against those on whose published work he made his splenetic attacks. With Surtees, George Paton, Walter Scott, and his nephew he corresponded good-humouredly to the end. He produced his works with every typographical advantage, and employed Bewick and Stothard to illustrate many of them. It is doubtful if any of his literary ventures proved remunerative. In person, according to his friend Robert Smith, Ritson resembled a spider. A caricature of him by Gillray represents him in a tall hat and a long closely buttoned coat.—LEE, SIDNEY, 1896, *Dictionary of National Biography, vol.* XLVIII, *p.* 330.

GENERAL

In Theron's form, mark Ritson next contend;
Fierce, meagre, pale, no commentator's
　　friend.
—MATHIAS, THOMAS JAMES, 1797, *The Pursuits of Literature, Eighth ed., p.* 100.

A man of acute observation, profound research, and great labour. These valuable attributes were unhappily combined with an eager irritability of temper, which induced him to treat antiquarian trifles with the same seriousness which men of the world reserve for matters of importance, and disposed him to drive controversies into personal quarrels, by neglecting, in literary debate, the courtesies of ordinary society. It ought to be said, however, by one who knew him well, that this irritability of disposition was a constitutional and physical infirmity, and that Ritson's extreme attachment to the severity of truth corresponded to the vigour of his criticisms upon the labours of others.— SCOTT, SIR WALTER, 1802-3, *Ancient Minstrelsy, Introduction.*

Hear how this puny worm lifts its feeble cry, to arraign the orders of nature, and scoff at the Omniscience, which, for wise purposes, though quite unknown to us, suffers it to crawl upon the earth. . . . Before taking leave of this nauseous performance, a few words remain to be added upon the *style,* in which so many absurdities are delivered. We do not mean to go farther than the external qualities,—the matchless ludicrousness of the orthography and typography. . . . We now most joyfully leave the "Essay on Abstinence from Animal Food" to that oblivion which awaits it; and from which its singularities, however gross and wicked, are of too dull a cast to save it. —SMITH, SIDNEY, AND BROUGHAM, HENRY LORD, 1803, *Ritson on Abstinence From Animal Food, Edinburgh Review, vol.* 2, *pp.* 135, 136.

Ritson is the oddest, but most honest of all our antiquarians.—SOUTHEY, ROBERT, 1803, *To S. T. Coleridge, March* 14; *Life and Correspondence.*

Mr. Joseph Ritson, unilluminated by a particle of taste or fancy, and remarkable only for the increasing drudgery with which he dedicated his life to one of the humblest departments of literary antiquities, and for the bitter insolence and foul abuse with which he communicated his dull acquisitions to the public. . . . Whoever is acquainted with that strange, but not totally useless, book ["Bibliographia Poetica"], will wonder how it was possible for a man, with such a fund of materials before him, to compile a work so utterly lifeless and stupid, so uncheared by one single ray of light, or one solitary flower admitted even by chance from the numerous and varied gardens of poetry over which he had been travelling! But, poor unhappy spirit, thou art gone! Perhaps thy restless temper was diseased: and mayst thou find peace in the grave!— BRYDGES, SIR SAMUEL EGERTON, 1805, *Censura Literaria, vol.* I, *p.* 54.

SYCORAX was this demon; and a cunning and clever demon was he! I will cease speaking metaphorically, but SYCORAX was a man of ability in his way. He taught literary men, in some measure, the value of careful research and faithful quotation; in other words, he taught them to speak the truth as they found her; and doubtless for this he merits not the name of demon, unless you allow me the privilege of a Grecian. That SYCORAX loved the truth must be admitted; but that he loved no one else so much as himself to speak the truth, must also be admitted.—DIBDIN, THOMAS FROGNALL, 1811, *The Bibliomania; or, Book-Madness.*

Ritson, the late antiquary of poetry (not to call him poetical) amazed the world by his vituperative railing at two authors of the finest taste in poetry, Warton and Percy; he carried criticism, as the discerning few had first surmised, to insanity itself; the character before us only approached it.—DISRAELI, ISAAC, 1812-13, *The Influence of a Bad Temper in Criticism, Calamities of Authors.*

As to the rabid Ritson, who can describe his vagaries? What great arithmetician can furnish an index to his absurdities, or what great decipherer furnish a key to the principles of these absurdities? In his very title-pages,—nay, in the most obstinate of ancient technicalities,—he showed his cloven foot to the astonished reader. Some of his many works were printed in *Pall-Mall;* now, as the world is pleased to pronounce that word *Pel-Mel,* thus and no otherwise (said Ritson) it shall be spelled for ever. Whereas, on the contrary, some men would have said: The spelling is well enough, it is the public pronunciation which is wrong. . . . Volumes would not suffice to exhaust the madness of Ritson upon this subject. And there was this peculiarity in his madness, over and above its clamorous ferocity,— that, being no classical scholar (a meagre self-taught Latinist and no Grecian at all), though profound as a black-letter scholar, he cared not one straw for ethnographic relations of words, nor for unity of analogy, which are the principles that generally have governed reformers of spelling. He was an attorney and moved constantly under the *monomaniac* idea that an action lay on behalf of misused letters, mutes, liquids, vowels, and diphthongs, against somebody or other (John Doe, was it, or Richard Roe?) for trespass on any rights of theirs which an attorney, might trace, and of course for any direct outrage upon their persons. Yet no man was more systematically an offender in both ways than himself,—tying up one leg of a quadruped word and forcing it to run upon three, cutting off noses and ears if he fancied that equity required it, and living in eternal hot water with a language which he pretended eternally to protect.—DE QUINCEY, THOMAS, 1847–60, *Orthographic Mutineers; Works, ed. Masson, vol.* XI, pp. 441, 442.

A man of ample reading and excellent taste in selection, and who, real scholar as he was, always drew from original sources.—LOWELL, JAMES RUSSELL, 1871, *Library of Old Authors, My Study Windows, p.* 359.

Neither Percy nor Warton escaped the strictures of Ritson, that "black-letter dog," a tame and affected pedant of no critical importance, but far more careful as an editor than either of them.—GOSSE, EDMUND, 1888, *A History of Eighteenth Century Literature, p.* 325.

I do not wonder that Ritson and Percy quarrelled. It was his misfortune that Ritson quarrelled with everybody. Yet Ritson was a scrupulously honest man; he was so vulgarly sturdy in his honesty that he would make all folk tell the truth even though the truth were of such a character as to bring the blush of shame to the devil's hardened cheek.—FIELD, EUGENE, 1895, *The Love Affairs of a Bibliomaniac, p.* 101.

Joseph Ritson possessed all the enthusiasm, and even more than the share of eccentricity, which so often accompanies the genius of the antiquary. . . . Violent in all his notions,—religious, moral, and political, as well as critical,— he was always ready to fall upon others whose opinions were at variance with truth, or at least with his own view of it. As his learning was large and strictly accurate, and his style incisive, he was respected and disliked; and at different times Warburton, Johnson, Warton, and Steevens all felt the edge of his criticism. It will readily be supposed that Percy's ideas of the duties of an editor did not commend themselves to Ritson.—COURTHOPE, W. J., 1895, *A History of English Poetry, vol.* I, p. 428.

Samuel Hopkins
1721–1803

A Congregational clergyman of Newport, Rhode Island, the founder of what has been called Hopkinsian Divinity, which differed from Calvinism in maintaining the free agency of sinners, the moral inability of the unregenerate, and ascribing the essence of sin to the disposition and purpose of the mind. His views had great influence in the modification of contemporary thought. He was a strong opponent of slavery, and his influence procured the passage of a law prohibiting the importation of slaves into Rhode Island. The "System of Doctrine contained in Divine Revelation" is his principal work. Others are, "The True State of the Unregenerate;" "Nature of True Holiness;" "The Duty and Interest of American States to Emancipate their Slaves." *See* "Life" by Park; Mrs. Stowe's "Minister's Wooing;" Sprague's "Annals of the American Pulpit."—ADAMS, OSCAR FAY, 1897, *A Dictionary of American Authors, p.* 194.

PERSONAL

His appearance was that of a man who had nothing to do with the world. I can well recollect the impression which he made on me when a boy, as he rode on horseback in a plaid gown, fastened by a girdle round his waist, and with a study cap on his head instead of a wig. His delivery in the pulpit was the worst I ever met with. Such tones never came from any human voice within my hearing. He was the very ideal of bad delivery. Then I must say, the matter was as often uninviting as the manner. . . . . His manners had a bluntness, partly natural, partly the result of long seclusion in the country. We cannot wonder that such a man should be set down as hard and severe. But he had a true benevolence, and what is more worthy of being noted, he was given to a facetious style of conversation.—CHANNING, WILLIAM ELLERY, 1836, *Christian Worship, Discourse at Newport, R. I., July* 27; *Works, vol.* IV, *p.* 348, *note.*

As to his personal appearance, my recollection is, that he was rather above the middle height, somewhat inclined to a plethoric habit, with a thoughtful and intelligent expression of countenance. He wore a black cap, and seemed to me very aged and infirm. I remember to have thought his preaching exceedingly dry and abstract, and such I believe was the estimate formed of it by those whose age and acquirements rendered them more competent judges than I was. I understand that some of his sermons were written out, but he usually preached from short notes. The effect of his preaching was that nearly all the young people of the town went to other churches. I distinctly recollect that there was a larger proportion of aged people in his congregation than I remember ever to have seen in any other; and there was a corresponding gravity and solemnity in their appearance.—PITMAN, BENJAMIN H., 1851, *Letter to William B. Sprague, Aug.* 18; *Annals of the American Pulpit, vol.* I, *p.* 433.

Nothing in the history of Samuel Hopkins is more honorable to him, than his early, fearless, uncompromising and indefatigable testimony against the slave trade and against slavery. We commend the consideration of his heroic example, and the study of his works on this subject, to those pastors and doctors, who, within the last three years, in their zeal for compromise and political expediency, have shown themselves recreant to the cause of liberty. That honest old man, with all his metaphysics, had a "throb under the left breast;" and, with all his logic, it was impossible for him to deduce from the Scriptures, or from his own theory of the nature of virtue, any apology for so atrocious a thing as the system of slavery. Without the gift of eloquence, without any advantage of station or office, without wealth, without personal influence, save in a restricted range, he made himself felt, and was willing to be hated, as a defender of the needy and the captive. His influence in this respect has acted upon thousands of minds who were never conscious that the influence which moved them came from so obscure a source. Guided by no impracticable or Jacobinical theory, impelled only by the Divine instinct of equity and love, he demanded, as with an inspired earnestness, justice for the wronged and liberty for all.—BACON, LEONARD, 1852, *Prof. Park's Memoir of Hopkins, New Englander, vol.* 10, *p.* 470.

He was so infirm, during at least a part of the time after I knew him, that he was unable to walk to the house of God without help. He was rather tall and somewhat corpulent, as well as infirm; and I well remember that a coloured man used to put his shoulder under the Doctor's arm, and thus walk with him to his pulpit, and then home again after the service. I think I never heard him preach but once, and then his voice and manner, owing I suppose to his bodily infirmities, were extremely feeble; but I think that, in his best state, he had not much animation in the pulpit. I visited him very often, and always found him in his study, and always received from him a cordial welcome. He was pleasant and instructive in conversation, and seemed to be living under a habitual sense of the Divine presence. He was evidently deeply affected that so little apparent success had attained his ministry, and I think he had great fears as to what would be the condition of his society after his removal from them. — BRADLEY, JOSHUA, 1853, *Letter to William B. Sprague, July* 15; *Annals of the American Pulpit, vol.* I, *p.* 435.

He was a good man. His own phrase to express the sum total of virtue was "disinterested benevolence," and he lived it as faithfully as he preached it. He secured the personal esteem and love of those of his neighbors who differed most widely from him in his theological views. His great mental trait was that which was so clearly marked upon his daily life that he received the nick-name Old Honesty. He was humble, and honest in expressing a depreciatory opinion of his own services. He was honest in his theological convictions, and thorough in carrying them out into their manifold ramifications. So honest was he, that he did not stop always to select language not likely unnecessarily to offend.—FOSTER, FRANK H., 1886, *The Eschatology of the New England Divines, Bibliotheca Sacra, vol. 43, p.* 711.

GENERAL

The celebrity of the author, who, with Edwards and Bellamy, completes the American triumvirate of eminent writers in the same strain of divinity, would have rendered this work ["System of Doctrines"] much more popular and useful, had he kept clear of a bold and grating statement,—that "God has foreordained all the moral evil which does take place," and which he endeavours to defend with more ingenuity than success.—WILLIAMS, EDWARD, 1800, *The Christian Preacher.*

His system, however fearful, was yet built on a generous foundation. He maintained that all holiness, all moral excellence, consists in benevolence, or disinterested devotion to the greatest good. . . He taught that sin was introduced into the creation, and is to be everlastingly punished, because evil is necessary to the highest good. . . . True virtue, as he taught, was an entire surrender of personal interest to the benevolent purposes of God. Self-love he spared in none of its movements.— CHANNING, WILLIAM ELLERY, 1836, *Christian Worship, Discourse at Newport, R. I., July* 27.

We have chosen to speak of Dr. Hopkins as a philanthropist, rather than a theologian. Let those who prefer to contemplate the narrow sectarian, rather than the universal man, dwell upon his controversial works, and extol the ingenuity and logical acumen with which he defended his own dogmas, and assailed those of others. We honor him, not as the founder of a new sect, but as the friend of all mankind; the generous defender of the poor and oppressed. Great as unquestionably were his powers of argument, his learning, and skill in the use of the weapons of theologic warfare, these by no means constitute his highest title to respect and reverence. As the product of an honest and earnest mind, his doctrinal dissertations have at least the merit of sincerity. They were put forth in behalf of what he regarded as truth; and the success which they met with, while it called into exercise his profoundest gratitude, only served to deepen the humility and self-abasement of their author.—WHITTIER, JOHN G., 1849, *Old Portraits and Modern Sketches, p.* 162.

Hopkins sought to add to the five points of Calvinism the rather heterogeneous ingredient that holiness consists in pure, disinterested benevolence, and that all regard for self is necessarily sinful.—HILDRETH, RICHARD, 1849-54, *History of the United States of America, vol.* II, *p.* 597.

Few theologians of our country have exerted a wider special influence than Samuel Hopkins, a descendant of Governor Hopkins, of Connecticut, and the chief of the Calvinistic sect of Christians known as *Hopkinsians.* . . . Dr. Hopkins was an inefficient preacher. His pen, and not his tongue, was the chief utterer of those sentiments which have made his name famous as a Calvinistic theologian.—LOSSING, BENSON J., 1855-86, *Eminent Americans, p.* 240.

Hopkinsianism is Calvinism, in distinction from every form and shade of Arminianism; and yet not Calvinism, in precisely the sense of Calvin, or of the Westminster Confession of faith. It is a modification of some of the points of old Calvinism, presenting them, as its abettors think, in a more reasonable, consistent, and scriptural point of light. These modifications originated in New England, more than a hundred years ago. They commenced with the first President Edwards, and were still further unfolded in the teachings of his pupils and followers, Hopkins, Bellamy, West, the younger Edwards, Dr. Emmons, and Dr. Spring. The name "Hopkinsian" is derived from Dr. Samuel Hopkins of Newport, R. I., and was fastened upon those who sympathized with him, not by himself, but by an opponent.— POND, ENOCH, 1862, *Hopkinsianism, Bibliotheca Sacra, vol.* 19, *p.* 633.

The progress of theology during the

thirty years which followed the Revolution is illustrated by the works of many men of mark in their profession, and by two men of original though somewhat crotchety religious genius, Samuel Hopkins and Nathaniel Emmons.— WHIPPLE, EDWIN PERCY, 1886, *American Literature and Other Papers, ed. Whittier, p. 29.*

He expected men to study his books till they got the great sweep and purpose of the whole, and interpret single expressions by his general meaning. If one will read him thus, and do him the justice now and then to re-state his thought in modern styles of expression, the grandeur of his fearless consistency will impress, as much as the deep solicitude and heart-searching faithfulness of this preacher-theologian will move and profit in the reading.— FOSTER, FRANK H., 1886, *The Eschatology of the New England Divines, Bibliotheca Sacra, vol.* 43, *p.* 712.

No one can read Hopkins's writings without perceiving how saturated he has become with Edwards's thought. Whether he is the truest interpreter of Edwards may be doubted, however, for his mind was cast in a different mould. Nor does it appear that Edwards admitted him, after all, to complete intellectual intimacy; for Hopkins is silent as the grave about Edwards's more recondite philosophical or theological speculations. . . . Dr. Hopkins passed his life shut up to his own reflections, within the narrow precincts of his theological system. He had learned to think vigorously for himself, but he had a strange incapacity for seeing how other people thought. He showed no concern at the great revulsion of feeling which was all around him in his later years. He had no anticipation of a truth to be revealed to the coming generation which would shake the principles to whose advocacy he had devoted his life.—ALLEN, ALEXANDER V. G., 1891, *The Transition in New England Theology, Atlantic Monthly, vol.* 68, *pp.* 769, 777.

Samuel Adams
1722–1803

Patriot and orator; a second cousin of President John Adams; born in Boston, Sept. 27, 1722; graduated at Harvard College in 1740; and became a merchant, but was not successful in business, and soon abandoned it. In 1765 he was chosen to represent Boston in the General Court of Massachusetts, in which he distinguished himself by his courage, energy, and oratorical talents, and acquired great influence. Before the Revolution he was an unflinching advocate of the popular cause, and took such an active part in political meetings that he was one of the two leading patriots who were excepted from a general pardon offered in 1775. He was a member of the first Continental Congress, which met in Sept., 1774, and he signed the Declaration of Independence in 1776. He remained in Congress about eight years, was afterwards elected to the Senate of Massachusetts, and was a member of the State convention which ratified the Federal Constitution in 1788. His political affinities connected him with the Republicans (or Jeffersonian) party. He was elected Governor of Massachusetts in 1794, was re-elected twice, and retired to private life in 1797. He died Oct. 2, 1803. In religion he was a decided Calvinist.—ADAMS, CHARLES KENDALL, ed., 1897, *Johnson's Universal Cyclopædia, vol.* I, *p.* 43.

PERSONAL

The Cromwell of New England.—DECIUS, 1779, *London Morning Post; Moore's Diary of the Revolution, vol.* II, *p.* 144.

If ever a man sincerely an idolater of republicanism, it was Samuel Adams; and never a man united more virtues to give respect to his opinions. He has the excess of republican virtues,—untainted probity, simplicity, modesty, and, above all, firmness. He will have no capitulation with abuses. He fears as much the despotism of virtue and talents as the despotism of vice. Cherishing the greatest love and respect for Washington, he voted to take from him the command at the end of a certain time. He recalled that Cæsar could not have succeeded in overturning the Republic but by prolonging the command of the army. The event has proved that the application was false; but it was by a miracle, and the safety of a country should never be risked on the faith of a miracle.—BRISSOT DE WARVILLE, JEAN P., 1790? *New Travels in the United States.*

The dignity of his manners was well

expressed by the majesty of his countenance,—an index of a mind never debased by grovelling ideas nor occupied in contemplating low pursuits. Yet this appearance was accompanied with a suavity of temper, qualifying him for those charities and graces so highly ornamental to the most sublime and dignified character. Few are there who better discharge the social relations of life than our departed friend; neither would it be easy to find a more tender husband, more affectionate parent, or more faithful friend. He would easily relax from severe care and study, to enjoy the delight of private conversation. Nor did he ever omit any patronage or kindness due to any in the circle of his acquaintance which was in his power to execute. So that some who disliked his political conduct loved and revered him as a neighbor and friend.—THACHER, THOMAS, 1803, *A Tribute of Respect to the Memory of Samuel Adams, LL. D., A. A. S.*

It has been lately announced to the public, that one of the earliest patriots of the Revolution has paid his last debt to Nature. I had hoped that some other gentleman, better qualified for the task, would have undertaken to call the attention of the House to this interesting event. It cannot indeed be a matter of deep regret that one of the first statesman of our country has descended to the grave full of years and full of honors; that his character and fame are put beyond the reach of that time and chance to which everything mortal is exposed. But it becomes this House to cherish a sentiment of veneration for such men, since such men are rare, and to keep alive the spirit to which we owe the Constitution under which we are now deliberating. . . . I feel myself in every way unequal to the attempt of doing justice to the merits of our departed countryman. Called upon by the occasion to say something, I could have not have said less. I would not, by any poor eulogium of mine, enfeeble the sentiments which pervades the House, but content myself with moving the following resolutions—*Resolved unanimously,* That this House is penetrated with a full sense of the eminent services rendered to his country in the most arduous times by the late Samuel Adams, deceased, and that the members thereof wear crape on the left arm for one month in testimony for the national gratitude and reverence towards the memory of that undaunted and illustrious patriot.— RANDOLPH, JOHN, 1803, *Speech before Congress, Oct.* 19.

Altho' my high reverence for Samuel Adams was returned by habitual notices from him which highly flattered me, yet the disparity of age prevented intimate and confidential communications. I always considered him as more than any other member the fountain of our important measures. And altho' he was neither an eloquent nor easy speaker, whatever he said was sound, and commanded the profound attention of the House.—JEFFERSON, THOMAS, 1819, *Letter to Benjamin Waterhouse, Jan.* 31; *Writings, ed. Ford, vol.* x, *p.* 124.

He attached an exclusive value to the habits and principles in which he had been educated, and wished to adjust wide concerns too closely after a particular model. One of his colleagues who knew him well, and estimated him highly, described him, with goood-natured exaggeration, in the following manner: "Samuel Adams would have the State of Massachusetts govern the Union, the town of Boston govern Massachusetts, and that he should govern the town of Boston, and then the whole would not be intentionally ill-governed." —TUDOR, WILLIAM, 1823, *The Life of James Otis, p.* 274.

No single man did so much to promote the success of the Revolution.—McMASTER, JOHN BACH, 1883, *A History of the People of the United States, vol.* I, *p.* 179.

In character and career he was a singular combination of things incongruous. He was in religion the narrowest of Puritans, but in manner very genial. He was perfectly rigid in his opinions, but in his expression of them, often very compliant. He was the most conservative of men, but was regarded as were the "abolition fanatics" in our time, before the emancipation proclamation. Who will say that his uprightness was not inflexible? Yet a wilier fox than he in all matters of political manœuvring our history does not show. In business he had no push or foresight, but in politics was a wonder of force and shrewdness. In a voice full of trembling he expressed opinions, of which the audacity would have brought him at once to the halter if he could have been seized. Even in his young manhood his hair had become gray and his hand shook as if with paralysis; but he lived, as we shall see, to his eighty-second year, his work rarely interrupted by sickness, serving as governor of Massachusetts for several successive terms after he had lived his three score and ten years, almost the last survivor among the great pre-revolutionary figures. . . . There is another character in our history to whom was once given the title, "Father of America,"— a man to a large extent forgotten, his reputation overlaid by that of those who followed him,—no other than this man of the town-meeting, Samuel Adams. As far as the *genesis* of America is concerned, Samuel Adams can more properly be called the "Father of America" than Washington.—HOSMER, JAMES K., 1885, *Samuel Adams (American Statesmen), pp.* 357, 374.

"The American Cato;" "The Cromwell of New England;" "The Father of America;" "The Last of the Puritans;" "The Man of the Revolution."—FREY, ALBERT R., 1888, *Sobriquets and Nicknames, p.* 369.

Samuel was stern, serious, and deeply in earnest. He seldom smiled and never laughed. He was uncompromisingly religious, conscientious, and morally unbending. In his life there was no soft sentiment. The fact that he ran a brewery can be excused when we remember that the best spirit of the times saw nothing inconsistent in the occupation; and further than this we might explain in extenuation that he gave the business indifferent attention and the quality of his brew was said to be very bad. In religion he swerved not nor wavered. He was a Calvinist and clung to the five points with a tenacity at times seemingly quite unnecessary. . . . Adams' home life was simple to the verge of hardship. All through life he was on the ragged edge financially, and in his latter years he was for the first time relieved from pressing obligations by an afflicting event—the death of his only son, who was a surgeon in Washington's army. The money paid to the son by the Government for his services gave the father the only financial competency he ever knew. Two daughters survived him, but with him died the name. . . . The grave of Samuel Adams is viewed by more people than that of any other American patriot. In the old Granary Burying Ground, in the very centre of Boston, on Tremont Street, there where travel congests, and two living streams meet all day long, you look through the iron fence, so slender that it scarce impedes the view, and not twenty feet from the curb is a simple metal disc set on an iron rod driven into the ground and on it this inscription. "This marks the grave of Samuel Adams." For many years the grave was unmarked, and the disc that now denotes it was only recently placed in position by the Sons of the Revolution.— HUBBARD, ELBERT, 1898, *Little Journeys to the Homes of American Statesmen, pp.* 120, 142, 143.

GENERAL

As a writer, he was indefatigable when he thought his literary efforts could tend to promote his liberal and patriotic views; and although most of his productions have suffered that oblivion, to which the best efforts of temporary politics are generally destined, those which remain, or of which a knowledge is yet preserved, give abundant proof of the strength and fervour of his diction, the soundness of his politics, the warmth of his heart, and the piety and sincerity of his devotion. As an orator, he was peculiarly fitted for the times and circumstances on which he had fallen. His language was pure, concise and impressive; he was more logical than figurative; and his arguments were addressed rather to the understanding than the feelings: yet these he could often deeply interest, when the importance and dignity of his subject led him to give free vent to the enthusiasm and patriotic ardour, of which his heart was always full; and if we are to judge by the fairest of all tests, the effect upon his hearers, few speakers of ancient or modern times, could be named as superior to him —SANDERSON, JOHN, 1820–27, *Signers to the Declaration of Independence, vol.* I, *p.* 57.

Samuel Adams possessed a calm, solid, and yet polished mind. There is a wonderful lucidness in his thought and phraseology; everything about his composition is plain, forcible, and level to the simplest comprehension. Above all the men of his day, he was distinguished for sound practical judgment. All prominent statesmen looked to him for counsel. He aided Otis in preparing state papers; and a direction to the printers, attached to some of Josiah Quincy's manuscripts, reads—"Let

Samuel Adams, Esq., correct the press.'' In fact there were few, if any, important documents published between 1764 and 1769, in Boston, that were not revised by the cool and solid judgment of the New England *Phocion.* . . . One great secret of the power of his popular address, probably, lay in the unity of his purpose and the energy of his pursuit. He passionately loved freedom, and subordinated every thing to its attainment. This kind of inspiration is a necessary pre-requisite to eminent success. Samuel Adams had more logic in his composition than rhetoric, and was accustomed to convince the judgment rather than inflame the passions; and, yet, when the occasion demanded, he could give vent to the ardent and patriotic indignation of which his heart was often full.—MAGOON, E. L., 1848, *Orators of the American Revolution,* pp. 102, 113.

His pen was early employed in political discussion, and the soundness of his judgment, and purity of his thoughts, made him very popular, even before public affairs called his patriotism into activity. —LOSSING, BENSON J., 1855-86, *Eminent Americans, p.* 76.

His state papers and essays in the public journals, which would fill volumes, contain the most advanced political doctrines of the times as they presented themselves to thinkers and actors for decision and application. It is impossible to touch upon the history of Massachusetts without meeting his name. He took a leading part in the Congress that separated us from England; and, having from the beginning cast in his lot with his country, never shrunk from the labour, the sacrifices, or the perils which his decision involved.— GREENE, G. W., 1866, *Wells's Life and Services of Samuel Adams, North American Review, vol.* 102, *p.* 615.

It is probable that he was one of the most voluminous writers whom America has as yet produced. Some twenty-five signatures have been identified as used by him in the newspapers at different times. At the same moment that he filled the papers, he went on with his preparation of documents for the town and the Assembly till one wonders how a single brain could have achieved it all. If those writings only which can be identified were published, the collection would present a formidable array of polemical documents, embracing all the great issues out of whose discussion grew our independence. They were meant for a particular purpose, to shatter British oppression, and when that purpose was secured, their author was perfectly careless as to what became of them. Like cannon-balls which sink the ship, and then are lost in the sea, so the bolts of Samuel Adams, after riddling British authority in America, must be sought by diving beneath the oblivion that has rolled over them. Of the portion that has been recovered, these pages have given specimens enough to justify a high estimate of the genius and accomplishments of their author.—HOSMER, JAMES K.. 1885, *Samuel Adams (American Statesmen), p.* 360.

No other American had so good an opportunity to mould the form of a democracy in its best condition, and Adams made the most of his opportunity. A Calvinistic Congregationalist in religion, he applied to politics the principles of equality upon which he insisted in church order. Boston was somewhat leavened with aristocratic and Tory tendencies; against both he fought with a vigour which finally triumphed. To him fell a work in the North like that done by Thomas Jefferson in the South. Democratic principles carried too far become communistic; but extreme Federalism endangers the rights of the people. In the latter Adams saw the greater danger; and his work, fortunately, came at a time when the centrifugal force was more needed than the centripetal. . . . His work was that of a strong personal force, a pioneer, a destroyer of oppression, and upbuilder of liberty. He was the central figure in the town-meeting; he framed and voiced its policy; he drew up important instructions or appeals to home and foreign officers or legislators; and his pen was almost constantly in his hand, for he wrote stirring articles for the people's newspaper in Boston. His signatures were many; now he was ''Vindex,'' now ''Valerius Poplicola,'' now ''A Son of Liberty,'' but the purport of his utterances was ever the same. In his speeches, epistles, or memorials he put the spirit before the letter, the matter before the manner.—RICHARDSON, CHARLES F.,1887, *American Literature,* 1607-1885, *vol.* I, *p.* 179.

One of the greatest citizens that Massachusetts has ever produced, the man who has been well described as preëminently "the man of the town meeting,"—Samuel Adams. The limitations of this great man, as well as his powers, were those which belonged to him as chief among the men of English race who have swayed society through the medium of the ancient folk mote.—FISKE, JOHN, 1888, *The Critical Period of American History,* 1783–1789, *p.* 318.

The first colonial orator in point of time was Samuel Adams, but the record of his speeches is not abundant. The central figure of the Boston town-meeting he fought toryism and federalism with equal vigor; but reporters did not frequent town-meetings, or think the utterances of even a leader worth preserving. For their literary merit the speeches of Adams would not have been recorded. They were the straightforward, energetic sentiments of an earnest man who had no time to choose his words. Back of these, however, was the tremendous force of a strong personal character, fired with enthusiasm for freedom. His pen served him as often as his voice, and in the people's newspaper in Boston and in the Providence Gazette he published predictions and opinions which both New England and Old might read, causing him to be excluded from the general offer of pardon to the patriots made by the Throne the year before the Revolution broke out. His name belongs as much to political literature as to oratory, by reason of such contributions to the public press. . . . In point of time the name of Samuel Adams heads the roll of American orators and statesmen, and in immediately effecting the purpose they had in mind none have surpassed him. His was a practical oratory which carried its point at the time and with contemporaries, even though it has not been perpetuated as a model to succeeding generations. It ended in action and the action which it secured was the establishment of a new and free nation on the western continent. Measured by what it accomplished it must be admitted to be among the greatest achievements of human speech, and in its final result it is as yet unmeasured.—SEARS, LORENZO, 1895, *The History of Oratory, pp.* 306, 309.

It is as an orator that he deserves mention in a history of American literature, though only fragments of his fiery oratory have come down to us. Tradition, however, mentions him as a speaker to be compared with Otis and Quincy.—PATTEE, FRED LEWIS, 1896, *A History of American Literatvre, p.* 68.

This sleepless, crafty, protean politician, for nearly a third of a century, kept flooding the community with his ideas, chiefly in the form of essays in the newspapers, —thereby constantly baffling the enemies of the Revolutionary movement, and conducting his followers victoriously through those battles of argument which preceded and then for a time accompanied the battles of arms. . . . Whether in oral or in written speech, his characteristics were the same,—simplicity, acuteness, logical power, and strict adaptation of means to the practical end in view. Nothing was for effect—everything was for effectiveness. He wrote pure English, and in a style severe, felicitous, pointed, epigrammatic. Careful as to facts, disdainful of rhetorical excesses, especially conscious of the strategic folly involed in mere overstatement, an adept at implication and at the insinuating light stroke, he had never anything to take back or to apologize for. . . . Perhaps no long public career was ever more perfectly self-consistent than his. From boyhood to old age, his master principle was individualism.— TYLER, MOSES COIT, 1897, *The Literary History of the American Revolution,* 1763– 1783, *vol.* II, *pp.* 9, 12, 13.

Joseph Priestley
1733–1804

Joseph Priestley was born, a cloth-dresser's son, at Fieldhead in Birstall parish, Leeds, 13th March 1733. After four years at a Dissenting academy at Daventry, in 1755 he became Presbyterian minister at Needham Market, and wrote "The Scripture Doctrine of Remission," denying that Christ's death was a sacrifice, and rejecting the Trinity and Atonement. In 1758 he removed to Nantwich, and in 1761 became a tutor at Warrington Academy. In yearly visits to London he met Franklin, who supplied him with books for his "History of Electricity" (1767). In 1764 he was made LL.D. of Edinburgh, and in 1766 F. R. S. In 1767 he became minister of a chapel at Mill Hill, Leeds, where he took up the study of chemistry. In 1774, as literary companion, he accompanied Lord Shelburne on a continental tour, and published "Letters to a Philosophical Unbeliever." But at home he was branded as an atheist in spite of his "Disquisition relating to Matter and Spirit" (1777), affirming from revelation our hope of resurrection. He was elected to the French Academy of Sciences in 1772 and to the St. Petersburg Academy in 1780. . He became in that year minister of a chapel at Birmingham. His "History of Early Opinions concerning Jesus Christ" (1786) occasioned renewed controversy. His reply to Burke's "Reflections on the French Revolution" led a Birmingham mob to break into his house and destroy its contents (1791). He now settled at Hackney, and in 1794 removed to America, where he was heartily received; at Northumberland, Pa., he died 6th February 1804, believing himself to hold the doctrines of the primitive Christians, and looking for the second coming of Christ. Priestley is justly called the father of pneumatic chemistry; good authorities (see "Nature," XLII. 1890) defend the priority of his discovery of oxygen (1774) and of the composition of water (1781), and deny Lavoisier's claim to be considered an independent discoverer. See Rutt's edition of Priestley's "Works" (1831-32), including Autobiographical Memoir; and Martineau's "Essay."—PATRICK AND GROOME, *eds.*, 1897, *Chambers's Biographical Dictionary, p.* 762.

PERSONAL

This morning an express arrived at the Secretary of State's office from Birmingham, with an account that a great number of persons, to the amount of some hundreds, who were in opposition to the Revolutionists, had assembled on Thursday last before the house where the Society dined, and broke all the windows. They then pulled part of the house down, and proceeded to the different meeting-houses, which they laid level with the ground. After which, they broke into the house of Dr. Priestley, took everything out, burnt his books, drank the wine, and other liquor found in his cellars, and, when the express came away, were demolishing the house to the foundation. The whole town was in an uproar. . . . A messenger was dispatched to His Majesty at Windsor with the above particulars.—LONDON CHRONICLE, 1791, *July* 14-16.

Seeing, as I passed, a house in ruins, on inquiry I found it was Dr. Priestley's. I alighted from my horse, and walked over the ruins of that laboratory which I had left home with the expectation of reaping instruction in; of that laboratory, the labours of which have not only illuminated mankind, but enlarged the sphere of science itself; which has carried its master's fame to the remotest corners of the civilized world; and will now, with equal celerity, convey the infamy of its destruction to the disgrace of the age, and the scandal of the British name.—YOUNG, ARTHUR, 1791, *Tour through Warwickshire.*

When I wrote my last, little did I forsee what soon after happened; but the will of God be done. The company were hardly gone from the inn, before a drunken mob rushed into the house, and broke all the windows. They then set fire to our meeting-house, and it is burned to the ground. After that they gutted, and, some say, burned the old meeting. In the meantime, some friends came to tell me that I and my house were threatened, and another brought a chaise to convey me and my wife away. I had not presence of mind to take even my MSS.; and after we were gone, the mob came and demolished everything, household goods, library, and apparatus. Indeed, they say the house itself is almost demolished, but happily no fire could be got, so that many things, but I know not what, will be saved. We thought that when it was day, the mob would disperse, and therefore we kept in the neighbourhood; but finding they rather increased, and grew more outrageous with liquor, we were advised to go off, and are now on our way to Heath. My wife behaves with wonderful courage. The recollection of my lost MSS. pains me the most, especially my Notes on the New Testament, which I wanted only five days of getting all transcribed. But, I doubt not, all will be for good in the end. I can hardly ever live at Birmingham again. —PRIESTLEY, JOSEPH, 1791, *To Rev. T. Lindsey, July* 15; *Memoirs, ed. Rutt, vol.* I, *p.* 123.

Sir, and most illustrious associate, the

Academy of Sciences have charged me to express the grief with which they are penetrated at the recital of the persecution of which you have been lately the victim. They all feel how much loss the sciences have experienced by the destruction of those labours which you had prepared for their aggrandizement. It is not you, Sir, who have reason to complain. Your virtue and your genius still remain undiminished, and it is not in the power of human ingratitude to forget what you have done for the happiness of mankind.—CONDORCET, M., 1791, *Letter to Dr. Priestley, July* 30; *Memoirs, ed. Rutt, vol.* I, *p.* 127.

His love to man was great, his usefulness greater. I have been informed by the faculty that his experimental discoveries on air, applied to medical purposes, have preserved the lives of thousands; and, in return, he can scarcely preserve his own. A clergyman attended this outrage, and was charged with examining and even *pocketing* the manuscripts. I think he paid the Doctor a compliment, by showing a regard for his works. I will farther do him the justice to believe he never meant to keep them, to invade the Doctor's profession by turning philosopher, or to sell them, though valuable; but only to exchange them with the minister for preferment.—HUTTON, WILLIAM, 1791, *A Narrative of the Riots in Birmingham, Life of Hutton by Jewitt, p.* 228.

The mighty dead
Rise to new life, whoe'er from earliest time
With conscious zeal had urg'd Love's wondrous plan,
Coadjutors of God. To *Milton's* trump
The odorous groves of earth, reparadis'd,
Unbosom their glad echoes: inly hush'd,
Adoring *Newton* his serener eye
Raises to heaven: and he, of mortal kind
Wisest, he first who mark'd the ideal tribes
Down the fine fibres from the sentient brain
Roll subtly surging. Pressing on his steps,
Lo! *Priestley* there, patriot, and saint, and sage,
Whom that my fleshly eye hath never seen,
A childish pang of impotent regret
Hath thrill'd my heart. Him from his native land
Statesmen, blood-stain'd, and priests idolatrous,
By dark lies madd'ning the blind multitude,
Drove with vain hate: calm, pitying he retir'd,
And mus'd expectant on these promis'd years.
—COLERIDGE, SAMUEL TAYLOR, 1794, *Religious Musings.*

I *have* seen Priestley. I love to see his name repeated in your writings. I love and honor him, almost profanely.—LAMB, CHARLES, 1796, *To Coleridge, Letters, ed. Ainger, vol.* I, *p.* 10.

I have lived much among the friends of Priestley, and learned from them many peculiar opinions of that man, who speaks all he thinks. No man has studied Christianity more, or believes it more sincerely.—SOUTHEY, ROBERT, 1797, *To John May, June* 26; *Life and Correspondence, ch.* v.

Yours is one of the few lives precious to mankind, and for the continuance of which every thinking man is solicitous. Bigots may be an exception.—JEFFERSON, THOMAS, 1801, *Letter to Joseph Priestley, March* 21; *Writings, ed. Ford, vol.* VIII, *p.* 21.

THIS TABLET
Is consecrated to the Memory of the
REV. JOSEPH PRIESTLEY, LL.D.
*by his affectionate Congregation,
in Testimony
of their Gratitude for his faithful Attention
to their spiritual Improvement,
and for his peculiar Diligence in training up their
Youth to rational Piety and genuine Virtue;
of their Respect for his great and
various Talents,
which were uniformly directed to the noblest
Purposes ;
and of their Veneration
for the pure, benevolent, and holy Principles,
which through the trying Vicissitudes of Life,
and in the awful hour of Death,
animated him with the hope of a blessed
Immortality.
His Discoveries as a Philosopher
will never cease to be remembered and admired
by the ablest Improvers of Science.
His Firmness as an Advocate of Liberty,
and his Sincerity as an Expounder of the
Scriptures,
endeared him to many
of his enlightened and unprejudiced
Contemporaries.
His Example as a Christian
will be instructive to the Wise, and interesting
to the Good,
of every Country, and in every Age.
He was born at Fieldhead, near Leeds, in
Yorkshire, March 24, A. D., 1733,
Was chosen a Minister of this Chapel,
Dec. 31, 1780.
Continued in that office Ten Years and Six Months.
Embarked for America, April 7, 1794.
Died at Northumberland, in Pennsylvania,
Feb. 6, 1804.*
—PARR, SAMUEL, *Inscription on Tablet at Birmingham.*

On Monday morning, the 6th of February, after having lain perfectly still till four o'clock in the morning, he called to me, but in a fainter tone than usual, to give him some wine and tincture of bark. I asked him how he felt. He answered, he had no pain, but appeared fainting away gradually. About an hour after, he asked me for some chicken-broth, of which he took a tea-cup full. His pulse was quick, weak, and fluttering, his breathing, though easy, short. About eight o'clock he asked me to give him some egg and wine. After this, he lay quite still till ten o'clock when he desired me and Mr. Cooper to bring him the pamphlets we had looked out the evening before. He then dictated as clearly and distinctly as he had ever done in his life, the additions and alterations he wished to have made in each. Mr. Cooper took down the substance of what he said, which, when he had done, I read to him. He said Mr. Cooper had put it in his own language; he wished it to be put in his. I then took a pen and ink to his bed-side. He then repeated over again, nearly word for word, what he had before said; and when I had done, I read it over to him. He said, "That is right; I have now done." About half an hour after he desired, in a faint voice, that we would move him from the bed on which he lay to a cot, that he might be with his lower limbs horizontal, and his head upright. He died in about ten minutes after we had moved him, but breathed his last so easy, that neither myself nor my wife, who were both sitting close to him, perceived it at the time. He had put his hand to his face, which prevented our observing it. —PRIESTLEY, JOSEPH, JR., 1805–7, *Memoirs of Dr. Joseph Priestley.*

Dr. Priestley, after he had abjured the Holy Ghost, and satisfied himself that Jesus Christ was nothing more than a man; that the scriptural writers were no more inspired than himself; and that the soul of man had no existence, retained the same devout passion for preaching, praying, and catechising, which he acquired while he believed in the Trinity and the immateriality of the sentient principle of his nature. . . . We have already said, that we believe him to have been sincere in the singular profession of faith which he promulgated; and therefore, we are constrained to respect his endeavours to confirm and recommend it. But it is impossible not to regret the presumption and infatuation by which he seems to have been guided; and we are afraid that the theological speculations of a man of great learning, sagacity, industry, and devotion, are at this day an offence to the serious, and a jest to the profane. —JEFFREY, FRANCIS LORD, 1806, *Memoirs of Dr. Priestley, Edinburgh Review, vol. 9, pp.* 137, 161.

Priestley was a good man, though his life was too busy to leave him leisure for that refinement and ardour of moral sentiment, which have been felt by men of less blameless life. Frankness and disinterestedness in the avowal of his opinion, were his point of honour. In other respects his morality was more useful than brilliant. But the virtue of the sentimental moralist is so over precarious and ostentatious, that he can seldom be entitled to look down with contempt on the steady, though homely, morals of the household. — MACKINTOSH, SIR JAMES, 1807, *Journal, Sep.* 13; *Life, ed. Mackintosh, vol.* I, *ch.* vii.

A list of folks that kicked a dust,
On this poor globe, from Ptol. the First.
.   .   .   .
The Fathers, ranged in goodly row,
A decent, venerable show,
Writ a great while ago, they tell us,
And many an inch o'ertop their fellows.
.   .   .   .
Sermons, or politics, or plays.
Papers and books, a stranged mixed olio,
From shilling touch to pompous folio;
Answer, remark, reply, rejoinder,
Fresh from the mint, all stamped and coined here.
.   .   .   .
Forgotten rhymes and college themes,
Wormeaten plans and embryo schemes,
A mass of heterogeneous matter,
A chaos dark, nor land nor water.
.   .   .   .
—BARBAULD, ANNA LÆTITIA, 1825, *An Inventory of the Furniture in Dr. Priestley's Study.*

Every person of sober mind, whilst commiserating Dr. Priestley as an unfortunate man, and esteeming him as a very ingenious one, could view him in no other light than as the victim of his own folly and misguided passions.—DE QUINCEY, THOMAS, 1831–57, *Dr. Samuel Parr, Works, vol.* v, *p.* 118.

In nothing did Dr. Priestley's mental

and moral freedom more nobly manifest itself than in his *well-proportioned* love of truth. With all his diversity of pursuit, he did not think all truth of equal importance, or deem the diffusion of useful knowledge an excuse for withholding the more useful. With all his ardour of mind, he did not look at an object till he saw nothing else, and it became his universe. He made his estimate deliberately; and he was not to be dazzled, or flattered, or laughed out of it. In his laboratory, he thought no better of chemistry than in his pulpit; and in the drawing-rooms of the French Academicians, no worse of Christianity than by the firesides of his own flock. He was never anxious to appear in either less or more than his real character.—MARTINEAU, JAMES, 1833–90, *Dr. Priestley, Essays, Reviews and Addresses, vol. I, p. 38.*

His character is a matter of no doubt, and it is of a high order. That he was a most able, most industrious, most successful student of nature, is clear; and that his name will for ever be held in grateful remembrance by all who cultivate physical science, and placed among those of its most eminent masters, is unquestionable. That he was a perfectly conscientious man in all the opinions which he embraced, and sincere in all he published respecting other subjects, appears equally beyond dispute. He was, also, upright and honourable in all his dealings, and justly beloved by his family and friends as a man spotless in all the relations of life. That he was governed in his public conduct by a temper too hot and irritable to be consistent either with his own dignity, or with an amiable deportment, may be freely admitted; and his want of self-command, and want of judgment in the practical affairs of life, was manifest above all in his controversial history; for he can be charged with no want of prudence in the management of his private concerns. His violence and irritability, too, seems equally to have been confined to his public life, for in private all have allowed him the praise of a mild and attractive demeanour; and we have just seen its great power in disarming the prejudices of his adversaries.—BROUGHAM, HENRY LORD, 1845–55, *Lives of Philosophers of the Time of George III., p. 89.*

I was intimately acquainted with Dr. Priestley: and a more amiable man never lived; he was all gentleness, kindness, and humility. He was once dining with me, when some one asked him (rather rudely) "How many books he had published?" He replied, "Many more, sir, than I should like to read."—ROGERS, SAMUEL, 1855, *Recollections of Table-Talk, ed. Dyce, p. 122.*

A man of admirable simplicity, gentleness, and kindness of heart, united with great acuteness of intellect. I can never forget the impression produced on me by the serene expression of his countenance. He, indeed, seemed present with God by recollection and with man by cheerfulness. —SCHIMMELPENNICK, MARY ANNE, 1859, *Life, ed. Hankin.*

The sources of information concerning the life of Joseph Priestley are numerous and detailed. His philosophical writings, his theological controversies, his liberal political essays, his notable discoveries in chemistry, and even his misfortunes in the Birmingham riots of 1791, that caused his eventual expatriation, kept him constantly before the public. Being both affectionately admired and cordially hated, persecuted by his own townsmen yet highly esteemed by continental savants, bitterly assailed by the public press and yet the frequent recipient of substantial testimonials of esteem from active and influential friends, contemporary publications portrayed his acts, his opinions, and his remarkable talents. Since his death many men of letters have placed on record their estimate of Priestley's philosophy, of his theological system, of his political tenets, and of his contributions to science, and, finally, every extended dictionary of biography and every encyclopædia, in three languages, for three-quarters of a century, has contained a sketch of his life and labors.—BOLTON, HENRY CARRINGTON, 1892, *Scientific Correspondence of Joseph Priestley, p.* 1.

His statue, modelled from Fuseli's portrait, was placed in the Oxford Museum by a committee co-operating with Prince Albert; his name figures on the great frieze surrounding the Palais d'Industrie in the Champs Elysées; and Birmingham erected a statue to him in 1874, the centenary of the discovery of oxygen. When this statue was inaugurated, my mother, who was born in Pennsylvania, was probably the only person living in England who could personally recall Joseph Priestley.

She was seven years old when he died. He had taught her to read, and her memory of him remained perfectly clear and vivid. The delicate features of the old man, framed in thin locks of silvery hair, are recorded in the portrait by Artaud before me as I write. This presentment, rather than any of those by Flaxman, is what my mother affirmed to be the real grandfather she remembered.—BELLOC, BESSIE RAYNER, 1894-95, *In a Walled Garden, p.* 25.

He composed in shorthand; his rapid pen never left his meaning doubtful; a turn for epigram is the chief ornament of his style. He had little humour, but enjoyed a remarkable faculty for making the best of things. His home affections were strong. He provided a maintenance for his younger brother Joshua at Birstall. Domestic management he left to his wife, speaking of himself as a lodger in her house. To the faults of his memory he often alludes; it is curious that he never learned the American currency, and would say to a shopkeeper, "You will give me the proper change, for I do not know it." . . . In person Priestley was slim but large-boned; his stature about five feet nine, and very erect. His countenance is best seen in profile, and the right and left profiles differ remarkably; the front face is heavy. He wore a wig till he settled in Northumberland, which did not boast of a hairdresser.— GORDON, ALEXANDER, 1896, *Dictionary of National Biography, vol.* XLVI, *p.* 366.

SCIENTIFIC WORK

Gentlemen, it is with great satisfaction I enter upon this part of my office, to confer, in your name, the prize-medal of this year upon a member of this Society, so worthy of that distinction. It is with singular pleasure I acquaint you that the Rev. Joseph Priestley, Doctor of Laws, has been found at this time the best entitled to this public mark of your approbation, on account of the many curious and useful experiments contained in his "Observations on Different Kinds of Air," read at the Society in March, 1772, and inserted in the last complete volume of your Transactions. And indeed, Gentlemen, when you reflect on the zeal which our worthy brother has shewn to serve the public, and to do credit to your Institution, by his numerous, learned, and valuable communications, you will, I imagine,

be inclined to think that we have been rather slow than precipitate in acknowledging so much merit.—PRINGLE, SIR JOHN, 1773, *President's Address to the Royal Society.*

He had great merit in the contrivance of his apparatus, which was simple and neat, to a degree that has never been equalled; and the indefatigable industry with which he pursued his researches, would entitle him to still higher praise, if he had combined with it the patience and forecast by which so much labour may be saved. The truth is, however, that he was always too much occupied with making experiments to have leisure, either to plan them beforehand with philosophical precision, or to combine their results afterwards into systematic conclusions. He was so impatient to be doing; that he could spare no time for thinking; and erroneously imagined, that science was to be forwarded rather by accumulating facts, than by meditating on those that were ascertained. —JEFFREY, FRANCIS LORD, 1806, *Memoirs of Dr. Priestley, Edinburgh Review, vol.* 9, *p.* 150.

Dr. Priestley drew no conclusion of the least value from his experiments. But Mr. Watt, after thoroughly weighing them, by careful comparison with other facts, arrived at the opinion that they proved the composition of water. This may justly be said to have been the discovery of that great truth in chemical science. I have examined the evidence, and am convinced that he was the first discoverer, in point of time, although it is very possible that Mr. Cavendish may have arrived at the same truth from his own experiments, without any knowledge of Mr. Watt's earlier process of reasoning.—BROUGHAM, HENRY LORD, 1835, *Discourse of Natural Theology, p.* 106, *note.*

Whose researches were devoted almost exclusively to the chemistry of the gases. Their results are recorded in six volumes of "Experiments and Observations on different kinds of Airs," which were published between 1775 and 1786, and which appear to have enjoyed an uncommon degree of popularity. They are written in a light and agreeable style, detailing his successes and his failures with equal candour and openness, and laying open his entire chemical mind to the observation of his readers. He was very ingenious in devising experiments, and dexterous in his manipulations; and though the processes which he followed and the means which he had at his command were generally insufficient to secure that minute and rigorous accuracy which is equally necessary for the establishment of great truths and the exclusion of great errors, yet it may be safely asserted that few persons have contributed so great a number of valuable facts to the science of chemistry. He affected no profound philosophical views, and the character of his mind was altogether unequal to them; he generally adopted at once the most obvious conclusions which his experiments appeared to justify, and he modified or abandoned them upon further investigation with almost equal facility.—CROKER, JOHN WILSON, 1845, *Quarterly Review, vol. 77, p.* 119.

Priestley's reputation as a man of science rests upon his numerous and important contributions to the chemistry of gaseous bodies; and to form a just estimate of the value of his work—of the extent to which it advanced the knowledge of fact and the development of sound theoretical views—we must reflect what chemistry was in the first half of the eighteenth century. . . . It is a trying ordeal for any man to be compared with Black and Cavendish, and Priestley cannot be said to stand on their level. Nevertheless, his achievements are not only great in themselves, but truly wonderful, if we consider the disadvantages under which he laboured. Without the careful scientific training of Black, without the leisure and appliances secured by the wealth of Cavendish, he scaled the walls of science as so many Englishmen have done before and since his day; and trusting to mother wit to supply the place of training, and to ingenuity to create apparatus out of washing tubs, he discovered more new gases than all his predecessors put together had done. He laid the foundations of gas analysis; he discovered the complementary actions of animal and vegetable life upon the constituents of the atmosphere; and, finally, he crowned his work, this day one hundred years ago, by the discovery of that "pure dephlogisticated air" to which the French chemists subsequently gave the name of oxygen. . . . That Priestley's contributions to the knowledge of chemical fact were of the greatest importance, and that they richly deserved all the praise that has been awarded to them is unquestionable; but it must, at the same time, be admitted that he had no comprehension of the deeper significance of his work; and, so far from contributing anything to the theory of the facts which he discovered, or assisting in their rational explanation, his influence to the end of his life was warmly exerted in favour of error.—HUXLEY, THOMAS HENRY, 1874, *Joseph Priestley, Macmillan's Magazine, vol.* 30, *pp.* 477, 478.

Priestley is mainly remembered by his theological controversies and his contributions to the history of pneumatic chemistry. I have nothing to tell you of his merits as a controversialist, except to say that some of his argumentative pieces are among the most forcible and best written of his literary productions. It is on his chemical work that his reputation will ultimately rest: this will continue to hand down his name when all traces of his other labours are lost. He has frequently been styled the *Father of Pneumatic Chemistry;* and although we may question the propriety of the appellation when we call to mind the labours of Van Helmont, of Boyle, and of Hales, there is no doubt that Priestley did more to extend our knowledge of gaseous bodies than any preceding or successive investigator. . . . The knowledge which Priestley, as he tells us, imparted to the French chemists was used by them with crushing effect against his favourite theory. The discovery of oxygen was the death blow to phlogiston. Here was the thing which had been groped for for years, and which many men had even stumbled over in the searching, but had never grasped. Priestley indeed grasped it, but he failed to see the magnitude and true importance of what he had found. It was far otherwise with Lavoisier. He at once recognised in Priestley's new air the one fact needed to complete the overthrow of Stahl's doctrine; and now every stronghold of phlogistonism was in turn made to yield. Priestley, however, never surrendered, even when nearly every phlogistian but he had given up the fight or gone over to the enemy. When age compelled him to leave his laboratory he continued to serve the old cause in his study, and almost his last publication was his "Doctrine of Phlogiston Established."— THORPE,

THOMAS E., 1874-94, *Joseph Priestley, Essays in Historical Chemistry, pp.* 35, 51.

Foremost in the number of those who after Black distinguished themselves as pneumatic chemists, was Dr. J. Priestley. His first discovery, made in 1772, was nitric oxide gas, which he soon employed in the analysis of air. . . . Besides nitric oxide and nitrogen, Priestley first made known sulphurous acid gas, gaseous ammonia and hydrochloric acid, and carbon monoxide; and he it was who, by showing that the condition of ammoniacal gas and of common air is altered by the transmission of electric sparks, led to Berthollet's analysis of ammonia, and Cavendish's discovery of the composition of nitric acid. —BUTLER, F. H., 1877, *Chemistry, Encyclopœdia Britannica, Ninth ed., vol.* V, *p.* 400.

Priestley was just the man who was wanted in the early days of chemical science. By the vast number, variety and novelty of his experimental results, he astonished scientific men—he forcibly drew attention to the science in which he laboured so hard; by the brilliancy of some of his experiments he obliged chemists to admit that a new field of research was opened before them, and the instruments for the prosecution of this research were placed in their hands; and even by the unsatisfactoriness of his reasoning he drew attention to the difficulties and contradictions of the theories which then prevailed in chemistry. That the work of Priestley should bear full fruit it was necessary that a greater than he should interpret it, and should render definite that which Priestley had but vaguely shown to exist. The man who did this, and who in doing it really established chemistry as a science, was Lavoisier.—MUIR, M. M. PATTISON, 1883, *Heroes of Science, Chemists, p.* 75.

Priestley's eminent discoveries in chemistry were due to an extraordinary quickness and keenness of imagination combined with no mean logical ability and manipulative skill. But, owing mainly to lack of adequate training, he failed to apprehend the full or true value of his great results. Carelessness and haste, not want of critical power, led him, at the outset, to follow the retrograde view of Stahl rather than the method of Boyle, Black, and Cavendish. The modification of the physical properties of bodies by the hypothetical electricity doubtless led him to welcome the theory of a "phlogiston" which could similarly modify their chemical properties. Priestley was content to assign the same name to bodies with different properties, and to admit that two bodies with precisely the same properties, in other respects different in composition ("Considerations . . . on Phlogiston," 1st edit. p., 17). Though often inaccurate, he was not incapable of performing exact quantitative experiments, but he was careless of their interpretation. . . . Priestley is unjust to himself in attributing most of his discoveries to chance.—HARTOG, P. J., 1896, *Dictionary of National Biography, vol.* XLVI, *p.* 375.

GENERAL

Of Dr. Priestley's theological works, he (Johnson) remarked, that they tended to unsettle everything, and yet settled nothing. —MAXWELL, WILLIAM, 1770, *Boswell's Life of Johnson, ed. Hill, vol.* II, *p.* 142.

It is a mortifying proof of the infirmity of the human mind, in the highest improvement of its faculties in the present life, that such fallacies in reasoning, such misconstruction of authorities, such distorted views of facts and opinions, should be found in the writings of a man, to whom, of all men in the present age, some branches of the experimental sciences are the most indebted.—HORSLEY, SAMUEL, 1783, *Letters in Answer to Priestley.*

The Bishop (Percy) wishes Mr. Pinkerton would carefully read Dr. Priestley's "Institutes of Natural and Revealed Religion," in 2 vols. 8vo, before he decides that all of that school have given up the Old Testament, as Mr. Pinkerton seems to hint in a former letter; but indeed he wishes Mr. Pinkerton would read them on other accounts.—PERCY, THOMAS, *To John Pinkerton, Feb.* 28, 1787; *Nichols's Illustrations of Literary History, vol.* VIII, *p.* 135.

The religious tenets of Dr. Priestley appear to me erroneous in the extreme; but I should be sorry to suffer any difference of sentiment to diminish my sensibility to virtue, or my admiration of genius. From him the poisoned arrow will fall pointless. His enlightened and active mind, his unwearied assiduity, the extent of his researches, the light he has poured into almost every department of science, will be the admiration of that period, when the greater part of those who have favoured, or those who have opposed him will be alike forgotten.—HALL, ROBERT, 1791, *Christianity Consistent With a Love of Freedom.*

I do not wonder at Johnson's displeasure when the name of Dr. Priestley was mentioned; for I know no writer who has been suffered to publish more pernicious doctrines. I shall instance only three. First, "Materialism;" by which *mind* is denied to human nature; which, if believed, must deprive us of every elevated principle. Secondly, "Necessity;" or the doctrine that every action, whether good or bad, is included in an unchangeable and unavoidable system; a notion utterly subversive of moral government. Thirdly, that we have no reason to think that the *future* world (which, as he is pleased to *inform* us, will be adapted to our *merely improved* nature), will be materially different from *this;* which, if believed, would sink wretched mortals into despair, as they could no longer hope for the "rest that remaineth for the people of God," or for that happiness which is revealed to us as something beyond our present conceptions, but would feel themselves doomed to a continuation of the uneasy state under which they now groan. I say nothing of the petulant intemperance with which he dares to insult the venerable establishments of his country. As a specimen of his writings, I shall quote the following passage, which appears to me equally absurd and impious, and which might have been retorted upon him by the men who were prosecuted for burning his house. . . . My illustrious friend was particularly resolute in not giving countenance to men whose writings he considered as pernicious to society. I was present at Oxford when Dr. Price, even before he had rendered himself so generally obnoxious by his zeal for the French revolution, came into a company where Johnson was, who instantly left the room. Much more would he have reprobated Dr. Priestley. Whoever wishes to see the perfect delineation of this "Literary Jack of all Trades" may find it in an ingenious tract, entitled "A Small Whole-Length of Dr. Priestley," printed for Rivingtons, in St. Paul's Churchyard. —BOSWELL, JAMES, 1791-93, *Life of Samuel Johnson, ed. Hill, vol.* IV, *pp.* 274, 275, *note.*

Let Dr. Priestley be confuted where he is mistaken; let him be exposed where he is superficial; let him be repressed where he is dogmatical; let him be rebuked where he is censorious. But let not his attainments be depreciated, because they are numerous almost without parallel. Let not his talents be ridiculed, because they are superlatively great. Let not his morals be vilified, because they are correct without austerity, and exemplary without ostentation; because they present, even to common observers, the innocence of a hermit, and the simplicity of a patriarch; and because a philosophic eye will at once discover in them the deep-fixed root of virtuous principle, and the solid trunk of virtuous habit.—PARR, SAMUEL, 1792, *Letter from Irenopolis to the Inhabitants of Eleutheropolis.*

To thee the slander of a passing age
Imports not. Scenes like these hold little
 space
In his large mind, whose ample stretch of
 thought
Grasps future periods.—Well canst thou
 afford
To give large credit for that debt of fame
Thy country owes thee. Calm thou canst
 consign it
To the slow payement of that distant day,—
If distant,—when thy name, to Freedom's
 joined,
Shall meet the thanks of a regenerate land.
—BARBAULD, ANNA LÆTITIA, 1792, *To Dr. Priestley, Dec. 29.*

In his "History of the Corruptions of Christianity," Dr. Priestley threw down his two gauntlets to Bishop Hurd and Mr. Gibbon. I declined the challenge in a letter exhorting my opponent to enlighten the World by his philosophical discoveries, and to remember that the merit of his predecessor Servetus is now reduced to a single passage, which indicates the smaller circulation of the blood through the lungs, from and to the heart. Instead of listening to this friendly advice, the dauntless philosopher of Birmingham continues to fire away his double battery against those who believe too little and those who believe too much. From my replies he has nothing to hope or fear; but his Socinian shield has repeatedly been pierced by the spear of the mighty Horsley, and his trumpet of sedition may at length awaken the magistrates of a free country. —GIBBON, EDWARD, 1793, *Autobiography, note.*

Though king-bred rage with lawless Tumult
rude
Have driv'n our *Priestley* o'er the ocean swell;
Though Superstition and her wolfish brood
Bay his mild radiance, impotent and fell;
Calm in his halls of brightness he shall dwell!
For lo! Religion at his strong behest
Disdainful rouses from the Papal spell,
And flings to Earth her tinsel-glittering vest,
Her mitred state and cumbrous pomp unholy;
And Justice wakes to bid th' oppression wail,
That ground th' ensnared soul of patient
Folly;
And from her dark retreat by Wisdom won,
Meek Nature slowly lifts her matron veil
To smile with fondness on her gazing son!
—COLERIDGE, SAMUEL TAYLOR, 1794,
Sonnet to Priestley, Dec. 11.

I am at present re-re-reading Priestley's
Examination of the Scotch Doctors: how
the rogue strings 'em up! three together!
You have no doubt read that clear, strong,
humorous, most entertaining piece of
reasoning. If not, procure it, and be exquisitely amused. I wish I could get more
of Priestley's works.—LAMB, CHARLES,
1797, *To Coleridge, Jan.* 2; *Letters, ed.
Ainger, vol.* I, *p.* 57.

If I *may* write, let Proteus Priestley tell,
He writes on *all* things, but on nothing well;
Who, as the dæmon of the day decrees,
Air, books, or water makes with equal ease.
May not I strive amid this motley throng,
All pale and pensive as I muse along?
—MATHIAS, THOMAS JAMES, 1797, *The
Pursuits of Literature, Eighth ed., p.* 50.

The attack of Dr. Priestley, however,
gave him [Beattie] no concern. He appears, indeed, by his correspondence with
his friends to have formed, at first, the
resolution of replying to it; and he speaks
as if he had already prepared his materials,
and of being altogether in such a state of
forwardness, and to be fully ready for the
task. On farther consideration, however,
he abandoned the idea, and he no doubt
judged wisely. For, while Dr. Priestley's
"Examination" is now never heard of,
the "Essay on Truth" remains a classical
work, of the highest reputation and
authority.—FORBES, SIR WILLIAM, 1806,
*An Account of the Life and Writings of
James Beattie, vol.* II, *p.* 96.

Dr. Priestley has written more, we
believe, and on a greater variety of subjects, than any other English author; and
probably believed, as his friend Mr. Cooper
appears to do at this moment, that his
several publications were destined to make

an æra in the respective branches of
speculation to which they bore reference.
We are not exactly of that opinion: But
we think Dr. Priestley a person of no common magnitude in the history of English literature.—JEFFREY, FRANCIS LORD,
1806–44, *Priestley, Contributions to the
Edinburgh Review, vol.* iii, *p.* 338.

No man living had a more affectionate
respect for him. In religion, in politics,
in physics, no man has rendered more
service.—JEFFERSON, THOMAS, 1807, *To
Thomas Cooper, July* 9; *Writings, ed.
Ford, vol.* IX, *p.* 102.

His work ["Notes on all the Books of
Scripture"] contains many invaluable notes
and observations, particularly on the philosophy, natural history, geography, and
chronology of the Scriptures; and to these
subjects few men in Europe were better
qualified to do justice.—CLARKE, ADAM,
1810–26, *Comment on the Bible.*

As to his theological creed, it could not
justify the usage he received; for though
he led the way to an open determined
avowal of socinianism, no patron of liberty
of conscience will impute this to him as a
civil crime; nor should the friends of the
orthodox creed condemn him for the frankness which rendered him the real, though
unintentional friend of the truth, which
has triumphed ever since Priestley tore
the mask of concealment from error, and
bade it be honest. The reflections which
he poured upon evangelical sentiments,
were often bitter enough, indeed; but the
same may be said of the charges brought
against him and his creed; and it was
Horsley rather than Priestley, who enlisted the depraved passions of men, and
the cruel prejudices of party politics, to
contend in the arena, which should have
been occupied solely by the authority of
revelation, and the evidence of unimpassioned argument.— BOGUE, DAVID, AND
BENNETT, JAMES, 1812, *History of Dissenters from the Revolution in* 1688 *to the
year* 1808, *vol.* IV, *p.* 433.

The celebrated natural philosopher,
Joseph Priestley, criticised at the same
time both Hume and his antagonists. He
may be said to have been more successful
with the latter, whose *instinctive principles*
he justly styled *qualitates occultæ.* In opposition to Hume he alleged a proof of the
existence of the Divinity, which was un-
tenable. He was a rank Determinist; and,

consistently with his principles, controverted, as Hartley had done, the doctrine of free agency, and endeavoured to establish a system of materiality of the soul.— TENNEMAN, WILLIAM GOTTLIEB, 1812-52, *A Manual of the History of Philosophy, tr. Johnson, ed. Morell.*

Neglecting accordingly, all the presumptions for a future state, afforded by a comparison of the course of human affairs with the moral judgments and moral feelings of the human heart; and overlooking, with the same disdain, the presumptions arising from the narrow sphere of human knowledge, when compared with the indefinite improvement of which our intellectual powers seem to be susceptible, this acute but superficial writer attached himself exclusively to the old and hackneyed pneumatological argument; tacitly assuming as a principle, that the future prospects of man depend entirely on the determination of a *physical* problem, analogous to that which was then dividing chemists about the existence or non-existence of phlogiston. In the actual state of science, these speculations might well have been spared.—STEWART, DUGALD, 1815-21, *First Preliminary Dissertation, Encyclopædia Britannica.*

Charmed with the discoveries of science, and eager, by prompt and unreserved communication, to diffuse as far as possible, their beneficial influence, he was yet supremely attracted to the discoveries of revelation. Hence his unvarying purpose, "by labour and patience, through evil report, and through good report," and even when flesh and heart were failing, to promote, in the most enlarged sense of the expression, "the greatest good of the greatest number;" a sentiment with which he had the honour, by one of his earliest publications, to inspire that philosopher and philanthropist, who has lately left the world, after devoting himself in death, as in life, to its service; but whose memory will remain, unless, again, in the dispensations of an inscrutable Providence, "darkness shall cover the earth, and gross darkness the people."—RUTT, JOHN TOWIL, 1832, *Life and Correspondence of Joseph Priestley, vol.* I, *pt.* ii, *p.* 533.

There can be no doubt that versatility was the great characteristic of Dr. Priestley's genius. Singularly quick of apprehension, he made all his acquisitions with facility and rapidity; and hence he derived a confidence in the working-power of his own mind, and a general faith in the sufficiency of the human faculties as instruments of knowledge, which led him on to achievement after achievement in the true spirit of intellectual enterprise.—MARTINEAU, JAMES, 1833-90, *Dr. Priestley, Essays, Reviews and Addresses, vol.* I, *p.* 17.

He is one of the most voluminous writers of any age or country, and probably he is of all voluminous writers the one who has the fewest readers.— BROUGHAM, HENRY LORD, 1845-55, *Lives of Philosophers of the Times of George III, p.* 74.

Priestley's mind was objective to an extreme; he could fix his faith upon nothing, which had not the evidence of sense in some way or other impressed upon it. Science, morals, politics, philosophy, religion, all came to him under the type of the sensational. The most spiritual ideas were obliged to be cast into a material mould before they could commend themselves to his judgment or conscience. His intellect was rapid to extraordinary degree; he saw the bearings of a question according to his own principles at a glance, and embodied his thoughts in volumes whilst many other men would hardly have sketched out their plan. All this, though admirable in the man of *action*, was not the temperament to form the solid metaphysician, nay, it was precisely opposed to that deep reflective habit, that sinking into one's own inmost consciousness, from which alone speculative philosophy can obtain light and advancement.—MORELL, J. D., 1846-7, *An Historical and Critical View of the Speculative Philosophy of Europe in the Nineteenth Century, p.* 101.

Dr. Priestley's metaphysical creed embraces four leading doctrines: he adopted the theory of vibrations, the association of ideas, the scheme of philosophical necessity, and the soul's materiality. On all these topics he has furnished us with extended dissertations; and, whatever opinions may be ascertained of any or all of them, there are few persons but will readily admit the Doctor has displayed both great zeal and great ability in defence of them.—BLAKEY, ROBERT, 1848, *History of the Philosophy of Mind, vol.* III.

His style is idiomatic, compact, incisive, and vigorous. He is eminently easy to follow; he usually describes the progress of his thoughts, explains by what circumstances he was led to take such and such a view, and thus introduces us from the known to the unknown by an easy gradation.—MINTO, WILLIAM, 1872-80, *Manual of English Prose Literature, p. 474.*

Priestley possessed one of those restless intellects which are incapable of confining themselves to any single task, and, unfortunately, incapable in consequence of sounding the depths of any philosophical system. Urged partly by his natural bent, and partly, it may be, constrained by the pressure of poverty, he gave to the world a numerous series of dissertations which, with the exception of his scientific writings, bear the marks of hasty and superficial thought. As a man of science he has left his mark upon the intellectual history of the century; but, besides being a man of science, he aimed at being a metaphysician, a theologian, a politician, a classical scholar, and a historian. With an amazing intrepidity he plunged into tasks the effective performance of which would have demanded the labours of a lifetime. With the charge of thirty youths on his hands he proposes to write an ecclesiastical history, and soon afterwards observes that a fresh translation of the Old Testament would "not be a very formidable task." He carried on all manner of controversies, upon their own ground, with Horsley and Bradcock, with his friend Price, with Beattie and the Scotch philosophers, with Gibbon and the sceptics, and yet often laboured for six hours a day at his chemical experiments. So discursive a thinker could hardly do much thorough work, nor really work out or co-ordinate his own opinions. Pushing rationalism to conclusions which shocked the orthodox, he yet retained the most puerile superstitions. He disbelieved in the inspiration of the Apostles, and found fault with St. Paul's reasoning, but had full faith in the phophecies, and at a late period of his life expected the coming of Christ within twenty years. Nelson's victories were to fulfill the predictions contained in the 19th chapter of Isaiah, and he suspected that Napoleon was the deliverer promised to Egypt. In his youth he had become convinced, as he tells us, of the falsity of the doctrines of the Atonement and the inspiration of the Bible, and

"of all idea of supernatural interference except" (a singular exception!) "for the purpose of miracles." Near half a century's familiarity with theological speculation failed to emancipate his mind from the bondage of half-truths. It would be in vain, therefore, to anticipate any great force or originality in Priestley's speculations. At best, he was a quick reflector of the current opinions of his time and class, and able to run up hasty theories of sufficient apparent stability to afford a temporary refuge amidst the storm of conflicting elements.—STEPHEN, LESLIE, 1876, *History of English Thought in the Eighteenth Century, vol. I, p. 430.*

If we choose one man as a type of the intellectual energy of the century, we could hardly find a better than Joseph Priestley, though his was not the greatest mind of the century. His versatility, eagerness, activity, and humanity; the immense range of his curiosity, in all things physical, moral, or social; his place in science, in theology, in philosophy, and in politics; his peculiar relation to the Revolution, and the pathetic story of his unmerited sufferings, may make him the hero of the eighteenth century.—HARRISON, FREDERIC, 1883, *The Choice of Books and Other Literary Pieces, p. 369.*

The style of this author is adequate to his thought. There is little flexibility or vivacity; the diction is heavy, and occasionally the preacher bestows on us the tediousness and prolixity too frequently associated with sermons. He has usually something to prove, and, if he does not prove it, the fault is not in the manner but in the matter of statement.—BONAR, JAMES, 1895, *English Prose, ed. Craik, vol. IV, p. 438.*

His labours culminated in the "History of Early Opinions concerning Jesus Christ" (1786). Writing as a sectary, he damaged at the outset his claim to scrutinise in the scientific spirit the course of thought in Christian antiquity; but he was one of the first to open the way to the study of doctrinal development, and while proclaiming his own bias with rare frankness, he submitted his historical judgments to the arbitrament of further research. His account of the origin of Arianism, as a novel system, has stood the test. What was special in his method was the endeavour, discarding the speculations of the fathers, to penetrate to the mind of the common Christian people. He broke entirely with the old application of the principle of private judgment, maintaining that a purely modern interpretation of Scripture is, *ipso facto*, discredited, and the meaning attached to it by the earliest age, if ascertainable, must be decisive. A good summary of his position is in his "Letters" (1787) to Alexander Geddes the Roman catholic scholar, who had addressed him as his "fellow-disciple in Jesus."— GORDON, ALEXANDER, 1896, *Dictionary of National Biography, vol.* XLVI, *p.* 362.

Alexander Hamilton
1757–1804

Alexander Hamilton was born in the Island of Nevis, in the West Indies, January 11, 1757. His father was a merchant from Scotland; his mother was the daughter of a French Huguenot; and the sons appear to have inherited, in equal measure, the vigour and endurance of the one race and the address and vivacity of the other. His education was not at all systematic, but his active mind instinctively found its proper stimulants, and he began to show his great natural powers at an early age. While attending to his studies at Columbia College, in New York city, the war broke out, and he entered the patriot army as a captain of artillery. In 1777 he was made aide-de-camp to General Washington, and distinguished himself by his ability in correspondence as well as by active personal service in the field. At the close of the war he commenced the practice of law in New York. His chief work, as an author, was a series of papers entitled "The Federalist," of which he wrote the greater number—an elaborate exposition of the Constitution of the United States. These papers, though necessarily abstruse in character, are perspicuous in style and powerful in reasoning. He was the first secretary of the treasury, and in that position he displayed unrivalled skill. . . . After six years' service Hamilton retired from office, and resumed the practice of his profession. As he had opposed Aaron Burr, first in his endeavours to become president, and afterwards in his canvass for the office of governor of New York, that unscrupulous demagogue, maddened by defeat, challenged him to fight a duel. Hamilton fell at the first fire, and died the next day, July 12, 1804.—UNDERWOOD, FRANCIS H., 1872, *A Hand-Book of English Literature, American Authors, p.* 29.

PERSONAL

Hamilton has a very boyish, giddy manner.—MACLAY, WILLIAM, 1790, *Sketches of Debate in the First Senate of the United States, p.* 238.

In every relation which you have borne to me I have found that my confidence in your talents, exertions, and integrity has been well placed. I the more freely tender this testimony of my approbation because I speak from opportunities of information which cannot deceive me and which furnish satisfactory proof of your title to public regard.— WASHINGTON, GEORGE, 1795, *Letter to Hamilton on his Resignation.*

The son of the camp-girl.—CALLENDER, J. T., 1800, *The Prospect Before the United States.*

On my expected interview with Colonel Burr, I think proper to make some remarks explanatory of my conduct, motives, and views. I was certainly desirous of avoiding this interview for the most cogent of reasons. First—My religious and moral principles are strongly opposed to the practice of duelling; and it would ever give me pain to shed the blood of a fellow creature in a private combat forbidden by the laws. Secondly—My wife and children are extremely dear to me, and my life is of the utmost importance to them in various views. Thirdly—I feel a sense of obligation toward my creditors, who, in case of accident to me, by the forced sale of my property, may be in some degree sufferers. I did not think myself at liberty, as a man of probity, lightly to expose them to hazard. Fourthly—I am conscious of no ill-will to Colonel Burr distinct from political opposition, which, as I trust, has proceeded from pure and upright motives. Lastly—I shall hazard much, and can possibly gain nothing, by the issue of the interview. . . . I have resolved, if our interview is conducted in the usual manner, and it pleases God to give me the opportunity, to reserve and throw away my first fire, and I have thoughts even of reserving my second fire,

EDMOND MALONE

ALEXANDER HAMILTON

and thus giving a double opportunity to Colonel Burr to pause and reflect. It is not, however, my intention to enter into any explanations on the ground. Apology, from principle, I hope, rather than pride, is out of the qustion. To those who, with me, abhorring the practice of duelling, may think that I ought on no account to have added to the number of bad examples, I answer that my *relative* situation, as well in public as private, enforcing all the considerations which constitute what men of the world denominate honor, imposed on me (as I thought) a peculiar necessity not to decline the call.—HAMILTON, ALEXANDER, 1804, *Paper Prepared the Evening Before his Duel with Aaron Burr.*

Brethren of the Cincinnati—there lies our chief! Let him still be our model. Like him, after long and faithful public services, let us cheerfully perform the social duties of private life. Oh! he was mild and gentle. In him there was no offence; no guile. His generous hand and heart were open to all. Gentleman of the bar—you have lost your brightest ornament. Cherish and imitate his example. While, like him, with justifiable, and with laudable zeal, you pursue the interests of your clients, remember, like him, the eternal principle of justice. Fellow-citizens—you have long witnessed his professional conduct, and felt his unrivalled eloquence. You know how well he performed the duties of a citizen—you know that he never courted your favor by adulation or the sacrifice of his own judgment. You have seen him contending against you, and saving your dearest interests as it were, in spite of yourselves. And you now feel and enjoy the benefits resulting from the firm energy of his conduct. Bear this testimony to the memory of my departed friend. *I charge you to protect his fame.* It is all he has left—all that these poor orphan children will inherit from their father. — MORRIS, GOUVERNEUR, 1804, *Funeral Oration by the Dead Body of Hamilton.*

The tears that flow on this fond recital will never dry up. My heart, penetrated with the remembrance of the man, grows liquid as I write, and I could pour it out like water. I could weep too for my country, which, mournful as it is, does not know the half of its loss. It deeply laments, when it turns its eyes back, and

sees what Hamilton was; but my soul stiffens with despair when I think what Hamilton would have been. . . . No man ever more disdained duplicity, or carried frankness further than he. . . . Virtue so rare, so pure, so bold, by its very purity and excellence inspired suspicion as a prodigy. His enemies judged of him by themselves; so splendid and arduous were his services, they could not find it in their hearts to believe that they were disinterested. . . . The name of Hamilton would have honoured Greece in the age of Aristides. May heaven the guardian of our liberty, grant that our country may be fruitful of Hamiltons, and faithful to their glory!—AMES, FISHER, 1804, *Sketch of the Character of Alexander Hamilton.*

Melancholy, most melancholy news for America—the premature death of her greatest man, Major-General Hamilton! . . . His most stupendous talents which set him above rivalship, and his integrity, with which intrigue had not the hardihood to tamper, held him up as the nation's hope and as the terror of the unprincipled. —MASON, JOHN M., 1804, *Letter to a Friend in Scotland, Aug. 11.*

TO THE MEMORY OF
ALEXANDER HAMILTON
THE CORPORATION OF TRINITY HAVE
ERECTED THIS
MONUMENT
IN TESTIMONY OF THEIR RESPECT
FOR
THE PATRIOT OF INCORRUPTIBLE INTEGRITY
THE SOLDIER OF APPROVED VALOUR
THE STATESMAN OF CONSUMMATE WISDOM
WHOSE TALENTS AND VIRTUES WILL BE
ADMIRED
BY
GRATEFUL POSTERITY
LONG AFTER THIS MARBLE SHALL HAVE
MOULDERED TO
DUST
HE DIED JULY 12TH, 1804, AGED 47.
—INSCRIPTION ON TOMB, *Trinity Churchyard, New York.*

The model of eloquence and the most fascinating of orators. With all his failings, he possessed a high and ennobled spirit, and acquired an influence from his overwhelming talents which death alone swept away.—STORY, JOSEPH, 1810, *Letter to Mrs. Story, Feb. 7; Life and Letters, vol.* I, *p.* 196.

Bastard brat of a Scotch peddler.— ADAMS, JOHN, 1813, *Letter to Thomas Jefferson.*

Of Mr. Hamilton I ought, perhaps, to speak with some restraint, though my feelings assure me that no recollection of political collisions could control the justice due to his memory. That he possessed intellectual powers of the first order, and the moral qualifications of integrity and honor in a captivating degree, has been decreed to him by a sufferage now universal.—MADISON, JAMES, 1831, *Letter to J. K. Paulding, April; Writings of James Madison, vol. IV, p. 176.*

He was under middle size, thin in person, but remarkably erect and dignified in his deportment. His bust, seen in so many houses, and the pictures and prints of him, make known, too generally, the figure of his face, to make an attempt at description expedient. His hair was turned back from his forehead, powdered, and collected in a club behind. His complexion was exceedingly fair, and varying from this only by the almost feminine rosiness of his cheeks. His might be considered, as to figure and color, an uncommonly handsome face. When at rest, he had rather a severe and thoughtful expression; but when engaged in conversation, it easily assumed an attractive smile. . . . The eloquence of Hamilton was said to be persuasive and commanding; the more likely to be so, as he had no guide but the impulse of a great and rich mind, he having had little opportunity to be trained at the bar, or in popular assemblies. Those who could speak of his manner from the best opportunities to observe him in public and private, concurred in pronouncing him a frank, amiable, high-minded, open-hearted gentleman. He was capable of inspiring the most affectionate attachment; but he could make those whom he opposed, fear and hate him cordially. He was capable of intense and effectual application, as is abundantly proved by his public labours. But he had a rapidity and clearness of perception, in which he may not have been equalled. One who knew his habits of study, said of him, that when he had a serious object to accomplish, his practice was to reflect on it previously; and when he had gone through this labour, he retired to sleep, without regard to the hour of the night, and having slept six or

seven hours, he rose, and having taken strong coffee, seated himself at his table, where he would remain six, seven, or eight hours; and the product of his rapid pen required little correction for the press. . . . In private and friendly intercourse, he is said to have been exceedingly amiable, and to have been affectionately beloved.—SULLIVAN, WILLIAM, 1834, *Familiar Letters on the Public Men of the Revolution.*

Among his brethren Hamilton was indisputably preëminent. This was universally conceded. He rose at once to the loftiest heights of professional eminence, by his profound penetration, his power of analysis, the comprehensive grasp and strength of his understanding, and the firmness, frankness, and integrity of his character. We may say of him, in reference to his associates, as was said of Papinian, *omnes longo post se intervallo reliquerit.*—KENT, JAMES, 1836, *Address before the Law Association, New York, Oct. 21.*

In Hamilton's death the Federalists and the country experienced a loss second only to that of Washington. Hamilton possessed the same rare and lofty qualities, the same just balance of soul, with less, indeed, of Washington's severe simplicity and awe-inspiring presence, but with more of warmth, variety, ornament, and grace. If the Doric in architecture be taken as the symbol of Washington's character, Hamilton belonged to the same grand style as developed in the Corinthian,—if less impressive, more winning. If we add Jay for the Ionic, we have a trio not to be matched, in fact, not to be approached, in our history, if, indeed, in any other. Of earth-born Titans, as terrible as great,— now angels, and now toads and serpents, —there are everywhere enough. Of the serene benign sons of the celestial gods, how few at any time have walked the earth!—HILDRETH, RICHARD, 1849–52, *History of the United States of America, vol. II, p. 526.*

His wife survived him, in widowhood, fifty years. She died on the 9th of November, 1854, at the age of ninety-seven years and three months.—LOSSING, BENSON J., 1855–86, *Eminent Americans, p. 214.*

As General Greene one day, on his way to Washington's headquarters, was passing through a field,—then on the outskirts of the city, now in the heart of its busiest quarters, and known as "the Park,"—he paused to notice a provincial company of artillery, and was struck with its able performances, and with the tact and talent of its commander. He was a mere youth, apparently about twenty years of age, small in person and stature, but remarkable for his alert and manly bearing. It was Alexander Hamilton.—IRVING, WASHINGTON, 1855, *Life of Washington, vol.* II, *p.* 237.

Two peculiar charms belong to the life of Hamilton as compared with his contemporary soldiers and statesmen,—his youth and his gifts of expression. The variety of his services, his exalted patriotism, and his untarnished honor endeared his genius to the highest order of minds; while his errors, however they may diminish his glory to the eye of the moralist and the Christian, add yet another effective element to his nature as a subject for delineation. His were errors of passion, not of calculation, and prove him weak, not inhuman. This weakness contrasted with the moral consistency of Washington, this yielding to the wiles of love and the sophistry of a false code of honor, associated as it is with the pre-eminent merits and transcendant abilities of Hamilton, gives an extraordinary pathos to the drama of his life. Circumstances here blend with character, tears and triumph, admiration with sorrow, to produce the highest tragedy of human existence.—TUCKERMAN, HENRY T., 1858, *Alexander Hamilton, North American Review, vol.* 86, *p.* 371.

Alexander Hamilton was of small stature, not above five feet five inches, according to my recollection. His countenance, without being handsome, was full of intelligence, and his powers of conversation distinguished. I heard him at the bar on one occasion plead before the Supreme Court of the United States the constitutional right of Congress to tax carriages and other excisable articles, in opposition to a party in Virginia; and no advocate that I ever heard acquitted himself so well. Talleyrand-Périgord sat not far from me as a listener.—BRECK, SAMUEL, 1862–77, *Recollections, ed. Scudder, p.* 210.

He had a good heart, but with it the pride and the natural arrogance of youth, combined with an almost over-weening consciousness of his powers, so that he was ready to find fault with the administration of others, and to believe that things might have gone better if the direction had rested with himself. Bold in the avowal of his own opinions, he was fearless to provoke, and prompt to combat opposition. It was not his habit to repine over lost opportunities. His nature inclined him rather to prevent what seemed to him coming evils by timely action.—BANCROFT, GEORGE, 1874, *History of the United States, vol.* X, *p.* 409.

It is a highly interesting fact, that A. D. 1797, one of the foremost men of the United States, a person who valued himself upon his moral principle, and was accepted by a powerful party at his own valuation in that particular, should have felt it to be a far baser thing to cheat men of their money than to despoil women of their honor. In this pamphlet he puts his honorable wife to an open shame, and publishes to the world the frailty of the woman who had gratified him; and this to refute a calumny which few would have credited. His conduct in this affair throws light upon his political course. He could be false to women for the same reason that he could disregard the will of the people. He did not look upon a woman as a person and an equal with whom faith was to be kept, any more than he recognized the people as the master and owner whose will was law. Original in nothing, he took his morals from one side of the Straits of Dover, and his politics from the other.—PARTON, JAMES, 1874, *Life of Thomas Jefferson, p.* 534.

I frankly acknowledge that I began this work with a deep admiration both for the character and the intellect of Hamilton, and that sentiment has strengthened as I have proceeded in the study of his career. . . . Hamilton was a man who excited no moderate feelings either of affection or animosity. His adherents worshipped him as a kind of human deity; his opponents assailed him as if he had been an incarnate fiend. He was loved as man has seldom been loved, and hated as a man free from the charge of any fearful crime against his fellow-men has seldom been hated. The language of moderation has never yet been used concerning him.—MORSE, JOHN T., JR., 1876, *The Life of Alexander Hamilton, vol.* I, *Preface, pp.* viii, ix.

There is something very attractive to us as we contemplate him during those early years of which we have written. We confess that we like to think of him as he there appears,—constant to the purpose of a noble life. The world was all before him. He was not the creature of circumstance, nor its servant. He chose his path, and never turned back. We are pleased when we think of him as the earnest student,—the boy that was willing to risk his life, though not his character, to exalt his station,—as the youth that knew himself, confided in his own understanding and strength, and yet never ventured beyond his ability,—as one who depended not on genius alone, but brought to his aid on every occasion the practical experience of actual knowledge,—and as the friend whose ardor no adversity could chill and whose faithfulness no reverse of fortune could alienate.—SHEA, GEORGE, 1879, *The Life and Epoch of Alexander Hamilton, p.* 430.

In person Hamilton was well made, of light and active build, but very small, much below the average height. His friends were wont to call him the "little lion;" and it is somewhat remarkable that his stature seems to have interfered so slightly, if at all, with his success as an orator. . . . The man was impressive. Inches of stature and of girth were lacking, but he was none the less full of dignity. In this, of course, his looks helped him. His head was finely shaped, symmetrical and massive. His eyes were dark, deep-set, and full of light and fire. He had a long, rather sharp nose, a well-shaped, close-set mouth, and a strong, firm jaw. The characteristics of the spare, clean-cut features are penetration and force. There is a piercing look about the face even in repose; and when Hamilton was moved a fire came into his eyes which we are told had a marvellous effect. But it was the soul which shone through his eyes, and animated his mobile countenance, that made him so effective in speech. As men listened to him, they felt profoundly the mastery of the strong nature, the imperious will, and the passionate energy which gave such force to his pathos, to his invective and to the even flow of clear, telling argument. . . . In private life Hamilton was much beloved and most attractive. He talked well and

freely. He was open-hearted and hospitable, full of high spirits and geniality. In his own family he was idolized by wife and children. The affection which he inspired in all who knew him was largely due to the perfect generosity of his nature, for he gave time and money with a lavish hand to all who sought his aid. He carried this habit into his business to his own detriment. He would often refuse to make any charge to poor clients, and never could be persuaded to accept anything beyond a reasonable and modest fee. He had in truth a contempt for money, and while he made a nation's fortune, he never made his own.—LODGE, HENRY CABOT, 1882, *Alexander Hamilton (American Statesmen), pp.* 272, 273, 274.

His temper was gentle; his manner engaging; his spirit, high and resolute, was raised above the influence both of cupidity and of fear; his parts were quick; his industry unwearied; his attainments various. He was at once a skilful officer, a brilliant pamphleteer, an active political leader, an impressive debater, a wise statesman, an able financier, a political economist of rare sagacity. In his veins was mingled the blood of two distinctly opposite races. In his mind and character were combined the choicest traits of each. From his father, a cool, deliberate, calculating Scotchman, he inherited the shrewdness, the logical habits of thought, which constitute the peculiar glory of the Scottish mind. From his mother, a lady of French extraction, and daughter of a Huguenot exile, he inherited the easy manners, the liveliness and vivacity, the keen sense of humor, the desire and ability to please, which so eminently distinguish the children of the Celtic race. Born within fifteen degrees of the equator, the rare powers of his mind ripened in him at a time when, in the natives of a colder climate, they have scarcely begun to bloom. Since the time of William of Orange the world had rarely seen an instance of so mature a mind in so young a lad.—MCMASTER, JOHN BACH, 1883, *A History of the People of the United States, vol.* I, *p.* 125.

Inseparably connected with the political history of the United States—above all other kindred events—is that memorable meeting of Alexander Hamilton and Aaron Burr at Weehawken (New Jersey) opposite the city of New York, on Wednesday morning, about seven o'clock, July 11, 1804, in which the former received his antagonist's bullet in a vital part, and from which he died at two o'clock Thursday afternoon. No event of the kind—so far as can be discovered by the author—in America, or elsewhere, ever produced such a general and profound sensation. The intelligence of the fall of the illustrious Hamilton, while it was received with marked feeling in Europe, even, fell like a crushing doom upon the American people. New York City was paralyzed, and the inhabitants of the whole country were plunged into the deepest mourning. Great multitudes of people thronged to New York to witness the melancholy ceremonies, and to take part in the funeral procession—which was very large and very impressive. This took place on Saturday, July 14. The funeral address was delivered by Gouverneur Morris, from a platform in front of Trinity Church, Broadway, in the presence of many thousands of grief-stricken people, among whom were four of the sons of the deceased, the eldest of whom was sixteen and the youngest between six and seven. . . . The weapons used by Hamilton and Burr are at present in the possession of a citizen of Rochester (New York). For more than fifty years they were in possession of the descendants of Hamilton, who gave them to the mother of the present possessor, also a descendant of Hamilton. In appearance they are very formidable. They are "horse-pistols" of English manufacture, and are exactly alike, so far as an ordinary observer can discover. The one from which Burr fired the fatal missile is marked by a cross filed under the lower part of the barrel. They do not in any respect resemble any modern arm. In handling them one is strongly impressed with the idea that they were evidently intended for use in duels where the participants "shot to kill" and not to obtain newspaper notoriety without the disagreeable shedding of blood. Although they evidently could not be manipulated so rapidly as the modern double-acting, self-cocking pistol, they are capable of fatal execution, as they carry a bullet of 56 calibre. They are sixteen inches long. —TRUMAN, BEN C., 1883, *The Field of Honor, pp.* 334, 354.

To the student, however, the military services of Alexander Hamilton shine out like new stars, giving an added lustre to his fame. He sees him in the fog and darkness covering that masterful retreat from Long Island. He hears him ask permission of his chief to retake Fort Washington with but a handful of men. Again he appears at Monmouth, correcting Lee's blunders and winning victory from defeat. Finally at Yorktown, with the dash of Ney, the magnetism of Napoleon, and the coolness of his own great Washington, he captures a redoubt with the loss of scarcely a man, and makes the surrender of Cornwallis a necessity. Such is the brief history of the "little lion" of Nevis on the field of battle. And this was accomplished while in stature and in age he was yet a boy.—HOTCHKISS, WILLIAM H., 1886, *Alexander Hamilton, ed. Dodge, p.* 142.

No name from the rolls of our struggle for independence and our binding together as a nation awakens more intense interest or opens wider fields for consideration than that of Hamilton. From the first appearance of the youthful student, to the tragic hour on the heights of Weehawken, the story has the attraction of romance, and in it can be found the kindling of influences potent not only for then but for all time. In the very beginning of his plan to found an institution of learning, Samuel Kirkland sought the counsel of Hamilton and received his approval. Hamilton was one of the first trustees, and in recognition of his encouragement the institution received his name. It is fitting that this College should call special attention to Alexander Hamilton. Soon after the establishment of prizes for English essays, the Faculty announced as a subject for the Senior class, "Alexander Hamilton as a Constitutional Statesman." The prize on this subject was awarded in a vigorous competition to Franklin H. Head of the Class of 1856, who evinced in College the marked ability he has shown so fully since. In 1863, the Senior prizes for essays having been withdrawn, Mr. Head established the prize called by his name, designating that the subject for this Prize Oration year by year should have reference to the character and career of Alexander Hamilton. . . . It is believed that these efforts grouped about the life of Hamilton will be of interest to many and will at least show how constant Hamilton College is to the memory of the great leader.—ROOT, OREN, 1896, *Alexander Hamilton, Thirty-one Orations Delivered at Hamilton College from 1864 to 1895, upon the Prize Foundation Established by Franklin Harvey Head, A. M., ed. Dodge, Introduction.*

The funeral took place from the house of John Church, in Robinson Street, near the upper Park. Express messengers had dashed out from New York the moment Hamilton breathed his last, and every city tolled its bells as it received the news. People flocked into the streets, weeping and indignant to the point of fury. Washington's death had been followed by sadness and grief, but was unaccompanied by anger, and a loud desire for vengeance. Moreover, Hamilton was still a young man. Few knew of his feeble health; and that dauntless resourceful figure dwelt in the high light of the public imagination, ever ready to deliver the young country in its many times of peril. His death was lamented as a national calamity. On the day of the funeral, New York was black. Every place of business was closed. The world was in the windows, on the housetops, on the pavements of the streets through which the cortège was to pass: Robinson, Beekman, Peal, and Broadway to Trinity Church. Those who were to walk in the funeral procession waited, the Sixth Regiment, with the colours and music of the several corps, paraded, in Robinson Street, until the standard of the Cincinnati, shrouded in crêpe, was waved before the open door of Mr. Church's house. The regiment immediately halted and rested on its reversed arms, until the bier had been carried from the house to the centre of the street, when the procession immediately formed. . . . When the procession after its long march reached Trinity Church the military formed in two columns, extending from the gate to the corners of Wall Street, and the bier was deposited before the entrance. Morris, surrounded by Hamilton's boys, stood over it, and delivered the most impassioned address which had ever leapt from that brilliant but erratic mind. It was brief, both because he hardly was able to control himself, and because he feared to incite the people to violence, but it was profoundly moving. . . . The bells tolled until sundown. The city and the people wore mourning for a month, the bar for six weeks. In due time the leading men of the parish decided upon the monument which should mark to future generations the cold and narrow home of him who had been so warm in life, loving as few men had loved, exulted in the wide greatness of the empire he had created.—ATHERTON, GERTRUDE FRANKLIN, 1902, *The Conqueror, Being the True and Romantic Story of Alexander Hamilton, pp. 532, 533, 534.*

STATESMAN

At the time when our government was organized we were without funds, though not without resources. To call them into action and establish order in the finances, Washington sought for splendid talents, for extensive information, and, above all, he sought for sterling, incorruptible integrity. All these he found in Hamilton. —MORRIS, GOUVERNEUR, 1804, *Funeral Oration by the dead body of Hamilton.*

I would hope and may not disbelieve, that Mr. Hamilton's attachment to the Union was of that stubborn, inflexible character which under no circumstances would have found him arrayed in arms against it. But in the events of Mr. Hamilton's life a comparison of his conduct with his opinions, in more than one instance, exhibits him in that class of human characters whose sense of rectitude itself is swayed by the impulses of the heart, and the purity of whose virtue is tempered by the baser metal of the ruling passion. This conflict between the influence of the sensitive and the reasoning faculty was perhaps never more strikingly exemplified than in the catastrophe which terminated his life, and in the picture of his soul unveiled by this posthumous paper.—ADAMS, JOHN QUINCY, 1800–15, *Federalism.*

This naturally brought Hamilton into his [Talleyrand] thoughts, and of him he spoke willingly, freely, and with great admiration. In the course of his remarks, he said that he had known, during his life, many of the more marked men of his time, but that he had never, on the whole, known one equal to Hamilton. I was much surprised, as well as gratified, by the remark; but still feeling that, as an American, I was, in some sort, a party concerned by patriotism in the compliment, I answered, —with a little reserve, perhaps with a little modesty,—that the great military commanders and the grest statesmen of Europe had dealt with much larger masses of men, and much wider interests than Hamilton ever had. "Mais, monsieur," the Prince instantly replied, "*Hamilton avait deviné l'Europe.*"—TICKNOR, GEORGE, 1818, *Journal.*

That he possessed intellectual powers of the first order, and the moral qualifications of integrity and honour in a captivating degree, has been decreed to him by a suffrage now universal. If his theory of government deviated from the republican standard, he had the candour to avow it, and the greater merit of co-operating faithfully in maturing and supporting a system which was not his choice.—MADISON, JAMES, 1831, *Letters, vol.* IV, *p.* 176.

He smote the rock of the national resources, and abundant streams of revenue gushed forth. He touched the dead corpse of the Public Credit, and it sprung upon its feet. The fabled birth of Minerva from the brain of Jove was hardly more sudden or more perfect than the financial system of the United States as it burst forth from the conception of Alexander Hamilton.— WEBSTER, DANIEL, 1831, *Speech at a Public Dinner in New York, Feb.*

Hamilton must be classed among the men who have best known the vital principles and fundamental conditions of a government,—not of a government such as this (France), but of a government worthy of its mission and of its name. There are not in the constitution of the United States an element of order, of force, or of duration, which he has not powerfully contributed to introduce into it and caused to predominate.—GUIZOT, FRANÇOIS PIERRE GUILLAUME, 1840, *An Essay on the Character of Washington and His Influence in the Revolution of the United States of America.*

Among all the remarkable men of the Revolution, we know of no one, who, for the attributes which usually mark genius, was more distinguished. He was endowed with a singularly comprehensive mind, which enabled him to originate forms of government and systems of administration, whilst he united with it an intrepidity and an energy equal to the task of putting them in execution. He was a politician and a statesman, without possessing those finer and more delicate feelings of lofty

morality, which, while they do honor to a public man, sometimes go far to impair his means of usefulness. To Hamilton, men appeared always as instruments to be moved, and not as accountable beings, and theories of government or modes of policy were regarded simply with reference to the ends which might be attained by applying them. The consequence was, that however bold the features of his system were, and however decidedly beneficial in its application to the interests of the country, there was always a slight taint of earthly morality about it, which deprived him of the share in the public confidence, which he may now be regarded as having deserved. Peculiarly fitted for the difficult duty of calling a government into being, he was capable, at the same time, of understanding the bearings, of the most comprehensive principles and of entering into its minutest practical detail. Yet there is this remarkable peculiarity about the history of Mr. Hamilton, that, whilst he acted a most important and honourable part in a critical period of our national affairs, there was not, probably, an instant of his life in which he enjoyed the perfect sympathy of the mass of the people of the United States.—ADAMS, CHARLES FRANCIS, 1841, *The Madison Papers, North American Review, vol.* 53, *p.* 70.

Where, among all the speculative philosophers in political science whom the world has seen, shall we find a man of greater acuteness of intellect, or more capable of devising a scheme of government which should appear theoretically, perfect? Yet Hamilton's unquestionable genius for political disquisition and construction was directed and restrained by a noble generosity, and an unerring perception of the practicable and the expedient, which enabled him to serve mankind without attempting to force them to his own plans, and without compelling them into his own views.—CURTIS, GEORGE TICKNOR, 1854, *History of the Origin, Formation and Adoption of the Constitution of the United States, vol.* I, *p.* 387.

In the career of Hamilton we trace the progress of the Constitution, from its first germ in the mind of the young soldier, through all the difficulties of its establishment, and the trials of its early years, until its administration passes from the control of its authors, to fall into the hands of the champions of an absolute democracy. But, apart from all political speculations, the story of Hamilton himself, his character, his services, and his fate, are well worthy of record and ought to be better known than they have hitherto been—especially in that England which he understood with the instinct of genius, and loved with the enthusiasm of a high and generous nature. Such knowledge can only tend to the honour of his name, and to the growth of kindly feelings between his country and our own.— RIETHMÜLLER, CHRISTOPHER JAMES, 1864, *Alexander Hamilton and His Contemporaries, Dedication, p.* IV.

It is idle to speculate on what "might have been;" but we may be permitted to conjecture that, had Hamilton lived, many of the evils which it has taxed the vitality of the States to survive, and others of equal magnitude, against which they still are struggling, would have been averted or mitigated. But when he fell, in a half-personal, half-political quarrel, in his thirty-fifth year [?] (1804), by the bullet of the infamous demagogue Aaron Burr, a blow was dealt to Western civilisation, only less vital and lasting than to that of Scotland by the assassination of the greatest of the Stuart kings; for Hamilton had no worthy successor, and the victory lay henceforth with the unscrupulous man of genius who, without serious let or hindrance, assumed the control of the national destinies. — NICHOL, JOHN, 1880–85, *American Literature, p.* 74.

Like Napoleon, Pitt, and so many others of his great contemporaries, Hamilton, instead of working his way slowly up, established his hold upon the government and direction of affairs from the day that he was admitted to a share in them, and leaped at a bound into a position which in quieter times men attain only after long years of patient struggle. His influence seems to have been due in great measure to the remarkable sincerity of his mind. His nature was profoundly truthful.— SEDGWICK, A. G., 1882, *Alexander Hamilton, The Nation, vol.* 34, *p.* 445.

There is one man in the political history of the United States whom Daniel Webster regarded as his intellectual superior. And this man was Alexander Hamilton; not so great a lawyer or orator as Webster, not so broad and experienced a statesman, but a more original genius, who gave shape to existing political institutions. He was one of those fixed stars which will forever blaze in the firmament of American lights, like Franklin, Washington, and Jefferson; and the more his works are critically examined, the brighter does his genius appear. No matter how great this country is destined to be,—no matter what illustrious statesmen are destined to arise, and work in a larger sphere with the eyes of the world upon them,—Alexander Hamilton will be remembered and will be famous for laying one of the corner-stones in the foundation of the American structure.—LORD, JOHN, 1885, *Beacon Lights of History, vol.* IV, *p.* 367.

Alexander Hamilton was, next to Franklin, the most consummate statesman among the band of eminent men who had been active in the Revolution, and who afterward labored to convert a loose confederation of States into a national government. His mind was as plastic as it was vigorous and profound. It was the appropriate intellectual expression of a poised nature whose power was rarely obtrusive, because it was half concealed by the harmonius adjustment of its various faculties. It was a mind deep enough to grasp principles, and broad enough to regard relations, and fertile enough to devise measures. Indeed, the most practical of our early statesmen was also the most inventive. He was as ready with new expedients to meet unexpected emergencies as he was wise in subordinating all expedients to clearly defined principles. In intellect he was probably the most creative of our early statesmen, as in sentiment Jefferson was the most widely influential. —WHIPPLE, EDWIN PERCY, 1886, *American Literature and Other Papers, ed. Whittier, p.* 14.

One cannot note the disappearance of this brilliant figure, to Europeans the most interesting in the early history of the Republic, without the remark that his countrymen seem to have never, either in his lifetime or afterwards, duly recognized his splendid gifts.—BRYCE, JAMES, 1888, *The American Commonwealth, vol.* I, *p.* 641.

Hamilton's work went to the making of the American State, but personally he may be said to have failed; for when death overtook him he had no political future, and could have had none, unless he could have readjusted himself entirely to the conditions of American public life.— SUMNER, WILLIAM GRAHAM, 1890, *Alexander Hamilton (Makers of America), Preface, p.* iv.

There are two points which should be clearly understood; the first, that Hamilton's character as a private individual was currupt, and as a politician full of plots, and bitterness, and not always free from treachery; the second, and his views of government and democratic institutions were such that, had they secured predominance, would have been fatal to the Republic. At the present moment the tendencies most likely to work mischief are Hamiltonian. — POWELL, E. P., 1891, *Popular Leaders Past and Present, The Arena, vol.* 3, *p.* 579.

No emergency found him at a loss, and his creative intellect brought victory out of disaster. The symmetry of his nature and the genuine modesty of his character veiled the extent and power of his resources; he sought not his own prosperity, but that of the measures in which he believed, and was careless though others got the credit of his success. Practical in his objects and clear in their expounding, he conquered opposition, partly by lucid and temperate reasoning, and partly by a magnetic force of intellectual passion. —HAWTHORNE, JULIAN, AND LEMMON, LEONARD, 1891, *American Literature, p.* 31.

His promptness rivalled occasion, and serried obstinacy yielded to his intrepid assaults. It was not his own success he sought, but the triumph of a mighty cause. Had he preferred power, which is transient, to influence, which endures; had he been a partisan rather than a patriot, a self-seeker rather than the trustee of a future beyond even his hope or ken; had he been duplex, where he was open, lucid and sincere; then he had not impressed his individuality upon a whole America as the truest translator of her predestinate nationality. . . . He was neither sophist nor paralogist. He dwelt above manipulation, and compromise, and expedient, and formula, and all mere passports. He sought the underlying principles and the ultimate reality. His soul went into his plea. With warmth and grace, but with a peculiar logical simplicity—a clearness that became clarity— and with the unshaken courage of one

compelled by conviction, he summoned his facts and marshaled his reasons. His was the strategy of unambushed truth and the elastic energy of a direct will. . . . With pen as with voice he was a chief of assemblies. He was a sharp sword and two-edged. He was the exponent and champion of frank and fearless argument. Malignity might vituperate, but he did not pause. Malice might misrepresent him, but he never sulked. Cunning was not in him, nor little envy, nor treachery. He met each new issue as it arose, and his enemies themselves being judges he was never put to the worst in free and open encounter. . . . Life, fortune, honor were to that sacredly rendered, ungrudgingly, unweariedly, unregrettingly, and, thank God, with absolute success. *He had no secrets from his country!*—STRYKER, M. WOOLSEY, 1895, *Address at the Hamilton Club, Brooklyn, N. Y., Jan.* 11, *pp.* 9, 10, 11.

Certainly one of the greatest figures in our history is the figure of Alexander Hamilton. American historians, though compelled always to admire him, often in spite of themselves, have been inclined, like the mass of men in his own day, to look at him askance. They hint, when they do not plainly say, that he was not "American." He rejected, if he did not despise, democratic principles; advocated a government as strong, almost, as a monarchy; and defended the government which was actually set up, like the skilled advocate he was, only because it was the strongest that could be had under the circumstances. He believed in authority, and he had no faith in the aggregate wisdom of masses of men. He had, it is true, that deep and passionate love of liberty, and that steadfast purpose in the maintenance of it, that mark the best Englishmen everywhere; but his ideas of government stuck fast in the old-world politics, and his statesmanship was of Europe rather than of America. And yet the genius and the steadfast spirit of this man were absolutely indispensable to us. No one less masterful, no one less resolute than he to drill the minority, if necessary, to have their way against the majority, could have done the great work of organization by which he established the national credit, and with the national credit the national government itself. — WILSON,

WOODROW, 1896, *Mere Literature and Other Essays, p.* 188.

The most precocious statesman of America, if not of the world.—BRONSON, WALTER C., 1900, *A Short History of American Literature, p.* 49.

THE FEDERALIST

No constitution of government ever received a more masterly and successful vindication. I know not, indeed, of any work on the principles of free government that is to be compared, in instruction and intrinsic value, to this small and unpretending volume of the *Federalist;* not even if we resort to Aristotle, Cicero, Machiavel, Montesquieu, Milton, Locke, or Burke. It is equally admirable in the depth of its wisdom, the comprehensiveness of its views, the sagacity of its reflections, and the fearlessness, patriotism, candour, simplicity, and elegance, with which its truths are uttered and recommended. Mr. Justice Story acted wisely in making the Federalist the basis of his Commentary.— KENT, JAMES, 1826-54, *Commentaries upon American Law.*

His are easily distinguished by their superior comprehensiveness, practicalness, originality, and condensed and polished diction.—GRISWOLD, RUFUS WILMOT, 1846, *The Prose Writers of America, p.* 91.

The Federalist originally appeared in the columns of the New York Daily Advertiser. The papers were collected and published in two neat duodecimo volumes, by J. & A. M'Lean, New York, 1788; another edition appeared during Hamilton's Lifetime, in 1802, from the press of George F. Hopkins, New York. The papers were also included in an edition of Hamilton's works, in three vols., by Williams & Whiting, New York, 1810. In 1818, an edition was published by Jacob Gideon at Washington, which embraced the revisions by Madison of his papers.—DUYCKINCK, EVERT A. AND GEORGE L., 1855-65-75, *Cyclopædia of American Literature,* ed. *Simons, vol.* I, *p.* 439, *note.*

It was from him that the Federalist derived the weight and the power which commanded the careful attention of the country, and carried conviction to the great body of intelligent men in all parts of the Union.—CURTIS, GEORGE TICKNOR, 1855, *History of the Origin, Formation and Adoption of the Constitution of the United States, vol.* I, *p.* 417.

On the whole, the "Federalist" is a very remarkable instance of statesmanlike ability, in which a certain amount of pedantry and affectation may well be pardoned in consideration of the clearness with which the conditions of a great political crisis are appreciated. Hamilton, whose influence is most perceptible, was by far the ablest representative of what may be called the English theory of government in the United States; and took no inconsiderable share in carrying into execution the plan which he had so ably defended.—STEPHEN, LESLIE, 1876, *History of English Thought in the Eighteenth Century, vol.* II, *p.* 260.

These are, perhaps, the ablest political essays in the English language; and they are like some of the great speeches of Burke, in that they were intended to effect an immediate purpose only and yet have served ever since as a perpetual storehouse of political wisdom.—MATTHEWS, BRANDER, 1896, *An Introduction to the Study of American Literature, p.* 221.

The effect was immediate and far-reaching. The "Federalist" did more than any other writing to secure the adoption and support of the Constitution throughout the country. It is a profound disquisition on the principles of our government, and has since been quoted as of the highest authority on constitutional questions. But it is more than a political and controversial treatise. Its masterly style raises it to the rank of real literature. Most of the controversial writings of the Revolutionary Period have been forgotten. Having served their temporary purpose, they have been swept into oblivion. But the "Federalist" endures as one of the masterpieces of the human reason. Its sustained power is wonderful. The argument, clothed in elevated, strong, and sometimes eloquent language, moves forward with a mighty momentum that sweeps away everything before it. It is hardly surpassed in the literature of the world as a model of masterful popular reasoning. By this production Hamilton won for himself a foremost place in the literature of his time.—PAINTER, F. V. N., 1897, *Introduction to American Literature, p.* 87.

As a series of formal essays, the "Federalist" groups itself roughly with the "Tatler," the "Spectator," and those numerous descendants of theirs which fill the literary records of eighteenth-century England. It differs, however, from all these, in both substance and purpose. The "Tatler," the "Spectator," and their successors dealt with superficial matters in a spirit of literary amenity : the "Federalist" deals, in an argumentative spirit as earnest as that of any Puritan divine, with political principles paramount in our history ; and it is so wisely thoughtful that one may almost declare it the permanent basis of sound thinking concerning American constitutional law. Like all the educated writing of the eighteenth century, too, it is phrased with a rhythmical balance and urbane polish which gave it claim to literary distinction. After all, however, one can hardly feel it much more significant in a history of pure letters than are the opinions in which a little later Judge Marshall and Judge Story developed and expounded the constitutional law which the "Federalist" commented on. Its true character appears when we remember the most important thing published in England during the same years,—the poetry of Robert Burns. The contrast between Burns and the "Federalist" tells the whole literary story. Just as in the seventeenth century the only serious literature of America was a phase of that half-historical, half-theological sort of work which had been a minor part of English literature generations before ; so in the eighteenth century the chief product of American literature was an extremely ripe example of such political pamphleteering as in England had been a minor phase of letters during the period of Queen Anne. Pure letters in America were still to come.—WENDELL, BARRETT, 1900, *A Literary History of America, p.* 118.

GENERAL

That great man, whose remarkable career was finished at the point when most men are just ready for action, was a reader and inquirer in political economy in his twentieth year. In his twenty-fifth year, in such leisure as the camp of the Revolution afforded, he matured a scheme for a Bank of the United States, and became a correspondent of Morris on that subject. And, finally, at the age of thirty-four, he produced, as Secretary of the Treasury, his great reports on the Public Credit, on a National Bank, and on Manufactures, the most powerful and comprehensive

discussion of the national finances every made under our government, and the subject, it may be remembered, of one of Mr. Webster's noblest periods. Those reports bear the evidence throughout of much reading and reflection upon the experiences of nations, and of careful meditation on the speculations and theories of previous writers. . . . Both the knowledge of economic questions and the power of dealing with them exhibited by Hamilton in these discussions warrant us in setting him down as a writer who, under other conditions and freed from the pressure of public business, might have been expected to make some positive contribution to the development of economic theory. But his few crowded years left him little opportunity for such pursuits, and it would now be hard to say that he left any impression on the thought of the world, by his dealing with this subject. His reports have continued to be the arsenal from which the advocates of special measures have again and again drawn forth weapons now well worn ; but systematic political economy cannot be said to owe to him any recognized principle, any discovery in method, or indeed any influence save the stimulus which his example must always afford to the student of financial history.—DUNBAR, CHARLES F., 1876, *Economic Science in America,* 1776–1876, *North American Review, vol.* 122, *pp.* 130, 131.

The greatness of his political has obscured the memory of his literary fame : he was one of the best writers of his time. He wrote in the periodic style, sonorous, often weighty and austere. He was only forty-seven when he died ; yet his literary productions fill many volumes, his clear intelligence instructed his age. He helped to form the Constitution, and, although not pleased with some of its provisions, defended it in the "Federalist" with great force and propriety. His pen was never at rest ; he spared few of his contemporaries ; his integrity was undoubted, his patriotism sincere ; his influence upon the fate of his country incalculable.—LAWRENCE, EUGENE, 1880, *A Primer of American Literature, p.* 42.

During our rapid advance in wealth and influence they [Hamilton's writings] have shown the adaptive power which belongs to principles rather than expedients. Their effect has been far-reaching and permanent, and the memory of their author shall be as lasting as the Union which he helped to form.—LANG, PHILIP A., 1880, *Alexander Hamilton, ed. Dodge, p.* 112.

If we compare Hamilton with the other writers of that period when every distinguished man did more or less political writing, and when there was no other native literature, it is a simple matter to fix his position. He was easily first. Not only have his writings alone survived for the general reader out of the wilderness of essays and pamphlets of the last century on similar subjects, but the "Federalist" has become a text-book in America and an authority in Europe. Hamilton, in this capacity, will, however, bear a severer test,—that of abstract merit. His writings deal exclusively with the great questions of that day, and have lost their living interest. Yet as specimens of political literature, as disquisitions on constitutions and the art of government, and as masterpieces of reasoning, they are not only the best produced here, but they will take high rank among the best efforts of other countries. One quality which raised Hamilton in this regard beyond his contemporaries on both sides of the Atlantic was his freedom from the didactic tone which so mars the writings of the latter half of the last century. His style was simple, nervous, and modern in feeling, and anyone who has tried to condense one of his arguments will appreciate the statement that the thought is compressed to the last point consistent with clearness. Yet forcible and convincing as all Hamilton's essays are, pure as is the style, and vigorous and rapid as is the flow of thought, they are hard reading. Admiring them as models in their way and as great intellectual efforts, one is forced to confess them dry to the last degree.—LODGE, HENRY CABOT, 1884, *Studies in History,* p. 168.

The writings of Hamilton, like those of nearly all the politicians whose names are here under consideration, had no real literary motive. They were produced in the course of the life of a statesman, and all, whether written with greater or less care, were designed to further the ends of statecraft or of political management. . . . His rank as an author depends finally upon his contributions to "The Federalist"—a weighty and potent book,

which, however, like Adam Smith's "Wealth of Nations," scarcely belongs within the border line of true literature.—RICHARDSON, CHARLES F., 1887, *American Literature,* 1607–1885, *vol.* I, *pp.* 201, 203.

In the exposition of his views touching the several vast fields of thought here brought under consideration,—constitutional law, municipal law, the long line of colonial charters, colonial laws and precedents, international polity as affecting the chief nations of Christendom, justice in the abstract and justice in the concrete, human rights both natural and conventional, the physical and metaphysical conditions underlying the great conflict then impending,—it must be confessed, that this beardless philosopher, this statesman not yet out of school, this military strategist scarcely rid of his roundabout, exhibits a range and precision of knowledge, a ripeness of judgment, a serenity, a justice, a massiveness both of thought and of style, which would perhaps make incredible the theory of his authorship of these pamphlets, were not this theory confirmed by his undoubted exhibition in other ways, at about the same period of his life, of the same astonishing qualities: as in his "Remarks on the Quebec Bill," published in 1775; in his letters under the signature of "Publius," published in 1778; in his essays over the signature of "The Continentalist," published in 1781; above all, in his personal letter to James Duane written in 1780, and containing a powerful statement of the defects of the articles of confederation, and an almost miraculous forecast of the very incidents and sequences of the process by which, some seven or eight years afterward, the articles of confederation were actually developed into the constitution of the United States.—TYLER, MOSES COIT, 1897, *The Literary History of the American Revolution,* 1763–1783, *vol.* I, *p.* 390.

From his time to the present, in peace and war, notwithstanding temporary embarrassments and occasional panics, the finances of the government have been sound, and its obligations accepted wherever offered. In the long line of honest and able secretaries who have administered the treasury, Hamilton stands as the first and greatest financier.—GILMAN, DANIEL C., 1897, *Library of the World's Best Literature, ed. Warner, vol.* xii, *p.* 6895.

Charlotte Lennox
1720–1804

Born (Charlotte Ramsay), in New York, 1720. To England, 1735(?). Being unprovided for at her father's death, went on the stage for a short time. Married to—Lennox, 1748(?). Friendship with Dr. Johnson and Richardson. Edited "The Ladies' Museum," 1760–61. Play, "The Sister" (dramatized from her novel "Henrietta"), produced at Covent Garden, 18 Feb. 1769; "Old City Manners" (adapted from Jonson, Chapman and Marston's "Eastward Hoe!"), Drury Lane, 9 Nov. 1775 Ill health and distress in later years. Pension from Royal Literary Fund, 1803. Died, in London, 4 Jan. 1804. *Works:* "Poems on Several Occasions," (anon.) 1747; "The Life of Harriot Stuart" (anon.) 1751 (1750); "The Female Quixote" (anon.), 1752; "Shakespear Illustrated" (3 vols., anon.), 1753–54; "Philander" (anon.), 1758; "Henrietta" (anon.), 1758; "Sophia" 1762; "The Sisters," 1769; "Old City Manners," 1775; "Euphemia," 1790; "Memoirs of Henry Lennox," 1804. She *translated:* "Memoirs of the Countess of Berci," 1756; "Memoirs of the Duke of Sully," 1756; "Memoirs for the History of Madame de Maintenon," 1757; Brumoy's "Greek Theatre" (with Johnson and others), 1759; the Duchess de la Vallière's "Meditations," 1774.—Sharp, R. Farquharson, 1897, *A Dictionary of English Authors, p.* 167.

PERSONAL

A poetess and deplorable actress.—Walpole, Horace, 1748, *To George Montagu, Sept.* 3; *Letters, ed. Cunningham, vol.* II, *p.* 126.

He (Dr. Johnson) gave us an account of Mrs. Lennox. Her "Female Quixote" is very justly admired here. But Mrs. Thrale says that though her books are generally approved, nobody likes her. I find she, among others, waited on Dr. Johnson upon her commencing writing, and he told us that at her request he carried her to Richardson. "Poor Charlotte Lennox!" continued he. "When we came to the house she desired me to leave her; 'for,' says she, 'I am under great restraint in your presence; but if you leave me alone with Richardson, I'll give you a very good account of him;' however, I fear poor Charlotte was disappointed, for she gave me no account at all."—D'Arblay, Mme. (Fanny Burney), 1778, *Diary, Aug.* 26.

Mrs. Lenox, a lady now well known in the literary world, had written a novel intitled, "The Life of Harriot Stuart," which in the spring of 1751, was ready for publication. One evening at the club, Johnson proposed to us the celebrating the birth of Mrs. Lenox's first literary child, as he called her book, by a whole night spent in festivity. Upon his mentioning it to me, I told him I had never sat up a whole night in my life; but he continuing to press me, and saying, that I should find great delight in it, I, as did all the rest of our company, consented. The place appointed was the Devil tavern, and there, about the hour of eight, Mrs. Lenox and her husband, and a lady of her acquaintance, now living, as also the club, and friends to the number of near twenty, assembled. Our supper was elegant, and Johnson had directed that a magnificent hot apple-pie should make a part of it, and this he would have stuck with bay-leaves, because, forsooth, Mrs. Lenox was an authoress, and had written verses; and further, he had prepared for her a crown of laurel, with which, but not till he had invoked the muses by some ceremonies of his own invention, he encircled her brows. The night passed, as must be imagined, in pleasant conversation, and harmless mirth, intermingled at different periods with the refreshments of coffee and tea. About five Johnson's face shone with meridian splendour, though his drink had been only lemonade; but the far greater part of us had deserted the colours of Bacchus, and were with difficulty, rallied to partake of a second refreshment of coffee, which was scarcely ended when the day began to dawn. This phenomenon began to put us in mind of our reckoning; but the waiters were all so overcome with sleep, that it was two hours before we could get a bill, and it was not till near eight that the creaking of the street-door gave the signal for our departure.—Hawkins, Sir John, 1787, *Life of Samuel Johnson, p.* 285.

GENERAL

On the evening of Saturday, May 15, he was in fine spirits at our Essex Head Club. He told us, "I dined yesterday at Mrs. Garrick's with Mrs. Carter, Miss Hannah

More, and Miss Fanny Burney. Three such women are not to be found: I know not where I could find a fourth, except Mrs. Lennox, who is superiour to them all."— JOHNSON, SAMUEL, 1784, *Life by Boswell, ed. Hill, vol.* IV, *p.* 317.

But her (Dorothy Osborne's) favourite books were those ponderous French Romances which modern readers know chiefly from the pleasant satire of Charlotte Lennox.—MACAULAY, THOMAS BABINGTON, 1838, *Sir William Temple, Edinburgh Review, Critical and Miscellaneous Essays.*

A very ingenious, deserving, and not very fortunate woman, who wrote the clever novel of the "Female Quixote," and a somewhat silly book about Shakespeare, to which Johnson, a great friend of her's, was suspected to have contributed. . . . Though with too much sentiment, it ["Sister"] is both amusing and interesting; and the Strawberry-hill critics who abused it, and afterwards pronounced Burgoyne's "Heiress" "the finest comedy in the English language," might have had the justice to discover that three of the characters of the fashionable General were stolen from this very "Sister" of poor Mrs. Lennox.—FORSTER, JOHN, 1848–54, *The Life and Times of Oliver Goldsmith, vol.* II, *pp.* 145, 146.

It ["Female Quixote"] certainly is a very amusing book. . . . The story is rather wire-drawn, but rather full of humor.—MINTO, WILLIAM, 1894, *The Literature of the Georgian Era, ed. Knight, pp.* 117, 118.

The "Female Quixote," published in 1752, and perpetuated by Mrs. Barbauld, is precious for preserving to the world the best impression we have of what the old, old romances of the Calprénede and Scudéry school really were; sparing us an effort which even I am incapable of—that is, wading through the black volumes like those beloved of the old nurse in the Wortley family, and even of Lady Mary herself and her contemporaries. It is an agreeable and ingenious satire upon the old romances, and I really think it is written in a modern spirit, and that Arabella, the heroine, has more good stuff in her than other imaginary ladies of the time who have been more praised. She is supposed to have been brought up in the country and secluded from all society, but allowed to amuse herself in an old library furnished with the works of these voluminous authors. Of course she imbibes their views of life, and when she comes out into the world, possessed of beauty and fortune, it is with a pronounced ignorance of every circumstance of real life and manners. She fancies every man who speaks to her to be secretly in love with her, and is in constant apprehension of being forcibly carried off.—HALE, SUSAN, 1898, *Men and Manners of the Eighteenth Century, p.* 45.

William Paley
1743–1805

Born, at Peterborough, July 1743. Educated at Giggleswick Grammar School (of which his father was head-master). To Christ's Coll., Camb., as Sizar, Oct. 1759; Scholar and Exhibitioner, Dec. 1759; B. A., 1763; M. A., 1766. Schoolmaster at Greenwich, 1763-66. Ordained Deacon, 1766; Priest, 21 Dec. 1767. Fellow of Christ's Coll., Camb., June 1766. Prælector, 1767-69; Hebrew Lecturer, 1768-70; Tutor, March 1771. Preacher at Whitehall, 1771-76. Rector of Musgrave, Cumberland, May 1775 to 1777. Married (i) Jane Hewitt, 6 June 1776. Vicar of Dalston, Cumberland, 1776-93. Vicar of Appleby, 1777 to Aug. 1782. Prebendary of Carlisle, 1780 to Jan. 1795. Archdeacon and Rector of Great Salkeld, Aug. 1782 to May 1805. Chancellor of the Diocese, 1785 to Jan. 1795. Wife died, May 1791. Vicar of Aldingham, May 1792 to March 1795; Vicar of Stanwix, 1793 to March 1795. Prebendary of St. Pancras, St. Paul's Cathedral, Aug. 1794. Sub-dean of Lincoln, Jan. 1795. D. D. Camb., 1795. Rector of Bishop-Wearmouth, March 1795. Resided there till his death. Married (ii), Miss Dobinson, 14 Dec. 1795. Died, at Lincoln, 25 May 1805. Buried in Carlisle Cathedral. *Works:* "A Defence of the 'Considerations on the propriety of requiring a subscription to Articles of faith'" (anon.) 1774; "Caution recommended in the use . . . of Scripture Language," 1777; "Advice addressed to the Young Clergy of the Diocese of Carlisle," 1781; "A Distinction of

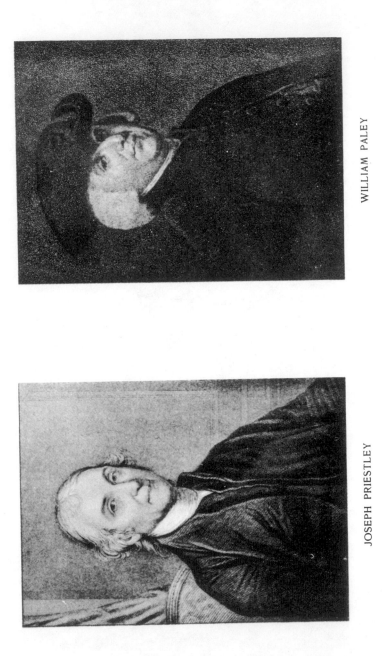

WILLIAM PALEY

From Original Engraving in Stipple.

JOSEPH PRIESTLEY

Engraving by C. Cook.

Orders in the Church defended," 1782; "Principles of Moral and Political Philosophy," 1785; "The young Christian instructed," 1790; "Horæ Paulinæ," 1790 (2nd edn. same year); "The Use and propriety of local and occasional preaching," 1790; "Reasons for Contentment," 1792; "View of the Evidences of Christianity," 1794 (2nd edn. same year); "Dangers incidental to the Clerical Character," 1795; "A Sermon preached at the Assizes at Durham," 1795; "A Short Memoir of the Life of Edward Law., D. D. 1800; "Natural Theology," 1802. *Posthumous:* "Sermons on Several Subjects," 1808; "Sermons and Tracts," 1808; "Sermons on Various Subjects," (2 vols.), 1825. *Collected Works* in 8 vols., 1805-08; in 5 **v**ols, 1819; etc., etc. *Life:* by G. W. Meadley, 2nd edn., 1810.—SHARP, R. FARQUHARSON, 1897, *A Dictionary of English Authors,* p. 220.

PERSONAL

His delivery was fluent, his language strong and perspicuous, though mixed sometimes with provincial, but expressive words and phrases, which, however, were purposely used as uncommon, and likely to be remembered. His general manner, also, was strikingly impressive; and he treated everything with such force and animation, that the driest topics became interesting. By all these means, he secured not only the attendance of his pupils without the aid of punishments, but also their admiration whilst he lectured, and their regret when he had done. . . . In person, Dr. Paley was above the common size, and rather inclined to corpulence in his latter years. The expression of his countenance is well delineated in Mr. Romney's exquisite portrait of him, taken after he was appointed archdeacon of Carlisle. Dr. Paley is understood to have left a very competent fortune amongst his family: for though he had never levied the utmost value of his preferments, and had always lived in a style suitable to his station, he had been through life, to use his own phrase, *an economist upon a plan.*— MEADLEY, GEORGE WILSON, 1809, *Memoirs of William Paley,* pp. 75, 225.

A man singularly without guile, and yet often misunderstood or misrepresented; a man who was thought to have no learning, because he had no pedantry, and who was too little of a quack to be reckoned a philosopher; who would have been infallibly praised as a useful writer on theory of government, if he had been more visionary, and would have been esteemed a deeper divine, if he had not been always so intelligible.—BLUNT, J. J., 1828, *Works and Character of Paley, Quarterly Review, vol.* 38, *p.* 335.

The greatest divine of the period is Dr. William Paley, a man of remarkable vigour and clearness of intellect, and originality of character. His acquirements as a scholar and churchman were grafted on a homely, shrewd, and benevolent nature, which no circumstances could materially alter. There was no doubt of obscurity either about the man or his works; he stands out in bold relief among his brother divines, like a sturdy oak on a lawn or parterre—a little hard and cross-grained, but sound, fresh, and massive—dwarfing his neighbours with his weight and bulk, and his intrinsic excellence.—CHAMBERS, ROBERT, 1876, *Cyclopædia of English Literature, ed. Carruthers.*

Paley was above the average height, and in later life stout. He was curiously clumsy, made grotesque gesticulations, and talked, as Meadley and Best agree, with broad north-country accent. His son only admits "a want of refinement." His voice was weak, though deep; and he overcame the awkward effect of his pulpit appearances by his downright sincerity. His son apologises for his abrupt conclusions by saying that he stopped when he had no more to say. . . . He was given to brooding over his books, often writing and teaching his sons at the same time, and turning every odd moment to account. . . . He was the incarnation of strong common-sense, full of genial good humour, and always disposed to take life pleasantly. As a lawyer, the profession for which he thought himself suited, he would probably have rivalled the youger Law, who became Lord Ellenborough. He had no romance, poetic sensibility, or enthusiasm; but was thoroughly genial and manly. He was a very affectionate father and husband, and fond, like Sydney Smith, of gaining knowledge from every one who would talk to him. He only met one person in his life from whom he could extract nothing.—STEPHEN, LESLIE, 1895, *Dictionary of National Biography, vol.* XLIII, *pp.* 104, 105.

PRINCIPLES OF MORAL AND POLITICAL PHILOSOPHY
1785

Paley, who had not read a great deal, had certainly read Puffendorf: he has borrowed from him several minor illustrations. . . . Their minds were in some respects alike; both phlegmatic, honest, and sincere, without warmth or fancy; yet there seems a more thorough good-nature and kindliness of heart in our countryman. . . . They do not, indeed, resemble each other in their modes of writing: one was very laborious, the other very indolent; one sometimes misses his mark by circuity, the other by precipitance.—HALLAM, HENRY, 1837–39, *Introduction to the Literature of Europe, pt.* iv, *ch.* iv, *par.* 49.

The work of Dr. Paley embraces the Principles of Political as well as Moral Philosophy; but, able and judicious as in many respects that portion of the book is, the space allotted to it, being little more than one-third of two moderate-sized and widely-printed octavo volumes, shows how far it must be from explaining the whole even of the principles of the science. Of Political Economy it has almost nothing; it only gives the principles of government in their most general form; it makes no application of them to any constitution but that of England; it derives from the constitution of no other country any illustration of them; and it may justly be regarded rather as an illustration of the doctrines of Moral Philosophy, and an appendix to the main body of the work, than as a treatise on Political Science.—BROUGHAM, HENRY LORD, 1840–44, *Political Philosophy, Introduction, pt.* i.

Of what value, let me ask, is Paley's "Moral Philosophy"? What is its imagined use? Is it that in substance it reveals any new duties, or banishes as false any old ones? No; but because the known and admitted duties—duties recognized in *every* system of ethics—are here placed (successfully or not) upon new foundations, or brought into relation with new principles not previously perceived to be in any relation whatever. This, in fact, is the very meaning of a theory or contemplation, when A, B, C, old and undisputed facts, have their relations to each other developed. It is not, therefore, for any practical benefit in action, so much as for

the satisfaction of the understanding, when reflecting on a man's own actions, the wish to see what his conscience or his heart prompts reconciled to general laws of thinking—this is the particular service performed by Paley's "Moral Philosophy." It does not so much profess to tell *what* you are to do, as the *why* and the *wherefore;* and, in particular, to show how one rule of action may be reconciled to some other rule of equal authority, but which, apparently, is in hostility to the first. Such then, is the utmost and highest aim of the Paleyian or the Ciceronian ethics, as they exist.—DE QUINCEY, THOMAS, 1853, *Literary Reminiscences, ch.* xxiii.

Paley is a hard-headed North-countryman, whose chief mental sustenance has been a severe course of Cambridge mathematics. He is throughout a systematiser, not an original thinker; and his system begins by expelling as far as possible everything that is not as solid and tangible as a proposition in Euclid. Moreover, his ethical treatise is, in fact, intended for educational purposes. In such works, clearness and order are the cardinal virtues, and originality, if not a vice, is of equivocal advantage. Paley primarily is a condenser and a compiler; though he modestly enough claims to be "more than a mere compiler." He gives a lucid summary of the most generally accepted system; and if there is any gleam of originality in his writing, it is, for the most part, such as occasionally results from a rearrangement of old materials. . . . Paley, with his undeniable merits as a reasoner, was not the man to desert the paths into which he had been guided. He has simply given a compact statement of what may be called the orthodox theory.—STEPHEN, LESLIE, 1876, *History of English Thought in the Eighteenth Century, vol.* II, *p.* 121.

It has been, I think, the fortuue of this work to be of late years very unduly depreciated, partly because, in consequence of the singular charm and lucidity of its style, it has been so widely read, studied, and criticised that all its weak points have been fully disclosed, and partly also because the particular type of the utilitarian theory of ethics which it teaches has been generally abandoned. It is, however, both in form and substance, one of the masterpieces of the eighteenth century, and the author was much too shrewd a man not to know that the doctrines which he taught were not likely under George III. to lead a clergyman to the bench.—LECKY, WILLIAM EDWARD HARTPOLE, 1887, *A History of England in the Eighteenth Century, vol.* v, *ch.* xix, *p.* •171.

HORÆ PAULINÆ
1790

He proceeds with infinite acuteness and ingenuity to produce most striking instances of *undesigned* coincidences in the documents in question. Many of his sentiments and expressions are eminently happy.—GREEN, THOMAS, 1810, *Diary of a Lover of Literature.*

He is singularly ingenious in hitting on a casual argument where a common mind would have overlooked it. He makes his deduction just as far as that instance bears him out, and no farther; and, on proper occasions, he presses his reasonings with convincing force.—ORME, WILLIAM, 1824, *Bibliotheca Biblica.*

Paley's "Horæ Paulinæ" is perhaps the most original and ingenious of his productions which may be called strictly professional; but his "Moral Philosophy" and "Natural Theology" will probably make his name longer known to posterity.— DIBDIN, THOMAS FROGNALL, 1824, *The Library Companion, p.* 88, *note.*

It would not be in the power of the most suspicious lawyer, at the Old Bailey, to subject two witnesses to stricter crossexamination than that by which Paley has tried the testimony of St. Paul and St. Luke. This is the light in which the "Horæ Paulinæ" is to be viewed: it is a close, and rigorous, and searching series of questions, addressed to two men deponents to certain facts, and addressed, too, by a most acute advocate, in open court, before an intelligent tribunal.— BLUNT, J. J., 1828, *Works and Character of Paley, Quarterly Review, vol.* 38, *p.* 317.

The "Horæ Paulinæ" is remarkably adapted for the profitable exercise of the minds of law-students. It is pronounced by one of the highest authorities upon such matters, Dr. Whately, to be "an incomparable specimen of reasoning,"—and of that kind of reasoning, moreover, with which lawyers are peculiarly conversant, and in which they do and ought to excel. Independently of the pre-eminent value

and importance of such an undertaking, in a religious point of view, such an interesting and masterly exhibition of logical acuteness ought to be familiar to all capable of appreciating and profiting by it. —WARREN, SAMUEL, 1835–45, *Popular and Practical Introduction to Law Studies, pp.* 224, 225.

EVIDENCES OF CHRISTIANITY
1793

Mr. Paley's book has been universally well received, and the first edition is already gone. As he wrote and published it at my desire, I have just given him a prebend of St. Paul's as a mark of my approbation and gratitude. It has given me much pleasure to find that this book has been much read and approved at Cambridge, where I think it will do essential service.—PORTEUS, BEILBY, 1793, *Letter to Hannah More, Memoirs, ed. Roberts, vol.* I, *p.* 424.

It is almost superfluous to name a work so universally known as Dr. Paley's "View of the Evidences of Christianity," which is probably, without exception, the most clear and satisfactory statement of the historical proofs of the Christian religion ever exhibited in any age or country.—HALL, ROBERT, 1800, *Modern Infidelity Considered with Respect to its Influence on Society, Preface.*

We regard Dr. Paley's writings on the "Evidences of Christianity" as of so signally decisive a character, that we could be content to let them stand as the essence and the close of the great argument on the part of its believers; and should feel no despondency or chagrin if we could be prophetically certified that such an efficient Christian reasoner would never henceforward arise. We should consider the grand fortress of proof as now raised and finished—the intellectual capitol of that empire which is destined to leave the widest boundaries attained by the Roman very far behind. . . . It is impossible to hear, with the slightest degree of respect or patience the expressions of doubt or anxiety about the truth of Christianity, from any one who can delay a week to obtain the celebrated "View of its Evidences," or fail to read it through again and again. It is of no use to say what would be our opinion of the moral and intellectual state of his mind, if after this he remained still undecided.—FOSTER, JOHN, 1809, *Paley as a Theologian, Critical Essays, ed. Ryland, vol.* I, *pp.* 236, 238.

I am glad you can speak so respectfully of Paley's Evidences as you do in your Preface. I have a sneaking regard for him, as a good, tough North of England man, not spoiled by his cleverness as a lawyer. But I have been fighting against him all my days; I cannot help thinking he has done much to demoralise Cambridge, and to raise up a set of divines who turn out a bag infidel on Sundays to run him down, fixing exactly where he shall run, and being exceedingly provoked if he finds any holes and corners which they do not happen to know of. I do not mean that Paley was at all like these disciples; but I have a spite against him for their sakes.— MAURICE, FREDERICK DENISON, 1863, *To Rev. Charles Kingsley, Aug.* 11; *Life, ed. Maurice, vol.* II, *p.* 450.

Paley was an able writer on the proofs of Christianity, yet bases his ethical system on the skeptical, materialistic view of obligation. He found in his spiritual philosophy, no higher inspiration, no weightier law for the duties of ordinary life, than came to Hume in absolute unbelief, generalizing a transient law of action, from the unsubstantial fleeting facts afloat about him,—the gains and losses that fall to us under them. The belief and unbelief of England often strike hands on this question of morals, intimate as it is to daily life and character.—BASCOM, JOHN, 1874, *Philosophy of English Literature, p.* 309.

The task is so judiciously performed that it would probably be difficult to get a more effective statement of the external evidences of Christianity than Paley has here presented. The general position, however, that the action of the first preachers of Christianity was due "solely" to their belief in the occurrence of certain miraculous events is on the same level as the view that "the proper business of a revelation" is to certify future rewards and punishments. It betrays a defective analysis of the religious consciousness. For the rest, his idea of revelation depends upon the same mechanical conception of the relation of God to the world which dominates his "Natural Theology," and he seeks to prove the divine origin of Christianity by isolating it from the general history of mankind,

whereas later writers find their chief argument in the continuity of the process of revelation.—SETH, ANDREW, 1885, *Encyclopædia Britannica, Ninth ed., vol.* XVIII, *p.* 186.

All his works, the most famous and characteristic of which is his "Evidences," exhibit a peculiar hard-headedness of thought and the utmost lucidity of expression.—SAINTSBURY, GEORGE, 1886, *Specimens of English Prose Style, p.* 244.

The evidences of the truth of the Christian religion, and the proofs of the Being of a God had never been presented in a form that seemed to bring them so nearly within the grasp of the ordinary human understanding. Yet after 100 years Paley's work on the subject seems to have many defects. In particular the Argument from Design is, as he gave it, founded too narrowly on the analogies of physical mechanism. The very facts of physiology, so carefully and minutely described (such as the phenomena of seeing and hearing), and the facts of biology as to the growth of life in the world, are all translated into terms of mechanical adaptation and compared to the watch or the windlass. He bore the stamp of his time. It is fairer to point to such defects in philosophical argument than to treat Paley's reasoning as discredited throughout by an *arrière-pensée.* No doubt like most men he did not refuse advancement, and he may even have courted it. But the social optimism which made him think that the labourers of England had nearly every reason in 1791 to be contented with their condition is of a piece with the metaphysical optimism which made him regard the organisation of living beings as nearly perfect. It seems also true that his theology, which gave character to to his utilitarianism, qualified his optimism. The world is a place of probation, and therefore is not perfect. Christianity would make men perfectly happy; but it has not been universally accepted. Paley is theologian first and philosopher afterwards.—BONAR, J., 1895, *English Prose, ed. Craik, vol.* IV, *p.* 498.

NATURAL THEOLOGY
1802

As a collection of striking facts and powerful arguments for the existence of a wise and beneficient Creator, this publication is certainly entitled to a very favourable reception. . . . Dr. Paley's chief excellence consists in the judicious disposition of his forces, and the skill and confidence with which he has extended his array to every point which atheism has affected to menace. . . . The language of this book is by no means remarkable for dignity or elegance. Perspicuity and conciseness, seem to have been the only accomplishments of style which the author was ambitious of acquiring; and to these his praise must be confined. There is a great carelessness of composition throughout the whole volume, and a colloquial homeliness of diction, upon some occasions, that does not seem altogether suitable either to the gravity of the subject, or the dignity of the writer.—JEFFREY, FRANCIS LORD, 1803, *Natural Theology, Edinburgh Review, vol. I, pp.* 304, 305.

It may be affirmed that a more important and generally useful work has scarcely at any time been published than the "Natural Theology."—JOYCE, JEREMIAH, 1804, *A Full and Complete Analysis of Dr. Paley's Natural Theology, p.* iii.

His "Natural Theology" will open the heart, that it may understand, or at least receive, the Scriptures, if anything can. It is philosophy in its highest and noblest sense; scientific, without the jargon of science; profound, but so clear that its depth is disguised.—BLUNT, J. J., 1828, *Works and Character of Paley, Quarterly Review, vol.* 38, *p.* 312.

His "Natural Theology" is the wonderful work of a man who, after sixty, had studied anatomy in order to write it; and it could only have been surpassed by one who, to great originality of conception and clearness of exposition, added the advantage of a high place in the first class of physiologists.—MACKINTOSH, SIR JAMES, 1830, *Dissertations on the Progress of Ethical Philosophy.*

Paley's "Theology" has been to me a treasure of instruction and delight: the concluding chapter of the Goodness of God is invaluable, especially where he speaks of the alleviations afforded to those who suffer under the most painful diseases, and the compensation of delight which results from the first interval of ease. My imperfect recollection injures the subject; but on lately reading his life by his son, his faith and patience appeared more exalted when I found that this testimony to the Divine goodness, in affording support, was written in the few intervals of ease afforded during a dreadful disorder, which proved fatal not long after.—GRANT, ANNE, 1832, *Letters, Sept.* 19; *Memoir and Correspondence, ed. Grant, vol.* III, *p.* 213.

His "Natural Theology" is the best work on the sublimest subject of human contemplation—the wisdom of God in the works of nature—that exists in our language.—ALISON, SIR ARCHIBALD, 1853–59, *History of Europe,* 1815–52, *vol.* I, *ch.* v.

I do not think I hardly ever admired a book more than Paley's "Natural Theology." I could almost formerly have said it by heart.—DARWIN, CHARLES, 1859, *To John Lubbock, Nov.* 15; *Life and Letters, ed. Darwin, vol.* II, *p.* 15.

So wonderful for its beauty, for its skilful statement, for its common sense, so valuable as a logical basis for the Christian faith, that the world will not willingly let it die.—WELSH, ALFRED H., 1883, *Development of English Literature and Language, vol.* II, *p.* 184.

GENERAL

I have enclosed a little work of that great and good man Archdeacon Paley; it is entitled "Motives of Contentment," addressed to the poorer part of our fellowmen. The twelfth page I particularly admire, and the twentieth. The reasoning has been of some service to *me,* who am of the race of the Grumbletonians.—COLERIDGE, SAMUEL TAYLOR, 1793, *To Mrs. Evans, Feb.* 5; *Letters, ed. Coleridge, vol.* I, *p.* 47.

The name of Dr. Paley, though scarcely to be reckoned among those of the *great* theologians and philosophers of England, is probably associated with as large and an enviable a portion of public approbation, as that of any living ecclesiastic. With less learning and less originality than some of his distinguished predecessors, it would be difficult, perhaps, to point out his superior in soundness of judgment, or in vigilant and comprehensive sagacity. . . . Almost all the writings of Dr. Paley relate to the highest and most important questions upon which human reason can be exercised, and appear to have been composed with suitable caution and deliberation. They are elaborate, rather than ingenious; and seem to have been diligently meditated, and carefully arranged, rather than to have been conceived in any fervour of imagination, or poured forth in any conviction of their infallibility. The utmost pains are taken, therefore, to render everything intelligible and precise; and more anxiety is shown that nothing necessary shall be omitted, than that all superfluity should be excluded. All cavil is prevented by a jealous strictness of expression; and a few homely illustrations are commonly sufficient to expose those illusions, by which a false philosophy is supported in so many of her unsubstantial speculations.— JEFFREY, FRANCIS LORD, 1803, *Natural Theology, Edinburgh Review, vol.* I, *pp.* 287, 288.

No reader of Dr. Paley's former works will open his Sermons with any expectation of what we usually call eloquence. . . . In speaking of the effect which we have felt in reading parts of these Sermons, from the cool and somewhat austere manner in which the most interesting subjects are presented, we have described something different from the usual course of our experience: from our manner of accounting for it, we shall not be misunderstood to approve, in general, of so cold a manner of exhibiting the subjects of supreme consequence; for popular addresses we condemn it totally. . . . It would be ridiculous in us to affect to recommend a volume written by Dr. Paley. It will be extensively read; its readers will receive many useful and striking thoughts; and we earnestly wish they may study the New Testament enough to be saved from any injurious impression of what we cannot allow ourselves to regard as unimportant errors.—FOSTER, JOHN, 1809, *Paley as a Theologian, Critical Essays, ed. Ryland, vol.* I, *pp.* 241, 243, 251.

Paley's writings have done more for the moral improvement of mankind than perhaps the writings of any other man that ever existed. The doctrines laid down and established by this wise and able writer may be considered as the principia of moral physiology!—WINDHAM, WILLIAM, 1810, *Speech, Feb.* 9.

To prove the existence of God, as Paley has attempted to do, is like lighting a lantern to seek for the sun. If you look hard by your lantern, you may miss your search.—CARLYLE, THOMAS, 1826, *Note Books, Life by Froude, vol.* I, *p.* 306.

This excellent writer, who after Clarke and Butler, ought to be ranked among the brightest ornaments of the English Church in the eighteenth century, is, in the history of philosophy, naturally placed after Tucker, to whom with praiseworthy liberality, he owns his extensive obligations. It is a mistake to suppose that he owed his system to Hume, a thinker too refined, and a writer perhaps too elegant, to have naturally attracted him. . . . The natural frame of Paley's understanding fitted it more for business and the world than for philosophy; and he accordingly enjoyed with considerable relish the few opportunities which the latter part of his life afforded of taking a part in the affairs of his county as a magistrate. . . . His style is as near perfection in its kind as any in our language. Perhaps no words were ever more expressive and illustrative than those in which he represents the art of life to be that of rightly "setting our habits."—MACKINTOSH, SIR JAMES, 1830, *Dissertation on the Progress of Ethical Philosophy.*

There is no name in the English Church, perhaps, that should stand higher than his; there are few in the vast circles of English literature whose just fame shall be more extensively or permanently recorded. —BARNES, ALBERT, 1838–55, *Address Delivered before the Society of Inquiry in Amherst College, Aug.* 21; *Essays and Reviews, vol.* II, *p.* 217.

Nothing can drop from the pen of such a writer, so remarkable for his clearness and excellent sense, that can be without its importance, particularly where the subject has any immediate connection with the business of human life. . . . Johnson and Paley, Locke and Butler, immediately occur as the great masters of moral, metaphysical, and religious instruction,—Locke the votary of truth; and Paley, the very genius of good sense. — SMYTH, WILLIAM, 1839, *Lectures on Modern History, Lectures* xxiv, xxix.

His mind was essentially English and English in its best mood. He was not remarkable for his learning, though far from being ill-informed; but the bent of his mind was not toward scholarship. He was eminently practical in his ideas; his thoughts, descending from the clouds, ever turned to some object of actual importance in real life. His mind was not of the most elevated cast; and accoraingly he made *utility* the great object of life and measure of actions. He will never be a favourite, accordingly, with that handful of men who nevertheless alone do great things in the world, who aim at the noble and generous in all things, and let the useful take care of itself. But, while his disposition precluded him from rising to the highest rank in literature, which never is to be attained but by the influence of lofty feelings, whithin his limits, and in a lower sphere, he was very admirable and eminently useful.—ALISON, SIR ARCHIBALD, 1853–59, *History of Europe*, 1815–1852, *vol.* I, *ch.* v.

All the theological works of all the numerous bishops whom he (Pitt) made and translated are not, when put together, worth fifty pages of the "Horæ Paulinæ," of the "Natural Theology," or of the "View of the Evidences of Christianity." But on Paley the all-powerful minister never bestowed the smallest benefice.—MACAULAY, THOMAS BABINGTON, 1859, *William Pitt, Critical and Miscellaneous Essays.*

No Englishman will refuse to join with Coleridge in "the admiration" he expresses "for the head and heart" of Paley, "the incomparable grace, propriety, and persuasive facility of his writings." But Paley had unfortunately dedicated his powers to a factitious thesis; his demonstration, however perfect, is in unreal matter.—PATTISON, MARK, 1860, *Religious Thought in England, Essays, ed. Nettelship, vol.* II, *p.* 50.

His intellect was clear and steady. He is a shining example of the form of practical good sense characteristic of Englishmen. He did not hunt after paradoxes and subtleties, nor did he throw himself with eagerness into original investigations. He liked to walk on sure ground, and made abundant use of the labours of others. . . . His writings contain little or nothing to satisfy the emotions; occasionally we cross a pleasant vein of irony or sarcasm, and we are constantly entertained with homely facts, but high-flown sentiment is totally wanting. . . . Although Paley's language is not studiously varied, he never seems to be in want of words, and the combinations are often agreeably fresh. His preference is for homely words; but he does not scruple to use the most technical terms,

and now and then even quotes Latin, trusting to make himself intelligible to the ordinary capacity by the power of his homely illustrations. . . . The chief thing worth noticing about Paley's sentences is that they are not constructed upon a few favourite forms, or with any leaning to a favourite rhythm. His is not a "formed" style; he is studious to express himself in simple language, without regard to measure of fluent melody. It might be expected that, having no misleading desire for euphonious combinations, he would adopt the best arrangement for emphasis. But it is not so; he had not much natural turn for point, and does not seem to have been aware of the advantage of calling special attention to a word by its position.—MINTO, WILLIAM, 1872–80, *Manual of English Prose Literature, pp.* 489, 490, 491.

No works of a theological or philosophical nature have been so extensively popular among the educated classes of England as those of Paley. His perspicacity of intellect and simplicity of style are almost unrivalled. Though plain and homely, and often inelegant, he had such vigour and discrimination, and such a happy vein of illustration, that he is always read with pleasure and instruction. No reader is ever at a loss for his meaning, or finds him too difficult for comprehension. He had the rare art for popularising the most recondite knowledge, and blending the business of life with philosophy. The principles inculcated in some of his works have been disputed, particularly his doctrine of expediency as a rule of morals, which has been considered as trenching on the authority of revealed religion, and also lowering the standard of public duty. The system of Paley certainly would not tend to foster the great and heroic virtues. —CHAMBERS, ROBERT, 1876, *Cyclopædia of English Literature, ed. Carruthers.*

Men received preferment neither from their abilities nor from their deserts, but through the interest of their friends. Paley was incomparably the ablest of living divines. But no one ever dreamed of offering him a bishopric. "Paley is a great man," said George III., "will never be a bishop—will never be a bishop."— WALPOLE, SPENCER, 1878, *A History of England from the Conclusion of the Great War in* 1815, *vol.* I, *p.* 173.

The crystal clearness and matchless grace of Paley's periods, which were the envy of Coleridge, continue to attract readers, in spite of his antiquated science and dangerous philosophy.—MATHEWS, WILLIAM, 1881, *Literary Style, p.* 7.

Paley's works, whether judiciously or not we need not pause to inquire, are still text-books at the universities, but the scepticism against which he sets his forces in array was not of the kind to which we are now accustomed, which takes much of the force from his defence. They are still however eminently readable in a merely literary point of view, and extracts might be made, in which the reader would find much happiness of expression and force of illustration, without any of the disadvantages of antiquated polemics.—OLIPHANT, MARGARET O. W., 1882, *Literary History of England, XVIII and XIX Centuries, vol.* III, *p.* 306.

The face of the world has changed so greatly since Paley's day that we are apt to do less than justice to his undoubted merits. He is nowhere original, and nowhere profound, but he justly claims to be "something more than a mere compiler." His strong reasoning power, his faculty of clear arrangement and forcible statement, place him in the first rank of expositors and advocates. He masses his arguments, it has been said, with a general's eye. His style is perfectly perspicuous, and its "strong home-touch" compensates for what is lacking in elasticity and grace. Paley's avoidance of ultimate speculative questions commended him to his own generation, and enabled him to give full scope to the shrewd practical understanding in which his strength lay.—SETH, ANDREW, 1885, *Encyclopœdia Britannica, Ninth edition, vol.* XVIII, *p.* 186.

Paley may very well be taken as characteristic of the theological style of the forty years preceding, and between Paley's literary form and the sapless legal style of Clarke, in the age of Anne, there is so little difference that we are tempted to regard these two as typical of their respective groups. If, then, we can say that in the generation of Swift leading theologians wrote like Clarke, and in the age of Burke like Paley, we are almost justified by that very circumstance in conjecturing that the contributions of eighteenth-century divinity to literature are so small that they are hardly worth considering.—GOSSE, EDMUND, 1888, *A History of Eighteenth Century Literature, p.* 396.

Paley is the most prominent instance among modern writers of a man who paragraphed on the theory of emphasis. His mechanical devices for securing prominence were numerous—different kinds of type, numerals, etc. But the man that takes up only mechanical means for securing emphasis, usually perishes by the same means: he loses in proportion what he gains in emphasis. Paley is a shining illustration of this fact.—LEWIS, EDWIN HERBERT, 1894, *The History of the English Paragraph, p.* 125.

Nobody has surpassed Paley as a writer of text-books. He is an unrivalled expositor of plain arguments, though he neither showed nor claimed much originality.—STEPHEN, LESLIE, 1895, *Dictionary of National Biography, vol.* XLIII, *p.* 105.

He was not, like Butler, an original thinker, but he was possessed of remarkable tact and common sense, and for lucidity of style is almost unrivalled. . . . An examination of Paley will show that he anticipates the hypothesis of evolution and the theory of indefinite, fortuitous variation, and shapes his argument accordingly. In his theological opinions Paley may be called a latitudinarian, although in his whole cast of thought he was at a wide remove from the school bearing that name. —FISHER, GEORGE PARK, 1896, *History of Christian Doctrine, pp.* 388, 389.

English theology in the later eighteenth century had, in fact, ceased to be speculative at all; and its philosophic impotence is peculiarly evident in the pages of its most luminous and persuasive exponent, Paley. Nowhere are the virtues and the vices of the mechanical modes of thought more easy to study than in the work of this accomplished senior wrangler, who made theology as transparently coherent as a proposition of Euclid, and as devoid of all appeal to the deeper instincts of man.—HERFORD, C. H., 1897, *The Age of Wordsworth, p.* 28.

As an apologist and expositor, Paley has been accused of a too business-like and profit-and-loss view of religion; but those who call him interested perhaps use an unfair presumption, and his popularity has no doubt suffered from his having served for generations as a class-textbook in the University of Cambridge. As a philosopher in things divine and human, he has a little too much of the merely forensic competence of the advocate about him. But this same competence extends (it may not be in the most interesting manner) to his work as literature. Paley gets the full value out of the plain style, for purposes to which it is far better adapted than anything more imaginative could possibly be. His arguments, if far lower and less noble, are much more easily intelligible than Butler's; his style is perfectly clear; he sees his point and his method distinctly and seldom or never fails to prove the one to the best of the other.—SAINTSBURY, GEORGE, 1898, *A Short History of English Literature*, p. 633.

Christopher Anstey

1724–1805.

Christopher Anstey, poet, was son of the Rev. Christopher Anstey, rector of Brinkley, Cambridgeshire, where he was born in 1724-5. He was educated at Eton and King's College, Cambridge. He was originally designed for the church, but his degrees being withheld from him, he retired into privacy "upon a competent fortune." He was rusticated from the university. . . . He entered the army, and having married a daughter of Cabert of Allbury Hall, Herts, he obtained a seat in parliament for Hertford by his father-in-law's influence. One of the most glaring of current literary blunders is the common statement that the "New Bath Guide," of Christopher Anstey was in a great measure built on Smollett's novel of "Humphrey Clinker." The facts are that the "New Bath Guide" was published in 1766, whilst "Humphrey Clinker" was not written until 1770, and was first published in 1771. . . . The "Election Ball, in Poetical Letters from Mr. Inkle at Bath to his wife at Gloucester," sustained the reputation won by the "Guide." It seems to us even more brilliant in its wit, and finely touched as verse. Other productions in verse and prose have long passed into oblivion. The poetical works were collected in 1808 (2 vols) by the author's son John, himself author of "The Pleader's Guide," in the same vein with the "New Bath Guide." He died on 3d August, 1805.—GROSART, A. B., 1875, *Encyclopædia Britannica, Ninth edition, vol.* II, *p.* 83.

PERSONAL

M. S.

CHRISTOPHERI ANSTEY, ARM.
ALUMNI ETONENSIS,
ET COLLEGII REGALIS APUD CANTABRI-
GIENSES OLIM SOCII,
POETÆ,
LITERIS ELEGANTIORIBUS ADPRIMÈ ORNATI,
ET INTER PRINCIPES POETARUM,
QUI IN EODEM GENERE FLORUERUNT,
SEDEM EXIMIAN TENENTIS.
ILLE ANNUM CIRCITER
MDCCLXX.
RUS SUUM IN AGRO CANTABRIGIENSI
MUTAVIT BATHONIÂ,
QUEM LOCUM EI PRÆTER OMNE DUDUM
ARRISISSE
TESTIS EST, CELEBERRIMUM ILLUD POEMA,
TITULO INDE DUCTO INSIGNITUM:
IBI DEINCEPS SEX ET TRIGINTA ANNOS
COMMORATUS,
OBIIT A. D. MDCCCV.
ET ÆTATIS SUÆ
OCTOGESIMO PRIMO.
—INSCRIPTION ON CENOTAPH, *Westminster Abbey*.

Mr. Anstey was often with me, and you will believe he was very droll and entertaining; but what recommends him more, is his great attention to his family. He has eight children. He instructs his boys in the Greek and Latin, so that they are fitted for the upper forms of Eton School, where their education is finished. He has a house in the Crescent, at which he resides the greatest part of the year. Mrs. Anstey is a very sensible, amiable woman, and does not deal in the gossip of the place. — MONTAGU, ELIZABETH, 1779, *Letter to Mrs. Robinson, June* 13; *A Lady of the Last Century*, ed. *Doran*, p. 249.

THE NEW BATH GUIDE

1766

Have you read the "New Bath Guide?" It is the only thing in fashion, and is a new and original kind of humour.—GRAY, THOMAS, 1766, *Letter to Thomas Wharton, Aug.* 26, *Works; ed. Gosse, vol.* III, *p.* 245.

It is a set of letters in verse, in all kind of verses, describing the life at Bath, and incidentally everything else; but so much wit, so much humour, fun, and poetry, so much originality, never met together before. Then the man has a better ear than Dryden or Handel. *Apropos* to Dryden, he has burlesqued his St. Cecilia, that you will never read it again without laughing. There is a description of a milliner's box in all the terms of landscape, *painted lawns and chequered shades*, a Moravian ode, and a Methodist ditty, that are incomparable, and the best names that ever were composed. — WALPOLE, HORACE, 1766, *To George Montagu, June* 20; *Letters, ed. Cunningham, vol.* IV, *p.* 504.

The very ingenious scheme of describing the various effects produced upon different members of the same family by the same objects, was not original, though it has been supposed to be so. Anstey the facetious author of the "New Bath Guide," has employed it six or seven years before "Humphrey Clinker" appeared. But Anstey's diverting satire was but a light sketch compared to the finish and elaborate manner in which Smollett has, in the first place, identified his characters, and then fitted them with language, sentiments, and powers of observation, in exact correspondence with their talents, temper, condition, and disposition. — SCOTT, SIR WALTER, 1821, *Tobias Smollett.*

Is not the fashion as well as faction of the time thus reflected to us vividly? *Now*, all excepting Christopher Anstey are forgotten, of these admired ones; nor is it likely that even Anstey would have been noticed with anything but a sneer, if, besides being a scholar and a wit, he had not also been a member of parliament. Beyond the benches of the Houses, too, or the gossip of St. James's, this affluence reached. It was social rank that had helped Anstey, for this poem of the "New Bath Guide," to no less a sum than two hundred pounds; it was because Goldsmith had no other rank than as a man of letters, depressed and at that time very slowly rising, that his "Traveller" had obtained for him only twenty guineas. — FORSTER, JOHN, 1848–54, *The Life and Times of Oliver Goldsmith, vol.* II, *p.* 25.

The versification of this is remarkably graceful, and the spirit of good-humoured raillery is admirably kept up. The similarity of the metre and the subject of Moore's "Fudge Family in Paris," suggests a comparison which may be worked

out not at all unfavorable to Anstey. — CREASY, SIR EDWARD, 1850–75, *Memoirs of Eminent Etonians, p.* 550.

Perhaps the best description of Bath in its heyday of fashion and popularity a century ago, is to be found in the verse of Anstey, burlesque although it be. "The New Bath Guide," written in a light and tripping manner, well adapted to the subject and little previously known, had an immense vogue in its day; a vogue all the greater that some of the characters were supposed to be real, and the poignancy of personal satire was added to general pleasantry. It is so far forgotten by the general reader, that the extracts upon which I may venture will probably be as good as new. I do not apologize for a few omissions rendered necessary by the better manners of our times. — MITFORD, MARY RUSSELL, 1851, *Recollections of a Literary Life, p.* 328.

"The New Bath Guide" does not rise or aspire to rise above a rattling vivacity, and has been far surpassed in brilliancy by later productions in the same style; but it is entitled to be remembered as the earliest successful attempt of its class. — CRAIK, GEORGE L., 1861, *A Compendious History of English Literature and of the English Language, vol.* II, *p.* 307.

GENERAL

Since the *first* edition of the "Bath Guide," never was a duller goose than Anstey!—WALPOLE, HORACE, 1786, *To the Countess of Ossory, Sept.* 28; *Letters, ed. Cunningham, vol.* IX, *p.* 68.

His other works hardly required the investigation of their date. In the decline of life he meditated a collection of his letters and poems; but letters recovered from the repositories of dead friends are but melancholy readings; and, probably overcome by the sensations which they excited, he desisted from his collection. —CAMPBELL, THOMAS, 1819, *Specimens of the British Poets.*

A painter and a poet were, perhaps, never more similar to each other in their talents than the contemporaries Bunbury and Anstey. There is in both an admirable power of seizing the ludicrous and the grotesque in their descriptions of persons and incidents in familiar life; and this accompanied by an elegance which might have seemed scarcely compatible with that power. There is in both an absence of any extraordinary elevation or vigour ; which we do not regret, because we can hardly conceive but that they would be less pleasing if they were in any respect different from what they are. Each possesses a perfect facility and command over his own peculiar manner, which has secured him from having any successful imitator. Yet as they were both employed in representing the fortuitous and transient follies, which the face of society had put on in their own day, rather than in portraying the broader and more permanent distinctions of character and manners, it may be questioned whether they can be much relished out of their own country, and whether even there, the effect must not be weakened as fatuity and absurdity shall discover new methods of fastening ridicule upon themselves.

They border more nearly on farce than comedy. They have neither of them any thing of fancy, that power which can give a new and higher interest to the laughable itself, by mingling it with the marvellous, and which has placed Aristophanes so far above all his followers. . . . On the whole, he has the rare merit of having discovered a mode of entertaining his readers, which belongs exclusively to himself.—CARY, HENRY FRANCIS, 1821–24–45, *Lives of English Poets, pp.* 188, 190.

Anstey never repeated the success of the "New Bath Guide." His reputation as a rhymester and humorist attracted attention to his subsequent performances, but they have neither the freshness nor the vivacity of his first effort.—DOBSON, AUSTIN, 1885, *Dictionary of National Biography, vol.* II, *p.* 39.

Arthur Murphy
1730–1805.

Born in county Roscommon, Ireland ; educated at St. Omer's college (1740–47), and spent two years in Cork in business. He then went to London and entered upon his career as literary man, dramatist, and actor. From 1752 to 1754 he published a periodical called "The Gray's Inn Journal," and afterwards a political Journal "The Test," both unsuccessful. As an actor he appeared at Covent Garden and Drury Lane Theatres, but did not meet with much favor. He now adopted the study of law and began practice in 1757, but once more with little success. He had already published a farce "The Apprentice," which had some popularity, and now occupied himself entirely in writing farces and comedies. In this he gained some wealth and a high reputation as a dramatist. Among the most successful of his pieces were, "The Upholsterer;" "The Way to Keep Him;" "All in the Wrong;" and "Know your Own Mind." In 1792 he published an essay on Dr. Johnson, and soon after a translation of Tacitus : his life of Garrick was printed in 1801. A few years before his death a pension of £200 and the office of commissioner of bankrupts were bestowed on him by the English government.—PECK, HARRY THURSTON, ed., 1898, *The International Cyclopædia, vol.* X, *p.* 202.

PERSONAL

As one with various disappointments sad,
Whom dulness, only, kept from being mad,
Apart from all the rest great Murphy came—
Common to fools and wits, the rage of fame.
What tho' the sons of nonsense hail him sire,
Auditor, author, manager and squire!
His restless soul's ambition stops not there ;
To make his triumphs perfect, dub him Player.
In person tall, a figure form'd to please,
If symmetry could charm, deprived of ease ;
When motionless he stands, we all approve ;
What pity 'tis the Thing was made to move!
. . . .
Still in extremes, he knows no happy mean,
Or raving mad, or stupidly serene.
In cold-wrought scenes the lifeless actor flags ;

In passion, tears the passion into rags.
Can none remember? Yes—I know all must—
When in the Moor he ground his teeth to dust,
When o'er the stage he folly's standard bore,
Whilst Common-Sense stood trembling at the door.
—CHURCHILL, CHARLES, 1761, *The Rosciad.*

A manner so studied, so vacant a face,
These features the mind of our Murphy disgrace,
A mind unaffected, soft, artless, and true,
A mind which, though ductile, has dignity too.
Where virtues ill-sorted are huddled in heaps,
Humanity triumphs, and piety sleeps ;
A mind in which mirth may with merit reside,
And Learning turns Frolic, with Humor, his guide.

31 C

Whilst wit, follies, faults, its fertility prove,
Till the faults you grow fond of, the follies
    you love,
And corrupted at length by the sweet con-
    versation,
You swear there's no honesty left in the
    nation.
—PIOZZI, HESTER LYNCH, 1773? *The
Streatham Portraits, Autobiography,* ed.
Hayward, p. 254.

Though apparently formed to captivate the sex, having every advantage which a fine face, a tall and graceful person, and dignified gentlemanly manners could give, Arthur Murphy was never induced to enter the marriage-state. Politely declining a romantic proposal made to him in early life, by the brother of a lady he had never seen, there is no record of any second negotiation. With some faults of temper, which probably proved the source of all his disappointments, he seems to have possessed a warm affectionate heart and a generous unselfish spirit. His attachments were cordial and steady, and totally free from any sordid consideration respecting money; his liberality did not render him unjust; he died poor, but devoid of debt; and, though he might have repented many acts of imprudence, there was no transaction of his life of which he had cause to be ashamed. Nor was the lustre of Murphy's talents obscured by folly of any kind; he put forth no absurd pretentions—displayed no over-weening vanity; securing in society the respect of his associates, and making a distinguished figure without any ambition to shine.—
DUNHAM, S. ASTLEY, 1838, *ed., Eminent Literary and Scientific Men of Great Britain and Ireland, vol.* III, *p.* 339.

I knew Murphy long and intimately; I was introduced to him by the Piozzis at Streatham. On the first night of any of his plays, if the slightest symptoms of disapprobation were shown by the audience, Murphy always left the house, and took a walk in Covent-Garden Market: then, after having composed himself, he would return to the theatre.—ROGERS, SAMUEL, 1855, *Recollections of Table Talk,* ed. *Dyce, p.* 106.

GENERAL

The attempt to naturalize the works of Tacitus has been justly considered, by the best scholars, as an achievement of great difficulty; and if Mr. Murphy has not altogether succeeded in preserving the style and manner of his author, which, terse and condensed as they are, are scarcely susceptible of transfusion, he has, however, presented the English reader with a faithful though a rather paraphrastic interpretation of a most useful and masterly historian, at the same time supplying many of the chasms which time had effected in the original.—DRAKE, NATHAN, 1810, *Essays Illustrative of the Rambler, Adventurer and Idler, vol.* II, *p.* 251.

Murphy's plays of "All in the Wrong" and "Know Your Own Mind," are admirably written; with sense, spirit, and conception of character, but without any great effect of the humourous, or that truth of feeling which distinguishes the boundary between the absurdities of natural character and the gratuitous fictions of the poet's pen. The heroes of these two plays, Millamour and Sir Benjamin Constant, are too ridiculous in their caprices to be tolerated, except in farce; and yet their follies are so flimsy, so motiveless, and fine-spun, as not to be intelligible, or to have any effect in their only proper sphere. Both his principle pieces are said to have suffered by their similarity, first, to Colman's "Jealous Wife," and next to the "School for Scandal," though in both cases he had the undoubted priority. It is hard that the fate of plagiarism should attend upon originality; yet it is clear that the elements of the "School for Scandal" are not sparingly scattered in Murphy's comedy of "Know Your Own Mind," which appeared before the latter play, only to be eclipsed by it.—HAZLITT, WILLIAM, 1818, *Lectures on the English Comic Writers, Lecture* viii.

Had the reputation of Murphy rested solely upon his tragic writings, he would have had little title to lasting fame. Notwithstanding his admiration for Shakspeare, and his capability of appreciating all the beauties of that exquisite genius, he made no attempt to pursue the same bold track, contenting himself with the turgid, pompous declamation which were the characteristics of the serious drama of his time. . . . No man ever did more for the cause of morality, in composing for the theatre, than the writer now under review; there is not a simple passage in any one of his plays that can justly give offence to the most fastidious reader; his wit is of a chaste and refined description, and he delighted in displaying the female character in its most charming point of view. During his public career he had to contend against prejudices occasioned by the strong part which he took in politics, and against the attack of hosts of newspaper writers, who envied him his talents, and hated him for his success; but though he did not disdain to defend himself when thus assailed, the hostilities which ensued led to nothing more than a petty kind of warfare, not worthy of a chronicle.—DUNHAM, S. ASTLEY, 1838, ed., *Eminent Literary and Scientific Men of Great Britain and Ireland,* vol. III, pp. 328, 336.

The translation [Tacitus] wants the compression of the original, and is too paraphrastic. The English language would not well admit of the brevity of Tacitus

without rendering the narration abrupt and obscure. The translation is distinguished for elegance and strength and dignity, and gives the sense of the original with fidelity.—KENT, JAMES, 1840–53, *A Course of English Reading,* ed. *Oakley.*

The comedies of Murphy have not in all cases lost the spirit of the originals from which he took them. Several of them were acted early in the present century. His tragedies are among the worst that have obtained any reputation. "Zenobia," however, was played as late as 1815, and the "Grecian Daughter" many years later. Totally devoid of invention, Murphy invariably took his plots from previous writers. He showed, however, facility and skill in adapting them to English tastes.—KNIGHT, JOSEPH, 1894, *Dictionary of National Biography,* vol. XXXIX, p. 336.

Mungo Park

1771–1806?

Traveler, born at Fowlshiels, Scotland, Sept. 10, 1771; studied surgery at Edinburgh, and was 1792–93 assistant surgeon in India. Under the auspices of the African Association, London, he was the pioneer in the modern exploration of Africa. He journeyed up the Gambia (1795), suffering extreme hardships, and being a prisoner for some time in the hands of a Moorish king. Escaping on July 1, 1796, he reached the upper Niger, the great object of his search, at Segu, and followed the river toward Timbuctoo as far as Silla, where he was compelled to turn back. After seven months' illness and great hardships he reached the mouth of the Gambia, having been nineteen months in the interior. This journey was described in his book, "Travels in the Interior of Africa." The British Government sent him (1805) to descend the Niger from the upper river, and trace its entire course. Most of his party died of fever, and before the Niger was reached only five white men were left out of forty-four. The party set sail down the river, at first in two canoes, but soon built a little schooner, with which they descended the Niger some 1,500 miles, where they were treacherously attacked by a large party of natives, and Park and all his company perished in the attempt to escape by swimming. The journals he sent home and information collected by Clapperton and Lander have given all the facts that are known of his last expedition. —ADAMS, CYRUS C., rev., 1897, *Johnson's Universal Cyclopædia,* vol. VI, p. 448.

PERSONAL

It grieves me to the heart to write anything that may give you uneasiness; but such is the will of Him who *doeth all things well!* Your brother Alexander, my dear friend, is no more! He died of the fever at Sansanding, on the morning of the 28th of October; for particulars I must refer you to your father. I am afraid that, impressed with a woman's fears and the anxieties of a wife, you may be led to consider my situation as a great deal worse than it really is. It is true, my

dear friends, Mr. Anderson and George Scott, have both bid adieu to the things of this world; and the greater part of the soldiers have died on the march during the rainy season; but you may believe me, I am in good health. The rains are completely over, and the healthy season has commenced, so that there is no danger of sickness; and I have still a sufficient force to protect me from any insult in sailing down the river, to sea. . . . I think it not unlikely but I shall be in England before you receive this.—You may be sure that I feel happy at turning my face towards home. We this morning have done with all intercourse with the natives; and the sails are now hoisting for our departure for the coast.—PARK, MUNGO, 1805, *Letter to Mrs. Park from Sansanding, Nov. 19.*

It might have been expected, that a person who had been so much accustomed to literary and scientific society, and who had lately been in some degree admitted into the fashionable circles of the metropolis, in which he had become an object of much interest and attention, would have felt great repugnance to the solitude and obscurity of a small market town. But this does not appear to have been the case. General society, for which indeed he was not particularly suited, was not much to his taste; and during every period of his life, he always looked forward to a state of complete retirement and seclusion in the country, as the object and end of all his labours. He had great enjoyment however in his own domestic circle, and in the society of select friends. . . . In his person he was tall, being about six feet high, and perfectly well proportioned. His countenance and whole appearance were highly interesting; and his frame active and robust, fitted for great exertions and the endurance of great hardships. His constitution had suffered considerably from the effects of his first journey into Africa, but seems afterwards to have been restored to its original vigour, of which his last expedition afforded the most ample proofs. Park's family consisted of three sons and one daughter, all of whom, together with Mrs. Park, their mother, are now living. He also left a mother, four brothers (of whom one is lately dead), and three sisters. —WHISHAW, JOHN, 1815, *The Journal of a Mission to the Interior of Africa in the Year 1805, by Mungo Park, to which is Prefixed an Account of His Life, pp.* 32, 84.

His character will be best understood by a careful examination of his life; but it may be useful to remark, in conclusion, that, although his natural prudence seems partly to have forsaken him during his second journey, few men have possessed in a higher degree the virtues of a traveller—intrepidity, enthusiasm, perseverance, veracity, prudence; his manners, likewise, though somewhat too stiff and reserved, must upon the whole have been agreeable, since he was able both in civilized and savage countries to gain and preserve many friends.—ST. JOHN, JAMES AUGUSTUS, 1832, *The Lives of Celebrated Travellers, vol.* III, *p.* 65.

During this autumn Scott formed the personal acquaintance of Mungo Park, the celebrated victim of African discovery. On his return from his first expedition, Park endeavoured to establish himself as a medical practitioner in the town of Hawick, but the drudgeries of that calling in such a district soon exhausted his ardent temper, and he was now living in seclusion in his native cottage at Fowlsheils on the Yarrow, nearly opposite Newark Castle. . . . His thoughts had always continued to be haunted with Africa. He told Scott, that whenever he awoke suddenly in the night, owing to a nervous disorder with which he was troubled, he fancied himself still a prisoner in the tent of Ali; but when the poet expressed some surprise that he should design again to revisit those scenes, he answered, he would rather brave Africa and all its horrors, than wear out his life in long and toilsome rides over the hills of Scotland, for which remuneration was hardly enough to keep soul and body together. Towards the end of the autumn, when about to quit his country for the last time, Park paid Scott a farewell visit and slept at Ashestiel. Next morning his host accompanied him homewards over the wild chain of hills between the Tweed and the Yarrow. Park talked much of his new scheme, and mentioned his determination to tell his family that he had some business for a day or two in Edinburgh, and send them his blessing from thence, without returning to take leave. He had married not long before a pretty and amiable woman; and when they reached the *Williamhope ridge,* "the autumnal mist floating heavily and slowly down the valley of the Yarrow," presented to Scott's imagination "a striking emblem of the troubled and uncertain prospect which his undertaking afforded." He remained, however, unshaken, and at length they reached the spot at which they had agreed to separate. A small ditch divided the moor from the road, and, in going over it, Park's horse stumbled, and nearly fell. "I am afraid, Mungo," said the Sheriff, "that is a bad omen." To which he answered, smiling, "*Freits* (omens) follow those who look to them."—LOCKHART, JOHN GIBSON, 1836, *Life of Sir Walter Scott, ch.* xiii.

What Ledyard wanted to complete his character, the famous Mungo Park eminently possessed. He had not so large a grasp of mind as Ledyard, but he was in no need of it. He had quite enough for his purpose, and not any of a doubtful sort to distract it. But who needs to be told what a thorough man for his purpose he was, what sufferings he went through with the simplest and most touching courage, what successes he achieved, and what a provoking, mortal mischance befell him after all? It was not so mortifying a one as Bruce's, who broke his neck down his own staircase; but it was sadder by a great deal, so far from home and on the threshold of the greatest of his adventures. —HUNT, LEIGH, 1849, *A Book for a Corner, p.* 176.

TRAVELS

But the essential merit of this book, and that which has conferred a lasting distinction on the name of its author, consists in the authentic and important information which it contains. Considered in this point of view, it must unquestionably be regarded as the greatest accession to the general stock of geographical knowledge, which was ever yet made by any single traveller. The claim of Park to this distinction will be apparent from a short view of his principal discoveries.—WHISHAW, JOHN, 1815, *The Journal of a Mission to the Interior of Africa in the Year* 1805, *by Mungo Park, to which is Prefixed an Account of his Life, p.* 16.

It is difficult for imagination to conceive a project of a more commanding, or, to a daring and contemplative spirit, a more attractive aspect, than that which Park returned to Africa, resolved to execute, or perish in the attempt. It was perfectly new, and it was vast to sublimity. It combined, in a singular manner, a definiteness of principle with a boundlessness of scope. Nothing could be more precise than the law of its execution, to follow with undeviating fidelity the course—indeed, to go with the stream—of a noble river, the directions of which had been perfectly ascertained, to a great distance, by the traveller himself; but then, no

man could tell him whither this river was to carry him, in what wilderness of lakes or sands it might desert him, or into what ocean it might, with the pride of accumulated waters, bear him down. On any hypothesis, immensity of scene was before him.—FOSTER, JOHN, 1815, *Mungo Park, Critical Essays, ed. Ryland, vol.* II, *p.* 289.

We now lay aside this interesting volume; and bid a mournful farewell to that amiable and illustrious man, whose last sufferings and exploits it is destined to record;—sufferings, borne with an unaffected cheerfulness of magnanimity, which must both exalt and endear him to all who are capable of being touched with what is generous and noble in character,— and exploits performed with a mildness and modesty, and ardour with which they were conjoined. In Mungo Park, we are not afraid to say, that the world has lost a great man,—and one who was as well qualified, as he was undoubtedly inclined, to have been one of its greatest benefactors. The account which is here given of him, is in the highest degree interesting,—not merely to those who care about Africa, but to all who take delight in the spectacle of unbounded courage and heroic ardour, unalloyed with any taint of ferocity, selfishness, or bigotry.—BROUGHAM, HENRY LORD, 1815, *Park's Last Journey and Life, Edinburgh Review, vol.* 24, *p.* 490.

Park,—a man of the most peculiar and splendid qualifications. His journey was unquestionably the most important ever performed by a European.—MURRAY, HUGH, 1817, *Historical Account of Discoveries and Travels in Africa.*

Few books of travels have acquired so speedy and extensive a reputation as this of Park's. It was sought for with an eagerness which might have done credit to a novel; and the reader—whilst his imagination was exalted by the remoteness, the eminent perils, and strange scenes of the journey—could not help feeling something like affection for a person so kindly, so resolute, and yet so unassuming. It still continues one of the most popular works of its class, and the qualities, both of its subject and manner, well deserve this pre-eminence. In pursuing it we follow the traveller with a keen anxiety; we participate in all his toils and dangers, and hairbreadth escapes, portrayed with a brief and touching simplicity, which at once awakens our sympathies by its indubitable air of truth; we are instructed and entertained by his delineation of those vast countries and the rude tribes which people them; we admire his modest though unshaken fortitude; we love the honesty and benevolent candour everywhere displayed by him. Many travellers have possessed more learning, more philosophy, and greater intellectual endowments; but none has ever known better the secret of concentrating our attention and calling forth our esteem. It required not only extraordinary strength of mind to accomplish this undertaking; no common powers of fancy and judgment were also requisite to describe it so agreeably.—CARLYLE, THOMAS, 1820-23, *Edinburgh Encyclopædia, Montaigne and other Essays, p.* 234.

Park was the first of the devoted band who returned to tell what he had seen, and his narrative was received with extreme eagerness. To this day, though many have gone, and some have returned like him, to give us knowledge, and then gone back to perish, Park's name is the most tenderly spoken, and every fragment of his experience, and of information about him, is still caught up with a stronger interest than any of his successors have ever commanded.—MARTINEAU, HARRIET, 1851, *History of England, A. D.,* 1800-1815, *p.* 536.

Thus perished Mungo Park, in the thirty-fifth year of his age; a man whose natural enthusiasm, scientific acquirements, undaunted intrepidity, patience of suffering, and inflexible perseverance—in short, every quality requisite for a traveller in the path he adopted, have never been surpassed, and who, had he survived, would no doubt have reaped those laurels, which more fortunate successors in the same career have won. To these qualities in his public character, it is pleasing to be able to add those of amiable simplicity of manners, constancy of affection, and sterling integrity in private life.—CLEVELAND, CHARLES D., 1853, *English Literature of the Nineteenth Century, p.* 70.

The style is simple and manly, and replete with a fine moral feeling.—CHAMBERS, ROBERT, 1876, *Cyclopædia of English Literature, ed. Carruthers.*

The journal of Mungo Park lacks the diffuseness and the inflated style which is so objectional a feature in Bruce's narrative. It is simple, straightforward, and possesses all the qualities of truthful history. It was at once received with favor, and still ranks among our most valuable narratives of travel in Africa.—BALDWIN, JAMES, 1883, *English Literature and Literary Criticism, Prose, p.* 129.

In lecturing and writing on the question of the innateness of conscience, or the moral sense in man, I have found no testimony as to the moral condition of the lower strata of humanity more explicit, instructive, and evidential than that given in the records of Mungo Park's "Travels in Africa," which I have not seen for more than sixty years, but which in my childhood I read with delight and wonder.—PEABODY, A. P., 1888, *Books That Have Helped Me, p.* 43.

Although Park was not spared to solve the problem which he had set himself, his discoveries and his observations enabled others to finish what he had begun; he was the first European in modern times to strike the Niger river, and he drew a correct inference when he convinced himself that the Niger "could flow nowhere but into the sea." In his travels he proved himself an explorer of untiring perseverance and inflexible resolution. His heroic efforts served to stimulate the enthusiasm of travellers who during the next twenty years followed in his footsteps, and they roused a keen public interest in African discovery and development. After James Bruce, who, like himself, was a Scotsman, he was the second great African traveller of British origin. The unaffected style and simple narration made use of by Park in the "Travels" increased the popularity of what would have been in any case a much-read book. The accuracy of the general narrative has never been impugned; but, owing to an unfortunate mistake in reckoning thirty-one days in April, the observations of longitude and latitude are not to be depended upon. The work was translated into both French and German the year after publication, and subsequently into most European languages; it has passed through a great number of editions, the quarto edition of 1799 being the best.—CARR, WILLIAM, 1895, *Dictionary of National Biography, vol.* XLIII, *p.* 221.

Henry Kirke White

1785–1806

Poet; born at Nottingham, England, Mar. 21, 1785; was the son of a butcher; was apprenticed to a stocking-weaver, and afterwards to an attorney, in whose office he found time to study the classics and several modern languages, as well as English literature, drawing, and music; began to write verses for magazines in his fifteenth year; gained several prizes offered by publishers of periodicals; printed a volume, "Clifton Grove, a Sketch in Verse, with other Poems," (1803), which won for him the high regard of Southey and other men of letters, by whom he was encouraged to study for the ministry; obtained a sizarship at St. John's College, Cambridge, 1804; was for two years at the head of his class, and became a tutor in mathematics, but destroyed his health by excessive study, and died of consumption at Cambridge, Oct. 19, 1806. His papers were placed in the hands of Southey, who published his "Remains, etc., with an Account of his Life" (2 vols., 1807; vol. III., 1822), which obtained for him a permanent place in English literature.—BEERS, HENRY A., *rev.*, 1897, *Johnson's Universal Cyclopædia, vol. VIII, p. 744.*

PERSONAL

The books which I now read with attention, are Blackstone, Knox's "Essays," Plutarch, Chesterfield's "Letters," four large volumes, Virgil, Homer and Cicero, and several others. . . . I have finished Rollin's "Ancient History," Blair's "Lectures," Smith's "Wealth of Nations," Hume's "England" and "British Nepos" lately. . . . With a little drudgery, I read Italian—Have got some good Italian works, as "Pastor Fido," etc. I taught myself, and have got a grammar.—WHITE, HENRY KIRKE, 1800, *Letters to his Brother Neville, June* 26; *Remains, ed. Southey, vol. I, pp.* 66, 67.

It is not possible to conceive a human being more amiable in all the relations of life. He was the confidential friend and adviser of every member of his family; this he instinctively became; and the thorough good sense of his advice is not less remarkable, than the affection with which it is always communicated. To his mother he is as earnest in beseeching her to be careful of her health, as he is in labouring to convince her that his own complaints were abating; his letters to her are always of hopes, of consolation, and of love. To Neville he writes with the most brotherly intimacy, still, however, in that occasional tone of advice which it was his nature to assume, not from any arrogance of superiority, but from earnestness of pure affection. To his younger brother he addresses himself like the tenderest and wisest parent; and to two sisters, then too young for any other communication, he writes to direct their studies, to enquire into their progress, to encourage and to improve them.—SOUTHEY, ROBERT, 1807, *The Remains of Henry Kirke White, with an Account of his Life, vol. I, p.* 54.

I have been very much interested lately with the "Remains" of H. K. White, which, however, left a very melancholy impression on my mind. Was there no patron for such a man but Simeon and Wilberforce, who, with the best intentions in the world, seem to have encouraged his killing himself by religious enthusiasm? I am afraid that sort of people do not recollect that enthusiasm, like other potent draughts, should be tempered to the strength of the patient. A dram which hardly warms the veins of a rough-nerved Scotchman will drive to frenzy a more sensitive system. I wish Simeon and Levi would confine their operations to hard-headed *Cantabs*, and make no excursions to Nottingham for crimping young poets. —SCOTT, SIR WALTER, 1808, *To Southey, Feb.* 26; *Familiar Letters, vol. I, p.* 96.

Unhappy White! while life was in its spring,
And thy young muse just waved her joyous wing,
The spoiler came; and all thy promise fair
Has sought the grave, to sleep forever there.
Oh! what a noble heart was here undone,
When Science's self destroyed her favorite son!
Yes, she too much indulged thy fond pursuit,
She sowed the seeds, but death has reaped the fruit.
'Twas thine own Genius gave the final blow,
And helped to plant the wound that laid thee low.

—BYRON, LORD, 1809, *English Bards and Scotch Reviewers.*

Butcher-basket-born Kirke White!—BEDDOES, THOMAS LOVELL, 1824, *Letters.*

That most gifted youth, Henry Kirke White, whose sincere and ardent piety was equaled only by his genius, his learning, and his uncommon ardor in the pursuit of knowledge.— CLEVELAND, CHARLES D., 1853, *English Literature of the Nineteenth Century*, p. 70.

GENERAL

Hail! gifted youth, whose passion-breathing lay
Portrays a mind attun'd to noblest themes.
—OWEN, ARTHUR, 1803, *Sonnet to H. K. White on his Poems Lately Published.*

He seldom discovered any sportiveness of imagination, though he would very ably and pleasantly rally any one of his friends for any little peculiarity; his conversation was always sober and to the purpose. That which is the most remarkable in him, is his uniform *good sense*, a faculty perhaps less common than genius. There never existed a more dutiful son, a more affectionate brother, a warmer friend, nor a devouter Christian. Of his powers of mind it is superfluous to speak; they were acknowledged wherever they were known. It would be idle too to say what hopes were entertained for him, and what he might have accomplished in literature. — SOUTHEY, ROBERT, 1807, *The Remains of Henry Kirke White, with an Account of His Life*, p. 59.

There are, I think, among these "Remains," a few of the most exquisite pieces in the whole body of English poetry. Conjoined with an easy and flowing fancy, they possess the charm of a peculiar moral delicacy, often conveyed in a happy and inimitable simplicity of language.—BRYDGES, SIR SAMUEL EGERTON, 1809, *Censura Literaria, vol.* IX, p. 393.

Setting aside his bigotry, he surely ranks next to Chatterton. It is astonishing how little he was known; and at Cambridge no one thought or heard of such a man till his death rendered all notice useless. For my own part, I should have been most proud of such an acquaintance: his very prejudices were respectable.—BYRON, LORD, 1811, *Letter to Mr. Dallas*, *Aug.* 27.

To Chatterton . . . he is not to be compared. Chatterton has the force of a young poetical Titan, who threatens to take Parnassus by storm. White is a boy differing from others more in aptitude to follow than in ability to lead. The one is complete in every limb, active, self-confident, and restless from his own energy. The other, gentle, docile, and animated rather than vigorous. He began, as most youthful writers have begun, by copying those whom he saw to be the objects of popular applause in his own day. He has little distinct character of his own. We may trace him by turns to Goldsmith, Chatterton, and Coleridge.—CARY, HENRY FRANCIS, 1821-24-45, *Lives of English Poets*, p. 418.

His talents were unusually precocious, and their variety was as astonishing as their extent. Besides the Poetical pieces in this volume, and his scholastic attainments, his ability was manifested in various other ways. His style was remarkable for its clearness and elegance, and his correspondence and prose pieces show extensive information. To great genius and capacity, he united the rarest and more important gifts of a sound judgment and common sense. . . . Kirke White's poetry is popular because it describes feelings, passions, and associations, which all have felt, and with which all can sympathize. It is by no means rich in metaphor, nor does it evince great powers of imagination; but it is pathetic, plaintive, and agreeable; and emanating directly from his own heart, it appeals irresistibly to that of his reader.— NICOLAS, SIR HARRIS, 1837, *The Poetical Works of Henry Kirke White, Memoir.*

Few writers of verses have been more overrated than Henry Kirke White, and it is a shame, that while there has never appeared in this country a single edition of the poetical writings of Landor, Kenyon, Milnes, Miss Barrett, and others of similar merit, there have been more impressions of White than there have been of Milton, or Pope, or Coleridge. . . . He was scarcely equal to the Davidsons of New York, and it would be almost as absurd to compare him with Keats or Chatterton as to compare Robert Montgomery with Milton. I doubt whether if he had lived to the maturest age, he would have produced any thing in poetry above elegant mediocrity.—GRISWOLD, RUFUS W., 1844, *The Poets and Poetry of England in the Nineteenth Century*, p. 214.

Kirke White's promises were endorsed by the respectable name of Mr. Southey, but surely with no authority from Apollo.

They have the merit of a traditional piety, which, to our mind, if uttered at all, had been less objectionable in the retired closet of a diary, and in the sober raiment of prose. They do not clutch hold of the memory with the drowning pertinacity of Watts; neither have they the interest of his occasional simple, lucky beauty.— LOWELL, JAMES RUSSELL, 1845, *Edgar Allan Poe, Graham's Magazine, Feb.*

The torch of his inspiration was certainly kindled at the inner shrine; but it was darkly destined that his fair dawn was to have no meridian, and with a heart full of youthful promise and of lofty aspirations—devoted to the noblest and purest objects of humanity—he died while his feet were yet on the threshold of manhood. Three, at least, of the great magnates of literature lamented his fate, and were loud in his praises. On examining his posthumous papers, Coleridge and Southey alike expressed their astonishment at so much genius united to so much industry; and Byron, in a truculent satire, wherein almost nobody was spared, truthstricken, suspended the lash, to scatter flowers liberally on his early grave.— MOIR, DAVID MACBETH, 1850-51, *Sketches of the Poetical Literature of the Past Half Century.*

In coming to the consideration of his works and genius, it is extremely difficult, so to speak, to *insulate* ourselves from all considerations connected with his lovely character, his brief laborious life, and his premature end. That he was a man of high talents, of powers of fancy and eloquence of a rare order, as well as indomitable energy, and great assimilative and acquisite capacity, must be conceded by all. But there are not a few who deny him the possession of original genius, and who even in the uniform good taste and good sense which he discovered at so early an age find an argument in favour of their hypothesis.—GILFILLAN, GEORGE, 1856, *ed., The Poetical Works of Henry Kirke White and James Grahame, p.* xix.

A protégé of Simeon, who fell a victim to over study, whose memory Byron embalmed in some beautiful lines, whose death Southey deemed a loss to our literature—hymns, sonnets, and lyric pieces, written before he had reached his twentieth year, all distinguished by plaintive tenderness and pleasing fancy, though without

the certain indications of great genius which we have in the equally early writings of Cowley or of Chatterton.—ANGUS, JOSEPH, 1865, *The Handbook of English Literature, p.* 269.

He wrote a number of sonnets, nearly all of which were composed while he was a hopeless consumptive. With one or two exceptions, they are pitched in a plaintive minor key; and although they are too uniformly sad to be thoroughly enjoyable, they are so gracefully poetic, and there is so little of selfish or morbid repining in them, that their soft murmurs awaken pleasant emotions, even while they touch our sympathies and suffuse our eyes with tender sorrow.—DESHLER, CHARLES D., 1879, *Afternoons With the Poets, p.* 233.

The lad, in every way lacking pith and substance, and ripening prematurely in a heated atmosphere, drooped and died. —DOWDEN, EDWARD, 1880, *Southey (English Men of Letters), p.* 124.

His splendid poem, the "Star of Bethlehem," is destined to live in the memories and hearts of all lovers of sacred song.— SAUNDERS, FREDERICK, 1885, *Evenings with the Sacred Poets, p.* 388.

Both withdrew from a profession that was distasteful to them; both loved unhappily—the lady being, curiously enough, in each case named *Fanny;* both had the foreknowledge of their approaching death, and both suffered in consequence from a penetrating melancholy, amounting at times to a refined despair, the outcome of baffled hopes and thwarted ambition. Both died young. The trumpeter of their fame had his clarion already at his lips, but hurrying death stopped their ears, so that they did not hear the blast. It would seem as if their lives and memories had been handed on together, as if our knowledge of the one is not complete without a knowledge of the other. Keats seems to have taken up the thread of Kirke White's inspiration, or to have woven it into the fabric of his own genius; he seems unconsciously to have become the sequel, the completion, the consummation of White. He did not so much *eclipse*, as pass into, comprehend, and, as it were *re-issue* him. Much of Keats's verse seems an echo, a remembrance of Henry's, but a remembrance that is given with a more satisfying expression, a more artistic utterance. . . . White, like Keats, is peculiarly the child of this century, though he died on its very threshold. There is in both cases the same self-destroying heart—and brain-consuming "passion for the unattainable." Henry possessed the genuine *fin-de-siècle* temperament, without being in any sense a sickly, sentimental, self-absorbed nineteenth century *poseur*. Like Tasso, he battled with his agony. His pain struck music from him; and until death seized him, his brave, high-minded courage enabled him to conceal the "torture of his despair." Nearly a hundred years have passed since he died, and while the name of Keats is upon many lips, the world only occasionally hears of Henry. But his genius cannot perish, and from time to time there will be breathed upon the air an echo of what he himself calls his "faint, neglected song."—LAW, ALICE, 1894, *A Forerunner of Keats, Westminster Review, vol.* 142, *p.* 291.

Any one who will now study Kirke White's poems in themselves, as literature, without prejudice, must inevitably come to the conclusion that they are worthless, and disfigured by every fault that can be laid to the charge of poetry. They are not even promising. They are tedious, grotesque, inharmonious, dull. And yet they have a place in the Aldine edition of British poets.—BENSON, ARTHUR CHRISTOPHER, 1896, *Essays, p.* 180.

He was a poetaster, and nothing more. The "genius" attributed to him in Byron's well-known and noble though rather rhetorical lines may be discovered on an average in about half a dozen poets during any two or three years of any tolerable poetic period. His best things are imitations of Cowper in his sacred mood, such as the familiar "Star of Bethlehem," and even these are generally spoilt by some feebleness or false note. At his worst he is not far from Della Crusca.—SAINTSBURY, GEORGE, 1896, *A History of Nineteenth Century Literature, p.* 108.

"Oft in Sorrow, Oft in Woe."—Kirke White's marching song of the Christian Life has no such lilting tune attached to it as "Onward Christian Soldiers," but being older it has probably helped more souls than its recent rival.—STEAD, W. T., 1897, *Hymns that Have Helped, p.* 169.

Few men have owed more in the way of reputation to their misfortunes than Kirke White. His continual struggles against adverse circumstances in the pursuit of knowledge, together with the amiability of his disposition and the piety of his life, secured for him many friends, who, in their admiration for his character, discovered evidence of Genius in his verse which those uninfluenced by his personality are unable to detect. It would of course be absurd to look for maturity in the work of a youth of twenty years, but Genius could scarcely have written as much as this youth wrote without betraying itself, however crudely, in some thought or phrase of obvious originality or latent power. Kirk White's poems display no such evidence as we expect to find in the work of Genius, however young. He lacked originality and imagination; and while unable to invent new forms of beauty, showed no freshness in his views of old forms of truth. He had ambition, but he had nothing to say, nor was there anything felicitous in his manner of saying nothing. Among the "Fragments," gathered from the backs of old mathematical papers, there are one or two which are calculated to excite expectation, but it may be doubted whether he would ever have justified the claims made on his behalf even if Time had dealt more gently with him. . . . Of Kirk White's shorter poems his lines "To Love" have been perhaps most frequently quoted, though they can scarcely be said to rise above the level of valentine verse.—MILES, ALFRED H., 1897, *The Poets and the Poetry of the Century ; Sacred, Moral and Religious Verse, pp.* 81, 83.

Southey's charitable judgment, which Byron echoed, has not stood the test of time. White's verse shows every mark of immaturity. In thought and expression it lacks vigour and originality. A promise of weirdness in an early and prophetic lyric, "A Dance of Consumptives" (from an unfinished "Eccentric Drama") was not fulfilled in his later compositions. The metrical dexterity which is shown in the addition to Waller's "Go, lovely Rose," is not beyond a mediocre capacity. Such popularity as White's work has enjoyed is to be attributed to the pathetic brevity of his career and to the fervour of the evangelical piety which inspired the greater part of his writings in both verse and prose.—LEE, SIDNEY, 1900, *Dictionary of National Biography, vol.* LXI, *p.* 50.

Elizabeth Carter

1717–1806

Elizabeth Carter (1717–1806), a celebrated lady scholar, and translator of the work of Epictetus, was the daughter of the Rev. Dr. Carter of Deal in Kent, and was born in that town, December 16, 1717. . . . Miss Carter learned Greek and Latin from her father, and was specially proficient in Greek, so that Dr. Johnson said concerning a celebrated scholar, that he "understood Greek better than any one whom he had ever known except Elizabeth Carter." She learned also Hebrew, French, German Italian, Spanish, Portuguese, and lastly some Arabic. She studied astronomy, ancient geography, and ancient and modern history. In 1734 some of her verses appeared in the "Gentleman's Magazine" under the signature "Eliza," Carr the editor being a friend of her father. In 1738 she published a small collection of poems, and next year she translated from the French an attack on Pope's "Essay on Man" by M. Crousaz. In 1739 appeared her translation from the Italian of Algarotti's "Newtonianismo per le Dame," calling it "Sir Isaac Newton's Philosophy explained for the use of the Ladies, in Six Dialogues on Light and Colors." Her translation of Epictetus was undertaken in 1749 to please her friends Dr. Secker (afterwards archbishop of Canterbury) and Miss Talbot, to whom the translation was sent, sheet by sheet, as it was done. This work was published by guinea subscription in 1758. In 1763 Miss Carter printed a second collection of poems. . . . Miss Carter never married, and lived to the age of eighty-nine. She died in Clarges street, Piccadilly, 1806; and her nephew the Rev. Montagu Pennington, published her "Memoirs" in 1808.—BAYNES, THOMAS SPENCER, ed., 1877, Encyclopædia Britannica, Ninth edition, vol. v, p. 124.

PERSONAL

For the most part of the time we are entirely alone. . . . Our friend, you know, has talents which must distinguish her in the largest circles; but there it is impossible for one fully to discover either the beauties of her character or the extent and variety of her understanding, which always improves on a more accurate examination and on a nearer view. . . . The charm is inexpressibly heightened when it is complicated with the affections of the heart.— MONTAGU, ELIZABETH, 1764, Letter to Mrs. Vesey, A Lady of the Last Century, ed. Doran, p. 136.

Mrs. Carter has in her person a great deal of what the gentlemen mean when they say such a one is a "poetical lady;" however, independently of her great talents and learning, I like her much; she has affability, kindness, and goodness; and I honour her heart even more than her talents.—MORE, HANNAH, 1775, Letter to One of Her Sisters, Memoirs, ed. Roberts, vol. I, p. 39.

This ardent thirst after knowledge was at length crowned with complete success, and her acquirements became, even very early in life, such as are rarely met with. What she once gained, she never afterwards lost, an effect, indeed, to be expected from the intense application by which she acquired her learning, and which is often by no means the case with those, the quickness of whose faculties renders labour almost useless.—PENNINGTON, MONTAGU, 1808, Memoirs of Mrs. Carter.

Though history and classical learning were, in profane literature, the favourite studies of Mrs. Carter, the sciences were not neglected; she had paid some attention to mathematics, and in astronomy and ancient geography she had made no common progress. What she studied, however, with still superior ardour and delight, and with an effect on her manners and conduct of the most indelible kind, was religion. Her piety, indeed, was the most decided feature of her character, and its intensity continued undiminished to the last moment of her life. Nothwithstanding these various, laborious, and important pursuits, she found leisure for amusements, and for the display of a cheerful and even gay disposition. Of dancing she was particularly fond, and entered, indeed, with singular naiveté and vivacity into all the innocent diversions of youth and high spirits. What enabled her to partake of so much relaxation was the habit which she had acquired of rising every morning between four and five o'clock, a practice that was continued, to a certain extent, even in very advanced life, for at no time, if in health, was she known to lie later than seven.—DRAKE, NATHAN, 1810, Essays,

Illustrative of the Rambler, Adventurer and Idler, vol. II, *p.* 74.

Miss Fanshawe says, in one of her letters to me, written soon after the death of this venerated person, that she appears to her to have been half an angel and half a sage; differing from most of her sex, in having laid down a plan in the outset of life to which she adhered steadily to the end; writing Greek in the face of the world without compunction, never losing a friend, and never making an enemy.—GRANT, ANNE, 1830, *Letters, Nov.* 13; *Memoir and Correspondence, ed. Grant, vol.* III, *p.* 165.

We were startled at reading somewhere the other day that, in her youth, she had not only the wisdom of a Pallas, but the look of a Hebe. Healthy no doubt she was, and possessed of a fine constitution. She was probably also handsome; but Hebe and a hook nose are in our minds impossible associations. — HUNT, LEIGH, 1847, *British Poetesses; Men, Women and Books, vol.* II, *p.* 119.

Her regular rule was, when in health, to read two chapters in the Bible before breakfast; a sermon, some Hebrew, Greek, and Latin, and after breakfast something in every language with which she was acquainted; thus never allowing herself to forget what she had once attained. These occupations were of course varied according to circumstances, and when she took exercise before breakfast her course of reading was necessarily deferred till later in the day. Her constitution must have been strong to have enabled her to take the very long walks to which she accustomed herself; but she suffered greatly from headaches, not improbably arising from her over-exertion of body and mind in early youth, and the not allowing herself sufficient repose to recruit her overworked strength. At one time of her life she was wont to sit up very late, and as she soon became drowsy, and would sleep soundly in her chair, many were the expedients she adopted to keep herself awake, such as pouring cold water down her dress, tying a wet bandage round her head, &c. She was a great snuff-taker, though she endeavoured to break herself of the habit to please her father. She suffered so much, however, in the attempt, that he kindly withdrew his prohibition. —HALE, SARAH JOSEPHA, 1852, *Woman's Record, p.* 244.

Genial, happy, old lady! We believe her when she declared that she had never regretted not having looked for interest in married life. We love her sapient sayings, and gentle, holy memory. We reverence her as the very pattern of a high-minded, active, and more than contented Old Maid.—THOMSON, KATHERINE (GRACE WHARTON), 1861, *Mrs. Elizabeth Carter and Miss Talbot, Celebrated Friendships, vol.* II, *p.* 170.

After the third edition of her poems, Mistress Carter wrote no more for the press; but she appears to have taken much delight in the productions of contemporary genius, and it is interesting to find that she lived to welcome and applaud "The Lay of the Last Minstrel." How amazed would she and many others of her time have been to behold the slight esteem in which it is the present fashion to hold that glorious "Lay!" And perchance, modest as she was, it would also have surprised not a little the translator of "Epictetus," and the greatest female scholar of her period, could she know that her very name, as well as the records of her triumphs, is almost unknown to a generation which has scarce patience for its own pedants, and cares less than nothing for the pedants of former days.—WALFORD, L. B., 1891, *A Learned Lady; Elizabeth Carter, Blackwood's Magazine, vol.* 149, *p.* 519.

She was more remarkable for her linguistic acquirements than for original work, and is said to have known not only Greek and Latin, but Hebrew, French, Italian, Spanish and German as well. With all these accomplishments she retained to the last a fund of delightful modesty and good sense, and bore with dignified equanimity the unpleasant notoriety that her learning sometimes brought her. —THOMSON, CLARA LINKLATER, 1900, *Samuel Richardson, A Biographical and Critical Study, p.* 113.

GENERAL

The judgments of this most excellent woman appears to have been at once original, candid and sound. They are expressed in language perspicuous, strong, and elegant; and are the result of a mind acting on the most mature deliberation, and enlightened by the nicest powers of distinction. . . . A mind more clear.

more extensive, and better regulated than Mrs. Carter's does not occur in the annals of genius and learning.—BRYDGES, SIR SAMUEL EGERTON, 1808, *Censura Literaria, vol.* VIII, *p.* 197.

The poetry of Mrs. Carter is such as might have been expected from the elegance of her classical learning, and the purity of her moral principles. Her language is clear and correct, her versification sweet and harmonious, while the sentiment is always dignified, or devotional, and even sometimes sublime. Of splendid imagination, of the creative powers which form the character of a first-rate poet, she has exhibited few proofs; yet are her productions far beyond mediocrity, and, though not breathing the fire and energy of exalted genius, will be ever highly valued by those to whom the union of taste, piety, and erudition, is dear.—DRAKE, NATHAN, 1810, *Essays, Illustrative of the Rambler, Adventurer, and Idler, vol.* II, *p.* 86.

I have the headache myself, caught perhaps by reading Mrs. Carter's letters, which tell of nothing else.—PIOZZI, HESTER LYNCH, 1817, *To Sir James Fellowes, June* 26; *Autobiography, Letters and Literary Remains, ed. Hayward, p.* 389.

This lady's poetical writings display but little imagination, and have none of those strong thoughts and sublime ideas which betoken lofty genius: but her verses exhibit great classical purity, and are remarkable for an unusual sweetness of versification. They embody, too, a cheerful serenity very highly calculated to improve the reader's mind; for although Miss Carter translated Epictetus, she by no means followed his philosophy.—ROWTON, FREDERIC, 1848, *The Female Poets of Great Britain, p.* 178.

Her literary fame was chiefly founded upon her translation of Epictetus, and this one work sufficed, as it well may do, for a lifetime. For of all her other literary efforts,—her translations from the French, and the Italian,—her contributions as "Eliza" to *The Gentleman's Magazine,*—her odes and elegies, the fame thereof has long since been entombed with her bones. — THOMSON, KATHERINE (GRACE WHARTON), 1848, *The Literary Circles of the Last Century, Fraser's Magazine, vol.* 37, *p.* 76.

The character of her poetry is such as might have been expected from the elegance of her classical learning, the purity of her moral principles, and her consistent piety. While, to high imagination, or to great creative power, she can lay no claim, her language is clear and correct, her versification sweet and harmonious, and her sentiments all that the moralist or the Christian could wish—pure, dignified, devotional, and sometimes rising to the sublime.—CLEVELAND, CHARLES D., 1853, *English Literature of the Nineteenth Century, p.* 59.

Her sound and comprehensive mind, highly cultured as it was, could produce nothing contemptible: but it wanted that essential qualification of the true poet, active originality, the power of conceiving, and of shaping new conceptions.—WILLIAMS, JANE, 1861, *The Literary Women of England, p.* 215.

Although superseded by later workers in the same field, Elizabeth Carter still holds an honourable place beside the Daciers, the Sarah Fieldings, and other women scholars, and will ever remain in our memories as the English translator of Epictetus.—EDWARDS, M. BETHAM-1880, *Six Life Studies of Famous Women, p.* 225.

Mrs. Carter was more celebrated for the solidity of her learning than for any brilliant intellectual qualities; and it is as a Greek scholar and translator of Epictetus that she is now best remembered. She used to relate with pleasure that Dr. Johnson had said, speaking of some celebrated scholar, that "he understood Greek better than any one he had ever known, except Elizabeth Carter." Her poems have ceased to be read and are not of very high order, the "Dialogue between the Body and the Mind" being perhaps the most successful. Her letters display considerable vigour of thought, and now and then a transient flash of humour. Though by no means a woman of the world, she possessed a large amount of good sense, and, though more learned than her fellows, was a thoroughly sociable and amiable woman. — BARKER, G. F. RUSSELL, 1887, *Dictionary of National Biography, vol.* IX, *p.* 196.

One of the most accomplished women of the century.—ABBEY, CHARLES J., 1887, *The English Church and Its Bishops,*1700–1800, *vol.* II, *p.* 49.

She belongs in spirit as well as in time to the last century. Among women she is perhaps its greatest scholar. Her distinction in her own age was due full as much to her learning as to her purely literary achievements. — LOUNSBURY, THOMAS R., 1891, *Studies in Chaucer, vol.* III, *p.* 262.

Samuel Horsley
1733-1806

A learned and eloquent prelate of the Church of England; born in London, 1733; died at Brighton, Oct. 4, 1806. His father was a minister, and personally supervised his education till he entered Trinity College, Cambridge, where he graduated LL.B. in 1758. His first charge in the ministry was Newington in Surrey. In 1767 he was elected to the Royal Society, and was secretary of that body from 1773 to 1784, when he resigned his membership, on account of difficulties with the president. He was an able classical scholar and mathematician, published works in both departments, and edited "Works of Sir Isaac Newton," in 5 vols., 1779-85. His ministerial career was a brilliant one. After filling other positions, he was appointed in 1781 archdeacon of St. Alban's. Whilst holding his position, he entered (1783) upon his famous controversy with Dr. Priestley. His "Letters" on this subject are full of learning and keen argument. In clear and solid reasoning he was more than a match for his opponent; and Gibbon describes his achievements by saying that "his spear pierced the Socinian's shield." The dispute was carried on with great heat, and not a little acrimony on both sides. For his services in stopping the tide of Socinianism, he was rewarded by Thurlow with a prebend's stall in Gloucester, and with the see of St. David's, in 1788. In Parliament, Bishop Horsley was an energetic supporter of Mr. Pitt. In 1793 he was translated to the see of Rochester, and rewarded with the deanery of Westminster for the famous sermon preached there on the anniversary of the execution of Charles I., and a few days after Louis XVI. was guillotined. In 1802 he was transferred to the see of St. Asaph. Bishop Horsley was a man of overbearing temper, but a keen reasoner, sound scholar, and eloquent orator. His sermons are among the very best specimens of English pulpit eloquence. Among his works not already referred to may be mentioned a "Commentary on Hosea" (1801, 2d ed. 1804), the posthumous work on the "Psalms translated from the Hebrew," etc. (1815, 2 vols, 4th ed., 1845), "Biblical Criticism of Fourteen Historical Books of the Old Testament," etc. (1820, 4 vols. 2d ed. 1844, 2 vols.), a collected edition of Horsley's "Theological Works" (London, 1830, 9 vols.), and his "Sermons," complete in 1 vol. (London, 1839).— SHAFF-HERZOG, *eds.*, 1883, *Encyclopædia of Religious Knowledge, vol.* II, *p.* 1023.

PERSONAL

No man of the age, perhaps, possessed more of what is generally understood by the term of *recondite* learning, or was more profoundly versed in classical chronology. He was extremely eloquent, and his voice was deep and full-toned; his enunciation also was distinct, and his delivery in all respects commanding and highly impressive. His manner was rather dictatorial, but he was, nevertheless, an argumentative speaker, equally clear and strong. His mind grasped all the learning of the ancient and modern world, and his heart was as warm and generous towards all whom he had the ability to serve, as his head was capable of advocating their cause. His charity to the distressed was even more than prudent; he often wanted himself when he gave away; and in money affairs no one was more careless than the bishop, and no one so easily imposed upon. Though he was irascible, passionate, and easily moved to anger, yet he had a very large amount of human kindness; he was a devoted father and husband, and always bent both his mind and body to partake of the amusements of children, of whom he was particularly fond.—DANIELL, J. W., 1874, *Bishop Horsley, Good Words, vol.* 15, *p.* 827.

Horsley is described as somewhat irritable in temperament and dictatorial in manner; apart from polemics he was notably generous, and so charitable as to be easily imposed upon. His intellectual force was great, and his learning admirably digested. As a speaker and preacher his deep-toned and flexible voice gave dire effect to his strong argumentative powers.

—GORDON, ALEXANDER, 1891, *Dictionary of National Biography, vol.* XXVII, *p.* 385.

SERMONS

His sermons are fine specimens of commanding eloquence, and contain many deep and original views of Scripture facts and prophecies.—WILLIAMS, EDWARD, 1800, *The Christian Preacher.*

In the evening I read two of Bishop Horsley's sermons upon the Forty-fifth Psalm. There are four, but I had already read the two previous ones. They have a very high reputation in this country, and are undoubtedly discourses of great learning and ingenuity. But they are dogmatical and bigoted; and their object is to inculcate doctrines so odious that I could not believe them if I would. Here are four sermons to explain one psalm, and, if the Bishop's exposition is correct, the psalm has been waiting three thousand years to be made at last intelligible by him.- - ADAMS, JOHN QUINCY, 1817, *Journal, April* 12; *Memoirs, ed. C. F. Adams, vol.* III, *p.* 498.

Confining our view to Horsley in his literary character, I must say that he is far beyond the reach of Dr. Parr's hostility. As a polematic and a champion of his own Church, he was above the competition of any contemporary divine. As a theologian, he reconciled the nearly contradictory merits of novelty and originality with well-meditated orthodoxy; and I may venture to assert that his "Sermons" produced a greater impression than any English book of pure divinity for the last century. In saying this, I do not speak of the sale; what that might be I know not; I speak of the strength of the impression diffused through the upper circles, as apparent in the reverential terms which, after the appearance of that work, universally marked the sense of cultivated men in speaking of Bishop Horsley—even of those who had previously viewed him with some dislike in his character of controversialist.—DE QUINCEY, THOMAS, 1831–57, *Dr. Samuel Parr, Collected Writings, ed. Masson, vol.* V, *p.* 32.

Lord Chancellor Thurlow, being detained by a thunderstorm at a country inn, and asking the hostess whether she had any books in the house, is said to have tossed aside the Bible she brought him, and to have sworn at Horsley's "Sermons,"— which last, however, to cure idleness by short distraction, his lordship began to read, and was so enthralled by the unknown divine that he read on, long after the rain was over, and carried it with him to the carriage steps—whence he threw the book back to the hostess, wishing he might be —something unpleasant—if he didn't make that fellow a bishop; and he was as good as his word.—JACOX, FRANCIS, 1872, *Enthralling Books, Aspects of Authorship, p.* 338.

GENERAL

It is most sincerely regretted by me, that the dispositions of Bishop Horsley should have been warped either by pride, ambition, or selfishness, to such an excessive obliquity as displays itself throughout his writings. The native vigour of his faculties, his various knowledge, his elegant and nervous style, and his ingenuity of invention might have been happily employed to the advancement of science, and to the confirmation and recommendation of the Christianity of the Scriptures.— WAKEFIELD, GILBERT, 1792, *Memoirs Written by Himself.*

It is not a little extraordinary that Bishop Horsley, the apologist of tyranny, the patron of passive obedience, should affect to admire the British constitution, whose freedom was attained by a palpable violation of the principles for which he contends. . . . Whatever bears the semblance of "reasoning," in Bishop Horsley's discourse, will be found, I trust, to have received a satisfactory answer; but to animadvert with a becoming severity on the temper it displays, is a less easy task. To render him the justice he deserves in that respect would demand all the fierceness of his character. . . . It is time to turn from this disgusting picture of sanctimonious hypocrisy and priestly insolence, to address a word to the reader on the following pamphlet. The political sentiments of Dr. Horsley are in truth of too little consequence in themselves to engage a moment's curiosity, and deserve attention only as they indicate the spirit of the times.—HALL, ROBERT, 1793, *An Apology for the Freedom of the Press, Preface.*

In my opinion, the controversy so ably maintained by this learned Prelate against the Heresiarch Priestley, is his peculiar praise. Bishop Horsley reminds me of the celebrated Divine, Charles Leslie. He has often the same strength, the same acuteness, and sometimes the same coarseness of manner. But the argument is cogent, and the arms are irresistible. In theological controversy, Charles Leslie and Bishop Horsley always appear to me, "Æacidæ similes, Vulcaniaque arma capessunt."—MATHIAS, THOMAS JAMES, 1797, *The Pursuits of Literature, Eighth ed., p.* 412.

Much original, deep, devout, and evangelical matter, with much that is bold, hazardous, speculative, and rash. Bishop Horsley's powers of mind were of a high order; and his sermons and his other works will render assistance to the student chiefly in the way of criticism. He had the integrity and candour to speak decidedly against the ignorance of many who opposed what they called Calvinistic views. — BICKERSTETH, EDWARD, 1844, *The Christian Student.*

Horsley was a man of a masculine mind, great learning, and quick intelligence. He was also master of a clear style and much power of logical argumentation. His attack upon Priestley was a very damaging one.—PERRY, GEORGE G., 1864, *The History of the Church of England, vol.* III, *p.* 434.

Horsley had an arrogance and dogmatism even fiercer than Warburton's, without anything like Warburton's genius for style. His sermons procured him respect from many that disapproved of his violence as a polemic; they are distinguished by breadth of view and clear racy expression. —MINTO, WILLIAM, 1872-80, *Manual of English Prose Literature, p.* 469.

As a critic and scholar, he had few equals; and his disquisitions on the prophets Isaiah and Hosea, his translation of the Psalms, and his "Biblical Criticisms" (in four volumes), justly entitled him to the honour of the mitre. His "Sermons," in three volumes, are about the best in the language: clear, nervous, and profound,

he entered undauntedly upon the most difficult subjects, and dispelled, by research and argument, the doubt that hung over several passages of Scripture.— CHAMBERS, ROBERT, 1876, *Cyclopædia of English Literature, ed.Carruthers.*

In Horsley we may find an example of what religious writing became in the latter part of the century, earnest and conscientious, rich in scholarship and robust in thought, but moving rather with judicial formality and dignified reverence than by any instinct of enthusiastic piety.—CRAIK, HENRY, 1895, *ed., English Prose, Introduction, vol.* IV, *p.* 6.

As a master of English prose Samuel Horsley had few equals in his own day. The reputation he gained among his contemporaries and their immediate successors was quite out of proportion to the bulk of his writings, but not at all out of proportion to their merits. He was in fact regarded in the early part of the nineteenth century as, in point of abilities and attainments, far above all other writers and speakers on the side of the Church. Men of the most widely differing sentiments agree in this. . . . He writes in a remarkably pure, luminous, and dignified style; his matter is weighty, his argumentative power convincing, his learning profound, and his satire, though always kept within the bounds of decency and courtesy, most cutting. There is a robustness and manliness about his tone of mind which is reflected in his style; he takes a lofty line, which some might think supercilious, but it is certainly justified by his merits; it is that of a judge summing up, not that of an advocate pleading his cause. His sentiments are always those of the marked high churchman, and in many points he anticipates the men of the Oxford movement. His sermons are the finest specimens of pulpit eloquence which the age produced, and they are still unrivalled in their way. —OVERTON, J. H., 1895, *English Prose, ed. Craik, vol.* IV, *pp.* 447, 448.

Charlotte Smith
1749-1806

Poet and novelist, was born at London, May 4, 1749. Married Benjamin Smith, Feb. 23, 1765. Published "Elegiac Sonnets and other Essays," 1784; second edition same year, and a fifth edition 1789. Translated "Manon Lescaut," 1785, and wrote the "Romance of Real Life," 1786. Her first novel, "Emmeline," published 1788; "The Old Manor House," 1793. Other works by Charlotte Smith are: 1. "Ethelinde, or the Recluse of the Lake," 5 vols. 1790; 2nd edit. 1814. 2. "The Banished Man," 4 vols. 1794. 3. "Montalbert," 1795. 4. "Marchmont." 5. "Rural Walks." 6. "Rambles Farther," 1796. 7. "Minor Morals interspersed with Sketches," 2 vols. 1798; other editions, 1799, 1800, 1816, 1825. 8. "The Young Philosopher," a novel, 1798. 9. "The Solitary Wanderer," 1799. 10. "Beachy Head," a poem, 1807.—MOULTON, CHARLES WELLS, 1902.

PERSONAL

But every one, whether of sad or gay temperament, must regret that the tone of melancholy which pervades Mrs. Smith's compositions was derived too surely from the circumstances and feelings of the amiable authoress. We are indeed, informed by Mrs. Dorset that the natural temper of her sister was lively and playful; but it must be considered that the works on which she was obliged, often reluctantly, to labour, were seldom undertaken from free choice. Nothing saddens the heart so much as that sort of literary labour which depends upon the imagination, when it is undertaken unwillingly, and from a sense of compulsion. The galley-slave may sing when he is unchained, but it would be uncommon equanimity which could induce him to do so when he is actually bound to his oar. If there is a mental drudgery which lowers the spirits and lacerates the nerves, like the toil of the slave, it is that which is exacted by literary composition when the heart is not in unison with the work upon which the head is employed. Add to the unhappy author's task, sickness, sorrow, or the pressure of unfavourable circumstances, and the labour of the bondsman becomes light in comparison.—SCOTT, SIR WALTER, 1823? CHARLOTTE SMITH, *Miscellanies*.

SONNETS

I did not see Charlotte Smith's "Sonnets" until after I had published my own; but when I met with them they filled me with delight, and to this day I equally admire them.—BRYDGES, SIR SAMUEL EGERTON, 1834, *Autobiography, vol. I, p. 63.*

I will, however, first prelude my examples from her by two sonnets from an earlier writer, Charlotte Smith, whose productions in this stanza are not only numerous, but of such elegance and merit as to command the homage of all who are interested in the history of its growth and development.— DESHLER, CHARLES D., 1879, *Afternoons With the Poets, p. 253.*

The unmitigable woe with which Mrs. Smith's poems are filled, together with their factitious and second-hand phraseology, renders them unpalatable to a generation so much healthier than that in which they were produced; yet we must respect the opinion of so admirable a critic as Wordsworth, who described her as a "a lady to whom English verse is under greater obligations than are likely to be either acknowledged or remembered." "She wrote little," he continues, "and that little unambitiously, but with true feeling for rural Nature, at a time when Nature was not much regarded by English Poets; for in point of time her earlier writings preceded, I believe, those of Cowper and Burns." Her Sonnets, about which some of their old sweetness still lingers, like the perfume of dried flowers, have been repeatedly praised by Dyce.— MAIN, DAVID M., 1879, *ed., A Treasury of English Sonnets, p. 358.*

When Bowles first published his sonnets he was accused of having imitated those of Charlotte Smith. In what high estimation this lady's work was still held nearly thirty years after her death, may be gathered from the fact that the late Rev. Alexander Dyce included no fewer than nine of her sonnets in his Selection, whereas he only gives one by Keats, and entirely omits those of Shelley and Byron.—WADDINGTON, SAMUEL, 1882, *English Sonnets by Poets of the Past, p. 229.*

GENERAL

A lady to whom English verse is under greater obligations than are likely to be either acknowledged or remembered. She wrote little, and that little unambitiously, but with true feeling for rural Nature, at a time when Nature was not much regarded by English Poets; for in point of time her earlier writings preceded, I believe, those of Cowper and Burns.— WORDSWORTH, WILLIAM, 1833, *St. Bees' Heads, note.*

Some of her novels will last, and her sonnets with them, each perhaps aided by the other. There is nothing great in her; but she is natural and touching, and has hit, in the music of her sorrows, upon some of those chords, which have been awakened equally, though not so well, in all human bosoms.—HUNT, LEIGH, 1847, *British Poetesses, Men, Women and Books, vol.* II, *p.* 119.

Did you ever read any of Charlotte Smith's novels? Except that they want cheerfulness, nothing can exceed the beauty of the style. Whenever Erskine had a great speech to make he used to read her works, that he might catch their grace of composition.—MITFORD, MARY RUSSELL, 1854, *To Mrs. Jennings, Nov.* 29; *Life, ed. L'Estrange, vol.* II, *p.* 358.

Her poetical compositions are distinguished by an easy grace. A sweet melancholy, never morbid though settled, but chastened by a hopeful piety, sheds a touching charm over her verses. She had a keen perception of natural beauty, and her descriptions of rural scenery or cultivated gardens are ever true and full of sentiment. Some of her sonnets are among the best of the second class in our language, and a volume of them, we are told, "passed through eleven editions, besides being translated into French and Italian." We have given a longer sketch of this interesting lady than of some others, because her writings, though marked with elegance, judgment and natural beauty, have fallen into such undeserved neglect, that they are rarely found except in libraries of collectors.— BETHUNE, GEORGE WASHINGTON, 1848, *The British Female Poets.*

Few women have ever possessed greater advantages of capacity and ability, of acquirement and influence. Her faculties were of no common kind. Her mind had naturally great scope, comprising the high imaginative power of an inborn poet, with the accuracy of detail and sound common sense which constitute the woman of business and worldly wisdom. To her belonged also that attribute of noble natures, pervading sincerity; the thoughts and feelings of her every-day existence being the opinions and sentiments of her prose and poetry. There is that charm in her poetry which belongs only to genius. The tone is too monotonous, the spirit too querulous; it wants the exulting and exalting notes of the caroller who soars to the skies and dwells blissfully in the turf, yet it has a sort of ravishment like the nightingale's strains, ever pleasing though plaintive.—WILLIAMS, JANE, 1861, *The Literary Women of England, p.* 224.

She was among the most prolific novelists of her time, but only one work, "The Old Manor House," enjoyed more than a passing reputation, or has any claim to particular mention here. The chief merit of Charlotte Smith's novels lies in their descriptions of scenery, an element only just entering into the work of the novelist. —TUCKERMAN, BAYNARD, 1882, *A History of English Prose Fiction, p.* 257.

As a novelist she shows skill in portraying character, but the deficiencies of the plots render her novels tedious. Her English style is good.—LEE, ELIZABETH, 1898, *Dictionary of National Biography, vol.* LIII, *p.* 29.

Charles James Fox
1749–1806

Third son of the first Lord Holland, was born in London, 24th January 1749, and educated at Eton and Hertford College, Oxford, spending his vacations in the gayest circles of the French capital. Even as a schoolboy he led an irregular life, but was distinguished for ability; at nineteen his father had him brought into parliament as member for Midhurst. Soon after he attained his majority he came forward as a supporter of Lord North, and was made a lord of Admirality. In 1772 he resigned, but next year was named a commissioner of the Treasury. Dismissed from that post in 1775 after another quarrel with Lord North, he passed over to the ranks of the opposition, and during the American war was the most formidable opponent of the coercive measures of government. After the downfall of North (1782), Fox was one of the secretaries of State till the death of the Marquis of Rockingham. In 1783 the North and Fox coalition was formed, and Fox resumed his former office; but the rejection of his India Bill by the House of Lords led to the resignation of his government. Now Pitt came into power, and the long contest between him and Fox began. The sudden illness of the king in 1788 and the need for a regency recalled Fox from a visit to Gibbon at Lausanne and to Italy. The regency, the trial of Warren Hastings, and the French

CHARLES JAMES FOX

WILLIAM PITT

*From an Engraving Published
by A. Fullarton Co.*

*Engraving by H. Meyer.
Original Picture by J. Hoppner, R. A.*

Revolution gave ample scope to the talents and energies of Fox, who employed his influence to modify, if not to counteract, the policy of his great rival. He was a strenuous opponent of the war with France, and an advocate of non-intervention. After Pitt's death in January 1806, Fox, recalled to office, set on foot negotiations for a peace with France. He was on the point of introducing a bill for the abolition of the slave-trade, when he died at Chiswick, 13th September 1806. He was buried, near Pitt, in Westminster Abbey. Fox was a hard liver, addicted to gambling and drinking; his bearing towards his opponents was generous: Burke called him "the greatest debater the world ever saw."—PATRICK AND GROOME, *eds.*, 1897, *Chambers's Biographical Dictionary, p. 375.*

PERSONAL

I believe there never was a person yet created who had the faculty of reasoning like him. His judgments are never wrong; his decision is formed quicker than any man's I ever conversed with; and he never seems to mistake but in his own affairs.—CARLISLE, EARL OF, 1772? *Letter to George Selwyn, George Selwyn and His Contemporaries, vol.* III, *p.* 23.

Fox is a most extraordinary man; here is a man . . . who has divided the Kingdom with Cæsar; so that it was a doubt whether the nation should be ruled by the sceptre of George the Third, or the tongue of Fox.—JOHNSON, SAMUEL, 1784, *Life by Boswell, ed. Hill, vol.* IV, *p.* 337.

I beg you would assure him that my expressions of esteem for him are not mere professions. I really think him a *great* man, and I should not think so, if I did not believe he was at bottom, and would prove himself, *a good* one.—FRANKLIN, BENJAMIN, 1783, *Letter to David Hartley, Works, ed. Sparks, vol.* X, *p.* I.

Mr. Fox is in a very bad state of health. His rapid journeys to England, on the news of the king's illness, have brought on him a violent complaint in the bowels, which will, it is imagined, prove mortal. However, if it should, it will vindicate his character from the general report that he has no bowels, as has been most strenuously asserted by his creditors.—MONTAGU, ELIZABETH, 1788, *Letter, Dec.; A Lady of the Last Century, p.* 346.

I have eat, and drank, and conversed, and sat up all night with Fox in England; but it never has happened, perhaps it never can happen again, that I should enjoy him, as I did that day, alone, from ten in the morning till ten at night. We had little politics; though he gave me in a few words such a character of Pitt as one great man should give of another his rival; much of books, from my own, on which he

flattered me very pleasantly, to Homer and the Arabian Nights; much about the country, my garden, (which he understands far better than I do); and, upon the whole, I think he envies me, and would do so were he minister.—GIBBON, EDWARD, 1788, *Correspondence, Oct.* 4, *p.* 331.

He, too, is fall'n, who Britain's loss supplied,
With him our fast-reviving hopes have died;
Not one great people only raise his urn,
All Europe's far-extending regions mourn.
"These feelings wide, let sense and truth unclue,
To give the palm where Justice points it's due:"
Yet let not canker'd Calumny assail,
Or round our statesmen wind her gloomy veil.
Fox! o'er whose corse a mourning world must weep,
Whose dear remains in honor'd marble sleep;
For whom, at last, e'en hostile nations groan,
While friends and foes alike his talents own;
Fox shall in Britain's future annals shine,
Nor e'en to Pitt the patriot's palm resign;
Which envy, wearing Candor's sacred mask,
For Pitt, and Pitt alone, has dared to ask.
—BYRON, LORD, 1806, *On the Death of Mr. Fox.*

Mr. Fox, though not an adept in the use of political wiles, was very unlikely to be the dupe of them. He was conversant in the ways of man, as well as in the contents of books. He was acquainted with the peculiar language of states, their peculiar forms, and the grounds and effects of their peculiar usages. From his earliest youth he had investigated the science of politics on the greater and smaller scale; he had studied it in the records of history, both popular and rare,—in the conferences of ambassadors,—in the archives of royal cabinets,—in the minuter detail of memoirs —and in collected or straggling anecdotes of the wrangles, intrigues, and cabals, which, springing up in the secret recesses of courts, shed their baneful influence on the determination of sovereigns, the fortune of favourites and the tranquility of kingdoms.—PARR, SAMUEL, 1807, *Character of Charles James Fox, Works, vol.* IV, *p.* 40.

Genius and taste, and talent gone,
Forever tombed beneath the stone,
Where—taming thought to human pride—
The mighty chiefs sleep side by side.
Drop upon Fox's grave the tear,
'Twill trickle to his rival's bier.
O'er Pitt's the mournful requiem sound,
And Fox's shall the notes rebound.
The solemn echo seems to cry,—
"Here let their discord with them die.
Speak not for those a separate doom
Whom fate made brothers in the tomb;
But search the land of living men,
Where wilt thou find their like again?"
—SCOTT, SIR WALTER, 1808, *Marmion, Canto I., Introduction.*

I have never seen Mr. Fox more perfectly happy than when we were quite alone. He was so utterly divested of a wish to shine, or of any appetite for flattery, that he in no manner required, what is called, company, to enliven or animate him. A lover of nature, and consequently an enemy to art, he held, I think, above every quality, sincerity, and unaffectedness ; and, being also of a character singularly domestic and amiable, he found in his little circle all he wished and wanted. To his other attainments he had added very considerable knowledge in Botany ; and without making it a primary object, enjoyed every pursuit connected with agriculture, in a high degree.—TROTTER, JOHN BERNARD, 1812, *Memoirs of the Latter Years of Charles James Fox, p.* 35.

In London mixed society Fox conversed little ; but at his own house in the country, with his intimate friends, he would talk on forever, with all the openness and simplicity of a child : he has continued talking to me for half-an-hour after he had taken up his bed-room candle.—I have seen it somewhere stated that Fox liked to talk about great people : nothing can be more untrue ; he hardly ever alluded to them.—ROGERS, SAMUEL, 1855, *Recollections of Table-Talk, ed. Dyce, p.* 74.

Nature bestowed on Mr. Fox the qualities which are certain to command distinction in popular assemblies. He possessed in the highest degree the temperament of the orator, which, equal to the poet's in the intensity of feeling, is diametrically opposed to the poet's in the direction to which its instincts impel it. . . . Mr. Fox might have spent the night in a gaming-house, hurried off to Newmarket at daybreak, returned just in time to open a debate in the House of Commons—but who shall say that during those hours he had found no intervals in which his reason was arranging a course of argument, and his memory suggesting the appropriate witticism or the felicitous allusion? . . . Those, indeed, notably err, who, judging only by the desultory social habits and dissipated tastes of Mr. Fox, conclude that his faculties attained their strength without the necessary toil of resolute exertion. —LYTTON, EDWARD BULWER LORD, 1855–68, *Pitt and Fox, Miscellaneous Prose Works, vol.* I, *pp.* 224, 225.

There is one man, Charles Fox, happy from his cradle, who learned everything without study, whom his father trained in prodigality and recklessness, whom, from the age of twenty-one, the public voice proclaimed as the first in eloquence and the leader of a great party, liberal, humane, sociable, faithful to these generous expectations, whose very enemies pardoned his faults, whom his friends adored, whom labour never wearied, whom rivals never embittered, whom power did not spoil ; a lover of converse, of literature, of pleasure, who has left the impress of his rich genius in the persuasive abundance, in the fine character, the clearness and continuous ease of his speeches.—TAINE, H. A., 1871, *History of English Literature, tr. Van Laun, vol.* II, *bk.* iii, *ch.* iii, *p.* 80.

It was an end which would better have become a serious Christian. But it is not for us to pass sentence on a man so benevolent in his dispositions and designs. We may rather be surprised at his possessing so much virtue, not having the gift of faith. We may hope that his good deeds, his gratitude to all who had ever served him, his constant uneasiness till he had repaid their kindness, his uniform longing for peace, and his general philanthropy, have been taken into account by the Merciful Judge who makes allowances for all. "Perhaps no human being," said Gibbon, "was ever more perfectly exempt from the taint of malevolence, vanity, or falsehood."—EARLE, JOHN CHARLES, 1871, *English Premiers, vol.* I, *p.* 332.

Our first great statesman of the modern

school. . . . He was not a political adventurer, but a knight-errant roaming about in search of a tilt, or, still better, of a *mêleê;* and not much caring whether his foes were robbers or true men, if only there were enough of them. He was one who, in a venal age, looked to something besides the main chance; who, when he had set his mind or his fancy on an enterprise, never counted the odds that he faced, or the hundreds a year that he forfeited. But with all these generous gifts, his education and his circumstances almost proved too much for him; and it was the instinct of moral self-preservation which drove him to detach himself from his early surroundings, and find safety in uncompromising hostility to that evil system which had come so near to spoiling him. "Are wills so weak? Then let not mine wait long.

Hast thou so rare a poison? Let me be
Keener to slay thee, lest thou poison me."

Such is the temper in which, fortunately for mankind, rare and noble natures have often revolted against that world whose blighting influence they had begun to feel; and such was the mood of Charles Fox when, sick of a prison-house whose secrets had so early been familiar to him, he dissolved his partnership with Sandwich and Wedderburn, and united himself to Burke and Chatham and Savile in their crusade against the tyranny which was trampling out English liberty in the colonies, and the corruption which was undermining it at home.—TREVELYAN, GEORGE OTTO, 1880, *The Early History of Charles James Fox, pp.* 1, 452.

While there is so much to admire and love in the character of Fox . . . there is no man of his own or perhaps of any age who presented in himself more to be accepted and at the same time more to be avoided as an example. His habits of life would have ruined him before he had matured if he had not contracted them innocently, and if they had not been afterward controlled to some extent by intellectual endowments of the very highest order. Happily the number of parents who train children as Fox was trained is very limited, and unhappily the number born with such marvelous endowments is still more limited. He is therefore to be contemplated rather as a phenomenon than model, reminding one of the Pyramid of Cheops, so imposing in its dimensions, so

unique in all its proportions, but fitly built in a wilderness, and not a model upon which a school of architecture can ever be founded.—BIGELOW, JOHN, 1881, *The Early History of Charles James Fox, Harper's Magazine, vol.* 62, *p.* 433.

The early days of Fox were his worst days. Indeed, in the opening years of his life it is not so easy to discover the great liberal of the future. Yet like all the rest of Fox's career his early life was typical. He inherited the doctrines of his father, who was, perhaps, as bad an example as could be found of all the political vices of the eighteenth century in England. Offices and blunders were the creed of the first Lord Holland; and his son, making himself master of these and backed by bought majorities, astonished the House of Commons by his brilliant, youthful rhetoric, attacking what was right with the same success which he won in later years when he denounced what was wrong. It was the way of the world into which Charles Fox was born, and he took up all the ways of that world with equal extravagance and success.—LODGE, HENRY CABOT, 1881, *The Early Days of Fox, The International Review, vol.* 10, *p.* 281.

That a man of whom all this can be truly said should have taken a high and honourable place in English history, and should have won for himself the perennial love and loyalty of some of the best Englishmen of his time, is not a little surprising, for a life such as I have described would with most men have destroyed every fibre of intellectual energy and of moral worth. But in truth there are some characters which nature has so happily compounded that even vice is unable wholly to degrade them, and there is a charm of manner and of temper which sometimes accompanies the excesses of a strong animal nature that wins more popularity in the world than the purest and the most self-denying virtue. Of this truth Fox was an eminent example. With a herculean frame, with iron nerves, with that happy vividness and buoyancy of temperament that can ever throw itself passionately into the pursuits and the impressions of the hour, and can then cast them aside without an effort, he combined one of the sweetest of human tempers, one of the warmest of human hearts. Nothing in his career is more remarkable than the spell which he cast over men who in character and principles were as unlike as possible to himself. —LECKY, WILLIAM EDWARD HARTPOLE, 1882, *A History of England in the Eighteenth Century, vol.* III, *ch.* xiii, *p.* 507.

In the duel between Fox (who was a very stout man) and Adam, so soon as the ground had been measured, Fitzgerald (second of the former) said, "You must stand sideways, Mr. Fox, as much as you can." "Why so?" asked the statesman; "I am as thick one way as the other." —TRUMAN, BEN C., 1884, *The Field of Honor, p.* 554.

"Carlo Khan." "A Hercules." "The Last of the Romans." "The Man of the People." "Niger." "The Young Cub."— FREY, ALBERT R., 1888, *Sobriquets and Nicknames, p.* 407.

As a young man Fox was strongly built; his frame was large, and he had a handsome face, bright eyes, high colour, and black hair. He soon became very stout, and his enemies considered that in manhood his swarthy countenance had a "saturnine" aspect, but his smile was always pleasant. From childhood he was courted for his gaiety, originality, and genius. He was perfectly good-natured, eager, warm-hearted, and unselfish. With great natural abilities, a singular quickness of apprehension, and a retentive memory, he combined the habit of doing all things with his might. He was, as he said, a "very painstaking man," and even when secretary of state wrote copies for a writing-master to improve his handwriting. He delighted in literature and art, his critical faculty was acute, and his taste cultivated. Poetry was to him "the best thing after all," and he declared that he loved "all the poets."—HUNT, WILLIAM, 1889, *Dictionary of National Biography, vol.* XX, *p.* 95.

Indeed we can only account for his great successes as an orator, his amazing repute, and his exceptional popularity, when we sum up a half score of contributory causes, which lie outside of the cold print of the Parliamentary record; among these, we count—his Holland wealth and training, his environments of rank and luxury, his picturesque bearing, his *bonhomie*, his scorn of the rank he held, his accessibility to all, his outspoken, democratic sympathies, that warmed him into outbursts

of generous passion, his fearlessness, his bearding of the king, his earnestness whenever afoot, his very shortcomings too, and the crowding disabilities that grew out of his trust—his simplicities—his lack of forethought, his want of moneyed prudence, his free-handedness, his little, unfailing, every-day kindnesses—these all backed his speeches and put a tender under-tone, and a glow, and a drawing power in them, which we look for vainly in the rhetoric or the argumentation.— MITCHELL, DONALD G., 1895, *English Lands Letters and Kings, Queen Anne and The Georges, p.* 191.

It was surely in an evil hour for himself that Burke became connected with Charles Fox. Charles Fox had fine impulses, though love of his own country was not one of them. It is not less certain that he was a most powerful debater, if in the reports of his speeches little of the fire is left. His social charms were also evidently great, and won him ardent friends. But his character had been formed at the gambling table, and Napoleon was right in saying that he would never, if he could help it, employ a gambler. The recklessness of the gambling table was brought by Fox into the arena of public life. . . . Fox, indolent, and ostentatiously ignorant of economy and finance, while he aspired to the government of a great commercial country, would, of course, welcome the industry and knowledge of Burke; while Burke would be drawn to Fox by Fox's lovable qualities, perhaps by his high connections, perhaps by the very dissimilarity of their character and gifts. Fox's violence in his opposition to North, which went almost to the length of treason, had the effect, as a good observer remarked, of confirming the obstinacy of the Government and prolonging the American war. Burke, as Fox's associate, must in some measure share the blame.—SMITH, GOLDWIN, 1896, *Burke, Cornhill Magazine, vol.* 74, *pp.* 22, 23.

SPEECHES

Vehement in his elocution, ardent in his language, prompt in his invention of arguments, adroit in its use, comprehensive in his view of the given subject, and equal to his political rival in the power of agitating the passions; but offending continually by the tautology of his diction and the repetition of his arguments. He feels this himself so much, as to think it necessary to vindicate it in private. And he so feels also his own inferiority in the selection of appropriate terms, that he says, "although he himself is never in want of words, Mr. Pitt is never without the best words possible."—ABBOT, CHARLES (LORD COLCHESTER),1795, *Diary and Correspondence, vol.* I, *p.* 23.

Paramount as he is in ability and in *political* eloquence beyond any man.—MATHIAS, THOMAS JAMES, 1797, *The Pursuits of Literature, Eighth ed., p.* 252.

Fox is the most illustrious model of a Parliamentary Leader, on the side of liberty, that this country has produced. This character is the appropriate glory of England, and Fox is the proper example of this character. . . . Fox, as an orator, appeared to come immediately from the forming hand of nature. He spoke well, because he felt strongly and earnestly. His oratory was impetuous as the current of the river Rhone; nothing could arrest its course. His voice would insensibly rise to too high a key; he would run himself out of breath. Everything showed how little artifice there was in his eloquence. Though on all great occasions he was throughout energetic, yet it was by sudden flashes and emanations that he electrified the heart, and shot through the blood of his hearer. I have seen his countenance lighted up with more than mortal ardour and goodness; I have been present when his voice has become suffocated with the sudden bursting forth of a torrent of tears.—GODWIN, WILLIAM, 1806, *Morning Chronicle, William Godwin, ed. Paul, vol.* II, *pp.* 153, 156.

For ourselves, we think we never heard any man who dismissed us from the argument on a debated topic with such a feeling of satisfied and final conviction, or such a competence to tell why we were convinced. There was, in the view in which subjects were placed by him, something like the daylight, that simple clearness which makes things conspicuous and does not make them glare, which adds no colour or form, but purely makes visible in perfection the real colour and form of all things round; a kind of light less amusing than that of magnificent lusters or a thousand coloured lamps, and less fascinating and romantic than that of the moon,

but which is immeasurably preferred when we are bent on sober business, and not at leisure, or not in the disposition to wander delighted among beautiful shadows and delusions. It is needless to say that Fox possessed in a high degree wit and fancy; but superlative intellect was the grand distinction of his eloquence; the pure force of sense, of plain, downright sense was so great, that it would have given a character of sublimity to his eloquence, even if it had never once been aided by a happy image or a brilliant explosion. The grandeur of plain sense would not have been deemed an absurd phrase, by any man who had heard one of Fox's best speeches. —FOSTER, JOHN, 1808, *Personal Virtue in its Relation to Political Eminence, Critical Essays, ed. Ryland, vol.* I, *p.* 158.

Pitt I never heard: Fox but once, and then he struck me as a debater, which to me seems as different from an orator as an improvisatore, or a versifier, from a poet.—BYRON, LORD, 1813, *Journal, Life by Moore.*

This extraordinary person, then, in rising generally to speak, had evidently no more premeditated the particular language he should employ, nor frequently the illustrations and images by which he should discuss and enforce his subject, than he had contemplated the hour he was to die; and his exalted merit as a debater in Parliament did not, therefore, consist in the length, variety, or roundness of his periods; but in the truth and vigour of his conceptions; in the depth and extent of his information; in the retentive powers of his memory, which enabled him to keep in constant view, not only all he had formerly read and reflected on, but everything said at the moment, and even at other times, by the various persons whose arguments he was to answer; in the faculty of spreading out his matter so clearly to the grasp of his own mind, as to render it impossible he should ever fail in the utmost clearness and distinctness to others; in the exuberant fertility of his invention, which spontaneously brought forth his ideas at the moment, in every possible shape by which the understanding might sit in the most accurate judgment upon them; whilst, instead of seeking afterwards to enforce them by cold, premeditated illustrations, or by episodes, which, however beautiful, only distract attention, he was accustomed to repass his subject, not *methodically*, but in the most *unforeseen* and fascinating review, enlightening every part of it, and binding even his adversaries in a kind of spell for the moment of involuntary assent. . . . He possessed, above all men I ever knew, the most gentle and yet the most ardent spirit—a rare and happy combination! He had nourished in his mind all the manly and generous sentiments, which are the true supports of the social world; he was trembling alive to every kind of private wrong or suffering; and from the habitual and fervent contemplation of the just principles of government, he had the most bitter and unextinguishable contempt for the low arts of political intrigue, and an indignant abhorrence of every species of tyranny, oppression, and injustice.—ERSKINE, LORD, 1815, *Fox's Speeches, Letter to the Editor, vol.* I.

Fox was heedless of method; having the complete command of good words, he never sought for better; if those which occurred expressed his meaning clearly and forcibly, he paid little attention to their arrangement or harmony. This detracts from the merit of his speeches when they are read; but, when they were delivered, it perhaps added to their effect, as it tended greatly to make the hearers believe that he was above art, and spoke from conviction. . . . The moment of his grandeur was, when he had stated the argument of his adversary, with much greater strength than his adversary had done, and with greater than his hearers thought possible, he seized it with the strength of a giant, and tore and trampled it to destruction.—BUTLER, CHARLES, 1822, *Reminiscences, vol.* I, *pp.* 158, 160.

We of 1858, that can only *read* him, hearing Fox described as *forcible*, are disposed to recollect Shakspere's Mr. Feeble amongst Falstaff's recruits, who also is described as *forcible*—viz. as the "most forcible Feeble." And, perhaps, a better description could not be devised for Fox himself: so feeble was he in matter, so forcible in manner; so powerful for instant effect, so impotent for posterity. In the Pythian fury of his gestures, in his screaming voice (for Fox's voice was shrill as a woman's), in his directness of purpose, Fox would now remind you of some demon steam-engine on a railroad, some Fire-king or Salmoneus,

that had counterfeited Jove's thunderbolts,—hissing, bubbling, snorting, fuming. Demonias gas, you think, gas from Acheron, must feed that dreadful system of convulsions.—DE QUINCEY, THOMAS, 1858, *Schlosser's Literary History, Works, ed. Masson, vol.* XI, *p.* 35.

While Fox, in the simplicity and the vehemence of his reasoning, might bear comparison with Demosthenes, his speeches as a whole show more distinctly perhaps than those of any other speaker the difference between Greek and British oratory. A speech of Demosthenes resembles a beautiful Greek temple; it is composed of reasoning, of elegant diction, of appeals to the patriotism and public spirit of his hearers, all of the same pure material. We admire the purity, and harmony, the unity and grace of the structure. A speech of Fox resembles rather a cathedral of Gothic architecture. The strength of the buttresses, the grandeur of the arches, the painted glass, the fretted aisle, these multiplied and fanciful ornaments, fill the mind with admiration and delight. . . . Pitt used to say that, when he thought that he had himself done better than usual, he found Fox, in reply, surpass his ordinary vigour, and exceed the best of his former efforts. Wilberforce is reported to have declared himself always convinced for the moment by Pitt or by Fox, and inclined to give the palm to that one of these two orators who had last spoken.—RUSSELL, EARL, 1866, *The Life and Times of Charles James Fox, vol.* III, *pp.* 388, 389.

Though a statesman of the first order, yet it was oratory which gave to Fox an indisputable preëminence among his contemporaries. He was born with the oratorical temperament; from youth upwards, his ambition was to become a great speaker. He was endowed with an understanding of exceeding quickness, with an imagination of great brilliancy, with feeling of great mobility and tenderness; he had read much in the ancient and modern languages; a retentive memory enabled him to utilize his vast stores of information and illustrations, while his logical disposition led him to marshal in faultless symmetry and imposing array all the arguments he adduced to prove a case or enforce a proposition. His constant appeal was to the intellect, and his aim was to convince by reasoning. He was as practical as

Demosthenes. He had none of Cicero's besetting anxiety to demonstrate, when pleading a cause or advocating a policy, that he was an unrivalled master of fine language. No contemporary orator was his parallel. Chatham was a greater adept in dramatic effects. Burke was far more ornate and profound. William Pitt poured forth sentences infinitely superior in finish and melody. Lord North was more uniformly witty; Charles Townshend and Sheridan were more uniformly brilliant. None, however, among the elder or younger generation of speakers succeeded in making an audience feel, as Fox did, that they were listening to arguments which could not be refuted, and to common sense it was hardly possible to gainsay.—RAE, WILLIAM FRASER, 1873, *Wilkes, Sheridan, Fox; The Opposition under George the III., p.* 420.

Fox was a great speaker, and, in the words of Burke, the greatest debater the world ever saw. Not place or power, but reputation as an orator, was the object of his ambition, as he declares in one of his earliest letters to an intimate friend and relation. He inspired affection rather than admiration. In his worst days an observer said of his party, "There are only forty of them, but every one of them is ready to be hanged for Fox." In his earliest days, Lord Mansfield being asked who that young man was whom he saw in Westminster Hall, answered, "That is the son of old Harry Fox, with twice his parts and half his sagacity." . . . The errors of Fox—his coalition with Lord North, and his India Bill—were grave; but the warmth of his feelings and his passionate love of liberty should obtain for his memory indemnity for these or even greater faults. His affectionate temper, combined with his love of liberty, won him the attachment of devoted friends. His memory ought to be consecrated in the heart of every lover of freedom throughout the globe.—RUSSELL, JOHN EARL, 1874, *Recollections and Suggestions, 1813–1873, pp.* 219, 220.

Fox delivered his speeches without previous preparation, and their power lay not in rhetorical adornments, but in the vigour of the speaker's thoughts, the extent of his knowledge, the quickness with which he grasped the significance of each point in debate, the clearness of his conceptions,

and the remarkable plainness with which he laid them before his audience. Even in his longest speeches he never strayed from the matter in hand; he never rose above the level of his hearers' understanding, was never obscure, and never bored the house. Every position that he took up he defended with a large number of shrewd arguments, plainly stated and well ordered. The training in elocution that he had received at Eton and his practice as an amateur actor gave him confidence and ease, while the accuracy and readiness of his memory supplied him with a store of quotations, and rendered him never at loss for a word. At the same time he does not appear to have been particularly fluent until he became warmed with his subject; then he spoke with a stormy eloquence which carried his hearers with him. His voice was naturally poor, and though he generally modulated it skilfully, he was apt when excited to speak with shrillness. His action was ungraceful. His attempts at pathos generally failed; he was prone to invective, and is said to have been the wittiest speaker of his time. Although some of his speeches introducing subjects to the house are magnificent, he especially excelled in reply; for great as he was as an orator, he was certainly greater in debate. —HUNT, WILLIAM, 1889, *Dictionary of National Biography, vol.* XX, *p.* 96.

Pre-eminently does he stand out as the first English statesman of ministerial rank who appreciated the power of the Platform, and who systematically used it. Whether or not it was that he liked it for the qualities which rendered him so much more fascinating to some men than the House of Commons, its freedom, its enthusiasm, its applause, certain it is that he was constantly addressing public meetings, so constantly, indeed, as to earn for himself the name of "The man of the people."—JEPHSON, HENRY, 1891, *The Platform, Its Rise and Progress, vol.* I, *p.* 224.

It may be said once for all that Fox was the most transcendant of all debaters, the most genial of all associates, the most beloved of all friends. He was moreover, after Burke, the most lettered politician in a generation that affected literature. . . . It has been said that his private life was conspicuously disordered. And yet even when it was blamable it was lovable, and it mellowed into an exquisite evening. Whether we see him plunged in Theocritus after a bout at faro which has left him penniless; or cheerfully watching the baliffs remove his last stick of furniture; or drinking with the jockey of Norfolk; or choosing wild waistcoats at Paris; or building with his own hands his little greenhouse at St. Anne's ; or sauntering down its cool glades with a book and a friend; or prone without either under a tree in the long summer afternoons; or watching the contests of Newmarket with the rapt frenzy of a boy; or chatting before the races with Windham on the horses of the ancients and the precise meaning of *argutum caput;* or corresponding with Gilbert Wakefield about innumerable other niceties of classical reading; or, when crippled and aged, playing trapball with the children and with more than a child's keenness; or speechless of generous tears in the House of Commons when quivering under the harsh severance of Burke; or placid on his deathbed reassuring his wife and nephew;—he stills exercises over us something of the unbounded fascination which he wielded over his contemporaries. — ROSEBERY, LORD, 1891, *Pitt (Twelve English Statesmen), pp.* 28, 32.

HISTORY

The goodness of his heart, and the grandeur of his mind—the just medium of his opinions between the crown and democracy, and his warm love of true and rational liberty, are, however, indelibly recorded in a work, which perhaps came out too soon after his death to be justly appreciated; and as it promoted the views of none of the parties of the day, it is rather to be considered a classic, whose wholesome tendency and purity of principle, will benefit posterity, than amend the present generation.—TROTTER, JOHN BERNARD, 1812, *Memoirs of the Latter Year of Charles James Fox, p.* 41.

The superiority of Mr. Fox to Sir James as an orator is hardly more clear than the superiority of Sir James to Mr. Fox as an historian. Mr. Fox with a pen in his hand, and Sir James on his legs in the House of Commons, were, we think, each out of his proper element. They were men, it is true, of far too much judgment and ability to fail scandalously in any undertaking to which they brought the whole

power of their minds. The "History of James II." will always keep its place in our libraries as a valuable book; and Sir James Mackintosh succeeded in winning and maintaining a high place among the parliamentary speakers of his time. Yet we could never read a page of Mr. Fox's writing, we could never listen for a quarter of an hour to the speaking of Sir James, without feeling that there was a constant effort, a tug up hill. Nature, or habit which had become nature, asserted its rights. Mr. Fox wrote debates. Sir James Mackintosh spoke essays. . . . While Mr. Fox winnowed and sifted his phraseology with a care, which seems hardly consistent with the simplicity and elevation of his mind, and of which the effect really was to debase and enfeeble his style, he was little on his guard against those more serious improprieties of manner into which a great orator, who undertakes to write history is in danger of falling. There is about the whole book a vehement, contentious, replying manner. Almost every argument is put in the form of an interrogation, an ejaculation, or a sarcasm. The writer seems to be addressing himself to some imaginary audience; to be tearing in pieces a defence of the Stuarts which has just been pronounced by an imaginary Tory. — MACAULAY, THOMAS BABINGTON, 1834, *Mackintosh's History of the Revolution in England in 1688, Critical and Miscellaneous Essays.*

It was also during the early progress of printing the first volume of these (Typographical) Antiquities, at Mr. Savage's, in Bedfordbury, Covent Garden, that I used to see the sheets of Mr. Fox's "Historical Work" hanging up in every direction through the dwelling-house and adjacent yard. It will be supposed that five thousand copies of a quarto volume, with five hundred more upon a larger paper, and yet another two hundred and fifty of an elephantine size, were not likely to be carried through the press where the premises were small, without seeming to suffocate every passage and corridor of the building. . . . It was doubtless the boldest experiment ever made with a large paper speculation: but it succeeded. In due course, what at first came forth as a rapid and overboiling torrent, at a high price subsided into a quiet channel, and became obtainable on very moderate terms. Yet, considering the extraordinary number of copies printed, I do not consider this book of the commonest possible occurrence. As the work of an Author whose name can never perish, it must necessarily form "part and parcel" of every well ordered library. Why is it not dressed in "rank and file" with the octavo HUMES, ROBERTSONS, and GIBBONS?—DIBDIN, THOMAS FROGNALL, 1836, *Reminiscences of a Literary Life, vol.* I, *pp.* 276, 277, *note.*

Has been greatly undervalued; but it will be properly estimated in future times. —ROGERS, SAMUEL, 1855, *Recollections of Table-Talk, ed. Dyce, p.* 97.

His History as he has left it, is simply a disquisition on English politics, from the time of Henry VII. to the death of Charles II., together with a narrative of the reign of James II. until the death of Monmouth. Here he paused, probably from the constant interruption of business, indolence, or pleasure. He evidently wanted sufficient steadiness to produce any laborious work, and the whole result of his inquiries is this imperfect fragment. The History has good sense, a clear manner, and an evident sincerity and honesty of execution; but it is wholly wanting in imagination, interest, and grace. Fox's style is that of a debater, plain, pointed, and inharmonious. His language does not flow easily, and wants the delicate graces of the fine writer. His narrative is sometimes interesting, on account of its clearness, but something more than simplicity is needed, to keep up for a long period the attention of the reader. And Fox must be remembered rather as one who desired to become an historian, than as having given any proofs of historical power.— LAWRENCE, EUGENE, 1855, *Lives of the British Historians, vol.* II, *p.* 365.

Incomparably the most important book relating to the art of government which appeared during his lifetime was the "Wealth of Nations," but Fox once owned that he had never read it, and the history which was his own serious composition added nothing to his reputation.—LECKY, WILLIAM EDWARD HARTPOLE, 1882, *A History of England in the Eighteenth Century, vol.* III, *ch.* xiii, *p.* 508.

GENERAL

We are no admirers of Mr. Fox's poetry. His *Vers de Société* appears to us flat and insipid. To write verses was the only thing which Mr. Fox ever attempted to do, without doing it well. In that single instance he seems to have mistaken his talent.—SMITH, SYDNEY, 1809, *Characters of Fox, Edinburgh Review, vol.* 14, *p.* 355.

Some specimens of his own verses have been circulated in private, and printed in collections. They were occasional, and on trifling subjects, but sufficient to prove the exquisite correctness of his ear and judgment, the delicacy of his feelings, and his great familarity with the best models of composition.—LODGE, EDMUND, 1821–34, *Portraits of Illustrious Personages of Great Britain, vol.* VIII, *p.* 201.

Charles Fox's "Fragment of History" falls far short of the expectations which that distinguished statesman's genius had raised regarding it. Probably the failure arose from the difference between the processes of speaking and of writing: yet Burke equally excelled in both!—Pitt has given no specimens, by which we may be led to believe that he could have been pre-eminent as an author. The matter of all his speeches is now dead: the spirit evaporated with the tones of his voice. We can cite no general wisdom,—nothing applicable beyond the occasion. Without this there may be talent; without a power of generalisation there cannot be genius. —BRYDGES, SIR SAMUEL EGERTON, 1834, *Autobiography, vol.* I, *p.* 320.

Fox, so pre-eminent as a debater, appears with small distinction in his authorship.—CROKER, JOHN WILSON, 1842, *Correspondence Between Mr. Pitt and the Duke of Rutland, Quarterly Review, vol.* 70, *p.* 289.

William Pitt
1759–1806

William Pitt generally called the Younger Pitt, the second son of the earl of Chatham, born May 28 1759. In 1780 he entered into public life, and took his seat in the House of Commons as member for Appleby. The opposition against the party in power, the cabinet of Lord North, consisted of two factions—one led by Rockingham and

Fox, and the other by Lord Shelburne. Pitt joined the latter which mostly consisted of old friends of his father, and his speeches made such an impression that Lord Shelburne, when he became first lord of the treasury in July 1782, offered him a place in the cabinet as chancellor of the exchequer. Lord North although at one time driven from power by Rockingham and Fox, now formed a coalition with them against the cabinet of Lord Shelburne, and in 1783 Lord Shelburne had to give in his resignation, and Pitt with him. But in the very next session, when Fox brought in his bill for transferring the government of India from the E. I. Co. to Parliament—that is to say, to the ministry—the coalition was defeated and the cabinet compelled to retire. Pitt was called upon to form the new cabinet, and after dissolving Parliament and gaining a majority at the general election of 1784, he established himself firmly in the most powerful position which a subject can occupy in England, and he maintained himself in this position without interruption for 14 years. The principal feature of his administration is his war with France, but no English historian has yet been able to give sufficient reason for this war which England began in 1793 and continued to 1815. It seems to have been a whim, a chimera of the minister ; he would imitate his great father in this point too. But his war administration was weak and confused, and when losses and disasters followed, the chimera grew into a mania. In 1801 he retired from office. In Feb. he resigned, and in May the Peace of Amiens was concluded. In 1804, however, he was recalled, and the war was renewed. But the surrender of the Austrian army at Ulm, the battle of Austerlitz, the Peace of Presburg filled the haughty but impotent minister with such chagrin that he died from disappointment, Jan. 23, 1806.—BARNARD AND GUYOT, 1885, *Johnson's New General Cyclopaedia, vol.* II, *p.* 1079.

PERSONAL

THIS MONUMENT
IS ERECTED BY PARLIAMENT TO
WILLIAM PITT,
SON OF WILLIAM, EARL OF CHATHAM,
IN TESTIMONY OF GRATITUDE
FOR THE EMINENT PUBLIC SERVICES
AND OF REGRET FOR THE IRREP-
ARABLE LOSS
OF THAT GREAT AND DISINTERESTED
MINISTER.
HE DIED ON JANUARY 23, 1806, IN THE
47TH YEAR OF HIS AGE.
—INSCRIPTION ON MONUMENT, *Westminster Abbey.*

Pitt . . . was merely a statesman, he was formed to seize occasions to possess himself of power, and to act with consummate craft upon every occurrence that arose. He belonged to ancient Carthage —he belonged to modern Italy—but there is nothing in him that expressly belongs to England.—GODWIN, WILLIAM, 1806, *Morning Chronicle, William Godwin, ed. Paul, vol.* II, *p.* 157.

Mr. Pitt, had received regular and systematic instruction in the principles of the Christian religion, in the doctrine and discipline of the Church of England, and in every branch of general ecclesiastical history. His knowledge on these subjects was accurate and extensive. He was completely armed against all sceptical assaults, as well against all fanatical illusion ; and in truth he was not merely a faithful and dutiful, but a learned member of our Established Church.—WELLESLEY, LORD, 1836, *Letter, Nov.*

Plain in feature, but with clear, grey, watchful eyes—with high and massive forehead, in which what phrenologists call the perceptive organs were already prominently marked—with lips which when in repose were expressive much of reserve, more of pertinacity and resolve, but in movement were singularly flexible to the impulse of the manlier passions, giving a noble earnestness to declamation and a lofty disdain to sarcasm—this young man sate amongst the Rockingham Whigs, a sojourner in their camp, not a recuit to their standard. He had, indeed, offered himself to their chief, but that provident commander had already measured for his uniform some man of his own inches, and did not think it worth while to secure the thews of a giant at the price of wasting a livery and disappointing a dwarf.—LYTTON, EDWARD BULWER LORD, 1855-68, *Pitt and Fox, Miscellaneous Prose Works, vol.* I, *p.* 229.

The impression left by the great Minister on all who knew him was indeed on several points, of no common kind. It is the more striking, since, in many cases, we find it come forth incidentally. "Pitt, the most forgiving and easy-tempered of men,"—so says Lord Malmesbury while treating of another subject. "Pitt is the most upright political character I every knew or heard of,"—so writes Wilberforce to Bankes. The observation of Rose upon another feature of his character is no less weighty:--"With respect to Mr. Pitt, I can say with the sincerest truth, that in an intercourse almost uninterrupted during more than twenty years I never saw him once out of temper, nor did ever one unpleasant sentence pass between us."— STANHOPE, PHILIP HENRY EARL, 1861–62, *Life of the Right Honourable William Pitt, vol.* IV, *p.* 403.

In all descriptions of Pitt's appearance in the House of Commons, a certain aloofness fills an odd space; he is "a thing apart," different somehow from other members. Fox was the exact opposite,— he was "a good fellow;" he rolled into the House, fat, good-humored, and popular. Pitt was spare, dignified, and reserved; when he entered the House, he walked to the place of the Premier without looking to the right or to the left, and he sat at the same place. He was ready to discuss important business with all proper persons, upon all necessary occasions; but he was not ready to discuss business unnecessarily with any one, nor did he discuss anything but business with any save a very few intimate friends, with whom his reserve at once vanished, and his wit and humor at once expanded, and his genuine interest in all really great subjects was at once displayed.—BAGEHOT, WALTER, 1861, *William Pitt, Works, ed. Morgan, vol.* III, *p.* 163.

His was one of those minds which dawns at rare intervals upon the world, yet with the exception of his lofty intellect, and his splendid sense of independence, which commanded the homage of all, he possessed few of the qualities which Englishmen admire in their rulers, and many of the faults which they detest. He was intensely proud, and, save in the presence of his family, where he was warmly loved, stiff, cold, and ungenial. When he appeared in public, even when he was cheered and fêted, his harsh features seldom relaxed their haughty, repellent expression. Kings bowed and smiled, but Pitt, the commoner, the son of a newly-created peer, took scant pains not to show that he held such homage in contempt. His conduct was irreproachable. . . .

He seemed never to forget that he was so rigidly virtuous, so highly honourable, so pure and disinterested, and endowed with such splendid talents; from the lofty pedestal of his superiority he never descended, he always spoke and acted as if the world were at his feet, and he the only man who should stand upright. He wanted humility, toleration, charity; had he possessed these great virtues, he would have been one of the noblest characters in history. As it was, his circle of friends was small, though intensely devoted, whilst that of his enemies was both numerous and powerful. His austerity alienated the sympathies of what is called society. . . . On the bead-roll of English Ministers, there have been men more popular, more kindly, more generous, but none more able, more straightforward, or more worthy of the high position he held, than the great, the disinterested, the austere William Pitt. — EWALD, ALEXANDER CHARLES, 1877, *Ministers and Maxims, Temple Bar, vol.* 51, *pp.* 229, 230.

Pitt, however, will always be measured and weighed by Englishmen according to two different modes of reckoning. Interpreted by his personal character, by the pureness, the loftiness,the public spirit and disinterestedness of his life, he stands on a higher pedestal than ever his genius for organization and administration has raised for him. To have been the least self-seeking politician that had wielded supreme power up to his own times—to have established and handed down a grand tradition of republican honour and simplicity in English statesmanship—is in itself a nobler triumph than the praise of his followers, or the success of his intrigues, or the votes of parliament, or the monument in Westminster Abbey.—SERGEANT, LEWIS, 1882, *William Pitt (English Political Leaders), p.* 192.

His friendship, although like all worthy friendship, not lavishly given, was singularly warm and was enthusiastically returned. Nothing in history is more credible and interesting than his affectionate and lifelong intimacy with Wilberforce, so widely differing from him in his views of life. Hardened politicians such as Rose and Farnborough were softened by their intercourse with him, and cherished his memory to the end of their lives with something of religious adoration.

This indeed was the posthumous feeling which he seems to have inspired more than any person in history. Even Sidmouth, who had loved him little during the last lustre of his life, shared this, and boasted that he had destroyed every letter of Pitt's which could cause the slightest detriment to Pitt's reputation. Canning, Pitt loved as a son. There is nothing more human in Pitt's life than the account of his affectionate solicitude and absorption at Canning's marriage. Canning's love for Pitt was something combined of the sentiments of a son, a friend, and a disciple. — ROSEBERY, LORD, 1891, *Pitt (Twelve English Statesmen)*, p. 264.

He had the genius of command, and was one of the greatest Parliamentary leaders England has ever seen; but it may be questioned if his public efficiency would not have been enhanced, had he possessed some of that "subordinate" experience he so haughtily repudiated, and had his long public life been more tempered by some of the teachings of Opposition. He came to regard rule and office almost as his right. . . . The life of this great statesman must be judged after taking into account, not only his actions and his motives, but also the times in which he lived, with all their difficulties and all their emergencies. In his review his "personal purity, disinterestedness, integrity, and love of country" stand out conspicuous. His aims, his gifts, and his powers were great, and William Pitt must forever be regarded as a very noble figure in the public life of England.—GIBSON, EDWARD, 1898 (LORD ASHBOURNE), *Pitt; Some Chapters of his Life and Times*, pp. 364, 368.

SPEECHES

In his luminous and comprehensive speeches in Parliament Pitt has explained his motives and unfolded his views, his objects, and his designs.—GIFFORD, JOHN, 1809, *History of the Political Life of Pitt*.

Before Mr. Pitt had a seat in parliament, he had been a constant attendant in the gallery of the house of commons, and near the throne in the house of lords, upon every important debate; and whenever he heard a speech of any merit on the side opposite to his own opinions, he accustomed himself to consider, as it proceeded, in what manner it might be answered; and when the speaker accorded with his own sentiments, he then observed his mode of

arranging and enforcing his ideas, and considered whether any improvement could have been made, or whether any argument had been omitted. To this habit, and to the practice already mentioned of reading Greek and Latin into English, joined to his wonderful natural endowments, may be attributed that talent for reply, and that command of language, for which he was from the first so highly distinguished. At whatever length he spoke, he avoided repetition and it was early and justly observed of him, that "he never failed to put the best word in the best place."—TOMLINE, GEORGE, 1821, *Memoirs of the Life of the Right Honourable William Pitt, vol.* I, p. 31.

Mackintosh said that Pitt's speeches are miserably reported. He was himself present at the speech on the Slave Trade in '92 (which Mr. Fox declared was the finest he had ever heard), and the report, he says, gives no idea whatever of its merits. —MOORE, THOMAS, 1823, *Diary, Memoirs, ed. Russell, vol.* IV, p. 76.

Pitt, tall and slender, had an air at once melancholy and sarcastic. His delivery was cold, his intonation monotonous, his action scarcely perceptible. At the same time, the lucidness and the fluency of his thoughts, the logic of his arguments, suddenly irradiated with flashes of eloquence, rendered his talent something above the ordinary line. . . . Ill dressed, without pleasure, without passion, greedy of power, he despised honours, and would not be any thing more than William Pitt.— CHATEAUBRIAND, FRANÇOIS RENÉ VICOMTE, 1837, *Sketches of English Literature, vol.* II, *pp.* 277, 278.

His declamation was admirable, mingling with and clothing the argument, as to be good for any thing declamation always must; and no more separable from the reasoning than the heat is from the metal in a stream of lava. Yet, with all this excellence, the last effect of the highest eloquence was for the most part wanting; we seldom forgot the speaker, or lost the artist in the work.—BROUGHAM, HENRY LORD, 1839–43, *Statesmen who Flourished in the Time of George III.*

The almost unanimous judgment of those who were in the habit of listening to that remarkable race of men, placed Pitt, as a speaker, above Burke, above Windham, above Sheridan, and not below Fox. His declamation was copious, polished, and splendid. In power of sarcasm he was probably not surpassed by any speaker, ancient or modern; and of this formidable weapon he made merciless use. In two parts of the oratorical art which are of the highest value to a minister of state he was singularly expert. No man knew better how to be luminous or how to be obscure.—MACAULAY, THOMAS BABINGTON, 1859, *William Pitt, Encyclopædia Britannica; Critical and Miscellaneous Essays.*

The early speeches of Pitt were masterpieces. Eloquence was his heritage, and the House of Commons the predestined theatre for its display. The lucidity of his exposition, the vigour of his declamation, the sting of his sarcasm, the regular flow and careful finish of his sentences, were as notable and striking when he first entered Parliament as they were after he had become its acknowledged ornament. His oratory had neither spring nor autumn. His mind never seemed to have been youthful. No one knew him as a mediocre speaker; it was difficult to believe that he ever had been a boy.—RAE, WILLIAM FRASER, 1873, *Wilkes, Sheridan, Fox; The Opposition Under George the Third,* p. 423.

All his classicism was but a weapon to smite with, or from which to forge the links of those shining parentheses by which he strangled an opponent. Nothing beyond or below the cool, considerate humanities of the cultured, self-poised gentleman (unless we except some rare outbreak of petulance) belongs to this great orator, who could thrust one through with a rapier held by the best rules of fence; and who never did or could say a word so warm as to touch a friend or make an enemy forget his courtliness.

—MITCHELL, DONALD G., 1895, *English Lands Letters and Kings, Queen Anne and the Georges,* p. 194.

GENERAL

Of the letters thus printed in the course of the present summer, we have had the honour to receive a copy, and we feel no hesitation in saying that—written though many of them were, in the very height of the session, or the utmost hurry of business—they appear to us models in that kind of composition. We can scarcely praise them more highly than by saying that they rival Lord Bolingbroke's celebrated diplomatic correspondence, of which, as we know from other sources, Mr. Pitt was a warm admirer. They never strain at any of those rhetorical ornaments, which, when real business is concerned, become only obstructions, but are endowed with a natural grace and dignity—a happy choice of words, and a constant clearness of thought. Although scarce ever divided into paragraphs, they display neither confusion, nor yet abrupt transition of subjects, but flow on, as it were, in an even and continuous stream.—CROKER, JOHN WILSON, 1842, *Correspondence Between Mr. Pitt and the Duke of Rutland, Quarterly Review, vol. 70, p. 291.*

If it is impossible now to read his private letters, written in the darkest hours of his official adversities, without a throbbing of the heart at the calm fortitude and indomitable hopefulness of their tone, it may be easily conceived how overpowering was the influence of these qualities over the minds of the small men, and the superficial men, and the congenial men, and the affectionate idolators, by whom he was surrounded.—MARTINEAU, HARRIET, 1851, *History of England, A. D. 1800–1815,* p. 32.

Clara Reeve
1729–1807

Born at Ipswich, the daughter of the rector of Freston, translated Barclay's "Argenis" (1772), and wrote "The Champion of Virtue, a Gothic Story" (1777), renamed "The Old English Baron," which was avowedly an imitation of Walpole's "Castle of Otranto." She wrote four other novels and "The Progress of Romance" (1785).
—PATRICK AND GROOME, *eds.,* 1897, *Chambers's Biographical Dictionary,* p. 782.

GENERAL

Have you seen "The Old Baron," a Gothic story, professedly written in imitation of Otranto, but reduced to reason and probability? It is so probable, that any trial for murder at the Old Bailey would make a more interesting story. Mrs. Barbauld's "Fragment" was excellent.

This is a *caput mortuum.*—WALPOLE, HORACE, 1778, *To Rev. William Mason, April 8; Letters, ed. Cunningham, vol.* VII, *p.* 51.

The yet unsated pleasure which I had received from repeated perusals of the "English Baron," excited an affectionate regard for its author, and solicitude for her fame.—ANNA, SEWARD, 1786, *The Gentleman's Magazine, vol.* 56, *pt.* i, *p.* 16.

This romance ["The Old English Baron"] is announced as an attempt to unite the most attractive and interesting circumstances of the ancient romance, with the incidents and feelings of real life. The latter, however, are sometimes too accurately represented, and the most important and heroic characters in the work exhibit a natural anxiety about settlements, stocking of farms, and household furniture, which ill assimilates with the gigantic and awful features of the romance.—DUNLOP, JOHN, 1814-45, *The History of Fiction, p.* 414.

The various novels of Clara Reeve are all marked by excellent good sense, pure morality, and a competent command of those qualities which constitute a good romance. They were, generally speaking, favourably received at the time, but none of them took the same strong possession of the public mind as "The Old English Baron," upon which the fame of the author may be considered as now exclusively rested. . . . In no part of "The Old English Baron," or of any other of her works, does Miss Reeve show the possession of a rich or powerful imagination. Her dialogue is sensible, easy, and agreeable, but neither marked by high flights of fancy, nor strong bursts of passion. Her apparition is an ordinary fiction, of which popular superstition used to furnish a thousand instances, when nights were long, and a family, assembled around a Christmas log, had little better to do than to listen to such tales. Miss Reeve has been very felicitously cautious in showing us no more of Lord Lovel's ghost than she needs must —he is a silent apparition, palpable to the sight only, and never brought forward into such broad daylight as might have dissolved our reverence. And so far, we repeat, the authoress has used her own power to the utmost advantage, and gained her point by not attempting to step beyond it. But we cannot allow that the rule which, in her own case, has been well and wisely adopted, ought to circumscribe a bolder and a more imaginative writer.— SCOTT, SIR WALTER, 1821, *Clara Reeve.*

That the "Old English Baron" was only *seventy* years ago esteemed by critics an excellent work of fiction, and became very popular, are facts that most forcibly declare the advance made during the last two generations in education and general intelligence.—JEAFFRESON, JOHN CORDY, 1858, *Novels and Novelists, vol.* I, *p.* 274.

As in Walpole's book [in the "Champion of Virtue"], there are a murder and a usurpation, a rightful heir defrauded of his inheritance and reared as a peasant. There are a haunted chamber, unearthly midnight groans, a ghost in armor, and a secret closet with its skeleton. The tale is infinitely tiresome, and is full of that edifying morality, fine sentiment and stilted dialogue—that "old perfumed, powdered D'Arblay conversation," as Thackeray called it—which abound in "Evelina," "Thaddeus of Warsaw," and almost all the fiction of the last quarter of the last century. Still it was a little unkind in Walpole to pronounce his disciple's performance tedious and insipid, as he did.—BEERS, HENRY A., 1898, *A History of English Romanticism in the Eighteenth Century, p.* 243.

John Home

1722-1808

Born, at Leith, 22 Sept. 1722. Educated at Leith Grammar School, and at Edinburgh Univ. Licensed Probationer of Presbyterian Church, 4 April 1745. Enlisted as Volunteer during Rebellion of 1745-46. Minister of Athelstaneford, 11 Feb. 1747. Tragedy "Agis" refused by Garrick, 1747. Tragedy "Douglas" refused by Garrick, 1755; performed in Edinburgh, 14 Dec. 1756; produced at Covent Garden, 14 March 1757. Pension of £100 from Princess of Wales, 1857. Returned to Scotland. Indicted by Presbytery; resigned ministry, 7 June, 1757. Tutor to Prince of Wales, 1757. Sec. to Lord Bute, 1757. "Agis" produced by Garrick at Drury Lane, 21

Feb. 1758. "The Siege of Aquileia" produced at Drury Lane, 21 Feb. 1760. Pension of £300 from George III., 1760. Conservator to Scots Privileges at Campvere, Holland (sinecure), 1763–70. "The Fatal Discovery" produced at Drury Lane, 23 Feb. 1769. Married Mary Home, 1770. "Alonzo" produced at Drury Lane, 27 Jan. 1773. To Bath with Hume, April 1776; to Edinburgh with him, July 1776. "Alfred," produced, at Drury Lane, 21 Jan. 1778. Enlisted in South Fusiliers, 1778. Died, at Murchiston, 5 Sept. 1808. *Works:* "Douglas" (anon.), 1757; "Agis" (anon.), 1758; "The Siege of Aquileia" (anon.), 1760; "Dramatick Works," 1760; "The Fatal Discovery" (anon.), 1769; "Alonzo" (anon.), 1773; "Alfred" (anon.), 1778; "The History of the Rebellion in . . . 1745" 1802. *Collected Works:* ed. by H. Mackenzie (3 vols.), 1822. *Life:* by H. Mackenzie, 1822.—SHARP, R. FARQUHARSON, 1897, *A Dictionary of English Authors, p.* 135.

PERSONAL

John Home was an admirable companion, and most acceptable to all strangers who were not offended with the levities of a young clergyman, for he was very handsome and had a fine person, about 5 feet 10½ inches, and an agreeable, catching address; he had not much wit, and still less humor, but he had so much sprightliness and vivacity, and such an expression of benevolence in his manner, and such an unceasing flattery of those he liked (and he never kept company with anybody else), —the kind commendations of a lover, not the adulation of a sycophant, —that he was truly irresistible, and his entry to a company was like opening a window and letting the sun into a dark room.—CAR-LYLE, ALEXANDER, 1746–48–1860, *Autobiography, p.* 181.

His temper was of that warm susceptible kind which is caught with the heroic and the tender, and which is more fitted to delight in the world of sentiment than to succeed in the bustle of ordinary life. This is a disposition of mind well suited to the poetical character, and, accordingly, all his earliest companions agree that Mr. Home was from his childhood delighted with the lofty and heroic ideas which embody themselves in the description or narrative of poetry. . . . Mr. Home's favourite amusement was angling.—MAC-KENZIE, HENRY, 1812–22, *Account of the Life of Mr. John Home, Home's Works, vol.* I, *pp.* 6, 31.

It is said that the only approaches to a disagreement in the long and intimate friendship existing between these "two Humes" were regarding the relative merits of claret and port, and in relation to the spelling of their name, the philosopher in early life having adopted the orthograhy indicated by the pronunciation, the poet and preacher always clinging to the old and invariable custom of his family. David carried the discussion so far that on his death-bed he added a codicil to his will, written with his own hand, to this effect: "I leave to my friend Mr. John Home, of Kilduff, ten dozen of my old claret at his choice; and one other bottle of that other liquor called port. I also leave him six dozen of port, provided that he attests, under his hand, signed John *Hume,* that he has himself alone finished that bottle at a sitting. By this concession he will at once terminate the only difference that ever arose between us concerning temporal matters." It is to be inferred that this is a joke which got into the head of one Scotchman without a surgical operation. — HUTTON, LAURENCE, 1891, *Literary Landmarks of Edinburgh, p.* 26.

Now he became part of Edinburgh society. A welcome addition he proved, with his hearty laugh, his unfailing good-humour; and he was happy once more in the company of his old friends Hume and Blair, Ferguson and Robertson. He and Hume enjoyed a banter, and a favourite subject was their names, which were pronounced alike, and had been spelt the same till the historian changed his paternal surname of "Home to Hume". . . . Home's exuberant praise of everybody and everything was not empty flattery, but sheer good-heartedness; and even his vanity over his achievements was likeable.—GRAHAM, HENRY GREY, 1901, *Scottish Men of Letters in the Eighteenth Century, p.* 73.

DOUGLAS
1754

On Wednesday, February the 2d, 1757, the Presbytery of Glasgow came to the following resolution. They having seen a printed paper, intituled, "An admonition and exhortation of the reverend Presbytery of Edinburgh;" which, among other "evils" prevailing, observing the following "melancholy" but "notorious" facts: that one who is a minister of the church of Scotland did "himself" write and compose a "stage-play," intituled, "The tragedy of Douglas" and got it to be acted at the theatre of Edinburgh; and that he with several other ministers of the church were present; and "some" of them "oftener than once," at the acting of the said play before a numerous audience. The presbytery being "deeply affected" with this new and strange appearance, do publish these sentiments, &c.—RESOLUTION BY THE PRESBYTERY OF GLASGOW, 1757, *Disraeli's Curiosities of Literature.*

With great pleasure I have more than once perused your tragedy. It is interesting, affecting, pathetic. The story is simple and natural; but what chiefly delights me, is to find the language so pure, correct, and moderate. For God's sake, read Shakespeare, but get Racine and Sophocles by heart. It is reserved to you, and you alone, to redeem our stage from the reproach of barbarism.—HUME, DAVID, 1756, *Letter to John Home.*

I can now give you the satisfaction of hearing that the play, though not near so well acted in Covent Garden as in this place, is likely to be very successful. Its great intrinsic merit breaks through all obstacles. When it shall be printed (which shall be soon) I am persuaded it will be esteemed the best, and by French critics the only tragedy of our language.—HUME, DAVID, 1757, *Letter to Adam Smith.*

The extraordinary merits of this performance, which is now become to Scotchmen a subject of national pride.—STEWART, DUGALD, 1796–1801, *Account of the Life and Writings of William Robertson.*

The "Douglas" of Home is not recommended by his species of merit. In diction and character it does not rise above other productions of the period. But the interest turns upon a passion which finds a response in every bosom; for those who are too old for love, and too young for ambition, are all alike awake to the warmth and purity of maternal and filial affection. The scene of the recognition of Douglas's birth possesses a power over the affections, which when supported by adequate representation, is scarce equalled in the circle of Drama. It is remarkable that

the ingenious author was so partial to this theatrical situation, as to introduce it in several of his other tragedies.—SCOTT, SIR WALTER, 1814–23, *The Drama.*

I think nobody can bestow too much praise on "Douglas." There has been no English tragedy worthy of the name since it appeared.—WILSON, JOHN, 1822, *Noctes Ambrosianæ, April.*

His great dramatic essay was a grievous offence against the laws of his church, to the practical duties of which he had again surrendered himself. Had it not been that Sarah Ward was willing to help author and friends, even the reading of "Douglas" would never have come off. Sarah lent her sitting room in the Canongate, to Home; and Digges was present and silent, for once, with Mrs. Ward, to enact audience. The characters were thus cast; and a fine group of intellectual persons, sitting as they could best catch the light, in an obscure room of the Cannongate, cannot well be imagined. Lord Randolph (or Barnard, according to the original cast) was read by Robertson; Glenalvon, by the greater historian, David Hume; Old Norval, by the famous Dr. Caryle, the minister of Musselburgh; and Douglas, by Home, in right of authorship. Lady Randolph was allotted to Professor Ferguson; and the part of Anna was read by Dr. Blair, the minister of the High Church, and author of the once popular sermons! But the Presbyteries of Edinburgh and Glasgow speedily denounced author, play, dramatists, and dramas generally, as instruments and children of Satan; and excommunicated, not only Home, but actors and audiences, and all abettors and approvers! The triumph of the play compensated for every thing. The nation confirmed the sentiment of the critic in the pit, whose voice was heard in the ovation of the first night, exultingly exclaiming, "Weel, lads, what do ye think o' Wully Shakspeare, noo?"—DORAN, JOHN, 1863, *Annals of the English Stage, vol. I, p.* 414.

The indisputable merits of the play cannot blind us to the fact that "Douglas" is the child of "Merope."—WARD, A.W., 1878, *Drama, Encyclopædia Britannica, Ninth edition, vol.* VII.

All the dramatic capital of "Douglas" is exhausted in telling a sentimental tale; for characters there are none. There is, it is true, some poetry in the piece; but it is poetry of a weak type, pretty, but not beautiful, mildly interesting, but not rousing with new and great thoughts.—WALKER, HUGH, 1893, *Three Centuries of Scottish Literature, vol.* II, *p.* 111.

A sort of affection, mingled with contempt, and connected with the universally known "My name is Norval," keeps in twilight rather than utter darkness the once famous "Douglas" of Home. But it is pretty certain that most audiences, and almost all modern readers, would be affected by it with the same sort of *fou rire* as that which Thackeray, by a slight anachronism, ascribes to General Lambert and Mr. George Warrington at an early performance of the play.—SAINTSBURY, GEORGE, 1898, *A Short History of English Literature, p.* 637.

"Douglas" was successful—though it only ran a usual nine nights at first. On the third night the Duke of Cumberland handed twenty guineas to the elated author, his pride not objecting to take what an author out-at-elbows would blush now to have offered. Society found a charm about the play which struck a finer note than the turgid dramas which were fashionable at that time; there were true touches of nature, a chord of human tragedy, a vein of poetry, which, though the play does not appeal strongly to us to-day, made it, by contrast with the bombast and fustian then in vogue, deserving of the honour it won. The fastidious Mr. Gray wrote to his friend Horace Walpole that the author of "Douglas" "seems to have retrieved the true language of the stage, which has been lost for a hundred years, and there is one scene (between Lady Randolph and the stranger) so masterly that it strikes one blind to all its defects." It was played with success in Ireland; and Thomas Sheridan, the manager, munificiently sent from Dublin a gold medal—worth £10—as a mark of admiration of the author. This Dr. Johnson stigmatised in his sweeping way not merely as a piece of impudence, but as an act of folly in rewarding a play "without ten good lines." English praise was high, but the enthusiasm of Scotsmen was boundless. The drama was proclaimed "the first of English tragedies"—though really and chronologically it was only the first of Scottish tragedies. The delighted

dramatist absorbed the flattery and believed it all. He had not that modest self-estimate shown by Dr. Samuel Johnson, who, when he was informed that young Mr. Pott, the poet, had pronounced "Irene" "the finest tragedy of modern days," growled out, "If Pott says so, Pott lies."—GRAHAM, HENRY GREY, 1901, *Scottish Men of Letters in the Eighteenth Century, p.* 67.

The literary merits are not so apparent to modern readers as they were to his contemporaries, but which had its own literary importance as a precursor of the romantic revival which was ere long to make itself more distinctly felt. . . . The excellence, as literature, of Home's tragedy has not been accepted by posterity; and its importance as an instrument in affecting thought may well be doubted. —CRAIK, SIR HENRY, 1901, *A Century of Scottish History, vol.* I, *pp.* 438, 442.

GENERAL

Let them with Home, the very prince of verse,
Make something like a tragedy in Erse.
—CHURCHILL, CHARLES, 1764, *The Journey.*

Mr. Home, author of the tragedy of "Douglas," is also to be numbered in the list of Scotish song writers; but it must be confessed that "The Banks of the Dee" has lost much of its popularity, though surely nothing of its merit, since the "valiant Jemmy" failed to "quell the proud rebels." That Jemmy's ghost now wanders on those banks, instead of his person, might be no improper or unpathetic subject for a second part.— RITSON, JOSEPH, 1794–1869, *An Historical Essay on Scotish Song, p.* 70.

Home's other tragedies are all very indifferent,—most of them quite bad. Mr. Mackenzie should not have disturbed their slumbers.—WILSON, JOHN, 1822, *Noctes Ambrosianæ, April.*

The work of Home was not entirely such as might have been expected from one who was not only an actor in the scene, but the author of a tragedy like "Douglas," elegant enough to have pleased on the French stage, and yet affecting enough to succeed on ours. The "History of the Rebellion" was a work which had been meditated so long, that it was delivered to the world too late,—when the writer was no longer what he once was. But I recommend it to **your** perusal, because it has all the marks of authenticity; possesses, I think, more merit than is generally supposed; treats of a very remarkable event in our history; and is, after all, entertaining, and not long.—SMYTH, WILLIAM, 1839, *Lectures on Modern History, Lec.* xxviii.

So much of the flavour of Home's work has evaporated that the reader of the present day almost inevitably asks what is the secret of the extraordinary popularity he enjoyed in his own time. As far as Scotland is concerned, the explanation might be supposed to lie, and no doubt did in part lie, in the feeling of patriotism. Home was the representative Scot of literature, and the honour of his country was bound up with his. But he was scarcely less warmly received in England; and a Scot living in England under the Bute administration was not the person to arouse a prejudice in favour of himself. The explanation of the popularity must therefore be sought within Home's writings, and not in external circumstances. It was probably due to the fact that his dramas appeal to sentiment; and thus, in an age when the appeal to reason had been somewhat overdone, they caught the fancy of the multitude. So long as the love of melodrama survives, and it is perennial, work such as Home's is sure of a temporary popularity. . . . Home was a man who could harp with success upon one string; but he could do nothing more. However foreign it might be to his plot, he must either enlist the spirit of sentiment or fail. To the true heroic he could

not rise. He had glimmerings of it in his soul, his heart warmed to it, but he could not express it. Now that the glitter of novelty is gone, it is easy to see that a niggard nature had denied him the wreath of the *vates sacer.* Johnson, whose scornful disbelief in Home is well known, though he expressed his opinion in exaggerated language, was essentially right. But a literary reputation is rarely achieved without some more or less real foundation; and Home's power was real within the limits of sentiment. He was master of a kind of pathos cognate to, yet different from, that of "East Lynne." He could at least make a martial figure stalk with a gallant bearing across the stage, and he could fill his mouth with sounding phrases. It ought in justice to be added that he has occasional lines of a high order.—WALKER, HUGH, 1893, *Three Centuries of Scottish Literature, vol.* II, *pp.* 109, 113.

No mortal now can go over any of Home's laborious tragedies except "Douglas;" and one may apply to them the verdict which the Marquis of Wellesley passed on Dr. Johnson's Latin verses—"All of them are bad, but some of them are worse than others." We need not, however, superciliously laugh at Home's defunct tragedies, for they admirably suited the taste of the age. All dramatists gave the same sort of produce for the stage, and society, strange to say, admired it.—GRAHAM, HENRY GREY, 1901, *Scottish Men of Letters in the Eighteenth Century, p.* 69.

Richard Hurd
1720–1808

Prelate and writer, named the "Beauty of Holiness" on account of his comeliness and piety, was born at Congreve, Staffordshire, January 13, 1720, and became a fellow of Emmanuel College, Cambridge, in 1742. In 1750 he became a Whitehall preacher, in 1774 Bishop of Lichfield and Coventry, and in 1781 of Worcester. He died May 28, 1808. Among his works are "Commentary on Horace's Ars Poetica" (1749); "Dissertations on Poetry" (1755–57); "Dialogues on Sincerity, &c." (1759), his most popular book; "Letters on Chivalry and Romance" (1762); "Dialogues on Foreign Travel" (1764); and "An Introduction to the Prophecies" (1722). See Hurd's Works (8 vols. 1811) and "Memoir" by Kilvert (1860).—PATRICK AND GROOME, *eds.,* 1897, *Chambers's Biographical Dictionary, p.* 514.

PERSONAL

He is grown pure and plump, just of the proper breadth for a celebrated town-preacher.—GRAY, THOMAS, 1765, *To Rev. William Mason; Letters, ed. Gosse, vol.* III, *p.* 224.

Of Dr. Hurd, Bishop of Worcester, Johnson said to a friend, "Hurd, Sir, is one of a set of men who account for every thing systematically; for instance, it has been a fashion to wear scarlet breeches; these men would tell you, that according to causes and effects, no other wear could at that time have been chosen." He, however, said of him at another time to the same gentleman, "Hurd, Sir, is a man whose acquaintance is a valuable acquisition."—JOHNSON, SAMUEL, 1783, *Life by Boswell*, ed. Hill, vol. IV, p. 219.

His appearance and air are dignified, placid, grave, and mild, but cold and rather distancing. He is extremely well-bred nevertheless. . . . Piety and goodness are so marked in his countenance, which is truly a fine one, that he has been named, and very justly, "The Beauty of Holiness." Indeed, in face, manner, demeanour, and conversation, he seems precisely what a bishop should be, and what would make a looker-on, were he not a Bishop, and a see vacant, call out,—take Dr. Hurd! that is the man!—D'ARBLAY, MADAME (FANNY BURNEY), 1786–7, *Diary*, Dec. 23, Jan. 2.

Hurd had acquired a great name by several works of slender merit, was a gentle plausible man, affecting a singular decorum that endeared him highly to devout old ladies.—WALPOLE, HORACE, 1797, *Journal of the Reign of King George the Third*.

Let me be allowed to boast that, from the commencement of my typographic life to the day of his death, I had the honour of uninterruptedly enjoying his Lordship's patronage. . . . I had often the satisfaction of attending this good prelate officially, when he was only Mr. Hurd, in the business of his various learned works; and uniformly experienced the same gratifying affability, which was not lessened by the progressive dignities to which he was advanced. After Dr. Hurd became a Bishop, I have frequently been honoured with an invitation to his hospitable dinners, with a very small but select party of his Lordship's friends, when the culinary feast, neatly elegant as it always was, formed the least part of the treat. The rich stores of a capacious and highly-cultivated mind were opened with the utmost placidity of manner, and were a never-failing source of instruction and delight.—NICHOLS, JOHN, 1812, *Literary Anecdotes*, vol. VI, p. 600.

Hurd was a man of strict integrity, and very kind to those of whom he approved; but he was distant and lofty, and not at all admired by those who did not estimate him in a literary capacity. Indeed he paid

no attention to them; for in one of his letters to Warburton he made use of a common phrase of his, "I am here perfectly quiet, for I have delightfully bad roads about me."—CRADOCK, JOSEPH, 1826–28, *Memoirs*.

In person, Bishop Hurd was below the middle size, of slight make, but well proportioned, his features not marked, but regular and pleasing, and his whole aspect intelligent, thoughtful, and in later life venerable. This idea is fully conveyed in the portraits of him extant, by Gainsborough and others. Although he reached so advanced an age, his health seems never to have been good; and, notwithstanding his temperate and abstemious mode of living, we find in his letters frequent complaints of his suffering from attacks of gout, dizziness, and lowness of spirits, as well as of languor and indolence arising from these causes. . . . His moral character was distinguished by undeviating integrity, and exact propriety, arising from *principle*, rather than from *sentiment*. It was said of him by an unfriendly judge, that he was "a cold, correct, gentleman," each word being intended as emphatic; and, with due allowance for the quarter from whence it came, this judgment seems not destitute of truth. Another jocularly called him "an old maid in breeches," a sarcasm which, though it attributes to him, perhaps not unjustly, some share of primness and precision, bears testimony to the scrupulous correctness of his character. This constitution of mind, whilst it rendered him less generally amiable, exempted him from many of the temptations to which warmer tempers are exposed. . . . As a Preacher, his manner was calm, dignified, and impressive. His discourses, though not marked by force and energy, had yet a mild persuasiveness, and a tone of gentle insinuation, which, joined to frequent originality of thought, and constant exactness of method, peculiarly recommended him to his cultivated and refined audience at Lincoln's Inn.—KILVERT, FRANCIS, 1860, *Memoirs of the Life and Writings of the Right Rev. Richard Hurd*, pp. 194, 197, 201.

Hurd was a man who, having many qualities that obtain respect, and none that attach regard, has been more hardly treated by the biographers than he deserved to be. That he provoked a peculiar animosity among his contemporaries may well be understood. For if men ill brooked the domineering arrogance of Warburton, they were little likely to tolerate the irritable superciliousness of Warburton's toady. The "terse, neat, little, thin man," as one of his college contemporaries describes him, was sadly deficient in the warmth and geniality which the impetuous and choleric Warburton possessed in excess. This contrast of character promoted the intimacy which sprang up between the two.—PATTISON, MARK, 1863–89, *Life of Bishop Warburton, Essays,* ed. *Nettleship, vol.* II, *p.* 145.

The Bishop of Worcester, chiefly from his connection with Warburton, enjoyed high reputation in his day, but he was emphatically an over-estimated man, and though his manners were courtly and dignified in the presence of royalty, they were extremely cold and proud to those whom he considered his inferiors. Some literary claims indeed may fairly be allowed him. His discourses on "Prophecy" are still known and valued.—PERRY, GEORGE G., 1864, *The History of the Church of England, vol.* III, *p.* 445.

Hurd is a man for whom, though he has attracted a recent biographer, animated by the ordinary biographer's enthusiasm, it is difficult to find a good word. He was a typical specimen of the offensive variety of University don; narrow-minded, formal, peevish, cold-blooded, and intolerably conceited. As Johnson said of "Hermes" Harris, he was "a prig, and a bad prig." Even Warburton, it is said, could never talk to him freely. In his country vicarage he saw nobody, kept his curate at arm's length, and never gave an entertainment except on one occasion, when Warburton, who was staying with him, rebelled against the intolerable solitude. As a bishop, he never drove a quarter of a mile without his episcopal coach and his servants in full liveries. His elevation to the bench was justified by his fame— for which there are, perhaps, some grounds—as an elegant writer of Addisonian English and a good critic of Horace.—STEPHEN, LESLIE, 1876, *History of English Thought in the Eighteenth Century, vol.* I, *p.* 348.

GENERAL

It is a pleasure to have anybody one esteems agree with one's own sentiments,

as you do strongly with mine about Mr. Hurd. It is impossible not to own that he has sense and great knowledge—but sure he is a most disagreeable writer! He loads his thoughts with so many words, and those couched in so hard a style, and so void of all veracity, that I have no patience to read him. In one point, in the "Dialogues" you mention, he is perfectly ridiculous. He takes infinite pains to make the world believe, upon *his* word, that they are the genuine productions of the speakers, and yet does not give himself the least trouble to counterfeit the style of any one of them.—WALPOLE, HORACE, 1760, *To Rev. Henry Zouch, Feb.* 4; *Letters,* ed. *Cunningham, vol.* III, *p.* 289.

I have now seen the whole of the "Letter on Chivalry," and am wonderfully taken with them. . . . They cannot but please all persons of taste, greatly. They are the petit-piece to that noble work, "The Dialogues." . . . In which there is all the correctness of Addison's style, and a strength of reasoning, under the direction of judgment far superior.— WARBURTON, WILLIAM, 1762–70, *Letters from a Late Eminent Prelate, Letters,* clv, ccxxviii.

In this interval, I published at London my "Natural History of Religion," along with some other small pieces: its public entry was rather obscure, except only that Dr. Hurd wrote a pamphlet against it, with all the illiberal petulance, arrogance, and scurrility, which distinguish the Warburtonian school. This pamphlet gave me some consolation for the otherwise indifferent reception of my performance.— HUME, DAVID, 1776, *My Own Life, p.* 21.

To grapple with the unwieldy was among the frolics of Warburton, whilst your Lordship toiled in chasing the subtle. He often darkened the subject, and you perplexed it. He, by the boldness and magnitude of his conceptions, overwhelmed our minds with astonishment, and you, by the singularity and nicety of your quibbles, benumbed them with surprize. In him, we find our intellectual powers expanded and invigorated by the full and vivid representation which he sometimes holds up, both of common and uncommon objects, while you, my Lord, contrive to cramp and to cripple them by all the tedious formalities of minute and scrupulous analysis. He scorned every appearance of soothing the reader into attention, and you failed in almost every attempt to decoy him into conviction. He instructed, even where he did not persuade, and you, by your petulant and contemptuous gibes, disgusted every man of sense, whom you might otherwise have amused by your curious and showy conceits.—PARR, SAMUEL, 1789, *Tracts by Warburton and a Warburtonian, Dedication.*

The assassination of Jortin by Dr. Hurd, now Bishop of Worcester (see the "Delicacy of Friendship"), is a base and malignant act, which cannot be erazed by time or expiated by *secret* pennance.—GIBBON, EDWARD, 1793, *Autobiography, p.* 304, *note.*

Bishop Hurd, with the hand of a master, has opened the general View of the subject of prophecy, and freed it from the intricacies of speculation, and shewn its time, nature, end, and intent.—MATHIAS, THOMAS JAMES, 1797, *The Pursuits of Literature, Eighth ed., p.* 204.

The most distinguished of our philosophical critics.—DRAKE, NATHAN, 1804, *Essays Illustrative of the Tatler, Spectator, and Guardian, vol.* II, *p.* 145.

His Horace, his "Dialogues," and three volumes of "Sermons," with a "Life of Bishop Warburton," are the principal works he left behind him, for as to the "Delicacy of Friendship," it has been dragged into notice without his consent, and in all probability contrary to his wishes. His merit as a writer has been variously estimated, and literary men have gone into opposite extremes. It must be acknowledged that his veneration for the author of the "Divine Legation" seduced him into excessive panegyric, both of the work itself and of the author, and caused him to depreciate the merits and labours of all who had the fortune to differ in their opinions. With much ingenuity in criticism, there will be discovered some unecessary refinement, and, in this instance, the character of the two prelates will descend to posterity as perfectly congenial.—BRYDGES, SIR SAMUEL EGERTON, 1808, *Censura Literaria, vol.* VIII, *p.* 224.

Subtle and sophistical, elegant, but never forcible, his heart was cold, though his admiration was excessive. He wanted that power of real genius, which is capable of being fired by the contemplation of excellence, till it partakes of the heat and flame of its object. On the other hand, he wanted nothing of that malignity which is incident to the coolest tempers, of that cruel and anatomical faculty, which, in dissecting the characters of an antagonist, can lay bare, with professional indifference, the quivering fibres of an agonized victim. For this purpose his instrument was irony; and few practitioners have ever adopted that or any other, more unfeelingly than did the biographer of Warburton, even when the ground of complaint was almost imperceptible, as in the cases of Leland and Jortin.—WHITAKER, T. D., 1812, *Hurd's Edition of Bishop Warburton's Works, Quarterly Review, vol.* 7, *p.* 385.

Then Hurd, the future shield, scarcely the sword of Warburton, made his first sally; a dapper, subtle, and cold-blooded champion, who could dexterously turn about the polished weapon of irony.—DISRAELI, ISAAC, 1814, *Warburton, Quarrels of Authors.*

This elegantly-written and learned volume ["Prophecies"] has long been known and duly appreciated by the public. The subject is here opened in the most masterly and instructive manner by Bishop Hurd.—HORNE, THOMAS HARTWELL, 1818–39, *A Manual of Biblical Bibliography.*

Never were my humble expectations more miserably disappointed [ed. Addison]. It seemed to me as a sad "potatoeroasting" performance from such a quarter. — DIBDIN, THOMAS FROGNALL, 1824, *The Library Companion, p.* 605, *note.*

Hurd has, perhaps, the merit of being the first who in this country aimed at philosophical criticism : he had great ingenuity, a good deal of reading, and a facility in applying it; but he did not feel very deeply, was somewhat of a coxcomb, and having always before his eyes a model neither good in itself nor made for him to emulate, he assumes a dogmatic arrogance, which, as it always offends the reader, so far the most part stands in the way of the author's own search for truth.—HALLAM, HENRY, 1837–39, *Introduction to the Literature of Europe, pt.* iv, *ch.* v, *par.* 26, *note.*

An upright and scholarly, but formal

and censorious man, whom Johnson called a "word-picker," and franker contemporaries "an old maid in breeches."—DOBSON, AUSTIN, 1883, *Fielding (English Men of Letters)*, *p.* 141, *note*.

Hurd was a cold and "correct" writer, no less arrogant than his master, little less learned, and if anything even more vapid and perverted as a would-be leader of literary taste; in style he seems a kind of ice-bound Addison.—GOSSE, EDMUND, 1888, *A History of Eighteenth Century Literature*, *p.* 281.

He is best known to the present generation by his impertinent notes on Addison's "Works." By reprinting them, Mr. Bohn did much to spoil what was otherwise an excellent edition of that author.—HILL, GEORGE BIRKBECK, 1891, *Boswell's Life of Johnson*, *vol.* IV, *p.* 219.

We must regard Hurd as a strong influence. (1) He was a follower of the Warton school of criticism, and spoke much more boldly and decisively than Warton for Romantic tastes. (2) Besides helping in the general movement, he joined the Wartons in dethroning Pope by exalting the imaginative poets. (3) He came just at the time to accelerate the speed of the Romantic movement. Hurd's learning and authoritative position counted for much; and the emphasis with which he spoke is remarkable, coming so early as 1762. The critical judgments on poetry made by Matthew Arnold are really a simple re-statement of what Joseph Warton and Hurd laid down a hundred years before.—PHELPS, WILLIAM LYON, 1893, *The Beginnings of the English Romantic Movement*, *p.* 115.

Richard Porson

1759-1808.

Born, at East Ruston, Norfolk, 25 Dec. 1759. Early education at village schools, and by the curate of the parish. At Eton, Aug. 1774 to 1778. To Trin. Coll., Camb., Oct. 1778; Scholar, 1780; Craven Scholar, 1781; B A., 1782; Chancellor's Prize Medal, 1782; Fellow of Trin. Coll., 1782; M. A., 1785. Obliged to give up Fellowship, owing to his not having taken holy orders, July 1792. Annuity purchased for him by his friends. Settled in rooms in the Temple, 1792. Regius Prof. of Greek, Cambridge, Nov. 1792. Continued to reside in London. Pursued classical studies. Contrib. to "Maty's Review," "Gentleman's Mag." "Monthly Review," "Morning Chronicle," etc. Married Mrs. Lunan, Nov. 1796; she died, 12 April 1797. Principal Librarian of newly-founded London Institution, April 1806. Died, in London, 25 Sept. 1808. Buried in chapel of Trin. College, Cambridge. *Works:* "Letters to Mr. Archdeacon Travis" (from "Gentleman's Mag."), 1790; Edition of Toup's "Emendationes in Suidam," 1790; Edition (anon.) of Æschylus, 1794; Editions of Euripides' "Hecuba," 1797, "Orestes," 1798, "Phœnissæ," 1799, and "Medea," 1801; Edition of Homer's "Iliad" and "Odyssey" (with Grenville and others), 1800. *Posthumous:* "Ricardi Porsoni Adversaria," ed. by J. H. Monk and C. J. Blomfield, 1812; "Tracts and Miscellaneous Criticisms," ed. by T. Kidd, 1815; "Aristophanica," ed. by P. P. Dobree, 1820; Edition of the "Lexicon of Photius," ed. by P. P. Dobree (2 vols.), 1822; "The Devil's Walk," ed. by H. W. Montagu [1830]; "Correspondence," ed. by H. R. Luard, 1867.—SHARP, R. FARQUHARSON, 1897, *A Dictionary of English Authors*, *p.* 230.

PERSONAL

I have been furnished with many opportunities of observing Porson, by a near inspection. He has been at my house several times, and once for an entire summer's day. Our intercourse would have been frequent, but for three reasons: 1. His extreme irregularity, and inattention to times and seasons, which did not at all comport with the methodical arrangement of my time and family. 2. His gross addiction to that lowest

and least excusable of all sensualities, immoderate drinking. And, 3. The uninteresting insipidity of his society; as it is impossible to engage his mind on any topic of mutual inquiry, to procure his opinion on any author or any passage of an author, or to elicit any conversation of any kind to compensate for the time and attendance of his company. And as for Homer, Virgil, and Horace, I never could hear of the least critical effort on them in his life. He is, in general, devoid of all human affections; but such as are of the misanthropic quality; nor do I think that any man exists for whom his propensities rise to the lowest pitch of affection and esteem.—WAKEFIELD, GIL-BERT, 1801?–1813, *Correspondence with C. J. Fox, p.* 99.

Two famous men of a preceding generation, Porson, the Grecian and Simeon, the Methodist, came within my sight, but nothing more, while I was at the university. They were both remarkable for their appearance, and on that account their portraits are still, as it were, before me in the mind's eye. Porson, when I saw him, was in cap and gown, a thin milddle-sized figure, with lank black hair and cheeks of the palest cast. He walked at a stealthy pace, and seemed to have a book which he hugged parentally under his arm.—CANNING, STRATFORD (STRATFORD DE REDCLIFFE), 1806–80–88, *Life, ed. Lane-Poole, vol.* I, *p.* 25.

In giving a relation of the facts concerning the illness of Mr. Porson, I cannot let the opportunity escape me, our official situations bringing us a good deal together, of lamenting in common with his most intimate friends, the loss of so pleasing and so valuable an acquaintance; for to the most gigantic powers of learning and criticism were united the manners of a gentleman, and the inoffensive habits of a child; and I am sorry to have occasion to observe, in concluding this narrative, that, especially since the Professor's decease, there should be found persons, who have used no common industry in representing his failings in such pointed terms, as totally to shade the numerous good qualities which were inherent in his nature; so that it cannot but be remarked with pity, that those persons should be deficient in one of those excellent qualities, which he possessed in an eminent degree, *never speaking ill of any one.*—SAVAGE, JAMES, 1808, *The Librarian, Dec.* 1, *vol.* I, *p.* 281.

Porson had a very lofty mind, and was tenacious of his proper dignity. Where he was familiar and intimate, he was exceedingly condescending and good-natured. He was kind to children, and would often play with them, but he was at no pains to conceal his partiality, where there were several in one family. In one which he often visited, there was a little girl of whom he was exceedingly fond; he often brought her trifling presents, wrote in her books, and distinguished her on every occasion, but she had a brother to whom, for no assignable reason, he never spoke, nor would in any respect, notice. He was also fond of female society, and though too frequently negligent of his person, was of the most obliging manners and behaviour, and would read a play, or recite, or do any thing that was required. . . . Much has been said of his irregularities.—That odious theme is left to others. With all his errors and eccentricities he who wrote this, loved him much, bowed with reverence to his talents, and admiration to his learning, and acknowledged with gratitude the delight and benefit he received from his society and conversation. Yet Porson by no means excelled in conversation; he neither wrote nor spoke with facility. His elocution was perplexed and embarrassed, except where he was exceedingly intimate; but there was strong indication of intellect in his countenance, and whatever he said was manifestly founded on judgment, sense, and knowledge. Composition was no less difficult to him. Upon one occasion, he undertook to write a dozen lines upon a subject which he had much turned in his mind, and with which he was exceedingly familiar. But the number of erasures and interlineations was so great as to render it hardly legible; yet, when completed, it was, and is, a memorial of his sagacity, acuteness, and erudition.—BELOE, WIL-LIAM, 1817, *The Sexagenarian, vol.* 1, *pp.* 217, 218.

I remember to have seen Porson at Cambridge, in the hall of our college, and in private parties, but not frequently; and I never can recollect him except as drunk and brutal, and generally both; I mean in an evening, for in the hall he dined at the Dean's table, and I at the Vice-master's, so that I was not near him; and he then and there appeared sober in his demeanour, nor did I ever hear of excess or outrage on his part in public,—commons, college, or chapel; but I have seen him in a private party of undergraduates, many of them freshmen and strangers, take up a poker to one of them, and heard him use language as blackguard as his action. I have seen Sheridan drunk, too, with all the world; but his intoxication was that of Bacchus, and Porson's that of Silenus. Of all the disgusting brutes, sulky, abusive, and intolerable, Porson was the most bestial, as far as the few times that I saw him went, which were only at William Bankes's (the Nubian discoverer's) rooms. I saw him once go away in a rage, because nobody knew the name of the "Cobbler of Messina," insulting their ignorance with the most vulgar terms of reprobation. He was tolerated in this state amongst the young men for his talents, as the Turks think a madman inspired, and bear with him. He used to recite, or rather vomit, pages of all languages, and could hiccup Greek like a Helot; and certainly Sparta never shocked her children with a grosser exhibition than this man's intoxication.—BYRON, LORD, 1818, *Letter to Mr. Murray, Feb.* 20; *Life, Letters and Journals, ed. Moore, p.* 374.

The Fieldings to dinner. Talked of Porson; one of his *scherzi*, the translation of "Three blue beans in a blue bladder;" τρεῖς κυαγοὶ κναμοὶ &c. The coolness with which he received the intelligence (which Raine trembled to communicate to him) of the destruction by fire of his long laboured "Photius," he merely quoted "To each his sufferings, all are men," adding, "let us speak no more on the subject," and the next day patiently begun his work all again.— MOORE, THOMAS, 1827, *Diary, Sept.* 12; *Memoirs, Journal and Correspondence, vol.* V, *p.* 203.

I was at first greatly struck with the acuteness of his understanding and his multifarious acquaintance with every branch of polite literature and classical attainments. I also found him extremely modest and humble, and not vain-glorious of his astonishing erudition and capacity. I was not less struck with his memory. Taking tea one afternoon in his company at Dockerell's coffee-house, I read a pamphlet written by Ritson against Tom Warton. I was pleased with the work, and after I had read it I gave it to Porson, who began it, and I left him perusing it, On the ensuing day he drank tea with me, with several other friends, and the conversation happened to turn on Ritson's pamphlet. I alluded to one particular part about Shakspeare, which had greatly interested me, adding, to those who had not read it, "I wish I could convey to you a specific idea of the remainder." Porson

repeated a page and a half, word for word. I expressed my surprise and said, "I suppose you studied the whole evening at the coffee-house and got it by heart?" "Not at all; I do assure you that I only read it once."—COXE, WILLIAM, 1828? *Life and Posthumous Works.*

There is one quality of the mind in which it may be confidently maintained that Mr. Porson had no superior—I mean, the most pure and inflexible love of truth. Under the influence of this principle, he was cautious, and patient, and persevering in his researches; and scrupulously accurate in stating facts as he found them. All who were intimate with him bear witness to this noble part of his character, and his works confirm the testimony of his friends.—TURTON, THOMAS, 1829, *A Vindication of the Literary Character of the Late Professor Porson, by Crito Cantabrigiensis.*

His head was remarkably fine; an expansive forehead, over which was smoothly combed (when in dress) his shining brown hair. His nose was Roman, with a keen and penetrating eye, shaded with long lashes. His mouth was full of expression; and altogether his countenance indicated deep thought. His stature was nearly six feet.—GORDON, PRYSE LOCKHART, 1830; *Personal Memoirs, vol.* I, *p.* 288.

I was once or twice in company with Porson at college. His gift was a surprising memory; he appeared to me a mere linguist, without any original powers of mind. He was vain, petulant, arrogant, overbearing, rough and vulgar. He was a great Greek scholar; but this was a department which very few much cultivated, and in which therefore he had few competitors. What are the extraordinary productions which he has left to posterity? Where is the proof that he has left of energetic sentiments, of deep sagacity, of powerful reasoning, or of high eloquence? Admit that he has shown acuteness in verbal criticism, and verbal emendation;—what is that? He was one of those men, whose eccentricities excited a false notice.—BRYDGES, SIR SAMUEL EGERTON, 1834, *Autobiography, vol.* I, *p.* 58.

I first saw Porson at the sale of Toup's library in 1784, and was introduced to him soon after. I was on the most intimate terms with him for the last twenty years of his life. In spite of all his faults and failings, it was impossible not to admire his integrity and his love of truth. . . . At one period of his life he was in such straitened circumstances, that he would go without dinner for a couple of days. However, when a dinner came his way, he would eat very heartily (mutton was his favourite dish), and lay in, as he used to say, a stock of provisions. He has subsisted for three weeks upon a guinea. —MALTBY, WILLIAM, 1854, *Porsoniana.*

When Porson dined with me, I used to keep him within bounds; but I frequently met him at various houses where he got completely drunk. He would not scruple to return to the dining-room, after the company had left it, pour into a tumbler the drops remaining in the wine-glasses, and drink off the omnium gatherum. I once took him to an evening party at William Spencer's, where he was introduced to several women of fashion, Lady Crewe, &c., who were very anxious to see the great Grecian. How do you suppose he entertained them? Chiefly by reciting an immense quantity of old forgotten Vauxhall songs. He was far from sober, and at last talked so oddly, that they all retired from him, except Lady Crewe, who boldly kept her ground. I recollect her saying to him, "Mr. Porson, *that* joke you have borrowed from Joe Miller," and his rather angry reply, "Madam, it is *not* in Joe Miller; you will not find it either in the preface or in the body of that work, no, nor in the index." I brought him home as far as Piccadilly, where, I am sorry to add, I left him sick in the middle of the street.—ROGERS, SAMUEL, 1855, *Recollections of Table-Talk*, ed. *Dyce, p.* 217.

Great as were Porson's deviations from the even tenour of sobriety, great as were his disagreements with the social habits of the generality of mankind, great also must have been his merit, which, with such aberrations and eccentricities, secured him, not only the praise, but the regard, of all men of learning and intellect that had intercourse with him. Whoever knew Richard Porson, felt that he knew a man of high and noble mind, who, with all his irregularities, and all his inclination to sarcasm and jest, had a sincere love of truth and honesty, and who, with an utter contempt for pretence and presumption,

was ever ready to do justice to genuine worth. His life is an example, and an admonition, how much a man may injure himself by indulgence in one unhappy propensity, and how much an elevated mind may suffer by long association with those of an inferior order. A Porson cannot day after day descend to the level of a Hewardine, without finding it difficult at length to recover his original position above it.—WATSON, JOHN SLEBY, 1861, *The Life of Richard Porson, p.* 387.

The humour of Professor Porson lay in parodies, imitations, and hoaxes, ready wit and repartee; in his oddities of dress and demeanour; and his disregard for certain decencies of society is very deplorable, though at the same time mirthful in its very extravagances. . . . He had for some time become notorious at Cambridge. His passion for smoking, which was then going out among the younger generations, his large and indiscriminate potations, and his occasional use of the poker with a very refractory controversialist, had caused his company to be shunned by all except the few to whom his wit and scholarship were irresistible. When the evening began to grow late, the Fellows of Trinity used to walk out of the common room, and leave Porson to himself, who was sometimes found smoking by the servants next morning, without having apparently moved from the spot where he had been left overnight. . . . The most remarkable feature in Porson's love of liquor was, that he could drink anything. Port wine, indeed, was his favourite beverage. But, in default of this, he would take whatever he could lay his hands on. He was known to swallow a bottle of spirits of wine, an embrocation, and when nothing better was forthcoming, he would even drench himself with water. . . . Porson was very odd in his eating. At breakfast, he frequently ate bread and cheese; and he then took his porter as copiously as Johnson took his tea.— TIMBS, JOHN, 1866, *English Eccentrics and Eccentricities, pp.* 150, 154, 155.

Great linguists have always been noted for their power both of retention and reproduction. Porson declared that he could repeat Smollett's "Roderick Random" from beginning to end, and that he would undertake to learn by heart a copy of the London "Morning Chronicle" in a week. One day he called upon a friend who chanced to be reading Thucydides, and who asked him the meaning of a certain word. Porson, on hearing the word did not look at the book, but at once repeated the passage. His friend asked how he knew that the word was in the passage. "Because," replied the great linguist, "the word occurs only twice in Thucydides; once on the right-hand page in your edition, and once on the left. I observed on which side you looked, and accordingly knew to which passage you referred."—MATHEWS, WILLIAM, 1881, *Literary Style*, p. 158.

This human monument of learning happened to be travelling in the same coach with a coxcomb who sought to air his pretended learning by quotations from the ancients. At last old Porson asked: "Pri' thee, sir, whence comes that quotation?" "From Sophocles," quoth the vain fellow. "Be so kind as to find it for me?" asked Porson, producing a copy of Sophocles from his pocket. Then the coxcomb, not at all abashed, said that he meant not Sophocles, but Euripides. Whereupon Porson drew from another pocket a copy of Euripides and challenged the upstart to find the quotation in question. Full of confusion, the fellow thrust his head out of the window of the coach and cried to the driver: "In Heaven's name, put me down at once; for there is an old gentleman in here that hath the Bodleian Library in his pocket!"—FIELD, EUGENE, 1895, *The Love Affairs of a Bibliomaniac*, p. 34.

The irony which pervades so much of Porson's writings, and the fierce satire which he could occasionally wield, were intimately connected with this love of accuracy and candour. They were the weapons which he employed where he discovered the absence of those qualities. He was a man of warm and keen feelings, a staunch friend, and also a good hater. In the course of life he had suffered, or believed himself to have suffered, some wrongs and many slights. These, acting on his sensitive temperament, tinged it with cynicism, or even with bitterness. He once described himself (in 1807) as a man who had become "a misanthrope from a morbid excess of sensibility." In this, however, he was less than just to himself.

He was, indeed, easily estranged, even from old acquaintances, by words or acts which offended him. But his native disposition was most benevolent. To those who consulted him on matters of scholarship he was liberal of his aid. Stephen Weston says "he told you all you wanted to know in a plain and direct manner, without any attempt to display his own superiority, but merely to inform you." Nor was his liberality confined to the imparting of his knowledge. Small though his means were, the strict economy which he practiced enabled him to spare something for the needs of others.—JEBB, R. C., 1896, *Dictionary of National Biography*, vol. XLVI, p. 159.

GENERAL

Mr. Porson . . . is a giant in literature, a prodigy in intellect, a critic whose mighty achievements leave imitation panting at a distance behind them, and whose stupendous powers strike down all the restless and aspiring suggestions of rivalry into silent admiration and passive awe.—PARR, SAMUEL, 1793, *Answer to Combe's Statement*, Works, vol. III, p. 518.

I consider Mr. Porson's answer to Archdeacon Travis as the most acute and accurate piece of criticism which has appeared since the days of Bentley. His strictures are founded in argument, enriched with learning, and enlivened with wit; and his adversary neither deserves nor finds any quarter at his hands. The evidence of the three heavenly witnesses would now be rejected in any court of justice: but prejudice is blind, authority is deaf, and our vulgar bibles will ever be polluted by this spurious text, "*sedet æternumque sedebit.*"—GIBBON, EDWARD, 1793, *Autobiograghy*, note.

Mr. Professor Porson's "Letters to Archdeacon Travis" are conspicuous for their erudition, acuteness, accuracy, virulence, bitterness, and invective.—MATHIAS, THOMAS JAMES, 1797, *The Pursuits of Literature*, Eighth ed., p. 143.

PORSON.—Removed alike from the crowd and the *coterie*, I have always avoided, with timid prudence, the bird-cage walk of literature. I have withholden from Herman and some others, a part of what is due to them; and I regret it. Sometimes I have been arrogant, never have I been malicious. Unhappily, I was educated in a school of criticism where the exercises were too gladitorial. Looking at my elders in it, they appeared to me so ugly, in part from their contortions, and in part from their scars, that I suspected that it must be a dangerous thing to wield a scourge of vipers; and I thought it no very creditable appointment to be linkboy or pander at an ally leading down to the Furies. Age and infirmity have rendered me milder than I was. I am loth to fire off my gun in the warren which lies before us; loth to startle the snug little creatures, each looking so comfortable at the mouth of its burrow, or skipping about at short distances, or frisking and kicking up the sand along the thriftless heath.—LANDOR, WALTER SAVAGE, 1828, *Imaginary Conversations, Third Series, Works, vol.* IV, *p.* 49.

This Greek professor, Porson—whose knowledge of English was so limited that his total cargo might have been embarked on board a walnut-shell on the bosom of a slop basin, and insured for three halfpence—astonishes me, that have been studying English for thirty years and upwards, by the strange discoveries that he announces in this field. One and all, I fear, are mares' nests.—DE QUINCEY, THOMAS, 1847–58, *Notes on Walter Savage Landor, Works, ed. Masson, vol.* XI, *p.* 421.

I read Porson's "Letters" to Archdeacon Travis, and compared the collected letters with the "Gentleman's Magazine," in which they originally appeared. The book has a little suffered from the awkwardness of turning what were letters to Sylvanus Urban into letters to Archdeacon Travis; but it is a masterly work. A comparison between it and the Phalaris would be a comparison between Porson's mind and Bentley's mind; Porson's more sure-footed, more exact, more neat, Bentley's far more comprehensive and inventive. While walking, I read Bishop Burgess's trash in answer to Porson, Home, and read Turton's defence of Porson against Burgess; an impenetrable dunce, to reason with whom is like kicking a woolpack. Was there ever such an instance of the binding power of bigotry as the fact that some men, who were not absolute fools, continued, after reading Porson and Turton, to believe in the authenticity of the text of the Three Witnesses?—MACAULAY, THOMAS BABINGTON, 1850, *Journal, Dec.* 25; *Life and Letters.*

Richard Porson was one of the profoundest Greek scholars and the greatest verbal critic that any age or country has produced. He possessed every quality which is necessary to the information of a scholar—a stupendous memory, unwearied application, great acuteness, strong sound sense, and a lively perception both of the beautiful and the ludicrous. Besides these qualifications he enjoyed the rare faculty of conjecturing from the imperfect data of corrupt readings the very words of the author whose text he sought to restore; in the last particular we know of no one, with the single exception of Bentley, who can be named in comparison with him, and in some points we should not hesitate to place Porson before the great Aristarchus of criticism.—HAWES, SIDAY, 1857, *English Encyclopædia, ed. Knight, Biography, vol.* IV, *f.* 940.

With the single exception of Porson, not one of the English scholars has shown an appreciation of the beauties of his native language. — BUCKLE, HENRY THOMAS, 1857, *History of Civilization in England, vol.* I, *p.* 587, *note.*

The delicacy of whose Greek scholarship almost amounted to a sense. —ARNOLD, THOMAS, 1862–87, *A Manual of English Literature, p.* 276.

Giant as he was, Porson had but small hands, that played with words as with marbles, and delighted in nothing so much as in good penmanship. One is astonished in reading through his edition of Euripides, to see how he wrote note upon note, all about words, and less than words—syllables, letters, accents, punctuation. He ransacked Codex A and Codex B, Codex Cantabrigiensis and Codex Cottonianus, to show how this noun should be in the dative, not in the accusative; how that verb should have the accent paroxytone, not perispomenon; and how by all the rules of prosody there should be an iambus, not a spondee, in this place or in that. Nothing can be more masterly of its kind than the preface to the "Hecuba," and supplement to it. The lad who hears enough of this wonderful dissertation from his tutors at last turns wistful eyes towards it, expecting to find some magical criticism on Greek tragedy. Behold it is a treatise on certain Greek metres. Its talk is of cæsural pauses, penthemimeral and hepthemimeral, of isochronous feet, of enclitics and cretic terminations; and the grand doctrine it promulgates is expressed in the cannon regarding the pause which, from the discoverer, has been named the Porsonian, that when the iambic trimeter, after a word of more than one syllable, has the cretic termination, included either in one word or two, then the fifth foot must be an iambus! The young student throws down the book thus prefaced, and wonders if this be all that giants of Porsonian height can see or care to speak about in Greek literature. Nor was Porson alone; he had disciples even worse.—DALLAS, E. S., 1866, *The Gay Science, vol.* I, *p.* 17.

In some respects the greatest of modern Greek scholars. . . . In claiming for Porson the very high place he has always occupied among Greek scholars, it is with those who went before him that he must be compared, if we would judge fairly of the advances he made in the knowledge of the language. In learning he was superior to Valckenaer, in accuracy to Bentley. It must be remembered that in his day the science of comparative philology had scarcely any existence; even the comparative value of MSS. was scarcely considered in editing an ancient author. With many editors MSS. were treated as of pretty much the same value, whether they were really from the hand of a trustworthy scribe, or what Bentley calls "scrub manuscripts" or "scoundrel copies" Thus, if we are to find fault with Porson's way of editing, it is that he does not make sufficient difference between the MSS. he uses, or point out the relative value of the early copies whether in MS. or print.—LUARD, H. R., 1885, *Encyclopædia Britannica, Ninth edition, vol.* XIX, *pp.* 537, 540.

Richard Porson, the profound scholar, linguist, and wit, reared many monuments of classic learning, which have however crumbled away, leaving his name familiar to us only as a writer of *jeux d'esprit;* but these are admirable. He was full of the sunshine of wit; and though sarcastic and personal, as the nature of his *bonmots* compelled, he had no bitterness in his reflections, and uttered them with a good-natured laugh.—BALLOU, MATURIN M., 1886, *Genius in Sunshine and Shadow, p.* 277.

Johnson had observed very rightly that "the justness of a happy restoration strikes at once, and the moral precept may be well applied to criticism, 'quod dubitas en feceris.'" Of no emendations is this more true than of Porson's. Unlike those of such critics as Bentley and Wakefield—for, immeasurable as was Bentley's superiority to Wakefield in point of ability and attainments, in temper and taste he was as rash and coarse—they are seldom or never superfluous. If they do not succeed in satisfying us that the word restored is the exact word lost, they afford us the still higher satisfaction of feeling that nothing which could be recovered could be an improvement on what has been supplied. . . . Porson's perception, indeed, of what stupidity, carelessness, or ignorance, had disguised or obscured in the text of an ancient poet, resembled clairvoyance. And even when he failed, his fine and delicate sense of the niceties of rhythm, his exquisite taste, his refined good sense, his sobriety, his tact, kept him at least from going far astray, and from making himself and his author ridiculous, as Bentley habitually did.—COLLINS, JOHN CHURTON, 1895, *The Porson of Shakspearian Criticism, Essays and Studies, pp.* 289, 291.

He possessed in almost the highest degree that power of divination, based on accurate knowledge, which distinguishes the scholar, and it is, as has been said, nearly certain that he would have been a brilliant writer in English on any subject he chose to take up.—SAINTSBURY, GEORGE, 1896, *A History of Nineteenth Century Literature, p.* 406.

Textual criticism was the work to which Porson's genius was mainly devoted. His success in it was due primarily to native acumen, aided—in a degree perhaps unequalled—by a marvellous memory, richly stored, accurate, and prompt. His emendations are found to rest both on a wide and exact knowledge of classical Greek, and on a wonderful command of passages which illustrate his point. He relied comparatively little on mere "divination," and usually abstained from conjecture where he felt that the remedy must remain purely conjectural. His lifelong love of mathematics has left a clear impress on his criticism; we see it in his precision and in his close reasoning. Very many of his emendations are such as at once appear certain or highly probable. Bentley's cogent logic sometimes (as in his Horace) renders a textual change plausible, while our instinct rebels; Porson, as a rule, merely states his correction, briefly gives his proofs, and convinces. His famous note on the "Medea," vv.139 *f.*, where he disengages a series of poetical fragments from prose texts, is a striking example of his method, and has been said also to give some idea of the way in which his talk on such subjects used to flow. Athenæus, so rich in quotations from the poets, afforded a field in which Porson did more, perhaps, than all former critics put together. He definitely advanced Greek scholarship in three principal respects: (1) by remarks on countless points of Greek idiom and usage; (2) by adding to the knowledge of metre, and especially of the iambic trimeter; (3) by emendation of texts. Then, as a master of precise and lucid phrase, alike in Latin and in English, he supplied models of compact and pointed criticism. A racy vigour and humour often animate his treatment of technical details. He could be trenchantly severe, when he saw cause; but his habitual weapon was irony, sometimes veiled, sometimes frankly keen, always polished, and usually genial. Regarding the correctness of texts as the most valuable office of the critic, he lamented that, in popular estimation, it stood below "literary" criticism.—JEBB, R.C.,1896, *Dictionary of National Biography, vol.*XLVI, *p.*162.

Fisher Ames
1758–1808.

Born at Dedham, Mass., April 9, 1758: died at Dedham, July 4, 1808. A noted American orator, statesman, and political writer. He was graduated from Harvard College in 1774, began the practice of law at Dedham in 1781, was a member of the Massachusetts ratifying committee in 1788, and was a Federal member of Congress from Massachusetts 1789–97. He declined the presidency of Harvard College in 1804. He wrote the "Laocoon" and other essays to rouse the opposition against France.—SMITH, BENJAMIN E., *ed.*, 1894–97, *The Century Cyclopedia of Names, p.* 49.

PERSONAL

The manly genius, ardent thought,
    The love of truth and wit refined,
The eloquence that wonders wrought,
    And flash'd its light on every mind.
These gifts were thine, immortal Ames!
    Of motive pure, of life sublime;
Their loss our flowing sorrow claims,—
    Their praise survives the wreck of time.
—GARDINER, J. S. J., 1808, *Verses Sung in King's Chapel, Boston, July* 6.

His spotless youth brought blessings to the whole remainder of his life. It gave him the entire use of his faculties, and all the fruit of his literary education. Its effects appeared in that fine edge of moral feeling which he always preserved; in his strict and often austere temperance; in his love of occupation, that made activity a delight; in his distaste for publick diversions, and his preference of simple pleasures. Beginning well, he advanced with unremitted steps in the race of virtue, and arriving at the end of life in peace and honour. . . . Mr. Ames in person a little exceeded the middle height, was well proportioned, and remarkably erect. His features were regular, his aspect respectable and pleasing, his eye expressive of benignity and intelligence. His head and face are shown with great perfection in the engraving prefixed to his works. In his manners he was easy, affable, cordial, inviting confidence, yet inspiring a respect. He had that refined spirit of society, which observes the forms of a real, but not studied politeness, and paid a more delicate regard to the propriety of conversation and behaviour.—KIRKLAND, JOHN THORNTON, 1809, *Life of Fisher Ames.*

His writings sufficiently exhibited him as a most cheerful and fascinating friend, a brilliant political essayist, an eloquent and fearless orator, and a patriot without reproach or suspicion. . . . In all his private relations, in his friendships, his pursuits, his successes, Mr. Ames had the good fortune which a happy temper, sound judgment, and fidelity are very apt to secure. The friends he had (and of what character they were his letters sufficiently show) he "grappled to him with hooks of steel." The honors which he won abroad were made thrice dear by the sympathy of a chosen circle at home. Of the law he had a noble conception, yet, on account of his health, he seems to have given himself to the practice of it as a matter of necessity, and with a divided love. Yet he had no reason to be dissatisfied with the results of his labors. His fortune was never ample, yet he became independent, and when he was no longer compelled to labor for his daily bread, his mind instinctively turned to those broad and varied studies whence he could draw the most important lessons for his country.—BROWN, S. G., 1855, *Works of Fisher Ames, North American Review, vol.* 80, *p.* 233.

In person Mr. Ames was above middle stature and well formed. His countenance was very handsome, and his eye blue in colour, and expressive. His features were not strongly marked. His forehead was neither high nor broad. His mouth was beautifully shaped, and was one of his finest features; his hair was black, and he wore it short, and in the latter years of his life unpowdered. He was exceedingly erect in walking, and when speaking he raised his head slightly. It is said that his expression was usually mild and complacent when in debate, and if he meant to be severe, it was seen in good-natured sarcasm, rather than in acrimonious words.—HARDWICKE, HENRY, 1896, *History of Oratory and Orators, p.* 340.

SPEECHES

Fisher Ames, among the great men of his day, was the orator of genius and elaborate beauty.—MAGOON, E. L., 1848, *Orators of the American Revolution, p.* 315.

He was decidedly one of the most splendid rhetoricians of the age. Two of his speeches, in a special manner—that on Jay's treaty, and that usually called his "Tomahawk Speech," (because it included some resplendent passages on Indian massacres)—were the most brilliant and fascinating specimens of eloquence I have ever heard; yet have I listened to some of the most celebrated speakers in the British parliament—among others, to Wilberforce and Mackintosh, Plunket, Brougham and Canning; and Dr. Priestley, who was familiar with the oratory of Pitt the father and Pitt the son, and also with that of Burke and Fox, made to myself the acknowledgement, that, in his own words, the speech of Ames, on the British Treaty, was "the most bewitching piece of parliamentary oratory he had ever listened to."—CALDWELL, CHARLES, 1853–55, *Autobiography.*

Mr. Ames possessed uncommon vigor of mind; his memory was stored with literary treasures; his fancy was active, furnishing illustrative images that were as much to the purpose as his logic. And such was the effect of his oratory, even upon deliberate bodies, that on one occasion Congress adjourned on motion of Ames's chief opponent in debate, for the alleged reason that the members ought not to be called upon to vote while under the spell of his extraordinary eloquence. The speeches of Mr. Ames that have been preserved fully sustain his great reputation, being vigorous and logical in statement, and adorned with the graces of a lively and learned style. His letters, also, are fresh and charming.— UNDERWOOD, FRANCIS H., 1872, *A Hand-Book of English Literature, American Authors, p.* 34.

If Ames does not quite rival the sublimest flights of Burke, he never is carried by the pursuit of an apt but offensive metaphor to a point that is scarcely short of the disgusting. His perfect taste is never at fault. In felicity of illustration, in playfulness of fancy, in readiness of wit, in neatness of raillery, in delicacy of irony, and in keenness of sarcasm, he is not unworthy to be placed in the company of the great Irishman.— QUINCY, EDMUND, 1872, *Fisher Ames, The Nation, vol.* 14, *p.* 76.

Though known to us only as a political orator and newspaper writer, was one of the most poetical minds of his age. His language avoids sonorous and pretentious words, but is rich in tropes and metaphors, which stimulate the attention and aid the apprehension of the reader. The simple words are the result of studious self-control; the figurative expression is the native temperament of the man. The effect is of power well in the leash, and more impressive for the restraint. . . . But, with all his beauty and earnestness, he lacked the massive individuality, the overwhelming torrent of feeling, the towering strength that should be within the scope of the greatest statesman.— HAWTHORNE, JULIAN AND LEMMON, LEONARD, 1891, *American Literature, p.* 34.

Ames, a man of fine mind and high character, hating exaggeration and rant, had an oratorical style that was nervous, tastefully ornate, and intense with restrained passion.—BRONSON, WALTER C., 1901, *A Short History of American Literature, p.* 78.

GENERAL

The traditional reputation of Ames for eloquence, handed down by his friends and fellow politicians, has not expired in his published writings. . . . The quick and forgetive fancy of Ames led to that condensation of expression which is the peculiarity of his writings. He thought in figures. . . . Well grounded in the principles of conservatism, and with a deeply founded respect for the Constitution, Ames mingled with his convictions the restless anticipations of mind given to despondency. For a new state, he was something of a croker; a man constitutionally timid. There were "the fears of the brave" in his composition; but, if he doubted of affairs, it was with a patriotic motive and acute philosophic argument to support him. . . . The letters of Ames are sharply written, with point and occasional felicities of expression, but they are not elaborate or highly finished compositions, rarely partaking of the essay character of some of Webster's epistles.—DUYCKINCK, EVERT A., AND GEORGE L., 1855-65-75, *Cyclopædia of American Literature, ed. Simons, vol.* I, *pp.* 486, 487.

In all the writings of this period, there are none that exceed those of Fisher Ames in vigor of thought and expression. He was remarkable for the aptness of his classical illusions and for the frequency and beauty of his comparisons. These are so numerous, indeed, that the reader would weary of them as needless ornament, were it not for the intense earnestness that everywhere breathes through the glowing periods.—HART, JOHN S., 1872, *A Manual of American Literature, p.* 85.

His literary style is quiet, and evidently elaborated with much care.—RICHARDSON, CHARLES F., 1887, *American Literature, 1607-1885, vol.* I, *p.* 209.

Thomas Paine
1737-1809

Born, at Thetford, Norfolk, 29 Jan. 1737. Educated at Thetford Grammar School. At sea, 1755-56. In London, working as staymaker, 1756-58. Removed to Dover, 1758; to Sandwich, 1759. Married (i.) Mary Lambert, 17 Sept. 1759. She died, at Margate, 1760. Returned to Thetford, as Excise Officer, July 1761; to Grantham, Dec. 1762; to Alford, Aug. 1764. Dismissed from Office, Aug. 1765; restored, Feb. 1768; sent to Lewes; dismissed again, April 1774. Married (ii.) Elizabeth Ollive, 26 March 1771; separated from her, June 1774. To Philadelphia, Nov. 1774, with introduction to Franklin [?]. Contrib. to "Pennsylvania Journal," 1775-76. Editor of "Pennsylvania Mag.," Jan. 1775 to Aug. 1776. Took part in American War of Independence. Sec. to Committee of Foreign Affairs, April 1777 to Jan. 1779. Clerk to Pennsylvania Assembly, Nov. 1779 to Dec. 1780. M. A., Pennsylvania Univ., 4 July 1780. Sec. to Col. Laurens on Mission to France, Feb. to Aug., 1781. Presented with estate of New Rochelle, 1784. Visit to England in connection with his invention of an iron bridge, 1787-90. To Paris, 1790. French citizen, Aug. 1793; Mem. of Convention, Sept. 1793. On Committee to form Republican Constitution, Oct. 1793. Imprisoned in Paris, Dec. 1793 to Nov. 1794. Returned to America, Oct. 1802. Contrib. to "The Prospect," 1804-05. Died, in New York, 8 July, 1809. *Works:* "The Case of the Officers of Excise" (anon.), [1772]; "Common Sense" (anon.), 1776; "Large Additions to Common Sense" (anon.), 1776; "Epistle to the People called Quakers," 1776; "Dialogue between Gen. Montgomery and an American Delegate," 1776; "The American Crisis" (13 nos.; anon.), 1776-83; "The Public Good," 1780; "Letter addressed to the Abbé Raynal," 1782; "Thoughts on the Peace," 1783; "Letter to the Earl of Shelburne," 1783; "Dissertation on Government," 1786; "Prospects on the Rubicon" (anon.), 1787; (another edn., called: "Prospects on the War," 1793); "Letter to Sir G. Staunton," 1788; "The Rights of Man" (2 pts.), 1791-92; "Address and Declaration of the Friends of Universal Peace and Liberty" [1791]; "Letter to the Abbé Sièyes," 1792; "Four Letters on Government," 1792; "Address to the

Republic of France" [1792]; "Letter addressed to the Addressers," 1792; "Speech in Convention on bringing Louis Capet to trial," 1792; "Lettre . . . au Peuple françois" [1792]; "Opinion . . . concernant le judgment de Louis XVI.," 1792; "Works," 1792; "Miscellaneous Articles," 1792; "Reasons for wishing to preserve the life of Louis Capet" [1793]; "Prospects on the War and Paper Currency," 1793; "Rational and Revealed Religion" (anon.), 1794; "The Age of Reason," pt. i., 1794; pt. ii, 1795; pt. iii., 1811; "Letter to the French Convention," 1794; "Dissertations on First Principles of Government," 1795; "The Decline and Fall of the English System of Finance," 1796; "Letter to George Washington," 1796; "Agrarian Justice opposed to Agrarian Law," 1797; "Lettre . . . sur les Cultes," 1797; "Letter to the Hon. T. Erskine," 1797; "Letter to Camille Jourdan," 1797; "Atheism Refuted," 1798; "Maritime Compact," 1801; "Letter to Samuel Adams," 1802; "Letter to Citizens of the United States," 1802; "Letter to the People of England," 1804; "To the French Inhabitants of Louisiana," 1804; "To the Citizens of Pennsylvania," 1805; "On the Causes of Yellow Fever," 1805; "On Constitutions, Governments and Charters," 1805; "Observations on Gunboats," 1806; "Letter to A. A. Dean," 1806; "On the Political and Military Affairs of Europe," 1806; "To the People of New York," 1807; "On Governor Lewis's Speech," 1807; "On Mr. Hale's Resolutions," 1807; "Three Letters to Morgan Lewis," 1807; "On the question, Will there be War?" 1807; "Essay on Dreams," 1807. *Posthumous:* "Reply to the Bishop of Llandaff," 1810; "The Origin of Freemasonry," 1811; "Miscellaneous Letters and Essays," 1819; "Miscellaneous Poems," 1819. *Collected Works:* ed. by M. D. Conway, 1894.—SHARP, R. FARQUHARSON, 1897, *A Dictionary of English Authors, p.* 219.

PERSONAL

Dear Son, The bearer, Mr. Thomas Paine, is very well recommended to me, as an ingenious, worthy young man. He goes to Pennsylvania with a view of settling there. I request you to give him your best advice and countenance, as he is quite a stranger there. If you can put him in a way of obtaining employment as a clerk, or assistant tutor in a school, or assistant surveyor, (of all which I think him very capable), so that he may procure a subsistence at least, till he can make acquaintance and obtain a knowledge of the country, you will do well, and much oblige your affectionate father.—FRANKLIN, BENJAMIN, 1774, *Letter to Richard Bache, Sept.* 30; *Works, ed. Sparks, vol.* VIII, *p.* 137.

Philadelphia, Feb. 10, 1782.—The subscribers, taking into consideration the important situation of affairs at the present moment, and the propriety and even necessity of informing the people and rousing them into action; considering also the abilities of Mr. Thomas Paine as a writer, and that he has been of considerable utility to the common cause by several of his publications: They are agreed that it will be much for the interest of the United States that Mr. Paine be engaged in their service for the purpose above mentioned. They are therefore agreed that Mr. Paine be offered a salary of $800 per annum, and that the same be paid him by the Secretary

of Foreign Affairs. The salary to commence from this day, and to be paid by the Secretary of Foreign Affairs out of monies to be allowed by the Superintendent of Finance for secret services. The subscribers being of opinion that a salary publicly and avowedly given for the above purpose would injure the effect of Mr. Paine's publications, and subject him to injurious personal reflections.—MORRIS, ROBERT, LIVINGSTON, ROBERT, WASHINGTON, GEORGE.

Dear Sir, I have learned since I have been at this place, that you are at Bordentown. Whether for the sake of retirement or economy, I know not. Be it for either, for both, or whatever it may, if you will come to this place, and partake with me, I shall be exceedingly happy to see you. Your presence may remind Congress of your past services to this country; and if it is in my power to impress them, command my best services with freedom, as they will be rendered cheerfully by one who entertains a lively sense of the importance of your works, and who, with much pleasure, subscribes himself, Your sincere friend.—WASHINGTON, GEORGE, 1783, *Letter to Paine from Rocky Hill, Sept.* 10.

The villain Paine came over to the Crown and Anchor; but, finding that his pamphlet had not set a straw on fire, and that the 14th of July was as little in fashion as the ancient gunpowder-plot, he dined at another tavern with a few quaking conspirators; and probably is returning to Paris, where he is engaged in a controversy with the Abbe Sieyes, about the "plus or minus" of the rebellion.—WALPOLE, HORACE, 1791, *To the Miss Berrys, July* 26; *Letters, ed. Cunningham, vol.* IX, *p.* 332.

I lodge with my friend Paine—we breakfast, dine, and sup together. The more I see of his interior, the more I like and respect him. I cannot express how kind he is to me; there is a simplicity of manner, a goodness of heart, and a strength of mind in him, that I never knew a man before possess.— FITZGERALD, LORD EDWARD, 1792, *Letter to his Mother, Oct.* 30; *Moore's Life and Death of Lord Edward Fitzgerald.*

The crime of ingratitude I trust will never stain our national character. You are considered by all your countrymen as one who has not only rendered important services to them, but also as one, who, on a more extensive scale, has been the friend of human rights, and a distinguished and able advocate in favor of public liberty. *To the worth and welfare of Thomas Paine the American people can never be indifferent.* — MONROE, JAMES, 1794, *Letter to Thomas Paine.*

That infamous wretch "Tom Paine" the Democrat, whom we all execrate, and who is now, with or without a head in France, I hope in the late fashion of that country.—MATHIAS, THOMAS JAMES, 1794, *The Pursuits of Literature, p.* 78.

I met this interesting personage at the lodgings of the son of a late patriotic American governour [Trumbull]. . . . He was dressed in a snuff-coloured coat, olive velvet vest, drab breeches, coarse hose. His shoe buckles of the size of a half dollar. A bob tailed wig covered that head which worked such mickle woe to courts and kings. If I should attempt to describe it, it would be in the same stile and principle with which the veteran soldier bepraiseth an old standard: the more tattered, the more glorious. It is probable that this was the same identical wig under the shadow of whose curls he wrote "Common Sense," in America, many years before. He was a spare man, rather under size; subject to the extreme of low, and highly exhilarating spirits; often sat reserved in company; seldom mingled in common chit-chat: But when a man of sense and elocution was present, and the company numerous, he delighted in advancing the most unaccountable, and often the most whimsical paradoxes; which he defended in his own plausible manner. If encouraged by success, or the applause of the company, his countenance was animated with an expression of feature which, on ordinary occasions one would look for in vain, in a man so much celebrated for acuteness of thought; but if interrupted by extraneous observation, by the inattention of his auditory, or in an irritable moment, even by the accidental fall of the poker, he would retire into himself, and no persuasion could induce him to proceed upon the most favourite topic.—TYLER, ROYALL, 1797, *The Algerine Captive.*

That the said Elizabeth Pain had ever since lived separate from him the said Thos. Pain, and never had any issue, and the said Thomas Pain had many years quitted this kingdom and resided (if living) in parts beyond the seas, but had not since been heard of by the said Elizabeth Pain, nor was it known for certain whether he was living or dead.—PAINE, ELIZABETH, 1800, *Release to Francis Mitchener, Oct.* 14.

I have received your letter calling for information relative to the life of Thomas Paine. It appears to me that this is not the moment to publish the life of that man in this country. His own writings are his best life, and these are not read at present. The greater part of readers in the United States will not be persuaded, as long as their present feelings last, to consider him in any other light than as a drunkard and a deist. The writer of his life who should dwell on these topics, to the exclusion of the great and estimable traits of his real character, might indeed please the rabble of the age, who do not know him; the book might sell, but it would only tend to render the truth more obscure for the future biographer than it was before. But if the present writer should give us Thomas Paine *complete* in all his character, as one of the most benevolent and disinterested of mankind, endowed with the clearest perception, an uncommon share of original genius, and the greatest breadth of thought; if this piece of biography should analyze his literary labors and rank him, as he ought to be ranked, among the brightest and most undeviating luminaries of the age in which he has lived, yet with a mind assailable by flattery, and receiving through that weak side a tincture of vanity which he was too proud to conceal; with a mind, though strong enough to bear him up and to rise elastic under the heaviest hand of oppression, yet unable to endure the contempt of his former friends and fellow-laborers, the rulers of the country that had received his first and greatest services; a mind incapable of looking down with serene compassion, as it ought, on the rude scoffs of their imitators, a new generation that knows him not; a mind that shrinks from their society, and unhappily seeks refuge in low company, or looks for consolation in the sordid, solitary bottle, till it sinks at last so far below its native elevation as to lose all respect for itself and to forfeit that of his best friends, disposing these friends almost to join with his enemies, and wish, though from different motives, that he would hasten to hide himself in the grave—if you are disposed and prepared to write his life *thus entire*, to fill up the picture to which these hasty strokes of outline give but a rude sketch with great vacuities, your book may be a useful one for another age, but it will not be relished, nor scarcely tolerated, in this. . . . You ask what company he kept. He always frequented the best, both in England and France, till he became the object of calumny in certain American papers (echoes of the English court papers) for his adherence to what he thought the cause of liberty in France—till he conceived himself neglected and despised by his former friends in the United States. From that moment he gave himself very much to drink, and, consequently, to companions less worthy of his better days. It is said that he was always a peevish ingrate. This is possible. So was Lawrence Sterne, so was Torquato Tasso, so was J. J. Rousseau. But Thomas Paine, as a visiting acquaintance and as a literary friend, the only points of view from which I knew him, was one of the most instructive men I have ever known.—BARLOW, JOEL, 1809, *Letter to James Cheetham, Life and Letters,* ed. Todd, pp. 236, 238.

Paine had no good qualities. Incapable of friendship, he was vain, envious, malignant; in France cowardly, and every where tyrannical. In his private dealings he was unjust, never thinking of paying for what he had contracted, and always cherishing deadly resentments against those who by law compelled him to do justice. To those who had been kind to him he was more than ungrateful, for to ingratitude, as in the case of Mr. Munroe, he added mean and detestable fraud. He was guilty of the worst species of seduction; the alienation of a wife and children from a husband, and a father. Filthy and drunken, he was a compound of all the vices.—CHEETHAM, JAMES, 1809, *Life of Thomas Paine, p.* 313.

I have lived a honest and useful life to mankind; my time has been spent in doing good; I die in perfect composure and resignation to the will of my God.—PAINE, THOMAS, 1809, *Will.*

Mr. Paine in his person was about five feet ten inches high, and rather athletic; he was broad shouldered, and latterly stooped a little. His eye, of which the painter could not convey the exquisite meaning, was full, brilliant, and singularly piercing; it had in it the "muse of fire." In his dress and person he was generally very cleanly, and wore his hair cued, with side curls, and powdered, so that he looked altogether like a gentleman of the old French school. His manners were easy and gracious; his knowledge was universal and boundless; in private company and among his friends his conversation had every fascination that anecdote, novelty and truth could give it. In mixt company and among strangers he said little, and was no public speaker.—RICKMAN, THOMAS C., 1819, *The Life of Thomas Paine.*

Paine lies in a little hole under the grass and weeds of an obscure farm in America. There, however, he shall not lie, unnoticed, much longer. He belongs to England. His fame is the property of England; and if no other people will show that they value that fame, the people of England will. Yes, amongst the pleasures that I promise myself, that of seeing the name of Paine honoured in every part of England; where base corruption caused him, while alive, to be burnt in effigy.—COBBETT, WILLIAM, 1819, *On the Remains of Thomas Paine.*

Paine, I regret to own it, was a native of England; at his outset a Quaker, and a stay-maker of Thetford, in Norfolk.—STANHOPE, PHILIP HENRY EARL (LORD

MAHON), 1836-54, *History of England from the Peace of Utrecht to the Peace of Versailles, vol.* VI, *p.* 93.

About this period, the notorious Tom Paine arrived at Nantes, in the Alliance frigate, as Secretary of Colonel Laurens, Minister Extraordinary from Congress; and he took up his quarters at my boarding-place. He was coarse and uncouth in his manners, loathsome in his appearance, and a disgusting egotist; rejoicing most in talking of himself, and reading the effusions of his own mind. Yet, I could not repress the deepest emotions of gratitude towards him, as the instrument of Providence in accelerating the declaration of our Independence. . . . On his arrival's being announced, the Mayor, and some of the most distinguished citizens of Nantes, called upon him to render their homage of respect. I often officiated as interpreter, although humbled and mortified at his filthy appearance, and awkward address. Besides, as he has been roasted alive at L'Orient, for the ———, and well basted with brimstone, he was absolutely offensive, and perfumed the whole apartment. He was soon rid of his respectable visitors, who left the room with marks of astonishment and disgust. I took the liberty, on his asking for the loan of a clean shirt, of speaking to him frankly of his dirty appearance and brimstone odor; and I prevailed upon him to stew, for an hour, in a hot bath. This, however, was not done without much entreaty; and I did not succeed, until, receiving a file of English newspapers, I promised, after he was in the bath he should have the reading of them, and not before. He at once consented, and accompanied me to the bath, where I instructed the keeper, in French (which Paine did not understand) gradually to increase the heat of the water, until *"le Monsieur serait bien bouilli."* He became so much absorbed in his reading, that he was nearly parboiled before leaving the bath, much to his improvement and my satisfaction.—WATSON, ELKANAH, 1842-56, *Men and Times of the Revolution, ed. W. C. Watson, p.* 127.

Poverty was his mother—Necessity his master. He had more brains than books; more sense than education; more courage than politeness; more strength than polish. He had no veneration for old mistakes—no admiration for ancient lies. He loved the truth for the truth's sake, and for man's sake. . . . The result of his investigations was given to the world in the "Age of Reason." From the moment of its publication he became infamous. He was caluminated beyond measure. To slander him was to secure the thanks of the Church. All his services were instantly forgotten, disparaged or denied. He was shunned as though he had been a pestilence. Most of his old friends forsook him. He was regarded as a moral plague, and at the bare mention of his name the bloody hands of the Church were raised in horror. He was denounced as the most despicable of men. Not content with following him to his grave, they pursued him after death with redoubled fury, and recounted with infinite gusto and satisfaction the supposed horrors of his death-bed; gloried in the fact that he was forlorn and friendless, and gloated like fiends over what they supposed to be the agonizing remorse of his lonely death. It is wonderful that all his services were thus forgotten. It is amazing that one kind word did not fall from some pulpit; that some one did not accord to him, at least—honesty. Strange, that in the general denunciation some one did not remember his labor for liberty, his devotion to principle, his zeal for the rights of his fellow-men. . . . He had made it impossible to write the history of political freedom with his name left out. He was one of the creators of light; one of the heralds of the dawn. He hated tyranny in the name of kings, and in the name of God, with every drop of his noble blood. He believed in liberty and justice, and in the sacred doctrine of human equality. Under these divine banners he fought the battle of his life. In both worlds he offered his blood for the good of man. In the wilderness of America, in the French Assembly, in the sombre cell waiting for death, he was the same unflinching, unwavering friend of his race; the same undaunted champion of universal freedom. And for this he has been hated; for this the Church has violated even his grave.—INGERSOLL, ROBERT G., 1874, *The Gods and Other Lectures, pp.* 122, 135.

Poor Paine! His errors were, for the most part, those of his age; and they were aggravated by his circumstances, his defective education, and the ardor of his temperament. But his merits, which were real and not small, were peculiarly his own. He loved the truth for its own sake; and he stood by what he conceived to be the truth when all the world around him reviled it. . . . It becomes us, however, to deal charitably with the faults of a benefactor who wrote, "The Crisis" and "Common Sense," who conceived the planing-machine and the iron bridge. A glorious monument in his honor swells aloft in many of our great towns. The principle of his arch now sustains the marvellous railroad depots that half abolish the distinction between in-doors and out. —PARTON, JAMES, 1874, *Life of Thomas Jefferson, pp.* 591, 592.

A somewhat extended study of the French Revolution, during the extraordinary period in which Paine was so intimately connected with it, fails to show anything to the prejudice of his personal or political character, but, on the other hand, it reveals many things eminently creditable to him.—WASHBURNE, E. B., 1880, *Thomas Paine and the French Revolution, Scribner's Monthly, vol.* 20, *p.* 771.

The bones of Thomas Paine were landed in Liverpool November 21, 1819. The monument contemplated by Cobbett was never raised. There was much parliamentary and municipal excitement. A Bolton town-crier was imprisoned nine weeks for proclaiming the arrival. In 1836 the bones passed with Cobbett's effects into the hands of a Receiver (West). The Lord Chancellor refusing to regard them as an asset, they were kept by an old day-laborer in 1844, when they passed to B. Tilley, 13 Bedford Square, London, a furniture dealer. In 1849 the empty coffin was in possession of J. Chennell Guildford. The silver plate bore the inscription "Thomas Paine, died June 8, 1809, aged 72." In 1854, Rev. R. Ainslie (Unitarian) told E. Truelove that he owned "the skull and the right hand of Thomas Paine," but evaded subsequent inquiries. The removal caused excitement in America. Of Paine's gravestone the last fragment was preserved by his friends of the Bayeaux family, and framed on their wall. In November, 1839, the present marble monument at New Rochelle was erected.—CONWAY, MONCURE DANIEL, 1892, *The Life of Thomas Paine, vol.* II, *p.* 427, *note.*

At eight o'clock on the morning of June 8, 1809, Paine died quietly and at peace in the seventy-third year of his age. He had expressed a wish to be buried in the Quaker cemetery, for the Quakers were the only Christian sect he held in respect; but the request was denied. Two days after his death his body was carried for burial to his farm at New Rochelle, twenty-five miles away. The Bonnevilles, good Willett Hicks, and two negroes were his mourners, and followed him to the journey's end. A stone was placed to mark the grave; and ten years later William Cobbett, once a mistaken vilifier of Paine and afterwards his eulogist, had his bones removed and carried to England, intending to raise a monuent to him in his native land. But the old outcry was heard again. A town-crier was sent to jail for proclaiming the arrival of the infidel's bones. Cobbett relinquished his design, and no one in the world to-day knows the resting place of Thomas Paine. . . . Paine was a religious man. His convictions were few and profound. So strong was his faith that it led him into the very intolerance he detested, and made him ridicule where he ought to have shown respect. . . . In private life Paine was uncorrupted by the worst vices of his generation. He was never abstemious, and during the Reign of Terror he drank to excess; but, if there be any truth in the accounts of drunkenness of his later years, it lies in the very occasional indulgence at a time when gentlemen slept under the table and awoke still gentlemen. The stories of his filthy habits are slander, though towards the close of his life, he became more careless of his dress, and maybe did not brush his coat after each pinch of snuff. He was always gentle to children and to animals. In manner he was kindly, and in conversation intelligent; but he was intolerant of contradiction, and not disinclined to assume the god in a gathering of friends. Like most vain men, Paine had little pride. His repeated requests for money for his services grate harshly enough, but their origin was not in meanness. . . . His tasks were not all done wisely, but they were done bravely. Too often his light was darkness; but he walked steadfastly in its path, and the goal which he sought was the happiness of his fellow-men.—SEDGWICK, ELLERY, 1899, *Thomas Paine, pp.* 139, 144, 145, 147.

COMMON SENSE
1776

This day was published, and is now selling by Robert Bell, in Third Street, price two shillings, "Common Sense," addressed to the inhabitants of North America.—PENNSYLVANIA JOURNAL, 1776, *Jan.* 10.

A few more of such flaming arguments as were exhibited at Falmouth and Norfolk, added to the sound doctrine and unanswerable reasoning contained in the pamphlet "Common Sense," will not leave numbers at a loss to decide upon the propriety of separation.—WASHINGTON, GEORGE, 1776, *Letter to Joseyh Reed, Jan.* 31; *Writings, ed. Ford, vol.* III, *p.* 396.

A pamphlet that had prodigious effects.—FRANKLIN, BENJAMIN, 1787, *Letter to M. de Veillard.*

Speaking a language which the colonists had felt but not thought, its popularity, terrible in its consequences to the parent country, was unexampled in the history of the press.—CHEETHAM, JAMES, 1809, *Life of Thomas Paine, p.* 46.

A pamphlet whose effect was such, that it is quite a feature in this memorable contest. You may now read it, and wonder how a performance not marked, as you may at first sight suppose, with any particular powers of eloquence, could possibly produce effects so striking.—SMYTH, WILLIAM, 1839, *Lectures on Modern History, Lecture* xxxiii.

Nor is our England without her missionaries. She has her life-saving Needham; to whom was solemnly presented a "civic sword,"—long since rusted into nothingness. Her Paine: rebellious Staymaker; unkempt; who feels that he, a single Needleman, did, by his "Common Sense" Pamphlet, free America;—that he can and will free all this World; perhaps even the other.—CARLYLE, THOMAS, 1837, *The French Revolution, vol.* II, *ch.* iii.

In '76 or '77 I was present, at Providence, Rhode Island, in a social assembly of most of the prominent leaders of the State. I recollect that the subject of independence was cautiously introduced by an ardent Whig, and the thought seemed to excite the abhorrence of the whole circle. A few weeks after, Paine's "Common Sense" appeared, and passed through the continent like an electric spark. It everywhere flashed conviction; and aroused a

determined spirit, which resulted in the Declaration of Independence, upon the 4th of July ensuing. The name of Paine was precious to every Whig heart, and had resounded throughout Europe.—WATSON, ELKANAH, 1842-56, *Men and Times of the Revolution, ed. W. C. Watson, p.* 127.

He was the first to perceive the destiny of the New World. No other pamphlet ever accomplished such wonderful results. It was filled with argument, reason, persuasion, and unanswerable logic. It opened a new world. It filled the present with hope and the future with honor. Everywhere the people responded, and in a few months the Continental Congress declared the colonies free and independent States. A new nation was born. It is simple justice to say that Paine did more to cause the Declaration of Independence than any other man. Neither should it be forgotten that his attacks upon Great Britain were also attacks upon monarchy; and while he convinced the people that the colonies ought to separate from the mother country, he also proved to them that a free government is the best that can be instituted among men. In my judgment, Thomas Paine was the best political writer that ever lived.—INGERSOLL, ROBERT G., 1874, *The Gods and Other Lectures, p.* 124.

Had in him the seeds of something like genius. . . . Though Burke moves in an intellectual sphere altogether superior to that in which Paine was able to rise, and though the richness of Burke's speculative power is as superior to Paine's meager philosophy as his style is superior in the amplitude of its rhetoric, it is not to be denied that Paine's plain-speaking is more fitted to reach popular passions, and even that he has certain advantages in point of argument.—STEPHEN, LESLIE, 1876, *History of English Thought in the Eighteenth Century, vol.* II, *p.* 261.

Like all his works, this pamphlet was written in clear, racy, vivid English, and with much power of popular reasoning; and, like most of his works, it was shallow, violent, and scurrilous.—LECKY, WILLIAM EDWARD HARTPOLE, 1882, *A History of England in the Eighteenth Century, vol.* III, *p.* 489.

No other pamphlet published during the Revolution is comparable with "Common

Sense" for interest to the reader of to-day, or for value as an historical document. Therein as in a mirror is beheld the almost incredible England, against which the colonies contended. And therein is reflected the moral, even religious, enthusiasm which raised the struggle above the paltriness of a rebellion against taxation to a great human movement,—a war for an idea. The art with which every sentence is feathered for its aim is consummate.—Conway, Moncure Daniel, 1892, *The Life of Thomas Paine, vol.* I, p. 66.

Colonial resolution had been screwed to the sticking point by Tom Paine, the stormy petrel of three countries, with his pamphlet "Common Sense," issued in the nick of time, coarsely but forcibly written and well spiced with rhetoric about the "royal brute."—Smith, Goldwin, 1893, *The United States, An Outline of Political History*, 1492–1871, p. 87.

THE AMERICAN CRISIS
1776–83

Under that cloud, by Washington's side, was silently at work the force that lifted it. Marching by day, listening to the consultations of Washington and his generals, Paine wrote by the camp fires; the winter storms, the Delaware's waves, were mingled with his ink; the half-naked soldiers in their troubled sleep dreaming of their distant homes, the skulking deserter creeping off in the dusk, the pallid face of the heavy hearted commander, made the awful shadows beneath which was written that leaflet which went to the Philadelphia printer along with Washington's last foreboding letters to his relatives in Virginia. It was printed on December 19th, and many copies reached the camp above Trenton Falls on the eve of that almost desperate attack on which Washington had resolved. . . . America has known some utterances of the lips equivalent to decisive victories in the field,—as some of Patrick Henry's, and the address of President Lincoln at Gettysburg. But of utterances by the pen none have achieved such vast results as Paine's "Common Sense" and his first "Crisis." Before the battle of Trenton the half-clad, disheartened soldies of Washington were called together in groups to listen to that thrilling exhortation. . . . Not a chord of faith, or love, or hope was left untouched. The

very faults of the composition, which the dilettanti have picked out, were effective to men who had seen Paine on the march, and knew these things were written in sleepless intervals of unwearied labors. . . . The pamphlet was never surpassed for true eloquence—that is, for the power that carries its point. With skilful illustration of lofty principles by significant details, all summed with simplicity and sympathy, three of the most miserable weeks ever endured by men were raised into epical dignity. The wives, daughters, mothers, sisters, seemed stretching out appealing hands against the mythically monstrous Hessians. The great commander, previously pointed to as "a mind that can even flourish upon care," presently saw his dispirited soldiers beaming with hope, and bounding to the onset,—their watchword : *These are the times that try men's souls!* Trenton was won, the Hessians captured, and a New Year broke for America on the morrow of that Christmas Day, 1776.— Conway, Moncure Daniel, 1892, *The Life of Thomas Paine, vol.* I, pp. 85, 86.

In the terrible hour of blackest disaster, poverty, suffering, and despair, when Washington was retreating before Lord Howe, defeated, and the country was beginning to feel the cause hopeless, Paine wrote the first number of "Crisis." Washington had it read at the head of every army corps ; and at every pinch of affairs throughout the war, the words of Paine were looked for, to inspirit the soldiers and arouse the flagging patriotism of the people. Franklin could not have done this work. His logic of prudence and honesty and courage would have failed to touch the souls that were discouraged. It needed words of fire and logic that rang like the blows of a berserker's sword on his shield.—Powell, E. P., 1893, *Study of Thomas Paine, The Arena, vol.* 8, p. 723.

THE RIGHTS OF MAN
1791–92

Mr. Paine's answer to Burke will be a refreshing shower to their minds. It would bring England itself to reason and revolution if it was permitted to be read there.—Jefferson, Thomas, 1791, *Letter to Benjamin Vaughan, May* 11 ; *Writings, ed. Ford, vol.* V, p. 334.

With respect to Paine's book, the first impression was seized by the government, and the circulation of it stopped as much as possible, but still many copies have got abroad, and, as I am just informed, have done much mischief. Your help, therefore, is as much wanted and as strongly called for as ever. I will venture to say, that the eyes of many are fixed on *you* at this important crisis. —PORTEUS, BEILBY, 1793, *Letter to Hannah More, Memoirs,* ed. *Roberts, vol.* I, *p.* 424.

I have had the ill or good fortune to provoke two great men of this age to the publication of their opinions : I mean Citizen Thomas Paine, and his Grace the * * * of * * * I am not so great a leveller as to put these two great men on a par, either in the state, or the republic of letters; but "the field of glory is a field for all." It is a large one, indeed; and we all may run, God knows where, in chase of glory, over the boundless expanse of that wild heath whose horizon always flies before us. I assure his Grace, (if he will yet give men leave to call him so), whatever may be said on the authority of the clubs or the bar, that Citizen Paine (who, they will have it, hunts with me in couples, and who only moves as I drag him along) has a sufficient activity in his own native benevolence to dispose and enable him to take the lead for himself. He is ready to blaspheme his God, to insult his king, and to libel the Constitution of his country, without any provocation from me or any encouragement from his Grace. —BURKE, EDMUND, 1795, *A Letter to William Elliot, Works, vol.* I, *p.* iii.

The book was characteristic of the man. Its purpose was, through the debasing principle of envy, which is after all the main principle of a leveller, to reduce all mankind to one standard, to write up a sort of *confusion made easy,* by addressing the baser to war against the better passions of our nature, by pulling down superior station, talents, virtues, and distinctions to the level of the lowest. It was an open declaration of hostility to all the institutions which we in England had been accustomed to consider as our ornament and pride; not a reform of the real or imaginary abuses of government, but a pretty plain recommendation to pull it down altogether for the pleasure of building afresh on the republican model—good perhaps in the eyes of an American, but at variance with the habits, the feelings, the

opinions, the honest convictions and prejudices of an Englishman. —PRIOR, SIR JAMES, 1824, *Memoir of the Life and Character of the Right Hon. Edmund Burke, vol.* II, *p.* 113.

This work should be read by every man and woman. It is concise, accurate, natural, convincing, and unanswerable. It shows great thought; and intimate knowledge of the various forms of government; deep insight into the very springs of human action, and a courage that compels respect and admiration. The most difficult political problems are solved in a few sentences. The venerable arguments in favor of wrong are refuted with a question—answered with a word. For forcible illustration, apt comparison, accuracy and clearness of statement, and absolute thoroughness, it has never been excelled. —INGERSOLL, ROBERT G., 1874, *The Gods and Other Lectures, p.* 130.

AGE OF REASON
1794–95–1811

How exceedingly superficial and frivolous are the hacknied objections to Christianity, and how entirely they arise from the grossest ignorance of the subject, will appear from my animadversions on Mr. Paine's boasted work. He would have written more to the purpose, if he had been acquainted with the writings of Voltaire, and other better informed unbelievers. But he seems entirely unread on the subject, and thereby to be acquainted with the ground on which either the friends or the enemies of Christianity must stand. Had he been better acquainted with the Scriptures which are a constant subject of his ridicule, he might have made a more plausible attack upon them. —PRIESTLEY, JOSEPH, 1794, *Letters to a Philosophical Unbeliever in Answer to Mr. Paine's Age of Reason.*

Read Tom Paine's "Age of Reason,"— God defend us from such poison. —WILBERFORCE, WILLIAM, 1794, *Journal, Life by R. I. and S. Wilberforce, vol.* II, *p.* 61.

This volume, the hornbook of vulgar infidelity, is now before us, and we have doubted how far we ought to refer to it, or what use to make of it. It has passed utterly out of the world's thoughts, and we have a repugnance, not easily to be overcome, in bringing it to light again. Its blasphemies are enough to sicken the heart; but still it may not be useless, in one view, to show the Christian reader to what dregs infidelity, beginning with refinement and high-bred speculation, will at last come.—READ, W. B., 1843, *The Life and Character of Thomas Paine, North American Review, vol.* 57, *p.* 49.

Perhaps the most blasphemous and mischievous book that was ever issued from the English press.—PERRY, GEORGE G., 1864, *The History of the Church of England, vol.* III, *p.* 436.

That hasty pamphlet of his which he named "The Age of Reason," written to alleviate the tedium of his Paris prison, differs from other deistical works only in being bolder and honester. It contains not a position which Franklin, John Adams, Jefferson, and Theodore Parker would have dissented from; and, doubtless, he spoke the truth when he declared that his main purpose in writing it was to "inspire mankind with a more exalted idea of the Supreme Architect of the Universe." I think his judgment must have been impaired before he could have consented to publish so inadequate a performance.—PARTON, JAMES, 1874, *Life of Thomas Jefferson, p.* 591.

The man who was the most influential assailant of the orthodox faith was Thomas Paine. He was the arch infidel, the infidel *par éminence,* whom our early and later theologians have united in holding up as a monster of iniquity and unbelief. The truth is that Paine was a dogmatic, well-meaning iconoclast, who attacked religion without having any religious experience or any imaginative perception of the vital spiritual phenomena on which religious faith is based. Nobody can read his "Age of Reason," after having had some preparatory knowledge derived from the study of the history of religions, without wondering at its shallowness. Paine is, in a spiritual application of the phrase, color-blind. He does not seem to know what religion is. The reputation he enjoyed was due not more to his masterly command of all the avenues to the average popular mind than to the importance to which he was lifted by his horrified theological adversaries. His merit as a writer against religion consisted in his hard, almost animal, common-sense, to whose tests he subjected the current theological dogmas.—WHIPPLE, EDWIN PERCY, 1886, *American Literature and Other Papers.*

Is popular only with the lower classes, unable to perceive its cheap and unscholarly critical method and its vulgar temper.—RICHARDSON, CHARLES F., 1887, *American Literature, 1607–1885, vol.* I, *p.* 211.

As an exponent of religious views, had a position in his day somewhat similar to that of Robert Ingersoll with us. He made a determined and vigorous attack upon a faith of whose true character he was irremediably ignorant. He was devoid of Ingersoll's quick wit and poetic genius; but he had his rough and ready knowledge of human nature, his love of destruction, his hard common sense, his spiritual color-blindness, and, perhaps, more than his earnestness. As in Ingersoll's case, too, the consternation which his attacks upon religion produced among clergymen and church members greatly increased his weight and importance as an "infidel." His "Age of Reason," is a shallow production, but it had its effect when it was written. Religion, it needs hardly be said, sustained no permanent injury at Paine's hands.—HAWTHORNE, JULIAN, AND LEMMON, LEONARD, 1891, *American Literature, p.* 27.

The "Age of Reason" went everywhere, into holes and corners, among backwoodsmen and pioneers, and did more execution among plain moral men than many a book that was more worthy of acceptance. It is a pity that his disciples should be content with repeating his denials, instead of building on the rational foundations which he laid. For instance, they might while adding to his criticism of the Scriptures, have shown their high moral bearing and their spiritual glow. They might have carried out further his "enthusiasm for humanity," showing that man had more in him than Paine suspected. They might have justified by more scientific reasons his belief in God and in immortality. They might have been truly rationalists as he wanted to be, but could not be at that period. But they were satisfied in saying over and over again, what he said as well as he could, but not as well as they can. He was simply a precursor, but he was a precursor of such men as Colenso and Robertson Smith, and a large host of scholars beside.—FROTHINGHAM, OCTAVIUS BROOKS, 1891, *Recollections and Impressions, p.* 252.

Paine's book has done as much to modify human belief as any ever written. It is one of the very few religious works of the last century which survives in unsectarian circulation. It requires a scholarly perception to recognize in its occasional expressions, by some called "coarse," the simple Saxon of Norfolkshire. . . . Paine's book is the uprising of the human HEART against the Religion of Inhumanity. . . . But here is one man, a prisoner, preparing for his long silence. He alone can speak for those slain between the throne and the altar. In these outbursts of laughter and tears, these outcries that think not of literary style, these appeals from surrounding chaos to the starry realm of order, from the tribune of vengeance to the sun shining for all, this passionate horror of cruelty in the powerful which will brave a heartless heaven or hell with its immortal indignation,—in all these the unfettered mind may hear the wail of enthralled Europe, sinking back choked with its blood, under the chain it tried to break. So long as a link remains of the same chain, binding reason or heart, Paine's "Age of Reason" will live. It is not a mere book—it is a man's heart.—CONWAY, MONCURE DANIEL, 1892, *The Life of Thomas Paine, vol. II, pp.* 184, 198, 222.

"The Age of Reason" damaged Paine's reputation in America, where the name of "Tom Paine" became a stench in the nostrils of the godly, and a synonym for atheism and blasphemy. His book was denounced from a hundred pulpits, and copies of it were carefully locked away from the sight of "the young," whose religious beliefs it might undermine. It was, in effect, a crude and popular statement of the deistic argument against Christianity. . . . The contest between skepticism and revelation has long since shifted to other grounds. Both the philosophy and the temper of "The Age of Reason" belong to the eighteenth century. But Paine's downright pugnacious method of attack was effective with shrewd, half-educated doubters; and in America well-thumbed copies of his book passed from hand to hand in many a rural tavern or store, where the village atheist wrestled in debate with the deacon or the schoolmaster.—BEERS, HENRY A., 1895, *Initial Studies in American Letters.*

A crude but often acute and forcible exposition of deism.—HERFORD, C. H., 1897, *The Age of Wordsworth, p.* 8.

GENERAL

That the early, unsolicited, and continued labors of Mr. Thomas Paine, in explaining and enforcing the principles of the late revolution by ingenious and timely publications upon the nature of liberty, and civil government, have been well received by the citizens of these States, and merit the approbation of Congress; and that in consideration of these services, and the benefits produced thereby, Mr. Paine is entitled to a liberal gratification from the United States.—RESOLUTION OF CONGRESS, 1785, *August 25th.*

I have frequently with pleasure reflected on your services to *my* native and *your* adopted country. Your "Common Sense," and your "Crisis," unquestionably awakened the public mind, and led the people loudly to call for a declaration of our national independence. I therefore esteemed you as a warm friend to the liberty and lasting welfare of the human race. But when I had heard you had turned your mind to a defence of infidelity, I felt myself much astonished and more grieved, that you had attempted a measure so injurious to the feelings and so repugnant to the true interest of so great a part of the citizens of the United States. The people of New England, if you will allow me to use a Scripture phrase, are fast returning to their first love. Will you excite among them the spirit of angry controversy at a time when they are hastening to amity and peace? I am told that some of our newspapers have announced your intention to publish an additional pamphlet upon the principles of your "Age of Reason." Do you think that your pen, or the pen of any other man, can unchristianize the mass of our citizens, or have your hopes of converting a few of them to assist you in so bad a cause? We ought to think ourselves happy in the enjoyment of opinion, without the danger of persecution by civil or ecclesiastical law. Our friend, the President of the United States, has been culminated for his liberal sentiments by men who have attributed that liberality to a latent design to promote the cause of infidelity. This, and all other slanders, have been made without the least shadow of proof.

Neither religion nor liberty can long subsist in the tumult of altercation and amidst the noise and violence of faction. *Felix qui cautus.* Adieu.— ADAMS, SAMUEL, 1802, *Letter to Thomas Paine, Works, vol.* III, *p.* 372.

Nobody now-a-days would trouble himself to read Tom Paine.—MCCARTHY, JUSTIN, 1872, *Science and Orthodoxy in England, Modern Leaders, p.* 242.

When our children's children shall celebrate America's *second* centennial, a hundred years from now, they will write in largest letters, upon their national banner, this sentence, which all intelligent American citizens will then enthusiastically recognize and applaud: "Thomas Paine—The Patriot, Philanthropist and Theologian of Two Hundred years ago."— SCHERMERHORN, MARTIN K., 1876, *Centennial Lecture on Thomas Paine, p.* 18.

What other last-century writer on political and religious issues survives in the hatred and devotion of a time engaged with new problems? What power is confessed in that writer who was set in the place of a decadent Satan, hostility to him being a sort of sixth point of Calvinism, and fortieth article of the Church? Large indeed must have been the influence of a man still perenially denounced by sectarians after heretical progress has left him comparatively orthodox, and retained as the figure-head of "Free thought" after his theism has been abandoned by its leaders. "Religion," said Paine, "has two principal enemies, Fanaticism and Infidelity." It was his strange destiny to be made a battle-field between these enemies. In the smoke of the conflict the man has been hidden. In the catalogue of the British Museum Library I counted 327 entries of books by or concerning Thomas Paine, who in most of them is a man-shaped or devil-shaped shuttlecock tossed between fanatical and "infidel" rackets. Here surely were phenomena enough to attract the historic sense of a scientific age, yet they are counterpart of an historic suppression of the most famous author of his time. The meagre references to Paine by other than controversial writers are perfunctory; by most historians he is either wronged or ignored. Before me are two histories of "American Slavery" by eminent members of Congress; neither mentions that Paine was the first political writer who advocated and devised a scheme of emancipation. Here is the latest "Life of Washington" (1889), by another member of Congress, who manages to exclude even the name of the man who, as we shall see, chiefly converted Washington to the cause of independence. And here is a history of the "American Revolution" (1891), by John Fiske, who, while recognizing the effect of "Common Sense," reveals his ignorance of that pamphlet, and of all Paine's works, by describing it as full of scurrilous abuse of the English people,—whom Paine regarded as fellow-sufferers with the Americans under royal despotism.—CONWAY, MONCURE DANIEL, 1892, *The Life of Thomas Paine, vol.* I, *Preface, p.* ix.

Paine is the only English writer who expresses with uncompromising sharpness the abstract doctrine of political rights held by the French revolutionists. His relation to the American struggle, and afterwards to the revolution of 1789, gave him a unique position, and his writings became the sacred books of the extreme radical party in England. Attempts to suppress them only raised their influence, and the writings of the first quarter of the century are full of proofs of the importance attached to them by friends and foes. Paine deserves whatever credit is due to absolute devotion to a creed believed by himself to be demonstrably true and beneficial. He showed undeniable courage, and is free from any suspicion of mercenary motives. He attached an excessive importance to his own work, and was ready to accept the commonplace that his pen had been as efficient as Washington's sword. He attributed to the power of his reasoning all that may more fitly be ascribed to the singular fitness of his formulæ to express the political passions of the time. Though unable to see that his opponents could be anything but fools and knaves, he has the merit of sincerely wishing that the triumph should be won by reason without violence. With a little more "human nature," he would have shrunk from insulting Washington or encouraging a Napoleonic invasion of his native country. But Paine's bigotry was of the logical kind which can see only one side of a question, and imagines that all political and religious questions are as simple as the first propositions of Euclid.

This singular power of clear, vigorous exposition made him unequalled as a pamphleteer in revolutionary times, when compromise was an absurdity. He also showed great shrewdness and independence of thought in his criticisms of the Bible. He said, indeed, little that had not been anticipated by the English deists and their French disciples; but he writes freshly and independently, if sometimes coarsely. —STEPHEN, LESLIE, 1895, *Dictionary of National Biography, vol.* XLIII, *p.* 78.

The coarse and violent expression, as well as the unpopular matter, of Paine's works may have led to his being rather unfairly treated in the hot fights of the Revolutionary period; but the attempts which have recently been made to whitewash him are a mere mistake of reaction, or paradox, or pure stupidity. The charges which used to be brought against his moral character matter little; for neither side in these days had, or in any days has, a monopoly of loose or of holy living. But two facts will always remain; first, that Paine attacked subjects which all require calm, and some of them reverent, treatment, in a tone of the coarsest violence; and, secondly, that he engaged in questions of the widest reach, and requiring endless thought and reading, with the scanty equipments and the superabundant confidence of a self-educated man.—SAINTSBURY, GEORGE, 1896, *A History of Nineteenth Century Literature, p.* 31.

When we consider the dignity, the elevation, and the reasonableness of so much that he says in his argument for the separation of the Colonies from England, and of many passages even in the "Age of Reason," one hardly knows how to account for the ribaldry which belongs to so many of his later writings: ribald about old friends and benefactors; ribald about religion; ribald about the public which had honored him. Jealous, morbid, crazed by his vanities—his clever mind at intervals blazing through the clouds and foulnesses which his own dissipations and selfish arrogance had created; dying at last, after long stages of drunkenness, and, as many report, with a nose as bloated as Bardolph's.—MITCHELL, DONALD G., 1897, *American Lands and Letters, The Mayflower to Rip-Van-Winkle, p.* 115.

Anna Seward

1747–1809

The "Swan of Lichfield," born in 1747 at Eyam rectory, Derbyshire, lived from seven at Lichfield, where her father, himself a poet, became a canon. He died in 1790, but she lived on in the bishop's palace, dear to her friends and correspondents, Mrs. Piozzi, Hayley, Southey, Scott, and died 23d March 1809. She published her poetical novel, "Louisa," in 1782; her "Sonnets" in 1799; her Life of Dr. Darwin in 1804; but bequeathed to Walter Scott the care of the collected edition of her poems (1810). Her . . . letters fill six volumes (1811–13).—PATRICK AND GROOME, eds., 1897, *Chambers's Biographical Dictionary, p.* 843.

PERSONAL

The great command of literary anecdotes which Miss Seward possessed, her ready perception both of the serious and ludicrous, and her just observation and original taste, rendered her society delightful. She entered into every topic with the keenness and vivacity of youth, and it was difficult to associate the idea of advanced years either with her countenance or conversation. The possessor of such quick feelings seldom escapes the portion of pain with which all earthly good are alloyed and tempered. With the warmest heart of her friends, and an unbounded enthusiasm in their service, Miss Seward united a sensibility to coldness, or to injuries real or supposed, which she permitted to disturb her more than was consistent with prudence or with happiness. The same tone of mind rendered her jealous of critical authority, when exercised over her own productions, or those of her friends.—SCOTT, SIR WALTER, 1810, *ed., The Poetical Works of Anna Seward, Memoir.*

Miss Seward had not the art of making friends, except among the little circle whom she flattered, and who flattered her. I never saw her myself, but judge only from the manner in which she was spoken of. My friend Shaw, whom she noticed, thought her the greatest of poetesses. She both gave offence and provoked ridicule by her affectation, and bad taste, and pompous pretensions.—BRYDGES, SIR SAMUEL EGERTON, 1834, *Autobiography, vol.* I, *p.* 57.

Anna Seward,—the most successful of unendowed poetesses,—appears before us, in or about her thirtieth year—still in all the freshness of her beauty. Let us follow her into her father's library, as she limps along—for she is lame from the fracture of her knee, years ago—yet she is still, though bent, tall, elegant, and even stately. She seats herself before a table, and with the finest and fairest of hands opens a book. We gaze upon her oval face as she upraises it to look at the old man beside her in his easy chair. That face is full of harmony, as it is of expression. The features are small, regular and delicate; there is something very firm, though very sweet, in the mouth. Her eyes, of auburn, are of the same hue and shade precisely as her hair, which is drawn up from her high forehead, and gathered under a knot of pearls. Around her long, fair throat is a string of pearls sewn to a small band of black velvet; over her shoulder she wears a loose bodice, which is edged with sable fur, leaving her bust exposed in the folds of her loose and short-waisted dress. Large white muslin cambric sleeves fall over her delicate arms.—THOMSON, KATHERINE (GRACE WHARTON), 1862, *The Literature of Society, vol.* II, *p.* 263.

Johnson could not appreciate the deep, sensitive nature of Miss Seward, and Boswell hated her, and speaks very disparagingly of her, with his usual coarseness. We can hardly forgive Scott for one of his letters, criticising her little weaknesses, after she was dead. No truer heart ever beat in the breast of any woman.—BUTTERWORTH, HEZEKIAH, 1876, *Anna Seward and Major André, The Galaxy, vol.* 21, *p.* 175.

Her admirers were wont to call her "The Swan of Lichfield," and she herself seems to have imagined the title not unmerited. Her chief foible, indeed, must have been this poetry. She could never have earned such hearty esteem from men like Sir Walter Scott, and have avoided so successfully the numberless jealousies which writing people have to encounter, had she not

in all her private relations shown herself a much more perfect mistress of her conduct than she was of the poet's pen.—ROBERTSON, ERIC S., 1883, *English Poetesses, p.* 98.

GENERAL

Misses Seward and Williams, and half-a-dozen more of these harmonious virgins, have no imagination, no novelty. Their thoughts and phrases are like their gown, old remnants cut and turned.—WALPOLE, HORACE, 1786, *To the Countess of Ossory, Nov.* 4; *Letters, ed. Cunningham, vol.* IX, *p.* 73.

I had the satisfaction of hearing that Miss Seward's "Louisa" made you weep; I remember the difficulty I had to make you promise to read it; the same repugnance I have had to combat in a dozen other people; all were as unwilling as if it had been a sermon, or something that was to do them good; but when they *had* read it, all who had any taste for imagery, sentiment, and poetry thanked me for having compelled them to enjoy this pleasure, and I expected *you* would have had the same gratitude. Miss Seward's imagination is bright and glowing; she is rich in expression, and admirable at description; but to counterbalance all these excellences, she has one fault, which is of great magnitude, but which may not perhaps be so great an offence in your eyes as I confess it is in mine: what it is I shall not mention, and in case it does not strike you, I am willing you should call me mean and malignant for suggesting it: a little envy is natural, if not pardonable; when I see Mrs. Pepys, I will tell her my objections.—MORE, HANNAH, 1784, *Letter to Mr. Pepys, July* 17; *Memoirs, ed. Roberts, vol.* I, *p.* 194.

I am now doing penance for my ill-breeding, by submitting to edit her posthumous poetry, most of which is absolutely execrable. This, however, is the least of my evils, for when she proposed this bequest to me, which I could not in decency refuse, she combined it with a request that I would publish her whole literary correspondence. This I declined on principle, having a particular aversion at perpetuating that sort of gossip; but what availed it? Lo! to ensure the publication, she left it to an Edinburgh bookseller; and I anticipate the horror of seeing myself advertised for a live poet like a wild beast on a painted streamer, for I understand all her friends are depicted therein in body, mind, and manners. So much for the risks of sentimental correspondence.—SCOTT, SIR WALTER, 1810, *Letter to Joanna Baillie, March* 18; *Life by Lockhart, ch.* xix.

Have you seen Miss Seward's "Letters?" The names of her correspondents are tempting, but, alas! though addressed to all the eminent literati of the last half century, all the epistles bear the signature of Anna Seward.. To tell you the truth, I was always a little shocked at the sort of reputation she bore in poetry. Sometimes affected, sometimes *fade*, sometimes pedantic, and sometimes tinselly, none of her works were ever simple, graceful, or natural; and I never heard her praised but I fancied the commendation would end in, "It is very well—for a woman!" What I have seen of her letters confirms me in this idea. They are affected, sentimental, and lackadaisical to the highest degree; and her taste is even worse than her execution. —MITFORD, MARY RUSSELL, 1811, *To Sir William Elford, Aug.* 11; *Life, ed. L'Estrange, vol.* I, *p.* 121.

I have returned for entertainment to a book you will not hold in high respect, even Anna Seward's "Letters" . . . and now I must apologise to her memory for the disgust with which I was wont to regard her pedantry, quaint, new-coined phrases, violent prejudices, and some small defects of female delicacy. Yet, after all, she amuses me much, now that the country and rainy weather have made me less critical, and more grateful for entertainment. She is so sincere and friendly, so capable of tasting the beauties of nature and of poetry, that I try hard to forget her injustice to Cowper, and preference of Chatterton to Burns. . . . Her poetry, on which she prided herself, I cannot taste at all; and her Darwin I cannot endure.—GRANT, ANNE, 1820, *To Mrs. Fletcher, July* 26; *Memoir and Correspondence, ed. Grant, vol.* II, *pp.* 244, 245.

She was endowed with considerable genius, and with an ample portion of that fine enthusiasm which sometimes may be taken for it; but her taste was far from good, and her numerous productions (a few excepted) are disfigured by florid ornament and elaborate magnificence.—DYCE, ALEXANDER, 1825, *Specimens of British Poetesses.*

It cannot be denied that she sometimes showed flashes of genius; but never in continuity. She believed that poetry rather lay in the diction than in the thought; and I am not acquainted with any literary letters, which exhibit so much corrupt judgment, and so many false beauties as her's. Her sentiments are palpably studied, and disguised, and dressed up. Nothing seems to come from the heart, but all to be put on. I understand the André family say, that in the "Monody on Major André," all about his attachment, and Honora Sneyd, &c., is a nonsensical falsehood, of her own invention. Among her numerous sonnets, there are not above five or six which are good; and I cannot doubt that Dr. Darwin's hand is in many of her early poems. The inequalities of all her compositions are of the nature of patchwork.—BRYDGES, SIR SAMUEL EGERTON, 1834, *Autobiography, vol.* I, *p.* 57.

She was a woman whose talents, if her language had not been distorted by false notions of excellence in composition, might have retained for her the high station among female writers, which in her palmy days it was allowed that she had won. Though not always a judicious critic, she was never unjust or ungenerous in her censures; and if she frequently mistook glittering faults for beauties, no beauty ever escaped her observation.—SOUTHEY, ROBERT, 1836-7, *The Life of William Cowper, vol.* II, *p.* 45.

In the course of this autumn [1810] appeared the Poetical Works of Miss Seward, in three volumes, with a Prefatory Memoir of her Life by Scott. This edition had, as we have seen, been enjoined by her last will—but his part in it was an ungrateful one, and the book was among the most unfortunate that James Ballantyne printed, and his brother published, in deference to the personal feelings of their partner. He had been, as was natural, pleased and flattered by the attentions of the Lichfield poetess in the days of his early aspirations after literary distinction; but her verses, which he had with his usual readiness praised to herself beyond their worth, appeared when collected a formidable monument of mediocrity. Her Correspondence, published at the same time by Constable, was considered by him with still greater aversion.—LOCKHART, JOHN GIBSON, 1836, *Life of Sir Walter Scott, ch.* xxii.

Affected and superfluous.—HUNT, LEIGH, 1847, *Men, Women and Books*.

Anna Seward, yclept the Swan of Lichfield, was the Sappho of that era of ribbons and gumflowers, and a fitting one for such a Juvenal as Hayley, and such a Lucretius as Darwin. She wrote with fluency, and poured out a cataract of verse.—MOIR, D. M., 1850-1, *Sketches of the Poetical Literature of the Past Half-Century, p. 12*.

Miss Seward's own poetry, with much more sentimentality and much less sense and substance, belongs with the same school with Darwin's. Hers is the feeble commonplace of the same labored, tortuous, and essentially unnatural and untrue style out of which he, with his more powerful and original genius, has evolved for himself a distinctive form or dialect. —CRAIK, GEORGE L., 1861, *A Compendious History of English Literature and of the English Language, vol. II, p. 402*.

If anything could be more absurd than the poems themselves in their form, conception, and execution, it would be Miss Seward's criticisms of them. Indeed it is scarcely possible to believe that such a work as her "Life of Dr. Darwin" could have been written in the present century; its stilted style, its unnatural verbiage, its pompous solemnity, are so out of keeping with our modern habits of thought, feeling, and expression.—STORY, WILLIAM WETMORE, 1890, *Conversations in a Studio, vol. I, p. 258*.

Miss Seward's poetry belongs to the school represented by William Hayley and satirised by Gifford in the "Baviad." . . . Her work abounds in every sort of affectation. . . . At times she shows an appreciation of natural scenery, and now and then turns a good line.— LEE, ELIZABETH, 1889, *Dictionary of National Biography, vol. LI, p. 281*.

Thomas Holcroft
1745–1809

Dramatist and miscellaneous writer, was born 10th December, 1745 (old style), in Orange Court, Leicester Fields, London. . . . On the expiry of his term of engagement as stable boy he returned to assist his father, who had again resumed his trade of shoemaker in London; but after marrying in 1765, he procured the office of teacher in a small school in Liverpool. His subsequent career, like his earlier life, was hard and checkered, but it must suffice to state that, after failing in an attempt to set up a private school, he followed for several years the profession of an actor, often at a very meagre salary, and that he was more successful as a dramatist and novelist, but suffered much and frequent anxiety from pecuniary embarrassments and repeated disappointments. He died 23d March, 1809, from enlargement of the heart, brought on, it is supposed, by the failure of several of his dramatic pieces. He was a member of the Society for Constitutional Reform, and on that account was, in 1794, indicted of high treason, but acquitted. The best known dramas of Holcroft are "Duplicity," "The School for Arrogance," "The Road to Ruin," and "The Deserted Daughter." Among his novels may be mentioned "Alwyn," and "Hugh Trevor." He was also the author of "Travels from Hamburg through Westphalia, Holland and the Netherlands to Paris," and of some volumes of verse, and translated several works from the French and German with considerable elegance. . . . His "Memoirs written by himself and continued down to the time of his death, from his diary, notes, and other papers," by William Hazlitt, appeared in 1815, and has gone into several editions.—BAYNES, THOMAS SPENCER, ed., 1880, *Encyclopædia Britannica, Ninth ed., vol. XII, pp. 59, 60*.

PERSONAL

There is a fierceness and dogmatism of conversation in Holcroft for which you receive little compensation either from the veracity of his information, the closeness of his reasoning, or the splendour of his language. He talks incessantly of metaphysics, of which he appears to me to know nothing, to have read nothing. He is ignorant as a scholar, and neglectful of the smaller humanities of a man.—COLERIDGE, SAMUEL TAYLOR, 1794, *To Robert Southey, Dec. 17; Letters, ed. E. H. Coleridge, vol. I, p. 114*.

The relaxations in which Mr. Holcroft indulged were few and regular. He was fond of riding, and for some years kept a horse, which had generally high blood in its veins. . . . His love for the arts sometimes subjected him to temptations which were not consistent with strict economy. . . . It may be supposed, that that part of Mr. Holcroft's time which he could spare from his studies, was chiefly devoted to the society of literary friends. He, however, gave few dinner-parties, and those were not ostentatious, and consequently not expensive. When a friend dined with him, a bottle of wine was usually produced after dinner; but, with respect to himself, he was extremely abstemious in the use of liquor, and the habits of his friends were rather those of philosophers than Bacchanalians. —HAZLITT, WILLIAM, 1816, *Memoirs of the Late Thomas Holcroft, Written by Himself, and Continued to the Time of his Death, p. 185.*

Holcroft's "Memoirs" are valuable as showing strength of endurance in the man, which is worth more than all the talent in the world.—BYRON, LORD, 1816, *Letter to Murray, Oct.* 5; *Life by Moore, p. 324.*

I own I could never think so considerably of myself as to decline the society of an agreeable or worthy man upon difference of opinion only. The impediments and the facilitations to a sound belief are various and inscrutable as the heart of man. Some believe upon weak principles; others cannot feel the efficacy of the strongest. One of the most candid, most upright, and single-meaning men I ever knew, was the late Thomas Holcroft. I believe he never said one thing, and meant another, in his life; and, as near as I can guess, he never acted otherwise than with the most scrupulous attention to conscience. Ought we to wish the character false, for the sake of a hollow compliment to Christianity?— LAMB, CHARLES, 1823, *The Tombs in the Abbey.*

The name of Holcroft at once gives rise to a crowd of recollections to those who are conversant with the history of the times, and that particular circle of literary men of which my father was one. The son of a shoemaker, he rose to eminence through the energy of his character, and the genius with which nature had endowed him. To think of Holcroft as his friends remember him, and to call to mind whence at this day he principally derives his fame

as an author, present a singular contrast. He was a man of stern and irascible character, and from the moment that he espoused liberal principles, he carried them to excess. He was tried for life as a traitor on account of his enthusiasm for the objects of the French Revolution. He believed that truth must prevail by the force of its own powers, but he advocated what he deemed truth with vehemence. He warmly asserted that death and disease existed only through the feebleness of man's mind, that pain also had no reality. Rectitude and Courage were the gods of his idolatry, but the defect of his temper rendered him a susceptible friend. His comedy, "The Road to Ruin," will always maintain its position on the English stage, so long as there are actors who can fitly represent its leading characters. He was a man of great industry, unwearied in his efforts to support his family.— SHELLEY, MARY WOLLSTONECRAFT, 1851, *Fragmentary Notes, Paul's Life of Godwin, vol.* I, *p.* 25.

Holcroft was a stern and conscientious man, with an irascible temper, great energy, and marvellous industry. . . . As an actor he was harsh and unsympathetic, and he appears to have taken no further part on the stage after his performance of Figaro. In spite of his poverty and many adverse circumstances, Holcroft with great tenacity of purpose contrived to educate himself creditably, and to acquire a competent knowledge of French, German, and Italian. His career, however, was one continuous struggle against misfortune, and owing to his many rash speculations and his "picture-dealing insanity" his affairs were perpetually in an embarrassed condition.—BARKER, G. F. RUSSELL, 1891, *Dictionary of National Biography, vol.* XXVII, *p.* 117.

GENERAL

You appear to have seen Holcroft's pamphlet; which certainly displays much ability and good-writing, but most of all the extreme vanity and self-importance of the author, which is equally ridiculous and disgusting. He thinks it impossible that any court or jury in the world could have resisted the force of his combined eloquence and philosophy; and actually told us that he would gladly have given one of his hands for the opportunity of making his defence, which by the way would certainly have hanged him, however favourable his judges might have been beforehand.—RITSON, JOSEPH, 1795, *Letters, Jan.* 16; *vol.* II, *p.* 62.

Upon the whole, we think that this book is a great deal too long, and that it has attained this magnitude by the most intrepid and extensive application of the approved receipts for bookmaking that has yet come under our consideration. If everything were deducted that has no relation to the present state of the countries which the author proposes to describe, and everything which is transcribed from books that might as well have been consulted at home, the publication, we are persuaded, would be reduced to one third of its present bulk. The lofty pretensions, too, with which the author sets out, and the solemnity with which he continually speaks of his labours, form a ridiculous contrast with the insignificance of the matters upon which he rested his attention. . . . Of the style and language of the book, a tolerable judgment may be formed from the extracts we have already given. Its ruling vice is affectation, which is frequently combined with a greater degree of grammatical inaccuracy than is usual, even in works of this description.—JEFFREY, FRANCIS LORD, 1804, *Holcroft's Travels from Hamburgh to Paris, Edinburgh Review, vol.* 4, *pp.* 98, 99.

This ["Road to Ruin"] comedy ranks among the most successful of modern plays. There is merit in the writing, but much more in that dramatic science, which disposes character, scenes, and dialogue, with minute attention to theatric exhibition: for the author has nicely considered, that it is only by passing the ordeal of a theatre with safety, that a drama has the privilege of being admitted to a library. The nice art with which the conversations in this play are written, will, by a common reader, pass unadmired and unnoticed. Some of the most important speeches consist of no more than one line. The grand skill has been to make no skill evident—to force a reader to forget the author, but to remember his play, and his distinct character. . . . "The Road to Ruin" is a complete **drama**; resting its power on itself alone, without adventitious aid.—INCHBALD, MRS. ELIZABETH, 1806–9, *The British Theatre, The Road to Ruin, Introduction.*

Mr. Holcroft, in his "Road to Ruin," set the example of that style of comedy, in which the *slang* phrases of jockey-noblemen and the humours of the four-in-hand club are blended with the romantic sentiments of distressed damsels and philosophic waiting-maids, and in which he has been imitated by the most successful of our living writers, unless we make a separate class for the school of Cumberland.—HAZLITT, WILLIAM, 1818, *Lectures on the English Comic Writers, Lecture* viii.

Becomes one of the best and most voluminous translators upon record. If ever one happens to take up an English version of a French or German book of that period—"Memoirs of Baron Trenck," or "Caroline de Litchfield"—and if that version have in it the zest and savor of original writing, we shall be sure to find the name of Thomas Holcroft in the title-page. . . . His comedies, "Duplicity," "The School for Arrogance," and "The Road to Ruin," evinced talent (I had well nigh written genius) of the highest order. The serious parts above all are admirable. Perhaps no scenes have ever drawn so many tears as those between the father and the son in the last-mentioned play. The famous "Good Night" is truly the one touch of nature that makes the whole world kin; and although I have seen it played as well as any thing can be played by Munden and Elliston, I have always felt that the real merit belonged to the author. His greater novels, too, "Anna St. Ives" and "Hugh Trevor," were full of powerful writing; and he seemed destined to a long course of literary prosperity.—MITFORD, MARY RUSSELL, 1851, *Recollections of a Literary Life, p.* 82.

Thomas Holcroft is one of the best forgotten men in English literature. Less than a hundred years ago he was a celebrity—a prolific writer of plays, novels and books of travel, the intimate of Hazlitt and Godwin, the hero of a political trial. Now-a-days, when "The Road to Ruin," his one work that has lived, is occasionally revived, the eye of the unlearned playgoer dubiously scans the bill in search of the author's name. For the student of the stage Holcroft's work must always retain a certain interest. He was not in any sense a great writer; but his plays were at least worthy of all the consideration bestowed upon them in their time, while

"The Road to Ruin" is one of the dozen or so plays of its century which have survived. Holcroft may be regarded as the founder of the modern school of melodrama. He was the first, too, to hastily adapt a French success to the exigencies of the English stage, after the fashion now in vogue.—HIBBERT, HENRY GEORGE, 1892, *The Author of "The Road to Ruin," The Theatre*, vol. 28, p. 132.

A curiosity of literature and a rather typical figure of the time.—SAINTSBURY, GEORGE, 1896, *A History of Nineteenth Century Literature*, p. 38.

Robert Tannahill
1774–1810

One of the most popular of the song-writers of Scotland since Burns, was a native of Paisley, born in 1774. He was bred a weaver; and his favourite pursuit was to recover old and neglected airs, to which he adapted new words. "I would I were a weaver," says Falstaff; "I could sing all manner of songs." He continued to work, with some exceptions, in his native town, where, at the beginning of this century, he made an acquaintance with Robert Archibald Smith, a musical composer, who set some of his songs to original music, and adapted others to old airs. In 1807, Tannahill collected his songs into a volume, which was decidedly successful. The higher success, which he more prized, was to find his songs universally known and sung amongst all classes. But the poet was the victim of a morbid melancholy which embittered his existence. His means were above his wants; he had no special unhappiness. But he died, as Ophelia died,—"Where a willow grows aslant a brook"—perhaps "chanting snatches of old tunes." This event occurred in 1810, near Paisley.—KNIGHT, CHARLES, 1847–48, *Half-Hours With the Best Authors*, vol. IV, p. 161.

PERSONAL

Tannahill used to declare, that one of the most gratifying tributes he ever had paid to his genius, was while taking a solitary walk, in the cool of a summer's evening, he had his musings interrupted by the sweet voice of a country girl, who, on his approaching nearer the spot, he discovered was singing one of his compositions—

"We'll meet beside the dusky glen on yon burn side."

This, he said, was one of the sweetest and delightful moments of his life; he beheld in it a promise of future fame, and hailed it as a pledge of the rising popularity of his Songs: but the highest tribute ever paid to the genius of Tannahill, was the visit which James Hogg, the Ettrick Shepherd, paid him, not long before his death. There was something romantic in this pilgrimage of the Mountain Bard, to feel, and see,—to converse and enjoy the fellowship of one whose heart, like his own, was gifted with the "magic voice of song:" they spent the night in each other's company. Tannahill convoyed Hogg, on the following morning, half way to Glasgow, where they parted. It was a melancholy adieu which Tannahill gave him—"Farewell," he cried, "we shall never meet again,—farewell, I shall never see you more!"—RYAN, RICHARD, 1826, *Poetry and Poets*, vol. II, p. 246.

As with the generality of people of his rank, the poet's education was limited to reading, writing, and accounts. At an early age he was sent to the loom,—then a profitable calling,—at which he distinguished himself by his industry. . . . He was possessed of a correct musical ear, and played well on the German flute. His favourite pursuit was to recover old or neglected airs, and unite them to appropriate words. The airs he hummed over while plying the shuttle, and as the words arose in his mind, he jotted them down at a rude desk which he had attached to his loom, and which he could use without rising from his seat. Thus did he contrive to relieve the monotonous dulness of his daily occupation, by combining with it the exercise of his more gentle craft,—weaving threads and verses alternately. . . . The melancholy to which Tannahill had been occasionally subject, now became deep and habitual. He evinced a proneness to imagine that his best friends were disposed to injure him, and a certain jealous fear of his claims to genius being impugned. These imaginary grievances were confided to his faithful adviser Smith, who found it impossible to convince him of the hallucination under which he laboured. His eyes sank, his countenance became pale, and his body emaciated. The strange and incoherent texture of some poetical pieces which he wrote about this time, betrayed the state of his mind. In short, it became apparent that a breaking up of his mental and bodily powers was at hand. He now set himself to destroy all his manuscripts; not a scrap which he could possibly collect was allowed to escape the flames. This is the more to be regretted, since the corrections and additions he had made for a second edition of his works, and some unpublished pieces of much merit, all of which fell a prey to the flames, would have added greatly to his reputation.—RAMSAY, PHILIP A., 1838, *ed., The Works of Robert Tannahill, Memoir, pp.* xv, xxxiv.

The victim of dissappointments which his sensitive temperament could not endure, Tannahill was naturally of an easy and cheerful disposition. As a child, his exemplary behaviour was so conspicuous that mothers were satisfied of their children's safety if they learned that they were in company with *"Bob* Tannahill." Inoffensive in his own dispositions, he entertained every respect for the feelings of others. He enjoyed the intercourse of particular friends, but avoided general society; in company he seldom talked, and only with a neighbour; he shunned the acquaintance of persons of rank, because he disliked patronage, and dreaded superciliousness. His conversation was simple; he possessed, but seldom used, considerable powers of satire; but he applied his keenest shafts of sarcasm against the votaries of cruelty. In performing acts of kindness he took delight, but he was scrupulous of accepting favours; he was strong in the love of independence, and had saved twenty pounds at the period of his death. His general appearance did not indicate intellectual superiority; his countenance was calm and meditative; his eyes were grey, and his hair a light brown. In person, he was under the middle size. Not ambitious of general learning, he confined his reading chiefly to poetry.—ROGERS, CHARLES, 1855-57-70, *The Scottish Minstrel, The Songs of Scotland Subsequent to Burns, p.* 133.

Robert Tannahill, a Scotch weaver, whose songs in their artless sweetness, their simplicity of diction, their tenderness of sentiment, have long since won distinction, came up to Edinburgh very poor in purse, but rich in the future that poetic aspirations imaged forth. He put his manuscripts into Constable's hands, offering the whole of them at a very small price. Day after day he waited for an answer, with a mind alternating between hope and fear. Constable, who always distrusted his own judgment in such matters, and who, perhaps, at the moment had no one else to consult, eventually returned the poems. Tannahill in a madness of despair put a period to his existence, adding one to those "young shadows" who hover round the shrine of genius, as if to warn all but the boldest from attempting to approach it.—CURWEN, HENRY, 1873, *A History of Booksellers, p.* 122.

The good people of Paisley have cherished the memory of Tannahill. The house in which he was born has inserted in its front wall a granite memorial-stone recording the circumstance. His brother, when old age compelled him to cease from labour, was provided with a competency by his fellow-citizens, who long ago formed a Tannahill Club, which always celebrated the anniversary of the poet's birth. The centenary of the "prince of Paisley poets," as he has been called, was celebrated with the utmost enthusiasm by the inhabitants of Paisley. A general holiday was held, and the town was decorated with flags and flowers. More than 15,000 persons assembled on the Braes o' Gleniffer to listen to addresses spoken in the poet's honour, and to the singing of his own sweet songs—songs that are a priceless heritage to his native land.—WILSON, JAMES GRANT, 1876, *The Poets and Poetry of Scotland, vol.* I, *p.* 502.

Poor Tannahill! Paisley truly has good reason to be proud of her handloom weaver, who knew to mingle the whir of his busy loom, not with the jarring notes of political fret or atheistic pseudo-philosophy, but with the sweet music of Nature in the most melodious season of the year. Sad to think that the author of this song, one of the most lovable, kindly, and human-hearted of mortals, and who, in spite of the deficiencies of his early culture, had achieved a reputation second only to Burns among the song-writers of his tuneful fatherland, should have bade farewell to the sweet light of the sun and the fair greenery of his native· glens at the early age of thirty-six—drowning himself, poor fellow! in a pool not far from the place of his birth.—BLACKIE, JOHN STUART, 1889, *Scottish Song, p.* 49.

GENERAL

Tannahill could achieve only a song; but as the songs which he did achieve were very genuine ones, with the true faculty in them, Scotland seems to be in no danger of forgetting them.—MILLER, HUGH, 1856, *Essays, p.* 449.

The poems of this ill-starred son of genius are greatly inferior to his songs. They have all a common-place artificial character. His lyrics, on the other hand, are rich and original, both in description and in sentiment. His diction is copious and luxuriant, particularly in describing natural objects and the peculiar features of the Scottish landscape. His simplicity is natural and unaffected, and though he appears to have possessed a deeper sympathy with nature than with the workings of human feeling, or even the passion of love, he is often tender and pathetic.— CHAMBERS, ROBERT, 1876, *Cyclopædia of English Literature, ed. Carruthers.*

If, as was said by Fletcher of Saltoun, song-writers are to be classed among lawgivers, then may we hail Tannahill as one of the foremost Scottish legislators— ruling by the sceptre of song.—WILSON, JAMES GRANT, 1876, *The Poets and Poetry of Scotland, vol.* I, *p.* 501.

For delicacy and refinement of feeling and expression, comes nearest to Burns of all our song-writers. His range was narrow, even compared with Hogg and Lady Nairne; for he had not the imagination of the one, nor the humour of the other; yet he possessed that sensitive tenderness of the poetic instinct, capable of touching the finest cords in nature to which the human soul has ever responded, in a degree which Burns alone excelled. Like all their contemporaries he was greatly Burns's inferior in passion, both as to range and intensity. . . . We have already remarked that his poetic range is a narrow one; out of it he produced nothing of self-sustaining merit, and his poems which are not songs are very commonplace. As a specialist his fame is secure, and as living at the present day as when he first delighted his admiring countrymen. His songs, though true to universal nature, have certain local features which make their perfect enjoyment dependent on that sensitiveness to the influences of locality which characterises the Scotch mind, and in consequence he is not so highly appreciated anywhere as in Scotland, nor, in Scotland, anywhere as in Paisley, of which he is the poetic divinity.—ROSS, J., 1884, *The Book of Scottish Poems, pp.* 707, 708.

Setting aside Burns, there is no song-writer more popular in Scotland than Tannahill. His memory is cherished with the deepest affection of his own West country. A gathering, at which the finest of his songs are sung, is annually held on the Braes of Gleniffer, and is attended by crowds from Glasgow, Paisley, and other towns in the neighbourhood. And he thoroughly merits the place he has won in his countrymen's hearts. A poet of the people, he has not received due recognition at the hands of literary critics. He has lines than which there are none sweeter in the Scottish tongue; a lyric could not be "more lightly, musically made" than "Gloomy Winter's now awa'." He has a curiously fine sense of words, his lyrics are as finished in their diction as they are true and touching in their sentiment and spontaneous in their flow. In one respect he may, perhaps, be said to have excelled Burns; namely, in his delicate aptness of descriptive phrase when dealing with nature. . . . An exquisite artist was lost by the death of the Paisley weaver. He had not a wide range, he had almost no sense of humour, no satiric or narrative faculty. His gift was purely lyrical, and, the gift, was in its way perfect. His love-songs, so pure and tender, so graceful in form, so musical, so admirably adapted to be sung, with the fragrance of the woodland braes he loved so well still clinging to the lines, are almost as little likely as the songs of Burns to lose their hold on Scotchmen's hearts. —WHYTE, WALTER, 1896, *The Poets of the Century, Southey to Shelley, ed. Miles, pp.* 74, 75.

With a more original gift of song than Cunningham, Robert Tannahill owed nothing to Scott, who was but slightly his senior, and not very much to Burns. . . . His language is not, any more than Burns's, free from occasional intrusions of discordant Anglicism; but in his own dialect he has an exquisite delicacy, and at times subtlety, of phrase. His love-songs are fine examples of the Scottish gift of painting passion by the human and sympathetic traits of landscape. — HERFORD, C. H., 1897, *The Age of Wordsworth, p.* 197.

Tannahill versified early, and some poetical epistles to his friends—e. g. "Epistle to James Barr," written in 1804 —are not without vigor and occasional epigrammatic points, though they are too discursive and diffuse to be generally effective. "The Soldier's Return, an Interlude," contains several good songs —some of which helped to win Tannahill his fame—but he has no dramatic quality. . . . In sentimental song Tannahill ranks almost with the greatest of Scottish song-writers, approaching Lady Nairne and Burns himself in such dainty and winning lyrics as "Bonnie Wood o' Craigielee," "Sleepin' Maggie," "Braes o' Gleniffer," "Gloomy Winter's noo awa'," "The Lass o' Arranteenie," "Cruikston Castle's lonely wa's," and "Jessie the Flower o' Dunblane."—BAYNE, THOMAS, 1898, *Dictionary of National Biography, vol.* LV, *p.* 358.

Mary Tighe

1772–1810

Mary Tighe, the daughter of the Rev. William Blachford, by Theodosia, the daughter of William Tighe, of Rosanna, Co. Wicklow, Ireland, was married to Henry Tighe, M. P., of Woodstock, Co. Wicklow, and died March 24 1810, after an illness of six years. Perhaps she is better known to many as the subject of Moore's touching lyric, "I saw Thy Form in Youthful Prime," and Mrs. Hemans's "Grave of a Poetess," than by her own exquisite verses. Her poem of "Psyche, or the Legend of Love" (founded on the story of Cupid and Psyche as related in the Golden Ass of Apuleius), was privately printed (100 copies) by C. Whittingham, London, 1805, 12mo. After her death appeared: "Psyche, with other Poems, by the Late Mrs. Henry Tighe" (with portrait), 1811.—ALLIBONE, S. AUSTIN, 1871, *A Critical Dictionary of English Literature, p.* 2419.

PERSONAL

Thou hast left sorrow in thy song,
　A voice not loud but deep!
The glorious bowers of earth among,
　How often didst thou weep?
Where couldst thou fix on mortal ground
　Thy tender thoughts and high?—
Now peace the woman's heart hath found,
　And joy the poet's eye.
—HEMANS, FELICIA DORTHEA, 1828, *The Grave of a Poetess.*

Perhaps no writer of merit has been more neglected by her own friends than Mrs. Tighe. With every means of giving to the public a good memoir of her, I believe no such is in existence. . . . The very servants who had lived years in the family had never heard the name of Mrs. Tighe, the poetess, mentioned! These present Tighes had been marrying the daughters of lords—this a daughter of the Duke of Richmond, and Dan Tighe, a daughter of Lord Crofton. They were ashamed, probably, that any of their name should have degraded herself by writing poetry, which a man or woman without an acre may do. When I reached the church at Innerstiogue, the matter received a most striking confirmation. There, sure enough, was the monument, in a small mausoleum in the church-yard. It is a recumbent figure, laid on a granite altar-shaped basement. The figure is of a freestone resembling Portland stone, and is lying on its side, as on a sofa, being said, by the person who showed it, to be the position in which she died, on coming in from a walk. The execution of the whole is very ordinary, and if really by Flaxman, displays none of his genius. I have seen much better things by a common-stone-mason. There is a little angel sitting at the head, but this has never been fastened down by cement. The monument was, no doubt, erected by the widower of the poetess, who was a man of classical taste, and, I believe, much attached to her. There is no inscription yet put upon the tomb, though one, said to be written by her husband, has long been cut in stone for the purpose. In the wall at the back of the monument, aloft, there is an oblong-square hole left for this inscription, which I understood was lying about at the house, but no single effort had been made to put it up, though it would not require an hour's work, and though Mrs. Tighe has been dead six-and-thirty years! This was decisive! If these two gentlemen, nephews of the poetess, who are enjoying the two splendid estates of the family, Woodstock and Rosanna, show thus little respect to the only one of their name that ever lifted it above the mob, it is not to be expected that they will show much courtesy to strangers. Well is it that Mrs. Tighe raised her own monument, that of immortal verse, and wrote her own epitaph in the hearts of all the pure and loving, not on a stone which sordid relatives, still fonder of earth than stone, may consign to the oblivion of a lumber room.—HOWITT, WILLIAM, 1846, *Homes and Haunts of the Most Eminent British Poets, vol.* I, *pp.* 461, 471.

PSYCHE

Tell me the witching tale again,
  For never has my heart or ear
Hung on so sweet, so pure a strain,
  So pure to feel, so sweet to hear.

.   .   .   .

Still be the song to Psyche dear,
  The song, whose gentle voice was given
To be, on earth, to mortal ear,
  An echo of her own, in heaven.
—MOORE, THOMAS, 1805? *To Mrs. Henry Tighe on Reading Her "Psyche."*

Sorrow seems to be the muse of song, and from Philomela to Mrs. Tighe the most plaintive notes are the most melodious. I have read "Psyche;" I am sorry that Mrs. Tighe chose such a story: it is both too mystical and too much exhausted. For the first three cantos I felt a sort of languid elegance and luscious sweetness, which had something of the same effect as if I had been overpowered by perfumes; but the three last are of such exquisite beauty that they quite silence me. They are beyond all doubt the most faultless series of verses ever produced by a woman.—MACKINTOSH, SIR JAMES, 1812, *Journal, Memoirs, ed. by his Son, vol.* II, *p.* 195.

The greater part of the poem itself is little worth, except as a strain of elegance; but now and then we meet with a fancy not unworthy a pupil of Spenser.—HUNT, LEIGH, 1847, *Men, Women and Books.*

She is chiefly known by her splendid poem of "Psyche," which for gorgeousness of colouring and refinement of imagination, is scarcely behind the best verse of Moore, while it is certainly more chaste and spiritual in its sentiment.—ROWTON, FREDERIC, 1848, *The Female Poets of Great Britain, p.* 200.

Her imagination is warm, and her descriptions often voluptuous, though always refined. Perhaps she has been somewhat diffuse; but, taking her altogether she is not equalled in classical elegance by any English female, and not excelled (in that particular) by any male English poet. She has that rare quality for a poetess of not sparing the *pumice-stone,* her verses being sedulously polished to the highest degree. She shows also her great taste in omitting obsolete words, the affectation of which so frequently disfigures imitations of the great master of English allegory.—BETHUNE, GEORGE WASHINGTON, 1848, *The British Female Poets.*

An adventurous and elaborate effort, full of power and beauty which wanted only a little more of artistic skill and concentration to have entitled it to a place among first-class productions.—MOIR, D. M., 1850–51, *Sketches of the Poetical Literature of the Past Half-Century.*

Displays everywhere an imagination, immature, indeed, and wanting in vigor, but yet both rich and delicate, such as might have shown forth in Spenser himself if he had been a woman, or, as compared to that which we have in the "Fairy Queen," something like what moonlight is to sunshine.—CRAIK, GEORGE L., 1861, *A Compendious History of English Literature and of the English Language, vol.* II, *p.* 541.

A very fair and gentle representative of poetry, Mary Tighe, the daughter of a clergyman, the wife of an Irish M. P., is another of the rare instances of literary production in Ireland. She was the author of a poem called "Psyche," an extremely sweet and melodious rendering of the classical legend, the external form of which, in a slim and sumptuous quarto, with creamy pages as thick as velvet enshrining in big margins a limpid stream of elaborate verse, gives a very just idea of its merit. It is one of those essays in art which at any time it would be cruel to judge rigorously, all the more as it is the composition of a gentle creature who died young and knew nothing of the world —which, with a humane sense of the claims of weakness, generally does receive such gentle efforts tenderly.—OLIPHANT, MARGARET O. W., 1882, *Literary History of England, XVIII. and XIX. Centuries, vol.* III *p.* 213.

The poem is written in the Spenserian stanza, and has decided merit. The verse is melodious, and the tale is told with pleasing directness and simplicity. It has suffered equally from excessive praise and undue disparagement. Mackintosh considered the last three cantos to be of exquisite beauty, and "beyond all doubt the most faultless series of verses ever produced by a woman."—LEE, ELIZABETH, 1898, *Dictionary of National Biography, vol.* LVI, *p.* 388.

GENERAL

Many of the pictures in this ["Psyche"], the chief production of her muse, are conceived in the true spirit of poetry, while over the whole composition is spread the richest glow of purified passion. It is a poem, however, to be read as a whole, and cannot well be appreciated by any detached passages. A luxurious, dreamy sweetness pervades the descriptions, and gives them a peculiar charm, while the elegance of the easy-flowing language attests the complete power of the poet over her theme. Some of her minor pieces, also, are exceedingly beautiful; and the lines "On Receiving a Branch of Mezereon," are scarcely exceeded, for beauty and pathos, by anything of the kind in the language —CLEVELAND, CHARLES D., 1853, *English Literature of the Nineteenth Century, p.* 86.

Mrs. Tighe ought not to be omitted in an enumeration of the writers who were read by Keats, and from whom consequently his poetry may be supposed to have taken some of its colour.—MAIN, DAVID M., 1879, *ed., A Treasury of English Sonnets, p.* 393.

Charles Brockden Brown

1771–1810

Charles Brockden Brown was born in Philadelphia, Jan. 17, 1771, and died in the same city, of consumption, Feb. 22, 1810. By his own statement, made in a letter just before his death, we learn that he never had more than one continuous half-hour of perfect health. In spite of his short life and his ill-health he accomplished much. At first he studied law, but abandoned it for literature. He was a frequent contributor to the magazines of the time and was himself editor of the "Monthly Magazine and American Review" (1799), and the "Literary Magazine and American Register" (1803-8). His first published work, "The Dialogue of Alcuin" (1797), dealt with questions of marriage and divorce, and he was also the author of several essays on political, historical, and geographical subjects. His novels followed each other with astonishing rapidity: "Sky Walk; or the Man Unknown to Himself" (1798, not published), "Wieland; or the Transformation" (1798), "Ormond; or the Secret Witness" (1799), "Arthur Mervyn; or Memoirs of the year 1793" (1799-1800), "Edgar Huntly; or Memoirs of a Sleep-Walker" (1801), "Jane Talbot" (1801), and "Clara Howard or the Enthusiasm of Love" (1801). They met with an equally astonishing success, and constitute the first important contribution to American fiction.—CARPENTER, GEORGE RICE, 1898, *ed., American Prose, p.* 84.

PERSONAL

Acted as if he had no use for money. . . . Without system in every thing. . . . Was negligent of personal appearance, even to slovenliness. . . . In mixed company often silent and absent. . . . Fitful and irregular.—DUNLAP, WILLIAM, 1815, *Life of Charles Brockden Brown, vol.* I, *pp.* 56, 57.

We believe Brown to have been one of the purest of men. The intellectual so predominated in him, and he seems so to have loathed the sensual, that perhaps he was not aware of the great strength of certain temptations over others.—DANA, RICHARD HENRY, 1827-50, *The Novels of Charles Brockden Brown, Poems and Prose Writings, vol.* II, *p.* 335.

His religious views were unsettled in the early period of his life, but in the preface of his Magazine he emphatically professes his faith in Christianity. His moral character was unexceptionable. He was much beloved by his friends and relatives, and was liberal notwithstanding his poverty, receiving his sisters-in-law,

JOEL BARLOW

Engraving by A. B. Durand.
Painting by Robert Fulton.

CHARLES BROCKDEN BROWN

Engraving by I. B. Forrest. From a
Miniature by William Dunlap in 1806.

on their father's death, into his own family. In person, Brown was tall and strongly framed, but extremely thin. His complexion was pale and sallow, his hair straight and black. The expression of his face was strongly marked with melancholy. "I saw him," says Sully, the painter, "a little before his death. I had never known him—never heard of him—never read any of his works. He was in a deep decline. It was in the month of November—our Indian summer—when the air is full of smoke. Passing a window one day, I was caught by the sight of a man, with a remarkable physiognomy, writing at a table in a dark room. The sun shone directly upon his head. I never shall forget it. The dead leaves were falling then —it was Charles Brockden Brown."— DUYCKINCK, EVERT A., AND GEORGE L., 1855–65–75, *Cyolopædia of American Literature,* ed. *Simons, vol.* I, *p.* 611.

Mr. Brown's character was one of great amiability and moral excellence, and his manners were distinguished by a gentleness and unaffected simplicity. His great colloquial powers made him a most agreeable companion; and his unwearied application is attested by the large amount of his works, the whole number of which, including his editorial labors, must be equal to twenty-four volumes,—a vast amount to be produced in the brief compass of a little more than ten years.— CLEVELAND, CHARLES D., 1859, *A Compendium of American Literature, p.* 178.

He had little of the spirit of adventure, and on one occasion said he would rather consort with a ploughman or an old market-woman forever, than expose himself to the hundredth part of the perils which beset the heels of a Ledyard or a Park. He was careless of money, and slovenly in dress, but he was habitually careful in his diet. He abstained from spirituous liquors long before temperance societies were established, and he wrote papers in one of his magazines on the deleterious effects of intemperance, and of the use of greasy articles of food.—SMITH, GEORGE BARNETT, 1878, *Brockden Brown, Fortnightly Review, vol.* 30, *p.* 408.

Truly he was a man of letters, in the fullest sense of the phrase; and though consumption ended his career at the age of thirty-nine, he had his share of the labor of life.—HAWTHORNE, JULIAN AND LEMMON, LEONARD, 1891, *American Literature, p.* 25.

WIELAND
1798

This powerful and original romance, excited attention and brought the author into the notice of all readers of works of this description. Few novels or romances have been written, which seize so strongly upon the imagination and feelings of the reader, hurry him from the realities which surround him, bury in oblivion his joys or sorrows, and fix his whole attention on the images which the author presents before him, as "Wieland."—DUNLAP, WILLIAM, 1815, *Life of Charles Brockden Brown, vol.* II, *p.* 12.

This novel is the history of a fanatic, whose religious mania incited him to murder his wife and children, and at last to commit suicide, and is one of the most masterly stories that has ever been told of the human soul.—SCHERR, J., 1874, *A History of English Literature, tr. M. V., p.* 307.

In the hands of a tiro, the materials of which "Wieland" is composed would have resulted in a melodrama of the commonest and most pinchbeck order; but being infused by the spirit and power of genius, they are transformed into a gloomy and awful tragedy, in which the reader forgets for a time the incredibility of the incidents and the impossibility of the situations. "Wieland" upon the whole, deservedly ranks as Brown's completest work of fiction.—SMITH, GEORGE BARNETT, 1878, *Brockden Brown, Fortnightly Review, vol.* 30, *p.* 414.

Brown's early life was unmistakably gloomy. From a temperament delicate and fine, but morbid,—in which the intellectual overbalanced the physical forces, —sprang his first book, which, though stimulated from across the water, was wholly within the range of his mood and spirit. It contained, however, not a hint of the new American life, not a spark of that humor which afterward flashed freely in American literature. Except for an awful sense of solitude,—the gloom of primeval nature,—there was scarcely a touch of our glorious scenery. No social element is represented.—MORSE, JAMES HERBERT, 1883, *The Native Element in American Fiction, The Century, vol.* 26, *p.* 289.

In spite of confusion and turgidity, the story has power. The end is ludicrously weak. The chapters in which the mind of Wieland is gradually possessed by delusion could have been written only by one who had genuinely felt a sense of what hideously mysterious things may lie beyond human ken. Some such sense as this, in terrible serious form, haunted the imagination of Puritans. In a meretricious form it appears in the work of Poe. In a form alive with beauty it reveals itself throughout the melancholy romances of Hawthorne. In Poe's work and in Hawthorne's, it is handled with something like mastery, and few men of letters have been much further from mastery of their art than Charles Brockden Brown; but the sense of horror which Brown expressed in "Wieland" is genuine. To feel its power you need only compare it with the similar feeling expressed in Lewis's "Monk," in the "Mysteries of Udolpho," or even in "Caleb Williams" itself.—WENDELL, BARRETT, 1900, *A Literary History of America*, p. 163.

ORMOND
1799

The appearance of these two novels ["Wieland," and "Ormond"], constitutes an epoch in the ornamental literature of America. They are the first decidedly successful attempts in the walk of romantic fiction. They are still farther remarkable as illustrating the character and state of society on this side of the Atlantic, instead of resorting to the exhausted springs of European invention. These circumstances, as well as the uncommon powers they displayed both of conception and execution, recommended them to the notice of the literary world, although their philosophical method of dissecting passion and analyzing motives of action placed them somewhat beyond the reach of vulgar popularity.—PRESCOTT, WILLIAM H., 1834, *Charles Brockden Brown, Biographical and Critical Miscellanies*, p. 26.

"Ormond" is mainly remarkable for the analytical power shown in the author's one fine female character, Constantia Dudley, who, reduced from affluence to poverty, braves all the threats and seductions of the hypocritical Lovelace, from whom the book takes its name. Brown's plots are, as a rule, methodless and improbable: his bursts of passion are dulled by intervening tediousness; and his style, generally rough, is sometimes further deformed by pedantic circumlocutions; but he leaves us, despite his acknowledged obligations to Godwin, with the impression of an original power cramped by the necessities of hasty work, unhappily because prematurely quenched, and of a writer who has been unduly forgotten.—NICHOL, JOHN, 1880–85, *American Literature*, p. 162.

ARTHUR MERVYN
1799–1800

"Arthur Mervyn" is, of all his books, the most wandering and forgetful in narrative, continually throwing out false clews and leaving behind unsolved mysteries, leading with elaborate pains up to situations which amount to nothing. With something of Poe's sombre imagination, Brown lacked Poe's fine economy of literary structure. The strength of "Arthur Mervyn" is in its episodes,—its vivid pictures of Philadelphia ravaged by the yellow fever, its glimpses of the debtors' prison, anticipating "Little Dorrit."—BATES, KATHARINE LEE, 1897, *American Literature*, p. 89.

EDGAR HUNTLY
1801

"Edgar Huntly," the scene of which is laid in a then thinly-settled part of Pennsylvania, is full of vivid, if somewhat over-colored, descriptions of the solitudes of mountain and forest. We are taken, perhaps for the first time in fiction, into the midst of the perils of our frontier life; we encounter the panther and the Indian, the latter surrounded with none of Cooper's tinge of romance, but depicted as the mere wily and bloodthirsty savage. This choice of a native theme was a deliberate one, for Brown says in his preface that he is the first to call forth the reader's sympathy by substituting for puerile superstitions, Gothic castles, and chimeras,—the conventional machinery of the English romances,—"the incidents of Indian hostility and the perils of the Western wilderness." In this story he distantly suggests Cooper, in his fondness for psychological problems, and in the morbid strain that runs through many of his books, he still more faintly fore-shadows Poe and the yet greater Hawthorne.—PANCOAST, HENRY S., 1898, *An Introduction to American Literature*, p. 110.

GENERAL

Brown owes his reputation to his novels. He wrote them indeed principally for his amusement, and preferred publishing them when unfinished to labouring upon them after they had lost their interest to himself: they are proofs or signs of power rather than the result of its complete and steady exertion; but they shew the character of his mind and will justify our curiosity to examine it. In attempting this, we do not feel as if we were bringing forward a deserving but neglected author; he has received honourable notice from distinguished men abroad, and his countrymen discerned his merits without waiting till a foreign glory had shone on and revealed them. Still he is very far from being a popular writer. There is no call, as far as we know, for a second edition of any of his works. He is rarely spoken of but by those who have an habitual curiosity about everything literary, and a becoming pride in all good writing which appears amongst ourselves. They have not met with the usual success of leaders, in matters of taste, since, with all their admiration, they have not been able to extend his celebrity much beyond themselves. . . . We should not pronounce Brown a man of genius, nor deny him that distinction, from his style. It might have been acquired by care and study, but it is the result only and never betrays the process.— VERPLANCK, GULIAN CROMMELIN, 1819, *Charles Brockden Brown, North American Review, vol.* 9, *pp.* 63, 76.

The very want of variety has given such an air of truth to what he is about, showing such an earnest singleness of purpose, that perhaps no writer ever made his readers more completely forget that they were not reading a statement of some serious matter of fact; and so strong is this impression, that we even become half reconciled to improbabilities which so vex us in fiction, though often happening in daily life. This enables us, also, to bear better with his style; for, along with something like a conviction that the man who had vivacity of genius enough for such inventions could never have delivered himself with such dull poverty and pedantry of phrase, we at last are almost driven to the conclusion, that, however extraordinary they may be, they are nevertheless facts; for the man never could have made

them, and things must have happened pretty much as he tells us they did.— DANA, RICHARD HENRY, 1827–50, *The Novels of Charles Brockden Brown, Poems and Prose Writings, vol.* II, *p.* 329.

He may be rather called a philosophical than a poetical writer; for, though he has that intensity of feeling which constitutes one of the distinguishing attributes of the latter, yet in his most tumultuous bursts of passion we frequently find him pausing to analyze and coolly speculate on the elements which have raised it. This intrusion, indeed, of reason, *la raison froide*, into scenes of the greatest interest and emotion, has sometimes the unhappy effect of chilling them altogether.—PRESCOTT, WILLIAM H., 1834, *Charles Brockden Brown, Biographical and Critical Miscellanies, p.* 38.

We have long been ashamed that one who ought to be the pride of the country, and who is, in the highest qualities of the mind, so far in advance of our other novelists, should have become almost inaccessible to the public. It has been the custom to liken Brown to Godwin. But there was no imitation, no second-hand in the matter. They were congenial natures, and whichever had come first might have lent an impulse to the other. Either mind might have been conscious of the possession of that peculiar vein of ore without thinking of working it for the mint of the world, till the other, led by accident, or overflow of feeling, showed him how easy it was to put the reveries of his solitary hours into words and upon paper for the benefit of his fellow men. . . . Brown is great as ever human writer was in showing the self-sustaining force of which a lonely mind is capable. He takes one person, makes him brood like the bee, and extract from the common life before him all its sweetness, its bitterness, and its nourishment.—OSSOLI, MARGARET FULLER, 1845–59, *Papers on Literature and Art,* ed. *Fuller, pp.* 322, 324.

He had more genius than talent, and more imagination than fancy. It has been said that he outraged the laws of art by gross improbabilities and inconsistencies, but the most incredible of his incidents had parallels in true history, and the metaphysical unity and consistency of his novels are apparent to all readers familiar with psychological phenomena. His works, generally written with great rapidity, are incomplete, and deficient in method. He disregarded rules, and cared little for criticism. But his style was clear and nervous, with little ornament, free of affectations, and indicated a singular sincerity and depth of feeling.—GRISWOLD, RUFUS WILMOT, 1845, *ed.*, *Intellectual History, Condition and Prospects of the Country, The Prose Writers of America,* p. 29.

So deficient, indeed, in constructive design and unity of purpose, are his writings, that, with the exception of his essays and other argumentative papers, they resemble the sketches that litter an artist's studio more than elaborate and finished works. His fictions might aptly be designated as studies in Romance. He left many fragmentary narratives, scenes and dialogues—some founded upon history, some upon observation, and others apparently the result of an inventive mood. At one time he had no less than five novels commenced, sketched out, or partially written.—TUCKERMAN, HENRY T., 1857, *Essays Biographical and Critical, p.* 372.

In romantic narrative, Brown was often successful, but he failed in the delineation of character.—CHAMBERS, ROBERT, 1876, *Cyclopædia of English Literature,* ed. *Carruthers.*

Some of his novels have been republished in this country, but copies of these it is now difficult to meet with. Yet a public which so liberally admired Hawthorne, ought to know something about a writer of kindred and more potent genius. If Hoffmann's Night-pieces and Fancy Pieces after the manner of Jacques Callot must rank first in the literature of the Weird, Brockden Brown comes second, and he adds to the weird such elements of psychological subtlety as give him a place to which Hoffmann had no claim in the literature of spiritual analysis. To a daring imagination—the most singular and flexible, perhaps, yet witnessed amongst American writers—Charles Brockden Brown united a placid temperament and a contemplative intellect. Such a combination of seeming discordant, and yet sharply defined qualities, is almost unique. Deep-rooted melancholy, and the pathos of an apparently disordered mind, distinguish the works of this author, and yet few men were happier in their lives, or more

profoundly enjoyed the simple fact of existence. He coveted no complex pleasures or recreations; his greatest solace was Nature; and he extracted happiness from those commonplace pursuits which by most men of genius would have been deemed monotonous and insupportable. His creations are dire, astounding, terrible—his life was sedate, tranquil, serene.— SMITH, GEORGE BARNETT, 1878, *Brockden Brown, Fortnightly Review, vol.* 30, *p.* 399.

In 1800 he was the best writer of fiction of his time; he led the way to the general diffusion of the novel. His scenery was all American: he loved to paint sometimes the golden air of autumn, the evening sinking over the Schuylkill, rich in unrivalled colors, the splendors of a clime to which Europe offered no parallel; but oftener the city street, the plague-stricken homes, the stately mansion. In this rare setting his sombre, mysterious characters move dark and dreadful, scarcely human in their objects, always governed by some immutable law. . . . He was the morning-star that beckoned in the day.— LAWRENCE, EUGENE, 1880, *A Primer of American Literature, pp.* 48, 49.

Brown, in his depth of insight into the morbid phenomena of the human mind, really anticipated Hawthorne; but hurried as he was by that most malignant of literary devils, the printer's, he produced no such masterpieces of literary art as "The Scarlet Letter," "The Blithedale Romance," and "The Marble Faun." Brown is one of the most melancholy instances of a genius arrested in its orderly development by the pressure of circumstances. In mere power his forgotten novels rank very high among the products of the American imagination. And it should be added that though he is unread, he is by no means unreadable. . . . With all his faults, Brown does not deserve to be the victim of the bitterest irony of criticism, that, namely, of not being considered worth the trouble of a critical examination. His writings are contemptuously classed among dead books, interesting to the antiquary alone. Still, they have that vitality which comes from the presence of genius, and a little stirring of the ashes under which they are buried would reveal sparks of genuine fire.—WHIPPLE, EDWIN PERCY, 1886, *American Literature and Other Papers, ed. Whittier, pp.* 28, 29.

Brockden Brown introduced the weird, the romantic, the appalling, the "native American," and made a failure, on the whole.—RICHARDSON, CHARLES F., 1887, *American Literature, 1607–1885, vol.* I, *p.* 263.

Charles Brockden Brown, of Philadelphia, had all the qualities which would have recommended him to Goethe's particular detestation, being slipshod in style and exhibiting a sovereign disregard of reality. His works abound in psychological curiosities and super-ingenious mysteries, exulting, like those of his romantic compeers, in all the calamities from which in the Prayer Book we ask God to deliver us. — BOYESEN, HJALMAR HJORTH, 1892–94, *Literary and Social Silhouettes, p.* 59.

Brown's romances are not wanting an inventive power; in occasional situations that are intensely thrilling, and in subtle analysis of character; but they are fatally defective in art. The narrative is by turns abrupt and tiresomely prolix, proceeding not so much by dialogue as by elaborate dissection and discussion of motives and states of mind, interspersed with the author's reflections. The wild improbabilities of plot and the unnatural and even monstrous developments of character are in startling contrast with the old-fashioned preciseness of the language; the conversations, when there are any, being conducted in that insipid dialect in which a fine woman was called an "elegant female." —BEERS, HENRY A., 1895, *Initial Studies in American Letters, p.* 65.

Judged by the standards set by Poe and Hawthorne, his work is crude and defective in art. The story is at times tediously spun out; character is dissected with disgusting minuteness; the plots are glaringly improbable; the characters either monsters or angels. He is not even a "clumsy Poe," as some have called him, so vastly inferior is his art to his who produced the "Fall of the House of Usher." Brown's excellences are his graphic portrayals of action and his descriptions of wild nature. He had the art of stimulating expectations;—it is hard to lay down one of his romances unfinished; one reads on and on in a sort of ghastly dream until at length the end of the book completes the hideous nightmare.—PATTEE, FRED LEWIS, 1896, *A History of American Literature, p.* 104.

The first imaginative writer worth mentioning in America. . . . He was also the first to exert a positive influence, across the Atlantic, upon British literature, laying thus early a few modest strands towards an ocean-cable of thought. As a result of this influence concealed doors opened in lonely houses, fatal epidemics laid cities desolate, secret plots were organized, unknown persons from foreign lands died in garrets leaving large sums of money; the honor of innocent women was occasionally endangered, though usually saved in time; people were subject to somnambulism and general frenzy; vast conspiracies were organized with small aims and smaller results. His books, published between 1798 and 1801, made their way across the ocean with a promptness that now seems inexplicable; and Mrs. Shelley in her novel of "The Last Man" founds her description of an epidemic on "'the masterly delineations of the author of 'Arthur Mervyn.'"' Shelley himself recognized his obligations to Brown; and it is to be remembered that Brown himself was evidently familiar with Godwin's philosophical writings, and that he may have drawn from those of Mary Wollstonecraft his advanced views as to the rights and education of women, a subject on which his first book, "Alcuin," provided the earliest American protest. . . . There is so much of monotony in the general method, that one novel seems to stand for all; and the same modes of solution reappear so often—somnambulism, ventriloquism, yellow fever, forged letters, concealed money, secret closets—that it not only gives a sense of puerility, but makes it very difficult to recall, as to any particular passage, from which book it came. —HIGGINSON, THOMAS WENTWORTH, 1898, *American Prose, ed. Carpenter, pp.* 84, 88.

The style, also, is a combination of crudeness and power. It is often stiff and sometimes ludicrously stilted; but everywhere it has strength; and in passages of exciting description and narration it rises to a very high degree of power. In these scenes of horror—the maniac Wieland about to kill his sister; Huntly groping about in the black pit; the midnight burial of Watson in the cellar; Ormond's deliberate and gloating assault upon his trembling victim in the lonely house; the loathsome scenes in the pestilence-stricken city—Brown is in his element, and by them he has made a permanent contribution to the literature of terror. Inferior to Hawthorne in subtle spiritual suggestiveness, to Poe in brilliancy, intensity, and enveloping atmosphere of poetic gloom, he is perhaps superior to them and to the whole contemporary English school of terror in Defoe-like sense of reality and in sheer mass of overwhelming horror.— BRONSON, WALTER C., 1900, *A Short History of American Literature*, p. 99.

Richard Cumberland
1732–1811

Born, at Trinity Coll., Dublin, 19 Feb. 1732. Educated at a school at Bury St. Edmunds, 1738–44; at Westminster School, 1744–46. To Trinity Coll., Cambridge, 1747; B. A., 1750; Fellowship, 1752; M. A., 1754. Private Secretary to Lord Halifax in Board of Trade; and afterwards Crown Agent to Nova Scotia. Married Elizabeth Ridge, 19 Feb. 1759. Ulster Secretary to Lord-Lieutenant of Ireland, 1761. Clerk of Reports in Board of Trade, 1762. Began to write plays. "The Summer's Tale" produced, 1765; "The Brothers" at Covent Garden, 1769; "The West Indian," 1771; "The Fashionable Lover," Jan. 1772; "The Choleric Man," 1774; "The Battle of Hastings," 1778. Secretary to Board of Trade, 1776. On secret mission to Spain, 1780–81. On abolition of Board of Trade, he retired to Tunbridge Wells. Great literary activity; many plays produced, including: "The Walloons," 20 April 1782; "The Jew," 1794; "The Wheel of Fortune," 1795, etc. Edited "The London Review" 1809. Died, at Tunbridge Wells, 7 May 1811. Buried in Westminster Abbey. *Works:* "An Elegy, written on St. Mark's Eve" (anon.), 1754; "The Banishment of Cicero," 1761; "The Summer's Tale" (anon.), 1765; "A Letter to the Bishop of O—d," (anon.), 1767; "Amelia" (anon.), 1768; "The Brothers" (anon.), 1770; "The West Indian" (anon.), 1771; "Timon of Athens, altered from Shakespeare," 1771; "The Fashionable Lover" (anon.), 1772; "The Note of Hand" (anon.), 1774; "The Choleric Man," 1775; "The Widow of Delphi" (anon.), 1775; "Odes," 1776; "The Battle of Hastings," 1778; "Calypso," 1779; "Anecdotes of Eminent Painters in Spain," 1782; "A Letter to Richard, Lord Bishop of Landaff," 1783; "The Mysterious Husband," 1783; "The Carmelite," 1784; "Character of the late Lord Viscount Sackville," 1785; "The Natural Son," 1785; "The Observer" (anon.), 1785; "An accurate . . . Catalogue of the several Paintings in the King of Spain's Palace at Madrid," 1787; "Arundel" (anon.), 1789; "The Impostors," 1789; "A Volume of Comedies," 1791; "Curtius rescued from the Gulph" (anon.), 1792; "Calvary," 1792; "The Armourer" (anon.), 1793; "The Box-Lobby Challenge," 1794; "The Jew," 1794; "First Love," 1795; "Henry," (anon.), 1795; "The Wheel of Fortune," 1795; "False Impressions," 1797; "The Days of Yore," 1798; "Joanna of Montfaucon" (adapted from Von Kotzebue,) 1800; "A Poetical Version of certain Psalms of David," 1801; "A Few Plain Reasons why we should believe in Christ," 1801; "The Tailor's Daughter," 1804; "A Melo-Dramatic Piece" (1805); "A Hint to Husbands," 1806; "Memoirs," 1806; "The Jew of Mogadore," 1808; "John de Lancaster," 1809; "Retrospection," 1811. *Posthumous:* "Posthumous Dramatic Works" (2 vols.), 1813. He *translated:* Lucan's "Pharsalia," 1760; "Aristophanes' Clouds," 1797.—SHARP, R. FARQUHARSON, 1897, *A Dictionary of English Authors*, p. 71.

PERSONAL

Mr. Cumberland is unquestionably a man of very great abilities; it is his misfortune to rate them greatly above their value; and to suppose that he has no equal.— DAVIES, THOMAS, 1780, *Memoirs of the Life of David Garrick, vol.* II, p. 275.

Sneer—"He is envious as any old maid verging on the desperation of six-and-thirty; and then the insidious humility with which he seduces you to give a free opinion on any of his works, can only be exceeded by the petulant arrogance with which he is sure to reject your observations. . . . Then his affected contempt of all the newspapers strictures; though, at the same time, he is the sorest man alive, and shrinks like scorched parchment from the fiery ordeal of true criticism; yet is he so covetous of popularity, that he had

rather be abused than not mentioned at all."
—SHERIDAN, RICHARD BRINSLEY, 1781,
The Critic.

It is a delicate and ardous task I have
had in hand, and I trust that now, as
heretofore, I shall be read and judged with
candour. I have not knowingly trans-
gressed, or even strained, the truth, to
which I pledged myself; but fairly and
sincerely stated how I have employed my
faculities, what I have been and what I
am. Man hath no need, no right, no interest to know of man more than I have
enabled every one to know of me. I have
no undivulged evil in my heart; but with
unabated affection for my friends, and
good will towards my fellow creatures, I
remain the reader's most devoted servant.
—CUMBERLAND, RICHARD, 1806, *Memoirs
Written by Himself, vol.* II, *p.* 405.

The person you now see deposited, is
Richard Cumberland, an author of no small
merit; his writings were chiefly for the
stage, but of strict moral tendency—they
were not without their faults, but these
were not of a gross description. He wrote
as much as any, and few wrote better;
and his works will be held in the highest
estimation, so long as the English language
is understood. He considered the theatre
as a school for moral improvement, and
his remains are truly worthy of mingling
with the illustrious dead which surround
us. In his subjects on Divinity, you find
the true Christian spirit; and may God,
in his mercy, assign him the true Christian
reward!—VINCENT, DR., DEAN OF WEST-
MINSTER, 1811, *Funeral Sermon.*

In youth, Mr. Cumberland must have
been handsome; in age, he possessed a
pleasing external appearance, and the
polite ease of a gentleman accustomed to
the best company. In society he was eloquent, well-informed, and full of anecdote;
a willing dealer in the commerce of praise,
or—for he took no great pains to ascertain
its sincerity—we should rather say, of
flattery. His conversation often showed
the author in his strong and in his weak
points. . . . In the little pettish sub-
acidity of temper which Cumberland sometimes exhibited, there was more of humorous sadness than of ill-will, either to his
critics or his contemporaries.—SCOTT, SIR
WALTER, 1824, *Richard Cumberland.*

Richard Cumberland put forth occasionally metrical compositions, but they were

vapid stuff. He had a vast memory, and a
great facility of feeble verbiage; but his
vanity, his self-conceit, and his supercilious airs, offended everybody. He was a
tall, handsome man, with a fair, regular-
featured face, and the appearance of good
birth. For many years he resided at
Tunbridge Wells, where he affected a sort
of dominion over the Pantiles, and paid
court, a little too servile, to rank and title.
He wrote some good comedies, and was a
miscellaneous writer of some popularity;
but in every department he was of a
secondary class,—in none he had originality. He was one of Johnson's literary
club, and therefore could render himself
amusing by speaking of a past age of
authors and eminent men. Sheridan represented him as *Sir Fretful Plagiary.* He
was a most fulsome and incontinent flat-
terer of those who courted him.—BRYDGES,
SIR SAMUEL EGERTON, 1834, *Autobiography, vol.* I, *p.* 189.

Cumberland was a most agreeable companion, and a very entertaining converser.
His theatrical anecdotes were related with
infinite spirit and humour. . . . When
Cumberland was composing any work, he
never shut himself in his study : he always
wrote in the room where his family sat,
and did not feel the least disturbed by the
noise of his children at play beside him.—
ROGERS, SAMUEL, 1855, *Recollections of
Table-Talk, ed. Dyce, pp.* 36, 37.

His sensitiveness to criticism made Garrick call him a "man without a skin," but
he explains that there was then "a filthy
nest of vipers" in league against every
well-known man.—STEPHEN, LESLIE, 1888,
Dictionary of National Biography, vol.
XIII, *p.* 291.

To the last Cumberland is described as
an agreeable and even fascinating companion, though he was so fond of flattery
himself that he supposed it to be acceptable to others, even in the most exuberant
proportions. Certain it is that, although
he was not altogether happy in his temperament, he made many friends; and
though time has dealt hardly with his
reputation, one piece of good fortune can
never be taken from him, namely, the
prospect of going down to posterity astride
the epitaph in Goldsmith's "Retaliation"
as "The Terence of England, the mender of
hearts."—PASTON, GEORGE, 1901, *Little
Memoirs of the Eighteenth Century, p.* 1.

GENERAL

Here Cumberland lies, having his part,
The Terence of England, the mender of
    hearts;
A flattering painter, who made it his care
To draw men as they ought to be, not as
    they are.
His gallants are all faultless, his women
    divine,
And comedy wonders at being so fine;
Like a tragedy-queen he has dizen'd her out,
Or rather, like tragedy giving a rout.
His fools have their follies so lost in a crowd
Of virtues and feelings, that folly grows
    proud,
And coxcombs alike in their failings alone,
Adopting his portraits, are pleas'd with their
    own.
Say, where has our poet this malady caught,
Or, wherefore his characters thus without
    fault ?
Say, was it that vainly directing his view,
To find out men's virtues, and finding them
    few,
Quite sick of pursuing each troublesome elf,
He grew lazy at last, and drew from himself?
—GOLDSMITH, OLIVER, 1774, *The Retalia-*
tion.

With all the merit which "The Brothers"
possesses, and which is of no small account, it is instructive to observe with
how much judgment Mr. Cumberland corrected in his second play all those faults
he had committed in the first. The
language of "The West Indian" is wholly
refined, and every idea it contains perfectly delicate. The youthful parts are
there rendered brilliant, as well as interesting; and wit and humour are not confined, as here, to the mean or the vulgar,
but skilfully on persons of pleasing forms
and polite manners. — INCHBALD, MRS.
ELIZABETH, 1806-9, *The Brothers, A Com-*
edy ; The British Theatre, Remarks.

We will pronounce no general judgment
on the literary merits of Mr. Cumberland ;
but our opinion of them certainly has not
been raised by the perusal of these "Memoirs." There is no depth of thought,
nor dignity of sentiment about him ;—he is
too frisky for an old man, and too gossiping
for an historian. His style is too negligent
even for the most familiar composition ;
and though he has proved himself, upon
other occasions, to be a great master of
good English, he has admitted a number of
phrases into this work, which, we are inclined to think, would scarely pass current even in conversation. . . . Upon
the whole, however, this volume is not the

work of an ordinary writer ; and we should
probably have been more indulgent to its
faults, if the excellence of some of the
author's former productions had not sent
us to its perusal with expectations perhaps somewhat extravagant.—JEFFREY,
FRANCIS LORD, 1806-1844, *Memoirs of*
Cumberland, Contributions to the Edinburgh
Review, vol. IV, *p.* 413.

The "Observer," though the sole labour
of an individual, is yet rich in *variety,* both
of subject and manner ; in this respect,
indeed, as well as in literary interests, and
in fertility of invention, it may be classed
with the "Spectator" and "Adventurer ;"
if inferior to the latter in grandeur of
fiction, or to the former in delicate irony
and dramatic unity of design, it is wealthier
in its literary fund than either, equally
moral in its views, and as abundant in the
creation of incident. I consider it,
therefore, with the exception of the papers just mentioned, as superior, *in its*
powers of attraction, to every other periodical composition.—DRAKE, NATHAN, 1810,
Essays Illustrative of the Rambler, Adven-
turer and Idler, vol. II, *p.* 393.

He could not easily endure a rival in any
branch of literature, but, without entering into his failings, it may easily be conceded that he had not in his time many
equals. His talents were so various, his
productions so numerous, and of many of
them it may truly be asserted, that they
were so valuable and so instructive, that
who can call to memory without a sigh
that his latter hours were darkened by
poverty.—BELOE, WILLIAM, 1817, *The*
Sexagenarian, vol. II, *p.* 222.

It ["West Indian"] is a classical comedy ; the dialogue spirited and elegant ;
the characters well conceived, and presenting bold features, though still within
the line of probability ; and the plot regularly conducted, and happily extricated.
. . . The drama must have been Cumberland's favourite style of composition, for
he went on, shooting shaft after shaft at
the mark which he did not always hit, and
often effacing by failures the memory of
triumphant successes. His plays at last
amounted to upwards of fifty, and intercession and flattery were sometimes necessary to force their way to the stage. . . .
He had a peculiar taste in love affairs,
which induced him to reverse the usual
and natural practice of courtship, and to

throw upon the softer sex the task of wooing, which is more gracefully, as well as naturally, the province of the man.—SCOTT, SIR WALTER, 1824, *Richard Cumberland.*

Cumberland was the last, and the best of the Sentimental School. His Genius was of too masculine a character to submit entirely to the fetters which the popular prejudices would impose upon it; and his taste too pure, to relish the sickly viands with which the public appetite was palled.—NEELE, HENRY, 1827-29, *Lectures on English Poetry*, p. 153.

Cumberland's worthless epics of "Calvary," "Richard the First," "The Exodiad."—CRAIK, GEORGE L., 1861, *A Compendious History of English Literature and of the English Language, vol.* II. *p.* 415.

He aimed without success at Fielding's constructive excellence, and imitated that great master's humor, only to reproduce his coarseness.—TUCKERMAN, BAYARD, 1882, *A History of English Prose Fiction,* p. 247.

There were few departments of literature in which this worthy writer did not do fair journeyman's work, and amid other work he employed himself as a writer of comedies. He who shoots often must hit sometimes. The "West Indian" has merit in it; but his characters are all endowed with a superhuman morality. Cumberland understood stage effect,—particularly of the emotional kind. But he was overemotional.—CRAWFURD, OSWALD, 1883, ed., *English Comic Dramatists*, p. 256.

Were I to be discovered on Primrose Hill, or any other eminence, reading "Henry," I should blush no deeper than if the book had been "David Grieve." . . . Cumberland has, of course, no place in men's memories by virtue of his plays, poems, or novels. Even the catholic Chambers gives no extracts from Cumberland in the "Encyclopedia." What keeps him for ever alive is—first, his place in Goldsmith's great poem, "Retaliation;" secondly, his memoirs to which Sir Walter refers so unkindly; and thirdly, the tradition, the well-supported tradition—that he was the original "Sir Fretful Plagiary." On this last point we have the authority of Croker, and there is none better for anything disagreeable. Croker says he knew Cumberland well for the last dozen years of his life, and that to his last day

he resembled "Sir Fretful."—BIRRELL, AUGUSTINE, 1894, *Essays about Men, Women and Books, pp.* 51, 52.

A rather curious person, and better known to literature as Sir Fretful Plagiary, but a scholar, a skilful playwright, and no contemptible man of letters.—SAINTSBURY, GEORGE, 1898, *A Short History of English Literature,* p. 639.

As a writer, Cumberland was not great; he was not even of the second rank, if we count men like Goldsmith and Sheridan in that degree; but he frequently wrote with effect, and invariably as a scholar and a gentleman. Like too many people, he tried to succeed in too many things, and has in consequence just missed high distinction, alike as a poet, a novelist, and a dramatist. Goldsmith's comparison of him with Terence might pass muster as a compliment, but certainly could not be defended on the score of accuracy. No doubt the later dramatist's methods were framed on those of Terence but in all the latter's great literary qualities Cumberland was but a shadow of him. Where is that pure and perfect style which have caused some eminent critics to class Terence with Cicero, Cæsar, and Lucretius? Where the fine individualisation of character, the cosmopolitanism, the metrical skill, the coruscating wit, the exquisite pathos? Cumberland's "Memoirs" are garrulous, but interesting, though some of his stories and recollections require taking with a considerable grain of salt. But he is so overshadowed by his contemporaries, that something less than justice has been done to his literary powers. In private life he was all that was excellent and sincere, he had varied stores of information, which he was never backward in imparting; and he was ever moved by a genuine consideration for the claims and feelings of others.—SMITH, GEORGE BARNETT, 1900, *The English Terence, Fortnightly Review, vol.* 73, *p.* 256.

Richard Cumberland, playright, novelist, poet, essayist, and editor, civil servant and amateur diplomatist, belongs to that numerous body of authors who have had to pay for temporary popularity by permanent neglect. His comedies have not held the stage like those of his contemporaries, Sheridan and Goldsmith; his novels are no longer read like those of his model, Henry Fielding; his "Observer" essays have not become a classic like the "Spectator" and the "Rambler;" his poems are dead; his pamphlets are forgotten; and even his delightful "Memoirs" have hardly taken the place they deserve in the biographical literature of his period.—PASTON, GEORGE, 1901, *Little Memoirs of the Eighteenth Century, p.* 57.

Thomas Percy
1729–1811

Bishop of Dromore, 1729–1811. Born, at Bridgnorth, Shropshire, 13 April, 1729. Early education at Bridgnorth Grammar School. Matric., Christ Church, Oxford, 7 July 1746; B. A., 1750; M. A., 1753. Vicar of Easton-Maudit, Northamptonshire, 1753–82. Rector of Wilby, 1756–82. Married Anne Gutteridge, 1759. Active literary life. Chaplain to George II., 1769. D. D., Camb., 1770. Dean of Carlisle, 1778–82. Bishop of Dromore, 1782. Suffered from blindness in last years of life. Died at Dromore, 30th Sept. 1811. Buried at Dromore Cathedral. *Works:* "Hau Kiou Choaun; or, the Pleasing History" (from the Chinese; 4 vols., anon.), 1761; "Miscellaneous Pieces relating to the Chinese" (2 vols., anon.), 1762; "Five Pieces of Runic Poetry from the Islandic Language" (anon.), 1763; "The Song of Solomon, newly translated" (anon.), 1764; "Reliques of Ancient English Poetry" (3 vols.), 1765; "A Letter describing the ride to Hulme Abbey from Alnwich" (anon.), [1765]; "Four Essays" (anon.), 1767; "A Key to the New Testament," 1769; "A Sermon" [on John xiii, 35], 1769; "Northern Antiquities" (anon.), 1770; "The Hermit of Warkworth" (anon.), 1771; "The Matrons" (anon.), 1772; "Life of Dr. Oliver Goldsmith" (anon.), 1774; "A Sermon" [on Prov. xxii, 6], 1790; "An Essay on the Origin of the English Stage," 1793. He *translated:* P. H. Mallet's "Northern Antiquities," 1770; and *edited:* Surrey's "Poems," 1763; the "Household Book of the Earl of Northumberland," 1768.—SHARP, R. FARQUHARSON, 1897, *A Dictionary of English Authors, p.* 226.

PERSONAL

He is a man very willing to learn, and very able to teach; a man out of whose company I never go without having learned something. It is sure that he vexes me sometimes, but I am afraid it is by making me feel my own ignorance. So much extention of mind, and so much minute accuracy of inquiry, if you survey your whole circle of acquaintance, you will find so scarce, if you find it at all, that you will value Percy by comparison. Lord Hailes is somewhat like him; but Lord Hailes does not, perhaps, go beyond him in research; and I do not know that he equals him in elegance. Percy's attention to poetry has given grace and splendour to his studies of antiquity. A mere antiquarian is a rugged being.—JOHNSON, SAMUEL, 1778, *Letter to Boswell, April* 23; *Boswell's Life of Johnson.*

No bishop in this kingdom exercises the various functions of his office with more ability, diligence, and universal approbation—STURROCK, R. W., 1787, *Letter to James Macpherson, Aug.* 21; *Nichols's Literary Illustrations, vol.* VIII, *p.* 241.

I have had a letter from the Bishop of Dromore of seven sides of paper, the object of which was, to induce me to add to my "Noble Authors" some meditations by a foolish Countess of Northumberland, and to set me to inquire after a MS. Tract of Earl Algernon; with neither of which I have complied or shall. The Bishop having created himself a Percy, is gone mad about that family, tho' the Percys are more remembered for having lost their heads, than for ever having had a head that was a loss to lose.—WALPOLE, HORACE, 1793, *Letter to Miss Berry, Oct.* 16; *Berry Correspondence, ed. Lewis, vol.* I, *p.* 398.

His episcopal functions were most faithfully and efficiently discharged, securing him (as we are told) the respect and love of all denominations; but this is no more than might have been expected from a man of his integrity of character and genuine religious feelings—one who was, in a word, actuated by a high sense of duty.—PICKFORD, J., 1867, *Bishop Percy's Folio Manuscript, Life, p.* l.

Percy had natually a hot temper, but this cooled down with time, and the trials of his later life were accepted with Christian meekness. One of his relations, who as a boy could just recollect him, told Mr. Pickford "that it was quite a pleasure to see even then his gentleness, amiability, and fondness for children. Every day used to witness his strolling down to a pond in the palace garden, in order to feed his swans, who were accustomed to come at the well-known sound of the old man's voice." He was a pleasing companion and a steady friend. His duties, both in the retired country village and in the more elevated positions of dean and bishop, were all performed with a wisdom and ardour that gained him the confidence of all those with whom he was brought in contact. The praise given to him in the inscription on the tablet to his memory in Dromore Cathedral does not appear to have gone beyond the truth. It is there stated that he resided constantly in his diocese, and discharged "the duties of his sacred office with vigilance and zeal, instructing the ignorant, relieving the necessitous, and comforting the distressed with pastoral affection." He was revered for his piety and learning, and beloved for his universal benevolence, by all ranks and religious denominations. — WHEATLEY, HENRY B., 1891, ed. *Percy's Reliques of Ancient English Poetry, General Introduction, vol. I, p.* lxxix.

RELIQUES OF ANCIENT ENGLISH POETRY
1765

You have heard me speak of Mr. Percy. He was in treaty with Mr. James Dodsley for the publication of our best old ballads in three volumes. He has a large folio MS. of ballads which he showed me, and which, with his own natural and acquired talents, would qualify him for the purpose as well as any man in England. I proposed the scheme to him myself, wishing to see an elegant edition and good collection of this kind.—SHENSTONE, WILLIAM, 1761, *Letter to Graves, March* 1.

The reader is here presented with select remains of our ancient English Bards and Minstrels, an order of men, who were once greatly respected by our ancestors, and contributed to soften the roughness of a martial and unlettered people by their songs and by their music. The greater part of them are extracted from an ancient folio manuscript, in the Editor's possession, which contains near two hundred Poems, Songs, and Metrical Romances.

This MS. was written about the middle of the last century; but contains compositions of all times and dates, from the age prior to Chaucer, to the conclusion of the reign of Charles I. This manuscript was shown to several learned and ingenious friends, who thought the contents too curious to be consigned to oblivion, and importuned the possessor to select some of them and give them to the press. As most of them are of great simplicity, and seem to have been merely written for the people, he was long in doubt, whether, in the present state of improved literature, they could be deemed worthy the attention of the public. At length the importunity of his friends prevailed, and he could refuse nothing to such judges as the Author of the Rambler and the late Mr. Shenstone.—PERCY, THOMAS, 1765, *Reliques of Ancient English Poetry, Preface.*

This ingenious work, which revived the taste for our old poets, is too well known to require being here particularized.— BRYDGES, SIR SAMUEL EGERTON, 1800, ed. *Phillips's Theatrum Poetarum Anglicanorum, Preface, p.* lxx.

I remember well the spot where I read these volumes for the first time. It was beneath a huge platanus tree, in the ruins of what had been intended for an old-fashioned arbor in the *garden* I have mentioned. The summer-day sped onward so fast, that notwithstanding the sharp appetite of thirteen, I forgot the hour of dinner, was sought for with anxiety, and was still found entranced in my intellectual banquet. To read and to remember was in this instance the same thing, and henceforth I overwhelmed my school-fellows, and all who would hearken to me, with tragical recitations from the ballads of Bishop Percy. The first time, too, I could scrape a few shillings together, which were not common occurrences with me, I bought unto myself a copy of these beloved volumes; nor do I believe I ever read a book half so frequently, or with half the enthusiasm.—SCOTT, SIR WALTER, 1808, *Autobiography, Life by Lockhart, vol. I, ch.* i.

The late Bishop of Dromore, if he merit no other distinction, is entitled to the proud praise of being the Father of Poetical Taste, in that department of literature which he has the exclusive merit of having first brought into public notice. His

"Reliques" is a publication that reflects lasting honor upon his name; and it has proved the germ of a rich harvest in the same field of the muses.—DIBDIN, THOMAS FROGNALL, 1817, *The Bibliographical Decameron, vol.* III, *p.* 339.

A collection singularly heterogeneous, and very unequal in merit, but from the publication of which, in 1765, some of high name have dated the revival of a genuine feeling for true poetry in the public mind.—HALLAM, HENRY, 1837–39, *Introduction to the Literature of Europe, pt.* ii, *ch.* v, *par.* 78.

I never take up these three heavily-bound volumes, the actual last edition, at which Dr. Johnson was wont to scoff, without feeling a pleasure quite apart from that excited by the charming book itself; although to that book, far more than to any modern school of minstrelsy we owe the revival of the taste for romantic and lyrical poetry, which had lain dormant since the days of the Commonwealth. This pleasure springs from a very simple cause. The associations of these ballads with the happiest days of my happy childhood.— MITFORD, MARY RUSSELL, 1851, *Recollections of a Literary Life, p.* 1.

Perhaps the publication which was as yet at once the most remarkable product of this new taste, and the most effective agent in its diffusion, was Percy's celebrated "Reliques of Ancient English Poetry," which first appeared in 1765. The reception of this book was the same that what is natural and true always meets with when brought into fair competition with the artificial.—CRAIK, GEORGE L., 1861, *A Compendious History of English Literature and of the English Language, vol.* II, *p.* 308.

The publication of the "Reliques," then, constitutes an epoch in the history of the great revival of taste, in whose blessings we now participate. After 1765, before the end of the century, numerous collections of old ballads, in Scotland and England, by Evans, by Pinkerton, Herd, Ritson, were made. The noble reformation, that received so great an impulse in 1765, advanced thenceforward steadily. The taste that was awakened never slumbered again. The recognition of our old life and poetry that the "Reliques" gave, was at last gloriously confirmed and established by Walter Scott.—HALES, JOHN W.,

1868, *Bishop Percy's Folio Manuscript, The Revival of Ballad Poetry in the Eighteenth Century, vol.* II, *p.* xxix.

The "Reliques of Ancient English Poetry," published in 1765 by Bishop Thomas Percy, produced a purer and more lasting effect than Macpherson's "Ossian." They are the fruit of the industry of a loving and careful collector, and proved to every susceptible mind that the essence of poetry is not to be found in formalism, and in sober reflection, but in true and strong feelings. In Percy's "Reliques" we again meet with undisguised nature, with simple feeling, and with energetic action; they are the poetic reflection of an age of national heroes and whose traditions are closely interwoven with English thought and feeling. Hence the powerful and rapid influence these ancient relics of minstrelsy acquired in England and Scotland, an influence which may be traced in the development of English poetry down to our own days.—SCHERR, J., 1874, *A History of English Literature, tr. M. V., p.* 167.

So ready and inflammable was the material prepared for these living coals, unraked from the ashes of departed years. The "Reliques" were largely composed of the lyrics of earlier and later writers. The ballads yielded the key-note, and then gave place to the melody of more modern verse, the most free and national in its character. Lyric poetry, less ambitious than other forms, more close to the individual sentiment, is wont to be the refuge of the most genuine, simple and passionate strains; to be most deeply infused with the national temper.—BASCOM, JOHN, 1874, *Philosophy of English Literature, p.* 224.

Percy's "Reliques" is commonly mentioned as the turning-point in the taste of the last century, but it was quite as much the result, as the cause, of the renewed interest in old ballads. Percy did more completely what had been done feebly before. Still, it is well to bear in mind the date of the publication, 1765, as mnemonic point, for this was by far the most important of the collections. A copy of the book fell into the hands of Bürger (1748–94), who translated many of the ballads into German, and was inspired by it to write his own "Lenore." . . . It would be fair to say that Percy's "Reliques" had more influence in Germany than in England. Bürger and his fellow-poets of the "Hainbund," who were all young men with a confused hatred of tyrants and great affection for the full moon, took to writing more ballads after the old pattern, as illustrated by Percy's "Reliques" and explained by Herder, and soon Herder established the new lines in which German thought was destined to run, substituting the intelligent study of the past for the faithful following of academic rules.—PERRY, THOMAS SERGEANT, 1883, *English Literature in the Eighteenth Century, pp.* 422, 423.

In undertaking the supervision of a new edition of the"Reliques of Ancient English Poetry," I felt that no safer or better guidance could be followed than that of Bishop Percy himself; and as he always strove, in the several editions published by himself, to embody therein the sum of the knowledge of his times, so I, following at a distance, have endeavoured, by gathering from many quarters particulars published since his death, to make his book still more worthy of the great reputation it has acquired.—WHEATLEY, HENRY B., 1891, *ed. Percy's Reliques of Ancient English Poetry, Preface, vol.* I, *p.* ix.

It was an epoch-making book, and is usually spoken of as one of the chief causes of the great re-awakening in English poetry. But the course of our studies in the ballad revival proves that Percy's book was fully as much a result as it was a cause of the Romantic movement. — PHELPS, WILLIAM LYON, 1893, *The Beginnings of the English Romantic Movement, p.* 129.

Percy was a critic of admirable poetical taste and literary skill, but he was not altogether proof against the temptations to which these qualities exposed him.· In the collection of ballads which he "edited" from the MS. in his possession, he did not scruple to alter and supplement the original text whenever he thought that by so doing he could improve the general effect. By these practices he roused the wrath of an able and relentless antagonist.—COURTHOPE, W. J., 1895, *A History of English Poetry, vol.* I, *p.* 428.

Percy not only rescued, himself, a number of ballads from forgetfulness; what was equally important, his book prompted others to hunt out and publish similar relics before it was too late. It was the occasion of collections like Herd's (1769), Scott's (1802–03), and Motherwell's (1827), and many more, resting on purer texts and edited on more scrupulous principles than his own. Furthermore, his ballads helped to bring about a reform in literary taste and to inspire men of original genius. Wordsworth, Coleridge, Southey, Scott, all acknowledged the greatest obligations to them. Wordsworth said that English poetry had been "absolutely redeemed" by them. "I do not think there is a writer in verse of the present day who would not be proud to acknowledge his obligations to the 'Reliques.' I know that it is so with my friends; and for myself, I am happy in this occasion to make a public avowal of my own." Without the "Reliques," "The Ancient Mariner," "The Lady of the Lake," "La Belle Dame sans Merci," "Stratton Water,"and"The Haystack in the Floods" might never have been. Perhaps even the "Lyrical Ballads" might never have been, or might have been something quite unlike what they are.—BEERS, HENRY A., 1898, *A History of English Romanticism in the Eighteenth Century, p.* 299.

GENERAL

Dr. Percy was so abashed by the ridicule flung upon his labours from the ignorance and insensibility of the persons with whom he lived, that, though while he was writing under a mask he had not wanted resolution to follow his genius into the regions of true simplicity and genuine pathos (as is evinced by the exquisite ballad of "Sir Cauline," and by many other pieces), yet when he appeared in his own person and character as a poetical writer, he adopted, as in the tale of the "Hermit of Warkworth," a diction scarcely in any one of its features distinguishable from the vague, the glossy, and unfeeling language of his day. I mention this remarkable fact with regret, esteeming the genius of Dr. Percy in this kind of writing superior to that of any other man by whom in modern times it has been cultivated.— WORDSWORTH, WILLIAM, 1815, *Poems, Essay Supplementary to the Preface.*

Percy was not, perhaps, a man of much originality of genius, or great strength, or richness of mind. Johnson was probably right when he said, "He runs about with little weight upon his mind." Yet he was unquestionably endowed with certain rare qualities. He had ardent enthusiasm, an enthusiasm which, like that of Scott, was the same in kind, although different in direction, from that of his warlike ancestors; he had a vivid sympathy with the old writers, and could think their thoughts, feel their passions, and talk their language;

he had invincible diligence, an enormous memory, and had written some ballads of his own, such as "Sir Cauline," which entitle him to an independent and considerable poetical reputation.— GILFILLAN, GEORGE, 1858, ed. *Reliques of Ancient English Poetry, Life of Thomas Percy, p.* 9.

James Grahame
1765-1811

Born at Glasgow, April 22, 1765. His father was a successful lawyer, and, by a very common error, he conceived that no other profession could be so suitable or so advantageous for his son. James, dutiful, and shrinking from opposition, as he did all through life, obeyed the parental wish, and after completing his literary course at the university of his native city, went in 1784 to Edinburgh, where he studied law, first to qualify himself for the business of writer to the signet, and subsequently for the Scottish bar, of which he was elected a member in 1795. His inclinations, however, were all for retirement and literature; and finally, when he had reached the mature age of forty-four, he took orders in the English Church, and became curate first at Shipton, Glouchestershire and then at Sedgefield in the county of Durham. He did not long enjoy an office which he adorned by his pious and eloquent ministrations. Ill health compelled him to try the renovating effects of his native air, but he died shortly after his return, September 14, 1811. The works of Grahame consist of a dramatic poem "Mary Queen of Scots" (published in 1801), "The Sabbath" (1804), "British Georgics" (1804), "The Birds of Scotland" (1806), and "Poems on the Abolition of the Slave Trade" (1810).—BAYNES, THOMAS SPENCER, *ed.*, 1880, *Encyclopædia Britannica, Ninth Edition, vol.* XI, *p.* 31.

PERSONAL

Yet, well I loved thee, even as one might love
An elder brother, imaged in the soul
With solemn features, half-creating awe,
But smiling still with gentleness and peace.
Tears have I shed when thy most mournful
    . voice
Did trembling breathe forth that touching air,
By Scottish shepherd haply framed of old,
Amid the silence of his pastoral hills,
Weeping the flowers on Flodden-field that
    died.
Wept too have I, when thou didst simply read
From thine own lays, so simply beautiful,
Some short pathetic tale of human grief,
Or orison or hymn of deeper love,
That might have won the skeptic's sullen
    heart
To gradual adoration, and belief
Of Him who died for us upon the cross.
—WILSON, JOHN, 1811, *Lines Sacred to the Memory of the Rev. James Grahame.*

Poor Grahame, gentle, and amiable, and enthusiastic, deserves all you can say of him; his was really a hallowed harp, as he was himself an Israelite without guile. How often have I teazed him, but never out of his good-humour, by praising Dundee and laughing at the Covenanters!— SCOTT, SIR WALTER, 1811, *Letter to Joanna Baillie; Life by Lockhart, ch.* xxiii.

I propose to send to one of the periodical works a biographical notice of the life and writings of my poor friend Grahame. But so small a part of James's value lay in his poetry, that I feel it difficult to express my real sentiments about it. . . . One of the most endearing circumstances which I remember of Grahame was his singing. I shall never forget one summer evening that we agreed to sit up all night, and go together to Arthur's Seat, to see the sun rise. We sat, accordingly, all night in his delightful parlor—the seat of so many happy remembrances! We then went and saw a beautiful sunrise. I returned home with him, for I was living in his house at the time. He was unreserved in all his devoutest feelings before me; and from the beauty of the morning scenery, and the recent death of his sister, our conversation took a serious turn, on the proofs of infinite benevolence in the creation, and the goodness of God. As I retired to my own bed, I overheard his devotions—not his prayer, but a hymn which he sung, and with a power and inspiration beyond himself, and everything else. At that time he was a strong voiced and commanding-looking man.

The remembrance of his large, expressive features when he climbed the hill, and of his organ-like voice in praising God, is yet fresh, and ever pleasing in my miud. But it is rendered a sad recollection from contrasting his then energy with the faltering and fallen man which he afterwards became.—CAMPBELL, THOMAS, 1812, *Life and Letters*, ed., *Beattie, vol.* I, *ch.* xxv.

Tall, solemn, large-featured, and very dark, he was not unlike one of the independent preachers of the commonwealth. He is styled "sepulchral Grahame" by Byron. Neither the bar, at which he practised a few years, nor Whig principles, in the promotion of which he was most ardent (but with which he meant only the general principles of liberty), were the right vocation of a pensive nature, whose delight was in religion and poetry. . . . With the softest of human hearts, his indignation knew no bounds when it was roused by what he held to be oppression, especially of animals or the poor, both of whom he took under his special protection. He and a beggar seemed always to be old friends. The merit of his verse consists in its expressing the feelings of his own heart. It all breathes a quiet, musing benevolence, and a sympathy with the happiness of every living creature. Contention, whether at the bar or in the church, had no charms for one to whom a Scotch tune was a pleasure for a winter evening, and who could pass the whole summer days in cultivating the personal acquaintance of birds in their own haunts, and to whom nothing was a luxury that excluded the etherial calm of indolence. Yet his virtue was by no means passive. He was roused into a new nature by abhorrence of cruelty, and could submit to anything in the cause of duty —COCKBURN, HENRY THOMAS LORD, 1852, *Life of Lord Jeffrey.*

GENERAL

We have a new poet come forth amongst us—James Graham, author of a poem called the "Sabbath," which I admire very much.—SCOTT, SIR WALTER, 1805, *To Miss Seward, March* 21 ; *Life by Lockhart, ch.* xiii.

The greater part of it ["The Sabbath"] is written in a heavy and inelegant manner. The diction throughout is tainted with vulgarity, and there is no selection of words, images, or sentiments, to conciliate the favour of the fastidious reader.

The author has evidently some talents for poetical compositions, and is never absolutely absurd, tedious, or silly ; but he has no delicacy of taste or imagination ; he does not seem to feel the force of the sanction against poetical mediocrity, and his ear appears to have no perception of the finer harmony of versification. If he be a young man, we think there are considerable hopes of him : but if this be the production of maturer talents, we cannot in our conscience exhort him to continue to the service of the muses. . . It contains a good deal of doctrine and argumentation, indeed, both in the text and in the notes ; but nothing that is not either very trite or very shallow and extravagant. . . . The whole publication, indeed, though not entitled to stand in the first rank of poetical excellence, is respectably executed, and may be considered as very creditable, either to a beginner, or to one who does not look upon poetry as his primary vocation.— JEFFREY, FRANCIS LORD, 1805, *The Sabbath, Edinburgh Review, vol.* 5, *pp.* 441, 442.

Sweet are thy Sabbath lays, my gentle Grahame,
Pure as thy mind, and spotless as thy fame!
—GRANT, ANNE, 1808, *Inscribed in " The Sabbath," Memoir and Correspondence,* ed. *Grant, vol.* I, *p.* 137.

Moravians, rise! bestow some meet reward
On dull devotion—Lo! the Sabbath bard,
Sepulchral Grahame, pours his notes sublime,
In mangled prose, nor e'en aspires to rhyme,
Breaks into blank the Gospel of St. Luke,
And boldly pilfers from the Pentateuch ;
And, undisturb'd by conscientious qualms,
Perverts the Prophets and purloins the Psalms.
—BYRON, LORD, 1809, *English Bards and Scotch Reviewers.*

While the criticasters of his own country were pronouncing sentence of condemnation upon it, for its pious dulness and inanity, the "Sabbath" had found its way from one end of Great Britain to the other ;—it was in the mouths of the young, and in the hearts of the aged.—SOUTHEY, ROBERT, 1810, *Grahame's British Georgics, Quarterly Review, vol.* 3, *p.* 457.

O Bard of sinless life and holiest song!
. . . . . . Thou didst despise
To win the ear of this degenerate age
By gorgeous epithets, all idly heaped
On theme of earthly state, or, idler still,
By tinkling measures and unchastened lays,
Warbled to pleasure and her syren-train,

Profaning the best name of poesy.
With loftier aspirations, and an aim
More worthy man's immortal nature, Thou
That holiest spirit that still loves to dwell
In the upright heart and pure, at noon of night
Didst fervently invoke, and, led by her
Above the Aonian mount, sent from the stars
Of heaven such soul-subduing melody
As Bethlehem-shepherds heard when Christ
  was born.
—WILSON, JOHN, 1811, *Lines Sacred to
the Memory of the Rev. James Grahame.*

His taste was singular, and his manner
correspondent. The general tenor of his
style is homely, and frequently so prosaic
that its peculiar graces appear in their
full lustre from the contrast of meanness
that surrounds them. His readers may
be few; but whoever does read him will
probably be oftener *surprised* into admiration, than in the perusal of any one of his
contemporaries. The most lively, the
most lovely sketches of natural scenery,
of minute imagery, and of exquisite
incident, unexpectedly developed, occur
in his compositions, with ever-varying, yet
ever-assimilating features. — MONTGOM-
ERY, JAMES, 1833, *Lectures on General
Literature, Poetry, etc., p.* 159.

The blank verse of Grahame has some
resemblance in structure to that of Cowper
and of Wordsworth; but as an artist, he
was much inferior to and wants the correctness of either. Whether this arose
from deficiency of ear—which could not
well be, as he is said to have sung the
ballads and songs of our native land
mellifluously, and with a touching tenderness—or from some preconceived conviction of its effect in preventing monotony,
we have ever, here and there, a line that
halts, or that grates prosaically on the ear,
like an instrument out of tune. His pages
are never lighted up with wit or humour;
and it has been objected to him, that he
is too uniformly tender or solemn.—MOIR,
D. M., 1850–51, *Sketches of the Political
Literature of the Past Half-Century, p.* 26.

It ["British Georgics"] does not exhibit
any particular system of husbandry; it
amuses rather than instructs, and recommends the study of the science rather
than teaching of it. The work embraces
a mixed description, and is lavish on rural
modes and manners; the poetry is both
lame and tame, and never rises beyond a
feebleness of conception, and a descriptive
halt. The portion of practical knowledge

is very minute, with incidental notes of
new introductions. — DONALDSON, JOHN,
1854, *Agricultural Biography.*

Grahame's genius was limited in its
range but within that range was exquisitely
true and beautiful. He had no dramatic
power, has written no lyrics of merit, and
his vein of thought is far from profound.
He has been called the Cowper of Scotland, and resembles him in tenderness of
feeling, truth of natural description, and
ardent piety, but is vastly inferior in
strength of mind, force and continuity of
style, and, whatever he might do in
private, has in his poetry given no evidence
of possessing a particle of Cowper's refined and inimitable humour.—GILFILLAN,
GEORGE, 1856, *ed., The Poetical Works of
Henry Kirke White and James Grahame.*

We may add, before we leave these
northern scenes, to which for a time the
high flood of intellectual activity seemed
to have been transferred, the gentle name
of James Grahame, the author of the
"Sabbath." He was not a great poet,
nor is that a great poem, but it is very
national, and full of a tender sweetness—
and echo of Cowper on Scottish soil.
Grahame came to light among the early
band of the Edinburgh Reviewers, a
spectator and sympathiser, if no more—
adding a mild enthusiasm for the work of
his stronger and more daring friends to
his own gentle faculty. . . . His
poems are full of the atmosphere of a pure
and retired existence, with something,
however, that reminds the reader more of
a Scottish manse than an English parsonage; and he was always intensely national.
—OLIPHANT, MARGARET O. W., 1882,
*The Literary History of England XVIIIth-
XIXth Century, vol.* II, *pp.* 169, 170.

When married, Grahame discovered that
his wife thought but meanly of his poetry,
and this, no doubt, was his main reason
for publishing "The Sabbath" anonymously
in 1804. It charmed him to find Mrs.
Grahame in raptures over the descriptive
beauty, the vivid historical illustrations,
the moving, sentimental pictures, and the
deep religious earnestness of a poem that
is Scottish to the core; and he then avowed
the authorship. Three new editions were
called for in a year, and to these Grahame
added descriptive and thoughtful "Sabbath
Walks."—BAYNE, THOMAS, 1890, *Dictionary of National Biography, vol.* XXII, *p.* 366.

John Horne Tooke

1736-1812

Born [John Horne; adopted additional name of Tooke in 1782 as a compliment to a patron] at Westminster, 25 June 1736. Early educations at schools in Soho and in Kent. At Westminster School, 1744-46; at Eton, 1746-53. Matric. St. John's Coll., Camb., 1755; B. A., 1758; M. A., 1771. Ordained Vicar of New Brentford in 1760; but gave up orders in 1773, and took up pursuit of law. Imprisoned for libel, 1777-78. Tried on charge of high treason, but acquitted, 1794. M. P. for Old Sarum, Feb. 1801 to 1802. Died, at Wimbledon, 18 March 1812. Buried at Ealing. *Works:* "The Petition of an Englishman" (anon.), 1765; "A Sermon," 1769; "An Oration delivered at a . . . Meeting of the Freeholders of Middlesex" [1770]; "Letter to John Dunning, Esq.," 1778; "Letter to Lord Ashburton," 1782; " 'Επεα Πτεροεντα," 1786; "Letter to a Friend on the Reported Marriage of the Prince of Wales," 1787; "Two Pair of Portraits," 1788; "Letter on the Meeting at the Crown and Anchor Tavern," 1791; "Proceedings in an Action for Debt," 1792; "Letter on Parliamentary Reform," 1794; "Speeches . . . during the Westminster Election, 1796" [1796]; "Letter to the Editor of 'The Times,' " 1807. Life, by J. A. Graham, 1828. —SHARP, R. FARQUHARSON, 1897, *A Dictionary of English Authors, p.* 281.

PERSONAL

There is abundance of proof that Mr. Horne was now considered an admirable preacher, and that his eloquence only wanted cultivation to place him among the most successful of our English divines. But it was in orthodox and doctrinal discourses that he chiefly excelled, and he is accordingly reported to have distinguished himself greatly by his exhortations before confirmation, on which occasion, by mingling sound argument with kind and affectionate persuasion, he never failed to make a suitable impression on all who heard him. In short, he might not only have been greatly respected as a popular pastor, but was still in a fair way to become one of the pillars of the Anglican church, when a memorable event occurred in the political world, and proved an insurmountable, though not, perhaps, an unexpected obstacle to his future preferment. —STEPHENS, ALEXANDER, 1813, *Memoirs of John Horne Tooke.*

It would be but impertinent, however, to effect to call such a character as that of John Horne Tooke to account for this or the other particular culpability. It would be something like attending to criticize the transactions of a pagan temple, and excepting to one rite as ungraceful, perhaps, and to another practice as irreverent; like as if the *substance* of the service were of a quality to deserve that its particular parts should be corrected. His whole moral constitution was unsound, from the exclusion . . . of all respect to a future account, to be given to the Supreme Governor. Towards the conclusion of his life, he made calm and frequent references to his death, but not a word is here recorded expressive of anticipations beyond it.—FOSTER, JOHN, 1813, *Horne Tooke, Critical Essays, ed. Ryland, vol.* II, *p.* 191.

Mr. Horne Tooke was one of those who may be considered as connecting links between a former period and the existing generation. His education and accomplishments, nay, his political opinions, were of the last age; his mind, and the tone of his feeling were *modern.* There was a hard, dry materialism in the very texture of his understanding, varnished over by the external refinement of the old school. Mr. Tooke had great scope of attainments, and great versatility of pursuits; but the same shrewdness, quickness, cool self-possession, the same *literalness* of perception, the absence of passion and enthusiasm, characterised nearly all he did, said or wrote. He was without a rival (almost) in private conversation, an expert public speaker, a keen politician, a first-rate grammarian, and the finest gentleman (to say the least) of his own party. He had no imagination (or he would not have scorned it!)—no delicacy of taste, no rooted prejudices or strong attachments: his intellect was like a bow of polished steel, from which he shot sharp-pointed poisoned arrows at his friends in private, at his enemies in public. His mind (so to speak) had no *religion* in it, and very little even of the moral qualities of genius; but he was a man of the world, a scholar bred, and a most acute and powerful logician. He was also a wit and a formidable one: yet it may be questioned whether his wit was anything more than an excess of his logical faculty: it did not consist in the play of fancy, but in close and cutting combinations of the understanding.—HAZLITT, WILLIAM, 1825, *The Spirit of the Age.*

While the compositions of Junius have furnished a model of style, as bold and brilliant as it is classical, the Author has eluded discovery, and to this moment, as if disdaining applause, the motto emblazoned on the escutcheon of his fame, applies, "Statnominis umbra." This, it must be admitted, is an appalling circumstance, not only checking ambition, but assailing the enquirer at the entrance; like some ancient sepulchral inscription, at once rebuking the curiosity of the profane intruder, and sternly prohibiting his further advance. Knowing, however, that the avenues to the temple of truth are ever open, and that its votaries are not to be deterred from fair and manly discussion, the Author of the following Essay has ventured upon a disclosure of facts and circumstances, which will not suffer himself, at least, to doubt as to the identity of JUNIUS. He had the honor of the acquaintance of JOHN HORNE TOOKE; and from the opportunities which this afforded, aided by other circumstances, he has been enabled to furnish facts hitherto unknown; and to present others in a light so new, as to induce a probability that TOOKE and JUNIUS are the same.— GRAHAM, JOHN A., 1828, *Memoirs of John Horne Tooke, together with His Valuable Speeches and Writings; also containing Proofs Identifying Him as the Author of the Celebrated Letters of Junius, Preface, p.* v.

Horne Tooke was always making a butt of Mr. Godwin; who nevertheless, had that in him which Tooke could never have understood. I saw a good deal of Tooke at one time: he left upon me the impression of his being a keen, iron man.— COLERIDGE, SAMUEL TAYLOR, 1830, *Table-Talk, ed. Ashe, May* 8, *p.* 72.

I often dined with Tooke at Wimbledon; and always found him most pleasant and most witty. There his friends would drop in upon him without any invitation: Colonel Bosville would come frequently, bringing with him a dinner from London, —fish, &c.—Tooke latterly used to expect two or three of his most intimate friends to dine with him every Sunday; and I once offended him a great deal by not joining his Sunday dinner-parties for several weeks.—ROGERS, SAMUEL, 1855, *Recollections of Table-Talk, ed. Dyce.*

Had, for many years, been the dread of judges, ministers of State, and all constituted authorities. He was that famous Parson Horne who attacked the terrible Junius, after statesmen, judges, and generals had fled before him, and drove him back defeated and howling with his wounds. He it was who silenced Wilkes. Some years afterwards he fastened a quarrel on the House of Commons, which he bullied and baffled with his usual coolness and address.—MASSEY, WILLIAM, 1855-63, *History of England During the Reign of George the Third.*

Tooke's *change of name* originated as follows. When he was rising into celebrity, the estate of Purley, near Croydon, belonged to Mr. William Tooke, one of four friends who joined in supplying him with an income, when, after quitting the Church, he studied for the Law. One of Tooke's richer neighbours, in wresting from him his manorial rights by a lawsuit, had applied to Parliament, and nearly succeeded in effecting his purpose by means of an inclosure bill, which would have greatly depreciated the Purley estate. Tooke despondingly confided his aprehensions to Horne, who resolved at once to avert the blow, which he did in a very bold and very singular manner. The third reading of the Bill was to take place the next day, and Horne immediately wrote a violent libel on the Speaker of the House of Commons, in reference to it, and obtained its insertion in the *Public Advertiser.* As might be expected, the first Parliamentary proceeding the next day was the appearance of the adventurous libeller in the custody of the Serjeant-at-Arms. When called upon for his defence, he delivered a most remarkable speech, in which he pointed out the injustice of the Bill in question with so much success, that it was reconsidered, and the clauses which affected his friend's property expunged. In gratitude for his important service, Mr. Tooke, who had no family, made Horne his heir; and on his death in 1803, the latter became proprietor of Purley as one of the conditions of inheritance, he added the name of Tooke to his own, and from this time was known as John Horne Tooke. —TIMBS, JOHN, 1860, *A Century of Anecdote, p. 177.*

John Horne had a great and varied reputation while he lived, and long enough afterwards to be honoured with the most florid, and far from the least amusing, of those biographies of sixty years ago, which were adulatory, but never uncandid; absurd, but never dull. There we learn that though, like Pericles, he rarely laughed, like Alcibiades he could suit himself to the humors of other men; that he could enjoy his wine with Homer and Ennius, could draw a character with Tacitus, and was as ready to accept money from his friends as Pliny and Cicero; that during his career he was as artful in counsel as Ulysses, as cool in action as the Duke of Marlborough, and as self-confident as Michael Angelo; and that, when the end came, he was as ready to die, and as desirous to have a simple funeral, as Titus Pomponius Atticus. But, in truth, his character and powers were not of the heroic order; and the people who had parallel histories and similiar dispositions with Horne were to be found in his own country and his own half-century. He was the earliest, and for practical business by far the ablest, of a class of men to whom Englishmen owe a debt of gratitude which they are, not inexcusably, somewhat unwilling to acknowledge. Among the most lamentable results of a system of coercion and repression is the deteriorating effect which it produces upon those who brave it. When to speak or write one's mind on politics is to obtain the reputation, and render one's self liable to the punishment, of a criminal, social discredit, with all its attendant moral dangers, soon attaches itself to the more humble opponents of a ministry. . . . Honest, impracticable, insatiably contentious, and inordinately vain, he had thrown away almost all his chances and his friends.—TREVELYAN, GEORGE OTTO, 1880, *The Early History of Charles James Fox, pp. 439, 441.*

The man who appears to have contributed most largely to its formation was Horne, the Vicar of Brentford, afterwards better known as Horne Tooke, who had now

thrown aside the clerical profession, for which he was utterly unsuited, and flung himself unreservedly into political agitation. The great contributions to grammar and the science of language which have given him a permanent place in English literature belong to a later period of his life, and at this time he was known chiefly as one of the most violent agitators among the City politicians. He possessed some literary and still greater forensic ability, and was a man of undoubted energy, courage, honesty, and independence, but at the same time turbulent, vain, and quarrelsome, and very unscrupulous about the means he employed.—LECKY, WILLIAM EDWARD HARTPOLE, 1882, *A History of England in the Eighteenth Century, vol.* III, *ch.* xi, *p. 189.*

THE DIVERSIONS OF PURLEY
1786–1798–1805

The distance between what he has proved and what he wishes us to believe that he has proved, is enormous.—DUDLEY, EARL, 1812, *Reed's Memoirs of the Life of John Horne Tooke, Quarterly Review, vol.* 7, *p. 321.*

Horne Tooke's is certainly a wonderful work; but the great merit was the original thought. The light which shines through such impenetrable words as articles and pronouns is admirable,— "the" and "it." No single book, perhaps, ever so much illustrated language: yet, how much more might he have done, if he had known the collateral languages! Adelung's "Dictionary" alone would have yielded great assistance.—MACKINTOSH, SIR JAMES, 1812, *Life, vol.* II, *ch.* iii.

The great thing which Mr. Horne Tooke has done, and which he has left behind him to posterity, is his work on Grammar, oddly enough entitled "The Diversions of Purley." Many people have taken it up as a description of a game—others supposing it to be a novel. It is, in truth, one of the few philosophical works on Grammar that were ever written. The essence of it (and, indeed, almost all that is really valuable in it) is contained in his "Letter to Dunning," published about the year 1775. Mr. Tooke's work is truly elementary. . . . It is also a pity that Mr. Tooke spun out his great work with prolix and dogmatical dissertations on irrelevant matters; and after denying the old metaphysical theories of language, should attempt to found a metaphysical theory of his own on the nature and mechanism of language.—HAZLITT, WILLIAM, 1825, *The Spirit of the Age.*

Horne Tooke was pre-eminently a ready-witted man. He had that clearness which is founded on shallowness. He doubted nothing; and, therefore, gave you all that he himself knew, or meant, with great completeness. His voice was very fine, and his tones exquisitely discriminating. His mind had no progression of development. All that is worth anything (and that is but little) in the "Diversions of Purley" is contained in a short pamphlet-letter which he addressed to Mr. Dunning; then it was enlarged to an octavo, but there was not a foot of progression beyond the pamphlet; at last, a quarto volume, I believe, came out; and yet, verily, excepting newspaper lampoons and political insinuations, there was no addition to the argument of the pamphlet. It shows a base and unpoetical mind to convert so beautiful and so divine a subject as language into the vehicle or make-weight of political squibs. All that is true in Horne Tooke's book is taken from Lennep, who gave it for so much as it was worth, and never pretended to make a system of it. Tooke affects to explain the origin and whole philosophy of language by what is, in fact, only a mere accident of the history of one language, or one or two languages.— COLERIDGE, SAMUEL TAYLOR, 1830, *Table Talk, ed. Ashe, May 7, p.* 69.

He has made one of the driest subjects in the whole range of literature or science one of the most amusing and even lively of books; nor did any one ever take up the "Diversions of Purley" (as he has quaintly chosen to call it) and lay it down till some other avocation tore it from his hands. The success of this system has been such as its great essential merits, and its more superficial attractions combined, might have led us to expect. All men are convinced of its truth; and as every thing which had been done before was superseded by it, so nothing has since been effected unless in pursuing its views and building upon its solid foundations.—BROUGHAM, HENRY LORD, 1839-43, *Lives of Statesmen of the Time of George III.*

Whatever may be Horne Tooke's short-comings (and they are great), whether in details of etymology, or in the philosophy of grammar, or in matters more serious still, yet, with all this, what an epoch in many a student's intellectual life has been his first acquaintance with "The Diversions of Purley."—TRENCH, RICHARD CHENEVIX, 1851, *On the Study of Words, Preface.*

It is a matter of sincere regret with all who know the real merits of Horne Tooke, that his spleen and causticity of temper should have prevented him from becoming what his talents and labors might easily have made him—the father of modern English. Darwin says very truly of him, that he first let in light upon the chaos of English etymology, and displayed the wonders of formation in language—at least in the particles. His mistaken vocation was the eternal bar to real greatness: the life-long struggle with it embittered his life and his mind, already too fond of paradox, and made him the very Ishmael of literature and politics—his hand against every man's hand, and every man's hand against his.—DE VERE, M. SCHELE, 1853, *Outlines of Comparative Philology, p.* 192.

Dire have been the disappointments incurred by the "Diversions of Purley,"— one of the toughest books in existence. It has even cast a shade over one of our best story-books, "The Diversions of Hollycot," by the late Mrs. Johnston.— BURTON, JOHN HILL, 1860, *His Functions, The Book-Hunter, pt.* ii.

Him who yet remains the greatest philologist that has made the English language his peculiar study, Horne Tooke. —WHITE, RICHARD GRANT, 1870, *Words and Their Uses.*

The main interest of the "Diversions" to the general reader lies in the witty intermixture of political thrusts and declamations. — MINTO, WILLIAM, 1872-80, *Manual of English Prose Literature, p.* 487.

The philology is eccentric and old-fahioned, and the book "diverting" to its author rather than its readers: but it is very unlike a work on which a revolutionary accused of high treason was likely to have been engaged.—OLIPHANT, MARGARET O. W., 1882, *The Literary History of England, XVIIIth-XIXth Century, vol.* II, p. 225.

As a philologist, Horne Tooke deserves credit for seeing the necessity of studying Gothic and Anglo-Saxon, and learnt enough to be much in advance of Johnson in that direction; although his views were inevitably crude as judged by a later standard. His philology was meant to subserve a characteristic philosophy. Locke, he said, had made a happy mistake when he called his book an essay upon human understanding, instead of an essay upon grammar. Horne Tooke, in fact, was a thorough nominalist after the fashion of Hobbes; he especially ridiculed the "Hermes" of Harris, and Monboddo, who had tried to revive Aristotelean logic; held that every word meant simply a thing; and that reasoning was the art of putting words together. Some of his definitions on this principle became famous; as that truth means simply what a man "troweth," and that right means simply what is ruled, whence it follows that right and wrong are as arbitrary as right and left, and may change places according to the legislator's point of view.—STEPHEN, LESLIE, 1899, *Dictionary of National Biography, vol.* LVII, *p.* 46.

GENERAL

Justice has scarcely been done to Horne, as a mob .politician and political writer. With all his violence he was generally in the right; and the best testimony to his sincerity is that he withdrew from active politics when he found that he was not likely to gain attention. In these City struggles it is plain that he was "pulling the strings," yet without any attempt to make himself conspicuous. In his appeals to the throne and the public there is an earnest ring, with a sarcastic, vigorous power, which excites admiration.—FITZGERALD, PERCY, 1888, *The Life and Times of John Wilkes, vol.* II, *p.* 164.

Joel Barlow
1754–1812

Born at Reading, Conn., 1754: died near Cracow, Poland, Dec. 24, 1812. An American poet and politician, one of the "Hartford Wits." He resided abroad, chiefly in France, 1788–1805, where he identified himself with the Girondist party; was consul to Algiers 1795–97; and was United States minister to France 1811–12. Author of "The Vision of Columbus" (1787: enlarged as "The Columbiad," 1807), "Hasty Pudding," and "Advice to the Privileged Orders" (Part I. 1791, Part II. 1795).— SMITH, BENJAMIN E., *ed.*, 1894–97, *The Century Cyclopedia of Names, p.* 121.

PERSONAL

In private life, our author was highly esteemed for his amiable temperament, and many social excellences. His manners were generally grave and dignified, and he possessed but little facility of general conversation; but with his intimate friends he was easy and familiar, and upon topics which deeply interested him he conversed with much animation. His mind was rather of a philosophical than a poetical cast, and better adapted to those studies which require patient investigation and profound thought than to the lighter and more fanciful labors of the Muse. Still, as a poet, he held no humble place among the authors of his day; while, as an ardent patriot, a sincere philanthropist, a zealous republican, and a friend and patron of science and art, he must ever stand among the most distinguished men of his age and country. — EVEREST, CHARLES W., 1843, *Poets of Connecticut, p.* 80.

We had in Paris at this period a few Americans. . . . In order to reach the apartment of Mr. Barlow, I was obliged to pass through the door of a great gambling establishment that occupied the floor immediately below his. This door was attended by a porter, who kept it locked, so that to get admittance I had to announce myself as a visitor to Mr. Barlow. A man ought to be cheaply lodged to be induced to reside behind such a barrier. The poet's poverty consented rather than his will. Barlow was a very estimable man, and I am happy to say that prosperous circumstances soon removed him from this attic prison to comfortable quarters, and a few years after he was enabled to display the suitable magnificence of an ambassador in one of the best hotels in the city when he represented our republic at Bonaparte's court.—BRECK, SAMUEL, 1862–77, *Recollections, ed. Scudder, p.*171.

The life of Joel Barlow is still unwritten. Political prejudice may have something to do with this, but to one who has pored over his private papers, read the letters written to him, by him, and about him, by all the celebrated people of his time, there is something ludicrous in opening an Encyclopædia and reading "Joel Barlow was an American poet." Barlow was a poor poet, but a very great man, and so posterity will one day rate him. Impracticable he may have been, for his wishes and aspirations were far before the possibilities of his time ; yet in hurrying to Wilna, that he might force from the reluctant Napoleon some acknowledgement of the rights and sufferings of impoverished American citizens, he laid down his life for his people as deliberately as if, like Warren, he had exposed it upon the first battle-field. The record of the terrible privations and sufferings which led to his death in a peasant's hut near Zarnovitch, Dec. 26, 1812, still survives, and will one day justify my words. —DALL, CAROLINE H., 1876, *A Centennial "Posie," The Unitarian Review, vol. 6, p.* 158.

Barlow left Paris for Wilna on the 26th of October in his private carriage, yet travelling night and day and with relays of horses at the post-towns to expedite his progress. . . . The perilous journey had been made in vain, and the treaty was doomed to still further delay. It now only remained for Barlow to extricate himself from his dangerous position and to reach the frontiers before the fleeing army and the pursuing Cossacks should close every avenue of escape. . . . On reaching Zarrow, an obscure village near Cracow, the poet was seized with a sudden and fatal attack of pneumonia, the result, no doubt, of privation and exposure. He was borne to a little Jewish cottage, the only inn that the village afforded, and there died December 26, 1812. His remains were interred in the little churchyard of the village where he died. It is rarely that an American visits his grave, and the government has never taken interest enough in its minister to erect a memorial slab above his dust : but wifely devotion has supplied the omission, and a plain monument of marble, on which are inscribed his name, age and station and the circumstances of his death, marks the poet's place of sepulture.—TODD, CHARLES BURR, 1880, *A Forgotten American Worthy, Lippincott's Magazine, vol.* 26, *pp.* 77, 78.

This Barlow is memorable as the only one of our countrymen who has been guilty of the folly of attempting to produce an American epic poem. But a better title to immortality is the infamous part he bore in enticing innocent Frenchmen to buy and settle the lands of the Scioto Company on the Ohio. Towards Adams, Barlow felt the same contempt which any man who admires poetry must feel towards the scribbler who defiled the English language by writing the "Columbiad," and, when he heard that John Adams was chosen President he poured out his thoughts on the political position in a letter to Abraham Baldwin, a brother-in-law and a Member of Congress. The letter abounded in obscure passages, but the one selected by the prosecutors of Lyon contained an expression of surprise that the answer of the House to the President's speech of April third, 1797, had not been "an order to send him to a madhouse."—MCMASTER, JOHN BACH, 1885, *History of the People of the United States, vol.* II, *p.* 399.

THE COLUMBIAD
1787–1807

America.—An epic poet has already appeared in that hemisphere, Barlow, author of the "Columbiad,"—not to be compared with the works of more polished nations. —BYRON, LORD, 1807, *Memoranda of Readings, Nov.* 30 ; *Life, Letters and Journals, ed. Moore, ch.* v.

The author's talents are evidently respectable ; and, severely as we have been obliged to speak of his taste and his diction in a great part of the volume, we have no hesitation in saying, that we consider him as a giant, in comparison with many of the puling and paltry rhymsters, who disgrace our English literature by their occasional success. As an Epic poet, we do think his case is desperate ; but, as a philosophical and moral poet, we think he has talents of no ordinary value ; and, if he would pay some attention to purity of style, and simplicity of composition, and cherish in himself a certain fastidiousness of taste,—which is not yet to be found, we are afraid, even among the better educated of the Americans,—we have no doubt that he might produce something which English poets would envy, and English critics applaud. In the meantime, we think it quite certain, that his present work will have no success in this country.

Its faults are far too many, and too glaring, to give its merits any chance of being distinguished; and indeed no long poem was ever redeemed by the beauty of particular passages—especially if its faults were owing to affectation, and its beauties addressed rather to the judgment than to the heart or the imagination. — JEFFREY, FRANCIS LORD, 1809, *Barlow's Columbiad, Edinburgh Review, vol.* 15, *p.* 39.

The "Columbiad" is not, in our opinion, so pleasing a poem in its present form as in that in which it was originally written. . . . Barlow, in his later poetry, attempted to invigorate his style, but, instead of drawing strength and salubrity from the pure wells of ancient English, he corrupted and debased it with foreign infusions. The imposing but unchaste glitter which distinguished the manner of Darwin and his imitators, appears likewise to have taken strong hold on his fancy, and he has not scrupled to bestow on his poem much of this meretricious decoration. But, notwithstanding the bad taste in which his principal work is composed, notwithstanding he cannot be said to write with much pathos or many of the native felicities of fancy, there is yet enough in the poetry of Mr. Barlow to prove that, had he fixed his eye on purer models, he might have excelled, not indeed in epic or narrative poetry nor in the delineation of passion and feeling, but in that calm, lofty, sustained style, which suits best with topics of morality and philosophy, and for which the vigor and spirit of his natural manner, whenever he permits it to appear, show him to have been well qualified.—BRYANT, WILLIAM CULLEN, 1818–84, *Early American Verse, Prose Writings,* ed. *Godwin, vol.* I, *p.* 51.

The strangest epic composition ever issued from the press.—MONTGOMERY, JAMES, 1833, *Lectures on General Literature, Poetry, etc., p.* 144.

The poem, having no unity of fable, no regular succession of incidents, no strong exhibition of varied character, lacks the most powerful charms of a narrative; and has, besides, many dull and spiritless passages, that would make unpopular a work of much more faultless general design. The versification is generally harmonious, but mechanical and passionless, the language sometimes incorrect, and the similes often inappropriate and inelegant. Yet

there are in it many bursts of eloquence and patriotism, which should preserve it from oblivion. The descriptions of nature and of personal character are frequently condensed and forceful; and passages of invective, indignant and full of energy.— GRISWOLD, RUFUS W., 1842–46, *The Poets and Poetry of America, p.* 25.

It may safely be affirmed that there is more genuine poetry in the bare *conception* of the Columbiad than is to be found in *all the works* of many pretentious bards of considerable note; and our author may well be pardoned for some imperfections in the execution of his plan. —BALDWIN, A. C., 1873, *Joel Barlow, The New Englander, vol.* 32, *p.* 430.

It is composed in a florid, declamatory style, and has little real poetic merit to recommend it.—BALDWIN, JAMES, 1882, *English Literature and Literary Criticism, Poetry, p.* 202.

All the poets of the United States were threatened with extinction or subordination when Joel Barlow appeared. He was, according to all accounts, an estimable man, cursed with the idea not only that he was a poet, but the greatest of American poets; and in 1808 he published, in a surperb quarto volume, "The Columbiad." It was also published in Paris and London. The London "Monthly Magazine" tried to prove not only that it was an epic poem, but that it was surpassed only by the Iliad, the Æneid, and "Paradise Lost." Joel Barlow is fairly entitled to the praise of raising mediocrity to dimensions almost colossal. "Columbia is, thank Heaven, still alive;" "The Columbiad" is, thank Heaven, hopelessly dead. There are some elderly gentlemen still living who declare that they have read "The Columbiad," and have derived much satisfaction from the perusal of the same; but their evidence cannot stand the test of cross-examination. They cannot tell what the poem is, what it teaches, and what it means. No critic within the last fifty years has read more than a hundred lines of it, and even this effort of attention has been a deadly fight with those merciful tendencies in the human organization which softly wrap the overworked mind in the blessedness of sleep. It is the impossibility of reading "The Columbiad" which prevents any critical estimate of its numberless demerits.—WHIPPLE, EDWIN PERCY, 1886,

American Literature and Other Papers,
ed. *Whittier, p.* 24.

Belton. Did you ever read Barlow's
"Columbiad," the great epic of the
American Revolution?

Mallett. All of it? *Gott bewahr!* I
have read a good deal of it, however, in
pure amusement, but it has all gone out
of my memory. But there is no foolish-
ness which is not to be found in verse, and
there is no verse so bad that it does not
find readers.—STORY WILLIAM WETMORE,
1890, *Conversations in a Studio, vol.* I,
p. 265.

Better would it have been, both for the
poem and for the poet, if, in his later revision of the work, he had attempted no
change in its essential character. . . . Of
course, never upon any plan could the poem
have taken the rank as a work of genius,
or have escaped the penalties of the
author's great literary defects. Under
any character, it would have had no tender
or delicate qualities, no lightness of touch,
no flashes of beauty, not a ripple of humor,
no quiet and dainty charm; a surfeit,
rather, of vehemence and proclamation,—
sonorous, metalic, rhetorical; forced description, manufactured sentiment, sublimity generated of pasteboard and starch;
and ever-rolling tattoo of declamation,
invective, eulogy; big, gaudy flowers of poetry which are also flowers of wax. Moreover, not even genius could have saved this
poem from the literary disaster involved in
its adoption of that conventional poetic
diction and of that worn-out metrical
form from which, after a whole century
of favor, English literature was just then
turning away in a recoil of weariness and
disgust. And yet, with all his limitations
as a poet, the author of "The Columbiad"
is entitled to the praise due to a sturdy
and effective ethical teacher in verse.
In didactic expression, the poem is often
epigrammatic, trenchant, and strong; nay,
in strenuous moral expositions and enforcement, it is at times even noble and
impressive.—TYLER, MOSES COIT, 1895,
Three Men of Letters, pp. 167, 168.

From a literary point of view, however,
it ranks among the curiosities of American literature. There are here and there
beautiful passages, but the poem is unwieldy, full of digressions and curious expressions.—PATTEE, FRED LEWIS, 1896,
A History of American Literature, p. 97.

Barlow's epic was thus a great and
serious labor, into which he put his life-
thought; but unfortunately it is a serious
labor for the reader too. . . . In
brief, "The Columbiad" is a stage-coach
epic, lumbering and slow. It is valuable
chiefly as a courageous attempt at greater
things in American literature; and it failed,
not because its author had no talent (for
he had a great deal), but because epics
demand genius.—BRONSON, WALTER C.,
1900, *A Short History of American Literature, pp.* 62, 63.

Even in its first form this turgid epic,
which few mortals now living have more
than glanced at, was the most ambitious
attempt at serious literature which had
appeared in the United States. To this
day, furthermore, a quarto edition of "The
Columbiad" is among the most impressive
books to look at in the world.—WENDELL,
BARRETT, 1900, *A Literary History of
America, p.* 127.

THE HASTY PUDDING

The most amusing and, perhaps, upon
the whole, the most popular poem he ever
composed, "Hasty-pudding," a mock
heroic in three cantos, which no genuine
Yankee ever read or ever can read without
interest. . . . In the whole poem,
there is such a commingling of stately,
grandiloquent diction, and ludicrous, rustic simplicity, as constitutes the soul of
wit, and the attention of the reader is
enchained from the beginning to the end.
—BALDWIN, A. C., 1873, *Joel Barlow,
The New Englander, vol.* 32, *pp.* 424, 425.

Of Barlow the poet a good deal may be
said. He sought to build his eternal fame
on "The Columbiad," an epic, but by the
irony of fate he is known in literature
only by an unambitious poem on hasty
pudding. . . . Deserves a rank among
mock heroics and pastorals, and every
New Englander ought to read it occasionally. The bard had the national fondness
for the national dish, and after seeking it in
the old world for many years in vain, suddenly unpromised joy expands his heart to
meet it in Savoy. His soul is soothed, his
cares have found an end. He greets his
long lost, unforgotten friend, and makes
both self and friend forever famous. Still
no part of "The Hasty Pudding," or any of
Barlow's poems, has proved sufficiently
worthy to gain a place in any of the popular

collections of poetry.—WHITNEY, ERNEST, 1886, *Joel Barlow, New Englander, vol.* 45, *pp.* 825, 828.

GENERAL

The critic, after a careful analysis of the character of Joel Barlow, would probably rank him, first, as philanthropist; second, as statesman; third, as Philosopher; and fourth, as poet. His philanthropy crops out in every line of his writings, in every act of his life. His letters to Washington, to the citizens of the United States, to Monroe, while abroad on the French mission, and his Fourth of July oration at Washington, give evidence of broad and liberal statesmanship. His philosophical turn was most apparent in his private letters and intercourse with familiar friends. As a poet he was certainly respectable. His "Hasty-Pudding" would be an addition to any literature, and in all his poems are passages that show the inspiration of the true poet. It is as the pioneer of American poetry, however, that he is worthy of the highest honor. He was not a voluminous writer.—TODD, CHARLES BURR, 1886, *Life and Letters of Joel Barlow, p.* 289.

Edmond Malone
1741–1812

Born, in Dublin, 4 Oct. 1741. Early education at private school in Dublin. To Trin. Col., Dublin, 1756; scholar, 1760; B. A., 1762. [Visit] To England, 1759. Student of Inner Temple, 1763. Friendship with Dr. Johnson begun, 1765. Travelled in France, 1766–67. Called to Irish Bar at King's Inns, 1767. Contrib. to Irish periodicals. Settled in London, May 1777. Resided there till his death. Mem. of Literary Club, 1782. Friendship with Boswell begun, 1785; assisted him in preparing "Life of Johnson" for press. Engaged in Shakespearean criticism. Hon. D. C. L., Oxford, 5 July 1793. Hon LL.D., Dublin, 1801. Unmarried. Died, in London, 25 May 1812. Buried in Kilbixy Churchyard. *Works:* "Attempt to ascertain the order in which the Plays of Shakespeare were written," 1778; "Supplement to Johnson's edn. of Shakespeare" (anon.), 1780; "Cursory Obseravtions on the Poems attributed to Thomas Rowley" (anon.), 1782. "A Second Appendix to Mr. Malone's Supplement," 1783; "A Dissertation on the three parts of 'King Henry VI.,'" 1787. "Letter to the Rev. R. Farmer," 1792; "An Enquiry into the Authenticity of certain papers" [the Ireland Forgeries], 1796; "An Account of the incidents from which the title and part of the story of Shakespeare's Tempest was derived" (priv. ptd.), 1808. "Biographical Memoir of W. Windham" (anon.), 1810. *Posthumous:* "Correspondence . . . with the Rev. J. Davenport," ed. by J. O. Halliwell, 1864; "Original Letters . . . to J. Jordan," ed. by J. O. Halliwell, 1864. He *edited:* "The Tragicall Hystory of Romeus and Juliet," 1780; Goldsmith's Works, 1780; Shakespeare's Works (11 vols.), 1790; Sir Joshua Reynolds' "Writings," 1797; Dryden's Works (4 vols.), 1800; the 1807 edn. of Boswell's "Life of Johnson;" Hamilton's "Parliamentary Logick," 1808. *Life:* by Sir James Prior, 1860.—SHARP, R. FARQUHARSON, 1897, *A Dictionary of English Authors, p.* 184.

PERSONAL

I have just dipped far enough into Mr. Malone's edition of Shakspeare to find he has not been sparing of his epithets whenever he has occasion to introduce me to the notice of his readers. In fact, I believe I originally gave him some little provocation. But I thought your countrymen had been remarkable rather for the suddenness of their anger than the duration of their malignity. Have the morals of this worthy editor been corrupted by his long residence amongst us?—RITSON, JOSEPH, 1790, *To Mr. Walker, Dec.* 14; *Letters, ed. Nicolas, vol.* I, *p.* 181.

I had the melancholy task of announcing to him the death of our excellent friend, Mr. Malone. I am unable to name in the large circle of Mr. Kemble's acquaintance, any gentleman for whom he had a more perfect esteem. He frequently alluded, in conversation to the elegance of his manners; and delighted to quote him, as one of the best illustrations of the old school. As a commentator upon Shakespeare, Mr. Kemble greatly preferred Mr. Malone; because he saw in him unwearied diligence and most scrupulous accuracy; with an utter rejection of that impertinent self-display which had discredited, on too many occasions, the wit, the learning, and the labour of some of his rivals.—BOADEN, JAMES, 1825, *Memoirs of the Life of John Philip Kemble, vol.* II, *p.* 544.

EDITIONS OF SHAKESPEARE

The heaviest of all books, Mr. Malone's "Shakspeare," in ten thick octavos, with notes, that are an extract of all the opium that is spread through the works of all the bad play-wrights of that age : mercy on the poor gentleman's patience!—WALPOLE, HORACE, 1791, *To the Miss Berrys, June* 14; *Letters, ed. Cunningham, vol.* IX, *p.* 326.

His pages abound with profound ignorance, idle conjectures, crude notions, feeble attempts at jocularity.—RITSON, JOSEPH, 1792, *Cursory Criticism.*

Hylactor means a dog with a clear and strong voice : One would think that "this dog" was one of Canidia's breed, which called from the sepulchre the actual remains of the dead to enchant and stupefy the living. This dog has been scratching up the earth about "Doctors Commons," and has torn up all "the Wills" of the actors who lived in Shakspeare's time, and carried them in his mouth to the printer of a late edition of that author.—MATHIAS, THOMAS JAMES, 1794, *The Pursuits of Literature, p.* 97.

Rival editors have recourse to necromancy to know from Shakspere himself who of them is the fittest to edit and illustrate him. Describe the meeting, the ceremonies of conjuration, the appearance of the spirit, the effect on the rival invokers. When they have resumed courage, the arbiter appointed by them asks the question. They listen,—Malone leaps up while the rest lay their heads at the same instant that the arbiter reëchoes the words of the spirit, "Let Malone!" The spirit shudders, then exclaims in the dread and angry utterance of the dead, "No! no! Let me alone, I said, inexorable boobies!" O that eternal bricker-up of Shakspere! Registers, memorandum-books—and that Bill, Jack, and Harry; Tom, Walter, and Gregory; Charles, Dick, and Jim, lived at that house, but that nothing more is known of them. But, oh! the importance when half a dozen players'-bills can be made to stretch through half a hundred or more of pages, though there is not one word in them that by any force can be made either to illustrate the times or life or writings

of Shakspere, or, indeed, of any time. And yet, no edition but this gentleman's name *burs* upon it—*burglossa* with a vengeance. Like the genitive plural of a Greek adjective, it is Malone, Malone, Malone, Μαλῶν, Μαλῶν, Μαλῶν.—COLERIDGE, SAMUEL TAYLOR, 1804, *Anima Poetæ, p.* 74.

Allied to this library in the general complexion of its literary treasures is that of Marcellus; while in the possession of numberless rare and precious volumes relating to the drama, and especially his beloved Shakespeare, it must be acknowledged that Marcellus hath somewhat the superiority. Meritorious as have been his labours in the illustration of our immortal bard, he is yet as zealous, vigilant, and anxious as ever to accumulate everything which may tend to the further illustration of him.—DIBDIN, THOMAS FROGNALL, 1811, *Bibliomania.*

Malone and Steevens were two laborious commentators on the meaning of words and phrases; one dull, the other clever ; but the dulness was accompanied by candor and a love of truth; the cleverness, by a total absence of both. Neither seems to have had a full discernment of Shakspeare's genius.—HALLAM, HENRY, 1837–39, *Introduction to the Literature of Europe, pt.* iii, *ch.* vi, *par.* 54.

Malone professes the same anxiety to adhere to the genuine text of Shakspere as Steevens had professed before him ; but he opened a wide field for editorial licence, in his principle of making up a text out of the folio edition and the previous quartos; and, to add to the apparent value of his own labours, he exaggerated, as others have since done, the real value of these quartos.—KNIGHT, CHARLES, 1845, *Studies of Shakspere, p.* 548.

Though not highly accomplished, he was a scholar, a man of good judgment, and, for his day, of good poetical taste. He was patient, indefatigably laborious, and modest—that is, as modest as it was possible for a Shakesperian critic and editor of the last century to be. Above all, he was honestly devoted to his task; he sought the glory of his author, not his own—except in so far as the latter was involved in the former. We of to-day can see that he committed many and great blunders ; but he saved the text of Shakespeare from wide and ruthless outrage, and by painful and well-directed investigation into the literature and manners contemporary with his author, cast new light upon his pages. To Edmund Malone the readers of Shakespeare during the last decade of the last century, and the first quarter of this, were indebted for the preservation of his works in a condition nearly approaching their original integrity. — WHITE, RICHARD GRANT, 1854, *Shakespeare's Scholar, p.* 19.

In the eighteenth century the persistent raillery of Voltaire ended in producing in England a certain waking up. Garrick, whilst correcting Shakespeare, played him, and acknowledged that it was Shakespeare that he played. They reprinted him at Glasgow. An imbecile, Malone, made commentaries on his plays, and, as a logical sequence, whitewashed his tomb. There was on this tomb a little bust, of a doubtful resemblance, and moderate as a work of art; but, what made it a subject of reverence, contemporaneous with Shakespeare. It is after this bust that all the portraits of Shakespeare have been made that we now see. The bust was whitewashed. Malone, critic and whitewasher of Shakespeare, spread a coat of plaster on his face, of idiotic nonsense on his work.—HUGO, VICTOR, 1864, *William Shakespeare, tr. Baillot, p.* 26.

He depended with greater fidelity than any of his predecessors on the early editions; and in Shakespearean biography and theatrical history he brought together more that was new and important than any predecessor or successor. But when he attempted original textual emendation, his defective ear became lamentably apparent. His intellect lacked the alertness characteristic of Steevens or Gifford.— LEE, SIDNEY, 1893, *Dictionary of National Biography, vol.* XXXV, *p.* 437.

GENERAL

From the perusal of Mr. Malone's Inquiry, it must appear evident to the meanest capacity that the commentator never dreamed of an opponent, although he ventured to peep into the court of Apollo during his drowsy fit: for after his conclusions are drawn upon each topic of discussion, his pages are so conceitedly interlarded with "Let us no longer hear of this"—"I trust we shall hear no more of that," and an hundred *et-ceteræ* of the same nature, that it should appear as if

Mr. Malone's fiat was irrevocable; whereas, from the perusal of Mr. Chalmer's Apology and Supplement, the facts in them exhibited and the just conclusions drawn, it is obvious that Malone was not only dreaming of Parnassus, but absolutely in a doze from the beginning to the termination of his boasted inquiry.—IRELAND, WILLIAM-HENRY, 1805, *Confessions, p.* 288.

In Malone was exhibited the character of all our dull and tasteless *Life writers, editors,* and *critics* for half a century past. —HURD, RICHARD, 1808? *Commonplace Book, ed. Kilvert, p.* 248.

Malone forms a striking example of a life devoted almost to one literary pursuit. The object indeed was not personal but national, having employed, more pens and given birth to more readers and admirers in our island than any other literary topic whatever. For this he forsook law, wealth, and probably station for unprofitable literature; and proved beyond most other men fitted for the occupation. . . . A few, not acquainted with the peculiarities of his line of studies, deemed them little more than dalliance with letters—a kind of agreeable disporting over the green fields of literature. They knew not the labours it involved; the occasional difficulties of access to the places where deposited; the interminable research, the exhausted patience, eyes, and frames of which I have in him endeavoured to depict an outline. None of his predecessors had attempted what he accomplished. Few of his successors have, on most points, added materially to our knowledge. When assailed for excess of accuracy by the idle or superficial, he disdained reply. He was studious, and selected an object of popular study; inquiring, and left nothing unexplored likely to afford information; reflective, and therefore usually accurate in drawing conclusions where positive testimony was at fault. His talents were steady and practical; his learning extensive; his critical judgments, as we have seen in the preceding pages, sound. He who could throw light upon the career of Shakspeare and Dryden—give us the first and best history of the Stage—and leave, for our study and guidance volumes at Oxford which no other spot supplies, must be considered no small benefactor to letters.—PRIOR, SIR JAMES, 1860, *Life of Edmond Malone, pp.* 322, 331.

Henry James Pye
1745–1813

Born, in London, 20 Feb. 1745.   Early education at home.   Matric., Magdalen Coll., Oxford, 12 July 1762; created M. A. 3 July 1766.   Married (i) Mary Hook, 1766. Created D. C. L., Oxford, 9 July 1773.   M. P. for Berkshire, 1784–90.   Appointed Poet Laureate, 1790.   Police Magistrate for Westminster, 1792.   Play "The Siege of Meaux" produced at Covent Garden, 19 May 1794; "Adelaide," Drury Lane, 25 Jan. 1800.   "A Prior Claim" (written with S. J. Arnold), Drury Lane, 29 Oct. 1805. Wife died, 1796.   Married (ii) Martha Corbett, Nov. 1801.   Died at Pinner, 11 Aug. 1813.   Works: "the Rosciad of Covent Garden" (anon. ; attrib. to Pye), 1762; "Beauty" (anon.), 1766; "Elegies (anon.), 1768; "The Triumph of Fashion" (anon.), 1771; "Farringdon Hill" (anon.), 1774.   "The Progress of Refinement," 1783; "Shooting" (anon.), 1784; "Aeriphorion," 1784; "Poems" (collected), 1787; "Amusement" 1790; "The Siege of Meaux," 1794; "The Democrat" (anon.), 1795; "War Elegies of Tyrtæus imitated," 1795; "Sketches on Various Subjects," (anon.), 1796; "Naucratia" 1798; "The Inquisitor" (with J. P. Andrews), 1798; "The Aristocrat" (anon.), 1799; "Carmen Seculare" 1800; "Adelaide," 1800; "Alfred," 1801; "Verses on Several Subjects," 1802; "A Prior Claim" (with S. J. Arnold), 1805; "Comments on the Commentators of Shakespeare," 1807; "Summary of the Duties of a Justice of the Peace out of Sessions," 1808.   He *translated:* "Six Olympic Odes of Pindar," 1775; Aristotle's "Poetics," 1788; Bürger's "Lenore," 1796; Homer's "Hymns and Epigrams," 1810; and edited: Francis's translation of the Odes of Horace, 1812.—SHARP, R. FARQUHARSON, 1897, *A Dictionary of English Authors, p.* 234.

PERSONAL

"Mr. Pye"—a celebrity whom even the encyclopædias scorn, and of whom we know nothing save that he was Poet-Laureate (!) before Southey took and vindicated the office. He was "a master of correct versification," Lord Beaconsfield says.—OLIPHANT, MARGARET O. W.,1882, *The Literary History of England, XVIIIth-XIXth Century, vol.* II, *p.* 313.

Byron said of him that he was eminently respectable in everything but his poetry. This, indeed, appears to have been the case, but certainly affords no reasonable explanation of his appointment to the office of Laureate. . . . As Pye was a pleasant, convivial man, it was somewhat peculiar that the Laureate's annual perquisite of a tierce of canary from the Royal cellar, should, during his tenure of the office, have been commuted for an annual payment of £27.—HAMILTON, WALTER, 1879, *The Poets Laureate of England, pp.* 203, 214.

He doubtless owed his good fortune to the support he had given the prime minister, Pitt, while he sat in the House of Commons. No selection could have more effectually deprived the post of reputable literary associations, and a satire, "Epistle to the Poet Laureate," 1790, gave voice to the scorn with which, in literary circles,

the announcement of his appointment was received. . . . Every year on the king's birthday he produced an ode breathing the most irreproachable patriotic sentiment, expressed in language of ludicrous tameness. His earliest effort was so crowded with allusions to vocal groves and feathered choir that George Steevens, on reading it, broke out into the lines :

> And when the *pie* was opened
> The birds began to sing;
> And wasn't that a dainty dish
> To set before the king?

—LEE, SIDNEY, 1896, *Dictionary of National Biography, vol.* XLVII, *pp.* 68, 69.

GENERAL

I have been rhyming as doggedly and as dully as if my name had been Henry James Pye.—SOUTHEY, ROBERT, 1814, *Letter to G. C. Bedford, Life and Correspondence, ch.* xix.

> The monarch, mute till then, exclaimed,
> "What! what!
> *Pye* come again? No more—no more of that!"

—BYRON, LORD, 1824, *The Vision of Judgment.*

We must admit that, as a poet, his Muse's chief attributes are Mediocrity and Morality. . . . An industrious student, a well-informed, cultivated, graceful writer ; but a poet he assuredly was not. Weighed in the balance of contemporaneous criticisms, he was found wanting; and Time has sanctioned the severe decree.—AUSTIN, WILLSHIRE STANTON, JR., AND RALPH, J., 1853, *Lives of the Poets-Laureate, pp.* 333, 345.

He was always made fun of as a poet, and, unfortunately for him, there was another poet in the House at the same time called Charles Small Pybus; hence the jest, "Pye et Parvus Pybus," which was in everyone's mouth. He was a voluminous author and diligent translator, but I do not recollect ever seeing a single book of his in a shop, or on a stall, or in a catalogue. Great Pye is dead—as dead as Parvus Pybus, M. P.—BIRRELL, AUGUSTINE, 1894, *Essays about Men, Women and Books, p.* 165.

Pye was devoted to the stage, and he tried his hand at writing some plays, but they are wholly forgotten. For a complete list of these we have to go to a foreign dictionary: English encyclopædias ignore this industrious, conscientious worker.

Pye's most ambitious work was an epic poem on King Alfred, but even he himself did not speak highly of his effort, and he had no hope that it would live. Indeed, Pye was as modest as Eusden had been egotistical. The contrast between them in this respect is well illustrated in their portraits. . . . Many of Pye's minor poems show graceful fancy and have considerable melody of versification and sparkle of style; but there is no originality of thought in them, no eloquent fervour, no imaginative strength. They are rhetorical efforts merely. His laureate odes are ardent and enthusiastic, even if they do not soar very high. He shows in them an earnest patriotism; and earnestness of itself is a form of strength and power. But Pye, with all his brilliancy of mind and his perseverance and industry, had not the making of a true poet, and his work has passed into oblivion.—HOWLAND, FRANCES, 1895, *The Laureates of England, p.* 142.

Alexander Wilson

1766–1813.

Born at Paisley, Scotland, July 6, 1766; died at Philadelphia, Aug. 23, 1813. A Scotch-American ornithologist.· In early life he was a weaver; was prosecuted and imprisoned for writing lampoons (in the dispute between the weavers and manufacturers at Paisley); emigrated to the United States in 1794; labored as a peddler, schoolmaster, and editor of an edition of "Rees's Cyclopædia;" and made many pedestrian and other expeditions through the country. He published "American Ornithology" (7 vols. 1808–1813; vols. 8 and 9 edited after his death; supplement by C. L. Bonaparte, 1825), poems (1791), "The Foresters" (1805), etc. His collected works were edited by Grosart (1876).—SMITH, BENJAMIN E., 1894–97, *The Century Cyclopædia of Names, p.* 1065.

PERSONAL

This Monument
covers the Remains of
Alexander Wilson,
Author of the
AMERICAN ORNITHOLOGY,
He was born in Renfrewshire, Scotland,
on the 6th of July, 1766;
Emigrated to the United States
in the year 1794;
and died in Philadelphia,
of the Dysentery,
on the 23d of August, 1813,
Aged 47.
—INSCRIPTION ON MONUMENT IN THE CEMETERY OF THE SWEDISH CHURCH, *Southwark, Philadelphia.*

The library of Wilson occupied but a small space. On casting my eyes, after his decease, over the ten or a dozen volumes of which it was composed, I was grieved to find that he had been the owner of only *one* work on Ornithology, and that was Bewick's "British Birds." For the use of the first volume of Turton's "Linnæus," he was indebted to the friendship of Mr. Thomas Say; the Philadelphia Library supplied him with "Latham."—ORD, GEORGE, 1825, *Life of Wilson.*

One fair morning I was surprised by the sudden entrance into our counting-room, at Louisville, of Mr. Alexander Wilson, the celebrated author of the "American Ornithology," of whose existence I had never until that moment been appraised. This happened in March 1810. How well do I remember him, as then he walked up to me! His long, rather hooked nose, the keenness of his eye, and his prominent cheek-bones, stamped his countenance with a peculiar character. His dress, too, was of a kind not usually seen in that part of the country; a short coat, trowsers, and a waistcoat of gray cloth. His stature was not above middle size. He had two volumes under his arm; and, as he approached the table at which I was working, I discovered something like astonishment in his countenance.—AUDUBON, JOHN JAMES, 1839? *American Ornithological Biography.*

Mr. Bradford, the same liberal patron who enabled me to study painting, enabled Wilson to publish the most interesting account of birds, and to illustrate it with the best representations of their forms and colours, that has ever appeared. Wilson was engaged by Mr. Bradford as tutor to his sons, and as editor of the American edition of Rees's "Cyclopædia," while at the same time he was advancing his "Ornithology" for publication. I assisted him to colour some of its first plates. We worked from birds which he had shot and stuffed, and I well remember the extreme accuracy of his drawings, and how carefully he had counted the number of scales on the tiny legs and feet of his subject. He looked like a bird; his eyes were piercing, dark, and luminous, and his nose shaped like a beak. He was of a spare bony form, very erect in his carriage, inclining to be tall; and with a light elastic step, he seemed perfectly qualified by nature for his extraordinary pedestrian achievements.— LESLIE, CHARLES ROBERT, 1860, *Autobiographical Recollections, ed. Taylor, ch.* xii.

His personal appearance was that of a modest, rather retiring man, of good countenance, not decidedly Scotch, but still with a cast of it, rather more like a New England Congregational clergyman in his black dress than any other description I can give. He was held in great esteem for probity, gentle manners, and accomplishments in his special branch of natural science.—BINNEY, HORACE, 1873, *Letter to James Grant Wilson, Feb.* 8; *The Poets and Poetry of Scotland, vol.* I, *p.* 420.

Thus closed a life and a work which, it is no exaggeration to say, are without a parallel. When Wilson's deprivations are borne in mind,—that his early instruction was scant and contemptible; that, as a boy,

he was put at an uncongenial occupation, which formed his means of livelihood through nearly half his days; that his was a lifelong struggle with difficulties, which only the sheer indomitable resolution of a man never cheerful or sanguine enabled him to surmount; that he was thirty years of age when, in a strange land, he effected his own education by becoming the instructor of others; that he was thirty-three when he began the study of ornithology, with scarcely any resources beyond his own powers of observation, and the practice of drawing without any previously suspected aptitude; that he was forty years old before an opportunity disclosed itself for the commencement of his work, forty-two when he first accomplished publication, and only forty-seven when his life was closed,—it must be admitted that few careers so brief have been equally productive.—GARDNER, DORSEY, 1876, *Wilson the Ornithologist, Scribner's Monthly vol.* 11, *pp.* 702.

POEMS

In his humor and feeling Wilson, as a poet, belongs to the family of Burns. He addresses his friends in verse with the old loving feeling of Scottish brotherhood, has his song for love and beauty, and his similar choice of subject in ludicrous tale or ballad, with a smarting sense of wrong and poverty; while an early observation in natural history, and his pursuit of descriptive poetry, belong especially to Wilson the naturalist. . . . In that fine descriptive poem of the "Foresters," in which he describes an October journey through Pennsylvania, and across the Alleghanies from Philadelphia to Niagara, the reader may have a true enjoyment of his poetic tastes and of his ardent love of nature and adventure.—DUYCKINCK, EVERT A., AND GEORGE L., 1855–65–75, *Cyclopædia of American Literature, ed. Simons, vol.* I, *pp.* 570, 571.

I have placed "Watty and Meg, or the Wife Reformed: a Tale" in the fore-front of the "Poems." It is *unique* in our literature. "Christ's Kirk on the Green" and the "Midden Fecht" have *bits* perhaps as effective in homely portraiture. But as a whole it stands alone for rough, coarse, realistic painting. It isn't altogether such a scene or incident as many would elect to paint, any more than one would those drinking groups which in Ostade and

Teniers give renown to a gallery; but having been chosen I know not where to look for such raciness, vigour, genuineness. Only a native-born Scotchman can take in the *flavour* of its thoroughly Scotch wording and *motif*. But he is an emasculated Scot who does not relish it all through. Hector Macneil's "Will and Jean" is a thin, vapid, namby-pamby production beside it.—GROSART, ALEXANDER B., 1876, *ed.*, *The Poems and Literary Prose of Alexander Wilson*, *Essay*, *vol.* II, *p.* x.

More famous though he certainly is in other fields, the great American ornithologist is also a claimant for a place of honour among the poets of his native country. . . . "Watty and Meg," from the popularity of its subject—the reform of a scolding wife by a threat of leaving her —has generally been placed first among Wilson's compositions. Nothwithstanding its high merits, however, of vividness and realism, it is handicapped heavily by the four-line trochaic measure in which it is written, and it does not appear unjust to say that it contains nothing which might not have been as well expressed in prose. The best qualities of Wilson's genius—the graphic touches by which whole scenes of the peasant life in Scotland are brought vividly before the eye, and a happiness of epithet which gives the freshness in individuality to its work—are to be found, with a higher quality of art, in his slightly longer piece, "The Laurel Disputed."— EYRE-TODD, GEORGE, 1896, *Scottish Poetry of the Eighteenth Century*, *vol.* II, *pp.* 284, 285.

He commended his wares even in poetic broadsides, and dealt not ungraciously with Scottish dialect at a time when Burns was singing; indeed his longest dialect poem was for some time attributed to Burns—only by the unwary, however. 'Tis hard to listen contentedly to the chirping of a sparrow, when a thrush (like Burns) fills the air with melody. But Wilson's verses, written on this side of the water, after he had made a tramp across the Alleghanies, are not to be scorned, and are without the grossness which belongs to many of his dialect poems.—MITCHELL, DONALD G., 1897, *American Lands and Letters, The Mayflower to Rip-Van-Winkle, p.* 199.

In Alexander Wilson's "The Foresters"

(1809), the humble home of a Pennsylvania Dutch farmer is pictured with courageous truth of detail. . . . In its neat perspective this sketch of a landscape as seen from a mountain-top resembles passages from Cowper.—BRONSON, WALTER C., 1900, *A Short History of American Literature, p.* 84.

AMERICAN ORNITHOLOGY
1808–13

"The Ornithology" of this naturalist, we look upon as quite a magnificent affair for America. The plates are good; colouring fine; typography capital; editorial matter excellent.—NEAL, JOHN, 1825, *American Writers*, *Blackwood's Magazine, vol.* 17, *p.* 204.

All his pencil or pen has touched is established incontestably: by the plate, description, and history he has always determined his bird so obviously as to defy criticism and prevent future mistake. . . . We may add, without hesitation, that such a work as he has published in a new country is still a *desideratum* in Europe. —BONAPARTE, CHARLES LUCIEN, 1825–33, *Wilson's American Ornithology.*

It is as an ornithologist that Wilson's fame will last for after ages. . . . Wilson was an observing naturalist; and, perhaps, Nature never had a more ardent pursuer. His object was to illustrate the different birds in their various states, as closely to the truth as possible, and to describe those parts of their manners which he could from actual observation, throwing aside all hearsay evidence and seldom indulging in any theories of classification, or the scale they hold in Nature. It is from these circumstances that his work derives its worth; the facts can be confidently quoted as authentic, and their value depended on in our reasonings upon their history—their migrations—their geographical distribution.—JARDINE, SIR WILLIAM, 1832, *ed. Wilson's American Ornithology, Life.*

There are few examples to be found in literary history of resolution equal to that of Wilson. Though he was made fully aware, both by his friends and his own reflections, of the difficulty of the enterprise in which he was engaged, his heart never for a moment failed him. By his agreement with his publisher, he bound himself to furnish the drawings and descriptions for the work, indeed everything, except the mechanical execution. To procure the materials, he was obliged to encounter heavy expenses; and the money which he received for *coloring the plates*, was the only revenue from which he defrayed them. It is easy to imagine the difficulties which he must have encountered; but his success was complete; and though he did not live to enjoy, he certainly anticipated, what has come to pass; that his work would always be regarded as a subject of pride by his adopted country, and would secure immortal 'honor for him whose name it bears.—PEABODY, WILLIAM B. O., 1834, *Alexander Wilson, Sparks' Library of American Biography, vol.* II, *p.* 168.

Alexander Wilson was the great pioneer in this branch of American science; and who that appreciates his chaste and eloquent style, his accurate and happy delineation of a class of the most lovely objects in nature, can fail to experience the greatest delight in reviewing the pages of the "American Ornithology?"—TOWNSEND, JOHN K., 1839, *Ornithology of the United States, Introduction.*

One of the most splendid works of Natural History ever produced. . . . No learned society gave it encouragement; no distinguished name in the world of science was its author. A poor Scotch peddler, who had left his native country in the hope of bettering his fortune, was the writer and the artist who, unaided except by the general public support, produced the most superb book of its class that the world had then seen. . . . Well did he deserve his hard-earned fame. As a writer he has a merit which seldom belongs to systematic naturalists; his descriptions are at once accurate and brilliant. He looks at Nature with the eye of a poet; he describes with an exactness which might satisfy the most rigid classifier.—KNIGHT, CHARLES, 1847–48, *Half-Hours with the Best Authors, vol.* II, *pp.* 137, 138.

The types, which were very beautiful, were cast in America; and though at that time paper was largely imported, he (Mr. Bradford) determined that the paper should be of American manufacture; and I remember that Amies, the papermaker, carried his patriotism so far that he declared that he would use only American rags in making it. The result was that the book far surpassed any other that had appeared in that country, and I apprehend, though it may have been equalled in typography, has not before or since been equalled in its matter or its plates. Bewick comes nearest to it; but his accounts of birds are not so full and complete, and his figures, admirably characteristic and complete as they are in form, have not the advantage of the much larger scale of Wilson's, or of colour. Unfortunately Wilson's book was necessarily expensive, and therefore not remunerative; but nothing discouraged him.—LESLIE, CHARLES ROBERT, 1860, *Autobiographical Recollections, ed. Taylor, ch.* xii.

Like Audubon, and like every great Ornithologist worthy of the name, Wilson was a poet as well as a man of science. He had an eye to see the beauty of the bird's life as well as of his plumage, and records the doings and ways of his little friends with the fondness of a lover and the imagination of an artist. Wilson's intense love for his subject and the intrinsic beauty of the theme itself seem to have had a transforming and educating influence on the man. When writing on some favorite bird he is no longer the mere scientific naturalist, but rises into the region of poetic fancy. There is nothing in Irving or Goldsmith finer, as mere literary efforts, than some of Wilson's descriptions of the birds of his acquaintance. —HART, JOHN S., 1872, *A Manual of American Literature, p.* 118.

His labors were not merely in a field in which he had to open a new path, but where the steps that had been taken were false and misleading, and in which there were but few fellow-travelers. His journeys, largely performed on foot, exceeded ten thousand miles. His work was unappreciated by those to whom he had the clearest right to appeal, and patronage was withheld by almost every incumbent of exalted position. Nevertheless, though discouraged by neglect, and hampered not merely by poverty, but by the necessity of succoring those in still deeper need than himself, he both laid the foundation for the study of natural history on this continent and bequeathed to his successors the outlines for its subsequent development; and he described the habits of American birds with fidelity to truth, graphic vigor, and a poetical realization of the beauties of

nature.—GARDNER, DORSEY, 1876, *Scribner's Monthly, vol.* 11, *p.* 703.

Wilson was no compiler ; he took his facts
from his own observations, or the accounts
of those who had known the birds for a
lifetime.—YOUMANS, WILLIAM JAY, 1896,
ed., *Pioneers of Science in America, p.* 98.

GENERAL

In the strictest sense of the term,
Wilson was a man of genius, his perceptions were quick, his impressions vivid ; a
bright glow of feeling breathes through
his compositions. In the professed walks
of poetry his attempts were not often
fortunate, but his prose writings partake
of the genuine poetic spirit; a lively
fancy, exuberance of thought, and minute
observation of the natural world, are
strongly indicated in whatever has flowed
from his pen.—SPARKS, JARED, 1827, *North
American Review, vol.* 24, *p.* 116.

Alexander Wilson was a remarkable
man. He was a great naturalist, a fair
poet, and an honest, upright gentleman,
bearing his hard won, tardy honors and
fame as gracefully as he had borne poverty
and obscurity. His "American Ornithology" must ever remain a classic.—COYLE,
HENRY, 1893, *Alexander Wilson, The
Chautauquan, vol.* 18, *p.* 184.

Wilson's life and writings will always
appeal to the general reader. Even to the
ornithologist, the personality of the man
and the vitality of his work are the chief
charms. The poem on the "Fish-Hawk"
is full of the strong, fresh breeze and
local color of the beaches, and that on
"The Bluebird"—"Wilson's Bluebird"—
breathes the free, open air of the country-side. — TROTTER, SPENCER, 1897,
Library of the World's Best Literature,
ed. *Warner, vol.* XXVII, *p.* 16018.

Charles Dibdin

1745-1814

Charles Dibdin was born in Southampton, England, in 1745. His mother was fifty
years old at the time of his birth, and he was her eighteenth child. He studied music,
and in 1761 went to London, where he composed ballads and tuned pianos. He also
wrote at this time an opera entitled "The Shepherd's Artifice," which was put upon
the stage at Covent Garden Theatre in 1763. He then became a professional actor
and composer, and produced "The Padlock," "The Deserter," "The Waterman,"
"The Quaker," and other pieces, all of which were brought out at Drury Lane Theatre
under Garrick's management, and in several of which Dibdin himself took part. In
1778 he became musical manager at Covent Garden, and a few years afterwards he
built the Surrey. In 1788 he published his "Musical Tour ;" and in 1789 he began an
entertainment called "The Whim of the Moment," in which he was the sole author
and performer. It was immensely successful, and in 1796 a small theatre, called
Sans Souci, was built for it. Here he performed for nine years, retiring from the
boards in 1805. In spite of his professional success, and a pension of £200 a year
which was awarded him in 1805, he was poor to the end of his days. He died on July
25, 1814. Dibdin wrote "A Complete History of the Stage," published in 1795, an
autobiography, from fifty to a hundred dramatic pieces, and something like a thousand
songs. His fame now rests upon his sea-songs, some of which, it is said, have been
quoted with good effect in cases of mutiny. "Poor Tom Bowling" was written on the
death of his eldest brother, captain of an Indiaman. A fine edition of the songs,
illustrated by Cruikshank, with a memoir by Thomas Dibdin, was published in 1850.—
JOHNSON, ROSSITER, 1875, *Little Classics, Authors, p.* 76.

PERSONAL

His form was of the manliest beauty,
  His heart was kind and soft,
Faithful, below, he did his duty,
  But now he's gone aloft.
—INSCRIPTION ON TOMB, *St. Martin's,
Camden Town.*

Charles Dibdin's method of composition,
or rather the absence of it, is illustrated

in the story of his lamenting his lack of a
new subject, while under the hairdresser's
hand, in a cloud of powder, in his rooms
in the Strand, preparing for his night's
"entertainment." The friend that was
with him suggested various topics—but all
of a sudden the jar of a ladder sounded
against the lamp-iron, and Dibdin exclaimed, "The lamplighter ! a good notion,"

—and at once began humming and fingering on his knee. As soon as his head was dressed, he stepped to the piano, finished off both music and words, and that very night sang "Jolly Dick, the Lamplighter" at the theatre, nor could he, we are assured, on critical authority, have well made a greater hit if the song had been the deliberate work of two authors—one for the words, another for the air—and had taken weeks to finish it, and been elaborated in studious leisure, instead of the distraction of dressing-room din.—JACOX, FRANCIS, 1872, *Aspects of Authorship, p.* 19.

He was popular with the public, but, thanks to the close monopoly which theatrical affairs were then subject to, he could not reach that public in the ordinary way. . . . Dibdin had quite as ill treatment as Burns, although his follies were not so great or so gross; but he was of tougher material, and did not drink, and so lived his evil days down; while the other perished miserably in the flower of his manhood.—DIBDIN, EDWARD RIMBAULT, 1886, *Dibdin at Sea, Temple Bar, vol.* 78, *p.* 348.

Dibdin's ambition seems to have been not so much in the direction of future fame as of universal recognition during his life-time. His appears to have been the kind of nature which is spurred on better by the shout of the multitude than by the "well done" of the conscience . . . Perhaps Dibdin might have been more content to work and live for posterity if the nation had only been capable of supplying him with funds for the needs of the present. Poet though he was, he had strong leanings towards the practical. If he had been asked to decide between the cabbage and the rose, he would have undoubtedly voted for the cabbage. While other composers might feel flattered by having their songs echoed through the streets on barrel organs and other mediums of musical torture, *he* only regretted that there could be no tangible participation in the popularity. His sea-songs had undoubtedly been a powerful influence for good, yet, with a depth of sarcasm, which he had always at command, he tells us that before 1802 the only symptom of acknowledgment he ever received was a hearty shake of the hand from Admiral Gardner, "when I gave him my vote for Westminster."—HADDEN, J. CUTHBERT, 1889, *Charles Dibdin, Gentleman's Magazine, vol.* 267, *pp.* 567, 568.

GENERAL

These "Songs" have been the solace of sailors in long voyages, in storms, in battles; and they have been quoted in mutinies to the restoration of order and discipline.—DIBDIN, THOMAS, 1850, *ed., Sea-Songs, Memoir.*

One man—a man without any great musical or nautical knowledge—has given poetic and musical utterance to the deep passion of the English nation for the sea, and done more to set up a standard type for the British sailor than any number of navy regulations. Wherever an English ship is found, beneath the tropical sun or in the ice of the poles, while an English sailor crosses the rolling deep, or Englishmen delight to speak of their country as the empress of the ocean, the name of Charles Dibdin will be known. His songs portray the sailor's strength and weakness, his valour afloat and his joviality ashore, the warmth of his heart and the force of his hand, his fidelity to King and flag,—in short, they lay open every throb of England's hearts of oak.—TOMPKINS, W. EARP, 1865, *Charles Dibdin the Ocean Minstrel, St. James's Magazine, vol.* 13, *p.* 480.

As a ballad writer, and as a composer of sea songs, Dibdin has made himself a name which will last as long as English poetry is read. . . . No man knew better how to please the popular taste.—BELLEW, J. C. M., 1866, *Poets' Corner, p.* 630.

The insertion of these ["Anchorsmiths"] grandly—simply, almost Homeric stanzas is due to the suggestion of Mr. W. E. Gladstone. — PALGRAVE, FRANCIS TURNER, 1875, *ed., The Children's Treasury of English Song, p.* 292, *note.*

Dibdin's fine "Anchorsmiths" I inserted in consequence of your praise of it some years ago. It is truly so much grander in style than his sea-songs, and so different in manner, that, except yourself, I have met with no one who knew it.—PALGRAVE, FRANCIS TURNER, 1875, *Letter to Mr. Gladstone, Oct.; Journals and Memories, ed. Palgrave, p.* 143.

The great merit of Dibdin's best songs, his sea-songs especially, words and music, in undeniable. His autobiography is dreary and egotistical in the extreme, and he is loose and inaccurate, whether by

defect of memory or by intentional distortion of truth. His sea-songs are full of generous sentiment and manly honesty. Somehow he cared less for a practical fulfillment of the ethics that he preached so well. He invented his own tunes, for the most part spirited and melodious, and in this surpassed Henry Carey beyond all comparison. They were admirably suited to his words. He boasted truly: "My songs have been the solace of sailors in long voyages, in storms, in battle; and they have been quoted in mutinies to the restoration of order and discipline." He brought more men into the navy in war time than all the press-gangs could. Exclusive of the "entertainments sans souci," commenced in 1797, with their 360 songs, he wrote nearly seventy dramatic pieces, and set to music production of other writers. He claimed nine hundred songs as his own, of which two hundred are repeatedly encored, ninety of them being sea-songs, and undoubtedly his master-work. He was a rapid worker. No one of his entertainments cost him more than a month; his best single songs generally half an hour, e. g. his "Sailor's Journal." Music and words came together.
—EBSWORTH, J. W., 1888, *Dictionary of National Biography, vol.* XV, *p.* 5.

Charles Dibdin—the author of half a hundred plays, and no less than fourteen hundred songs, to say nothing of a dozen or more novels, and a history of the stage. . . . In his day, his ballads and plays delighted countless thousands of his fellow countrymen; they stimulated good feelings, and were of immeasurable pleasure to our soldiers and sailors.—BRERETON, AUSTIN, 1888, *Tom Bowling, The Theatre, vol.* 20, *pp.* 136, 138.

There is perhaps a touch of cant and also of political purpose in it ["Tom Bowling"], here and there, but "The little cherub that sits up aloft" has grown into our literature, and embedded in it and in the popular estimation is the couplet—
"For my heart is my Poll's, and my rhino's my friend's,
And as for my life, 'tis the king's."
It is the philosophy of the true fighting British sailor now as it was in King George's day. Then again there are two verses which to the serious student of literature deserve all attention, for they show how the real, at times, trancends the ideal and the artificial, even in the most conventional periods of our literature.
"What argufies snivelling and piping your eye?
Why, what a damned fool you must be!"
—CRAWFURD, OSWALD, 1896, *ed., Lyrical Verse from Elizabeth to Victoria, p.* 433, *note.*

In all of these songs, whether the theme be his native land or the wind-swept seas that close it round, love is the poet's real inspiration; love of old England and her sovereign, love of the wealth-bringing ocean, love of the good ship that sails its waves. This fundamental affection for the things of which he sings has endeared the songs of Dibdin to the heart of the British sailor; and in this lies the proof of their genuineness. His songs are simple and melodious; there is a manly ring in their word and rhythm; they have the swagger and the fearlessness of the typical tar; they have, too, the beat of his true heart, his kindly waggery, his sturdy fidelity to his country and his king. There is nothing quite like them in any other literature.—WARNER, CHARLES DUDLEY, *ed.,* 1897, *Library of the World's Best Literature, vol.* VIII, *p.* 4621.

Charles Burney
1726-1814

Born, at Shrewsbury, 12 April 1726. Educated at Free School, Chester. To Shrewsbury, to study music, 1741 [?]. Articled as pupil to Dr. Arne, 1744; with him in London, 1744–47. Taken under patronage of Fulke Greville, 1747. Taught and composed music. Married Esther Sleepe, 1749. Organist of St. Dionis, Backchurch, 1749. Mem. of Roy. Soc. of Musicians, 3 Dec. 1749. Organist of Lynn Regis, 1751–60. Returned to London, 1760. Wife died, 1761. Married (privately) Mrs. Stephen Allen, 1767. Mus. Doc. degree, Oxford, June 1769. Travelled on Continent, 1770 and 1772. F. R. S., 1773. Organist of Chelsea Hospital, 1783. Mem. of Literary Club, 1784. Contrib. to "Monthly Review," 1790–93. Second wife died, Oct. 1796. Contrib. to Rees's "Encyclopædia," 1800–05. Crown pension granted, 1806. Foreign Member of Institut de France, 1810. Died, at Chelsea, 12 April 1814; buried in churchyard of Chelsea Hospital. *Works:* "Essay toward the History of the principal Comets, etc.," (anon.), 1769; "The Present State of Music in France and Italy," 1771; "The Present State of Music in Germany, the Netherlands, and the United Provinces," 1773; "History of Music," vol. i., 1776; vol. ii., 1782; vols. iii., iv., 1789; "Account of an Infant Musician," 1779; "An Account of the Musical Performances . . . in 1784 in Commemoration of Handel," 1785; "Memoir of the Life and Writings of Metastasio" (3 vols.), 1796. *Life:* by his daughter Frances, 1832.—SHARP, R. FARQUHARSON, 1897, *A Dictionary of English Authors*, p. 40.

PERSONAL

See next, happy contrast! in Burney combine
Every power to please, every talent to shine.
In professional science a second to none,
In social if second, through shyness alone.
So sits the sweet violet close to the ground,
Whilst holy-oaks and sunflowers flaunt it
    around.
His character formed free, confiding, and
    kind,
Grown cautious by habit, by station confined:
Though born to improve and enlighten our
    days,
In a supple facility fixes his praise;
And contented to soothe, unambitious to
    strike,
Has a faint praise from all men, from all
    men alike.
While thus the rich wines of Frontiniac im-
    part
Their sweets to our palate, their warmth to
    our heart,
All in praise of a liquor so luscious agree,
From the monarch of France to the wild
    Cherokee.
—PIOZZI, HESTER LYNCH, 1773? *The Streatham Portraits, Autobiography*, ed. *Hayward*, p. 256.

I never met with any person who had more decided talents for conversation, eminently seasoned with wit and humour, and these talents were so at command that he could exert them at will. He was remarkable for some sprightly story or witty *bon mot* just when he quitted a company, which seemed as much as to say, "There now, I have given you a dose which you may work upon in my absence." His society was greatly sought after by all classes, from the first nobility to the mere *homme de lettres*. He dressed expensively, always kept his carriage, and yet died worth about 15,000*l*, leaving a most capital library of curious books. His second wife was my wife's sister.—YOUNG, ARTHUR, 1820? *Autobiography*, ed., *Betham-Edwards*, p. 101.

Where the life has been as private as that of Dr. Burney, its history must necessarily be simple, and can have little further call upon the attention of the world, than that which may belong to a wish of tracing the progress of a nearly abandoned child, from a small village of Shropshire, to a man allowed throughout Europe to have risen to the head of his profession; and thence, setting his profession aside, to have been elevated to an intellectual rank in society, as a man of letters. "Though not first in the very line" with most of the eminent men of his day, Dr. Johnson and Mr. Burke, soaring above any contemporary mark, always, like senior wranglers excepted. And this height, to which, by means and resources all his own, he arose, the genius that impelled him to fame, the integrity that established his character, and the amiability that magnetized all hearts,—in the phrase of Dr. Johnson,—*to go forth to meet him*, were the only materials with which he worked his way.—D'ARBLAY, MME. (FANNY BURNEY), 1832, *Memoirs of Doctor Burney, Preface*, p. vii.

His mind, though not very powerful or capacious, was restlessly active; and, in the intervals of his professional pursuits, he had contrived to lay up much miscellaneous information. His attainments, the suavity of his temper, and the gentle simplicity of his manners, had obtained for him ready admission to the first literary circles.—MACAULAY, THOMAS BABINGTON, 1842, *Madame D'Arblay, Critical and Miscellaneous Essays*.

His place in social life was unique, being due to what Dr. Johnson implied to be an almost unique blending of a happy temper of mind, an affectionate disposition, gentle and attractive manners (having dignity in reserve should it be needed), with a very active and versatile intellect, and considerable acquirements. The charm of character and of manners, the "vivacity and readiness of wit," which made him the man of the eighteenth century who gained and *kept* the greatest number of friends, can now be brought before us only by the warmth of the praise of those friends; and of the love (rising to enthusiasm) of his children, to which the diaries that follow bear continuous testimony.— ELLIS, ANNIE RAINE, 1889, *ed., The Early Diary of Frances Burney, Preface, vol.* I, *p.* vii.

GENERAL

He [Johnson], gave much praise to his friend, Dr. Burney's elegant and entertaining "Travels," and told Mr. Seward that he had them in his eye, when writing his "Journey to the Western Islands of Scotland."—BOSWELL, JAMES, 1791-93, *Life of Samuel Johnson, ed. Hill, vol.* IV, *p.*215.

Dr. Burney's "History" is one continuous misrepresentation of English music and musicians, only rendered plausible by misquotation of every kind. . . . Burney carries his depreciation of English authors systematically throughout his work. . . . It is sufficient for my present purpose to say that Dr. Burney's "History" is written throughout in this strain. What with mistake, and what with misrepresentation, it can but mislead the reader as to English music or musicians; and from the slight search I have made into his early Italian authorities, I doubt whether even that portion is very reliable.—CHAPPELL, WILLIAM, 1855-59, *Popular Music of the Olden Time, Introduction, vol.* I, *pp.* vii, viii, ix.

Between the two rival histories, the public decision was loud and immediate in favour of Dr. Burney. Time has modified this opinion, and brought the merits of each work to their fair and proper level—adjudging to Burney the palm of style, arrangement, and amusing narrative, and to Hawkins the credit of minuter accuracy and deeper research, more particularly in parts interesting to the antiquary and the literary world in general.—RIMBAULT, EDWARD F., 1879, *A Dictionary of Music and Musicians, ed. Grove, vol.* I, *p.* 284.

The work was from the outset very successful, and was generally pronounced superior to the similar undertaking of Sir John Hawkins. . . . Both works are of the highest value, and form the foundation of nearly every English work on musical history which has appeared since; but Burney's is disfigured by the undue prominence he gives to the fashionable music of his own day, and the lack of appreciation he displays toward the compositions of the English schools of the preceding centuries. —SQUIRE, W. BARCLAY, 1886, *Dictionary of National Biography, vol.* VII, *p.* 417.

No list of his musical compositions is known to exist. His daughter admits that they were out of date even in her own day. No list of his many articles in the "Monthly Review," and the Cyclopædia of Abraham Rees, has ever been compiled; his "Tours" are less read than they might well be, and his "History of Music" has, in the very course and progress of Music, been superseded. The repute of his reputation survives.—ELLIS, ANNIE RAINE, 1889, *ed., The Early Diary of Frances Burney, Preface, vol.* I. *p.* vi.

Count Rumford
Sir Benjamin Thompson
1753-1814

Benjamin Thompson, Count Rumford. Born at Woburn, Mass., March 26, 1753: died at Auteuil, near Paris, Aug. 21, 1814. An American scientist and Bavarian administrator. Having been refused a commission in the Continental army, he offered his services to the British, and in 1776 was sent to England with despatches from General William Howe. Here he was given a place in the administrative service by Lord George Germaine, secretary of state for the colonies, and rose to the post of under-secretary of state (1780). He was elected a fellow of the Royal Society in 1779. On the retirement of his patron, he returned in 1781 to America, and raised in New York the "King's American Dragoons," of which he was commissioned lieutenant-colonel. He returned to England before the close of the war, and in 1784 accepted a confidential appointment with the rank of aide-de-camp and chamberlain at the Court of the Elector of Bavaria. He reorganized the military establishment of Bavaria, and introduced important economic and other reforms, with the result that he was rapidly promoted to the highest offices in the state, including those of commander-in-chief of the general Staff, minister of war, and superintendent of the police. He was created a count in the Holy Roman Empire in 1791. Owing to ill health he quitted Bavaria about 1798, and was for a time a private agent of Bavaria in England. He removed to Paris in 1802, and in 1804 married as his second wife the widow of the French chemist Lavoisier. The rest of his life was spent at his wife's villa in Auteuil. He gave $5,000 to the American Academy of Arts and Sciences and a like amount to the Royal Society of London to found prizes bearing his name for the most important discoveries in heat and light. He left to Harvard the funds with which the Rumford professorship of the physical and mathematical sciences as applied to the useful arts has been erected.— SMITH, BENJAMIN E., *ed.*, 1894–97, *The Century Cyclopedia of Names, p.* 993.

PERSONAL

Knight of the Dishclout, whereso'er I walk
I hear thee, Rumford, all the kitchen talk:
Note of melodious cadence on the ear,
Loud echoes, *Rumford here*, and *Rumford there!*
Lo, every parlour, drawing-room I see,
Boasts of thy stoves, and talks of nought but thee.
—WOLCOTT, JOHN (PETER PINDAR), 1801, *A Poetical Epistle to Benjamin Count Rumford.*

From this general view of the conduct of Major Thompson and his manner of leaving America, some may have received unfavorable impressions of his character. But he had never made politics his study, and never perhaps seriously considered the origin and progress of the contest; and if he had sought for employment against his countrymen, he had sufficient opportunities of being gratified. But he wished not to build his fame upon his exploits and dexterity in warlike achievements. He wished not to sacrifice his countrymen, that he might thereby become the hero of the British arms. But, believing that the benevolent plans which he has since adopted could never be executed but under the fostering hand of well-directed power, he sought a field for the exercise of his goodness and ingenuity where they could be executed, and where there was the most obvious demand. In doing this, success has attended his steps, and he has erected in the bosom of every poor man a temple to gratitude which will endure as long as benevolence and charity shall be considered Christian virtues.—BALDWIN, LOAMMI, 1805, *Literary Miscellany, vol.* I.

I am almost afraid to tell you the story, my good child, lest in future you should not be good; lest what I am about relating should set you a bad example, make you passionate, and so on. But I had been made very angry. A large party had been invited I neither liked nor approved of, and invited for the sole purpose of vexing me. Our house being in the centre of the garden, walled around, with iron gates, I put on my hat, walked down to the porter's lodge, and gave him orders, on his peril, not to let any one in. Besides I took away the keys. Madame went down, and when the company arrived, she talked with them —she on one side, they on the other, of the high brick wall. After that she goes and pours boiling water on some of my beautiful flowers. — RUMFORD, COUNT, 1806, *Letter to his Daughter.*

I wish here and now only to recall to your minds those of his most directly useful and beneficient works which have made his name known in every part of Europe. Who is ignorant of what he has done for relieving the scarcity in food : of his multiplied efforts for making food more healthful, more agreeable, and, above all, more economical; what service he has rendered to humanity in introducing the general use of the soups which go by his own name, and which have been so invaluable to so many thousands of persons exposed to the horrors of the prevailing scarcity? Who has not been made acquainted with his effective methods for suppressing mendicity; with his Houses of Industry, for work and instruction; with his means for improving the construction of chimneys, of lamps, of furnaces, of baths, of heating by steam; and, in fine, with his varied undertakings in the cause of domestic economy? In England, in France, in Germany, in all parts of the continent, the people are enjoying the blessings of his discoveries; and, from the humble dwelling of the poor even to the palaces of sovereigns, all will remember that his sole aim was to be always useful to his fellow-men.—DELESSERT, BENJAMIN, 1814, *Address Pronounced over the Grave of Count Rumford, Aug.* 24.

We have seen him here, in fact, for ten years honored by Frenchmen and foreigners, held in high regard by the lovers of science, sharing their labors, aiding with his advice the humblest artisans, and nobly serving the public by a constant succession of useful inventions. Nothing would have been lacking to the perfect enjoyment of his life, if the amenity of his manners had equalled his ardor in promoting the public welfare. But it must be confessed that he exhibited in conversation and intercourse, and in all his demeanor, a feeling which would seem most extraordinary in a man who was always so well treated by others, and who had himself done so much good to others. It was as if while he had been rendering all these services to his fellow-men he had no real love or regard for them. It would appear as if the vile passions which he had observed in the miserable objects committed to his care, or those other passions, not less vile, which his success and fame had excited among his rivals, had imbittered him towards human nature. So he thought it was not wise or good to intrust to men in the mass the care of their own well-being.— CUVIER, BARON, 1815, *Éloge on Count Rumford, Jan.* 9.

The sight of him very much reduced our enthusiasm. We found him a dry, precise man, who spoke of beneficence as a sort of discipline, and of the poor as we had never dared to speak of vagabonds. It was necessary, he said, to punish those who dispensed alms; we must compel the poor to work, etc. Our amazement was great on hearing such maxims. M. de Rumford established himself in Paris, where he married Madame Lavoisier, the widow of the celebrated chemist. I had relations with each of them, and never saw a more bizarre connection. Rumford was cold, calm, obstinate, egotistic, prodigiously occupied with the material element of life and the very smallest inventions of detail. He wanted his chimneys, lamps, coffee-pots, windows, made after a certain pattern, and he contradicted his wife a thousand times a day about the household management. Madame Lavoisier-Rumford (for so she was called during his life, and did not begin to bear the name of Rumford till after his death) was a woman of a resolute and willful character. A widow during twelve or fifteen years, she had the habit of following her own inclination, and with difficulty bore opposition. Her spirit was high, her soul strong, her character

masculine. Her second marriage was very soon vexed by the most grotesque scenes. Their separation was more of a blessing to both of them than was their union.—DE CANDOLLE, AUGUSTIN-PYRAMUS, 1842-62, *Mémoires et Souvenirs.*

His true character is rather to be inferred from his useful and philanthropic labors, and his numerous useful and scientific discoveries, than from the report of those who only knew him after his energy was impaired, and he had experienced disappointment and ingratitude. We, however, draw from the report of his French eulogist one prominent trait, which may not have been developed in the preceding pages; this was the love of order, and the strictest observance of method, in all his pursuits. This he called "the necessary auxiliary of genius, the only possible instrument of true happiness, and almost a subordinate divinity in this lower world." It is to this feature in his character, that we are to ascribe all his scientific attainments, and the high reputation he must ever hold in the eyes of posterity. From the time he landed in England, except a single short interval, until he bade adieu to Bavaria, he had been engaged in one continued series of important and engrossing employments, civil, military, and diplomatic; and yet, by a wise and skillful distribution of his time, he found leisure not only to devote himself to the most minute objects of domestic economy, but to enter into and accomplish philosophic investigations, that have become a portion of physical science, which no future discoveries can obliterate.—RENWICK, JAMES, 1845, *Count Rumford, Sparks' Library of American Biography, vol.* XV, *p.* 200.

It is hardly necessary to say that there was no ground whatever for the morbid fancy which the Countess connected with the loss of her father, nor was there any extraordinary circumstance attending his death. He was a lonely, and he was not a happy man. Having spent years of most thoughtful, wise, arduous labour for his fellow-men, and having advanced the welfare and comfort and happiness of millions of his race,—especially of the poor, the abject, and the forlorn among them,—he did not himself find serenity of heart, or satisfaction in society, or peace in his own fragment of a home. A fever came upon him which, after a rapid course of three days, ended fatally.—ELLIS, GEORGE E., 1871, *Memoir of Sir Benjamin Thompson, Count Rumford, p.* 613.

Men find pleasure in exercising the powers they possess, and Rumford possessed, in its highest and strongest form, the power of organization. In him flexible wisdom formed an amalgam with despotic strength. He held undoubtingly that "arrangement, method, provision for the minutest details, subordination, co-operation, and a careful system of statistics, will facilitate and make effective any undertaking, however burdensome and comprehensive." Pure love of humanity would at first sight seem to be the motive force of his action. Still, it has been affirmed by those who knew him that this was not the case. Fontenelle said of Dodard, that he turned his rigid observance of the fasts of the Church into a scientific experiment on the effects of abstinence, thereby taking the path which led at once to heaven and into the French Academy. In Rumford's case the pleasure of the administrator outweighed, it was said, that of the philanthropist.—TYNDALL, JOHN, 1883, *Count Rumford, Contemporary Review, vol.* 44, *p.* 48.

In the Maximilian Strasse, the finest street in Munich, there stands the bronze statue of an American who won renown in three countries of Europe,—England, Germany, and France. Born in Woburn, Mass., marrying in Concord, N. H., he was made a baronet by George III., and Count of the Holy Roman Empire by the Elector of Bavaria. He often dined with Napoleon, he corresponded with the Czar of Russia, and the Emperor of Austria, and he was on intimate terms with all the scientific men of his time. In London he founded the Royal Institution, and cured five hundred smoking chimneys. In Bavaria he suppressed the system of beggary and reformed the army. He taught the world how to cook, he discovered the principle of the correlation of forces, and he invented porcelain kettles.—ABBOTT, FRANCES M., 1893, *Count Rumford and his Daughter, New England Magazine, vol.* 15, *p.* 463.

GENERAL

This most valuable and important work, whose truly philosophick and benevolent author must feel a joy and self-satisfaction far superior to any praise which man can bestow.—MATHIAS, THOMAS JAMES, 1794-8, *The Pursuits of Literature, p.*224.

We profess to be of the daily increasing number of those who do not think very highly of Count Rumford's talents as a philosopher; and if our former prepossession required any confirmation (which it certainly did not), he has taken very great pains, in the elaborate performance now before us, to supply a variety of new proofs. . . . The merits of Count Rumford, too, have been so much a theme of conversation, and have had such an active influence in the fashionable world of science, that it is proper his pretensions should at length be sifted. But, above all, a paper filled with theoretical matter, abounding in pulses, vibrations, internal motions, and ethereal fluids, deserves to be exposed; the more, because these chimeras are mingled with a portion of induction, and have received the ill-deserved honour of a place in the Philosophical Transactions.—BROUGHAM, HENRY LORD, 1804, *Count Rumford on the Nature of Heat, Edinburgh Review, vol.* 4, *pp.* 399, 400.

The uncommon popularity which the Count enjoyed for some years seems to have produced a bad effect upon his disposition, or perhaps rather induced him to display without reserve those dispositions which he had hitherto been at some pains to conceal. Pomposity, and a species of literary arrogance quite unsuitable to the nature of experimental philosophy, for some years characterized his writings and injured their value. But in some of the last essays with which he favoured the world we find much valuable and curious information, respecting the heat evolved by different combustibles while burning,—a subject of great interest, which he prosecuted for many years, and at last elucidated with considerable success.— THOMSON, THOMAS, 1815, *Count Rumford, Annals of Philosophy, vol.* 5, *p.* 243.

His "Essays on Pauperism," and his plans for its relief and prevention, would alone entitle him to the blessings of mankind. Almost everything which is valuable in our modern systems of charity may be traced in his writings. When we add all that he did for science, and for the advancement of science, at the Royal Institution in London, and at Harvard, and at our American Academy, his claim to a statue seems to be far less equivocal, to say the least, than that of many of those who have lately received such commemoration. I trust we shall have a portrait of him, one of these days, in the gallery of our Historical Society, if nowhere else.— WINTHROP, ROBERT C., 1867, *Letter to George E. Ellis, Aug.* 19; *Memoir of Count Rumford, Preface, p.* vi.

We enter into the labors of Count Rumford every day of our lives, without knowing it or thinking of him. And he had his exceeding great reward. His homely efforts for the daily comfort of mankind led him to the discoveries which have made his name illustrious as a philosopher. His great contributions to science in the development of the correlation and indestructibility of forces, of the relations or rather the identity of force and heat, place him among the foremost discoverers in the world of science. By his experiments he overthrew the theories as to the nature of heat, which had been taken for granted by natural philosophers from the time of Aristotle, and established the true doctrine upon which every succeeding advance of knowledge in that direction rests, and without which none could have been made. The mighty and beneficent agents of light and heat were the objects of his intense study, that he might ascertain how they could best be made to answer the benevolent intentions of the Creator in promoting the happiness of mankind. And his forecasting mind provided fit honors to be bestowed, on either continent, after his death, on his successors in the same line of investigation and discovery.—QUINCY, EDMUND, 1871, *Count Rumford, Atlantic Monthly, vol.* 27, *p.* 521.

In spite of all the progress we have made in physical science, these essays, written for the most part during the last century, contain a great deal that is still suggestive and worthy of thoughtful reading both by popular students and experts in physical and social science.—WILLIAMS, W. MATTIEU, 1875, *Count Rumford's Complete Works, Nature, vol.* 11, *p.* 206.

The name and fame of Rumford, which were resonant in Europe at the beginning of this century, have fallen in England into general oblivion. To scientific men, however, his figure presents itself with singular impressiveness at the present day. This result is mainly due to the establishment, in recent times, of the grand scientific generalisation known as the Mechanical Theory of Heat. Boyle, and Hooke, and Locke, and Leibnitz, had already ranged themselves on the side of this theory. But by experiments conducted on a scale unexampled at the time, and by reasonings, founded on these experiments, of singular force and penetration, Rumford has made himself a conspicuous landmark in the history of the theory. His inference from his experiments was scored in favour of those philosophers who held that heat is a form of motion.—TYNDALL J., 1883, *Count Rumford, Contemporary Review, vol.* 44, *p.* 38.

Richard Brinsley Sheridan
1751–1816

Born, in Dublin, 30 Oct. 1751. Parents removed to London, 1758. Educated at Harrow, 1762-68. Parents removed to Bath, 1771. Eloped with Elizabeth Linley, 1772; secretly married to her at Calais. Formally married in London, 13 April 1773. Settled in London, spring of 1774. "The Rivals" produced at Covent Garden, 17 Jan. 1775; "St. Patrick's Day; or, The Scheming Lieutenant," Covent Garden, May 1775; "The Duenna," Covent Garden, 21 Nov. 1775. Purchased a share in Drury Lane Theatre, June 1776; Manager, Sept. 1776 to Feb. 1809. "A Trip to Scarborough" (adapted from Vanbrugh's "The Relapse") produced at Drury Lane, 24 Feb. 1777; "The School for Scandal," Drury Lane, 8 May 1777; "The Critic," Drury Lane, 30 Oct. 1779. M. P. for Stafford, 1780. Under Secretary of State, 1782. Concerned in impeachment of Warren Hastings, 1787-88. Intimacy with Prince of Wales begun, 1787. Wife died, 1792. Drury Lane Theatre rebuilt, 1792-94; new house opened, 21 April 1794. Married (ii.) Esther Ogle, 27 April 1795. "Pizarro" (adapted from Kotzebue's "Spaniards in Peru") produced at Drury Lane, 24 May 1799. Privy Councillor and Treasurer of Navy, 1799. Receiver of Duchy of Cornwall, 1804. Drury Lane Theatre burnt down, 24 Feb. 1809. Died, in London, 7 July 1816. Buried in Westminster Abbey. *Works:* "Clio's Protest" (under pseud.; "Asmodeo") [1771];

"The Rivals," 1775; "St. Patrick's Day; or, The Scheming Lieutenant," 1775; "The General Fast" (anon.) [1775?]; "The Duenna," 1775; "A Trip to Scarborough," 1777; "The School for Scandal," (anon.), 1777; "Verses to the Memory of Garrick," 1779; "The Critic," 1781; "The Legislative Independence of Ireland" (a speech), 1785; "Speech . . . against Warren Hastings," 1788; "A Comparative Statement of the two Bills for the better Government of the British Possessions in India," 1788; "Dramatic Works" [1795?]; "Pizarro," 1799; "Speech . . . on the Motion to address His Majesty" [1798]; "Speech . . . on the Union with Ireland," 1799; "Speech . . . on the Army Estimates," 1802. *Posthumous:* "Speeches" (5 vols.), 1816; "An Ode to Scandal," 2nd edn. 1819; "Speeches in the Trial of Warren Hastings," ed. by E. A. Bond (4 vols.), 1859–61. He *translated:* "The Love Epistles of Aristænetus" (with N. B. Halhed), 1771. *Collected Works:* ed. by F. Stainforth, 1874. *Life:* by T. Moore, 1825; by Mrs. Oliphant, 1883; by W. F. Rae, 1896.—SHARP, R. FARQUHARSON, 1897, *A Dictionary of English Authors, p.* 255.

PERSONAL

Mr. Sheridan has a very fine figure, and a good though I don't think a handsome face. He is tall, and very upright, and his appearance and address are at once manly and fashionable, without the smallest tincture of foppery or modish graces. In short, I like him vastly, and think him every way worthy his beautiful companion. . . . He evidently adores her, and she as evidently idolises him. The world has by no means done him justice.— D'ARBLAY, MME. (FANNY BURNEY), 1779, *Diary and Letters, vol.* I, *ch.* IV.

It was some Spirit, SHERIDAN! that breathed
O'er thy young mind such wildly-various power!
My soul hath marked thee in her shaping hour,
Thy temples with Hymettian flow'rets wreathed:
And sweet thy voice, as when o'er Laura's bier
Sad music trembled through Vauclusa's glade;
Sweet, as at dawn the love-lorn serenade
That wafts soft dreams to Slumber's listening ear.
Now patriot Rage and Indignation high
Swell the full tones! And now thy eye-beams dance
Meanings of Scorn and Wit's quaint revelry!
—COLERIDGE, SAMUEL TAYLOR, 1795, *To Richard Brinsley Sheridan.*

Sheridan is very little consulted at present; and it is said, will not have a seat in the cabinet. This is a distressing necessity. His habits of daily intoxication are probably considered as unfitting him for trust. The little that has been confided to him he has been running about to tell; and since Monday, he has been visiting Sidmouth. At a dinner at Lord Cowper's on Sunday last, where the Prince

was, he got drunk as usual, and began to speak slightingly of Fox. From what grudge this behaviour proceeds I have not learned. The whole fact is one to investigate with candour, and with a full remembrance of Sheridan's great services, in the worst times, to the principles of liberty.—HORNER, FRANCIS, 1806, *Memoirs and Correspondence, vol.* I, *p.* 357.

I find things settled so that £150 will remove all difficulty. I am absolutely undone and broken-hearted. I shall negotiate for the Plays successfully in the course of a week, when all shall be returned. I have desired Fairbrother to get back the Guarantee for thirty. They are going to put the carpets out of window, and brake into Mrs. S.'s room and *take me*—for God's sake let me see you.—SHERIDAN, RICHARD BRINSLEY, 1816, *Letter to Samuel Rogers, May* 15; *Moore's Memoirs of Sheridan. vol.* II, *p.* 454.

RICHARD BRINSLEY SHERIDAN
BORN, 1751.
DIED, 7th JULY, 1816.
THIS MARBLE IS THE TRIBUTE OF AN ATTACHED FRIEND,
PETER MOORE.
—INSCRIPTION ON GRAVE, 1816, *Westminster Abbey.*

Sheridan's worst can effect but few; his best will redound to the good of his country, and to the delight of thousands to come.—HUNT, LEIGH, 1816, *The Examiner, July* 14.

Long shall we seek his likeness—long in vain,
And turn to all of him which may remain,
Sighing that Nature form'd but one such man,
And broke the die—in moulding Sheridan.
—BYRON, LORD, 1816, *Monody on the Death of the Rt. Hon. R. B. Sheridan, Spoken at Drury-Lane Theatre.*

The orator,—dramatist,—minstrel,—who ran
Thro' each mode of the lyre and was master
   of all;—
Whose mind was an essence compounded
   with art
From the finest and best of all other men's
   powers;—
Who ruled, like a wizard, the world of the
   heart,
And could call up its sunshine or bring down
   its showers;—
Whose humor, as gay as the fire-fly's light,
Played round every subject and shone as it
   played;—
Whose wit in the combat, as gentle as bright,
Ne'er carried a heart-stain away on its
   blade;—
Whose eloquence—brightening whatever it
   tried,
Whether reason or fancy, the gay or the
   grave,—
Was as rapid, as deep and as brilliant a tide,
As ever bore Freedom aloft on its wave!
—MOORE, THOMAS, 1816, *Lines on the
Death of Sheridan.*

I must differ from Moore in his view of
Sheridan's heart. Notwithstanding his
passion for Miss Linley and his grief for
his father's death, who used him ill, I
question his having a "really good heart."
His making love to Pamela, Madame de
Genlis's daughter, so soon after his lovely
wife's death, and his marriage, in two
years, with a young girl as a *compliment*
to her remembrance, renders one very suspicious of the real depth of his passion. No
man of wit to the full extent of the word
can have a good heart, because he has by
nature less regard for the feelings of
others than for the brilliancy of his own
sayings. There must be more mischief
than love in the hearts of all radiant wits.
Moore's life of him wants courage.—HAY-
DON, BENJAMIN ROBERT, 1825, *To Miss
Mitford, Dec.* 10; *Life, Letters and Table
Talk, ed. Stoddard, p.* 226.

Sheridan was a man of quick but not
deep feelings; of sudden but not lasting
excitements. He was not one of those
who suffer a single passion to influence
the whole course of their lives. Even the
desire to dazzle by his wit, great as was
its power over him, was not always awake,
for we are told that he would sometimes
remain silent for hours in company, too
lazy to invent a smart saying for the
occasion, but idly waiting for the opportunity to apply some brilliant witticism
already in his memory. . . . His

griefs might have been violent, but they
were certainly brief, and he quickly
forgot them when he came to look again
at the sunny side of things. Even his
political disappointments do not seem in
the least to have soured his temper, or
abated his readiness to adopt new hopes
and new expedients.—BRYANT, WILLIAM
CULLEN, 1826-84, *The Character of Sheridan, Prose Writings, ed. Godwin, vol.* II,
p. 368.

I was present on the second of Hasting's
trial in Westminster Hall; when Sheridan
was listened to with such attention that
you might have heard a pin drop.—During one of those days, Sheridan, having
observed Gibbon among the audience, took
occasion to mention "The luminous author
of 'The Decline and Fall.'" After he had
finished one of his friends reproached him
with flattering Gibbon. "Why, what did
I say of him?" asked Sheridan.—"You
called him the luminous author," &c.,—
"Luminous! oh, I meant—voluminous."
. . . Sheridan did not display his admirable powers in company till he had been
warmed by wine. During the earlier part
of dinner he was generally heavy and silent:
and I have heard him, when invited to drink
a glass of wine, reply, "No, thank you;
I'll take—a little small beer." After
dinner, when he had had a tolerable
quantity of wine, he was brilliant indeed.
But when he went on swallowing too much,
he became downright stupid: and I once,
after a dinner-party at the house of
Edwards the bookseller in Pall Mall, walked
with him to Brookes's, when he had
absolutely lost the use of speech. . . .
Sheridan had very fine eyes, and he was
not a little vain of them. He said to me
on his death-bed, "Tell Lady Besborough
that my eyes will look up to the coffin-lid
as brightly as ever." . . . In his dealings with the world, Sheridan certainly
carried the "privileges of genius" so far
as they were ever carried by man.—
ROGERS, SAMUEL, 1855, *Recollections of
Table-Talk, pp.* 65, 69, 70, 71.

Poor Sherry! poor Sherry! drunkard,
gambler, spendthrift, debtor, godless and
worldly as thou wert, what is it that
shakes from our hand the stone we would
fling at thee? Almost, we must confess
it, thy very faults; at least those qualities
which seem to have been thy glory and thy
ruin; which brought thee into temptation;

to which, hadst thou been less brilliant, less bountiful, thou hadst never been drawn. What is it that disarms us when we review thy life, and wrings from us a tear when we should utter a reproach? Thy punishment; that bitter, miserable end; that long battling with poverty, debt, disease, all brought on by thyself; that abandonment in the hour of need, more bitter than them all; that awakening to the terrible truth of the hollowness of man and rottenness of the world!—THOMSON, KATHERINE AND J. C. (GRACE AND PHILIP WHARTON), 1860, *The Wits and Beaux of Society, p.* 329.

The account of Sheridan's death-bed is as nearly fabulous as any narration can be; but it is the current "copied" account, and passes muster with the rest. And now, we may fairly ask, if such "biographies" be true, how came this man, so abused, so run down, whose faults were so prodigious, whose merits were *nil*, to occupy the position he did when living? . . . How did it happen, then, that a man labouring under such a disadvantage of birth, and also described as a commonplace swindler, drunkard, and driveller, excelled in everything he attempted, and, from the obscure son of the Bath actor and schoolmaster, became minister of state and companion of princes? What dazzled fools does it make all his contemporaries that *they* admitted him unquestioned to a superiority which is now denied to have existed! What an extraordinary anomaly does that famous funeral in Westminster Abbey present, amid a crowd of onlookers so dense that they seemed "like a wall of human faces," if it was merely the carrying of a poor old tipsy gentleman to his grave by a group of foolish lords!—NORTON, HON. CAROLINE, 1861, *Sheridan and His Biographers, Macmillan's Magazine, vol.* 3, *p.* 177.

When Sheridan was dying, in the extremity of poverty, an article appeared from a generous enemy in the "Morning Post," saying that relief should be given before it was too late: "Prefer ministering in the chamber of sickness" to ministering at "the splendid sorrows that adorn the hearse"—"life and succor, against Westminster Abbey and a funeral." But it was too late; and Westminster Abbey and the funeral, with all the pomp that rank could furnish, was the alternative. It was this which suggested the remark of a French

journal: "France is the place for a man of letters to live in, and England the place for him to die in."—STANLEY, ARTHUR PENRHYN, 1867-96, *Historical Memorials of Westminster Abbey, p.* 317.

He was the contemporary of Beaumarchais, and resembled him in his talent and in his life. The two epochs, the two schools of drama, the two characters correspond. Like Beaumarchais, he was a lucky adventurer, clever, amiable, and generous, reaching success through scandal, who flashed up and shone in a moment, scaled with a rush the empyrean of politics and literature, settled himself, as it were, among the constellations, and, like a brilliant rocket, presently went out in the darkness. Nothing failed him; he attained all at the first leap, without apparent effort, like a prince who need only show himself to win a place. All the most surpassing happiness, the most brilliant in art, the most exalted in worldly position, he took as his birthright. The poor unknown youth, wretched translator of an unreadable Greek sophist, who at twenty walked about Bath in a red waistcoat and a cocked hat, destitute of hope, and ever conscious of the emptiness of his pockets, had gained the heart of the most admired beauty and musician of her time, and carried her off from ten rich, elegant, titled adorers, had fought with the best-hoaxed of the ten, beaten him, had carried by storm the curiosity and attention of the public. Then, challenging glory and wealth, he placed successively on the stage the most diverse and the most applauded dramas, comedies, farce, opera, serious verse; he bought and worked a large theatre without a farthing, inaugurated a reign of success and pecuniary advantages, and led a life of elegance amid the enjoyments of social and domestic joys, surrounded by universal admiration and wonder. Thence, aspiring yet higher, he conquered power, entered the House of Commons, showed himself a match for the first orators. . . . Whatever the business, whoever the man, he persuaded; none withstood him, every one fell under his charm. What is more difficult than for an ugly man to make a young girl forget his ugliness? There is one thing more difficult, and that is to make a creditor forget you owe him money. There is something more difficult still, and that is, to borrow money of a creditor who has come to demand it. . . . In the morning, creditors and visitors filled the rooms in which he lived; he came in smiling, with an easy manner, with so much loftiness and grace, that the people forgot their wants and their claims, and looked as if they had only come to see him. His animation was irresistible; no one had a more dazzling wit; he had an inexhaustible fund of puns, contrivances, sallies, novel ideas. Lord Byron, who was a good judge, said that he had never heard nor conceived of a more extraordinary conversation. Men spent nights in listening to him.— TAINE, H. A., 1871, *History of English Literature*, tr. *Van Laun, vol.* I, *bk.* iii, *ch.* i, *pp.* 524, 525.

He had been born in obscurity—he died in misery. Out of the humblest, unprovided, unendowed poverty he had blazed into reputation, into all the results of great wealth, if never to its substance; more wonderful still, he had risen to public importance and splendour, and his name can never be obliterated from the page of history; but had fallen again, down, down into desertion, misery, and the deepest degradation of a poverty for which there was neither hope nor help: till death wiped out all possibilities of further trouble or embarrassment, and Sheridan became once more in his coffin the great man whom his party delighted to honour—a national name and credit, one of those whose glory illustrates our annals. It may be permitted now to doubt whether these last mournful honours were not more than his real services to England deserved; but at the moment it was, no doubt, a fine thing that the poor, hopeless "Sherry" whom everybody admired and despised, whom no one but a few faithful friends would risk the trouble of helping, who had sunk away out of all knowledge into endless debts, and duns, and drink, should rise at an instant as soon as death had stilled his troubles into the Right Honourable, brilliant, and splendid Sheridan, whose enchanter's wand the stubborn Pitt had bowed under, and the noble Burke acknowledged with enthusiasm. It was a fine thing; but the finest thing was that death which in England makes all glory possible, and which restores to the troublesome bankrupt, the unfortunate prodigal, and all stray sons of fame, at one stroke, their

friends, their reputation, and the abundant tribute which it might have been dangerous to afford them living, but with which it is both safe and prudent to glorify their tomb.— OLIPHANT, MARGARET O. W., 1883, *Sheridan (English Men of Letters), p.* 194.

Perhaps Sheridan was never a wise man, he can hardly be called a good one, yet he was free from the worse vices of his condition and craft. He never exhibited envy of his favoured rivals; his temper was never soured by misfortune. People said he had stolen his wit and borrowed his plots, that his fertile soil was capable of one crop and no more. But he was too well versed in the infirmities of human nature to look for generosity where he was more likely to meet with malice, and too sensible or too indolent to be angry when his experience justified his insight. Sheridan's own infirmities were inconvenient certainly, but not noxious. . . . Sheridan had just that minimum of selfishness which perforce adheres to the profligate; he had few or none of the higher virtues which belong to the chivalrous spirit; but force of character he certainly possessed. It is a grave error to say that either the middle or the end of life found him deficient in strength.—CAINE, HALL, 1883, *Sheridan, The Academy, vol.* 24, *pp.* 171, 172.

Doubtless, in any attempt to judge of Sheridan as he was apart from his works, we must make considerable deductions from the mass of floating anecdotes that have gathered round his name. It was not without reason that his granddaughter Mrs. Norton denounced the unfairness of judging of the real man from unauthenticated stories about his indolent procrastination, his wrecklessness in money matters, his drunken feats and sallies, his wild gambling, his ingenious but discreditable shifts in evading and duping creditors. The real Sheridan was not a pattern of decorous respectability, but we may fairly believe that he was very far from being as disreputable as the Sheridan of vulgar legend. Against the stories about his reckless management of his affairs we must set the broad facts that he had no source of income but Drury Lane theatre, that he bore from it thirty years all the expenses of a fashionable life, and that the theatre was twice burnt to the ground during his proprietorship. Enough was lost in those fires to account ten times over for all his debts. His biographers always speak of his means of living as a mystery. Seeing that he started with borrowed capital, it is possible that the mystery is that he applied much more of his powers to plain matters of business than he affected or got credit for.—MINTO, WILLIAM, 1886, *Encyclopædia Britannica, Ninth edition, vol.* XXI, *p.* 836.

No man has ever lived in more worlds than Sheridan, or has ever shone with such brilliancy in all. In the world of fashion, in the company of wits, among authors, painters and poets, in the House of Commons, at the Court of the Prince Regent,—whatever society he frequented,—he moved a star. His charming manners, his handsome person, his gaiety, and, above all, his good nature, which was one of his principal characteristics, rendered him universally popular. But these engaging qualities were sometimes marred by the foibles and peculiarities which are most apt to attract attention and to serve as weapons in the hands of a man's enemies. In early manhood he became one of the chiefs of a political party when party strife ran high, and when virulent calumny and abuse, in an age more coarse than ours, were considered legitimate means of offence, and his memory has suffered accordingly. Moreover, from his youth, two impediments clogged and embarrassed his every step,— his poverty and his Irish origin. . . . Sheridan's conviviality has been more rigorously denounced than many a contemporary toper's sodden and unredeemed intemperance. Wine quickly disordered his high-strung nervous system ; and, while delighting the harder-headed drinkers around him with the sallies of his wit, two or three glasses were sufficient to overset the delicate poise of his brain. As a consequence, his cheerful and comparatively innocent indiscretions over the bottle have been more frequently in men's mouths than the results of deeper potations of his more stolid boon companions. In later life, alas! for a certain period, grief and accumulated misfortunes drove him into more serious lapses, but from the dominion of these, to his great credit be it said, he eventually redeemed himself.—DUFFERIN, MARQUESS OF, 1896, *Sheridan, A Biography by Rae, Introduction, vol.* I, *pp.* viii, xi.

He appears to have entered the world to demonstrate by his example and conduct the utter and contemptible absurdity of proclaiming that all men can remain equal, or ought to rest satisfied with their lot. It is unhappily true that a dead level in humanity does exist ; but it can only be found within the walls of an asylum for idiots. Sheridan's confidence in himself could not be repressed by penury, nor deadened by the predominance of those who were elevated above him by the accident of high birth or inherited wealth. When a boy he had resolved to rise to the top; he neither flinched nor failed in his upward course, and he lived to look down with serenity from the pinnacle of fame upon the applauding multitude below. It is inspiring to follow his steps; it is instructive to contemplate how he always despised the aid of unworthy means, and disdained employing any of the despicable tricks to which such men as his own Joseph Surface frequently resort for the attainment of their miserable ends. He was always dissatisfied and he was often imprudent ; but there is an imprudence which is sublime as well as a discontent which is noble, and their manifestation in his person constitutes one of his titles to esteem. —RAE, W. FRASER, 1896, *Sheridan, A Biography, vol.* I, *p.* 346.

It is impossible to close this rapid and slight sketch without one word at least on Mrs. Sheridan. One of the strong titles of Sheridan to the favour of posterity is to be found in the warm attachment of his family and his descendants to his memory. The strongest of them all lies in the fact that he could attract, and could retain through her too short life, the devoted affections of this admirable woman, whose beauty and accomplishments, remarkable as they were, were the least of her titles to praise. Mrs. Sheridan was certainly not strait-laced : not only did she lose at cards fifteen and twenty-one guineas on two successive nights, but she played cards, after the fashion of her day, on Sunday evenings. I am very far from placing such exploits among her claims on our love. But I frankly own to finding it impossible to read the accounts of her without profoundly coveting, across the gulf of all these years, to have seen and known her. Let her be judged by the incomparable verses (presented to us in these volumes) in which she opened the floodgates of her bleeding heart at a moment when she feared that she had been robbed, for the moment, of Sheridan's affections by the charms of another. Those verses of loving pardon proceed from a soul advanced to some of the highest Gospel attainments. She passed into her rest when still under forty; peacefully absorbed for days before her departure, in the contemplation of the coming world. — GLADSTONE, WILLIAM EWART, 1896, *Sheridan, Nineteenth Century, vol.* 39, *p.* 1041.

It might indeed be said that the low opinion of Sheridan's character is so general that hardly a single respectable man of his time is found to mention him without contempt or reproach. In every direction we hear of some trickeries and faithlessness.—FITZGERALD, PERCY, 1897, *The Real Sheridan, p.* 41.

Richard Brinsley Sheridan was the most distinguished member of a distinguished family. His grandfather was Dr. Sheridan, the friend and correspondent of Swift. His father was Thomas Sheridan, elocutionist, actor, manager, and lexicographer. His mother was Frances Sheridan, author of the comedy of "The Discovery" (acted by David Garrick), and of the novel "Miss Sidney Biddulph" (praised by Samuel Johnson). His three granddaughters, known as the beautiful Sheridans, became, one the Duchess of Somerset, another the Countess of Dufferin, and the third the Hon. Mrs. Norton (afterward Lady Stirling-Maxwell). His great-grandson is Lord Dufferin, author and diplomatist. Thus, in six generations of the family, remarkable power of one kind or another has been revealed. — MATTHEWS, BRANDER, 1897, *Library of the World's Best Literature, ed. Warner, vol.* XXIII, *p.* 13317.

SPEECHES

If you could bring over Mr. Sheridan, he would do something: he talked for five hours and a half on Wednesday, and turned everybody's head. One heard everybody in the streets raving on the wonders of that speech; for my part, I cannot believe it was so supernatural as they say—do you believe it was, Madam? I will go to my oracle, who told me of the marvels of the pamphlet, which assures us that Mr. Hastings is a prodigy of virtue and abilities; and, as you think so too, how should such a fellow as Sheridan, who has no diamonds to bestow, fascinate all the world?— Yet witchcraft no doubt, there has been, for when did simple eloquence ever convince a majority?—WALPOLE, HORACE, 1787, *To the Countess of Ossory, Feb.* 9; *Letters, ed. Cunningham, vol.* IX, *p.* 93.

Mr. Sheridan, I hear, did not quite satisfy the passionate expectation that had been raised; but it was impossible he could, when people had worked themselves into an enthusiasm of offering fifty—ay, *fifty* guineas for a ticket to hear him.—WALPOLE, HORACE, 1788, *To Thomas Barrett, June* 5; *'s, ed. Cunningham, vol.* IX, *p.* 127.

Yesterday the august scene was closed for this year. Sheridan surpassed himself and though I am far from considering him as a perfect orator, there were many beautiful passages in his speech on justice, filial love, &c.; one of the closest chains of argument I ever heard, to prove that Hastings was responsible for the acts of Middleton; and a compliment, much admired, to a certain historian of your acquaintance. Sheridan, in the close of his speech, sunk into Burke's arms; but I called this morning, he is perfectly well. A good Actor!—GIBBON, EDWARD, 1788, *To Lord Sheffield, June* 17; *Private Letters, ed. Prothero, vol.* II, *p.* 172.

Burke caught him in his arms as he sat down. . . . I have myself enjoyed that embrace on such an occasion, and know its value.—ELLIOT, SIR GILBERT, 1788, *Letter to His Wife.*

He possessed a ductility and versatility of talents, which no public man in our time has equalled; and these intellectual endowments were sustained by a suavity of temper, that seemed to set at defiance all attempts to ruffle or discompose it. Playing with his irritable or angry antagonist, Sheridan exposed him by sallies of wit, or attacked him by classic elegance of satire; performing this arduous task in the face of a crowded assembly, without losing for an instant either his presence of mind, his facility of expression, or his good humour. He wounded deepest, indeed, when he smiled; and convulsed his hearers with laughter, while the object of his ridicule or animadversion was twisting under the lash. Pitt and Dundas, who presented the finest marks for his attack, found by experience, that though they might repel, they could not confound, and still less could they silence or vanquish him. In every attempt that they made by introducing personalities, or illiberal reflections on his private life, and literary or dramatic occupations, to disconcert him, he turned their weapons on themselves. Nor did he, while thus chastising his adversary alter a muscle of his own countenance; which, as well as his gestures, seemed to participate and display the unalterable serenity of his intellectual formation. Rarely did he elevate his voice, and never except in subservience to the dictates of his judgment, with a view to produce a corresponding effect on his audience. Yet he was always heard, generally listened to with eagerness, and could obtain a hearing at almost any hour. Burke, who wanted Sheridan's nice tact, and his amenity of manner, was continually coughed down; and on those occasions lost his temper. Even Fox often tired the House by the repetitions which he introduced into his speeches. Sheridan never abused their patience. Whenever he rose they anticipated a rich repast of wit without acrimony, seasoned by allusions and citations the most delicate yet obvious in their application.—WRAXALL, SIR NATHANIEL WILLIAM, 1784-1836, *Posthumous Memoirs of His Own Time.*

The most deliberate criticism must allow his eloquence to be distinguished by strong sense and brilliant wit; by a vigour of argument not too ingenious for business, nor too subtle for conviction; by a great command of pure English words, and by a vivid power of imagination in those passages which aimed at grandeur and pathos, though they must be owned to be too artificial and ostentatious to produce the highest effect, and to be approved by a severe taste.—MACKINTOSH, SIR JAMES, 1812, *Journal, Feb.* 7; *Memoirs, ed. Mackintosh, vol.* II, *p.* 204.

From the charm'd council to the festive board,
Of human feelings the unbounded lord;
In whose acclaim the loftiest voices vied,
The praised—the proud—who made his praise their pride.
When the loud cry of trampled Hindostan
Arose to Heaven in her appeal from man,
His was the thunder—his the avenging rod,
The wrath—the delegated voice of God!
Which shook the nations through his lips—and blazed
Till vanquish'd senates trembled as they praised.
—BYRON, LORD, 1816, *Monody on the Death of the Rt. Hon. R. B. Sheridan, Spoken at Drury-Lane Theatre.*

His reputation as an orator may be said to rest substantially on his two speeches against Mr. Warren Hastings; and it unfortunately happens, as we have already hinted, that both of these are miserably reported in the parliamentary debates. When he delivered those far-famed philippics, he was a new man in St. Stephens'—the extent of his genius and the truth of his character were yet to be developed; and we must be permitted to doubt whether, if he had spoken the same words a few years later, the world would ever have heard so much about the matter.—CROKER, JOHN WILSON, 1826, *Memoirs of Sheridan, Quarterly Review, vol.* 33, *p.* 593.

His most celebrated speech was certainly the one upon the "Begum Charge" in the proceedings against Hastings; and nothing can exceed the accounts left us of its unprecedented success. . . . All men on all sides vied with each other in extolling so wonderful a performance. Nevertheless, the opinion has now become greatly prevalent that a portion of this success was owing to the speech having so greatly surpassed all the speaker's former efforts; to the extreme interest of the topics which the subject naturally presented, and to the artist-like elaboration and beautiful delivery of certain fine passages, rather than to the merits of the whole. Certain it is, that the repetition of great part of it, presented in the short-hand notes of the speech on the same charge in Westminster Hall, disappoints every reader who has heard of the success of the earlier effort. In truth, Mr. Sheridan's taste was very far from being chaste, or even moderately correct; he delighted in gaudy figures; he was attracted by glare, and cared not whether the brilliancy came from tinsel or gold, from broken glass or pure diamond; he overlaid his thoughts with epigrammatic diction; he "played to the galleries," and indulged them, of course, with an endless succession of claptraps. His worst passages by far were those which he evidently preferred himself. —BROUGHAM, HENRY LORD, 1839-43, *Lives of Statesmen of the Time of George III.*

The charge touching the spoliation of the Begums was brought forward by Sheridan, in a speech which was so imperfectly reported that it may be said to be wholly lost; but which was, without doubt, the most elaborately brilliant of all the productions of his ingenious mind. The impression which it produced was such as has never been equalled. He sat down, not merely amidst cheering, but amidst the loud clapping of hands, in which the Lords below the bar, and the strangers in the gallery, joined. The excitement of the House was such that no other speaker could obtain a hearing, and the debate was adjourned. The impression made by this remarkable display of eloquence on severe and experienced critics, whose discernment may be supposed to have been quickened by emulation, was deep and permanent. Mr. Windham, twenty years later, said that the speech deserved all its fame, and was, in spite of some faults of taste, such as were seldom wanting either in the literary or in the parliamentary performances of Sheridan, the greatest that had been delivered within the memory of man. Mr. Fox, about the same time, being asked by the late Lord Holland what was the best speech ever made in the House of Commons, assigned the first place, without hesitation, to the great oration of Sheridan on the Oude charge.—MACAULAY, THOMAS BABINGTON, 1841, *Warren Hastings, Critical and Miscellaneous Essays.*

There was, undoubtedly, some bombast in Mr. Sheridan's speeches; but they were marked by glowing eloquence, and not unfrequently by brilliant wit. Although some of his jokes were the result of great study, yet, as they were perfect in their kind, and that kind of the very highest, we may forgive the labour. Few men have possessed the power to make such a speech as that which dazzled the House of Commons on the Begum Charge; few ever wrote so good a comedy as "The School for Scandal." It is melancholy to reflect that the possessor of such talents should, as it were in mere wantonness, have thrown away the influence which he was so well qualified to exercise over the destiny of his country.—RUSSELL, LORD JOHN, 1853, ed., *Memoirs, Journal and Correspondence of Thomas Moore, vol.* II, *p.* 187, *note.*

Sheridan, like Whitefield, was a great rhetorician, not a great orator.—DICEY, A. V., 1884, *Sheridan, The Nation, vol.* 39, *p.* 137.

He cannot be called a classic orator.

His oriental exuberance of imagination is Asiatic rather than Greek. With a Celtic intellect that was always in extremes, joined to a native sense of humor he could not be reckoned with the grand orators of the Demosthenean type. Impetuous and heedless he plunged into the very errors he was quick to detect and expose. But for conjouring up a storm of eloquence that should bear his hearers away from their sober sense, stirring their emotions and moving their will his magnetic and impulsive oratory was surpassed by none and equalled by few.—SEARS, LORENZO, 1895, *The History of Oratory, p.* 295.

THE RIVALS
1775

I prefer Sheridan's "Rivals" to his "School for Scandal:" exquisite humour pleases me more than the finest wit.— ROGERS, SAMUEL, 1855, *Recollections of Table-Talk.*

In such a play as "The Rivals" the reader is kept in a state of continual hilarious delight by a profusion of sallies, rejoinders, blunders, contrasts, which seem to exhaust all the resources of the ludicrous. Mrs. Malaprop's "parts of speech" will raise the laughter of unborn generations, and the choleric generous old father will never find a more perfect representative than Sir Anthony Absolute.— ARNOLD, THOMAS, 1868–75, *Chaucer to Wordsworth, p.* 371.

After the lapse of a hundred years, "The Rivals" still remains, next to its author's greater work, the most popular comedy of the last century.—BAKER, H. BARTON, 1878, *Richard Brinsley Sheridan, Gentleman's Magazine, vol.* 243, *p.* 308.

"The Rivals" is artificial comedy, inclining on one side to farce, and, in the parts of Falkland and Julia, to the sentimental. But it is, on its own rather artificial plan, constructed with remarkable skill and tightness; and the characters of Sir Anthony Absolute, Mrs. Malaprop, Sir Lucius O'Trigger, and Bob Acres, with almost all the rest, combine fun with at least theatrical verisimilitude in a very rare way. Indeed, Sir Anthony and Mrs. Malaprop, though heightened from life, can hardly be said to be false to it, and though in the other pair the license of dramatic exaggeration is pushed to its farthest, it is not exceeded. The effect could not have been produced without the sparkling dialogue, but this alone could not have given it.—SAINTSBURY, GEORGE, 1898, *A Short History of English Literature, p.* 641.

"The Rivals," from the date of its first night's failure, has neither merited nor enjoyed a like measure of success as, throughout the world, has followed the "School for Scandal;" while I venture to think the incidents of the comedy are too fragile and farcical to bear such elaborate scenic treatment as we endeavoured to depict of last-century life, when Beau Nash reigned in the pumproom at Bath.— BANCROFT, SIR SQUIRE BANCROFT, 1896, *Sheridan, A Biography by Rae, vol.* II, *p.* 321.

THE DUENNA
1775

This drama has a charm for the public beyond its own intrinsic worth—it was written by Richard Brinsley Sheridan. If that name has no power over the reader's imagination, so as to give to every sentence a degree of interest, let him throw aside the book, and forbear to seek after literary pleasures, for he has not the taste to enjoy them. Although "The Duenna's" highest claim to notice depends, now, upon the reputation of its author, yet the author was first indebted to "The Duenna" for the honour of ranking among poets, and of receiving from the fashionable world all those animating caresses, so dear to a poet's heart. . . . Divested of all adventitious aid, the value of the opera consists in the beautiful poetry of many of the songs; for though it is a production of much ingenuity and skill, it does not give a presage, either in wit or incident, of such a work, from the same hand, as "The School for Scandal."—INCHBALD, MRS. ELIZABETH, 1806–9, *The British Theatre, vol.* II.

The "Duenna" is a perfect work of art. It has the utmost sweetness and point. The plot, the characters, the dialogue, are all complete in themselves, and they are all his own; and the songs are the best that ever were written, except those in the "Beggar's Opera." They have a joyous spirit of intoxication in them, and a strain of the most melting tenderness.— HAZLITT, WILLIAM, 1818, *Lectures on the English Comic Writers, Lecture* viii.

One of the very few operas in our language, which combines the merits of legitimate comedy with the attractions of poetry and song.—MOORE, THOMAS, 1825, *Memoirs of the Life of the Right Honourable Richard Brinsley Sheridan, vol.* I, *p.* 169.

The "Duenna" is partly a *pasticcio*, consisting of original music mingled with popular airs, glees, &c., adapted to new words; and it appears from the above passages in Sheridan's letters, that he himself had a hand in the selection and adaptation of the old music. Several of the original pieces were contributed by Thomas Linley, the composer's eldest son. These were, the overture; the songs, "Could I each fault remember," "Friendship is the bond of reason," and "Sharp is the woe;" the duet, "Turn thee round, I pray thee;" and the trio which concludes the first act. These are all charming things, and do honour to the genius of a young musician, who, but for his untimely fate, would undoubtedly have achieved the highest triumphs in his art.—HOGARTH, GEORGE, 1838, *Memoirs of the Musical Drama, vol.* II, *p.* 433.

The songs in his opera of the "Duenna" are as superior to the productions of the century before, as they are inferior to those of the Elizabethan age. They have the sharpness and the grace of a fine intaglio: Ovid might have been proud of them: they have as much tenderness as the best portions of his "Amores," and the *tour de malice* of his epigrammatic couplets. If Sheridan had turned his attention to the writing of lyrical dramas, Gay would have had a formidable rival for his "Beggar's Opera."—DONNE, WILLIAM BODHAM, 1854–58, *Essays on the Drama, p.* 117.

Not only in the drawing of character, but also in dialogue, is "The Duenna" inferior to Sheridan's better-known plays. In spite of all its brightness and lightness, it is impossible not to acknowledge that it does not contain his best work. It has few specimens of the recondite wit and quaint fancy which make "The School for Scandal" so brilliant and unequalled a comedy. If Sheridan's wit, like quicksilver, is always glistening, perhaps at times, like mercury it seems a little heavy. Now and again the dialogue vies in sparkle and point with the talk of its author's other plays, but not as often as might be wished.— MATTHEWS, BRANDER, 1880, *"Pinafore's" Predecessor, Harper's Magazine, vol.* 60, *p.* 504.

A lyric poet of somewhat limited powers.—CRAWFURD, OSWALD, 1896, *ed., Lyrical Verse from Elizabeth to Victoria, p.* 434, *note.*

With the progress of musical compositions, especially in connexion with the Drama, "The Duenna," greatly admired as it was on its first production, passed out of fashion; and in spite of the simplicity and the charm of many of the melodies composed for the work by Linley, in spite, above all, of the ingenuity, wit and humour of the piece, it may be doubted whether Sheridan's "Duenna," will ever be played again in its original form. . . . A justly admired composer of our time, Mr. J. L. Roeckel, has set to music Sheridan's ancient opera-book with such lyrical additions as the taste and fashion of the day seemed to render necessary, but with no change whatever in the original dialogue, and "The Duenna" with music by Roeckel will probably supersede "The Duenna" with music by Linley, just as the operatic version of Beaumarchais' "Barber of Seville" with music by Rossini has displaced the older operatic version of the same work with music by Paisiello.— EDWARDS, SUTHERLAND, 1896, *Sheridan, A Biography by Rae, vol.* I, *p.* 305.

SCHOOL FOR SCANDAL
1777

How is the Saint to-day? A gentleman who is as mad as myself about yᵉ School remark'd, that the characters upon the stage at yᵉ falling of the screen stand too long before they speak;—I thought so too yᵉ first night:—he said it was the same on yᵉ 2ⁿᵈ, and was remark'd by others;— tho' they should be astonish'd, and a little petrify'd, yet it may be carry'd to too great a length.—All praise at Lord Lucan's last night.—GARRICK, DAVID, 1777, *Letter to Mr. Sheridan, May* 12.

I have seen Sheridan's new comedy, and liked it much better than any I have seen since "The Provoked Husband." There is a great deal of wit and good situations; but it is too long, has two or three bad scenes that might easily be omitted, and seemed to me to want nature and truth of character; but I have not read it, and sat too high to hear it well.—WALPOLE,

HORACE, 1778, *To Rev. Wm. Mason, May* 16; *Letters, ed. Cunningham, vol.* VII, *p.* 67.

The "School for Scandal" is, if not the most original, perhaps the most finished and faultless comedy which we have. When it is acted you hear people all around you exclaiming: "Surely it is impossible for anything to be cleverer." The scene in which Charles sells all the old family pictures but his uncle's, who is the purchaser in disguise, and that of the discovery of Lady Teazle when the screen falls, are among the happiest and most highly wrought that comedy, in its wide and brilliant range, can boast. Besides the wit and ingenuity of this play, there is a genial spirit of frankness and generosity about it that relieves the heart as well as clears the lungs. It professes a faith in the natural goodness as well as habitual depravity of human nature. While it strips off the mask of hypocrisy it inspires a confidence between man and man. As often as it is acted it must serve to clear the air of that low, creeping, pestilent fog of cant and mysticism, which threatens to confound every native impulse, or honest conviction, in the nauseous belief of a perpetual lie, and the laudable profession of systematic hypocrisy.— HAZLITT, WILLIAM, 1818, *Lectures on the English Comic Writers, Lecture* viii.

Amidst the mortifying circumstances attendant upon growing old, it is something to have seen the "School for Scandal" in its glory. This comedy grew out of Congreve and Wycherley, but gathered some allays of the sentimental comedy which followed theirs. It is impossible that it should be now *acted*, though it continues, at long intervals, to be announced in the bills. Its hero, when Palmer played it at least, was Joseph Surface. When I remember the gay boldness, the graceful solemn plausibility, the measured step, the insinuating voice—to express it in a word— the downright *acted* villainy of the part,—so different from the pressure of conscious actual wickedness,—the hypocritical assumption of hypocrisy,—which made Jack so deservedly a favourite in that character, I must needs conclude the present generation of playgoers more virtuous than myself, or more dense. I freely confess that he divided the palm with me with his better brother; that, in fact, I liked him quite as well. . . . You did not believe in Joseph with the same faith with which you believed in Charles. The latter was a pleasant reality, the former a no less pleasant poetical foil to it. The comedy, I have said is incongruous; a mixture of Congreve with sentimental incompatibilities: the gaiety upon the whole is buoyant; but it required the consummate art of Palmer to reconcile the discordant elements.—LAMB, CHARLES, 1824? *On the Artificial Comedy of the Last Century.*

The beauties of this Comedy are so universally known and felt, that criticism may be spared the trouble of dwelling upon them very minutely. With but little interest in the plot, with no very profound or ingenious development of character, and with a group of personages, not one of whom has any legitimate claims on either our affection or esteem, it yet, by the admirable skill with which its materials are managed,—the happy contrivance of the situations, at once both natural and striking,—the fine feeling of the ridiculous that smiles throughout, and that perpetual play of wit which never tires, but seems, like running water, to be kept fresh by its own flow,—by all this general animation and effect, combined with a finish of the details almost faultless, it unites the suffrages, at once, of the refined and the simple, and is not less successful in ministering to the natural enjoyment of the latter, than is satisfying and delighting the most fastidious tastes among the former. —MOORE, THOMAS, 1825, *Memoirs of the Life of the Right Honourable Richard Brinsley Sheridan, vol. I, p. 245.*

Many of the situations are so exquisitely comic, though a large portion of the piece is passed in talk which does not advance the action, the habit of scandal and tale-bearing is so admirably ridiculed, and the tone of the whole is so brilliant and refined, that it is equally delightful when read or when acted.—SHAW, THOMAS B., 1847, *Outlines of English Literature, p. 404.*

The surpassing merits of the "School for Scandal" become the more brilliant, the more minutely they are scanned, and the more fairly the faults of the play are in juxtaposition with its beauties. Its merits are not so much to be sought in the saliency of any predominating excellence as in the harmonious combination of great varieties of excellence, in a unity of purpose sufficiently philosophical for the intellect of comedy, but not so metaphysical as to mar the airy playfulness of comic mirth. The satire it conveys is directed, not to rare and exceptional oddities in vice or folly, but to attributes of human society which universally furnish the materials and justify the ridicule of satire. It is one of the beauties of this great drama, that its moral purpose is not rigidly narrowed into the mere illustration of a maxim—that the outward plot is indeed carried on by personages who only very indirectly serve to work out the interior moral.—LYTTON, EDWARD BULWER LORD, 1863-68, *Caxtoniana, Miscellaneous Prose Works, vol. III, p. 457.*

Seems fairly to deserve the character generally given to it of being the most perfect comedy which has been composed since the time of Shakespeare. . . . The justice of the general verdict of its pre-eminent excellence is sufficiently confirmed by its remaining undisturbed after the lapse of little less than a century.— YONGE, CHARLES DUKE, 1872, *Three Centuries of English Literature, p. 78.*

Is perhaps the best existing English comedy of intrigue.—GOSSE, EDMUND, 1888, *A History of Eighteenth Century Literature, p. 337.*

Since the "School for Scandal" no English drama has been produced which has anything like the same hold on the stage. —HARRISON, FREDERIC, 1894, *Early Victorian Literature, p. 21.*

Sheridan is not of course to be likened to Molière : the Frenchman had a depth and a power to which the Irishman could not pretend. But a comparison with Beaumarchais is fair enough, and it can be drawn only in favor of Sheridan; for brilliant as the "Marriage of Figaro" is, it lacks the solid structure and the broad outlook of the "School for Scandal." Both the French wit and the Irish are masters of fence, and the dialogue of these comedies still scintillates as steel crosses steel. Neither of them put much heart into his plays; and perhaps the "School for Scandal" is even more artificial than the "Marriage of Figaro,"—but it is wholly free from the declamatory shrillness which to-day mars the masterpiece of Beaumarchais.—MATTHEWS, BRANDER, 1897, *Library of the World's Best Literature, ed. Warner, vol. XXIII, p. 13320.*

THE CRITIC
1779-81

I have read Sheridan's "Critic," but, not having seen it, for they say it is admirably acted, it appeared wondrously flat and old, and a poor imitation: it makes me fear I shall not be so much charmed with "The School for Scandal" on reading, as I was when I saw it.—WALPOLE, HORACE, 1779, *To Rev. Wm. Mason, Dec.* 11; *Letters, ed. Cunningham, vol.* VII, *p.* 291.

In some of its most admired passages little better than an exquisite cento of the wit of the satirists before him. Sheridan must have felt himself emphatically at home in a production of this kind, for there was every call in it upon the powers he abounded in,—wit, banter, and style, —and none upon his good nature.—HUNT, LEIGH, 1841, *ed. Sheridan's Dramatic Works, Critical Sketch.*

Sir Fretful, between his two tormenters, and the cheerful bustle and assured confidence of Mr. Puff, have held their ground when hundreds of sensational dramas have drooped and died. Never was a more wonderful literary feat. The art of puffing has been carried to a perfection unsuspected by Mr. Puff, and not one person in a thousand has the most remote idea who Cumberland was; but "The Critic" is as delightful as ever, and we listen to the gentlemen talking with as much relish as our grandfathers did. Nay, the simplest-minded audience, innocent of literature, and perhaps not very sure what it all means, will still answer to the touch and laugh till they cry over the poor author's wounded vanity and the woes of Tilburina. Shakspeare, it is evident, found the machinery cumbrous, and gave up the idea of making Sly and his mockers watch the progress of the "Taming of the Shrew," and Beaumont and Fletcher lose our interest altogether in their long-drawn-out by-play, though the first idea of it is comical in the highest degree. Nor could Fielding keep the stage with his oft-repeated efforts, notwithstanding the wit and point of many of his dialogues. But Sheridan at last, after so many attempts, found out the right vein.—OLIPHANT, MARGARET O. W., 1883, *Sheridan (English Men of Letters), p.* 97.

"The Critic" is perhaps the highest proof of Sheridan's skill as a dramatist, for in it he has worked out, with perfect success for all time, a theme which, often as it has been attempted, no other dramatist has ever succeeded in redeeming from tedious circumstantiality and ephemeral personalities. The laughable infirmities of all classes connected with the stage, —authors, actors, patrons, and audience, —are touched off with the lightest of hands; the fun is directed, not at individuals, but at absurdities that grow out of the circumstances of the stage as naturally and inevitably as weeds in a garden.— MINTO, WILLIAM, 1886, *Encyclopædia Britannica, Ninth edition, vol.* XXI, *p.* 835.

GENERAL

At the same age with Congreve, he composed comedies of similar, and one of almost equal, merit: like his great master, he neglected incident and character, and sought only brilliancy of dialogue: what he sought, he attained, even to excess; and his wit was fertile enough to betray him into the splendid fault of rendering his dialogue more dazzling and poignant than suited his own personages, or, indeed, any human conversation.—MACKINTOSH, SIR JAMES, 1812, *Journal, Feb.* 7; *Memoirs, ed. Mackintosh, vol.* II, *p.* 203.

Lord Holland told me a curious piece of sentimentality in Sheridan. The other night we were all delivering our respective and various opinions on him and other *hommes marquans,* and mine was this: "What ever Sheridan has done or chosen to do has been, *par excellence,* always the *best* of its kind. He has written the *best* comedy ('School for Scandal'), the *best* drama (in my mind, far before that St. Giles's lampoon, 'The Beggar's Opera,') the best farce ('the Critic'—it is only too good for a farce), and the best Address ('Monologue on Garrick'), and, to crown all, delivered the very best Oration (the famous Begum Speech) ever conceived or heard in this country." Somebody told S. this the next day, and on hearing it he burst into tears! Poor Brinsley! if they were tears of pleasure, I would rather have said these few, but most sincere, words than have written the Iliad or made his own celebrated Philippic. Nay, his own comedy never gratified me more than to hear that he had derived a moment's gratification from any praise of mine, humble as it must appear to "my elders and my betters."—BYRON, LORD, 1813, *Journal, Dec.* 17, 18.

The comedy of the fourth period is chiefly remarkable for exhibiting "The Rivals" and "The School for Scandal." Critics prefer the latter; while the general audience reap, perhaps, more pleasure from the former, the pleasantry being of a more general cast, the incident more complicated and varied, and the whole plot more interesting. In both these plays, the gentlemanlike ease of Farquhar is united with the wit of Congreve. Indeed, the wit of Sheridan, though equally brilliant with that of his celebrated predecessor, flows so easily, and is so happily elicited by the tone of the dialogue, that in admiring its sparkles, we never once observe the stroke of the flint which produces them. Wit and pleasantry seemed to be the natural atmosphere of this extraordinary man, whose history was at once so brilliant and so melancholy.—SCOTT, SIR WALTER, 1814–23, *The Drama.*

There is too much merely ornamental dialogue, and, with some very fine rhetorical situations, too much intermission in the action and business of the play; and, above all, there is too little real warmth of feeling, and too few indications of noble or serious passion, thoroughly to satisfy the wants of English readers and spectators—even in a comedy. Their wit [that of "The Rivals" and "The School for Scandal"] is the best of them.—JEFFREY, FRANCIS LORD, 1826, *Moore's Life of Sheridan, Edinburgh Review, vol.* 45, *p.* 7.

The dramas of Sheridan . . . have placed him at the head of the genteel comedy of England; and while truth of character and manners, chastised brilliancy of wit, humour devoid of the least stain of coarseness, exquisite knowledge of stage-effect, and consummate ease and elegance of idiomatic language are appreciated, there can be no doubt that the name of Sheridan will maintain its place.—CROKER, JOHN WILSON, 1826, *Memoirs of Sheridan, Quarterly Review, vol.* 33, *p.* 592.

No writers have injured the Comedy of England so deeply as Congreve and Sheridan. Both were men of splendid wit and polished taste. Unhappily they made all their characters in their own likeness. Their works bear the same relation to the legitimate drama which a transparency bears to a painting; no delicate touches; no hues imperceptibly fading into each other; the whole is lighted up with a universal glare. Outlines and tints are forgotten, in the common blaze which illuminates all. The flowers and fruits of the intellect abound; but it is the abundance of a jungle, not of a garden—unwholesome, bewildering, unprofitable from its very plenty, rank from its very fragrance. Every fop, every boor, every valet is a man of wit. The very butts and dupes, Tattle, Urkwould, Puff, Acres, outshine the whole Hôtel de Rambouillet. To prove the whole system of this school absurd, it is only necessary to apply the test which dissolved the enchanted Florimel—to place the true by the false Thalia, to contrast the most celebrated characters which have been drawn by the writers of whom we speak, with the Bastard in King John, or the Nurse in Romeo and Juliet.—MACAULAY, THOMAS BABINGTON, 1827, *Machiavelli, Edinburgh Review, Critical and Miscellaneous Essays.*

Sheridan is, indeed, a golden link which connects us with the Authors of better days. He has wit; pure, polished, genuine wit. He has humour; not, perhaps, of quite so pure an order, a little forced and overstrained, but its root is in Nature, whatever aberrations it may spread into in its branches. His dialogue is of matchless brilliancy; so brilliant as to enchain the attention, and to blind us to the grand defect of his Plays, their want of action, and of what is technically called, business. This defect alone shuts out Sheridan from taking his place by the side of the elder Dramatists, and assigns him his situation a step lower among the writers of the age of Charles. He is, however, free from their impurities of thought and language; their equal in wit, and their superior in genuine humour.—NEELE, HENRY, 1827–29, *Lectures on English Poetry, p.* 155.

Sheridan's defects as a dramatist answer to the defects of his mind and character. Acute in observing external appearances, and well informed in what rakes and men of fashion call life, he was essentially superficial in mind and heart. A man of great wit and fancy, he was singularly deficient in the deeper powers of humor and imagination. All his plays lack organic life. In plot, character, and incident, they are framed by mechanical, not conceived by vital, processes. They evince no genial enjoyment of mirth, no insight into the deeper springs of the ludicrous.

The laughter they provoke is the laughter of antipathy, not of sympathy. It is wit detecting external inconsistencies and oddities, not humor representing them in connection with the inward constitution whence they spring.—WHIPPLE, EDWIN P., 1848, *Essays and Reviews, vol.* II, *p.* 306.

The close of the last century gave birth to the finest prose comedy in the English, or perhaps any other language. In abstract wit, Congreve equals, and, in the opinion of some critics, even surpasses, Sheridan; but Congreve's wit is disagreeably cynical; Sheridan's wit has the divine gift of the Graces—charm. The smile it brings to our lips is easy and cordial; the smile which Congreve brings forth is forced and sardonic. In what is called *vis comica,* Farquhar, it is true, excels Sheridan by the rush of his animal spirits, by his own hearty relish of the mirth he creates. Sheridan's smile, though more polished than Farquhar's, has not less ease; but his laugh, though as genuine, has not the same lusty ring. It is scarcely necessary, however, to point out Sheridan's superiority to Farquhar in the quality of the mirth excited. If in him the *vis comica* has not the same muscular strength, it has infinitely more elegance of movement, and far more disciplined skill in the finer weapons at its command; and whatever comparison may be drawn between the general powers of Sheridan for comic composition and those of Farquhar and Congreve, neither of the two last-named has produced a single comedy which can be compared to the "School for Scandal."— LYTTON, EDWARD BULWER LORD, 1863–68, *Caxtoniana, Miscellaneous Prose Works, vol.* III, *p.* 454.

His comedies were comedies of society, the most amusing ever written, but merely comedies of society.—TAINE, H. A., 1871, *History of English Literature, tr.* Van Laun, *vol.* I, *bk.* iii, *ch.* i, *p.* 526.

Sheridan's Irish birth and Celtic temperament must be largely credited with the brightness and permanent attractiveness of his plays.—ARNOLD, THOMAS, 1878, *English Literature, Encyclopædia Britannica, Ninth edition.*

His comedies are a continual running fire of wit; not true to nature and utterly destitute of that highest kind of humour which approaches pathos, but full of happy turns of expression and admirably constructed with a view to stage representation. He is the last of our playwriters who have produced works both excellent as literature and also good acting dramas. NICOLL, HENRY J., 1882, *Landmarks of English Literature, p.* 152.

He had a fit of writing, a fit of oratory, but no impulse to keep him in either path long enough to make anything more than the dazzling but evanescent triumph of a day. His harvest was like a Southern harvest, over early, while it was yet but May; but he sowed no seed for a second ingathering, nor was there any growth or richness left in the soon exhausted soil.— OLIPHANT, MARGARET O. W., 1883, *Sheridan (English Men of Letters), p.* 199.

Sheridan's was a brilliant, shallow intellect, a shifty, selfish nature; his one great quality, his one great element of success as a dramatist, as an orator and as a man, was mastery of effect. His tact was exquisitely nice and fine. He knew how to say and how to do the right thing, at the right time, in the right way. This was the sum of him; there was no more. Without wisdom, without any real insight into the human heart, without imagination, with a flimsy semblance of fancy, entirely devoid of true poetic feeling, even of the humblest order, incapable of philosophic reflection, never rising morally above the satirizing of the fashionable vices and follies of his day, to him the doors of the great theatre of human life were firmly closed. His mind flitted lightly over the surface of society, now casting a reflection of himself upon it, now making it sparkle and ripple with a touch of his flashing wing. He was a surface man, and the name of the two chief agents in the plot of his principal comedy is so suitable to him as well as to their characters, that the choice of it would seem to have been instinctive and intuitive. He united the qualities of his Charles and Joseph Surface; having the wit, the charming manner, the careless good-nature of the one, with at least a capacity of the selfishness, the duplicity, the crafty design, but without the mischief and the malice, of the other.— WHITE, RICHARD GRANT, 1883, ed., *The Dramatic Works of Richard Brinsley Sheridan, Introduction.*

Compared even with Congreve himself, he stands high as a dialoguist, for though his wit is not quite so keen or so nimble, or his style quite so polished, his epigrams and jests seem to grow more naturally and unforcedly out of the circumstances of the play; his geniality, too, is much greater, and is contagious. After a play of Sheridan's we feel on better terms with human nature. His plots are admirable—not solutions of any of the problems of social life as, according to some critics, comedies should be, but easy, pleasant, and fluent, and full, as such ease and pleasantness implies, of much concealed art. The spirit of Sheridan's plays is so thoroughly modern, they are salted with so good and true a wit, have so much of honest stage-craft in them, and are so full of a humour which is wholly that of the present period, that a play of his adequately put upon the stage will hold its own to this day triumphantly against the most successful of modern pieces.—CRAWFURD, OSWALD, 1883, *ed., English Comic Dramatists, p.* 262.

There is more freedom, more freshness of impulse, more kindness, more joy, more nature in "The Rivals" than there is in the "School for Scandal;" but both are artificial; both reflect, in a mirror of artistic exaggeration, the hollow, feverish, ceremonious, bespangled, glittering, heart-breaking fashionable world, in which their author's mind was developed and in which they were created. The "School for Scandal," indeed, is completely saturated with artificiality, and the fact that it was intended to satirise and rebuke the faults of an insincere, scandal-mongering society does not—and was not meant to—modify that pervasive and predominant element of its character.—WINTER, WILLIAM, 1892, *Old Shrines and Ivy, p.* 225.

His wit was an incessant flame.—He sometimes displayed a kind of serious and elegant playfulness, not apparently arising to wit, but unobservedly saturated with it, which was unspeakably pleasing.—His wit is the wit of common sense.—Grace of manner, charm of voice, fluency of language, and, above all, a brilliancy of sarcasm, a wit and a humour; and again a felicity of statement that made him the delight of every audience and that excited the admiration of his very opponents themselves.—The wit displayed by Sheridan in Parliament was perhaps, from the suavity of his temper, much less sharp than brilliant.—JERROLD, WALTER, 1893, *ed.,*

Bon-Mots of R. Brinsley Sheridan, Introduction, p. 12.

Can any one see such plays acted, for instance, as Sheridan's, without being forcibly struck by the total absence of spontaneity and the absolute submission to social routine of the average society man and woman of those days. Sheridan's comedies are undoubtedly as true to their times on the one hand as they are to human nature on the other, but the humanity of them is thrown into vivid and strong relief by the artificiality of the elements in the midst of which the chief actors have their being. As for the literature, it is hardly necessary for me to defend the statement that it was conventional.— CRAWFORD, F. MARION, 1893, *The Novel, What it is, p.* 100.

The real risk to which "The School for Scandal" is more and more exposed as the years roll by, is lest it may be found trespassing on the borderlands of truth and reality, and evoking genuine feeling; for as soon as it does this, the surroundings must become incongruous and therefore painful. Too long ago, when Miss Ellen Terry used to act Lady Teazle at the Vaudeville with a moving charm still happily hers, I remember hearing behind me a youthful voice full of tears and terror (it was of course when Joseph Surface was making his insidious proposals to Lady Teazle) exclaim, "Oh, mother, I hope she won't yield!" and I then became aware of the proximity of some youthful creature to whom all this comic business (for one knew the screen was soon to fall) was sheer tragedy. It made me a little uncomfortable. To Sheridan, nearer to Congreve than we are now to Sheridan, it was all pure comedy. We see this from the boisterous laughter with which Charles Surface greets the *dénouement.* Charles was no doubt a rake, but he was not meant to be a heartless rake after the fashion of the Wildairs of an earlier day. Had he not refused five hundred pounds for a trumpery picture of his uncle, for whose fortune he was waiting? It was all comedy to Sheridan, and if it ever ceases to be all comedy to us, it will be the first blow this triumphant piece has ever received.— BIRRELL, AUGUSTINE, 1896, *The School for Scandal and the Rivals, Introduction.*

Sheridan brought the comedy of manners to the highest perfection, and "The

School for Scandal" remains to this day the most popular comedy in the English language. Some of the characters both in this play and in "The Rivals" have become so closely associated with our current speech that we may fairly regard them as imperishable. No farce of our time has so excellent a chance of immortality as "The Critic." A playwright of whom these things are commonplaces must have had brilliant qualities for his craft; but the secret in this case, I think, lies in the pervading humanity of Sheridan's work. That is the only preservative against decay.—IRVING, SIR HENRY, 1896, *Sheridan, A Biography by Rae, vol.* II, *p.* 322.

As a dramatist Sheridan carried the comedy of manners in this country to its highest pitch, and his popularity as a writer for the stage is exceeded by that of Shakespeare alone.—RAE, FRASER, 1897, *Dictionary of National Biography, vol.* LII, *p.* 84.

The fact that Sheridan has held the stage, while his far greater predecessor, Congreve, has disappeared from it, is due to an accident of time. Luckily for Sheridan's permanence, he began to write when that wave of squeamishness and reticence in regard to certain things . . . had fairly washed over England. . . . No one who knows them both can doubt that Sheridan helped himself from Congreve with a generous hand. It is probable that he consciously "refined" him: it is certain that he unconsciously vulgarised him. . . . In this matter of breeding Sheridan comes off ill. In the more important matter of intellect he comes off worse. Epigrams and witty remarks apart, in which Congreve can beat the whole of Sheridan with one act of "The Way of the World," there is a meaning, a thought, in Congreve's characters and oppositions of characters which Sheridan never approaches. In this respect, at least, Sheridan is by far the coarser of the two. . . . Congreve's plays are more genuine comedies than Sheridan's. Sheridan had an eye for fantastic accessories and little more in his plays: Congreve was concerned, not primarily perhaps, but because he could not help using his intellect and his knowledge of life, with essentials of character and human relations. . . . Sheridan, then, is popularly regarded as the great and permanent exemplar of witty old English comedy by an accident. He does not deserve this preeminence, which should have been Congreve's. But he does deserve to hold the stage, and to be revived at the expense of contemporary dramatists. His wit is superficial and intellectually coarse, but there is plenty of it. His characters are rather thin and farcical, but they are distinct and act funnily on one another. A few lapses excepted, he is gay and lively. He has a style and a manner. Above all, he is an ingenious and effective craftsman, and therefore a good friend and a stimulus to the players. He is a fair task master to them. If they act well, they are sure of their due effect: he does not stultify them with inconsistencies or negations.—STREET, G. S., 1900, *Sheridan and Mr. Shaw, Blackwood's Magazine, vol.* 167, *pp.* 832, 833, 834.

Adam Ferguson

1723–1816

Philosopher and historian, was born 20th June 1723, at Logierait in Perthshire, where his father was parish minister. He studied at St. Andrews and Edinburgh, and as chaplain to the Black Watch was present at Fontenoy (1745). In 1757 he succeeded David Hume as keeper of the Advocate's Library in Edinburgh, and was next professor, first of Natural Philosophy (1759), and subsequently (1764) of Moral Philosophy. He accompanied the young Earl of Chesterfield (1774) on his travels on the Continent, and acted as secretary to the commission sent out by Lord North to try to arrange the disputes with the North American colonies (1778–79). Ill health compelled him in 1785 to resign his professorship, in which he was succeeded by Dugald Stewart. He next travelled on the Continent, then lived at Neidpath Castle, and latterly at St. Andrews, where he died 22nd of February 1816. His works are an "Essay on Civil Society" (1766), "Institutes of Moral Philosophy" (1772), "History of the Roman Republic" (1782; long a standard authority), and "Moral and Political Science" (1792). —PATRICK AND GROOME, *eds.*, 1897, *Chambers's Biographical Dictionary, p.* 360.

PERSONAL

He had the manners of a man of the world, and the demeanor of a high-bred gentleman, insomuch that his company was much sought after; for though he conversed with ease, it was with a dignified reserve. If he had any fault in conversation, it was of a piece with what I have said of his temper, for the elevation of his mind prompted him to such sudden transitions and dark allusions that it was not always easy to follow him, though he was a very good speaker. He had another talent, unknown to any but his intimates, which was a boundless vein of humour, which he indulged when there were none others present, and which flowed from his pen in every familiar letter he wrote. He had the faults, however, that belonged to that character, for he was apt to be jealous of his rivals, and indignant against assumed superiority. His wife used to say that it was very fortunate that I was so much in Edinburgh, as I was a great peacemaker among them. She did not perceive that her own husband was the most difficult of them all.—CARLYLE, ALEXANDER, 1753–56–1860, *Autobiography*, p. 229.

His hair was silky and white; his eyes animated and light-blue; his cheeks sprinkled with broken red, like autumnal apples, but fresh and healthy; his lips thin, and the under one curled. A severe paralytic attack had reduced his animal vitality, though it left no external appearance, and he required considerable artificial heat. His raiment, therefore, consisted of half-boots, lined with fur; cloth breeches; a long cloth waistcoat, with capacious pockets; a single-breasted coat; a cloth greatcoat, also lined with fur, and a felt hat, commonly tied by a ribbon below the chin. His boots were black; but, with this exception, the whole coverings, including the hat, were of a quaker-gray color, or of a whitish-brown; and he generally wore the furred greatcoat even within doors. When he walked forth, he used a tall staff, which he commonly held at arm's length out towards the right side; and his two coats, each buttoned by only the upper button, flowed open below, and exposed the whole of his curious and venerable figure. His gait and air were noble; his gestures slow; his look full of dignity and composed fire. He looked like a philosopher from Lapland.—COCKBURN,

HENRY LORD, 1830–54, *Memorials of his Time, ch.* i.

He was none the less, in affection as well as in character, a thorough Celt, with all the impulsiveness and dash that belonged to the race; and in later days, when Jacobitism was only a romantic memory, he was wont to delight his friends by his singing of Jacobite songs. Alone amongst the philosophers he spoke the language, and was stirred by the traditions of Gaul, and retained for that race to the end of his life the passionate attachment which it never fails to inspire. . . . Amongst a galaxy of men—none of the first rank in intellect, but all of more than respectable calibre—he has a place all his own. He achieved it partly by his wide and varied experience of life. But it was aided by his Celtic temperament, which gave a freedom and a verve to his speculation which was lacking to others of his school. Morality was to him essentially a thing of great deeds upon a great stage. The type he sought for was that of Aristotle's great-souled man. The subtleties of free thinking would have vexed his soul as much as the subtleties of doctrine; but he was more than any of them—however little he would have avowed it—the type of a purely pagan morality. His stoicism was a picturesque fiction, indeed, and none confessed more frankly than he that in the affairs of ever day life he was nervous and irritable to the last degree.—CRAIK, SIR HENRY, 1901, *A Century of Scottish History, vol.* II, *pp.* 210, 216.

At ninety-three there was still wondrous freshness in the venerable face, with the ribstone-pippin complexion, the mild blue eyes, the soft, humorous mouth, the silvery hair. There was the old mental alertness about everything that was new, and the aged philosopher listened eagerly when the divinity student who attended him read out to him the newspapers. He was a young man when the Rebellion of '45 broke out, lived to read the bulletins of the battle of Waterloo. At last, in 1816, he died, his final words as he turned to his daughters by the bedside being the exclamation of bright assurance: "There *is* another world," and in a few minutes he was gone to see it. One of the best of a brilliant company of literary comrades, he was the last to die. He had seen his old friends pass away one by one, in fame, honour, and old age. After having lived in the bright old days of Scottish literature, he survived to see with unjealous eyes another brilliant day dawn which should rival the past.—GRAHAM, HENRY GREY, 1901, *Scottish Men of Letters of the Eighteenth Century, p.* 120.

GENERAL

It was provoking to hear those who were so ready to give loud praises to very shallow and imperfect English productions —to curry favor, as we supposed, with the booksellers and authors concerned,—taking every opportunity to undermine the reputation of Ferguson's book. "It was not a Roman history," said they (which it did not say it was). "This delineation of the constitution of the republic is well sketched; but for the rest, it is anything but history, and then it is so incorrect that it is a perfect shame." All his other books met with the same treatment, while, at the same time, there were a few of us who could not refrain from saying that Ferguson's was the best history of Rome; that what he had omitted was fabulous or insignificant, and what he had wrote was more profound in research into characters, and gave a more just delineation of them than any book now extant. The same thing was said of his book on Moral Philosophy, which we held to be the book that did the most honor of any to the Scotch philosophers, because it gave the most perfect picture of moral virtues, with all their irresistible attractions. His book on Civil Society ought only to be considered as a college exercise, and yet there is in it a turn of thought and a species of eloquence peculiar to Ferguson.—CARLYLE, ALEXANDER, 1753–56–1860, *Autobiography, p.* 230.

Read the first, and half the second, volume, quarto, of Dr. Ferguson's "Principles of Moral and Political Philosophy." He was Dugald Stewart's predecessor, and, as I attended his lecture, I heard the substance of his book. He has, in some degree, the Scotch fault of expressing common ideas in a technical form. He had adopted the very just, stoical principle, "that the state of the mind is of more importance to happiness than outward circumstances;" but he is so entirely and constantly occupied with it, as to forget everything else. There is something not unbecoming a moral teacher in his austere, dogmatic, sententious manner; and he contemplates human life with a cold sternness worthy of those magnanimous moralists whom he professes to follow. . . . It is not a pleasing, but it is an improving book; it elevates the moral sentiments.—MACKINTOSH, SIR JAMES, 1812, *Journal, April* 10; *Memoirs, ed. Mackintosh, vol.* II, *pp.* 243, 244.

Ferguson's "History of the Roman Republic" is not only well written, but meritorious for its researches into the constitution of Rome.—SPALDING, WILLIAM, 1852–82, *A History of English Literature, p.* 347.

In Roman history, Hooke, the friend of Pope, was first in the field; and to him succeeded Dr. Ferguson, with his dry book on the Roman republic.—ARNOLD, THOMAS, 1862–87, *A Manual of English Literature, p.* 486.

Ferguson's style and manner are not so subdued as those of the Scottish metaphysicians who preceded him. He has more of a leaping mode of composition, as if he had an audience before him, and is at times eloquent or magniloquent. I have an idea that, as Dugald Stewart drew his philosophy mainly from Reid, so he got his taste for social studies from Ferguson, who may also have helped to give him a livelier style,—the academic dignity, however, being entirely Stewart's own.—McCOSH, JAMES, 1874, *The Scottish Philosophy, p.* 260.

Ferguson's book has the superficial merits which were calculated for the ordinary mind. He possessed the secret of that easy gallicised style, which was more or less common to the whole Scott school, including Hume, Robertson, and Adam Smith. He makes elegant and plausible remarks, and the hasty reader does not perceive that the case is gained by the evasion, instead of the solution, of difficulties. Here and there we come across an argument or an illustration which seems to indicate greater acuteness. . . . Ferguson was in politics what Blair was in theology—a facile and dexterous declaimer, whose rhetoric glides over the surface of things without biting into their substance. He expounds well till he comes to the real difficulty, and then placidly evades the dilemma.—STEPHEN, LESLIE, 1876, *History of English Thought in the Eighteenth Century, vol.* II, *p.* 215.

A work ["History of the Roman Republic"] which under the guise of history is in truth a series of lectures on ethics and politics, with a strong leaven of stoicism. —CRAIK, SIR HENRY, 1901, *A Century of Scottish History, vol.* II, *p.* 216.

Jane Austen
1775–1817

No other English woman of letters ever lived a life so entirely uneventful. . . . Born on the 16th of December, 1775. In the year 1796 and '97, before she was twenty-three years old, she wrote the novel "Pride and Prejudice;" in 1797 and '98, "Sense and Sensibility," and "Northanger Abbey." These works, however, waited fifteen years for a publisher; and Jane, who wrote merely for her own amusement, seems to have possessed her soul in patience. In 1801 the family removed to Bath; in 1805 the Rev. George Austen died, and they again removed to Southampton. In 1809 they settled at Chawton, Hampshire; and in 1811 Jane was at length enabled to publish "Sense and Sensibility." It was followed in 1813 by "Pride and Prejudice." "Mansfield Park" appeared in 1814, and "Emma" in 1816. Jane Austen died on the 18th of July, 1817. After her death her early novel "Northanger Abbey," and "Persuasion," a mature work which has the same mellower quality as "Emma," together with a pathos peculiarly its own, were published.—CONE, HELEN GRAY, AND GILDER, JEANNETTE L., 1887, *Pen-Portraits of Literary Women, vol.* I, *p.* 195.

PERSONAL

There were twenty dances, and I danced them all, and without fatigue. I was glad to find myself capable of dancing so much and with so much satisfaction as I did; from my slender enjoyment of the Ashford balls, I had not thought myself equal to it, but in cold weather and with few couples I fancy I could just as well dance for a week together as for half an hour. —AUSTEN, JANE, 1799, *To her Sister, Dec.* 24; *Letters, ed. Brabourne.*

A friend of mine, who visits her now, says that she has stiffened into the most perpendicular, precise, taciturn piece of "single blessedness" that ever existed, and that, till "Pride and Prejudice" showed what a precious gem was hidden in that unbending case, she was no more regarded in society than a poker or a fire-screen, or any other thin upright piece of wood or iron that fills its corner in peace and quietness. The case is very different now; she is still a poker, but a poker of whom every one is afraid. It must be confessed that this silent observation from such an observer is rather formidable. . . . After all, I do not know that I can quite vouch for this account, though the friend from whom I received it is truth itself; but her family connections must render her disagreeable to Miss Austen, since she is the sister-in-law of a gentleman who is at law with Miss A.'s brother for the greater part of his fortune.—MITFORD, MARY RUSSELL, 1815,

Letter to Sir Wm. Elford, April 3; *Life,* ed. L'Estrange.

I remember Jane Austen, the novelist, a little child. . . . When I knew Jane Austen, I never suspected that she was an authoress; but my eyes told me she was fair and handsome, slight and elegant, but with cheeks a little too full. The last time I think that I saw her was at Ramsgate in 1803: perhaps she was then about twenty-seven years old. Even then I did not know she was addicted to literary composition.—BRYDGES, SIR SAMUEL EGERTON, 1834, *Autobiography, vol.* II, *p.* 41.

In person she was very attractive; her figure was rather tall and slender, her step light and firm, and her whole appearance expressive of health and animation. In complexion she was a clear brunette with a rich colour; she had full round cheeks, with mouth and nose small and well formed, bright hazel eyes, and brown hair forming natural curls close round her face. If not so regularly handsome as her sister, yet her countenance had a peculiar charm of its own to the eyes of most beholders. . . . She was not highly accomplished according to the present standard, . . . was fond of music, and had a sweet voice, both in singing and in conversation; in her youth she had received some instruction of the pianoforte; and at Chawton she practised daily, chiefly before breakfast. . . . She read French with facility, and knew something of Italian. In those

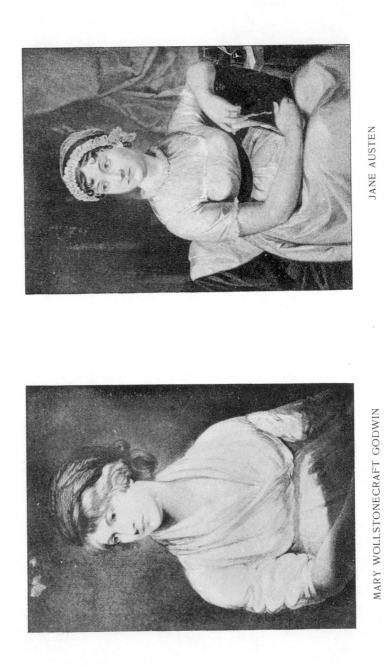

MARY WOLLSTONECRAFT GODWIN

From a Woodburytype after a Painting by Opie

JANE AUSTEN

After an Original Family Portrait.

days German was no more thought of than Hindostanee, as part of a Lady's education. . . . She was well acquainted with the old periodicals from the "Spectator" downwards. Her knowledge of Richardson's works was such as no one is likely again to acquire, now that the multitude and the merits of our light literature have called off the attention of readers from that great master.—LEIGH, J. E. AUSTEN, 1870, *A Memoir of Jane Austen, by her Nephew*, pp. 82, 83, 84.

During her whole life she remained to a great extent engrossed by the interests of her family and their limited circle of old and intimate friends. This was as it should be—so far, but there may be too much of a good thing. The tendency of strictly restricted family parties and sets—when their members are above small bickerings and squabblings—when they are really superior people in every sense, is to form "mutual admiration" societies, and neither does this more respectable and amiable weakness act beneficially upon its victims. . . . Fondly loved and remembered as Jane Austen has been, with much reason, among her own people, in their considerable ramifications, I cannot imagine her as greatly liked, or even regarded with anything save some amount of prejudice, out of the immediate circle of her friends, and in general society. . . . What I mean is, that she allowed her interests and sympathies to become narrow, even for her day, and that her tender charity not only began, but ended, in a large measure, at home.—KEDDIE, HENRIETTA (SARAH TYTLER), 1880, *Jane Austen and Her Works*, pp. 15, 16.

Jane is described as tall, slender, and remarkably graceful; she was a clear brunette with a rich colour, hazel eyes, fine features, and curling brown hair. Her domestic relations were delightful, and she was specially attractive to children. A vague record is preserved of an attachment for a gentleman whom she met at the seaside, and who soon afterwards died suddenly. But there is no indication of any serious disturbance of her habitual serenity.—STEPHEN, LESLIE, 1885, *Dictionary of National Biography*, vol. II, p. 259.

The precise locality of the gravestone is in the pavement of the fifth bay of the north aisle, counting from the west. It is a slab of black marble with the following inscription:—"In memory of JANE AUSTEN, youngest daughter of the late Revd. George Austen, formerly Rector of Steventon in this County. She departed this life on July 18, 1817, aged 41, after a long illness, supported with the patience and hope of a Christian. The benevolence of her heart, the sweetness of her temper, and the extraordinary endowments of her mind, obtained the regard of all who knew her, and the warmest love of her immediate connexions. Their grief is in proportion to their affection; they know their loss to be irreparable, but in their deepest affliction they are consoled by a firm, though humble, hope that her charity, devotion, faith, and purity have rendered her soul acceptable in the sight of her Redeemer."—ADAMS, OSCAR FAY, 1891-96, *The Story of Jane Austen's Life*, p. 220.

All the time that she was writing her three best novels she had no private study: she wrote in the general sittingroom at her little mahogany desk, and when visitors interrupted, a handkerchief or a newspaper was thrown over the tell-tale MSS. Very often her nephews and nieces rushed in, and she was always ready to break off from her writing to tell them long delightful fairy stories. . . . She was essentially a womanly woman. Everything that she did with her fingers was well done. She wrote a clear, firm hand, as easy to read as print.—HAMILTON, CATHERINE J., 1892, *Women Writers, First Series*, pp. 203, 204.

May we not be well content with Jane Austen as we have her, the central figure of a little loving family group, the dearest of daughters and sisters, the gayest and brightest of aunts, the most charming and incomparable of old maids?—REPPLIER, AGNES, 1892-95, *Essays in Miniature*, p. 170.

No book published in Jane Austen's lifetime bore her name on the title-page; she was never lionized by society; she was never two hundred miles from home; she died when forty-two years of age, and it was sixty years before a biography was attempted or asked for. She sleeps in the cathedral at Winchester, and not so very long ago a visitor, on asking the verger to see her grave, was conducted thither, and the verger asked, "Was she anybody in particular? so many folks ask where she's buried, you know!" But this is changed now, for when the verger took me to her grave and we stood by that plain black marble slab, he spoke intelligently of her life and work. And many visitors now go to the cathedral only because it is the resting-place of Jane Austen, who lived a beautiful, helpful life and produced great art, yet knew it not.—HUBBARD, ELBERT, 1897, *Little Journeys to the Homes of Famous Women, p.* 353.

PRIDE AND PREJUDICE
1796–1813

Read again, and for the third time at least, Miss Austen's very finely written novel of "Pride and Prejudice." That young lady had a talent for describing the involvements, and feelings, and characters of ordinary life, which is to me the most wonderful I every met with. The Big Bow-wow strain I can do myself like any now going; but the exquisite touch, which renders ordinary commonplace things and characters interesting, from the truth of the description and the sentiment, is denied to me. What a pity such a gifted creature died so early!—SCOTT, SIR WALTER, 1826, *Diary, March* 14; *Memoirs, ed. Lockhart, ch.* lxviii.

Why do you like Miss Austen so very much? I am puzzled on that point. What induced you to say that you would rather have written "Pride and Prejudice," or "Tom Jones," than any of the Waverly Novels? I had not seen "Pride and Prejudice" till I read that sentence of yours—then I got the book. And what did I find? An accurate daguerreotyped portrait of a commonplace face; a carefully fenced, high-cultivated garden, with neat borders and delicate flowers; but no glance of a bright, vivid physiognomy, no open country, no fresh air, no blue hill, no bonny beck. I should hardly like to live with her ladies and gentlemen, in their elegant but confined houses. . . . She (George Sand) is sagacious and profound—Miss Austen is only shrewd and observant. . . . You say I must familiarize my mind with the fact that "Miss Austen is not a poetess, has no 'Sentiment,' no eloquence, none of the ravishing enthusiasm of poetry,"—and then you add, I *must* "learn to acknowledge her as *one of the greatest artists, of the greatest painters of human character,* and one of the writers with the nicest sense of means to an end that ever lived." The last point only will I ever acknowledge. Can

there be a great artist without poetry?— BRONTË, CHARLOTTE, 1848, *Letters to G. H. Lewes, Life of Brontë by Gaskell, pp.* 313, 319.

She was only about twenty in her sheltered and happy life at home in the end of the old century, when she wrote what might have been the outcome of the profoundest prolonged observation and study of mankind—what is, we think, the most perfect of all her works—"Pride and Prejudice." —OLIPHANT, MARGARET O. W., 1882, *Literary History of England, XVIII and XIX Centuries, vol.* III, *p.* 184.

To say nothing of the supreme excellence of the dialogue, there is scarcely a page but has its little gem of exact and polished phrasing; scarcely a chapter which is not adroitly opened or artistically ended; while the whole book abounds in sentences over which the writer, it is plain, must have lingered with patient and loving craftsmanship. . . . Criticism has found little to condemn in the details of this capital novel.—DOBSON, AUSTIN, 1895, *ed., Pride and Prejudice, Introduction.*

Never was there a book written which has given more harmless pleasure to those who have come under its spell. As we open its pages, we bid adieu to a world of sordid cares and troublesome interests, and though we do not wander into fairy-land, for Miss Austen's world is always matter-of-fact, we do catch a breath of an air less severe than that which we habitually draw, and find, if not fairy-land, at least a touch of the lightness of fairy-land brought down to us.—JACK, ADOLPHUS ALFRED, 1897, *Essays on the Novel, p.* 254.

"Pride and Prejudice" is realistic in its narrowness of scope, in its lack of complicated plot, and in that it sets forth clearly and fully a limited section of life. It attempts to hold up no ideals; it deals for the most part with middle-class people; it has in it no literary atmosphere suggested either by the characters or by the author's allusions. And yet one forgets that he is reading a book; he feels as if he were making a visit among people in whom he had a human interest. He finds himself scheming with the fond mother in her matchmaking interests for her daughters five.—DYE, CHARITY, 1898, *The Story-Teller's Art, p.* 71.

Perhaps "Pride and Prejudice" is the

only one where the general design can be almost unreservedly praised, but even in this, which is undoubtedly the finest of her novels, there is one serious defect that is absent in none of them, namely, an inadequate sense of dramatic climax. It may be ungenerous to find fault with the author for the perfunctory manner in which she disposes of the minor figures in her story after the main interest has been exhausted. . . . It was entirely inexcusable that she should invariably fail to realise the opportunity of making emotional capital out of the supreme psychological moment of her *dénoûment.*— OLIPHANT, JAMES, 1899, *Victorian Novelists, pp.* 26, 27.

It is a dated society, and it is a dated woman, not the woman of all time, that we have portrayed; but it is a society and a woman portrayed with marvellous perfection. . . . Moreover, if we had a complete novel-form, we have an equally complete method. One can use the style of Jane Austen as a model for study in the schoolroom. There is repression in every detail; the plot is made simple; the adjective is cut out of the sentences; every detail of finish is subordinated to a requirement of sincerity, to a limited and selected variety. The humor is cultivated, genial; it is the humor of an observer—of a refined, satisfied observer—rather than the humor of a reformer; it is the humor of one who sees the incongruities, but never dreams of questioning the general excellence of the system as a whole. All this is the method of a completed ideal; a method of manifest limits, but within its limits absolutely true. Still further we may claim that this novel is not only an expression of a complete novel form; it is not only an expression of a complete literary method; it is also an embodiment of completed ideals.—STODDARD, FRANCIS HOVEY, 1900, *The Evolution of the English Novel, pp.* 53, 55.

May lay claim to being the most enjoyable book any woman ever wrote.—GREY, ROWLAND, 1901, *The Bores of Jane Austen, Fortnightly Review, vol.* 76, *p.* 43.

SENSE AND SENSIBILITY
1797–1811

I think the title of the book is misleading to modern ears. Sensibility in Jane Austen's day meant warm, quick feeling, not exaggerated or over keen, as it really does now; and the object of the book, in my belief, is not to contrast the sensibility of Marianne with the sense of Elinor, but to show how with equally warm, tender feelings the one sister could control her sensibility by means of her sense when the other would not attempt it. These qualities come still more prominently forward when Mrs. Dashwood and her daughters have found a home at Barton Cottage. . . . There can be little doubt that in "Sense and Sensibility" we have the first of Jane Austen's revised and finished works, and in several respects it reveals an inexperienced author. The action is too rapid, and there is a want of dexterity in getting the characters out of their difficulties. Mrs. Jennings is too vulgar, and in her, as in several of the minor characters, we see that Jane Austen had not quite shaken off the turn for caricature, which in early youth she had possessed strongly.—MALDEN, MRS. CHARLES, 1889, *Jane Austen (Famous Women), pp.* 60, 77.

To contend, however, for a moment that the present volume is Miss Austen's greatest, as it was her first published, novel, would be a mere exercise in paradox. There are, who swear by "Persuasion;" there are, who prefer "Emma" and "Mansfield Park;" there is a large contingent for "Pride and Prejudice;" and there is even a section which advocates the pre-eminence of "Northanger Abbey." But no one, as far as we can remember, has ever put "Sense and Sensibility" first, nor can I believe that its author did so herself. And yet it is she herself who has furnished the standard by which we judge it, and it is by comparison with "Pride and Prejudice," in which the leading characters are also two sisters, that we assess and depress its merit. The Elinor and Marianne of "Sense an Sensibility" are only inferior when they are contrasted with the Elizabeth and Jane of "Pride and Prejudice;" and even then, it is probably because we personally like the handsome and amiable Jane Bennet rather better than the obsolete survival of the sentimental novel represented by Marianne Dashwood. Darcy and Bingley again are much more "likeable" (to use Lady Queensberry's word) than the colourless Edward Ferrars and the stiff-jointed Colonel Brandon.— DOBSON, AUSTIN, 1896, *Sense and Sensibility, Introduction.*

NORTHANGER ABBEY
1797-1818

The behaviour of the General in "Northanger Abbey," packing off the young lady without a servant or the common civilities which any bear of a man, not to say gentleman, would have shown, is quite outrageously out of drawing and out of nature. —EDGEWORTH, MARIA, 1818, *Letters, vol.* I, *p.* 246.

I read Dickens' "Hard Times." One excessively touching, heartbreaking passage and the rest sullen socialism. The evils which he attacks he caricatures grossly, and with little humor. Another book of Pliny's letters. Read "Northanger Abbey;" worth all Dickens and Pliny together. Yet it was the work of a girl. She was certainly not more than twenty-six. Wonderful creature!—MACAULAY, THOMAS BABINGTON, 1854, *Journal, Aug.* 12; *Life and Letters, ed. Trevelyan.*

Her style deserves the highest commendation. It has all the form and finish of the eighteenth century, without being in the least degree stilted or unnatural. It has all the tone of good society without being in the least degree insipid. For a specimen of crisp, rich English, combining all the vigour of the masculine with all the delicacy of the feminine style, we suggest the opening chapter of "Northanger Abbey" as a model for any young lady writer of the present age.—KEBBEL, T. E., 1870, *Jane Austen, Fortnightly Review, vol.* 13, *p.* 193.

MANSFIELD PARK
1814

It is certainly not *incumbent* on you to dedicate your work now in the press to His Royal Highness; but if you wish to do the Regent that honour either now or at any future period I am happy to send you that permission, which need not require any more trouble or solicitation on your part. Your late works, Madam, and in particular "Mansfield Park," reflect the highest honour on your genius and your principles. In every new work your mind seems to increase its energy and power of discrimination. The Regent has read and admired all your publications.—CLARKE, J. S., *Librarian,* 1815; *Letter to Miss Austen, Nov.* 16.

Finished "Mansfield Park," which hurries with a very inartificial and disagreeable rapidity to its conclusions, leaving some opportunities for most interesting and beautiful scenes, particularly the detailed expression of the "how and the when" Edward's love was turned from Miss Crawford to Fanny Price. The great merit of Miss Austen is in the finishing of her characters; the action and conduct of her stories I think frequently defective.— MACREADY, W. C., 1836, *Diary, July* 10; *Reminiscences, ed. Pollock, p.* 393.

The longest, and, we think, least valuable of her books.—OLIPHANT, MARGARET, O. W., 1882, *Literary History of England, XVIII and XIX Centuries, vol.* III, *p.* 192.

How well I recall the greatest literary pleasure of my life, its time and place! A dreary winter's day without, within a generous heat and glow from the flaming grate, and I reclining at my ease on the library lounge, "Mansfield Park" in hand. Then succeed four solid hours of literary bliss, and an absorption so great that when I mechanically close the book at the last page it is only by the severest effort that I come back to the real world of pleasant indoors and bleak outdoors. I was amazed that I, a hardened fiction reader, should be so transported by this gentle tale of Miss Austen's, and yet I enjoyed to the full the after-taste of her perfect realistic art. This first enthusiasm, however, soon abated, and I began to see flaws, to note the prolixity and unevenness of the work, and to feel that it was almost school-girlish in tone and sentiment. While the verisimilitude is, indeed, fascinating, the realization is far from profound. And the characters are too one-sided for full human beings—are only puppets, each pulled by a single string. Edmund Bertram is, perhaps, the most woodeny of these marionettes. Lady Bertram, the languid beauty, seems often overdrawn. Mrs. Norris is a perfect busybody, but a pettiness so absolutely consistent at length rouses our suspicions and irritates us. We feel that human nature, outside of the madhouse, does not fulfill the single types so completely. But in Fanny Price we find no flaw or artistic presentment. Here comes before our eyes a real, a free, a complex human being. . . . I am acquainted with no more charming figure in fiction than Fanny; she is so completely, perfectly, deliciously feminine in instinct, feeling, manner and intelligence.—STANLEY, HIRAM M., 1897, *Essays on Literary Art, p.* 47.

EMMA
1816

We, therefore, bestow no mean compliment upon the author of "Emma," when we say that, keeping close to common incidents, and to such characters as occupy the ordinary walks of life, she has produced sketches of such spirit and originality, that we never miss the excitation which depends upon a narrative of uncommon events, arising from the consideration of minds, manners and sentiments, greatly above our own. In this class she stands almost alone; for the scenes of Miss Edgeworth are laid in higher life, varied by more romantic incident, and by her remarkable power of embodying and illustrating national character. But the author of "Emma" confines herself chiefly to the middling classes of society; her most distinguished characters do not rise greatly above well-bred country gentlemen and ladies; and those which are sketched with most originality and precision, belong to a class rather below that standard.—SCOTT, SIR WALTER, 1815, *Emma, Quarterly Review, vol.* 14, *p.* 193.

Finished Miss Austen's "Emma," which amused me very much, impressing me with a high opinion of her powers of drawing and sustaining character, though not satisfying me always with the end and aim of her labours. She is successful in painting the ridiculous to the life, and while she makes demands on our patience for the almost intolerable absurdities and tediousness of her well-meaning gossips, she does not recompense us for what we suffer from her conceited and arrogant nuisances by making their vices their punishments. We are not much better, but perhaps a little more prudent for her writings. She does not probe the vices, but lays bare the weaknesses of character; the blemish on the skin, and not the corruption at the heart, is what she examines. Mrs. Brunton's books have a far higher aim; they try to make us better, and it is an addition to previous faults if they do not. The necessity, the comfort, and the elevating influence of piety is continually inculcated throughout her works—which never appears in Miss Austen's.—MACREADY, W. C., 1834, *Diary, Feb.* 15; *Reminiscences, ed. Pollock, p.* 312.

I have likewise read one of Miss Austen's works—"Emma"—read it with interest and with just the degree of admiration which Miss Austen herself would have thought sensible and suitable. Anything like warmth or enthusiasm—anything energetic, poignant, heart-felt is utterly out of place in commending these works: all such demonstration the authoress would have met with a well-bred sneer, would have calmly scorned as outré and extravagant. She does her business of delineating the surface of the lines of genteel English people curiously well. There is a Chinese fidelity, a miniature delicacy in the painting. She ruffles her reader by nothing vehement, disturbs him by nothing profound. The passions are perfectly unknown to her; she rejects even a speaking acquaintance with that stormy sisterhood. Even to the feelings she vouchsafes no more than an occasional graceful but distant recognition— too frequent converse with them would ruffle the smooth elegance of her progress. Her business is not half so much with the human heart as with the human eyes, mouth, hands, and feet. What sees keenly, speaks aptly, moves flexibly, it suits her to study; but what throbs fast and full, though hidden, what the blood rushed through, what is the unseen seat of life and the sentient target of death— this Miss Austen ignores. She no more, with her mind's eye, beholds the heart of her race than each man, with bodily vision, sees the heart in his heaving breast. Jane Austen was a complete and most sensible lady, but a very incomplete and rather insensible (not senseless) woman. If this is heresy, I cannot help it.— BRONTË, CHARLOTTE, 1850, *Letter to W. S. Williams, April* 12; *Charlotte Brontë and her Circle, by Shorter, p.* 399.

"Emma," perhaps, is the work upon which most suffrages would meet as the most perfect of all her performances.— OLIPHANT, MARGARET O. W., 1882, *Literary History of England, XVIII and XIX Centuries, vol.* III, *p.* 192.

I have a great liking, witnessed by a periodical re-reading, for the pleasant scampishness and easy, go as you please narrative of "Gil Blas;" and I humbly claim to share in the learned's appreciation of Miss Austen, taking "Emma" as my first choice among the fruits of a genius so great and yet so ladylike, so almost young ladylike. — HAWKINS, ANTHONY HOPE,

1897, *My Favorite Novelist and His Best Book*, *Munsey's Magazine*, vol. 18, p. 351.

PERSUASION
1818

"Persuasion"—excepting the tangled, useless histories of the family in the first fifty pages—appears to me, especially in all that relates to poor Anne and her lover, to be exceedingly interesting and natural. The love and the lover admirably well drawn: don't you see Captain Wentworth, or rather don't you in her place feel him taking the boisterous child off her back as she kneels by the sick boy on the sofa? And is not the first meeting after their long separation admirably well done?—EDGEWORTH, MARIA, 1818, *Letters*, vol. I, p. 247.

The book shows broader sympathies, deeper observation, and perhaps more perfect symmetry, balance, poise, than the others. The always flexible, unobtrusive style, in which reduction of emphasis is carried sometimes to the verge of equivocation, concealing the author, yet instinct with her presence, in none of her books approximates more nearly to Cardinal Newman's definition—"a thinking out into language." In general, the qualities that appear in the others are in "Persuasion" perhaps more successfully fused than before.—CLYMER, W. B. SHUBRICK, 1891, *A Note on Jane Austen, Scribner's Magazine*, vol. 9, p. 384.

"Persuasion" represents the ripest development of Jane Austen's powers, that latest phase of her thoughts and feelings. It is a novel which, while not wanting in the several excellences of those which preceded it, has a mellower tone and a more finished grace of style than any of the others. It was written at a time when bodily strength had given place to weakness; and although her mind was more active than ever, her physical condition insensibly influenced her thought, giving this latest of her books that deeper note of feeling, that finer touch of sympathy and tenderness, which make "Persuasion" the greatest of all her works.—ADAMS, OSCAR FAY, 1891–96, *The Story of Jane Austen's Life*, p. 254.

It was Miss Austen's last story, and has more depth of feeling and pathos than most of hers. . . . The delicate miniature painting of the characters in these tales is apt not to be appreciated by the young, and the tone of county society of that day disgusts them; but as they grow older they perceive how much ability and insight is displayed in the work, and esteem the forbearance, sweetness, and self-restraint of such a heroine as Anne.—YONGE, CHARLOTTE M., 1893, *Anne Elliot, Great Characters of Fiction, ed. Townsend, pp.* 18, 19.

Of Anne Elliot, the heroine of "Persuasion," she wrote to a friend, "You may *perhaps* like her, as she is almost too good for me." She is too good for most of us, but not the less charming, and even the brilliancy of Elizabeth Bennet pales a little before the refined womanliness of this delightful English lady. Whether the future of Catherine Morland and Henry Tilney was wholly ideal may be doubted; we may even have secret reservations as to the absolute bliss of Emma and her Knightley; but there can be no sort of question as to the ultimate and unalloyed happiness of Anne Elliot and Captain Wentworth, who is another of those pleasant manly naval officers whom Miss Austen, drawing no doubt from material in her own family circles, depicts so sympathetically. — DOBSON, AUSTIN, 1897, *Northanger Abbey and Persuasion, Introduction*, p. xii.

GENERAL

Miss Austin's works may be safely recommended, not only as among the most unexceptionable of their class, but as combining, in an eminent degree, instruction with amusement, though without the direct effort at the former, of which we have complained as sometimes defeating its object. For those who cannot or will not *learn* anything from productions of this kind, she has provided entertainment which entitles her to thanks; for mere innocent amusement is in itself a good, when it interferes with no greater; especially as it may occupy the place of some other that may *not* be innocent. The Eastern monarch who proclaimed a reward to him who should deserve a new pleasure, would have deserved well of mankind had he stipulated that it should be blameless. Those, again, who delight in the study of human nature, may improve in the knowledge of it, and in the profitable application of that knowledge by the perusal of such fictions as those before us.—WHATELY, ARCHBISHOP, 1821, *Northanger Abbey and Persuasion, Quarterly Review*, vol. 24, p. 375.

By the way, did you know Miss Austen, authoress of some novels which have a great deal of nature in them?—nature in ordinary and middle life, to be sure, but valuable from its strong resemblance and correct drawing. I wonder which way she carried her pail.—SCOTT, SIR WALTER, 1822, *Letter to Miss Joanna Baillie, Memoirs, ed. Lockhart, ch.* lv.

All-perfect Austen. Here
Let one poor wreath adorn thy early bier,
That scarce allowed thy modest youth to claim
Its living portion of thy certain fame.
Oh, Mrs. Bennet! Mrs. Norris, too!
While memory survives we'll dream of you,
And Mr. Woodhouse, whose abstemious lip
Must thin, but not too thin, his gruel sip;
Miss Bates, our idol, though the village bore;
And Mrs. Elton, ardent to explore:
While the dear style flows on without pretence,
With unstained purity, and unmatched sense.
—CARLISLE, EARL OF, 1825, *The Keepsake.*

Our dinner-party this evening was like nothing but a chapter out of one of Miss Austen's novels. What wonderful books those are! She must have written down the very conversations she heard *verbatim*, to have made them so like, which is Irish.—KEMBLE, FRANCES ANN, 1831, *Records of a Girlhood, July* 31, p. 441.

My idol.—MITFORD, MARY RUSSELL, 1832, *Letter to Mrs. Trollope; What I Remember, by T. A. Trollope,* p. 496.

The delicate mirth, the gently hinted satire, the feminine, decorous humor of Jane Austen, who, if not the greatest, is surely the most faultless of female novelists. My Uncle Southey and my father had an equally high opinion of her merits, but Mr. Wordsworth used to say that though he admitted that her novels were an admirable copy of life, he could not be interested in productions of that kind; unless the truth of nature were presented to him clarified, as it were, by the pervading light of imagination, it had scarce any attractions in his eyes.—COLERIDGE, SARA, 1834, *Letter to Miss Emily Trevenen, Aug.; Memoirs and Letters, ed. by her Daughter,* p. 77.

It is the constant manner of Shakspeare to represent the human mind as lying, not under the absolute dominion of one domestic propensity, but under a mixed government, in which a hundred powers balance each other. Admirable as he was

in all parts of his art, we most admire him for this, that, while he has left us a greater number of striking portraits than all other dramatists put together, he has scarcely left us a single caricature. Shakspeare has had neither equal nor second. But among the writers who, in the point which we have noticed, have approached nearest to the manner of the great master, we have no hesitation in placing Jane Austen, a woman of whom England is justly proud. She has given us a multitude of characters, all, in a certain sense, commonplace, all such as we meet every day. Yet they are all as perfectly discriminated from each other as if they were the most eccentric of human beings.—MACAULAY, THOMAS BABINGTON, 1842, *Madame D'Arblay, Critical and Miscellaneous Essays.*

We should say that Fielding and Miss Austen are the greatest novelists in our language. . . . Miss Austen has been called a prose Shakspeare;—and, among others, by Macaulay. In spite of the sense of incongruity which besets us in the words *prose* Shakspeare, we confess the greatness of Miss Austen, her marvelous dramatic power, seems more than anything in Scott, akin to the greatest quality in Shakspeare. — LEWES, GEORGE HENRY, 1847, *Recent Novels, Fraser's Magazine, vol.* 36, p. 687.

Home, and finished "Persuasion." I have now read over again all Miss Austen's novels. Charming they are, but I found a little more to criticise than formerly. Yet there are in the world no compositions which approach nearer to perfection.—MACAULAY, THOMAS BABINGTON, 1851, *Journal, May* 1; *Life and Letters, ed. Trevelyan.*

She [Miss Milford] never taught *me* anything but a very limited admiration of Miss Austen, whose people struck me as wanting souls, even more than is necessary for men and women of the world. The novels are perfect as far as they go—that's certain. Only they don't go far, I think. It may be my fault.—BROWNING, ELIZABETH BARRETT, 1855, *To Mr. Ruskin, Nov.* 5; *Letters, ed. Kenyon, vol.* II, p. 217.

All in all, as far as my information goes, the best judges unanimously prefer Miss Austen to any of her contemporaries of the same order. They reckon her "Sense and Sensibility," her "Pride and Prejudice," her "Mansfield Park" and her "Emma" (which novels were published in her lifetime), and also her "Northanger Abbey" and her "Persuasion" (which were published posthumously) as not only better than anything else of the kind written in her day, but also among the most perfect and charming fictions in the language. I have known the most hard-headed men in ecstasies with them; and the only objection I have heard of as brought against them by ladies is, that they reveal too many of their secrets.—MASSON, DAVID, 1859, *British Novelists and Their Styles*, p. 189.

Miss Austen is, of all his successors, the one who most nearly resembles Richardson in the power of impressing reality upon her characters. There is a perfection in the exhibition of Miss Austen's characters which no one else has approached; and truth is never for an instant sacrificed in that delicate atmosphere of satire which pervades her works. . . . She has been accused of writing dull stories about ordinary people. But her supposed ordinary people are really not such very ordinary people. Let any one who is inclined to criticize on this score, endeavour to construct one character from among the ordinary people of his own acquaintance that shall be capable of interesting any reader for ten minutes. It will then be found how great has been the discrimination of Miss Austen in the selection of her characters and how skillful is her treatment in the management of them.—POLLOCK, W. F., 1860, *British Novelists, Fraser's Magazine, vol.* 61, pp. 30, 31.

By those who have studied character distinct from its outward manifestations, as expressed in conformity to uses and customs, there will be found in Miss Austen's novels an expression of firm and original courage as clear as if she had braved society, whether theoretically or practically. The boldness which will vindicate for persons of mediocre intellect souls to be saved and feelings to be tortured, and which by such vindication can interest and compel a jaded, hurrying public, eager for changing excitements, to pause and to listen—is surely no common quality; but it has within itself a promise and an assurance of enduring reputation. —CHORLEY, G. F., 1870, *Miss Austen*

and Miss Mitford, Quarterly Review, vol. 128, *p.* 203.

Jane Austen was the flower of a stock, full, apparently, through all its branches, of shrewd sense and caustic humour, which in her were combined with the creative imagination. . . . She possessed a real and rare gift, and she rendered a good account of it. If the censer which she held among the priests of art was not of the costliest, the incense was of the purest. If she cannot be ranked with the very greatest masters of fiction, she has delighted many, and none can draw from her any but innocent delight.—SMITH, GOLDWIN, 1870–81, *Austen-Leigh's Memoir of Jane Austen, Lectures and Essays.*

She was always very careful not to meddle with matters which she did not thoroughly understand. She never touched upon politics, law, or medicine; but with ships and sailors she felt herself at home, or at least could always trust to a brotherly critic to keep her right. It is said that no flaw has ever been found in her seamanship either in "Mansfield Park" or in "Persuasion."—CONANT, S. S., 1870, *Jane Austen, Harper's Magazine, vol.* 41, *p.* 227.

I am equally sure that Miss Austen cannot be third, any more than first or second: I think you were rather drawn away by a fashion when you put her there: and really old Spedding seems to me to have been the Stag whom so many followed in that fashion. She is capital as far as she goes: but she never goes out of the Parlour; if but Magnus Troil, or Jack Bunce, or even one of Fielding's Brutes, would but dash in upon the Gentility and swear a round Oath or two! I must think the "Woman in White," with her Count Fosco, far beyond all that. Cowell constantly reads Miss Austen at night after his Sanskrit Philology is done: it composes him, like Gruel: or like Paisiello's Music, which Napoleon liked above all other, because he said it didn't interrupt his Thoughts.— FITZGERALD, EDWARD, 1871, *Letters, vol.* I, *p.* 335.

Miss Austen is without a rival in the field she occupied. . . . It was a mere fragment of human life that Miss Austen saw with a clearness and an intelligence and a reproductive power that defy panegyric.—HALES, JOHN W., 1873, *Notes and Essays on Shakespeare, p.* 72.

The extraordinary skill which Miss Austen displayed in describing what Scott called "the involvements and feelings and characters of ordinary life," places her as a novelist above her predecessor, Miss Burney. But it is more doubtful whether she is entitled to rank above her contemporary Miss Edgeworth. In Macaulay's opinion Madame de Stael was certainly the first woman of her age; Miss Edgeworth the second; and Miss Austen the third. Yet Miss Austen has one advantage over Miss Edgeworth which is very important. In reading Miss Austen no one ever thinks of the moral of the story, everyone becomes insensibly the better person for perusing it.—WALPOLE, SPENCER, 1878, *A History of England from the Conclusion of the Great War in 1815, vol.* I, *p.* 378.

A distinguished English scholar said to a lecturer who had extolled the tales of Charlotte Brontë, "I am afraid you do not know that Miss Austen is the better novelist." If the scholar had explained doubtless he would have said, in comparing Miss Brontë or George Eliot with Miss Austen, —and the three are the chief of their sex in this form of English literature—that her distinction and superiority lie in her more absolute artistic instinct. She writes wholly as an artist, while George Eliot advocates views, and Miss Brontë's fiery page is often a personal protest. In Miss Austen, on the other hand, there is in kind, but infinitely less in degree, the same clear atmosphere of pure art which we perceive in Shakespeare and Goethe. It is a thread of exceeding fineness with which she draws us, but it is spun of pure gold. There are no great characters, no sweep of passion, no quickening of soul and exaltation of purpose and sympathy, upon her page, but there is the pure pleasure of a Watteau. . . . Miss Austen's art is not less in the choice than in the treatment. She does not, indeed, carve the Moses with Michael Angelo, but she moulds the delicate cup, she cuts the gem.—CURTIS, GEORGE WILLIAM, 1881, *Editor's Easy Chair, Harper's Magazine, vol.* 62, *p.* 309.

Like Wordsworth, she sought to show the charm that lies under the common things about us, and with a fine feminine humour, under sentences clear, simple, and exactly fitted to expression of a shrewd good sense, she came nearer to Fielding than any novelist who wrote before the reign of Queen Victoria. — MORLEY, HENRY, 1881, *Of English Literature in the Reign of Victoria, With a Glance at the Past, p.* 111.

Her humour flows gentle and spontaneous; it is no elaborate mechanism nor artificial fountain, but a bright natural stream, rippling and trickling over every stone and sparkling in the sunshine. . . . Her picnics are models for all future and past picnics. . . . Her machinery is simple but complete; events group themselves so vividly and naturally in her mind that, in describing imaginary scenes, we seem not only to read them, but to live them, to see the people coming and going: the gentlemen courteous and in top-boots, the ladies demure and piquant; we almost hear them talking to one another.— RITCHIE, ANNE ISABELLA THACKERAY, 1883, *A Book of Sibyls, pp.* 200, 201.

To-day, more than seventy long years have rolled away since the greater part of them ["Letters"] were written; no one now living can, I think, have any possible just cause of annoyance at their publication, whilst, if I judge rightly, the public never took a deeper or more lively interest in all that concerns Jane Austen than at the present moment. Her works, slow in their progress towards popularity, have achieved it with the greater certainty, and have made an impression the more permanent from its gradual advance. The popularity continues, although the customs and manners which Jane Austen describes have changed and varied so much as to belong in a great measure to another age.— BRABOURNE, EDWARD LORD, 1884, *ed., Letters of Jane Austen, Introduction, vol.* I, *p.* xii.

She never exhausts a scene by what is called word-painting. She indicates its main features, and describes the general effect it produces upon the spectator, rather than recapitulates the size, weight, and colour of its various component elements. To say that she has a strong insight into female character is almost superfluous. George Eliot does not enter more deeply into the workings of the female mind and heart than she does. Add to all these claims that our author's novels are perfectly unexceptionable from every point of view, and that they combine rational amusement with no small degree of instruction, and we have advanced tolerably sufficient grounds for the continuous favour with which they have been and are still regarded. The critic who said that these novels added a new pleasure to existence was not wide of the mark. In Miss Austen's later books, the most exacting may discover a maturity of thought and a felicity of expression seldom attained by members of her craft; and these augured still greater achievements in the future had her life been spared.— SMITH, GEORGE BARNETT, 1885, *More Views of Jane Austen, Gentleman's Magazine, vol.* 258, *p,* 44.

Even Jane Austen's novels, which strangely retain their hold on the public taste, are tedious to those who dare to think for themselves and forget Macaulay's verdict.—SANBORN, KATE, 1885, *The Wit of Women, p.* 33.

As to your own works (immortal, as I believe), I have but little that is wholly cheering to tell one who, among women of letters, was almost alone in her freedom from a lettered vanity. You are not a very popular author: your volumes are not found in gaudy covers on every bookstall; or, if found, are not perused with avidity by the Emmas and Catherines of our generation. . . . Your admirers, if not very numerous, include all persons of taste. . . . Your volumes neither excite nor satisfy the curiosities provoked by that modern and scientific fiction, which is greatly admired, I learn, in the United States as well as in France and at home. —LANG, ANDREW, 1886, *To Jane Austen, Letters to Dead Authors, pp.* 75, 76, 79.

The great literary artist to whom we are indebted, among other things, for a gallery of those clerical portraits, destined to last as long as the English language. . . . I am one of the regular Austen vassals, and consider her as without a rival among English writers, in her own line and within her own limits. I should not say, as Macaulay says, that she ranks next to Shakspeare, any more than I should put a first-rate miniature painter on the same level with Raphael or Titian. It is enough for me that she stands alone as a first-rate miniature painter in her own particular school of design.—DOYLE, SIR FRANCIS HASTINGS, 1886, *Reminiscences and Opinions, p.* 353.

It is a curious fact that Paris, to which the works of Jane Austen were lately as unknown as if she were an English painter, has just discovered her existence. Moreover, it has announced that she, and she only, is the founder of that realistic school which is construed to include authors so remote from each other as the French Zola and the American Howells. The most decorous of maiden ladies is thus made to originate the extreme of indecorum; and the good loyal Englishwoman, devoted to Church and King, is made sponsor for the most democratic recognition of persons whom she would have loathed as vulgar. There is something extremely grotesque in the situation; and yet there is much truth in the theory. It certainly looked at one time as if Miss Austen had thoroughly established the claim of her sex to the minute delineation of character and manners, leaving to men the bolder school of narrative romance. . . . But the curious thing is that of the leading novelists in the English tongues to-day it is the men, not the women, who have taken up Miss Austen's work, while the women show more inclination, if not to the "big bow-wow style" of Scott, at least to the novel of plot and narrative. Anthony Trollope among the lately dead, James and Howells among the living, are the lineal successors of Miss Austen. Perhaps it is an old-fashioned taste which leads me to think that neither of these does his work quite so well as she.—HIGGINSON, THOMAS WENTWORTH, 1887, *Women and Men, pp.* 156, 157.

I very early enjoyed Jane Austen's novels. I can sustain a competitive examination upon them now, having probably read each of the more important ones at least fifty times in my life.—HALE, EDWARD EVERETT, 1888, *Books That Have Helped Me, p.* 8.

Miss Austen is likely to remind the average reader more of Cowper than of Shakspeare. Her books seem redolent of the aroma of tea mixed in just the right proportion. They are comfortable— steeped in comfort. If there is no word in them that can bring a blush to the cheek of a young girl, there is likewise no word in them to "catch us by the throat" and to force us to acknowledge there are better things in the world than a comfortable income, a bright grate, and pleasant acquaintances. Nevertheless she was an

artist of the highest type.—EGAN, MAU-
RICE FRANCIS, 1889, *Lectures on English
Literature, p.* 146.

Her work displays creative imagination,
wonderful power of observing, fine feeling
for dramatic situation, and perfect command of her literary vehicle; but we cannot help feeling conscious of a certain lack
of weight which comes of her steady
avoidance of the heights and the depths of
human nature. We are charmed always,
but seldom, if ever, deeply moved.
Though in various respects Jane Austen
may be compared favourably with George
Sand, George Eliot, and Charlotte Brontë,
we feel that these writers have spells of
which she knew not the secret. It is in
virtue of their combination of veracious
and uncompromising realism with unfailing vivacity and ever-present grace that
the novels of Jane Austen are unique in
literature. — NOBLE, JAMES ASHCROFT,
1889, *Jane Austen, The Academy, vol.* 36,
p. 96.

Criticism is becoming the art of saying
fine things, and there are really no fine
things to be said about Jane Austen.—
SMITH, GOLDWIN, 1890, *Jane Austen
(Great Writers).*

Realism is nothing more and nothing less
than the truthful treatment of material,
and Jane Austen was the first and the
last of the English novelists to treat
material with entire truthfulness. Because she did this, she remains the most
artistic of the English novelists, and alone
worthy to be matched with the great
Scandinavian and Slavic and Latin artists.
—HOWELLS, W. D., 1891, *Criticism and
Fiction, p.* 73.

Nobody can read any of Miss Austen's
works without admiring her wonderful
closeness and keenness of humorous observation, the skill with which she displays
every turn in the motives of commonplace
character, and the exquisite quality of the
ridicule with which her fancy dances round
and round them as she holds them up to
our inspection. If you once make the
acquaintance of the Bennet family in
"Pride and Prejudice," you can never forget them, so distinctly is each individual
marked, and so keen and exquisite is the
revelation of their foibles. In mere art
of humorous portraiture, in a quieter and
less farcical style than Miss Burney's, Miss
Austen is an expert of classical finish.

But somehow, speaking for myself, I must
confess to a certain want of interest in
the characters themselves. Unless one is
really interested in the subjects of such
an elaborate art of portraiture, the gradual
revelation of them, touch after touch, is
apt to become tedious, however much one
may enjoy for a time the quick and delicate
play of the writer's gently malicious
humor. But this want of interest in the
characters of English middle-class provincial life is of course a personal defect.
—MINTO, WILLIAM, 1894, *The Literature
of the Georgian Era, ed. Knight, p.* 281.

The perfection of Miss Austen's workmanship has been seized upon by unfavourable critics and used as a weapon of
offence. She is perfect, they allege, only
as some are virtuous, because she has no
temptation; she lives in an abject world,
dead to poetry, visited by no breath of
romance, and is placidly contented with
her ant-hill, which she describes with
great accuracy and insight. It would be
unjust to this type of criticism to interpret
it merely as a complaint that one who
was of unsurpassed power in comedy and
satire did not forego her gifts and take
up with romance and tragedy. If it has
a meaning worth considering, it means
that even the comedy of life has in it
shades of pathos and passion to which she
is constitutionally blind. And this is to
mistake her art. The world of pathos and
passion is present in her work by implication; her delicious quiet mirth, so quiet as
to be inaudible to gross ears, is stirred by
the incongruity between the realities of
the world, as she conceives them, and
these realities as they are conceived by
the puppets. The kingdom of Lilliput has
its meaning only when it is seen through
the eyes of Gulliver. A rabbit fondling
its own harmless face affords no matter of
amusement to another rabbit, and Miss
Austen has had many readers who have
perused her works without a smile.
Sympathy with her characters she frequently has, identity never. Not in the
high-spirited Elizabeth Bennet, not in that
sturdy young patrician Emma, not even in
Anne Elliot of "Persuasion," is the real
Jane Austen to be found. She stands forever aloof. Those who wish to enjoy her
art must stand aloof too, and must not ask
to be hurried through her novels on a
personally conducted tour, with their

admirations and dislikes prepared for them.—RALEIGH, WALTER, 1894, *The English Novel, p.* 263.

She makes you slip into easy acquaintance with the people of her books as if they lived next door, and would be pulling at your bell to-morrow, or to-night. And you never confound them; by the mere sound of their voices you know which is Ellinor, and which is Marianne; and as for the disagreeable people in her stories, they are just as honestly and naturally disagreeable as any neighbor you could name—whether by talking too much, or making puns, or prying into your private affairs.—MITCHELL, DONALD G., 1895, *English Lands Letters and Kings, Queen Anne and the Georges, p.* 266.

One indeed of the most wonderful things about her is her earliness. . . . Irony is by no means a frequent feminine gift; and as women do not often possess it in any great degree, so they do not as a rule enjoy it. Miss Austen is only inferior among English writers to Swift, to Fielding, and to Thackeray—even if it be not improper to use the term inferiority at all for what is after all not much more than difference—in the use of this potent but most double-edged weapon. Her irony indeed is so subtle that it requires a certain dose of subtlety to appreciate it, and it is not uncommon to find those who consider such personages as Mr. Collins in "Pride and Prejudice" to be merely farcical, instead of, as they are in fact, preachers of the highest and most Shakespearian comedy. . . . the important thing for the purposes of this history is to observe again that she "set the clock," so to speak, of pure novel writing to the time which was to be nineteenth century time to this present hour. She discarded violent and romantic adventure. She did not rely in the very least degree on describing popular or passing fashions, amusements, politics; but confined herself to the most strictly ordinary life. Yet she managed in some fashion so to extract the characteristics of that life which are perennial and human, there can never be any doubt of fit readers in any age finding themselves at home with her, just as they find themselves at home with all the greatest writers of bygone ages. And lastly, by some analogous process she hit upon a style which, though again true to the ordinary speech of her

own day, and therefore now reviled as "stilted" and formal by those who have not the gift of literary detachment, again possesses the universal quality, and, save in the merest externals, is neither ancient nor modern.—SAINTSBURY, GEORGE, 1896, *A History of Nineteenth Century Literature, pp.* 129, 130.

The one prose-writer of this period whose genius has proved absolutely perdurable, who holds no lower a place in her own class than is held in theirs by Wordsworth, Coleridge, and Scott—for that impeccable Jane Austen, whose fame becomes every day more inaccessible to the devastating forces of time and shifting fashion. It has long been seen, it was noted even by Macaulay, that the only writer with whom Jane Austen can fairly be compared is Shakespeare. It is obvious that she has nothing of his width of range or sublimity of imagination; she keeps herself to that two-inch square of ivory of which she spoke in her proud and simple way. But there is no other English writer who possesses so much of Shakespeare's inevitability, or who produces such evidence of a like omniscience. Like Balzac, like Tourgenieff at his best, Jane Austen gives the reader an impression of knowing everything there was to know about her creations, of being incapable of error as to their acts, thoughts, or emotions. She presents an absolute illusion of reality; she exhibits an art consummate that we mistake it for nature. She never mixes her own temperament with those of her characters, she is never swayed by them, she never loses for a moment her perfect, serene control of them. Among the creators of the world, Jane Austen takes a place that is with the highest and that is purely her own.—GOSSE, EDMUND, 1897, *Short History of Modern English Literature, p.* 295.

Her conditions and temperament conspired to impose limitations which make her art perhaps more enduring than that of her great successors, since from very scarcity of material she was forced to individualize after much our present manner. But on account of these very limitations, her work has slight value as social evidence to the wider phases of contemporary life.—SCUDDER, VIDA D., 1898, *Social Ideals in English Letters, p.* 130.

The style of Jane Austen cannot be

separated from herself or her method. It is the natural easy flowing garment of her mind, delighting in inconsistencies and infinite detail. It is so peculiarly her own that one cannot trace in it with any degree of certainty the course of her reading. . . . The matter of observation, in passing through Jane Austen's imagination, was never violently disturbed; the particular bias it received was from a delicate and delightful irony; there was precisely that selection and recombination and heightening of incident and character that distinguish the comedy of manners from real life.—CROSS, WILBUR L., 1899, *The Development of the English Novel, pp.* 121, 124.

No doubt the quibs and cranks and trickeries of literary fashion will go on and on so long as printing is not one of the lost arts; but there will always be many, among whom I count myself one, to believe that Jane Austen's genius will assert itself triumphantly, however many these vacillations and counterchanges in literary taste, and however long they may last.—POLLOCK, WALTER HERRIES, 1899, *Jane Austen, Her Contemporaries and Herself, p.* 1.

After considering the short, feverish, genius-filled lives of such people as Marie Bashkirtseff or Aubrey Beardsley, what a rest it is to go back to the contemplation of a peaceful, homely, healthy existence like that of Jane Austen! It is, indeed, this peaceful, homely element in her writings that gives them the place they are rightfully reclaiming in English literature.—HARPER, JANET, 1900, *The Renascence of Jane Austen, Westminster Review, vol.* 153, *p.* 442.

It has sometimes occurred to me that it would be a very delightful thing if a magazine could be started which should be devoted entirely to Miss Austen, and to which only her sincere admirers should be allowed to contribute. We are never tired of talking about her; should we ever grow weary of reading or writing about her? For my own part I read every book or article that relates to her with the utmost eagerness, provided that the author displays a due sense of worship; but any criticism which is not of the most loving character is irritating, and, like other follies, it should be avoided. . . . The great men in literature have always appreciated her. The praise given her by Scott and Macaulay has been often quoted, and I recollect my mother telling me of a conversation with Lord Beaconsfield, who certainly expressed his admiration of the authoress, and who, I think, said that "Emma" was his favourite among the novels. But since I was young, Miss Austen's popularity with the general public has increased in a quite remarkable manner. Some thirty years ago I was starting on a journey with two companions, one of them about my own age, the other an older man. My contemporary went to the book-stall and proposed to buy "Emma," but his senior interposed and told him it was "awfully stupid." I looked upwards, but no lightning struck the impious head, nor did we even encounter a railway smash. Fate may have been merciful because the intending purchaser proved himself worthy, and "Emma" was after all properly honoured. There are not now, one may hope, many who can read the novel and decide that it is "awfully stupid," but my friend, though undoubtedly an extravagant sinner, was not altogether peculiar in his generation. —IDDESLEIGH, EARL OF, 1900, *A Chat about Jane Austen's Novels, The Nineteenth Century, vol.* 47, *p.* 811.

Timothy Dwight
1752–1817

Was born in Northampton, Massachusetts, in 1752. After graduating at Yale College, he was chosen tutor, which office he held for six years. In 1783 he was ordained over the Congregational church in Greenfield, Connecticut, and in 1795 was chosen president of Yale College, which post he held until his death, which occurred January 11, 1817. Dr. Dwight's published works are, "The Conquest of Canaan," a poem; "Greenfield Hill," a poem; "Travels in New England," four volumes; "Theology Explained and Defended," five volumes; and some versions of the Psalms. His "Theology" has passed through numerous editions in England as well as in our own country, and is very highy esteemed.—CLEVELAND, CHARLES DEXTER, 1868, *Lyra Sacra Americana, p.* 308.

PERSONAL

Of this American poet I am sorry to be able to give the British reader no account. I believe his personal history is as little known as his poetry on this side of the Atlantic. — CAMPBELL, THOMAS, 1819, *Specimens of the British Poets.*

As a poet President Dwight was little inferior to any of his contemporaries in America; but it was not on his poetry that his claims to the respect of mankind were based. As an instructor probably he was never surpassed in this country, and as a theologian he had no equal among the men of his time. An eloquent preacher, with a handsome person, an expressive countenance, polished and affable manners, brilliant conversational abilities, and vast stores of learning,—it was almost impossible that he should fail of success in any effort, and least of all in the administration of the important office which he so long and so honourably filled. When he died, the country was bereaved of a great and good man.—GRISWOLD, RUFUS W., 1842–46, *The Poets and Poetry of America,* p. 14.

Stately and majestic, and every way well proportioned. His features were regular; his eye black and piercing, yet benignant; and his countenance altogether indicative of a high order of mind. His voice was rich and melodious, adapted alike to music and oratory.— SPRAGUE, WILLIAM B., 1844, *Life of Timothy Dwight, Library of American Biography, ed. Sparks, vol.* 14, *p.* 230.

Pleasing as Dr. Dwight is as a poet, and learned and eloquent as he was as a divine, it is as President of Yale College that he was most valued, and honoured, and loved while living, and as such is embalmed in the hearts of the large number of scholars, divines, and statesmen still living, who were instructed by him in their collegiate course. He had the remarkable faculty of winning the affections and commanding the most profound respect of the young men who came under his influence, while he poured forth his instructions in a most impressive eloquence, from a mind stored with the treasures of ancient and modern learning. And knowing, as we do, that for the last twenty years of his life he could scarcely use his eyes at all, our wonder increases that he accomplished so much.—CLEVELAND, CHARLES D., 1859, *A Compendium of American Literature, p.* 103.

His influence was extensive and beneficent beyond that of any other man in New England; indeed, his enemies called him "old Pope Dwight." . . . Whenever he came to my house, the family thought it a privilege to gather round him to listen to his conversation. We sat round, and he talked. A question now and then would be asked, but nobody ever thought of talking much, only of hearing. He loved to talk, and we loved to listen. Whenever I wanted advice, I went to him as to a father, and told him everything.— BEECHER, LYMAN, 1863, *Autobiography, vol.* I, *p.* 328.

He was himself greater than anything he ever said or did; and for those who came near him, all that he did or said had an added import and fascination as proceeding from one so overpoweringly competent and impressive.—TYLER, MOSES COIT, 1895, *Three Men of Letters, p.* 99.

GENERAL

In his fictions he discovers much warmth of conception, and his numbers are very harmonious. His numbers, indeed, imitate pretty closely those of Pope, and therefore cannot fail to be musical; but he is chiefly to be commended for the animation with which he writes, and which rather increases as he proceeds, than suffer any abatement. . . . The composition, however, is not without a fault; and as we have candidly praised, we will censure with fidelity. By the motto which the author has chosen, we are led to suspect that he is young, and the chief blemish of his poem is one into which hardly anything but youth could have betrayed him. A little mature consideration would have taught him, that a subject nearly four thousand years old could not afford him a very fair opportunity for the celebration of his contemporaries.—COWPER, WILLIAM, 1788, *The Conquest of Canaan, Analytical Review; Works, ed. Southey, vol.* IV, *pp.* 355, 356.

Of Dr. Dwight we would speak with all the respect due to talents, to learning, to piety, and a long life of virtuous usefulness, but we must be excused from feeling any high admiration of his poetry. It seems to us modelled upon a manner altogether too artificial and mechanical. There is something strained, violent, and out of nature in all his attempts. His

"Conquest of Canaan" will not secure immortality to its author. In his work he has been considered by some critics as by no means happy in the choice of his fable. However this may be, he has certainly failed to avail himself of the advantages it offered him; his epic wants the creations and colorings of an inventive and poetical fancy—the charm which, in the hands of a genius, communicates an interest to the simplest incidents, and something of the illusion of reality to the most improbable fictions. The versification is remarkable for its unbroken monotony. Yet it contains splendid passages, which, separated from the body of the work, might be admired, but a few pages pall both on the ear and the imagination. It has been urged in its favor that the writer was young. The poetry of his maturer years does not, however, seem to possess greater beauties or fewer faults.—BRYANT, WILLIAM CULLEN, 1818–84, *Early American Verse, Prose Writings, ed. Godwin, vol.* I. *p.* 49.

Corresponding with the laws which the author prescribed to himself, in his "Conquest of Canaan," he made every thing too common. There is little that is really distinctive, little that is truly oriental about any of his persons or scenes. A certain equable current of unexceptionable, and oftentimes pleasing thoughts and expressions, flows through the poem. It is occasionally animated, and in description, sometimes picturesque and poetical. The versification, though generally monotonous, having too little variety in the pauses, is for the most part uncommonly smooth. In the expression of strong emotion, there is an avoidance of all offensive extravagance, if it do not reach the genuine ardour or pathos of the highest order of poetry. Having said thus much, we fear we have said all that is due to this poetical work; nor do we say this to deduct any thing from the high and well-deserved reputation of President Dwight. It is not the lot of a single man to excel in every thing; and it is often our misfortune to make a false estimate of our own powers, and to stake too much of our intellectual wealth on the race, in which we are unable to reach the goal.—WILLARD, S., 1818, *Life and Writings of President Dwight, North American Review, vol.* 7, *p.* 352.

The work before us ["Travels"] though the humblest in its pretences, is the most important of his writings, and will derive additional value from time, whatever may become of his poetry and of his sermons. . . . A wish to gratify those who, a hundred years hence, might feel curiosity concerning his native country, made him resolve to prepare a faithful description of its existing state. He made notes, therefore, and collected information on the spot. . . . The remarks upon natural history are those of an observant and sagacious man who makes no pretentions to science; they are more interesting, therefore, than those of a merely scientific traveller; and, indeed, science is not less indebted to such observers, than history to the faithful chroniclers and humbler annalists of former times.—SOUTHEY, ROBERT, 1823, *Quarterly Review, vol.* 30, *pp.* 1, 2.

No production of the transatlantic press has met with so favourable a reception in this country, and experienced so extensive a circulation, as this work ["Theology Explained"] of President Dwight. Nor is its popularity likely to be ephemeral. It bears the impress of a most powerful mind, and will pass down to posterity, both in the Old and New World, as the work of one of the master-spirits of the Christian Church.—ORME, ROBERT, 1824, *Bibliotheca Biblica.*

In Dwight's early poems we see a heat of honest enthusiasm sufficient to warm the faculties through life. These productions have been hardly dealt with. They are worth something more than to furnish a dull jest at epic failures. The "Conquest of Canaan," it should be remembered, was the production of a youth hardly out of college, and should be looked at as a series of poetic sketches, not over nice in rhetorical treatment or obedience to the laws of Aristotle. In that view it contains much pleasing writing, but the word epic should never be brought in contact with it. . . . "Greenfield Hill" is an idyllic poem of rare merit. A little more nicety of execution and a better comprehension of the design at the outset, would doubtless have improved it; but the spirit is there. — DUYCKINCK, EVERT A., AND GEORGE L., 1855–65–75, *Cyclopædia of American Literature, ed. Simons, vol.* I, *pp.* 373, 375.

Dr. Dwight was a well-meaning, amiable, indefatigable man, of remarkable talent,

but distinctly falling short of genius.—
NICHOL, JOHN, 1880–85, *American Literature, p.* 93.

He wrote "America," "The Conquest
of Canaan" (an epic), "Greenfield Hill,"
and "The Triumph of Infidelity." These
poems are not properly subjects of criticism, because they are hopelessly forgotten,
and no critical resurrectionist can give
them that slight appearance of vitality
which would justify an examination of
their merits and demerits. Yet they are
reasonably good of their kind, and "Greenfield Hill," especially, contains some descriptions which are almost worthy to be
called charming. Dwight, as a Latin
scholar, occasionally felt called upon to
show his learning in his rhymes. Thus in
one of his poems he characterizes one of
the most delightful of Roman lyrists as
"desipient" Horace. After a diligent exploration of the dictionary the reader finds
that *desipient* comes from a Latin word
signifying "to be wise," and that its English meaning is "trifling, foolish, playful."
It might be supposed that in the whole
range of English poetry there was no
descriptive epithet so ludicrously pedantic.
—WHIPPLE, EDWIN PERCY, 1886, *American Literature and Other Papers, ed.
Whittier, p.* 21.

Surely, "The Conquest of Canaan," with
its eleven dreadful books of conventional
rhymed pentameters,—all tending more or
less to disarrange and confuse the familiar
facts of Biblical history, as well as to
dilute, to render garrulous, and to cheapen,
the noble reticence, the graphic simplicity,
of the antique chronicle,—is such an epic
as can be grappled with, in these degenerate days, by no man who is not himself as
heroic as this verse assumes to be. . . .
A satire in verse, entitled "The Triumph
of Infidelity." . . . From title-page
to colophon, the intended method of the
satire is irony,—a method calling, of

course, for delicacy of movement, for arch
and mocking sprightliness, for grace and
levity of stroke, and obviously beyond the
quality of one who being, in the first place,
always dead-in-earnest, emphatic, and even
ponderous, and secondly quite guiltless of
humor, was above all things an intellectual
gladiator, and could hardly think of any
other way of dealing with an antagonist
than by the good old-fashioned one of
felling him to the floor. Probably there
can now be left for us on this planet few
spectacles more provocative of the melancholy and pallid form of mirth, than that
presented by these laborious efforts of the
Reverend Doctor Timothy Dwight to be
facetious at the expense of David Hume,
or to slay the dreadful Monsieur de Voltaire
in a duel of irony. . . . "Greenfield
Hill,"—that one of his larger poems which
almost attained to popular favor, and fairly
deserved to do so.—TYLER, MOSES COIT,
1895, *Three Men of Letters, pp.* 86, 91, 92.

In scholarship and force of character,
Dwight has had few superiors since
Edwards.—PATTEE, FRED LEWIS, 1896,
A History of American Literature, p. 96.

"The Conquest of Canaan" is an honest,
respectable piece of work, but of genius
or even of high talent it has not a glimmer.
The worst defect of this poem, next to its
hopeless mediocrity, is the incongruity
between the early, rude times depicted and
the conventional eighteenth-century manner throughout.—BRONSON, WALTER C.,
1900, *A Short History of American Literature, p.* 61.

Dwight also wrote a poem called
"Greenfield Hill," of which the name is
remembered. It is long, tedious, formal,
and turgid; but it indicates, like the good
President's travels, that he was touched
by a sense of the beauties of nature in his
native country. — WENDELL, BARRETT,
1900, *A Literary History of America,
p.* 123.

Francis Horner
1778–1817

Francis Horner was born at Edinburgh, 29th August 1778, a merchant's son of
mixed English and Scottish ancestry. From the High School he passed at fourteen to
the university; and, after three years there, spent two more with a clergyman in
Middlesex, to "unlearn" his broad native dialect. On his return (1797) he was called
to the Scottish bar, from which in 1802 he removed to the English; in 1806 he became
Whig member for St. Ives. He had made his mark in the House as a political economist, when, at thirty-eight, he died of consumption at Pisa, 8th February 1817. He

left little to preserve his name, beyond some contributions to the "Edinburgh Review," of which he was one of the founders. Yet, in Lord Cockburn's words, he was "possessed of greater public influence than any other private man." See his "Memoir and Correspondence" (1843).—PATRICK AND GROOME, *eds.*, 1897, *Chambers's Biographical Dictionary, p.* 504.

PERSONAL

Horner—*the* Horner, an Edinburgh Reviewer, an excellent speaker in the "Honourable House," very pleasing, too, and gentlemanly in company, as far as I have seen.—BYRON, LORD, 1813, *Journal, Nov.* 30; *Life, Letters and Journals of Lord Byron, ed. Moore.*

He had, indeed, qualifications eminently calculated to obtain and to deserve success. His sound principles—his enlarged views—his various and accurate knowledge—the even tenour of his manly and temperate eloquence—the genuineness of his warmth, when into warmth he was betrayed—and, above all, the singular modesty with which he bore his faculties, and which shed a grace and lustre over them all; these qualifications, added to the known blamelessness and purity of his private character, did not more endear him to his friends, than they commanded the respect of those to whom he was opposed in adverse politics; they ensured to every effort of his abilities an attentive and favouring audience; and secured for him, as the result of all, a solid and unenvied reputation.—CANNING, GEORGE, 1817, *Proceedings in the House of Commons, March* 3.

The only event which now appears interesting to me, is the scene in the House of Commons on Monday. Lord Morpeth opened it in a speech so perfect, that it might have been well placed as a passage in the most elegant English writer; it was full of feeling; every topic was skillfully presented, and contained, by a sort of prudence which is a part of taste, within safe limits; he slid over the thinnest ice without cracking it. Canning filled well what would have been the vacant place of a calm observer of Horner's public life and talents. Manners Sutton's most affecting speech was a tribute of affection from a private friend become a political enemy; Lord Lascelles, at the head of the country gentlemen of England, closing this affecting, improving, and most memorable scene by declaring, "that if the sense of the House could have been taken on this occasion, it would have been unanimous."

I may say without exaggeration, that never were so many words uttered without the least suspicion of exaggeration; and that never was so much honour paid in any age or nation to intrinsic claims alone. A Howard introduced, and an English House of Commons adopted, the proposition of thus honouring the memory of a man of thirty-eight, [?] the son of a shopkeeper, who never filled an office, or had the power of obliging a living creature, and whose grand title to this distinction was the belief of his virtue. How honourable to the age and to the House! A country where such sentiments prevail is not ripe for destruction.—MACKINTOSH, SIR JAMES, 1817, *Journal, March* 6; *Memoirs, ed. Mackintosh, vol.* II, *p.* 343.

Nor do I believe that there is or ever was, a great divided political assembly where so generous and just a testimony would have been borne unanimously to personal merit, joined especially as it was in that individual, with a stern and unaccommodating disdain of all sorts of baseness or falsehood.—JEFFREY, FRANCIS LORD, 1817, *Letter to John Allen, March* 14.

I thought his knowledge various, correct, and ready for use. In his language, he united the precision of a philosopher with the elegance of a scholar. He had cheerfulness without levity, and seriousness without austerity. He was sincere in his principles and steady in his attachments. But his manners were mild, his temper was benevolent, and, with a becoming zeal in the support of his own opinions, he was perfectly exempt from intolerance to those who thought differently from himself.—PARR, SAMUEL, 1817, *Letter to Mr. L. Horner, July* 25.

Francis Horner was a rising speaker, when he was taken off in the flower of his age. He was calm, rational, strong, and so argumentative and clear, as to fix the attention, and carry with him very frequently the conviction of a part of his audience against their will; yet he never rose to eloquence, and had always something of a professional manner.—BRYDGES, SIR SAMUEL EGERTON, 1824, *Recollections of Foreign Travel, July* 23.

It was the force of his character that raised him; and this character not impressed upon him by nature, but formed, out of no peculiarly fine elements, by himself. There were many in the House of Commons of far greater ability and eloquence. But no one surpassed him in the combination of an adequate portion of these with moral worth. Horner was born to show what moderate powers, unaided by any thing whatever except culture and goodness, may achieve, even when these powers are displayed amidst the competition and jealousy of public life.—COCK-BURN, HENRY LORD, 1830–54, *Memorials of His Time*, p. 296.

There was something very remarkable in his countenance—the commandments were written on his face, and I have often told him there was not a crime he might not commit with impunity, as no judge or jury who saw him, would give the smallest degree of credit to any evidence against him: there was in his look a calm settled love of all that was honourable and good —an air of wisdom and of sweetness; you saw at once that he was a great man, whom nature had intended for a leader of human beings; you ranged yourself willingly under his banners, and cheerfully submitted to his sway.—SMITH, SYDNEY, 1842, *Letter to Mr. L. Horner, Aug. 26.*

Francis Horner's was a short and singular life. He was the son of an Edinburgh shopkeeper; he died at thirty-nine: and when he died, from all sides of the usually cold House of Commons great statesmen and thorough gentlemen got up to deplore his loss. Tears are rarely parliamentary; all men are arid towards young Scotchmen: yet it was one of that inclement nation whom statesmen of the species Castlereagh and statesmen of the species Whitbread—with all the many kinds and species that lie between the two—rose in succession to lament. The fortunes and superficial aspect of the man make it more singular. He had no wealth, was a briefless barrister, never held an office, was a conspicuous member of the most unpopular of all Oppositions,—the opposition to a glorious and successful war. He never had the means of obliging any one. He was destitute of showy abilities: he had not the intense eloquence or overwhelming ardor which enthrall and captivate popular assemblies; his powers

of administration were little tried, and may possibly be slightly questioned. In his youthful reading he was remarkable for laying down, for a few months of study, enormous plans, such as many years would scarcely complete; and not especially remarkable for doing anything wonderful towards accomplishing those plans. Sir Walter Scott, who, though not illiberal in his essential intellect, was a keen partisan on superficial matters, and no lenient critic on actual Edinburgh Whigs, used to observe, "I will not admire your Horner : he always put me in mind of Obadiah's bull, who, though he never produced a calf, went through his business with such a grave demeanor that he always maintained his credit in the parish." It is no explanation of the universal regret, that he was a considerable political economist : no real English gentleman, in his secret soul, was ever sorry for the death of a political economist. . . . He may be useful, as drying machines are useful, but the notion of crying about him is absurd. The economical loss might be great, but it will not explain the mourning for Francis Horner. The fact is, that Horner is a striking example of the advantage of keeping an atmosphere.— BAGEHOT, WALTER, 1855–89, *The First Edinburgh Reviewers, Works*, ed. *Morgan, vol.* I, *pp.* 21, 22.

The plodding assiduity and eminent respectability of Horner enabled him to carry away from Edinburgh a well-earned esteem, although even his friends were obliged to admit that he owed nothing to talent or genius, and we are painfully struck by the truth of Scott's passing jibe, which found in Horner's solemn earnestness a certain reminiscence of Obadiah's bull.—CRAIK, SIR HENRY, 1901, *A Century of Scottish History, vol.* II, *p.* 252.

GENERAL

I cannot say that I thought Mr. Horner a man of genius. He seemed to me to be one of those men who have not very extended minds, but who know what they know very well—shallow streams, and clear because they are shallow.—COLE-RIDGE, SAMUEL TAYLOR, 1832, *Table-Talk*, ed. *Ashe, May* 2, *p.* 162.

His object was not to acquire fame for himself, but to confer benefits on his fellowmen; and his journals and correspondence not only afford evidence the most conclusive of his abilities, his public services, and his virtues, but as it were revive and continue, even after death, the exercise of his active duties. They instruct and benefit mankind, and more especially that country which he ever warmly loved.—MONTEAGLE, LORD, 1843, *Memoirs and Correspondence of Francis Horner, Edinburgh Review, vol.* 78, *p.* 299.

Mr. Horner is entitled to a high rank as a political economist. But he was more than this; he was a diligent student of intellectual philosophy, a man of great elevation of character, and unblemished purity in private life.—ALLIBONE, S. AUSTIN, 1854–58, *A Critical Dictionary of English Literature, vol.* I, *p.* 892.

He was a correct and forcible speaker, and though without the gift of eloquence or humour, exercised a remarkable influence in the House of Commons, owing to his personal character. Few men, with such small advantages at the outset of their career, ever acquired in such a short space of time so great a reputation among their contemporaries. As a political economist Horner ranks deservedly high, and though the bullion report, with which his name is identified, produced no immediate legislative results, its effect upon public opinion was so great that Peel was enabled to pass his bill for the gradual resumption of cash payments by the bank a few years afterwards.— BARKER, G. F. RUSSELL, 1891, *Dictionary of National Biography, vol.* XXVII, *p.* 370.

Matthew Gregory Lewis
1775–1818

Born, in London, 9 July 1775. At Westminster School, June 1783 to 1790. Matric., Ch. Ch., Oxford, 27 April 1790; B. A., 1794; M. A., 1797. Visit to Paris, 1791; to Weimar, autumn 1792–93. Attaché to British Embassy at the Hague, 1794. M. P., for Hindon, 1796–1802. Play, "The Castle Spectre," produced at Drury Lane, 14 Dec. 1797; "The East Indian" (afterwards called; "Rich and Poor"), Drury Lane, 24 April 1799; "Adelmorn," Drury Lane, 4 May 1801; "Alphonso," Covent Garden, 15 Jan. 1802; "The Captive," Covent Garden, 1803; "The Harper's Daughter," Covent Garden, 4 May 1803; "Rugantino," Covent Garden, 1805; "Adelgitha," Drury Lane, 1807; "The Wood Demon" (afterwards called "One o'clock"), Covent Garden, 1807; "Venoni," Drury Lane, 1 Dec. 1808; "Timour the Tartar," Covent Garden, 29 April, 1811. In West Indies, Jan. to March 1816. In Italy, May 1816 to Dec. 1817. In West Indies, Feb. to May 1818. Sailed for England, 4 May; died at sea, 14 May 1818. *Works:* "The Monk," (anon.), 1796: "Village Virtues" (anon.), 1796; "The Castle Spectre," 1798; "Tales of Terror," 1799 [?]; "The Love of Gain" (from Juvenal), 1799; "The East Indian," 1799; "Adelmorn," 1801 (2nd edn. same year); "Alfonso, King of Castile," 1801; "Tales of Wonder" (with Scott and Southey), 1801; "Adelgitha," 1806; "Feudal Tyrants," 1806; "Romantic Tales" 1808; "Venoni," 1809; "One o'clock," 1811; "Timour the Tartar," 1812; "Poems," 1812; "Koenigsmark the Robber" [1815]?. *Posthumous:* "Raymond and Agnes" [1820?]; "The Isle of Devils," 1827; "Journal of a West Indian Proprietor," 1834; "My Uncle's Garret Window," 1841. He *translated:* Schiller's "The Minister" ("Kabale and Liebe"), 1798; Kotzebue's "Rolla," 1799; Zschokke's "The Bravo of Venice" (Abellino), 1805. *Life:* "Life and Correspondence" (2 vols.), 1839.—SHARP, R. FARQUHARSON, 1897, *A Dictionary of English Authors, p.* 168.

PERSONAL

Talked of poor Monk Lewis: his death was occasioned by taking emetics for seasickness, in spite of the advice of those about him. He died lying on the deck. When he was told all hope was over, he sent his man down below for pen, ink, and paper; asked him to lend him his hat; and upon that, as he lay, wrote a codicil to his will. Few men, once so talked of, have ever produced so little sensation by their death. He was ruining his Negroes in Jamaica, they say, by indulgence, for which they suffered severely as soon as his back was turned; but he has enjoined it to his heirs, as one of the conditions of holding his estate, that the Negroes were to have three additional holidays in the year. —MOORE, THOMAS, 1818, *Diary, Sept.* 7; *Memoirs, Journal and Correspondence, ed. Russell, vol.* II, *p.* 183.

Lewis was a good man, a clever man,

but a bore. . . . My only revenge or con-solation used to be, setting him by the ears with some vivacious person who hated bores, especially, Me de Stael or Hobhouse, for example. But I liked Lewis: he was a jewel of a man had he been better set. I don't mean *personally*, but less *tiresome*, for he was tedious, as well as contradictory to every thing and every body. — BYRON, LORD, 1821, *Detached Thoughts*.

He did much good by stealth, and was a most generous creature. . . . Lewis was fonder of great people than he ought to have been, either as a man of talent or as a man of fashion. He had always dukes and duchesses in his mouth, and was pathetically fond of any one who had a title. You would have sworn he had been a *parvenu* of yesterday, yet he had lived all his life in good society. . . . Mat had queerish eyes—they projected like those of some insects, and were flattish on the orbit. His person was extremely small and boyish—he was indeed the least man I ever saw, to be strickly well and neatly made. . . . This boyishness went through life with him. He was a child, and a spoilt child, but a child of high imagination; and so he wasted himself on ghost-stories and German romances. He had the finest ear for rhythm I ever met with—finer than Byron's.—SCOTT, SIR WALTER, 1825, *Lockhart's Life of Scott, ch.* ix.

This good-natured fopling, the pet and plaything of certain fashionable circles.— LOCKHART, JOHN GIBSON, 1836, *Life of Sir Walter Scott, ch.* ix.

A very odd fellow! One of the best of men, if he had not had a trick of writing profane and indecent books. Excellent son; excellent master; and in the most trying circumstances; for he was the son of a vile brace of parents, and the master of a stupid, ungrateful gang of negroes.— MACAULAY, THOMAS BABINGTON, 1854, *Journal, Feb.* 16; *Life and Letters, ed. Trevelyan.*

Monk Lewis was a great favourite at Oaklands. One day after dinner, as the Duchess was leaving the room, she whispered something into Lewis's ear. He was much affected, his eyes filling with tears. We asked what was the matter. "Oh," replied Lewis, "the Duchess spoke so *very* kindly to me!"—"My dear

fellow," said Colonel Armstrong, "pray don't cry; I daresay she didn't mean it." —ROGERS, SAMUEL, 1855, *Recollections of Table-Talk, ed. Dyce.*

In poetry he is a good imitator of the worst style of a very ingenious but fan-tastic school of Germans. To many even then it was a matter of astonishment how a ludicrously little and overdressed manni-kin (the fac-simile of Lovel in "Evelina"), "with eyes projecting like those of some insects, and flattish in the orbits," should be the lion of London literary society, and how the Prince of Dandies should have a taste for the weird and wonderful, and be the first to transfer to English the spirit of some of the early German bards.— GILFILLAN, GEORGE, 1870, *Life of Sir Walter Scott, p.* 45.

When he was still a schoolboy, quarrels arose in his home, which resulted in a separation between his parents, and the pretty, proud, frivolous mother, left her husband's house. Henceforward, the precocious boy became her affectionate friend, protector, and champion, dividing his schoolboy means with her, when her thoughtless expenditure had exhausted her own, writing her long tender letters about all that was going on, sympathising, guid-ing, deferring to her opinion, confiding all his plans, literary and otherwise, to her. A more touching picture could not be than that of this curious pair, in themselves so imperfect, the faded, extravagant, foolish, but loving mother, and her fat little under-graduate, so sensible, so tender, so con-stant, so anxious to anticipate all her wants, scarcely betraying the conscious-ness that these wants are sometimes un-reasonable, and while he pours out all his heart to her, still remaining loyally just and faithful to the father, whose liberality he will not hear impugned.—OLIPHANT, MARGARET O. W., 1882, *Literary History of England, XVIII-XIX Century, vol.* III, *p.* 136.

THE MONK

There is one publication at the time too peculiar, and too important to be passed over in a general reprehension. There is nothing with which it may be compared. A legislator in our own parliament, a member of the House of Commons of Great Britain, an elected guardian and defender of the laws, the religion, and the good man-ners of the country, has neither scrupled nor blushed to depict, and to publish to the world, the arts of lewd and systematick seduction, and to thrust upon the nation the most open and unqualified blasphemy against the very code and volume of our religion. And all this, with his name, style, and title, prefixed to the novel or romance called "The Monk." And one of our publick theatres has allured the publick attention *still more* to this novel, by a scenick representation of an Episode in it.—MATHIAS, THOMAS JAMES, 1797, *The Pursuits of Literature, Eighth ed., p.* 239.

Himself (Lewis) a poet of no mean calibre. The ballads and little pieces, scattered throughout his novel of the "Monk," were, in their day, the most popular things known. They were chanted in the street and in the drawing-room; while the subject of the most terrific ("Alonzo and Imogene"), and many episodes in the novel, were represented on the stage.—DIBDIN, THOMAS FROGNALL, 1824, *The Library Companion, p.* 746, *note.*

The brushwood splendour of "The Monk's" fame.—LOCKHART, JOHN GIBSON, 1836, *Life of Sir Walter Scott, ch.* ix.

We should be disposed to say now that it is hardly up to the mark of a "penny dreadful," even in point of literary merit. The horrors are of the crudest description, and there is neither character nor force of writing to redeem them. Mrs. Radcliffe is incomparably superior. There must have been something in the contrast between the fat little boyish person, blubber lips and beady eyes, of the author and the atrocites he lisped forth so innocently, which tickled Society. It is scarcely possible to conceive any more serious reason for his fame. — OLIPHANT, MARGARET O. W., 1882, *Literary History of England, XVIII–XIX Century, vol.* III, *p.* 138.

Lewis's acquaintance with literature, and especially with the German resuscitations of feudalism, monasticism, ghosts, and hobgoblins, enabled him to fill his museum of atrocities with a large variety of articles of vertu, including the Inquisition, the wandering Jew, and the bleeding nun. But his imagination is gross, boyish, and vulgar, and his horrors rests mainly on a physical basis. He was foolish enough to throw over all the restraints that Mrs. Radcliffe had observed, and to attempt explicit climax.—RALEIGH, WALTER, 1894, *The English Novel, p.* 234.

"The Monk" used, and abused, the now familiar apparatus of Gothic romance. It had Spanish grandees, heroines of dazzling beauty, bravoes and forest banditti, foolish duennas and gabbling domestics, monks, nuns, inquisitors, magic mirrors, enchanted wands, midnight incantations, sorcerers, ghosts, demons; haunted chambers, wainscoted in dark oak; moonlit castles with ruined towers and ivied battlements, whose galleries rang with the shrieks and blasphemies of guilty spirits, and from whose portals issued, when the castle clock tolled one, the spectre of a bleeding nun, with dagger and lamp in hand. There were poisonings, stabbings, and ministrations of sleeping portions; beauties who masqueraded as pages, and pages who masqueraded as wandering harpers; secret springs that gave admittance to winding stairs leading down into the charnel vaults of convents, where erring sistes were immured by cruel prioresses and fed on bread and water among the loathsome relics of the dead. With all this, "The Monk" is a not wholly contemptible work. There is a certain narrative power about it which puts it much above the level of "The Castle of Otranto." And though it partakes of the stilted dialogue and false conception of character that abound in Mrs. Radcliffe's romances, it has neither the excess of scenery nor of sentiment which distinguishes that very prolix narrator.—BEERS, HENRY A., 1898, *A History of English Romanticism in the Eighteenth Century, p.* 410.

GENERAL

O! wonder-working Lewis! Monk or Bard,
Who fain would'st make Parnassus a church-
 yard;
Lo! wreaths of yew, not laurel, bind thy
 brow,
Thy muse a sprite, Apollo's sexton thou;
Whether on ancient tombs thou tak'st thy
 stand,
By gibbering spectres hailed, thy kindred
 band,
Or tracest chaste descriptions on thy page,
To please the females of our modest age;
All hail, M. P., from whose infernal brain
Thin-sheeted phantoms glide, a grisly train;
At whose command "grim women" throng
 in crowds,
And kings of fire, of water and of clouds,
With "small gray men," "wild yagers" and
 what not,
To crown with honor thee and Walter Scott!
—BYRON, LORD, 1809, *English Bards and Scotch Reviewers.*

As a man of truly original powers, M. G. Lewis was far behind either Godwin or Coleridge, and stood much on the level of his successor Maturin: but what his imagination lacked in grandeur was made up by energy: he was a high-priest of the intense school. Monstrous and absurd in many things, as were the writings of Lewis, no one could say that they were deficient in interest. Truth and nature, to be sure, he held utterly at arm's-length; but, instead, he had a life-in-death vigour, a spasmodic energy, which answered well for all purposes of astonishment.—MOIR, D. M., 1850–51, *Sketches of the Poetical Literature of the Past Half-Century*, p. 18.

One of his best novels was "The Bravo of Venice," published in 1804. . . . He contrives to make this hero respected, even admired to a degree; and artfully employs the poetry and witchery of Venice, that unique city in the world,—half land, half sea,—to give a tinge of appropriateness and even congruity to his wild romance. The "Bravo" is as good a specimen of the improbable and yet conceivable as any work of fiction earlier than Scott. —SIMONDS, WILLIAM EDWARD, 1894, *An Introduction to the Study of English Fiction*.

As Crabbe may serve to represent the extreme of naturalism in art, so "Monk" Lewis may serve to represent the other extreme, the extravagance of the romantic tendency.—DOWDEN, EDWARD, 1895, *New Studies in Literature*, p. 337.

Nothing can be worse in kind, and nothing, of its kind, can well be better than "Alonso the Brave." It was Lewis's *rôle* to fling the orts and refuse of German Romanticism about the soil of England. It was his luck rather than merit to have once or twice thrown them where they nourished good seed, and now and then to have grasped a flower among his handfuls of treasured weeds. His false ballads helped to elicit the true ones of Scott, and the respectable ones of Southey, and he introduced to the author of "Manfred" what he doubtless regarded as that capital "Tale of Wonder," Goethe's "Faust."— HERFORD, C. H., 1897, *The Age of Wordsworth*, p. 94.

It is a part of the irony of things that so robust a muse as Walter Scott's should have been nursed in infancy by a little creature like Lewis.—BEERS, HENRY A., 1898, *A History of English Romanticism in the Eighteenth Century*, p. 404.

Sir Samuel Romilly

1757–1818

Born at London, March 1, 1757: committed suicide Nov. 2, 1818. An English lawyer and philanthropist, of Huguenot descent. At 21 years of age he entered Gray's Inn. In 1806 he was appointed solicitor-general of the Grenville administration. He is famous from his labors for the reform of the criminal law, commencing in 1807. His plans were not realized during his lifetime. His speeches were published in 1820, and his autobiography in 1840.—SMITH, BENJAMIN E., ed., 1894–97, *The Century Cyclopedia of Names*, p. 865.

PERSONAL

Some women use their tongues—she *look'd* a lecture,
Each eye a sermon and her brow a homily,
An all-in-all-sufficient self-director,
Like the lamented late Sir Samuel Romilly,
The Law's expounder, and the State's corrector,
Whose suicide was almost an anomaly—
One sad example more that, "All is vanity,"
(The jury brought their verdict in "Insanity.")
— BYRON, LORD, 1818–24, *Don Juan*, Canto I.

In person, Sir Samuel Romilly was tall and justly proportioned, with a countenance regular and pleasing; but tinged with deep shades of thought, and susceptible of the greatest or tenderest emotions. His manners were distinguished by singular modesty, unaffected simplicity, and the kindest attention and regard to the wishes and feelings of others. His habits were temperate, studious, and domestic. No man ever indulged less in those pursuits which the world calls pleasure. He rose regularly at six o'clock; and was occupied, during the greater part of the day, and frequently to a late hour at night, either in study or laborious attendance to his professional and parliamentary duties. What little intervals of leisure could be snatched from his toils he anxiously devoted to domestic intercourse and enjoyments. Moderate in his own expences, he was generous, without ostentation, to the want of others; and the exquisite sensibility of his nature was never more strikingly displayed than in the fervent zeal with which his professional knowledge was always ready to be exerted for the destitute and oppressed, for those who might seem, in their poverty, to have been left without a friend. Even to the last, when sinking under the weight of domestic affliction, when anticipating as its probable result a wretched life of mental malady and darkness, he was still intent on the welfare and happiness of those around him. The religion of Sir Samuel Romilly was, like his life, pure, fervent, and enlightened. Unclouded by superstition or intolerance, it shone forth in pious gratitude to God, and in charity to all mankind—PETER, WILLIAM, 1820, *Memoirs of the Life of Sir Samuel Romilly.*

Sir *Samuel Romilly* was a very effective speaker on the topics which he handled : he was a most acute reasoner,—of extraordinary penetration and subtlety,—with occasional appeals to sentiment, and addresses to the heart; but still his manner was strictly professional (which is never a popular manner in parliament), and it had also something of a Puritan tone, which, with a grave, warm, pallid, puritanic visage and attitude, took off from the impression of a perfect orator, though it never operated to diminish the great attention and respect with which he was heard. The veneration for his character, the admiration of him as a profound lawyer, the confidence in the integrity of his principles, and his enlightened, as well as conscientious study of the principles of the constitution of his country, procured for all he said the most submissive attention; and they who thought him in politics a stern and bigoted republican, whose opinions were uncongenial to the mixed government of Great Britain, and therefore dissented *toto corde* from his positions, deductions, and general views of legislation and of state, never dared to treat lightly whatever came from his lips. He had a cold reserved manner, which repelled intimacy and familiarity; and, therefore, whatever he did, he did by his own sole strength.—BRYDGES, SIR S. E., 1824, *Recollection of Foreign Travel, July 23.*

He was, in the highest sense of the word, a philanthropist, loving mankind with wise and constant affection, not misled by any false sensibility, yet trembling alive to their best and truest interests. Without displacing for a moment the beautiful affections of domestic life, the welfare of his fellow creatures ever lay next to the heart of Sir Samuel Romilly; and the feelings which in weaker and meaner minds extend only round the small circle which blood or friendship draws, were in him diffused with undiminished warmth over the wide orbit of human existence.—ROSCOE, HENRY, 1830, *Eminent British Lawyers ; The Cabinet Cyclopædia, Biography, p. 404.*

It is fit that no occasion on which Sir Samuel Romilly is named should ever be passed over without an attempt to record the virtues and endowments of so great and so good a man, for the instruction of after-ages. Few persons have ever attained celebrity of name and exalted station, in any country, or in any age, with such unsullied purity of character, as this equally eminent and excellent person.—BROUGHAM, HENRY LORD, 1839–43, *Lives of Statesmen of the Time of George III, vol. i, p. 363.*

There are circumstances in Sir Samuel's history that render the state of his mind on the subject of religion so important—particularly as the editors profess to publish this work for the purposes of "*example* and *instruction*"—that we feel ourselves reluctantly obliged to say that, with our best diligence, we have not been able to discover throughout these volumes—his own share written, he says, for the instruction of his children—any distinct evidence that he was a *Christian* though there is abundant proof that he was a man of the kindest social and domestic feelings, and of the purest morality, that he believed in a future state of retribution, and had a full and well-reasoned conviction of the existence and transcendent attributes of the Deity. . . . In all other respects we willingly offer our testimony—*valeat quantum*—to his great talents, large acquirements, and deserved success—to his social and domestic virtues —to his integrity, benevolence, and honour—and, in short, to the most essential qualities that constitute the character of a *virtuous man.*—CROKER, JOHN WILSON,

1840, *Life of Sir Samuel Romilly, Quarterly Review, vol.* 66, *pp.* 574, 626.

SPEECHES

As Saturday drew near, my anxiety for Romilly's first public appearance had swallowed up every other concern. . . . Romilly's success was as great as his friends predicted. He spoke for three hours and a half, and his speech might be named as the model of the simple style. . . . The fact is, he kept every one chained in attention, and made the whole case (impeachment of Lord Melville) distinct to the dullest.—HORNER, FRANCIS, 1806, *Memoirs and Correspondence, May* 12, 13.

From the tenderness of his feelings, and from an anger never roused but by cruelty and baseness, as much as from his genius and his pure taste, sprung that original and characteristic eloquence which was the hope of the afflicted as well as the terror of the oppressor. If his oratory had not flowed so largely from this moral source, which years do not dry up, he would not perhaps have been the only example of an orator who, after the age of sixty, daily increased in polish, in vigour, and in splendour.—MACKINTOSH, SIR JAMES, 1830, *Second Preliminary Dissertation, Encyclopædia Britannica.*

As a speaker, Romilly habitually addressed himself rather to the reason than the passions, though he by no means lacked eloquence. He marshalled his premises, and deduced his conclusions with mathematical precision, and his diction was as chaste as his logic was cogent. The unerring instinct with which he detected and the unfailing felicity with which he exposed a fallacy, united to no small powers of sarcasm and invective, made him formidable in reply, while the effect of his easy and impressive elocution was enhanced by a tall and graceful figure, a melodious voice, and features of classical regularity. As an adept not only in the art of the advocate, but in the whole mystery of law and equity, he was without a superior, perhaps without a rival, in his day. He was also throughout life a voracious and omnivorous reader, and seized and retained the substance of what he read with unusual rapidity and tenacity. He was an indefatigable worker, rising very early and going to bed late. His favourite relaxation was a long walk. From intensity of conviction, aided perhaps by the melancholy of his temperament, he carried political antagonism to extreme lengths, even to the abandonment of a friendship with Perceval, which had been formed on circuit, and cemented by constant and confidential intercourse.—RIGG, J. M. 1897, *Dictionary of National Biography, vol.* XLIX, *p.* 190.

GENERAL

A charm, too, is spread over the whole work, and it leaves in the mind a feeling of affection for the author; and this because he displays himself without pretention, and because the picture he draws relates only to those moral feelings, those private virtues, which every one can imitate, and to that domestic life, the happiness of which, as it is derived from the purest and most amiable feelings, creates jealousy in the breast of no one. Mere men of the world will probably disbelieve it : in their eyes it will appear a romance, but one that will not offend them ; and, by the middling ranks, the most numerous class of society, these memoirs will be read with the same feeling as that which dictated their composition. . . . To me, these Memoirs appear a precious monument : and when I reflect that this laborious undertaking was the work of a man always occupied to the utmost extent, who gave up to it, as well as to all his legislative labours, that time from whence he might have derived very considerable professional advantages, it seems to me that it cannot fail to produce a lasting effect upon those who know how to profit by a great example, and to reflect upon what may be done with life by him who chooses to employ it.—DUMONT, PIERRE ÉTIENNE LOUIS, 1829, *Letter in Memoirs of the Life of Sir Samuel Romilly, ed. by His Sons, Preface, vol.* I, *pp.* xi, xii.

Romilly is one of the few lawyers who have left any thing like an autobiography. His sketch of his life is slight, designed only for his children, but suffices to disclose his modesty, his candor, his sincerity, his self scrutiny and the purity of his motives. . . . It has always been conceded that Romilly was the leader of the equity bar in his day. . . . Romilly's fame mainly depends on his efforts to reform the criminal code.— BROWNE, IRVING, 1878, *Short Studies of Great Lawyers, pp.* 121, 122, 124.

At this period of his life, Romilly's ambition was to follow his profession just as far as was necessary for his subsistence, and to aspire to fame by his literary pursuits. Accordingly, he began to exercise himself in prose composition, and, judging translation to be the most useful exercise for forming a style, he rendered into English the finest models of writing that the Latin language afforded. With the same view of improving his style, he read and studied the best English writers—Addison, Swift, Bolingbroke, Robertson, and Hume —noting down every peculiar propriety and happiness of expression which he met with, and which he was conscious he would not have used himself. Romilly's method of .improving himself in English composition bears a very close resemblance to that adopted by Buckle, the historian.—NICOLL, HENRY J., 1881, *Great Movements and Those Who Achieved Them.*

Sir Philip Francis
1740-1818

Sir Philip Francis, was born in Dublin, 22d October 1740. Leaving Ireland at twelve, he entered St. Paul's School in London, and at sixteen became a junior clerk in the secretary of state's office. In 1758 he was a secretary in the expedition against Cherbourg; in 1760 he was secretary on a mission to Portugal; in 1761 he acted as amanuensis to the elder Pitt; and in 1762 he was made first-clerk in the War Office. In 1773 Lord North made him a member of the Council of Bengal; in 1780 he fought a duel with Warren Hastings (with whom he was always at enmity), and was seriously wounded. In 1781 he returned home with a fortune largely acquired by playing whist. He entered parliament in 1784. He was energetic in the proceedings against Hastings, wrote many pamphlets, was eager to be governor-general of India, and was made a K. C. B. in 1806. He was devoted to the prince-regent and a warm supporter of the "Friends of the People." In 1816 Mr. John Taylor wrote a book identifying Francis with "Junius," but Francis never acknowledged having written the seventy "Letters," which appeared in the "Public Advertiser" (21st Jan. 1769—21st Jan. 1772), and were reprinted in 1812 with 113 additional letters. His young second wife, whom he married when seventy-four, was convinced that he must be Junius.—PATRICK AND GROOME, *eds.,* 1897, *Chambers's Biographical Dictionary, p.* 379.

PERSONAL

Nature had conferred on Francis talents such as are rarely dispensed to any individual—a vast range of ideas, a retentive memory, a classic mind, considerable command of language, energy of thought and expression, matured by age, and actuated by an inextinguishable animosity to Hastings. Francis indeed uniformly disclaimed any personal enmity to the *man,* only reprobating the measures of the *ruler of India;* and perhaps he might sincerely believe his assertion. But he always appeared to me, like the son of Livia, to deposit his resentments deep in his own breast; from which he drew them forth, if not augmented by time, at least in all their original vigour and freshness. Acrimony distinguished and characterized him in everything. Even his person, tall, thin, and scantily covered with flesh; his countenance, the lines of which were acute, intelligent, and yet full of meaning; the tones of his voice, sharp, distinct and sonorous; his very gestures, impatient, and irregular—eloquently bespoke the formation of his intellect. I believe I never saw him smile. . . . Bursting with bile, which tinged and pervaded all his speeches in Parliament, yet his irascibility never overcame his reason; nor compelled his friends, like those of Burke, to mingle regret with their admiration, and to condemn or to pity the individual whom they applauded as an orator. Francis, however inferior he was to Burke in all the flowers of diction, in exuberance of ideas borrowed from antiquity, and in the magic of eloquence, more than once electrified the house, by passages of pathos or of interest which arrested every hearer.—WRAXALL, SIR NATHANIEL, 1784-90, *Posthumous Memoirs of his own Time, p.* 49.

I was alone with him in his last moments. . . . Never was a death so worthy of such a life: his spirits composed, tranquil, and even cheerful, his mind apparently as strong as ever and his perception as quick. He expressed his gratitude for all my little attentions and cares during the last sad, solemn night, in the most touching manner. I was not aware at the time, though I now am, that he knew how short his time was. He showed great anxiety that I should not leave him for a moment, no doubt he anticipated my future regrets had I done so ; but he never expressed fear or anxiety on any other subject. Towards morning he fell into a trance, from which he revived and spoke to me, and took some refreshment. About ten he fell into a deep sleep, which lasted four hours. I was flattering myself with the hope of his waking much restored ; Mrs. Cholmondeley had just left me, when, on a sudden, the breathing I had been listening to so contentedly stopped. I undrew the curtain . . . not a sigh, not a motion, not a change of countenance. Heart, pulses and breath stopped at once without an effort. —FRANCIS, LADY, 1818, *Letter to a Friend, Francis Letters, vol.* II, *p.* 691.

Sir Philip Francis is best known to the public as the supposed author of the letters signed Junius. Whether he would deserve notice or respect if he were the real Junius, is a question which any one can answer who is intimately acquainted with Francis's career. . . . Yet, irrespective of the assumed connexion between Francis and Junius, there is much in Francis's life which deserves more attention than many readers may suppose. Though not one of the great men whose names shine in the annals of the eighteenth century, and though his place is in the second rank, yet Francis's career was as varied and interesting as that of many whose names precede and overshadow his on the roll of fame.—RAE, W. FRASER, 1889, *Sir Philip Francis, Temple Bar, vol.* 87, *p.* 171.

Francis, whether Junius or not, was a man of great ability and unflagging industry ; arrogant and vindictive in the extreme ; unscrupulous in gratifying his enmities by covert insinuations and false assertions, yet courageous in attacking great men ; rigid and even pedantic in his adherence to a set of principles which had their generous side ; really scornful of meanness and corruption in others ; and certainly doing much to vindicate the power of public opinion, although from motives which were not free from selfishness and the narrowest personal ambition. There may have been two such men, whose careers closely coincided during Francis's most vigorous period ; but it seems more probable that there was only one.—STEPHEN, LESLIE, 1889, *Dictionary of National Biography, vol.* XX, *p.* 179.

Junius

The signature appended to a famous series of letters on political subjects, which appeared in "The Public Advertiser," at various intervals between 1769 and 1772. They were 44 in number ; to which must be added 15 signed Philo-Junius, 113 under various signatures, and 72 privately addressed to Woodfall, the publisher of the "Advertiser," and to Wilkes. The first of those signed Junius appeared on January 21, 1769.—ADAMS, W. DAVENPORT, 1877, *Dictionary of English Literature, p.* 356.

AUTHORSHIP.

The following list of 51 names, embraces the personages to whom these celebrated letters have been attributed :

Adair, James, M. P.; Allen, Captain; Barré, Lieut.-Col. Isaac, M. P.; Bentinck, William Henry Cavendish; Bickerton, Mr.; Boyd, Hugh M'Aulay; Burke, Rt. Hon. Edmund; Burke, William ; Butler, John; Camden, Charles, Lord; De Lolme, John Lewis; Dunning, John, afterwards Lord Ashburton; Dyer, Samuel; Flood, Henry; Francis, Sir Philip; George III.; Gibbon, Edward ; Glover, Richard ; Grattan, Henry; Greatrakes, William; Grenville, George; Grenville, James; Hamilton, William Gerard ; Hollis, James ; Hollis, Thomas ; Jackson, Sir George ; Jones, Sir William ; Kent, John ; Lee, *Maj.-Gen. Charles ; Lloyd, Charles ; Lyttleton, Thomas ; Maclean, Laughlin ; Marshall, Rev. Edmund; Paine, Thomas; Pitt, William; Portland, William, Duke of ; Pownall, Thomas; Rich, Lieut.-Col. Sir Robert ; Roberts, John ; Rosenhagen, Rev. Philip ; Sackville, George, Viscount ; Shelburne, Earl of ; Stanhope, Philip Dormer; Suett, Richard ; Temple, Richard, Earl ; Tooke, John Horne ; Walpole, Horatio ; Wedderburn, Alexander; Wilkes, John; Wilmot, James, D.D.; Wray, Daniel.*

—FREY, ALBERT R., 1885, *Initials and Pseudonyms by William Cushing.*

Boswell: "Supposing the person who wrote *Junius* were asked whether he was the authour, might he deny it ?" *Johnson:* "I don't know what to say to this. If you were *sure* that he wrote *Junius*, would you, if he denied it, think as well of him afterwards? Yet it may be urged, that what a man has no right to ask, you may refuse to communicate; and there is no other effectual mode of preserving a secret and an important secret, the discovery of which may be very hurtful to you, but a flat denial; for if you are silent, or hesitate, or evade, it will be held equivalent to a confession. But stay, Sir, here is another case. Supposing the authour had told me confidentially that he had written *Junius*, and I were asked if he had, I should hold myself at liberty to deny it, as being under a previous promise, express or implied, to conceal it. Now what I ought to do for the authour, may I not do for myself?— JOHNSON, SAMUEL, 1784, *Life by Boswell, ed. Hill, vol.* IV., *p.* 353.

It has long been a question who was the author of the letters which appeared under the signature of "Junius" in 1769 and 1770. Many have ascribed them to Mr. Wm. Gerard Hamilton, who is certainly capable of having written them, but his style is very different. He would have had still more point than they exhibit, and certainly more Johnsonian energy. Besides, he has all his life been distinguished for political timidity and indecision. Neither would he, even under a mask, have entered into such decided warfare with many persons whom it might be necessary afterwards to have as colleagues. What is still more decisive, he could not have divested himself of the apprehension of a discovery, having long accustomed his mind to too refined a policy, and being very apt to suppose that many things are brought about by scheme and machination which are merely the offspring of chance. He would have suspected that even the penny post could not be safe; and that Sir W. Draper or any other antagonist would have managed so as to command every one of those offices within the bills of mortality. Many have supposed "Junius" to have been written by Mr. Hamilton's old friend, the well-known and deservedly celebrated Edmund Burke. Dr. Johnson being once asked whether he thought Burke capable of writing "Junius," said he thought him fully equal to it; but that he did not believe him the author because he himself had told him so; and he did not believe he would deliberately assert a falsehood.

Mr. Burke, however, it is extremely probable, had a considerable share in the production of those papers in furnishing materials, suggesting hints, constructing and amending sentences, &c., &c. He has acknowledged to Sir Joshua Reynolds *that he knew the author.* Sir Joshua with very great probabilty thinks that the late Mr. *Samuel Dyer* was the author, assisted by Mr. Burke and by Mr. William Burke, his cousin, now in India.— MALONE, EDMOND, 1791, *Maloniana, ed. Prior, p.* 419.

Sir,—I frankly assure you that I know nothing of Junius, except that I am *not* the author. When Junius began I was a boy, and knew nothing of politics or the persons concerned in them. I am, Sir, *not Junius,* but your very good wisher and obedient servant. — GRATTAN, HENRY, 1805, *Letter to Mr. Almon, Nov.* 4.

The question respecting the author of Junius's Letters, is thought, we believe, by philosophers, to be one of more curiosity than importance. We are very far from pretending that the happiness of mankind is materially interested in its determination; or that it involves any great and fundamental scientific truths. But it must be viewed as a point of literary history; and, among discussions of this description, it ranks very high. After all, are there many points of civil or military history really more interesting to persons living in the present times? Is the guilt of Queen Mary—the character of Richard III.—or the story of the Man in the Iron Mask, very nearly connected with the welfare of the existing generation? Indeed, we would rather caution, even the most profound of philosophers, against making too nice an inquiry into the practical importance of scientific truths; for assuredly there are numberless propositions, of which the curiosity is more easily described than the utility, in all the branches of science, and especially in the severer ones—the professors of which are the most prone to deride an inquiry like that about Junius. . . . That it proves Sir Philip to be Junius, we will not affirm; but this we can safely assert, that it accumulates such a mass of circumstantial evidence as renders it extremely difficult to believe he is not; and that, if so, many coincidences shall be found to have misled us in this case, our faith in all conclusions drawn from proofs of a similiar kind may henceforth be shaken.— BROUGHAM, HENRY LORD? 1817, *Junius, Edinburgh Review, vol.* 29, *pp.* 94, 96.

A cause, however ingeniously pleaded, is not therefore gained. You may remember the neatly-wrought chain of circumstantial evidence so artificially brought forward to prove Sir Philip Francis's title to the "Letters of Junius" seemed at first irrefragable; yet the influence of the reasoning has pased away, and Junius, in the general opinion, is as much unknown as ever.— SCOTT, SIR WALTER, 1822, *Fortunes of Nigel, Introductory, Epistle.*

And several people swore, from out the press,
They knew him perfectly; and one could swear
He was his father: upon which another
Was sure he was his mother's cousin's brother.
.   .   .   .
I've an hypothesis—'tis quite my own;
I never let it out till now, for fear
Of doing people harm about the throne,
And injuring some minister or peer,
On whom the stigma might perhaps be blown;
It is—my gentle public, lend thine ear!
'Tis that what Junius we are wont to call
Was really, truly, nobody at all.
—BYRON, LORD, 1824, *The Vision of Judgment.*

I will just state here, *en passant*, that I have strong reason to suspect that Lord George Sackville was the author of "Junius." He *may* have had a literary assistant, but I am convinced by a great variety of reasons, that *he* was substantially Junius.—CROKER, JOHN WILSON, 1824, *Letter to Lord Liverpool, Oct.* 13; *Correspondence, ed. Jennings, vol.* I, *p.* 273.

I persist in thinking that neither Mr. Burke nor Philip Francis was the author of the letter under the signature of Junius. I think the mind of the first so superior, and the mind of the latter so inferior, to that of Junius, as to put the supposition that either of them was Junius wholly out of the question.—BUTLER, CHARLES, 1828, *Letter to E. H. Barker, June* 14.

A new knight entered the lists with his vizor down, and with unreal devices on his shield, but whose arm was nerved with inborn vigour, and whose lance was poised with most malignant skill. Even now the dark shadow of Junius looms across that period of our annals with a grandeur no doubt much enhanced and heightened by the mystery. To solve that mystery has since employed the most patient industry, and aroused the most varied conjectures. . . . Strong as this, the "Franciscan," theory appears when separately viewed, it becomes, I think, far stronger still when compared with the other claims that have been urged. In no other can many strained inferences and many gratuitous assumptions fail to be observed. In no other do the feelings and the circumstances which must be ascribed to Junius, or the dates applying to the cessation of his letters, admit on all points, or even on most points, of simple explanations from the theory adduced. Even the claim on behalf of Lord George Sackville, which at first sight has dazzled many acute observers, will not, as I conceive, endure the light of a close and critical examination.—STANHOPE, PHILIP HENRY EARL (LORD MAHON), 1836–54, *History of England from the Peace of Utrecht to the Peace of Versailles, vol.* v, *pp.* 211, 225.

Before your last volume is published, I am desirous of stating to you some of the considerations which, more than seventeen years ago, led me to the belief I still entertain, that Walpole had a principal share in the composition and publication of the Letters of Junius: though I think it likely that Mason, or some other friend corrected the style, and gave precision and force to the most striking passages. . . . If we turn from a recollection of the words to a consideration of the peculiarities of the style of Junius, I think it will be agreed that the most remarkable of all is that species of irony which consists in equivocal compliment. Walpole also excelled in this; and prided himself upon doing so. Are we not justified in saying, that of all who, in the eighteenth century, cast their thoughts on public occurrences into the form of letters, Junius and Walpole are the most distinguished? That the works of no other prose writer of their time exhibit a zest for political satire equal to that which is displayed in the Letters of Junius, and the Memories and Political Letters of Walpole? and that the sarcasm of equivocal praise was the favourite weapon in the armoury of each, though it certainly appears to have been tempered, and sharpened, and polished with additional care for the hand of Junius?—GREY, CHARLES EDWARD, 1840, *To the Editor of Letters of Horace Walpole.*

The external evidence is, we think, such as would support a verdict in a civil, nay, in a criminal proceeding. The hand-writing of Junius is the very peculiar hand-writing of Francis, slightly disguised. As to the position, pursuits, and connexions of Junius, the following are the most important facts which can be considered as clearly proved: first, that he was acquainted with the technical forms of the Secretary of State's office; secondly, that he was intimately acquainted with the business of the war-office; thirdly, that he, during the year 1770, attended debates in the House of Lords, and took notes of speeches, particularly of the speeches of Lord Chatham; fourthly, that he bitterly resented the appointment of Mr. Chamier to the place of Deputy Secretary at War; fifthly, that he was bound by some strong tie to the first Lord Holland. Now, Francis passed some years in the Secretary of State's office. He was subsequently chief clerk of the war-office. He repeatedly mentioned that he had himself, in 1770, heard speeches of Lord Chatham; and some of those speeches were actually printed from his notes. He resigned his clerkship at the war-office from resentment at the appointment of Mr. Chamier. It was by Lord Holland that he was first introduced into the public service. Now here are five marks, all of which ought to be found in Junius. They are all five found in Francis. We do not believe that more than two of them can be found in any other person whatever. If this argument does not settle the question, there is an end of all reasoning on circumstantial evidence. The internal evidence seems to us to point the same way. The style of Francis bears a strong resemblance to that of Junius; nor are we disposed to admit, what is generally taken for granted, that the acknowledged compositions of Francis are very decidedly inferior to the anonymous letters. The argument from inferiority, at all events, is only which may be urged with at least equal force against every claimant that has ever been mentioned with the single exception of Burke, who certainly was not Junius. . . . To go no further than the letters which bear the signature of Junius;—

the letter to the king and the letters to Horne Tooke have little in common, except the asperity; and asperity was an ingredient seldom wanting either in the writings or in the speeches of Francis.—MACAULAY, THOMAS BABINGTON, 1841, *Warren Hastings, Critical and Miscellaneous Essays.*

It is here proper to remark that so far from having any theory of our own on Junius's identity, we are as entirely free from bias on the subject, and confess ourselves as profoundly ignorant of the authorship of those celebrated Letters, as if, instead of having for many years constantly had the question in our mind, and having read, we believe, nearly everything that has been written on the point, we had never bestowed a thought on the matter. We have indeed a strong impression that Junius was not any one of the numerous persons heretofore so confidently brought forward.—NICOLAS, SIR HARRIS, 1843, *Junius and His Works.*

It is my firm and deliberate conviction, that if Lord Temple were not the author of Junius, then the author has never yet been publicly named, and that he will still remain that mysterious *Umbra sine Nomine,* to exercise the ingenuity of some more successful inquirer.—SMITH, WILLIAM JAMES, 1852, *ed., The Grenville Papers.*

If not a member of the peerage, Junius must have had men of rank and station as his allies, and, as he himself confesses, persons about him who supplied him with the information he required, and whose importunities he was bound to obey. Among the political writers who may be considered as having played the principal part in this combination, Sir Philip Francis and Colonel Lachlan Macleane have the highest claims. We leave it to a jury of our readers to decide between them from the evidence which is now within their reach.—BREWSTER, SIR DAVID, 1853, *The Grenville Papers, North British Review,* vol. 19, p. 517.

We think more highly of Lord Temple than Mr. Smith does. He was a man of humour, energy, sense, and we think of sound judgment,—but no genius. There never was a Grenville who had a particle of genius:—not even my Lord, the most plausible of the family, nor Thomas Grenville, the best of them. Lord Temple would not if he could, and could not if he would, have written the Letters of Junius.

Junius, with twenty times the ability of Temple, wanted his nobleness and generosity. — DILKE, CHARLES WENTWORTH, 1853, *Junius, Papers of a Critic, vol.* II, *p.* 219.

My own impression is, that the "Letters of Junius" were written by Sir Philip Francis. In a speech, which I once heard him deliver, at the Mansion House, concerning the Partition of Poland, I had a striking proof that Francis possessed no ordinary powers of eloquence.—ROGERS, SAMUEL, 1855, *Recollections of Table-Talk, ed. Dyce.*

Wonder has been expressed at the manner in which the secret has been kept. But has it been so closely kept? May not an accurate guess, or a genuine betrayal, have been too hastily disregarded? Burke told Reynolds that he knew Junius. Boyd, according to Almon, as good as let out the secret to him. Lord Grenville and Mr. Thomas Grenville knew, or believed that they knew, Junius, and declared that he was neither of the persons to whom the letters have been popularly ascribed. The tradition in the Woodfall family is decidedly anti-Franciscan. Dr. Parr invariably stood out for Lloyd. Rosenhagen claimed the authorship. Burke has always been a favourite. . . . The name of Francis was never so much as suggested for the authorship for forty years. It is not mentioned by Almon, who, in his edition of 1806, passes seventeen claimants in review. It only occurs incidentally in Woodfall's complete edition of 1812, in the letter of "Veteran," March 23,1772, publicly calling on D'Oyly and Francis to "declare their reasons for quitting the War Office," to which (we now know) Francis would have been the last to direct public attention at the time. This edition revived inquiry, and led eventually to the "Junius Identified" of 1814. The credit of first starting the Franciscan theory is certainly due to Mr. Taylor, but its general acceptance to this hour is owing to its unhesitating adoption and eager advocacy by Earl Stanhope and Lord Macaulay, who agree in resting their case on similarity of handwriting and style.—HAYWARD, ABRAHAM, 1867, *More About Junius, Fraser's Magazine, vol.* 76, *pp.* 809, 810.

As to the Junius question in general, there is a little bit of the philosophy of horse-racing which may be usefully applied. A man who is so confident of his horse that he places him far above any other, may nevertheless, and does, refuse to give odds against all the field: for many small adverse chances united make a big chance for one or other of the opponents. I suspect Mr. Taylor has made it at least 20 to 1 for Francis against any one competitor who has been named: but what the odds may be against the whole field is more difficult to settle. What if the real Junius should be some person not yet named?— DE MORGAN, AUGUSTUS, 1871, *A Budget of Paradoxes, p.* 312.

During the whole of the present century the public mind of England has been constantly inquiring by whom the Junius letters were written. The claims of all the competitors, with one exception, have been disproved. However strong the circumstantial evidence has borne at different times in favor of different aspirants, some fatal fact would thrust itself forward to overthrow the claimants one by one, until all have dropped out of the controversy. . . . If Sir Philip Francis were now living, and on trial for libelling the Duke of Grafton, and all the facts and circumstances that sixty years of earnest and enlightened scrutiny had developed had been given to an intelligent jury, the probabilities are that that jury would be unable to agree upon a verdict which pronounced Francis guilty of writing the libel. No jury would hesitate to find that the libel itself was the most scorching and atrocious to be found in any language in the world's history.—WEED, THURLOW, 1873, *The Letters of Junius, The Galaxy, vol.* 15, *p.* 609.

Probably no English book, except the plays of Shakespeare, has been submitted to such a minute and exhaustive criticism as the "Letters of Junius;" and although the sufficiency of the evidence tracing them to Francis is still much disputed, it may, I think, be truly said that rival candidates have almost disappeared from the field. — LECKY, WILLIAM EDWARD HARTPOLE, 1882, *A History of England in the Eighteenth Century, vol.* III, *ch.*xi, *p.*267.

England has hitherto had her mystery in "Junius;" but she will enjoy it no more, for there can be no longer any shadow of doubt that the "Letters" were written by Sir Philip Francis.—SMITH, GOLDWIN, 1894, *Junius Revealed, Sketch, May* 16.

I do not venture to identify Amyand with Junius; but the facts which I am about to set forth deserve consideration. . . . I have written more than once that I do not know who Junius was; as my ignorance still continues, I will not affirm that Claudius Amyand ever used "Junius" as a signature. In six articles on "The Franciscan Myth," the first of which appeared in the *Athenœum* for December 25th, 1897, I have proved that Francis could not be Junius, unless he were the same man who denounced George III. and Lord Mansfield as Junius, and defended them in his own person as Britannicus in the *Public Advertiser.* I am unable to admit that when Henry Sampson Woodfall, William Pitt, and Lord Grenville stated, from personal knowledge, that Junius was not Francis, they are unworthy of belief. . . . It certainly requires no ordinary courage or the excuse of invincible ignorance to reject conclusions at which Macaulay, Mr. Leslie Stephen, and Mr. Lecky have arrived; yet the critic who is neither over-weighted nor misled by prepossessions or forgone conclusions may decline to admit the infallibility of any writer.—RAE, W. FRASER, 1899, *Junius, Athenœum, pt.* i, *pp.* 434, 435.

GENERAL

How comes this Junius to have broke through the cobwebs of the law, and to range uncontrolled, unpunished, through the land? The myrmidons of the Court have been long, and are still, pursuing him in vain. They will not spend their time upon me, or you, or you: no; they disdain such vermin, when the mighty boar of the forest, that has broke through all their toils, is before them. But, what will all their efforts avail? No sooner has he wounded one, than he lays down another dead at his feet. For my part, when I saw his attack upon the King, I own my blood ran cold. . . . In short, after carrying away our Royal Eagle in his pounces, and dashing him against a rock, he has laid you prostrate. King, Lords, and Commons are but the sport of his fury. Were he a member of this house, what might not be expected from his knowledge, his firmness, and integrity! He would be easily known by his contempt of all danger, by his penetration, by his vigour. Nothing would escape his vigilance and activity. Bad ministers could conceal nothing from his sagacity; nor could promises nor threats induce him to conceal any thing from the public.—BURKE, EDMUND, 1770, *Speech in the House of Commons, Nov.* 27.

Junius bursts into notice with a blaze of impudence which has rarely glared upon the world before, and drew the rabble after him as a monster makes a show. When he had once provided for his safety by impenetrable secrecy, he had nothing to combat but truth and justice, enemies whom he knows to be feeble in the dark. Being then at liberty to indulge himself in all the immunities of invisibility, out of the reach of danger, he has been bold; out of the reach of shame he has been confident. As a rhetorician, he has the art of persuading when he seconded desire; as a reasoner, he has convinced those who had no doubt before; as a moralist, he has taught that virtue may disgrace; and as a patriot, he has gratified the mean by insults on the high. . . . It is not by his liveliness of imagery, his pungency of periods, or his fertility of allusion, that he detains the cits of London and the boors of Middlesex. Of style and sentiment they take no cognizance.—JOHNSON, SAMUEL, 1771, *Thoughts on the Late Transactions Respecting Falkland's Islands.*

I dedicate to you a collection of letters, written by one of yourselves for the common benefit of us all. They would never have grown to this size, without your continued encouragement and applause. To me they originally owe nothing, but a healthy sanguine constitution. Under *your* care they have thriven. To *you* they are indebted for whatever strength or beauty they possess. When kings and ministers are forgotten, when the force and direction of personal satire is no longer understood, and when measures are only felt in their remotest consequences, this book will, I believe, be found to contain principles worthy to be transmitted to posterity. When you leave the unimpaired, hereditary freehold to your children, you do but half your duty. Both liberty and property are precarious, unless the possessors have sense and spirit enough to defend them. This is not the language of vanity. If I am a vain man, my gratification lies within a narrow circle. I am the sole depositary of my own secret, and it shall perish with me.—JUNIUS, 1772, *Letters, Dedication to the English Nation.*

The classic purity of their language, the exquisite force and perspicuity of their argument, the keen severity of their reproach, the extensive information they evince, their fearless and decisive tone, and, above all, their stern and steady attachment to the purest principles of the constitution, acquired for them, with an almost electric speed, a popularity which no series of letters have since possessed, nor, perhaps, ever will; and, what is of far greater consequence, diffused among the body of the people a clearer knowledge of their constitutional rights than they had ever before attained, and animated them with a more determined spirit to maintain them inviolate. Enveloped in the cloud of a fictitious name, the writer of these philippics, unseen himself, beheld with secret satisfaction the vast influence of his labours, and enjoyed, though, as we shall afterwards observe, not always without apprehension, the universal hunt that was made to detect him in his disguise. He beheld the people extolling him, the court execrating him, and ministers and more than ministers trembling beneath the lash of his invisible hand.—GOOD, JOHN MASON, 1812, *Essay on Junius and His Writings.*

It is a signal testimony to the eminence of the powers displayed in these Letters, that, at the distance of nearly half a century from their first coming forth—that after a great number of subsequent political censors had each had his share of attention, and perhaps admiration, and are now in a great measure forgotten—and that in times like the present, superabounding with strange events, and flagrant examples of political depravity of their own —they should still hold such a place in public estimation, that the appearance of an edition enlarged and illustrated from the store of materials left by the original publisher, will be regarded as an interesting event in the course of our literature. An interest that has thus continued to subsist in vigour after the loss of all temporary stimulants, and that is capable of so lively an excitement at this distant period, by a circumstance tending to make us a little better acquainted with the author's character, and to put us in more complete possession of his writings, gives assurance that this memorable work may maintain its fame to an indefinite

period, and will go down with that portion of our literature, which, in the language of pride and poetry, we call immortal.— FOSTER, JOHN, 1813, *Junius, Critical Essays, ed. Ryland, vol.* II, *p.* 72.

The author is now considered as an English classic: yet, if we reflect on his very intemperate language, the virulence of his abuse, and the unsupported nature of some of the charges which he has adduced, we should rather be disposed to exclude him from ordinary perusal, as one who would mislead his admirers. He certainly writes with animation, frequently with elegance, generally with force and perspicuity. He argues plausibly, but does not always impress conviction: he evinces a knowledge of the constitution, though he sometimes misrepresents its principles: he is an advocate for liberty, but occasionally carries it to the verge of licentiousness. A ministerial author says, "If we allow him only his merit, where will be his praise?" We answer, that his praise will be that of an ingenious and able writer, and an intelligent politician. At the same time he deserves severe censure for his seditious spirit, the foulness of his reproaches, and his transgression of the bounds of truth. —COOTE, CHARLES, 1823, *Goldsmith's History of England, Continuation, vol.* III, *p.* 190.

The style of Junius is a sort of metre, the law of which is a balance of thesis and antithesis. When he gets out of this aphorismic metre into a sentence of five or six lines long, nothing can exceed the slovenliness of the English. Horne Tooke and a long sentence seem the only two antagonists that were too much for him. Still the antithesis of Junius is a real antithesis of images or thought, but the antithesis of Johnson is rarely more than verbal. — COLERIDGE, SAMUEL TAYLOR, 1833, *Table Talk, ed. Ashe, July* 3, *p.* 238.

The style of this writer, it is true, has many faults, and grave ones. It has point without aim, and vigour without agility. Wit alone can long bear up the shafts of sarcasm; and the wit of Junius had only one leg to stand on, a stiff and swollen one. His flashy and figured invectives, like court-dresses, would fit half the court as well as they fitted the person they were made for; if, indeed, like the prefaces of Sallust and Cicero, they were not kept ready until the author had found or

contrived a place for their exhibition.—
LANDOR, WALTER SAVAGE, 1839, *The Examiner, June* 30; *Letters, ed. Wheeler, p.* 250.

No man can read a page of any letter
without perceiving that the writer has
but one way of handling every subject, and that he constructs his sentences
with the sole design of saying the most
bitter things he can in the most striking way, without ever regarding in the
least degree their being applicable or
inapplicable to the object of the attack.
The consequence is, that the greater part
of this invective will just suit one bad man
or wicked minister as well as another. It is
highly probable that whoever he may be,
he had often attacked those with whom he
lived on intimate terms, or to whom he
was under obligations. This affords an
additional reason for his dying unrevealed.
That he was neither Lord Asburton, nor
any other lawyer, is proved by what we
have said of his gross ignorance of law.
To hold that he was Mr. Francis is libelling
that gentlemen's memory; and although
much external evidence concurs in pointing towards him, he certainly never wrote
anything of the same kind in his own
character.— BROUGHAM, HENRY LORD,
1839–43, *Lives of Statesmen of the Time
of George III, vol.* I, *p.* 207.

The passage of time has had no very
favorable effect upon the reputation of
that writer, particularly since it has given
to another and impartial generation the
opportunity to estimate the value of his
patriotism, and to weigh the motives of
his censures. It may be doubted, whether
the same sort of papers, if written at the
present day, would produce one half of the
effect they did when the novelty and boldness of the manner contributed so large a
share to their success.—ADAMS, CHARLES
FRANCIS, 1842, *The Elder Pitt, North
American Review, vol.* 55, *p.* 419.

As Wilkes was one of the worst specimens of a popular leader, so was Junius of
a popular political writer. One is ashamed
to think of the celebrity so long enjoyed
by a publication so worthless. No great
question of principle is discussed in it; it
is remarkable that on the subject of the
impressment of seamen, which is a real
evil of the most serious kind, and allowed
to be so even by those who do not believe
that it is altogether remediable, Junius
strongly defends the existing practice.

All the favourite topics of his letters are
purely personal or particular; his appeals
are never to the best part of our nature,
often to the vilest. If I wished to prejudice a good man against popular principles, I could not do better than to put into
his hands the letters of Junius.—ARNOLD,
THOMAS, 1842, *Introductory Lectures on
Modern History, p.* 333.

At last "the great boar of the forest,"
who had gored the King and almost all his
Court, and seemed to be more formidable
than any "blatant beast," was conquered,
—not by the spear of a knight-errant, but
by a little provender held out to him, and he
was sent to whet his tusks in a distant land.
This certainly was a very great deliverance
for Lord Mansfield, who had long been
afraid at breakfast to look into the *Daily
Advertiser,* less he should find in it some
new accusation, which he could neither
passively submit to nor resent without discredit; and although he might call the
mixture of bad law and tumid language
poured out upon him *ribaldry* it had an
evident effect in encouraging his opponents in parliament, and in causing shakes
of the head, shrugs of the shoulders,
smiles and whispers in private society,
which could not escape his notice.—
CAMPBELL, JOHN LORD, 1849, *Lives of the
Chief Justices of England, vol.* II, *p.* 492.

That Junius can only be described with
truth as a political adventurer there is no
doubt. It is plain enough that his own
personal success in life was involved in
that of the party whose cause he adopted,
or, to speak still more accurately, in the
fall of the party which he attacked. And
it is equally true that he was utterly unscrupulous in his use of means; that his
sincerity, even when he was sincere, was
apt to assume the form of the most ignoble
rancor, and that no ties of friendship, or
party, or connection, seem to have restrained his virulence. All this is but too
deducible from the published anonymous
writings only. . . . But when all this
has been said, there remains a residue of
a higher order, which must in justice to
him be fairly weighed in the balance.
Notwithstanding all his sins against
justice and truth, Junius was assuredly
actuated at bottom by a strong and
ardent public spirit. He was throughout
a genuine lover of his country. He was
earnest in behalf of her honor and of her

liberties. He saw clearly that her road to the accomplishment of a higher destiny lay through the maintenance of that honor and the extension of those liberties. He hated with an honest hatred the meanness of principle and venality of conduct which characterized but too strongly the governments against which he fought, and tarnished the political genius of his time. And very remarkable was the success which attended his struggle against them. Great indeed were the practical victories achieved by the efforts of this nameless, obscure agitator. Freedom of the press and the personal freedom of the subject owe probably more to the writings of Junius than to the eloquence of Chatham or Burke, the law of Camden and Dunning. It is not too much to say that after the appearance of those writings, a new tone on these great subjects is found to prevail in our political literature.—PARKES, J., AND MERIVALE, H., 1852–67, *Memoirs of Sir Philip Francis.*

Sir Philip Francis, who, under his early disguise of Junius, had such a success as no writer of libels ever will have again. It is our private opinion that this success rested upon a great delusion which has never been exposed. The general belief is that Junius was read for his elegance; we believe no such thing. The pen of an angel would not, upon such a theme as personal politics, have upheld the interest attached to Junius, had there been no other cause in co-operation. Language, after all, is a limited instrument; and it must be remembered that Junius, by the extreme narrowness of his range, which went entirely upon matters of fact and personal interests, still further limited the compass of that limited instrument. For it is only in the expression and management of general ideas that any room arises for conspicuous elegance. The real truth is this: the interest in Junius travelled downwards; he was read in the lower ranks, because in London it speedily became known that he was read with peculiar interest in the highest. This was already a marvel; for newspaper patriots, under the signatures of Publicola, Brutus, and so forth, had become a jest and a byword to the real practical statesman; and any man at leisure to write for so disinterested a purpose as "his country's good" was presumed of course to write in a garret. But

here for the first time a pretended patriot, a Junius Brutus, was read even by statesmen, and read with agitation. Is any man simple enough to believe that such a contagion could extend to cabinet ministers and official persons overladen with public business on so feeble an excitement as a little reputation in the art of constructing sentences with elegance,—an elegance which, after all, excluded eloquence and every other *positive* quality of excellence? That this can have been believed shows the readiness with which men swallow marvels. The real secret was this:—Junius was read with the profoundest interest by members of the cabinet, who would not have paid half-a-crown for all the wit and elegance of this world, simply because it was most evident that some traitor was amongst them, and that, either directly by one of themselves, or through some abuse of his confidence by a servant, the secrets of office were betrayed. — DE QUINCEY, THOMAS, 1859, *Rhetoric, Collected Writings, ed. Masson, vol.* x, *p.* 117.

Attacked the Government in letters which, rancorous and unscrupulous as was their tone, gave a new power to the literature of the Press by their clearness and terseness of statement, the finish of their style, and the terrible vigor of their invective.—GREEN, JOHN RICHARD, 1874, *A Short History of the English People, p.* 738.

Though containing occasional passages of weighty invective and of brilliant epigram, these early letters are, I think, of very little value, and it was only by slow degrees that the writer learnt the secret of true dignity of style, and exchanged the tone of simple scurrility for that measured malignity of slander in which he afterwards excelled. . . . As a popular political reasoner he was truly admirable. He introduced, indeed, little or nothing new or original into controversy, but he possessed to supreme perfection the art of giving the arguments on his side their simplest, clearest, and strongest expression; disengaging them from all extraneous matter, making them transparently evident to the most cursory reader. In this, as in most other respects, he is a curious contrast to Burke, who is always redundant, and who delights in episodes, illustrations, ramifications, general reflections, various lights, remote and indirect

JOHN WOLCOT

RICHARD PORSON

Engraving by C. Heath.
Painting by J. R. Smith.

Engraving by H. Adlard.
Painting by J. Hoppner, R. A.

consequences. Junius never for a moment loses sight of the immediate issue, and he flies swift and direct as an arrow to its heart. The rapid march of the eighteenth century is apparent in his style, and it is admirably suited for a class of literature which, if it impresses at all, must impress at a glance. He possessed the easy air of good society, and his letters, if not those of a great statesman, are at least unquestionably those of a man who had a real and experimental knowledge of public business, who had mixed with active politicians, who knew the anecdotes which circulated in political society. . . . A reader who knows Junius as we know him now, must indeed have an extraordinary estimate of the value of a brilliant style if he can regard him with the smallest respect. He wisely attacked for the most part men whose rank and position prevented them from descending into the arena, and who were at the same time intensely and often deservedly unpopular. His encounter with Horne was the one instance in which he met a really able and practised writer; and although the character of Horne was a very vulnerable one, he appears to me to have had in this controversy a great advantage over his opponent.—LECKY, WILLIAM EDWARD HARTPOLE, 1882, *A History of England in the Eighteenth Century, vol.* III, *ch.* xi, *pp.* 253, 257, 264.

The "Letters of Junius," with which he is credited, are perhaps more famous than excellent, but still excellent.— SAINTSBURY, GEORGE, 1886, *Specimens of English Prose Style, p.* 242.

If Junius could have exercised a greater command of his feelings, he might have provided a still better feast of malignity.

This he could have done by well-contrived admissions, palliations and excuses; and by keeping within the ordinary limits of human nature in his attributing of vices. In that case, we might have had no compunctions in going along with him; our pleasure of malignity would have been unalloyed.—BAIN, ALEXANDER, 1888, *English Composition and Rhetoric, Part Second, p.* 251.

The literary value of Junius seems to have been absurdly overrated. The letters are vigorous, of course, but their malignity is atoned for or relieved by no philosophical enthusiasm, while the indignation itself appears to be personal first and patriotic afterwards. It is an instance of the difficulty which attends contemporary criticism that Johnson, so eminent a judge of language, thought that Junius was Burke. To us it seems amazing that brass should thus be mistaken for gold. At the same time the *Letters* have "polish," a quality for which Francis preserved an exaggerated affection; the balance and modulation of their merciless sentences may still please the ear.—GOSSE, EDMUND, 1888, *A History of Eighteenth Century Literature, p.* 363.

They are the work of a man who was a practical politician first and a man of letters afterwards, and his writings are distinguished by a political sagacity and precision of criticism which only a close acquaintance with the practice of politics can give. His motives indeed were not of a high order; personal spite entered largely into them, and many of his letters were written merely to revenge real or fancied wrongs.—POLLARD, A. F., 1897, *ed., Political Pamphlets, Introduction, p.* 22.

John Wolcot

Peter Pindar

1738–1819

Born, at Dodbrooke, Devonshire, 1738; baptized, 9 May. Educated at Kingsbridge Free School; at Bodmin Grammar School, and in France. For seven years assistant to his uncle, an apothecary in practice in Cornwall. M. D., Aberdeen, 1767. In Jamaica, practising as surgeon and physician, 1767–69. Returned to England, 1769. Ordained Deacon and Priest, 1769; returned to Jamaica. Vicar of Vere, Jamaica, 1772. Returned to England, Dec. 1772. Practised medicine in Truro, 1773–79. Settled in London, 1781. Prolific writer of satires, under pseudonym "Peter Pindar." Died, in London, 14 Jan. 1819. Buried in St. Paul's, Covent Garden. *Works:* "Persian Love Elegies," 1773; [*the following all pubd. under pseud.* "*Peter Pindar :*"] "A

Poetical   .   .   .   Epistle to the Reviewers," 1778; "Poems on various Subjects,"
1778; "Lyric Odes to the Royal Academicians," 1782; "Lyric Odes for the Year,"
1785; "The Louisad," 1785–95; "Farewell Odes," 1786; "A Poetical and Congratulatory Epistle to James Boswell," 1786; "Bozzy and Piozzi," 1786; "Ode upon Ode,"
1787; "An Apologetic Postscript to 'Ode upon Ode,'" 1787; "Congratulatory Epistle
to Peter Pindar," 1787; "Instructions to a Celebrated Laureat," 1787; "Brother Peter
to Brother Tom," 1788; "Peter's Pension," 1788; "Sir Joseph Banks and the Emperor
of Morocco," 1788; "Epistle to his pretended Cousin Peter," 1788; "The King's
Ode," (anon.), 1788; "Peter's Prophecy," 1788; "Lyric Odes to the Academicians,"
1789; "Subjects for Painters," 1789; "A Poetical Epistle to a Falling Minister,"
1789; "Expostulatory Odes," 1789; "Works" (2 vols.), 1789–92; "A Benevolent
Epistle to Sylvanus Urban," 1790; "Advice to the Future Laureat," 1790; "Letter
to the Most Insolent Man alive," 1790; "Complimentary Epistle to James Bruce, 1790;
"The Rights of Kings," 1791; "Odes to Mr. Paine," 1791; "The Remonstrance,"
1791; "A Commiserating Epistle to G. Lowther," 1791; "More Money," 1792; "The
Tears of St. Margaret," 1792; "Odes of Importance," 1792; "Odes to Kien Long,"
1792; "A Pair of Lyric Epistles," 1792; "A Poetical   .   .   Epistle to the Pope,"
1793; "Pathetic Odes," 1794; "Pindariana," 1794; "Celebration; or, the Academic
Procession to St. James's," 1794; "Works" (4 vols.), 1794–96; "Hair-Powder," 1795;
"The Convention Bill," 1795; "The Cap," 1795; "The Royal Visit to Exeter," 1795;
"Liberty's Last Squeak," 1795; "The Royal Tom," 1795; "An Admirable Satire on
Burke's Defence of his Pension," 1796; "One Thousand, Seven Hundred, and Ninety-
six" 1797; "An Ode to the Livery of London," 1797; "Tales of the Hoy" [1798];
"Nil Admirari," 1799; "Lord Auckland's Triumph," 1800; "Out at Last," 1801;
"Odes to Inns and Outs," 1801; "A Poetical Epistle to Benjamin, Count Rumford,"
1801; "Tears and Smiles," 1801; "The Island of Innocence," 1802; "Pitt and his
Statute," 1802; "The Middlesex Election," 1802; "The Horrors of Bribery," 1802;
"Great Cry and Little Wool," 1804; "An Instructive Epistle to the Lord Mayor,"
1804; "Tristia," 1806; "One More Peep at the Royal Academy," 1808; "The Fall of
Portugal," 1808; "Works" (4 vols.), 1809; "Carlton House Fête," 1811; "Works"
(5 vols.), 1812; "An Address to be spoken at the Opening of Drury-Lane Theatre"
(anon.), 1813; "Royalty Fog-bound," 1814; "The Regent and the King," 1814;
"Midnight Dreams," 1814; "Tom Halliard," [1815?]. He *edited:* Pilkington's
"Dictionary of Painters," 1799; "The Beauties of English Poetry," 1804.—SHARP,
R. FARQUHARSON, 1897, *A Dictionary of English Authors, p. 302.*

PERSONAL

The concealed author of "Lyrick Odes,"
by Peter Pindar, Esquire, is one Woolcot,
a clergyman, who abjured the gown, and
now lives in Great Queen Street, Lincoln's
Inn Fields, under the character of a
physician.   He is likewise author of a
scurrilous epistle lately published, addressed to James Boswell, Esq., March
4th, 1786.   He is noted for impudence,
lewdness, and almost every species of
profligacy. — MALONE, EDMOND, 1783,
Maloniana, ed. Prior, p. 364.

A bloated mass, a gross, blood-boltered clod,
A foe to man, a renegade from God,
From noxious childhood to pernicious age,
Separate to infamy in every stage.   .   .   .
Come, then, all filth, all venom, as thou art,
Rage in thy eye, and rancour in thy heart;
Come with thy boasted arms, spite, malice,
    lies,
Smut, scandal, execrations, blasphemies:
I brave them all! Lo, here I fix my stand,

And dare the utmost of thy tongue and hand;
Prepared each threat to baffle or to spurn,
Each blow with tenfold vigour to return.
—GIFFORD, WILLIAM, 1800, *Epistle to
Peter Pindar.*

Dined with Thelwall.   A large party.
The man whom we went to see, and, if we
could, admire, was Dr. Wolcott, better
known as Peter Pindar.   He talked about
the artists, said that West could paint
neither ideal beauty nor from nature,
called Opie the Michael Angelo of old age,
complained of the ingratitude of certain
artists who owed everything to himself,
spoke contemptuously of Sir Walter Scott,
who, he said, owed his popularity to hard
names.   He also declaimed against rhyme
in general, which he said was fit only for
burlesque.   .   .   .   As Peter Pindar was
blind, I was requested to help him to his
wine, which was in a separate pint bottle,
and was not wine at all, but brandy, . . .

I referred to his own writings. He said he recollected them with no pleasure. "Satire is a bad trade."—ROBINSON, HENRY CRABB, 1811, *Diary, May* 9, *pp.* 210, 211.

He always sat in a room facing the south. Behind the door stood a square piano-forte, on which there generally lay his favourite Cremona violin; on the left, a mahogany table with writing materials. Everything was in perfect order. . . . Facing him, over the mantlepiece, hung a fine landscape by Richard Wilson. . . . In writing, except a few lines haphazard, the Doctor was obliged to employ an amanuensis. Of all his acquisitions, music to him remained alone unaltered. . . . He even composed light airs for amusement. — REDDING, CYRUS, 1856, *Fifty Years' Recollections.*

He was as little fitted for a doctor of medicine as for a doctor of divinity. He could better epigrammatize than prescribe, preferred ridiculing to healing, and had a keener eye for mental or personal obliquities than for corporal infirmities. . . . Wolcot's vanity is irrepressible. Peter is always the prominent picture. He writes to everybody about himself, and he is the central orb round which kings and subjects, and indeed the whole creation, move. His pension, his prophecy, his paintings, his praise, his censure, and his criticisms are to annihilate all other topics. The desire to silence such a critic was quite natural. Nobody likes to be laughed at, and it is not all laughter, for he sometimes uses a whip of scorpions, and lashes sore places with the delight of a Mephistopheles. That in those libel-hunting days he should have escaped unscathed can only be attributed to the fear of giving wider circulation to his incisive jokes, many of which remain indelibly associated with the blunderings and stutterings of the "Good King George."—BOWRING, SIR JOHN, 1872, *Autobiographical Recollections, pp.* 360, 363.

Wolcot was buried in the Church of St. Paul, Covent Garden, at his own request that he might "lie as near as possible to the bones of old Hudibras Butler." His grave is believed to be under the floor of the vestry-room; but there is no tablet to his memory.—HUTTON, LAURENCE, 1885, *Literary Landmarks of London, p.* 321.

In appearance Wolcot was "a thick squat man with a large dark and flat face, and no speculation in his eye." He possessed considerable accomplishments, being a fair artist and good musician, and, despite the character of his compositions, his friends described him as of a "kind and hearty disposition." He was probably influenced in his writings by no real animosity towards royalty, and himself confessed that "the king had been a good subject to him, and he a bad one to the king."— CARR, WILLIAM, 1900, *Dictionary of National Biography, vol.* LXII, *p.* 292.

GENERAL

There is an obscure person, stiling himself Peter Pindar, of whom I shall say a few words. This man certainly possesses a mind by no means uninformed, and a species of humour; but it is exhausted by a repetition of the *same* manner, and nearly the *same* ideas, even to disgust. He has the power of rhyming ludicrously, and is sometimes even gifted with poetry; and finally, he is puffed up with a vanity and self-conceited importance, almost without a parallel. This *obscure* man has contrived, by these qualifications, to thrust himself upon the publick notice, and become the scorn of every man of character and of virtue. Such is the blasphemy, such is the impiety, the obscenity, the impudence and the contempt of all decent respect, which pervade his numerous pamphlets in verse, that the reader is ill repaid by the lively sallies of humour which frequently animate this mass of crudities. I form my judgment *from his works,* and not from any acquaintance whatever with the man. . . . Posterity (if it can be supposed that such trash should exist) will be astonished, that the present age could look with patience on such malignant ribaldry.—MATHIAS, THOMAS JAMES, 1794-96, *The Pursuits of Literature, pp.* 51, 52.

I cannot tell you how much I admire and despise Peter; he is every way original, and most original in this respect, that I know not that ever any other object at once excited my contempt and admiration. His humour is most peculiar, most unaffected, most irresistible. Yet, for what end Providence intrusted a weapon so dangerous in the hands of one who avows his disregard of everything sacred and venerable, is very difficult for us to conjecture. I am the more fully convinced of the bad tendency of his writings, from the amusement I derive from them, forearmed as I am by a disgust at his want of principle and decency. "Bozzy and Piozzi," however, is above praise and beyond censure: there the satire is so just, so pointed, so characteristic, that one can laugh without self-reproach. The "Lousiad," however, I regard with a mixture of contempt and disgust.—GRANT, ANNE, 1802, *To Miss Dunbar, May* 4; *Letters from the Mountains, ed. Grant, vol.* II.

The most unsparing calumniator of his time.—SCOTT, SIR WALTER, 1827, *Diary, Jan.* 17, *Memoirs, ed. Lockhart, ch.* lxxiii.

There are a few fables of Peter Pindar in the exact style of La Fontaine, and I think them among the best in the language. —ADAMS, JOHN QUINCY, 1829, *Memoirs, vol.* 8, *p.* 133.

Wolcot had an eye for little that was grave in life, except the face-makings of absurdity and pretension; but these he could mimic admirably, putting on at one and the same time their most nonchalant and matter-of-course airs, while he fetched out into his countenance the secret nonsense. He echoes their words, with some little comment of approval, or change in their position; some classical inversion, or exaltation, which exposes the pretension in the very act of admitting it, and has an irresistibly ludicrous effect.—HUNT, LEIGH, 1846, *Wit and Humour, p.* 351.

Dr. Wolcot was certainly one of the most original poets England has produced; his production displaying not merely wit and smartness, but a profound knowledge of the world and of the human heart, combined with a sound and cultivated understanding. His serious poems evince the same command of language and originality of ideas as are displayed in his satires, though he excelled in the latter.— CLEVELAND, CHARLES D., 1853, *English Literature of the Nineteenth Century, p.*111.

I am not sure that I do not prefer Wolcot (Peter Pindar) to Churchill.—ROGERS, SAMUEL, 1855, *Recollections of Table-Talk.*

The most voluminous, and one of the best, of the humourous poets who have written in the English language.—PARTON, JAMES, 1856, *ed., The Humorous Poetry of the English Language, p.* 687.

Wolcot was equal to Churchill as a satirist, as ready and versatile in his powers, and possessed of a quick sense of the ludicrous, as well as a rich vein of fancy and humour. Some of his songs and serious effusions are tender and pleasing; but he could not write long without sliding into the ludicrous and burlesque. His critical acuteness is evinced in his "Odes to the Royal Academicians," in various passages scattered throughout his works; while his ease and felicity, both of expression and illustration, are remarkable.— CHAMBERS, ROBERT, 1876, *Cyclopædia of English Literature, ed. Carruthers.*

At this distance the fun and sport and spontaneous overflowing laughter of the satirist, and the perfect and laughable distinctness of the figure he sets before us, are far more conspicuous than any political mischief that could have been in them. The story of the Dumpling, over which the inquisitive king puzzled his brains to know how the apples got into it, and the visit of his Majesty to Whitbread's brewery, are still as amusing as when they were written; and few of the personages in grave historical biography stand out with half the force which characterises this careless lighthearted picture, in which the fun is so much more prominent than the satire.—OLIPHANT, MARGARET O. W., 1882, *The Literary History of England, XVIIIth—XIXth Century, vol.* II, *p.* 184.

Neither Charles the Second at the hands of Marvell, nor George the Fourth at the hands of Moore, received anything like the steady fire of lampoon which Wolcot for years poured upon the most harmless and respectable of English monarchs. George the Third had indeed no vices,—unless a certain parsimony may be dignified by that name,—but he had many foibles of the kind that is more useful to the satirist than even vice. Wolcot's extreme coarseness, his triviality of subject, and a vulgarity of thought which is quite a different thing from either, are undeniable. But "The Lousiad" (a perfect triumph of cleverness expended on what the Greeks called rhyparography), the famous pieces on George and the Apple Dumplings and on the King's visit to Whitbread's Brewery, with scores of other things of the same kind (the best of all, perhaps, being the record of the Devonshire Progress), exhibit incredible felicity and fertility in the lower kinds of satire.—SAINTSBURY, GEORGE, 1896, *A History of Nineteenth Century Literature, p.* 22.

William Hayley
1745–1820

The friend and biographer of Cowper, and grandson of William Hayley, dean of Chichester, was born in that city on the 9th November, 1745. . . . After some years' private tuition he pursued his studies at Eton and at Trinity College, Cambridge. In 1766 he procured a certificate of admission to the Middle Temple, London, but a short trial of legal studies was sufficient to dissipate the unexperienced preference which he had cherished for the profession of law. After his marriage in 1769, he stayed for some years chiefly in London, but in 1774 he retired to his patrimonial estate of Eartham in Sussex, resolved to spend the remainder of his days in rural quiet, with only such an amount of literary activity as might defy ennui and give a zest to life. Hayley made more than one attempt to succeed as a dramatic author, but first won fame by his poetical "Essays on Painting," "History and Epic Poetry," and by his poem the "Triumph of Temper." . . . On the death of Warton, Hayley was offered the laureateship, but declined it. In 1792 he made the acquaintance of the poet Cowper; and this acquaintance ripened into a friendship which remained unbroken until Cowper's death in 1800. This bereavement was separated by only a week from that caused by the death of Hayley's natural son Thomas Alphonso, who had given great promise of excellence as a sculptor; and, shrinking from the associations now connected with Eartham, Hayley retired to what he called a "marine hermitage," which he had built at Feltham, and there resided till his death, November 20, 1820. Besides the "life of Cowper," published in 1803, Hayley was the author of a number of works in prose, which were not, however, so successful as his early poetical productions. . . . The "Memoirs of Hayley," 2 vols., for writing which, to be published posthumously, he received a considerable allowance during the last twelve years of his life, appeared in 1823.—Baynes, Thomas Spencer, ed., 1880, *Encyclopædia Britannica, Ninth edition, vol.* xi, *p.* 484.

PERSONAL

He was considerably above the middle stature, had a countenance remarkably expressive of intellect and feeling, and a commanding air and deportment that reminded the beholder rather of a military officer, than of the character he assumes in the close of his epistolary addresses (he used to sign himself *the Hermit*). The deplorable infirmity, however, of his early years, had left a perceptible lameness, which attended him through life, and induced a necessity of adventitious aid, towards procuring him the advantage of a tolerably even walk. As to his personal qualities, of a higher order, these were cheerfulness and sympathy in a very eminent degree; so eminent, indeed, that as no afflictions of his own could divest him of the former, so neither could the afflictions of others find him destitute of the latter. His temper also was singularly sweet and amiable, being not only free from ebullitions of anger, but from all those minor defects which it is needless to enumerate, and to which social peace and harmony are so repeatedly sacrificed.— Johnson, John, 1823, ed., *Memoirs of the Life and Writings of William Hayley.*

The book [Hayley's "Memoirs"] itself is to me the most miserable, meagre, affected, ill-arranged string of commonplaces I ever yawned over. You are more tenderhearted and indulgent than I am. I cannot give Hayley credit for all the feeling he pretends to. Feeling does not thrust itself into notice so perpetually: feeling does not flow into verse, or even words, at the first moment of excitement, though I know that, when it subsides into calm melancholy, poetry is its natural language. Hayley wrote epitaphs upon his dearest friends before their eyes were well closed—a sort of poetical carrion crow! I never could have endured that man, with all his tender epitaphs. I daresay he helped to drive his poor wife mad —"his pitiably irritable Eliza." There is something very unsatisfactory even in his attention to the poor youth, his son. How strange that he should choose only to visit him in the day-time, making Felpham his own residence. But all the particulars of Hayley's life did not bear telling.— Bowles, Caroline A., 1824, *To Robert Southey, June* 20; *The Correspondence of Robert Southey with Caroline Bowles, ed. Dowden, p.* 64.

He made this residence a delightful spot. Gibbon called it the little Paradise of Eartham. "His place (said the historian) though small, is as elegant as his mind, which I value much more highly;" and communicating to Lord Sheffield a wish which Hayley had expressed to become acquainted with him; he adds, that this was "no vulgar compliment." Hayley is now estimated only by his writings, and these, because they were greatly overrated in their day, have perhaps, been depreciated since in proportion. But the person of whom Gibbon could speak thus, must have been no ordinary man. Literary acquirements like his were rare at that time, and are not common now; and these were not his only accomplishments. All who knew him, concur in describing his manners as in the highest degree winning, and his conversation as delightful. It is said that few men have ever rendered so many essential acts of kindness to those who stood in need of them. His errors were neither few nor trifling; but his good qualtities greatly preponderated. He was a most affectionate father, a most warm and constant friend; and his latter days of infirmity and pain were distinguished by no common degree of cheerful fortitude and Christian resignation.—SOUTHEY, ROBERT, 1836-7, *The Life of William Cowper, vol.* II, *p.* 45.

If Hayley was always romancing, as it were, which his position in life allowed; always living in a fool's paradise of ever-dispelled, ever-renewed self-deceptions about the commonest trifles; seeing all men and things athwart a fog of amiability; it was not in the main a worse world than common, and sometimes it was a useful life to others. The pension his bustling energy obtained for Cowper outweighs many an absurdity and inanity. He was surely an endurable specimen, for variety sake, among corn-law and game-preserving squires. A sincere, if conventional love of literature, independence of the great world, and indifference to worldly distinctions, are, after all, not criminal foibles. Pertinacious, wrongheaded, and often foolish in his actions; weakly, greedy of applause, as ready to lavish it; prone to exaggeration of word and thought; without reticence; he was also an agreeable companion, really kind-hearted and generous; though vanity mixed itself with all

he did; for ever going out of his way to befriend some one, to set in motion some well-intended, ill-considered scheme. For Blake,—let us remember, to the hermit's honour,—Hayley continued to entertain unfeigned respect. And the self-tutored, willful visionary must have been a startling phenomenon to so conventional a mind. During the artist's residence at Felpham his literary friend was constantly on the alert to advance his fortunes.—GILCHRIST, ALEXANDER, 1861-63, *Life of William Blake, vol.* I, *p.* 156.

Hayley was a mediocre poet, who had for a time obtained distinction above his merits. Afterwards his star had declined, but having an excellent heart, he had not been in the least soured by the downfall of his reputation. He was addicted to a pompous rotundity of style; perhaps he was rather absurd; but he was thoroughly good-natured, very anxious to make himself useful, and devoted to Cowper, to whom, as a poet, he looked up with an admiration unalloyed by any other feeling.—SMITH, GOLDWIN, 1880, *Cowper (English Men of Letters), p.* 120.

Hayley, though a bad poet, was a good friend.—STEPHEN, LESLIE, 1887, *Dictionary of National Biography, vol.* XII, *p.* 400.

GENERAL

There are just appeared three new "Epistles on History," addressed to Mr. Gibbon by Mr. Hayley. They are good poems, I believe, weight and measure, but, except some handsome new similes, have little poetry and less spirit. In short, they are written by Judgment, who has set up for herself, forgetting that her business is to correct verses, and not to write them.—WALPOLE, HORACE, 1780, *To Rev. William Mason, May; Letters, ed. Cunnnigham, vol.* VII, *p.* 361.

Who is this Mr. Hayley? His poetry has more merit than that of most of his contemporaries; but his whiggism is so bigoted, and his Christianity so fierce, that he almost disgusts one with two very good things.—ROBERTSON, WILLIAM, 1781, *Letter to Gibbon.*

I hope you like Mr. Hayley's poem; he rises with the subject, and since Pope's death, I am satisfied that England has not seen so happy a mixture of strong sense and flowing numbers. Are you not delighted with his address to his mother? I understand that she was, in plain prose, every thing that he speaks her in verse.— GIBBON, EDWARD, 1782, *To his Stepmother, Private Letters, ed. Prothero, vol.* II, *p.* 17.

The epistles of Mr. Hayley on Painting, History, and Epic Poetry, would perhaps more properly have been thrown under the title Historical, had I thought it worth while thus to designate a column for the admission of a single writer. They inculcate however so much elegant and judicious criticism, and diffuse so much light over their respective subjects, that they may not unaptly find a place in the didactic compartment. The versification of these pieces is peculiarly smooth, correct, and flowing, but not unfrequently deficient in energy and compression. The characters are in general justly drawn, and several display a warmth of fancy and of beauty in illustration highly worthy of applause.—DRAKE, NATHAN, 1798–1820, *Literary Hours, vol.* II, *No.* xxix, *p.* 114.

Behold!—ye tarts! one moment spare the text—
Hayley's last work, and worst—until his next;
Whether he spin poor couplets into plays,
Or damn the dead with purgatorial praise,
His style in youth or age is still the same,
For ever feeble and for ever tame.
Triumphant first see "Temper's Triumphs" shine!
At least I'm sure they triumph'd over mine.
Of "Music's Triumphs," all who read may swear
That luckless music never triumph'd there.
—BYRON, LORD, 1809, *English Bards and Scotch Reviewers.*

As Hayley was too much extolled at the beginning of his poetical course, so was he undeservedly neglected or ridiculed at the close of it. The excessive admiration he at first met with, joined to that flattering self-opinion which a solitary life is apt to engender, made him too easily satisfied with what he had done. Perhaps he wrote worse after his acquaintance with Cowper; for, aiming at a simplicity which he had not power to support, he became flat and insipid. He had at no time much force of conception or language. Yet if he never elevates he frequently amuses his reader. His chief attraction consists in setting off some plain and natural thought or observation, by a sparkling and ingenious similitude, such as we commonly find in the Persian poets. To this may be added a certain sweetness of numbers peculiar to

himself, without the spirit and edge of Pope, or the boldness of Dryden, and fashioned as I think to his own recitation, which though musical, was somewhat too pompous and monotonous. He was desirous that all his rhymes should be exact; but they are sometimes so only according to his own manner of pronouncing them. He holds about the same rank among our poets that Bertaut does among the French; but differs from him in this; that, whereas Bertaut was the earliest of a race analogous to the school of Dryden and Pope, so Hayley was the latest of the correspondent class among ourselves.—CARY, HENRY FRANCIS, 1821-24-45, *Lives of English Poets, p.* 344.

The vain and silly egotism, and the tiresome load of epithets which clogs his style with sickly affectation, revolt me so much, that I have barely candour enough left to give Hayley credit for kindness of heart, and steadiness of attachment.—GRANT, ANNE, 1823, *Letters, Sept.* 2; *Memoir and Correspondence, ed. Grant, vol.* III, *p.* 16.

On the 18th of the month, the tragedy of "Lord Russel," by Mr. Hayley, was also represented at this theatre. He had written this, and one other tragedy, "Marcella," for a private theatre, and it remained to be tried how compositions, so very sober and regular, would gratify the taste of a public auditory. I believe it answered the most sanguine expectations. The characters interested by their virtue: but the muse of Hayley was not, I think, vigorous enough for tragedy; his verses were too uniform in their structure, and his diction rather feeble and flat.—BOADEN, JAMES, 1825, *Memoirs of the Life of John Philip Kemble, vol.* I, *p.* 182.

If Hayley had not a high invention and forcible intellect, his mind was copiously enriched with multifarious acquisitions from study, a retentive memory, and a susceptible heart. He wanted compression; but his moral sentiments were always amiable and abundant, though languid; and surely the range of literature he had mastered, alone entitled him not only to respect but to distinction.—BRYDGES, SIR SAMUEL EGERTON, 1834, *Autobiography, vol.* I, *p.* 131.

Whether or not any of Hayley's "Essays" have had the specific effect which he hoped to produce, they imparted, by help of the copious notes wherewith he elucidated them, much information in an agreeable form: his translated specimens of Dante, which were introduced in these notes, revived among us a taste for the Italian poets; and Spanish literature had been so long and so utterly neglected in this country, that he may be truly said to have introduced the knowledge of it to his contemporaries. . . . Perhaps the "Essays" were read more for the sake of the notes than of the poetry; but the poetry was praised in the highest terms.—SOUTHEY, ROBERT, 1836-7, *The Life of William Cowper, vol.* II, *p.* 25.

If Hayley was formerly over-rated, he is now under-valued.—ROGERS, SAMUEL, 1855, *Recollections of Table-Talk, ed.* Dyce.

Hayley's masterpiece, "The Triumphs of Temper," published in 1781, was the "hit" of the day. Its author was a man of considerable culture and intellectual refinement, and, as his "Epistle to Romney" shows, of no contemptible artistic taste. It is impossible to read his warblings, with whatever amount of critical disdain for the warbler, without conceiving a genuine liking for the man. His nature had all the simplicity in which his art was so lamentably to seek, and his disposition was as modest as his Muse was pretentious. His geniality and good nature break out irresistibly even in his metrical attack upon Hume, and even in his letters to the egregious Miss Anna Seward he cannot heartily abuse even his rough Johnson, but is continually slipping in admiring epithets which his fair but fiercer correspondent amusingly entreats him to recall. But Johnson, omnivorous reader though he was, declared himself unable to get beyond the first two pages of "The Triumphs of Temper," and posterity perhaps has never got so far. Its readability even to a seasoned critic is strictly limited to its interest as a deliberate imitation, sometimes declining into a downright parody, of its illustrious model. . . . Hayley is always faultlessly smooth in his versification, and careful in his workmanship, never slovenly, never inelegant. The errors of his poetic creed stand therefore conclusively proved in the hopeless reprobation of one, who, if poets could be saved by "correctness" alone, would occupy a high position among the blest.—TRAILL, HENRY DUFF, 1896, *Social England, vol.* V, *pp.* 440, 441.

His verse itself is impossible and intolerable to any but the student of literary history, who knows that all things are possible, and finds the realisation of all in its measure interesting.— SAINTSBURY, GEORGE, 1896, *A History of Nineteenth Century Literature, p.* 18.

Arthur Young
1741–1820

Writer on agriculture, was born at Whitehall, but spent his boyhood, as indeed most of his life, at Bradfield near Bury St. Edmunds, his father being rector and a prebendary of Canterbury. In 1763 he rented a small farm of his mother's, on which he made 3,000 unsuccessful experiments; during 1766–71 held a good-sized farm in Essex (ruin the result); from 1776 to 1778 was in Ireland; resumed farming at Bradfield; and in 1793 was appointed secretary to the Board of Agriculture, with a salary of £600. Blind from 1811, he died in London, and was buried at Bradfield. Young, by his writings, was one of the first to elevate agriculture to a science. They include "A Tour through the Southern Counties" (1768), "A Tour through the North of England" (1771), "The Farmer's Tour through the East of England" (1770–71), "Tour in Ireland" (1780), "Travels in France during 1787–88–89–90" (a very memorable view of the state of France just before the Revolution, 1792–94), "The Farmer's Kalendar" (215th ed. 1862), and "Agricultural Surveys" of eight English counties, besides many papers in "The Annals of Agriculture," which he edited. See A. W. Hutton's edition of the "Tour in Ireland" with bibliography by J. P. Anderson (1892); M. Betham-Edwards's edition of the "Travels in France" (1890); and her edition of his "Autobiography" (1897).—PATRICK AND GROOME, *eds.*, 1897, *Chambers's Biographical Dictionary, p.* 990.

PERSONAL

He was not a walking blue-book, but a highly sensitive, enthusiastic, impulsive, and affectionate man of flesh and blood, whose acquaintance one would have been glad to cultivate. . . . Young's devoted and unflagging zeal, and his sanguine confidence in his principles is equally attractive, whatever the inconsistencies or rashness of his speculations.—STEPHEN, LESLIE, 1896, *Arthur Young, National Review, vol.* 27, *pp.* 489, 499.

Whilst Arthur Young's famous "Travels in France" have become a classic, little is known of the author's life, a life singularly interesting and singularly sad. Whether regarded as the untiring experimentalist and dreamer of economic dreams, as the brilliant man of society and the world, or as the blind, solitary victim of religious melancholia, the figure before us remains unique and impressive. . . . The religious melancholia of his later years is explicable on several grounds: to the influence of his friend, the great Wilberforce; to the crushing sorrow of his beloved little daughter "Bobbin's" death; lastly, perhaps, to exaggerated self-condemnation for foibles of his youth. Few lives have been more many-sided, more varied; few, indeed have been more fortunate and unfortunate at the same time.—BETHAM-EDWARDS, M., 1898, *ed., The Autobiography of Arthur Young, Introductory Note.*

Young was a great favourite in society. Vivacious, high-spirited, and well informed, he was an agreeable companion. His characteristics are abundantly manifested in his writings, and there is no lack of material for forming a mental picture of his personality. . . . His tall slim figure, thin features, aquiline nose, and hawk eyes are in keeping with the restless activity of his character. He rose at 5 A. M., bathed in the open air; on one occasion—undaunted experimentalist—he broke the ice in the pond to bathe, and rolled his body in the snow to test the effect.—HIGGS, HENRY, 1900, *Dictionary of National Biography, vol.* LXIII, *p.* 362.

GENERAL

To the works of Arthur Young the world is more indebted for the diffusion of agricultural knowledge than to any writer who has yet appeared. If great zeal, indefatigable exertions, and an unsparing expense in making experiments can give a man a claim to the gratitude of agriculturists, Arthur Young deserves it more than most men. We will not assert that in all cases his conclusions were correct, or his judgment unimpeachable; but even his blunders, if he committed any, have tended to the benefit of agriculture, by exciting discussion and criticism.—KIRWAN, RICHARD, 1808? *Transactions of the Irish Academy.*

The works of Arthur Young did incomparably more than those of any other individual to introduce a taste for agriculture and to diffuse a knowledge of the art in this and other countries. They are written in an animated, forcible, pure English style, and are at once highly entertaining and instructive. Though sometimes rash and prejudiced, his statements and inferences may in general be depended upon. His activity, perseverance, and devotedness to agriculture were unequalled. His Tours, especially those in Ireland and in France, which are both excellent, are his most valuable publications.—MCCULLOCH, JOHN RAMSAY, 1845, *Literature of Political Economy.*

I am a *worshipper* of Arthur Young's, and from me you will hear only his praises. I think him the most truthful writer and fuller of information upon any subject than any other author. In his 150 volumes that he wrote and edited, like Shakespeare, and *another book,* you find everything, or something *à propos* to every subject. He is the only man of eminence of my time that I unfortunately was not acquainted with; I did not then appreciate his merits. Since I have turned my attention to agriculture, I look upon him as the real source of information upon all matters; his correctness, his accuracy, has never been impunged. I have a duplicate of his works, one at Lowther and another in London, and some odd ones both at Barnes and Whitehaven. His agricultural tours in France and Italy I consider the only works that give an intelligible account of those countries. His tour in Ireland has given me the idea that his views of Ireland were nearer the truth than any other work.—LONSDALE, EARL OF, 1849, *Letter to Mr. Croker, Sept.* 4; *Correspondence and Diaries of John Wilson Croker, ed. Jennings, vol.* III, *p.* 201.

He projected nothing new or original, nor devised any different scheme of agriculture in any point; but he collected a huge mass of miscellaneous information, which had no small effect on the progress of agriculture.—DONALDSON, JOHN, 1854, *Agricultural Biography.*

It is a somewhat remarkable fact, that a man so distinguished in agriculture, so full of information, so earnest in advocacy of improved methods of culture, so doggedly industrious, should yet never have undertaken farming on his own account save at a loss. I attribute this very much to his zeal for experiments. If he could establish, or controvert, some popular theory by the loss of his crop, he counted it no loss, but a gain to husbandry. Such men are benefactors; such men need salaries; and if any such are afloat with us, unprovided for, I beg to recommend them for clerkships in the Agricultural Bureau at Washington; and if the Commissioner shall hit upon one Arthur Young among the score of his *protégés*, the country will be better repaid than it usually is. —MITCHELL, DONALD G., 1864, *Wet Days at Edgewood, p.* 254.

But the substantial and decisive reply to Burke came from his former correspondent, the farmer at Bradfield in Suffolk. Arthur Young published his "Travells in France" some eighteen months after the "Reflections" (1792), and the pages of the twenty-first chapter in which he closes his performance, as a luminous criticism of the most important side of the Revolution, are worth a hundred times more than Burke, Mackintosh, and Paine all put together. Young afterwards became panic-stricken, but his book remained. There the writer plainly enumerates without trope or invective the intolerable burdens under which the great mass of the French people had for long years been groaning. MORLEY, JOHN, 1888 *Burke (English Men of Letters), p.* 236.

It is as a social and political observer that Young is now best known to the reading public, and the books which have established his reputation in these departments—his "Tour in Ireland" and "Travels in France"—are still full of interest and instruction. . . . His master passion was the devotion of agriculture, which constantly showed itself. He strongly condemned the *métayer* system then widely prevalent in France, as "perpetuating poverty and excluding instruction," as, in fact, the curse and ruin of the country. Some of his phrases have been often quoted by the advocates of peasant proprietorship as favoring their view. "The magic of property turns sand to gold." Give a man the secure possession of a bleak rock, and he will turn it into a garden; give him a nine years' lease of a garden, and he will convert it into a desert. But these sentences, in which the epigrammatic form exaggerates a truth, and which might seem to represent the possession of capital as of no importance in agriculture, must not be taken as conveying his approbation of the system of small properties in general. He approved it only when the subdivision was strictly limited, and even then with great reserves; and he remained to the end what J. S. Mill calls him, "the apostle of *la grande culture*."—INGRAM, JOHN KELLS, 1889, *Encyclopaedia Britannica, vol.* XXIV, *pp.* 793, 794.

His "Survey of France" has permanent attraction for its picture of the state of that country just before, and in the earliest days of the Revolution. And though his writing is extremely incorrect and unequal, though its literary effect is much injured by the insertion of statistical details which sometimes turn it for pages together into a mere set of tables, he has constant racy phrases, some of which have passed into the most honourable state of all—that of unidentified quotation—while more deserve it.—SAINTSBURY, GEORGE, 1896, *A History of Nineteenth Century Literature, p.* 28.

As a writer Young contributed nothing of permanent importance towards the advancement of political economy; but he remains the greatest of English writers on agriculture. . . . He was indefatigable in observation, inquiries, researches, and experiments, collecting by hand the seeds of artificial grasses and sowing them himself, pointing out to the country as a whole practices which were successful in particular neighbourhoods at home and abroad, endeavouring, with the aid of Priestley, to discover the chemistry of soils and to apply science to practice, incessantly attempting new methods, new rotations of crops, and stirring up a widespread and intelligent interest in the development of agricultural science. He thought the most useful feature of his tours was his teaching upon the correct courses of crops. His works were much esteemed at home and abroad, and especially in the two great agricultural countries of Europe—France and Russia.—HIGGS, HENRY, 1900, *Dictionary of National Biography*.

Thomas Brown

1778–1820

Born at Kilmabreck, Kirkcubrightshire, Scotland, Jan. 9, 1778: died at Brompton, near London, April 2, 1820. A noted Scottish physician, philosopher, and poet, colleague of Dugald Stewart from 1810. His works include "An Inquiry into the Relation of Cause and Effect" (1818), "Lectures on the Physiology of the Human Mind" (1820), "Poems" (1804), "Paradise of Coquettes" (1814), "The War-fiend" (1817), "Agnes" (1818), "Emily" (1819), etc. He is chiefly notable from his support of Hume's theory of causation.—SMITH, BENJAMIN E., ed., 1894–97, *The Century Cyclopedia of Names*, p. 187.

PERSONAL

I see Dr. Thomas Brown now and then, who is as witty, amusing, and metaphysical, and as good a son and brother, as ever.—GRANT, ANNE, 1813, *To Mrs. Lowell, May 23; Memoirs and Correspondence*, ed. Grant, vol. II, p. 18.

He seldom began to prepare any of his lectures till the evening of the day before it was delivered He was often writing at his desk, when he heard the hour of twelve. When he hurried off to deliver what he had written. When his lecture was over, if the day was favourable, he generally took a walk, or employed his time in light reading, till his favorite beverage, tea, restored him again to a capacity for exertion.—WELSH, DAVID, 1825, *Account of the Life and Writings of Thomas Brown*, p. 194.

Even those who have never seen him can form a pretty lively image of him at this time, when his talents have reached all the maturity of which they are capable, and his reputation is at its height. In person, he is about the middle size; his features are regular, and in the expression of his countenance, and especially of his eye, there is a combination of sweetness and calm reflection. His manner and address are somewhat too fastidious, not to say finical and feminine, for a philosopher; but the youths who wait on his lectures are disposed to overlook this, when they fall under the influence of his gentleness, so fitted to win, and of the authority which he has to command. Expectation was on the tip-toe, and he fully met and gratified it. His amiable look, his fine elocution, his acuteness and ingenuity, his skill in reducing a complex subject into a few elements, his show of originality and independence, the seeming comprehensiveness of his system, and, above all, his fertility of illustration, and the glow, like that of stained glass, in which he set forth

42 C

his refined speculations, did more than delight his youthful audience,—it entranced them; and, in their ecstasies, they declared that he was superior to all the philosophers who had gone before him, and, in particular, that he had completely superseded Reid, and they gave him great credit, in that he generously refrained from attacking and overwhelming Stewart. He had every quality fitted to make him a favourite with students. His eloquence would have been felt to be too elaborate by a younger audience, and regarded as too artificial and sentimental by an older audience, but exactly suited the tastes of youths between sixteen and twenty.—McCosh, JAMES, 1874, *The Scottish Philosophy*, p. 322.

GENERAL

We must ackowledge that, in the writings of Dr. Brown, there are too many obscure and difficult passages. After making due allowance for the imperfect state in which his manuscripts may have been left, for the abstruse and shadowy nature of many of his topics, and even for an occasional mysticism and unattainable aim in some of his thoughts, there still remain too many sentences to remind us, by contrast, of the unabating transparency of Mr. Stewart's elocution. On the whole, we must allow, that our author's is often a hard style to read, and, as we should have thought, a much harder one to hear. He seems frequently not to have adapted his sentences to the capacity of the ear. The attention is stormed and borne along, rather by the force and brilliancy of the expressions, by the earnest energy of the writer, and by the novelty, splendour, and importance, of his well selected topics, than by the clearness and distinctness of each successive position, and a certain smooth and resistless current of diction, of which Adam Smith, Paley, and Godwin in his philosophical works, occur to us just now as three of the most remarkable instances.—GILMAN, S., 1825, *Character and Writings of Dr. Brown, North American Review, vol.* 21, *p.* 45.

His first tract on Causation appeared to me the finest model of discussion in Mental Philosophy since Berkeley and Hume: with this superiority over the latter, that its aim is that of a philosopher who seeks to enlarge knowledge, not that of a skeptic, the most illustrious of whom have no better end than that of displaying their powers in confounding and darkening every truth; so that their very happiest efforts cannot be more leniently described than as brilliant fits of debauchery.—MACKINTOSH, SIR JAMES, 1830, *Second Preliminary Dissertation Encyclopædia Britannica.*

Thomas Brown was an intimate friend of mine, and used to dine with me regularly every Sunday in Edinburgh. He was a Lake poet, a profound metaphysician, and one of the most virtuous men that lived. As a metaphysician, Dugald Stewart was a humbug to him. Brown had real talents for the thing. You must recognize in reading Brown, many of those arguments with which I have so often reduced you to silence in metaphysical discussions. Your discovery of Brown is amusing. Go on! You will detect Dryden if you persevere; bring to light John Milton, and drag William Shakspeare from his ill-deserved obscurity!—SMITH, SYDNEY, 1836, *Letter to Sir George Philips, Feb.* 28; *Memoir, ed. Lady Holland.*

Neither his poetry nor his lectures, however, are destined to any permanent fame; and the latter, as might have been anticipated from his hasty preparations, have already lost the place they for a short time obtained among the text-books of our colleges and universities.—PARKMAN, F., 1840, *Life and Writings of Thomas Brown, Christian Examiner, vol.* 29, *p.* 217.

As a writer, Brown must be regarded as eminently successful. Inferior to Stewart in classic chasteness of diction, and philosophic elegance of style, yet his mind was of that poetic order which can throw a luxuriance, perhaps we might say a redundancy of imagery and illustration, around every subject that it undertakes. From this, mainly, has arisen the great popularity of his lectures, which have not only passed through many editions, but are now, after more than twenty years, in

almost as great request as they were at first. . . . That Brown possessed splendid abilities, and that his writings generally are marked with superior excellence, every candid reader must admit. The most distinctive feature of his mind is generally allowed to have been *the power of analysis,* in which he greatly transcended all philosophers of the Scottish school who preceded him.—MORELL, J. D., 1846–53, *An Historical and Critical View of Speculative Philosophy of Europe in the Nineteenth Century.*

Brown, in his great work, ["Cause and Effect"]—one of the greatest which this century has produced.—BUCKLE, HENRY THOMAS. 1862–66, *History of Civilization in England, vol.* III, *p.* 333, *note.*

The psychology of Brown may be summarily described as a combination of the Scottish philosophy of Reid and Stewart, and of the analyses by Condillac, Destutt de Tracy, and the higher philosophers of the sensational school of France, together with views of the association of ideas derived from a prevailing British school. To Reid and Stewart he was indebted more than he was willing to allow, and it would have been better for his ultimate reputation had he imbibed more of their spirit, and adhered more closely to their principles. He admits everywhere with them the existence of principles of irresistible belief; for example, he comes to such a principle when he is discussing the beliefs in our personal identity, and in the invariability of the relation between cause and effect. But acknowledging, as he does, the existence of intuitive principles he makes no inquiry into their nature and laws and force, or the relation in which they stand to the faculties. In this respect so far from being an advance on Reid and Stewart, he is rather a retrogression. His method is as much that of Condillac, Destutt de Tracy, and the ideologists of France, as that of Reid and Stewart.—McCOSH, JAMES, 1874, *The Scottish Philosophy, p.* 325.

The fame achieved by the Lectures when published surpassed even what they had attained when delivered. It is no exaggeration to say that never before or since has a work of metaphysics been so popular. In 1851 the book had reached its 19th edition in England, and in America its success was perhaps greater. Since that time, however, its popularity has declined with almost equal rapidity, judgments on its merits are now as severe as they were formerly favorable, and the name of Brown may be said to be a dead letter in the annals of philosophy. . . . On the whole, it will be seen from this brief statement of what was new in Brown's philosophy that it occupies an intermediate place between the earlier Scottish school and the later analytical or associational psychology. To the latter Brown really belonged, but he had preserved certain doctrines of the older school which were out of harmony with his fundamental view. He still retained a small quantum of intuitive beliefs, and did not appear to see that the very existence of these could not be explained by his theory of mental action. This intermediate or wavering position accounts for the comparative neglect into which his works have now fallen. They did much to excite thinking, and advanced many problems by more than one step, but they did not furnish a coherent system, and the doctrines which were then new have since been worked out with greater consistency and clearness.—ADAMSON, ROBERT, 1876, *Encyclopædia Britannica, Ninth edition, vol.* IV, *pp.* 348, 349.

That he should have accomplished the amount of literary work that he did during his short life is amazing. Little of it can be said now to live, with the exception, perhaps, of his "Lectures on the Philosophy of the Human Mind," which are not only to be valued as an elucidation of mental science, but also as an interesting monument of the brilliant genius and indefatigable industry of a most amiable and deserving man. The fault of the work is its prolixity, and that the same ground is traced over and over again, in lecture after lecture, with tedious iteration. However, the defect, so to call it, has certainly this counterbalancing advantage, that it impresses what the writer has to teach on the mind of the reader with such singular clearness, that it is well-nigh impossible to mistake his sense. It should, too, in fairness be remembered that the lectures were prepared merely for oral delivery. They were never corrected by the author for the press; but were printed off from his manuscripts after his death, with all their blemishes and mistakes, and published precisely as he wrote them.—COPNER, JAMES, 1885, *Sketches of Celibate Worthies, p.* 272.

In spite of his original and suggestive work in detail, Brown thus failed to create a perfectly coherent system of thought. This defect impaired, and within a generation totally destroyed, his influence upon the course of speculation.—HERFORD, C. H., 1897, *The Age of Wordsworth, p.* 5, *note.*

Joseph Rodman Drake
1795–1820

A native of New York, began to contribute poetical compositions to the periodicals at a very early age. The first four of the Croaker Pieces (published in New York Evening Post, March 10–20, 1819), were written by him; after the fourth number, Fitz-Greene Halleck was admitted as a partner, and the literary firm was henceforth Croaker & Co. The lively satire of these sallies gave them a great reputation at the time of their publication. Drake's longest poem is "The Culprit Fay;" his best-known composition, "The American Flag." Their poetical merit is unquestionably of a high order. In 1836 a collection of Drake's poetical pieces was published by Commodore Dekay, son-in-law of the author.—ALLIBONE, S. AUSTIN, 1854–58, *A Critical Dictionary of English Literature, vol.* I, *p.* 519.

PERSONAL

I officiated as groomsman, though much against my will. . . . He is, perhaps, the handsomest man in New York—a face like an angel, a form like an Apollo, and, as I well knew that his person was the true index of his mind, I felt myself during the ceremony as committing a crime in aiding and assisting in such a sacrifice.—HALLECK, FITZ-GREENE, 1817, *Life and Letters.*

Green be the turf above thee,
Friend of my better days!
None knew thee but to love thee,
Nor named thee but to praise.

. . . .

While memory bids me weep thee,
Nor thoughts nor words are free,
The grief is fixed too deeply
That mourns a man like thee.

—HALLECK, FITZ-GREENE, 1820, *On the Death of Joseph Rodman Drake.*

The spirit, force, and at the same time simplicity of expression, with his artless manner, gained him many friends. He had that native politeness which springs from benevolence, which would stop to pick up the hat or the crutch of an old servant, or walk by the side of the horse of a timid lady. When he was lost to his friends one of them remarked that it was not so much his social qualities which engaged the affections as a certain inner grace or dignity of mind, of which they were hardly conscious at the time. . . . Drake's person was well formed and attractive; a fine head, with a peculiar blue eye, pale and cold in repose, but becoming dark and brilliant under excitement. His voice was full-toned and musical; he was a good reader, and sang with taste and feeling, though rarely.— LAWSON, JAMES, 1855, *Duyckinck's Cyclopædia of American Literature,* vol. I, p. 929.

There may be poetry as well as propriety in hiding the remains of a departed Poet, on the summit of a barren and useless sandy knoll, in the midst of a wide-spread salt marsh, with a lazy stream flowing *in the distance,* and it may, by an amazing stretch of imagination, be a very appropriate continuation of the imaginary compliment, to let the grave which such a spot contains, thenceforward take care of itself and become obscured, in every direction, by the bushes and weeds which surround it.—DAWSON, HENRY B., 1865–72, *The Grave of J. Rodman Drake, M. D., Historical Magazine, Third Series,* vol. I, p. 107.

He was buried at Hunt's Point; and as Halleck returned from the funeral, he said to DeKay, "There will be less sunshine for me hereafter, now that Joe is gone." A low monument of marble, surmounted by a quadrangular pyramid, rises above the grave where the poet's remains have reposed for sixty-five years. The inscription is on one side, and reads thus: "Sacred to the memory of Joseph R. Drake, M. D., who died September 21, 1820.

"None knew him but to love him,
  None named him but to praise."

These lines were afterward slightly varied and improved by their author.—WILSON, JAMES GRANT, 1885, *Bryant and His Friends,* p. 305.

For many years Drake's grave was waste and neglected: the stone was overgrown, lichened, disjointed, broken; a fallen tree had thrown the tapering shaft to the ground. Now a Catholic club of the vicinage has beneficently assumed care of it, the monument is cleansed and renovated, and the brush is cleared away from its base. The steep little pathway is evidently trodden by many pilgrim feet, and we find a garland of myrtle crowning the obelisk, while fresh field-flowers— gathered, we hope, from the near-by fields where he loved to roam—lie upon the pedestal and are still aglitter with the dew of the morning. The poet's grave is fitly placed amid the scenes he loved and sung. Yonder "his own romantic Bronx" lazily skirts the "green bank side" where he wrote; southward stands the venerable mansion he so often visited, where we may see the room he and Halleck habitually occupied; and all about the old place lie shores and scenes which inspired portions of his charming "Culprit Fay" and are portrayed in its imagery. Even in the desolate old cemetery we realize some of his poetic phrases: we feel the breeze "fresh springing from the lips of morn," we see the hum-bird with "his sun-touched wings," we hear the carol of the finch and the "winding of the merry locust's horn" above the grave where the poet rests, reckless of these that once thrilled his senses and stirred his soul to song.—WOLFE, THEODORE F., 1898, *Literary Haunts and Homes, American Authors,* p. 102.

THE CULPRIT FAY

"The Culprit Fay" was written, begun, and finished in three days. The copy you have is from the original, without the least alteration. It is certainly the best thing of the kind in the English language, and is more strikingly original than I had supposed it possible for a modern poem to be.—HALLECK, FITZ-GREENE, 1817, *Life and Letters,* p. 183.

It is a well-versified and sufficiently fluent composition, without high merit of any kind. Its defects are gross and superabundant. Its plot and conduct, considered in reference to its scene, are absurd. Its originality is none at all. Its imagination (and this was the great feature insisted upon by its admirers) is but a "counterfeit presentment,"—but the shadow of the shade of that lofty quality which is, in fact, the soul of the

Poetic Sentiment, but a drivelling *effort to be fanciful*, an effort resulting in a species of hop-skip-and-go-merry rodomontade, which the uninitiated feel it a duty to call ideality, and to admire as such, while lost in surprise at the impossibility of performing at least the latter half of the duty with anything like satisfaction to themselves. And all this we not only asserted, but without difficulty *proved*. Dr. Drake has written some beautiful poems, but "The Culprit Fay" is not of them.—POE, EDGAR ALLAN, 1842, *Graham's Magazine; Works, eds. Stedman and Woodberry, vol.* VIII, *p.* 264.

A poem of more exquisite fancy—as happily conceived as it is artistically executed—we have hardly had since the days of Milton's "Comus."—CLEVELAND, CHARLES D., 1859, *A Compendium of American Literature, p.* 401.

Discovers exquisite fancy and rare poetic beauty.—SAUNDERS, FREDERICK, 1865, *A Festival of Song, p.* 124.

It does not by any labored structure reveal that its origin was deliberate and not spontaneous. No poem done of set purpose ever flowed more freely and more easily; and as we read its tuneful measures we never think of denying the right of the fairy folk to dwell on the beautiful banks of the Hudson.—MATTHEWS, BRANDER, 1896, *An Introduction to the Study of American Literature, p.* 89.

GENERAL

As an exercise of that delicate imagination which we term fancy, "The Culprit Fay," although the work of a youth schooled in fairy-lore and the metres of Coleridge, Scott, and Moore, boded well for his future. "The American Flag" is a stirring bit of eloquence in rhyme. The death of this spirited and promising writer was justly deplored. His talent was healthy; had he lived, American authorship might not so readily have become, in Griswold's time, a vent for every kind of romantic and sentimental absurdity.— STEDMAN, EDMUND CLARENCE, 1885, *Poets of America, p.* 40.

Drake is, on the whole, less remembered by his own poems than by the beautiful tribute which Halleck made to his memory. —WHIPPLE, EDWIN PERCY, 1886, *American Literature and Other Papers, ed. Whittier, p.* 51.

Drake's services to nascent American poetry also included the composition of a spirited lyric to "The American Flag," familiar in the anthologies, and long a favorite with the school-boys of the nation. Its tropes are somewhat strained, and its sensational scheme narrowly escapes bombast; but on the whole—like a greater poem, Shelley's "Cloud"—it avoids the pathetic and produces an honest and stirring effect upon the reader.—RICHARDSON, CHARLES F., 1888, *American Literature, 1607–1888, vol.* II. *p.* 26.

A commonplace of American criticism is to compare Keats with a certain Joseph Rodman Drake. They both died at twenty-five and they both wrote verse. The parallel ends there. Keats was one of the great writers of the world. Drake was a gentle imitative bard of the fourth or fifth order, whose gifts culminated in a piece of pretty fancy called "The Culprit Fay." Every principle of proportion is outraged in a conjunction of the names of Drake and Keats. To compare them is like comparing a graceful shrub in your garden with the tallest pine that fronts the tempest on the forehead of Rhodope. —GOSSE, EDMUND, 1889, *Has America Produced a Poet? Questions at Issue, p.* 76.

Drake's poety should not be read as if it had been written in our day, when poets are so plentiful that every versifier has their art at his finger-ends: it should be read as it was read when it was written, in the first two decades of the century, when poets were few among us, and their skill so limited and uncertain as to disconcert and irritate later readers. He had no American models whom he could study to advantage, only such rude workmen in verse as Dwight, Trumbull, and Freneau; and the only English models whom he knew, or for whom he seemed to care, were Moore and Scott. He could not have had a more manly master than Scott, though he might have found a more deliberate one, for Scott improvised rather than composed. Like Scott, Drake wrote too rapidly, and too carelessly; for whatever its merits, and they are considerable, since poetic invention is one of them, and spirited metrical movement is another, "The Culprit Fay" is an improvisation and nothing more—an improvisation which needed much, but never had any, correction. It is charming, however, for just what it is, being one of the pillars upon which the reputation of Drake rests, the other being his lyric, "The American Flag," which is still the standard sheet in our Heaven of Song. No one but a poet could have written these two poems, to remember which is to remember Joseph Rodman Drake. — STODDARD, RICHARD HENRY, 1895, *Joseph Rodman Drake, The Critic, vol.* 27, *p.* 84.

He wrote several pretty things, among them a poem published after his death, entitled "The Culprit Fay." This conventional tale of some tiny fairies, supposed to haunt the Hudson River, is so much better than American poetry had previously

been that one is at first disposed to speak of it enthusiastically. An obvious comparison puts it in true perspective. Drake's life happened nearly to coincide with that of Keats. Both left us only broken fragments of what they might have done, had they been spared; but the contrast between these fragments tells afresh the story of American letters. Amid the full fervour of European experience Keats produced immortal work; Drake, whose whole life was passed amid the national inexperience of New York, produced only pretty fancies. — WENDELL, BARRETT, 1900, *A Literary History of America, p.* 195.

John Keats

1795–1821

Born, in London 31 Oct. 1795. At school at Enfield, at irregular periods between 1801 and 1810. His mother removed to Edmonton, 1806. Apprenticed to surgeon at Edmonton, 1810. To London 1814. Studied medicine at St. Thomas's and Guy's Hospitals. Appointed Dresser at Guy's, March 1816. Licentiate of Apothecaries' Hall, 25 July 1816. Contrib. to "The Examiner," 1816–17. Friendship with Leigh Hunt and Haydon begun about this time. Abandoned medical career, 1817. Visit to Oxford, Sept. to Oct. 1817. Contrib. poems to "The Champion," 1817; wrote dramatic criticism for it, Dec. 1817 to Jan. 1818. At this period resided mainly with his brothers at Hampstead. Walking tour with Charles Armitage Brown in Northern England and Scotland, June to Aug. 1818. Engaged to Fanny Brawne, Dec. 1818. One brother married and went to America, June 1818; the other died, Dec. 1818. Lived at Shanklin and Winchester successively during early part of 1819; settled in Westminster, Oct. 1819. Contrib. "Ode to a Nightingale" to "Annals of the Fine Arts," 1819; "La Belle Dame Sans Merci" to "The Indicator," 1820. Consumption set in, Feb. 1820. Sailed with Joseph Severn to Italy, Sept. 1820; arrived at Naples in Oct.; at Rome in Nov. Died, in Rome, 23 Feb. 1821. Buried in Old Protestant Cemetery there. *Works:* "Poems," 1817; "Endymion," 1818; "Lamia; Isabella; the Eve of St. Agnes," 1820. *Posthumous:* "Life, Letters and Literary Remains," ed. by R. Monckton Milnes, 1848; "Letters to Fanny Brawne," ed. by H. Buxton Forman, 1878; "Letters," ed. by H. Buxton Forman, 1895. *Collected Works:* ed. by H. Buxton Forman (4 vols.), 1883. Life: by Lord Houghton, revised edn. 1867; by W. M. Rossetti, 1887; by Sidney Colvin, 1887.—SHARP, R. FARQUHARSON, 1897, *A Dictionary of English Authors, p.* 154.

PERSONAL

He is gone. He died with the most perfect ease—he seemed to go to sleep. On the 23rd, about four, the approaches of death came on. "Severn—I—lift me up. I am dying—I shall die easy. Don't be frightened: be firm, and thank God it has come." I lifted him up in my arms. The phlegm seemed boiling in his throat, and increased until eleven, when he gradually sunk into death, so quiet that I still thought he slept. I cannot say more now. I am broken down by four nights' watching, no sleep since, and my poor

Keats gone. Three days since the body was opened: the lungs were completely gone. The doctors could not imagine how he had lived these two months. I followed his dear body to the grave on Monday [February 26th], with many English. . . . The letters I placed in the coffin with my own hand. — SEVERN, JOSEPH, 1821, *Journal, Feb.* 27.

The genius of the lamented person to whose memory I have dedicated these unworthy verses was not less delicate and fragile than it was beautiful; and where canker-worms abound, what wonder if its

JOHN KEATS

MATTHEW GREGORY LEWIS

Engraving by G. J. Anderton.
Original Painting by J. Severn.

From Engraving Published by
Henry Colburn in 1839.

young flower was blighted in the bud?
The savage criticism on his "Endymion"
which appeared in the "Quarterly Review"
produced the most violent effect on his
susceptible mind; †he agitation thus
originated ended in a rupture of a blood-
vessel in the lungs; a rapid consumption
ensued; and the succeeding acknowledg-
ments from more candid critics of the
true greatness of his powers were ineffectual to heal the wound thus wantonly
inflicted.—SHELLEY, PERCY BYSSHE, 1821,
Adonais, Preface.

But now thy youngest, dearest one, has per-
  ish'd,
The nursling of thy widowhood, who grew,
Like a pale flower by some sad maiden cher-
  ish'd,
And fed with true love tears instead of dew.
Most musical of mourners, weep anew!
Thy extreme hope, the loveliest and the last,
The bloom whose petals, nipt before they
  blew,
Died on the promise of the fruit, is waste;
The broken lily lies—the storm is overpast.
—SHELLEY, PERCY BYSSHE, 1821, *Adon-
ais, An Elegy on the Death of John Keats.*

I have just this moment heard of poor
Keats's death. We are unlucky in our
butts. It would appear very cruel if any
jokes now appeared on the pharmacopolical
part of "Endymion." And indeed when
I heard that the poor devil was in a con-
sumpticn, I was something sorry that I
annoyed him at all of late. If I were able
I should write a dirge over him, as a kind
of *amende honorable;* but my Muse, I am
afraid, does not run in the mournful. If
you print my hymn strike out the hemistich
concerning him, substituting anything you
like—such as "Pale is the cheek of Leigh
Hunt, the tea-drinking king of the
Cockneys." I hope I am in time, for it
would annoy me if it appeared that we
were attacking any one who had it not in
his power to reply—particularly an old
enemy after his death.—MAGINN, WIL-
LIAM, 1821, *Letter to Blackwood, April* 10;
*William Blackwood and His Sons, ed. Oli-
phant, vol.* I, *p.* 375.

Keats was a victim to personal abuse and
the want of power to bear it. . . . He began life full of hope. . . . He expected
the world to bow at once to his talents, as
his friends had done. . . . Goaded by
ridicule, he distrusted himself and flew to
dissipation. For six weeks he was hardly
ever sober. . . . He told me that he once

covered his tongue and throat, as far as he
could reach, with Cayenne pepper, in order
to enjoy "the delicious coolness of claret
in all its glory." . . . He had great enthusiasm for me, and so had I for him, but
he grew angry latterly because I shook my
head at his proceedings. I told him, I
begged of him to bend his genius to some
definite object. I remonstrated on his
absurd dissipation, but to no purpose. The
last time I saw him was at Hampstead,
lying on his back in a white bed, helpless,
irritable, and hectic. He had a book, and
enraged at his own feebleness, seemed as
if he were going out of the world with
a contempt for this, and no hopes of a
better. He muttered as I stood by him
that if he did not recover, he would "cut
his throat." I tried to calm him, but to no
purpose. . . . Poor dear Keats!—HAYDON,
BENJAMIN ROBERT, 1821, *Letter to Miss
Mitford, Apr.* 21; *Life, Letters and Table
Talk, ed. Stoddard, pp.* 207, 208, 209.

John Keats, who was kill'd off by one
  critique
  Just as he really promised something great,
If not intelligible. without Greek
  Contrived to talk about the gods of late,
Much as they might have been supposed to
  speak.
Poor fellow! His was an untoward fate;
  'Tis strange the mind, that very fiery par-
    ticle,
Should let itself be snuff'd out by an article.
—BYRON, LORD, 1823, *Don Juan, Canto,* xi.

It was nevertheless on the same day,
sitting on the bench in Well Walk at Hemp-
stead, nearest the heath (the one against
the wall), that he told me, with unaccus-
tomed tears in his eyes, that his "heart
was breaking."—HUNT, LEIGH, 1828, *Lord
Byron and Some of his Contemporaries, vol.*
I, *p.* 440.

One night at eleven o'clock, he came
into the house in a state that looked like
fierce intoxication. Such a state in him,
I knew, was impossible; it therefore was
the more fearful. I asked hurriedly,
"What is the matter? you are fevered."
"Yes, yes," he answered, "I was on the
outside of the stage this bitter day till I
was severely chilled—but now I don't feel
it. Fevered!—of course, a little." He
mildly and instantly yielded, a property in
his nature towards any friend, to my request that he should go to bed. I followed
with the best immediate remedy in my
power. I entered his chamber as he leapt

into bed. On entering the cold sheets, before his head was on the pillow, he slightly coughed, an I heard him say, "That is blood from my mouth." I went towards him; he was examining a single drop of blood upon the sheet. "Bring me the candle, Brown, and let me see this blood." After regarding it steadfastly, he looked up in my face with a calmness of countenance that I can never forget, and said, "I know the colour of that blood —it is arterial blood—I cannot be deceived in that colour—that drop of blood is my death-warrant—I must die."— BROWN, CHARLES ARMITAGE, 1841 ? *Houghton MSS.*

And Keats the real
Adonis with the hymeneal
Fresh vernal buds half sunk between
His youthful curls, kissed straight and sheen
In his Rome-grave, by Venus queen.
—BROWNING, ELIZABETH BARRETT, 1844, *A Vision of Poets.*

Jean Paul says that some souls fall from heaven like flowers, but that ere the pure and fresh buds have had time to open, they are trodden in the dust of the earth, and lie soiled and crushed beneath the foul tread of some brutal hoof. It was the fate of John Keats to illustrate, in some respects, this truth. He experienced more than the ordinary share of the world's hardness of heart, and had less than the ordinary share of sturdy strength to bear it. In him, an imagination and fancy of much natural capacity, were lodged in a frame too weak to sustain the shocks of life, and too sensitive for the development of high and sturdy thought. The great defect of his nature was a lack of force. —WHIPPLE, EDWIN P., 1845, *English Poets of the Nineteenth Century, American Review, July ; Essays and Reviews.*

He had a soul of noble integrity, and his common sense was a conspicuous part of his character. Indeed his character was, in the best sense, manly. . . . With his friends, a sweeter tempered man I never knew than was John Keats. Gentleness was indeed his proper characteristic, without one particle of dulness, or insipidity, or want of spirit. . . . In his letters he talks of *suspecting* everybody. It appeared not in his conversation. On the contrary, he was uniformly the apologist for poor frail human nature, and allowed for people's faults more than any man I every knew, and especially for

the faults of his friends. But if any act of wrong or oppression, of fraud or falsehood, was the topic, he rose into sudden and animated indignation.—BAILEY, BENJAMIN, 1848, *Letter to Lord Houghton, Houghton MSS.*

Keats, when he died, had just completed his four-and-twentieth year. He was under the middle height; and his lower limbs were small in comparison with the upper, but neat and well-turned. His shoulders were very broad for his size; he had a face in which energy and sensibility were remarkably mixed up; and eager power, checked and made patient by ill health. Every feature was at once strongly cut, and delicately alive. If there was any faulty expression it was in the mouth, which was not without something of a character of pugnacity. The face was rather long than otherwise ; the upper lip projected a little over the under ; the chin was bold, the cheeks sunken ; the eyes mellow and glowing ; large, dark, and sensitive. At the recital of a noble action, or a beautiful thought, they would suffuse with tears, and his mouth trembled. In this there was ill health as well as imagination, for he did not like these betrayals of emotion ; and he had great personal as well as moral courage. He once chastised a butcher, who had been insolent, by a regular stand-up fight. His hair, of a brown color, was fine, and hung in natural ringlets. The head was a puzzle for the phrenologists, being remarkably small in the skull ; a singularity which he had in common with Byron and Shelley, whose hats I could not get on. Keats was sensible of the disproportion above noticed, between his upper and lower extremities ; and he would look at his hand, which was faded and swollen in the veins, and say that it was the hand of a man of fifty. He was a seven months' child.—HUNT, LEIGH, 1850–60, *Autobiography, vol. II, ch.* xvi.

He had that fine compactness of person which we regard as the promise of longevity, and no mind was ever more exultant in youthful feeling. I cannot summon a sufficient reason why in one short year he should have been thus cut off, "with all his imperfections on his head." . . . Those bright falcon eyes, which I had known only in joyous intercourse, while revelling in books and Nature, or while he was reciting his own poetry, now beamed an unearthly brightness and a penetrating steadfastness that could not be looked at. It was not the fear of death,—on the contrary, he earnestly wished to die,—but it was the fear of lingering on and on, that now distressed him; and this was wholly on my account. . . . There were few Englishmen at Rome who knew Keats's works, and I could scarcely persuade any one to make the effort to read them, such was the prejudice against him as a poet; but when his gravestone was placed, with his own expressive line, "Here lies one whose name was writ in water," then a host started up, not of admirers, but of scoffers, and a silly jest was often repeated in my hearing, "Here lies one whose name was writ in water, and *his works in milk and water ;*" and this I was condemned to hear for years repeated, as though it had been a pasquinade.—SEVERN, JOSEPH, 1863, *On the Vicissitudes of Keats's Fame, Atlantic Monthly, vol.* 11, *pp.* 401, 402, 404.

A lady, whose feminine acuteness of perception is only equalled by the vigour of her understanding, thus describes Keats as he appeared about this time (1818) at Hazlitt's lectures:—"His eyes were large and blue, his hair auburn; he wore it divided down the centre, and it fell in rich masses on each side his face; his mouth was full, and less intellectual than his other features. His countenance lives in my mind as one of singular beauty and brightness; it had the expression as if he had been looking on some glorious sight. The shape of his face had not the squareness of a man's, but more like some women's faces I have seen—it was so wide over the forehead and so small at the chin. He seemed in perfect health, and with life offering all things that were precious to him."—MILNES, RICHARD MONCKTON, 1869, *ed., The Poetical Works of John Keats, Memoir, p.* xxvii.

The young Endymion sleeps Endymion's sleep;
The shepherd-boy whose tale was left half told!
The solemn grove uplifts its shield of gold
To the red rising moon, and loud and deep
The nightingale is singing from the steep;
It is midsummer, but the air is cold;
Can it be death? Alas, beside the fold
A shepherd's pipe lies shattered near his sheep.
—LONGFELLOW, HENRY WADSWORTH, 1873, *Keats, A Book of Sonnets.*

In the early part of his school-life John gave no extraordinary indications of intellectual character; but it was remembered of him afterwards, that there was ever present a determined and steady spirit in all his undertakings: I never knew it misdirected in his required pursuit of study. He was a most orderly scholar. . . . Not the less beloved was he for having a highly pugnacious spirit, which, when roused, was one of the most picturesque exhibitions—off the stage—I ever saw. One of the transports of that marvellous actor, Edmund Kean—whom, by the way, he idolized—was its nearest resemblance; and the two were not very dissimilar in face and figure. . . . His passion at times was almost ungovernable; and his brother George, being considerably the taller and stronger, used frequently to hold him down by main force, laughing when John was in one of his moods, and was endeavoring to beat him. It was all, however, a wisp-of-straw conflagration; for he had an intensely tender affection for his brothers, and proved it upon the most trying occasions. He was not merely the "favorite of all," like a pet prize-fighter, for his terrier courage; but his high-mindedness, his utter unconsciousness of a mean motive, his placability, his generosity, wrought so general a feeling in his behalf, that I never heard a word of disapproval from any one, superior or equal, who had known him. . . . The character and expression of Keats's features would arrest even the casual passenger in the street. . . . Reader, alter in your copy of the "Life of Keats," vol. i., page 103, "eyes" *light hazel,* "hair" *lightish brown and wavy.* — CLARKE, CHARLES COWDEN, 1874-78, *Keats, Recollections of Writers, pp.* 122, 123, 133, 154.

I confess there is something in the personality of Keats, some sort of semi-physical aroma wafted from it, which I cannot endure; and I fear these letters will be very redolent of this. What a curious thing is that undefinable flavour of personality—suggestion of physical quality, odour of the man in his unconscious and spontaneous self-determination, which attracts or repels so powerfully, and is the very root of love or dislike.—SYMONDS, JOHN ADDINGTON, 1878, *Letter to Edmund Gosse, Feb.* 16; *Life by Brown, vol.* II, *p.* 147.

So when I saw beside a Roman portal
"In this house died John Keats"—for tears
    that sprung
I could no further read.   O bard immortal!
Not for thy fame's sake—but so young, so
    young;
Such beauty vanished, spilled such heavenly
    wine,
All quenched that power of deathless song
    divine!
—GILDER, RICHARD WATSON, 1885, *An
Inscription in Rome, Lyrics and Other
Poems*, p. 101.

From this point (1819) forwards nothing but misery remains to be recorded of John Keats.   The narrative becomes depressing to write and depressing to read. The sensation is like that of being confined in a dark vault at noonday.   One knows indeed, that the sun of the poet's genius is blazing outside, and that, on emerging from the vault, we shall be restored to light and warmth; but the atmosphere within is not the less dark and laden, nor the shades the less murky.   In tedious wretchedness, racked and dogged with the pang of body and soul, exasperated and protesting, raging now, and now ground down into patience and acceptance, Keats gropes through the valley of the shadow of death.—ROSSETTI, WILLIAM MICHAEL, 1887, *Life of John Keats (Great Writers)*, p. 40.

Ah, grave of graves! what pathos round it
    clings!
To this sad bourne from coming age to age,
While the tired earth endures its sufferings,
Will wandering feet make worship's pil-
    grimage!
Thou, hoary Rome,
In bosoming him hast higher glory won,
Although for Pantheon
Thou gav'st him naught, save that wherein
    the sun
Beams morn by morn, an everlasting dome.
—SCOLLARD, CLINTON, 1888, *At the Grave
of Keats, Old and New World Lyrics*, p. 5.

The new Endymion thou, enamored so
  Of thy supernal themes, some goddess,
    proud
    And jealous, doomed thee to a deathless
      swoon,
As he on myrtled Latmos long ago
  Wast doomed.   I will not think thee in
    thy shroud,
    But sleeping quietly and waking soon.
—BLANDEN, CHARLES G., 1889, *Thoughts
of Keats.*

Unluckily Keats died, and his death was absurdly attributed to a pair of reviews which may have irritated him, and which were coarse and cruel even for that period of robust reviewing.   But Keats knew very well the value of these critiques, and probably resented them not much more than a foot-ball player resents being "hacked" in the course of the game.   He was very willing to see Byron and Wordsworth "trounced," and as ready as Peter Corcoran in his friend's poem to "take punishment" himself.   The character of Keats was plucky, and his estimate of his own genius was perfectly sane.   He knew that he was in the thick of a literary "scrimmage," and he was not the man to flinch or to repine at the consequences.— LANG, ANDREW, 1889, *Letters on Literature*, p. 197.

Although the legend as to the cause of the premature death of Keats has thus to be dismissed as an impassioned hallucination of Shelley's, perpetuated by Byron's epigrammatic version of it, those two articles on Keats's "Endymion" on its first appearance,—the *Blackwood* article of August, 1818, and the *Quarterly* article of September, 1818,—retain an infamous kind of interest in English literary history, and cannot be allowed to be forgotten. The recollection of them suggests various reflections.   They exemplify for us, in the first place, the horrible iniquity, the utter detestability, of the practice of carrying the rancour of party politics into the business of literary criticism.   Almost avowedly, it was because young Keats was a friend of Leigh Hunt, and was supposed to share the political opinions of Hunt and a few other Londoners of prominent political notoriety at the time, that the two periodicals in question made their simultaneous onslaught on "Endymion." They had vowed exterminating war against Hunt and his political associates, and were lying in wait for every new appearance in the field of a straggler from that camp; and what did it matter to them *who* emerged next, or in what guise?   Keats had emerged,—in reality no party politician at all, but in very fibre of his nature a poet and that only,—Keats had emerged and they bludgeoned *him!* — MASSON, DAVID, 1892, *The Story of Gifford and Keats, The Nineteenth Century*, vol. 31, p. 603.

Of no other English poet has the popular idea been so wide of the mark; about no other English poet have so many clouds of misunderstanding gathered and hung to the lasting concealment of the man. . . . Above all English poets Keats has been the victim of his feeble brethren, who mitigate their own sense of baffled ambition with the remembrance of his woes at the hands of the Philistine reviewers, and of those sentimental hangers on at the court of poetry who mistake the king's robe for the king's majesty, and whose solemn genuflections are the very mockery of homage. Instead of the real Keats, virile, manly, courageous, well-poised, and full of noble ambitions, the world has fashioned for itself a weakly sentimental, sensuous maker of over-ripe verse, without large ideas of his art, and sensitive to the very death under the lash of a stupid and vulgar criticism. It was no small offence against the memory of this peculiarly rich and sane nature that these misconceptions were permitted to become traditions. Although Lord Houghton, Mr. Arnold, Professor Colvin, and other students and critics of Keats have done much to rescue his fame from the hands of those who have accomplished what blundering critics were unable to effect, there is still much to be done before the world, which takes its impressions, rapidly and at second hand, is set right concerning one of the most promising men of the age.—MABIE, HAMILTON WRIGHT, 1892–93, *Essays in Literary Interpretation, p.* 138.

Let us suppose he does not sleep, but wakes—wakes, and harkens to what sounds soever of earthly detraction or praise may reach him, throned among his fellow "inheritors of unfulfilled renown," whose place is "far in the unapparent." For he died full of thwarted aims and balked ambitions, his life a splendid fragment like his own "Hyperion;" and perhaps it is not wildly fanciful to think of the eager spirit of Adonais as taking some posthumous interest in the progress and consummation of his own terrestrial fame. He will have seen that fame gradually disentangled from minor accidents and incidents which at first did much to perplex it and hinder it from having free way; disentangled from "Cockney Schools," real or imaginary; from irrelevant prejudices arising out of political and personal considerations; from warring theories of literary art. He will have seen his influence operating as a potent factor in the artistic evolution of the most eminent of present day poets. He will have seen the main and essential facts of his life laid before the world by a distinguished and genial *dilettante,* whose biography of him was not indeed a work of high talent, but was inspired by sympathy and directed by good taste. In a word, he will have seen almost everything come to pass which, living, he could have hoped for. Unfortunately, however, this is not all; would it were! He will have seen Haydon's "Journal" go forth to posterity, perpetuating a slander which went unrebuked and undenied till yesterday. He will have seen the passionate letters to his somewhat mundane goddess catalogued in sale lists, and knocked down under the auctioneer's hammer. He will have seen the effigy of his warm and palpitating heart held up to the stare of a world that with gaping mouth and craning neck presses forward into every sanctuary where there is a secret to be ravished and a veil to be rent in twain. He will have seen the yelping pack of scandal, never so joyous as when they can scent some fallen greatness, or run down any noble quarry. He will have seen the yet uncleaner creature, the thing of teeth and claws, that lives by scratching up the soil from over the bones of the buried and laying corruption bare. He will have seen the injudicious and uncritical worshipper. He will have seen the painstaking modern editor.—WATSON, WILLIAM, 1893, *Excursions in Criticism, p.* 25.

FANNY BRAWNE

Mr. Severn tells me that Mrs. and Miss Brawne felt the keenest regret that they had not followed him and Keats to Rome; and, indeed, I understand that there was some talk of a marriage taking place before the departure. Even twenty years after Keats's death, when Mr. Severn returned to England, the bereaved lady was unable to receive him on account of the extreme painfulness of the associations connected with him.—FORMAN, HARRY BUXTON, 1877, *Letters of John Keats to Fanny Brawne, Introduction, p.* lxii.

Her ways and presence at first irritated and after a little while completely fascinated him. From his first sarcastic account of her written to his brother, as well as from Severn's mention of her likeness to the draped figure in Titian's picture of Sacred and Profane Love, and from the full-length silhouette of her that has been preserved, it is not difficult to realize her aspect and presence. A brisk and blooming very young beauty, of the far from uncommon English hawk blonde type, with aquiline nose and retreating forehead, sharp-cut nostril and gray-blue eye, a slight, shapely figure, rather short than tall, a taking smile, and good hair, carriage and complexion—such was Fanny Brawne externally, but of her character we have little means of judging. She was certainly high-spirited, inexperienced, and self-confident; as certainly, though kind and constant to her lover, in spite of prospects that before long grew dark, she did not fully realise what manner of man he was. Both his men and women friends, without thinking unkindly of her, were apparently of one opinion in holding her no mate for him either in heart or mind, and in regarding the attachment as unlucky.—COLVIN, SIDNEY, 1887, *Keats (English Men of Letters)*, p. 129.

Though she was inexperienced and self-confident, she was constant and kind to her lover in spite of prospects which soon grew very dark. She never, however, fully realized what manner of man he was, though some of the things said by his friends, who did not approve of her or of his frenzy of passion for her, were most unkind and entirely unjustified. As I have been guilty in previous writings of repeating at least one such unkind remark, I most cheerfully acknowledge that better evidence has convinced me that she loved Keats dearly, and when he was dead tenderly cherished his memory.—SPEED, JOHN GILMER,* 1895, *The Real John Keats, McClure's Magazine, vol.* 5, p. 468.

Fanny Brawne was a poor creature upon which to stake love and life, and Keats knew this to be true in the lucid intervals of his infatuation. . . . These *terrible* love-letters. Each is a drop of life-blood, and their leap from the anguished heart actually appalls us. No eyes but hers should ever have rested upon the pages. It was nothing short of vivisection for her to turn them over to public examination and judgment. And this was done, in effect, by her preservation of them, aware as she was, what use would be made of them when they escaped from her keeping. We

*Grand-nephew of Keats.

cannot, and we do not care to, forgive her.—HERRICK, MARY VIRGINIA TERHUNE (MARION HARLAND), 1898, *Where Ghosts Walk, pp.* 171, 179.

LOVE LETTERS

The thirty-seven letters of Keats to Fanny Brawne I have read with great pain inasmuch as from them I now understand *for the first* time the sufferings and death of the Poet.—He did not confide to me this serious passion and it now seems to me *but for this cause he might have lived many* years—I can now understand his want of courage to speak as it was consuming him in body and mind. . . . Perhaps I view the work more painfully as I was not aware of such torment existing in the Poet's mind and as I saw him struck down from health and vigour to sickness and death you will not wonder at my emotion now that I find the fatal cause.—SEVERN, JOSEPH, 1878, *Letter to Harry Buxton Forman, Feb.* 5; *The Poetical Works and Other Writings of John Keats, vol.* IV, *pp.* 218, 219.

The character of the letters is such as obtains in similar productions, only it is intensified a thousand-fold. I know of nothing comparable with them in English literature—know nothing that is so unselfish, so longing, so adoring—nothing that is so mad, so pitiful, so utterly weak and wretched. John Keats was a great genius, but he had not one particle of common-sense—for himself. Few men of genius ever do have; it is only the Master Shakespeare and the Masters Milton and Wordsworth, who are able to cope with the world. Why, a boy might have told Keats that the way to woo and win a woman was not to bare his heart before her, as he did before Fanny Brawne, and not to let her know, as he did, that he was her captive. If he had had the least glimmer of common-sense, he never would have surrendered at discretion. . . . Miss Fanny Brawne made John Keats ridiculous in the eyes of his friends in his lifetime, and now she (through her representatives) makes him ridiculous in the eyes of the world. She (and they) have had fifty-seven years in which to think about it—she forty-four years as maid and wife; they thirteen years as her children. Why did she keep his letters all those years? What *could* she keep them for but to minister to her vanity, and to remind her that once upon a time a crazy young English poet was desperately in love with her, was her captive and her slave? What else could she keep them for? She revered the memory of Keats, did she? This is how she revered it!—STODDARD, RICHARD HENRY, 1878, *John Keats and Fanny Brawne, Appleton's Journal, vol.* 19, *pp.* 381, 382.

What! shall thy heart's rich blood poured
    out so deep
Be made a merchandise without redress,
Nor any voice the world's base deed confess
Which prints and sells a poet's love so cheap?
My curse upon this prying, prurient age!
    And curst the eyes not closed in angry
    shame!
For him whom English air and critic pen
Twice baffled, ere his splendid youthful gage
    Had measured half the heaven of love and
    fame,
This shameless book has murdered once
    again!
—ALBEE, JOHN, 1878, *Keats' Love-Letters.*

A man who writes love-letters in this strain is probably predestined, one may observe, to misfortune in his love-affairs; but that is nothing. The complete enervation of the writer is the real point for remark. We have the tone, or rather the entire want of tone, the abandonment of all reticence and all dignity, of the merely sensuous man, of the man who "is passion's slave." Nay, we have them in such wise that one is tempted to speak even as *Blackwood* or the *Quarterly* were in the old days wont to speak, one is tempted to say that Keats's love-letter is the love-letter of a surgeon's apprentice. It has in its relaxed self-abandonment something underbred and ignoble, as of a youth ill brought up, without the training which teaches us that we must put some constraint upon our feelings, and upon the expression of them. It is the sort of love-letter of a surgeon's apprentice which one might hear read out in a breach of promise case, or in the Divorce Court. The sensuous man speaks in it, and the sensuous man of a badly bred and badly trained sort. That many who are themselves, also, badly bred and badly trained should enjoy it, and should even think it a beautiful and characteristic production of him whom they call their "lovely and beloved Keats," does not make it better. —ARNOLD, MATTHEW, 1880, *The English Poets, ed. Ward, vol.* IV, *p.* 429.

While admitting that neither his love-letters nor the last piteous outcries of his wailing and shrieking agony would ever have been made public by merciful or respectful editors, we must also admit that, if they ought never to have been published, it is no less certain that they ought never to have been written; that a manful kind of man or even a manly sort of boy, in his love-making or in his suffering, will not howl and snivel after such a lamentable fashion. — SWINBURNE, ALGERNON CHARLES, 1882–86, *Keats, Encyclopædia Britannica, Miscellanies, p.* 212.

Keats seems to me, throughout his love-letters, unbalanced, wayard, and profuse; he exhibts great fervour of temperament, and abundant caressingness, without the inner depth of tenderness and regard. He lives in his mistress, for himself. As the letters pass further and further into the harsh black shadows of disease, he abandons all self-restraint, and lashes out right and left; he wills that his friends should have been disloyal to him, as the motive of his being disloyal to them. To make allowance for all this is possible, and even necessary; but to treat it as not needing that any allowance should be made would seem to me futile.—ROSSETTI, WILLIAM MICHAEL, 1887, *Life of John Keats (Great Writers), p.* 45.

ENDYMION
1818

Knowing within myself the manner in which this Poem has been produced, it is not without a feeling of regret that I make it public. What manner I mean, will be quite clear to the reader, who must soon perceive great inexperience, immaturity, and every error denoting a feverish attempt, rather than a deed accomplished. —KEATS, JOHN, 1818, *Endymion, Preface.*

Reviewers have been sometimes accused of not reading the works which they affected to criticise. On the present occasion we shall anticipate the author's complaint, and honestly confess that we have not read his work. Not that we have been wanting in our duty—far from it—indeed, we have made efforts almost as superhuman as the story itself appears to be, to get through it; but with the fullest stretch of our perseverance, we are forced to confess that we have not been able to struggle beyond the first of the four books of which this Poetic

Romance consists. We should extremely lament this want of energy, or whatever it may be, on our parts, were it not for one consolation—namely, that we are no better acquainted with the meaning of the book through which we have so painfully toiled, than we are with that of the three which we have not looked into. It is not that Mr. Keats (if that be his real name, for we almost doubt that any man in his senses would put his real name to such a rhapsody) it is not, we say, that the author has not powers of language, rays of fancy, and gleams of genius:—he has all these; but he is unhappily a disciple of the new school of what has been somewhere called Cockney poetry; which may be defined to consist of the most incongruous ideas in the most uncouth language. . . . Of the story we have been able to make out but little; it seems to be mythological, and probably relates to the loves of Diana and Endymion; but of this, as the scope of the work has altogether escaped us, we cannot speak with any degree of certainty; and must therefore content ourselves with giving some instances of its diction and versification.—GIFFORD, WILLIAM, 1818, *Keats's Endymion, Quarterly Review, vol.* 19, *pp.* 204, 205.

Warmly as I admire the poetry of Keats, I can imagine that an intelligent man might read the "Endymion" with care, yet think that it was not genuine poetry; that it showed a sheer misuse of abundant fancy and rhythmical power. For its range is narrow; like the artificial comedy it has a world of its own, and this world is more harmonious within itself, made up of light rich materials; but it is not deep enough or wide enough to furnish satisfaction for the general heart and mind. —COLERIDGE, HENRY NELSON, 1843? *ed., S. T. Coleridge's Biographia Literaria, Introduction.*

As reasonably, and as hopefully in regard to human sympathies, might a man undertake an epic poem upon the loves of two butterflies. The modes of existence in the two parties to the love-fable of the "Endymion," their relations to each other and to us, their prospects finally, and the obstacles to the *instant* realisation of these prospects,—all these things are more vague and incomprehensible than the reveries of an oyster. Still, the unhappy subject, and its unhappy expansion, must be laid to the account of childish years and childish inexperience.—DE QUINCEY, THOMAS, 1845–57, *Gilfillan's Literary Portraits, Works, ed. Masson, vol.* XI, *p.* 392.

Let any man of literary accomplishment, though without the habit of writing poetry, or even much taste for reading it, open "Endymion" at random, (to say nothing of the later and more perfect poems), and examine the characteristics of the page before him, and I shall be surprised if he does not feel that the whole range of literature hardly supplies a parallel phenomenon. As a psychological curiosity, perhaps Chatterton is more wonderful; but in him the immediate ability displayed is rather the full comprehension of and identification with the old model, than the effluence of creative genius. In Keats, on the contrary, the originality in the use of his scanty materials, his expansion of them to the proportions of his own imagination, and above all, his field of diction and expression extending so far beyond his knowledge of literature, is quite inexplicable by any of the ordinary processes of mental education. If his classical learning had been deeper, his seizure of the full spirit of Grecian beauty would have been less surprising; if his English reading had been more extensive, his inexhaustible vocabulary of picturesque and mimetic words could more easily be accounted for; but here is a surgeon's apprentice, with the ordinary culture of the middle classes, rivalling in æsthetic perceptions of antique life and thought the most careful scholars of his time and country, and reproducing these impressions in a phraseology as complete and unconventional as if he had mastered the whole history and the frequent variations of the English tongue, and elaborated a mode of utterance commensurate with his vast ideas.—MILNES, RICHARD MONCKTON (LORD HOUGHTON), 1848–67, *Life and Letters of John Keats, p.* 330.

"Endymion" bears us along in a whirl of imaginative creation; and the beauties with which it is lavishly strewn scarcely leave time for the thought that the construction wants perspicacity—a thought which will intrude at last.—FORMAN, HARRY BUXTON, 1883, *ed., The Poetical Works and other Writings of John Keats.*

Luscious and luxuriant in intention—for I cannot suppose that Keats aimed at being exalted or ideal—the poem becomes mawkish in result: he said so himself, and we need not hesitate to repeat it. Affectations, conceits, and puerilities, abound, both in thought and in diction: however willing to be pleased, the reader is often disconcerted and provoked. The number of clever things said cleverly, of rich things richly, and of fine things finely, is however abundant and superabundant; and no one who peruses "Endymion" with a true sense for poetic endowment and handling can fail to see that it is peculiarly the work of a poet.— ROSSETTI, WILLIAM MICHAEL, 1887, *Life of John Keats (Great Writers), p.* 178.

"Endymion" discloses to the reader of to-day the strength and the weakness which Keats saw in it before the garish light of criticism fell upon it. It has the freshness of feeling and perception, the glow of imagination, the profusion and riot of imagery, the occasional overripeness, the occasional perfection of expression, the lack of sustained and cumulative power, which one would expect from so immature a mind: as a finished product it has very great blemishes; as the work of a young poet it overflows with promise. One wonders not so much at the brutality of the critics as at their stupidity.— MABIE, HAMILTON WRIGHT, 1892–93, *Essays in Literary Interpretation, p.* 159.

LAMIA
1820

Perhaps there is no poet, living or dead, except Shakspeare, who can pretend to anything like the felicity of epithet which characterizes Keats. One word or phrase is the essence of a whole description or sentiment. It is like the dull substance of the earth struck through by electric fires, and converted into veins of gold and diamonds. For a piece of perfect and inventive description, that passage from "Lamia," where, Lycius gone to bid the guests to his wedding, Lamia, in her uneasy excitement, employs herself and her demon powers in adorning her palace, is unrivaled. — HOWITT, WILLIAM, 1846, *Homes and Haunts of the Most Eminent British Poets, vol.* I, p. 482.

Is, on the whole, the finest of his longer poems.—BROOKE, STOPFORD A., 1896, *English Literature, p.* 242.

No one can deny the truth of Keats's own criticism on "Lamia" when he says, "I am certain there is that sort of fire in it which must take hold of people in some way—give them either pleasant or unpleasant sensation." There is, perhaps, nothing in all his writing so vivid, or that so burns itself in upon the mind, as the picture of the serpent-woman awaiting the touch of Hermes to transform her, followed by the agonized process of the transformation itself. . . . This thrilling vividness of narration in particular points, and the fine melodious vigour of much of the verse, have caused some students to give "Lamia" almost the first, if not the first, place among Keats's narrative poems. But surely for this it is in some parts too feverish and in others too unequal. It contains descriptions not entirely successful, as, for instance, that of the palace reared by Lamia's magic, which will not bear comparison with other and earlier dream-palaces of the poet's building.—COLVIN, SIDNEY, 1887, *Keats (English Men of Letters), p.* 166.

EVE OF ST. AGNES
1820

To the description before us, it would be a great injury either to add or diminish. It falls at once gorgeously and delicately upon us, like the colours of the painted glass. Nor is Madeline hurt by all her encrusting jewlery and rustling silks. Her gentle, unsophisticated heart is in the midst, and turns them into so many ministrants to her loveliness.— HUNT, LEIGH, 1820, *The Indicator.*

The glory and charm of the poem is in the description of the fair maiden's antique chamber, and of all that passes in that sweet and angel-guarded sanctuary: every part of which is touched with colours at once rich and delicate—and the whole chastened and harmonised, in the midst of its gorgeous distinctness, by a pervading grace and purity, that indicate not less clearly the exaltation than the refinement of the author's fancy.—JEFFREY, FRANCIS LORD, 1820–44, *Keats's Poems, Contributions to the Edinburgh Review, vol.* III, p. 116.

The loose versification of many of his works has induced belief that he lacked energy proportionate to the vividness of his conceptions; but the opinion is wrong. Many of his sonnets possess a Miltonic vigour, and his "Eve of St. Agnes," is as highly finished, almost, as the masterpieces of Pope.—GRISWOLD, RUFUS W., 1844, *The Poets and Poetry of England in the Nineteenth Century, p.* 302.

What a gorgeous gallery of poetic pictures that "Eve of St. Agnes" forms, and yet how slim the tissue that lies below! How thin the canvas on which the whole is painted! For vigorous sense, one deep-thoughted couplet of Dryden would make the whole kick the beam. And yet what can be more exquisite in their way than those pictures of the young poet! Even the old worn out gods of Grecian mythology become life-like when he draws them. They revive in his hands, and become vital once more.—MILLER, HUGH, 1856–62, *Essays, p.* 452.

"The Eve of St. Agnes," aiming at no doubtful success, succeeds in evading all casual difficulty in the line of narrative; with no shadow of pretence to such interest as may be derived from stress of incident or depth of sentiment, it stands out among all other famous poems as a perfect and unsurpassable study in pure color and clear melody—a study in which the figure of Madeline brings back upon the mind's eye, if not as moonlight recalls a sense of sunshine, the nuptial picture of Marlow's Hero, and the sleeping presence of Shakespeare's Imogen. Besides this poem should always be placed the less famous but not less precious "Eve of St.. Mark" a fragment unexcelled for the simple perfection of its perfect simplicity, exquisite alike in suggestion and in accomplishment.—SWINBURNE, ALGERNON CHARLES, 1882–86, *Keats, Encyclopædia Britannica, Miscellanies, p.* 213.

"The Eve of St. Agnes" is *par excellence* the poem of "glamour." It means next to nothing; but means that little so exquisitely, and in so rapt a mood of musing or of trance, that it tells as an intellectual no less than a sensuous restorative. Perhaps no reader has ever risen from "The Eve of St. Agnes" dissatisfied. After a while he can question the grounds of his satisfaction, and may possibly find them wanting; but he has only to peruse the poem again, and the same spell is upon him.—ROSSETTI, WILLIAM MICHAEL, 1887, *Life of John Keats (Great Writers), p.* 183.

Pure and passionate, surprising by its fine excess of color and melody, sensuous in every line, yet free from the slightest taint of sensuality, is unforgettable and unsurpassable as the dream of first love. —VAN DYKE, HENRY, 1895, *The Influence of Keats, The Century, vol.* 50, *p.* 912.

HYPERION
1820

His fragment of "Hyperion" seems actually inspired by the Titans, and is as sublime as Æschylus. — BYRON, LORD, 1821, *Observations upon an Article in Blackwood's Magazine, note.*

Keats's new volume has arrived to us, and the fragment called "Hyperion" promises for him that he is destined to become one of the first writers of the age. —SHELLEY, PERCY BYSSHE, 1820, *Correspondence of Leigh Hunt, vol.* I, *p.* 158.

Though there are passages of some force and grandeur, it is sufficiently obvious, from the specimen before us, that the subject is too far removed from all the sources of human interest, to be successfully treated by any modern author. Mr. Keats has unquestionably a very beautiful imagination, a perfect ear for harmony, and a great familiarity with the finest diction of English poetry; but he must learn not to misuse or misapply these advantages; and neither to waste the good gifts of nature and study on intractable themes, nor to luxuriate too recklessly on such as are more suitable.— JEFFREY, FRANCIS LORD, 1820–44, *Keats's Poems, Contributions to the Edinburgh Review, vol.* III, *p.* 119.

The very midsummer madness of affectation, of false vapoury sentiment, and of fantastic effeminacy, seemed to me combined in Keats's "Endymion," when I first saw it, near the close of 1821. The Italian poet Marino had been reputed the greatest master of gossamery affectation in Europe. But *his* conceits showed the palest of rosy blushes by the side of Keats's bloody crimson. Naturally I was discouraged at the moment from looking further. But about a week later, by pure accident, my eye fell upon his "Hyperion." The first feeling was that of incredulity that the two poems could, under change of circumstances or lapse of time, have emanated from the same mind. The "Endymion" trespasses so strongly against good sense and just feeling that, in order to secure its pardon, we need the whole weight of the imperishable "Hyperion;" which, as Mr. Gilfillan truly says, "is the greatest of poetical torsos." The first belongs essentially to the vilest collection of waxwork filigree or gilt gingerbread, the other presents the majesty, the austere beauty, and the simplicity of a Grecian temple enriched with Grecian sculpture.—DE QUINCEY, THOMAS, 1845–57, *Gilfillan's Literary Portraits, Works,* ed. Masson, vol. XI, p. 389.

One of the great disappointments in Literature is the coming upon the stars which show that the "Hyperion" of Keats is a fragment.—CALVERT, GEORGE H., 1874, *Brief Essays and Brevities,* p. 217.

As a *story*, "Endymion" deserves all that its worst enemies ever said of it. "Hyperion" shows a remarkable advance, but it is well that Keats left it a fragment, for it is plain that, with his effeminate notion of Apollo, he could never have invented any kind of action which would have interested the reader in learning how the old Titan Sun-God was turned out of his kingdom.—COURTHOPE, WILLIAM JOHN, 1885, *The Liberal Movement in English Literature,* p. 184.

But though Keats sees the Greek world from afar, he sees it truly. The Greek touch is not his, but in his own rich and decorated English way he writes with a sure insight into the vital meaning of Greek ideas. . . . With a few slips and inequalities, and one or two instances of verbal incorrectness, "Hyperion," as far as it was written, is indeed one of the grandest poems in our language, and in its grandeur seems one of the easiest and most spontaneous.—COLVIN, SIDNEY, 1887, *Keats (English Men of Letters),* pp. 153, 155.

The opening promises well; we are conscious at once of a new musical blank verse, a music both sweet and strong, alive with imagination and tenderness. There and throughout the poem are passages in which Keats, without losing his own individuality, is as good as Milton, where Milton is as good as Virgil; and such passages rank with the best things that Keats ever did; but in other places he seems a little overshadowed by Milton, while definite passages of the "Paradise Lost" are recalled, and in some places the imitation seems frigid.—BRIDGES, ROBERT, 1894, *Poems of John Keats,* ed. Drury, Introduction, vol. I, p. xli.

ODES
1820

I have come to that pass of admiration for him now, that I dare not read him, so discontented he makes me with my own work; but others must not leave unread, in considering the influence of trees upon the human soul, that marvellous ode to Psyche.—RUSKIN, JOHN, 1860, *Modern Painters,* pt. vi, ch. ix.

If one may say a word *obiter*, out of the fulness of one's heart—I am often inclined to think for all-in-all,—that is, for thoughts most mortally compacted, for words which come forth, each trembling and giving off light like a morning-star, and for the pure beauty of the spirit and strength and height of the spirit,—which, I say, for all-in-all, I am often inclined to think ["Ode on Melancholy"], reaches the highest height yet touched in the lyric line.—LANIER, SIDNEY, 1881, *The English Novel,* p. 95.

The "Ode to a Nightingale," one of the finest masterpieces of human work in all time and for all ages.—SWINBURNE, ALGERNON CHARLES, 1882–86, *Keats, Encyclopædia Britannica, Miscellanies,* p. 211.

I make bold to name one of our shorter English lyrics that still seems to me, as it seemed to me ten years ago, the nearest to perfection, the one I would surrender last of all. What should this be save the "Ode to a Nightingale," so faultless in its varied unity and in the cardinal qualities of language, melody, and tone? A strain that has a dying fall; music wedded to ethereal passion, to the yearning that floods all nature.— STEDMAN, EDMUND CLARENCE, 1884, *Keats, The Century, vol.* 27, p. 600.

The "Ode on a Grecian Urn" wonderfully enshrines the poet's kinship with Greece, and with the spirit of her worship. There is all the Greek measure and moderation about it also; a calm and classic grace, with severe loveliness of outline. In form it is perfect. There is an exquisiteness of expression—not that which is often mistakenly so designated, but a translucence, as of silver air, or limpid water, that both reveals and glorifies all fair plants, or pebbles, or bathing lights. —NOEL, RODEN, 1886, *Keats, Essays on Poetry and Poets,* p. 169.

In the five odes there is naturally some diversity in the degrees of excellence.

. . . Considered intellectually, we might form a kind of symphony out of them, and arrange it thus—1, "Grecian Urn;" 2, "Psyche;" 3, "Autumn;" 4, "Melancholy;" 5, "Nightingale;" and, if Keats had left us nothing else, we should have in this symphony an almost complete picture of his poetic mind, only omitting, or representing deficiently, that more instinctive sort of enjoyment which partakes of gaiety. Viewing all these wondrous odes together, the predominant quality which we trace in them is an extreme susceptibility to delight, close-linked with after thought—pleasure with pang—or that poignant sense of ultimates, a sense delicious and harrowing, which clasps the joy in sadness, and feasts upon the very sadness in joy. The emotion throughout is the emotion of beauty. Beauty intensely perceived, intensely loved, questioned of its secret like the sphinx, imperishable and eternal, yet haunted (as it were) by its own ghost, the mortal throes of the human soul. As no poet had more capacity for enjoyment than Keats, so none exceeded him in the luxury of sorrow. Few also exceeded him in the sense of the one moment irretrievable; but this conception in its fulness belongs to the region of morals yet more than of sensation, and the spirit of Keats was almost an alien in the region of morals.—ROSSETTI, WILLIAM MICHAEL, 1887, *Life of John Keats (Great Writers), p.* 194.

When the young poet wrought so unaware
From purest Parian, washed by Grecian seas,
And stained to amber softness by the breeze
Of Attic shores, his Urn, antiquely fair,—
And brimmed it at the sacred fountain,where
The draughts he drew were sweet as Castaly's,—
Had he foreseen what souls would there appease
Their purer thirsts, he had not known despair!
About it long processions move and wind,
Held by its grace,—a chalice choicely fit
For Truth's and Beauty's perfect interfuse,
Whose effluence the exhaling years shall find
Unwasted: for the poet's name is writ
(Firmer than marble) in Olympian dews!
—PRESTON, MARGARET J., 1887, *Keats' Greek Urn, The Century, vol.* 33, *p.* 586.

SONNETS

"Nature's Eremite:" like a solitary thing in Nature.—This beautiful Sonnet was the last word of a poet deserving the title "marvellous boy" in a much higher sense than Chatterton. If the fulfilment may ever safely be prophesied from the promise, England appears to have lost in Keats one whose gifts in Poetry have rarely been surpassed.—PALGRAVE, FRANCIS TURNER, 1861, *The Golden Treasury.*

Do you remember that last sonnet? Let us repeat it solemnly, and let the words wander down with the waters of the river to the sea. . . . How the star-sheen on the tremulous tide, and that white death-like "mask," haunt the imagination! Had the poet, who felt the grass grow over him ere he was five-and-twenty, been crowned with a hundred summers, could he have done anything more consummate? I doubt it.—SKELTON, JOHN (SHIRLEY), 1862, *Nugæ Criticæ, p.* 236.

Though Keats has never been and probably never will be a really popular poet, his influence on other poets and on poetic temperaments generally has been quite incalculable. Some of his sonnets are remarkable for their power and beauty, while others are indifferent and a few are poor. With all his love for the beauty of isolated poetic lines—music condensed into an epigram more concise than the Greeks ever uttered—as, for example, his own splendid verse,
There is a budding morrow in mid-night—
and with all that sense of verbal melody which he manifested so remarkably in his odes, it is strange that in his sonnets he should so often be at fault in true harmony.—SHARP, WILLIAM, 1886, *Sonnets of this Century, Introduction, p.* lv.

The sonnet on Chapman's Homer stands alone in its perfection among boyish productions and high up among the great sonnets of the language.—LODGE, HENRY CABOT, 1897, *Certain Accepted Heroes and Other Essays, p.* 130.

As well rounded and compact a poetic unit ["Chapman's Homer"] as our literature can show.—JOHNSON, CHARLES F., 1898, *Elements of Literary Criticism, p.* 19.

GENERAL

Sir,—We regret that your brother ever requested us to publish this book, or that our opinion of its talent should have led us to acquiesce in undertaking it. We are, however, much obliged to you for relieving us from the unpleasant necessity of declining any further connexion with it, which we must have done, as we think the curiosity is satisfied, and the sale has dropped. By far the greater number of persons who have purchased it from us have found fault with it in such plain terms, that we have in many cases offered to take the book back rather than be annoyed with the ridicule which has, time after time, been showered upon it. In fact, it was only on Saturday last that we were under the mortification of having our own opinion of its merits flatly contradicted by a gentleman, who told us he considered it "no better than a take in." These are unpleasant imputations for any one in business to labour under, but we should have borne them and concealed their existence from you had not the style of your note shewn us that such delicacy would be quite thrown away. We shall take means without delay for ascertaining the number of copies on hand, and you shall be informed accordingly. Your most, &c.— OLLIER, C. AND J., 1817, *Letter to George Keats, April 29.*

To witness the disease of any human understanding, however feeble, is distressing; but the spectacle of an able mind reduced to a state of insanity is of course ten times more afflicting. It is with such sorrow as this that we have contemplated the case of Mr. John Keats. This young man appears to have received from nature talents of an excellent, perhaps even of a superior order—talents which, devoted to the purposes of any useful profession, must have rendered him a respectable if not an eminent citizen. His friends, we understand, destined him to the career of medicine, and he was bound apprentice some years ago to a worthy apothecary in town. But all has been undone by a sudden attack of the malady to which we have alluded. . . . We venture to make one small prophecy, that his bookseller will not a second time venture 50*l.* on anything he can write. It is a better and a wiser thing to be a starved apothecary than a starved poet; so back to the shop Mr. John, back to "plasters, pills, and ointment-boxes," &c. But, for Heaven's sake, young Sangrado, be a little more sparing of extenuatives and soporifics in your practice than you have been in your poetry.—LOCKHART, JOHN GIBSON? 1818, *The Cockney School of Poetry, No. 4; Blackwood's Magazine, vol. 3, pp. 519, 524.*

His feelings are full, earnest and original, as those of the olden writers were and are; they are made for all time, not for the drawing-room and the moment. Mr. Keats always speaks of, and describes nature, with an awe and a humility, but with a deep and almost breathless affection.—He knows that Nature is better and older than he is, and he does not put himself on an equality with her. You do not see him, when you see her. The moon and the mountainous foliage of the woods, and the azure sky, and the ruined and magic temple; the rock, the desert, and the sea; the leaf of the forest, and the embossed foam off the most living ocean, are the spirits of his poetry; but he does not bring them in his own hand, or obtrude his person before you, when you are looking at them. . . . In the structure of his verse, and the sinewy quality of his thoughts, Mr. Keats greatly resembles old Chapman, the nervous translator of Homer. His mind has "thews and limbs like to its ancestors." Mr. Gifford, who knows something of the old dramatists, ought to have paused before he sanctioned the abuse of a spirit kindred with them. If he could not feel, he ought to know better.—REYNOLDS, JOHN HAMILTON, 1818, *West of England Journal and General Advertiser, Oct. 6.*

No more Keats, I entreat:—flay him alive;—if some of you don't, I must skin him myself. There is no bearing the drivelling idiotism of the manikin.—BYRON, LORD, 1820, *Letter to Mr. Murray, Oct. 12.*

Mr. Keats, we understand, is still a very young man; and his whole works, indeed, bear evidence enough of the fact. They are full of extravagance and irregularity, rash attempts at originality, interminable wanderings, and excessive obscurity. They manifestly require, therefore, all the indulgence that can be claimed for a first attempt:—But we think it no less plain that they deserve it: For they are flushed all over with the rich lights of fancy; and so coloured and bestrewn with the flowers of poetry, that even while perplexed and bewildered in their labyrinths, it is impossible to resist the intoxication of their sweetness, or to shut our hearts to the enchantments they so lavishly present. — JEFFREY, FRANCIS LORD, 1820-44, *Keats's Poems, Contributions to the Edinburgh Review, vol. III, p. 102.*

> . . . till the Future dares
> Forget the Past, his fate and fame shall be
> An echo and a light unto eternity!　. . .
> 　He is made one with Nature: there is
> 　　heard
> 　His voice in all her music, from the moan
> 　Of thunder to the song of night's sweet
> 　　bird;
> 　He is a presence to be felt and known
> 　In darkness and in light, from herb and
> 　　stone,
> 　Spreading itself where'er that Power may
> 　　move
> 　Which has withdrawn his being to its own;
> 　Which wields the world with never wearied
> 　　love,
> Sustains it from beneath, and kindles it
> 　above. . . .
> 　　. . . burning through the inmost veil of
> 　　Heaven,
> The soul of Adonais, like a star,
> Beacons from the abode where the Eternal
> 　are.

—SHELLEY, PERCY BYSSHE, 1821, *Adonais, An Elegy on the Death of John Keats,*
st. i, xlii, lv.

Mr. Keats is also dead. He gave the
greatest promise of genius of any poet of
his day. He displayed extreme tenderness, beauty, originality and delicacy of
fancy; all he wanted was manly strength
and fortitude to reject the temptations of
singularity in sentiment and expression.
Some of his shorter and later pieces are,
however, as free from faults as they are
full of beauties.— HAZLITT, WILLIAM,
1824, *Select British Poets.*

> Thy clear, strong tones will oft bring sudden
> 　bloom
> Of hope secure, to him who lonely cries,
> Wrestling with the young poet's agonies,
> Neglect and scorn, which seem a certain
> 　doom:
> Yes! the few words which, like great thunder-drops,
> Thy large heart down to earth shook doubtfully,
> Thrilled by the inward lightening of its
> 　might,
> Serene and pure, like gushing joy of light,
> Shall track the eternal chords of Destiny,
> After the moon-led pulse of ocean stops.

—LOWELL, JAMES RUSSELL, 1841, *To the*
Spirit of Keats.

Keats was born a poet of the most poetical kind. All his feelings came to him
through a poetical medium, or were
speedily coloured by it. He enjoyed a
jest as heartily as any one, and sympathized
with the lowliest commonplace; but the
next minute his thoughts were in a garden

of enchantment, with nymphs, and fauns
and shapes of exalted humanity:

> Elysian beauty, melancholy grace.

It might be said of him, that he never beheld an oak-tree without seeing the Dryad.
His fame may now forgive the critics who
disliked his politics, and did not understand his poetry. Repeated editions of
him in England, France, and America,
attest its triumphant survival of all
obloquy; and there can be no doubt that
he has taken a permanent station among
the British Poets, of a very high, if not
thoroughly mature, description.—HUNT,
LEIGH, 1844, *Imagination and Fancy, p.* 283.

Had there been no such thing as literature, Keats would have dwindled into a
cipher. Shelley, in the same event, would
hardly have lost one plume from his crest.
It is in relation to literature, and to the
boundless questions as to the true and the
false arising out of literature and poetry,
that Keats challenges a fluctuating interest,—sometimes an interest of strong
disgust, sometimes of deep admiration.
There is not, I believe, a case on record
throughout European Literature where
feelings so repulsive of each other have
centered in the same individual.— DE
QUINCEY, THOMAS, 1845-57, *Gilfillan's Literary Portraits, Works, ed. Masson, vol.*
XI, *p.* 388.

By the by, beg, borrow, steal, or buy
Keats' "Letters and Poems;" most wonderful bits of Poems, written off hand
at a sitting, most of them: I only wonder
that they do not make a noise in the
world.—FITZGERALD, EDWARD, 1849, *Letters, vol.* I, *p.* 195.

> What was his record of himself, ere he
> 　Went from us? "Here lies one whose name
> 　　was writ
> 　In water." While the chilly shadows flit
> 　Of sweet St. Agnes' Eve, while basil
> 　　springs—
> His name, in every humble heart that sings
> Shall be a fountain of love, verily.

—ROSSETTI, CHRISTINA, 1849, *On Keats,*
New Poems, p. 23.

> The song of a nightingale sent thro' a slumbrous valley,
> Low-lidded with twilight, and tranced with
> 　the dolorous sound,
> Tranced with a tender enchantment; the
> 　yearning of passion
> That wins immortality even while panting
> 　delirous with death.

—MEREDITH, GEORGE, 1851, *Works, vol.*
XXXI, *p.* 140.

Keats, the most Grecian of all, rejected the
metre of Grecians ;
Poesy breathed over *him*, breathed constantly,
tenderly, freshly.
—LANDOR, WALTER SAVAGE, 1853, *English Hexameters.*

Every one of Keats's poems was a sacrifice of vitality; a virtue went away from
him into every one of them; even yet, as
we turn the leaves, they seem to warm and
thrill our fingers with the flush of his fine
senses, and the flutter of his electrical
nerves, and we do not wonder he felt that
what he did was to be done swiftly. . . .
Keats certainly had more of the penetrative and sympathetic imagination which
belongs to the poet, of that imagination
which identifies itself with the momentary
object of its contemplation, than any man
of these later days. It is not merely that
he has studied the Elizabethans and caught
their turn of thought, but that he really
sees things with their sovereign eye, and
feels them with their electrified senses.
His imagination was his bliss and bane.
. . . To me one of the most interesting
aspects of Keats is that in him we have an
example of the *renaissance* going on almost
under our eyes, and that the intellectual
ferment was in him kindled by a purely
English leaven. He had properly no
scholarship, any more than Shakespeare
had, but like him he assimilated at a touch
whatever could serve his purpose. His
delicate senses absorbed culture at every
pore.—LOWELL, JAMES RUSSELL, 1854–
90, *Keats, Prose Writings, Riverside ed.,
vol.* I, *pp.* 232, 243, 244.

 . . . The man who never stepped
In gradual progress like another man,
But, turning grandly on his central self,
Ensphered himself in twenty perfect years
And died, not young (the life of a long life
Distilled to a mere drop, falling like a tear
Upon the world's cold cheek to make it burn
For ever).
—BROWNING, ELIZABETH BARRETT, 1856,
Aurora Leigh, bk. i.

Keats drinks the beauty of nature
violently; but has no more real sympathy
with her than he has with a bottle of
claret. His palate is fine; but he "bursts
joy's grape against it," gets nothing but
misery, and a bitter taste of dregs out of
his desperate draught.—RUSKIN, JOHN,
1856, *Modern Painters, pt.* iv, *ch.* xvi.

Keats, both in verbal form and in the
higher qualities of poetry, is constantly

reminding us of the more imaginative
works of Chaucer.—MARSH, GEORGE P.,
1859, *Lectures on the English Language,
First Series, p.* 23, *note.*

Spenser's manner is no more Homeric
than is the manner of the one modern inheritor of Spenser's beautiful gift; the
poet, who evidently caught from Spenser
his sweet and easy-slipping movement, and
who has exquisitely employed it; a
Spenserian genius, nay, a genius by natural
endowment, richer probably than even
Spenser; that light which shines so unexpected and without fellow in our century,
an Elizabethan born too late, the early
lost and admirably gifted Keats.—ARNOLD,
MATTHEW, 1861, *Lectures on Homer, p.* 68.

 While I sit in silence,
  Comes from mile on mile hence,
From English Keats's Roman grave, a voice
 that lightens toil.
—BUCHANAN, ROBERT, 1866, *To David in
Heaven.*

Wrote in a manner which carried the
reader back to the time when those charming passages of lyrical enthusiasm were
produced which we occasionally find in the
plays of Shakespeare, in those of Beaumont
and Fletcher, and in Milton's "Comus."
The verses of Keats are occasionally disfigured, especially in his "Endymion," by
a flatness almost childish, but in the finer
passages they clothe the thought in the
richest imagery and in words each of
which is a poem. Lowell has justly called
Keats "over-languaged," but there is
scarce a word that we should be willing to
part with in his "Ode to the Nightingale,"
and that on a "Grecian Urn," and the
same thing may be said of the greater part
of his "Hyperion."—BRYANT, WILLIAM
CULLEN, 1870, *A New Library of Poetry
and Song, Introduction, vol.* I, *p.* 43.

Were it necessary, in this place, to
characterize Keats as a writer, I should
say that he was more intensely and exclusively poetical than any other. No one
can read his poems (including "Endymion"
and all others subsequently published)
without feeling at once that he is communing with a great poet. There can be
no mistake about his *quality*. It is above
all doubt; and if, like Lucifer, he has not
drawn after him a third part of the
heavens, he has had a radiant train of
followers, comprising (with the exception
of the great name of Wordsworth) all who

have since succeeded in distinguishing themselves in the same sphere of art.— PROCTER, BRYAN WALLER, 1874, *Recollections of Men of Letters*, p. 202.

He hath quaffed
Glory and Death in one immortal draught;
Surely among the undying men of old
Numbered art thou, great Heart.
—DE VERE, AUBREY, 1874, *To Keats, Alexander the Great and Other Poems*, p. 402.

Keats died at twenty-five, and yet, to men past sixty he is fresh, freshening.— CALVERT, GEORGE H., 1874, *Brief Essays and Brevities*, p. 216.

No one regards the poet's quivering string,
Since thine was hushed, who brought the myrtle here
    From perfect Arcadie, whose verse
    Young earth's freshness could rehearse.
No eventide was thine,
But like the young athlete from the bath,
    For one brief hour,
You stood in the arena yet uncrowned,
Doubtful, although beyond all venturers strong:
Yes, strong to guide Hyperion's coursers round
The love-inscribèd zodiac of all time:
Thou youth, who in the gardens Athenine,
The noblest sage had leant upon with pride,
And called thee Musagætes, and thy lyre
    Wreathed with the bay
    Of the god of day.
—SCOTT, WILLIAM BELL, 1875, *To the Memory of Keats.*

The spirit of art was always vividly near and precious to Keats. He fashioned it exuberantly into a thousand shapes, now of gem-like exquisiteness, now mere sightly or showy trinkets; and of these the scrupulous taste will even pronounce the cheapest, and rightly pronounce them, to be trumpery. Still, there is the feeling of art, however provoking its masquerade; recognizable here as clearly as it is in the formative fine art, wrought by a cunning hand, in a period of great and overblown development and impending decadence— such as the late cinquecento or the earlier French rococo. Not indeed that, in Keats's case, there is any taint of decadence— but on the contrary the wanton and tangled wilfulnesses of a beautiful precocity, and a beautiful immaturity. Clearer and clearer did the true and high promptings of art become to him as he advanced, and more immediate and certain his response

to them. He might have said at the last with Nero "*Qalis artifex pereo !*"—ROSSETTI, WILLIAM MICHAEL, 1878, *Lives of Famous Poets*, p. 360.

Yet later, lingering briefly among men,
  He dropt before the world's feet those few flowers
    Whose color and odor brave all blight of years,
And the rare radiance of whose bloom, since then,
  Pathos, their sweet attendant, ever dowers
    With the soft silver dews of pitying tears!
—FAWCETT, EDGAR, 1878, *Fantasy and Passion*, p. 186.

His faults are numerous and glaring. The mythology which supplied him with his *mise en scène* is elementary and almost puerile. His stories are lacking in human interest. In fact, he does hardly anything but describe, and he describes with an exuberance which is unluckily not incompatible with the most painful monotony. The enthusiasm for nature which is the soul of his verse is certainly sincere, and yet Keats writes with effort. His naïveté is not feigned, but there is something in it of deliberation, and therefore of exaggeration. In short, there is affectation in him, and I cannot regard as wholly unjust the reproach of cockneyism which critics used to throw at this poet and his friends. Yet, with all these faults, Keats is very far from being an ordinary person ; his posthumous popularity is very far from being inexplicable, and the influence which he still exercises is very far from being a mere matter of coterie and *engouement*. He has a special feeling, a feeling of extraordinary intensity, for nature and for beauty. It seems as though he saw woods, streams, fields for the first time, so full of novelty and of the marvellous is the spectacle to him. There is at once sensuousness and religion in his communion with the life of all things. There would seem to be a perfume which gets in his head, an intoxication to which he gives himself up, a ritual into whose mysteries he is trying to break, a baptism, a whelming in the eternal *natura naturans*. Wordsworth himself, as we shall see, can lay claim to a deeper understanding of nature : but it is easy to understand that his idyllic piety, his patriarchal philosophizing, must have at last seemed terribly groveling to a generation which had drunk the heady philtres of Keats's descriptive poetry. — SCHERER, EDMOND, 1880–91, *Wordsworth and Modern Poetry in England, Essays on English Literature, tr. Saintsbury, p.* 192.

O pang-dowered Poet, whose reverberant lips
And heart-strung lyre awoke the Moon's
　eclipse,—
Thou whom the daisies glory in growing
　o'er,—
Their fragrance clings around thy name, not
　writ
But rumour'd in water, while the fame of it
Along Time's flood goes echoing evermore.
—ROSSETTI, DANTE GABRIEL, 1881, *John Keats, Five English Poets, Ballads and Sonnets.*

Among the poets who appeared in the first two decades of this century, as among all poets, readers will choose their favourites according to their sympathies. But putting aside personal preferences, every one must allow that none of the poets of that time was more "radiant with genius," and more rich in promise, than the short-lived Keats.—SHAIRP, JOHN CAMPBELL, 1881, *Modern English Poetry, Aspects of Poetry, p.* 149.

In his first book there was little fore-taste of anything greatly or even genuinely good; but between the marshy and sandy flats of sterile or futile verse there were undoubtedly some few purple patches of floral promise. The style was frequently detestable—a mixture of sham Spenserian and mock Wordsworthian, alternately florid and arid. His second book, "Endymion," rises in its best passages to the highest level of Barnfield and of Lodge, the two previous poets with whom, had he published nothing more he might have probably have been classed; and this, among minor minstrels, is no unenviable place. His third book raised him at once to a foremost rank in the highest class of English poets. Never was any one of them but Shelley so little of a marvellous boy and so suddenly revealed as a marvellous man. Never has any poet suffered so much from the chaotic misarrangement of his poems in every collected edition. The rawest and the rankest rubbish of his fitful spring is bound up in one sheaf with the ripest ears, flung into one basket with the richest fruits, of his sudden and splendid summer.—SWINBURNE, ALGERNON CHARLES, 1882–86, *Keats, Encyclopædia Britannica; Miscellanies, p.* 210.

He would have been among the very greatest of us if he had lived. There is something of the innermost soul of poetry in almost everything he ever wrote.— TENNYSON, ALFRED LORD, 1883, *Criticisms on Poets and Poetry, Memoir, ed. by his Son, vol.* II, *p.* 286.

The sixth to come was like unto a drooping flower, or a spirit among men that went in and out none knew how. He, too, sang a song, whereof no man could say certainly whether it were his or the lark's. He went forward with a wand in his hand, but no helmet was on his head, and over his heart no breast-plate. One blow from the true-men he received, and it went in about the third rib, near the heart, and for awhile he fainted; but presently recovering himself he stood up and turned his eyes wistfully to the path, and in a moment disappearing was lost in a thicket, and was seen again of none till he came forth at the top.—CAINE, HALL, 1883, *The Fable of the Critics, Cobwebs of Criticism, p.* ix.

The genius of Greek poetry was alien to the English mind until it revealed itself to the young imagination of Keats, who wore it in his heart of hearts, not because he was a scholar,—for a scholar he was not, —but because he was a Greek. There are a thousand faults in "Endymion," but the unpardonable fault of falsehood is not one of them. It is true, everywhere true to the spirit of Greek pastoral poetry, of which it was the first, and is the last, example in English song. How thoroughly the genius of Keats was possessed with the beautiful mythology of Greece, and how rapidly it matured his wonderful genius, which in writing "Endymion" outgrew the lush luxuriance of manner which is the worst defect of that poem, we see in his Odes "To Psyche," and "On a Grecian Urn,"—exquisite productions in the purest style of art,—and in the fragment of "Hyperion," wherein magnificence of conception and severity of expression are alike conspicuous, and where, for the first time, the epical height of the Greeks is attained by an English poet. The secret of "Hyperion" and "Endymion" inhered in the temperament of Keats, who *was* a Greek, as one of his friends declared.— STODDARD, RICHARD HENRY, 1884, *Selections from the Poetical Works of A. C. Swinburne, Introduction, p.* ix.

As regards verbal expression, a close test of original power, he certainly outranks any poet since Shakspere.—STEDMAN, EDMUND CLARENCE, 1884, *Keats, The Century, vol.* 27, *p.* 600.

So far as the general reading public are concerned, Hunt was the discoverer of Keats, and not only his discoverer, but his faithful interpreter, pointing out lovingly, by means of his "signpost criticism," (as it has been called somewhat disparagingly by those who profess to need no guidance the along byways of literature), those magical facilities of insight and expression which even in his earliest and crudest work testified that here was a poet of the true royal line.—NOBLE, JAMES ASHCROFT, 1886, *The Sonnet in England and other Essays, p,* 107.

By power, as well as by temperament and aim, he was the most Shakspearean spirit that has lived since Shakspeare.—COLVIN, SIDNEY, 1887, *Keats* (*English Men of Letters*), *p,* 215.

In no poetry is the personality of the writer more manifest than in his: in none does the ideal creation spring more eivdently from introspection and self-consciousness. His character determined his method of compositioin, as his method of composition imposed a limitation on his genius. A certain morbidness of fancy—due, probably in great part, to physical causes—haunted him, which did not, indeed, like the imagination of Shelley, force him to take ideas for facts, but which, producing in him a kind of incessant love-longing, drove him to shun the realities of life, and to find an asylum in the regions of imagination.—COURTHORPE, WILLAM JOHN, 1887, *Keats' Place in English Poetry, The National Review, vol,* 10, *p.*16.

A fair-formed image of immortal youth
  Breasting the steep hillside of life's endeavor;
A white-robed herald of eternal truth
  Shouting a message from the gods forever.
—WILSON, ROBERT BURNS, 1887, *Keats, The Century, vol.* 34, *p.* 110.

Probably the very finest lyric ["La Belle Dame san Merci."] in the English language.—PATMORE, COVENTRY, 1889–98, *Principle in Art, p.* 76.

Keats, "the Elizabethan born out of due time," as he has been called, kept himself indeed unspotted from the contagion of science. Yet his passion for nature

moving though it did on lines traced by Spenser, has a far greater intensity, a far more fiery self-abandonment to the intoxication of earth, than would have been possible in the sixteenth century.—SYMONDS, JOHN ADDINGTON, 1890, *Essays Speculative and Suggestive, vol.* II, *p.* 270.

Thou silent singer 'neath the grass,
Still sing to me those sweeter songs unsung,
"Pipe to the spirit ditties of no tone,"
Caressing thought with wonderments of phrase
Such as thy springtide rapture knew to win.
Ay, sing to me thy unborn summer songs,
And the ripe autumn lays that might have been;
Strong wine of fruit mature, whose flowers alone we know.
—MITCHELL, S. WEIR, 1891, *The Grave of Keats, Collected Poems, p.* 307.

It was on the trinity of truth, beauty, and pleasure that Keats built, and built lastingly.—CHENEY, JOHN VANCE, 1891, *The Golden Guess, p.* 28.

Probably no English poet who has used the Spenserian stanza, first assimilated so fully the spirit of Spenser, before using the stanza, as did Keats; and to this fact may be partly attributed his effective use of it as an organ for his imagination in its "lingering, loving, particularizing mood."—CORSON, HIRAM, 1892, *A Primer of English Verse, p,* 124.

Not since Spenser had there been a purer gift of poetry among English-speaking peoples; not since Milton a line of nobler balance of sound, thought, and cadence. There is no magic of colour in written speech that is not mixed in the diction of "The Eve of Saint Agnes,"—a vision of beauty, deep, rich, and glowing as one of those dyed windows in which the heart of the Middle Ages still burns. While of the odes, so perfect in form, so ripe with thought, so informed and irradiated by the vision and the insight of the imagination, what remains to be said save that they furnish us with the tests and standards of poetry itself? They mark the complete identification of thought with form, of vision with faculty, of life with art.—MABIE, HAMILTON WRIGHT, 1892–3, *Essays in Literary Interpretation, p.* 164.

He was one of the greatest of English poets; he led a life in which there was no doubt a vast deal of keen and exquisite pleasure, but little or no happiness; thrown, for the most part, among a set of clever, small men, he towers above them, a man by no means clever but very great; though not unfortunate in the worst and bitterest sense of the word, though he had no struggles with immediate adversity and want, he yet suffered much; he lavished the strength of a tender and noble heart upon a rather commonplace young woman, who evidently had no suspicion that she was worshipped—she, ordinary little piece of pretty Eve's flesh —by one of earth's immortal sons. Among these clever, small men, Hunt, Reynolds, and the rest, by whom he was surrounded, and with whom in popular estimation he was scarce distinguishably merged, he held before his eyes a lofty and splendid ideal of excellence in the art which he had chosen, or which nature had chosen for him. He saw this ideal at first with blurred and faltering vision, but ever more clearly as his eyes were purged with the euphrasy and rue of human experience; he added to the store of the world's beauty, he increased the sum of man's happiness, and doing this was rewarded with contempt and ribald mockery, was condemned to read things written about himself which if uttered in oral intercourse would be recognised by everybody as gross insult and brutal outrage; spending himself in the service of man, his recompense was not seldom such scorn and contumely as might appropriately be reserved for an enemy of one's species. Worn out by suffering and discouragement, and perhaps in part by the yet more shattering pangs of immoderate joy, he sinks in premature death.—WATSON, WILLIAM, 1893, *Excursions in Criticism, p. 23.*

We honor in the lad who passed so long unobserved among the inhabitants of Hampstead, a poet, and nothing but a poet, but one of the very greatest poets that the modern world has seen. . . . Keats lives, as he modestly assured his friends would be the case, among the English poets. Nor among them, merely, but in the first rank of them—among the very few of whom we instinctively think whenever the characteristic versemen of our race are spoken of.—GOSSE, EDMUND, 1894, *Address at the Keats Monument, July* 16.

I am inclined to think that Mr. Matthew Arnold, a critic with whose judgments I rarely find myself in dissent, makes a somewhat misleading remark when he insists that Keats's master passion was not the passion of the sensuous or sentimental poet, but was an intellectual or spiritual passion. If the words sensuous and sentimental were intended in an opprobrious sense, the remark might be useful; but if they are used in the literal meaning, and then contrasted with intellectual and spiritual, their tendency is to withdraw the reader of Keats from the main characteristics of his poetry.—MINTO, WILLIAM, 1894, *The Literature of the Georgian Era, ed. Knight, p.* 304.

Upon thy tomb 'tis graven, "Here lies one
  Whose name is writ in water." Could
    there be
A flight of Fancy fitlier feigned for thee,
A fairer motto for her favorite son?
For, as the wave, thy varying numbers run—
  Now crested proud in tidal majesty,
  Now tranquil as the twilight reverie
Of some dim lake the white moon looks upon
While teems the world with silence. Even
    there,
  In each Protean rainbow-tint that stains
The breathing canvas of the atmosphere,
  We read an exhalation of thy strains.
Thus, on the scroll of Nature, everywhere,
  Thy name, a deathless syllable, remains.
—TABB, JOHN B., 1894, *Keats, Poems.*

In spite of this earnestness and philosophy, it is certainly true that Keats' mind was of a luxurious habit; and it must have been partly due to this temperament that he showed so little severity towards himself in the castigation of his poems, though that was, as I said before, chiefly caused by the prolific activity of his imagination, which was always providing him with fresh material to work on. In this respect he is above all poets an example of what is meant by inspiration: the mood which all artists require, covet, and find most rare was the common mood with him; and I should say that being amply supplied with this, what as an artist he most lacked was self-restraint and self-castigation,—which was indeed foreign to his luxurious temperament, unselfish and devoted to his art as he was,—the presence of which was most needful to watch, choose, and reject the images which crowded on him as he thought or wrote.—BRIDGES, ROBERT, 1894, *Poems of John Keats, ed. Drury, Introduction, vol.* I, *p.* ci.

One would like to know whether a first reading in the letters of Keats does not generally produce something akin to a severe mental shock. It is a sensation which presently becomes agreeable, being in that respect like a plunge into cold water, but it is undeniably a shock. Most readers of Keats, knowing him, as he should be known, by his poetry, have not the remotest conception of him as he shows himself in his letters. Hence they are unprepared for this splendid exhibition of virile intellectual health. Not that they think of him as morbid,—his poetry surely could not make this impression,—but rather that the popular conception of him is, after all these years, a legendary Keats, the poet who was killed by reviewers, the Keats of Shelley's preface to the Adonais, the Keats whose story is written large in the world's book of Pity and of Death. When the readers are confronted with a fair portrait of the real man, it makes them rub their eyes. Nay, more, it embarrasses them. To find themselves guilty of having pitied one who stood in small need of pity is mortifying. In plain terms, they have systematically bestowed (or have attempted to bestow) alms on a man whose income at its least was bigger than any his patrons could boast. Small wonder that now and then you find a reader, with large capacity for the sentimental, who looks back with terror to his first dip into the letters.— VINCENT, LEON H., 1894, *A Reading in the Letters of John Keats, Atlantic Monthly, vol.* 74, *p.* 399.

The perfection of Keats's art, the sureness of success with which he translated into words, feelings that but for him those who underwent them would have abandoned as inexpressible, make rather startling the suggestion that there was anything to which he was inadequate because for it "he was not ripe." Indeed it is the very ripeness of Keats's art at its best that distinguishes it above the work of so many generations of his elders, and makes it so astonishing as the work of a youth, so far is it removed, in its security and ease of mastery, from the struggles for expression of immaturity, from the mere glibness of precocity. It is the sense rather of overripeness than of unripeness that it gives of a sensibility hectic and excessive.— SCHUYLER, MONTGOMERY, 1895, *The Centenary of Keats, The Forum, vol.* 20, *p.* 362.

Setting aside his rapid progress, Keats is the best illustration of the natural development of a poet. Beginning and ending his intemperate period with the too ample verge and room, the trailing fringe and sampler-like embroidery of "Endymion," he was soon writing the most perfect odes in the language; he elaborated in a few months a style, the like of which greater men have failed to achieve even in half a century of uninterrupted work.— DAVIDSON, JOHN, 1895, *Sentences and Paragraphs, p.* 12.

He gave to that end the best that he had to give, freely, generously, joyously pouring himself into the ministry of his art. He did not dream for a moment that the gift was perfect. Flattery could not blind him to the limitations and defects of his early work. He was his own best and clearest critic. But he knew that so far as it went his poetic inspiration was true. He had faithfully followed the light of a pure and elevating joy in the opulent, manifold beauty of nature, and in the eloquent significance of old-world legends, and he believed that it had already led him to a place among the poets whose verse would bring delight, in far-off years, to the sons and daughters of mankind. . . . The poetry of Keats, small in bulk and slight in body as it seems at first sight to be, endures, and will endure, in English literature, because it is the embodiment of the spirit of immortal youth.—VAN DYKE, HENRY, 1895, *The Influence of Keats, The Century, vol.* 50, *pp.* 911, 912.

His landscape seems to me of quite equal importance with the human side of his work; it was, indeed, the region in which he felt that his art, as yet unqualified through youthful inexperience to deal powerfully with human character and interests, attained the highest mastery. Keats, sharing with Shelley an intense appreciation of Nature, has a music in his verse more solemn, if less aerial. He neither views the landscape through the colours of personal feeling like Byron, nor with Wordsworth thinks of it as allied with human sympathy, or as penetrated by spiritual life, nor, with Shelley, wearies us with a crude pantheism. Hence his pictures are more powerfully true to actuality; he grasps the scene more vividly, emblazons it more richly: the object, seen in thought, has the salience, the relief, of Nature; the melody never pausing, and the word the *"inevitable"* word. Hence, what Arnold named his "fascinating felicity."—PALGRAVE, FRANCIS TURNER, 1896, *Landscape in Poetry,* p. 210.

Nothing is more interesting, even in the endless and delightful task of literary comparison, than to contrast the work of Shelley and Keats, so alike and yet so different. A little longer space of work, much greater advantages of means and education, and a happier though less blameless experience of passion, enabled Shelley to produce a much larger body of work than Keats has to his name, even when this is swollen by what Mr. Palgrave has justly stigmatised as "the incomplete and inferior work" withheld by Keats himself, but made public by the cruel kindness of admirers. And this difference in bulk probably coincides with a difference in the volume of genius of the two writers. Further, while it is not at all improbable that if Shelley had lived he would have gone on writing better and better, the same probability is, I think, to be more sparingly predicated of Keats.—SAINTSBURY, GEORGE, 1896, *A History of Nineteenth Century Literature,* p. 87.

Short as was the life of John Keats, and small as was the actual bulk of his production, there is no one of his contemporaries who holds more distinctly or securely his place as the legitimate successor of the greatest among the English poets before him and as the necessary precursor of those who have followed. . . . He had in common with the poets of Greece and of England at its greatest time a certain enchanting directness and simplicity of expression: while from both he differed in his comparative indifference to humanity. Keats shared with the Greeks that pagan sensuousness which revels in the delights of the senses untroubled by moral meaning or responsibility; like the Elizabethans he possessed the perception and appreciation of natural beauty entirely apart from its ministry to man; while from both he differed—and in so far fell below both—by the capability to rest upon a passionate satisfaction in sensuous beauty for its own sake and as an end sufficient in itself. . . . There is no stronger link between the poetry of the Elizabethan time and that of the Victorian school than John Keats; and the more closely this

statement is examined the more suggestive and the more accurate in substantial effect it is found to be.—BATES, ARLO, 1896, ed., *Poems by John Keats, Introduction,* pp. xxii, xxiv, xxviii.

I might cite page on page from Keats, and yet hold your attention; there is something so beguiling in his witching words; and his pictures are finished—with only one or two or three dashes of his pencil.—MITCHELL, DONALD G., 1897, *English Lands Letters and Kings, The Later Georges to Victoria,* p. 231.

Nearly all people who read poetry have a favoritism for Keats; he is in many respects the popular hero of English literature. He was young, and chivalrously devoted to his art; he has a mastery of expression almost unparalleled; he is neither obscure nor polemic; and he has had from the first a most fecundating influence on other minds: in Hood, in Tennyson, in Rossetti and Matthew Arnold, in Lanier and Lowell, in Yeats and Watson, one feels the breath and touch of Keats like an incantation. . . . Now, what is the outstanding extraneous feature of Keats's poetry? It is perhaps the musical and sculptural effect which he can make with words: a necromancy which he exercises with hardly a rival, even "among the greatest;" and among these he justly hoped to stand. Observe that a facility of this sort cannot be a natural endowment, since we must still, as Sir Philip Sidney bewails, "be put to school to learn our mother-tongue;" and that it implies ascetic diligence in the artist compassing it. Moreover, Keats's craftsmanship is no menace to him. It is true that he carries, in general, no such hindering burden of thought along his lyre as Donne, Dryden, Wordsworth, Browning; but neither, once having learned his strength, does he ever fall into the mere teasing ecstasy of symbolic sound, as Shelley does often, as Swinburne does more often than not. Keats, unlike Shelley or a cherub, is not all wing; he "stands foursquare" when he wills, or moves like the men of the Parthenon frieze, with a health and joyous gravity entirely carnal.—GUINEY, LOUISE IMOGEN, 1897, *Library of the World's Best Literature,* ed. *Warner, vol.* XV, *pp.* 8497, 8498.

It is enough for me that we find in Keats some odes of exquisite passion and charm, a delight in glow and colour that touches us like a canvas by Giorgione, a few short lyrics which stand in the everlasting lyrical triumphs of our tongue, a promise of command over the melody of verse, a power of painting in winged words which (if he had lived another twenty or thirty years) might have placed him well in the rank of poets somewhere below Milton and Shakespeare. *Might have done* this, if only promise were always followed by performance; if we could be sure that the nature of Keats as a man, his brain, and hold on truths and realities, equalled his mastery over language; if we did not too often feel (even in his best and latest work) that the instrument wherefrom he wrung forth such luscious music, seemed endowed with magic gifts to dash itself free from the hands and consciousness of him who held it.—HARRISON, FREDERIC, 1899, *Lamb and Keats, The Contemporary Review, vol.* 76, *p.* 67.

"The Cap and Bells" is a melancholy example of what a great poet can produce who is consumed by a hopeless passion and wasted by disease. . . . In his first sonnet on Fame, Keats, in a saner mood, puts by the temptation which would withdraw him from the high serenity of conscious worth. In the second, wherein he seems almost to be seeing Fanny Brawne, mocking behind the figure of Fame, he shows a more scornful attitude. There is little doubt that notwithstanding his close companionship with poets living and dead Keats never could long escape from the allurements of this "wayward girl," yet it may surely be said that his escape was most complete when he was fulfilling the highest law of his nature and creating those images of beauty which have given him Fame while he sleeps.—SCUDDER, HORACE E., 1899, *The Complete Poetical Works and Letters of John Keats, Cambridge ed., Biographical Sketch, pp.* xxiii, xxiv.

Hester Lynch Piozzi
Mrs. Thrale
1740–1821.

Born [Hester Lynch Salusbury], at Bodvel, Carnarvonshire, 16 Jan. 1741. Contrib. to "St. James's Chronicle" while still a young girl. Married to Henry Thrale, 11 Oct. 1763. Friendship with Johnson begun, 1764. Husband died, 4 April 1781. Intimacy with Gabriel Piozzi begun, 1780; married to him in London (at Roman Catholic Church), 23 July, in Bath (at Anglican Church), 25 July 1784. In Italy, 1784–87. Lived at Streatham, 1787–95; in Wales, 1795 to 1809. Husband died, March 1809; after that she resided mainly in Bath. Died, 2 May 1821. *Works:* "Anecdotes of the late Samuel Johnson," 1786; "Letters to and from the late Samuel Johnson," 1788; "Observations and Reflections made in the course of a Journey through France, Italy, and Germany" (2 vols.), 1789 (another edn. same year); "British Synonymy," 1794; "Retrospection" (2 vols.), 1801. *Posthumous:* "Two Letters . . . to W. A. Conway," 1843; "Autobiography, Letters, and Literary Remains," ed. by A. Hayward (2 vols.), 1861 (2nd edn. same year). She *edited:* "The Arno Miscellany," 1784. *Life:* by L. B. Seeley, 1891.—SHARP, R. FARQUHARSON, 1897, *A Dictionary of English Authors, p.* 228.

PERSONAL

Madam,—If I interpret your letter aright, you are ignominiously married: if it is yet undone let us *once* more *talk* together. If you have abandoned your children and your religion, God forgive your wickedness; if you have forfeited your fame and your country, may your folly do no further mischief. If the last act is yet to do, I who have loved you, esteemed you, reverenced you, and *served you;* I who long thought you the first of womankind, entreat that, before your fate is irrevocable, I may once more

see you. I was, I once was, Madam, most truly yours.—JOHNSON, SAMUEL, 1784, *Letter to Mrs. Thrale, July* 2.

The party was select and very agreeable, but rendered especially interesting by the announcement in the evening of "Mrs. Piozzi." It seemed almost as if a portrait by Sir Joshua had stepped out of its frame, when the little old lady, dressed *point de vice* in black satin, with dark glossy ringlets under her neat black hat, highly roughed, not the end of a ribbon or lace out of its place, with an unfaltering step entered the room. And was this really "the Mrs. Thrale," the stage monitress of "The Three Warnings," the indefatigable tea-maker of the Great Insatiable? She was instantly the center on which every eye was fixed, engrossing the attention of all. I had the satisfaction of a particular introduction to her, and was surprised and delighted with her vivacity and good-humour. The request that she would read to us from Milton was readily complied with, and I was given to understand she piqued herself on her superiority in giving effect to the great poet's verse.—MACREADY, W. C., 1815-75, *Reminiscences, ed. Pollock, p.* 82.

She was, in truth, a most wonderful character for talents and eccentricity, for wit, genius, generosity, spirit, and powers of entertainment. She had a great deal both of good and not good, in common with Madame de Staël Holstein. They had the same sort of highly superior intellect, the same depth of learning, the same general acquaintance with science, the same ardent love of literature, the same thirst for universal knowledge, and the same buoyant animal spirits, such as neither sickness, sorrow, nor even terror, could subdue. Their conversation was equally luminous, from the sources of their own fertile minds, and from their splendid acquisitions from the works and acquirements of others. Both were zealous to serve, liberal to bestow, and graceful to oblige; and both were truly highminded in prizing and praising whatever was admirable that came in their way. Neither of them was delicate nor polished, though each was flattering and caressing; but both had a fund inexhaustible of good humour, and of sportive gaiety, that made their intercourse with those they wished to please attractive, instructive, and delightful; and though not either of them had the smallest real malevolence in their compositions, neither of them could ever withstand the pleasure of uttering a repartee, let it wound whom it might, even though each would serve the very person they goaded with all the means in their power. Both were kind, charitable, and munificent, and therefore beloved; both were sarcastic, careless, and daring, and therefore feared. — D'ARBLAY, MME (FANNY BURNEY), 1821, *Diary and Letters, ed. Barrett, vol.* IV, *p.* 462.

The world was most wrong in blaming Mrs. Thrale for marrying Piozzi; he was a very handsome, gentlemanly, and amiable person, and made her a very good husband. In the evening he used to play to us most beautifully on the piano. Her daughters never would see her after that marriage; and (poor woman) when she was at a very great age, I have heard her say that "she would go down upon her knees to them, if they would only be reconciled to her." —ROGERS, SAMUEL, 1855, *Recollections of Table-Talk, ed. Dyce, p.* 45.

She was a woman of great vivacity and independence of character. She had a sensitive and passionate, if not a very tender nature, and enough literary culture to appreciate Johnson's intellectual power, and on occasion to play a very respectable part in conversation. She had far more Latin and English scholarship than fell to the lot of most ladies of her day, and wit enough to preserve her from degenerating like some of the "blues," into that most offensive of beings—a feminine prig.— STEPHEN, LESLIE, 1879, *Samuel Johnson, (English Men of Letters), p.* 81.

The public sentiment of Great Britain has never got over the sense of outrage it experienced when it was discovered that the widow of an English brewer had actually had the audacity to take for her second husband an Italian music master.—LOUNSBURY, THOMAS R., 1892, *The Nation, vol.* 54, *p.* 415.

GENERAL

Two days ago appeared Madame Piozzi's "Anecdotes of Dr. Johnson."—I am lamentably disappointed—in her, I mean; not in him. I had conceived a favourable opinion of her capacity. But this new book is wretched; a high-varnished preface to a heap of rubbish, in a very vulgar style, and too void of method even for such a farrago. Her panegyric is loud in praise of her hero; and almost every fact she relates disgraces him.—WALPOLE, HORACE, 1786, *To Sir Horace Mann, March* 28; *Letters, ed. Cunningham, vol.* IX, *p.* 46.

See Thrale's grey widow with a satchel roam.
And bring in pomp laborious nothings home.
—GIFFORD, WILLIAM, 1797, *The Baviad and Mœviad.*

Read the first volume of Mrs. Piozzi's "Travels in Italy." Tolerably amusing, but for a pert flippancy and ostentation of learning. — GREEN, THOMAS, 1810, *Diary of a Lover of Literature.*

Her mind, despite her masculine acquirements, was thoroughly feminine, she had more tact than genius, more sensibility and quickness of perception than depth, comprehensiveness, or continuity of thought. But her very discursiveness prevented her from becoming wearisome; her varied knowledge supplied an inexhaustible store of topics and illustrations; her lively fancy placed them in attractive lights; and her mind has been well likened to a kaleidoscope which, whenever its glittering and heterogeneous contents are moved or shaken, surprises by some new combination of color or of form. She professed to write as she talked; but her conversation was doubtless better than her books; her main advantages being a well-stored memory, fertility of images, aptness of allusion, and *apropos.*—HAYWARD, A., 1861, *ed., Autobiography, Letters and Literary Remains of Mrs. Piozzi (Thrale), p.* 155.

There were no morbid sensibilities in Mrs. Piozzi's composition. She can tell all her sorrows without ever a tear. A mark of exclamation looks better than a blot. And yet she had suffered; but it had been with such suffering as makes the soul hard rather than tender. The pages with which she ends this narrative of her life are curiously characteristic.—NORTON, CHARLES ELIOT, 1861, *Original Memorials of Mrs. Piozzi, Atlantic Monthly, vol.* 7, *p.* 621.

She was a minute and clever observer of men and manners, but deficient in judgment, and not particular as to the accuracy of her relations. — CHAMBERS, ROBERT, 1876, *Cyclopædia of English Literature, ed. Carruthers.*

Of Mrs. Piozzi's verses, by far the best-known and best-written are to be found in "The Three Warnings," a tale so neatly told that Johnson was credited by some with a share in its production. There never was any real reason for thus robbing the authoress of credit, and even Boswell writes that he "cannot withhold from Mrs. Thrale the praise of being the author of that admirable poem, 'The Three Warnings.'" The piece first appeared along with Johnson's fairy-tale called "The Fountains," in the "Miscellanies" published by Mrs. Williams in 1766.— ROBERTSON, ERIC S., 1883, *English Poetesses, p.* 60.

Mrs Piozzi wrote wittily, describing scenes vividly, relating anecdotes with humor and point, never allowing her English prejudices to interfere with her judgment or to spoil her enjoyment of the scenes so new to her. Her knowledge of Italian must have been very thorough, she detected so readily the slightest differences in the dialect of each of the cities she visited. Her book remains a most valuable record of Italian society in the eighteenth century. It is delightfully written, and leaves an impression of extreme accuracy. It still remains for our nineteenth century to produce a book which will read as well a hundred years hence. — STILLMAN, M. S., 1892, *Mrs. Piozzi in Italy, The Nation, vol.* 54, *p.* 343.

Mrs. Elizabeth Inchbald

1753–1821.

Born [Elizabeth Simpson], at Stanningfield, Suffolk, 15 Oct. 1753. Left home in April 1772, with intention of going on the London stage. Married to Joseph Inchbald, 9 June 1772. First appeared on the stage at Bristol, 4 Sept. 1772. Acting with her husband in Scotland, 1772–76. In Paris, July to Sept. 1776. Acting with her husband in England, 1776–79; he died, suddenly, 6 June 1779. Friendship with Mrs. Siddons and J. P. Kemble. Continued to act at York till 1780. At Covent Garden, Oct. 1780 to July 1782; at Haymarket, July to Sept, 1782; in Dublin, Nov. 1782 to spring of 1783; returned to Covent Garden, 1783. Play, "The Mogul Tale," produced at Haymarket, 1784. Plays produced at Haymarket, Covent Garden, and Drury Lane, 1784–1805. Contrib. to "Edinburgh Review." Retired from stage, 1789. Died, at Kensington House, 1 Aug 1821. Buried in Kensington Churchyard. *Works:* "Appearance is against them" (anon.), 1785; "I'll Tell you What," 1786; "The Widow's Vow" (anon.), 1786; "The Mogul Tale" (anon.), 1788; "Such Things Are," 1788 (2nd edn. same year); "The Midnight Hour" (from the French of Damaniant), 1787; "The Child of Nature" (from the French of Countess de Genlis), 1788; "Animal

Magnetism" (anon.), 1788; "The Married Man" (from the French of Néricault-Destouches), 1789; "Next Door Neighbours," 1791; "A Simple Story" (4 vols), 1791; "Everyone has his Fault," 1793; "The Wedding Day," 1794; "Nature and Art" (2 vols), 1796; "Wives as they Were, and Maids as they Are," 1797; "Lovers' Vows" (from the German of Kotzebue), 1798; "The Wise Men of the East" (from the German of Kotzebue), 1799; "To Marry or Not to Marry," 1805. She *edited:* "The British Theatre" (25 vols.), 1808; "The Modern Theatre" (10 vols), 1811; "A Collection of Farces" (7 vols.), 1815; and contributed "remarks" to plays by Addison, Cibber, Colman, Lillo, Machlin, Norton, Otway, Rowe, Shakespeare, Southerne, Thomson. *Life:* "Memoirs," by J. Boaden (2 vols.), 1833.—SHARP, R. FARQUHARSON, 1897, *A Dictionary of English Authors, p.* 144.

PERSONAL

Gloria in Excelsis Deo.
Sacred to the Memory
of
ELIZABETH INCHBALD,
Whose writings will be cherished
While truth, simplicity and feeling
Command public admiration :
And whose retired and exemplary life
Closed, as it existed,
In acts of charity and benevolence.
She died August 1st, 1821, aged 68 years,
Requiescat in Pace.
—INSCRIPTION ON GRAVE, 1821, *Kensington Churchyard.*

She was in truth a figure that could not be seen without astonishment at its loveliness—tall, slender, straight, of the purest complexion and most beautiful features. Her hair of a golden auburn, her eyes full at once of spirit and sweetness; a combination of delicacy that checked presumption and interest that captivated the fancy.
—BOADEN, JAMES, 1833, *ed., Memoirs and Correspondence of Mrs. Inchbald.*

At all times Mrs. Inchbald seems to have determined to retain her perfect independence, and to have chosen to have her time and property at her own disposal. She had an enthusiastic love of home, although that home was often, indeed generally, only a single, or at most a couple of rooms up two or three pairs of stairs, occasionally in the attic, where she was waited on by the servant of the house, or sometimes not waited on at all, for she not unfrequently speaks of fetching her own water, and dressing her own dinner; and she once kept a coroneted carriage waiting whilst she finished scouring her apartment. . . . At one time she took up her abode in a boarding-house; but she could not, she said, when there, command her appetite and be hungry at stated periods, like the rest of the boarders;

so she generally returned to her attic, her crust of bread, and liberty.—ELWOOD, MRS. A. K., 1842, *Memoirs of the Literary Ladies of England from the Commencement of the Last Century, vol.* I.

Living in mean lodgings, dressed with an economy allied to penury, without connections, and alone, her beauty, her talents, and the charm of her manners gave her entrance into a delightful circle of society. Apt to fall in love, and desirous to marry, she continued single, because the men who loved and admired her were too worldly to take an actress and a poor author, however lovely and charming for a wife. Her life was thus spent in an interchange of hardship and amusement, privation and luxury. Her character partook of the same contrast: fond of pleasure, she was prudent in her conduct; penurious in her personal expenditure, she was, generous to others. Vain of her beauty, we are told that the gown she wore was not worth a shilling, it was so coarse and shabby. Very susceptible to the softer feelings, she could yet guard herself against passion; and though she might have been called a flirt, her character was unimpeached. I have heard that a rival beauty of her day pettishly complained that when Mrs. Inchbald came into a room, and sat in a chair in the middle of it as was her wont, every man gathered round it, and it was vain for any other woman to attempt to gain attention. Godwin could not fail to admire her: she became and continued to be a favourite. Her talents, her beauty, her manners, were all delightful to him He used to describe her as a piquante mixture between a lady and a milkmaid, and added that Sheridan declared she was the only authoress whose society pleased him.—SHELLEY, MARY WOLLSTONECRAFT, 1851, *Fragmentary Notes, Paul's Life of Godwin, vol.* I, *p.* 73.

She was very beautiful, and gifted with

original genius, as her plays and farces and novels (above all, the "Simple Story") testify; she was not an actress of any special merit, but of respectable mediocrity. She stuttered habitually, but her delivery was never impeded by this defect on the stage. . . . Mrs Inchbald was a person of a very remarkable character, lovely, poor, with unusual mental powers, and of irreproachable conduct. . . . Mrs. Inchbald had a singular uprightness and unworldliness, and a childlike directness and simplicity of manner, which, combined with her personal loveliness, and halting, broken utterance, gave to her conversation, which was both humorous and witty, a most peculiar and comical charm.—KEMBLE, FRANCES ANN, 1879, *Records of a Girlhood, pp.* 212, 213.

Elizabeth Inchbald was an admirable woman, a heroine in her way, not, indeed, after the manner of Miss Pinkerton, the Semiramis of Hammersmith, but a warm, human personality, all the more lovable for some feminine foibles. She was an actress and authoress of no mean celebrity, she attained competency and fame, but the thought that remains with us, as we rise from the perusal of her diary and "Memoirs," is how ill fame and fortune supply the want of love in a woman's life, what a void they still leave unsatisfied; yet the prevailing note in her life is of cheerfulness and bright vivacity.—MANSON, EDWARD, 1897, *Elizabeth Inchbald, The Westminster Review, vol.* 148, *p.* 346.

A SIMPLE STORY
1791

But there were no "Waverly Novels" in those days, no Jane Austen, no Maria Edgeworth; and the "Simple Story" was highly prized by its contemporaries. . . . But nobody now-a-days suggests of a female novelist that "it is as if Venus had written books." The reader will remember how this Venus wrote to Godwin when his wife lay yet unburied.—OLIPHANT, MARGARET O. W., 1882, *The Literary History of England, XVIIIth-XIXth Century, vol.* II, *p.* 227.

The "Simple Story," appeared in February and a second edition was ordered in March. It has become a classic, and nothing need here be said in praise of its pathos, its knowledge of human nature, and the epigrammatic touches in which it abounds. The novel brought her not only

money and fame, but a flock of new friends. . . . In literature, as in life, it is not always the most famous or distinguished persons that are the most interesting. Elizabeth Inchbald cannot claim high rank in the former class, but her character, her letters, and her "Simple Story" leave her with few rivals in the latter.—MAYER, GERTRUDE TOWNSHEND, 1894, *Women of Letters, vol.* II, *pp.* 32, 58.

Built upon the unpromising motive of displaying "the improper education of the unthinking Miss Milner" is a powerful picture of passion, even prophetic of "Jane Eyre" than any other English novel of the eighteenth century.—HERFORD, C. H., 1897, *The Age of Wordsworth, p.* 101.

Though marred by the author's anxiety to attribute to the influence of early education the gradual moral decay of her heroine, it contains the strongest situation that had yet appeared in the English novel—the conflict between religious prejudice and love, such as we have on a grander scale in Charles Reade's "Cloister and the Hearth."—CROSS, WILBUR L., 1899, *The Development of the English Novel, p.* 87.

GENERAL

If Mrs. Radcliffe touched the trembling chords of the imagination, making wild music there, Mrs Inchbald has no less power over the spring of the heart. She not only moves the affections, but melts us into "all the luxury of woe." Her "Nature and Art" is one of the most pathetic and interesting stories in the world. It is indeed too much so; the distress is too naked, and the situation hardly to be borne with patience.—HAZLITT, WILLIAM, 1818, *Lecture on the English Novelists.*

As a dramatist, she is distinguished for a certain ingenuity and vivacity of dialogue; her wit however is infrequent, and the intrigues of her comedies often present the unnatural combinations of farce. Her plays, with few exceptions, still retain the stage. Her talents as a novelist were by no means inferior; and had she devoted her whole attention to this department of literature she would undoubtedly have produced works of lasting celebrity.—DURIVAGE, F. A., 1833, *Memoirs of Mrs. Inchbald, North American Review vol.* 37, *p.* 466.

In 1789, when she retired from the

stage, her reputation was at its highest. She had published an edition of plays with prefaces, and now she got fifty guineas by merely looking over a catalogue of fifty farces, drawing her pen across one or two, and writing the names of others in their places. The catalogue was then printed with "SELECTED BY MRS. INCHBALD" on the title-page.—HAMILTON, CATHARINE J., 1892, *Women Writers, First Series*, p. 41.

The scene where William [in "Nature and Art"], as a judge, condemns to death the girl he had deceived and deserted is great, not from the boisterous strength of the situation, but from the strength of its telling. That and the character of Miss Milner in "A Simple Story" entitled Mrs. Inchbald to a very high place among the novelists proper of her day.—RALEIGH, WALTER, 1894, *The English Novel*, p. 248.

Percy Bysshe Shelley
1792-1822

Born, at Field Place, near Horsham, Sussex, 4 Aug. 1792. Educated privately, 1798-1802; at a school at Brentford, 1802-04; at Eton, July 1804 to 1809. Wrote poetry while at Eton. Matric., University Coll., Oxford, 10 April 1810. Expelled (with Hogg) from Oxford for publication of "The Necessity of Atheism," 25 March 1811. Married (i.) Harriet Westbrook, 28 Aug. 1811. Lived for a few weeks with Hogg in Edinburgh; thence to Keswick, Nov. 1811. Friendship formed there with Southey. Friendship with Godwin begun, Jan. 1812. In Dublin, spring of 1812; at Lynmouth, June to Sept. 1812; in Carnarvonshire, Sept. 1812 to Feb. 1813; in Ireland, Feb. to April 1813; to London, April 1813. Removed to Bracknell, July 1813; in Edinburgh, winter 1813-14; returned to Bracknell, spring of 1814. On account of his having been married in Scotland as a minor, he remarried his wife in London, 24 March 1814. Estrangement from his wife, and meeting with Mary Godwin, 1814. To Continent with Mary Godwin, 28 July 1814; returned with her to England, Sept. 1814. Friendship with Byron begun, 1816. At Geneva with him, summer of 1816. Mrs. Shelley committed suicide, Dec. 1816. He married (ii.) Mary Godwin, 30 Dec. 1816; settled with her at Marlow, spring of 1817. Friendship with Keats begun, 1817. Removed to Italy, March 1818. Drowned, 8 July 1822. His body cremated on the shore near Via Reggio, 16 Aug. 1822. His ashes buried in old Protestant Cemetery, Rome, Dec. 1822. *Works:* "Zastrozzi" (under initials: P. B. S.), 1810; "Original Poetry: by Victor and Cazire" (no copy known [?]), 1810; "Posthumous Fragments of Margaret Nicholson," 1810 (priv. ptd., ed. by H. B. Forman, 1877); "St. Irvyne" (anon.), 1811; "Poetical Essay on the Existing State of Things," 1811; "The Necessity of Atheism," 1811; "An Address to the Irish People," 1812; "Proposals for an Association," 1812; "Declaration of Rights," 1812; "Letters to Lord Ellenborough" [1812]; "The Devil's Walk," 1812; "Queen Mab," 1813; "A Vindication of Natural Diet" (anon.), 1813; "A Refutation of Deism" (anon.), 1814; "Alastor," 1816; "Proposal for putting reform to the Vote" (anon.), 1817; "History of a Six Weeks' Tour through a Part of France" (with his wife; anon.), 1817; "Laon and Cythna," 1818 [1817] (recalled; and reissued as "The Revolt of Islam," 1817); "Address to the People on the Death of Princess Charlotte" [1818]; "Rosalind and Helen," 1819; "The Cenci," 1819; "Prometheus Unbound," 1820; "Œdipus Tyrannus" (anon.), 1820; "Epipsychidion" (anon.), 1821; "Adonais," 1821; "Hellas," 1822. *Posthumous:* "Posthumous Poems," ed. by Mrs. Shelley [1824]; "The Masque of Anarchy," ed. by Leigh Hunt, 1832; "The Shelley Papers" (from "Athenæum") 1833; "Essays, etc.," ed. by Mrs. Shelley, 1840; "The Dæmon of the World," ed. by H. B. Forman (priv. ptd.), 1876; "Notes on Sculptures in Rome and Florence" (ed. by H. B. Forman; priv. ptd.), 1879. *Collected Works;* ed. by H. Buxton Forman (8 vols.), 1880 [1876-80]. *Life:* by Prof. Dowden, 1886.— SHARP, R. FARQUHARSON, 1897, *A Dictionary of English Authors*, p. 254.

PERSONAL

I went to Godwin's. Mr. Shelley was there. I had never seen him before. His youth and a resemblance to Southey, particularly in his voice, raised a pleasing impression, which was not altogether destroyed by his conversation, though it is vehement, and arrogant, and intolerant.

44 C

He was very abusive towards Southey, whom he spoke of as having sold himself to the Court. And this he maintained with the usual party slang. . . . Shelley spoke of Wordsworth with less bitterness, but with an insinuation of his insincerity, etc.—ROBINSON, HENRY CRABB, 1817, *Diary, Nov. 6.*

Midst others of less note, came one frail
   Form,
A phantom among men, companionless
As the last cloud of an expiring storm
Whose thunder is its knell; he, as I guess,
Had gazed on Nature's naked loveliness,
Actæon-like, and now he fled astray
With feeble steps o'er the world's wilderness,
And his own thoughts, along that rugged way
Pursued, like raging hounds, their father
   and their prey.
.   .   .   .
He came at last, neglected and apart;
A herd-abandoned deer struck by the hunter's
   dart,
All stood aloof.
—SHELLEY, PERCY BYSSHE, 1821, *Adonais, st.* xxxi, xxxiii, xxxiv.

The author of the "Prometheus Unbound," has a fire in his eye, a fever in his blood, a maggot in his brain, a hectic flutter in his speech, which mark out the philosophic fanatic. He is sanguine-complexioned, and shrill-voiced. As is often observable in the case of religious enthusiasts, there is a slenderness of constitutional stamina, which renders the flesh no match for the spirit. His bending, flexible form appears to take no strong hold of things, does not grapple with the world about him, but slides from it like a river,—
"And in its liquid texture mortal wound
Receives no more than can the fluid air."
—HAZLITT, WILLIAM, 1821, *On Paradox and the Commonplace, Table-Talk, p.* 355.

I cannot grieve for you, beloved Shelley! I grieve for thy friends—for the world—for thy child—most for myself, enthroned in thy love, growing wiser and better beneath thy gentle influence, taught by you the highest philosophy—your pupil, friend, lover, wife, mother of your children! The glory of the dream is gone. I am a cloud from which the light of sunset has passed. Give me patience in the present struggle. *Meum codium cor!* Good-night!
"I would give
All that I am to be as thou now art;
But I am chain'd to time, and cannot thence
   depart."
—SHELLEY, MARY GODWIN, 1823, *Journal, May* 31.

Ten years ago the indiscretions of Shelley had rendered his name an unmentionable one to ears polite.—MADDEN, R. R., 1833, *Infirmities of Genius, vol.* I, *p.* 5.

Jackson talks much of Shelley. He knew him well; says that he was a perfect child in his habits. He remembers Shelley telling him how fine a death he thought it would be to be shipwrecked in the bay of Spezzia. Poor lad! He learned to know too well.—APPLETON, THOMAS GOLD, 1834, *Life and Letters, p.* 194.

"You should have known Shelley," said Byron, "to feel how much I must regret him. He was the most gentle, most amiable, and *least* worldly-minded person I ever met; full of delicacy, disinterested beyond all other men, and possessing a degree of genius, joined to a simplicity as rare as it is admirable. He had formed to himself a *beau-idéal* of all that is fine, high-minded, and noble, and he acted up to this ideal even to the very letter. He had a most brilliant imagination, but a total want of worldly wisdom. I have seen nothing like him, and never shall again, I am certain. I never can forget the night that his poor wife rushed into my room at Pisa, with a face as pale as marble, and terror impressed on her brow, demanding, with all the tragic impetuosity of grief and alarm, where was her husband? Vain were all our efforts to calm her; a desperate sort of courage seemed to give her energy to confront the horrible truth that awaited her; it was the courage of despair. I have seen nothing in tragedy or on the stage so powerful, or so affecting, as her appearance; and it often presents itself to my memory. I knew nothing then of the catastrophe, but the vividness of her terror communicated itself to me, and I feared the worst,—which fears were, alas! too soon fearfully realized."
—BLESSINGTON, MARGUERITE COUNTESS, 1834, *Conversations with Lord Byron, ch.* iv.

The qualities that struck any one newly introduced to Shelley, were,—First, a gentle and cordial goodness that animated his intercourse with warm affection and helpful sympathy. The other, the eagerness and ardour with which he was attached to the cause of human happiness and improvement; and the fervent eloquence with which he discussed subjects.

His conversation was marked by its happy abundance, and the beautiful language with which he clothed his poetic ideas and philosophical notions. To defecate life of its misery and its evil was the ruling passion of his soul : he dedicated to it every power of his mind, every pulsation of his heart. He looked on political freedom as the direct agent to affect the happiness of mankind ; and thus any new-sprung hope of liberty inspired a joy and an exultation more intense than he could have felt for any personal advantage.—SHELLEY, MARY GODWIN, 1839, *Shelley's Poetical Works, Preface.*

Possessing one of the most richly gifted minds ever framed by Providence to adorn and bless the world, and a heart whose sympathies comprehended all nature and mankind in the broad sphere of its love, he was still the most unpopular poet of his time—although he indicated, perhaps, more than any other, the tendencies of its imaginative literature, and expressed with more fulness, precision, and beauty, the subtle spirituality of its tone of thought. His character and his writings were elaborately misrepresented. Persons infinitely inferior to him, we will not say in genius, but in honesty, in benevolence, in virtue, in the practice of those duties of love and self-sacrifice which religion enjoins, still contrived to experience for him a mingled feeling of pity and aversion, unexampled even in the annals of the Pharisees. The same sympathizing apologists for the infirmities of ,genius, who shed tears and manufactured palliatives for Burns and Byron, fell back on the rigor and ice of their morality when they mentioned the name of Shelley. His adversaries were often in ludicrous moral contrast to himself. Venal politicians, fattening on public plunder, represented themselves as shocked by his theories of government. Roués were apprehensive that his refined notions of marriage would encourage libertinism. Smooth, practical atheists preached morality and religion to him from quarterly reviews, and defamed him with an arrogant stupidity, and a sneaking injustice, unparalleled in the effronteries and fooleries of criticism. That pure and pious poet, Thomas Moore, conceived it incumbent on himself to warn his immaculate friend Lord Byron, from being led astray by Shelley's principles.

. . . Men who could not write a single sentence unstained with malignity, selfishness or some other deadly sin, gravely rebuked him for infidelity, and volunteered their advice as to the manner by which he might become a bad christian and a good hypocrite. But Shelley happened to be an honest man as well as a poet, and was better contented with proscription, however severe, than with infamy, however splendid. This was a peculiarity of his disposition which made his conduct so enigmatical to the majority of his enemies. —WHIPPLE, EDWIN P., 1845, *English Poets of the Nineteenth Century, Essays and Reviews.*

Can we imagine the case of an angel touched by lunacy? Have we ever seen the spectacle of a human intellect, exquisite by its functions of creation, yet in one chamber of its shadowy house already ruined before the light of manhood had cleansed its darkness? Such an angel, such a man—if ever such there were—such a lunatic angel, such a ruined man, was Shelley whilst yet standing on the earliest threshold of life. . . . Something of a similar effect arises to myself when reviewing the general abstract of Shelley's life—so brief, so full of agitation, so full of strife. When one thinks of the early misery which he suffered, and of the insolent infidelity which, being yet so young, he wooed with a lover's passion, then the darkness of midnight begins to form a deep, impenetrable background, upon which the phantasmagoria of all that is to come may arrange itself in troubled phosphoric streams, and in sweeping processions of woe. Yet, again, when one recurs to his gracious nature, his fearlessness, his truth, his purity from all fleshliness of appetite, his freedom from vanity, his diffusive love and tenderness, suddenly out of the darkness reveals itself a morning of May, forests and thickets of roses advance to the foreground, and from the midst of them looks out "the eternal child," cleansed from his sorrow, radiant with joy, having power given him to forget the misery which he suffered, power given him to forget the misery which he caused, and leaning with his heart upon that dove-like faith against which his erring intellect had rebelled.—DE QUINCEY, THOMAS, 1845–57, *Gilfillan's Literary Portraits, Works,* ed. *Masson, vol.* XI, *pp.* 358, 376.

Innocent and careless as a boy, he possessed all the delicate feelings of a gentleman, all the discrimination of a scholar, and united, in just degrees, the ardor of the poet with the patience and forbearance of the philosopher. His generosity and charity went far beyond those of any man (I believe) at present in existence. He was never known to speak evil of any enemy, unless that enemy had done some grievous injustice to another; and he divided his income of only one thousand pounds with the fallen and the afflicted. This is the man against whom such clamors have been raised by the religious and the loyal, and by those who live and lap under their tables.—LANDOR, WALTER SAVAGE, 1846, *Imaginary Conversations.*

Shelley, indeed, was a good and noble creature. He had, spite of his skepticism, clearly and luminously stamped on his front the highest marks of a Christian; for the grand distinction appointed by Christ was—love. Shelley was a Christian in spite of himself. We learn from all who knew him that the Bible was his most favorite book. He venerated the character of Christ, and no man more fully carried out his precepts. His delight was to do good, to comfort and assist the poor. It was his zeal for truth and for the good of mankind which led him, in his indignation against those who oppressed them and imposed upon them, to leap too far in his attack on those enemies, and pass the borders which divide truth from error. For his conscientious opinion he sacrificed ease, honor, the world's esteem, fortune, and friendship. Never was there so generous a friend, so truly and purely poetical a nature. Others are poets in their books and closets; the poet's soul in him was the spirit of all hours and all occasions.— HOWITT, WILLIAM, 1846, *Homes and Haunts of the Most Eminent British Poets.*

His features were small—the upper part of his face not strictly regular—the eyes unusually prominent, too much so for beauty. His mouth was moulded after the finest modelling of Greek art, and wore an habitual expression of benevolence, and when he smiled, his smile irradiated his whole countenance. His hands were thin, and expressed feeling to the fingers' ends; . . . his hair, profuse, silken, and naturally curling, was at a very early period interspersed with gray. . . .

He did not look so tall as he was, being nearly five feet eleven, for his shoulders were a little bent by study. . . . owing to his being near-sighted, and leaning over his books, and which increased the narrowness of his chest.—MEDWIN, THOMAS, 1847, *The Life of Percy Bysshe Shelley.*

Shelley, when he died, was in his thirtieth year. His figure was tall and slight, and his constitution consumptive. He was subject to violent spasmodic pains, which would sometimes force him to lie on the ground till they were over; but he had always a kind word to give to those about him, when his pangs allowed him to speak. . . . Though well-turned, his shoulders were bent a little, owing to premature thought and trouble. The same causes had touched his hair with gray; and though his habits of temperance and exercise gave him a remarkable degree of strength, it is not supposed that he could have lived many years. . . . His eyes were large and animated, with a dash of wildness in them; his face small, but well-shaped, particularly his mouth and chin, the turn of which was very sensitive and graceful. His complexion was naturally fair and delicate, with a color in the cheeks. He had brown hair which, though tinged with gray, surmounted his face well, being inconsiderable in quantity, and tending to a curl. His side-face upon the whole was deficient in strength, and his features would not have told well in a bust; but when fronting and looking at you attentively, his aspect had a certain seraphical character that would have suited John the Baptist, or the angel whom Milton describes as holding a reed "tipt with fire." —HUNT, LEIGH, 1850, *Autobiography.*

Shelley's figure was tall and almost unnaturally attenuated, so as to bend to the earth like a plant that had been deprived of its vital air; his features had an unnatural sharpness, and an unhealthy paleness, like a flower that has been kept from the light of day; his eyes had an almost superhuman brightness, and his voice a preternatural elevation of pitch and shrillness of tone;—all which peculiarities probably arose from some accidental circumstances connected with his early nurture and bringing up.—PATMORE, PETER GEORGE, 1854, *My Friends and Acquaintances.*

Both in appearance and in manners Shelley was the perfect gentleman.— ROGERS, SAMUEL, 1855, *Recollections of Table-Talk, ed. Dyce, p.* 236.

Brown's four novels, Schiller's "Robbers," and Goethe's "Faust," were, of all the works with which he was familiar, those which took the deepest root in his mind, and had the strongest influence in the formation of his character. He was an assiduous student of the great classical poets, and among these his favourite heroines were Nausicaa and Antigone. I do not remember that he greatly admired any of our old English poets, excepting Shakspeare and Milton. He devotedly admired Wordsworth and Coleridge, and in a minor degree Southey: these had great influence on his style, and Coleridge especially on his imagination; but admiration is one thing and assimilation is another; and nothing so blended itself with the structure of his interior mind as the creations of Brown. Nothing stood so clearly before his thoughts as a perfect combination of the purely ideal and possibly real, as Constantia Dudley. . . . He had a prejudice against theatres which I took some pains to overcome. I induced him one evening to accompany me to a representation of the "School for Scandal." When, after the scenes which exhibited Charles Surface in his jollity, the scene returned, in the fourth act, to Joseph's library, Shelley said to me,—"I see the purpose of this comedy. It is to associate virtue with bottles and glasses, and villainy with books." I had great difficulty to make him stay to the end. He often talked of "the withering and perverting spirit of comedy." I do not think he ever went to another.—PEACOCK, THOMAS LOVE, 1858, *Memoirs of Percy Bysshe Shelley, Fraser's Magazine, vol.* 57, *pp.* 657, 658.

After the fire was well kindled we repeated the ceremony of the previous day; and more wine was poured over Shelley's dead body than he had consumed during his life. This with the oil and salt made the yellow flames glisten and quiver. The heat from the sun and fire was so intense that the atmosphere was tremulous and wavy. The corpse fell open and the heart was laid bare. The frontal bone of the skull, where it had been struck with the mattock, fell off; and, as the back of the head rested on the redhot bottom bars of the furnace, the brains literally seethed, bubbled, and boiled, as in a cauldron, for a very long time. Byron could not face this scene, he withdrew to the beach and swam off to the *Bolivar.* Leigh Hunt remained in the carriage. The fire was so fierce as to produce a white heat on the iron, and to reduce its contents to grey ashes. The only portions that were not consumed were some fragments of bones, the jaw, and the skull; but what surprised us all was that the heart remained entire. In snatching this relic from the fiery furnace, my hand was severely burnt; and had any one seen me do the act I should have been put into quarantine. — TRELAWNY, EDWARD JOHN, 1858–78, *Records of Shelley, Byron and the Author, p.* 144.

At the commencement of Michaelmas term, that is, at the end of October, in the year 1810, I happened one day to sit next to a freshman at dinner; it was his first appearance in hall. His figure was slight, and his aspect remarkably youthful, even at our table, where all were very young. He seemed thoughtful and absent. He ate little, and had no acquaintance with any one. . . . His figure was slight and fragile, and yet his bones and joints were large and strong. He was tall, but he stooped so much, that he seemed of a low stature. His clothes were expensive, and made according to the most approved mode of the day; but they were tumbled, rumpled, unbrushed. His gestures were abrupt, and sometimes violent, occasionally even awkward, yet more frequently gentle and graceful. His complexion was delicate and almost feminine, of the purest red and white; yet he was tanned and freckled by exposure to the sun, having passed the autumn, as he said, in shooting. His features, his whole face, and particularly his head, were, in fact, unusually small; yet the last *appeared* of a remarkable bulk, for his hair was long and bushy, and in fits of absence, and in the agonies (if I may use the word) of anxious thought, he often rubbed it fiercely with his hands, or passed his fingers quickly through his locks unconsciously, so that it was singularly wild and rough. . . . His features were not symmetrical (the mouth, perhaps, excepted), yet was the effect of the whole extremely powerful. They breathed an animation, a fire, an enthusiasm, a vivid and preternatural intelligence, that I never met with in any other countenance. Nor was the moral expression less beautiful than the intellectual; for there was a softness, a delicacy, a gentleness, and especially (though this will surprise many) that air of profound religious veneration, that characterises the best works, and chiefly the frescoes (and into these they infused their whole souls), of the great masters of Florence and of Rome.—HOGG, THOMAS JEFFERSON, 1858, *The Life of Percy Bysshe Shelley*, *vol.* I, *pp.* 51, 54, 55.

The ashes of Shelley were deposited in the Protestant burial ground at Rome, by the side of his son William, and of his brother-poet Keats. An inscription in Latin, simply setting forth the facts, was written by Leigh Hunt, and Mr. Trelawny added a few lines from Shakspeare's "Tempest" (one of Shelley's favorite plays):—

"Nothing of him that doth fade,
But doth suffer a sea-change
Into something rich and strange."

The same gentleman also planted eight cypresses round the spot, of which seven were flourishing in 1844, and probably are still. And so the sea and the earth closed over one who was great as a poet, and still greater as a philanthropist; and of whom it may be said, that his wild, spiritual character, seems to have fitted him for being thus snatched from life under circumstances of mingled terror and beauty, while his powers were yet in their spring freshness, and age had not come to render the ethereal body decrepit, or to wither the heart which could not be consumed by fire.—SHELLEY, LADY, 1859, *ed. Shelley Memorials from Authentic Sources, p.* 219.

Shelley was a tall man,—nearly, if not quite, five feet ten in height. He was peculiarly slender, and . . . his chest had palpably enlarged after the usual growing period. He retained the same kind of straitness in the perpendicular outline on each side of him; his shoulders were the reverse of broad, but yet they were not sloping, and a certain squareness in them was naturally incompatible with anything feminine in his appearance. To his last days he still suffered his chest to collapse; but it was less a stoop than a peculiar mode of holding the head and shoulders,—the face thrown a little

forward, and the shoulders slightly elevated; though the whole attitude below the shoulders, when standing, was unusually upright, and had the appearance of litheness and activity. . . . He had an oval face and delicate features, not unlike those given to him in the well known miniature. His forehead was high. His fine, dark brown hair, when not cut close, disposed itself in playful and very beautiful curls over his brows and round the back of his neck. He had brown eyes, with a color in his cheek "like a girl's;" but as he grew older, his complexion bronzed. So far the reality agrees with the current descriptions; nevertheless they omit material facts. The outline of the features and face possessed a firmness and *hardness* entirely inconsistent with a feminine character. The outline was sharp and firm; the markings distinct, and indicating an energetic *physique*. The outline of the bone was distinctly perceptible at the temples, on the bridge of the nose, at the back portion of the cheeks, and in the jaw, and the artist could trace the principal muscles of the face. The beard, also, although the reverse of strong, was clearly marked, especially about the chin.— HUNT, THORNTON, 1863, *Shelley*, *Atlantic Monthly, vol.* 11, *pp.* 202, 203.

The lovers of Shelley as a man and a poet have done what they could to palliate his conduct in this matter. But a question of morals, as between man and society, cannot be reduced to any individual standard however exalted. Our partiality for the man only heightens our detestation of the error. The greater Shelley's genius, the nobler his character and impulses, so much the more startling is the warning. If we make our own inclinations the measure of what is right, we must be the sterner in curbing them. A woman's heart is too delicate a thing to serve as a fulcrum for the lever with which a man would overturn any system, however conventional. The misery of the elective-affinity scheme is that men are not chemical substances, and that in nine cases in ten the force of the attraction works more constantly and lasting upon the woman than the man.—NORTON, CHARLES ELIOT, 1865, *Shelley's Poetical Works, Memoir.*

Poor Shelley—gentle, tender, ethereal, and aspiring, sober and abstemious, a pale student, an abstract and highly metaphysical thinker, delicate as a woman in his organization, sensitive as a woman in his sympathies, loathing all that was coarse and low with a woman's shrinking, detesting all field-sports as barbarous and brutal.—GREG, W. R., 1873, *Kingsley and Carlyle, Literary and Social Judgments*, p. 131.

A more crystalline heart than Shelley's has rarely throbbed in human bosom. He was incapable of an untruth, or of deceit in any form. . . . Shelley's figure was a little above the middle height, slender, and of delicate construction, which appeared the rather from a lounging or waving manner in his gait, as though his frame was compounded barely of muscle and tendon; and that the power of walking was an achievement with him and not a natural habit. Yet I should suppose that he was not a valetudinarian, although that has been said of him on account of his spare and vegetable diet: for I have the remembrance of his scampering and bounding over the gorse-bushes on Hampstead Heath late one night,—now close upon us, and now shouting from the height like a wild school-boy. He was both an active and an enduring walker—feats which do not accompany an ailing and feeble constitution. His face was round, flat, pale, with small features; mouth beautifully shaped; hair bright brown and wavy; and such a pair of eyes as are rarely in the human or any other head,—intensely blue, with a gentle and lambent expression, yet wonderfully alert and engrossing; nothing appeared to escape his knowledge. Whatever peculiarity there might have been in Shelley's religions faith, I have the best authority for believing that it was confined to the early period of his life. The *practical* result of its course of *action*, I am sure, had its source from the "Sermon on the Mount." There is not one clause in that Divine code which his conduct towards his fellow mortals did not confirm and substantiate him to be—in action a follower of Christ.—CLARKE, CHARLES COWDEN, 1874-78, *Recollections of Writers*, pp. 151, 152.

Of all the poets who have illustrated the Literature of England, there is no one whose life presents so many difficulties to the biographer as Percy Bysshe Shelley. . . . He was one of the most extraordinary men that ever walked the earth, so

extraordinary, I think, that Shakespeare alone could have plucked out the heart of his mystery. He led at all times a dual life, and at most times a life of contradictions. To say that he was eccentric is to say nothing. He was as much out of place in this world as a being of another world would be, and he moved among its men and women like some strange creature of the elements. He neither understood himself, nor was understood by others, or at most by very few. The saintly Byron was warned against him by the clique in Murray's back parlor; but Byron defended him—after he was dead. He had a passion for reforming the world, and the world never wants to be reformed. Of course, it was too strong for him—the many are always too strong for the one. He learned the lesson which he states so tersely:

"Most wretched men
Are cradled into poetry by wrong:
They learn in suffering what they teach in song."

—STODDARD, RICHARD HENRY, 1876, *ed., Anecdote Biography of Percy Bysshe Shelley, Preface*, pp. xiii, xiv.

We must learn to think of Shelley not merely as gentle, dreamy, unworldly, imprudently disinterested, and ideally optimistic—though he was all this—but likewise as swift, prompt, resolute, irascible, strong-limbed and hardy, often very practical in his views of politics, and endowed with preternatural keenness of observation. There is but one formula for combining and harmonizing these apparent discrepancies: he was an elemental force whose essence is simplicity itself, but whose modes of operation are many and various. If we study the divers ways in which those who shared his society have striven to express that which they have felt to be inexpressible, we shall find that in the last analysis all amount to this.— GARNETT, RICHARD, 1878, *Shelley's Last Days, Fortnightly Review, vol.* 29, p. 851.

Hush! From the grave where I so oft
Have stood, 'mid ruined Rome,
I seem to hear a whisper soft
Wafted across the foam;
Bidding justest wrath be still,
Good feel lovingly for ill,
As exiles for rough paths that help them to
their home.

—AUSTIN, ALFRED, 1882, *Soliloquies in Song*, p. 145.

To prove that Shelley as a man was

deficient in passion we need mention one incident only in his life. Some time after his separation from Harriett, he proposed that she should return to him and take up a place as a member of his household, not as his wife, but side by side with the friend for whom she had been abandoned, and who still shared his bed. This extraordinary proposal arose out of the most self-oblivious generosity, but what a commentary it affords on Shelley's masculinity! The man who had no more acute sense than this implies of the beautiful relation of the sexes that is determined by healthy nature may have had the noblest heart, but he was deficient in one attribute. And the fractious men contemporary with him felt this in some uncertain way, though they could not realize it, and their slanderous accusations of licentiousness were the inapt and shameful speech in which their vague feeling expressed itself.—CAINE, HALL, 1883, *Cobwebs of Criticism, p.* 229.

Shelley, however free his theories, was a person on whose imagination a licentious image had never left a stain.—FROUDE, JAMES ANTHONY, 1883, *A Leaf from the Real Life of Byron, The Nineteenth Century, vol.* 14, *p.* 232.

Whilst Field Place and the Enthusiasts have committed indiscretions. that provoke remonstrance and demand correction, the extreme Shelleyan Socialists have placed his strongest title to social homage, on his courageous avowal of sentiments, that are unutterably distasteful to the great majority of conscientious and right-minded people. When a man is taken from the long roll of our mighty poets, and offered to the world's admiration as a rare example of all the human virtues, it is well for people to examine the grounds of such extraordinary commendation. Now that "Queen Mab," with its anti-matrimonial note, is put into the hands of our boys; now that "Laon and Cythna," with its monstrous doctrine, is seen on our drawing-room tables; now that the author of so reprehensible a book is proclaimed a being of unqualified goodness, who, under auspicious circumstances, "Might have been the Saviour of the World," it is time for the world to be told, that the recent efforts to win for Shelley a kind of regard, to which he is in no degree whatever entitled, are only part of a social movement, that, so far as the extreme Shelleyan

Socialists are concerned, is a movement for the Abolition of Marriage,—in accordance with the spirit and purpose of his Social Philosophy.—JEAFFRESON, JOHN CORDY, 1885, *The Real Shelley, vol.* II, *p.* 478.

Mary Shelley returned to England in the autumn of 1823. On February 21, 1851, she died. Shelley's son, Percy Florence, succeeded to the baronetcy on the death of his grandfather in April, 1844. In the monument, by Weekes, which Sir Percy and Lady Shelley have erected in the noble parish church of Christchurch, Hants, the feeling of Mary's heart, confided to the pages of her journal after her husband's death, is translated into monumental marble. In Boscombe Manor, Bournemouth, in an alcove devoted to that purpose, the portraits, relics, journals, note-books, and letters of Shelley and Mary, duly ordered by Lady Shelley's hands, are preserved with love and reverence. The murmur of pine woods, and the resonance and silvery flash of the waves of our English sea, are near to solemnize and to gladden the heart.—DOWDEN, EDWARD, 1886, *Life of Percy Bysshe Shelley, vol.* II, *p.* 538.

"Ariel;" "The Atheist;" "Glowry Scythrop;" "The Poet of Poets;" "The Snake."—FREY, ALBERT R., 1888, *Sobriquets and Nicknames, p.* 463.

What a set! what a world! is the exclamation that breaks from us as we come to an end of this history of "the occurrences of Shelley's private life." I used the French word *bête* for a letter of Shelley's; for the world in which we find him I can only use another French word, *sale.* Godwin's house of sordid horror, and Godwin preaching and holding the hat, and the green-spectacled Mrs. Godwin, and Hogg the faithful friend, and Hunt the Horace of this precious world, and, to go up higher, Sir Timothy Shelley, a great country gentleman, feeling himself safe while "the exalted mind of the Duke of Norfolk [the drinking Duke] protects me with the world," and Lord Byron with his deep grain of coarseness and commonness, his affectation, his brutal selfishness—what a set! . . . Mrs. Shelley, after her marriage and during Shelley's closing years, becomes attractive; up to her marriage her letters and journal do not please. Her ability is manifest, but she is not attractive. In the world discovered to us by Professor Dowden as surrounding Shelley up to 1817, the most pleasing figure is poor Fanny Godwin; after Fanny Godwin, the most pleasing figure is Harriet Shelley herself. — ARNOLD, MATTHEW, 1888, *Shelley, The Nineteenth Century, vol. 23, p. 34, Essays in Criticism, vol.* II.

Shelley's moral character was really no better than Byron's; but one was a cynic, and the other a sentimentalist who perhaps did not always carry his feelings into action. Without going back to Shelley's former life, it is sufficient to study his relations to Emilia Viviani, to Jane Williams, and, indeed, to all the women whom he met frequently, or to read his poem, "Epipsychidion," which inculcates the necessity of loving more than one woman in the interest of art and of the higher spiritual culture. — SCHUYLER, EUGENE, 1888-1901, *Italian Influences, p.* 143.

What Shelley was at first he remained to the last: a beautiful, effeminate, arrogant boy—constitutionally indifferent to money, generous by impulse, self-indulgent by habit, ignorant. to the end of all that it most behooves a responsible being to know, and so conceited that his ignorance was incurable; showing at every turn the most infallible sign of a feeble intellect, a belief in human perfectibility; and rushing at once to the conclusion, when he or others met with suffering, that some one, not the sufferer, was doing grievous wrong. — PATMORE, COVENTRY, 1889-98, *Principle in Art, p.* 87.

He never could clearly realise the aspect which his relations with Mary bore to the world, who merely saw in him a married man who had deserted his wife and eloped with a girl of sixteen. He thought people should understand all he knew, and credit him with all he did not tell them; that they should sympathise and fraternise with him, and honour Mary the more, not the less, for what she had done and dared. Instead of this, the world accepted his family's estimate of its unfortunate eldest son, and cut him. — MARSHALL, MRS. JULIAN, 1889, *The Life and Letters of Mary Wollstonecraft Shelley, vol.* I, *p.* 128.

Few, perhaps, if any, think of Shelley as often as I do; and to me his whole personality seems the most spiritual and the most sympathetic of the age. The personality of Byron startles, captivates, entrances; he flashes by us like a meteor—lover, noble, man of pleasure and of the world, solitary and soldier by turns, and a great poet always, let the poetasters and sciolists of the moment say what they will in their efforts to decry and to deny him. Shelley's has nothing of this dazzling and gorgeous romance, as he has nothing in his portraits of that haughty and fiery challenge which speaks in the pose of the head, and the glance of the eyes in every picture of Byron. Shelley's eyes gaze outward with wistful, dreamy tenderness; they are the eyes of contemplative genius, the eyes which behold that which is not seen by the children of men. That sweetness and spirituality which are in his physiognomy characterize the fascination which his memory, like his verse, must exercise over any who can understand his soul. Nothing is more unfitting to him than those wranglings over his remains which are called studies of his life and letters. The solemnity and beauty of his death and burial should surely have secured him repose in his grave. — RAMÉE, LOUISE DE LA (OUIDA), 1890, *A New View of Shelley, North American Review, vol.* 150, *p.* 247.

He cursed his father, deceived his friend, and deserted his wife; yet every literary critic for sixty years has hesitated to call him a bad man. His poetry is full of a more subtle and perilous poison even than Byron's; yet its latest editor has declared Shelley one who possessed the qualifications necessary for a saviour of the world. — DAWSON, W. J., 1892, *Quest and Vision, p.* 21.

Proper critical appreciation of Shelley's poetry, for example, does not involve any such reckless eulogy of Shelley's character as has been the recent vogue in America and England. Charity covers faults, but it never lies about them or excuses them. Ethics draws no distinction between the wife-murderer who cleans stables or keeps a dive, and the wife-murderer who writes a "Prometheus Unbound," or an "Ode to a Skylark." The right of the aristocrat is not available as a shield against the operation of moral responsibility. The glamour of genius cannot blind the eyes of God. — THOMPSON, MAURICE, 1893, *The Ethics of Literary Art, p.* 10.

At Shelley's birth,
The Lark, dawn-spirit, with an anthem loud
Rose from the dusky earth
To tell it to the Cloud,

That, like a flower night-folded in the gloom
  Burst into morning bloom.
At Shelley's death,
The Sea, that deemed him an immortal, saw
  A god's extinguished breath,
  And landward, as in awe,
Upbore him to the altar whence he came,
  And the rekindling flame.
—TABB, JOHN B., 1894, *To Shelley, Poems.*

Shelley was nineteen. He was not a youth, but a man. He had never had any youth. He was an erratic and fantastic child during eighteen years, then he stepped into manhood, as one steps over a door-sill. He was curiously mature at nineteen in his ability to do independent thinking on the deep questions of life and to arrive at sharply definite decisions regarding them, and stick to them—stick to them and stand by them at cost of bread, friendships, esteem, respect, and approbation. For the sake of his opinions he was willing to sacrifice all these valuable things, and did sacrifice them; and went on doing it, too, when he could at any moment have made himself rich and supplied himself with friends and esteem by compromising with his father, at the moderate expense of throwing overboard one or two indifferent details of his cargo of principles.—CLEMENS, SAMUEL LANGHORNE (MARK TWAIN), 1897, *In Defence of Harriet Shelley, How to Tell a Story and Other Essays, p.* 24.

There is a clique which had made what Mr. Rudyard Kipling would term "a little tin god" of Shelley; and the members of this absurd coterie, in affecting to raise their idol above ordinary human nature, really do his fame nothing but great disservice in depicting him as what that very caustic and sarcastic lady Miss Clairmont termed "an insipid idiot." — GRAHAM, WILLIAM, 1898, *Last Links with Byron, Shelley, and Keats, p.* xii.

He was, in the obvious sense of the word, a visionary, and his violent antagonisms were far more caused by his disgust with the contact of reality than by any genuine appreciation of the relative values of good and evil. He made no sane and conscious effort to understand things. He did not know how to strike injustice in its weakest part, or how best to help on the downtrodden. He wasted three-fourths of his energy on side-issues. He was always taking seriously the wrong people and the wrong ideas. He held Harriet Westbrook

for a victim of social oppression, whereas she was merely the average pretty girl in search of "bread-and-cheese and kisses." He accepted Mary Godwin as a sort of female seraph, and this essentially vulgar-souled, small minded, sentimental *poseuse* exploited him fifty times more ruthlessly than the poor little Methodist. This did not in the least prevent him from a still wider, if only momentary, aberration over the lovely nullity of Emilia Viviani, the attitudinising Italian girl from whom he was inveigled by the envious Mary, resolute to retain the monopoly of exploitation which she had won by the ruin of a better woman than herself. Intellectually or sexually—it makes little difference which —Shelley was the born child of illusion. To the very last he looked upon Godwin— Godwin, the most sordid of mediocrities— as a great thinker, and his conception of Byron as a supreme artist is one of the gems of criticism. Shelley's true brother is Blake, the inspired Cockney.—ADAMS, FRANCIS, 1899, *Essays in Modernity, p.* 171.

NECESSITY OF ATHEISM
1811

At a meeting of the Master and Fellows held this day, it was determined that Thomas Jefferson Hogg, and Percy Bysshe Shelley, commoners, be publicly expelled for contumaciously refusing to answer questions proposed to them, and for also repeatedly declining to disavow a publication entitled "The Necessity of Atheism." —RECORDS, UNIVERSITY OF OXFORD, 1811.

The importance of "The Necessity of Atheism" is rather biographical and illustrative than literary. It is true the little tract is put together cleverly, and apparently with perfect good faith; but from a strictly literary standpoint it could not be said that an irreparable loss would be sustained by its destruction. None the less its recovery seems to me a matter for great congratulation. So much hung upon this tract,—Shelley's expulsion and all its momentous issues,—so much has been said and written about it,—that to have it before us exactly as it issued from the Press at Worthing and was offered to the Oxford worthies and undergraduates was highly desirable.—FORMAN, HARRY BUXTON, 1880, *ed., The Prose Works of Percy Bysshe Shelley, vol.* I, *p.* xviii.

His "Essay on Christianity" is full of

noble views, some of which are held at the present day by some of the most earnest believers. At what time of his life it was written we are not informed; but it seems such as would insure his acceptance with any company of intelligent and devout Unitarians.—MACDONALD, GEORGE, 1882, *The Imagination and Other Essays*, p. 271, *note*.

QUEEN MAB
1813

An extravagant expression of his zeal for the improvement of the world, full of vague fantastic notions, but also, like all his poems, replete with delicate, lofty, and brilliant ideas. The book, published by a treacherous bookseller against the poet's wish, was condemned. Shelley had excited persecution specially by the notes he had added to the text. These notes, which contain an argument against Christianity, revealed great youthful incompetence; he forgot that it would be simple folly to deny the effects of Christianity in the history of the world. . . . It does not belong to a particular class; it is a series of sketches, lyrical, descriptive, polemic, didactic, in changing metres.— SCHERR, J., 1874, *A History of English Literature*, tr. M. V., p. 246.

We cannot include "Queen Mab," in spite of its sonorous rhetoric and fervid declamation, in the canon of his masterpieces. It had a *succès de scandale* on its first appearance, and fatally injured Shelley's reputation. As a work of art it lacks maturity and permanent vitality.—SYMONDS, JOHN ADDINGTON, 1879, *Shelley* (*English Men of Letters*), p. 69.

The poem is such a marvel as the production of youth of eighteen, it illustrates so fully the starting point and direction of Shelley's thought, it contains so many ideas which were his controlling mental qualities, it is on the whole so intensely Shelleyan, that I do not see why it cannot be regarded as one of his characteristic poems.—JOHNSON, CHARLES F., 1885, *Three Americans and Three Englishmen*, p. 108.

Ridiculed in so far as it was not ignored at the time of its appearance, it has in later times and in some quarters been absurdly overpraised; but, with all its defects and excesses of youth, an impartial criticism can hardly hesitate to pronounce it the most striking and powerful work of imagination, and by far the richest in promise, that has ever sprung from the brain of a poet who had not yet passed his twentieth year.—TRAILL, HENRY DUFF, 1896, *Social England, vol.* v, p. 586.

Despite the metaphysical speculations which disfigure "Queen Mab," passages of extraordinary beauty give no uncertain promise of the coming glories.—LODGE, HENRY CABOT, 1897, *Certain Accepted Heroes and Other Essays*, p. 130.

By it Shelley was long most widely known, and it remains one of the most striking of his works in popular apprehension. . . . The radical character of "Queen Mab," which was made a part of the evidence against his character, on the occasion of the trial which resulted in his being deprived of the custody of his children by Lord Eldon, was a main element in the contemporary obloquy in which his name was involved in England, though very few persons could ever have read the poem then; but it may be doubted whether in the end it did not help his fame by the fascination it exercises over a certain class of minds in the first stages of social and intellectual revolt or angry unrest so widespread in this century.—WOODBERRY, GEORGE EDWARD, 1901, *ed., Complete Poetical Works of Percy Bysshe Shelley, Cambridge ed.*, p. 2.

ALASTOR
1815

In "Alastor" we at last have the genuine, the immortal Shelley. It may indeed be said that the poem, though singularly lovely and full—charged with meaning, has a certain morbid vagueness of tone, a want of firm human body: and this is true enough. Nevertheless, "Alastor" is proportionately worthy of the author of "Prometheus Unbound" and "The Cenci," the greatest Englishman of his age.— ROSSETTI, WILLIAM MICHAEL, 1870–78–86, *Memoir of Percy Bysshe Shelley*, p. 57.

The first of his poems, which really was worthy of his powers—"Alastor"—was written in the first year of this union. It is the first real indication of the new voice which had awakened in English literature. It was like nothing else then existing; nor do we know to what to compare it in the past. Shelley had no story to tell, no character to disclose; his was pure poetry, music such as charmed the ear and filled the mouth with sweetness. Never was poet so eager to teach, or with so many wild assertions to make, or so strong a conviction of the possibility of influencing humanity and changing the world; but the soul of his poetry was the same as that of music, not definite, scarcely articulate, only melodious, ineffably sweet.—OLI-PHANT, MARGARET O. W., 1882, *Literary History of England, XVIII–XIX Century, vol. III, p. 46.*

THE REVOLT OF ISLAM
1817

The Poem which I now present to the world is an attempt from which I scarcely dare to expect success, and in which a writer of established fame might fail without disgrace. It is an experiment on the temper of the public mind as to how far a thirst for a happier condition of moral and political society survives, among the enlightened and refined, the tempests which have shaken the age in which we live. I have sought to enlist the harmony of metrical language, the ethereal combinations of the fancy, the rapid and subtle transitions of human passion, all those elements which essentially compose a poem, in the cause of a liberal and comprehensive morality; and in the view of kindling within the bosoms of my readers a virtuous enthusiasm for those doctrines of liberty and justice, that faith and hope in something good, which neither violence, nor misrepresentation, nor prejudice, can ever totally extinguish among mankind.—SHELLEY, PERCY BYSSHE, 1817, *The Revolt of Islam, Preface.*

Whatever its imperfections of plan and execution, it is not alone a marvellous well-head of poetry, but, in conception and tone, and in its womanly ideal embodied in Cythna, a remarkably original work: it was greatly unlike any poem that had preceded (so far as I know), and even the demon of imitation has left it solitary.—ROSSETTI, WILLIAM MICHAEL, 1870–78–86, *Memoir of Percy Bysshe Shelley, p. 77.*

Even in its amended form it probably presents a better key to the poet's wild opinions than any other of his works. It is a protest against the ordinary usages of society, which Shelley calls "custom." Cythna and Laon declare war against this custom. The reader finds some difficulty in following the fertile imagination of the poet through the phases of alternate suffering and victory which the hero and the heroine experience. He fails to comprehend the means which enabled Cythna to enthrone herself as the Goddess of Liberty, or to appreciate the causes which produced the sudden downfall of her authority. Her flight with Laon on the black Tartarian steed is absurdly unnatural; and her subsequent conduct, or the narrative of it, is grossly indecent. Custom, in short, or, to speak more correctly, the custom which had made matrimony a necessity, was the tyranny against which Shelley's eloquence is directed, and the poem is thus fitly dedicated, in some of the most beautiful verses Shelley ever wrote, to the lady who, for his sake, had broken the bands of custom.—WALPOLE, SPENCER, 1878, *A History of England from the Conclusion of the Great War in 1815, vol. I, p. 366.*

The storms are even better than the sunsets and dawns. The finest is at the beginning of the "Revolt of Islam." It might be a description of one of Turner's storm-skies. The long trains of tremulous mist that precede the tempest, the cleft in the storm-clouds, and seen through it, high above, the space of blue sky fretted with fair clouds, the pallid semicircle of the moon with mist on its upper horn, the flying rack of clouds below the serene spot —all are as Turner saw them; but painting cannot give what Shelley gives—the growth and changes of the storm.—BROOKE, STOPFORD A., 1880, *Some Thoughts on Shelley, Macmillan's Magazine, vol. 42, p. 129.*

As a poet, in richness of language, brilliancy of fancy, and natural melody of versification, Shelley stands second among English poets only to Shakespeare. Yet so wedded was he to the wilfulness of his own imagination, so negligent to the sympathies of his readers, and, consequently, of the true ends of the art of poetry, that, beyond the circle of his ardent admirers, his more ambitious compositions have made little impression on the mind of the nation. For one reader of "The Revolt of Islam," there are ten thousand readers of "Marmion."—COURTHOPE, WILLIAM JOHN, 1887, *Thoughts on Dowden's "Life of Shelley," National Review, vol. 8, p. 619.*

"The Revolt of Islam" is more genuinely and intensely lyrical in its character than is any other poem in which the stanza is used. The poem is the expression of a lofty, aspiring, but feverish and much-bewildered spirit, who, at times, brings out of the instrument employed all its capabilities of "brilliancy and magnificence of sound." But the reader of "The Revolt of Islam" cannot but feel that the instrument was constructed for the expression of other states and attitudes of mind and feeling than are generally exhibited in this poem.—CORSON, HIRAM, 1892, *A Primer of English Verse, p.* 111.

JULIAN AND MADDALO
1818

Is a Conversation or Tale, full of that thoughtful and romantic humanity, but rendered perplexing and unattractive by that veil of shadowy or of glittering obscurity, which distinguished Mr. Shelley's writings. The depth and tenderness of his feelings seems often to have interfered with the expression of them, as the sight becomes blind with tears. A dull, waterish vapour, clouds the aspect of his philosophical poetry, like that mysterious gloom which he has himself described as hanging over the Medusa's Head of Leonardo de Vinci.—HAZLITT, WILLIAM, 1824, *Shelley's Posthumous Poems, Edinburgh Review, vol.* 40, p. 499.

The familiarity of "Julian and Maddalo" is almost as foreign to that of "Beppo" as to that of the "Idiot Boy." It is a high-bred, poetic familiarity, equally remote from the cynicism verging on vulgarity of the one, and from the rusticity verging on ugliness of the other; a manner happily mediating between the abstract intensity of Shelley's ordinary verse and the rich concrete talk of Byron, under the "intoxication" of which it arose.—HERFORD, C. H., 1897, *The Age of Wordsworth, p.* 245.

PROMETHEUS UNBOUND
1819

PROMETHEUS UNBOUND. | A Lyrical Drama | in four acts | with other Poems | by | Percy Bysshe Shelley | Audisne hæc amphiarae, sub terram abdite? | London | C. and J. Ollier Vere Street Bond Street | 1820.—TITLE PAGE TO FIRST EDITION, 1820.

To our apprehensions, Prometheus is little else but absolute raving; and were we not assured to the contrary, we should take it for granted that the author was a lunatic—as his principles are ludicrously wicked, and his poetry a mélange of nonsense, cockneyism, poverty, and pedantry. —ANON, 1820, *Literary Gazette, Sept.* 9.

Shelley styles his new poem "Prometheus Unbound,"
And 'tis like to remain so while time circles round;
For surely an age would be spent in the finding
A reader so weak as to pay for the binding!
—HOOK, THEODORE EDWARD, 1820? *On Shelley's "Prometheus Unbound."*

In short, it is quite impossible that there shoud exist a more pestiferous mixture of blasphemy, sedition, and sensuality, than is visible in the whole structure and strain of this poem—which, nevertheless, and notwithstanding all the detestation its principles excite, must and will be considered by all that read it attentively, as abounding in poetical beauties of the highest order—as presenting many specimens not easily to be surpassed, of the moral sublime of eloquence—as overflowing with pathos, and most magnificent in description. Where can be found a spectacle more worthy of sorrow than such a man performing and glorying in the performance of such things?—ANON, 1820, *Prometheus Unbound, Blackwood's Magazine, vol.* 7, p. 680.

In Mr. Shelley's poetry, all is brilliance, vacuity, and confusion. We are dazzled by the multitude of words which sound as if they denoted something very grand or splendid: fragments of images pass in crowds before us; but when the procession has gone by, and the tumult of it is over, not a trace of it remains upon the memory. The mind, fatigued and perplexed, is mortified by the consciousness that its labour has not been rewarded by the acquisition of a single distinct conception; the ear, too, is dissatisfied; for the rhythm of the verse is often harsh and unmusical; and both the ear and the understanding are disgusted by new and uncouth words, and by the awkward and intricate construction of the sentences. The predominating characteristic of Mr. Shelley's poetry, however, is its frequent and total want of meaning.—ANON, 1821, *Shelley, Quarterly Review, vol.* 26, p. 169.

It contains passages of the sublimest grandeur, and the most wonderful richness of imagination; but the effect of the whole is so vaporous and unsubstantial, the images which he evokes are so unsolid, that not even the unsurpassable purity of the diction, and the unequalled variety of the lyric music, can preserve us from weariness and a painful sense of dreamy confusion.—SHAW, THOMAS B., 1847, *Outlines of English Literature, p.* 367.

"Prometheus Unbound" is the most ambitious of his poems. But it was written too fast. It was writen, too, in a state of over-excitement, produced by the intoxication of an Italian spring, operating upon a morbid system, and causing it to flush over with hectic and half-delirious joy. Above all, it was written twenty years too soon, ere his views had consolidated, and ere his thought and language were cast in their final mould. Hence, on the whole, it is a strong and beautiful disease. Its language is loose and luxuriant as a "Moenad's hair ;" its imagery is wilder and less felicitous than in some of his other poems. The thought is frequently drowned in a diarrhœa of words ; its dialogue is heavy and prolix ; and its lyrics have more flow of sound than beauty of image or depth of sentiment ;—it is a false gallop rather than a great kindling race. Compared with the "Prometheus" of Æschylus, Shelley's poem is wordy and diffuse ; lacks unity and simplicity ; above all, lacks whatever human interest is in the Grecian work. Nor has it the massive strength, the piled-up gold and gems, the barbaric but kingly magnificence of Keats' "Hyperion."— GILFILLAN, GEORGE, 1855, *A Third Gallery of Portraits, p.* 431.

The greatest and most attractive of all Shelley's longer poems. That drama is from beginning to end a great lyrical poem, or I should rather say a congeries of lyrics, in which perhaps more than anywhere else Shelley's lyrical power has highest soared.—SHAIRP, JOHN CAMPBELL, 1881, *Shelley as a Lyric Poet, Aspects of Poetry, p.* 245.

Of all Shelley's works, the "Prometheus Unbound" is that which combines the greatest amount of individual power and peculiarity. There is an airy grandeur about it, reminding one of the vast masses of cloud scattered about in broken, yet magnificently suggestive forms, all over the summer sky after a thunderstorm. The fundamental ideas are grand, the

superstructure, in many parts, so ethereal, that one hardly knows whether he is gazing on towers of solid masonry, rendered dim and unsubstantial by intervening vapour, or upon the golden turrets of cloudland, themselves born of the mist which surrounds them with a halo of glory.—MAC-DONALD, GEORGE, 1882, *The Imagination and other Essays, p.* 278.

The "Prometheus Unbound" gives perhaps the most perfect expression anywhere to be found of the thought and passion of a great period of English poetry. It fully initiates the earnest student into the ideals of the Revolution—those ideals which, in their development, are determining the trend of our modern life. There is no need to speak of the imaginative fervor and pure lyricism of the drama : few English poems can be more effective to quicken and train æsthetic sensitiveness. So far as difficulty is concerned, the student who can understand the "Faery Queene" can understand the "Prometheus Unbound." . . . The supreme æsthetic glory of the "Prometheus Unbound" is not its nature-descriptions nor its color-treatment, but its music. Never did melody so enfold the spirit of a poet. The form is transparent and supple as clear flame. Blank verse rises into the long, passionate swing of the anapæst, or is broken by the flute-like notes of short trochaic lines, or relieved by the half-lyrical effect of rhymed endings. The verse lends itself with equal beauty to the grandeur of sustained endurance, to the passionate yearning of love, to severe philosophic inquiry, to the ethereal notes of spirit-voices dying on the wind. The variety of metres is marvellous. Thirty-six distinct verse-forms are to be found, besides the blank verse. These forms are usually simple ; but at times the versification-scheme is as complex as that of the most elaborate odes of Dryden or Collins. Yet the artificial and labored beauty of the eighteenth century verse is replaced in Shelley by song spontaneous as that of his own skylark. The conventions, the external barriers of poetry, are completely swept away by the new democracy.— SCUDDER, VIDA D., 1892, *ed., Prometheus Unbound, Preface and Introduction, pp.* iii,1.

In the seventy-six years that have passed since Shelley conceived his "Prometheus," as he sat gazing over the sombre ruins of the Campagna, no one has ever ventured into that seventh heaven of invention.—HARRISON, FREDERIC, 1894, *English Literature of the Victorian Age, The Forum, vol.* 16, *p.* 710, *Early Victorian Literature, p.* 21.

"Prometheus Unbound" best combines the various elements of Shelley's genius in their most complete expression, and unites harmoniously his lyrically creative power of imagination and his "passion for reforming the world." It is the fruit of an outburst of poetic energy under the double stimulus of his enthusiastic Greek studies, begun under Peacock's influence, and of his delight in the beauty of Italy, whither he had removed for health and rest. It marks his full mastery of his powers.—WOODBERRY, GEORGE EDWARD, 1901, *ed. Complete Poetical Works of Percy Bysshe Shelley, Cambridge ed., p.* 160.

THE CENCI
1819

THE CENCI. | A Tragedy, | in five acts. | By Percy B. Shelley. | Italy. | Printed for C. and J. Ollier | Vere Street, Bond Street. | London. | 1819.—TITLE PAGE OF FIRST EDITION, 1819.

I have read the tragedy of "Cenci," and am glad to see Shelley at last descending to what really passes among human creatures. The story is certainly an unfortunate one, but the execution gives me a new idea of Shelley's powers. There are passages of great strength, and the character of Beatrice is certainly excellent.—GODWIN, WILLIAM, 1820, *Letter to Mrs. Shelley, March* 30; *Paul's Godwin, vol.* II, *p.* 272.

This is evidence enough that if Shelley had lived the "Cenci" would not now be the one great play written in the great manner of Shakespeare's men that our literature has seen since the time of these. The proof of power is here as sure and as clear as in Shelley's lyric work; he has shown himself, what the dramatist must needs be, as able to face the light of hell as of heaven, to handle the fires of evil as to brighten the beauties of things. This latter work indeed he preferred, and wrought at it with all the grace and force of thought and word which give to all his lyrics the light of a divine life; but his tragic truth and excellence are as certain and absolute as the sweetness and the glory of his songs. The mark of his hand, the

trick of his voice, we can always recognise in their clear character and individual charm; but the range is various from the starry and heavenly heights to the tender and flowering fields of the world wherein he is god and lord : with here such a flower to gather as the spinners' song of Beatrice, and here such a heaven to ascend as the Prologue to Hellas, which the zealous love of Mr. Garnett for Shelley has opened for us to enter and possess for ever; where the pleadings of Christ and Satan alternate as the rising and setting of stars in the abyss of luminous sound and sonorous light.—SWINBURNE, ALGERNON CHARLES, 1869, *Notes on the Text of Shelley, Fortnightly Review, vol.* 11, *p.* 561.

Is not only a poem of great beauty, but a drama of true power, abnormally revolting in its theme, but singularly pure and delicate in treatment.—WARD, ADOLPHUS WILLIAM, 1878, *Drama, Encyclopœdia Britannica, Ninth edition, vol.* VII, *p.* 379.

The greatest tragedy composed in English since the death of Shakespere.—SYMONDS, JOHN ADDINGTON, 1879, *Shelley (English Men of Letters), p.* 129.

Admiration is often expressed of his dramatic ability, and "The Cenci" has been spoken of as the greatest English tragedy since Shakespeare. In truth there seems to be little that is dramatic in it. It is a nightmare of a drama. We are plunged at once into the deepest gloom, and kept at the highest pitch of excitement all through till the final catastrophe. There is no relief except in the very last half-dozen lines, when we know that the women are to be executed. In rapidity of action "The Cenci" much resembles "Macbeth," but what a contrast in other respects ! Every one must feel the extreme beauty of the scene where Duncan is riding towards the castle and is met by Lady Macbeth, and Banquo tells us of the "temple-haunting martlet," and how it is increased by contrast with the horrors that are so soon to follow. The mutual relations of Beatrice and Count Cenci are wonderfully depicted, and Beatrice's character skilfully developed; but who could suppose that such a perfect monster as Cenci ever existed? His utter shamelessness and selfishness are superhuman. We feel, too, the fatal want of humour, but we are always on the solid ground, the sentiments are obvious enough, and the play had consequently some success, being the only one of Shelley's poems that reached a second edition in his lifetime.— SEATON, R. C., 1881, *Shelley, The Temple Bar, vol.* 61, *p.* 234.

The greatest English dramatic poem of the century.—PAYNE, WILLIAM MORTON, 1895, *Little Leaders, p.* 19.

ADONAIS
1821

ADONAIS | An Elegy on the Death of John Keats, | Author of Endymion, Hyperion, etc. | By | Percy B. Shelley | Ἀστήρ πρὶν μὲν ἔλαμπες ἐνι ζώοισιν ἐῶος. | Νῦν δὲ θανῶν, λάμπεις ἔσπερος ἐν φθίμενοις. | Plato. | Pisa | With the Types of Didot | MDCCCXXI. — TITLE PAGE OF FIRST EDITION, 1821.

There is much in the "Adonais" which seems now more applicable to Shelley himself, than to the young and gifted poet whom he mourned. The poetic view he takes of death, and the lofty scorn he displays towards his calumniators, are as a prophecy on his own destiny, when received among immortal names, and the poisonous breath of critics has vanished into emptiness before the fame he inherits.—SHELLEY, MARY WOLLSTONECRAFT, 1839, *ed. Shelley's Poetical Works, p.* 328.

There is, in reading his poem, a feeling of deeper sorrow for the poet that wrote than for him that was lamented.—REED, HENRY, 1850–55, *Lectures on English Literature from Chaucer to Tennyson, p.* 321.

An elegy only equalled in our language by "Lycidas," and in the point of passionate eloquence even superior to Milton's youthful lament for his friend.—SYMONDS, JOHN ADDINGTON, 1879, *Shelley* (*English Men of Letters*), *p.* 143.

As an utterance of abstract pity and indignation, "Adonaïs" is unsurpassed in literature; with its hurrying train of beautiful spectral images, and the irresistible current and thrilling modulation of its verse, it is perhaps the most perfect and sympathetic effect of Shelley's art; while its strain of transcendental consolation for mortal loss contains the most lucid exposition of his philosophy. But of Keats as he actually lived the elegy presents no feature, while the general impression it conveys of his character and fate is erroneous.—COLVIN, SIDNEY, 1887, *Keats* (*English Men of Letters*), *p.* 207.

"Adonais," perhaps the most widely read of the longer poems of Shelley, owes something of its charm to the fact noted by Mrs. Shelley. . . . The elegy has contributed much to the feeling that links these two poets in one memory, though in life they were rather pleasant than intimate friends.—WOODBERRY, GEORGE EDWARD, 1901, *ed. The Complete Poetical Works of Percy Bysshe Shelley, Cambridge ed., p.* 307.

GENERAL

There is no *Original Poetry* in this volume: ["Original Poetry by Victor and Cazire"]: there is nothing in it but downright scribble. It is really annoying to see the waste of paper which is made by such persons as the putters-together of these 64 pages. There is, however, one consolation for the critics who are obliged to read all this sort of trash. It is that the crime of publishing is generally followed by condign punishment in the shape of bills from the stationer and printer, and in the chilling tones of the bookseller, when, to the questions of the anxious rhymer how the book sells, he answers that not more than a half-a-dozen copies have been sold.—ANON, 1810–11, *The Poetical Register and Repository of Fugitive Poetry.*

I can no more understand Shelley than you can. His poetry is "thin-sown with profit or delight." . . . For his theories and nostrums, they are oracular enough, but I either comprehend 'em not, or there is "miching malice" and mischief in 'em; but, for the most part, ringing with their own emptiness. Hazlitt said well of 'em, "Many are the wiser or better for reading Shakspeare, but nobody was ever wiser or better for reading Shelley." — LAMB, CHARLES, 1824, *To Bernard Barton, Aug.* 24; *Life and Letters, ed. Talfourd.*

Mr. Shelley's style is to poetry what astrology is to natural science—a passionate dream, a straining after impossibilities, a record of fond conjectures, a confused embodying of vague abstractions,—a fever of the soul, thirsting and craving after what it cannot have, indulging its love of power and novelty at the expense of truth and nature, associating ideas by contraries, and wasting great powers by their application to unattainable objects. — HAZLITT, WILLIAM, 1824, *Shelley's Posthumous Poems, Edinburgh Review, vol.* 40, *p.* 494.

The disappearance of Shelley from the world, seems, like the tropical setting of that luminary (*aside* I hate that word) to which his poetical genius can alone be compared with reference to the companions of his day, to have been followed by instant darkness and owl-season; whether the vociferous Darley is to be the comet, or tender fullfaced L. E. L. the milk-and-watery moon of our darkness, are questions for the astrologers: if I were the literary weather-guesser for 1825 I would safely prognosticate fog, rain, blight in due succession for its dullard months.— BEDDOES, THOMAS LOVELL, 1824, *Letters, p.*33.

Percy Bysshe Shelley was a man of far superior powers to Keats. He had many of the faculties of a great poet. He was, however, we verily believe it now, scarcely in his right mind.—WILSON, JOHN, 1826, *Blackwood's Magazine, Preface, vol.* 19.

Shelley is one of the best *artists* of us all: I mean in workmanship of style.— WORDSWORTH, WILLIAM, 1827, *Miscellaneous Memoranda, Memoirs by Christopher Wordsworth, vol.* II, *p.* 484.

The strong imagination of Shelley made him an idolater in his own despite. Out of the most indefinite terms of a hard, cold, dark, metaphysical system, he made a gorgeous Pantheon, full of beautiful, majestic, and life-like forms. He turned atheism itself into a mythology, rich with visions as glorious as the gods that live in the marble of Phidias, or the virgin saints that smile on us from the canvass of Murillo. The Spirit of Beauty, the Principle of Good, the Principle of Evil, when he treated of them, ceased to be abstractions. They took shape and colour. They were no longer mere words, but "intelligible forms;" "fair humanities;" objects of love, of adoration, or of fear. As there can be no stronger sign of a mind destitute of the poetical faculty than that tendency which was so common among the writers of the French school to turn images into abstractions,—Venus, for example, into Love, Minerva into Wisdom, Mars into War, and Bacchus into festivity, —so there can be no stronger sign of a mind truly poetical than a disposition to reverse this abstracting process, and to make individuals out of generalities. Some of the metaphysical and ethical theories of Shelley were certainly most absurd and pernicious. But we doubt

whether any modern poet has possessed in an equal degree the highest qualities of the great ancient masters. The words bard and inspiration, which seems so cold and affected when applied to other modern writers, have a perfect propriety when applied to him. He was not an author, but a bard. His poetry seems not to have been an art, but an inspiration. Had he lived to the full age of man, he might not improbably have given to the world some great work of the very highest rank in design and execution. But, alas,

ὁ Δάφνις ἔβα ῥ́οον· ἔηνσε δίνα
Yὸν Μωσαις φιλον ἀνδρα, τὸν ὀυ Νύμφαισιν
ἀπεκθῆ

—MACAULAY, THOMAS BABINGTON, 1831, *Southey's Edition of the Pilgrim's Progress, Edinburgh Review, vol.* 54, *p.* 454.

Read the "Prometheus Unbound." How gorgeous it is! I do not think Shelley is read or appreciated now as enthusiastically as he was, even in my recollection, some few years ago. . . . At home spent my time in reading Shelley. How wonderful and beautiful the "Prometheus" is! The unguessed heavens and earth and sea are so many storehouses from which Shelley brings gorgeous heaps of treasure and piles them in words like jewels. I read "The Sensitive Plant" and "Rosalind and Helen." As for the latter—powerful enough, certainly—it gives me bodily aches to read such poetry.—KEMBLE, FRANCES ANN, 1832, *Records of a Girlhood, Jan.* 25, 27, *pp.* 496, 498.

Sun-treader, life and light be thine for ever!
Thou art gone from us; years go by and
   spring
Gladdens and the young earth is beautiful,
Yet thy songs come not, other bards arise,
But none like thee: they stand, thy majesties
Like mighty works which tell some spirit
   there
Hath sat regardless of neglect and scorn,
Till, its long task completed, it hath risen
And left us, never to return, and all
Rush in to peer and praise when all in vain.
  .   .   .   .   .   .
But thou art still for me who have adored
Tho' single, panting but to hear thy name
Which I believed a spell to me alone,
Scarce deeming thou wast as a star to men!
—BROWNING, ROBERT, 1833, *Pauline.*

The imaginative feelings of Byron and Shelley had but little similitude: those of Shelley were mystical and clouded; those of Byron, clear, distinct, direct, and bold. Shelley was more theoretical and abstract;

Byron, however imaginative, had it always mixed up with humanity,—human passions and human forms. Shelley had gleams of poetry; Byron was always poetical; Shelley never put a master's hand upon his subject; he could not mould it to his will.—BRYDGES, SIR SAMUEL EGERTON, 1834, *Autobiography, vol.* I, *p.* 329.

"The Ode to the Skylark" and "The Cloud," which, in the opinion of many critics, bear a purer poetical stamp than any other of his productions. They were written as his mind prompted, listening to the carolling of the bird aloft in the azure sky of Italy; or marking the cloud as it sped across the heavens,,while he floated in his boat on the Thames. No poet was ever warmed by a more genuine and unforced inspiration. His extreme sensibility gave the intensity of passion to his intellectual pursuits; and rendered his mind keenly alive to every perception of outward objects, as well as to his internal sensations. Such a gift is, among the sad vicissitudes of human life, the disappointments we meet, and the galling sense of our own mistakes and errors, fraught with pain; to escape from such, he delivered up his soul to poetry, and felt happy when he sheltered himself from the influence of human sympathies in the wildest regions of fancy.—SHELLEY, MARY GODWIN, 1839, *ed. Shelley's Poetical Works, Preface.*

If Coleridge is the sweetest of our poets, Shelley is at once the most ethereal and most gorgeous; the one who has clothed his thoughts in draperies of the most evanescent and most magnificent words and imagery. Not Milton himself is more learned in Grecisms, or nicer in etymological propriety; and nobody, through-·out, has a style so Orphic and primæval. His poetry is as full of mountains, seas, and skies, of light, and darkness, and the seasons, and all the elements of our being, as if Nature herself had written it, with the creation and its hopes newly cast around her; not, it must be confessed, without too indiscriminate a mixture of great and small, and a want of sufficient shade,—a certain chaotic brilliancy, "dark with excess of light."—HUNT, LEIGH, 1844, *Imagination and Fancy, p.* 268.

And Shelley, in his white ideal
All statue-blind.
—BROWNING, ELIZABETH BARRETT, 1844, *Vision of Poets.*

Had Shelley possessed humor, his might have been the third name in English poetry.—WHIPPLE, EDWIN P., 1845, *Wit and Humor, Literature and Life, p.* 112.

If ever mortal "wreaked his thoughts upon expression," it was Shelley. If ever poet sang (as a bird sings) impulsively, earnestly, with utter abandonment, to himself solely, and for the mere joy of his own song, that poet was the author of the "Sensitive Plant." Of art—beyond that which is the inalienable instinct of genius—he either had little or disdained all. He really disdained that Rule which is the emanation from Law, because his own soul was law in itself. His rhapsodies are but the rough notes, the stenographic memoranda of poems,—memoranda which, because they were all-sufficient for his own intelligence, he cared not to be at the trouble of transcribing in full for mankind. In his whole life he wrought not thoroughly out a single conception. For this reason it is that he is the most fatiguing of poets. Yet he wearies in having done too little, rather than too much; what seems in him the diffuseness of one idea, is the conglomerate concision of many; and this concision it is which renders him obscure. With such a man, to imitate was out of the question; it would have answered no purpose—for he spoke to his own spirit alone, which would have comprehended no alien tongue;—he was, therefore, profoundly original.—POE, EDGAR ALLAN, 1845? *Miss Barrett's "A Drama of Exile," Works of Poe, ed. Stedman and Woodberry, vol.* VI, *p.* 317.

Most purely poetic genius of his age.—HOWITT, WILLIAM, 1846, *Homes and Haunts of the Most Eminent British Poets, vol.* I, *p.* 494.

I turn to one whom I love still more than I admire; the gentle, the gifted, the ill-fated Shelley. . . . Poor Shelley! Thou were the warmest of philanthropists, yet doomed to live at variance with thy country and thy time. Full of the spirit of genuine Christianity, yet ranking thyself among unbelievers, because in early life thou hadst been bewildered by seeing it perverted, sinking beneath those precious gifts which should have made a world thine own, intoxicated with thy lyric enthusiasm and thick-coming fancies, adoring Nature as a goddess, yet misinterpreting her oracles, cut off from life just as thou

wert beginning to read it aright; O, most
musical, most melancholy singer; who that
has a soul to feel genius, a heart to grieve
over misguided nobleness, can forbear
watering the profuse blossoms of thy too
early closed spring with tears of sympathy,
of love, and (if we may dare it for one so
superior in intellect) of pity?—OSSOLI,
MARGARET FULLER, 1850? *Art, Literature and the Drama, p.* 78.

It is needless to disguise the fact, and
it accounts for all—his mind was diseased:
he never knew, even from boyhood, what
it was to breathe the atmosphere of
healthy life, to have the *mens sana in cor-
pore sano.* His sensibilities were over-
acute; his morality was thoroughly morbid;
his metaphysical speculations illogical, incongruous, incomprehensible—alike base-
less and objectless. The suns and systems
of his universe were mere nebulæ; his continents were a chaos of dead matter;
his oceans "a world of waters, and without a shore." . . . It is gratuitous
absurdity to call his mystical speculations
a search after truth; they are no such
thing; and are as little worth the attention of reasoning and responsible man as
the heterogeneous reveries of nightmare.
—MOIR, D. M., 1850–51, *Sketches of the
Poetical Literature of the Past Half-Century.*

I would rather consider Shelley's poetry
as a sublime fragmentary essay towards a
presentment of the correspondency of the
universe to Diety, of the natural to the
spiritual, and of the actual to the ideal,
than I would isolate and separately ap-
praise the worth of many detachable portions which might be acknowledged as
utterly perfect in a lower moral of view,
under the mere conditions of art.—
BROWNING, ROBERT, 1851, *Letters of Percy
Bysshe Shelley, Introductory Essay.*

See'st thou a Skylark whose glistening wing-
lets ascending
Quiver like pulses beneath the melodious
dawn?
Deep in the heart-yearning distance of heaven
it flutters—
Wisdom and beauty and love are the treas-
ures it brings down at eve.
—MEREDITH, GEORGE, 1851, *Works, vol.*
XXXI, *p.* 140.

In a literary point of view, there is no
doubt but every succeeding poem showed
the gradual clearing away of the mists and

vapors with which, in spite of his exquisite
rhythm, and a thousand beauties of detail,
his fine genius was originally clouded.—
MITFORD, MARY RUSSELL, 1851, *Recollections of a Literary Life, p.* 315.

Nature baptized him in ethereal fire,
And Death shall crown him with a wreath
of flame.
—HOLMES, OLIVER WENDELL, 1853, *After
a Lecture on Shelley.*

And it is worth remarking, that it is
Shelley's form of fever, rather than
Byron's, which has been of late years the
prevailing epidemic. Since Shelley's
poems have become known in England,
and a timid public, after approaching in
fear and trembling the fountain which
was understood to be poisoned, has begun
first to sip, and then, finding the magic
water at all events sweet enough, to quench
its thirst with unlimited draughts, the
Byron's Head has lost its customers.
Well—at least the taste of the age is more
refined, if that be matter of congratulation. And there is an excuse for preferring *eau sucré* to waterside porter,
heady with grains of paradise and quassia,
salt and *coccum indicum.* . . . Among
the many good-going gentleman and ladies,
Byron is generally spoken of with horror—
he is "so wicked," forsooth; while poor
Shelley, "poor dear Shelley," is "very
wrong, of course," but "so refined," "so
beautiful," "so tender"—a fallen angel,
while Byron is a satyr and a devil. We
boldly deny the verdict. Neither of the
two are devils; as for angels, when we
have seen one, we shall be better able to
give an opinion; at present, Shelley is in
our eyes far less like one of those old
Hebrews and Miltonic angels, fallen or
unfallen, than Byron is. And as for the
satyr, the less that is said for Shelley, on
that point, the better. If Byron sinned
more desperately and flagrantly than he,
it was done under the temptations of rank,
wealth, disappointed love, and under the
impulses of an animal nature, to which
Shelley's passions were

As moonlight unto sunlight, and as water
unto wine.

And, at all events, Byron never set to work
to consecrate his own sin into a religion,
and proclaim the worship of uncleanness
as the last and highest ethical development
of "pure" humanity. No—Byron may
be brutal, but he never cants. If at

moments he finds himself in hell, he never turns round to the world, and melodiously informs them that it is heaven, if they could but see it in its true light.—KINGSLEY, CHARLES, 1853, *Thoughts about Shelley and Byron, Fraser's Magazine, vol. 48, p.* 570.

Melodious Shelley caught thy softest song,
   And they who heard his music heard not thine;
Gentle and joyous, delicate and strong,
   From the far tomb his voice shall silence mine.

—LANDOR, WALTER SAVAGE, 1853, *To the Nightingale.*

Through cloud and wave and star his insight keen
   Shone clear, and traced a God in each disguise,
Protean, boundless. Like the buskined scene
   All Nature rapt him into ecstasies:
In him, alas! had Reverence equal been
   With Admiration, those resplendent eyes
Had wandered not through all her range sublime
To miss the one great marvel of all time.

—DE VERE, AUBREY, 1856, *Lines Composed Near Shelley's House at Lerici.*

It is impossible to deny that he loved with a great intensity; yet it was with a certain narrowness, and therefore a certain fitfulness. Possibly a somewhat wider nature, taking hold of other characters at more points,—fascinated as intensely but more variously, stirred as deeply but through more complicated emotions,—is requisite for the highest and most lasting feeling; passion, to be enduring, must be many-sided. Eager and narrow emotions urge like the gadfly of the poet, but they pass away; they are single; there is nothing to revive them. Various as human nature must be the passion which absorbs that nature into itself. Shelley's mode of delineating women has a corresponding peculiarity; they are well described, but they are described under only one aspect. Every one of his poems, almost, has a lady whose arms are white, whose mind is sympathizing, and whose soul is beautiful. She has many names,—Cythna, Asia, Emily; but these are only external disguises; she is indubitably the same person, for her character never varies. No character can be simpler; she is described as the ideal object of love in its most simple and elemental form; the pure object of the essential passion. She is a being to be

loved in a single moment, with eager eyes and gasping breath; but you feel that in that moment you have seen the whole,—there is nothing to come to afterwards. The fascination is intense, but uniform; there is not the ever-varying grace, the ever-changing charm, that alone can attract for all time the shifting moods of a various and mutable nature.—BAGEHOT, WALTER, 1856, *Percy Bysshe Shelley, Works, ed. Morgan, vol.* I, *p.* 117.

Let it not be supposed that I mean to compare the sickly dreaming of Shelley over clouds and waves with the masculine and magnificent grasp of men and things which we find in Scott.—RUSKIN, JOHN, 1856, *Modern Painters, pt.* iii, *sec.* ii. *ch.* iv, *note.*

Intense as is his ethical spirit, his desire to act upon man and society, his imagination cannot work with things as he finds them, with the actual stuff of historical life. His mode of thinking is not according to the terrestrial conditions of time, place, cause and effect, variety of race, climate, and costume. His persons are shapes, winged forms, modernized versions of Grecian mythology, or mortals highly allegorized; and their movements are vague, swift, and independent of ordinary physical laws. In the "Revolt of Islam," for example, the story is that of two lovers who career through the plains and cities of an imaginary kingdom on a Tartar horse, or skim over leagues of ocean in a boat whose prow is of moonstone. But for the *Cenci,* and one or two other pieces, one would say that Shelley had scarcely any aptitude for the historical.—MASSON, DAVID, 1860–74, *Wordsworth, Shelley, Keats and Other Essays, p.* 140.

Florence to the living Dante was not more cruelly unjust than England to the living Shelley. Only now, nearly forty years after his death, do we begin to discern his true glory. It is well that this glory is such as can afford to wait for recognition; that it is one of the permanent stars of heaven, not a rocket to be ruined by a night of storm and rain. I confess that I have long been filled with astonishment and indignation at the manner in which he is treated by the majority of our best living writers. Emerson is serenely throned above hearing him at all; Carlyle only hears him "shriek hysterically;" Mrs. Browning discovers him "blind with his white ideal;" Messrs. Ruskin and Kingsley treat him much as senior schoolboys treat the youngster who easily "walks over their heads" in class—with reluctant tribute of admiration copiously qualified with sneers, pinches, and kicks. Even Bulwer (who, intellectually worthless as he is, now and then serves well as a straw to show the way the wind blows among the higher and more educated classes), even Bulwer can venture to look down upon him with pity, to pat him patronisingly on the back, to sneer at him—in "Earnest Maltravers"—with a sneer founded upon a maimed quotation. . . . These distinctive marks of the highest poetry I find displayed in the works of Shelley more gloriously than in those of any other poet in our language. As we must study Shakespeare for knowledge of idealised human nature, and Fielding for knowledge of human nature unidealised, and Carlyle's "French Revolution" as the unapproached model of history, and Currer Bell's "Villette" to learn the highest capabilities of the novel, and Ruskin for the true philosophy of art, and Emerson for quintessential philosophy, so must we study, and so will future men more and more study Shelley for quintessential poetry.—THOMSON, JAMES ("B. V."), 1860–96, *Biographical and Critical Studies, pp.* 270, 280.

Since the seventeenth century, we have had no poet of the highest order, though Shelley, had he lived, would perhaps have become one. He had something of that burning passion, that sacred fire, which kindles the soul, as though it came fresh from the altar of the gods. But he was cut off in his early prime, when his splendid genius was still in its dawn.—BUCKLE, HENRY THOMAS, 1861, *History of Civilization in England, vol,* II, *p.* 397.

Emotion was found insufficient; ideas were called for. And so poor Shelley, poor Shelley! so disdained and cried down in his lifetime, succeeded Wordsworth in vogue. The *amende honorable* was made to him; he was proclaimed one of the glories of England. Men became passionately enamoured of his ethereal, subtle, intangible poetry, and the hollowness of his humanitarian dreams was forgiven him in virtue of the sublimity and beauty of his imagination. After which he shared the fate of his predecessors. As time went on his defects

became more apparent. There was not enough human heart-beat, not enough life, not enough of the dramatic within him. —SCHERER, EDMOND, 1863–91, *Taine's History of English Literature, Essays on English Literature, tr.* Saintsbury, *p.* 87.

The master-singer of our modern poets. —SWINBURNE, ALGERNON CHARLES, 1869, *Notes on the Text of Shelley, Fortnightly Review, vol.* 11, *p.* 539.

Has anyone since Shakspeare and Spenser lighted on such tender and such grand ecstasies?—TAINE, H. A., 1871, *History of English Literature, tr. Van Laun, vol.* II, *bk.* iv, *ch.* i, *p.* 267.

The most truly spiritual of all English poets, Shelley. . . . That Shelley was immeasurably superior to Byron in all the rarer qualities of the specially poetic mind appears to us so unmistakably assured a fact, that difference of opinion upon it can only spring from a more fundamental difference of opinion as to what it is that constitutes this specially poetic quality. . . . We feel that Shelley transports the spirit to the highest bound and limit of the intelligible; and that with him thought passes through one superadded and more rarefying process than the other poet is master of.—MORLEY, JOHN, 1871, *Byron, Critical Miscellanies, p.* 259.

This uncritical negligence, the want of minute accuracy in the details of his verse, seems to us intimately connected with the whole character of Shelley's mind, and especially with the lyrical sweep and intensity of his poetical genius. He had an intellect of the rarest delicacy and analytical strength, that intuitively perceived the most remote analogies, and discriminated with spontaneous precision the finest shades of sensibility, the subtilest differences of perception and emotion. He possessed a swift soaring and prolific imagination that clothed every thought and feeling with imagery in the moment of its birth, and instinctively read the spiritual meanings of material symbols. His fineness of sense was so exquisite that eye and ear and touch became, as it were, organs and inlets not merely of sensitive apprehension, but of intellectual beauty and ideal truth. Every nerve in his slight but vigorous frame seemed to vibrate in unison with the deeper life of nature in the world around him, and, like the wandering harp, he was swept to music by every breath of material beauty, every gust of poetical emotion. Above all, he had a strength of intellectual passion and a depth of ideal sympathy that in moments of excitement fused all the powers of his mind into a continuous stream of creative energy, and gave the stamp of something like inspiration to all the higher productions of his muse. His very method of composition reflects these characteristics of his mind. He seems to have been urged by a sort of irresistible impulse to write, and displayed a vehement and passionate absorption in the work that recalls the old traditions of poetical frenzy and divine possession.—BAYNES, THOMAS S., 1871, *Rossetti's Edition of Shelley, Edinburgh Review, vol* 133, *p.* 428.

I heard of an enthusiastic American who went about English fields hunting a lark with Shelley's poem in his hand, thinking no doubt to use it as a kind of guide-book to the intricacies and harmonies of the song. He reported not having heard any larks, though I have little doubt they were soaring and singing about him all the time, though of course they did not sing to his ear the song that Shelley heard. . . . Shelley's poem is perhaps better known and has a higher reputation among literary folk than Wordsworth's, but I like the latter best. Shelley's is too long, though no longer than the lark's song; but the lark cannot help it, and Shelley can.— BURROUGHS, JOHN, 1873, *The Birds of the Poets, Scribner's Monthly, vol.* 6, *p.* 568.

Shelley balloons it too much. He ascends easily, gracefully, and then is swayed by scented breezes from an exuberant imagination. It had been a gain could he oftener have dipped his mind deeper into the core of common things. He has too much elevation and not enough depth,—that is, not enough depth for *his* elevation.—CALVERT, GEORGE H., 1874, *Brief Essays and Brevities, p.* 217.

One cannot help thinking that Shelley's natural place in the world would be that of a spiritualised Spenser; and if that calm could have come to him which alone can furnish the poet with the opportunity he ought to have, there is no knowing but he might have given us a work rich enough to justify this fancy of him. As it is, between writhings and groanings, the paroxysms of a much-tried spirit, he wrote

those exquisite lyrics and poems, which we should be indeed loth to loose from our literature. — SMITH, GEORGE BARNETT, 1875, *Elizabeth Barrett Browning, Poets and Novelists, p.* 84.

Chaucer, Shakespeare, Milton, Shelley—these are, I believe, the four sublimest sons of song that England has to boast of among the mighty dead—say rather among the undying, the never-to-die. Let us remember also two exceptional phenomena, an "inspired ploughman," Burns, and an unparalleled poetess, Mrs. Browning, and be thankful for such a national destiny. There are plenty of others: but those four are, if I mistake not, *the* four. . . . The poetic ecstacy took him constantly upwards; and, the higher he got, the more thoroughly did his thoughts and words become one exquisite and intense unit. With elevation of meaning, and splendour and beauty of perception, he combined the most searching, the most inimitable loveliness of verse-music; and he stands at this day, and perhaps will always remain, the poet who, by instinct of verbal selection and charm of sound, comes nearest to expressing the half-inexpressible— the secret things of beauty, the intolerable light of the arcane. . . . To sum up, there is no poet—and no man either—in whose behalf it is more befitting for all natures, and for some natures more inevitable, to feel the privileges and the delights of enthusiasm. The very soul rushes out towards Shelley as an unapproached poet, and embraces him as a dearest friend. — ROSSETTI, WILLIAM MICHAEL, 1878, *Lives of Famous Poets, pp.* 309, 327, 328.

Whether we consider his minor songs, his odes, or his more complicated choral dramas, we acknowledge that he was the loftiest and the most spontaneous singer of our language. In range of power he was also conspicuous above the rest. Not only did he write the best lyrics, but the best tragedy, the best translations, and the best familiar poems of his century. As a satirist and humourist, I cannot place him so high as some of his admirers do; and the purely polemical portions of his poems, those in which he puts forth his antagonism to tyrants and religions and custom in all its myriad forms, seem to me to degenerate at intervals into poor rhetoric.—SYMONDS, JOHN ADDINGTON, 1879, *Shelley (English Men of Letters).*

The materials with which he works are impalpable abstractions where other poets use concrete images. His poetry is like the subtle veil woven by the witch of Atlas from "threads of fleecy mist,""'long lines of light," such as are kindled by the dawn and "starbeams." When he speaks of natural scenery the solid earth seems to be dissolved, and we are in presence of nothing but the shifting phantasmagoria of cloudland, the glow of moonlight on eternal snow, or the "golden lightning of the setting sun." The only earthly scenery which recalls Shelley to a more material mind is that which one sees from a high peak at sunrise, when the rising vapours tinged with prismatic colours shut out all signs of human life, and we are alone with the sky and the shadowy billows of the sea of mountains. Only in such vague regions can Shelley find fitting symbolism for those faint emotions suggested by the most abstract speculations, from which he alone is able to extract an unearthly music.—STEPHEN, LESLIE, 1879, *Hours in a Library, Cornhill Magazine, vol. 39, p, 294.*

The title of "the poet's poet," which has been bestowed for various reasons on very different authors, applies perhaps with a truer fitness to Shelley than to any of the rest. For all students of Shelley must in a manner feel that they have before them an extreme, almost an extravagant, specimen of the poetic character; and the enthusiastic love, or contemptuous aversion, which his works have inspired has depended mainly on the reader's sympathy or distaste for that character when exhibited in its unmixed intensity.—MYERS, FREDERIC W. H., 1880, *The English Poets* ed. Ward, vol. IV, p. 348.

On flaming chariot Shelley soars
  Through starry realms serene.
—BLACKIE, JOHN STUART, 1880, *Lays and Legends of Ancient Greece, Introduction.*

By instinct, intuition, whatever we have to call that fine faculty that feels truths before they are put into definite shape, Shelley was an evolutionist. He translated into his own pantheistic language the doctrine of the eternity of matter and the eternity of motion, of the infinite transformation of the different forms of matter into each other, without any creation or destruction of either matter or motion.—AVELING, EDWARD AND ELEANOR MARX, 1880, *Shelley and Socialism, To-Day, April.*

In choosing the Spenserian stanza for his great visionary poem, Shelley challenges comparison with Spenser himself, and with Byron; and it cannot be said that he appears to advantage in this comparison. . . . Compare the impetuous rapidity and pale intensity of Shelley's verse with the lulling harmony, the lingering cadence, the voluptuous color of Spenser's, or with the grandiose majesty of Byron's. The stanzas of the "Faerie Queene" have something of the wholesome old-world mellowness of Haydn's music; those of "Laon and Cythna" something of the morbid fever of Chopin's. . . . In "Adonais," indeed, a poem on which he bestowed much labor, he handles the stanza in a masterly manner, and endows it with an individual music beautiful and new; and even "Laon and Cythna" is full of exquisite passages, in which the very rhymes lend wings to his imagination, and become the occasion of sweet out-of-the-way modes of expression, full of ethereal poetry of the most Shelleyan kind.—TODHUNTER, JOHN A., 1880, *A Study of Shelley.*

When that mist cleared, O Shelley! what
    dread veil
Was rent for thee, to whom far-darkling
    Truth
Reigned soverign guide through thy brief
    ageless youth?
Was the Truth *thy* Truth, Shelley?—Hush!
    All-Hail,
Past doubt, thou gav'st it; and in Truth's
    bright sphere
Art first of praisers, being most praisèd here.
—ROSSETTI, DANTE GABRIEL, 1881, *Five English Poets, Ballads and Sonnets.*

Of Shelley he said: "He is often too much in the clouds for me. I admire his 'Alastor,' 'Adonais,' 'Prometheus Unbound,' and 'Epipsychidion,' and some of his short lyrics are exquisite. As for 'The Lover's Tale,' that was written before I had ever seen a Shelley, though it is called Shelleyan."—TENNYSON, ALFRED LORD, 1883, *Some Criticisms on Poets, Memoir, by his Son, vol. II, p. 285.*

Each poet gives what he has, and what he can offer; you spread before us fairy bread and enchanted wine, and shall we turn away, with a sneer, because, out of all the multitudes of singers, one is spiritual and strange, one has seen Artemis unveiled?—LANG, ANDREW, 1886, *Letters to Dead Authors, p.* 177.

After Milton, the next great poet who is eminently musical is Shelley. . . . In some of Shelley's lyrics no formal quality seems to exist except the music; a clear intellectual meaning is always present, but often there is scarcely any suggestion of distinct imagery. The power that he shows in these lyrics of giving music of verse an existence apart from all other formal qualities is what makes Shelley more of a musical poet than Coleridge or Keats; and no other poet of the same period can be compared with these in this quality of verse.—WHITTAKER, THOMAS, 1886, *The Musical and the Picturesque Elements in Poetry, Essays and Notices, p.* 103.

Shelley wrote even fewer sonnets than did Byron: but the few which Byron wrote he wrote well, and this cannot be said of Shelley. . . . It is strange that Shelley, the most poetic of poets, should have been unable to write a good sonnet *as* a sonnet; but probably the restrictions of the form pressed upon him with a special heaviness. Chopin, the Shelley of musical composers, wrote his beautiful mazurkas: looked at strictly as mazurkas they are unsatisfactory. In both instances, however, uncontrollable genius overbalanced propriety of form.—SHARP, WILLIAM, 1886, *Sonnets of this Century, p.* 312, *note.*

How shall we name the third class of men, who live for the ideal alone, and yet are betrayed into weakness and error, and deeds which demand an atonement of remorse; men who can never quite reconcile the two worlds in which we have our being, the world of material fact and the spiritual world above and beyond it; who give themselves away for love or give themselves away for light yet sometimes mistake bitter for sweet, and darkness for light; children who stumble on the sharp stones and bruise their hands and feet, yet who can wing their way with angelic ease through spaces of the upper air. These are they whom we say the gods love, and who seldom reach the four-score years of Goethe's majestic old age. They are dearer perhaps than any others to the heart of humanity, for they symbolise, in a pathetic way, both its weakness and its strength. We cannot class them with the exact and patient craftsmen;

they are ever half defeated and can have no claim to take their seats beside their conquerors. Let us name them lovers; and if at any time they have wandered far astray, let us remember their errors with gentleness, because they have loved much. It is in this third class of those who serve mankind that Shelley has found a place.—DOWDEN, EDWARD, 1887, *Last Words on Shelley, Fortnightly Review, vol.* 48, *p.* 481.

There is no longer, we imagine, any room for discussion of the position of Shelley as a lyric poet. He is second to no one in our language. If we want an exact definition of what we mean by "poetry," we turn to his. It was his natural language. He wrote as a bird flies. And his flights are only to be compared to the strong-pinioned eagle, which soars in ever-widening spirals into the empyrean. Both go out of mortal ken. How prodigal he is! Image on image, flight above flight, imagination on imagination, scaling the heavens, and when the amazed reader thinks the climax is reached, lo! the unconscious ease with which he soars to more aërial regions. If you attempt to turn this verse into prose, the meaning escapes. It is poetry. The unapproachable melody of it, also! It is as untranslatable as music. It is possible for a person, sensitive to harmony, to read pages and pages of his poetry, with exquisite delight, having only the vaguest consciousness of the poet's meaning, with that sense of enjoyment that one has in listening to an orchestra.— WARNER, CHARLES DUDLEY, 1887, *Shelley, The New Princeton Review, vol.* 4, *p.* 302.

I liked Shelley very much better, though his qualities were too ethereal in their exquisiteness to have any practical influence on my own work.—HAMERTON, PHILIP GILBERT, 1887, *Books which Have Influenced Me, p.* 55.

I remember, at a very early age, falling in with a little dumpy 16mo edition of Shelley, and finding a kind of fearful fascination in secretly reading it. Not that his ideas anywise influenced my mind. Shelley is a magician, not a thinker, and his creations are chiefly a wondrous dream-work set to the most exquisite music. That music never ceased to charm me, and for many months I carried the book about in my pocket and read it whenever I found myself alone. I was already quite as democratic as the poet, but rather shuddered at his atheism. But I could not read "The Cloud," or "The Skylark," or "The Lines to an Indian Air," or the dedication of "The Revolt of Islam," even when I only partly understood them, without bringing a moisture into my eyes. Yet the book did not do much for me, for it did not properly give me any thoughts.—SMITH, WALTER C., 1887, *Books which have Influenced Me, p.* 91.

Shelley, however, was not for long my idol. He so often seems to be singing in a falsetto voice; and when a man does that, he is pretty sure to shriek when he gets excited.—JESSOPP, AUGUSTUS, 1887, *Books that have Helped Me, The Forum, vol.* 4, *p.* 33.

Strange as it may seem, Shelley has given me very uniformly the delight of the invisible, the spiritual, resolving itself, in rapid, creative touch, into distinct, changeable, evanescent, beautiful form. No English poet quite equals him in making way for his thought where no way is; in leaving a vivid trail of light behind him where no light was. He completes the illusion of his own sight with marvelous facility, and leaves the distinct mirage of his vision where the elements must almost instantly swallow it up again. The gossamer web of the spider floats in the air, invisible save from some one position, from which it gleams through its whole length, a fluctuating silver thread. No poet ever cast in the air lighter conceptions, or made them, from his own outlook, more fascinatingly visible. To turn Nature, in all her manifold forms, in the inexhaustible vocabulary of the spirit, so that the image and the feeling it utters float off together as a living thing, this is the unwearied inspiration of Shelley. Yet no mind is more alien to me than that of Shelley in some of its aspects. Of logical incoherence, inconsequential narrative, and thoroughly mistaken opinion, Shelley is a supreme example. Deep and pure in his own affections, he missed the first principles of purity and strength in the living world of men. He wandered like a lost, not a fallen, angel among the evil passions of his kind, and understood nothing of their nature or their remedy. In his sympathetic rehearsal of the encounter of the serpent and the eagle, he takes part with the serpent, because the

facts symbolized are wholly misplaced in his mind. An error so deep as this would fatally have weakened another man—it weakened Byron; but Shelley escapes from it constantly into a region pure, creative, remote. In the freedom of his own free spirit, he mistook unlicensed activity for liberty, and resentfully struggled with, and cast off, those social restraints which are, after all, the flowing garments of virtue.—BASCOM, JOHN, 1888, *Books that have Helped Me, p.* 30.

It is his poetry, above everything else, which for many people establishes that he is an angel. Of his poetry I have not space now to speak. But let no one suppose that a want of humour and a self-delusion such as Shelley's have no effect upon a man's poetry. The man Shelley, in very truth, is not entirely sane, and Shelley's poetry is not entirely sane either. The Shelley of actual life is a vision of beauty and radiance, indeed, but availing nothing, effecting nothing. And in poetry, no less than in life, he is "a beautiful *and ineffectual* angel, beating in the void his luminous wings in vain."—ARNOLD, MATTHEW, 1888, *Shelley, The Nineteenth Century, vol.* 23, *p.* 39, *Esssays in Criticism, vol.* II.

Behold I send thee to the heights of song,
My brother! Let thine eyes awake as clear
As morning dew, within whose glowing
    sphere
Is mirrowed half a world; and listen long,
Till in thine ears, famished to keenness, throng
The bugles of the soul, till far and near
Silence grows populous, and wind and mere
Are phantom-choked with voices. Then be
    strong—
Then halt not till thou seest the beacons flare
Souls mad for truth have lit from peak to
    peak.
Haste on to breathe the intoxicating air—
Wine to the brave and poison to the weak—
Far in the blue where angels' feet have trod,
Where earth is one with heaven and man
    with God.
—MONROE, HARRIET, 1889, *With a Copy of Shelley, The Century, vol.* 39, *p.* 313.

With the exception of Shakespeare, no English poet ever possessed a greater wealth of language or a finer sense of harmony. What he lacked was a general idea of Nature, and a knowledge of the manner in which the great majority of mankind think and feel. Hence the "Revolt of Islam," "Prometheus Unbound," and the "Witch of Atlas," fail in what is most essential to epic and dramatic poets—design, action, manners, character. Shelley formed his idea of Nature and his conception of his subjects in a solitary and purely capricious spirit. Unless the reader is prepared to surrender his own thought and judgment to his author's imagination, and to reason, judge, and believe, for the moment, as the poet would have him, he cannot fail to perceive that, in the poems I have mentioned, the "parts do not mutually support and explain each other." — COURTHOPE, WILLIAM JOHN, 1889, *The Life of Alexander Pope ; Pope's Works*, eds. Elwin and Courthope, vol. V, p. 373.

His muse had only wings, and not feet. It could soar into ideal heights, but it could not walk on the earth.—STORY, WILLIAM WETMORE, 1890, *Conversations in a Studio*, vol. I, p. 233.

Shelley is more truly a son of Italy than any one of her own poets, for he had the sentiment and passion of her natural beauty, which cannot be said of the greatest of them. I think that Shelley can scarcely be well comprehended by those who are not intimately acquainted with Italian landscape. The exceeding truthfulness of his observation of and feeling for it cannot certainly be appreciated except by those who have lived amongst the sights and sounds which took so close a hold upon his imagination and his heart.—RAMÉE, LOUISE DE LA (OUIDA), 1890, *A New View of Shelley*, North American Review, vol. 150, p. 246.

A creature of impetuous breath,
Our torpor deadlier than death
He knew not; whatsoe'er he saith
   Flashes with life:
He spurreth men, he quickeneth
   To splendid strife.
And in his gusts of song he brings
Wild odours shaken from strange wings,
And unfamiliar whisperings
   From far lips blown,
While all the rapturous heart of things
   Throbs through his own.
—WATSON, WILLIAM, 1892, *Shelley's Centenary, Poems*, p. 142.

Shelley is none of those of whom we are sometimes told in these days, whose mission is too serious to be transmitted with the arts of language, who are too much occupied with the substance to care about the form. All that is best in his exquisite collection of verse cries out against this wretched heresy. With all his modernity, his revolutionary instinct, his disdain of the unessential, his poetry is of the highest and most classical technical perfection. No one, among the moderns, has gone further than he in the just attention to poetic form.—GOSSE, EDMUND, 1892, *Shelley in* 1892, Questions at Issue, p. 213.

In Christ's own town did fools of old condemn
A sinless maid to burn in felon's fire ;
She looked above; she spake from out the pyre
To skies that made a star for Bethlehem,
When, lo! the flames touching her garment's hem
Blossom'd to roses—warbled like a lyre—
Made every fagot-twig a scented brier,
And crowned her with a rose-bud diadem!
Brothers in Shelley, we this morn are strong :
Our Heart of Hearts hath conquered—conquered those
Once fain to work the world and Shelley wrong :
Their pyre of hate now bourgeons with the rose—
Their every fagot, now a sweet-brier, throws
Love's breath upon the breeze of Shelley's song!
—WATTS, THEODORE, 1892, *For the Shelley Centenary*.

He could not solve the mystery of life —its shame, its wrong, its anguish; and like many another pure and ardent spirit bruised himself in many a wild fluttering against the iron bars of insoluble problems. And then he flew to Nature. In her freshness and grandeur, in the hospitality of her silence, and the friendliness of her unchangingness, he took refuge, and hid himself in her starry pavilion against the windy tempest of life's futility and malice. He becomes her high-priest and confidant. He serves her with unquenchable devotion and delight. He thirsts for her beauty, and toils to mirror her glory in fit and perfect speech. At thirty he is gray-headed, and his face is lined and furrowed like an old man's. The spirit of sorrow never leaves him; his verse is one long lament, and underneath its utmost triumph the voice sobs quietly and the sick heart aches. Then suddenly the end comes, and Nature weaves her blackest tempest for a pall and opens the door of rest in the dim green depths of that unresting ocean he had loved so well. He dies with purpose, character, and work alike unfinished. We know what he did, but know not what he might have done or been. But life is only just begun at thirty, and ended thus in its beginning, surely merits the grace of charity, of sympathy, of pity. That meed of reverent feeling has never yet been denied by any who have drunk of the magic stream of his poetry, and never will be wanting so long as English literature endures, and with it the name of Shelley.—DAWSON, W. J., 1892, *Quest and Vision, p. 38.*

Now a hundred years agone among us came
Down from some diviner sphere of purer flame,
Clothed in flesh to suffer, maimed of wings to soar,
One whom hate once hailed as now love hails by name,
Chosen of love as chosen of hatred. Now no more
Ear of man may hear or heart of man deplore
Aught of dissonance or doubt that mars the strain
Raised at last of love where love sat mute of yore.
—SWINBURNE, ALGERNON CHARLES, 1892, *The Centenary of Shelley.*

Be then the poet's poet still! for none
Of them whose minstrelsy the stars have blessed
Has from expression's wonderland so won
The unexpressed,—
So wrought the charm of its elusive note
On us, who yearn in vain
To mock the paean and the plain
Of tides that rise and fall with sweet mysterious rote.
—STEDMAN, EDMUND CLARENCE, 1892, *Ariel, Atlantic Monthly, vol. 70, p. 146.*

The cause Shelley served is still in its struggle; but those to whom social justice is a watchword, and the development of the individual everywhere in liberty, intelligence, and virtue is a cherished hope, must be thankful that Shelley lived, that the substance of his work is so vital, and his influence, inspiring as it is beyond that of any of our poets in these ways, was, and is, so completely on the side of the century's advance. His words are sung by marching thousands in the streets of London. No poet of our time has touched the cause of progress in the living breath and heart-throb of men so close as that. Yet, remote as the poet's dream always seems, it is rather that life-long singing of the golden age, in poem after poem which most restores and inflames those who, whether they be rude or refined, are

the choicer spirits of mankind, and bring, with revolutionary violence or ideal imagination, the times to come.—WOODBERRY, GEORGE E., 1892, *Shelley's Work, The Century, vol. 44, p. 629.*

The star that burns on revolution smote
Wild heats and change on thine ascendant sphere,
Whose influence thereafter seemed to float
Through many a strange eclipse of wrath and fear,
Dimming awhile the radiance of thy love.
But still supreme in thy nativity,
All dark, invidious aspects far above,
Beamed one clear orb for thee,—
The star whose ministrations just and strong
Controlled the tireless flight of Dante's song.
—ROBERTS, CHARLES G. D., 1892–93, *Ave! An Ode for the Centenary of Shelley's Birth, st. xiii.*

The sovereign transmutation that the dull, hard stuff of Godwin's doctrines suffered in the crucible of Shelley's imagination is known to all readers of the poems. In the "Epipsychidion" the nightingale pours forth a song suggested to her by the croaking of the frog.—RALEIGH, WALTER, 1894, *The English Novel, p. 251.*

The common judgment of Shelley, at least as expressed in literary organs, has undergone a complete revolution since he was a living man. Nobody now would venture to publish an article about Shelley without copious protestations of admiration for the poet, whatever the opinion might be expressed about his conduct as a man. To acknowledge indifference to his poetry would be to set one's self against an overwhelming weight of authoritative opinion. To deny him equal rank with any poet of his generation would be heresy. Enjoyment of Shelley is often put forward as a test of poetic sensibility; if Shelley does not delight you, you are set down as not being capable of knowing what poetry is. He is now *par excellence* the poet's poet.—MINTO, WILLIAM, 1894, *The Literature of the Georgian Era, ed. Knight, p. 292.*

It ["Defence of Poetry"] expresses Shelley's deepest thoughts about poetry, and marks, as clearly as any writing of the last hundred years, the width of the gulf that separates the ideals of recent poetry from those of the century preceding the French Revolution. It may be compared with Sidney's "Apologie" on the one hand, and with Wordsworth's Preface to the "Lyrical Ballads," or the more abstract parts of Carlyle's critical writings upon the other. The fundamental conceptions of Shelley are the same as those of the Elizabethan critic and of his own great contemporaries. But he differs from Sidney and Wordsworth, and perhaps from Carlyle also, in laying more stress upon the outward form, and particularly the musical element, of poetry; and from Sidney in laying less stress upon its directly moral associations. He thus attains to a wider and truer view of his subject; and, while insisting as strongly as Wordsworth insists upon the kinship between the matter of poetry and that of truth or science, he also recognizes, as Wordsworth commonly did not, that there is a harmony between the imaginative conception of that matter and its outward expression, and that beautiful thought must necessarily clothe itself in beauty of language and of sound. There is not in our literature any clearer presentment of the inseparable connection between the matter and form of poetry, nor of the ideal element which, under different shapes, is the life and soul of both.—VAUGHAN, C. E., 1896, ed., *English Literary Criticism*, p. 160.

Shelley was heart and soul a freethinker; and free-thought is now in the ascendant wherever men think at all. He was an advocate of free love; and the failure of marriage has become so notorious as to be a commonplace of modern novel-writers. He was a pioneer of communism; and the vast spread of socialist doctrines is the every-day complaint of a capitalist press. He was a humanitarian; and humanitarianism, having survived the phase of ridicule and misrepresentation, is taking its place among the chief-motive powers of civilised society.—SALT, HENRY S., 1896, *Percy Bysshe Shelley, Poet and Pioneer*, p. 187.

He has had a vast influence; but it has been in the main the influence, the inspiration of his unsurpassed exciting power. No one has borrowed or carried further any specially Shelleian turns of phrase, rhythm, or thought. Those who have attempted to copy and urge further the Shelleian attitude towards politics, philosophy, ethics, and the like, have made it generally ludicrous and sometimes disgusting. He is, in his own famous words, "something remote and afar." His poetry is almost poetry in its elements, uncoloured by race, language, time, circumstance, or creed. He is not even so much a poet as Poetry accidentally impersonated and incarnate.—SAINTSBURY, GEORGE, 1896, *A History of Nineteenth Century Literature*, p. 88.

Happily, Shelley's treatment of Nature —his landscape would be too limiting a word—in those instances where he has concentrated his mind upon his object, I should myself hold, as in the case of Keats, on the whole, his most precious achievement in poetry. . . . Without adopting M. Arnold's judgment that Shelley's prose will prove his permanent memorial, I must here (with all due respect and apology) make the confession, probably unpopular, reached after long reluctance, that no true poet of any age has left us so gigantic a mass of wasted effort, exuberance so Asiatic, such oceans (to speak out) of fluent, well-intended platitude—such ineffectual beating of his wings in the persistent effort to scale heights of thought beyond the reach of youth;—youth closed so prematurely, so lamentably. Hence the difference between Shelley's best and what is not best is enormous; the sudden transition from mere prose rendered more prosaic by its presentation in verse, to the most ethereal and exquisite poetry, frequent; and hence, also, it is in his shorter and mostly later lyrics that we find Shelley's very finest, uniquest, most magically delightful work. Yet even here at times the matter is attenuated as the film of the soap-bubble, gaining through its very thinness its marvellous iridescent beauty. —PALGRAVE, FRANCIS TURNER, 1896, *Landscape in Poetry*, pp. 218, 219.

Shelley's love-poems may be very good evidence, but we know well that they are "good for this day and train only." We are able to believe that they spoke the truth for that one day, but we know by experience that they could not be depended on to speak it the next. That very supplication for a rewarming of Harriet's chilled love was followed so suddenly by the poet's plunge into an adoring passion for Mary Godwin that if it had been a check it would have lost its value before a lazy person could have gotten to the bank with it.—CLEMENS, SAMUEL LANGHORNE (MARK TWAIN), 1897, *In Defence of Harriet Shelley, How to Tell a Story and other Essays, p.* 81.

He took Parnassus by storm. His poetical productiveness would have been admirable as the result of a long life; as the work in the main of little more than five years, it is one of the greatest marvels in the history of the human mind.—GARNETT, RICHARD, 1897, *Dictionary of National Biography, vol.* LII, *p.* 38.

Shelley:—The early editions of Shelley's Poems and Prose Treatises were amongst the first of this class of books to attain high prices. Some may be noted here in chronological order:—"Zastrozzi: a Romance," 1810, was published at 5s. Bound and cut copies have sold for £5, 15s., and £12, 5s. An uncut copy, in calf, fetched £12, 5s. in 1890, and an uncut copy in morocco brought fifteen guineas in 1897 (Sir C. S. Forbes). The most interesting of these pamphlets is the one which was the cause of its author being expelled from University College, Oxford. "The Necessity of Atheism. Worthing. Printed by E. & W. Phillips. Sold in London and Oxford," n. d. (1811) f. 8vo, p. 13. Nearly all the copies were destroyed by the printers, and Mr. Slater values a clean copy at about £20, but probably it would realise much more than that. "St. Irvyne," 1811, morocco uncut, Sir C. S. Forbes, 1897, £16, 10s. "An Address to the Irish People" (Dublin, 1812) was published at 5d., and Mr. Slater values a copy at £8 to £12, but one was sold at Alfred Crampton's sale, 1896, for £42. "Queen Mab," 1813, in the original boards, was sold in 1891 for £22, 10s. "The Refutation of Deism," 1814, fetched £33 at an auction in 1887. The largest price, however, given for one of these pamphlets was £130 for "Œdipus Tyrannus," 1820, at Crampton's sale. The entire impression was destroyed except seven copies, only two or three of which were known to exist, but

a reprint on vellum appeared in 1876. The British Museum possesses a copy, presented by Lady Shelley.—WHEATLEY, HENRY B., 1898, *Prices of Books, p.* 259.

Shelley was a true child of the Revolution; he inherited its vehement temper, he shared its impassioned illusions, he was the apt pupil of its doctrines; among his brother poets he must therefore take precedence. His radical spirit expressed itself in two ways: in an unrestrained denunciation of the past with its tyrannical government of priests and kings, and in an unshakable faith for a future with its perfect humanity and exemption from government. Like Rousseau and his dreaming disciples, he broke absolutely with a historic method; he failed to connect the gap between past and future with a passable bridge. History for him was but a record of human misery and depravity; he could read it only with a shudder. From that his mind turned, with its incandescent idealism, to flash upon the screen of the future the radiant panorama of the Golden Age. Imagination bestrode his reason, as Dean Swift would say; blind faith and hope obscured his sense of fact; desire gave wings to his thoughts, and they flew until, to use his own phrase, they were "pinnacled dim in the intense inane." Shelley was a true apostle of the Revolution's method; he objectified his own ideals and called them realities.—HANCOCK, ALBERT ELMER, 1899, *The French Revolution and the English Poets, p.* 50.

Shelley's was the passion of weakness, but not the passion of strength. Here is the true cause of his essential inferiority to Byron; here is the reason, as Mr. Richard Holt Hutton well showed, why Shelley's poetry is not sublime. There is no sublimity without power and Shelley's power was only the pseudo-power which morbid and introspective people can discover in weakness.—TRENT, WILLIAM P., 1899, *The Authority of Criticism and other Essays, p.* 80.

Ann Ward Radcliffe

1764-1823

Born [Ann Ward], in London, 9 July 1764. Married William Radcliffe, 1787. Occupied with literature, 1789-1802. Spent last twenty years of her life practically in retirement. Died, 7 Feb. 1823. Buried in St. George's Burial Ground, Bayswater Road. *Works:* "The Castles of Athlin and Dunbayne," 1789; "A Sicilian Romance,"

1790; "The Romance of the Forest" (anon.), 1791; "The Mysteries of Udulpho," 1794; "A Journey . . . through Holland," 1795; "The Italian," 1797; "Poems," 1816. *Posthumous:* "Gaston de Blondeville," 1826.—SHARP, R. FARQUHARSON, 1897, *A Dictionary of English Authors, p.* 235.

PERSONAL

The tenor of Mrs. Radcliffe's private life seems to have been peculiarly calm and sequestered. She probably declined the sort of personal notoriety, which, in London society, usually attaches to persons of literary merit; and perhaps no author whose works were so universally read and admired, was so little personally known even to the most active of that class of people of distinction, who rest their peculiar pretensions to fashion upon the selection of literary society.—SCOTT, SIR WALTER, 1821, *Mrs. Ann Radcliffe.*

A beautiful little woman of delicate constitution and sequestered habits, as fond, as her own heroines of lonely sea-shores, picturesque mountains, and poetical mediations.—HUNT, LEIGH, 1849, *A Book for a Corner, p.* 104.

Mrs. Radcliffe appears to have possessed a cheerful and equable temper, and to have manifested no peculiarity except the sensitive aversion to notice which she shared with many other authoresses. For the last twelve years of her life she suffered from spasmodic asthma, and succumbed to a sudden attack on 7 Feb. 1823. She was interred at the chapel-of-ease in the Bays-water Road (the resting-place of Laurence Sterne and of Paul Sandby) belonging to St. George's Hanover Square.—GARNETT, RICHARD, 1896, *Dictionary of National Biography, vol.* XLVII, *p.* 121.

GENERAL

I have read some of the descriptive verbose tales, of which your Ladyship says I was the patriarch by several mothers. (Miss Reeve and Mrs. Radcliffe?) All I can say for myself is that I do not think my concubines have produced issue more natural for excluding the aid of anything marvellous.—WALPOLE, HORACE, 1794, *To Countess of Ossory, Sept.* 4; *Letters, ed. Cunningham, vol.* IX, *p.* 440.

Mrs. Charlotte Smith, Mrs. Inchbald, Mrs. Mary Robinson, Mrs. &c., &c., though all of them are very ingenious ladies, yet they are too frequently *whining* or *frisking* in novels, till our girls' heads turn wild with impossible adventures, and now and then are tainted with democracy.—Not so

the mighty magician of the Mysteries of Udolpho, bred and nourished by the Florentine Muses in their sacred solitary caverns, amid the paler shrines of Gothick superstition, and in all the dreariness of inchantment; a poetess whom Ariosto would with rapture have acknowledged, as the

La nudrita
Damigella Trivulzia al sacro speco.

—MATHIAS, THOMAS JAMES, 1795, *The Pursuits of Literature, p.* 58.

In the productions of Mrs. Radcliffe, the Shakspeare of Romance Writers, and who to the wild landscape of Salvator Rosa has added the softer graces of a Claude, may be found many scenes truly terrific in their conception, yet so softened down, and the mind so much relieved, by the intermixture of beautiful description, or pathetic incident, that the impression of the whole never becomes too strong, never degenerates into horror, but pleasurable emotion is ever the predominating result.—DRAKE, NATHAN, 1798–1820, *Literary Hours, vol.* I, *No.* xvii, *p.* 273.

In the writings of this author there is a considerable degree of uniformity and mannerism, which is perhaps the case with all the productions of a strong and original genius. Her heroines too nearly resemble each other, or rather they possess hardly any shade of difference. They have all blue eyes and auburn hair—the form of each of them has "the airy lightness of a nymph"—they are all fond of watching the setting sun, and catching the purple tints of evening, and the vivid glow or fading splendour of the western horizon. Unfortunately they are all likewise early risers. I say unfortunately, for in every exigency Mrs. Radcliffe's heroines are provided with a pencil and paper, and the sun is never allowed to rise or set in peace. Like Tilburina in the play, they are "inconsolable to the minuet in Ariadne," and in the most distressing circumstances find time to compose sonnets to sunrise, the bat, a sea-nymph, a lily, or a butterfly.—DUNLOP, JOHN, 1814–42, *The History of Fiction, vol.* II, *p.* 412.

Her descriptions of scenery, indeed, are vague and wordy to the last degree; they are neither like Salvator nor Claude, nor nature nor art; and she dwells on the effects of moonlight till we are sometimes weary of them; her characters are insipid, —the shadows of a shade, continued on, under different names, through all her novels; her story comes to nothing. But in harrowing up the soul with imaginary horrors, and making the flesh creep and the nerves thrill with fond hopes and fears, she is unrivalled among her fair country-women. Her great power lies in describ-ing the indefinable, and embodying a phantom. She makes her readers twice children. . . . All the fascination that links the world of passion to the world unknown is hers, and she plays with it at her pleasure: she has all the poetry of romance, all that is obscure, visionary, and objectless in the imagination.—HAZ-LITT, WILLIAM, 1818, *Lecture on the Eng-lish Novelists.*

Indeed, the praise may be claimed for Mrs. Radcliffe, of having been the first to introduce into her prose fictions a beautiful and fanciful tone of natural description and impressive narrative, which had hitherto been exclusively applied to poetry. Field-ing, Richardson, Smollett, even Walpole, though writing upon an imaginative sub-ject, are decidedly prose authors. Mrs. Radcliffe has a title to be considered as the first poetess of romantic fiction, that is, if actual rhythm shall not be deemed essential to poetry.—SCOTT, SIR WALTER, 1821, *Mrs. Ann Radcliffe.*

Up to the close of "The Italian," her mind seems gradually to have ascended; and perhaps she felt as if the next step might be downward. It may be that she was right. "Gaston de Blondeville,"—not given to the world till after her death, and written scarcely five years after "The Italian,"—though showing a surprising improvement in style, discovers, at the same time, a subsiding of those energies by which she had held us with such fearful mastery.—DANA, RICHARD HENRY, 1827-50, *Radcliffe's Gaston de Blondeville, Poems and Prose Writings, vol.* II, *p.* 317.

Miss Edgeworth would scarcely venture into the region of the picturesque, and Mrs. Radcliffe is good for nothing out of it, except, indeed, when she is in her horrors.—PRESCOTT, WILLIAM HICKLING, 1832, *English Literature of the Nineteenth Century, North American Review, vol.* 35, *p.* 188.

But all this, though impressive, and sometimes grand, is unnatural: such fictions could not last: they were not of God, and so they failed. The authoress lived long enough to see the fabric which she had reared melt away, and Nature resume her reign with the same ease and quietness that the moon succeeds the tempest.—CUNNINGHAM, ALLAN, 1833, *Biographical and Critical History of the Literature of the Last Fifty Years.*

We would not pass over, without a tribute of gratitude, Mrs. Radcliffe's wild and wondrous tales. When we read them, the world seems shut out, and we breathe only in an enchanted region, where lovers' lutes tremble over placid waters, moulder-ing castles rise conscious of deeds of blood, and the sad voices of the past echo through deep vaults and lonely galleries. There is always majesty in her terrors. She pro-duces more effect by whispers and slender hints than ever was attained by the most vivid display of horrors. Her conclusions are tame and impotent almost without example. But while her spells actually operate, her power is truly magical.—TALFOURD, THOMAS NOON, 1842, *On British Novels and Romances, Critical and Miscel-laneous Writings, p.* 17.

Mystery is the whole spell. Nothing can be poorer and more conventional than the personages: they are not human beings, nor even the types of classes; they have no more individuality than the pieces of a chessboard; they are merely counters; but the skill with which the author juggles with them gives them a kind of awful necromantic interest. The characters are mere abstract algebraical expressions, but they are made the exponents of such ter-rible and intense fear, suffering and sus-pense, that we sympathise with their fate as if they were real.—SHAW, THOMAS B., 1847, *Outlines of English Literature, p.* 372.

In her verses, she is a tinselled nymph in a pantomime, calling up commonplaces with a wand.—HUNT, LEIGH, 1847, *Men, Women and Books, vol.* II, *p.* 125.

Mrs. Radcliffe's romances are, indeed, of a wholly fantastic kind of Gothic, with no whit of foundation in actual knowledge of mediæval history. Her characters are but vague melodramatic phantoms that flit through her descriptions of scenery, and serve as agents for her terrific situations. There is something like treachery also to the true theory of her style in her habit of always solving the mystery at the end by purely natural explanations.— MASSON, DAVID, 1859, *British Novelists and Their Styles*, p. 187.

Whose name everybody knows, but whose works, great as their power and effect was in their day, are less known now than their merit deserves. The "Mysteries of Udolpho" is old-fahioned, but it is fine reading for those who have leisure to trace the meanderings of the threads so carefully entangled, and to follow the most ethereal of heroines through the piled-up troubles which make her reward all the sweeter when it comes: and that reward aways does come. . . . Her landscapes, even now, though literature has done a great deal since then in the pictorial art, are full of an elaborate and old-fashioned yet tender beauty. She is not familiar with them, nor playful, but always at the height of a romantic strain; not graphic, but refined and full of perception. There are scenes that remind us of the learned Poussin, and some that have a light in them not unworthy of Claude before he was put down from his throne by the braggart energy and rivalship of Turner—since when the modern spectator has scarcely had eyes for those serene horizons and gleaming moonlight seas. Perhaps of all others Mrs. Radcliffe's art is most like that of the gentle painter whom people call Italian Wilson. There is a ruined temple in the distance, a guitar laid against a broken column; but the lights, how mellow and soft, the skies how full of tempered radiance, the pastoral valleys unprofaned by ungracious foot— full of the light that never was on sea or shore!—OLIPHANT, MARGARET O. W., 1882, *The Literary History of England, XVIIIth-XIXth Century*, vol. II, pp. 232, 233.

But what Mrs. Radcliffe attempted, she carried out with a very great skill.— TUCKERMAN, BAYARD, 1882, *A History of English Prose Fiction*, p. 268.

A hundred years later, women touched the novel of plot and adventure with a bolder grasp, and Mrs. Radcliffe's romances seemed the joint offspring of "big bow-bow" and nightmare parentage. But they too moved with sweep and power; she was strong in description and invention; she

bridged the interval between the mediæval and modern novel, and painted landscape so well that even Byron sometimes borrowed from her.—HIGGINSON, THOMAS WENTWORTH, 1887, *Women and Men*, p. 160.

Mrs. Radcliffe sometimes writes powerfully and well, but sometimes she writes very badly. Her style is stiff and inflated; she is fond of fine words and involved sentences, and has a righteous detestation of calling a spade a spade. Her forte is description, she has a peculiar talent for drawing link after link of detail. She brings us into a suite of mysterious rooms, with high casements, a dagger eaten with rust on the floor, an old bedstead, a heap of lumber, and a dusty manuscript—each completes a chain of horrors.—HAMILTON, CATHARINE J., 1892, *Women Writers, First Series*, p. 152.

There is generally some mystery afloat; when one has been cleared up, we are not suffered long to breathe freely before we are caught in the toils of another. Yet all the time only human agents are at work; there is nothing improbable except the extraordinary combination of circumstances, nothing supernatural except in the superstitious imaginings of the personages of the story. Every thing that seemed as if it must be the work of spirits is carefully and fully explained as the story goes on. Mrs. Radcliffe has been censured for these explanations, as if they were a mistake in point of art, destroying the illusion and making us ashamed of ourselves for having been imposed upon. This censure I can regard only as an affectation, unless when it comes from a convinced believer in ghosts. Such persons might resent the explanation as casting doubts upon their cherished belief. But for other people I can see nothing that could be gained by leaving the mysterious incidents unexplained, except by the authoress, who would undoubtedly have saved herself an immense deal of trouble if she had made free use of ghosts and other supernatural properties, whenever she required them, without taking any pains to explain how the facts occurred. I read the story myself with a double interest; I enjoy the excitement of superstitious wonder and awe while the illusion lasts, and when the mystery is cleared up, and the excitement is gently subsiding, I am in a mood to get additional enjoyment from reflecting on the ingenuity of the complication that gave to the illusion for the moment the force of truth. Yet it was no less a person than Sir Walter Scott that set the fashion of objecting to Mrs. Radcliffe's explanations. — MINTO, WILLIAM, 1894, *The Literature of the Georgian Era, ed. Knight*, p. 126.

Her ignorance of the world at the time when she wrote was complete and many-sided. Human character she knew, not from observation but from dreams. The landscapes for which she is so justly famous are pictures of countries she never saw. There is nothing in her books that she did not create. And it is a testimony to the power of her art that her fancy first conceived a type of character that subsequently passed from art into life. The man that Lord Byron tried to be was the invention of Mrs. Radcliffe. — RALEIGH, WALTER, 1894, *The English Novel*, p. 228.

The actual literary value is, on the whole, low; though Mrs. Radcliffe is not without glimmerings. — SAINTSBURY, GEORGE, 1896, *A History of Nineteenth Century Literature*, p. 44.

It was, indeed, in the melodramatic manipulation of landscape that this artist was most original. "The scenes that savage Rosa dashed" seem to have been her model, and critics who were fond of analogy called her the Salvator Rosa of fiction. It is here that her influence on Byron and Chateaubriand is most apparent. Mrs. Radcliffe's scenery is not quite to our modern taste, any more than are Salvator's paintings. Her Venice by moonlight, her mountain gorges with their black pines and foaming torrents, are not precisely the Venice and the Alps of Ruskin; rather of the operatic stage. Still they are impressive in their way, and in this department she possessed genuine poetic feeling and a real mastery of the art of painting in distemper. — BEERS, HENRY A., 1898, *A History of English Romanticism in the Eighteenth Century*, p. 255.

Mrs. Radcliffe wrote for the story, and not for the characters, which are all types, and soon became conventional. There is always the young lover, a gentleman of high birth, usually in some sort of disguise, who, without seeing the face of the heroine, may fall in love with her "distinguished air of delicacy and grace" or "the sweetness and fine expression of her voice." The only variation in the heroine is that she may be either dark or fair. The beautiful creature is confined in a castle or a convent because she refuses to marry some one whom she hates. She finally has her own way and marries her lover. The tyrant is always the same man under different names; add to him a little softness, and he becomes the Byronic hero. — CROSS, WILBUR L., 1899, *The Development of the English Novel*, p. 106.

Does any one now read Mrs. Radcliffe, or am I the only wanderer in her windy corridors, listening timidly to groans and hollow voices, and shielding the flame of a lamp, which, I fear, will presently flicker out, and leave me in the darkness? People know the name of "The Mysteries of Udolpho;" they know that boys would say to Thackeray, at school, "Old fellow, draw us Vivaldi in the Inquisition." But have they penetrated into the chill galleries of the Castle of Udolpho? Have they shuddered for Vivaldi in face of the sable-clad and masked Inquisition? Certainly Mrs. Radcliffe, within the memory of man, has been extremely popular. The thick double-columned volume in which I peruse the works of the Enchantress belongs to a public library. It is quite the dirtiest, greasiest, most dog's-eared, and most bescribbled tome in the collection. Many of the books have remained, during the last hundred years, uncut, even to this day, and I have had to apply the paper knife to many an author, from Alciphron (1790) to Mr. Max Müller, and Dr. Birkbeck Hill's edition of Bozzy's "Life of Dr. Johnson." But Mrs. Radcliffe has been read diligently, and copiously annotated. . . . Mrs. Radcliffe does not always keep on her highest level, but we must remember that her last romance, "The Italian," is by far her best. She had been feeling her way to this pitch of excellence, and, when she had attained to it, she published no more. . . . "The Italian" is an excellent novel. The Prelude, "the dark and vaulted gateway," is not unworthy of Hawthorne, who, I suspect, had studied Mrs. Radcliffe. — LANG, ANDREW, 1900, *Mrs. Radcliffe's Novels, Cornhill Magazine, vol. 82, pp.* 23, 24, 33.

Charles Wolfe

1791–1823

Born, in Dublin, 14 Dec. 1791. At school at Bath, 1801; at Salisbury, 1803–05; at Winchester Col., 1806–09. To Dublin Univ., 1809; scholar, 1812; B. A., 1814. Ordained, Nov. 1817. Curate of Ballyclog, Tyrone, Dec. 1817 to Jan. 1818; of Castle Caulfield, Donoughmore, 1818–21. Ill-health from 1821. Died at Cove of Cork, 21 Feb. 1823. *Works:* "The Burial of Sir John Moore; with other poems," 1825; "Remains," ed. by J. A. Russell, with *memoir* (2 vols.), 1825.—SHARP, R. FARQUHARSON, 1897, *A Dictionary of English Authors, p.* 303.

PERSONAL

His habits and manner of life, as a clergyman, were exceedingly simple and primitive. He scarcely ever thought of providing a regular meal. His small cottage contained a few rushbottomed chairs, a rickety table, and two trunks: one for his papers and the other for his linen. The trunks also did service by covering the broken parts of the floor. The damp paper hung in loose folds from the mouldy walls of the closet where he slept. A dangerous place for a man of a consumptive habit. *Between* the parlour and the closet was the kitchen, the warmest and most comfortable apartment of the three. This was occupied by a disbanded soldier, his wife, and a numerous band of children, who kept house for the minister, whom they entertained as a lodger, taking possession of the "bit of potato garden" (which went with the cottage) as lords of the soil.—GIBSON, CHARLES B., 1864, *Charles Wolfe, Once a Week, vol.* 11, *p.* 504.

GENERAL

Charles Wolfe has been one of the few who have gained probable immortality from a casual gleam of inspiration thrown over a single poem, consisting of only a few stanzas, and these, too, little more than a spiritual version from the prose of another. But the lyric is indeed full of fervor and freshness; and his triumph is not to be grudged.—MOIR, D. M., 1850–51, *Sketches of the Poetical Literature of the Past Half-Century.*

The famous ode on "The Burial of Sir John Moore." . . . Almost immediately it took its place among the four or five best martial poems in our language, preeminent for simplicity, patriotic fervour, and manly pathos. It was presently discovered that this poem had been written some years before it was printed, by a young Irishman of much promise who died of a decline in his thirty-second year.

When this fact became known, public curiosity was attracted to his name, and an attempt was made by one of his early friends to collect what he had written. Only twelve short pieces, besides the ode, could be discovered; they were mostly songs of love and friendship, full of ardour, and not uninfluenced by the popular Irish manner of Moore.—GOSSE, EDMUND, 1880, *The English Poets, ed. Ward, vol.* IV, *p.*323.

The "single speech" accident of Charles Wolfe, the author of the "Burial of Sir John Moore," which everybody knows, and of absolutely nothing else that is worth a single person's knowing.—SAINTSBURY, GEORGE, 1896, *A History of Nineteenth Century Literature, p.* 124.

The Rev. Charles Wolfe, an obscure Irish clergyman, writes a short poem which a friend who had learned it recites to a casual travelling acquaintance. The latter publishes it in the "Newry Telegraph." Soon it is on the lips of Shelley and Byron, and now there is hardly a reader of the English language who has not read the "Burial of Sir John Moore." Few indeed are the "occasional" poems that possess so enduring a power to move the heart. Its note of pride and sorrow is tuned to that of all the lofty sorrows of the world, and the very music of the lines with their long, deep vowel sounds, like the burst of solemn passion in Beethoven's Funeral March, will carry their meaning and emotion to readers of many generations hence. Wolfe wrote but little poetry in his short life, and little of what he wrote can compare with the "Burial Ode." But the "Song" which he wrote under the influence of a strain of Irish music, to which he was keenly sensitive, has a remarkable intensity of feeling and sweetness of melody.—ROLLESTON, T. W., 1900, *A Treasury of Irish Poetry, eds. Brooke and Rolleston, p.* 51.

The poetical achievements of Wolfe fill but a few pages in the memorial volumes.

. . . Exclusive of some boyish productions, they number no more than fifteen pieces, all of them written almost at random, without any idea of publication, and preserved almost by accident. These, however, present the potentials of a poet of no mean order. The testimony of many contemporaries, afterwards eminent, confirms the impression which his other lyrics convey, that the lines on the burial of Sir John Moore are not, as has been represented, a mere freak of intellect, but the fruit of a temperament and genius essentially poetic.—FALKINER, C. LITTON, 1900, *Dictionary of National Biography,* vol. LXII, *p.* 296.

Robert Bloomfield
1766–1823

Robert Bloomfield (1766–1823)—farmer's boy, and, through the influence of the Duke of Grafton, government clerk, with a somewhat unhappy lot in both positions— "The Farmer's Boy" (1798), "Rural Tales" (1802), "Wild Flowers," and other pieces; volumes of cheerful description of rural life with much moral feeling and smoothness of versification: his great fault is his want of passion—his great excellence, the truth and reality of his delineations: some of his lines, those for example on the "Soldier's Home," Wilson thinks equal to Burns'.—ANGUS, JOSEPH, 1865, *The Handbook of English Literature, p.* 265.

PERSONAL

Bloomfield was dull in conversation; but humble, simple, mild, and unpretending. . . . I never saw a man more humble in manner, without losing his dignity, than Robert Bloomfield; but he was not easy in the company of men born and moving in a rank of society much above him; and I do not think he gained anything by suffering himself to be drawn into it.—BRYDGES, SIR SAMUEL EGERTON, 1834, *Autobiography, vol.* II, *pp.* 46, 172.

It is little to the credit of the age, that the latter days of a man whose name was at one time so deservedly popular, should have been past in poverty, and perhaps shortened by distress, that distress having been brought on by no misconduct or imprudence of his own.—SOUTHEY, ROBERT, 1836, *Lives of Uneducated Poets, p.* 163.

Having now become hypochondriacal and half blind, he retired to Shefford, where he died in great poverty on 19 Aug. 1823, leaving a widow and four children. Had he lived longer, he would probably have gone mad.—BULLEN, A. H., 1886, *Dictionary of National Biography, vol.* V, *p.* 237.

No British poet ever had a harder life than Robert Bloomfield, whose misfortune it was to suffer from poetry and poverty alike. He cannot be said to have been worsened by his gift of verse, such as it was, but he can hardly be said to have been bettered by it, since it neither developed his character nor strengthened his mind.

But perhaps it did all that could be expected, his mind being, as Lamb observed, a poor one, and his character a weak one. He was the creature of circumstances, crushed by inherited poverty, and cursed with a feeble constitution and constant illness. Nature does not make heroes out of sickly shoemakers only five feet four inches long, still less great poets.—STODDARD, RICHARD HENRY, 1892, *Under the Evening Lamp, p.* 116.

GENERAL

Such indeed are the merits of this work ["The Farmer's Boy"] that, in true *pastoral* imagery and simplicity, I do not think any production can be put in competition with it since the days of Theocritus. To that charming rusticity which particularises the Grecian are added the individuality, fidelity, and boldness of description which render Thomson so interesting to the lovers of Nature. Gresner possesses the most engaging sentiment, and the most refined simplicity of manners, but he wants that rustic wildness and naïveté in delineation characteristic of the Sicilian and of the composition before us. Warner and Drayton have much to recommend them, but they are very unequal, and are devoid of the sweet and pensive morality which pervade almost every page of the "Farmer's Boy;" nor can they establish any pretentions to that fecundity in painting the economy of rural life, which this poem, drawn from actual experience, so richly displays It is astonishing, indeed, what various and striking circumstances peculiar to the occupation of the British Farmer, and which are adapted to all the purposes of the pastoral Muse, had escaped our poets previous to the publication of Mr. Bloomfield's work.—DRAKE, NATHAN, 1798-1820, *Literary Hours, vol.* II, *No.* xxxix, *p.* 308.

Don't you think the fellow who wrote it (who is a shoemaker) has a poor mind? Don't you find he is always silly about *poor Giles,* and those abject kind of phrases which mark a man that looks up to wealth? None of Burns' poet dignity. What do you think? I have just opened him, but he makes me sick.—LAMB, CHARLES, 1800, *Letter to Manning, Nov.* 3.

I have received many honourable testimonies of esteem from strangers; letters without a name, but filled with the most cordial advice, and almost a parental anxiety, for my safety under so great a share of public applause. I beg to refer such friends to the great teacher, Time; and hope that he will hereafter give me my deserts, and no more.—BLOOMFIELD, ROBERT, 1801, *Rural Tales, Preface.*

Bloomfield, thy happy-omen'd name
Ensures continuance to thy fame;
Both sense and truth this verdict give,
While *fields* shall *bloom,* thy name shall live!
—WHITE, HENRY KIRKE, 1803, *Clifton Grove.*

How wise, how noble, was thy choice,
  To be the Bard of simple swains;
In all their pleasures to rejoice,
  And soothe with sympathy their pains;
To sing with feeling in thy strains
  The simple subjects they discuss,
And be, though free from classic chains,
  Our own more chaste Theocritus!
—BARTON, BERNARD, 1823, *To the Memory of Robert Bloomfield, London Magazine, vol.* 8, *Memoir.*

In his "Rural Tales," he has succeeded in the patriotic attempt to render the loves and joys, the sports and manners, of English peasants interesting. I recollect no poet before him who, by a serious, unaffected delineation of humble life, as it actually exists, had awakened strong sympathy, in people more prosperously circumstanced, towards the lower classes of the community.—MONTGOMERY, JAMES, 1833, *Lectures on General Literature, Poetry, etc.,* p. 165.

Beyond any example, save that of Clare, Bloomfield seemed to be a poet almost by intuition; for in point of taste, melody, and accuracy, his early verses, composed without almost a glimpse of education, were never excelled by his after efforts.—MOIR, D. M., 1850-51, *Sketches of the Poetical Literature of the Past Half-Century, p.* 32.

The success of the poem was immediate and complete. It was warmly received by the public, and praised in all quarters as a masterpiece of natural poetic simplicity and beauty. Twenty-six thousand copies were sold in the first three years of its issue, seven editions having been called for. The position secured by the "Farmer's Boy" on its first publication has been held until the present day. All lovers of poetry read it with delight. It is natural and graceful as the song of a bird "warbling his native woodnotes wild." When the English song-bird sings in captivity there seems to be a touch of pathos in his note; and one can hardly resist the same impression in reading these sweet rustic melodies in verse which came from the lips of the shoemaker-poet imprisoned in a London garret. Yet there is something much more stimulating in Boomfield's lines than this. They are sweet and joyous, and full of that glowing enthusiasm for beauty which all fine natures feel. Besides the editions sent forth in this country, the "Farmer's Boy" was printed at Leipsic, and was translated into French, Italian, and Latin.—WINKS, WILLIAM EDWARD, 1882, *Lives of Illustrious Shoemakers, p.* 99.

It was not in the nature of a man like Lamb to respect a man like Bloomfield. There was nothing in common between them, the one being a scholar and a thinker, the other an unlettered rustic, with a knack at versifying. The reputation of Burns, who died four years before, prepared the way for a self-made rhymester like Bloomfield, whose temporary vogue prepared the way in turn for a little school of self-made rhymsters who sprung up around him. There are tracts of literature wherein, as in old, neglected pastures, mushrooms are sometimes found, and with these mushrooms hundreds of other fungi which are often mistaken for them by the ignorant and the credulous. Byron described Churchill as the comet of a season. If I were to describe Bloomfield, it would be as a glow-worm, whose mild and fitful raidance twinkled awhile, and then went out in the darkness.—STODDARD, RICHARD HENRY, 1892, *Under the Evening Lamp,* p. 114.

We children who were used to the free range of woods and fields were homesick for the country in our narrow city yard, and I associate with this longing the "Farmer Boy" of Bloomfield, which my father got for me. It was a little book in blue cloth, and there were some mild woodcuts in it. I read it with a tempered pleasure and with a vague resentment of its trespass upon Thomson's ground in the division of its parts under the names of the seasons. I do not know why I need have felt this. I was not yet very fond of Thomson. I really liked Bloomfield better; for one thing, his poem was written in the heroic decasyllables which I preferred to any other verse.—HOWELLS, WILLIAM DEAN, 1895, *My Literary Passions,* p. 46.

Bloomfield's poetry is characterised by a smoothness and ease of versification which came quite natural to him. He had an ear for music which guided him in the formation of his verse. If his vocabulary was not extensive it was quite large enough for the themes upon which he wrote; and his choice of words is often felicitous. . . . But it is as a poet of Nature rather than of Humanity that Bloomfield claims recognition. His descriptions of natural scenery are both faithful and characteristic. His pictures of the farmer's boy engaged in various labours of the farm are those of one who draws direct from Nature, and who has himself experienced the life that he depicts. These show both minuteness of observation and fidelity of description, which entitle him to an honourable place among the earliest of modern worshippers at the so long neglected shrine of Nature.—MILES, ALFRED H., 1895, *The Poets and the Poetry of the Century, Crabbe to Coleridge, pp.* 155, 156.

One of those unfortunate "prodigy" poets whom mistaken kindness encourages. . . . His "Farmer's Boy," an estimable but much over-praised piece.—SAINTSBURY, GEORGE, 1896, *A History of Nineteenth Century Literature, p.* 107.

David Ricardo
1772–1823

Born, in England, 19 April 1772. Early education in England; in Holland, 1783–85. Began to assist his father in business on Stock Exchange, 1786. Married Priscilla Anne Wilkinson, 20 Dec. 1793. Mem. of newly founded Geological Soc., 1807. Bought the estate of Gatcombe Park, Gloucestershire, 1813. Retired from business, 1814. Sheriff, 1818. M. P. for Portarlington, Ireland, 1819–23. Visit to Continent, 1822. Died, at Gatcombe Park, 11 Sept. 1823. *Works:* "The High Price of Bullion a proof of the depreciation of Bank Notes," 1810 (3rd edn., same year); "Observations on some passages in . . . the Edinburgh Review," 1811; "Reply to Mr. Bosanquet's Practical Observations," 1811; "Essay on the Influence of a Low Price of Corn on the Profits of Stock," 1815 (2nd edn., same year); "Proposals for an Economical and Secure Currency," 1816 (2nd edn., same year); "On the Principles of Political Economy and Taxation," 1817; "On Protection to Agriculture," 1822 (4th edn., same year); "Plan for the Establishment of a National Bank," 1824. *Posthumous:* Letters to T. R. Malthus, 1887. *Collected Works:* ed. by McCulloch, 2nd edn., 1852.—SHARP, R. FARQUHARSON, 1897, *A Dictionary of English Authors, p.* 239.

PERSONAL

I do not remember that any public event of our own times has touched me so nearly, or so much with the feelings belonging to a private affliction, as the death of Mr. Ricardo. To me in some sense it was a private affliction, and no doubt to all others who knew and honoured his extraordinary talents. For great intellectual merit, wherever it has been steadily contemplated, cannot but conciliate some personal regard; and, for my part, I acknowledge that, abstracting altogether from the use to which a man of splendid endowments may apply them—or even supposing the case that he should deliberately apply them to a bad one—I could no more on that account withhold my good wishes and affection from his person, than, under any consideration of their terrific attributes, I could forbear to admire the power and the beauty of the serpent or the panther. . . . Mr. Ricardo, however, stood in no need of a partial or indulgent privilege; his privilege of intellect had a comprehensive sanction from all the purposes to which he applied it in the course of his public life; in or out of Parliament, as a senator, or as an author, he was known and honoured as a public benefactor. Though connected myself by private friendship with persons of the political party hostile to his, I heard amongst them all but one language of respect for his public conduct.—DE QUINCEY, THOMAS, 1823, *The Services of Mr. Ricardo to the Sciences of Political Economy, London Magazine.*

His speaking, his conduct, his manner, were all exceptionable and all suited to the man,—his high station among philosophers, his known opinions on political affairs, his kindly nature, and his genuine modesty. There was something about him, chiefly a want of all affectation as well as pretention in everything he said or did, that won the respect of each party. His matter was ever of high value. Whether you agreed or differed with him, you were well pleased to have it brought out and made to bear upon the question, if indeed the pursuit of right and truth was your object. His views were often, indeed, abundantly theoretical, sometimes too refined for his audience, occasionally extravagant, from his propensity to follow a right principle into all its consequences, without duly taking into account in practice the condition of things to which he was applying it, as if a mechanician were to construct an engine without taking into consideration the resistance of the air in which it was to work, or the strength and the weight and the friction of the parts of which it was to be made. . . . But while such were his errors, and those of a kind to excite very strong feelings in certain large and important classes in the House of Commons, he was uniformly and universally respected for the sterling qualities of his capacity and his character, which were acknowledged by all.— BROUGHAM, HENRY LORD, 1839-43, *Lives of Statesmen of the Time of George III.*

His benignity of character and simple but earnest manner in argument often made converts where his books had failed to do so.—HOLLAND, SIR HENRY, 1871, *Recollections of Past Life, p.* 241.

During this first period of my life, the habitual frequenters of my father's house were limited to a very few persons, most of them little known to the world, but whom personal worth, and more or less of congeniality with at least his political opinions (not so frequently to be met with then as since) inclined him to cultivate; and his conversations with them I listened to with interest and instruction. My being an habitual inmate of my father's study made me acquainted with the dearest of his friends, David Ricardo, who by his benevolent countenence, and kindliness of manner, was very attractive to young persons, and who, after I became a student of political economy, invited me to his house and to walk with him in order to converse on the subject.—MILL, JOHN STUART, 1873, *Autobiography.*

Miss Edgeworth visited the Ricardos at Gatcombe in 1821, and gives an account of his family and "delightfully pleasant house." She says that he was charming in conversation; perpetually starting new game, and never arguing for victory. He took part in charades, and represented a coxcomb very drolly. Altogether she thought him one of the most agreeable and least formal persons she ever met. . . . His family held, it appears, that any child "could impose upon him."—STEPHEN, LESLIE, 1896, *Dictionary of National Biography, vol.* XLVIII, *p.* 95.

GENERAL

Consolidating his views in one work, he gave to the world his excellent treatise on his favourite science, which, with Mr. Malthus's "Essay on the Principle of Population," divides the claim to a second place after the "Wealth of Nations," among the books which this country has produced upon the important science of economics.— BROUGHAM, HENRY LORD, 1839-43, *Lives of Statesmen of the Time of George III.*

This is a most able, original, and profound work. Its appearance formed a new era in the history of the science. Exclusive of many valuable correlative discussions, Mr. Ricardo has traced the source and limiting principle of exchangeable value, and has exhibited the laws which determine the distribution of the various products of art and industry among the various ranks and orders of society. . . . Mr. Ricardo was the first to perceive the error into which Smith had fallen, in supposing that the effects consequent upon an increase or diminution of the wages paid for the labour employed in the production of commodities were the same with those consequent upon an increase or diminution of the quantity of such labour.—McCulloch, John Ramsay, 1845, *Literature of Political Economy, p.* 16.

His book is the true manual of the demagogue,—seeking power by means of agrarianism, war, and plunder. Its lessons being inconsistent with those afforded by the study of all well-observed facts, and inconsistent even with themselves, the sooner they shall come to be discarded the better will it be, for the interests of landlord and tenant, manufacturer and mechanic, and mankind at large.—Carey, Henry C., 1858, *Principles of Social Science, vol.* iii, *p.* 154.

He was an economist only, not at all a social philosopher in the wider sense, like Adam Smith or John Mill. He had great acuteness, but little breadth. For any large treatment of moral and political questions he seems to have been alike by nature and preparation unfitted; and there is no evidence of his having had any but the most ordinary and narrow views of the great social problems. His whole conception of human society is material and mechanical, the selfish principle being regarded, after the manner of the Benthamites, as omnipotent, not merely in practical economy, but, as appears from his speech on the ballot and his tract on reform, in the whole extent of the social field. Roscher calls him "ein tiefer Menschenkenner;" it would be difficult to characterize him more inaptly. The same writer remarks on his "capitalistic" tone, which, he says, becomes, "mammonistic" in some of his followers; but the latter spirit is already felt as the pervading atmosphere of Ricardo's works. He shows no trace of that hearty sympathy with the working classes which breaks out in several passages of the "Wealth of Nations;" we ought, perhaps, with Held, to regard it as a merit in Ricardo that he does not cover with fine phrases his deficiency in warmth of social sentiment.—Ingram, John Kells, 1886, *Encyclopædia Britannica, Ninth ed., vol.* xx, *p.* 550.

There are few writers so open to misunderstanding, and few indeed whose real merits have been so completely thrust out of sight by other merits fancifully attributed to them. "The Principles of Political Economy and Taxation" has been invested with the portentiously solemn character of a complete scientific handbook, while its author has been praised alike by friend and foe for rigid logic, careful method, and an exactitude of definition, almost mathematical in its nature. To such an extent has this attitude been assumed that till some few years ago hardly any critic, however unfriendly, hesitated to give his assent to the proposition that Ricardo's conclusions, his premises once granted, were irrefutable. And yet it is hardly possible to doubt that the eulogies thus lavishly if carelessly bestowed are not those to which Ricardo is best entitled. It is doubtful, perhaps, whether he is entitled to some of them at all. So far is the work under consideration from being a perfect work that it is disfigured by blemishes and defects of very many kinds. Not only is it remarkable for infelicity of language, with all its fatal consequences of exaggeration and obscurity, but the grammar itself is halting and the accuracy often apparent, fallaciously apparent, rather than real.—Gonner, E. C. K., 1891, *ed. Ricardo's Political Economy, Introductory Essay, p.* xxiii.

English economists can hardly fail to be proud of Ricardo; and whether their pride takes the form of treating him as an Angel of Light or as the Prince of Darkness, they will probably all assign to him much greater influence than foreign economists would allow. Besides, if, as we are told, it is a pleasure to the young and vehement to be heterodox and to scoff at great names, it is a comfort to the staid and academic "stare super antiquas vias," to feel that they are building on the foundations that were laid by the fathers of their church.—Ashley, W. J., 1891, *The Rehabilitation of Ricardo, Economic Journal, vol.* i, *p.* 475.

With Ricardo's name is associated a progress in our science far more considerable than can be credited to Say. Ricardo is in fact by general consent recognised as the greatest economist of the nineteenth century. Like Malthus, he suffered much from the misconceptions of his too enthusiastic friends, but he had a still larger number of adversaries who attacked him when he wrote, and his recent adversaries have not been few. Among them it is grievous that we must mention two writers of such conspicuous merit as Jevons and Ferrara. . . . But after all, Ricardo's chief title to fame rests upon the "Principles of Political Economy" (1817), a work of originality and profundity so remarkable that it marks an epoch in the history of our science, though, to be sure, its good points are overstated by such enthusiastic partisans as MacCulloch and De Quincey. That it has defects is obvious to any conscientious and critical reader, but these are not often the ones which trivial-minded or incompetent critics have stretched its words and twisted its thoughts to fasten upon it. Ricardo certainly never dreamt of writing an exhaustive treatise, because, as is definitely recorded by him again and again in his letters, he was painfully aware of his disqualifications as a writer, indeed his modesty has overstated them.—COSSA, LUIGI, 1891–93, *An Introduction to the Study of Political Economy*, ed. *Dyer.*

Ever since the death of Ricardo there has been an increasing interest in him and his writings. For all deductive economists his theories have had a charm which those of no later writer possess. There are many whose reasoning is more perfect, many whose ideas are more clearly expressed; but few have attained the commanding position of Ricardo in economic theory. On the other hand, among a large class of economists with inductive and historical tendencies, any doctrine to which Ricardo's name is attached is discredited, and often treated with contempt. I have no desire to enter this controversy, which must rest as it is until a new spirit causes men to interpret the history of economic theory from a new standpoint. I only desire to discuss the interpretation of Ricardo's writings which has grown up among his followers and disciples, and from a position friendly to him and them. Few writers have a greater interest in deductive economics than I, and no one would be less willing to say anything that would reflect any discredit or lower in any way the high esteem in which Ricardo is held. Yet it seems to me that his friends in defending him have placed him in a false light, and have distorted the history of economic theory. Ricardo is too great a man to need any false praise; his merits will only be magnified if he is placed in his true historical position as an economist.—PETTAN, SIMON N., 1893, *The Interpretation of Ricardo, The Quarterly Journal of Economics, vol.* 7, *p.* 322.

Thomas Erskine

1750–1823

Thomas, Baron Erskine. Born at Edinburgh, Jan. 21, 1750: died at Almondell, near Edinburgh, Nov. 17, 1823. A British jurist and forensic orator. He was the youngest son of the tenth Earl of Buchan. He attained celebrity as a pleader in supporting charges of corruption advanced against Lord Sandwich, and subsequently distinguished himself especially in his defence of Stockdale (1789), Thomas Paine (1792), and Hardy, Horne Tooke, etc. (1794). He represented Portsmouth in the House of Commons from 1790 till raised to the peerage as Baron Erskine, of Restormel, on his being made lord chancellor in Lord Grenville's administration (Feb., 1806,—April, 1807.)—SMITH, BENJAMIN E., ed., 1894–97, *The Century Cyclopedia of Names, p.* 367.

PERSONAL

ERSKINE.—Mr. Barrister Erskine is famous for taking opium in great quantities (I have often heard him speak in praise of it), and if he proceeds in this manner, it is apprehended that his *political* faculties will die of too large a dose, of which there are *many* symptoms already. But *all* my observations are confined to his *political* conduct and career. They are not extended to his professional character, which is great, or to his private life, which

no man is inclined to respect more than myself. But his political doctrines are plunging and dangerous. Mr. Erskine has informed the publick, that He *has not the talents of a statesman*, which, in common with the kingdom at large, I readily admit as part of my political creed; though it is so very plain, as hardly to be an article of faith.—MATHIAS, THOMAS JAMES, 1794–98, *The Pursuits of Literature, p.* 363.

Although the new administration has been formed in general of the public men of the greatest talents and highest character of any in the country, yet there are some few appointments which have been received by the public with such dissatisfaction, and none the more than that of Erskine to be Lord Chancellor. The truth undoubtedly is, that he is totally unfit for the situation. His practice has never led him into courts of equity ; and the doctrines which prevail in them are to him almost like the law of a foreign country. It is true that he has a great deal of quickness and is capable of much application ; but, at his time of life, with the continual occupations which the duties of his office will give him, and the immense arrear of business left him by his tardy and doubting predecessor, It is quite impossible that he should find the means of making himself master of that extensive and complicated system of law, which he will have to administer.—ROMILLY, SIR SAMUEL, 1806, *Diary*, Feb. 8; *Memoirs by his Sons*, *vol.* II, *p.* 128.

The House of Commons was not his theatre of glory ; he was perpetually losing there the fame he won in Westminster Hall.—HORNER, FRANCIS, 1810, *Memoirs and Correspondence, vol.* II, *p.* 21.

Erskine, too! Erskine was there ; good, but intolerable. He jested, he talked, he did every thing admirably, but then he *would* be applauded for the same thing twice over. He would read his own verses, his own paragraph, and tell his own story, again and again —BYRON, LORD, 1812, *Detached Thoughts.*

He was a most zealous and efficient labourer in the cause of the Greeks, not that he had much knowledge or judgment —for what he wrote on the subject was vague and declamatory—but there was a charm about his name which was transferred to the cause, and the master-string of his mind, vanity, had been touched, its vibrations trembling to the very end of his existence.—BOWRING, SIR JOHN, 1823-72, *Autobiographical Recollections, p.* 400.

At such a moment, Tom Sheridan came up to me, and asked me, whether I had a mind for a high treat ? "I won't keep you long," said he, "you may rely upon that." He then led a few of us, among whom was George Gordon, the brother of Pryse Lockhart, a fellow of "infinite jest and most excellent fancy," to the opposite end of the building ; where, standing in an arm chair,

with the back foremost, we saw Thomas Erskine, the prince of pleaders, but the most unfortunate of politicians, with an audience of about a dozen dry Scotch Whigs, delivering, with almost insane expression, a whole Armata of political oratory. The thing was irresistible. We honoured the orator with the "Hear! hear!" very exactly imitated, of several well known voices in the House of Commons; and effected our retreat, undiscovered by the learned and honourable gentlemen.—BOADEN, JAMES, 1831, *The Life of Mrs. Jordan, vol.* II, *p.* 139.

Latterly Erskine was very poor ; and no wonder, for he always contrived to sell out of the funds when they were very low, and to buy in when they were very high. "By heaven," he would say, "I am a perfect kite, all paper ; the boys might fly me." Yet, poor as he was he still kept the best society.—ROGERS, SAMUEL, 1855, *Recollections of Table-Talk, ed. Dyce, p.* 53.

In singular contrast to Sir S. Romilly came Lord Erskine ; of whom indeed I saw much less, and at a time, when his faculties had undergone a decay more obvious to others than to himself. He was still eager and eloquent in speech ; but with a certain restless irritability, augmented, as I believe, by narrow worldly circumstances, and by what he deemed the neglect of his former political friends. His mind too, when I knew him, was clouded by little foibles and superstitions. I well recollect a dinner at Sir S. Romilly's, where his agitation was curiously shown in his reluctance to sit down as one of thirteen at table, and by the relief he expressed when the fourteenth guest came in. His life had been one of *meteoric* kind throughout, vanishing in mist as such lives are prone to do.—HOLLAND, SIR HENRY, 1871, *Recollections of Past Life, p.* 243.

Erskine was a man of undoubted genius, and yet was a great spendthrift of the personal pronoun, so much so that Cobbett, who was printing one of his speeches, stopped in the middle, stating that the remainder would be published when they got a new font with sufficient I's, and that it was proposed Erskine should take "the title of Baron Ego of Eye, in the county of Suffolk."—MORRILL, JUSTIN S., 1887, *Self-Consciousness of Noted Persons, p.* 125.

At first his arguments and authorities were laboriously prepared, and read from a manuscript volume. Till his day there were few classical allusions or graces of rhetoric in the king's bench. His oratory, never overloaded with ornament, but always strictly relevant and adapted to the needs of the particular case, set a new example, as his courtesy and good humour considerably mitigated the previous asperities of nisi prius practice.—HAMILTON, J. A., 1889, *Dictionary of National Biography, vol.* XVII, *p.* 438.

The life of Lord Erskine should exercise a salutary influence on the younger members of the legal profession. It should constantly remind them of the noble objects of that noble profession, and impress indelibly upon their minds the great truth, that its highest rewards can only be attained by the advocate who is honest and strictly faithful to the interests of clients. He should be, as Erskine was, imbued, deeply, with the principles of patriotism and a passionate love of his highly honourable profession. He should ever be, too, keenly alive to human suffering, and reflect that it often becomes his duty to remember the forgotten, to attend the neglected, and visit the forsaken.— HARDWICKE, HENRY, 1896, *History of Oratory and Orators, p.*235.

GENERAL

The style of Lord Erskine's speeches may be regarded as a model for serious forensic oratory: it is clear, animated, forcible, and polished; never loaded with meretricious ornament, never debased by colloquial vulgarisms. It is throughout sustained in a due and dignified elevation. The illustrations which it exhibits are borrowed rather from the intellectual than the material world; and its ornaments are rather those of sentiment than of diction. It receives little assistance from the quaintness of similes or the brilliancy of metaphors; and is addressed rather to the reason and to the passions than to the taste and imagination of the hearer. It seldom displays any attempt at wit, or even at humour; though occasional instances of the latter quality are to be found in the Speeches. Although the speeches of Lord Erskine cannot be compared with those of Mr. Burke, for the varied exposition of philosophical principles in which those extraordinary productions abound; yet they not unfrequently display a profound acquaintance with human nature, and with

the springs of human action.—ROSCOE, HENRY, 1830, *Eminent British Lawyers, p.* 382.

Erskine's rapidity and lightness of wing made him often take the first hasty view of his own mind, than search in books for technical knowledge and arbitrary authority. His arguments, therefore, are commonly addressed rather to the general condition of men's understandings than to professional auditors. All these distinctions may be exemplified and illustrated, by a comparison of his speeches with those of the other law lords in the Banbury case, as reported by Le Marchant.—BRYDGES, SIR SAMUEL EGERTON, 1834, *Autobiography, vol.* I, *p.* 296.

In considering the characteristics of his eloquence, it is observable that he not only was free from measured sententiousness and tiresome attempts at antithesis, but that he was not indebted for his success to riches of ornament, to felicity of illustration, to wit, to humour, or to sarcasm. His first great excellence was his devotion to his client, and in the whole compass of his orations, there is not a single instance of the business in hand,—the great work of persuading,—being sacrificed to raise a laugh or to excite admiration of his own powers. He utterly forgot himself in the character he represented. Through life he was often ridiculed for vanity and egotism,—but not from anything he ever said or did in conducting a cause in a court of justice. There, from the moment the jury were sworn, he thought of nothing but the verdict, till it was recorded in his favour. Earnestness and energy were ever present throughout his speeches—impressing his argument on the mind of his hearer with a force which seemed to compel conviction. He never spoke at a tiresome length; and throughout all his speeches no weakness, no dulness, no flagging is discoverable; and we have ever a lively statement of facts,—or reasoning pointed, logical, and triumphant.—CAMPBELL, JOHN LORD, 1845–48, *The Lives of the Lord Chancellors and Keepers of the Great Seal of England, vol.* VI, *p.* 514.

Though not a poet in the highest sense of the term, Mr Erskine was wont to indite stanzas with more success than usually inspires the gentle tinklings of orators and statesmen. From the date of his residence in college—when he wrote the clever

PERCY BYSSHE SHELLEY

LORD BYRON

Portrait by Miss Curran.

From a Painting by Alonzo Chappel.
After a Painting by Thomas Phillips.

parody to his barber upon Gray's ode, "Ruin seize thee, ruthless king," to the octo-syllabic stanzas by which he would fain in old age have whiled away farmers from the cruel sport of shooting rooks— he was never wholly innocent of rhyme.— TOWNSEND, WILLIAM C., 1846, *The Lives of Twelve Eminent Judges, vol.* I, *p.* 469.

The published Speeches of Thomas, Lord Erskine are among the finest specimens we have of English forensic oratory.— CHAMBERS, ROBERT, 1876, *Cyclopædia of English Literature, ed. Carruthers.*

In the long roll of names which have shed lustre on the British bar, there is no one about which clusters more of romance and undying interest than about that of Thomas Erskine. . . . A profound lawyer he was not, nor was he well equipped with the learning of the schools. It was not to its rhetorical qualities, to its beauty of diction, its richness of ornament or illustration, its wit, humor, or sarcasm, that his oratory owed its power and charm, but to its matchless strength and vigor. His first great excellence was his devotion to his client, to which all other considerations were made secondary. Self was forgotten in the character he personated. From the moment the jury were sworn he thought of nothing but the verdict till it was recorded in his favor. The earnestness, the vehemence, the energy of the advocate were ever present throughout his speeches, impressing the arguments upon the mind of the hearer with a force which seemed to compel conviction. He resisted every temptation to mere declamation which his luxuriant fancy cast in his path, and won his verdicts not more by what he said than by what he refrained from saying. Even in the longest of his speeches there is no weakness, no flagging; but the same earnestness of manner, the same lively statement of facts, the same luminous exposition of argument, from beginning to close. . . . Of all the lawyers that ever lived, Erskine seems to have made the closest approach to the ideal of a forensic advocate.—MATHEWS, WILLIAM, 1878, *Oratory and Orators, pp.* 346, 354, 358.

George Gordon Lord Byron

1788–1824

Born, in London, 22 Jan. 1788. Lame from birth. Early years spent with mother in Aberdeen. Educated at private schools there, and at Grammar School, 1794–98. Succeeded to title on death of grand-uncle, May 1798. To Newstead with his mother, autumn of 1799. Made ward in Chancery under guardianship of Lord Carlisle. To school at Nottingham. To London for treatment for lameness, 1799. To Dr. Glennie's school at Dulwich, 1799. At Harrow, summer of 1801 to 1805. To Trinity Coll., Cambridge, Oct. 1805; M. A., 4 July 1808. On leaving Cambridge, settled at Newstead. Took seat in House of Lords, 13 March 1809. Started on "grand tour," 2 July 1809, to Spain, Malta, Turkey, Greece. Returned to England, July 1811. Settled in St. James's Street, London, Oct. 1811. Spoke for first time in House of Lords, 27 Feb. 1812. Married Anne Isabella Milbanke, 2 Jan. 1815. Settled in Piccadilly Terrace, London, March 1815. Daughter born, 10 Dec. 1815. Separation from wife, Feb. 1816. Left England, 24 April 1816. To Belgium, Germany, Switzerland, Italy. Amour with Miss Clairmont, 1816–17. Daughter born by her, Jan. 1817 (died April 1822). Settled in Venice, 1817. Amour with Countess Guiccioli, April to Oct., 1819. To Ravenna, Christmas 1819. Prolific literary production. "Marino Faliero" performed at Drury Lane, spring of 1821. To Pisa, Oct. 1821. "The Liberal" published (4 nos. only), with Leigh Hunt and Shelley, 1823. Elected member of Greek Committee in London, 1823. Sailed from Genoa for Greece, 15 July 1823. Raising Suliote troops on behalf of Greeks against Turks at Missolonghi, Dec. 1823. Serious illness, Feb. 1824. Died, 19 April 1824. Buried in England, at Hucknall Torkard. *Works:* "Fugitive Pieces" (privately printed, all destroyed except two copies), 1806 (a facsimile privately reprinted, 1886); "Poems on Various Occasions" (anon., same as preceding, with omissions), 1807; "Hours of Idleness," 1807; "English Bards and Scotch Reviewers" (anon.), 1809 (2nd edn. same year); Poems contrib. to J. C. Hobhouse's "Imitations and Translations," 1809; "Childe Harold," cantos 1 and 2, 1812 (2nd–5th edns., same year); "The Curse of Minerva" (anon.), 1812; "The

Waltz'' (under pseud. of ''Horace Hornem''), 1813; ''The Giaour,'' 1813; ''The Bride of Abydos,'' 1813 (2nd-5th edns., same year); ''The Corsair,'' 1814; ''Ode to Napoleon Buonaparte'' (anon.), 1814; ''Lara'' (anon., with Rogers's ''Jacqueline''), 1814; ''Hebrew Melodies,'' 1815; ''Siege of Corinth'' (anon.), 1816; ''Parisina,'' 1816 (second edn., with preceding work, same year); ''Poems,'' 1816; ''Poems on his Domestic Circumstances,'' 1816; ''Prisoner of Chillon,'' 1816; ''Childe Harold,'' canto 3, 1816; ''Monody on the Death of Sheridan'' (anon.), 1816; ''Fare Thee Well!'' 1816; ''Manfred,'' 1817 (2nd edn., same year); ''The Lament of Tasso,'' 1817; ''Poems Written by Somebody'' (anon.), 1818; ''Childe Harold,'' canto 4, 1818; ''Beppo'' (anon.), 1818; ''Suppressed Poems,'' 1818; ''Three Poems not included in the Works of Lord Byron,'' 1818; ''Don Juan,'' cantos 1 and 2 (anon.), 1819; ''Mazeppa,'' 1819; ''Marino Faliero,'' 1820; ''Don Juan,'' cantos 3-5 (anon.), 1821; ''Prophecy of Dante'' (with 2nd. edn. of ''Marino Faliero''), 1821; ''Sardanapalus, The Two Foscari, and Cain,'' 1821; ''Letter . . . on the Rev. W. L. Bowles's Strictures on Pope,'' 1821; ''Werner,'' 1822; ''Don Juan,'' cantos 6-14 (anon.), 1823; ''The Liberal,'' with Leigh Hunt and Shelley (anon., 4 nos.), 1823; ''The Age of Bronze'' (anon.), 1823; ''The Island,'' 1823 (2nd. edn., same year); ''The Deformed Transformed,'' 1823; ''Heaven and Earth'' (anon.), 1824; ''Don Juan,'' cantos 15, 16 (anon.), 1824 (canto 17 of ''Don Juan,'' 1829, and ''Twenty Suppressed Stanzas,'' 1838, are spurious); ''Parliamentary Speeches,'' 1824; ''The Vision of Judgment'' (anon., reprinted from pt. i. of ''The Liberal''), 1824. *Posthumous:* ''Correspondence with a Friend'' (3 vols.), 1825; ''Letters and Journals,'' edited by T. Moore (2 vols.), 1830. *Collected Works:* in 8 vols., 1815-17; in 5 vols., 1817; in 8 vols., 1818-20; in 4 vols., 1828; ''Life and Works'' (17 vols.), 1832-35, etc. *Life:* ''Lord Byron and his Contemporaries,'' by Leigh Hunt, 1828; life by Moore, 1830; by Galt, 1830; by Jeaffreson, 1883; by Roden Noel (''Great Writers'' series), 1890.—SHARP, R. FARQUHARSON, 1897, *A Dictionary of English Authors, p.* 45.

PERSONAL

Of Lord Byron I can tell you only that his appearance is nothing that you would remark.—EDGEWORTH, MARIA, 1813, *Letters, vol.* I, *p.* 206.

I called on Lord Byron to-day, with an introduction from Mr. Gifford. Here, again, my anticipations were mistaken. Instead of being deformed, as I had heard, he is remarkably well built, with the exception of his feet. Instead of having a thin and rather sharp and anxious face, as he has in his picture, it is round, open, and smiling; his eyes are light, and not black; his air easy and careless, not forward and striking; and I found his manners affable and gentle, the tones of his voice low and conciliating, his conversation gay, pleasant, and interesting in an uncommon degree.—TICKNOR, GEORGE, 1815, *Journal, June* 20; *Life Letters and Journals, vol.* I, *p.* 58.

A countenance, exquisitely modeled to the expression of feeling and passion, and exhibiting the remarkable contrast of very dark hair and eye-brows, with light and expressive eyes, presented to the physiognomist the most interesting subject for the exercise of his art. The predominating expression was that of deep and

habitual thought, which gave way to the most rapid play of features when he engaged in interesting discussion; so that a brother poet compared them to the sculpture of a beautiful alabaster vase, only seen to perfection when lighted up from within. The flashes of mirth, gayety, indignation, or satirical dislike which frequently animated Lord Byron's countenance, might, during an evening's conversation, be mistaken by a stranger, for the habitual expression, so easily and happily was it formed for them all; but those who had an opportunity of studying his features for a length of time, and upon various occasions, both of rest and emotion, will agree with us that their proper language was that of melancholy.—SCOTT, SIR WALTER, 1816, *Childe Harold Canto* iii, *and Other Poems, Quarterly Review, vol.* 16, *p.* 176.

If you had seen Lord Byron, you could scarcely disbelieve him. So beautiful a countenance I scarcely ever saw—his teeth so many stationary smiles, his eyes the open portals of the sun—things of light and for light—and his forehead so ample, and yet so flexible, passing from marble smoothness into a hundred wreaths and lines and dimples correspondent to the

feelings and sentiments he is uttering.—
COLERIDGE, SAMUEL TAYLOR, 1816, *Letter, April* 10; *Life by Gillman*.

I was introduced, at the theatre, to Lord Byron.—What a grand countenance!—it is impossible to have finer eyes!—the divine man of genius!—He is yet scarcely twenty-eight years of age, and he is the first poet in England, probably in the world; when he is listening to music it is a countenance worthy of the *beau-ideal* of the Greeks. For the rest, let a man be ever so great a poet, let him besides be the head of one of the most ancient families in England, this is too much for our age, and I have learnt with pleasure that *Lord Byron is a wretch*. When he came into the drawing-room of Madame de Staël, at Copet, all the English ladies left it. Our unfortunate man of genius had the imprudence to marry,—his wife is very clever, and has renewed at his expense the old story of "Tom Jones and Blifil." Men of genius are generally mad, or at the least very imprudent! His lordship was so atrocious, as to take an actress into keeping for two months. If he had been a blockhead, nobody would have concerned themselves with his following the example of almost all young men of fashion; but it is well known that Mr. Murray, the bookseller, gives him two guineas a line for all the verses he sends him. He is absolutely the counterpart of M. de Mirabeau; the feodalists, before the Revolution, not knowing how to answer the "Eagle of Marseilles," discovered that he was a monster. — BEYLE, HENRI (COUNT DE STENDHAL), 1817, *Rome, Naples and Florence, June* 27.

Thou, whose true name the world yet knows not,
Mysterious spirit, man, angel, or devil.
—LAMARTINE, ALPHONSE MARIE LOUIS DE, 1820, *Meditation: L'Homme, A Lord Byron*.

I come at once to his lordship's charge against me, blowing away the abuse with which it is frothed, and evaporating a strong acid in which it is suspended. The residuum, then, appears to be, that "Mr. Southey, on his return from Switzerland (in 1817), scattered abroad calumnies, knowing them to be such, against Lord Byron and others." To this I reply with *a direct and positive denial*. If I had been told in that country that Lord Byron had

turned Turk, or monk of La Trappe,—that he had furnished a *harem*, or endowed a hospital, I might have thought the report, whichever it had been, possible, and repeated it accordingly, passing it, as it had been taken, in the small change of conversation, for no more than it was worth. In this manner I might have spoken of him as of Baron Gerambe, the Green Man, the Indian Jugglers, or any other *figurante* of the time being. There was no reason for any particular delicacy on my part in speaking of his lordship; and, indeed, I should have thought anything which might be reported of him would have injured his character as little as the story which so greatly annoyed Lord Keeper Guilford—that he had ridden a rhinoceros. He may ride a rhinoceros, and though every one would stare, no one would wonder. But making no inquiry concerning him when I was abroad, because I felt no curiosity, I heard nothing, and had nothing to repeat.—SOUTHEY, ROBERT, 1822, *To the Editor of the Courier, Jan.* 5.

Saw Lord Byron for the first time. The impression of the first few minutes disappointed me, as I had, both from the portraits and descriptions given, conceived a different idea of him. I had fancied him taller, with a more dignified and commanding air; and I looked in vain for the hero-looking sort of person with whom I had so long identified him in imagination. His appearance is, however, highly prepossessing; his head is finely shaped, and the forehead open, high, and noble; his eyes are gray and full of expression, but one is visibly larger than the other; the nose is large and well shaped, but from being a little *too thick*, it looks better in profile than in front-face; his mouth is the most remarkable feature in his face, the upper lip of Grecian shortness, and the corners descending; the lips full and finely cut. In speaking, he shows his teeth very much, and they are white and even; but I observed that even in his smile—and he smiles frequently—there is something of a scornful expression in his mouth that is evidently natural, and not, as many suppose, affected. This particularly struck me. His chin is large and well shaped, and finishes well the oval of his face. He is extremely thin; indeed, so much so that his figure has almost a boyish air; his face is peculiarly pale, but not the paleness of ill-health, as its character is that of fairness, the fairness of a dark-haired person—and his hair (which is getting rapidly gray) is of a very dark brown, and curls naturally: he uses a great deal of oil in it, which makes it look still darker. His countenance is full of expression, and changes with the subject of conversation; it gains on the beholder the more it is seen, and leaves an agreeable impression. I should say that melancholy was its prevailing character, as I noticed that when any observation elicited a smile—and they were many, as the conversation was gay and playful—it appeared to linger but for a moment on his lip, which instantly resumed its former expression of seriousness. His whole appearance is remarkably gentlemanlike, and he owes nothing of this to his toilet, as his coat appears to have been many years made, is much too large—and all his garments convey the idea of having been purchased ready-made, so ill do they fit him. There is a *gaucherie* in his movements, which evidently proceeds from the perpetual consciousness of his lameness, that appears to haunt him; for he tries to conceal his foot when seated, and when walking has a nervous rapidity in his manner. He is very slightly lame, and the deformity of his foot is so little remarkable that I am not now aware which foot it is.—BLESSINGTON, COUNTESS OF, 1823, *Conversations with Lord Byron, Genoa, April* 1.

Unlooked-for event! deplorable misfortune! But a short time has elapsed since the people of this deeply suffering country welcomed, with unfeigned joy and open arms, this celebrated individual to their bosoms; to-day, overwhelmed with grief and despair, they bathe his funeral couch with tears of bitterness, and mourn over it with inconsolable affliction. On Easter Sunday, the happy salutation of the day, "Christ is risen," remained but half pronounced on the lips of every Greek; and as they met, before even congratulating one another on the return of that joyous day, the universal demand was, "How is Lord Byron?" Thousands, assembled in the spacious plain outside of the city to commemorate the sacred day, appeared as if they had assembled for the sole purpose of imploring the Saviour of the world to restore to health him who was a partaker with us in our present struggle

for the deliverance of our native land. And how is it possible that any heart should remain unmoved, any lip closed upon the present occasion? Was ever Greece in greater want of assistance than when the ever-to-be-lamented Lord Byron, at the peril of his life, crossed over to Messolonghi? Then, and ever since he has been with us, his liberal hand has been opened to our necessities—necessities which our own poverty would have otherwise rendered irremediable. How many and much greater benefits did we not expect from him!—and to-day, alas! to-day, the unrelenting grave closes over him and our hopes! . . . All Greece, clothed in mourning and inconsolable, accompanies the procession in which it is borne; all ecclesiastical, civil and military honours attend it; all his fellow-citizens of Messolonghi and fellow-countrymen of Greece follow it, crowning it with their gratitude and bedewing it with their tears; it is blessed by the pious benedictions and prayers of our Archbishop, Bishop, and all our Clergy.—TRICOUPI, M. SPIRIDION, 1824, *Funeral Oration on Lord Noel Byron, April* 10; *Medwin's Conversations of Lord Byron, pp.* xci, xcviii.

I was told it all alone in a room full of people. If they had said the sun or the moon was gone out of the heavens, it could not have struck me with the idea of a more awful and dreary blank in the creation than the words, "Byron is dead."—WELSH, JANE, 1824, *Letter to Thomas Carlyle, Life by Froude, vol.* I, *p.* 173.

Poor Byron! alas, poor Byron! the news of his death came upon my heart like a mass of lead; and yet, the thought of it sends a painful twinge through all my being, as if I had lost a brother. O God! that so many souls of mud and clay should fill up their base existence to its utmost bound; and this the noblest spirit in Europe should sink before half his course was run. Late so full of fire and generous passion and proud purposes; and now for ever dumb and cold. Poor Byron! and but a young man, still struggling amidst the perplexities and sorrows and aberrations of a mind not arrived at maturity, or settled in its proper place in life. Had he been spared to the age of three-score and ten, what might he not have done! what might he not have been! But we shall hear his voice no more. I dreamed of seeing him and knowing him; but the curtain of everlasting night has hid him from our eyes. We shall go to him; he shall not return to us. Adieu. There is a blank in your heart and a blank in mine since this man passed away.—CARLYLE, THOMAS, 1824, *Letter to Jane Welsh, Life by Froude, vol.* I, *p.* 173.

I am extremely sorry I have not had it in my power to answer the kind letter with which you have honored me, before this, being so very unwell, and so much hurt at the severe loss of my much-esteemed and ever-to-be-lamented lord and master. You wish me, Sir, to give you some information in respect to my lord's manner and mode of life after his departure from Cephalonia, which I am very happy to say was that of a good Christian, and one who fears and serves God, in doing all the good that lay in his power, and avoiding all evil. And his charity was always without bounds; for his kind and generous heart could not see nor hear of misery, without a deep sigh, and striving in which way he could serve and soften misery, by his liberal hand, in the most effectual manner. . . . A greater friend to Christianity could not exist, I am fully convinced, in his daily conduct, not only making the Bible his first companion in the morning, but in regard to whatever religion a man might be of, whether Protestant, Catholic, friar, or monk, or any other religion, every priest, of whatever order, if in distress, was always most liberally rewarded, and with larger sums than any one who was not a minister of the gospel, I think, (would give). I think every thing, combined together, must prove, not only to you, Sir, but to the public at large, that my lord was not only a Christian, but a good Christian.— FLETCHER, WILLIAM, 1824, *Letter to Dr. Kennedy, May* 19; *Kennedy's Conversations on Religion with Lord Byron, pp.* 369, 372.

I met Lord B. for the first time at Metaxata, in Cephalonia, in the month of October, 1823. On calling, I found his Lordship had ridden out with Count Gamba; I resolved to wait for his return, and was shown his only public room, which was small and scantily furnished in the plainest manner. One table was covered for dinner, another and a chair were strewed with books, and many were ranged in order on the floor. . . . I presented a letter of introduction, and he sat down upon the sofa, still examining me; I felt the reception more poetical than agreeable: but he immediately commenced his fascinating conversation. . . . Whenever he commenced a sentence which showed that the subject had engaged his mind, and that his thoughts were sublime, he checked himself, and finished a broken sentence, either with an indifferent smile, or with this annoying tone. I thought he had adopted it to conceal his feelings, when he feared to trust his tongue with the sentiments of his heart. Often, it was evident, he did it to avoid betraying the author, or rather the poet. In mere satire and wit his genius ran wild, even in conversation. I left him quite delighted, charmed to find so great a man so agreeable, yet astonished that the author of "Childe Harold," the "Corsair," and "Manfred," should have said so little worth remembering.—FINLAY, GEORGE, 1824, *Letter to Colonel Stanhope, June; Broughton's Recollections of a Long Life.*

Honorable Lady,—After the ever to be lamented loss of your illustrious brother, with whose friendship I was so long honoured, my sole aim was to fulfil my duties towards his memory and towards those whom I knew were nearest and dearest to him when alive. . . . I collected all the words he uttered in those few hours in which he was certain of his danger. He said, "Poor Greece! Poor People! my poor family! Why was I not aware of this in time? but now it is too late." Speaking of Greece he said, "I have given her my time, my money, and my health—what could I do more? Now I give her my life." He frequently repeated that he was content to die, and regretted only that he was aware of it too late. He mentioned the names of many people and several sums of money, but it was not possible to distinguish clearly what he meant. He named his dear daughter —his sister—his wife—Hobhouse, and Kinnaird. "Why did I not go to England before I came here? I leave those that I love behind me—in other respects I am willing to die." After six o'clock in the evening of the 18th it is certain that he suffered no pain whatever. He died in a strange land and amongst strangers, but more loved—more wept—he could not have been. . . . Those who are acquainted only with his writings will lament the loss of so great a genius: but I knew his heart. If to have sincere companions of your sorrows will at all alleviate them, be assured that the grief of no one can be more deeply, more truly felt than that of —GAMBA, COUNT PIETRO, 1824, *To the Hon. Augusta Leigh, Aug.* 17.

I never met with any man who shines so much in conversation. He shines the more, perhaps, for not seeking to shine. His ideas flow without effort, without his having occasion to think. As in his letters, he is not nice about expressions or words;—there are no concealments in him no injunctions to secresy. He tells everything that he has thought or done without the least reserve, and as if he wished the whole world to know it; and does not throw the slightest gloss over his errors. . . . He hates argument, and never argues for victory. He gives every one an opportunity of sharing in the conversation, and has the art of turning it to subjects that may bring out the person with whom he converses. — MEDWIN, THOMAS, 1824, *Conversations of Lord Byron Noted During a Residence with his Lordship at Pisa in the Years* 1821 *and* 1822, *p.* 334.

I have just finished Lord Byron's "Conversations." . . . Fifty years hence our descendants will see which is remembered best, the author of the "Excursion," or of "Childe Harold." But he seems to me to have wanted the power of admiration, the organ of veneration; to have been a cold, sneering, vain, Voltairish person, charitable as far as money went, and liberal so far as it did not interfere with his aristocratic notions; but very derisive, very un-English, very scornful. Captain Medwyn speaks of his suppressed laugh. How unpleasant an idea that gives! The only thing that does him much credit in the whole book is his hearty admiration of Scott. . . . Well, I think this book will have one good effect, it will disenchant the ¦whole sex.—MITFORD, MARY RUSSELL, 1824, *Letter to B. R. Haydon, Nov.* 2.

It would be to little purpose to dwell upon the mere beauty of a countenance in which the expression of an extraordinary mind was so conspicuous. What serenity was sealed on the forehead, adorned with the finest chestnut hair, light, curling, and disposed with such art, that the art was hidden in the imitation of most pleasing nature! What varied expression in his eyes! They were of the azure colour of the heavens, from which they seemed to derive their origin. His teeth, in form, in colour, in transparency, resembled pearls; but his cheeks were too delicately tinged with the hue of the pale rose. His neck, which he was in the habit of keeping uncovered as much as the usages of society permitted, seemed to have been formed in a mould, and was very white. His hands were as beautiful as if they had been the works of art. His figure left nothing to be desired, particularly by those who found rather a grace than a defect in a certain light and gentle undulation of the person when he entered a room, and of which you hardly felt tempted to enquire the cause. Indeed it was scarcely perceptible,—the clothes he wore were so long. . . . His face appeared tranquil like the ocean on a fine spring morning; but, like it, in an instant became changed into the tempestuous and terrible, if a passion (a passion did I say?), a thought, a word, occurred to disturb his mind. His eyes then lost all their sweetness, and sparkled so that it became difficult to look on them. . . . What delighted him greatly one day annoyed him the next. — ALBRIZZI, COUNTESS, 1826, *Character of Byron.*

It appears, therefore, from a review of Byron's private character, that it was a common one, being mixed with many virtues and stained with some fashionable vices. We meet nothing in it to command our veneration: we find many things to pity and excuse, from the peculiarity of his situation; but we are not entitled to call him a virtuous, pious man. . . . We find, in fact, that he was like all those nominal Christians who are unregenerate: —he knew not its spirit. His conduct was not regulated by it, and he differed simply from many of those who hold in the world a very respectable character, in his having treated it with seeming ridicule in his writings, while they, perhaps, have done the same in conversation.—KENNEDY, DR. JAMES, 1827-30, *Conversations on Religion with Lord Byron and Others, held in Cephalonia, a Short Time Previous to his Lordship's Death, pp.* 340, 341.

Lord Byron's face was handsome; eminently so in some respects. He had a mouth and chin fit for Apollo; and when I first knew him, there were both lightness and energy all over his aspect. But his countenance did not improve with age, and there were always some defects in it. The jaw was too big for the upper part. It had all the wilfulness of a despot in it. The animal predominated over the intellectual part of his head, inasmuch as the face altogether was large in proportion to the skull. The eyes also were set too near one another; and the nose, though handsome in itself, had the appearance when you saw it closely in front, of being grafted on the face, rather than growing properly out of it. His person was very handsome, though terminating in lameness, and tending to fat and effeminacy; which makes me remember what a hostile fair one objected to him, namely, that he had little beard. . . . His lameness was only in one foot, the left; and it was so little visible to casual notice, that as he lounged about a room (which he did in such a manner as to screen it) it was hardly perceivable. But it was a real and even a sore lameness. Much walking upon it fevered and hurt it. It was a shrunken foot, a little twisted.—HUNT, LEIGH, 1828, *Lord Byron and Some of his Contemporaries, vol.* I, *pp.* 150, 151.

With the faults and foibles of Byron, Greece had nothing to do; she knew nothing of them; to her he was only "the great and noble." . . . Crossing the Gulf Salamis one day in a boat, with a rough mountain Captain and his men, I pulled out a volume of Byron's works and was reading; the wind blowing open the leaves, the Captain caught a glimpse of the portrait and recognised it. He begged to take the book, and looking for a moment, with melancholy, at the face of the noble lord, he kissed it and passed it to his men, who did the same saying, "Eeton megalos kai kalos" ("he was great and noble").—HOWE, SAMUEL G., 1828, *Historical Sketch of the Greek Revolution, p.* 198, *and note.*

Of his face the beauty may be pronounced to have been of the highest order, as combining at once regularity of features with the most varied and interesting expression. The same facility, indeed, of change observable in the movements of his mind was seen also in the free play of his features, as the passing thoughts within darkened or shone through them. His eyes, though of a light grey, were capable of all extremes of expression, from the most joyous hilarity to the deepest sadness, from the very sunshine of benevolence to the most concentrated scorn or rage. . . . But it was in the mouth and chin that the great beauty as well as expression of his fine countenance lay. . . . His head was remarkably small,—so much so as to be rather out of proportion with his face. The forehead, though a little too narrow, was high, and appeared more so from his having his hair (to preserve it, as he said), shaved over the temples; while the glossy, dark-brown curls, clustering over his head, gave the finish to its beauty. When to this is added, that his nose, though handsomely, was rather thickly shaped, that his teeth were white and regular, and his complexion colourless, as good an idea perhaps as it is in the power of mere words to convey may be conceived of his features. In height he was, as he himself has informed us, five feet eight inches and a half, and to the length of his limbs he attributed his being such a good swimmer. His hands were very white, and—according to his own notion of the size of hands as indicating birth—aristocratically small. The lameness of his right foot, though an obstacle to grace, but little impeded the activity of his movements; and from this circumstance, as well as from the skill with which the foot was disguised by means of long trowsers, it would be difficult to conceive a defect of this kind less obtruding itself as a deformity; while the diffidence which a constant consciousness of the infirmity gave to his first approach and address made, in him, even lameness a source of interest.—MOORE, THOMAS, 1830–31, *Life of Lord Byron, vol.* II, *pp.* 534, 535.

The young peer had great intellectual powers; yet there was an unsound part in his mind. He had naturally a generous and tender heart; but his temper was wayward and irritable. He had a head which statuaries loved to copy, and a foot the deformity of which the beggars in the streets mimicked. Distinguished at once by the strength and by the weakness of his intellect, affectionate yet perverse, a poor lord and a handsome cripple, he required if ever man required, the firmest and the most judicious training. But, capriciously as nature had dealt with him, the relative to whom the office of forming his character was intrusted was more capricious still. She passed from paroxysms of rage to paroxysms of fondness. At one time she stifled him with her caresses, at another time she insulted his deformity. He came into the world, and the world treated him as his mother treated him—sometimes with kindness, sometimes with severity, never with justice. It indulged him without discrimination, and punished him without discrimination. He was truly a spoiled child; not merely the spoiled child of his parents, but the spoiled child of nature, the spoiled child of fortune, the spoiled child of fame, the spoiled child of society. —MACAULAY, THOMAS BABINGTON, 1830, Moore's Life of Lord Byron, Critical and Miscellaneous Essays.

Perhaps the beauty of his physiogonomy has been more highly spoken of than it really merited. Its chief grace consisted, when he was in a gay humour, of a liveliness which gave a joyous meaning to every articulation of the muscles and features; when he was less agreeably disposed, the expression was morose to a very repulsive degree.—GALT, JOHN, 1830, The Life of Byron, ch. xlix.

No petit maître could pay more sedulous attention than he did to external appearance, or consult with more complacency the looking glass. Even when en negligé he studied the nature of the postures he assumed as attentively as if he had been sitting for his picture, and so much value did he attach to the whiteness of his hands, that, in order not to suffer "the winds of heaven to visit them too roughly," he constantly, and even within doors, wore gloves.—MILLINGEN, JULIUS, 1831, Memoirs of Affairs of Greece.

Mrs. Arkwright is here. I know few people as agreeable as she is, so fresh and original. She told me a great deal of Mr. Hodgson, Lord Byron's friend, and now the clergyman at Bakewell, and who, she says, is the most delightful man in the world. He was warmly attached to Lord Byron, and had lived with him in the closest intimacy for twenty-six years. He had no doubt that Lord Byron was insane; when Lady Byron left Lord Byron he sent for Mr. Hodgson, who found him perfectly mad.—GREVILLE, HENRY, 1832, Leaves from his Diary, p. 5.

It now remains to show how far the character of Byron was influenced by disease, and what the nature of that disease was. . . . In one place we read of his being subject to an hysterical affection, in another of his being carried out of a theatre in a convulsive swoon; elsewhere, of an apoplectic tendency, attended with temporary deprivation of sense and motion; at another time, of nervous twitches of the features, and the limbs following any emotion of anger, and from trivial excitement, and slight indisposition, of temporary aberrations of intellect, and delirium; but no where do we find the cause of these phenomena plainly and intelligibly pointed out, nor the real name given to his disorder, till his last and fatal attack. The simple fact is, he laboured under an epileptic diathesis, and on several occasions of mental emotion, even in his early years, he had slight attacks of this disease.— MADDEN, R. R., 1833, Infirmities of Genius, vol. II, pp. 128, 129.

Byron had the strangest and most perverse of all vanities—the desire to surprise the world by showing, that, after all his sublime and spiritual flights, he could, on nearer inspection, be the lowest, the coarsest, the most familiar, and the most sensual of the low: and this, it is said, he exhibited in the MS. autobiography which was burnt. This is a most incomprehensible fact,—even more incomprehensible than some of the mad Confessions of Rousseau. Byron's, perhaps, arose from the vanity of wishing to be considered a man of the world, and a man of fashion —a very mean and contemptible wish. I scorn hypocrisy; but who in a sane mind would blacken his own character with disgraceful vice beyond the truth? —BRYDGES, SIR SAMUEL EGERTON, 1834, Autobiography, vol. II, p. 229.

England will one day feel how ill it is— not for Byron but for herself—that the foreigner who lands upon her shores should search in vain in that Temple which should be her national Pantheon, for the Poet beloved and admired by all the nations of Europe, and for whose death Greece and Italy wept as if it had been that of the noblest of their own sons.— MAZZINI, JOSEPH, 1839, Byron and Goethe, Essays, ed. Clarke, p. 108.

Lord Byron had failings—many failings certainly, but he was untainted with any of the baser vices; and his virtues, his good qualities, were all of the higher order. He was honourable and open in all his dealings—he was generous, and he was kind. He was affected by the distress, and rarer still he was pleased with the prosperity of others. Tenderhearted he was to a degree not usual with our sex—and he shrunk, with feminine sensibility, from the sight of cruelty. . . . There was, indeed, something about him, not to be definitely described, but almost universally felt, which captivated those around him, and impressed them, in spite of occasional distrusts, with an attachment not only friendly but fixed. Part of this fascination may, doubtless, be ascribed to the entire self-abandonment, the incautious, it may be said the dangerous, sincerity of his private conversation; but his very weaknesses were amiable; and, as has been said of a portion of his virtues, were of a feminine character—so that the affection felt for him was as that for a favourite and sometimes froward sister. — BROUGHTON, LORD, 1844-55, *Travels in Albania, Appendix.*

Byron may almost be said to have had no character at all. Every attempt to bring his virtues or his vices within the boundaries of a theory, or to represent his conduct as guided by any predominant principle of good or evil, has been accompanied by blunders and perversions. His nature had no simplicity. He seems an embodied antithesis,—a mass of contradictions,—a collection of opposite frailties and powers. Such was the versatility of his mind and morals, that it is hardly possible to discern the connection between the giddy goodness and the brilliant wickedness which he delighted to exhibit. His habit of mystification, of darkly hinting remorse for sins he never committed, of avowing virtues he never practised, increases the difficulty. —WHIPPLE, EDWIN P., 1845, *Byron, Essays and Reviews.*

He died among strangers, in a foreign land, without a kindred hand to close his eyes; yet he did not die unwept. With all his faults and errors, and passions and caprices, he had the gift of attaching his humble dependents warmly to him. One of them, a poor Greek, accompanied his remains to England, and followed them to the grave. I am told, that during the ceremony, he stood holding on by a pew in an agony of grief, and when all was over, seemed as if he would have gone down into the tomb with the body of his master.— A nature that could inspire such attachments, must have been generous and beneficent. . . . His love for Miss Chaworth, to use Lord Byron's own expression, was "the romance of the most romantic period of his life," and I think we can trace the effect of it throughout the whole course of his writings, coming up every now and then, like some lurking theme which runs through a complicated piece of music, and links it all in a pervading chain of melody.—IRVING, WASHINGTON, 1849, *Newstead Abbey, The Crayon Miscellany, pp,* 296, 316.

Changeful! how little do you know
Of Byron when you call him so!
True as the magnet is to iron
Byron hath ever been to Byron.
His colour'd prints, in gilded frames,
Whatever the designs and names,
One image set before the rest,
In shirt with falling collar drest,
And keeping up a rolling fire at
Patriot, conspirator, and pirate.
—LANDOR, WALTER SAVAGE, 1853, *Last Fruit of An Old Tree.*

In external appearance Byron realised that ideal standard with which imagination adorns genius. He was in the prime of life, thirty-four; of middle height, five feet eight and a half inches; regular features, without a stain or furrow on his pallid skin, his shoulders broad, chest open, body and limbs finely proportioned. His small highly-finished head and curly hair had an airy and graceful appearance from the massiveness and length of his throat: you saw his genius in his eyes and lips. In short, Nature could do little more than she had done for him, both in outward form and in the inward spirit she had given to animate it. But all these rare gifts to his jaundiced imagination only served to make his one personal defect (lameness) the more apparent, as a flaw is magnified in a diamond when polished; and he brooded over that blemish as sensitive minds will brood until they magnify a wart into a wen. His lameness certainly helped to make him sceptical, cynical, and savage. There was no peculiarity in his dress, it was adapted to the climate: a tartan jacket braided—he said it was the Gordon pattern, and that his mother was of that race. A blue velvet cap with a gold band, and very loose nankeen trousers strapped down so as to cover his feet; his throat was not bare, as represented in drawings. . . . He would exist on biscuits and soda-water for days together. — TRELAWNY, EDWARD JOHN, 1858–78, *Records of Shelley, Byron and the Author, pp.* 18, 51.

All who knew Lord Byron personally, while thoroughly understanding the consequence of a fickleness nurtured by an excessively bad training,—that of a boy of fortune, with an impulsive and passionate nature, brought up among strangers, with traditions of wild life in his family —remember, also, that he had a strong sympathy with all that was beautiful and generous, strong tendencies of natural affection, and unquestionably a desire to do right. One of his besetting weaknesses was the excessive anxiety for approval. This betrayed him into impulsive courses, which he afterwards found a difficulty in sustaining, and his extravagant disappointment exhibited itself in ways which made him seem far more uncertain and changeful than he really was at heart. —HUNT, THORNTON, 1862, *ed., Correspondence of Leigh Hunt, vol.* I, *p.* 202.

The man in Byron is of nature even less sincere than that of the poet. Underneath this Beltenebros there is hidden a coxcomb. He posed all through his life. He had every affectation—the writer's, the roué's, the dandy's, the conspirator's. He was constantly writing, and he pretends to despise his writings. To believe himself, he was proud of nothing but his skill in bodily exercises. An Englishman, he affects Bonapartism; a peer of the realm, he speaks of the Universal Republic with the enthusiasm of a schoolboy of fifteen. He plays at misanthropy, at disillusion: he parades his vices; he even tries to make us believe that he has committed a crime or two. Read his letters—his letters written nominally to friends, but handed about from hand to hand in London. Read his journal—a journal kept ostensibly for himself, but handed over afterwards by him to Moore with authority to publish it. The littleness which these things show is amazing.—SCHERER, EDMOND, 1863–91, *Taine's History of English Literature, Essays on English Literature, tr. Saintsbury.*

What helps it now, that Byron bore,
With haughty scorn which mock'd the smart
Through Europe to the Ætolian shore
The pageant of his bleeding heart?
That thousands counted every groan,
And Europe made his woe her own?
—ARNOLD, MATTHEW, 1867, *Stanzas from the Grande Chartreuse.*

Occasionally, indeed, the fervour of the poet warmed his expression, and always the fire of genius kindled his eye; but in general, an affection of fashion pervaded his manner, and the *insouciance* of satiety spread a languor over his conversation. He was destitute of that simplicity of thought and manner which is the attendant of the highest intellect, and which was so conspicuous in Scott. He was always aiming at effect: and the effect he desired was rather that of fashion than of genius; he sought rather to astonish than impress. He seemed *blasé* with every enjoyment of life, affected rather the successful *roué* than the great poet, and deprecated beyond the cant of morality. The impression he wished to leave on the mind was that of a man who had tasted to the dregs of all the enjoyments of life, and above all of high life, and thought everything else mere balderdash and affectation.—ALISON, SIR ARCHIBALD, 1867–83, *Some Account of my Life and Writings, vol.* I, *p.* 142.

Personally, I know nothing but good of him. Of what he became in his foreign banishment, when removed from all his natural ties and hereditary duties, I, personally, am ignorant. In all probability he deteriorated; he would have been more than human if he had not. But when I was in the habit of familiarly seeing him, he was kindness itself. . . . Byron had one preëminent fault—a fault which must be considered as deeply criminal by every one who does not, as I do, believe it to have resulted from monomania. He had a morbid love of a bad reputation. There was hardly an offence of which he would not, with perfect indifference, accuse himself. An old school-fellow, who met him on the Continent, told me that he would continually write paragraphs against himself in the foreign journals, and delight in their republication by the English newspapers as in the success of a practical joke. When anybody had related anything discreditable of Byron, assuring me that it must be true, for he had heard it from himself, I have always felt that he could not have spoken with authority, and that, in all probability, the tale was a pure invention. If I could remember, and were willing to repeat, the various misdoings which I have from time to time heard him attribute to himself, I could fill a volume. But I never believed them. I very soon became aware of this strange idiosyncrasy. It puzzled me to account for it; but there it was—a sort of diseased and distorted vanity.— HARNESS, WILLIAM, 1869, *Life of Harness by L'Estrange, ed. Stoddard, pp.* 189, 191.

We talked of Byron and Wordsworth. "Of course," said Tennyson, "Byron's merits are on the surface. This is not the case with Wordsworth. You must love Wordsworth ere he will seem worthy of your love. As a boy I was an enormous admirer of Byron, so much so that I got a surfeit of him, and now I cannot read him as I should like to do. I was fourteen when I heard of his death. It seemed an awful calamity; I remember I rushed out of doors, sat down by myself, shouted aloud, and wrote on the sandstone: '*Byron is dead!*' "— TENNYSON, ALFRED LORD, 1869, *Some Opinions on Poetry, Memoir by his Son, vol.* II, *p.* 69.

O master, here I bow before a shrine;
  Before the lordliest dust that ever yet
Moved animate in human form divine.
Lo! dust indeed to dust. The mould is set
  Above thee, and the ancient walls are wet,
And drip all day in dark and silent gloom;
  As if the cold gray stones could not forget
Thy great estate shrunk to this sombre room,
But learn to weep perpetual tears above thy
  tomb.
—MILLER, JOAQUIN, 1870–84, *At Lord Byron's Tomb, Memorie and Rime, p.* 15.

Byron was *always* mean. He could pretend affection to Shelley in Italy, while he was secretly joining in the cry against him in England. He betrayed Leigh Hunt; he betrayed every hand that ever touched his. The only good thing that can be said of him is, that he finally came to despise himself; and he probably entered the Greek struggle, where he fell, from sheer desperation at the glimpse of his own degradation. As for this new revelation by Mrs. Stowe, I don't see that it should sink Byron another degree in the opinion of any one were it proved true; it would suggest the plea of diseased instincts, which is the best that can be offered for his crimes; but his cowardice,

his affectation, his deliberate meanness— pah!—CONWAY, M. D., 1870, *Southcoast Saunterings in England, Harper's Magazine, vol.* 40, *p.* 525.

I happened to be in London when Lord Byron's fame was reaching its height, and saw much of him in society. . . . Though he was far from being a great or ambitious talker, his presence at this time made the fortune of any dinner or drawing-room party for which it could be obtained; and was always known by a crowd gathered round him, the female portion generally predominating. I have seen many of these *epidemic* impulses of fashion in London society, but none more marked than this. There was a certain haughtiness or seeming indifference in his manner of receiving the homage tendered him, which did not however prevent him from resenting its withdrawal—an inconsistency not limited to the case of Lord Byron. Though brought into frequent intercourse by our common travels in the East, my intimacy with him went little beyond this. He was not a man with whom it was easy to cultivate friendship. He had that double or conflicting nature, well pictured by Dante, which rendered difficult any close or continued relations with him.— HOLLAND, SIR HENRY, 1871, *Recollections of Past Life, p.* 206.

Insincerity was the real darkness of Byron's life; he turned to the unholy love of women to assuage the anguish of a spirit, enraged, both with itself and the world.—SMITH, GEORGE BARNETT, 1876, *Dean Swift, The International Review, vol.* 3, *p.* 311.

Had he survived he might possibly have become, as H. E. W. surmises, King of Greece, and perhaps not altogether a bad one. How strange a vista of the possibilities of history is opened by such a suggestion! Against Byron's vices and miserable affectations, and the false *ring* of his whole character—which was so ludicrously exemplified by his writing "Fare thee well, and if for ever" on the back of an unpaid butcher's bill—must always be set the honour of his self-devotion and heroism in the Greek war. If he was somewhat of a Sardanapalus, it was a Sardanapalus who could fight for a noble cause not his own. Expressing once to Mazzini my own sense that Byron could scarcely take rank as a poet, compared to Shelley, the Italian

patriot replied: "Ah! but you forgot that Shelley was only a poet in words and feeling; Byron translated his poetry into action, when he went to fight for Greece."
—COBBE, FRANCES POWER, 1882, *Letter to the Temple Bar, vol.* 64, *p.* 318.

Vehement in all things, Byron was especially vehement in his friendships; and despite all that may be urged to the contrary, on the strength of cynical flippancies uttered to astonish his hearers, and bitter words spoken or written under the spur of sudden resentments or the torture of exasperating suspicions, it may be averred stoutly that in choosing his friends and dealing with them he was altogether controlled by his heart. . . . In the domain of the affections he was, from boyhood till his hair whitened, a man of so acute a sensibility that it may well be termed morbid. To this excessive sensibility, and the various kinds of emotionality that necessarily attended it, must be attributed the quickness with which his "passions" succeeded one another. . . . With women he was what they pleased to make or take him for. But he was most pleased with them when they treated him as nearly as possible like "a favorite and sometimes froward sister." The reader may smile, but must not laugh; it was as "a favorite and sometimes froward sister" that he was thought of and treated by Hobhouse and other men. What then more natural for him to like to be thought of and treated by women in the same way?
—JEAFFRESON, JOHN CORDY, 1883, *The Real Lord Byron, pp.* 4, 65, 172.

It is not too much to say that the character of Lord Byron, though untainted by the baser vices attributed to it during the poet's lifetime, consisted of a mass of miserable weaknesses and transparent affectations, relieved by certain amiable traits and some generous impulses. — CAINE, HALL, 1883, *Cobwebs of Criticism,* p. 101.

And lived he here? And could this sweet
   green isle
Volcanic stuff to his hot heart afford,
That he might nurse his wrath, and vent his
   bile
On gods and men, this proud, mistempered
   lord?
Alas! poor lord, to this soft leafy nest,
   Where only pure and heavenly thoughts
     should dwell,
He brought, and bore and cherished in his
   breast,

A home-bred devil, and a native hell.
Unhappy lord! If this be genius, then
  Grant me, O God, a muse with sober sweep,
That I may eat and drink with common men,
  Joy with their joys, and with their weeping weep:
Better to chirp mild loves in lowly bower,
Than soar through stormy skies, with hatred
   for my dower.
—BLACKIE, JOHN STUART, 1886, *Lord Byron and the Armenian Convent, Messis Vitae, p.* 164.

"The Balaam of Baron;" "Bard of Corsair;" "The Comus of Poetry;" "Damætas;" "Don José;" "Don Juan;" "A Literary Vassal;" "Lord Glenarvon;" "The Mocking Bird of our Parnassian Ornithology."
—FREY, ALBERT R., 1888, *Sobriquets and Nicknames, p.* 395.

"Well," said Mr. Stevenson's Attwater to Captain Davis, "you seem to me to be a very twopenny pirate!" And to me, Byron with all his pretensions and his fame seems a very twopenny poet and a farthing man. . . . His letters alone reveal the man; a man of malignant dishonour and declamatory affectation, and poetising conceit; a man who could not even act upon Luther's advice and "sin boldly," but must needs advertise his silly obscenities. Despicable, that is the word for him; and it is no Philistine Puritanism that so speaks. The vulgar aristocrat, the insolent plebeian, that Byron was, looks ludicrous by the side of his great contemporaries. Wordsworth, so impassioned, awful, and august; Shelley and Keats; Lamb, the well-beloved, that tragic and smiling patient; miraculous Coleridge; Landor, with his gracious courtesy and Roman wrath; how does Byron show by these? He did one thing well; he rid the world of a cad—by dying as a soldier. There was a strain of greatness in the man, and it predominated at the last.— JOHNSON, LIONEL, 1898, *Byron, The Academy, vol.* 53, *p.* 489.

Byron and Napoleon are "in the air." The cause is not far to seek. Ours is an age of co-operation rather than of ascendency; "the individual withers;" and public interest naturally recurs to the overwhelming personalities of the past. Among these there is none more original than Byron. As a meteoric force he was revolutionary; as a "human document" he is at once perplexing and paramount. To understand him aright it is needful to watch the development of his weird character, to get close up to him, both in his works and his letters—which are themselves literature. Such a study has, until now, been rendered extremely difficult by the mass of disordered material and the dearth of digested information. It has, practically, been confined to a few, the chief of whom was Disareli the younger, eminently qualified, alike by his poetic endowment and by his aristocratic perceptions. In one passage of "Vivian Grey," throughout "Venetia," is a real interpretation of Byron's nature.—SICHEL, WALTER, 1898, *The Two Byrons, The Fortnightly Review, vol.* 70, *p.* 231.

The real original reason of the outcry against Byron was simply that the women made such a ridiculous fuss about him that the men grew jealous, and were not satisfied until he was hounded out of England.—GRAHAM, WILLIAM, 1898, *Last Links with Byron, Shelley and Keats, Introduction, p.* xii.

The more I read in his letters and in the accounts of those who knew him best, the more I am convinced that the popular idea of Byron as a man whose life was bound up in his love affairs, whatever their nature, is the very reverse of the truth: that, on the contrary, his heart was very little concerned in them, and that his strongest emotions were his friendships with men whom he respected, whom he took for his intellectual peers. He seems to me to have longed to be understood, and liked, and affectionately regarded by his men friends with far more real feeling of the heart than is shown in any one of his affairs with women. He took women lightly, just a trifle in the Mohammedan way, and did not really care deeply about them in any other.—STREET, G. S., 1901, *Byron, 1816–1824, Blackwood's Magazine, vol.* 170, *p.* 764.

LADY BYRON

She is a very superior woman, and very little spoiled; which is strange in an heiress, a girl of twenty, a peeress that is to to be in her own right, an only child, and a savante, who has always had her own way. She is a poetess, a mathematician, a metaphysician; yet, withal, very kind, generous, and gentle, with very little pretension. Any other head would be turned with half her acquisitions and a

tenth of her advantages.—BYRON, LORD, 1815, *Journal.*

> Fare thee well! and if for ever
> Still for ever, fare *thee well* ;
> Even though unforgiving, never
> 'Gainst thee shall my heart rebel.
>
> . . . .
>
> Though my many faults defaced me,
> Could no other arm be found,
> Than the one which once embraced me,
> To inflict a cureless wound?

—BYRON, LORD, 1816, *Fare Thee Well, March* 17.

Lord and Lady Byron are, you know, separated. He said to Rogers that Lady Byron had parted with him, apparently in good friendship, on a visit to her father, and that he had no idea of their being about to part, when he received her decision to that effect. He stated that his own temper, naturally bad, had been rendered more irritable by the derangement of his fortune, and that Lady Byron was entirely blameless. The truth is, he is a very unprincipled fellow.—SMITH, SYDNEY, 1816, *To Francis Jeffrey, A Memoir of Sydney Smith by Lady Holland.*

Of Lady Byron,—highly informed and accomplished, richly endowed by both nature and fortune, yet dwelling meekly in the shade of retirement,—

"As mild and patient as the female dove,
When first her golden couplets are disclos'd;"

bearing with patience her own hard lot, and the published sarcasm of her malignant lord, devoting herself to her superior duties, a blessing to all around by her pious example, and liberal charity,—of her I have neither time nor room to speak as she deserves. Her injuries from him she never did nor will disclose. It should be observed that the most cordial intimacy has always subsisted between her and Mrs. Leigh, the half-sister of Lord Byron.—GRANT, ANNE, 1827, *Letters, Jan.* 16; *Memoir and Correspondence, ed. Grant, vol.* III, *p.* 86.

Lord Byron's was a marriage of convenience,—certainly at least on his own part. . . . He married for money, but of course he wooed with his genius; and the lady persuaded herself that she liked him, partly because he had a genius, and partly because it is natural to love those who take pains to please us. Furthermore, the poet was piqued to obtain his mistress, because she had a reputation for being delicate in such matters; and the lady was piqued to become his wife, not because she did not know the gentleman previously to marriage, but because she did, and hoped that her love and her sincerity, and her cleverness, would enable her to reform him. The experiment was dangerous, and did not succeed. . . . The "Farewell" that he wrote, and that set so many tender-hearted white handkerchiefs in motion, only resulted from his poetical power of assuming an imaginary position, and taking pity on himself in the shape of another man. He had no love for the object of it, or he would never have written upon her in so different a style afterwards.—HUNT, LEIGH, 1828, *Lord Byron and Some of His Contemporaries, vol.* I, *pp.* 9, 11.

True Jedwood justice was dealt out to him. First came the execution, then the investigation, and last of all, or rather not at all, the accusation.—MACAULAY, THOMAS BABINGTON, 1830, *Moore's Life of Lord Byron, Critical and Miscellaneous Essays.*

The accounts given me after I left Lord Byron, by the persons in constant intercourse with him, added to those doubts which had before transiently occurred to my mind as to the reality of the alleged disease; and the reports of his medical attendant were far from establishing the existence of anything like lunacy. Under this uncertainty, I deemed it right to communicate to my parents, that, if I were to consider Lord Byron's past conduct as that of a person of sound mind, nothing could induce me to return to him. It therefore appeared expedient, both to them and myself, to consult the ablest advisers. For that object, and also to obtain still further information respecting the appearances which seemed to indicate mental derangement, my mother determined to go to London. She was empowered by me to take legal opinions on a written statement of mine, though I had then reasons for reserving a part of the case from the knowledge even of my father and mother. Being convinced by the result of these inquiries, and by the tenor of Lord Byron's proceedings, that the notion of insanity was an illusion, I no longer hesitated to authorize such measures as were necessary in order to secure me from

being ever again placed in his power. Conformably with this resolution, my father wrote to him on the 2d of February to propose an amicable separation. Lord Byron at first rejected this proposal; but when it was distinctly notified to him, that, if he persisted in his refusal, recourse must be had to legal measures, he agreed to sign a deed of separation.—BYRON, LADY A. I. NOEL, 1830, *Letter to the Public, Feb.* 19.

She brought to Lord Byron beauty, manners, fortune, meekness, romantic affection, and every thing that ought to have made her to the most transcendent man of genius—*had he been what he should have been*—his pride and his idol. I speak not of Lady Byron in the commonplace manner of attesting character; I appeal to the gifted Mrs. Siddons and Joanna Baillie, to Lady Charlemont, and to other ornaments of their sex, whether I am exaggerating in the least when I say, that, in their whole lives, they have seen few beings so intellectual and well-tempered as Lady Byron. I wish to be as ingenuous as possible in speaking of her. Her manner, I have no hesitation to say, is cool at the first interview, but is modestly, and not insolently, cool: she contracted it, I believe, from being exposed by her beauty and large fortune, in youth, to numbers of suitors, whom she could not have otherwise kept at a distance. But this manner could have had no influence with Lord Byron; for it vanishes on nearer acquaintance, and has no origin in coldness. All her friends like her frankness the better for being preceded by this reserve. This manner, however, though not the slightest apology for Lord Byron, has been inimical to Lady Byron in her misfortunes.—CAMPBELL, THOMAS, 1830, *The New Monthly Magazine.*

Miss Milbank knew that he was reckoned a rake and a *roué;* and although his genius wiped off, by impassioaned eloquence in love-letters that were felt to be irresistible, or hid the worst stain of that reproach, still Miss Milbank must have believed it a perilous thing to be the wife of Lord Byron. . . . But still, by joining her life to his in marriage, she pledged her troth, and her faith, and her love, under probabilities of severe, disturbing, perhaps fearful trials in the future. . . . But I think Lady Byron ought not to have printed that Narrative. Death abrogates not the rights of a husband to his wife's silence, when speech is fatal . . . to his character as a man. Has she not flung suspicion over his bones interred, that they are the bones of a—monster?—WILSON, JOHN (CHRISTOPHER NORTH), 1830, *Noctes Ambrosianæ, Blackwood's Magazine, vol. 27, pp. 823, 824.*

Many excellent reasons are given for his being a bad husband; the sum of which is, that he was a very bad man. I confess I was rejoiced then, and am rejoiced now, that he was driven out of England by public scorn; because his vices were not in his passions, but in his principles.—WEBSTER, DANIEL, 1833, *Letter to George Ticknor, April 8.*

I have said enough to show him as he was, a thoroughly spoilt man. Lady Byron was equally spoilt in an opposite direction —self-willed, intolerant, jealous, and vindictive. She was a rigid Puritan: they are a brave and undaunted sect in self-reliance on their superiority over all other people, and fear nothing. Saints armed in righteousness prefer doing battle with great sinners, confident of their cause. Lady Byron, with the pertinacity of a zealot, plied the poet with holy texts from Scripture and moral maxims from pious writers. . . . Any one could live with him excepting an inflexible and dogmatic saint; not that he objected to his wife's piety, for he saw no harm in that, but her inflicting it on him. The lady's theory was opposed to this: her mission was to reform him by her example and teaching. She had a smattering of science, mathematics, and metaphysics— a toy pet from her childhood, idolized by her parents, and considered as a phenomenon by her country neighbours.—TRELAWNY, EDWARD JOHN, 1858-78, *Records of Shelley, Byron and the Author, pp. 40, 41.*

Never was a young creature led to the altar more truly as a sacrifice. She was rash, no doubt; but she loved him, and who was not, in the whole business, more rash than she? At the altar she did not know that she was a sacrifice: but before sunset of that winter day she knew it, if a judgment may be formed from her face and attitude of despair when she alighted from the carriage on the afternoon of her marriage-day. It was not the traces of tears which won the sympathy of the old butler who stood at the open door. The bridegroom jumped out of the carriage and walked away. The bride alighted, and came up the steps alone, with a countenance and frame agonized and listless with evident horror and despair. The old servant longed to offer his arm to the young, lonely creature, as an assurance of sympathy and protection. From this shock she certainly rallied, and soon. The pecuniary difficulties of her new home were exactly what a devoted spirit like hers was fitted to encounter. Her husband bore testimony, after the catastrophe, that a brighter being, a more sympathizing and agreeable companion, never blessed any man's home. When he afterwards called her cold and mathematical, and over-pious, and so forth, it was when public opinion had gone against him, and when he had discovered that her fidelity and mercy, her silence and magnanimity, might be relied on, so that he was at full liberty to make his part good, as far as she was concerned. . . . She loved him to the last with a love which it was not in his own power to destroy. She gloried in his fame; and she would not interfere between him and the public who adored him, any more than she would admit the public to judge between him and her. As we have said, her love endured to the last.—MARTINEAU, HARRIET, 1860-69, *Biographical Sketches, pp. 284, 287.*

She has been called, after his words, the moral Clytemnestra of her husband. Such a surname is severe: but the repugnance we feel to condemning a woman cannot prevent our listening to the voice of justice, which tells us that the comparison is still in favor of the guilty one of antiquity; for *she* driven to crime by fierce passion overpowering reason, at least only deprived her husband of physical life, and, in committing the deed, exposed herself to all its consequences; while Lady Byron left her husband at the very moment that she saw him struggling amid a thousand shoals in the stormy sea of embarrassments created by his marriage, and precisely when he more than ever required a friendly, tender, and indulgent hand to save him from the tempests of life. Besides, she shut herself up in silence a thousand times more cruel than Clytemnestra's poniard: *that* only killed the body; whereas Lady Byron's silence was destined to kill the soul,—and such a soul!—leaving the door open to calumny, and making it to be supposed that her silence was magnanimity destined to cover over frightful wrongs, perhaps even depravity. In vain did he, feeling his conscience at ease, implore some inquiry and examination. She refused, and the only favor she granted was to send him, one fine day, two persons to see whether he were not mad.—GUICCOLI, COUNTESS, 1868–69, *My Recollections of Lord Byron, tr. Jerningham, p.* 540.

Supposing Mrs. Stowe's narrative to have been really a "true story," and that we had meant to reveal the whole of our grandmother's history, I do not see what defence that is to Mrs. Stowe against the charge of repeating what was told her in a "private, confidential conversation." But it is not true that Lady Anne Blunt and I ever intended to publish correspondence of the nature mentioned. About three years ago a manuscript in Lady Noel Byron's handwriting was found among her papers, giving an account of some circumstances connected with her marriage, and apparently intended for publication after her death; but as this seemed not quite certain, no decision as to its publication was come to. In the event of a memoir being written, this manuscript might, perhaps, be included, but hitherto it has not been proposed to publish any other matter about her separation. This statement in Lady Byron's own handwriting does not contain any accusation of so grave a nature as that which Mrs. Stowe asserts was told her, and Mrs. Stowe's story of the separation is inconsistent with what I have seen in various letters, &c., of Lady Byron's. . . . I, for one, cannot allow that Mrs. Stowe's statement is substantially correct. —WENTWORTH, LORD, 1869, *Pall Mall Gazette, Sept.* 3.

It appears by Dr. Lushington's statements, that, when Lady Byron did speak, she had a story to tell that powerfully affected both him and Romilly,—a story supported by evidence on which they were willing to have gone to public trial. Supposing, now, she had imitated Lord Byron's example, and, avoiding public trial, had put her story into private circulation; as he sent "Don Juan" to fifty confidential friends, suppose she had sent a written

statement of her story to fifty judges as intelligent as the two that had heard it; or suppose she had confronted his autobiography with her own,—what would have been the result? The first result would have been Mrs. Leigh's utter ruin. The world may finally forgive the man of genius anything; but for a woman there is no mercy and no redemption. This ruin Lady Byron prevented by her utter silence and great self-command. Mrs. Leigh never lost position. Lady Byron never so varied in her manner toward her as to excite the suspicions even of her confidential old servant. To protect Mrs. Leigh effectually, it must have been necessary to continue to exclude even her own mother from the secret, as we are assured she did at first; for, had she told Lady Milbanke, it is not possible that so high-spirited a woman could have restrained herself from such outward expressions as would at least have awakened suspicion. There was no resource but this absolute silence.—STOWE, HARRIET BEECHER, 1870, *Lady Byron Vindicated, p.* 73.

If the case is looked at calmly, a simple explanation is not difficult to find. A woman who could ask such a husband in a voice of provoking sweetness "when he meant to give up his bad habit of making verses," a woman who never lost her temper, never gave up her point, and inflicted the most malignant stabs in the tenderest places with angelic coolness, possessed the power of goading a sensitive, impetuous man to frenzy. She had a maid, for example, to whom Byron entertained a violent aversion, because he suspected her of poisoning his wife's mind against him. Lady Byron listened to all his furious tirades with unruffled meekness, but never consented to send the woman away. She was quite as jealous of her dignity, quite as resentful of slights, real or supposed, as himself; and in their differences of opinion she had the inestimable advantage of a temper perfectly under control, and a command of all the sweet resignation of a martyr, combined with the most skilful ingenuity of provoking retort. Byron, with his liability to fits of uncontrollable passion, could never have been an easy man to live with; but if his wife had been a loving, warm-hearted woman, with the unconscious tact that such women have, the result would probably

have been very different.—MINTO, WIL-
LIAM, 1894, *The Literature of the Georgian
Era, ed. Knight, p.* 272.

HOURS OF IDLENESS
1807

The poesy of this young lord belongs to
the class which neither gods nor men are
said to permit. Indeed, we do not recollect to have seen a quantity of verse with
so few deviations in either direction from
that exact standard. His effusions are
spread over a dead flat, and can no more
get above or below the level, than if they
were so much stagnant water. As an
extenuation of this offence, the noble
author is peculiarly forward in pleading
minority. We have it in the title-page,
and on the very back of the volume; it
follows his name like a favourite part of
his *style.* Much stress is laid upon it in
the preface, and the poems are connected
with this general statement of his case, by
particular dates, substantiating the age at
which each was written. Now, the law
upon the point of minority we hold to be
perfectly clear. It is a plea available only
to the defendant; no plaintiff can offer it
as a supplementary ground of action. . . .
Whatever judgment may be passed on the
poems of this noble minor, it seems we
must take them as we find them, and be
content; for they are the last we shall
ever have from him. . . . What right
have we poor devils to be nice? We are
well off to have got so much from a man
of this Lord's station; who does not live
in a garret, but "has the sway" of
Newstead Abbey. Again, we say, let us
be thankful; and, with honest Sancho, bid
God bless the giver, nor look the gift
horse in the mouth.—BROUGHAM, HENRY
LORD, 1808, *Lord Byron's Poems, Edinburgh Review, vol.* 11, *pp.* 285, 289.

Yet though there were many, and those
not the worst judges, who discerned in
these juvenile productions, a depth of
thought and felicity of expression which
promised much at a more mature age, the
errors did not escape the critical lash;
and certain brethren of ours yielded to the
opportunity of pouncing upon a titled
author, and to that which most readily
besets our fraternity, and to which we
dare not pronounce ourselves wholly inaccessible, the temptation, namely, of shew-
ing our own wit, and entertaining our
readers with a lively article without much

respect to the feelings of the author, or
even to the indications of merit which the
work may exhibit.—SCOTT, SIR WALTER,
1816, *Childe Harold Canto* iii, *and other
Poems, Quarterly Review, vol.* 16, *p.* 174.

The "Hours of Idleness" were poorish
and pretentious verses, certainly with less
of promise in them than the first productions of most other great poets. Yet
they had some, and there was little excuse
for the smart but stupid "Edinburgh Review" article upon them. However, this
had the good effect of rousing Byron to
put forth his power.—NOEL, RODEN, 1896,
*The Poets and the Poetry of the Century,
Southey to Shelley, ed. Miles, p.* 375.

ENGLISH BARDS AND SCOTCH
REVIEWERS
1809

As to the *Edinburgh Reviewers,* it would
indeed require an Hercules to crush the
Hydra; but if the author succeeds in
merely "bruising one of the heads of the
serpent," though his own hand should suffer
in the encounter, he will be amply satisfied.—BYRON, LORD, 1809, *English Bards
and Scotch Reviewers, Preface.*

If I could envy any man for successful ill-nature, I should envy Lord Byron
for his skill in satirical momenclature.—
SMITH, SYDNEY, 1810, *To Lady Holland,
June; Memoir by Lady Holland.*

It is very abusive; but with few exceptions its satire is as weak as it is violent
and unjust.—STORY, WILLIAM WETMORE,
1890, *Conversations in a Studio, vol.* I,
p. 233.

A verse pamphlet clearly inspired.—
RHYS, ERNEST, 1897, *Literary Pamphlets,
vol.* I, *p.* 32.

Is the last angry reverberation of the
literary satire of Dryden and Pope. It is
a kind of inverted "Dunciad;" and novice
falls upon the masters of his day, as the
Augustan master upon the nonentities of
his, and emulates Pope's stiletto with a
vigorous bludgeon. Only those who, like
Rogers or Campbell, in some sort also
maintained the tradition of Pope, came off
without a gibe. But the invective, though
as a rule puerile as criticism, shows extraordinary powers of malicious statement, and bristles with the kind of epigram
which makes satire stick, when it is too
wildly aimed to wound.—HERFORD, C. H.,
1897, *The Age of Wordsworth, p.* 222.

CHILDE HAROLD
1812-16-18

You have written one of the most delightful poems I ever read. . . . I have been so fascinated with "Childe Harold," that I have not been able to lay it down. I would almost pledge my life on its advancing the reputation of your poetical powers, and of its gaining you great honour and regard, if you will do me the credit and favour of attending to my suggestions respecting some alterations and omissions which I think indispensable.—DALLAS, R. C., 1811, *Letter to Byron, July* 16; *Recollections of Lord Byron, pp.* 74, 75.

The Third Canto of "Childe Harold" exhibits, in all its strength and in all its peculiarities, the wild, powerful and original vein of poetry which, in the preceding cantos, first fixed the public attention upon the author. If there is any difference, the former seems to us to have been rather more sedulously corrected and revised for the publication, and the present work to have been dashed from the author's pen with less regard to the subordinate points of expression and versification. Yet such is the deep and powerful strain of passion, such the original tone and colouring of description, that the want of polish in some of its minute parts rather adds to than deprives the poem of its energy. — SCOTT, SIR WALTER, 1816, *Childe Harold Canto* iii, *and other Poems, Quarterly Review, vol.* 16, *p.* 189.

The effect was, accordingly, electric; his fame had not to wait for any of the ordinary gradations, but seemed to spring up, like the palace of a fairy tale, in a night. As he himself briefly described it in his memoranda, "I awoke one morning and found myself famous."—MOORE, THOMAS, 1830, *Life of Lórd Byron, vol.* I, *p.* 274.

The appearance of this admirable poem placed the author, instantly and forever, at the head of all the poets of his time.— SHAW, THOMAS B., 1847, *Outlines of English Literature, p.* 352.

Byron, who desired to please the public, took care to mix a good deal of tall talk in the most popular of his poems, "Childe Harold."— PATTISON, MARK, 1872-89, *Pope and His Editors, Essays, ed. Nettleship, vol.* II, *p.* 355.

"Childe Harold," even in its complete form, is no finished whole, no work of art in the higher sense; the requisite repose and depth were wanting alike for the creation and for the enjoyment of such a work. It is a string of pearls of opinions and thoughts on questions of philosophy and politics in a brilliant and highly poetical setting, and what many scarcely ventured to think, they found there set forth in bold and lofty expression. The dissatisfaction, so energetically uttered by the poet, on the part which England played in the affairs of the world, was felt and recognised with especial earnestness by a great part of the nation.—ELZE, KARL, 1870-72, *Lord Byron, p.* 125.

On taking up a fairly good version of "Childe Harold's Pilgrimage" in French or Italian prose, a reader whose eyes and ears are not hopelessly sealed against all distinction of good from bad in rhythm or in style will infallibly be struck by the vast improvement which the text has undergone in the course of translation. The blundering, floundering, lumbering and stumbling stanzas, transmuted into prose and transfigured into grammar, reveal the real and latent force of rhetorical energy that is in them: the gasping, ranting, wheezing, broken-winded verse has been transformed into really effective and fluent oratory. A ranter, of course, it is whose accents we hear in alternate moan and bellow from the trampled platform of theatrical misanthropy: but he rants no longer out of tune: and we are able to discern in the thick and troubled stream of his natural eloquence whatever of real value may be swept along in company with much drifting rubbish. It is impossible to express how much "Childe Harold" gains by being done out of wretchedly bad metre into decently good prose: the New Testament did not gain more by being translated out of canine Greek into divine English.— SWINBURNE, ALGERNON CHARLES, 1886, *Wordsworth and Byron, Miscellanies, p.* 75.

But no English poet has used the Spenserian stanza with the grand *vigor* with which Byron has used it in his "Childe Harold." His impetuous spirit imparts a character to the stanza quite distinct from its peculiar Spenserian character. Even the stanzas in which his gentler and more pensive moods are embodied, bear little or no similarity to the manner of Spenser.

—CORSON, HIRAM, 1892, *A Primer of English Verse, p.* 125.

Its cantos, here and there splendidly ablaze with Nature—its storms, its shadows, its serenities; and the sentiment —now morbid, now jubilant—is always his own, though it beguiles with honeyed sounds, or stabs like a knife.—MITCHELL, DONALD G., 1897, *English Lands Letters and Kings, The Later Georges to Victoria,* p. 238.

The demerits of "Childe Harold" lie on the surface; but it is difficult for the modern reader, familiar with the sight, if not the texture, of "the purple patches," and unattracted, perhaps demagnetized, by a personality once fascinating and always "puissant," to appreciate the actual worth and magnitude of the poem. We are "o'er informed;" and as with Nature, so with Art, the eye must be couched, and the film of association removed, before we can see clearly. But there is one characteristic feature of "Childe Harold" which association and familiarity have been powerless to veil or confuse—originality of design. "By what accident," asks the Quarterly Reviewer (George Agar Ellis), "has it happened that no other English poet before Lord Byron has thought fit to employ his talents on a subject so well suited to their display?" The question can only be answered by the assertion that it was the accident of genius which inspired the poet with a "new song." "Childe Harold's Pilgrimage" had no progenitors, and, with the exception of some feeble and forgotten imitations, it has had no descendants.—COLERIDGE, ERNEST HARTLEY, 1899, *ed., The Works of Lord Byron, Poetry, vol.* II, *p.* 13.

THE GIAOUR
1813

I suppose you have read Lord Byron's "Giaour,"—and which edition? because there are five, and in every one he adds about fifty lines; so that the different editions have rather the sisterly likeness which Ovid says the Nereids had, than the identity expected by the purchasers of the same work. And pray do you say Lord Byron, or Byron, in defiance of the *y* and our old friend in Sir Charles Grandison? And do you pronounce Giaour hard *g* or soft *g*? And do you understand the poem at first reading?—because Lord Byron and the Edinburgh Reviewers say you are very

stupid if you don't; and yet the same Reviewers have thought proper to prefix the story to help your apprehension. All these, unimportant as you may think them, are matters of discussion here.—BARBAULD, ANNA LÆTITIA, 1813, *Works, vol.* II, *p.* 96.

Poured forth for its amusement those Oriental tales, of which "The Giaour" alone retains sufficient vitality or perfume of true poetry to make its perusal at the present day desirable.—SYMONDS, JOHN ADDINGTON, 1880, *The English Poets, ed. Ward, vol.* IV, *p.* 247.

The "Giaour" is, as he truly called it, "a string of passages," not a work moving by a deep internal law of development to a necessary end; and our total impression from it cannot but receive from this, its inherent defect, a certain dimness and indistinctness. But the incidents of the journey and death of Hassan, in that poem, are conceived and presented with a vividness not to be surpassed; and our impression from them is correspondingly clear and powerful.—ARNOLD, MATTHEW, 1881, *Poetry of Byron, Preface.*

THE CORSAIR
1814

To me Byron's "Corsair" appears the best of all his works. Rapidity of execution is no sort of apology for doing a thing ill, but when it is done well, the wonder is so much the greater. I am told he wrote this poem at ten sittings—certainly it did not take him more than three weeks. —DUDLEY, EARL OF, 1818, *Letters.*

His "Corsair" is marred by classic elegancies: the pirates' song at the beginning is no truer than a chorus at the Italian opera; his scamps propound philosophical antitheses as balanced as those of Pope. A hundred times ambition, glory, envy, despair, and the other abstract personages, whose images in the time of the Empire the French used to set upon their drawing-room clocks, break in amidst living passions. The noblest passages are disfigured by pedantic apostrophes, and the pretentious poetic diction sets up its threadbare frippery and conventional ornaments. Far worse, he studies effect and follows the fashion.—TAINE, H. A., 1871, *History of English Literature, tr. Van Laun, vol.* II, *bk. iv, ch. ii, p.* 284.

Medora's song in the *Corsair*, "Deep in

my soul that tender secret dwells,'' though not flawless as a lyric, is one of his most beautiful expressions of this mournful sentiment in a subdued key.—MINTO, WILLIAM, 1876, *Encyclopædia Britannica, vol.* IV, *p.* 540.

PRISONER OF CHILLON
1816

Next day beautiful drive to Vevay, as you know. After visiting Chillon, where Lord Byron's name and *coat of arms* are cut upon Bonnivar's pillar, I read the poem again, and think it most sublime and pathetic. How can that man have perverted so much feeling as was originally given to him!—EDGEWORTH, MARIA, 1820, *Letters, vol.* II, *p.* 12.

Perhaps the first and most faultless of his poems.—REED, HENRY, 1850–55, *Lectures on English Literature from Chaucer to Tennyson, p.* 290.

No one of Byron's poems is so purely narrative, or has such a unity of lofty and tender interest, uninterrupted by a single distracting image. But this very perfection makes it tame and cold among the heat and animation of the rest: it is the only one in which Byron is left out.—OLIPHANT, MARGARET O. W., 1882, *Literary History of England, XVIII-XIX Century, vol.* III, *p.* 56.

Detained by bad weather at Ouchy, he wrote in two days "The Prisoner of Chillon," with its glorious introductory sonnet to Liberty. This tale is a very beautiful composition, having unity, graphic description, tenderness, and pathos. — NOEL, RODEN, 1890, *Life of Lord Byron (Great Writers), p.* 120.

MANFRED
1817

There are great faults, it must be admitted, in this poem;—but it is undoubtedly a work of genius and originality. Its worse fault, perhaps, is that it fatigues and overawes us by the uniformity of its terror and solemnity. Another is the painful and offensive nature of the circumstance on which its distress is ultimately founded.—JEFFREY, FRANCIS LORD, 1817–44, *Contributions to the Edinburgh Review, vol.* II, *p.* 386.

His [Goethe's] "Faust" I never read, for I don't know German; but Matthew Monk Lewis, in 1816, at Coligny, translated most of it to me *vivâ voce*, and I was naturally much struck with it; but it was the

"Staubach" and the "Jungfrau," and something else, much more than Faustus, that made me write "Manfred."—BYRON, LORD, 1820, *Letter to Mr. Murray, June* 7.

Last week, *le sentiment de malédiction* was upon me, about me, within me. I owe that to Lord Byron; I read through his "Manfred," in English, twice. Never, never shall I be so upset by any thing I read as I was by that. It has fairly made me ill. On Sunday I went out to see the sun set; it was as threatening as the fires of hell. I went into the church where the faithful were peacefully chanting the Hallelujah; I leaned against a pillar, and gazed at them with envy and scorn. I understood why Byron's Incantation ended thus:—

"O'er thy heart and brain together
Hath the word been passed,—now wither! ''

In the evening I dined with Edmond; I had to talk with Mrs. Morel about rooms and wall-papers. At nine o'clock I could stand it no longer; I was overcome by bitter, violent despair; my eyes were closed; my head tipped back, and I was consuming my own heart. To the gentle Lydia's consolations I dropped a few words of grief and irony. Adieu.—AMPÈRE, J. J., 1820, *Letter, May* 20, *Correspondence.*

Byron's tragedy, "Manfred," was to me a wonderful phenomenon, and one that closely touched me. This singular intellectual poet has taken my *Faustus* to himself, and extracted from it the strangest nourishment for his hypochondriac humour. He has made use of the impelling principles in his own way, for his own purposes, so that no one of them remains the same; and it is particularly on this account that I cannot enough admire his genius. The whole is in this way so completely formed anew that it would be an interesting task for the critic to point out, not only the alterations he has made, but their degree of resemblance with, or dissimilarity to, the original; in the course of which I cannot deny that the gloomy heat of an unbounded and exuberant despair becomes at last oppressive to us. Yet is the dissatisfaction we feel always connected with esteem and admiration. We find thus in this tragedy the quintessence of the most astonishing talent born to be its own tormentor.—GOETHE, JOHANN WOLFGANG, 1820, *Review of Manfred, tr. Hoppner.*

Lord Byron's "Manfred" is in parts

intensely poetical; yet the delicate mind naturally shrinks from the spirit which here and there reveals itself, and the basis on which the drama is built. From a perusal of it we should infer, according to the above theory, that there was right and fine feeling in the poet's mind, but that the central and consistent character was wanting. From the history of his life we know this to be the fact.—NEWMAN, JOHN HENRY, 1829–71, *Poetry with Reference to Aristotle's Poetics; Essays Critical and Historical, vol.* I, *p.* 22.

Into what mediocrity and platitude sinks the "Faust" of Goethe, compared to "Manfred!"—TAINE, H. A., 1871, *History of English Literature, tr. Van Laun, vol.* II, *bk.* iv, *ch.* ii, *p.* 295.

Byron's grandest poem is "Manfred." Henri Taine compares it with "Faust," and says that "Manfred" is the poem of individuality, and "Faust" the poem of humanity. I should call "Manfred" the poem of sentiment, and "Faust" the poem of ideas; "Manfred" the poem of nature, and "Faust" the poem of history. Both poems represent the disenchantment which is produced within the limits of human existence. Faust himself is weary after having thought, and Manfred after having lived. The one dies, as becomes a German doctor, after having studied medicine, alchemy, the theological sciences and philosophy, and having found them but ashes. The other expires after having felt, struggled, and loved in vain; after having ascended the gigantic ladder formed by the Alps, without finding anything more than the piercing wind eternally moaning, the white frost falling, the pines amid the snow-flakes, the cold desert of crystal fatal to life, the profound abyss where light is extinguished; beneath, men are like insects; above, the eagles fly in endless circles, breaking the immensity and the silence by their cries of hunger; a spectacle which reminds him of another desolation, the moonlight night in which he trod the ground of the Colosseum, the ruins overgrown with nettles, and heard nothing but owls, whose melancholy cries were an elegy over the ashes of the martyrs and gladiators of the past. . . . Byron *feels* the evil and Goethe *thinks* it.—CASTELAR, EMILIO, 1873–75, *Life of Lord Byron and other Sketches, tr. Arnold, pp.* 169, 176.

We read Jeffrey's awe-stricken applause and Wilson's enthusiastic appreciation, and find that even such an authority as Goethe declares Manfred's mouthings of mock despair to be an improvement on Hamlet's soliloquy, the extraordinary mistake takes away our breath. . . . The subject is one which only the most exceptional merit in the poetry could make tolerable; and the poetry is not exceptional, but below the highest level of Byron's power. To compare this *diablerie* with that of Goethe, or the songs of the spirits whom Manfred evokes, with the melody of Shelley's responses in the "Prometheus," is to put him at an extraordinary disadvantage. — OLIPHANT, MARGARET O. W., 1882, *Literary History of England, XVIII-XIX Century, vol.* III, *pp.* 60, 61.

DON JUAN
1819–1824

A foul blot on the literature of his country, an act of high treason on English poetry.—SOUTHEY, ROBERT, 1820, *Letter to Landor, Feb.* 20.

I do most cordially agree with you that *I* deserve quizzing for refusing to sell "Don Juan," and should not be spared in the article. The only apology I have to offer to *you* is this, that it proceeded partly from pique and partly from principle. When the book was published by Murray, I was just on the point of breaking with him. I had not had a letter from him for some months. He sent me copies of the book per mail, without either letter or invoice, so that when I received them I was not disposed to read it with a favourable eye. I did read it, and I declare solemnly to you, much as I admire the talent and genius displayed in it, I never in my life was so filled with utter disgust. It was not the grossness or blackguardism which struck me, but it was the vile, heartless, and cold-blooded way in which this fiend attempted to degrade every tender and sacred feeling of the human heart. I felt such a revolting at the whole book after I had finished it, that I was glad of the excuse I had, from Mr. Murray not writing me, for refusing to sell it. I was terribly laughed at by my friends here, and I daresay you will laugh as much still at my prudery and pique.—BLACKWOOD, WILLIAM, 1821, *Letter to Maginn; William Blackwood and His Sons, by Oliphant, vol.* I, *p.* 380.

How lamentably the *art* of versification is neglected by most of the poets of the present day!—by Lord Byron, as it strikes me, in particular, among those of eminence for other qualities. Upon the whole, I think the part of "Don Juan" in which Lambro's return to his home, and Lambro himself, are described, is the best, that is, the most individual, thing in all I know of Lord B's. works. The festal abandonment puts one in mind of Nicholas Poussin's pictures.—COLERIDGE, SAMUEL TAYLOR, 1824, *Table-Talk, ed. Ashe, June* 7, *p.* 39.

Lord Byron was the assassin of his own fame, and seemed to glory in the deliberate act of assassination. . . . Replete, it is true, with passages of extraordinary splendour and power, but debased with a far greater proportion of what was vulgar, common-place, and indecent. Latterly, indeed, these cantos became intolerably dull, and found few readers.—DIBDIN, THOMAS FROGNALL, 1824, *The Library Companion, p.* 744, *note.*

The most prodigal use did not exhaust his powers, nay, seemed rather to increase their vigour. Neither "Childe Harold," nor any of the most beautiful of Byron's earlier tales, contain more exquisite morsels of poetry than are to be found scattered through the cantos of "Don Juan," amidst verses which the author appears to have thrown off with an effort as spontaneous as that of a tree resigning its leaves to the wind.—SCOTT, SIR WALTER, 1824, *Death of Lord Byron, The Edinburgh Weekly Journal.*

I passed some hours over "Don Juan," and saw no reason to change the opinion which I formed twenty-five years ago. The first two cantos are Byron's masterpiece. The next two may pass as not below his average. Then begins the descent, and at last he sinks to the level of his own imitators in the Magazines.—MACAULAY, THOMAS BABINGTON, 1849, *Journal, Aug.* 3; *Life and Letters, ed. Trevelyan.*

No father would put "Don Juan" into his daughter's hands; nor would he consent that his son should read it until his principles were fixed, and his judgment clear and defined. It has received its worst condemnation by being reprinted and sold by certain booksellers who deal with the most corrupting literature, and by being found on the bookshelves of the rake

and the man of the world. And yet—("But yet the pity of it, Iago! O Iago, the pity of it, Iago!")—it contains noble poetry, most beautiful passages, and the best literary work that its author in his mature power was capable of.—FRISWELL, JAMES HAIN, 1869, *Essays on English Writers, p.* 322.

The admirable wit both of his letters, and of pieces like the "Vision of Judgment" and "Don Juan," where wit reaches as high as any English writer has ever carried it.—MORLEY, JOHN, 1870, *Byron, Fortnightly Review, vol.* 14, *p.* 656.

The poem, as will be remembered, begins with the meanest and foulest attack on his wife that ever ribald wrote, and put it in close neighborhood with scenes which every pure man or woman must feel to be the beastly utterances of a man who had lost all sense of decency. . . . Society revolted, however, and fought stoutly against the nauseous dose. Even his sister wrote to him that she heard such things said of it that *she* never would read it; and the outcry against it on the part of all women of his acquaintance was such that for a time he was quite overborne; and the Countess Guiccioli finally extorted a promise from him to cease writing it. Nevertheless there came a time when England accepted "Don Juan,"—when Wilson, in the Noctes Ambrosianæ, praised it as a classic, and took every opportunity to reprobate Lady Byron's conduct.—STOWE, HARRIET BEECHER, 1870, *Lady Byron Vindicated, pp.* 62, 64.

And then he wrote his masterpiece, "Don Juan." . . . There is a derangement of heart and mind in the style of "Don Juan," as in Swift. When a man jests amidst his tears, it is because he has a poisoned imagination. This kind of laughter is a spasm, and you see in one man a hardening of the heart, or madness; in another, excitement or disgust. Byron was exhausted, at least the poet was exhausted in him. The last cantos of "Don Juan" drag: the gaiety became forced, the escapades became digressions; the reader began to be bored. A new kind of poetry, which he had attempted, had given way in his hands: in the drama he only attained to powerful declamation, his characters had no life; when he forsook poetry, poetry forsook him; he went to Greece in search of action, and only found death.—TAINE, H. A., 1871, *History of English Literature, tr. Van Laun, vol. II, bk. iv, ch. ii, pp.* 301, 309.

In my opinion the poem of "Don Juan" could not have been written by any other author of the present century. The jests and turns which have been stigmatized as so many blots and sins of the author, are essentially portions of the poem, of its nature and character, and could not have been omitted or destroyed, except by radically damaging the poem itself.—PROCTER, BRYAN WALLER, 1874, *Recollections of Men of Letters, p.* 135.

The Immortal, the unprecedented and unrivalled masterpiece.—ROSSETTI, WILLIAM MICHAEL, 1878, *Lives of Famous Poets, p.* 301.

A sensitive man, and yet heroic, strong in spirit, but without fixed ideals of life, a rebel by nature who yet finds no greater soul to lead him, no faithful band to follow him in any definite effort for mankind, Byron is a modern likeness of him that in the legend afterwards became St. Christopher. Only Byron seeks the strongest without finding him, learns to despise the devil, and never meets the devil's master. Worn out with the search, the poet flings himself down in the woods of doubt and dreams "Don Juan." We look in vain for the right adjective with which to qualify this poem: it is so full of strength, so lavish of splendid resources, and yet in sum so disappointing. It has no true ending, and never could have had one. It is a mountain stream, plunging down dreadful chasms, singing through grand forests, and losing itself in a lifeless gray alkali desert. Here is romantic self-criticism pushed to its farthest consequences. Here is the self-confession of an heroic soul that has made too high demands on life, and that has found in its own experience and in the world nothing worthy of true heroism.—ROYCE, JOSIAH, 1885, *The Religious Aspect of Philosophy, p.* 119.

He could exhibit only two squeaking and disjointed puppets: there is, as far as I can remember, just one passage in the whole range of his writings which shows any power of painting any phase of any kind of character at all: and this is no doubt a really admirable (if not wholly original) instance of the very broadest comedy—the harangue addressed by Donna Julia to her intruding husband.—SWINBURNE, ALGERNON CHARLES, 1886, *Wordsworth and Byron, Miscellanies, p.* 85.

Some of Byron's most powerful writing is found in "Don Juan;" some of his tenderest; and the possible flexibility of the English language is often fully realized. But when he wrote this poem, his better nature was more or less eclipsed; but wherever it asserts itself, we feel its presence in the moulding of the verse, as much as we do in the sentiments expressed.—CORSON, HIRAM, 1892, *A Primer of English Verse, p.* 29.

If a novel in verse is a novel all the same, where is better reading (given liberty to skip when you like) than in "Don Juan?"—HAWKINS, ANTHONY HOPE, 1897, *My Favorite Novelist and His Best Book, Munsey's Magazine, vol.* 18, *p.* 351.

MARINO FALIERO
1820

"Marino Faliero," has, we believe, been pretty generally pronounced a failure by the public voice, and we see no reason to call for a revision of their sentence. It contains, beyond all doubt, many passages of commanding eloquence and some of genuine poetry, and the scenes, more particularly, in which Lord Byron has neglected the absurd greed of his pseudo-Hellenic writers, are conceived and elaborated with great tragic effect and dexterity. But the subject is decidedly ill-chosen. In the main tissue of the plot and in all the busiest and most interesting parts of it, it is, in fact, no more than another "Venice Preserved," in which the author has had to contend (nor has he contended successfully) with our recollections of a former and deservedly popular play on the same subject.—HEBER, REGINALD, 1822, *Lord Byron's Dramas, Quarterly Review, vol.* 27, *p.* 487.

Notwithstanding his predominant personality, has sometimes had the power of renouncing himself altogether, as may be seen in some of his dramatic pieces, particularly in his "Marino Faliero." In this piece one quite forgets that Lord Byron, or even an Englishman, wrote it. We live entirely in Venice, and entirely in the time in which the action takes place.—GOETHE, JOHANN WOLFGANG, 1830, *Conversations, ed. Eckermann, vol.* II, *p.* 253.

A composition that abounds in noble

passages and rests on a fine and original conception of character.—MORLEY, JOHN, 1870, *Byron, Fortnightly Review, vol.* 14, *p.* 659.

"Marino Faliero," one of Byron's less important works, may be cited as a fair example of his eloquence and concentrated passion. The theme of the drama is perfectly simple,—the conflict in Marino's breast between aristocratic pride and the love of liberty (predominant characteristics, be it observed, of the poet himself); and about this conflict the whole action of the play revolves, without any minor issues to dissipate the effect. The mind is held gripped to one emotion and one thought; we seem to hear the mighty pleading of a Demosthenes. There is no poem of Shelley's (with the possible exception of "The Cenci," where he resorts to monstrous and illegitimate means) which begins to leave on the mind so distinct and powerful an impression as this, yet the whole drama contains perhaps not a single line of the illusive charm to be found in passages on every page of Shelley's works. —MORE, PAUL ELMER, 1898, *The Wholesome Revival of Byron, Atlantic Monthly, vol.* 82, *p.* 802.

CAIN
1821

"Cain, a Mystery," was worse and worse. Byron dared to measure himself with Milton, and came off as poorly as Belial might have done from a contest with Michael. Crude metaphysics, as old as the hills, and as barren—bald, thread-bare blasphemies, and peurile ravings, formed the staple of the piece. The only tolerable touches, those of domestic love and the like, were visibly borrowed from Gesner's "Death of Abel:" and in short, one of the most audacious of all the insults that have ever been heaped upon the faith and feelings of a Christian land, was also one of the most feeble and ineffectual. Thank God! Cain was abandoned to the Radicals—and thank God, it was too radically dull to be popular even among them. —MAGINN, WILLIAM, 1822, *Odoherty on Werner, Blackwood's Magazine, vol.* 12, *p.* 711.

Though it abounds in beautiful passages, and shows more *power* perhaps than any of the author's dramatical compositions, we regret very much that it should ever have been published. It will give great

scandal and offence to pious persons in general—and may be the means of suggesting the most painful doubts and distressing perplexities, to hundreds of minds that might never otherwise have been exposed to such dangerous disturbance.—JEFFREY, FRANCIS LORD, 1822-44, *Contributions to the Edinburgh Review, vol.* II, *p.*362.

I said that I had lately been reading Byron's "Cain," and had been particularly struck by the third act, and the manner in which the murder is brought about. "It is, indeed, admirable," said Goethe. "Its beauty is such as we shall not see a second time in the world." "Cain," said I, "was at first prohibited in England; but now everybody reads it, and young English travellers usually carry a complete Byron with them." "It was folly" said Goethe; "for, in fact, there is nothing in the whole of 'Cain' which is not taught by the English bishops themselves."— ECKERMANN, JOHN PETER, 1827, *Conversations of Goethe, vol.* I, *p.* 419.

Like a lion impatiently beating against the iron bars of his cage, so Byron precipitates himself in this poem on the mysteries of revealed faith. He never, indeed, succeeds in bursting his cage; rather he remains in a state of indecision, and never comes to a positive conclusion in either direction. To Englishmen this scepticism was, with few exceptions, an insurmountable stone of offence. In England freedom of action is cramped by the want of freedom in thought; the converse is the case with us Germans, freedom of thought is restricted by the want of freedom in action. To us this scepticism presents nothing in the least degree fearful; we, like Faust, are afraid neither of the devil nor of hell.—ELZE, KARL, 1870-72, *Lord Byron, p.* 415.

"Cain" is the most complete and finished work of the poet, and we cannot contradict Shelley when he calls it the greatest of Byron's poems. Cain is a Titanic Manfred, a creation similar to Job and Prometheus. The spirit of Æschylus seems to breath in the poem, and with the exception of a few passages in "Paradise Lost" and in "Faust," modern poetry has produced nothing similar in boldness and in grandeur to Cain's flight with Lucifer through illimitable space, and the conversations of the two in Hades. In England the poem was appreciated by few at first, and Byron called it jestingly "the Waterloo of his popularity." But it is an æsthetic truth that the creation of Satan in "Cain" must be considered as one of the greatest achievements of modern poetry. There are altogether only four poets who have succeeded in portraying Satan: Vandel, Milton, Goethe, and Byron. Vandel's satan was created fourteen years before that of Milton; it is a powerful conception, and undoubtedly the greatest poetical figure which Holland has produced. Goethe's Mephisto is such a peculiar impersonation of the Satanic idea that he cannot be compared to the others. Byron's Satan ranks next to Milton's. Dante's detailed delineation only produces a somewhat ridiculous monster which leaves us perfectly indifferent, while Milton's and Byron's Satan is a colossal extention of the human form surrounded by a darkness as of thunder-clouds, and exciting our terror as well as a feeling of sympathy.—SCHERR, J., 1874, *A History of English Literature*, tr. *M. V.*, *p.* 236.

It may be true, Basrandes observes, that in Cain, Byron is dashing about like a wild beast in the cage of dogma; it may be true that this poem is simply an expression of man's monotonous fate in this world; but the power of personal force, the strength of the individual's will, must have been an inspiring influence to that younger generation whose fate it was to stand firm against the efforts of the Holy Alliance to crush out the spirit of liberty. Certainly the poem is another revelation of that fierce assertion of self-sufficiency which enabled Byron, in the later days, to take up the heritage of leadership left him by Rousseau.—HANCOCK, ALBERT ELMER, 1899, *The French Revolution and the English Poets*, *p.* 117.

LETTERS

The Letters, at least those which were sent from Italy, are among the best in our language. They are less affected than those of Pope and Walpole; they have more matter in them than those of Cowper. Knowing that many of them were not written merely for the person to whom they were directed, but were general epistles, meant to be read by a large circle, we expected to find them clever and spirited, but deficient in ease. We looked with vigilance for instances of stiffness in the language, and awkwardness in the transitions. We have been agreeably disappointed; and we must confess, that if the epistolary style of Lord Byron was artificial, it was a rare and admirable instance of that highest art which cannot be distinguished from nature.—MACAULAY, THOMAS ·BABINGTON, 1830, *Moore's Life of Lord Byron, Edinburgh Review, Critical and Miscellaneous Essays.*

His letters from Italy, alone,—things thrown off in every variety of mood, and some of them bearing strong evidence of the bottle,—display more genius than can be found in all the first two cantos of "Childe Harold."—WHIPPLE, EDWIN P., 1845, *Byron, Essays and Reviews.*

We are indebted to the poet's misfortune for all that series of delightful letters which in themselves form one of the most perfect biographies, and which reflect the whole contemporary life like the literary correspondence of Grimm. A slender thread of criticism and by-play links them together in Moore's Life, and with this are blended corollary recollections of observers and travellers, critics, and intimates; never, however, obscuring the splendid figure of the chief actor, embellishing his surroundings like living *coulisses,* shifting or shoving in landscapes or backgrounds, stories, and scenes, and throwing right upon him as he stands in the centre of the stage the whole affluence of their light. There is no better illuminated figure on the whole canvas of history. Turning to the memoirs of this man is like walking down a corridor of the Louvre, where the Pagan mythology shimmers before us in marble, and far at the end, queen-like and alone, stands the Venus of Milo. Turn down what corridor you will, an excess of illumination falls upon the head of Byron; it is cloudless save for one great cloud; it is put to the torture of endless light: it is the story of Regulus and the Carthaginian sun; it is the glare of the dog-star upon the bald ruins of the Parthenon. —HARRISON, JAMES ALBERT, 1875, *A Group of Poets and Their Haunts, p.* 33.

GENERAL

Byron, with eager indifference.—HUNT, LEIGH, 1814, *The Feast of the Poets.*

His verse, with all its lofty aspirations and endowments, is lost in the mazes of infidelity and despair; groping in a vast crowd of strange unearthly shapes conjured up by midnight fancy, it deifies only a morbid heroism, which it invests with the gloomy spell of varied passion. This atheistic inspiration was not altogether alien to German poetry at an earlier epoch; but a purer sphere was soon attained, the monstrosities of false tragic grandeur being banished to the extreme confines of the drama. In the higher regions of art it was speedily discovered that modern poetry cannot flow in transparent stream from the turbid eddy of forward passion; but founded on eternal hope, it must become a glorified admixture of Faith and Love, radiant as the rainbow after the storm, or the dawn of morn after the shades of night.—SCHLEGEL, FRIEDRICH, 1815-59, *Lectures on the History of Literature.*

"Parisina," is the most interesting and best conceived and best told story I ever read. I was never more affected.—MURRAY, JOHN, 1815, *William Blackwood and His Sons, by Oliphant, vol.* I, *p.* 49.

He has not the variety of Scott—nor the delicacy of Campbell—nor the absolute truth of Crabbe—nor the polished sparkling of Moore; but in force of diction, and inextinguishable energy of sentiment, he clearly surpasses them all.—JEFFREY, FRANCIS LORD, 1816-44, *Lord Byron's Poetry, Contributions to the Edinburgh Review, vol.* III, *p.* 164.

Lord Byron is a splendid and noble egotist.—He vists Classical shores; roams over romantic lands, and wanders through magnificent forests; courses the dark and restless waves of the sea, and rocks his spirit on the midnight lakes; but no spot is conveyed to our minds, that is not peopled by the gloomy and ghastly feelings of one proud and solitary man. It is as if he and the world were the only two things which the air clothed.—His lines are majestic vanities;—his poetry always is marked with a haughty selfishness;—he writes loftily, because he is the spirit of an ancient family;—he is liked by most of his readers, because he is a Lord. If a common man were to dare to be as moody, as contemptuous, and as misanthropical, the world would laugh at him. There must be a coronet marked on all his little pieces of poetical insolence, or the world would not countenance them.—REYNOLDS, JOHN HAMILTON, 1818, *West of England Journal and General Advertiser, Oct.* 6.

What, then, should be said of those for whom the thoughtlessness and inebriety of wanton youth can no longer be pleaded, but who have written in sober manhood, and with deliberate purpose?—men of diseased hearts and depraved imaginations, who, forming a system of opinions to suit their own unhappy course of conduct, have rebelled against the holiest ordinances of human society, and, hating that revealed religion, which, with all their efforts and bravadoes, they are unable entirely to disbelieve, labour to make others as miserable as themselves, by infecting them with a moral virus that eats into the soul! The school which they have set up may properly be called the Satanic School; for, though their productions breathe the spirit of Belial in their lascivious parts, and the spirit of Moloch in those loathsome images of atrocities and horrors which they delight to represent, they are more especially characterized by a satanic pride and audacious impiety, which still betrays the wretched feeling of hopelessness wherewith it is allied.—SOUTHEY, ROBERT, 1821, *The Vision of Judgment, Preface.*

The Pilgrim of Eternity, whose fame
Over his living head like Heaven is bent,
An early but enduring monument,
Came, veiling all the lightnings of his song
In sorrow.
—SHELLEY, PERCY BYSSHE, 1821, *Adonais, st.* XXX.

It seems, to my ear, that there is a sad want of harmony in Lord Byron's verses. Is it not unnatural to be always connecting very great intellectual power with utter depravity? Does such a combination often really exist *in rerum naturâ?*—COLERIDGE, SAMUEL TAYLOR, 1822, *Table Talk, ed. Ashe, Dec.* 29, *p.* 16.

Even I—albeit I'm sure I did not know it,
Nor sought of foolscap subjects to be king,—
Was reckon'd a considerable time,
The grand Napoleon of the realms of rhyme.
—BYRON, LORD, 1823, *Don Juan, Canto* X.

He has filled a leaf in the book of fame, but it is a very blotted leaf.—BARBAULD, ANNA LÆTITIA, 1824, *Works, vol.* II, *p.* 137.

There are things in Byron's poetry so exquisite, that fifty or five hundred years hence, they will be read, felt, and adored throughout the world. . . . No, no! give me Byron, with all his spite, hatred, depravity, dandyism, vanity, frankness, passion, and idleness, to Wordsworth, with all his heartless communion with woods and grass. — HAYDON, BENJAMIN ROBERT, 1824, *Letter to Mary Russell Mitford; Life, Letters and Table Talk, ed. Stoddard, pp.* 217, 218.

Lord Byron is to be regarded as a man, as an Englishman, and as a great talent. His good qualities belong chiefly to the man, his bad to the Englishman and the peer, his talent is incommensurable. . . . He is a great talent, a born talent, and I never saw the true poetical power greater in any man than in him. In the apprehension of external objects, and a clear penetration into past situations, he is quite as great as Shakspeare. But as a pure individuality, Shakspeare is his superior. This was felt by Byron, and on this account, he does not say much of Shakspeare, although he knows whole passages by heart. He would willingly have denied him altogether; for Shakspeare's cheerfulness is in his way, and he feels that he is no match for it. Pope he does not deny, for he had no cause to fear him. On the contrary, he mentions him, and shews him respect when he can, for he knows well enough that Pope is a mere foil to himself. — GOETHE, JOHANN WOLFGANG, 1825, *Conversations, ed. Eckermann, vol.* I, *p.* 209.

We ought too to look back with late repentance & remorse on our intoxicated praise, now cooling, of Lord Byron—such a man to be so spoken of when the world possessed Goëthe, Schiller, Shelley!— BEDDOES, THOMAS LOVELL, 1825, *Letters, p.* 58.

Byron—good generous hapless Byron! And yet when he died he was only a *Kraftmann* (*Powerman* as the Germans call them). Had he lived he would have been a poet.—CARLYLE, THOMAS, 1826, *Journal, Dec.* 3; *Life by Froude, vol.* I, *p.* 304.

As a poet, he stands among the most eminent that England has ever produced. Few, indeed (and, among those who live, we may say, fearless of contradiction, none), have possessed at the same time an energy and intellectual grasp like his, together with his facility and gracefulness.—CLINTON, GEORGE, 1826, *The Life and Writings of Lord Byron, p.* 1.

Byron seems to me deficient in *feeling.* Professor Wilson, I think, used to say that "Beppo" was his best poem; because all his faults were there brought to a height.

—WORDSWORTH, WILLIAM, 1827, *Miscellaneous Memoranda, Memoirs by Christopher Wordsworth, vol.* II, *p.* 483.

> With joint acclaim
> Let's hail the name
> Of our great Bard, whose mighty fame
> Must spread for aye,
> Ne'er to decay
> Till heaven and earth shall pass away.

—HOGG, JAMES, 1827, *Ode on the Death of Lord Byron, Blackwood's Magazine, vol.* 21, *p.* 521.

> He, from above descending, stooped to touch
> The loftiest thought; and proudly stooped, as though
> It scarce deserved his verse.

—POLLOK, ROBERT, 1827, *The Course of Time, bk.* iv.

Byron has been extolled as the sublimest of poets. There are passages in all his poems which I have thought charming, but mixed with so much that was disgusting that I never believed his popularity would be lasting. His versification is so destitute of sustained harmony, many of his thoughts are so strained, his sentiments so unamiable, his misanthropy so gloomy, his images so grossly indelicate, his libertinism so shameless, his merriment such grinning of a ghastly smile, that I have always believed his verses would soon rank with forgotten things. . . . This person has now been seven years dead, and the public interest in him has not abated. He was one of the wonders of his age, and was, like Napoleon Bonaparte, the torso of a Hercules. A "grand homme manqué" —a club-footed Apollo—in mind as in person. There are sublime and beautiful passages of detail in his poetry; and if he had finished his "Don Juan" it would have been a worthy companion to Voltaire's "Pucelle," in the Temple of Cloacina upon the summit of Parnassus. — ADAMS, JOHN QUINCY, 1830, *Memoirs, vol.* VIII, *pp.* 218, 248.

With Byron's own works in one's hand his character cannot possibly be a riddle to anybody. I dare say the devil may sometimes be painted blacker than he is; but Byron has a fancy for the character of Lucifer, and seems to me, on the contrary, *tres pauvre diable.* . . . Nobody was ever a more fanatical worshipper of his poetry than I was: time was that I devoured his verses (poison as they were to me) like "raspberry tarts;" I still know, and remember with delight, their exquisite beauty and noble vigor, but they don't agree with me. And, without knowing anything of his religious doubts or moral delinquencies, I cannot at all agree with Mr. Moore that upon the showing of his own works Byron was a "good man."— KEMBLE, FRANCES ANNE, 1831, *Letter, Jan. 12; Records of a Girlhood, pp.* 330, 331.

Byron was a paradox in every thing. He was at once a cold-blooded satirist and a man of sentiment; an aristocrat and a radical; a Platonist and an Epicurean; the most sublime and the most sensual of mortals; "half dust, half diety," to borrow his own phrase; but the most barefaced paradox, was his ostentatious defence in prose of Pope's poetical system, which, in his poetry, he had been all his life endeavoring to subvert. The key to Byron's eccentricities is to be found in his total want of principle, and his uncontrollable passions. To the last is to be referred, moreover, much of what is grand and striking in his poetry. Many were led to charge him with affectation. The history of his life, however, which may be called passion put into action, shows how uniformly he sacrificed to his passions all his worldly interests and better hopes. His poetry gains somewhat in effect by our conviction of this, for sincerity is essential to the full success of the poet as of the orator; and, in this point of view, the exhibition of actual vice is less detrimental to his interest than the affectation of it. Much stress has been laid on the mischievous tendency of Byron's philosophy. But, in truth, there is little in his writings to deserve that name. He had no principles to build on, and seems to have been incapable of forming any settled system, or even a systematic attack on any thing. He levelled his shafts pretty indiscriminately at whatever men prize most in this life, or look forward to with hope in the next. This sort of random aim was little better than shooting in the dark.—PRESCOTT, WILLIAM HICKLING, 1832, *English Literature of the Nineteenth Century, North American Review, vol.* 35, *p.* 176.

No modern author who can lay claim to the highest honors of Parnassus has written a greater quantity of perishable, perishing rhyme, than the noblest of them all.—MONTGOMERY, JAMES, 1833, *Lectures on General Literature, Poetry, etc., p.* 313.

Byron's "Heaven and Earth," . . .

is full of passages which none but he could have written; and it also affords some instances of the facility with which the noble bard could extract honey from any flower, or weed, however humble.—ELLIOTT, EBENEZER, 1833, *Spirits and Men, Preface.*

Lord Byron has abundance of wit, and extremely diversified wit, but of a kind that agitates and has a baneful influence. He has read Voltaire, and he frequently imitates him. In following the great English poet step by step, we are forced to acknowledge that he aims at effect, that he rarely loses sight of himself, that he is almost always in attitude; that he looks at himself with complacency; but the affectation of eccentricity, singularity, originality, belongs to the English character in general. If, however, Lord Byron has atoned for his genius by certain foibles, futurity will not concern itself about such paltry matters, or rather it will know nothing about them; the poet will hide the man, and will interpose talent between the man and future generations: through this divine veil posterity will discern nothing but the god.—CHATEAUBRIAND, FRANÇOIS RENÉ VICOMTE, 1837, *Sketches of English Literature, vol.* II, *p.* 344.

Byron and Goethe—the two names that predominate, and, come what may, ever will predominate, over our every recollection of the fifty years that have passed away. They rule;—the master-minds, I might almost say the tyrants, of a whole period of poetry; brilliant, yet sad; glorious in youth and daring, yet cankered by the worm i' the bud, despair. They are the two Representative Poets of two great schools; and around them we are compelled to group all the lesser minds which contributed to render the era illustrious. The qualities which adorn and distinguish their works are to be found, although more thinly scattered, in other poets their contemporaries; still theirs are the names that involuntarily rise to our lips whenever we seek to characterise the tendencies of the age in which they lived. . . . The day will come when Democracy will remember all that it owes to Byron. England too, will, I hope, one day remember the mission—so entirely English, yet hitherto overlooked by her—which Byron fulfilled on the Continent; the European rôle given by him to English literature, and the appreciation and sympathy for England which he awakened amongst us. Before he came, all that was known of English literature was the French translation of Shakespeare, and the anathema hurled by Voltaire against the "intoxicated barbarian." It is since Byron that we Continentalists have learned to study Shakespeare and other English writers. From him dates the sympathy of all the true-hearted amongst us for this land of liberty, whose true vocation he so worthily represented among the oppressed. He led the genius of Britain on a pilgrimage throughout all Europe.—MAZZINI, JOSEPH, 1839, *Byron and Goethe, Essays, ed. Clarke, pp.* 84, 107.

> And poor, proud Byron, sad as grave
> And salt as life; forlornly brave,
> And quivering with the dart he drave.

—BROWNING, ELIZABETH BARRETT, 1844, *A Vision of Poets.*

Few poets excel him in the instantaneous sympathy he creates, even among minds having no natural affinity with his own. He is eminently the poet of passion. In almost all the changes of his mood, the same energy of feeling glows in his verse. The thought or emotion uppermost in his mind at any one time, whether it be bad or good, seems to sway, for the moment, all the faculties of his nature. He has a passionate love for evil, a passionate love for nature, for goodness, for beauty, and, we may add, a passionate love for himself. When he sits in the place of the scoffer, his words betray the same inspiration from impulse,—the same passion, though condensed into bitterness and mockery.— WHIPPLE, EDWIN P., 1845, *Byron, Essays and Reviews.*

In Byron there is much to admire but nothing to imitate: for energy is beyond the limits of imitation. Byron could not have written better than he did. Altho' he seems negligent in many places, he was very assiduous in correcting his verses. His poetry took the bent of a wayward and perverted mind often weak, but oftener perturbed. Tho' hemp and flax and cotton are the stronger for being twisted, verses and intellects certainly are not. . . . It is unfortunate that Ariosto did not attract him (Byron) first. Byron had not in his nature amenity enough for it, and chose Berni in preference, and fell from Berni to Casti. But his scorching and dewless heat burnt up their flowery

meadows.—LANDOR, WALTER SAVAGE, 1845, *To Mrs. Paynter, Aug.* 3; *Letters, ed. Wheeler, p.* 146.

Lord Byron is altogether in my affection again. . . . I have read on to the end, and am quite sure of the great qualities which the last ten or fifteen years had partially obscured. Only a little longer life and all would have been gloriously right again. I read this book of Moore's too long ago; but I always retained my first feeling for Byron in many respects, . . . the interest in the places he had visited, in relics of him. I would at any time have gone to Finchley to see a curl of his hair or one of his gloves, I am sure —while Heaven knows that I could not get up enthusiasm enough to cross the room if at the other end of it all Wordsworth, Coleridge and Southey were condensed into the little China bottle yonder, after the Rosicrucian fashion . . . they seem to "have their reward" and want nobody's love or faith. Just one of those trenchant opinions which I found fault with Byron for uttering,—as "proving nothing!"—BROWNING, ROBERT, 1846, *Letters of Robert Browning and Elizabeth Barrett, 1845-1846, vol.* II, *p.* 453.

Ever so unfortunate, a man's folding his hands over it in melancholy mood, and suffering himself to be made a puppet by it, is a sadly weak proceeding. Most thoughtful men have probably some dark fountains in their souls, by the side of which, if there were time, and it were decorous, they could let their thoughts sit down and wail indefinitely. That long Byron wail fascinated men for a time, because there is that in huamn nature.— HELPS, SIR ARTHUR, 1847, *Friends in Council.*

The truth is, that what has put Byron out of favour with the public of late, is not his faults, but his excellencies. His artistic good taste, his classical polish, his sound shrewd sense, his hatred of cant, his insight into humbug, above all, his shallow, pitiable habit of being always intelligible; these are the sins which condemn him in the eyes of a mesmerizing, table-turning, spirit-rapping, Spiritualizing, Romanizing generation, who read Shelley in secret, and delight in his bad taste, mysticism, extravagance, and vague and pompous sentimentalism. The age is an effeminate one; and it can well afford to pardon the lewdness of the gentle and sensitive vegetarian, while it has no mercy for that of the sturdy peer, proud of his bull-neck and his boxing, who keeps bears and bull-dogs, drilled Greek ruffians at Missolonghi, and "had no objection to a pot of beer;" and who might, if he had reformed, have made a gallant English gentleman.—KINGSLEY, CHARLES, 1853, *Thoughts about Shelley and Byron, Fraser's Magazine, vol.* 48, *p.* 571.

It was not until the "Siebengebirge" or Seven Mountains rose to view, that the glories of the Rhine were revealed in all their matchless grandeur. No description I have ever read approaches the reality, save the verses of the most impassioned of poets. How wonderfully, how truthfully, has Byron pictured in glowing words the beauty of scenery which meets the eye on every side.—LE VERT, MADAME OCTAVIA WALTON, 1853, *Souvenirs of Travel, vol.* I, *p.* 130.

Had a larger amount of common sense than any poet of his day.—SMITH, ALEXANDER, 1863, *Dreamthorp, p.* 160.

Byron, doubtless, is no ordinary bard. He possesses fecundity, eloquence, wit. Yet these very qualites are confined within pretty narrow limits. The wit of "Beppo" and of "Don Juan" is of the kind that consists in dissonance; that is to say, in the serio-comic, in an apparent gravity which is contradicted every moment by drollery of phrase. In the same way Byron's fecundity is more apparent than real. He wrote a great deal—poems serious and poems comic, epics and dramas, visions and satires; but, speaking strictly, he never had more than a single subject—himself. No man has ever pushed egotism farther than he.—SCHERER, EDMOND, 1863–91, *Taine's History of English Literature, Essays on English Literature, tr. Saintsbury, p.* 91.

This shallowness has no part in Byron himself. His weariness was a genuine outcome of the influence of the time upon a character consumed by passion. His lot was cast among spent forces, and while it is no hyperbole to say that he was himself the most enormous force of his time, he was only half conscious of this, if indeed he did not always inwardly shrink from crediting his own power and strength, as so many strong men habitually do, in spite of noisy and perpetual self-assertion.

Conceit and persumption have not been any more fatal to the world, than the waste which comes of great men failing in their hearts to recognise how great they are.—MORLEY, JOHN, 1870, *Byron, Fortnightly Review, vol.* 14, *p.* 664.

The genius of Byron was of a more vigorous mould than that of Keats; but nothwithstanding his great popularity and the number of his imitators at one time, he made a less permanent impression on the character of English poetry. His misanthropy and gloom, his scoffing vein, and the fierceness of his animosities, after the first glow of admiration was over, had a repellant effect upon readers, and made them turn to more cheerful strains.—BRYANT, WILLIAM CULLEN, 1870, *A New Library of Poetry and Song, Introduction, vol.* I, *p.* 43.

Byron will be remembered longer by the lyrical pearls, which are scattered so copiously through his poems, gems which are familiar to every reader of his works, and can never be forgotten. It is in these that his muse takes her noblest flight; these are the portions of his poetry which are instinct with the most exquisite beauty, and exercise on us the most powerful spell; and we cannot imagine, that they will ever fail to fill their readers with rapture. . . . In Germany, Byron, like almost all English poets, found a second fatherland. His influence on our literature was confined indeed to one period only, nor has his poetry been interwoven, like Shakespeare's, for ever with our own; but if limited in duration, it was widely propagated and intense during its reign.—ELZE, KARL, 1870–72, *Lord Byron, pp.* 402, 428.

His ideas were banned during his life; it has been attempted to depreciate his genius since his death. To this day English critics are unjust to him. He fought all his life against the society from which he came; and during his life, as after his death, he suffered the pain of the resentment which he provoked, and the repugnance to which he gave rise. A foreign critic may be more impartial, and freely praise the powerful hand whose blows he has not felt. If ever there was a violent and madly sensitive soul, but incapable of being otherwise; ever agitated, but in an enclosure without issue; predisposed to poetry by its innate fire, but limited by its natural barriers to a single kind of poetry,—it was Byron's. . . . All styles appear dull, and all souls sluggish by the side of his. . . . No such great poet has had so narrow an imagination; he could not metamorphose himself into another. They are his own sorrows, his own revolts, his own travels, which, hardly transformed and modified, he introduces into his verses. He does not invent, he observes; he does not create, he transcribes —TAINE, H. A., 1871, *History of English Literature, tr. Van Laun, vol.* II, *bk.* iv, *ch.* ii, *pp.* 271, 274, 279.

The youth thus strangely educated, had at least one fountain of inspiration—the Bible. The study of the Prophets invigorated the poetic character of his nature. Their rugged genius is visible in some of his works, severe and steady as the simoom, monotonous as the desert, but solemn as immensity, and sublime as the idea of the Almighty; their semitical genius, expressed by Isaiah in his admirable works, is reproduced by Michael Angelo in the majestic features of his Moses, whose venerable beard, descending to his breast, seems to be stirred by the breezes of Sinai. —CASTELAR, EMILIO, 1873-75, *Life of Lord Byron and other Sketches, tr. Arnold, p.* 10.

The great thing in Byron is *genius*, that quality so perilous to define, so evanescent in its aroma, so impossible to mistake. If ever a man breathed whom we recognize (athwart much poor and useless work, when strictly tested) as emphatically the genius, that man was Byron; and, if ever genius made poetry its mouthpiece, covering with its transcendent utterances a multitude of sins whether against art or against the full stature of perfect manhood, Byron's is that poetry.—ROSSETTI, WILLIAM MICHAEL, 1878, *Lives of Famous Poets, p.* 307.

How to make a Satanic Poem like the late Lord Byron. Take a couple of fine deadly sins; and let them hang before your eyes until they become racy. Then take them down, dissect them, and stew them for some time in a solution of weak remorse; after which they are to be devilled with mock-despair.—MALLOCK, W. H., 1878, *Every Man his own Poet, or the Inspired Singer's Recipe Book, p.* 28.

Byron is probably the greatest poet that Britain has produced since the days of Dryden. He is, perhaps, the most thorough master of words that ever lived. His most beautiful passages bear comparison with the noblest poetry in the language; and his longest poems, full of faults as they are, are mangnificent monuments to his genius.—WALPOLE, SPENCER, 1878, *A History of England from the Conclusion of the Great War in* 1815, *vol.* I, *p.* 362.

The refrain of Carlyle's advice during the most active years of his criticism was, "Close thy Byron, open thy Goethe." We do so, and find that the refrain of Goethe's advice in reference to Byron is—"*Nocturnâ versate manu, versate diurnâ.*" He urged Eckermann to study English, that he might read him; remarking, "A character of such eminence has never existed before, and probably will never come again. . . . The English may think of him as they please; this is certain, they can show no (living) poet who is to be compared to him." . . . Dr. Elze ranks the author of "Harold" and "Juan" among the four greatest English poets, and claims for him the intellectual parentage of Lamartine and Musset, in France, of Espronceda, in Spain; of Puschkin, in Russia; with some modifications, of Heine, in Germany, of Berchet and others in Italy. So many voices of so various countries cannot be simply set aside: unless we wrap ourselves in an insolent insularism, we are bound at least to ask what is the meaning of their concurrent testimony. . . . We may learn much from him still, when we have ceased to disparage, as our fathers ceased to idolize, a name in which there is so much warning and so much example.—NICHOL, JOHN, 1880, *Byron (English Men of Letters), pp.* 205, 206, 212.

Wordsworth has an insight into permanent sources of joy and consolation for mankind which Byron has not; his poetry gives us more which we may rest upon than Byron's,—more which we can rest upon now, and which men may rest upon always. I place Wordsworth's poetry, therefore, above Byron's, on the whole, although in some points he was greatly Byron's inferior, and although Byron's poetry will always, probably, find more readers than Wordsworth's, and will give pleasure more easily. But these two, Wordsworth and Byron, stand, it seems to me, first and preëminent in actual performance, a glorious pair, among the English poets of this century. — ARNOLD, MATTHEW, 1881, *Poetry of Byron, Preface.*

It is by the vast strength and volume of his powers, rather than by any one perfect work, that he is to be estimated. He does not seem to have had any delicacy of ear for the refinements of metre, or to have studied the intricacies of it. But, when the impulse came, he poured himself forth with wonderful rapidity, home-thrusting directness, and burning elo-quence—eloquence that carries you over much that is faulty in structure, and imper-fect, or monotonous in metre. He him-self did not stay to consider the way he said things, so intent was he on the things he had to say. Neither any more does the reader. His cadences were few, but they were strong and impressive, and carried with them, for the time, every soul that heard them.—SHAIRP, JOHN CAMPBELL, 1881, *Modern English Poetry, Aspects of Poetry, p.* 146.

In early boyhood he had been possessed by Byron's poetry, but he could not read it in later life, except perhaps "The Vision of Judgment," and parts of "Childe Harold," and of "Don Juan." He would say: "Byron is not an artist or a thinker, or a creator in the higher sense, but a strong personality: he is endlessly clever, and is now unduly depreciated."—TENNY-SON, ALFRED LORD, 1883, *Some Criti-cisms on Poets, Memoir by his Son, vol.* II, *p.* 287.

Has stirred England more deeply than any other poet since the earlier years of the seventeenth century, who has influ-enced human kind outside England more widely and profoundly than any writer of our literature, and who, in whatever else of his aspirations he failed, will be found in the slowly moving ages to have achieved his ambition to be "remembered in his line with his land's language."—JEAF-FRESON, JOHN CORDY, 1883, *The Real Lord Byron, p.* 553.

The glory of Scott was the last red tints of a setting sun, and the glory of Words-worth the first mild radiance of a rising moon, when Byron came like a comet, and paled their ineffectual fires.—STODDARD, RICHARD HENRY, 1884, *Selections from the Poetical Works of A. C. Swinburne, Intro-duction, p.* x.

It is remarkable that the influence of Byron's poetry has been far greater on the Continent than it has been in England. No English poet, except Shakespeare, has been so much read or so much admired by foreigners. His works, or parts of them, have been translated into many European languages, and numerous foreign writers have been affected by their ideas and style. The estimate that has been formed of them is extraordinarily high. Charles Nodier said: "The appearance of Lord Byron in the field of European literature is one of those events the influence of which is felt by all peoples and through all genera-tions;" and his judgment in this respect by no means stands alone. The chief reason of this, independently of the splendour of his compositions, is to be found in his political opinions. Byron's poetry, like that of most of his English contemporaries—Wordsworth, Coleridge, Southey, and Shelley—was the outcome of the French Revolution; but whereas the three first-named of these poets, disgusted with the excesses of that movement, went over into the opposite camp, and the idealism of Shelley was too far removed from the sphere of practical politics to be a moving force, Byron became, almost unintentionally, the apostle of the princi-ples which it represented. . . . Thus his writings became a political power through-out Europe, and more so on the Continent than in England, in proportion as the loss of liberty was more keenly felt by foreign nations. Wherever aspirations for inde-pendence arose, Byron's poems were read and admired.—TOZER, H. F., 1885, *ed. Childe Harold's Pilgrimage.*

Byron wrote, as easily as a hawk flies, and as clearly as a lake reflects, the exact truth in the precisely narrowest terms; not only the exact truth, but the most central and useful one. Of course I could no more measure Byron's greater powers at that time than I could Turner's; but I saw that both were right in all things that *I* knew right from wrong in; and that they must henceforth be my masters, each in his own domain.—RUSKIN, JOHN, 1885, *Præterita, vol.* I, *p.* 258.

Perhaps the most powerful factor in Byron's poetical genius is his style. Alone among his contemporaries he understood how to swell the stream of English poetical diction as it had come down to him from the eighteenth century, so as to make it an adequate vehicle of expression for romantic thought and feeling. Wordsworth speaks the language of philosophers, Shelley of spirits, but Byron of men.— COURTHOPE, WILLIAM JOHN, 1885, *The Liberal Movement in English Literature*, p. 141.

May all the devastating force be spent?
Or all thy godlike energies lie shent?
Nay! thou art founded in the strength
  Divine:
The Soul's immense eternity is thine!
Profound Beneficence absorbs thy power,
While Ages tend the long-maturing flower:
Our Sun itself, one tempest of wild flame,
For source of joy, and very life men claim
In mellowing corn, in bird, and bloom of
  spring,
In leaping lambs, and lovers dallying.
Byron! the whirlwinds rended not in vain;
Aloof behold they nourish and sustain!
In the far end we shall account them gain.
—NOEL, RODEN, 1885, *Byron's Grave, Songs of the Heights and Deeps*, p. 178.

The tragic power of Crabbe is as much above the reach of Byron as his singularly vivid though curiously limited insight into certain shades of character.—SWINBURNE, ALGERNON CHARLES, 1886, *Wordsworth and Byron, Miscellanies*, p. 89.

The genius of Byron was not one from which we might have expected good sonnet-work. He is greater in mass than in detail, in outlines than in delicate side-touches—in a word, he is like a sculptor who hews a Titan out of a huge block, one whom we would never expect to be able, or to care, to delicately carve a canoe. That Byron could write sonnets, and that he could even write an exceptionaly fine one, is evident from that which I have quoted.—SHARP, WILLIAM, 1886, *Sonnets of this Century*, p. 281, *note*.

The next influence on my mind was that of Byron, and his power over me was much increased by the injudicious and unjust hostility of one of my tutors, who hated Byron as the clergy hated him during his lifetime. My tutor was always expressing contempt for the poet, whose works he had not read and was incompetent to appreciate. This only made me read them more and think them more magnificent than ever. At this day I am not aware that Byron ever exercised any bad influence over me. His gloom, which was in great part unreal, did not prove to be infectious in my case, but his clear, direct, and manly

use of the English language was very valuable as a part of education. As to his immorality, it was more in his life than in his writings, and his enemies made the most of it whilst they tolerated without protest the immoralities of more favoured authors.— HAMERTON, PHILIP GILBERT, 1887, *Books which have Influenced Me*, p. 54.

His style is remarkable for its strength and elasticity, for its immensely powerful sweep, tireless energy, and brilliant illustrations.—MEIKLEJOHN, J. M. D., 1887, *The English Language: Its Grammar, History and Literature*, p. 344.

Which is the better and stronger is a question that can hardly be determined now. It is certain that Byron's star has waned, and that Wordsworth's has waxed; but it is also certain that there are moments in life when the "Ode to Venice" is almost as refreshing and as precious as the ode on the "Intimations," and when the epic mockery of "Don Juan" is to the full as beneficial as the chaste philosophy of "The Excursion" and the "Ode to Duty."— HENLEY, WILLIAM ERNEST, 1890, *Views, and Reviews*, p. 60.

The loose, the ungrammatical.—GOSSE, EDMUND, 1891, *Is Verse in Danger? The Forum*, vol. 10, p. 521.

Now, at least two or three of these had great genius; Shelley and Villon especially set a lasting fascination in their works, and although Byron does not wear so well, he compels a slowly relaxing attention as he retreats in the romantic distance.— THOMPSON, MAURICE, 1893, *The Ethics of Literary Art*, p. 75.

Wordsworth tried the moral lesson and spoiled some of his best work with botany and the Bible. A good many smaller men than he have tried the same thing since, and have failed. Perhaps "Cain" and "Manfred" have taught the human heart more wisdom than "Matthew" or the unfortunate "idiot boy" over whom Byron was so mercilessly merry. And yet Byron probably never meant to teach any one anything in particular, and Wordsworth meant to teach everybody, including and beginning with himself. — CRAWFORD, MARION, 1893, *What is a Novel? The Forum*, vol. 14, p. 594.

One poet, and one alone, of that great early group, can to-day reach our affections through our amusement. If Byron lives, he lives by virtue of wit. The sorrowful recklessness of his irony bears the stamp of living power, unknown to his heroics or his sentimental tears. Byron alone among his comrades is great as a humorist; for alone among his comrades he was a realist. What he saw was doubtless often unworthy; but it had the merit of existing.—SCUDDER, VIDA D., 1895, *The Life of the Spirit in the Modern English Poets, p.* 203.

Poor Byron showed in his life the struggle for good as well as evil, even if the evil predominated. He had so nursed his weaknesses and enjoyed a selfish indulgence in all coveted experiences, with no detaining hand or gentle voice to draw him back, that his passions, prejudices, and viciousness overcame him. He was a wanderer over the land, with a "might have been." There is little doubt that Byron deeply loved Mary Chaworth, and when fate placed her beyond his reach, his whole future was embittered, and he had not the strength of character to rise above it. He was defiant, with a will that could not be forced. . . . The originality of his conceptions, the vigor of his thoughts, the boldness of his imagination, together with beauty and sublime harmony, stand to-day unrivalled.—WARREN, INA RUSSELLE, 1896, *Magazine of Poetry, vol.* 8, *p.* 168.

Byron's landscape style resembles that of Scott in its direct painting, in its rapid motion, but, as a rule, with very superior though very unequal power. In fact, to digress for a moment, perhaps no English poet has equaled Byron, whether in his grasp and sweep of subject, his free sympathy with mankind, or in what we might call his initial force. In narrative, how straight to the mark does his energy go, compared with the bewildering discursiveness of the "Revolt of Islam," or "Endymion," the tortuous progress, never ending, still beginning, of the "Ring and the Book!" In this movement, this directness of power, and here only, Byron's style was doubtless affected by Scott. . . . Even in his early lines it is impossible not to recognise the hand of a mighty master—unless indeed we are enslaved and bound to limit our taste by partisan favouritism and coterie decrees: as if Parnassus could not afford space for many styles;—or as if a man should worship crimson and

therefore despise blue. . . . When successful, his work retains its original freshness, its stimulating power, its largeness of sentiment, its humanity veiled under cynicism. What has been condemned as mere calculated and spurious sensibility was, in truth, the clumsy turbid expression of genuine feeling, by an artist who could rarely put in his deepest, finest tints with success—who had little command of *gradation.* . . . Byron's love of landscape was a passion, deep and sincere perhaps as that of any poet.—PALGRAVE, FRANCIS TURNER, 1896, *Landscape in Poetry, pp.* 188, 189, 195.

Byron, then, seems to me a poet distinctly of the second class, and not even of the best kind of second, inasmuch as his greatness is chiefly derived from a sort of parody, a sort of imitation, of the qualities of the first. His verse is to the greatest poetry what melodrama is to tragedy, what plaster is to marble, what pinchbeck is to gold. He is not indeed an impostor; for his sense of the beauty of nature and of the unsatisfactoriness of life is real, and his power of conveying this sense to others is real also. He has great, though uncertain, and never very *fine,* command of poetic sound, and a considerable though less command of poetic vision. But in all this there is a singular touch of illusion, of what his contemporaries had learnt from Scott to call gramarye. The often cited parallel of the false and true Florimels in Spenser applies here also. The really great poets do not injure each other in the very least by comparison, different as they are. Milton does not "kill" Wordsworth; Spenser does not injure Shelley; there is no danger in reading Keats immediately after Coleridge. But read Byron in close juxtaposition with any of these, or with not a few others, and the effect, to any good poetic taste, must surely be disastrous; to my own, whether good or bad, it is perfectly fatal. The light is not that which never was on land or sea; it is that which is habitually just in front of the stage: the roses are rouged, the cries of passion even sometimes (not always) ring false. I have read Byron again and again; I have sometimes, by reading Byron only and putting a strong constraint upon myself, got nearly into the mood to enjoy him. But let eye or ear once catch sight or sound of real poetry, and the enchantment vanishes.—SAINTSBURY, GEORGE, 1896, *A History of Nineteenth Century Literature, p.* 80.

Byron had splendid powers of humour, and the most poetic satire that we have example of, fusing at times to hard irony. He had no strong comic sense, or he would not have taken an anti-social position, which is directly opposed to the Comic; and in his philosophy, judged by philosophers, he is a comic figure, by reason of this deficiency.—MEREDITH, GEORGE, 1897, *An Essay on Comedy and the Uses of the Comic Spirit, p.* 76.

Byron has always been, to many competent judges, one of the greatest poets of any age or country. To say that you do not like his poetry because you do not like the life he led is the same as saying you dislike a house because you do not like the architect who planned or the carpenter or mason who built it.—ABBEY, HENRY, 1897, *Byron—The Man and His Work, Literary World, vol.* 28, *p.* 126.

To acquire a right feeling for Byron and his poetry is a discipline in equity. It is easy to yield to a sense of his power, to the force and sweep of his genius; it is easy to be repelled by his superficial insincerity, his license, his cynicism, his poverty of thought, his looseness of construction, his carelessness in execution. To know aright the evil and the good is difficult. It is difficult to feel justly towards this dethroned idol (presently, perhaps, to be re-enthroned), an idol in whose composition iron and clay are mingled with fine gold. . . . We must take him or leave him as he is,—the immortal spoilt by his age, great and petty, weak and strong, exalted and debased. A glorious wave that curls upon the sea-beach, though it leave sea-wrack and refuse on the sands, is more stimulating, more health-giving, than a pitcher of such salt water in one's dressing-room, even if it be free from every floating weed. . . . He was a democrat among aristocrats and an aristocrat among democrats; a sceptic among believers and a believer among sceptics. And yet his line of advance was not a *via media*, nor was it determined by a spirit of moderation or critical balance.—DOWDEN, EDWARD, 1897, *The French Revolution and English Literature, pp.* 261, 262, 264.

There are still a few faithful, like the well-known Greek scholar of whom it was remarked in my hearing that he never quoted any English save Byron and the Bible.—MORE, PAUL ELMER, 1898, *The Wholesome Revival of Byron, Atlantic Monthly, vol.* 82, *p.* 801.

His poetry had no repose; all is revolt. He is inspired by no faith, human or divine. There is passion, but little love, affection, or tenderness. No large views of human life or destiny soften the hard lines of his horizon; no enthusiasms, except it be for liberty or for inanimate nature, pierce its darkness. There is only the scorching light of the volcano, whose eruptive fire intensifies the blackness of the surrounding darkness, which in part is itself its own product, and casts a lurid glare on a narrow circle of the wilderness it has itself bared and blasted.—PROTHERO, ROWLAND EDMUND, 1898, *Childhood and School Days of Byron, The Nineteenth Century, vol.* 43, *p.* 62.

As we should expect in a man "proud as Lucifer and beautiful as Apollo," the personal note in Byron is supreme. It is the note of a struggling Titian's tempest-anger, tempest-mirth; and yet his best work reached the very pinnacle of poetic glory. He has the distinction of having made English letters appreciated in Europe.—GEORGE, ANDREW J., 1898, *From Chaucer to Arnold, Types of Literary Art, p.* 652.

But Byron the poet? Emphatically, he was *not* a poet; not if Shakespeare and Milton are poets. He was a magnificent satirist; the "Vision of Judgment," "Don Juan," and "Beppo" are very glories of wit, indignation, rhetoric; accomplished to the uttermost, marvellous and immortal; filled with scathing laughter, rich with a prodigal profusion of audacious fancy and riot of rhyme. Here the man is himself, eloquent and vehement of speech, alive and afire. No coarseness, cruelty, insolence, can blind us to the enduring excellence of these writings, to their virility and strength. *This* Byron is deathless. But the Byron of love lyrics and tragedies, and romantic tales, is a poet of infinite tediousness in execrable verse; in the severely courteous French phrase, he "does not permit himself to be read." And he is not read; no one now reads "Lara," or "Parisina," or "The Corsair," or "The Giaour," or "The Bride of Abydos," or "The Siege of Corinth," or

"The Island," or the weary, weary plays. They are dead, and past resurrection; their passion is as poor and tawdry a thing as that of "Frankenstein" or "The Mysteries of Udolpho;" their garish theatricality is laughable, and we can scarce believe that these things of nought were once preferred to the noble simplicities and rough, true music of Scott.—JOHNSON, LIONEL, 1898, *Byron, The Academy, vol.* 53, *p.* 489.

Mr. Swinburne may criticise his verbal workmanship, but Byron will still remain a great artist, inclining, perhaps, a little too much to rhetorical force at the expense of poetico-musical form. His affluence must be held to compensate for his lack of finish. Byron's lack of philosophical insight and of sane judgment is balanced by great penetration and scope in some particular directions. His attitude towards nature is marked by sympathy with all that is lonely, self-contained, and vast.—JOHNSON, CHARLES F., 1898, *Elements of Literary Criticism, p.* 118.

On the continent of Europe there can be no Byronic revival, for the reason that there has never been a decline. English critics might do what they would to "bear" the market—our readers will perhaps remember Mr. Saintsbury's exploit in this line—Byron stock has always stood well in the literary and academic bourses of Germany and France. His poetry is very seriously studied at the universities; dissertations on Byron and Shakspere, treatsies on "Byron der Uebermensch," and the like, have abounded.—KITTREDGE, GEORGE LYMAN, 1898, *Two New Editions of Byron, The Nation, vol.* 67, *p.* 132.

There is very little truth in Byron's work: his characters are nothing—mere photographs of his own postures; his action is largely melodrama; his workmanship is often hurried and slovenly to the last degree; and yet Byron impressed himself upon his generation as no one else could. The sheer force of his personality, perverse, unhealthy, but intense, burned his work into men's minds. The emotion was for the most part not sane or well-grounded, and his work, therefore, has largely lost its interest; but for a time it had immense power.—WINCHESTER, C. T., 1899, *Some Principles of Literary Criticism, p.* 88.

Charles Robert Maturin
1782-1824

Born, in Dublin, 1782. To Trin. Coll., Dublin, as scholar, 1798; B. A., 1800. Married Henrietta Kingsbury, 1802. Ordained Curate of Loughrea; afterwards of St. Peter's, Dublin. Kept a school, and also engaged in literature. Tragedy "Bertram" produced at Drury Lane, 9 May 1816; "Manuel," Drury Lane, 8 March 1817; "Fredolfo," Covent Garden, 12 May 1817. Lived for some time in London. Died, in Dublin, 30 Oct. 1824; buried in St. Peter's, Dublin. *Works:* "The Fatal Revenge" (under pseudonym: "Dennis Jasper Murphy"), 1807; "The Wild Irish Boy" (anon.), 1808; "The Milesian Chief" (anon.), 1812; "Bertram," 1816 (7th edn. same year); "Manuel" (anon.), 1817; "Women" (anon.), 1818; "Sermons," 1819; "Fredolfo," 1819; "Melmoth the Wanderer" (anon.), 1820; "The Universe" (probably written by J. Wills), 1821; "Six Sermons on the Errors of the Roman Catholic Church," 1824; "The Albigenses" (anon.), 1824. *Life:* in 1892 edn. of "Melmoth."—SHARP, R. FARQUHARSON, 1897, *A Dictionary of English Authors, p.* 191.

PERSONAL

Walter Scott, however, was the *first* who mentioned him, which he did to me, with great commendation, in 1815; and it is to this casualty, and two or three other accidents, that this very clever fellow owed his first and well-merited public success.—BYRON, LORD, 1817, *Letter to Mr. Moore, March* 31; *Life by Moore.*

Unhappy Maturin,—what a life was his! Of his death I fear to ask. What makes me more particularly think of him just now is a drawing in chalk that I saw of him immediately before Mary's illness. A young man of the name of Bewick, who is, I think, from Ireland, came to town, wishing to take portraits of people here who were known to the public. The great Well-known, the Arch-Critic, and many others sat to him; and when all more worthy subjects were exhausted, he wrote to ask permission to take a likeness of me, and brought all the portraits he had to show me. Those of Maturin and Lady Morgan astonished me,—they were so very like the pictures that existed in my imagination of those worthies. The earnest melancholy look of Maturin, while strongly marked by genius, is like that of one who had not only supped full of horrors, but dined and breakfasted on them: I never saw character more strongly portrayed in a countenance.—GRANT, ANNE, 1825, *Letter, Mar.* 23; *Memoir and Correspondence, ed. Grant, vol.* III, *p.* 57.

The curate of St. Peter's was exceedingly vain both of his person and accomplishments; and as his income would not allow him to attract attention by the splendour of his dress and manners, he seldom failed to do so by their singularity. Mr. Maturin was tall, slender, but well-proportioned, and, on the whole, a good figure, which he took care to display in a well-made black coat, tightly buttoned, and some odd light-coloured stocking-web pantaloons, surmounted, in winter, by a coat of prodigious dimensions, gracefully thrown on, so as not to obscure the symmetry it affected to protect. The Rev. Gentleman sang and danced, and prided himself on performing the movements and evolutions of the quadrille, certainly equal to any other divine of the Established Church, if not to any private lay gentleman of the three kingdoms. It often happened, too, that Mr. Maturin either laboured under an attack of gout, or met with some accident, which compelled the use of a slipper or a bandage, on one foot or one leg, and, by an unaccountable congruity of mischances, he was uniformly compelled on these occasions to appear in the public thoroughfares of Dublin, where the melancholy spectacle of a beautiful limb in pain never failed to excite the sighs and sympathies of all the interesting persons who passed as well as to prompt their curiosity to make audible remarks or inquiries respecting the possessor.— RYAN, RICHARD, 1826, *Poetry and Poets, vol.* I, *p.* 64.

Could not endure to have children near him during his hours of literary composition. At such times he was particularly sensitive, and pasted a wafer on his forehead as a token to the members of his family that he was not to be interrupted. He said if he lost the thread of his ideas

even for a moment, they were gone from him altogether.—BALLOU, MATURIN M., 1886, *Genius in Sunshine and Shadow, p.* 110.

BERTRAM
1816

It is grand and powerful; the language most animated and poetical; and the characters sketched with a masterly enthusiasm.—SCOTT, SIR WALTER, 1814, *Letter to Daniel Terry, Memoirs, ed. Lockhart, ch.* xxxiv.

I want words to describe the mingled horror and disgust with which I witnessed the opening of the fourth act, considering it as a melancholy proof of the depravation of the public mind. The shocking spirit of jacobinism seemed no longer confined to politics. The familiarity with atrocious events and characters appeared to have poisoned the taste, even where it had not directly disorganized the moral principles, and left the feelings callous to all the mild appeals, and craving alone for the grossest and most outrageous stimulants.—COLERIDGE, SAMUEL TAYLOR, 1817, *Biographia Literaria.*

Crudities and absurdities abound, but there are outbursts of wild poetry amidst the rant. Coleridge's critique brings into a piquant juxtaposition the subtle Romanticism of the poets, and the crude Radcliffian premonitions which here still lingered.—HERFORD, C. H., 1897, *The Age of Wordsworth, p.* 97.

MELMOTH THE WANDERER
1820

"Melmoth" is not altogether so mad as some reviewers pronounced it, yet sufficiently so to excuse thousands for closing their eyes against the poetic invention and buoyancy of fancy everywhere visible.— CUNNINGHAM, ALLAN, 1833, *Biographical and Critical History of the Literature of the Last Fifty Years.*

Although far too long, marvellously involved with tales within tales, and disfigured in parts by the rant and the gush of its class, "Melmoth" is really a powerful book, which gave something more than a passing shudder to its own generation (it specially influenced Balzac), and which has not lost its force even now. But the usual novel of this kind, which was written in vast numbers, was simply beneath contempt.—SAINTSBURY, GEORGE, 1896, *A*

History of Nineteenth Century Literature,
p. 126.

The work of renovation began with
Charles Robert Maturin, in his time a well-
known Irish clergyman and *littérateur.*
The tale in which he displayed his finer
imaginative power is "Melmoth the
Wanderer" (1820). He eliminated from
the Radcliffe romance the "sentimental
Miss who luxuriates in the rich and weeping softness of a watery landscape," and
depended on fear as his sole motive. In
many scenes, resembling the punishments
in the lower circles of Dante's "Inferno,"
he reached, if not terror, the borderland
where horror becomes terror. Such is the
incarceration of a young monk among
serpents, whose "cold and bloating" forms
crawl over him, and the starvation and
madness of lovers in a subterranean prison.
But the incoherency and extreme length
of the romance have long since overwhelmed it; one of the last references to
it being Thackeray's, who compared
Goethe's eye to Melmoth's.—CROSS, WIL-
BUR, L., 1899, *The Development of the Eng-*
lish Novel, p. 159.

GENERAL

It ["Manuel"] is the absurd work of a
clever man.—BYRON, LORD, 1817, *Letter*
to Mr. Murray, June 14.

We observe, with pleasure, that Mr.
Maturin has put his genius under better
regulation [in "Women"] than in his
former publications, and retrenched that
luxuriance of language, and too copious
use of ornament, which distinguishes the
authors and orators of Ireland, whose
exuberance of imagination sometimes
places them in the predicament of their
honest countrymen who complained of
being run away with by his legs.—SCOTT,
SIR WALTER, 1818, *Women; or Pour et*
Contre, Edinburgh Review, vol. 30, *p.* 256.

The author of "Montorio" and of "Bertram" is unquestionably a person gifted
with no ordinary powers. He has a quick
sensibility—a penetrating and intuitive
acuteness—and an unrivalled vigour and
felicity of language, which enable him at
one time to attain the happiest condensation of thought, and at others to pour forth
a stream of eloquence rich, flowing, and
deep, chequered with images of delicate
loveliness, or darkened by broad shadows
cast from objects of stern and adamantine
majesty. Yet, in common with many

other potent spirits of the present time,
he fails to excite within us any pure and
lasting sympathy. We do not, on reading
his works, feel that we have entered on a
precious and imperishable treasure. They
dazzle, they delight, they surprise, and
they weary us—we lay them down with a
vague admiration for the author, and try
to shake off their influence as we do the
impressions of a feverish dream.—TAL-
FOURD, THOMAS NOON, 1842, *Maturin,*
Critical and Miscellaneous Writings, p. 43.

Was verily and indeed a man of genius.
—DE QUINCEY, THOMAS, 1854, *Letter to*
his Daughter Emily, Oct. ; Life and Writ-
ings, ed. Page, ch. xviii.

Above all, however, there were the
works of Maturin,—those startling and
enthralling, however sombre and repellent
fictions, which, with all their defects of
art, and taste, and insufficiency of purpose, lift the mystery and terror and
physical agencies of Mrs. Radcliffe into an
imaginative grandeur worthy of Shelley or
Novalis. There were "The Albigenses,"
with its masterly contrasts of the hunted
people and their hunters; "The Fatal
Revenge," with its terrible capacities and
convulsions of the human soul; and "Melmoth," with its amazing pictures of guilt,
malignity, and suffering, and its girl of the
Indian seas—its Immalee, loveliest conception of youth, purity, and ardour.—
BERNARD, BAYLE, 1874, *The Life of Sam-*
uel Lover, p. 157.

The name of Maturin has almost died
altogether from the recollection of the
reader, and it is with difficulty that the
student can find any of the many works
which he poured forth, and which, indeed,
are little worth the trouble of looking for.
His high-flown productions and romantic
theatrical figure might, however, have
thrown at least an amusing tragi-comic
light upon his surroundings had any record of them been attainable.—OLIPHANT,
MARGARET O. W., 1882, *Literary History*
of England, XVIII-XIX Century, vol. III.

He never overcame his tendency to
absurd extravagance of expression and
wild improbability, though we can understand why it was that the great critics of
the time continued to hope that he would
tone down. — MINTO, WILLIAM, 1894, *The*
Literature of the Georgian Era, ed. Knight,
p. 286.

DATE DUE

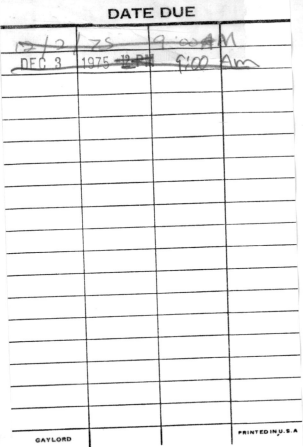

12/2/75		9:00 AM	
DEC 3 1975 12 PM		9:00 Am	

GAYLORD | | | PRINTED IN U.S.A